AFAQ

ACTION DIRECTE CONTRE LE CAPITAL
DIRECT ACTION AGAINST CAPITAL
ACCIÓN DIRECTA CONTRA EL CAPITAL

"An Anarchist FAQ", Version 12.0

Copyright © 1995-2007
The Anarchist FAQ Editorial Collective:
Iain McKay, Gary Elkin, Dave Neal, Ed Boraas

Catalogue records for this book are available from the British Library and from the Library of Congress.

ISBN   9781902593906

Library of Congress Control Number   2007939197

First published 2008 by:

AK Press   AK Press
PO Box 12766   674-A 23rd Street
Edinburgh   Oakland
Scotland   CA 94612-1163
EH8 9YE   USA

www.akuk.com   www.akpress.org

ak@akedin.demon.co.uk   akpress@akpress.org

Design, layout and typesetting by:

Euan Sutherland
www.agitcollage.org

Printed in Canada

An Anarchist FAQ

AFAQ volume one
Iain McKay

AK PRESS
EDINBURGH · OAKLAND · WEST VIRGINIA

Contents

An Anarchist FAQ: After ten years 7

Introduction 10

Introduction to Volume 1 12

Section A: What is anarchism? 18

An overview of what anarchism stands for, where it comes from and what anarchists have done. Presents a summary of the major schools of anarchism as well as important anarchist and related thinkers.

A.1 What is anarchism? 19
A.2 What does anarchism stand for? 26
A.3 What types of anarchism are there? 58
A.4 Who are the major anarchist thinkers? 82
A.5 What are some examples of "Anarchy in Action"? 94

Section B: Why do anarchists oppose the current system? 120

Why anarchists are against hierarchy, capitalism and the state. What they are and how they affect liberty. On the negative nature and impact of social hierarchies and economic classes.

B.1 Why are anarchists against authority and hierarchy?.............................. 121
B.2 Why are anarchists against the state? 139
B.3 Why are anarchists against private property? 157
B.4 How does capitalism affect liberty? 169
B.5 Is capitalism empowering and based on human action? 182
B.6 But won't decisions made by individuals with their own money be the best?.... 184
B.7 What classes exist within modern society?... 185

Section C: What are the myths of capitalist economics? 196

Why capitalist economics is an ideology, not a science. Why anarchists think capitalism is exploitative. Exposes the extremely negative effects of trying to run a society along the lines recommended in economics textbooks.

C.1 What is wrong with economics? 199
C.2 Why is capitalism exploitative?... 227
C.3 What determines the distribution between labour and capital? 259
C.4 Why does the market become dominated by Big Business?..................... 262
C.5 Why does Big Business get a bigger slice of profits?.............................. 270
C.6 Can market dominance by Big Business change? 274
C.7 What causes the capitalist business cycle?.. 275
C.8 Is state control of money the cause of the business cycle? 286
C.9 Would laissez-faire capitalism reduce unemployment?........................... 302
C.10 Is "free market" capitalism the best way to reduce poverty? 324
C.11 Doesn't neo-liberalism in Chile prove that the free market benefits everyone? 342
C.12 Doesn't Hong Kong show the potentials of "free market" capitalism? 353

Section D: How do statism and capitalism affect society? 360

How economics and politics cannot be separated and outlines the impact of each on the other. It indicates how wealth influences society and discusses the media, imperialism, nationalism, state intervention and technology.

D.1 Why does state intervention occur? 361
D.2 What influence does wealth have over politics? 375
D.3 How does wealth influence the mass media?...380
D.4 What is the relationship between capitalism and the ecological crisis? 386
D.5 What causes imperialism? 388
D.6 Are anarchists against Nationalism? 403
D.7 Are anarchists opposed to National Liberation struggles?.................................405
D.8 What causes militarism and what are its effects?..408
D.9 Why does political power become concentrated under capitalism?.....................411
D.10 How does capitalism affect technology?..419
D.11 Can politics and economics be separated from each other? 424

Section E: What do anarchists think causes ecological problems? 434

An overview of the roots of the ecological crisis and why anarchists reject many commonly proposed solutions as inadequate (when they do not make it worse).

E.1 What are the root causes of our ecological problems?.....................................436
E.2 What do eco-anarchists propose instead of capitalism?...................................442
E.3 Can private property rights protect the environment?......................................446
E.4 Can laissez-faire capitalism protect the environment? 459
E.5 Can ethical consumerism stop the ecological crisis? 467
E.6 What is the population myth? 471

Section F: Is "anarcho"-capitalism a form of anarchism? 478

No, it is not. If you know about anarchism and its history, you will already know why.

F.1 Are "anarcho"-capitalists really anarchists? 481
F.2 What do "anarcho"-capitalists mean by freedom?...486
F.3 Why do "anarcho"-capitalists place little or no value on equality? 493
F.4 What is the right-"libertarian" position on private property?.............................503
F.5 Will privatising "the commons" increase liberty?...508
F.6 Is "anarcho"-capitalism against the state?...510
F.7 How does the history of "anarcho"-capitalism show that it is not anarchist? 519
F.8 What role did the state take in the creation of capitalism? 528

Appendix: The Symbols of Anarchy 550

This explains why anarchists carry Black and Black and Red Flags and use the circled-A. What they mean and where they originate from.

1 What is the history of the Black Flag? 550
2 Why the red-and-black flag?...554
3 Where does the circled-A come from? 555

An Anarchist FAQ: After ten years

It is now ten years since "An Anarchist FAQ" (AFAQ) was officially released. A lot has happened over that time, unfortunately finishing it has not been one of them!

Over that decade, AFAQ has changed considerably. It was initially conceived as a energy-saving device to stop anarchists having to continually make the same points against claims that "anarcho"-capitalism was a form of anarchism. As would be expected, the quality of the initial versions and sections were pretty mixed. Most of it was extremely good (even if we do say so ourselves!) and has required little change over the decade (mostly we have built upon and expanded the original material). A few bits were less good and have been researched more and rewritten. We have also, of course, made mistakes and corrected them when we have been informed about them or have discovered them ourselves. In general, though, our initial work has stood up well and while we were occasionally wrong on a few details, the general thrust of even these areas has been proven correct. Overall, our aim to produce an FAQ which reflected the majority of anarchist thought, both currently and historically from an international perspective, has been a success as shown by the number of mirrors, links and translations AFAQ has seen (being published by AK Press confirms this).

Since the official release, AFAQ has changed. When we released it back in 1996, we had already decided to make it a FAQ about anarchism rather than an FAQ on why anarchism is anti-capitalist. However, the first versions still bore the marks of its origins. We realised that this limited it somewhat and we have slowly revised the AFAQ so that it has become a resource about anarchism (indeed, if it were to be started again the section on "anarcho"-capitalism would be placed into an appendix, where it belongs). This means that the aim of AFAQ has changed. I would say that it has two related goals:

1. To present the case for anarchism, to convince people they should become anarchists.

2. To be a resource for existing anarchists, to use to bolster their activism and activities by presenting facts and arguments to allow them to defend anarchism against those opposed to it (Marxists, capitalists, etc.).

The second goal explains why, for example, we spend a lot of time refuting capitalist economics and Marxism/Leninism (partly, because many of the facts and arguments are in academic books which are unavailable to the general public). We hope that AFAQ has proved useful to our comrades as much as we hope we have convinced non-anarchists, at best, to become anarchists, or at worst, to take our ideas seriously. Hopefully, the two aims are mutually complementary.

Not only has AFAQ changed over the last ten years, so has the anarchist and general political landscape on the internet. When AFAQ was being initially created, the number of anarchists on-line was small. There were not that many anarchist webpages and, relatively speaking, right-wing "libertarians" were unopposed in arguing that "anarcho"-capitalism was a form of anarchism (the only FAQ was Caplan's biased and inaccurate "Anarchist Theory FAQ"). As a non-American, I was surprised that this oxymoron even existed (I still am, as are all the anarchists I mention it to). Anarchism has always been a **socialist** theory and the concept of an "anarchism" which supported the economic system anarchism was born opposing is nonsense. Arguing with its supporters and reading up on it convinced me that the only real link it has with anarchism is simply its attempted appropriation of the name. [1] Hence the pressing need for a **real** anarchist FAQ, a need AFAQ successfully met.

Luckily, over the 1990s things changed. More anarchists went online, anarchist organisations created a web presence and the balance of forces changed to reflect reality (i.e. there are far more anarchists than "anarcho"-capitalists). The anti-capitalist movement helped, putting anarchists back in the news (the BBC even linked to AFAQ for those interested in finding out what anarchists wanted!) Even in the USA, things got better and after Seattle genuine anarchism could no longer be ignored. This produced some articles by "anarcho"-capitalists, explaining how there are two forms of anarchism and that the two have nothing or little in common (if that is the case, why call your ideology anarchism?). Anarchist organisations and activism increased and the awareness that anarchism was anti-hierarchy, anti-state **and** anti-capitalist increased. As an added bonus, some genuine individualist anarchists appeared, refuting the claim that "anarcho"-capitalism was merely a form of "updated" individualist anarchism. All these developments were welcomed, as were the words of praise and encouragement we received for our work on AFAQ from many anarchists (including, it must be stressed, individualist ones). Today, genuine anarchism in all its forms has a much greater profile, as has anarchist opposition to "anarcho"-capitalism and its claims. We hope AFAQ played a role, however small, in that process.

Of course, the battle is not over. On Wikipedia, for example, right-"libertarians" are busy trying to rewrite the history of anarchism. Some anarchists have tried to counteract this attempt, and have meant with differing degrees of success. We urge you to get involved, if you have the time and energy as numbers, sadly, do seem to count. This is because we anarchists are up against people who, apparently, do not have a life and so can wage a war of attrition against those who try and include relevant facts to the entries (such as the obvious anti-capitalism of "traditional" anarchism, that anarchism is **not** compatible with government or hierarchy – hence an-**archy**! – or that calling yourself an anarchist does not necessarily make it so). It is a shame that such a promising project has been derailed by ideologues whose ignorance of the subject matter is matched only by their hatred of AFAQ which they deny is a "credible" or valid reference on anarchism.

I am not surprised that AFAQ is hated by the "libertarian" right (nor will I be surprised if it is equally hated by the authoritarian left). After all, it presents the case for genuine anarchism, exposes the claims of a capitalist "anarchism" for the nonsense they are and shows how deeply authoritarian right-wing "libertarianism" actually is. That the FAQ can be called "biased" by these people goes without saying (it is, after all, a FAQ about anarchism written by anarchists). What seems funny is that they just do not comprehend that anarchists take offence to their pretensions of labelling their ideology "anarchism," that we would seek to refute such claims and that their notion that "anarcho"-capitalism is anarchist is far more biased. Let us hope that more academics will pay attention to this and the obvious fact that there is a very long list of anarchists, famous and not-so-famous, who consider the whole concept an oxymoron.

Equally unsurprising is the attempt to deny that AFAQ is a valid reference on Wikipedia. This boils down to the claim that the authors are "nobodies." Given that Kropotkin always stressed that anarchism was born from the people, I take that intended insult as a badge of pride. I have always taken the position that it is not who says something that counts, but what they say. In other words, I would far sooner quote a "nobody" who knows what they are talking about than a "somebody" who does not. As AFAQ indicates with its many refutations of straw man arguments against anarchism, there are plenty of the latter. Ultimately, the logical conclusion of such an argument is that anarchists are not qualified to discuss anarchism, an inherently silly position but useful if you are seeking to turn anarchism into something it is not.

Given that even such an usually reliable expert as the late, great, Paul Avrich made mistakes, this position is by far the most sensible. Between what a suitably qualified "expert" writes and what actual anarchists say and do, I always go for the latter. Any serious scientist would do so, but sadly many do not – instead, we get ideology. A classic example is Eric Hobsbawm's thesis on **"Primitive Rebels"** which he decided to illustrate, in part, with the example of Spanish anarchism. As we recount as part of our appendix on "Marxism and Spanish Anarchism" while being undoubtedly a "somebody" and immensely qualified to write on the subject, his account was utter nonsense. This was proven beyond doubt when an anthropologist interviewed the survivors of the Casas Viejas massacre. Their account of the event had only appeared previously in anarchist papers at the time and both, needless to say, refuted Hobsbawm.

So, to be called a "nobody" is quite a complement, given how many of the "somebodies" have not stopped being ignorant of anarchism from putting pen to paper and exposing that ignorance to the world (the worse recent example of this, outside of Marxism, must be George Monbiot's terrible comments in his **"Age of Consent"**). So, when it comes to saying what anarchism is, I turn to anarchists. This is what the "experts" should be doing anyway if they were doing their job.

Are we "qualified" to write about anarchism? Well, the collective has always been made up of anarchists, so we have an anarchist FAQ written by anarchists. It has always been a popular site, given the number of mirrors, translations and links it has been given (one mirror called it "world famous"). It is being published by AK Press, one of the leading anarchist publishers in the world.

I am the main editor and contributor to AFAQ. While one contributor to Wikipedia claimed I am an American academic, this is not the case. I have a "real" job and work on AFAQ in my spare time (I do despair when people, particularly leftists, assume that wage slaves are incapable of producing works like AFAQ). I have been always been an anarchist since becoming politically aware which means I have been an anarchist activist for approximately 20 years (time flies when you are having fun!). I have been a member of numerous anarchist groups and have contributed to many anarchist publications and websites. As can be seen from my personal webpage [2], I regularly contribute articles to **Freedom** (the leading English-language anarchist newspaper). Rarely does an issue come out without something by me it in. Moreover, some of the longer articles have appeared in **Black Flag** (before and after I joined its editorial committee). My works have also been published in **Scottish Anarchist**, **Anarcho-Syndicalist Review** and **Free Voices** and some have been translated into other languages. I am also an invited columnist for the www.infoshop.org and www.anarkismo.net webpages (neither of which I am otherwise involved with). In addition, I have been invited to speak at anarchist conferences in Scotland and Ireland, as well as by Marxist parties to debate the merits of anarchism. Due to family commitments, my specifically anarchist activities are pretty much limited to writing these days, but I remain a reasonably active trade unionist.

I will leave it up to the reader to decide whether we are "qualified" to write about anarchism or not!

But as I said, I always consider what is said more important than who says it. The fact that AFAQ is so popular with anarchists is what counts and I hope that we continue to be. We are always looking for help and suggestions, so if you want to get involved or want something added or changed, please contact us – we consider AFAQ as a resource for anarchists and we want it to reflect what anarchists think and do. [3] However, if you do want something changed or added be prepared to do some or all of the work yourself as we have our own plans on future developments and may not be able to provide the time or energy for other changes. Also, if you spot a mistake or a typo, please inform us as no matter how often we check errors do creep in. We take our task seriously and correct all errors when informed of them (differences in interpretation or terminology are not, of course, errors). [4]

Speaking personally, I have enjoyed being part of this project. I have learned a lot and have gained a better understanding of many anarchist thinkers and historical events. For example, I can now understand why Daniel Guerin was so interested in Proudhon and why it has been a crying shame that Voltairine de Cleyre's works have been unavailable for 8 decades. As such, my understanding and appreciation of anarchism has been enriched by working on AFAQ and I hope that others have had a similar experience reading it. On the negative side, I've had to read some terrible books and articles but very few, if any, of those were anarchist. But this is minor. The work has been worth it and while it has taken longer than any of us had imagined at the start, I'm glad that we are still working on it ten years later as AFAQ is much improved for all that time and energy. If nothing else, this work has reinforced my belief in the positive ideas and ideals of anarchism and confirmed why I became an anarchist so long ago. And, let me be honest, I would not do it unless I enjoyed it!

What of the future? Obviously, we know that AFAQ is not the final word on anarchism (we have always stressed that this is **An** Anarchist FAQ and not "The Anarchist FAQ," although some do call it that). The immediate aim is to revise the existing main sections of AFAQ for publication, which we are slowly doing. In the process some previous work is being added to and, in some cases, totally revised. After ten years, our knowledge of many subjects has expanded considerably. We have also asked a couple of individualist anarchist comrades to have a look over section G and hopefully their input will flesh out that section when it comes to be revised (for all its flaws, individualist anarchism deserves far more than to be appropriated by the right and social anarchists should be helping its modern supporters attempts to reclaim their radical tradition). [5] Once the revision of the main body of AFAQ is complete, the appendix on the Russian Revolution will be finished and then all the appendices will be revised.

After that, AFAQ will be added to once new information becomes available and new anarchist social movements and ideas develop. We have not covered everything nor does AFAQ discuss all developments within anarchism in all countries. If you think we have missed something, then contact us and we can arrange to include the subject and issues missing. As noted above, though, do **not** expect us to do all the work for you. This is a resource for the movement and, as such, we expect fellow anarchists to help out beyond merely suggesting things they expect **others** to do!

Hopefully, after summarising 19th and 20th century anarchism, the anarchists of the 21st century will use that to build and develop new ideas and movements and create both viable anarchist alternatives under statism and capitalism and, eventually, a free society. Whether we do so or not is, ultimately, up to us. Let us hope we can rise to the challenge! I do hope that anarchists can rise above the often silly arguments that we often inflict on each other and concentrate on the 90%+ that unites us rather than the often insignificant differences some consider so important. One thing is sure, if we do not then the worse will happen.

Finally, another personal note. On the way to work, I go past a little park. This little oasis of green in the city is a joy to behold, more so since someone has added this piece of graffiti to one of its walls:

*"Resistance is **never** futile! Have a nice day, y'all. Love Friday, XXX"*

With that in mind, we dedicate the ten year anniversary release of "An Anarchist FAQ" to all those "nobodies," all those anarchists who are not famous or have the appropriate "qualifications", but whose activity, thoughts, ideas, ideals, dreams and hopes give the "somebodies" something to write about (even if they fail to get some, or even all of it, right).

Iain McKay

Notes

1. While "anarcho"-capitalism has some overlap with individualist anarchism, it lacks the radical and socialist sensibility and aims of the likes of Tucker which makes the latter anarchist, albeit a flawed and inconsistent form. Unlike the former, individualist anarchism **can** become consistent anarchism by simply applying its own principles in a logical manner.

2. Under my pseudonym "Anarcho" (given what's on it, I'm surprised I bother using "Anarcho" these days as it is obvious who writes the articles). It is available here: http://anarchism.ws/writers/anarcho.html

3. Apologies for those who sent emails over the years and never received a reply – some were lost and, given how much busy we are, emails are always the first to suffer.

4. For a discussion of one early incident, mentioned in the Wikipedia entry on AFAQ, see my article (*"An Anarchist FAQ, David Friedman and Medieval Iceland"* on my webpage). Suffice to say, once we became aware of his new criticism this year (Friedman did not bother to inform us directly), we sped up our planned revision and expansion of that section and corrected the few mistakes that had remained. In summary, it can be said our original critique remained valid in spite of some serious errors in details caused by a failure to check sources in a rush to officially release it. We learned our lesson and try not to make the same mistake again (and have not, as far as I am aware).

5. A few people have said that AFAQ does not give equal billing to individualist anarchism. However, in terms of numbers and influence it has always been very much a minority trend in anarchism outside of America. By the 1880s, this was probably the case in America as well and by the turn of the 20th century it was definitely the case (as noted by, among others, Paul Avrich). As such, it is hardly a flaw that AFAQ has presented the majority position on anarchism (social anarchism), particularly as this is the position of the people involved.

Introduction

"Proletarians of the world, look into the depths of your own beings, seek out the truth and realise it yourselves: you will find it nowhere else" – Peter Arshinov **The History of the Makhnovist Movement**

This FAQ was written by anarchists across the world in an attempt to present anarchist ideas and theory to those interested in it. It is a co-operative effort, produced by a (virtual) working group and it exists to present a useful organising tool for anarchists on-line and, hopefully, in the real world. It desires to present arguments on why you should be an anarchist as well as refuting common arguments against anarchism and other proposed solutions to the social problems we face.

As anarchist ideas seem so at odds with "common-sense" (such as "of course we need a state and capitalism") we need to indicate **why** anarchists think like we do. Unlike many political theories, anarchism rejects flip answers and instead bases its ideas and ideals in an in-depth analysis of society and humanity. In order to do both anarchism and the reader justice we have summarised our arguments as much as possible without making them simplistic. We know that it is a lengthy document and may put off the casual observer but its length is unavoidable.

Readers may consider our use of extensive quoting as being an example of a *"quotation [being] a handy thing to have about, saving one the trouble of thinking for oneself."* (A.A. Milne) This is not the case of course. We have included extensive quotations by many anarchist figures for three reasons. Firstly, to indicate that we are **not** making up our claims of what certain anarchists thought or argued for. Secondly, and most importantly, it allows us to link the past voices of anarchism with its present adherents. And lastly, the quotes are used for their ability to convey ideas succinctly rather than as an appeal to "authority."

In addition, many quotes are used in order to allow readers to investigate the ideas of those quoted and to summarise facts and so save space. For example, a quote by Noam Chomsky on the development of capitalism by state protection ensures that we base our arguments on facts without having to present all the evidence and references Chomsky uses. Similarly, we quote experts on certain subjects (such as economics, for example) to support and bolster our analysis and claims.

We should also indicate the history of this FAQ. It was started in 1995 when a group of anarchists got together in order to write an FAQ refuting the claims of certain "libertarian" capitalists to being anarchists. Those who were involved in this project had spent many an hour on-line refuting claims by these people that capitalism and anarchism could go together. Finally, a group of net-activists decided the best thing was to produce an FAQ explaining why anarchism hates capitalism and why "anarcho" capitalists are not anarchists. However, after the suggestion of Mike Huben (who maintains the ***"Critiques of Libertarianism"*** web-page) it was decided that a pro-Anarchist FAQ would be a better idea than an anti-"anarcho"-capitalist one. So the Anarchist FAQ was born. It still bears some of the signs of its past-history. For example it gives the likes of Ayn Rand, Murray Rothbard, and so on, far too much space outside of Section F – they really are not that important. However, as they present extreme examples of everyday capitalist ideology and assumptions, they do have their uses – they state clearly the authoritarian implications of capitalist ideology which its more moderate supporters try to hide or minimise.

We think that we have produced a useful on-line resource for anarchists and other anti-capitalists to use. Perhaps, in light of this, we should dedicate this anarchist FAQ to the many on-line "libertarian" capitalists who, because of their inane arguments, prompted us to start this work. Then again, that would give them too much credit. Outside the net they are irrelevant and on the net they are just annoying. As you may guess, sections F and G contain the bulk of this early anti-Libertarian FAQ and are included purely to refute the claim that an anarchist can be a supporter of capitalism that is relatively common on the net (in the real world this would not be required as almost all anarchists think that "anarcho"-capitalism is an oxymoron and that its supporters are not part of the anarchist movement).

So, while coming from a very specific reason, the FAQ has expanded into more than we originally imagined. It has become a general introduction about anarchism, its ideas and history. Because anarchism recognises that there are no easy answers and that freedom must be based on individual responsibility the FAQ is quite in-depth. As it also challenges a lot of assumptions, we have had to cover a lot of ground. We also admit that some of the "frequently asked questions" we have included are more frequently asked than others. This is due to the need to include relevant arguments and facts which otherwise may not have been included.

We are sure that many anarchists will not agree 100% with what we have written in the FAQ. That is to be expected in a movement based upon individual freedom and critical thought. However, we are sure that most anarchists will agree with most of what we present and respect those parts with which they do disagree with as genuine expressions of anarchist ideas and ideals. The anarchist movement is marked by wide-spread disagreement and argument about various aspects of anarchist ideas and how to apply them (but also, we must add, a wide-spread tolerance of differing viewpoints and a willingness to work together in spite of minor disagreements). We have attempted to reflect this in the FAQ and hope we have done a good job in presenting the ideas of all the anarchist tendencies we discuss.

We have no desire to write in stone what anarchism is and is not. Instead the FAQ is a starting point for people to read and learn for themselves about anarchism and translate that learning into direct action and self-activity. By so doing, we make anarchism a living theory, a product of individual and social self-activity. Only by applying our ideas in practice can we find their strengths and limitations and so develop anarchist theory in new directions and in light of new experiences. We hope that the FAQ both reflects and aids this process of self-activity and self-education.

We are sure that there are many issues that the FAQ does not address. If you think of anything we could add or feel you have a question and answer which should be included, get in contact with us. The FAQ is not our "property" but belongs to the whole anarchist movement and so aims to be an organic, living creation. We desire to see it grow and expand with new ideas and inputs from as many people as possible. If you want to get involved with the FAQ then contact us. Similarly, if others (particularly anarchists) want to distribute all or part of it then feel free. It is a resource for the movement. For this reason we have "copylefted" An Anarchist FAQ (see http://www.gnu.org/copyleft/copyleft.html for details). By so doing we ensure that the FAQ remains a free product, available for use by all.

One last point. Language has changed a lot over the years and this applies to anarchist thinkers too. The use of the term "man" to refer to humanity is one such change. Needless to say, in today's world such usage is inappropriate as it effectively ignores half the human race. For this reason the FAQ has tried to be gender neutral. However, this awareness is relatively recent and many anarchists (even the female ones like Emma Goldman) used the term "man" to refer to humanity as a whole. When we are quoting past comrades who use "man" in this way, it obviously means humanity as a whole rather than the male sex. Where possible, we add "woman", "women", "her" and so on but if this would result in making the quote unreadable, we have left it as it stands. We hope this makes our position clear.

So we hope that this FAQ entertains you and makes you think. Hopefully it will produce a few more anarchists and speed up the creation of an anarchist society. If all else fails, we have enjoyed ourselves creating the FAQ and have shown anarchism to be a viable, coherent political idea.

We dedicate this work to the millions of anarchists, living and dead, who tried and are trying to create a better world. An Anarchist FAQ was officially released on July 19th, 1996 for that reason – to celebrate the Spanish Revolution of 1936 and the heroism of the Spanish anarchist movement. We hope that our work here helps make the world a freer place.

The following self-proclaimed anarchists are (mostly) responsible for this FAQ:
Iain McKay (main contributor and editor)
Gary Elkin
Dave Neal
Ed Boraas

We would like to thank the following for their contributions and feedback:

Andrew Flood
Mike Ballard
Francois Coquet
Jamal Hannah
Mike Huben
Greg Alt
Chuck Munson
Pauline McCormack
Nestor McNab
Kevin Carson
Shawn Wilber
and our comrades on the
anarchy, oneunion and organise! mailing lists.

Introduction to Volume 1

As many anarchists have noted, our ideal must be one of the most misunderstood and misrepresented political theories on the planet. "An Anarchist FAQ" (AFAQ) aims to change this by presenting the basics of anarchist theory and history, refuting the most common distortions and nonsense about it and providing anarchists with a resource they can use to aid their arguments and struggles for freedom. This is important, as much of the ground covered in AFAQ was provoked by having to critique other theories and refute attacks on anarchism.

Anarchism has changed over the years and will continue to evolve and change as circumstances do likewise and new struggles are fought and (hopefully) won. It is not some fixed ideology, but rather a means of understanding an evolving world and to change it in libertarian directions. As such, AFAQ seeks to place specific aspects of anarchism into their historical context. For example, certain aspects of Proudhon's ideas can only be understood by remembering that he lived at a time when the vast majority of working people were peasants and artisans. Many commentators (particularly Marxist ones) seem to forget this (and that he supported co-operatives for large-scale industry). Much the same can be said of Bakunin, Tucker and so on. I hope AFAQ will help anarchism continue to develop to meet new circumstances by summarising what has gone before so that we can build on it.

We also seek to draw out what anarchists have in common while not denying their differences. After all, individualist-anarchist Benjamin Tucker would have agreed with communist-anarchist Peter Kropotkin when he stated that anarchism was the *"no government form of socialism."* While some anarchists seem to take more time in critiquing and attacking their comrades over (ultimately) usually minor differences than fighting oppression, I personally think that this activity while, at times, essential is hardly the most fruitful use of our limited resources – particularly when it is about possible future developments (whether it is on the economic nature of a free society or our attitude to a currently non-existing syndicalist union!). So we have discussed the differences between anarchist schools of thought as well as within them, but we have tried to build bridges by stressing where they agree rather than create walls.

Needless to say, not all anarchists will agree with what is in AFAQ (it is, after all, as we have always stressed "An Anarchist FAQ", not "The Anarchist FAQ" as some comrades flatteringly call it). From my experience, most anarchists agree with most of it even if they have quibbles about certain aspects of it. I know that comrades do point others to it (I once saw a Marxist complain that anarchists always suggested he read AFAQ, so I explained to him that this was what having a "Frequency Asked Questions" was all about). So AFAQ is only a guide, you need to discover anarchism for yourself

and develop and apply it in your own way. Hopefully AFAQ will help that process by presenting an overview of anarchism and indicating what it is, what it is not and where to find out more.

Some may object to the length of many of the answers and that is a valid point. However, some questions and issues cannot be dealt with quickly and be considered as remotely convincing. For example, simply stating that anarchists think that capitalism is exploitative and that claims otherwise are wrong may be both correct and short but it hardly a convincing reply to someone aware of the various defences of profit, interest and rent invented by capitalist economists. Similarly, stating that Marxist ideology helped destroy the Russian Revolution is, again, both correct and short but it would never convince a Leninist who stresses the impact of civil war on Bolshevik practice. Then there is the issue of sources. We have tried to let anarchists speak for themselves on most issues and that can take space. Some of the evidence we use is from books and articles the general reader may not have easy access so we have tried to present full quotes to show that our use is correct (the number of times I've tracked down references only to discover they did not say what was suggested is, sadly, quite numerous).

Moreover, refuting distortions and inventions about anarchism can be lengthy simply because of the necessity of providing supporting evidence. Time and again, the same mistakes and straw man arguments are regurgitated by those unwilling or unable to look at the source material (Marxists are particularly bad at this, simply repeating *ad nauseum* the assertions of Marx and Engels as if they were accurate). Assumptions are piled onto assumptions, assertions repeated as if they were factual. AFAQ seeks to address these and present evidence to refute them once and for all. Simply saying that some statement is false may be correct, but hardly convincing unless you already know a lot about the subject. So I hope that readers will understand and find even the longest answers interesting and informative (one of the advantages of a FAQ format is that people can simply go to the sections they are interested in and skip others).

This volume covers what anarchism is, where it comes from, what it has done, what it is against (and why) as well as what anarchism is not (i.e., showing why "anarcho"-capitalism is not a form of anarchism).

The latter may come as a surprise to most. Few anarchists, never mind the general population, have heard of that specific ideology (it is US based, in the main) and those who have heard of it may wonder why we bothered given its obvious non-anarchist nature. Sadly, we need to cover this ground simply because some academics insist in listing it alongside genuine forms of anarchism and that needs to be exposed for the nonsense it is. Few serious thinkers would list fascism along side socialism, regardless of whether its supporters call their ideology "National Socialism" or "National Syndicalism" (unsurprisingly, right-"libertarians" do precisely that). No one took the Soviet bloc states seriously when they described themselves as "peoples' democracies" nor considered their governments democratic. Anarchism seems to be excluded from such common-sense and so we find academics discussing "anarcho"-capitalists along side anarchism simply, I suspect, because they **call** themselves "anarchists." That almost all anarchists reject their claims to being anarchists does not seem to be a sufficient warning about taking such statements at face value! For obvious reasons, we have not wasted space in explaining why another US based ideology, "National Anarchism," is not anarchism. While some individual anarchists were racist, the notion that anarchism has anything in common with those who aim for racially pure nationalist communities is ridiculous. Even academics have not fallen for **that**, although for almost all genuine anarchists "anarcho"-capitalism makes as little sense as "anarcho"-nationalism.

Then there is the history of AFAQ. As indicated in the original introduction, AFAQ was prompted by battles with "anarcho"-capitalists on-line in the early 1990s. However, while AFAQ may have started as a reply to the "anarcho"-capitalists it is no longer that. It would be a mistake to think that they are more significant than they actually are or that many anarchists bother with them (most, I am sure, have never heard of it). I did consider whether it was wiser to simply exclude section F from the book but, in the end, I decided it should remain. Partly, for the reasons above and partly because it does serve another, more useful, purpose. Neo-liberalism is based, in many ways, on right-"libertarian" dogmas so critiquing those helps our struggle against "actually existing" capitalism and the current attacks by the ruling class.

I do not wish anarchism to go the same way that "libertarian" has gone in the US (and, to a lesser extent, in the UK). Between the 1890s and 1970s, libertarian was simply a pseudonym for anarchist or similar socialist theories. However, the American free-market right appropriated the label in the 1970s and now it means supporters of minimal state (or private-state) capitalism. Such is the power having ideas that bolster the wealthy! The change in "libertarian" is such that some people talk about "libertarian anarchism" – as if you can have an "authoritarian anarchism"! That these people include "anarcho"-capitalists simply shows how ignorant of anarchism they actually are and how alien the ideology is to our movement (I've seen quite a few of them proclaim anarchism is simply a "new" form of Marxism, which shows their grasp of the subject). Equally bizarrely, these self-proclaimed "libertarian anarchists" are also those who most fervently defend the **authoritarian** social relationships inherent within capitalism! In other words, if "authoritarian anarchists" **could** exist then the "libertarian anarchists" would be them!

As AFAQ explains, being opposed to the state is a necessary, but not sufficient, condition for being an anarchist. Not only is this clear from the works of anarchist thinkers and anarchism as a social movement, but also from the nature of the idea itself. To be an anarchist you must also be a socialist (i.e. opposed to capitalist property and the exploitation of labour). It is no coincidence that Godwin and Proudhon independently analysed private property from a libertarian perspective and drew similar conclusions or that Kropotkin and Tucker considered themselves socialists. To deny this critique is to deny anarchism as a movement and as a socio-political

theory never mind its history and the aims of anarchists across the years.

Furthermore, as AFAQ stresses, to be a **consistent** anarchist you must recognise that freedom is more than simply the ability to change masters. Anarchism means "no authority" (an-archy) and to support social relationships marked by authority (hier-**archy**) produces a self-contradictory mess (such as supporting forms of domination, such as wage labour, which are essentially identical to those produced by the state – and, sometimes, admitted as such!). Anarchism is, fundamentally, a theory of organisation based on individuals associating together without restricting, and so denying and limiting, their freedom and individuality. This means that a consistent anarchism is rooted in free association within a context of self-management, decentralisation and "bottom-up" decision-making (i.e., it is rooted in political, economic and social equality). While it is possible to be an anarchist while opposing exploitation but not all forms of hierarchical social relationships, it is hardly logical nor a convincing position.

AFAQ also seeks to go into subjects anarchists have, traditionally, been weak on, such as economics (which is ironic, as Proudhon made his name by his economic critiques). In this sense, it is a resource for anarchists both in terms of our own history and ideas but also on subjects which we inevitably come across in our struggles (hopefully, the critiques we provide of capitalism, neo-liberalism and so forth will also be useful to other radicals). We have tried to indicate if the quoted source is an anarchist or libertarian. If in doubt, please look at the bibliography on the webpage. This breaks references down into libertarian (anarchist and non-anarchist) thinkers (or sympathetic accounts of anarchism) and non-libertarians (which, needless to say, includes right-"libertarians"). It should go without saying that quoting an expert on one subject does not mean anarchists subscribe to their opinions on other matters. Thus if we quote, say, a Keynesian or post-Keynesian economist on how capitalism works it does not imply we support their specific political recommendations.

Some have criticised AFAQ for not including some of the more recent developments within anarchism, which is fair enough. I have asked on numerous occasions for such critics to contribute a section on these and, of course, for referenced corrections for any mistakes others think we have done. Nothing has been forthcoming and we have usually discovered mistakes ourselves and corrected them (although a steady flow of emails pointing out typos has come our way). We have always been a small collective and we cannot do everything. This also explains why important social events like, say, the turn of the century Argentinean revolt against neo-liberalism is not discussed in section A.5 (this is a wonderful example of anarchist ideas being spontaneously applied in practice during a mass revolt). Suffice to say, anarchistic tendencies, ideas and practices develop all the time and anarchism is growing in influence but if we continually added to AFAQ to reflect this then it would never have become ready for publication! As it is, we have excluded most of the appendices from the book version (these remain available on the website along with a lengthy links page).

I would like to thank everybody who has helped and contributed (directly and indirectly, knowingly and unknowingly) to AFAQ. As for authorship, AFAQ started as a collective effort and remained so for many years. I have been the only person involved from the start and have done the bulk of the work on it. Moreover, the task of getting it ready and revised for publication has fallen to me. I have enjoyed it, in the main. This explains why the book has my name on it rather than a collective. I feel I have earned that right. As such, I claim responsibility for any typos and examples of bad grammar that remain. I have substantially revised AFAQ for publication and while I have tried to find them all, I am sure I have failed (particularly in sections that were effectively rewritten). I hope these do not detract from the book too much.

Finally, on a personal note I would like to dedicate this book to my partner and two lovely children. They are a constant source of inspiration, love, support and hope (not to mention patience!). If this work makes the world we live in better for them then it has been more than worthwhile. For, when it comes down to it, anarchism is simply about making the world a freer and better place. If we forget that, then we forget what makes us anarchists in the first place.

Iain McKay
www.anarchistfaq.org

A Summation

"No question, the word anarchy freaks people. Yet anarchy – rule by no one – has always struck me as the same as democracy carried to its logical and reasonable conclusions. Of course those who rule – bosses and politicians, capital and the state – cannot imagine that people could rule themselves, for to admit that people can live without authority and rulers pulls out the whole underpinnings of their ideology. Once you admit that people can – and do, today, in many spheres of their lives – run things easier, better and more fairly than the corporation and the government can, there's no justification for the boss and the premier. I think most of us realise and understand that, in our guts, but schools, culture, the police, all the authoritarian apparatuses, tell us we need bosses, we need to be controlled 'for our own good.' It's not for our own good – it's for the good of the boss, plain and simple."

"Anarchism is a demand for real freedom and real autonomy"

"But I also remain convinced that something like an anarchist future, a world of no bosses or politicians, one in which people, all people, can live full and meaningful lives, is possible and desirable. We see glimpses of it all around us in our day-to-day lives, as people organise much of their lives without depending on someone to tell them what to do. We see it in that spirit of revolt – a spirit that is often twisted by anger and despair, but nonetheless shows us that people have not given up. We see it in the political activism, the social lives, the demands for decency and respect and autonomy people put forward, the desire to be individuals while still being part of a community.

"No, I don't think bowling leagues are the anarchist utopia, but they, like much of our lives outside of the workplace, are organised without hierarchy and oppression; the most meaningful, truly human parts of our lives already work best when organised on anarchist principles. Yet I also believe that in its function as critique and as a vision of the future – perhaps the only one that doesn't end in our extinction as a species, or, as Orwell put it, as a jackboot smashing a human face, forever – anarchism is not only desirable but possible and necessary."

Mark Leier: **The Case for Anarchy**

Section A
What is Anarchism?

Section A – What is Anarchism?..18

A.1 What is anarchism?...19
A.1.1 What does "anarchy" mean?...19
A.1.2 What does "anarchism" mean?..21
A.1.3 Why is anarchism also called libertarian socialism?...............................22
A.1.4 Are anarchists socialists?...23
A.1.5 Where does anarchism come from?..25

A.2 What does anarchism stand for?...26
A.2.1 What is the essence of anarchism?..27
A.2.2 Why do anarchists emphasise liberty?...28
A.2.3 Are anarchists in favour of organisation?...29
A.2.4 Are anarchists in favour of "absolute" liberty?...................................31
A.2.5 Why are anarchists in favour of equality?...31
A.2.6 Why is solidarity important to anarchists?..33
A.2.7 Why do anarchists argue for self-liberation?......................................34
A.2.8 Is it possible to be an anarchist without opposing hierarchy?.....................36
A.2.9 What sort of society do anarchists want?..37
A.2.10 What will abolishing hierarchy mean and achieve?.................................39
A.2.11 Why are most anarchists in favour of direct democracy?...........................40
A.2.12 Is consensus an alternative to direct democracy?.................................42
A.2.13 Are anarchists individualists or collectivists?..................................43
A.2.14 Why is voluntarism not enough?..44
A.2.15 What about "human nature"?..46
A.2.16 Does anarchism require "perfect" people to work?.................................48
A.2.17 Aren't most people too stupid for a free society to work?........................50
A.2.18 Do anarchists support terrorism?...51
A.2.19 What ethical views do anarchists hold?...54
A.2.20 Why are most anarchists atheists?..56

A.3 What types of anarchism are there?..58
A.3.1 What are the differences between individualist and social anarchists?.............59
A.3.2 Are there different types of social anarchism?....................................63
A.3.3 What kinds of green anarchism are there?..65
A.3.4 Is anarchism pacifistic?..67
A.3.5 What is Anarcha-Feminism?...69
A.3.6 What is Cultural Anarchism?...73
A.3.7 Are there religious anarchists?...74
A.3.8 What is "anarchism without adjectives"?...76
A.3.9 What is anarcho-primitivism?..78

A.4 Who are the major anarchist thinkers?.......................................82
A.4.1 Are there any thinkers close to anarchism?..86
A.4.2 Are there any liberal thinkers close to anarchism?................................88
A.4.3 Are there any socialist thinkers close to anarchism?..............................90
A.4.4 Are there any Marxist thinkers close to anarchism?................................92

A.5 What are some examples of "Anarchy in Action"?.............................94
A.5.1 The Paris Commune...95
A.5.2 The Haymarket Martyrs...97
A.5.3 Building the Syndicalist Unions...99
A.5.4 Anarchists in the Russian Revolution...101
A.5.5 Anarchists in the Italian Factory Occupations....................................107
A.5.6 Anarchism and the Spanish Revolution...112
A.5.7 The May-June Revolt in France, 1968..114

Section A
What is Anarchism?

Modern civilisation faces three potentially catastrophic crises: (1) social breakdown, a shorthand term for rising rates of poverty, homelessness, crime, violence, alienation, drug and alcohol abuse, social isolation, political apathy, dehumanisation, the deterioration of community structures of self-help and mutual aid, etc.; (2) destruction of the planet's delicate ecosystems on which all complex forms of life depend; and (3) the proliferation of weapons of mass destruction, particularly nuclear weapons.

Orthodox opinion, including that of Establishment "experts," mainstream media, and politicians, generally regards these crises as separable, each having its own causes and therefore capable of being dealt with on a piecemeal basis, in isolation from the other two. Obviously, however, this "orthodox" approach isn't working, since the problems in question are getting worse. Unless some better approach is taken soon, we are clearly headed for disaster, either from catastrophic war, ecological Armageddon, or a descent into urban savagery – or all of the above.

Anarchism offers a unified and coherent way of making sense of these crises, by tracing them to a common source. This source is the principle of **hierarchical authority**, which underlies the major institutions of all "civilised" societies, whether capitalist or "communist." Anarchist analysis therefore starts from the fact that all of our major institutions are in the form of hierarchies, i.e. organisations that concentrate power at the top of a pyramidal structure, such as corporations, government bureaucracies, armies, political parties, religious organisations, universities, etc. It then goes on to show how the authoritarian relations inherent in such hierarchies negatively affect individuals, their society, and culture. In the first part of this FAQ (**sections A to E**) we will present the anarchist analysis of hierarchical authority and its negative effects in greater detail.

It should not be thought, however, that anarchism is just a critique of modern civilisation, just "negative" or "destructive." Because it is much more than that. For one thing, it is also a proposal for a free society. Emma Goldman expressed what might be called the "anarchist question" as follows: *"The problem that confronts us today … is how to be one's self and yet in oneness with others, to feel deeply with all human beings and still retain one's own characteristic qualities."* [**Red Emma Speaks**, pp. 158-159] In other words, how can we create a society in which the potential for each individual is realised but not at the expense of others? In order to achieve this, anarchists envision a society in which, instead of being controlled *"from the top down"* through hierarchical structures of centralised power, the affairs of humanity will, to quote Benjamin Tucker, *"be managed by individuals or voluntary associations."* [**Anarchist Reader**, p. 149] While later sections of the FAQ (**sections I and J**) will describe anarchism's positive proposals for organising society in this way, "from the bottom up," some of the constructive core of anarchism will be seen even in the earlier sections. The positive core of anarchism can even be seen in the anarchist critique of such flawed solutions to the social

question as Marxism and right-wing "libertarianism" (**sections F and H**, respectively).

As Clifford Harper elegantly puts it, *"[l]ike all great ideas, anarchism is pretty simple when you get down to it – human beings are at their best when they are living free of authority, deciding things among themselves rather than being ordered about."* [**Anarchy: A Graphic Guide**, p. vii] Due to their desire to maximise individual and therefore social freedom, anarchists wish to dismantle all institutions that repress people:

> *"Common to all Anarchists is the desire to free society of all political and social coercive institutions which stand in the way of the development of a free humanity."* [Rudolf Rocker, **Anarcho-Syndicalism**, p. 9]

As we'll see, all such institutions are hierarchies, and their repressive nature stems directly from their hierarchical form.

Anarchism is a socio-economic and political theory, but not an ideology. The difference is **very** important. Basically, theory means you have ideas; an ideology means ideas have you. Anarchism is a body of ideas, but they are flexible, in a constant state of evolution and flux, and open to modification in light of new data. As society changes and develops, so does anarchism. An ideology, in contrast, is a set of "fixed" ideas which people believe dogmatically, usually ignoring reality or "changing" it so as to fit with the ideology, which is (by definition) correct. All such "fixed" ideas are the source of tyranny and contradiction, leading to attempts to make everyone fit onto a Procrustean Bed. This will be true regardless of the ideology in question – Leninism, Objectivism, "Libertarianism," or whatever – all will all have the same effect: the destruction of real individuals in the name of a doctrine, a doctrine that usually serves the interest of some ruling elite. Or, as Michael Bakunin puts it:

> *"Until now all human history has been only a perpetual and bloody immolation of millions of poor human beings in honour of some pitiless abstraction – God, country, power of state, national honour, historical rights, judicial rights, political liberty, public welfare."* [**God and the State**, p. 59]

Dogmas are static and deathlike in their rigidity, often the work of some dead "prophet," religious or secular, whose followers erect his or her ideas into an idol, immutable as stone. Anarchists want the living to bury the dead so that the living can get on with their lives. The living should rule the dead, not vice versa. Ideologies are the nemesis of critical thinking and consequently of freedom, providing a book of rules and "answers" which relieve us of the "burden" of thinking for ourselves.

In producing this FAQ on anarchism it is not our intention to give you the "correct" answers or a new rule book. We will explain a bit about what anarchism has been in the past, but we will focus more on its modern forms and why **we** are anarchists today. The FAQ is an attempt to provoke thought and analysis on your part. If you are looking for a new ideology, then sorry, anarchism is not for you.

While anarchists try to be realistic and practical, we are not "reasonable" people. "Reasonable" people uncritically accept what the "experts" and "authorities" tell them is true, and so they will always remain slaves! Anarchists know that, as Bakunin wrote:

"[a] person is strong only when he stands upon his own truth, when he speaks and acts from his deepest convictions. Then, whatever the situation he may be in, he always knows what he must say and do. He may fall, but he cannot bring shame upon himself or his causes." [quoted in Albert Meltzer, **I couldn't Paint Golden Angels**, p. 2]

What Bakunin describes is the power of independent thought, which is the power of freedom. We encourage you not to be "reasonable," not to accept what others tell you, but to think and act for yourself!

One last point: to state the obvious, this is **not** the final word on anarchism. Many anarchists will disagree with much that is written here, but this is to be expected when people think for themselves. All we wish to do is indicate the **basic** ideas of anarchism and give our analysis of certain topics based on how we understand and apply these ideas. We are sure, however, that all anarchists will agree with the core ideas we present, even if they may disagree with our application of them here and there.

A.1
What is anarchism?

Anarchism is a political theory which aims to create anarchy, *"the absence of a master, of a sovereign."* [P-J Proudhon, **What is Property**, p. 264] In other words, anarchism is a political theory which aims to create a society within which individuals freely co-operate together as equals. As such anarchism opposes all forms of hierarchical control – be that control by the state or a capitalist – as harmful to the individual and their individuality as well as unnecessary.

In the words of anarchist L. Susan Brown:

"While the popular understanding of anarchism is of a violent, anti-State movement, anarchism is a much more subtle and nuanced tradition then a simple opposition to government power. Anarchists oppose the idea that power and domination are necessary for society, and instead advocate more co-operative, anti-hierarchical forms of social, political and economic organisation." [**The Politics of Individualism**, p. 106]

However, "anarchism" and "anarchy" are undoubtedly the most misrepresented ideas in political theory. Generally, the words are used to mean "chaos" or "without order," and so, by implication, anarchists desire social chaos and a return to the "laws of the jungle."

This process of misrepresentation is not without historical parallel. For example, in countries which have considered government by one person (monarchy) necessary, the words "republic" or "democracy" have been used precisely like "anarchy," to imply disorder and confusion. Those with a vested interest in preserving the status quo will obviously wish to imply that opposition to the current system cannot work in practice, and that a new form of society will only lead to chaos. Or, as Errico Malatesta expresses it:

"since it was thought that government was necessary and that without government there could only be disorder and confusion, it was natural and logical that anarchy, which means absence of government, should sound like absence of order." [**Anarchy**, p. 16]

Anarchists want to change this "common-sense" idea of "anarchy," so people will see that government and other hierarchical social relationships are both harmful **and** unnecessary:

"Change opinion, convince the public that government is not only unnecessary, but extremely harmful, and then the word anarchy, just because it means absence of government, will come to mean for everybody: natural order, unity of human needs and the interests of all, complete freedom within complete solidarity." [**Op. Cit.**, pp. 16]

This FAQ is part of the process of changing the commonly-held ideas regarding anarchism and the meaning of anarchy. But that is not all. As well as combating the distortions produced by the "common-sense" idea of "anarchy", we also have to combat the distortions that anarchism and anarchists have been subjected to over the years by our political and social enemies. For, as Bartolomeo Vanzetti put it, anarchists are *"the radical of the radical – the black cats, the terrors of many, of all the bigots, exploiters, charlatans, fakers and oppressors. Consequently we are also the more slandered, misrepresented, misunderstood and persecuted of all."* [Nicola Sacco and Bartolomeo Vanzetti, **The Letters of Sacco and Vanzetti**, p. 274]

Vanzetti knew what he was talking about. He and his comrade Nicola Sacco were framed by the US state for a crime they did not commit and were, effectively, electrocuted for being foreign anarchists in 1927. So this FAQ will have to spend some time correcting the slanders and distortions that anarchists have been subjected to by the capitalist media, politicians, ideologues and bosses (not to mention the distortions by our erstwhile fellow radicals like liberals and Marxists). Hopefully once we are finished you will understand why those in power have spent so much time attacking anarchism – it is the one idea which can effectively ensure liberty for all and end all systems based on a few having power over the many.

A.1.1 What does "anarchy" mean?

The word **"anarchy"** is from the Greek, prefix **an** (or **a**), meaning *"not," "the want of," "the absence of,"* or *"the lack of"*, plus **archos**, meaning *"a ruler," "director", "chief," "person in charge,"* or *"authority."* Or, as Peter Kropotkin put it, Anarchy comes from the Greek words meaning *"contrary to authority."* [**Anarchism**, p. 284]

While the Greek words **anarchos** and **anarchia** are often taken to mean *"having no government"* or *"being without a government,"* as can be seen, the strict, original meaning of anarchism was not simply *"no government."* **"An-archy"** means *"without a ruler,"* or more generally, *"without authority,"* and it is in this sense that anarchists have continually used the word. For example, we find Kropotkin arguing that anarchism *"attacks not only capital, but also the main sources of the power of capitalism: law, authority, and the State."* [**Op. Cit.**, p. 150] For anarchists, anarchy means *"not necessarily absence of order, as is generally supposed, but an absence of rule."* [Benjamin Tucker, **Instead of a Book**, p. 13] Hence David Weick's excellent summary:

> *"Anarchism can be understood as the **generic** social and political idea that expresses negation of **all** power, sovereignty, domination, and hierarchical division, and a will to their dissolution ... Anarchism is therefore more than anti-statism ... [even if] government (the state) ... is, appropriately, the central focus of anarchist critique."* [**Reinventing Anarchy**, p. 139]

For this reason, rather than being purely anti-government or anti-state, anarchism is primarily a movement against **hierarchy.** Why? Because hierarchy is the organisational structure that embodies authority. Since the state is the "highest" form of hierarchy, anarchists are, by definition, anti-state; but this is **not** a sufficient definition of anarchism. This means that real anarchists are opposed to all forms of hierarchical organisation, not only the state. In the words of Brian Morris:

> *"The term anarchy comes from the Greek, and essentially means 'no ruler.' Anarchists are people who reject all forms of government or coercive authority, all forms of hierarchy and domination. They are therefore opposed to what the Mexican anarchist Flores Magón called the 'sombre trinity' – state, capital and the church. Anarchists are thus opposed to both capitalism and to the state, as well as to all forms of religious authority. But anarchists also seek to establish or bring about by varying means, a condition of anarchy, that is, a decentralised society without coercive institutions, a society organised through a federation of voluntary associations."* ["Anthropology and Anarchism," pp. 35-41, **Anarchy: A Journal of Desire Armed**, no. 45, p. 38]

Reference to "hierarchy" in this context is a fairly recent development – the "classical" anarchists such as Proudhon, Bakunin and Kropotkin did use the word, but rarely (they usually preferred "authority," which was used as short-hand for "authoritarian"). However, it's clear from their writings that theirs was a philosophy against hierarchy, against any inequality of power or privileges between individuals. Bakunin spoke of this when he attacked *"official"* authority but defended *"natural influence,"* and also when he said:

> *"Do you want to make it impossible for anyone to oppress his fellow-man? Then make sure that no one shall possess power."* [**The Political Philosophy of Bakunin**, p. 271]

As Jeff Draughn notes, *"while it has always been a latent part of the 'revolutionary project,' only recently has this broader concept of anti-hierarchy arisen for more specific scrutiny. Nonetheless, the root of this is plainly visible in the Greek roots of the word 'anarchy.'"* [**Between Anarchism and Libertarianism: Defining a New Movement**]

We stress that this opposition to hierarchy is, for anarchists, not limited to just the state or government. It includes all authoritarian economic and social relationships as well as political ones, particularly those associated with capitalist property and wage labour. This can be seen from Proudhon's argument that *"**Capital** ... in the political field is analogous to **government** ... The economic idea of capitalism, the politics of government or of authority, and the theological idea of the Church are three identical ideas, linked in various ways. To attack one of them is equivalent to attacking all of them ... What capital does to labour, and the State to liberty, the Church does to the spirit. This trinity of absolutism is as baneful in practice as it is in philosophy. The most effective means for oppressing the people would be simultaneously to enslave its body, its will and its reason."* [quoted by Max Nettlau, **A Short History of Anarchism**, pp. 43-44] Thus we find Emma Goldman opposing capitalism as it meant *"that man [or woman] must sell his [or her] labour"* and, therefore, *"that his [or her] inclination and judgement are subordinated to the will of a master."* [**Red Emma Speaks**, p. 50] Forty years earlier Bakunin made the same point when he argued that under the current system *"the worker sells his person and his liberty for a given time"* to the capitalist in exchange for a wage. [**Op. Cit.**, p. 187]

Thus "anarchy" means more than just "no government," it means opposition to all forms of authoritarian organisation and hierarchy. In Kropotkin's words, *"the origin of the anarchist conception of society ... [lies in] the criticism ... of the hierarchical organisations and the authoritarian conceptions of society; and ... the analysis of the tendencies that are seen in the progressive movements of mankind."* [**Op. Cit.**, p. 158] For Malatesta, anarchism *"was born in a moral revolt against social injustice"* and that the *"specific causes of social ills"* could be found in *"capitalistic property and the State."* When the oppressed *"sought to overthrow both State and property – then it was that anarchism was born."* [**Errico Malatesta: His Life and Ideas**, p. 19]

Thus any attempt to assert that anarchy is purely anti-state is a misrepresentation of the word and the way it has been used by the anarchist movement. As Brian Morris argues, *"when one examines the writings of classical anarchists ... as well as the character of anarchist movements ... it is clearly evident that it has never had this limited vision [of just being against the state]. It has always challenged all forms of authority and exploitation, and has been equally critical of capitalism and religion as it has been of the state."* [**Op. Cit.**, p. 40]

And, just to state the obvious, anarchy does not mean chaos nor do anarchists seek to create chaos or disorder. Instead, we wish to create a society based upon individual freedom and voluntary co-operation. In other words, order from the bottom up, not disorder imposed from the top down by authorities. Such a society would be a true anarchy, a society without rulers.

While we discuss what an anarchy could look like in section I, Noam Chomsky sums up the key aspect when he stated that in a truly free society *"any interaction among human beings that is more than personal – meaning that takes institutional forms of one kind or another – in community, or workplace, family, larger society, whatever it may be, should be under direct control of its participants. So that would mean workers' councils in industry,* popular democracy in communities, interaction between them, free associations in larger groups, up to organisation of international society." [**Anarchism Interview**] Society would no longer be divided into a hierarchy of bosses and workers, governors and governed. Rather, an anarchist society would be based on free association in participatory organisations and run from the bottom up. Anarchists, it should be noted, try to create as much of this society today, in their organisations, struggles and activities, as they can.

A.1.2 What does "anarchism" mean?

To quote Peter Kropotkin, Anarchism is *"the no-government system of socialism."* [**Anarchism**, p. 46] In other words, *"the abolition of exploitation and oppression of man by man, that is the abolition of private property [i.e. capitalism] and government."* [Errico Malatesta, **Towards Anarchism,"**, p. 75]

Anarchism, therefore, is a political theory that aims to create a society which is without political, economic or social hierarchies. Anarchists maintain that anarchy, the absence of rulers, is a viable form of social system and so work for the maximisation of individual liberty and social equality. They see the goals of liberty and equality as mutually self-supporting. Or, in Bakunin's famous dictum:

> *"We are convinced that freedom without Socialism is privilege and injustice, and that Socialism without freedom is slavery and brutality."* [**The Political Philosophy of Bakunin**, p. 269]

The history of human society proves this point. Liberty without equality is only liberty for the powerful, and equality without liberty is impossible and a justification for slavery.

While there are many different types of anarchism (from individualist anarchism to communist-anarchism – see section A.3 for more details), there has always been two common positions at the core of all of them – opposition to government and opposition to capitalism. In the words of the individualist-anarchist Benjamin Tucker, anarchism insists *"on the abolition of the State and the abolition of usury; on no more government of man by man, and no more exploitation of man by man."* [cited by Eunice Schuster, **Native American Anarchism**, p. 140] All anarchists view profit, interest and rent as **usury** (i.e. as exploitation) and so oppose them and the conditions that create them just as much as they oppose government and the State.

More generally, in the words of L. Susan Brown, the *"unifying link"* within anarchism *"is a universal condemnation of hierarchy and domination and a willingness to fight for the freedom of the human individual."* [**The Politics of Individualism**, p. 108] For anarchists, a person cannot be free if they are subject to state or capitalist authority. As Voltairine de Cleyre summarised:

> *"Anarchism ... teaches the possibility of a society in which the needs of life may be fully supplied for all, and in which the opportunities for complete development of mind and body shall be the heritage of all ... [It] teaches*

that the present unjust organisation of the production and distribution of wealth must finally be completely destroyed, and replaced by a system which will insure to each the liberty to work, without first seeking a master to whom he [or she] must surrender a tithe of his [or her] product, which will guarantee his liberty of access to the sources and means of production ... Out of the blindly submissive, it makes the discontented; out of the unconsciously dissatisfied, it makes the consciously dissatisfied ... Anarchism seeks to arouse the consciousness of oppression, the desire for a better society, and a sense of the necessity for unceasing warfare against capitalism and the State."* [**Anarchy! An Anthology of Emma Goldman's Mother Earth**, pp. 23-4]

So Anarchism is a political theory which advocates the creation of anarchy, a society based on the maxim of *"no rulers."* To achieve this, *"[i]n common with all socialists, the anarchists hold that the private ownership of land, capital, and machinery has had its time; that it is condemned to disappear: and that all requisites for production must, and will, become the common property of society, and be managed in common by the producers of wealth. And ... they maintain that the ideal of the political organisation of society is a condition of things where the functions of government are reduced to minimum ... [and] that the ultimate aim of society is the reduction of the functions of government to nil – that is, to a society without government, to an-archy"* [Peter Kropotkin, **Op. Cit.**, p. 46]

Thus anarchism is both positive and negative. It analyses and critiques current society while at the same time offering a vision of a potential new society – a society that fulfils certain human needs which the current one denies. These needs, at their most basic, are liberty, equality and solidarity, which will be discussed in section A.2.

Anarchism unites critical analysis with hope, for, as Bakunin (in his pre-anarchist days) pointed out, *"the urge to destroy is a creative urge."* One cannot build a better society without understanding what is wrong with the present one.

However, it must be stressed that anarchism is more than just a means of analysis or a vision of a better society. It is also rooted in struggle, the struggle of the oppressed for their freedom. In other words, it provides a means of achieving a new system based on the needs of people, not power, and which places the planet before profit. To quote Scottish anarchist Stuart Christie:

> *"Anarchism is a movement for human freedom. It is concrete, democratic and egalitarian ... Anarchism began – and remains – a direct challenge by the underprivileged to their oppression and exploitation. It opposes both the insidious growth of state power and the pernicious ethos of possessive individualism, which, together or separately, ultimately serve only the interests of the few at the expense of the rest.*
>
> *"Anarchism is both a theory and practice of life. Philosophically, it aims for the maximum accord between the individual, society and nature. Practically, it aims for us to organise and live our lives in such a way as to*

make politicians, governments, states and their officials superfluous. In an anarchist society, mutually respectful sovereign individuals would be organised in non-coercive relationships within naturally defined communities in which the means of production and distribution are held in common.

"Anarchists are not dreamers obsessed with abstract principles and theoretical constructs ... Anarchists are well aware that a perfect society cannot be won tomorrow. Indeed, the struggle lasts forever! However, it is the vision that provides the spur to struggle against things as they are, and for things that might be ...

"Ultimately, only struggle determines outcome, and progress towards a more meaningful community must begin with the will to resist every form of injustice. In general terms, this means challenging all exploitation and defying the legitimacy of all coercive authority. If anarchists have one article of unshakeable faith, it is that, once the habit of deferring to politicians or ideologues is lost, and that of resistance to domination and exploitation acquired, then ordinary people have a capacity to organise every aspect of their lives in their own interests, anywhere and at any time, both freely and fairly.

"Anarchists do not stand aside from popular struggle, nor do they attempt to dominate it. They seek to contribute practically whatever they can, and also to assist within it the highest possible levels of both individual self-development and of group solidarity. It is possible to recognise anarchist ideas concerning voluntary relationships, egalitarian participation in decision-making processes, mutual aid and a related critique of all forms of domination in philosophical, social and revolutionary movements in all times and places." [**My Granny made me an Anarchist**, pp. 162-3]

Anarchism, anarchists argue, is simply the theoretical expression of our capacity to organise ourselves and run society without bosses or politicians. It allows working class and other oppressed people to become conscious of our power as a class, defend our immediate interests, and fight to revolutionise society as a whole. Only by doing this can we create a society fit for human beings to live in.

It is no abstract philosophy. Anarchist ideas are put into practice everyday. Wherever oppressed people stand up for their rights, take action to defend their freedom, practice solidarity and co-operation, fight against oppression, organise themselves without leaders and bosses, the spirit of anarchism lives. Anarchists simply seek to strengthen these libertarian tendencies and bring them to their full fruition. As we discuss in section J, anarchists apply their ideas in many ways within capitalism in order to change it for the better until such time as we get rid of it completely. Section I discusses what we aim to replace it with, i.e. what anarchism aims for.

A.1.3 Why is anarchism also called libertarian socialism?

Many anarchists, seeing the negative nature of the definition of *"anarchism,"* have used other terms to emphasise the inherently positive and constructive aspect of their ideas. The most common terms used are *"free socialism," "free communism," "libertarian socialism,"* and *"libertarian communism."* For anarchists, libertarian socialism, libertarian communism, and anarchism are virtually interchangeable. As Vanzetti put it:

"After all we are socialists as the social-democrats, the socialists, the communists, and the I.W.W. are all Socialists. The difference – the fundamental one – between us and all the other is that they are authoritarian while we are libertarian; they believe in a State or Government of their own; we believe in no State or Government." [Nicola Sacco and Bartolomeo Vanzetti, **The Letters of Sacco and Vanzetti**, p. 274]

But is this correct? Considering definitions from the **American Heritage Dictionary**, we find:

LIBERTARIAN: *one who believes in freedom of action and thought; one who believes in free will.*

SOCIALISM: *a social system in which the producers possess both political power and the means of producing and distributing goods.*

Just taking those two first definitions and fusing them yields:

LIBERTARIAN SOCIALISM: *a social system which believes in freedom of action and thought and free will, in which the producers possess both political power and the means of producing and distributing goods.*

(Although we must add that our usual comments on the lack of political sophistication of dictionaries still holds. We only use these definitions to show that "libertarian" does not imply "free market" capitalism nor "socialism" state ownership. Other dictionaries, obviously, will have different definitions – particularly for socialism. Those wanting to debate dictionary definitions are free to pursue this unending and politically useless hobby but we will not).

However, due to the creation of the Libertarian Party in the USA, many people now consider the idea of *"libertarian socialism"* to be a contradiction in terms. Indeed, many "Libertarians" think anarchists are just attempting to associate the "anti-libertarian" ideas of "socialism" (as Libertarians conceive it) with Libertarian ideology in order to make those "socialist" ideas more "acceptable" – in other words, trying to steal the "libertarian" label from its rightful possessors.

Nothing could be further from the truth. Anarchists have been using the term "libertarian" to describe themselves and their ideas since the 1850's. According to anarchist historian Max Nettlau, the revolutionary anarchist Joseph Dejacque published **Le Libertaire, Journal du Mouvement Social** in New York between 1858 and 1861 while the use of the term *"libertarian communism"* dates from

November, 1880 when a French anarchist congress adopted it. [Max Nettlau, **A Short History of Anarchism**, p. 75 and p. 145] The use of the term "Libertarian" by anarchists became more popular from the 1890s onward after it was used in France in an attempt to get round anti-anarchist laws and to avoid the negative associations of the word "anarchy" in the popular mind (Sébastien Faure and Louise Michel published the paper **Le Libertaire – The Libertarian** – in France in 1895, for example). Since then, particularly outside America, it has **always** been associated with anarchist ideas and movements. Taking a more recent example, in the USA, anarchists organised *"The Libertarian League"* in July 1954, which had staunch anarcho-syndicalist principles and lasted until 1965. The US-based "Libertarian" Party, on the other hand has only existed since the early 1970's, well over 100 years after anarchists first used the term to describe their political ideas (and 90 years after the expression "libertarian communism" was first adopted). It is that party, not the anarchists, who have "stolen" the word. Later, in Section B, we will discuss why the idea of a "libertarian" capitalism (as desired by the Libertarian Party) is a contradiction in terms.

As we will also explain in Section I, only a libertarian-socialist system of ownership can maximise individual freedom. Needless to say, state ownership – what is commonly **called** "socialism" – is, for anarchists, not socialism at all. In fact, as we will elaborate in Section H, state "socialism" is just a form of capitalism, with no socialist content whatever. As Rudolf Rocker noted, for anarchists, socialism is *"not a simple question of a full belly, but a question of culture that would have to enlist the sense of personality and the free initiative of the individual; without freedom it would lead only to a dismal state capitalism which would sacrifice all individual thought and feeling to a fictitious collective interest."* [quoted by Colin Ward, *"Introduction"*, Rudolf Rocker, **The London Years**, p. 1]

Given the anarchist pedigree of the word "libertarian," few anarchists are happy to see it stolen by an ideology which shares little with our ideas. In the United States, as Murray Bookchin noted, the *"term 'libertarian' itself, to be sure, raises a problem, notably, the specious identification of an anti-authoritarian ideology with a straggling movement for 'pure capitalism' and 'free trade.' This movement never created the word: it appropriated it from the anarchist movement of the [nineteenth] century. And it should be recovered by those anti-authoritarians ... who try to speak for dominated people as a whole, not for personal egotists who identify freedom with entrepreneurship and profit."* Thus anarchists in America should *"restore in practice a tradition that has been denatured by"* the free-market right. [**The Modern Crisis**, pp. 154-5] As we do that, we will continue to call our ideas libertarian socialism.

A.1.4 Are anarchists socialists?

Yes. All branches of anarchism are opposed to capitalism. This is because capitalism is based upon oppression and exploitation (see sections B and C). Anarchists reject the *"notion that men cannot work together unless they have a driving-master to take a percentage of their product"* and think that in an anarchist society

"the real workmen will make their own regulations, decide when and where and how things shall be done." By so doing workers would free themselves *"from the terrible bondage of capitalism."* [Voltairine de Cleyre, *"Anarchism"*, **Exquisite Rebel**, p. 75 and p. 79]

(We must stress here that anarchists are opposed to **all** economic forms which are based on domination and exploitation, including feudalism, Soviet-style "socialism" – better called "state capitalism" – , slavery and so on. We concentrate on capitalism because that is what is dominating the world just now).

Individualists like Benjamin Tucker along with social anarchists like Proudhon and Bakunin proclaimed themselves *"socialists."* They did so because, as Kropotkin put it in his classic essay *"Modern Science and Anarchism,"* *"[s]o long as Socialism was understood in its wide, generic, and true sense – as an effort to **abolish** the exploitation of Labour by Capital – the Anarchists were marching hand-in-hands with the Socialists of that time."* [**Evolution and Environment**, p. 81] Or, in Tucker's words, *"the bottom claim of Socialism [is] that labour should be put in possession of its own,"* a claim that both *"the two schools of Socialistic thought ... State Socialism and Anarchism"* agreed upon. [**The Anarchist Reader**, p. 144] Hence the word *"socialist"* was originally defined to include *"all those who believed in the individual's right to possess what he or she produced."* [Lance Klafta, *"Ayn Rand and the Perversion of Libertarianism,"* in **Anarchy: A Journal of Desire Armed**, no. 34] This opposition to exploitation (or usury) is shared by all true anarchists and places them under the socialist banner.

For most socialists, *"the only guarantee not to be robbed of the fruits of your labour is to possess the instruments of labour."* [Peter Kropotkin, **The Conquest of Bread**, p. 145] For this reason Proudhon, for example, supported workers' co-operatives, where *"every individual employed in the association ... has an undivided share in the property of the company"* because by *"participation in losses and gains ... the collective force [i.e. surplus] ceases to be a source of profits for a small number of managers: it becomes the property of all workers."* [**The General Idea of the Revolution**, p. 222 and p. 223] Thus, in addition to desiring the end of exploitation of labour by capital, true socialists also desire a society within which the producers own and control the means of production (including, it should be stressed, those workplaces which supply services). The means by which the producers will do this is a moot point in anarchist and other socialist circles, but the desire remains a common one. Anarchists favour direct workers' control and either ownership by workers' associations or by the commune (see section A.3 on the different types of anarchists).

Moreover, anarchists also reject capitalism for being authoritarian **as well as** exploitative. Under capitalism, workers do not govern themselves during the production process nor have control over the product of their labour. Such a situation is hardly based on equal freedom for all, nor can it be non-exploitative, and is so opposed by anarchists. This perspective can best be found in the work of Proudhon (who inspired both Tucker and Bakunin) where he argues that anarchism would see *"[c]apitalistic and proprietary exploitation stopped everywhere [and] the wage system abolished"* for *"either the workman ... will be simply the employee of the proprietor-capitalist-promoter; or he will participate.... In the first case the* workman is subordinated, exploited: his permanent condition is one of obedience ... In the second case he resumes his dignity as a man and citizen ... he forms part of the producing organisation, of which he was before but the slave ... we need not hesitate, for we have no choice ... it is necessary to form an ASSOCIATION among workers ... because without that, they would remain related as subordinates and superiors, and there would ensue two ... castes of masters and wage-workers, which is repugnant to a free and democratic society." [**Op. Cit.**, p. 233 and pp. 215-216]

Therefore **all** anarchists are anti-capitalist ("If labour owned the wealth it produced, there would be no capitalism" [Alexander Berkman, **What is Anarchism?**, p. 44]). Benjamin Tucker, for example – the anarchist most influenced by liberalism (as we will discuss later) – called his ideas "Anarchistic-Socialism" and denounced capitalism as a system based upon "the usurer, the receiver of interest, rent and profit." Tucker held that in an anarchist, non-capitalist, free-market society, capitalists will become redundant and exploitation of labour by capital would cease, since "labour ... will ... secure its natural wage, its entire product." [**The Individualist Anarchists**, p. 82 and p. 85] Such an economy will be based on mutual banking and the free exchange of products between co-operatives, artisans and peasants. For Tucker, and other Individualist anarchists, capitalism is not a true free market, being marked by various laws and monopolies which ensure that capitalists have the advantage over working people, so ensuring the latter's exploitation via profit, interest and rent (see section G for a fuller discussion). Even Max Stirner, the arch-egoist, had nothing but scorn for capitalist society and its various "spooks," which for him meant ideas that are treated as sacred or religious, such as private property, competition, division of labour, and so forth.

So anarchists consider themselves as socialists, but socialists of a specific kind – *libertarian socialists*. As the individualist anarchist Joseph A. Labadie puts it (echoing both Tucker and Bakunin):

> "It is said that Anarchism is not socialism. This is a mistake. Anarchism is voluntary Socialism. There are two kinds of Socialism, archistic and anarchistic, authoritarian and libertarian, state and free. Indeed, every proposition for social betterment is either to increase or decrease the powers of external wills and forces over the individual. As they increase they are archistic; as they decrease they are anarchistic." [**Anarchism: What It Is and What It Is Not**]

Labadie stated on many occasions that "all anarchists are socialists, but not all socialists are anarchists." Therefore, Daniel Guérin's comment that "Anarchism is really a synonym for socialism. The anarchist is primarily a socialist whose aim is to abolish the exploitation of man by man" is echoed throughout the history of the anarchist movement, be it the social or individualist wings. [**Anarchism**, p. 12] Indeed, the Haymarket Martyr Adolph Fischer used almost exactly the same words as Labadie to express the same fact – "every anarchist is a socialist, but every socialist is not necessarily an anarchist" – while acknowledging that the movement was "divided into two factions; the communistic anarchists and the Proudhon or middle-class anarchists." [**The Autobiographies of the Haymarket Martyrs**, p. 81]

So while social and individualist anarchists do disagree on many issues – for example, whether a true, that is non-capitalist, free market would be the best means of maximising liberty – they agree that capitalism is to be opposed as exploitative and oppressive and that an anarchist society must, by definition, be based on associated, not wage, labour. Only associated labour will "decrease the powers of external wills and forces over the individual" during working hours and such self-management of work by those who do it is the core ideal of real socialism. This perspective can be seen when Joseph Labadie argued that the trade union was "the exemplification of gaining freedom by association" and that "[w]ithout his union, the workman is much more the slave of his employer than he is with it." [**Different Phases of the Labour Question**]

However, the meanings of words change over time. Today "socialism" almost always refers to **state** socialism, a system that all anarchists have opposed as a denial of freedom and genuine socialist ideals. All anarchists would agree with Noam Chomsky's statement on this issue:

> "If the left is understood to include 'Bolshevism,' then I would flatly dissociate myself from the left. Lenin was one of the greatest enemies of socialism." [**Marxism, Anarchism, and Alternative Futures**, p. 779]

Anarchism developed in constant opposition to the ideas of Marxism, social democracy and Leninism. Long before Lenin rose to power, Mikhail Bakunin warned the followers of Marx against the "Red bureaucracy" that would institute "the worst of all despotic governments" if Marx's state-socialist ideas were ever implemented. Indeed, the works of Stirner, Proudhon and especially Bakunin all predict the horror of state Socialism with great accuracy. In addition, the anarchists were among the first and most vocal critics of and opposition to the Bolshevik regime in Russia.

Nevertheless, being socialists, anarchists do share **some** ideas with **some** Marxists (though none with Leninists). Both Bakunin and Tucker accepted Marx's analysis and critique of capitalism as well as his labour theory of value (see section C). Marx himself was heavily influenced by Max Stirner's book **The Ego and Its Own**, which contains a brilliant critique of what Marx called "vulgar" communism as well as state socialism. There have also been elements of the Marxist movement holding views very similar to social anarchism (particularly the anarcho-syndicalist branch of social anarchism) – for example, Anton Pannekoek, Rosa Luxembourg, Paul Mattick and others, who are very far from Lenin. Karl Korsch and others wrote sympathetically of the anarchist revolution in Spain. There are many continuities from Marx to Lenin, but there are also continuities from Marx to more libertarian Marxists, who were harshly critical of Lenin and Bolshevism and whose ideas approximate anarchism's desire for the free association of equals.

Therefore anarchism is basically a form of socialism, one that stands in direct opposition to what is usually defined as "socialism" (i.e. state ownership and control). Instead of "central planning," which many people associate with the word "socialism," anarchists advocate free association and co-operation between individuals, workplaces and communities and so oppose "state" socialism as a form of state capitalism in which "[e]very man [and woman] will be a wage-receiver, and the State the only wage payer." [Benjamin

Tucker, **The Individualist Anarchists**, p. 81] Thus anarchists reject Marxism (what most people think of as "socialism") as just "[t]he idea of the State as Capitalist, to which the Social-Democratic fraction of the great Socialist Party is now trying to reduce Socialism." [Peter Kropotkin, **The Great French Revolution**, vol. 1, p. 31] The anarchist objection to the identification of Marxism, "central planning" and State Socialism/Capitalism with socialism will be discussed in section H.

It is because of these differences with state socialists, and to reduce confusion, most anarchists just call themselves "anarchists," as it is taken for granted that anarchists are socialists. However, with the rise of the so-called "libertarian" right in the USA, some pro-capitalists have taken to calling themselves "anarchists" and that is why we have laboured the point somewhat here. Historically, and logically, anarchism implies anti-capitalism, i.e. socialism, which is something, we stress, that all anarchists have agreed upon (for a fuller discuss of why "anarcho"-capitalism is not anarchist see section F).

A.1.5 Where does anarchism come from?

Where does anarchism come from? We can do no better than quote **The Organisational Platform of the Libertarian Communists** produced by participants of the Makhnovist movement in the Russian Revolution (see Section A.5.4). They point out that:

"The class struggle created by the enslavement of workers and their aspirations to liberty gave birth, in the oppression, to the idea of anarchism: the idea of the total negation of a social system based on the principles of classes and the State, and its replacement by a free non-statist society of workers under self-management.

"So anarchism does not derive from the abstract reflections of an intellectual or a philosopher, but from the direct struggle of workers against capitalism, from the needs and necessities of the workers, from their aspirations to liberty and equality, aspirations which become particularly alive in the best heroic period of the life and struggle of the working masses.

"The outstanding anarchist thinkers, Bakunin, Kropotkin and others, did not invent the idea of anarchism, but, having discovered it in the masses, simply helped by the strength of their thought and knowledge to specify and spread it." [pp. 15-16]

Like the anarchist movement in general, the Makhnovists were a mass movement of working class people resisting the forces of authority, both Red (Communist) and White (Tsarist/Capitalist) in the Ukraine from 1917 to 1921. As Peter Marshall notes "anarchism ... has traditionally found its chief supporters amongst workers and peasants." [**Demanding the Impossible**, p. 652] Anarchism was created in, and by, the struggle of the oppressed for freedom. For Kropotkin, for example, "Anarchism ... originated

in everyday struggles" and "the Anarchist movement was renewed each time it received an impression from some great practical lesson: it derived its origin from the teachings of life itself." [**Evolution and Environment**, p. 58 and p. 57] For Proudhon, "the proof" of his mutualist ideas lay in the "current practice, revolutionary practice" of "those labour associations ... which have spontaneously ... been formed in Paris and Lyon ... [show that the] organisation of credit and organisation of labour amount to one and the same." [**No Gods, No Masters**, vol. 1, pp. 59-60] Indeed, as one historian argues, there was "close similarity between the associational ideal of Proudhon ... and the program of the Lyon Mutualists" and that there was "a remarkable convergence [between the ideas], and it is likely that Proudhon was able to articulate his positive program more coherently because of the example of the silk workers of Lyon. The socialist ideal that he championed was already being realised, to a certain extent, by such workers." [K. Steven Vincent, **Pierre-Joseph Proudhon and the Rise of French Republican Socialism**, p. 164]

Thus anarchism comes from the fight for liberty and our desires to lead a fully human life, one in which we have time to live, to love and to play. It was not created by a few people divorced from life, in ivory towers looking down upon society and making judgements upon it based on their notions of what is right and wrong. Rather, it was a product of working class struggle and resistance to authority, oppression and exploitation. As Albert Meltzer put it:

"There were never theoreticians of Anarchism as such, though it produced a number of theoreticians who discussed aspects of its philosophy. Anarchism has remained a creed that has been worked out in action rather than as the putting into practice of an intellectual idea. Very often, a bourgeois writer comes along and writes down what has already been worked out in practice by workers and peasants; he [or she] is attributed by bourgeois historians as being a leader, and by successive bourgeois writers (citing the bourgeois historians) as being one more case that proves the working class relies on bourgeois leadership." [**Anarchism: Arguments for and against**, p. 18]

In Kropotkin's eyes, "Anarchism had its origins in the same creative, constructive activity of the masses which has worked out in times past all the social institutions of mankind – and in the revolts ... against the representatives of force, external to these social institutions, who had laid their hands on these institutions and used them for their own advantage." More recently, "Anarchy was brought forth by the same critical and revolutionary protest which gave birth to Socialism in general." Anarchism, unlike other forms of socialism, "lifted its sacrilegious arm, not only against Capitalism, but also against these pillars of Capitalism: Law, Authority, and the State." All anarchist writers did was to "work out a general expression of [anarchism's] principles, and the theoretical and scientific basis of its teachings" derived from the experiences of working class people in struggle as well as analysing the evolutionary tendencies of society in general. [**Op. Cit.**, p. 19 and p. 57]

However, anarchistic tendencies and organisations in society have existed long before Proudhon put pen to paper in 1840 and declared himself an anarchist. While anarchism, as a specific political theory, was born with the rise of capitalism (Anarchism *"emerged at the end of the eighteenth century ... [and] took up the dual challenge of overthrowing both Capital and the State."* [Peter Marshall, **Op. Cit.**, p. 4]) anarchist writers have analysed history for libertarian tendencies. Kropotkin argued, for example, that *"from all times there have been Anarchists and Statists."* [**Op. Cit.**, p. 16] In **Mutual Aid** (and elsewhere) Kropotkin analysed the libertarian aspects of previous societies and noted those that successfully implemented (to some degree) anarchist organisation or aspects of anarchism. He recognised this tendency of actual examples of anarchistic ideas to predate the creation of the "official" anarchist movement and argued that:

> *"From the remotest, stone-age antiquity, men [and women] have realised the evils that resulted from letting some of them acquire personal authority ... Consequently they developed in the primitive clan, the village community, the medieval guild ... and finally in the free medieval city, such institutions as enabled them to resist the encroachments upon their life and fortunes both of those strangers who conquered them, and those clansmen of their own who endeavoured to establish their personal authority."* [**Anarchism**, pp. 158-9]

Kropotkin placed the struggle of working class people (from which modern anarchism sprung) on par with these older forms of popular organisation. He argued that *"the labour combinations ... were an outcome of the same popular resistance to the growing power of the few – the capitalists in this case"* as were the clan, the village community and so on, as were *"the strikingly independent, freely federated activity of the 'Sections' of Paris and all great cities and many small 'Communes' during the French Revolution"* in 1793. [**Op. Cit.**, p. 159]

Thus, while anarchism as a political theory is an expression of working class struggle and self-activity against capitalism and the modern state, the ideas of anarchism have continually expressed themselves in action throughout human existence. Many indigenous peoples in North America and elsewhere, for example, practised anarchism for thousands of years before anarchism as a specific political theory existed. Similarly, anarchistic tendencies and organisations have existed in every major revolution – the New England Town Meetings during the American Revolution, the Parisian 'Sections' during the French Revolution, the workers' councils and factory committees during the Russian Revolution to name just a few examples (see Murray Bookchin's **The Third Revolution** for details). This is to be expected if anarchism is, as we argue, a product of resistance to authority then any society with authorities will provoke resistance to them and generate anarchistic tendencies (and, of course, any societies without authorities cannot help but being anarchistic).

In other words, anarchism is an expression of the struggle against oppression and exploitation, a generalisation of working people's experiences and analyses of what is wrong with the current system and an expression of our hopes and dreams for a better future. This struggle existed before it was called anarchism, but the historic anarchist movement (i.e. groups of people calling their ideas anarchism and aiming for an anarchist society) is essentially a product of working class struggle against capitalism and the state, against oppression and exploitation, and **for** a free society of free and equal individuals.

A.2

What does anarchism stand for?

These words by Percy Bysshe Shelley gives an idea of what anarchism stands for in practice and what ideals drive it:

> *The man*
> *Of virtuous soul commands not, nor obeys:*
> *Power, like a desolating pestilence,*
> *Pollutes whate'er it touches, and obedience,*
> *Bane of all genius, virtue, freedom, truth,*
> *Makes slaves of men, and, of the human frame,*
> *A mechanised automaton.*

As Shelley's lines suggest, anarchists place a high priority on liberty, desiring it both for themselves and others. They also consider individuality – that which makes one a unique person – to be a most important aspect of humanity. They recognise, however, that individuality does not exist in a vacuum but is a **social** phenomenon. Outside of society, individuality is impossible, since one needs other people in order to develop, expand, and grow.

Moreover, between individual and social development there is a reciprocal effect: individuals grow within and are shaped by a particular society, while at the same time they help shape and change aspects of that society (as well as themselves and other individuals) by their actions and thoughts. A society not based on free individuals, their hopes, dreams and ideas would be hollow and dead. Thus, *"the making of a human being ... is a collective process, a process in which both community and the individual* **participate**." [Murray Bookchin, **The Modern Crisis**, p. 79] Consequently, any political theory which bases itself purely on the social or the individual is false.

In order for individuality to develop to the fullest possible extent, anarchists consider it essential to create a society based on three principles: **liberty**, **equality** and **solidarity**. These principles are shared by all anarchists. Thus we find, the communist-anarchist Peter Kropotkin talking about a revolution inspired by *"the beautiful words, Liberty, Equality and Solidarity."* [**The Conquest of Bread**, p. 128] Individualist-anarchist Benjamin Tucker wrote of a similar vision, arguing that anarchism *"insists on Socialism ... on true Socialism, Anarchistic Socialism: the prevalence on earth of Liberty, Equality, and Solidarity."* [**Instead of a Book**, p. 363] All three principles are interdependent.

Liberty is essential for the full flowering of human intelligence, creativity, and dignity. To be dominated by another is to be denied the chance to think and act for oneself, which is the only way to grow and develop one's individuality. Domination also stifles innovation and personal responsibility, leading to conformity and mediocrity. Thus the society that maximises the growth of individuality will necessarily be based on voluntary association, not coercion and authority. To quote Proudhon, *"All associated and all free."* Or, as

Luigi Galleani puts it, anarchism is *"the autonomy of the individual within the freedom of association"* [**The End of Anarchism?**, p. 35] (See further section A.2.2 – Why do anarchists emphasise liberty?).

If liberty is essential for the fullest development of individuality, then equality is essential for genuine liberty to exist. There can be no real freedom in a class-stratified, hierarchical society riddled with gross inequalities of power, wealth, and privilege. For in such a society only a few – those at the top of the hierarchy – are relatively free, while the rest are semi-slaves. Hence without equality, liberty becomes a mockery – at best the "freedom" to choose one's master (boss), as under capitalism. Moreover, even the elite under such conditions are not really free, because they must live in a stunted society made ugly and barren by the tyranny and alienation of the majority. And since individuality develops to the fullest only with the widest contact with other free individuals, members of the elite are restricted in the possibilities for their own development by the scarcity of free individuals with whom to interact. (See also section A.2.5 – Why are anarchists in favour of equality?)

Finally, solidarity means mutual aid: working voluntarily and co-operatively with others who share the same goals and interests. But without liberty and equality, society becomes a pyramid of competing classes based on the domination of the lower by the higher strata. In such a society, as we know from our own, it's "dominate or be dominated," "dog eat dog," and "everyone for themselves." Thus "rugged individualism" is promoted at the expense of community feeling, with those on the bottom resenting those above them and those on the top fearing those below them. Under such conditions, there can be no society-wide solidarity, but only a partial form of solidarity within classes whose interests are opposed, which weakens society as a whole. (See also section A.2.6 – Why is solidarity important to anarchists?)

It should be noted that solidarity does not imply self-sacrifice or self-negation. As Errico Malatesta makes clear:

> *"we are all egoists, we all seek our own satisfaction. But the anarchist finds his greatest satisfaction in struggling for the good of all, for the achievement of a society in which he [sic] can be a brother among brothers, and among healthy, intelligent, educated, and happy people. But he who is adaptable, who is satisfied to live among slaves and draw profit from the labour of slaves, is not, and cannot be, an anarchist."* [**Errico Malatesta: His Life and Ideas**, p. 23]

For anarchists, **real** wealth is other people and the planet on which we live. Or, in the words of Emma Goldman, it *"consists in things of utility and beauty, in things which help to create strong, beautiful bodies and surroundings inspiring to live in … [Our] goal is the freest possible expression of all the latent powers of the individual … Such free display of human energy being possible only under complete individual and social freedom,"* in other words *"social equality."* [**Red Emma Speaks**, pp. 67-8]

Also, honouring individuality does not mean that anarchists are idealists, thinking that people or ideas develop outside of society. Individuality and ideas grow and develop within society, in response to material and intellectual interactions and experiences, which people actively analyse and interpret. Anarchism, therefore, is a **materialist** theory, recognising that ideas develop and grow from social interaction and individuals' mental activity (see Michael Bakunin's **God and the State** for the classic discussion of materialism versus idealism).

This means that an anarchist society will be the creation of human beings, not some deity or other transcendental principle, since *"[n]othing ever arranges itself, least of all in human relations. It is men [sic] who do the arranging, and they do it according to their attitudes and understanding of things."* [Alexander Berkman, **What is Anarchism?**, p. 185]

Therefore, anarchism bases itself upon the power of ideas and the ability of people to act and transform their lives based on what they consider to be right. In other words, liberty.

A.2.1 What is the essence of anarchism?

As we have seen, *"an-archy"* implies *"without rulers"* or *"without (hierarchical) authority."* Anarchists are not against "authorities" in the sense of experts who are particularly knowledgeable, skilful, or wise, though they believe that such authorities should have no power to force others to follow their recommendations (see section B.1 for more on this distinction). In a nutshell, then, anarchism is anti-authoritarianism.

Anarchists are anti-authoritarians because they believe that no human being should dominate another. Anarchists, in L. Susan Brown's words, *"believe in the inherent dignity and worth of the human individual."* [**The Politics of Individualism**, p. 107] Domination is inherently degrading and demeaning, since it submerges the will and judgement of the dominated to the will and judgement of the dominators, thus destroying the dignity and self-respect that comes only from personal autonomy. Moreover, domination makes possible and generally leads to exploitation, which is the root of inequality, poverty, and social breakdown.

In other words, then, the essence of anarchism (to express it positively) is free co-operation between equals to maximise their liberty and individuality.

Co-operation between equals is the key to anti-authoritarianism. By co-operation we can develop and protect our own intrinsic value as unique individuals as well as enriching our lives and liberty for *"[n]o individual can recognise his own humanity, and consequently realise it in his lifetime, if not by recognising it in others and co-operating in its realisation for others … My freedom is the freedom of all since I am not truly free in thought and in fact, except when my freedom and my rights are confirmed and approved in the freedom and rights of all men [and women] who are my equals."* [Michael Bakunin, quoted by Errico Malatesta, **Anarchy**, p. 30]

While being anti-authoritarians, anarchists recognise that human beings have a social nature and that they mutually influence each other. We cannot escape the "authority" of this mutual influence, because, as Bakunin reminds us:

> *"The abolition of this mutual influence would be death. And when we advocate the freedom of the masses, we*

are by no means suggesting the abolition of any of the natural influences that individuals or groups of individuals exert on them. What we want is the abolition of influences which are artificial, privileged, legal, official." [quoted by Malatesta, **Anarchy**, p. 51]

In other words, those influences which stem from hierarchical authority.

This is because hierarchical systems like capitalism deny liberty and, as a result, people's *"mental, moral, intellectual and physical qualities are dwarfed, stunted and crushed"* (see section B.1 for more details). Thus one of *"the grand truths of Anarchism"* is that *"to be really free is to allow each one to live their lives in their own way as long as each allows all to do the same."* This is why anarchists fight for a better society, for a society which respects individuals and their freedom. Under capitalism, *"[e]verything is upon the market for sale: all is merchandise and commerce"* but there are *"certain things that are priceless. Among these are life, liberty and happiness, and these are things which the society of the future, the free society, will guarantee to all."* Anarchists, as a result, seek to make people aware of their dignity, individuality and liberty and to encourage the spirit of revolt, resistance and solidarity in those subject to authority. This gets us denounced by the powerful as being breakers of the peace, but anarchists consider the struggle for freedom as infinitely better than the peace of slavery. Anarchists, as a result of our ideals, *"believe in peace at any price – except at the price of liberty. But this precious gift the wealth-producers already seem to have lost. Life … they have; but what is life worth when it lacks those elements which make for enjoyment?"* [Lucy Parsons, **Liberty, Equality & Solidarity**, p. 103, p. 131, p. 103 and p. 134]

So, in a nutshell, Anarchists seek a society in which people interact in ways which enhance the liberty of all rather than crush the liberty (and so potential) of the many for the benefit of a few. Anarchists do not want to give others power over themselves, the power to tell them what to do under the threat of punishment if they do not obey. Perhaps non-anarchists, rather than be puzzled why anarchists are anarchists, would be better off asking what it says about themselves that they feel this attitude needs any sort of explanation.

A.2.2 Why do anarchists emphasise liberty?

An anarchist can be regarded, in Bakunin's words, as a *"fanatic lover of freedom, considering it as the unique environment within which the intelligence, dignity and happiness of mankind can develop and increase."* [**Michael Bakunin: Selected Writings**, p. 196] Because human beings are thinking creatures, to deny them liberty is to deny them the opportunity to think for themselves, which is to deny their very existence as humans. For anarchists, freedom is a product of our humanity, because:

> *"The very fact … that a person has a consciousness of self, of being different from others, creates a desire to act freely. The craving for liberty and self-expression is a*

very fundamental and dominant trait." [Emma Goldman, **Red Emma Speaks**, p. 439]

For this reason, anarchism *"proposes to rescue the self-respect and independence of the individual from all restraint and invasion by authority. Only in freedom can man [sic!] grow to his full stature. Only in freedom will he learn to think and move, and give the very best of himself. Only in freedom will he realise the true force of the social bonds which tie men together, and which are the true foundations of a normal social life."* [**Op. Cit.**, pp. 72-3]

Thus, for anarchists, freedom is basically individuals pursuing their own good in their own way. Doing so calls forth the activity and power of individuals as they make decisions for and about themselves and their lives. Only liberty can ensure individual development and diversity. This is because when individuals govern themselves and make their own decisions they have to exercise their minds and this can have no other effect than expanding and stimulating the individuals involved. As Malatesta put it, *"[f]or people to become educated to freedom and the management of their own interests, they must be left to act for themselves, to feel responsibility for their own actions in the good or bad that comes from them. They'd make mistakes, but they'd understand from the consequences where they'd gone wrong and try out new ways."* [**Fra Contadini**, p. 26]

So, liberty is the precondition for the maximum development of one's individual potential, which is also a social product and can be achieved only in and through community. A healthy, free community will produce free individuals, who in turn will shape the community and enrich the social relationships between the people of whom it is composed. Liberties, being socially produced, *"do not exist because they have been legally set down on a piece of paper, but only when they have become the ingrown habit of a people, and when any attempt to impair them will meet with the violent resistance of the populace … One compels respect from others when one knows how to defend one's dignity as a human being. This is not only true in private life; it has always been the same in political life as well."* In fact, we *"owe all the political rights and privileges which we enjoy today in greater or lesser measures, not to the good will of their governments, but to their own strength."* [Rudolf Rocker, **Anarcho-syndicalism**, p. 75]

It is for this reason anarchists support the tactic of ***"Direct Action"*** (see section J.2) for, as Emma Goldman argued, we have *"as much liberty as [we are] willing to take. Anarchism therefore stands for direct action, the open defiance of, and resistance to, all laws and restrictions, economic, social, and moral."* It requires *"integrity, self-reliance, and courage. In short, it calls for free, independent spirits"* and *"only persistent resistance"* can *"finally set [us] free. Direct action against the authority in the shop, direct action against the authority of the law, direct action against the invasive, meddlesome authority of our moral code, is the logical, consistent method of Anarchism."* [**Red Emma Speaks**, pp. 76-7]

Direct action is, in other words, the application of liberty, used to resist oppression in the here and now as well as the means of creating a free society. It creates the necessary individual mentality and social conditions in which liberty flourishes. Both are essential as liberty develops only within society, not in opposition to it. Thus

Murray Bookchin writes:

*"What freedom, independence, and autonomy people have in a given historical period is the product of long social traditions and … a **collective** development – which is not to deny that individuals play an important role in that development, indeed are ultimately obliged to do so if they wish to be free."* [**Social Anarchism or Lifestyle Anarchism**, p. 15]

But freedom requires the right **kind** of social environment in which to grow and develop. Such an environment **must** be decentralised and based on the direct management of work by those who do it. For centralisation means coercive authority (hierarchy), whereas self-management is the essence of freedom. Self-management ensures that the individuals involved use (and so develop) all their abilities – particularly their mental ones. Hierarchy, in contrast, substitutes the activities and thoughts of a few for the activities and thoughts of all the individuals involved. Thus, rather than developing their abilities to the full, hierarchy marginalises the many and ensures that their development is blunted (see also section B.1).

It is for this reason that anarchists oppose both capitalism and statism. As the French anarchist Sébastien Faure noted, authority *"dresses itself in two principal forms: the political form, that is the State; and the economic form, that is private property."* [cited by Peter Marshall, **Demanding the Impossible**, p. 43] Capitalism, like the state, is based on centralised authority (i.e. of the boss over the worker), the very purpose of which is to keep the management of work out of the hands of those who do it. This means *"that the serious, final, complete liberation of the workers is possible only upon one condition: that of the appropriation of capital, that is, of raw material and all the tools of labour, including land, by the whole body of the workers."* [Michael Bakunin, quoted by Rudolf Rocker, **Op. Cit.**, p. 50]

Hence, as Noam Chomsky argues, a *"consistent anarchist must oppose private ownership of the means of production and the wage slavery which is a component of this system, as incompatible with the principle that labour must be freely undertaken and under the control of the producer."* [*"Notes on Anarchism"*, **For Reasons of State**, p. 158]

Thus, liberty for anarchists means a non-authoritarian society in which individuals and groups practice self-management, i.e. they govern themselves. The implications of this are important. First, it implies that an anarchist society will be non-coercive, that is, one in which violence or the threat of violence will not be used to "convince" individuals to do anything. Second, it implies that anarchists are firm supporters of individual sovereignty, and that, because of this support, they also oppose institutions based on coercive authority, i.e. hierarchy. And finally, it implies that anarchists' opposition to "government" means only that they oppose centralised, hierarchical, bureaucratic organisations or government. They do not oppose self-government through confederations of decentralised, grassroots organisations, so long as these are based on direct democracy rather than the delegation of power to "representatives" (see section A.2.9 for more on anarchist organisation). For authority is the opposite of liberty, and hence any form of organisation based on the delegation of power is a threat to the liberty and dignity of the

people subjected to that power.

Anarchists consider freedom to be the only social environment within which human dignity and diversity can flower. Under capitalism and statism, however, there is no freedom for the majority, as private property and hierarchy ensure that the inclination and judgement of most individuals will be subordinated to the will of a master, severely restricting their liberty and making impossible the *"full development of all the material, intellectual and moral capacities that are latent in every one of us."* [Michael Bakunin, **Bakunin on Anarchism**, p. 261] That is why anarchists seek to ensure *"that real justice and real liberty might come on earth"* for it is *"all false, all unnecessary, this wild waste of human life, of bone and sinew and brain and heart, this turning of people into human rags, ghosts, piteous caricatures of the creatures they had it in them to be, on the day they were born; that what is called 'economy', the massing up of things, is in reality the most frightful spending – the sacrifice of the maker to the made – the loss of all the finer and nobler instincts in the gain of one revolting attribute, the power to count and calculate."* [Voltairine de Cleyre, **The First Mayday: The Haymarket Speeches 1895-1910**, pp, 17-18]

(See section B for further discussion of the hierarchical and authoritarian nature of capitalism and statism).

A.2.3 Are anarchists in favour of organisation?

Yes. Without association, a truly human life is impossible. Liberty **cannot** exist without society and organisation. As George Barrett pointed out:

"To get the full meaning out of life we must co-operate, and to co-operate we must make agreements with our fellow-men. But to suppose that such agreements mean a limitation of freedom is surely an absurdity; on the contrary, they are the exercise of our freedom.

"If we are going to invent a dogma that to make agreements is to damage freedom, then at once freedom becomes tyrannical, for it forbids men to take the most ordinary everyday pleasures. For example, I cannot go for a walk with my friend because it is against the principle of Liberty that I should agree to be at a certain place at a certain time to meet him. I cannot in the least extend my own power beyond myself, because to do so I must co-operate with someone else, and co-operation implies an agreement, and that is against Liberty. It will be seen at once that this argument is absurd. I do not limit my liberty, but simply exercise it, when I agree with my friend to go for a walk.

"If, on the other hand, I decide from my superior knowledge that it is good for my friend to take exercise, and therefore I attempt to compel him to go for a walk, then I begin to limit freedom. This is the difference between free agreement and government." [**Objections to Anarchism**, pp. 348-9]

As far as organisation goes, anarchists think that *"far from creating authority, [it] is the only cure for it and the only means whereby each of us will get used to taking an active and conscious part in collective work, and cease being passive instruments in the hands of leaders."* [Errico Malatesta, **Errico Malatesta: His Life and Ideas**, p. 86] Thus anarchists are well aware of the need to organise in a structured and open manner. As Carole Ehrlich points out, while anarchists *"aren't opposed to structure"* and simply *"want to abolish **hierarchical** structure"* they are *"almost always stereotyped as wanting no structure at all."* This is not the case, for *"organisations that would build in accountability, diffusion of power among the maximum number of persons, task rotation, skill-sharing, and the spread of information and resources"* are based on *"good social anarchist principles of organisation!"* [*"Socialism, Anarchism and Feminism"*, **Quiet Rumours: An Anarcha-Feminist Reader**, p. 47 and p. 46]

The fact that anarchists are in favour of organisation may seem strange at first, but it is understandable. *"For those with experience only of authoritarian organisation,"* argue two British anarchists, *"it appears that organisation can only be totalitarian or democratic, and that those who disbelieve in government must by that token disbelieve in organisation at all. That is not so."* [Stuart Christie and Albert Meltzer, **The Floodgates of Anarchy**, p. 122] In other words, because we live in a society in which virtually all forms of organisation are authoritarian, this makes them appear to be the only kind possible. What is usually not recognised is that this mode of organisation is historically conditioned, arising within a specific kind of society – one whose motive principles are domination and exploitation. According to archaeologists and anthropologists, this kind of society has only existed for about 5,000 years, having appeared with the first primitive states based on conquest and slavery, in which the labour of slaves created a surplus which supported a ruling class.

Prior to that time, for hundreds of thousands of years, human and proto-human societies were what Murray Bookchin calls *"organic,"* that is, based on co-operative forms of economic activity involving mutual aid, free access to productive resources, and a sharing of the products of communal labour according to need. Although such societies probably had status rankings based on age, there were no hierarchies in the sense of institutionalised dominance-subordination relations enforced by coercive sanctions and resulting in class-stratification involving the economic exploitation of one class by another (see Murray Bookchin, **The Ecology of Freedom**).

It must be emphasised, however, that anarchists do **not** advocate going "back to the Stone Age." We merely note that since the hierarchical-authoritarian mode of organisation is a relatively recent development in the course of human social evolution, there is no reason to suppose that it is somehow "fated" to be permanent. We do not think that human beings are genetically "programmed" for authoritarian, competitive, and aggressive behaviour, as there is no credible evidence to support this claim. On the contrary, such behaviour is socially conditioned, or **learned**, and as such, can be **unlearned** (see Ashley Montagu, **The Nature of Human Aggression**). We are not fatalists or genetic determinists, but believe in free will, which means that people can change the way they do things, including the way they organise society.

And there is no doubt that society needs to be better organised, because presently most of its wealth – which is produced by the majority – and power gets distributed to a small, elite minority at the top of the social pyramid, causing deprivation and suffering for the rest, particularly for those at the bottom. Yet because this elite controls the means of coercion through its control of the state (see section B.2.3), it is able to suppress the majority and ignore its suffering – a phenomenon that occurs on a smaller scale within all hierarchies. Little wonder, then, that people within authoritarian and centralised structures come to hate them as a denial of their freedom. As Alexander Berkman puts it:

> *"Any one who tells you that Anarchists don't believe in organisation is talking nonsense. Organisation is everything, and everything is organisation. The whole of life is organisation, conscious or unconscious … But there is organisation and organisation. Capitalist society is so badly organised that its various members suffer: just as when you have a pain in some part of you, your whole body aches and you are ill…, not a single member of the organisation or union may with impunity be discriminated against, suppressed or ignored. To do so would be the same as to ignore an aching tooth: you would be sick all over."* [**Op. Cit.**, p. 198]

Yet this is precisely what happens in capitalist society, with the result that it is, indeed, *"sick all over."*

For these reasons, anarchists reject authoritarian forms of organisation and instead support associations based on free agreement. Free agreement is important because, in Berkman's words, *"[o]nly when each is a free and independent unit, co-operating with others from his own choice because of mutual interests, can the world work successfully and become powerful."* [**Op. Cit.**, p. 199] As we discuss in section A.2.14, anarchists stress that free agreement has to be complemented by direct democracy (or, as it is usually called by anarchists, self-management) within the association itself otherwise "freedom" become little more than picking masters.

Anarchist organisation is based on a massive decentralisation of power back into the hands of the people, i.e. those who are directly affected by the decisions being made. To quote Proudhon:

> *"Unless democracy is a fraud and the sovereignty of the People a joke, it must be admitted that each citizen in the sphere of his [or her] industry, each municipal, district or provincial council within its own territory … should act directly and by itself in administering the interests which it includes, and should exercise full sovereignty in relation to them."* [**The General Idea of the Revolution**, p. 276]

It also implies a need for federalism to co-ordinate joint interests. For anarchism, federalism is the natural complement to self-management. With the abolition of the State, society *"can, and must, organise itself in a different fashion, but not from top to bottom … The future social organisation must be made solely from the bottom upwards, by the free association or federation of workers, firstly in their unions, then in the communes, regions, nations and finally in* a great federation, international and universal. Then alone will be realised the true and life-giving order of freedom and the common good, that order which, far from denying, on the contrary affirms and brings into harmony the interests of individuals and of society." [Bakunin, **Michael Bakunin: Selected Writings**, pp. 205-6] Because a "truly popular organisation begins ... from below" and so "federalism becomes a political institution of Socialism, the free and spontaneous organisation of popular life." Thus libertarian socialism "is federalistic in character." [Bakunin, **The Political Philosophy of Bakunin**, pp. 273-4 and p. 272]

Therefore, anarchist organisation is based on direct democracy (or self-management) and federalism (or confederation). These are the expression and environment of liberty. Direct (or participatory) democracy is essential because liberty and equality imply the need for forums within which people can discuss and debate as equals and which allow for the free exercise of what Murray Bookchin calls "the creative role of dissent." Federalism is necessary to ensure that common interests are discussed and joint activity organised in a way which reflects the wishes of all those affected by them. To ensure that decisions flow from the bottom up rather than being imposed from the top down by a few rulers.

Anarchist ideas on libertarian organisation and the need for direct democracy and confederation will be discussed further in sections A.2.9 and A.2.11.

A.2.4 Are anarchists in favour of "absolute" liberty?

No. Anarchists do not believe that everyone should be able to "do whatever they like," because some actions invariably involve the denial of the liberty of others.

For example, anarchists do not support the "freedom" to rape, to exploit, or to coerce others. Neither do we tolerate authority. On the contrary, since authority is a threat to liberty, equality, and solidarity (not to mention human dignity), anarchists recognise the need to resist and overthrow it.

The exercise of authority is not freedom. No one has a "right" to rule others. As Malatesta points out, anarchism supports "freedom for everybody ... with the only limit of the equal freedom for others; which does **not** mean ... that we recognise, and wish to respect, the 'freedom' to exploit, to oppress, to command, which is oppression and certainly not freedom." [**Errico Malatesta: His Life and Ideas**, p. 53]

In a capitalist society, resistance to all forms of hierarchical authority is the mark of a free person – be it private (the boss) or public (the state). As Henry David Thoreau pointed out in his essay on **"Civil Disobedience"** (1847)

"Disobedience is the true foundation of liberty. The obedient must be slaves."

A.2.5 Why are anarchists in favour of equality?

As mentioned in above, anarchists are dedicated to social equality because it is the only context in which individual liberty can flourish. However, there has been much nonsense written about "equality," and much of what is commonly believed about it is very strange indeed. Before discussing what anarchist **do** mean by equality, we have to indicate what we **do not** mean by it.

Anarchists do **not** believe in "equality of endowment," which is not only non-existent but would be **very** undesirable if it could be brought about. Everyone is unique. Biologically determined human differences not only exist but are "a cause for joy, not fear or regret." Why? Because "life among clones would not be worth living, and a sane person will only rejoice that others have abilities that they do not share." [Noam Chomsky, **Marxism, Anarchism, and Alternative Futures**, p. 782]

That some people **seriously** suggest that anarchists means by "equality" that everyone should be **identical** is a sad reflection on the state of present-day intellectual culture and the corruption of words – a corruption used to divert attention from an unjust and authoritarian system and side-track people into discussions of biology. "The uniqueness of the self in no way contradicts the principle of equality," noted Erich Fromm, "The thesis that men are born equal implies that they all share the same fundamental human qualities, that they share the same basic fate of human beings, that they all have the same inalienable claim on freedom and happiness. It furthermore means that their relationship is one of solidarity, not one of domination-submission. What the concept of equality does not mean is that all men are alike." [**The Fear of Freedom**, p. 228] Thus it would be fairer to say that anarchists seek equality **because** we recognise that everyone is different and, consequently, seek the full affirmation and development of that uniqueness.

Nor are anarchists in favour of so-called "equality of outcome." We have **no** desire to live in a society were everyone gets the same goods, lives in the same kind of house, wears the same uniform, etc. Part of the reason for the anarchist revolt against capitalism and statism is that they standardise so much of life (see George Reitzer's **The McDonaldisation of Society** on why capitalism is driven towards standardisation and conformity). In the words of Alexander Berkman:

"The spirit of authority, law, written and unwritten, tradition and custom force us into a common groove and make a man [or woman] a will-less automation without independence or individuality ... All of us are its victims, and only the exceptionally strong succeed in breaking its chains, and that only partly." [**What is Anarchism?**, p. 165]

Anarchists, therefore, have little to desire to make this "common grove" even deeper. Rather, we desire to destroy it and every social relationship and institution that creates it in the first place.

"Equality of outcome" can only be introduced and maintained by force, which would **not** be equality anyway, as some would have more power than others! "Equality of outcome" is particularly hated by anarchists, as we recognise that every individual has different needs, abilities, desires and interests. To make all consume the same would be tyranny. Obviously, if one person needs medical treatment and another does not, they do not receive an "equal" amount of medical care. The same is true of other human needs. As Alexander Berkman put it:

"equality does not mean an equal amount but equal **opportunity** ... Do not make the mistake of identifying equality in liberty with the forced equality of the convict camp. True anarchist equality implies freedom, not quantity. It does not mean that every one must eat, drink, or wear the same things, do the same work, or live in the same manner. Far from it: the very reverse in fact."

"Individual needs and tastes differ, as appetites differ. It is **equal opportunity to satisfy** them that constitutes true equality.

"Far from levelling, such equality opens the door for the greatest possible variety of activity and development. For human character is diverse ... Free opportunity of expressing and acting out your individuality means development of natural dissimilarities and variations." [**Op. Cit.**, pp. 164-5]

For anarchists, the "concepts" of "equality" as "equality of outcome" or "equality of endowment" are meaningless. However, in a hierarchical society, "equality of opportunity" and "equality of outcome" **are** related. Under capitalism, for example, the opportunities each generation face are dependent on the outcomes of the previous ones. This means that under capitalism "equality of opportunity" without a rough "equality of outcome" (in the sense of income and resources) becomes meaningless, as there is no real equality of opportunity for the off-spring of a millionaire and that of a road sweeper. Those who argue for "equality of opportunity" while ignoring the barriers created by previous outcomes indicate that they do not know what they are talking about – opportunity in a hierarchical society depends not only on an open road but also upon an equal start. From this obvious fact springs the misconception that anarchists desire "equality of outcome" – but this applies to a hierarchical system, in a free society this would not the case (as we will see).

Equality, in anarchist theory, does not mean denying individual diversity or uniqueness. As Bakunin observes:

"once equality has triumphed and is well established, will various individuals' abilities and their levels of energy cease to differ? Some will exist, perhaps not so many as now, but certainly some will always exist. It is proverbial that the same tree never bears two identical leaves, and this will probably be always be true. And it is even more truer with regard to human beings, who are much more complex than leaves. But this diversity is hardly an evil. On the contrary ... it is a resource of the human race. Thanks to this diversity, humanity is a collective whole in which the one individual complements all the others and needs them. As a result, this infinite diversity of human

individuals is the fundamental cause and the very basis of their solidarity. It is all-powerful argument for equality." ["All-Round Education", **The Basic Bakunin**, pp. 117-8]

Equality for anarchists means **social** equality, or, to use Murray Bookchin's term, the **"equality of unequals"** (some like Malatesta used the term **"equality of conditions"** to express the same idea). By this he means that an anarchist society recognises the differences in ability and need of individuals but does not allow these differences to be turned into power. Individual differences, in other words, "would be of no consequence, because inequality in fact is lost in the collectivity when it cannot cling to some legal fiction or institution." [Michael Bakunin, **God and the State**, p. 53]

If hierarchical social relationships, and the forces that create them, are abolished in favour of ones that encourage participation and are based on the principle of "one person, one vote" then natural differences would not be able to be turned into hierarchical power. For example, without capitalist property rights there would not be means by which a minority could monopolise the means of life (machinery and land) and enrich themselves by the work of others via the wages system and usury (profits, rent and interest). Similarly, if workers manage their own work, there is no class of capitalists to grow rich off their labour. Thus Proudhon:

"Now, what can be the origin of this inequality?

"As we see it, ... that origin is the realisation within society of this triple abstraction: capital, labour and talent.

"It is because society has divided itself into three categories of citizen corresponding to the three terms of the formula ... that caste distinctions have always been arrived at, and one half of the human race enslaved to the other ... socialism thus consists of reducing the aristocratic formula of capital-labour-talent into the simpler formula of labour! ... in order to make every citizen simultaneously, equally and to the same extent capitalist, labourer and expert or artist." [**No Gods, No Masters**, vol. 1, pp. 57-8]

Like all anarchists, Proudhon saw this integration of functions as the key to equality and freedom and proposed self-management as the means to achieve it. Thus self-management is the key to social equality. Social equality in the workplace, for example, means that everyone has an equal say in the policy decisions on how the workplace develops and changes. Anarchists are strong believers in the maxim "that which touches all, is decided by all."

This does not mean, of course, that expertise will be ignored or that everyone will decide everything. As far as expertise goes, different people have different interests, talents, and abilities, so obviously they will want to study different things and do different kinds of work. It is also obvious that when people are ill they consult a doctor – an expert – who manages his or her own work rather than being directed by a committee. We are sorry to have to bring these points up, but once the topics of social equality and workers' self-management come up, some people start to talk nonsense. It is common sense that a hospital managed in a socially equal way will **not** involve non-medical staff voting on how doctors should perform an operation!

In fact, social equality and individual liberty are inseparable. Without the collective self-management of decisions that affect a group (equality) to complement the individual self-management of decisions that affect the individual (liberty), a free society is impossible. For without both, some will have power over others, making decisions **for** them (i.e. governing them), and thus some will be more free than others. Which implies, just to state the obvious, anarchists seek equality in **all** aspects of life, not just in terms of wealth. Anarchists *"demand for every person not just his [or her] entire measure of the wealth of society but also his [or her] portion of social power."* [Malatesta and Hamon, **No Gods, No Masters**, vol. 2, p. 20] Thus self-management is needed to ensure both liberty **and** equality.

Social equality is required for individuals to both govern and express themselves, for the self-management it implies means *"people working in face-to-face relations with their fellows in order to bring the uniqueness of their own perspective to the business of solving common problems and achieving common goals."* [George Benello, **From the Ground Up**, p. 160] Thus equality allows the expression of individuality and so is a necessary base for individual liberty.

Section F.3 ("Why do 'anarcho'-capitalists place little or no value on equality?") discusses anarchist ideas on equality further. Noam Chomsky's essay *"Equality"* (contained in **The Chomsky Reader**) is a good summary of libertarian ideas on the subject.

A.2.6 Why is solidarity important to anarchists?

Solidarity, or mutual aid, is a key idea of anarchism. It is the link between the individual and society, the means by which individuals can work together to meet their common interests in an environment that supports and nurtures both liberty and equality. For anarchists, mutual aid is a fundamental feature of human life, a source of both strength and happiness and a fundamental requirement for a fully human existence.

Erich Fromm, noted psychologist and socialist humanist, points out that the *"human desire to experience union with others is rooted in the specific conditions of existence that characterise the human species and is one of the strongest motivations of human behaviour."* [**To Be or To Have**, p.107]

Therefore anarchists consider the desire to form "unions" (to use Max Stirner's term) with other people to be a natural need. These unions, or associations, must be based on equality and individuality in order to be fully satisfying to those who join them – i.e. they must be organised in an anarchist manner, i.e. voluntary, decentralised, and non-hierarchical.

Solidarity – co-operation between individuals – is necessary for life and is far from a denial of liberty. Solidarity, observed Errico Malatesta, *"is the only environment in which Man can express his personality and achieve his optimum development and enjoy the greatest possible wellbeing."* This *"coming together of individuals for the wellbeing of all, and of all for the wellbeing of each,"* results in *"the freedom of each not being limited by, but complemented – indeed finding the necessary **raison d'etre** in – the freedom*

of others." [**Anarchy**, p. 29] In other words, solidarity and co-operation means treating each other as equals, refusing to treat others as means to an end and creating relationships which support freedom for all rather than a few dominating the many. Emma Goldman reiterated this theme, noting *"what wonderful results this unique force of man's individuality has achieved when strengthened by co-operation with other individualities ... co-operation – as opposed to internecine strife and struggle – has worked for the survival and evolution of the species. ... only mutual aid and voluntary co-operation ... can create the basis for a free individual and associational life."* [**Red Emma Speaks**, p. 118]

Solidarity means associating together as equals in order to satisfy our common interests and needs. Forms of association not based on solidarity (i.e. those based on inequality) will crush the individuality of those subjected to them. As Ret Marut points out, liberty needs solidarity, the recognition of common interests:

> *"The most noble, pure and true love of mankind is the love of oneself. **I** want to be free! **I** hope to be happy! **I** want to appreciate all the beauties of the world. But my freedom is secured **only** when all other people around me are free. I can only be happy when all other people around me are happy. I can only be joyful when all the people I see and meet look at the world with joy-filled eyes. And **only** then can I eat my fill with pure enjoyment when I have the secure knowledge that other people, too, can eat their fill as I do. And for that reason it is a question of **my own contentment**, only of **my own self**, when I rebel against every danger which threatens my freedom and my happiness ... "* [Ret Marut (a.k.a. B. Traven), **The BrickBurner** magazine quoted by Karl S. Guthke, **B. Traven: The life behind the legends**, pp. 133-4]

To practice solidarity means that we recognise, as in the slogan of **Industrial Workers of the World**, that *"an injury to one is an injury to all."* Solidarity, therefore, is the means to protect individuality and liberty and so is an expression of self-interest. As Alfie Kohn points out:

> *"when we think about co-operation ... we tend to associate the concept with fuzzy-minded idealism ... This may result from confusing co-operation with altruism ... Structural co-operation defies the usual egoism/altruism dichotomy. It sets things up so that by helping you I am helping myself at the same time. Even if my motive initially may have been selfish, our fates now are linked. We sink or swim together. Co-operation is a shrewd and highly successful strategy – a pragmatic choice that gets things done at work and at school even more effectively than competition does ... There is also good evidence that co-operation is more conductive to psychological health and to liking one another."* [**No Contest: The Case Against Competition**, p. 7]

And, within a hierarchical society, solidarity is important not only because of the satisfaction it gives us, but also because it is necessary to resist those in power. Malatesta's words are relevant here:

"the oppressed masses who have never completely resigned themselves to oppression and poverty, and who … show themselves thirsting for justice, freedom and wellbeing, are beginning to understand that they will not be able to achieve their emancipation except by union and solidarity with all the oppressed, with the exploited everywhere in the world." [**Anarchy**, p. 33]

By standing together, we can increase our strength and get what we want. Eventually, by organising into groups, we can start to manage our own collective affairs together and so replace the boss once and for all. *"**Unions** will … multiply the individual's means and secure his assailed property."* [Max Stirner, **The Ego and Its Own**, p. 258] By acting in solidarity, we can also replace the current system with one more to our liking: *"in union there is strength."* [Alexander Berkman, **What is Anarchism?**, p. 74]

Solidarity is thus the means by which we can obtain and ensure our own freedom. We agree to work together so that we will not have to work for **another**. By agreeing to share with each other we increase our options so that we may enjoy **more**, not less. Mutual aid is in my self-interest – that is, I see that it is to my advantage to reach agreements with others based on mutual respect and social equality; for if I dominate someone, this means that the conditions exist which allow domination, and so in all probability I too will be dominated in turn.

As Max Stirner saw, solidarity is the means by which we ensure that our liberty is strengthened and defended from those in power who want to rule us: *"Do you yourself count for nothing then?"*, he asks. *"Are you bound to let anyone do anything he wants to you? Defend yourself and no one will touch you. If millions of people are behind you, supporting you, then you are a formidable force and you will win without difficulty."* [quoted in Luigi Galleani's **The End of Anarchism?**, p. 79 – different translation in **The Ego and Its Own**, p. 197]

Solidarity, therefore, is important to anarchists because it is the means by which liberty can be created and defended against power. Solidarity is strength and a product of our nature as social beings. However, solidarity should not be confused with "herdism," which implies passively following a leader. In order to be effective, solidarity must be created by free people, co-operating together as **equals**. The "big WE" is **not** solidarity, although the desire for "herdism" is a product of our need for solidarity and union. It is a "solidarity" corrupted by hierarchical society, in which people are conditioned to blindly obey leaders.

A.2.7 Why do anarchists argue for self-liberation?

Liberty, by its very nature, cannot be given. An individual cannot be freed by another, but must break his or her own chains through their own effort. Of course, self-effort can also be part of collective action, and in many cases it has to be in order to attain its ends. As Emma Goldman points out:

"History tells us that every oppressed class [or group or individual] gained true liberation from its masters by its own efforts." [**Red Emma Speaks**, p. 167]

This is because anarchists recognise that hierarchical systems, like any social relationship, shapes those subject to them. As Bookchin argued, *"class societies organise our psychic structures for command or obedience."* This means that people **internalise** the values of hierarchical and class society and, as such, *"the State is not merely a constellation of bureaucratic and coercive institutions. It is also a state of mind, an instilled mentality for ordering reality … Its capacity to rule by brute force has always been limited … Without a high degree of co-operation from even the most victimised classes of society such as chattel slaves and serfs, its authority would eventually dissipate. Awe and apathy in the face of State power are products of social conditioning that renders this very power possible."* [**The Ecology of Freedom**, p. 159 and pp. 164-5] Self-liberation is the means by which we break down both internal **and** external chains, freeing ourselves mentally as well as physically.

Anarchists have long argued that people can only free themselves by their own actions. The various methods anarchists suggest to aid this process will be discussed in section J ("What Do Anarchists Do?") and will not be discussed here. However, these methods all involve people organising themselves, setting their own agendas, and acting in ways that empower them and eliminate their dependence on leaders to do things for them. Anarchism is based on people *"acting for themselves"* (performing what anarchists call *"**direct action**"* – see section J.2 for details).

Direct action has an empowering and liberating effect on those involved in it. Self-activity is the means by which the creativity, initiative, imagination and critical thought of those subjected to authority can be developed. It is the means by which society can be changed. As Errico Malatesta pointed out:

"Between man and his social environment there is a reciprocal action. Men make society what it is and society makes men what they are, and the result is therefore a kind of vicious circle. To transform society men [and women] must be changed, and to transform men, society must be changed … Fortunately existing society has not been created by the inspired will of a dominating class, which has succeeded in reducing all its subjects to passive and unconscious instruments of its interests. It is the result of a thousand internecine struggles, of a thousand human and natural factors …

"From this the possibility of progress … We must take advantage of all the means, all the possibilities and the opportunities that the present environment allows us to act on our fellow men [and women] and to develop their consciences and their demands … to claim and to impose those major social transformations which are possible and which effectively serve to open the way to further advances later … We must seek to get all the people … to make demands, and impose itself and take for itself all the improvements and freedoms it desires as and when it reaches the state of wanting them, and the power to

demand them … we must push the people to want always more and to increase its pressures [on the ruling elite], until it has achieved complete emancipation." [**Errico Malatesta: His Life and Ideas**, pp. 188-9]

Society, while shaping all individuals, is also created by them, through their actions, thoughts, and ideals. Challenging institutions that limit one's freedom is mentally liberating, as it sets in motion the process of questioning authoritarian relationships in general. This process gives us insight into how society works, changing our ideas and creating new ideals. To quote Emma Goldman again: "True emancipation begins … in woman's soul." And in a man's too, we might add. It is only here that we can "begin [our] inner regeneration, [cutting] loose from the weight of prejudices, traditions and customs." [**Op. Cit.**, p. 167] But this process must be self-directed, for as Max Stirner notes, "the man who is set free is nothing but a freed man … a dog dragging a piece of chain with him." [**The Ego and Its Own**, p. 168] By changing the world, even in a small way, we change ourselves.

In an interview during the Spanish Revolution, the Spanish anarchist militant Durutti said, "we have a new world in our hearts." Only self-activity and self-liberation allows us to create such a vision and gives us the confidence to try to actualise it in the real world.

Anarchists, however, do not think that self-liberation must wait for the future, after the "glorious revolution." The personal is political, and given the nature of society, how we act in the here and now will influence the future of our society and our lives. Therefore, even in pre-anarchist society anarchists try to create, as Bakunin puts it, "not only the ideas but also the facts of the future itself." We can do so by creating alternative social relationships and organisations, acting as free people in a non-free society. Only by our actions in the here and now can we lay the foundation for a free society. Moreover, this process of self-liberation goes on all the time:

"Subordinates of all kinds exercise their capacity for critical self-reflection every day – that is why masters are thwarted, frustrated and, sometimes, overthrown. But unless masters are overthrown, unless subordinates engage in political activity, no amount of critical reflection will end their subjection and bring them freedom." [Carole Pateman, **The Sexual Contract**, p. 205]

Anarchists aim to encourage these tendencies in everyday life to reject, resist and thwart authority and bring them to their logical conclusion – a society of free individuals, co-operating as equals in free, self-managed associations. Without this process of critical self-reflection, resistance and self-liberation a free society is impossible. Thus, for anarchists, anarchism comes from the natural resistance of subordinated people striving to act as free individuals within a hierarchical world. This process of resistance is called by many anarchists the **"class struggle"** (as it is working class people who are generally the most subordinated group within society) or, more generally, **"social struggle."** It is this everyday resistance to authority (in all its forms) and the desire for freedom which is the key to the anarchist revolution. It is for this reason that "anarchists emphasise over and over that the class struggle provides the only means for the workers [and other oppressed groups] to achieve control over their destiny." [Marie-Louise Berneri, **Neither East Nor West**, p. 32]

Revolution is a process, not an event, and every "spontaneous revolutionary action" usually results from and is based upon the patient work of many years of organisation and education by people with "utopian" ideas. The process of "creating the new world in the shell of the old" (to use another **I.W.W.** expression), by building alternative institutions and relationships, is but one component of what must be a long tradition of revolutionary commitment and militancy.

As Malatesta made clear, "to encourage popular organisations of all kinds is the logical consequence of our basic ideas, and should therefore be an integral part of our programme … anarchists do not want to emancipate the people; we want the people to emancipate themselves…, we want the new way of life to emerge from the body of the people and correspond to the state of their development and advance as they advance." [**Op. Cit.**, p. 90]

Unless a process of self-emancipation occurs, a free society is impossible. Only when individuals free themselves, both materially (by abolishing the state and capitalism) and intellectually (by freeing themselves of submissive attitudes towards authority), can a free society be possible. We should not forget that capitalist and state power, to a great extent, is power over the minds of those subject to them (backed up, of course, with sizeable force if the mental domination fails and people start rebelling and resisting). In effect, a spiritual power as the ideas of the ruling class dominate society and permeate the minds of the oppressed. As long as this holds, the working class will acquiesce to authority, oppression and exploitation as the normal condition of life. Minds submissive to the doctrines and positions of their masters cannot hope to win freedom, to revolt and fight. Thus the oppressed must overcome the mental domination of the existing system before they can throw off its yoke (and, anarchists argue, direct action is the means of doing both – see sections J.2 and J.4). Capitalism and statism must be beaten spiritually and theoretically before it is beaten materially (many anarchists call this mental liberation **"class consciousness"** – see section B.7.4). And self-liberation through struggle against oppression is the only way this can be done. Thus anarchists encourage (to use Kropotkin's term) **"the spirit of revolt."**

Self-liberation is a product of struggle, of self-organisation, solidarity and direct action. Direct action is the means of creating anarchists, free people, and so "Anarchists have always advised taking an active part in those workers' organisations which carry on the **direct** struggle of Labour against Capital and its protector, – the State." This is because "[s]uch a struggle … better than any indirect means, permits the worker to obtain some temporary improvements in the present conditions of work, while it opens his [or her] eyes to the evil that is done by Capitalism and the State that supports it, and wakes up his [or her] thoughts concerning the possibility of organising consumption, production and exchange without the intervention of the capitalist and the state," that is, see the possibility of a free society. Kropotkin, like many anarchists, pointed to the Syndicalist and Trade Union movements as a means of developing libertarian ideas within existing society (although he, like most anarchists, did not limit anarchist activity exclusively to them). Indeed, any movement which "permit[s] the working men [and women] to realise their solidarity and to feel the community of their interests … prepare[s] the way for these conceptions" of communist-anarchism, i.e. the overcoming the spiritual domination of existing society within the minds of the oppressed. [**Evolution and Environment**, p. 83 and p. 85]

For anarchists, in the words of a Scottish Anarchist militant, the *"history of human progress [is] seen as the history of rebellion and disobedience, with the individual debased by subservience to authority in its many forms and able to retain his/her dignity only through rebellion and disobedience."* [Robert Lynn, **Not a Life Story, Just a Leaf from It**, p. 77] This is why anarchists stress self-liberation (and self-organisation, self-management and self-activity). Little wonder Bakunin considered *"rebellion"* as one of the *"three fundamental principles [which] constitute the essential conditions of all human development, collective or individual, in history."* [**God and the State**, p. 12] This is simply because individuals and groups cannot be freed by others, only by themselves. Such rebellion (self-liberation) is the **only** means by which existing society becomes more libertarian and an anarchist society a possibility.

A.2.8 Is it possible to be an anarchist without opposing hierarchy?

No. We have seen that anarchists abhor authoritarianism. But if one is an anti-authoritarian, one must oppose all hierarchical institutions, since they embody the principle of authority. For, as Emma Goldman argued, *"it is not only government in the sense of the state which is destructive of every individual value and quality. It is the whole complex authority and institutional domination which strangles life. It is the superstition, myth, pretence, evasions, and subservience which support authority and institutional domination."* [**Red Emma Speaks**, p. 435] This means that *"there is and will always be a need to discover and overcome structures of hierarchy, authority and domination and constraints on freedom: slavery, wage-slavery [i.e. capitalism], racism, sexism, authoritarian schools, etc."* [Noam Chomsky, **Language and Politics**, p. 364]

Thus the consistent anarchist must oppose hierarchical relationships as well as the state. Whether economic, social or political, to be an anarchist means to oppose hierarchy. The argument for this (if anybody needs one) is as follows:

> *"All authoritarian institutions are organised as pyramids: the state, the private or public corporation, the army, the police, the church, the university, the hospital: they are all pyramidal structures with a small group of decision-makers at the top and a broad base of people whose decisions are **made for them** at the bottom. Anarchism does not demand the changing of labels on the layers, it doesn't want different people on top, it wants **us** to clamber out from underneath."* [Colin Ward, **Anarchy in Action**, p. 22]

Hierarchies *"share a common feature: they are organised systems of command and obedience"* and so anarchists seek *"to eliminate hierarchy per se, not simply replace one form of hierarchy with another."* [Bookchin, **The Ecology of Freedom**, p. 27] A hierarchy is a pyramidally-structured organisation composed of a series of grades, ranks, or offices of increasing power, prestige, and (usually) remuneration. Scholars who have investigated the hierarchical form have found that the two primary principles it embodies are domination and exploitation. For example, in his classic article *"What Do Bosses Do?"* (**Review of Radical Political Economy**, Vol. 6, No. 2), a study of the modern factory, Steven Marglin found that the main function of the corporate hierarchy is not greater productive efficiency (as capitalists claim), but greater control over workers, the purpose of such control being more effective exploitation.

Control in a hierarchy is maintained by coercion, that is, by the threat of negative sanctions of one kind or another: physical, economic, psychological, social, etc. Such control, including the repression of dissent and rebellion, therefore necessitates centralisation: a set of power relations in which the greatest control is exercised by the few at the top (particularly the head of the organisation), while those in the middle ranks have much less control and the many at the bottom have virtually none.

Since domination, coercion, and centralisation are essential features of authoritarianism, and as those features are embodied in hierarchies, all hierarchical institutions are authoritarian. Moreover, for anarchists, any organisation marked by hierarchy, centralism and authoritarianism is state-like, or "statist." And as anarchists oppose both the state and authoritarian relations, anyone who does not seek to dismantle **all** forms of hierarchy cannot be called an anarchist. This applies to capitalist firms. As Noam Chomsky points out, the structure of the capitalist firm is extremely hierarchical, indeed fascist, in nature:

> *"a fascist system … [is] absolutist – power goes from top down … the ideal state is top down control with the public essentially following orders.*
>
> *"Let's take a look at a corporation … [I]f you look at what they are, power goes strictly top down, from the board of directors to managers to lower managers to ultimately the people on the shop floor, typing messages, and so on. There's no flow of power or planning from the bottom up. People can disrupt and make suggestions, but the same is true of a slave society. The structure of power is linear, from the top down."* [**Keeping the Rabble in Line**, p. 237]

David Deleon indicates these similarities between the company and the state well when he writes:

> *"Most factories are like military dictatorships. Those at the bottom are privates, the supervisors are sergeants, and on up through the hierarchy. The organisation can dictate everything from our clothing and hair style to how we spend a large portion of our lives, during work. It can compel overtime; it can require us to see a company doctor if we have a medical complaint; it can forbid us free time to engage in political activity; it can suppress freedom of speech, press and assembly – it can use ID cards and armed security police, along with closed-circuit TVs to watch us; it can punish dissenters with 'disciplinary*

layoffs' (as GM calls them), or it can fire us. We are forced, by circumstances, to accept much of this, or join the millions of unemployed … In almost every job, we have only the 'right' to quit. Major decisions are made at the top and we are expected to obey, whether we work in an ivory tower or a mine shaft." ["For Democracy Where We Work: A rationale for social self-management", **Reinventing Anarchy, Again**, Howard J. Ehrlich (ed.), pp. 193-4]

Thus the consistent anarchist must oppose hierarchy in all its forms, including the capitalist firm. Not to do so is to support **archy** – which an anarchist, by definition, cannot do. In other words, for anarchists, "[p]romises to obey, contracts of (wage) slavery, agreements requiring the acceptance of a subordinate status, are all illegitimate because they do restrict and restrain individual autonomy." [Robert Graham, "The Anarchist Contract, **Reinventing Anarchy, Again**, Howard J. Ehrlich (ed.), p. 77] Hierarchy, therefore, is against the basic principles which drive anarchism. It denies what makes us human and "divest[s] the personality of its most integral traits; it denies the very notion that the individual is **competent** to deal not only with the management of his or her personal life but with its most important context: the **social** context." [Murray Bookchin, **Op. Cit.**, p. 202]

Some argue that as long as an association is voluntary, whether it has a hierarchical structure is irrelevant. Anarchists disagree. This is for two reasons. Firstly, under capitalism workers are driven by economic necessity to sell their labour (and so liberty) to those who own the means of life. This process re-enforces the economic conditions workers face by creating "massive disparities in wealth … [as] workers … sell their labour to the capitalist at a price which does not reflect its real value." Therefore:

> "To portray the parties to an employment contract, for example, as free and equal to each other is to ignore the serious inequality of bargaining power which exists between the worker and the employer. To then go on to portray the relationship of subordination and exploitation which naturally results as the epitome of freedom is to make a mockery of both individual liberty and social justice." [Robert Graham, **Op. Cit.**, p. 70]

It is for this reason that anarchists support collective action and organisation: it increases the bargaining power of working people and allows them to assert their autonomy (see section J).

Secondly, if we take the key element as being whether an association is voluntary or not we would have to argue that the current state system must be considered as "anarchy." In a modern democracy no one forces an individual to live in a specific state. We are free to leave and go somewhere else. By ignoring the hierarchical nature of an association, you can end up supporting organisations based upon the denial of freedom (including capitalist companies, the armed forces, states even) all because they are "voluntary." As Bob Black argues, "[t]o demonise state authoritarianism while ignoring identical albeit contract-consecrated subservient arrangements in the large-scale corporations which control the world economy is fetishism at its worst." [The Libertarian as Conservative, **The Abolition of Work and other essays**, p. 142] Anarchy is more than being free to pick a master.

Therefore opposition to hierarchy is a key anarchist position, otherwise you just become a "voluntary anarchist" – which is hardly anarchistic. For more on this see section A.2.14 (Why is voluntarism not enough?).

Anarchists argue that organisations do not need to be hierarchical, they can be based upon co-operation between equals who manage their own affairs directly. In this way we can do without hierarchical structures (i.e. the delegation of power in the hands of a few). Only when an association is self-managed by its members can it be considered truly anarchistic.

We are sorry to belabour this point, but some capitalist apologists, apparently wanting to appropriate the "anarchist" name because of its association with freedom, have recently claimed that one can be both a capitalist and an anarchist at the same time (as in so-called "anarcho" capitalism). It should now be clear that since capitalism is based on hierarchy (not to mention statism and exploitation), "anarcho"-capitalism is a contradiction in terms. (For more on this, see Section F)

A.2.9 What sort of society do anarchists want?

Anarchists desire a decentralised society, based on free association. We consider this form of society the best one for maximising the values we have outlined above – liberty, equality and solidarity. Only by a rational decentralisation of power, both structurally and territorially, can individual liberty be fostered and encouraged. The delegation of power into the hands of a minority is an obvious denial of individual liberty and dignity. Rather than taking the management of their own affairs away from people and putting it in the hands of others, anarchists favour organisations which minimise authority, keeping power at the base, in the hands of those who are affected by any decisions reached.

Free association is the cornerstone of an anarchist society. Individuals must be free to join together as they see fit, for this is the basis of freedom and human dignity. However, any such free agreement must be based on decentralisation of power; otherwise it will be a sham (as in capitalism), as only equality provides the necessary social context for freedom to grow and development. Therefore anarchists support directly democratic collectives, based on "one person one vote" (for the rationale of direct democracy as the political counterpart of free agreement, see section A.2.11 – Why do most anarchists support direct democracy?).

We should point out here that an anarchist society does not imply some sort of idyllic state of harmony within which everyone agrees. Far from it! As Luigi Galleani points out, "[d]isagreements and friction will always exist. In fact they are an essential condition of unlimited progress. But once the bloody area of sheer animal competition – the struggle for food – has been eliminated, problems of disagreement could be solved without the slightest threat to the social order and individual liberty." [**The End of Anarchism?**, p. 28] Anarchism aims to "rouse the spirit of initiative in individuals and in groups."

These will *"create in their mutual relations a movement and a life based on the principles of free understanding"* and recognise that ***"variety, conflict even, is life and that uniformity is death."*** [Peter Kropotkin, **Anarchism**, p. 143]

Therefore, an anarchist society will be based upon co-operative conflict as *"[c]onflict, per se, is not harmful … disagreements exist [and should not be hidden] … What makes disagreement destructive is not the fact of conflict itself but the addition of competition."* Indeed, *"a rigid demand for agreement means that people will effectively be prevented from contributing their wisdom to a group effort."* [Alfie Kohn, **No Contest: The Case Against Competition**, p. 156] It is for this reason that most anarchists reject consensus decision making in large groups (see section A.2.12).

So, in an anarchist society associations would be run by mass assemblies of all involved, based upon extensive discussion, debate and co-operative conflict between equals, with purely administrative tasks being handled by elected committees. These committees would be made up of mandated, recallable and temporary delegates who carry out their tasks under the watchful eyes of the assembly which elected them. Thus in an anarchist society, *"we'll look after our affairs ourselves and decide what to do about them. And when, to put our ideas into action, there is a need to put someone in charge of a project, we'll tell them to do [it] in such and such a way and no other … nothing would be done without our decision. So our delegates, instead of people being individuals whom we've given the right to order us about, would be people … [with] no authority, only the duty to carry out what everyone involved wanted."* [Errico Malatesta, **Fra Contadini**, p. 34] If the delegates act against their mandate or try to extend their influence or work beyond that already decided by the assembly (i.e. if they start to make policy decisions), they can be instantly recalled and their decisions abolished. In this way, the organisation remains in the hands of the union of individuals who created it.

This self-management by the members of a group at the base and the power of recall are essential tenets of any anarchist organisation. The **key** difference between a statist or hierarchical system and an anarchist community is who wields power. In a parliamentary system, for example, people give power to a group of representatives to make decisions for them for a fixed period of time. Whether they carry out their promises is irrelevant as people cannot recall them till the next election. Power lies at the top and those at the base are expected to obey. Similarly, in the capitalist workplace, power is held by an unelected minority of bosses and managers at the top and the workers are expected to obey.

In an anarchist society this relationship is reversed. No one individual or group (elected or unelected) holds power in an anarchist community. Instead decisions are made using direct democratic principles and, when required, the community can elect or appoint delegates to carry out these decisions. There is a clear distinction between policy making (which lies with everyone who is affected) and the co-ordination and administration of any adopted policy (which is the job for delegates).

These egalitarian communities, founded by free agreement, also freely associate together in confederations. Such a free confederation would be run from the bottom up, with decisions following from the elemental assemblies upwards. The confederations would be

run in the same manner as the collectives. There would be regular local regional, "national" and international conferences in which all important issues and problems affecting the collectives involved would be discussed. In addition, the fundamental, guiding principles and ideas of society would be debated and policy decisions made, put into practice, reviewed, and co-ordinated. The delegates would simply *"take their given mandates to the relative meetings and try to harmonise their various needs and desires. The deliberations would always be subject to the control and approval of those who delegated them"* and so *"there would be no danger than the interest of the people [would] be forgotten."* [Malatesta, **Op. Cit.**, p. 36]

Action committees would be formed, if required, to co-ordinate and administer the decisions of the assemblies and their congresses, under strict control from below as discussed above. Delegates to such bodies would have a limited tenure and, like the delegates to the congresses, have a fixed mandate – they are not able to make decisions on behalf of the people they are delegates for. In addition, like the delegates to conferences and congresses, they would be subject to instant recall by the assemblies and congresses from which they emerged in the first place. In this way any committees required to co-ordinate join activities would be, to quote Malatesta's words, *"always under the direct control of the population"* and so express the *"decisions taken at popular assemblies."* [**Errico Malatesta: His Life and Ideas**, p. 175 and p. 129]

Most importantly, the basic community assemblies can overturn any decisions reached by the conferences and withdraw from any confederation. Any compromises that are made by a delegate during negotiations have to go back to a general assembly for ratification. Without that ratification any compromises that are made by a delegate are not binding on the community that has delegated a particular task to a particular individual or committee. In addition, they can call confederal conferences to discuss new developments and to inform action committees about changing wishes and to instruct them on what to do about any developments and ideas.

In other words, any delegates required within an anarchist organisation or society are **not** representatives (as they are in a democratic government). Kropotkin makes the difference clear:

> *"The question of true delegation versus representation can be better understood if one imagines a hundred or two hundred men [and women], who meet each day in their work and share common concerns … who have discussed every aspect of the question that concerns them and have reached a decision. They then choose someone and send him [or her] to reach an agreement with other delegates of the same kind…. The delegate is not authorised to do more than explain to other delegates the considerations that have led his [or her] colleagues to their conclusion. Not being able to impose anything, he [or she] will seek an understanding and will return with a simple proposition which his mandatories can accept or refuse. This is what happens when true delegation comes into being."* [**Words of a Rebel**, p. 132]

Unlike in a representative system, **power** is not delegated into the hands of the few. Rather, any delegate is simply a mouthpiece for the association that elected (or otherwise selected) them in the first place. All delegates and action committees would be mandated and subject to instant recall to ensure they express the wishes of the assemblies they came from rather than their own. In this way government is replaced by anarchy, a network of free associations and communities co-operating as equals based on a system of mandated delegates, instant recall, free agreement and free federation from the bottom up.

Only this system would ensure the *"free organisation of the people, an organisation from below upwards."* This *"free federation from below upward"* would start with the basic *"association"* and their federation *"first into a commune, then a federation of communes into regions, of regions into nations, and of nations into an international fraternal association."* [Michael Bakunin, **The Political Philosophy of Bakunin**, p. 298] This network of anarchist communities would work on three levels. There would be *"independent Communes for the territorial organisation, and of federations of Trade Unions [i.e. workplace associations] for the organisation of men [and women] in accordance with their different functions … [and] free combines and societies … for the satisfaction of all possible and imaginable needs, economic, sanitary, and educational; for mutual protection, for the propaganda of ideas, for arts, for amusement, and so on."* [Peter Kropotkin, **Evolution and Environment**, p. 79] All would be based on self-management, free association, free federation and self-organisation from the bottom up.

By organising in this manner, hierarchy is abolished in all aspects of life, because the people at the base of the organisation are in control, **not** their delegates. Only this form of organisation can replace government (the initiative and empowerment of the few) with anarchy (the initiative and empowerment of all). This form of organisation would exist in all activities which required group work and the co-ordination of many people. It would be, as Bakunin said, the means *"to integrate individuals into structures which they could understand and control."* [quoted by Cornelius Castoriadis, **Political and Social Writings**, vol. 2, p. 97] For individual initiatives, the individual involved would manage them.

As can be seen, anarchists wish to create a society based upon structures that ensure that no individual or group is able to wield power over others. Free agreement, confederation and the power of recall, fixed mandates and limited tenure are mechanisms by which power is removed from the hands of governments and placed in the hands of those directly affected by the decisions.

For a fuller discussion on what an anarchist society would look like see section I. Anarchy, however, is not some distant goal but rather an aspect of current struggles against oppression and exploitation. Means and ends are linked, with direct action generating mass participatory organisations and preparing people to directly manage their own personal and collective interests. This is because anarchists, as we discuss in section I.2.3, see the framework of a free society being based on the organisations created by the oppressed in their struggle against capitalism in the here and now. In this sense, collective struggle creates the organisations as well as the individual attitudes anarchism needs to work. The struggle against oppression is the school of anarchy. It teaches us not only how to be anarchists but also gives us a glimpse of what an anarchist society would be like, what its initial organisational framework could be and the experience of managing our own activities which is required for

such a society to work. As such, anarchists try to create the kind of world we want in our current struggles and do not think our ideas are only applicable "after the revolution." Indeed, by applying our principles today we bring anarchy that much nearer.

A.2.10 What will abolishing hierarchy mean and achieve?

The creation of a new society based upon libertarian organisations will have an incalculable effect on everyday life. The empowerment of millions of people will transform society in ways we can only guess at now.

However, many consider these forms of organisation as impractical and doomed to failure. To those who say that such confederal, non-authoritarian organisations would produce confusion and disunity, anarchists maintain that the statist, centralised and hierarchical form of organisation produces indifference instead of involvement, heartlessness instead of solidarity, uniformity instead of unity, and privileged elites instead of equality. More importantly, such organisations destroy individual initiative and crush independent action and critical thinking. (For more on hierarchy, see section B.1 – "Why are anarchists against authority and hierarchy?").

That libertarian organisation can work and is based upon (and promotes) liberty was demonstrated in the Spanish Anarchist movement. Fenner Brockway, Secretary of the British Independent Labour Party, when visiting Barcelona during the 1936 revolution, noted that *"the great solidarity that existed among the Anarchists was due to each individual relying on his [sic] own strength and not depending upon leadership…. The organisations must, to be successful, be combined with free-thinking people; not a mass, but free individuals"* [quoted by Rudolf Rocker, **Anarcho-syndicalism**, p. 67f]As sufficiently indicated already, hierarchical, centralised structures restrict freedom. As Proudhon noted: *"the centralist system is all very well as regards size, simplicity and construction: it lacks but one thing – the individual no longer belongs to himself in such a system, he cannot feel his worth, his life, and no account is taken of him at all."* [quoted by Martin Buber, **Paths in Utopia**, p. 33]

The effects of hierarchy can be seen all around us. It does not work. Hierarchy and authority exist everywhere, in the workplace, at home, in the street. As Bob Black puts it, *"[i]f you spend most of your waking life taking orders or kissing ass, if you get habituated to hierarchy, you will become passive-aggressive, sado-masochistic, servile and stupefied, and you will carry that load into every aspect of the balance of your life."* [*"The Libertarian as Conservative,"* **The Abolition of Work and other essays**, pp. 147-8]

This means that the end of hierarchy will mean a **massive** transformation in everyday life. It will involve the creation of individual-centred organisations within which all can exercise, and so develop, their abilities to the fullest. By involving themselves and participating in the decisions that affect them, their workplace, their community and society, they can ensure the full development of their individual capacities.

With the free participation of all in social life, we would quickly see the end of inequality and injustice. Rather than people existing to make ends meet and being used to increase the wealth and power of the few as under capitalism, the end of hierarchy would see (to quote Kropotkin) *"the well-being of all"* and it is *"high time for the worker to assert his [or her] right to the common inheritance, and to enter into possession of it."* [**The Conquest of Bread**, p. 35 and p. 44] For only taking possession of the means of life (workplaces, housing, the land, etc.) can ensure *"liberty and justice, for liberty and justice are not decreed but are the result of economic independence. They spring from the fact that the individual is able to live without depending on a master, and to enjoy ... the product of his [or her] toil."* [Ricardo Flores Magón, **Land and Liberty**, p. 62] Therefore liberty requires the abolition of capitalist private property rights in favour of **"use rights."** (see section B.3 for more details). Ironically, the *"abolition of property will free the people from homelessness and nonpossession."* [Max Baginski, *"Without Government,"* **Anarchy! An Anthology of Emma Goldman's Mother Earth**, p. 11] Thus anarchism promises *"both requisites of happiness – liberty and wealth."* In anarchy, *"mankind will live in freedom and in comfort."* [Benjamin Tucker, **Why I am an Anarchist**, p. 135 and p. 136]

Only self-determination and free agreement on every level of society can develop the responsibility, initiative, intellect and solidarity of individuals and society as a whole. Only anarchist organisation allows the vast talent which exists within humanity to be accessed and used, enriching society by the very process of enriching and developing the individual. Only by involving everyone in the process of thinking, planning, co-ordinating and implementing the decisions that affect them can freedom blossom and individuality be fully developed and protected. Anarchy will release the creativity and talent of the mass of people enslaved by hierarchy.

Anarchy will even be of benefit for those who are said to benefit from capitalism and its authority relations. Anarchists *"maintain that **both** rulers and ruled are spoiled by authority; **both** exploiters and exploited are spoiled by exploitation."* [Peter Kropotkin, **Act for Yourselves**, p. 83] This is because *"[i]n any hierarchical relationship the dominator as well as the submissive pays his dues. The price paid for the 'glory of command' is indeed heavy. Every tyrant resents his duties. He is relegated to drag the dead weight of the dormant creative potential of the submissive all along the road of his hierarchical excursion."* [For Ourselves, **The Right to Be Greedy**, Thesis 95]

A.2.11 Why are most anarchists in favour of direct democracy?

For most anarchists, direct democratic voting on policy decisions within free associations is the political counterpart of free agreement (this is also known as **"self-management"**). The reason is that *"many forms of domination can be carried out in a 'free.' non-coercive, contractual manner ... and it is naive ... to think that mere opposition to political control will in itself lead to an end of oppression."* [John P. Clark, **Max Stirner's Egoism**, p. 93] Thus the relationships we create **within** an organisation are as important

in determining its libertarian nature as its voluntary nature (see section A.2.14 for more discussion).

It is obvious that individuals must work together in order to lead a fully human life. And so, *"[h]aving to join with other humans"* the individual has three options: *"he [or she] must submit to the will of others (be enslaved) or subject others to his will (be in authority) or live with others in fraternal agreement in the interests of the greatest good of all (be an associate). Nobody can escape from this necessity."* [Errico Malatesta, **Life and Ideas**, p. 85]

Anarchists obviously pick the last option, association, as the only means by which individuals can work together as free and equal human beings, respecting the uniqueness and liberty of one another. Only within direct democracy can individuals express themselves, practice critical thought and self-government, so developing their intellectual and ethical capacities to the full. In terms of increasing an individual's freedom and their intellectual, ethical and social faculties, it is far better to be sometimes in a minority than be subject to the will of a boss all the time. So what is the theory behind anarchist direct democracy?

As Bertrand Russell noted, the anarchist *"does not wish to abolish government in the sense of collective decisions: what he does wish to abolish is the system by which a decision is enforced upon those who oppose it."* [**Roads to Freedom**, p. 85] Anarchists see self-management as the means to achieve this. Once an individual joins a community or workplace, he or she becomes a "citizen" (for want of a better word) of that association. The association is organised around an assembly of all its members (in the case of large workplaces and towns, this may be a functional sub-group such as a specific office or neighbourhood). In this assembly, in concert with others, the contents of his or her political obligations are defined. In acting within the association, people must exercise critical judgement and choice, i.e. manage their own activity. Rather than promising to obey (as in hierarchical organisations like the state or capitalist firm), individuals participate in making their own collective decisions, their own commitments to their fellows. This means that political obligation is not owed to a separate entity above the group or society, such as the state or company, but to one's fellow "citizens."

Although the assembled people collectively legislate the rules governing their association, and are bound by them as individuals, they are also superior to them in the sense that these rules can always be modified or repealed. Collectively, the associated "citizens" constitute a political "authority", but as this "authority" is based on horizontal relationships between themselves rather than vertical ones between themselves and an elite, the "authority" is non-hierarchical ("rational" or "natural," see section B.1 – "Why are anarchists against authority and hierarchy?" – for more on this). Thus Proudhon:

> *"In place of laws, we will put contracts [i.e. free agreement]. – No more laws voted by a majority, nor even unanimously; each citizen, each town, each industrial union, makes its own laws."* [**The General Idea of the Revolution**, pp. 245-6]

Such a system does not mean, of course, that everyone participates in every decision needed, no matter how trivial. While any decision can be put to the assembly (if the assembly so decides, perhaps prompted by some of its members), in practice certain activities (and so purely functional decisions) will be handled by the association's elected administration. This is because, to quote a Spanish anarchist activist, *"a collectivity as such cannot write a letter or add up a list of figures or do hundreds of chores which only an individual can perform."* Thus the need *"to **organise the administration.**"* Supposing an association is *"organised without any directive council or any hierarchical offices"* which *"meets in general assembly once a week or more often, when it settles all matters needful for its progress"* it still *"nominates a commission with **strictly administrative functions.**"* However, the assembly *"prescribes a definite line of conduct for this commission or gives it an **imperative mandate**"* and so *"would be **perfectly anarchist.**"* As it *"follows that **delegating** these tasks to qualified individuals, who are **instructed in advance how to proceed,** … does not mean an abdication of that collectivity's own liberty."* [Jose Llunas Pujols, quoted by Max Nettlau, **A Short History of Anarchism**, p. 187] This, it should be noted, follows Proudhon's ideas that within the workers' associations *"all positions are elective, and the by-laws subject to the approval of the members."* [Proudhon, **Op. Cit.**, p. 222]

Instead of capitalist or statist hierarchy, self-management (i.e. direct democracy) would be the guiding principle of the freely joined associations that make up a free society. This would apply to the federations of associations an anarchist society would need to function. *"All the commissions or delegations nominated in an anarchist society,"* correctly argued Jose Llunas Pujols, *"must be subject to replacement and recall at any time by the permanent suffrage of the section or sections that elected them."* Combined with the *"imperative mandate"* and *"purely administrative functions,"* this *"make[s] it thereby impossible for anyone to arrogate to himself [or herself] a scintilla of authority."* [quoted by Max Nettlau, **Op. Cit.**, pp. 188-9] Again, Pujols follows Proudhon who demanded twenty years previously the *"implementation of the binding mandate"* to ensure the people do not *"adjure their sovereignty."* [**No Gods, No Masters**, vol. 1, p. 63]

By means of a federalism based on mandates and elections, anarchists ensure that decisions flow from the bottom-up. By making our own decisions, by looking after our joint interests ourselves, we exclude others ruling over us. Self-management, for anarchists, is essential to ensure freedom within the organisations so needed for any decent human existence.

Of course it could be argued that if you are in a minority, you are governed by others (*"Democratic rule is still rule"* [L. Susan Brown, **The Politics of Individualism**, p. 53]). Now, the concept of direct democracy as we have described it is not necessarily tied to the concept of majority rule. If someone finds themselves in a minority on a particular vote, he or she is confronted with the choice of either consenting or refusing to recognise it as binding. To deny the minority the opportunity to exercise its judgement and choice is to infringe its autonomy and to impose obligation upon it which it has not freely accepted. The coercive imposition of the majority will is contrary to the ideal of self-assumed obligation, and so is contrary to direct democracy and free association. Therefore, far from being a denial of freedom, direct democracy within the context

of free association and self-assumed obligation is the only means by which liberty can be nurtured (*"Individual autonomy limited by the obligation to hold given promises."* [Malatesta, quoted by quoted by Max Nettlau, **Errico Malatesta: The Biography of an Anarchist**]). Needless to say, a minority, if it remains in the association, can argue its case and try to convince the majority of the error of its ways.

And we must point out here that anarchist support for direct democracy does not suggest we think that the majority is always right. Far from it! The case for democratic participation is not that the majority is always right, but that no minority can be trusted not to prefer its own advantage to the good of the whole. History proves what common-sense predicts, namely that anyone with dictatorial powers (by they a head of state, a boss, a husband, whatever) will use their power to enrich and empower themselves at the expense of those subject to their decisions.

Anarchists recognise that majorities can and do make mistakes and that is why our theories on association place great importance on minority rights. This can be seen from our theory of self-assumed obligation, which bases itself on the right of minorities to protest against majority decisions and makes dissent a key factor in decision making. Thus Carole Pateman:

> *"If the majority have acted in bad faith … [then the] minority will have to take political action, including politically disobedient action if appropriate, to defend their citizenship and independence, and the political association itself … Political disobedience is merely one possible expression of the active citizenship on which a self-managing democracy is based … The social practice of promising involves the right to refuse or change commitments; similarly, the practice of self-assumed political obligation is meaningless without the practical recognition of the right of minorities to refuse or withdraw consent, or where necessary, to disobey."* [**The Problem of Political Obligation**, p. 162]

Moving beyond relationships within associations, we must highlight how different associations work together. As would be imagined, the links between associations follow the same outlines as for the associations themselves. Instead of individuals joining an association, we have associations joining confederations. The links between associations in the confederation are of the same horizontal and voluntary nature as within associations, with the same rights of "voice and exit" for members and the same rights for minorities. In this way society becomes an association of associations, a community of communities, a commune of communes, based upon maximising individual freedom by maximising participation and self-management.

The workings of such a confederation are outlined in section A.2.9 (What sort of society do anarchists want?) and discussed in greater detail in section I (What would an anarchist society look like?).

This system of direct democracy fits nicely into anarchist theory. Malatesta speaks for all anarchists when he argued that *"anarchists deny the right of the majority to govern human society in general."* As can be seen, the majority has no right to enforce itself on a minority – the minority can leave the association at any time and so, to use Malatesta's words, do not have to *"submit to the decisions of the majority before they have even heard what these might be."* [**The Anarchist Revolution**, p. 100 and p. 101] Hence, direct democracy within voluntary association does not create "majority rule" nor assume that the minority must submit to the majority no matter what. In effect, anarchist supporters of direct democracy argue that it fits Malatesta's argument that:

> *"Certainly anarchists recognise that where life is lived in common it is often necessary for the minority to come to accept the opinion of the majority. When there is an obvious need or usefulness in doing something and, to do it requires the agreement of all, the few should feel the need to adapt to the wishes of the many.... But such adaptation on the one hand by one group must be on the other be reciprocal, voluntary and must stem from an awareness of need and of goodwill to prevent the running of social affairs from being paralysed by obstinacy. It cannot be imposed as a principle and statutory norm ... "* [**Op. Cit.**, p. 100]

As the minority has the right to secede from the association as well as having extensive rights of action, protest and appeal, majority rule is not imposed as a principle. Rather, it is purely a decision making tool which allows minority dissent and opinion to be expressed (and acted upon) while ensuring that no minority forces its will on the majority. In other words, majority decisions are not binding on the minority. After all, as Malatesta argued:

> *"one cannot expect, or even wish, that someone who is firmly convinced that the course taken by the majority leads to disaster, should sacrifice his [or her] own convictions and passively look on, or even worse, should support a policy he [or she] considers wrong."* [**Errico Malatesta: His Life and Ideas**, p. 132]

Even the Individual Anarchist Lysander Spooner acknowledged that direct democracy has its uses when he noted that *"[a]ll, or nearly all, voluntary associations give a majority, or some other portion of the members less than the whole, the right to use some **limited** discretion as to the **means** to be used to accomplish the ends in view."* However, only the unanimous decision of a jury (which would *"judge the law, and the justice of the law"*) could determine individual rights as this *"tribunal fairly represent[s] the whole people"* as *"no law can rightfully be enforced by the association in its corporate capacity, against the goods, rights, or person of any individual, except it be such as **all** members of the association agree that it may enforce"* (his support of juries results from Spooner acknowledging that it *"would be impossible in practice"* for **all** members of an association to agree) [**Trial by Jury**, p. 130-1f, p. 134, p. 214, p. 152 and p. 132]

Thus direct democracy and individual/minority rights need not clash. In practice, we can imagine direct democracy would be used to make most decisions within most associations (perhaps with super-majorities required for fundamental decisions) plus some combination of a jury system and minority protest/direct action to evaluate/protect minority claims/rights in an anarchist society. The actual forms of freedom can only be created through practical experience by the people directly involved.

Lastly, we must stress that anarchist support for direct democracy does not mean that this solution is to be favoured in all circumstances. For example, many small associations may favour consensus decision making (see the next section on consensus and why most anarchists do not think that it is a viable alternative to direct democracy). However, most anarchists think that direct democracy within free association is the best (and most realistic) form of organisation which is consistent with anarchist principles of individual freedom, dignity and equality.

A.2.12 Is consensus an alternative to direct democracy?

The few anarchists who reject direct democracy within free associations generally support consensus in decision making. Consensus is based upon everyone on a group agreeing to a decision before it can be put into action. Thus, it is argued, consensus stops the majority ruling the minority and is more consistent with anarchist principles.

Consensus, although the "best" option in decision making, as all agree, has its problems. As Murray Bookchin points out in describing his experience of consensus, it can have authoritarian implications:

> *"In order ... to create full consensus on a decision, minority dissenters were often subtly urged or psychologically coerced to decline to vote on a troubling issue, inasmuch as their dissent would essentially amount to a one-person veto. This practice, called 'standing aside' in American consensus processes, all too often involved intimidation of the dissenters, to the point that they completely withdrew from the decision-making process, rather than make an honourable and continuing expression of their dissent by voting, even as a minority, in accordance with their views. Having withdrawn, they ceased to be political beings – so that a 'decision' could be made. ... 'consensus' was ultimately achieved only after dissenting members nullified themselves as participants in the process.*
>
> *"On a more theoretical level, consensus silenced that most vital aspect of all dialogue, **dissensus**. The ongoing dissent, the passionate dialogue that still persists even after a minority accedes temporarily to a majority decision, ... [can be] replaced ... by dull monologues – and the uncontroverted and deadening tone of consensus. In majority decision-making, the defeated minority can resolve to overturn a decision on which they have been defeated – they are free to openly and persistently articulate reasoned and potentially persuasive disagreements. Consensus, for its part, honours no minorities, but mutes them in favour of the metaphysical 'one' of the 'consensus' group."* ["Communalism: The Democratic Dimension of Anarchism", **Democracy and Nature**, no. 8, p. 8]

Bookchin does not *"deny that consensus may be an appropriate form of decision-making in small groups of people who are thoroughly familiar with one another."* But he notes that, in practical terms, his own experience has shown him that *"when larger groups try to make decisions by consensus, it usually obliges them to arrive at the lowest common intellectual denominator in their decision-making: the least controversial or even the most mediocre decision that a sizeable assembly of people can attain is adopted – precisely because everyone must agree with it or else withdraw from voting on that issue"* [**Op. Cit.**, p.7]

Therefore, due to its potentially authoritarian nature, most anarchists disagree that consensus is the political aspect of free association. While it is advantageous to try to reach consensus, it is usually impractical to do so – especially in large groups – regardless of its other, negative effects. Often it demeans a free society or association by tending to subvert individuality in the name of community and dissent in the name of solidarity. Neither true community nor solidarity are fostered when the individual's development and self-expression are aborted by public disapproval and pressure. Since individuals are all unique, they will have unique viewpoints which they should be encouraged to express, as society evolves and is enriched by the actions and ideas of individuals.

In other words, anarchist supporters of direct democracy stress the *"**creative** role of dissent"* which, they fear, *"tends to fade away in the grey uniformity required by consensus."* [**Op. Cit.**, p. 8]

We must stress that anarchists are **not** in favour of a mechanical decision making process in which the majority just vote the minority away and ignore them. Far from it! Anarchists who support direct democracy see it as a dynamic debating process in which majority and minority listen to and respect each other as far possible and create a decision which all can live with (if possible). They see the process of participation within directly democratic associations as the means of creating common interests, as a process which will encourage diversity, individual and minority expression and reduce any tendency for majorities to marginalise or oppress minorities by ensuring discussion and debate occurs on important issues.

A.2.13 Are anarchists individualists or collectivists?

The short answer is: neither. This can be seen from the fact that liberal scholars denounce anarchists like Bakunin for being "collectivists" while Marxists attack Bakunin and anarchists in general for being "individualists."

This is hardly surprising, as anarchists reject both ideologies as nonsense. Whether they like it or not, non-anarchist individualists and collectivists are two sides of the same capitalist coin. This can best shown be by considering modern capitalism, in which "individualist" and "collectivist" tendencies continually interact, often with the political and economic structure swinging from one pole to the other. Capitalist collectivism and individualism are both one-sided aspects of human existence, and like all manifestations of imbalance, deeply flawed.

For anarchists, the idea that individuals should sacrifice themselves for the "group" or "greater good" is nonsensical. Groups are made up of individuals, and if people think only of what's best for the group, the group will be a lifeless shell. It is only the dynamics of human interaction within groups which give them life. "Groups" cannot think, only individuals can. This fact, ironically, leads authoritarian "collectivists" to a most particular kind of "individualism," namely the *"cult of the personality"* and leader worship. This is to be expected, since such collectivism lumps individuals into abstract groups, denies their individuality, and ends up with the need for someone with enough individuality to make decisions – a problem that is "solved" by the leader principle. Stalinism and Nazism are excellent examples of this phenomenon.

Therefore, anarchists recognise that individuals are the basic unit of society and that only individuals have interests and feelings. This means they oppose "collectivism" and the glorification of the group. In anarchist theory the group exists only to aid and develop the individuals involved in them. This is why we place so much stress on groups structured in a libertarian manner – only a libertarian organisation allows the individuals within a group to fully express themselves, manage their own interests directly and to create social relationships which encourage individuality and individual freedom. So while society and the groups they join shapes the individual, the individual is the true basis of society. Hence Malatesta:

> *"Much has been said about the respective roles of individual initiative and social action in the life and progress of human societies … [E]verything is maintained and kept going in the human world thanks to individual initiative…. The real being is man, the individual. Society or the collectivity – and the **State** or government which claims to represent it – if it is not a hollow abstraction, must be made up of individuals. And it is in the organism of every individual that all thoughts and human actions inevitably have their origin, and from being individual they become collective thoughts and acts when they are or become accepted by many individuals. Social action, therefore, is neither the negation nor the complement of individual initiatives, but is the resultant of initiatives, thoughts and actions of all individuals who make up society … [T]he question is not really changing the relationship between society and the individual … [I]t is a question of preventing some individuals from oppressing others; of giving all individuals the same rights and the same means of action; and of replacing the initiative to the few [which Malatesta defines as a key aspect of government/ hierarchy], which inevitably results in the oppression of everyone else … "* [**Anarchy**, pp. 38-38]

These considerations do not mean that "individualism" finds favour with anarchists. As Emma Goldman pointed out, *"'rugged individualism' … is only a masked attempt to repress and defeat the individual and his individuality. So-called Individualism is the social and economic **laissez-faire**: the exploitation of the masses by the [ruling] classes by means of legal trickery, spiritual debasement and systematic indoctrination of the servile spirit … That corrupt and perverse 'individualism' is the straitjacket of individuality … [It] has inevitably resulted in the greatest modern slavery, the crassest class distinctions driving millions to the breadline. 'Rugged individualism' has meant all the 'individualism' for the masters, while the people are regimented into a slave caste to serve a handful of self-seeking 'supermen.'" [**Red Emma Speaks**, p. 112]

While groups cannot think, individuals cannot live or discuss by themselves. Groups and associations are an essential aspect of individual life. Indeed, as groups generate social relationships by their very nature, they help **shape** individuals. In other words, groups structured in an authoritarian way will have a negative impact on the freedom and individuality of those within them. However, due to the abstract nature of their "individualism," capitalist individualists fail to see any difference between groups structured in a libertarian manner rather than in an authoritarian one – they are both "groups". Because of their one-sided perspective on this issue, "individualists" ironically end up supporting some of the most "collectivist" institutions in existence – capitalist companies – and, moreover, always find a need for the state despite their frequent denunciations of it. These contradictions stem from capitalist individualism's dependence on individual contracts in an unequal society, i.e. **abstract** individualism.

In contrast, anarchists stress **social** "individualism" (another, perhaps better, term for this concept could be **"communal individuality"**). Anarchism "insists that the centre of gravity in society is the individual – that he [sic] must think for himself, act freely, and live fully. … If he is to develop freely and fully, he must be relieved from the interference and oppression of others. … [T]his has nothing in common with … 'rugged individualism.' Such predatory individualism is really flabby, not rugged. At the least danger to its safety, it runs to cover of the state and wails for protection….Their 'rugged individualism' is simply one of the many pretences the ruling class makes to mask unbridled business and political extortion." [Emma Goldman, **Op. Cit.**, pp. 442-3]

Anarchism rejects the **abstract** individualism of capitalism, with its ideas of "absolute" freedom of the individual which is constrained by others. This theory ignores the social context in which freedom exists and grows. "The freedom we want," Malatesta argued, "for ourselves and for others, is not an absolute metaphysical, abstract freedom which in practice is inevitably translated into the oppression of the weak; but it is a real freedom, possible freedom, which is the conscious community of interests, voluntary solidarity." [**Anarchy**, p. 43]

A society based on abstract individualism results in an inequality of power between the contracting individuals and so entails the need for an authority based on laws above them and organised coercion to enforce the contracts between them. This consequence is evident from capitalism and, most notably, in the "social contract" theory of how the state developed. In this theory it is assumed that individuals are "free" when they are isolated from each other, as they allegedly were originally in the "state of nature." Once they join society, they supposedly create a "contract" and a state to administer it. However, besides being a fantasy with no basis in reality (human beings have **always** been social animals), this "theory" is actually a justification for the state's having extensive powers over society; and this in turn is a justification of the capitalist system, which requires a strong state. It also mimics the results of the capitalist economic relations upon which this theory is

built. Within capitalism, individuals "freely" contract together, but in practice the owner rules the worker for as long as the contract is in place. (See sections A.2.14 and B.4 for further details).

Thus anarchists reject capitalist "individualism" as being, to quote Kropotkin, *"a narrow and selfish individualism"* which, moreover, is *"a foolish egoism which belittles the individual"* and is *"not individualism at all. It will not lead to what was established as a goal; that is the complete broad and most perfectly attainable development of individuality."* The hierarchy of capitalism results in *"the impoverishment of individuality"* rather than its development. To this anarchists contrast *"the individuality which attains the greatest individual development possible through the highest communist sociability in what concerns both its primordial needs and its relationships with others in general."* [**Selected Writings on Anarchism and Revolution**, p. 295, p. 296 and p. 297] For anarchists, our freedom is enriched by those around us when we work with them as equals and not as master and servant.

In practice, both individualism and collectivism lead to a denial of both individual liberty and group autonomy and dynamics. In addition, each implies the other, with collectivism leading to a particular form of individualism and individualism leading to a particular form of collectivism.

Collectivism, with its implicit suppression of the individual, ultimately impoverishes the community, as groups are only given life by the individuals who comprise them. Individualism, with its explicit suppression of community (i.e. the people with whom you live), ultimately impoverishes the individual, since individuals do not exist apart from society but can only exist within it. In addition, individualism ends up denying the "select few" the insights and abilities of the individuals who make up the rest of society, and so is a source of self-denial. This is Individualism's fatal flaw (and contradiction), namely *"the impossibility for the individual to attain a really full development in the conditions of oppression of the mass by the 'beautiful aristocracies'. His [or her] development would remain uni-lateral."* [Peter Kropotkin, **Anarchism**, p. 293]

True liberty and community exist elsewhere.

A.2.14 Why is voluntarism not enough?

Voluntarism means that association should be voluntary in order maximise liberty. Anarchists are, obviously, voluntarists, thinking that only in free association, created by free agreement, can individuals develop, grow, and express their liberty. However, it is evident that under capitalism voluntarism is not enough in itself to maximise liberty.

Voluntarism implies promising (i.e. the freedom to make agreements), and promising implies that individuals are capable of independent judgement and rational deliberation. In addition, it presupposes that they can evaluate and change their actions and relationships. Contracts under capitalism, however, contradict these implications of voluntarism. For, while technically "voluntary" (though as we show in section B.4, this is not really the case), capitalist contracts result in a denial of liberty. This is because the social relationship of wage-labour involves promising to obey in return for payment. And as Carole Pateman points out, *"to promise to obey is to deny or to limit, to a greater or lesser degree, individuals' freedom and equality and their ability to exercise these capacities [of independent judgement and rational deliberation]. To promise to obey is to state, that in certain areas, the person making the promise is no longer free to exercise her capacities and decide upon her own actions, and is no longer equal, but subordinate."* [**The Problem of Political Obligation**, p. 19] This results in those obeying no longer making their own decisions. Thus the rational for voluntarism (i.e. that individuals are capable of thinking for themselves and must be allowed to express their individuality and make their own decisions) is violated in a hierarchical relationship as some are in charge and the many obey (see also section A.2.8). Thus any voluntarism which generates relationships of subordination is, by its very nature, incomplete and violates its own justification. This can be seen from capitalist society, in which workers sell their freedom to a boss in order to live. In effect, under capitalism you are only free to the extent that you can choose whom you will obey! Freedom, however, must mean more than the right to change masters. Voluntary servitude is still servitude. For if, as Rousseau put it, sovereignty, *"for the same reason as makes it inalienable, cannot be represented"* neither can it be sold nor temporarily nullified by a hiring contract. Rousseau famously argued that the *"people of England regards itself as free; but it is grossly mistaken; it is free only during the election of members of parliament. As soon as they are elected, slavery overtakes it, and it is nothing."* [**The Social Contract and Discourses**, p. 266] Anarchists expand on this analysis. To paraphrase Rousseau:

> Under capitalism the worker regards herself as free; but she is grossly mistaken; she is free only when she signs her contract with her boss. As soon as it is signed, slavery overtakes her and she is nothing but an order taker.

To see why, to see the injustice, we need only quote Rousseau:

> *"That a rich and powerful man, having acquired immense possessions in land, should impose laws on those who want to establish themselves there, and that he should only allow them to do so on condition that they accept his supreme authority and obey all his wishes; that, I can still conceive … Would not this tyrannical act contain a double usurpation: that on the ownership of the land and that on the liberty of the inhabitants?"* [**Op. Cit.**, p. 316]

Hence Proudhon's comment that *"Man may be made by property a slave or a despot by turns."* [**What is Property?**, p. 371] Little wonder we discover Bakunin rejecting *"any contract with another individual on any footing but the utmost equality and reciprocity"* as this would *"alienate his [or her] freedom"* and so would be a *"a relationship of voluntary servitude with another individual."* Anyone making such a contract in a free society (i.e. anarchist society) would be *"devoid of any sense of personal dignity."* [**Michael Bakunin: Selected Writings**, pp. 68-9] Only self-managed associations can create relationships of equality rather than of subordination between its members.

Therefore anarchists stress the need for direct democracy in voluntary associations in order to ensure that the concept of "freedom" is not a sham and a justification for domination, as it is under capitalism. Only self-managed associations can create relationships of equality rather than of subordination between its members.

It is for this reason that anarchists have opposed capitalism and urged *"workers to form themselves into democratic societies, with equal conditions for all members, on pain of a relapse into feudalism."* [Proudhon, **The General Idea of the Revolution**, p. 277] For similar reasons, anarchists (with the notable exception of Proudhon) opposed marriage as it turned women into *"a bonded slave, who takes her master's name, her master's bread, her master's commands, and serves her master's passions … who can control no property, not even her own body, without his consent."* [Voltairine de Cleyre, *"Sex Slavery"*, **The Voltairine de Cleyre Reader**, p. 94] While marriage, due to feminist agitation, in many countries has been reformed towards the anarchist ideal of a free union of equals, it still is based on the patriarchal principles anarchists like Goldman and de Cleyre identified and condemned (see section A.3.5 for more on feminism and anarchism).

Clearly, voluntary entry is a necessary but not a sufficient condition to defend an individual's liberty. This is to be expected as it ignores (or takes for granted) the social conditions in which agreements are made and, moreover, ignores the social relationships created by them (*"For the worker who **must sell** his labour, it is impossible to remain **free**."* [Kropotkin, **Selected Writings on Anarchism and Revolution**, p. 305]). Any social relationships based on abstract individualism are likely to be based upon force, power, and authority, **not** liberty. This of course assumes a definition of liberty according to which individuals exercise their capacities and decide their own actions. Therefore, voluntarism is **not** enough to create a society that maximises liberty. This is why anarchists think that voluntary association **must** be complemented by self-management (direct democracy) **within** these associations. For anarchists, the assumptions of voluntarism imply self-management. Or, to use Proudhon's words, *"as individualism is the primordial fact of humanity, so association is its complementary term."* [**System of Economical Contradictions**, p. 430]

To answer the second objection first, in a society based on private property (and so statism), those with property have more power, which they can use to perpetuate their authority. *"Wealth is power, poverty is weakness,"* in the words of Albert Parsons. This means that under capitalism the much praised "freedom to choose" is extremely limited. It becomes, for the vast majority, the freedom to pick a master (under slavery, quipped Parsons, the master *"selected … his own slaves. Under the wage slavery system the wage slave selects his master."*). Under capitalism, Parsons stressed, *"those disinherited of their natural rights must hire out and serve and obey the oppressing class or starve. There is no other alternative. Some things are priceless, chief among which are life and liberty. A freeman [or woman] is not for sale or hire."* [**Anarchism**, p. 99 and p. 98] And why should we excuse servitude or tolerate those who desire to restrict the liberty of others? The "liberty" to command is the liberty to enslave, and so is actually a denial of liberty.

Regarding the first objection, anarchists plead guilty. We **are** prejudiced against the reduction of human beings to the status of robots. We are prejudiced in favour of human dignity and freedom.

We are prejudiced, in fact, in favour of humanity and individuality. (Section A.2.11 discusses why direct democracy is the necessary social counterpart to voluntarism (i.e. free agreement). Section B.4 discusses why capitalism cannot be based on equal bargaining power between property owners and the propertyless).

A.2.15 What about "human nature"?

Anarchists, far from ignoring "human nature," have the only political theory that gives this concept deep thought and reflection. Too often, "human nature" is flung up as the last line of defence in an argument against anarchism, because it is thought to be beyond reply. This is not the case, however. First of all, human nature is a complex thing. If, by human nature, it is meant "what humans do," it is obvious that human nature is contradictory – love and hate, compassion and heartlessness, peace and violence, and so on, have all been expressed by people and so are all products of "human nature." Of course, what is considered "human nature" can change with changing social circumstances. For example, slavery was considered part of "human nature" and "normal" for thousands of years. Homosexuality was considered perfectly normal by the ancient Greeks yet thousands of years later the Christian church denounced it as unnatural. War only become part of "human nature" once states developed. Hence Chomsky:

> "Individuals are certainly capable of evil … But individuals are capable of all sorts of things. Human nature has lots of ways of realising itself, humans have lots of capacities and options. Which ones reveal themselves depends to a large extent on the institutional structures. If we had institutions which permitted pathological killers free rein, they'd be running the place. The only way to survive would be to let those elements of your nature manifest themselves.

> "If we have institutions which make greed the sole property of human beings and encourage pure greed at the expense of other human emotions and commitments, we're going to have a society based on greed, with all that follows. A different society might be organised in such a way that human feelings and emotions of other sorts, say, solidarity, support, sympathy become dominant. Then you'll have different aspects of human nature and personality revealing themselves." [**Chronicles of Dissent**, p. 158]

Therefore, environment plays an important part in defining what "human nature" is, how it develops and what aspects of it are expressed. Indeed, one of the greatest myths about anarchism is the idea that we think human nature is inherently good (rather, we think it is inherently sociable). How it develops and expresses itself is dependent on the kind of society we live in and create. A hierarchical society will shape people in certain (negative) ways and produce a "human nature" radically different from a libertarian one. So *"when we hear men [and women] saying that Anarchists imagine men [and women] much better than they really are, we merely wonder how intelligent people can repeat that nonsense. Do we not say continually that the only means of rendering men [and women] less rapacious and egotistic, less ambitious and less slavish at the same time, is to eliminate those conditions which favour the growth of egotism and rapacity, of slavishness and ambition?"* [Peter Kropotkin, **Act for Yourselves**, p. 83]

As such, the use of "human nature" as an argument against anarchism is simply superficial and, ultimately, an evasion. It is an excuse not to think. *"Every fool,"* as Emma Goldman put it, *"from king to policemen, from the flatheaded parson to the visionless dabbler in science, presumes to speak authoritatively of human nature. The greater the mental charlatan, the more definite his insistence on the wickedness and weakness of human nature. Yet how can any one speak of it to-day, with every soul in prison, with every heart fettered, wounded, and maimed?"* Change society, create a better social environment and then we can judge what is a product of our natures and what is the product of an authoritarian system. For this reason, anarchism *"stands for the liberation of the human mind from the dominion of religion; the liberation of the human body from the dominion of property; liberation from the shackles and restraint of government."* For *"[f]reedom, expansion, opportunity, and above all, peace and repose, alone can teach us the real dominant factors of human nature and all its wonderful possibilities."* [**Red Emma Speaks**, p. 73]

This does not mean that human beings are infinitely plastic, with each individual born a **tabula rasa** (blank slate) waiting to be formed by "society" (which in practice means those who run it). As Noam Chomsky argues, *"I don't think its possible to give a rational account of the concept of alienated labour on that assumption [that human nature is nothing but a historical product], nor is it possible to produce something like a moral justification for the commitment to some kind of social change, except on the basis of assumptions about human nature and how modifications in the structure of society will be better able to conform to some of the fundamental needs that are part of our essential nature."* [**Language and Politics**, p. 215] We do not wish to enter the debate about what human characteristics are and are not "innate." All we will say is that human beings have an innate ability to think and learn – that much is obvious, we feel – and that humans are sociable creatures, needing the company of others to feel complete and to prosper. Moreover, they have the ability to recognise and oppose injustice and oppression (Bakunin rightly considered *"**the power to think** and **the desire to rebel**"* as *"precious faculties."* [**God and the State**, p. 9]).

These three features, we think, suggest the viability of an anarchist society. The innate ability to think for oneself automatically makes all forms of hierarchy illegitimate, and our need for social relationships implies that we can organise without the state. The deep unhappiness and alienation afflicting modern society reveals that the centralisation and authoritarianism of capitalism and the state are denying some innate needs within us. In fact, as mentioned earlier, for the great majority of its existence the human race **has** lived in anarchic communities, with little or no hierarchy. That modern society calls such people "savages" or "primitive" is pure arrogance. So who can tell whether anarchism is against "human nature"? Anarchists have accumulated much evidence to suggest that it may not be.

As for the charge the anarchists demand too much of "human nature," it is often **non** anarchists who make the greatest claims on it. For *"while our opponents seem to admit there is a kind of salt of the earth – the rulers, the employers, the leaders – who, happily enough, prevent those bad men – the ruled, the exploited, the led – from becoming still worse than they are"* we anarchists *"maintain that **both** rulers and ruled are spoiled by authority"* and *"**both** exploiters and exploited are spoiled by exploitation."* So *"there is [a] difference, and a very important one. **We** admit the imperfections of human nature, but we make no exception for the rulers. **They** make it, although sometimes unconsciously, and because we make no such exception, they say that we are dreamers."* [Peter Kropotkin, **Op. Cit.**, p. 83] If human nature is so bad, then giving some people power over others and hoping this will lead to justice and freedom is hopelessly utopian.

Moreover, as noted, Anarchists argue that hierarchical organisations bring out the worse in human nature. Both the oppressor and the oppressed are negatively affected by the authoritarian relationships so produced. *"It is a characteristic of privilege and of every kind of privilege,"* argued Bakunin, *"to kill the mind and heart of man … That is a social law which admits no exceptions … It is the law of equality and humanity."* [**God and the State**, p. 31] And while the privileged become corrupted by power, the powerless (in general) become servile in heart and mind (luckily the human spirit is such that there will always be rebels no matter the oppression for where there is oppression, there is resistance and, consequently, hope). As such, it seems strange for anarchists to hear non-anarchists justify hierarchy in terms of the (distorted) "human nature" it produces.

Sadly, too many have done precisely this. It continues to this day. For example, with the rise of "sociobiology," some claim (with very little **real** evidence) that capitalism is a product of our "nature," which is determined by our genes. These claims are simply a new variation of the "human nature" argument and have, unsurprisingly, been leapt upon by the powers that be. Considering the dearth of evidence, their support for this "new" doctrine must be purely the result of its utility to those in power – i.e. the fact that it is useful to have an "objective" and "scientific" basis to rationalise inequalities in wealth and power (for a discussion of this process see **Not in Our Genes: Biology, Ideology and Human Nature** by Steven Rose, R.C. Lewontin and Leon J. Kamin).

This is not to say that it does not hold a grain of truth. As scientist Stephen Jay Gould notes, *"the range of our potential behaviour is circumscribed by our biology"* and if this is what sociobiology means *"by genetic control, then we can scarcely disagree."* However, this is not what is meant. Rather, it is a form of *"biological determinism"* that sociobiology argues for. Saying that there are specific genes for specific human traits says little for while *"[v]iolence, sexism, and general nastiness **are** biological since they represent one subset of a possible range of behaviours"* so are *"peacefulness, equality, and kindness."* And so *"we may see their influence increase if we can create social structures that permit them to flourish."* That this may be the case can be seen from the works of sociobiologists themselves, who *"acknowledge diversity"* in human cultures while *"often dismiss[ing] the uncomfortable 'exceptions' as temporary and unimportant aberrations."* This is surprising, for if you believe that *"repeated, often genocidal warfare has shaped our genetic destiny, the existence of nonaggressive peoples is embarrassing."* [**Ever Since Darwin**, p. 252, p. 257 and p. 254]

Like the social Darwinism that preceded it, sociobiology proceeds by first projecting the dominant ideas of current society onto nature (often unconsciously, so that scientists mistakenly consider the ideas in question as both "normal" and "natural"). Bookchin refers to this as *"the subtle projection of historically conditioned human values"* onto nature rather than *"scientific objectivity."* Then the theories of nature produced in this manner are transferred **back** onto society and history, being used to "prove" that the principles of capitalism (hierarchy, authority, competition, etc.) are eternal **laws,** which are then appealed to as a justification for the status quo! *"What this procedure does accomplish,"* notes Bookchin, *"is reinforce human social hierarchies by justifying the command of men and women as innate features of the 'natural order.' Human domination is thereby transcribed into the genetic code as biologically immutable."* [**The Ecology of Freedom**, p. 95 and p. 92] Amazingly, there are many supposedly intelligent people who take this sleight-of-hand seriously.

This can be seen when "hierarchies" in nature are used to explain, and so justify, hierarchies in human societies. Such analogies are misleading for they forget the institutional nature of human life. As Murray Bookchin notes in his critique of sociobiology, a *"weak, enfeebled, unnerved, and sick ape is hardly likely to become an 'alpha' male, much less retain this highly ephemeral 'status.' By contrast, the most physically and mentally pathological human rulers have exercised authority with devastating effect in the course of history."* This *"expresses a power of hierarchical **institutions** over persons that is completely reversed in so-called 'animal hierarchies' where the absence of institutions is precisely the only intelligible way of talking about 'alpha males' or 'queen bees.'"* [*"Sociobiology or Social Ecology"*, **Which way for the Ecology Movement?**, p. 58] Thus what makes human society unique is conveniently ignored and the real sources of power in society are hidden under a genetic screen.

The sort of apologetics associated with appeals to "human nature" (or sociobiology at its worse) are natural, of course, because every ruling class needs to justify their right to rule. Hence they support doctrines that defined the latter in ways appearing to justify elite power – be it sociobiology, divine right, original sin, etc. Obviously, such doctrines have always been wrong … until now, of course, as it is obvious our current society truly conforms to "human nature" and it has been scientifically proven by our current scientific priesthood!

The arrogance of this claim is truly amazing. History hasn't stopped. One thousand years from now, society will be completely different from what it is presently or from what anyone has imagined. No government in place at the moment will still be around, and the current economic system will not exist. The only thing that may remain the same is that people will still be claiming that their new society is the "One True System" that completely conforms to human nature, even though all past systems did not.

Of course, it does not cross the minds of supporters of capitalism that people from different cultures may draw different conclusions from the same facts – conclusions that may be **more** valid. Nor does it occur to capitalist apologists that the theories of the "objective" scientists may be framed in the context of the dominant ideas of the society they live in. It comes as no surprise to anarchists, however, that scientists working in Tsarist Russia developed a theory of evolution based on **co-operation** within species, quite unlike their counterparts in capitalist Britain, who developed a theory based on **competitive struggle** within and between species. That the latter theory reflected the dominant political and economic theories of British society (notably competitive individualism) is pure coincidence, of course.

Kropotkin's classic work **Mutual Aid**, for example, was written in response to the obvious inaccuracies that British representatives of Darwinism had projected onto nature and human life. Building upon the mainstream Russian criticism of the British Darwinism of the time, Kropotkin showed (with substantial empirical evidence) that "mutual aid" within a group or species played as important a role as "mutual struggle" between individuals within those groups or species (see Stephan Jay Gould's essay *"Kropotkin was no Crackpot"* in his book **Bully for Brontosaurus** for details and an evaluation). It was, he stressed, a *"factor"* in evolution along with competition, a factor which, in most circumstances, was far more important to survival. Thus co-operation is just as "natural" as competition so proving that "human nature" was not a barrier to anarchism as co-operation between members of a species can be the best pathway to advantage individuals.

To conclude. Anarchists argue that anarchy is not against "human nature" for two main reasons. Firstly, what is considered as being "human nature" is shaped by the society we live in and the relationships we create. This means a hierarchical society will encourage certain personality traits to dominate while an anarchist one would encourage others. As such, anarchists *"do not so much rely on the fact that human nature will change as they do upon the theory that the same nature will act differently under different circumstances."* Secondly, change *"seems to be one of the fundamental laws of existence"* so *"who can say that man [sic!] has reached the limits of his possibilities."* [George Barrett, **Objections to Anarchism**, pp. 360-1 and p. 360]

For useful discussions on anarchist ideas on human nature, both of which refute the idea that anarchists think human beings are naturally good, see Peter Marshall's *"Human nature and anarchism"* [David Goodway (ed.), **For Anarchism: History, Theory and Practice**, pp. 127-149] and David Hartley's *"Communitarian Anarchism and Human Nature"*. [**Anarchist Studies**, vol. 3, no. 2, Autumn 1995, pp. 145-164]

A.2.16 Does anarchism require "perfect" people to work?

No. Anarchy is not a utopia, a "perfect" society. It will be a **human** society, with all the problems, hopes, and fears associated with human beings. Anarchists do not think that human beings need to be "perfect" for anarchy to work. They only need to be free. Thus

Christie and Meltzer:

> *"[A] common fallacy [is] that revolutionary socialism [i.e. anarchism] is an 'idealisation' of the workers and [so] the mere recital of their present faults is a refutation of the class struggle ... it seems morally unreasonable that a free society ... could exist without moral or ethical perfection. But so far as the overthrow of [existing] society is concerned, we may ignore the fact of people's shortcomings and prejudices, so long as they do not become institutionalised. One may view without concern the fact ... that the workers might achieve control of their places of work long before they had acquired the social graces of the 'intellectual' or shed all the prejudices of the present society from family discipline to xenophobia. What does it matter, so long as they can run industry without masters? Prejudices wither in freedom and only flourish while the social climate is favourable to them.... What we say is ... that once life can continue without imposed authority from above, and imposed authority cannot survive the withdrawal of labour from its service, the prejudices of authoritarianism will disappear. There is no cure for them other than the free process of education."*

[The Floodgates of Anarchy, pp. 36-7]

Obviously, though, we think that a free society will produce people who are more in tune with both their own and others individuality and needs, thus reducing individual conflict. Remaining disputes would be solved by reasonable methods, for example, the use of juries, mutual third parties, or community and workplace assemblies (see section I.5.8 for a discussion of how could be done for anti-social activities as well as disputes).

Like the "anarchism-is-against-human-nature" argument (see section A.2.15), opponents of anarchism usually assume "perfect" people – people who are not corrupted by power when placed in positions of authority, people who are strangely unaffected by the distorting effects of hierarchy, privilege, and so forth. However, anarchists make no such claims about human perfection. We simply recognise that vesting power in the hands of one person or an elite is never a good idea, as people are not perfect.

It should be noted that the idea that anarchism requires a "new" (perfect) man or woman is often raised by the opponents of anarchism to discredit it (and, usually, to justify the retention of hierarchical authority, particularly capitalist relations of production). After all, people are not perfect and are unlikely ever to be. As such, they pounce on every example of a government falling and the resulting chaos to dismiss anarchism as unrealistic. The media loves to proclaim a country to be falling into "anarchy" whenever there is a disruption in "law and order" and looting takes place.

Anarchists are not impressed by this argument. A moment's reflection shows why, for the detractors make the basic mistake of assuming an anarchist society without anarchists! (A variation of such claims is raised by the right-wing "anarcho"-capitalists to discredit real anarchism. However, their "objection" discredits their own claim to be anarchists for they implicitly assume an anarchist society without anarchists!). Needless to say, an "anarchy" made up of people who still saw the need for authority, property and statism would soon become authoritarian (i.e. non-anarchist) again. This is because even if the government disappeared tomorrow, the same system would soon grow up again, because *"the strength of the government rests not with itself, but with the people. A great tyrant may be a fool, and not a superman. His strength lies not in himself, but in the superstition of the people who think that it is right to obey him. So long as that superstition exists it is useless for some liberator to cut off the head of tyranny; the people will create another, for they have grown accustomed to rely on something outside themselves."* [George Barrett, **Objections to Anarchism**, p. 355]

Hence Alexander Berkman:

> *"Our social institutions are founded on certain ideas; as long as the latter are generally believed, the institutions built on them are safe. Government remains strong because people think political authority and legal compulsion necessary. Capitalism will continue as long as such an economic system is considered adequate and just. The weakening of the ideas which support the evil and oppressive present day conditions means the ultimate breakdown of government and capitalism."* [**What is Anarchism?**, p. xii]

In other words, anarchy needs **anarchists** in order to be created and survive. But these anarchists need not be perfect, just people who have freed themselves, by their own efforts, of the superstition that command-and-obedience relations and capitalist property rights are necessary. The implicit assumption in the idea that anarchy needs "perfect" people is that freedom will be given, not taken; hence the obvious conclusion follows that an anarchy requiring "perfect" people will fail. But this argument ignores the need for self-activity and self-liberation in order to create a free society. For anarchists, *"history is nothing but a struggle between the rulers and the ruled, the oppressors and the oppressed."* [Peter Kropotkin, **Act for Yourselves**, p. 85] Ideas change through struggle and, consequently, in the struggle against oppression and exploitation, we not only change the world, we change ourselves at the same time. So it is the struggle for freedom which creates people capable of taking the responsibility for their own lives, communities and planet. People capable of living as equals in a free society, so making anarchy possible.

As such, the chaos which often results when a government disappears is not anarchy nor, in fact, a case against anarchism. It simple means that the necessary preconditions for creating an anarchist society do not exist. Anarchy would be the product of collective struggle at the heart of society, not the product of external shocks. Nor, we should note, do anarchists think that such a society will appear "overnight." Rather, we see the creation of an anarchist system as a process, not an event. The ins-and-outs of how it would function will evolve over time in the light of experience and objective circumstances, not appear in a perfect form immediately (see section H.2.5 for a discussion of Marxist claims otherwise).

Therefore, anarchists do not conclude that "perfect" people are necessary for anarchism to work because the anarchist is *"no liberator with a divine mission to free humanity, but he is a part of that humanity struggling onwards towards liberty."* As such, *"[i]f,*

then, by some external means an Anarchist Revolution could be, so to speak, supplied ready-made and thrust upon the people, it is true that they would reject it and rebuild the old society. If, on the other hand, the people develop their ideas of freedom, and they themselves get rid of the last stronghold of tyranny – the government – then indeed the revolution will be permanently accomplished." [George Barrett, **Op. Cit.**, p. 355]

This is not to suggest that an anarchist society must wait until **everyone** is an anarchist. Far from it. It is highly unlikely, for example, that the rich and powerful will suddenly see the errors of their ways and voluntarily renounce their privileges. Faced with a large and growing anarchist movement, the ruling elite has always used repression to defend its position in society. The use of fascism in Spain (see section A.5.6) and Italy (see section A.5.5) show the depths the capitalist class can sink to. Anarchism will be created in the face of opposition by the ruling minorities and, consequently, will need to defend itself against attempts to recreate authority (see section H.2.1 for a refutation of Marxist claims anarchists reject the need to defend an anarchist society against counter-revolution).

Instead anarchists argue that we should focus our activity on convincing those subject to oppression and exploitation that they have the power to resist both and, ultimately, can end both by destroying the social institutions that cause them. As Malatesta argued, *"we need the support of the masses to build a force of sufficient strength to achieve our specific task of radical change in the social organism by the direct action of the masses, we must get closer to them, accept them as they are, and from within their ranks seek to 'push' them forward as much as possible."* [**Errico Malatesta: His Life and Ideas**, pp. 155-6] This would create the conditions that make possible a rapid evolution towards anarchism as what was initially accepted by a minority *"but increasingly finding popular expression, will make its way among the mass of the people"* and *"the minority will become the People, the great mass, and that mass rising up against property and the State, will march forward towards anarchist communism."* [Kropotkin, **Words of a Rebel**, p. 75] Hence the importance anarchists attach to spreading our ideas and arguing the case for anarchism. This creates conscious anarchists from those questioning the injustices of capitalism and the state.

This process is helped by the nature of hierarchical society and the resistance it naturally developed in those subject to it. Anarchist ideas develop spontaneously through struggle. As we discuss in section I.2.3, anarchistic organisations are often created as part of the resistance against oppression and exploitation which marks every hierarchical system and can., potentially, be the framework of a few society. As such, the creation of libertarian institutions is, therefore, always a possibility in any situation. A peoples' experiences may push them towards anarchist conclusions, namely the awareness that the state exists to protect the wealthy and powerful few and to disempower the many. That while it is needed to maintain class and hierarchical society, it is not needed to organise society nor can it do so in a just and fair way for all. This is possible. However, without a conscious anarchist presence any libertarian tendencies are likely to be used, abused and finally destroyed by parties or religious groups seeking political power over the masses (the Russian Revolution is the most famous example of this process).

It is for that reason anarchists organise to influence the struggle and spread our ideas (see section J.3 for details). For it is the case that only when anarchist ideas *"acquire a predominating influence"* and are *"accepted by a sufficiently large section of the population"* will we *"have achieved anarchy, or taken a step towards anarchy."* For anarchy *"cannot be imposed against the wishes of the people."* [Malatesta, **Op. Cit.**, p. 159 and p. 163]

So, to conclude, the creation of an anarchist society is not dependent on people being perfect but it is dependent on a large majority being anarchists and wanting to reorganise society in a libertarian manner. This will not eliminate conflict between individuals nor create a fully formed anarchist humanity overnight but it will lay the ground for the gradual elimination of whatever prejudices and anti-social behaviour that remain after the struggle to change society has revolutionised those doing it.

A.2.17 Aren't most people too stupid for a free society to work?

We are sorry to have to include this question in an anarchist FAQ, but we know that many political ideologies explicitly assume that ordinary people are too stupid to be able to manage their own lives and run society. All aspects of the capitalist political agenda, from Left to Right, contain people who make this claim. Be it Leninists, fascists, Fabians or Objectivists, it is assumed that only a select few are creative and intelligent and that these people should govern others. Usually, this elitism is masked by fine, flowing rhetoric about "freedom," "democracy" and other platitudes with which the ideologues attempt to dull people's critical thought by telling them want they want to hear.

It is, of course, also no surprise that those who believe in "natural" elites always class themselves at the top. We have yet to discover an "objectivist", for example, who considers themselves part of the great mass of "second-handers" (it is always amusing to hear people who simply parrot the ideas of Ayn Rand dismissing other people so!) or who will be a toilet cleaner in the unknown "ideal" of "real" capitalism. Everybody reading an elitist text will consider him or herself to be part of the "select few." It's "natural" in an elitist society to consider elites to be natural and yourself a potential member of one!

Examination of history shows that there is a basic elitist ideology which has been the essential rationalisation of all states and ruling classes since their emergence at the beginning of the Bronze Age (*"if the legacy of domination had had any broader purpose than the support of hierarchical and class interests, it has been the attempt to exorcise the belief in public competence from social discourse itself."* [Bookchin, **The Ecology of Freedom**, p. 206]). This ideology merely changes its outer garments, not its basic inner content over time.

During the Dark Ages, for example, it was coloured by Christianity, being adapted to the needs of the Church hierarchy. The most useful "divinely revealed" dogma to the priestly elite was "original sin": the notion that human beings are basically depraved and incompetent creatures who need "direction from above," with priests as the conveniently necessary mediators between ordinary humans and "God." The idea that average people are basically stupid and thus incapable of governing themselves is a carry over from this doctrine, a relic of the Dark Ages.

In reply to all those who claim that most people are "second-handers" or cannot develop anything more than "trade union consciousness," all we can say is that it is an absurdity that cannot withstand even a superficial look at history, particularly the labour movement. The creative powers of those struggling for freedom is often truly amazing, and if this intellectual power and inspiration is not seen in "normal" society, this is the clearest indictment possible of the deadening effects of hierarchy and the conformity produced by authority. (See also section B.1 for more on the effects of hierarchy). As Bob Black points outs:

> *"You are what you do. If you do boring, stupid, monotonous work, chances are you'll end up boring, stupid, and monotonous. Work is a much better explanation for the creeping cretinisation all around us than even such significant moronising mechanisms as television and education. People who are regimented all their lives, handed to work from school and bracketed by the family in the beginning and the nursing home in the end, are habituated to hierarchy and psychologically enslaved. Their aptitude for autonomy is so atrophied that their fear of freedom is among their few rationally grounded phobias. Their obedience training at work carries over into the families **they** start, thus reproducing the system in more ways than one, and into politics, culture and everything else. Once you drain the vitality from people at work, they'll likely submit to hierarchy and expertise in everything. They're used to it."* [**The Abolition of Work and other essays**, pp. 21-2]

When elitists try to conceive of liberation, they can only think of it being **given** to the oppressed by kind (for Leninists) or stupid (for Objectivists) elites. It is hardly surprising, then, that it fails. Only self-liberation can produce a free society. The crushing and distorting effects of authority can only be overcome by self-activity. The few examples of such self-liberation prove that most people, once considered incapable of freedom by others, are more than up for the task.

Those who proclaim their "superiority" often do so out of fear that their authority and power will be destroyed once people free themselves from the debilitating hands of authority and come to realise that, in the words of Max Stirner, *"the great are great only because we are on our knees. Let us rise."*

As Emma Goldman remarks about women's equality, *"[t]he extraordinary achievements of women in every walk of life have silenced forever the loose talk of women's inferiority. Those who still cling to this fetish do so because they hate nothing so much as to see their authority challenged. This is the characteristic of all authority, whether the master over his economic slaves or man over women. However, everywhere woman is escaping her cage, everywhere she is going ahead with free, large strides."* [**Vision on Fire**, p. 256] The same comments are applicable, for example, to the very successful experiments in workers' self-management during the Spanish Revolution.

Then, of course, the notion that people are too stupid for anarchism to work also backfires on those who argue it. Take, for example, those who use this argument to advocate democratic government rather than anarchy. Democracy, as Luigi Galleani noted, means *"acknowledging the right and the competence of the people to select their rulers."* However, *"whoever has the political competence to choose his [or her] own rulers is, by implication, also competent to do without them, especially when the causes of economic enmity are uprooted."* [**The End of Anarchism?**, p. 37] Thus the argument for democracy against anarchism undermines itself, for *"if you consider these worthy electors as unable to look after their own interests themselves, how is it that they know how to choose for themselves the shepherds who must guide them? And how will they be able to solve this problem of social alchemy, of producing the election of a genius from the votes of a mass of fools?"* [Malatesta, **Anarchy**, pp. 53-4]

As for those who consider dictatorship as the solution to human stupidity, the question arises why are these dictators immune to this apparently universal human trait? And, as Malatesta noted, *"who are the best? And who will recognise these qualities in them?"* [**Op. Cit.**, p. 53] If they impose themselves on the "stupid" masses, why assume they will not exploit and oppress the many for their own benefit? Or, for that matter, that they are any more intelligent than the masses? The history of dictatorial and monarchical government suggests a clear answer to those questions. A similar argument applies for other non-democratic systems, such as those based on limited suffrage. For example, the Lockean (i.e. classical liberal or right-wing libertarian) ideal of a state based on the rule of property owners is doomed to be little more than a regime which oppresses the majority to maintain the power and privilege of the wealthy few. Equally, the idea of near universal stupidity bar an elite of capitalists (the "objectivist" vision) implies a system somewhat less ideal than the perfect system presented in the literature. This is because most people would tolerate oppressive bosses who treat them as means to an end rather than an end in themselves. For how can you expect people to recognise and pursue their own self-interest if you consider them fundamentally as the *"uncivilised hordes"*? You cannot have it both ways and the *"unknown ideal"* of pure capitalism would be as grubby, oppressive and alienating as "actually existing" capitalism.

As such, anarchists are firmly convinced that arguments against anarchy based on the lack of ability of the mass of people are inherently self-contradictory (when not blatantly self-servicing). If people are too stupid for anarchism then they are too stupid for any system you care to mention. Ultimately, anarchists argue that such a perspective simply reflects the servile mentality produced by a hierarchical society rather than a genuine analysis of humanity and our history as a species. To quote Rousseau:

> *"when I see multitudes of entirely naked savages scorn European voluptuousness and endure hunger, fire, the sword, and death to preserve only their independence, I feel that it does not behove slaves to reason about freedom."* [quoted by Noam Chomsky, **Marxism, Anarchism, and Alternative Futures**, p. 780]

A.2.18 Do anarchists support terrorism?

No. This is for three reasons.

Terrorism means either targeting or not worrying about killing innocent people. For anarchy to exist, it must be created by the mass of people. One does not convince people of one's ideas by blowing them up. Secondly, anarchism is about self-liberation. One cannot blow up a social relationship. Freedom cannot be created by the actions of an elite few destroying rulers **on behalf of** the majority. Simply put, a *"structure based on centuries of history cannot be destroyed with a few kilos of explosives."* [Kropotkin, quoted by Martin A. Millar, **Kropotkin**, p. 174] For so long as people feel the need for rulers, hierarchy will exist (see section A.2.16 for more on this). As we have stressed earlier, freedom cannot be given, only taken. Lastly, anarchism aims for freedom. Hence Bakunin's comment that *"when one is carrying out a revolution for the liberation of humanity, one should respect the life and liberty of men [and women]."* [quoted by K.J. Kenafick, **Michael Bakunin and Karl Marx**, p. 125] For anarchists, means determine the ends and terrorism by its very nature violates life and liberty of individuals and so cannot be used to create an anarchist society. The history of, say, the Russian Revolution, confirmed Kropotkin's insight that *"[v]ery sad would be the future revolution if it could only triumph by terror."* [quoted by Millar, **Op. Cit.**, p. 175]

Moreover anarchists are **not** against individuals but the institutions and social relationships that cause certain individuals to have power over others and abuse (i.e. use) that power. Therefore the anarchist revolution is about destroying structures, not people. As Bakunin pointed out, *"we wish not to kill persons, but to abolish status and its perquisites"* and anarchism *"does not mean the death of the individuals who make up the bourgeoisie, but the death of the bourgeoisie as a political and social entity economically distinct from the working class."* [**The Basic Bakunin**, p. 71 and p. 70] In other words, ***"You can't blow up a social relationship"*** (to quote the title of an anarchist pamphlet which presents the anarchist case against terrorism).How is it, then, that anarchism is associated with violence? Partly this is because the state and media insist on referring to terrorists who are **not** anarchists as anarchists. For example, the German Baader-Meinhoff gang were often called "anarchists" despite their self-proclaimed Marxist-Leninism. Smears, unfortunately, work. Similarly, as Emma Goldman pointed out, *"it is a known fact known to almost everyone familiar with the Anarchist movement that a great number of [violent] acts, for which Anarchists had to suffer, either originated with the capitalist press or were instigated, if not directly perpetrated, by the police."* [**Red Emma Speaks**, p. 262]

An example of this process at work can be seen from the current anti-globalisation movement. In Seattle, for example, the media reported "violence" by protestors (particularly anarchist ones) yet this amounted to a few broken windows. The much greater **actual** violence of the police against protestors (which, incidentally, started **before** the breaking of a single window) was not considered worthy of comment. Subsequent media coverage of anti-globalisation demonstrations followed this pattern, firmly connecting anarchism with violence in spite of that the protesters have been the ones to suffer the greatest violence at the hands of the state. As anarchist activist Starhawk notes, *"if breaking windows and fighting back when the cops attack is 'violence,' then give me a new word, a word a thousand times stronger, to use when the cops are beating non-resisting people into comas."* [**Staying on the Streets**, p. 130]

Similarly, at the Genoa protests in 2001 the mainstream media presented the protestors as violent even though it was the state who killed one of them and hospitalised many thousands more. The presence of police agent provocateurs in creating the violence was unmentioned by the media. As Starhawk noted afterwards, in Genoa *"we encountered a carefully orchestrated political campaign of state terrorism. The campaign included disinformation, the use of infiltrators and provocateurs, collusion with avowed Fascist groups…, the deliberate targeting of non-violent groups for tear gas and beating, endemic police brutality, the torture of prisoners, the political persecution of organisers … They did all those openly, in a way that indicates they had no fear of repercussions and expected political protection from the highest sources."* [**Op. Cit.**, pp. 128-9] This was, unsurprisingly, not reported by the media.

Subsequent protests have seen the media indulge in yet more anti-anarchist hype, inventing stories to present anarchists are hate-filled individuals planning mass violence. For example, in Ireland in 2004 the media reported that anarchists were planning to use poison gas during EU related celebrations in Dublin. Of course, evidence of such a plan was not forthcoming and no such action happened. Neither did the riot the media said anarchists were organising. A similar process of misinformation accompanied the anti-capitalist May Day demonstrations in London and the protests against the Republican National Congress in New York. In spite of being constantly proved wrong after the event, the media always prints the scare stories of anarchist violence (even inventing events at, say Seattle, to justify their articles and to demonise anarchism further). Thus the myth that anarchism equals violence is perpetrated. Needless to say, the same papers that hyped the (non-existent) threat of anarchist violence remained silent on the actual violence of, and repression by, the police against demonstrators which occurred at these events. Neither did they run apologies after their (evidence-less) stories of doom were exposed as the nonsense they were by subsequent events.

This does not mean that Anarchists have not committed acts of violence. They have (as have members of other political and religious movements). The main reason for the association of terrorism with anarchism is because of the ***"propaganda by the deed"*** period in the anarchist movement.

This period – roughly from 1880 to 1900 – was marked by a small number of anarchists assassinating members of the ruling class (royalty, politicians and so forth). At its worse, this period saw theatres and shops frequented by members of the bourgeoisie targeted. These acts were termed *"propaganda by the deed."* Anarchist support for the tactic was galvanised by the assassination of Tsar Alexander II in 1881 by Russian Populists (this event prompted Johann Most's famous editorial in **Freiheit**, entitled *"At Last!"*, celebrating regicide and the assassination of tyrants). However, there were deeper reasons for anarchist support of this tactic: firstly, in revenge for acts of repression directed towards working class people; and secondly, as a means to encourage people to revolt by showing that their oppressors could be defeated.

Considering these reasons it is no coincidence that propaganda by the deed began in France after the 20 000-plus deaths due to the French state's brutal suppression of the Paris Commune, in which many anarchists were killed. It is interesting to note that while the anarchist violence in revenge for the Commune is relatively well known, the state's mass murder of the Communards is relatively unknown. Similarly, it may be known that the Italian Anarchist Gaetano Bresci assassinated King Umberto of Italy in 1900 or that Alexander Berkman tried to kill Carnegie Steel Corporation manager Henry Clay Frick in 1892. What is often unknown is that Umberto's troops had fired upon and killed protesting peasants or that Frick's Pinkertons had also murdered locked-out workers at Homestead.

Such downplaying of statist and capitalist violence is hardly surprising. *"The State's behaviour is violence,"* points out Max Stirner, *"and it calls its violence 'law'; that of the individual, 'crime.'"* [**The Ego and Its Own**, p. 197] Little wonder, then, that anarchist violence is condemned but the repression (and often worse violence) that provoked it ignored and forgotten. Anarchists point to the hypocrisy of the accusation that anarchists are "violent" given that such claims come from either supporters of government or the actual governments themselves, governments *"which came into being through violence, which maintain themselves in power through violence, and which use violence constantly to keep down rebellion and to bully other nations."* [Howard Zinn, **The Zinn Reader**, p. 652]

We can get a feel of the hypocrisy surrounding condemnation of anarchist violence by non-anarchists by considering their response to state violence. For example, many capitalist papers and individuals in the 1920s and 1930s celebrated Fascism as well as Mussolini and Hitler. Anarchists, in contrast, fought Fascism to the death and tried to assassinate both Mussolini and Hitler. Obviously supporting murderous dictatorships is not "violence" and "terrorism" but resisting such regimes is! Similarly, non-anarchists can support repressive and authoritarian states, war and the suppression of strikes and unrest by violence ("restoring law and order") and not be considered "violent." Anarchists, in contrast, are condemned as "violent" and "terrorist" because a few of them tried to revenge such acts of oppression and state/capitalist violence! Similarly, it seems the height of hypocrisy for someone to denounce the anarchist "violence" which produces a few broken windows in, say, Seattle while supporting the actual violence of the police in imposing the state's rule or, even worse, supporting the American invasion of Iraq in 2003. If anyone should be considered violent it is the supporter of state and its actions yet people do not see the obvious and *"deplore the type of violence that the state deplores, and applaud the violence that the state practises."* [Christie and Meltzer, **The Floodgates of Anarchy**, p. 132]

It must be noted that the majority of anarchists did not support this tactic. Of those who committed "propaganda by the deed" (sometimes called *"attentats"*), as Murray Bookchin points out, only a *"few … were members of Anarchist groups. The majority … were soloists."* [**The Spanish Anarchists**, p. 102] Needless to say, the state and media painted all anarchists with the same brush. They still do, usually inaccurately (such as blaming Bakunin for such acts even though he had been dead years before the tactic was even discussed in anarchist circles or by labelling non-anarchist groups anarchists!).

All in all, the "propaganda by the deed" phase of anarchism was a failure, as the vast majority of anarchists soon came to see. Kropotkin can be considered typical. He *"never liked the slogan **propaganda by deed**, and did not use it to describe his own ideas of revolutionary action."* However, in 1879 while still *"urg[ing] the importance of collective action"* he started *"expressing considerable sympathy and interest in **attentats**"* (these *"collective forms of action"* were seen as acting *"at the trade union and communal level"*). In 1880 he *"became less preoccupied with collective action and this enthusiasm for acts of revolt by individuals and small groups increased."* This did not last and Kropotkin soon attached *"progressively less importance to isolated acts of revolt"* particularly once *"he saw greater opportunities for developing collective action in the new militant trade unionism."* [Caroline Cahm, **Kropotkin and the Rise of Revolutionary Anarchism**, p. 92, p. 115, p. 129, pp. 129-30, p. 205] By the late 1880s and early 1890s he came to disapprove of such acts of violence. This was partly due to simple revulsion at the worse of the acts (such as the Barcelona Theatre bombing in response to the state murder of anarchists involved in the Jerez uprising of 1892 and Emile Henry's bombing of a cafe in response to state repression) and partly due to the awareness that it was hindering the anarchist cause.

Kropotkin recognised that the *"spate of terrorist acts"* of the 1880s had caused *"the authorities into taking repressive action against the movement"* and were *"not in his view consistent with the anarchist ideal and did little or nothing to promote popular revolt."* In addition, he was *"anxious about the isolation of the movement from the masses"* which *"had increased rather than diminished as a result of the preoccupation with"* propaganda by deed. He *"saw the best possibility for popular revolution in the ... development of the new militancy in the labour movement. From now on he focussed his attention increasingly on the importance of revolutionary minorities working among the masses to develop the spirit of revolt."* However, even during the early 1880s when his support for individual acts of revolt (if not for propaganda by the deed) was highest, he saw the need for collective class struggle and, therefore, *"Kropotkin always insisted on the importance of the labour movement in the struggles leading up to the revolution."* [**Op. Cit.**, pp. 205-6, p. 208 and p. 280]

Kropotkin was not alone. More and more anarchists came to see "propaganda by the deed" as giving the state an excuse to clamp down on both the anarchist and labour movements. Moreover, it gave the media (and opponents of anarchism) a chance to associate anarchism with mindless violence, thus alienating much of the population from the movement. This false association is renewed at every opportunity, regardless of the facts (for example, even though Individualist Anarchists rejected "propaganda by the deed" totally, they were also smeared by the press as "violent" and "terrorists"). In addition, as Kropotkin pointed out, the assumption behind propaganda by the deed, i.e. that everyone was waiting for a chance to rebel, was false. In fact, people are products of the system in which they live; hence they accepted most of the myths used to keep that system going. With the failure of propaganda by deed, anarchists turned back to what most of the movement had been doing anyway: encouraging the class struggle and the process of self-liberation. This turn back to the roots of anarchism can be seen from the rise in anarcho-syndicalist unions after 1890 (see section A.5.3). This position flows naturally from anarchist theory, unlike the idea of individual acts of violence:

> *"to bring about a revolution, and specially the Anarchist revolution[, it] is necessary that the people be conscious of their rights and their strength; it is necessary that they be ready to fight and ready to take the conduct of their affairs into their own hands. It must be the constant preoccupation of the revolutionists, the point towards which all their activity must aim, to bring about this state of mind among the masses ... Who expects the emancipation of mankind to come, not from the persistent and harmonious co-operation of all men [and women] of progress, but from the accidental or providential happening of some acts of heroism, is not better advised that one who expected it from the intervention of an ingenious legislator or of a victorious general ... our ideas oblige us to put all our hopes in the masses, because we do not believe in the possibility of imposing good by force and we do not want to be commanded ... Today, that which ... was the logical outcome of our ideas, the condition which our conception of the revolution and reorganisation of society imposes on us ... [is] to live among the people and to win them over to our ideas by actively taking part in their struggles and sufferings."* [Errico Malatesta, *"The Duties of the Present Hour"*, pp. 181-3, **Anarchism**, Robert Graham (ed.), pp. 180-1]

Despite most anarchists' tactical disagreement with propaganda by deed, few would consider it to be terrorism or rule out assassination under all circumstances. Bombing a village during a war because there **might** be an enemy in it is terrorism, whereas assassinating a murdering dictator or head of a repressive state is defence at best and revenge at worst. As anarchists have long pointed out, if by terrorism it is meant "killing innocent people" then the state is the greatest terrorist of them all (as well as having the biggest bombs and other weapons of destruction available on the planet). If the people committing "acts of terror" are really anarchists, they would do everything possible to avoid harming innocent people and never use the statist line that "collateral damage" is regrettable but inevitable. This is why the vast majority of "propaganda by the deed" acts were directed towards individuals of the ruling class, such as Presidents and Royalty, and were the result of previous acts of state and capitalist violence.

So "terrorist" acts have been committed by anarchists. This is a fact. However, it has nothing to do with anarchism as a socio-political theory. As Emma Goldman argued, it was *"not Anarchism, as such, but the brutal slaughter of the eleven steel workers [that] was the urge for Alexander Berkman's act."* [**Op. Cit.**, p. 268] Equally, members of **other** political and religious groups have also committed such acts. As the Freedom Group of London argued:

*"There is a truism that the man [or woman] in the street seems always to forget, when he is abusing the Anarchists, or whatever party happens to be his **bete noire** for the moment, as the cause of some outrage just perpetrated. This indisputable fact is that homicidal outrages have, from time immemorial, been the reply of goaded and desperate classes, and goaded and desperate individuals, to wrongs from their fellowmen [and women], which they felt to be intolerable. Such acts are the violent recoil from violence, whether aggressive or repressive ... their cause lies not in any special conviction, but in the depths of ... human nature itself. The whole course of history, political and social, is strewn with evidence of this."* [quoted by Emma Goldman, **Op. Cit.**, p. 259]

Terrorism has been used by many other political, social and religious groups and parties. For example, Christians, Marxists, Hindus, Nationalists, Republicans, Moslems, Sikhs, Fascists, Jews and Patriots have all committed acts of terrorism. Few of these movements or ideas have been labelled as "terrorist by nature" or continually associated with violence – which shows anarchism's threat to the status quo. There is nothing more likely to discredit and marginalise an idea than for malicious and/or ill-informed persons to portray those who believe and practice it as "mad bombers" with no opinions or ideals at all, just an insane urge to destroy.

Of course, the vast majority of Christians and so on have opposed terrorism as morally repugnant and counter-productive. As have the vast majority of anarchists, at all times and places. However, it seems that in our case it is necessary to state our opposition to terrorism time and time again.

So, to summarise – only a small minority of terrorists have ever been anarchists, and only a small minority of anarchists have ever been terrorists. The anarchist movement as a whole has always recognised that social relationships cannot be assassinated or bombed out of existence. Compared to the violence of the state and capitalism, anarchist violence is a drop in the ocean. Unfortunately most people remember the acts of the few anarchists who have committed violence rather than the acts of violence and repression by the state and capital that prompted those acts.

A.2.19 What ethical views do anarchists hold?

Anarchist viewpoints on ethics vary considerably, although all share a common belief in the need for an individual to develop within themselves their own sense of ethics. All anarchists agree with Max Stirner that an individual must free themselves from the confines of existing morality and question that morality – *"I decide whether it is the **right thing** for me; there is no right **outside** me."* [**The Ego and Its Own**, p. 189]

Few anarchists, however, would go so far as Stirner and reject **any** concept of social ethics at all (saying that, Stirner does value some universal concepts although they are egoistic ones). Such extreme moral relativism is almost as bad as moral absolutism for most anarchists (moral relativism is the view that there is no right or wrong beyond what suits an individual while moral absolutism is that view that what is right and wrong is independent of what individuals think).

It is often claimed that modern society is breaking up because of excessive "egoism" or moral relativism. This is false. As far as moral relativism goes, this is a step forward from the moral absolutism urged upon society by various Moralists and true-believers because it bases itself, however slimly, upon the idea of individual reason. However, as it denies the existence (or desirability) of ethics it is but the mirror image of what it is rebelling against. Neither option empowers the individual or is liberating.

Consequently, both of these attitudes hold enormous attraction to authoritarians, as a populace that is either unable to form an opinion about things (and will tolerate anything) or who blindly follow the commands of the ruling elite are of great value to those in power. Both are rejected by most anarchists in favour of an evolutionary approach to ethics based upon human reason to develop the ethical concepts and interpersonal empathy to generalise these concepts into ethical attitudes within society as well as within individuals. An anarchistic approach to ethics therefore shares the critical individual investigation implied in moral relativism but grounds itself into common feelings of right and wrong. As Proudhon argued:

"All progress begins by abolishing something; every reform rests upon denunciation of some abuse; each new idea is based upon the proved insufficiency of the old idea."

Most anarchists take the viewpoint that ethical standards, like life itself, are in a constant process of evolution. This leads them to reject the various notions of *"God's Law,"* *"Natural Law,"* and so on in favour of a theory of ethical development based upon the idea that individuals are entirely empowered to question and assess the world around them – in fact, they require it in order to be truly free. You cannot be an anarchist and blindly accept **anything**! Michael Bakunin, one of the founding anarchist thinkers, expressed this radical scepticism as so:

"No theory, no ready-made system, no book that has ever been written will save the world. I cleave to no system. I am a true seeker."

Any system of ethics which is not based on individual questioning can only be authoritarian. Erich Fromm explains why:

*"Formally, authoritarian ethics denies man's capacity to know what is good or bad; the norm giver is always an authority transcending the individual. Such a system is based not on reason and knowledge but on awe of the authority and on the subject's feeling of weakness and dependence; the surrender of decision making to the authority results from the latter's magic power; its decisions can not and must not be questioned. **Materially**, or according to content, authoritarian ethics answers the question of what is good or bad primarily in terms of the interests of the authority, not the interests of the subject; it is exploitative, although the subject may*

derive considerable benefits, psychic or material, from it." [**Man For Himself**, p. 10]

Therefore Anarchists take, essentially, a scientific approach to problems. Anarchists arrive at ethical judgements without relying on the mythology of spiritual aid, but on the merits of their own minds. This is done through logic and reason, and is a far better route to resolving moral questions than obsolete, authoritarian systems like orthodox religion and certainly better than the "there is no wrong or right" of moral relativism.

So, what are the source of ethical concepts? For Kropotkin, *"nature has thus to be recognised as the **first ethical teacher of man.** The social instinct, innate in men as well as in all the social animals, – this is the origin of all ethical conceptions and all subsequent development of morality."* [**Ethics**, p. 45]

Life, in other words, is the basis of anarchist ethics. This means that, essentially (according to anarchists), an individual's ethical viewpoints are derived from three basic sources:

1)   from the society an individual lives in. As Kropotkin pointed out, *"Man's conceptions of morality are completely dependent upon the form that their social life assumed at a given time in a given locality … this [social life] is reflected in the moral conceptions of men and in the moral teachings of the given epoch."* [**Op. Cit.**, p. 315] In other words, experience of life and of living.

2)   A critical evaluation by individuals of their society's ethical norms, as indicated above. This is the core of Erich Fromm's argument that *"Man must accept the responsibility for himself and the fact that only using his own powers can he give meaning to his life … **there is no meaning to life except the meaning man gives his life by the unfolding of his powers, by living productively."*** [**Man for Himself**, p. 45] In other words, individual thought and development.

3)   The feeling of empathy – *"the true origin of the moral sentiment … [is] simply in the feeling of sympathy."* [*"Anarchist Morality"*, **Anarchism**, p. 94] In other words, an individual's ability to feel and share experiences and concepts with others.

This last factor is very important for the development of a sense of ethics. As Kropotkin argued, *"[t]he more powerful your imagination, the better you can picture to yourself what any being feels when it is made to suffer, and the more intense and delicate will your moral sense be … And the more you are accustomed by circumstances, by those surrounding you, or by the intensity of your own thought and your imagination, to **act** as your own thought and imagination urge, the more will the moral sentiment grow in you, the more will it became habitual."* [**Op. Cit.**, p. 95]

So, anarchism is based (essentially) upon the ethical maxim *"treat others as you would like them to treat you under similar circumstances."* Anarchists are neither egoists nor altruists when it come to moral stands, they are simply **human.**

As Kropotkin noted, *"egoism"* and *"altruism"* both have their roots in the same motive – *"however great the difference between the*

two actions in their result of humanity, the motive is the same. It is the quest for pleasure." [**Op. Cit.**, p. 85]

For anarchists, a person's sense of ethics must be developed by themselves and requires the full use of an individual's mental abilities as part of a social grouping, as part of a community. As capitalism and other forms of authority weaken the individual's imagination and reduce the number of outlets for them to exercise their reason under the dead weight of hierarchy as well as disrupting community, little wonder that life under capitalism is marked by a stark disregard for others and lack of ethical behaviour.

Combined with these factors is the role played by inequality within society. Without equality, there can be no real ethics for *"Justice implies Equality … only those who consider **others** as their **equals** can obey the rule: 'Do not do to others what you do not wish them to do to you.' A serf-owner and a slave merchant can evidently not recognise … the 'categorical imperative' [of treating people as ends in themselves and not as means] as regards serfs [or slaves] because they do not look upon them as equals."* Hence the *"greatest obstacle to the maintenance of a certain moral level in our present societies lies in the absence of social equality. Without **real** equality, the sense of justice can never be universally developed, because **Justice implies the recognition of Equality.**"* [Peter Kropotkin, **Evolution and Environment**, p. 88 and p. 79]

Capitalism, like any society, gets the ethical behaviour it deserves. In a society which moves between moral relativism and absolutism it is little wonder that egoism becomes confused with egotism. By disempowering individuals from developing their own ethical ideas and instead encouraging blind obedience to external authority (and so moral relativism once individuals think that they are without that authority's power), capitalist society ensures an impoverishment of individuality and ego. As Erich Fromm puts it:

*"The failure of modern culture lies not in its principle of individualism, not in the idea that moral virtue is the same as the pursuit of self-interest, but in the deterioration of the meaning of self-interest; not in the fact that people are **too much concerned with their self-interest,** but that they are **not concerned enough with the interest of their real self; not in the fact that they are too selfish, but that they do not love themselves.**"* [**Man for Himself**, p. 139]

Therefore, strictly speaking, anarchism is based upon an egoistic frame of reference – ethical ideas must be an expression of what gives us pleasure as a whole individual (both rational and emotional, reason and empathy). This leads all anarchists to reject the false division between egoism and altruism and recognise that what many people (for example, capitalists) call "egoism" results in individual self-negation and a reduction of individual self-interest. As Kropotkin argues:

"What was it that morality, evolving in animal and human societies, was striving for, if not for the opposition to the promptings of narrow egoism, and bringing up humanity in the spirit of the development of altruism? The very expressions 'egoism' and 'altruism' are incorrect, because there can be no pure altruism without an admixture of

personal pleasure – and consequently, without egoism. It would therefore be more nearly correct to say that ethics aims at **the development of social habits and the weakening of the narrowly personal habits.** *These last make the individual lose sight of society through his regard for his own person, and therefore they even fail to attain their object, i.e. the welfare of the individual, whereas the development of habits of work in common, and of mutual aid in general, leads to a series of beneficial consequences in the family as well as society."* [**Ethics**, pp. 307-8]

Therefore anarchism is based upon the rejection of moral absolutism (i.e. *"God's Law," "Natural Law," "Man's Nature," "A is A"*) and the narrow egotism which moral relativism so easily lends itself to. Instead, anarchists recognise that there exists concepts of right and wrong which exist outside of an individual's evaluation of their own acts.

This is because of the social nature of humanity. The interactions between individuals do develop into a social maxim which, according to Kropotkin, can be summarised as *"[i]s it useful to society? Then it is good. Is it hurtful? Then it is bad."* Which acts human beings think of as right or wrong is not, however, unchanging and the *"estimate of what is useful or harmful … changes, but the foundation remains the same."* [*"Anarchist Morality"*, **Op. Cit.**, p. 91 and p. 92]

This sense of empathy, based upon a critical mind, is the fundamental basis of social ethics – the 'what-should-be' can be seen as an ethical criterion for the truth or validity of an objective 'what-is.' So, while recognising the root of ethics in nature, anarchists consider ethics as fundamentally a **human** idea – the product of life, thought and evolution created by individuals and generalised by social living and community.

So what, for anarchists, is unethical behaviour? Essentially anything that denies the most precious achievement of history: the liberty, uniqueness and dignity of the individual.

Individuals can see what actions are unethical because, due to empathy, they can place themselves into the position of those suffering the behaviour. Acts which restrict individuality can be considered unethical for two (interrelated) reasons.

Firstly, the protection and development of individuality in all enriches the life of every individual and it gives pleasure to individuals because of the diversity it produces. This egoist basis of ethics reinforces the second (social) reason, namely that individuality is good for society for it enriches the community and social life, strengthening it and allowing it to grow and evolve. As Bakunin constantly argued, progress is marked by a movement from *"the simple to the complex"* or, in the words of Herbert Read, it *"is measured by the degree of differentiation within a society. If the individual is a unit in a corporate mass, his [or her] life will be limited, dull, and mechanical. If the individual is a unit on his [or her] own, with space and potentiality for separate action … he can develop – develop in the only real meaning of the word – develop in consciousness of strength, vitality, and joy."* [*"The Philosophy of Anarchism,"* **Anarchy and Order**, p. 37]

This defence of individuality is learned from nature. In an ecosystem, diversity is strength and so biodiversity becomes a source of basic

ethical insight. In its most basic form, it provides a guide to *"help us distinguish which of our actions serve the thrust of natural evolution and which of them impede them."* [Murray Bookchin, **The Ecology of Freedom**, p. 442]

So, the ethical concept *"lies in the feeling of sociality, inherent in the entire animal world and in the conceptions of equity, which constitutes one of the fundamental primary judgements of human reason."* Therefore anarchists embrace *"the permanent presence of a* **double tendency** *– towards greater development on the one side, of* **sociality**, *and, on the other side, of a consequent increase of the intensity of life which results in an increase of happiness for the* **individuals**, *and, in progress – physical, intellectual, and moral."* [Kropotkin, **Ethics**, pp. 311-2 and pp. 19-20]

Anarchist attitudes to authority, the state, capitalism, private property and so on all come from our ethical belief that the liberty of individuals is of prime concern and that our ability to empathise with others, to see ourselves in others (our basic equality and common individuality, in other words).

Thus anarchism combines the subjective evaluation by individuals of a given set of circumstances and actions with the drawing of objective interpersonal conclusions of these evaluations based upon empathic bounds and discussion between equals. Anarchism is based on a humanistic approach to ethical ideas, one that evolves along with society and individual development. Hence an **ethical** society is one in which *"[d]ifference among people will be respected, indeed fostered, as elements that enrich the unity of experience and phenomenon … [the different] will be conceived of as individual parts of a whole all the richer because of its complexity."* [Murray Bookchin, **Post Scarcity Anarchism**, p. 82]

A.2.20 Why are most anarchists atheists?

It is a fact that most anarchists are atheists. They reject the idea of god and oppose all forms of religion, particularly organised religion. Today, in secularised western European countries, religion has lost its once dominant place in society. This often makes the militant atheism of anarchism seem strange. However, once the negative role of religion is understood the importance of libertarian atheism becomes obvious. It is because of the role of religion and its institutions that anarchists have spent some time refuting the idea of religion as well as propagandising against it.

So why do so many anarchists embrace atheism? The simplest answer is that most anarchists are atheists because it is a logical extension of anarchist ideas. If anarchism is the rejection of illegitimate authorities, then it follows that it is the rejection of the so-called Ultimate Authority, God. Anarchism is grounded in reason, logic, and scientific thinking, not religious thinking. Anarchists tend to be sceptics, and not believers. Most anarchists consider the Church to be steeped in hypocrisy and the Bible a work of fiction, riddled with contradictions, absurdities and horrors. It is notorious in its debasement of women and its sexism is infamous. Yet men are treated little better. Nowhere in the bible is there an acknowledgement that human beings have inherent rights to life, liberty, happiness, dignity, fairness, or self-government. In the bible, humans are sinners, worms, and slaves (figuratively and literally, as it condones slavery). God has all the rights, humanity is nothing. This is unsurprising, given the nature of religion. Bakunin put it best:

> "The idea of God implies the abdication of human reason and justice; it is the most decisive negation of human liberty, and necessarily ends in the enslavement of mankind, both in theory and in practice.

> "Unless, then, we desire the enslavement and degradation of mankind … we may not, must not make the slightest concession either to the God of theology or to the God of metaphysics. He who, in this mystical alphabet, begins with A will inevitably end with Z; he who desires to worship God must harbour no childish illusions about the matter, but bravely renounce his liberty and humanity.

> "If God is, man is a slave; now, man can and must be free; then, God does not exist." [**God and the State**, p. 25]

For most anarchists, then, atheism is required due to the nature of religion. "To proclaim as divine all that is grand, just, noble, and beautiful in humanity," Bakunin argued, "is to tacitly admit that humanity of itself would have been unable to produce it – that is, that, abandoned to itself, its own nature is miserable, iniquitous, base, and ugly. Thus we come back to the essence of all religion – in other words, to the disparagement of humanity for the greater glory of divinity." As such, to do justice to our humanity and the potential it has, anarchists argue that we must do without the harmful myth of god and all it entails and so on behalf of "human liberty, dignity, and prosperity, we believe it our duty to recover from heaven the goods which it has stolen and return them to earth." [**Op. Cit.**, p. 37 and p. 36]

As well as the theoretical degrading of humanity and its liberty, religion has other, more practical, problems with it from an anarchist point of view. Firstly, religions have been a source of inequality and oppression. Christianity (like Islam), for example, has always been a force for repression whenever it holds any political or social sway (believing you have a direct line to god is a sure way of creating an authoritarian society). The Church has been a force of social repression, genocide, and the justification for every tyrant for nearly two millennia. When given the chance it has ruled as cruelly as any monarch or dictator. This is unsurprising:

> "God being everything, the real world and man are nothing. God being truth, justice, goodness, beauty, power and life, man is falsehood, iniquity, evil, ugliness, impotence, and death. God being master, man is the slave. Incapable of finding justice, truth, and eternal life by his own effort, he can attain them only through a divine revelation. But whoever says revelation, says revealers, messiahs, prophets, priests, and legislators inspired by God himself; and these, as the holy instructors of humanity, chosen by God himself to direct it in the path of salvation, necessarily exercise absolute power. All men

> owe them passive and unlimited obedience; for against the divine reason there is no human reason, and against the justice of God no terrestrial justice holds." [Bakunin, **Op. Cit.**, p. 24]

Christianity has only turned tolerant and peace-loving when it is powerless and even then it has continued its role as apologist for the powerful. This is the second reason why anarchists oppose the church for when not being the source of oppression, the church has justified it and ensured its continuation. It has kept the working class in bondage for generations by sanctioning the rule of earthly authorities and teaching working people that it is wrong to fight against those same authorities. Earthly rulers received their legitimisation from the heavenly lord, whether political (claiming that rulers are in power due to god's will) or economic (the rich having been rewarded by god). The bible praises obedience, raising it to a great virtue. More recent innovations like the Protestant work ethic also contribute to the subjugation of working people.

That religion is used to further the interests of the powerful can quickly be seen from most of history. It conditions the oppressed to humbly accept their place in life by urging the oppressed to be meek and await their reward in heaven. As Emma Goldman argued, Christianity (like religion in general) "contains nothing dangerous to the regime of authority and wealth; it stands for self-denial and self-abnegation, for penance and regret, and is absolutely inert in the face of every [in]dignity, every outrage imposed upon mankind." [**Red Emma Speaks**, p. 234]

Thirdly, religion has always been a conservative force in society. This is unsurprising, as it bases itself not on investigation and analysis of the real world but rather in repeating the truths handed down from above and contained in a few holy books. Theism is then "the theory of speculation" while atheism is "the science of demonstration." The "one hangs in the metaphysical clouds of the Beyond, while the other has its roots firmly in the soil. It is the earth, not heaven, which man must rescue if he is truly to be saved." Atheism, then, "expresses the expansion and growth of the human mind" while theism "is static and fixed." It is "the absolutism of theism, its pernicious influence upon humanity, its paralysing effect upon thought and action, which Atheism is fighting with all its power." [Emma Goldman, **Op. Cit.**, p. 243, p. 245 and pp. 246-7]

As the Bible says, "By their fruits shall ye know them." We anarchists agree but unlike the church we apply this truth to religion as well. That is why we are, in the main, atheists. We recognise the destructive role played by the Church, and the harmful effects of organised monotheism, particularly Christianity, on people. As Goldman summaries, religion "is the conspiracy of ignorance against reason, of darkness against light, of submission and slavery against independence and freedom; of the denial of strength and beauty, against the affirmation of the joy and glory of life." [**Op. Cit.**, p. 240]

So, given the fruits of the Church, anarchists argue that it is time to uproot it and plant new trees, the trees of reason and liberty.

That said, anarchists do not deny that religions contain important ethical ideas or truths. Moreover, religions can be the base for strong and loving communities and groups. They can offer a sanctuary from the alienation and oppression of everyday life and offer a guide to action in a world where everything is for sale. Many aspects of, say, Jesus' or Buddha's life and teachings are inspiring and worth following. If this were not the case, if religions were simply a tool of the powerful, they would have long ago been rejected. Rather, they have a dual-nature in that contain both ideas necessary to live a good life as well as apologetics for power. If they did not, the oppressed would not believe and the powerful would suppress them as dangerous heresies.

And, indeed, repression has been the fate of any group that has preached a radical message. In the middle ages numerous revolutionary Christian movements and sects were crushed by the earthly powers that be with the firm support of the mainstream church. During the Spanish Civil War the Catholic church supported Franco's fascists, denouncing the killing of pro-Franco priests by supporters of the republic while remaining silent about Franco's murder of Basque priests who had supported the democratically elected government (Pope John Paul II is seeking to turn the dead pro-Franco priests into saints while the pro-Republican priests remain unmentioned). The Archbishop of El Salvador, Oscar Arnulfo Romero, started out as a conservative but after seeing the way in which the political and economic powers were exploiting the people became their outspoken champion. He was assassinated by right-wing paramilitaries in 1980 because of this, a fate which has befallen many other supporters of liberation theology, a radical interpretation of the Gospels which tries to reconcile socialist ideas and Christian social thinking.

Nor does the anarchist case against religion imply that religious people do not take part in social struggles to improve society. Far from it. Religious people, including members of the church hierarchy, played a key role in the US civil rights movement of the 1960s. The religious belief within Zapata's army of peasants during the Mexican revolution did not stop anarchists taking part in it (indeed, it had already been heavily influenced by the ideas of anarchist militant Ricardo Flores Magón). It is the dual-nature of religion which explains why many popular movements and revolts (particularly by peasants) have used the rhetoric of religion, seeking to keep the good aspects of their faith will fighting the earthly injustice its official representatives sanctify. For anarchists, it is the willingness to fight against injustice which counts, not whether someone believes in god or not. We just think that the social role of religion is to dampen down revolt, not encourage it. The tiny number of radical priests compared to those in the mainstream or on the right suggests the validity of our analysis.

It should be stressed that anarchists, while overwhelmingly hostile to the idea of the Church and an established religion, do not object to people practising religious belief on their own or in groups, so long as that practice doesn't impinge on the liberties of others. For example, a cult that required human sacrifice or slavery would be antithetical to anarchist ideas, and would be opposed. But peaceful systems of belief could exist in harmony within in anarchist society. The anarchist view is that religion is a personal matter, above all else – if people want to believe in something, that's their business, and nobody else's as long as they do not impose those ideas on others. All we can do is discuss their ideas and try and convince them of their errors.

To end, it should noted that we are not suggesting that atheism is somehow mandatory for an anarchist. Far from it. As we discuss in section A.3.7, there are anarchists who do believe in god or some form of religion. For example, Tolstoy combined libertarian ideas with a devoute Christian belief. His ideas, along with Proudhon's, influence the Catholic Worker organisation, founded by anarchists Dorothy Day and Peter Maurin in 1933 and still active today. The anarchist activist Starhawk, active in the current anti-globalisation movement, has no problems also being a leading Pagan. However, for most anarchists, their ideas lead them logically to atheism for, as Emma Goldman put it, *"in its negation of gods is at the same time the strongest affirmation of man, and through man, the eternal yea to life, purpose, and beauty."* [**Red Emma Speaks**, p. 248]

A.3
What types of anarchism are there?

One thing that soon becomes clear to any one interested in anarchism is that there is not one single form of anarchism. Rather, there are different schools of anarchist thought, different types of anarchism which have many disagreements with each other on numerous issues. These types are usually distinguished by tactics and/or goals, with the latter (the vision of a free society) being the major division.

This means that anarchists, while all sharing a few key ideas, can be grouped into broad categories, depending on the economic arrangements that they consider to be most suitable to human freedom. However, all types of anarchists share a basic approach. To quote Rudolf Rocker:

> *"In common with the founders of Socialism, Anarchists demand the abolition of all economic monopolies and the common ownership of the soil and all other means of production, the use of which must be available to all without distinction; for personal and social freedom is conceivable only on the basis of equal economic advantages for everybody. Within the Socialist movement itself the Anarchists represent the viewpoint that the war against capitalism must be at the same time a war against all institutions of political power, for in history economic exploitation has always gone hand in hand with political and social oppression. The exploitation of man by man and the domination of man over man are inseparable, and each is the condition of the other."* [**Anarcho-Syndicalism**, pp. 62-3]

It is within this general context that anarchists disagree. The main differences are between ***"individualist"*** and ***"social"*** anarchists, although the economic arrangements each desire are not mutually exclusive. Of the two, social anarchists (communist-anarchists, anarcho-syndicalists and so on) have always been the vast majority, with individualist anarchism being restricted mostly to the United States. In this section we indicate the differences between these main trends within the anarchist movement. As will soon become clear, while social and individualist anarchists both oppose the state and capitalism, they disagree on the nature of a free society (and how to get there). In a nutshell, social anarchists prefer communal solutions to social problems and a communal vision of the good society (i.e. a society that protects and encourages individual freedom). Individualist anarchists, as their name suggests, prefer individual solutions and have a more individualistic vision of the good society. However, we must not let these difference cloud what both schools have in common, namely a desire to maximise individual freedom and end state and capitalist domination and exploitation.

In addition to this major disagreement, anarchists also disagree over such issues as syndicalism, pacifism, "lifestylism," animal rights and a whole host of other ideas, but these, while important, are only different aspects of anarchism. Beyond a few key ideas, the anarchist movement (like life itself) is in a constant state of change, discussion and thought – as would be expected in a movement that values freedom so highly.

The most obvious thing to note about the different types of anarchism is that *"[n]one are named after some Great Thinker; instead, they are invariably named either after some kind of practice, or, most often, organisational principle … Anarchists like to distinguish themselves by what they do, and how they organise themselves to go about doing it."* [David Graeber, **Fragments of An Anarchist Anthropology**, p. 5] This does not mean that anarchism does not have individuals who have contributed significantly to anarchist theory. Far from it, as can be seen in section A.4 there are many such people. Anarchists simply recognise that to call your theory after an individual is a kind of idolatry. Anarchists know that even the greatest thinker is only human and, consequently, can make mistakes, fail to live up to their ideals or have a partial understanding of certain issues (see section H.2 for more discussion on this). Moreover, we see that the world changes and, obviously, what was a suitable practice or programme in, say, industrialising France of the 1840s may have its limitations in 21st century France!

Consequently, it is to be expected that a social theory like anarchism would have numerous schools of thought and practice associated with it. Anarchism, as we noted in section A.5, has its roots in the struggles of working class people against oppression. Anarchist ideas have developed in many different social situations and, consequently, have reflected those circumstances. Most obviously, individualist anarchism initially developed in pre-industrial America and as a result has a different perspective on many issues than social anarchism. As America changed, going from a predominantly pre-capitalist rural society to an industrialised capitalist one, American anarchism changed:

> *"Originally the American movement, the native creation which arose with Josiah Warren in 1829, was purely individualistic; the student of economy will easily understand the material and historical causes for such development. But within the last twenty years the communist idea has made great progress, owning primarily to that concentration in capitalist production which has driven the American workingman [and woman] to grasp at the idea of solidarity, and, secondly, to the expulsion of active communist propagandists from*

Europe." [Voltairine de Cleyre, **The Voltairine de Cleyre Reader**, p. 110]

Thus rather than the numerous types of anarchism being an expression of some sort of "incoherence" within anarchism, it simply shows a movement which has its roots in real life rather than the books of long dead thinkers. It also shows a healthy recognition that people are different and that one person's dream may be another's nightmare and that different tactics and organisations may be required at different social periods and struggles. So while anarchists have their preferences on how they think a free society will, in general, be like and be created they are aware that other forms of anarchism and libertarian tactics may be more suitable for other people and social circumstances. However, just because someone calls themselves or their theory anarchism does not make it so. Any genuine type of anarchism must share the fundamental perspectives of the movement, in other words be anti-state and anti-capitalist.

Moreover, claims of anarchist "incoherence" by its critics are usually overblown. After all, being followers of Marx and/or Lenin has not stopped Marxists from splitting into numerous parties, groups and sects. Nor has it stopped sectarian conflict between them based on whose interpretation of the holy writings are the "correct" ones or who has used the "correct" quotes to bolster attempts to adjust their ideas and practice to a world significantly different from Europe in the 1850s or Russia in the 1900s. At least anarchists are honest about their differences!

Lastly, to put our cards on the table, the writers of this FAQ place themselves firmly in the "social" strand of anarchism. This does not mean that we ignore the many important ideas associated with individualist anarchism, only that we think social anarchism is more appropriate for modern society, that it creates a stronger base for individual freedom, and that it more closely reflects the sort of society we would like to live in.

A.3.1 What are the differences between individualist and social anarchists?

While there is a tendency for individuals in both camps to claim that the proposals of the other camp would lead to the creation of some kind of state, the differences between individualists and social anarchists are not very great. Both are anti-state, anti-authority and anti-capitalist. The major differences are twofold.

The first is in regard to the means of action in the here and now (and so the manner in which anarchy will come about). Individualists generally prefer education and the creation of alternative institutions, such as mutual banks, unions, communes, etc. They usually support strikes and other non-violent forms of social protest (such as rent strikes, the non-payment of taxes and so on). Such activity, they argue, will ensure that present society will gradually develop out of government into an anarchist one. They are primarily evolutionists, not revolutionists, and dislike social anarchists' use of direct action to create revolutionary situations. They consider revolution as being in contradiction to anarchist principles as it involves the expropriation of capitalist property and, therefore, authoritarian means. Rather they seek to return to society the wealth taken out of society by property by means of an new, alternative, system of economics (based around mutual banks and co-operatives). In this way a general "social liquidation" would be rendered easy, with anarchism coming about by reform and not by expropriation.

Most social anarchists recognise the need for education and to create alternatives (such as libertarian unions), but most disagree that this is enough in itself. They do not think capitalism can be reformed piece by piece into anarchy, although they do not ignore the importance of reforms by social struggle that increase libertarian tendencies within capitalism. Nor do they think revolution is in contradiction with anarchist principles as it is not authoritarian to destroy authority (be it state or capitalist). Thus the expropriation of the capitalist class and the destruction of the state by social revolution is a libertarian, not authoritarian, act by its very nature as it is directed against those who govern and exploit the vast majority. In short, social anarchists are usually evolutionists **and** revolutionists, trying to strengthen libertarian tendencies within capitalism while trying to abolish that system by social revolution. However, as some social anarchists are purely evolutionists too, this difference is not the most important one dividing social anarchists from individualists.

The second major difference concerns the form of anarchist economy proposed. Individualists prefer a market-based system of distribution to the social anarchists need-based system. Both agree that the current system of capitalist property rights must be abolished and that use rights must replace property rights in the means of life (i.e. the abolition of rent, interest and profits – "usury," to use the individualist anarchists' preferred term for this unholy trinity). In effect, both schools follow Proudhon's classic work **What is Property?** and argue that possession must replace property in a free society (see section B.3 for a discussion of anarchist viewpoints on property). Thus property *"will lose a certain attribute which sanctifies it now. The absolute ownership of it – 'the right to use or abuse' – will be abolished, and possession, use, will be the only title. It will be seen how impossible it would be for one person to 'own' a million acres of land, without a title deed, backed by a government ready to protect the title at all hazards."* [Lucy Parsons, **Freedom, Equality & Solidarity**, p. 33]

However, within this use-rights framework, the two schools of anarchism propose different systems. The social anarchist generally argues for communal (or social) ownership and use. This would involve social ownership of the means of production and distribution, with personal possessions remaining for things you use, but not what was used to create them. Thus *"your watch is your own, but the watch factory belongs to the people." "Actual use,"* continues Berkman, *"will be considered the only title – not to ownership but to possession. The organisation of the coal miners, for example, will be in charge of the coal mines, not as owners but as the operating agency … Collective possession, co-operatively managed in the interests of the community, will take the place of personal ownership privately conducted for profit."* [**What is Anarchism?**, p. 217]

This system would be based on workers' self-management of their work and (for most social anarchists) the free sharing of the product of that labour (i.e. an economic system without money). This is because *"in the present state of industry, when everything is interdependent, when each branch of production is knit up with all the rest, the attempt to claim an individualist origin for the products of industry is untenable."* Given this, it is impossible to *"estimate the share of each in the riches which **all** contribute to amass"* and, moreover, the *"common possession of the instruments of labour must necessarily bring with it the enjoyment in common of the fruits of common labour."* [Kropotkin, **The Conquest of Bread**, p. 45 and p. 46] By this social anarchists simply mean that the social product which is produced by all would be available to all and each individual who has contributed productively to society can take what they need (how quickly we can reach such an ideal is a moot point, as we discuss in section I.2.2). Some social anarchists, like mutualists for example, are against such a system of libertarian (or free) communism, but, in general, the vast majority of social anarchists look forward to the end of money and, therefore, of buying and selling. All agree, however, that anarchy will see *"Capitalistic and proprietary exploitation stopped everywhere"* and *"the wage system abolished"* whether by *"equal and just exchange"* (like Proudhon) or by the free sharing (like Kropotkin). [Proudhon, **The General Idea of the Revolution**, p. 281]

In contrast, the individualist anarchist (like the mutualist) denies that this system of use-rights should include the product of the workers labour. Instead of social ownership, individualist anarchists propose a more market based system in which workers would possess their own means of production and exchange the product of their labour freely with other workers. They argue that capitalism is not, in fact, a truly free market. Rather, by means of the state, capitalists have placed fetters on the market to create and protect their economic and social power (market discipline for the working class, state aid for the ruling class in other words). These state created monopolies (of money, land, tariffs and patents) and state enforcement of capitalist property rights are the source of economic inequality and exploitation. With the abolition of government, **real** free competition would result and ensure the end of capitalism and capitalist exploitation (see Benjamin Tucker's essay **State Socialism and Anarchism** for an excellent summary of this argument).

The Individualist anarchists argue that the means of production (bar land) are the product of individual labour and so they accept that people should be able to sell the means of production they use, if they so desire. However, they reject capitalist property rights and instead favour an *"occupancy and use"* system. If the means of production, say land, is not in use, it reverts back to common ownership and is available to others for use. They think this system, called mutualism, will result in workers control of production and the end of capitalist exploitation and usury. This is because, logically and practically, a regime of "occupancy and use" cannot be squared with wage labour. If a workplace needs a group to operate it then it must be owned by the group who use it. If one individual claims to own it and it is, in fact, used by more than that person then, obviously, "occupancy and use" is violated. Equally, if an owner employs others to use the workplace then the boss can appropriate the product of the workers' labour, so violating the maxim that labour should receive its full product. Thus the principles of individualist anarchism point to anti-capitalist conclusions (see section G.3).

This second difference is the most important. The individualist fears being forced to join a community and thus losing his or her freedom (including the freedom to exchange freely with others). Max Stirner puts this position well when he argues that *"Communism, by the abolition of all personal property, only presses me back still more into dependence on another, to wit, on the generality or collectivity ... [which is] a condition hindering my free movement, a sovereign power over me. Communism rightly revolts against the pressure that I experience from individual proprietors; but still more horrible is the might that it puts in the hands of the collectivity."* [**The Ego and Its Own**, p. 257] Proudhon also argued against communism, stating that the community becomes the proprietor under communism and so capitalism and communism are based on property and so authority (see the section *"Characteristics of communism and of property"* in **What is Property?**). Thus the Individualist anarchist argues that social ownership places the individual's freedom in danger as any form of communism subjects the individual to society or the commune. They fear that as well as dictating individual morality, socialisation would effectively eliminate workers' control as "society" would tell workers what to produce and take the product of their labour. In effect, they argue that communism (or social ownership in general) would be similar to capitalism, with the exploitation and authority of the boss replaced with that of "society."

Needless to say, social anarchists disagree. They argue that Stirner's and Proudhon's comments are totally correct – but only about authoritarian communism. As Kropotkin argued, *"before and in 1848, the theory [of communism] was put forward in such a shape as to fully account for Proudhon's distrust as to its effect upon liberty. The old idea of Communism was the idea of monastic communities under the severe rule of elders or of men of science for directing priests. The last vestiges of liberty and of individual energy would be destroyed, if humanity ever had to go through such a communism."* [**Act for Yourselves**, p. 98] Kropotkin always argued that communist-anarchism was a **new** development and given that it dates from the 1870s, Proudhon's and Stirner's remarks cannot be considered as being directed against it as they could not be familiar with it.

Rather than subject the individual to the community, social anarchists argue that communal ownership would provide the necessary framework to protect individual liberty in all aspects of life by abolishing the power of the property owner, in whatever form it takes. In addition, rather than abolish **all** individual "property," communist anarchism acknowledges the importance of individual possessions and individual space. Thus we find Kropotkin arguing against forms of communism that *"desire to manage the community after the model of a family ... [to live] all in the same house and ... thus forced to continuously meet the same 'brethren and sisters' ... [it is] a fundamental error to impose on all the 'great family' instead of trying, on the contrary, to guarantee as much freedom and home life to each individual."* [**Small Communal Experiments and Why They Fail**, pp. 8-9] The aim of anarchist-communism is, to again quote Kropotkin, to place *"the product reaped or manufactured at the disposal of all, leaving to each the liberty to consume them as he pleases in his own home."* [**The Place of Anarchism in the Evolution of Socialist Thought**, p. 7] This ensures individual expression of tastes and desires and so individuality – both in consumption **and** in production, as social anarchists are firm supporters of workers' self-management.

Thus, for social anarchists, the Individualist Anarchist opposition to communism is only valid for state or authoritarian communism and ignores the fundamental nature of communist-anarchism. Communist anarchists do not replace individuality with community but rather use community to defend individuality. Rather than have "society" control the individual, as the Individualist Anarchist fears, social anarchism is based on importance of individuality and individual expression:

> *"Anarchist Communism maintains that most valuable of all conquests – individual liberty – and moreover extends it and gives it a solid basis – economic liberty – without which political liberty is delusive; it does not ask the individual who has rejected god, the universal tyrant, god the king, and god the parliament, to give unto himself a god more terrible than any of the proceeding – god the Community, or to abdicate upon its altar his [or her] independence, his [or her] will, his [or her] tastes, and to renew the vow of asceticism which he formally made before the crucified god. It says to him, on the contrary, 'No society is free so long as the individual is not so! ...'"* [**Op. Cit.**, pp. 14-15]

In addition, social anarchists have always recognised the need for voluntary collectivisation. If people desire to work by themselves, this is not seen as a problem (see Kropotkin's **The Conquest of Bread**, p. 61 and **Act for Yourselves**, pp. 104-5 as well as Malatesta's **Errico Malatesta: His Life and Ideas**, p. 99 and p. 103). This, social anarchists, stress does not in any way contradict their principles or the communist nature of their desired society as such exceptions are rooted in the "use rights" system both are based in (see section I.6.2 for a full discussion). In addition, for social anarchists an association exists solely for the benefit of the individuals that compose it; it is the means by which people co-operate to meet their common needs. Therefore, **all** anarchists emphasise the importance of free agreement as the basis of an anarchist society. Thus all anarchists agree with Bakunin:

> *"Collectivism could only imposed only on slaves, and this kind of collectivism would then be the negation of humanity. In a free community, collectivism can only come about through the pressure of circumstances, not by imposition from above but by a free spontaneous movement from below."* [**Bakunin on Anarchism**, p. 200]

If individualists desire to work for themselves and exchange goods with others, social anarchists have no objection. Hence our comments that the two forms of anarchism are not mutually exclusive. Social anarchists support the right of individuals **not** to join a commune while Individualist Anarchists support the rights of individuals to pool their possessions as they see fit, including communistic associations. However, if, in the name of freedom, an individual wished to claim property rights so as to exploit the labour of others, social anarchists would quickly resist this attempt to recreate statism in the name of "liberty." Anarchists do not respect the "freedom" to be a ruler! In the words of Luigi Galleani:

> "No less sophistical is the tendency of those who, under the comfortable cloak of anarchist individualism, would welcome the idea of domination … But the heralds of domination presume to practice individualism in the name of their ego, over the obedient, resigned, or inert ego of others." [**The End of Anarchism?**, p. 40]

Moreover, for social anarchists, the idea that the means of production can be sold implies that private property could be reintroduced in an anarchist society. In a free market, some succeed and others fail. As Proudhon argued, in competition victory goes to the strongest. When one's bargaining power is weaker than another then any "free exchange" will benefit the stronger party. Thus the market, even a non-capitalist one, will tend to magnify inequalities of wealth and power over time rather than equalising them. Under capitalism this is more obvious as those with only their labour power to sell are in a weaker position than those with capital but individualist anarchism would also be affected.

Thus, social anarchists argue, much against its will an individualist anarchist society would evolve away from fair exchanges back into capitalism. If, as seems likely, the "unsuccessful" competitors are forced into unemployment they may have to sell their labour to the "successful" in order to survive. This would create authoritarian social relationships and the domination of the few over the many via "free contracts." The enforcement of such contracts (and others like them), in all likelihood, "opens … the way for reconstituting under the heading of 'defence' all the functions of the State." [Peter Kropotkin, **Anarchism**, p. 297]

Benjamin Tucker, the anarchist most influenced by liberalism and free market ideas, also faced the problems associated with all schools of abstract individualism – in particular, the acceptance of authoritarian social relations as an expression of "liberty." This is due to the similarity of property to the state. Tucker argued that the state was marked by two things, aggression and "the assumption of authority over a given area and all within it, exercised generally for the double purpose of more complete oppression of its subjects and extension of its boundaries." [**Instead of a Book**, p. 22] However, the boss and landlord also has authority over a given area (the property in question) and all within it (workers and tenants). The former control the actions of the latter just as the state rules the citizen or subject. In other words, individual ownership produces the same social relationships as that created by the state, as it comes from the same source (monopoly of power over a given area and those who use it).

Social anarchists argue that the Individualist Anarchists acceptance of individual ownership and their individualistic conception of individual freedom can lead to the denial of individual freedom by the creation of social relationships which are essentially authoritarian/statist in nature. "The individualists," argued Malatesta, "give the greatest importance to an abstract concept of freedom and fail to take into account, or dwell on the fact that real, concrete freedom

is the outcome of solidarity and voluntary co-operation." [**The Anarchist Revolution**, p. 16] Thus wage labour, for example, places the worker in the same relationship to the boss as citizenship places the citizen to the state, namely of one of domination and subjection. Similarly with the tenant and the landlord.

Such a social relationship cannot help but produce the other aspects of the state. As Albert Meltzer points out, this can have nothing but statist implications, because "the school of Benjamin Tucker – by virtue of their individualism – accepted the need for police to break strikes so as to guarantee the employer's 'freedom.' All this school of so-called Individualists accept … the necessity of the police force, hence for government, and the prime definition of anarchism is **no government.**" [**Anarchism: Arguments For and Against**, p. 8] It is partly for this reason social anarchists support social ownership as the best means of protecting individual liberty.

Accepting individual ownership this problem can only be "got round" by accepting, along with Proudhon (the source of many of Tucker's economic ideas), the need for co-operatives to run workplaces that require more than one worker. This naturally complements their support for "occupancy and use" for land, which would effectively abolish landlords. Without co-operatives, workers will be exploited for "it is well enough to talk of [the worker] buying hand tools, or small machinery which can be moved about; but what about the gigantic machinery necessary to the operation of a mine, or a mill? It requires many to work it. If one owns it, will he not make the others pay tribute for using it?" This is because "no man would employ another to work for him unless he could get more for his product than he had to pay for it, and that being the case, the inevitable course of exchange and re-exchange would be that the man **having received less than the full amount.**" [Voltairine de Cleyre, "Why I am an Anarchist", **Exquisite Rebel**, p. 61 and p. 60] Only when the people who use a resource own it can individual ownership not result in hierarchical authority or exploitation (i.e. statism/capitalism). Only when an industry is co-operatively owned, can the workers ensure that they govern themselves during work and can get the full value of the goods they make once they are sold.

This solution is the one Individualist Anarchists **do** seem to accept and the only one consistent with all their declared principles (as well as anarchism). This can be seen when French individualist E. Armand argued that the key difference between his school of anarchism and communist-anarchism is that as well as seeing "ownership of the consumer goods representing an extension of [the worker's] personality" it also "regards ownership of the means of production and free disposal of his produce as the quintessential guarantee of the autonomy of the individual. The understanding is that such ownership boils down to the chance to deploy (as individuals, couples, family groups, etc.) the requisite plot of soil or machinery of production to meet the requirements of the social unit, provided that the proprietor does not transfer it to someone else or reply upon the services of someone else in operating it." Thus the individualist anarchist could "defend himself against … the exploitation of anyone by one of his neighbours who will set him to work in his employ and for his benefit" and "greed, which is to say the opportunity for an individual, couple or family group to own more than strictly required for their normal upkeep." ["Mini-Manual of the Anarchist Individualist", pp. 145-9, **Anarchism**, Robert Graham (ed.), p. 147 and pp. 147-8]

The ideas of the American individualist anarchists logically flow to the same conclusions. "Occupancy and Use" automatically excludes wage labour and so exploitation and oppression. As Wm. Gary Kline correctly points out, the US Individualist anarchists *"expected a society of largely self-employed workmen with no significant disparity of wealth between any of them."* [**The Individualist Anarchists**, p. 104] It is this vision of a self-employed society that logically flows from their principles which ensures that their ideas are truly anarchist. As it is, their belief that their system would ensure the elimination of profit, rent and interest place them squarely in the anti-capitalist camp alongside social anarchists.

Needless to say, social anarchists disagree with individualist anarchism, arguing that there are undesirable features of even non-capitalist markets which would undermine freedom and equality. Moreover, the development of industry has resulted in **natural** barriers of entry into markets and this not only makes it almost impossible to abolish capitalism by competing against it, it also makes the possibility of recreating usury in new forms likely. Combine this with the difficulty in determining the exact contribution of each worker to a product in a modern economy and you see why social anarchists argue that the only real solution to capitalism is to ensure community ownership and management of the economy. It is this recognition of the developments within the capitalist economy which make social anarchists reject individualist anarchism in favour of communalising, and so decentralising, production by freely associated and co-operative labour on a large-scale rather than just in the workplace.

For more discussion on the ideas of the Individualist anarchists, and why social anarchists reject them, see section G – "Is individualist anarchism capitalistic?"

A.3.2 Are there different types of social anarchism?

Yes. Social anarchism has four major trends – mutualism, collectivism, communism and syndicalism. The differences are not great and simply involve differences in strategy. The one major difference that does exist is between mutualism and the other kinds of social anarchism. Mutualism is based around a form of market socialism – workers' co-operatives exchanging the product of their labour via a system of community banks. This mutual bank network would be *"formed by the whole community, not for the especial advantage of any individual or class, but for the benefit of all ... [with] no interest ... exacted on loans, except enough to cover risks and expenses."* Such a system would end capitalist exploitation and oppression for by *"introducing mutualism into exchange and credit we introduce it everywhere, and labour will assume a new aspect and become truly democratic."* [Charles A. Dana, **Proudhon and his "Bank of the People"**, pp. 44-45 and p. 45]

The social anarchist version of mutualism differs from the individualist form by having the mutual banks owned by the local community (or commune) instead of being independent co-operatives. This

would ensure that they provided investment funds to co-operatives rather than to capitalistic enterprises. Another difference is that some social anarchist mutualists support the creation of what Proudhon termed an ***"agro-industrial federation"*** to complement the federation of libertarian communities (called communes by Proudhon). This is a *"confederation ... intended to provide reciprocal security in commerce and industry"* and large scale developments such as roads, railways and so on. The purpose of *"specific federal arrangements is to protect the citizens of the federated states [sic!] from capitalist and financial feudalism, both within them and from the outside."* This is because *"political right requires to be buttressed by economic right."* Thus the agro-industrial federation would be required to ensure the anarchist nature of society from the destabilising effects of market exchanges (which can generate increasing inequalities in wealth and so power). Such a system would be a practical example of solidarity, as *"industries are sisters; they are parts of the same body; one cannot suffer without the others sharing in its suffering. They should therefore federate, not to be absorbed and confused together, but in order to guarantee mutually the conditions of common prosperity ... Making such an agreement will not detract from their liberty; it will simply give their liberty more security and force."* [**The Principle of Federation**, p. 70, p. 67 and p. 72]

The other forms of social anarchism do not share the mutualists support for markets, even non-capitalist ones. Instead they think that freedom is best served by communalising production and sharing information and products freely between co-operatives. In other words, the other forms of social anarchism are based upon common (or social) ownership by federations of producers' associations and communes rather than mutualism's system of individual co-operatives. In Bakunin's words, the *"future social organisation must be made solely from the bottom upwards, by the free association or federation of workers, firstly in their unions, then in the communes, regions, nations and finally in a great federation, international and universal"* and *"the land, the instruments of work and all other capital may become the collective property of the whole of society and be utilised only by the workers, in other words by the agricultural and industrial associations."* [**Michael Bakunin: Selected Writings**, p. 206 and p. 174] Only by extending the principle of co-operation beyond individual workplaces can individual liberty be maximised and protected (see section I.1.3 for why most anarchists are opposed to markets). In this they share some ground with Proudhon, as can be seen. The industrial confederations would *"guarantee the mutual use of the tools of production which are the property of each of these groups and which will by a reciprocal contract become the collective property of the whole ... federation. In this way, the federation of groups will be able to ... regulate the rate of production to meet the fluctuating needs of society."* [James Guillaume, **Bakunin on Anarchism**, p. 376]

These anarchists share the mutualists support for workers' self-management of production within co-operatives but see confederations of these associations as being the focal point for expressing mutual aid, not a market. Workplace autonomy and self-management would be the basis of any federation, for *"the workers in the various factories have not the slightest intention of handing over their hard-won control of the tools of production to a superior power calling itself the 'corporation.'"* [Guillaume, **Op. Cit.**, p. 364] In addition to this industry-wide federation, there would also be cross-industry and community confederations to look after tasks which are not within the exclusive jurisdiction or capacity of any particular industrial federation or are of a social nature. Again, this has similarities to Proudhon's mutualist ideas.

Social anarchists share a firm commitment to common ownership of the means of production (excluding those used purely by individuals) and reject the individualist idea that these can be "sold off" by those who use them. The reason, as noted earlier, is because if this could be done, capitalism and statism could regain a foothold in the free society. In addition, other social anarchists do not agree with the mutualist idea that capitalism can be reformed into libertarian socialism by introducing mutual banking. For them capitalism can only be replaced by a free society by social revolution.

The major difference between collectivists and communists is over the question of "money" after a revolution. Anarcho-communists consider the abolition of money to be essential, while anarcho-collectivists consider the end of private ownership of the means of production to be the key. As Kropotkin noted, collectivist anarchism *"express[es] a state of things in which all necessaries for production are owned in common by the labour groups and the free communes, while the ways of retribution [i.e. distribution] of labour, communist or otherwise, would be settled by each group for itself."* [**Anarchism**, p. 295] Thus, while communism and collectivism both organise production in common via producers' associations, they differ in how the goods produced will be distributed. Communism is based on free consumption of all while collectivism is more likely to be based on the distribution of goods according to the labour contributed. However, most anarcho-collectivists think that, over time, as productivity increases and the sense of community becomes stronger, money will disappear. Both agree that, in the end, society would be run along the lines suggested by the communist maxim: **"From each according to their abilities, to each according to their needs."** They just disagree on how quickly this will come about (see section I.2.2).

For anarcho-communists, they think that *"communism – at least partial – has more chances of being established than collectivism"* after a revolution. [**Op. Cit.**, p. 298] They think that moves towards communism are essential as collectivism *"begins by abolishing private ownership of the means of production and immediately reverses itself by returning to the system of remuneration according to work performed which means the re-introduction of inequality."* [Alexander Berkman, **What is Anarchism?**, p. 230] The quicker the move to communism, the less chances of new inequalities developing. Needless to say, these positions are **not** that different and, in practice, the necessities of a social revolution and the level of political awareness of those introducing anarchism will determine which system will be applied in each area.

Syndicalism is the other major form of social anarchism. Anarcho-syndicalists, like other syndicalists, want to create an industrial union movement based on anarchist ideas. Therefore they advocate decentralised, federated unions that use direct action to get reforms under capitalism until they are strong enough to overthrow it. In many ways anarcho-syndicalism can be considered as a new version of collectivist-anarchism, which also stressed the importance of anarchists working within the labour movement and creating unions which prefigure the future free society.

Thus, even under capitalism, anarcho-syndicalists seek to create *"free associations of free producers."* They think that these associations would serve as *"a practical school of anarchism"* and they take very seriously Bakunin's remark that the workers' organisations must create *"not only the ideas but also the facts of the future itself"* in the pre-revolutionary period.

Anarcho-syndicalists, like all social anarchists, *"are convinced that a Socialist economic order cannot be created by the decrees and statutes of a government, but only by the solidaric collaboration of the workers with hand and brain in each special branch of production; that is, through the taking over of the management of all plants by the producers themselves under such form that the separate groups, plants, and branches of industry are independent members of the general economic organism and systematically carry on production and the distribution of the products in the interest of the community on the basis of free mutual agreements."* [Rudolf Rocker, **Anarcho-syndicalism**, p. 55]

Again, like all social anarchists, anarcho-syndicalists see the collective struggle and organisation implied in unions as the school for anarchism. As Eugene Varlin (an anarchist active in the First International who was murdered at the end of the Paris Commune) put it, unions have *"the enormous advantage of making people accustomed to group life and thus preparing them for a more extended social organisation. They accustom people not only to get along with one another and to understand one another, but also to organise themselves, to discuss, and to reason from a collective perspective."* Moreover, as well as mitigating capitalist exploitation and oppression in the here and now, the unions also *"form the natural elements of the social edifice of the future; it is they who can be easily transformed into producers associations; it is they who can make the social ingredients and the organisation of production work."* [quoted by Julian P. W. Archer, **The First International in France, 1864-1872**, p. 196]

The difference between syndicalists and other revolutionary social anarchists is slight and purely revolves around the question of anarcho-syndicalist unions. Collectivist anarchists agree that building libertarian unions is important and that work within the labour movement is essential in order to ensure *"the development and organisation ... of the social (and, by consequence, anti-political) power of the working masses."* [Bakunin, **Michael Bakunin: Selected Writings**, p. 197] Communist anarchists usually also acknowledge the importance of working in the labour movement but they generally think that syndicalistic organisations will be created by workers in struggle, and so consider encouraging the **"spirit of revolt"** as more important than creating syndicalist unions and hoping workers will join them (of course, anarcho-syndicalists support such autonomous struggle and organisation, so the differences are not great). Communist-anarchists also do not place as great an emphasis on the workplace, considering struggles within it to be equal in importance to other struggles against hierarchy and domination outside the workplace (most anarcho-syndicalists would agree with this, however, and often it is just a question of emphasis). A few communist-anarchists reject the labour movement as hopelessly reformist in nature and so refuse to work within it, but these are a small minority.

Both communist and collectivist anarchists recognise the need for anarchists to unite together in purely anarchist organisations. They think it is essential that anarchists work together as anarchists to clarify and spread their ideas to others. Syndicalists often deny the importance of anarchist groups and federations, arguing that revolutionary industrial and community unions are enough in themselves. Syndicalists think that the anarchist and union movements can be fused into one, but most other anarchists disagree. Non-syndicalists point out the reformist nature of unionism and urge that to keep syndicalist unions revolutionary, anarchists must work within them as part of an anarchist group or federation. Most non-syndicalists consider the fusion of anarchism and unionism a source of potential **confusion** that would result in the two movements failing to do their respective work correctly. For more details on anarcho-syndicalism see section J.3.8 (and section J.3.9 on why many anarchists reject aspects of it). It should be stressed that non-syndicalist anarchists do **not** reject the need for collective struggle and organisation by workers (see section H.2.8 on that particular Marxist myth).

In practice, few anarcho-syndicalists totally reject the need for an anarchist federation, while few anarchists are totally anti-syndicalist. For example, Bakunin inspired both anarcho-communist and anarcho-syndicalist ideas, and anarcho-communists like Kropotkin, Malatesta, Berkman and Goldman were all sympathetic to anarcho-syndicalist movements and ideas.

For further reading on the various types of social anarchism, we would recommend the following: mutualism is usually associated with the works of Proudhon, collectivism with Bakunin's, communism with Kropotkin's, Malatesta's, Goldman's and Berkman's. Syndicalism is somewhat different, as it was far more the product of workers' in struggle than the work of a "famous" name (although this does not stop academics calling George Sorel the father of syndicalism, even though he wrote about a syndicalist movement that already existed. The idea that working class people can develop their own ideas, by themselves, is usually lost on them). However, Rudolf Rocker is often considered a leading anarcho-syndicalist theorist and the works of Fernand Pelloutier and Emile Pouget are essential reading to understand anarcho-syndicalism. For an overview of the development of social anarchism and key works by its leading lights, Daniel Guérin's excellent anthology **No Gods No Masters** cannot be bettered.

A.3.3 What kinds of green anarchism are there?

An emphasis on anarchist ideas as a solution to the ecological crisis is a common thread in most forms of anarchism today. The trend goes back to the late nineteenth century and the works of Peter Kropotkin and Elisée Reclus. The latter, for example, argued that a *"secret harmony exists between the earth and the people whom it nourishes, and when imprudent societies let themselves violate this harmony, they always end up regretting it."* Similarly,

no contemporary ecologist would disagree with his comments that the *"truly civilised man [and women] understands that his [or her] nature is bound up with the interest of all and with that of nature. He [or she] repairs the damage caused by his predecessors and works to improve his domain."* [quoted by George Woodcock, *"Introduction"*, Marie Fleming, **The Geography of Freedom**, p. 15]

With regards Kropotkin, he argued that an anarchist society would be based on a confederation of communities that would integrate manual and brain work as well as decentralising and integrating industry and agriculture (see his classic work **Fields, Factories, and Workshops**). This idea of an economy in which *"small is beautiful"* (to use the title of E.F. Schumacher's Green classic) was proposed nearly 70 years before it was taken up by what was to become the green movement. In addition, in **Mutual Aid** Kropotkin documented how co-operation within species and between them and their environment is usually of more benefit to them than competition. Kropotkin's work, combined with that of William Morris, the Reclus brothers (both of whom, like Kropotkin, were world-renowned geographers), and many others laid the foundations for the current anarchist interest in ecological issues.

However, while there are many themes of an ecological nature within classical anarchism, it is only relatively recently that the similarities between ecological thought and anarchism has come to the fore (essentially from the publication of Murray Bookchin's classic essay *"Ecology and Revolutionary Thought"* in 1965). Indeed, it would be no exaggeration to state that it is the ideas and work of Murray Bookchin that has placed ecology and ecological issues at the heart of anarchism and anarchist ideals and analysis into many aspects of the green movement.

Before discussing the types of green anarchism (also called eco-anarchism) it would be worthwhile to explain exactly **what** anarchism and ecology have in common. To quote Murray Bookchin, *"both the ecologist and the anarchist place a strong emphasis on spontaneity"* and *"to both the ecologist and the anarchist, an ever-increasing unity is achieved by growing differentiation. **An expanding whole is created by the diversification and enrichment of its parts.**"* Moreover, *"[j]ust as the ecologist seeks to expand the range of an eco-system and promote free interplay between species, so the anarchist seeks to expand the range of social experiments and remove all fetters to its development."* [**Post-Scarcity Anarchism**, p. 36]

Thus the anarchist concern with free development, decentralisation, diversity and spontaneity is reflected in ecological ideas and concerns. Hierarchy, centralisation, the state and concentrations of wealth reduce diversity and the free development of individuals and their communities by their very nature, and so weakens the social eco-system as well as the actual eco-systems human societies are part of. As Bookchin argues, *"the reconstructive message of ecology ... [is that] we must conserve and promote variety"* but within modern capitalist society *"[a]ll that is spontaneous, creative and individuated is circumscribed by the standardised, the regulated and the massified."* [**Op. Cit.**, p. 35 and p. 26] So, in many ways, anarchism can be considered the application of ecological ideas to society, as anarchism aims to empower individuals and communities, decentralise political, social and economic power so ensuring that individuals and social life develops freely and so becomes increasingly diverse in nature. It is for this reason Brian Morris argues that *"the only political tradition that complements and, as it were, integrally connects with ecology – in a genuine and authentic way – is that of anarchism."* [**Ecology and Anarchism**, p. 132]

So what kinds of green anarchism are there? While almost all forms of modern anarchism consider themselves to have an ecological dimension, the specifically eco-anarchist thread within anarchism has two main focal points, **Social Ecology** and **"primitivist"**. In addition, some anarchists are influenced by **Deep Ecology**, although not many. Undoubtedly Social Ecology is the most influential and numerous current. Social Ecology is associated with the ideas and works of Murray Bookchin, who has been writing on ecological matters since the 1950's and, from the 1960s, has combined these issues with revolutionary social anarchism. His works include **Post-Scarcity Anarchism**, **Toward an Ecological Society**, **The Ecology of Freedom** and a host of others.

Social Ecology locates the roots of the ecological crisis firmly in relations of domination between people. The domination of nature is seen as a product of domination within society, but this domination only reaches crisis proportions under capitalism. In the words of Murray Bookchin:

> *"The notion that man must dominate nature emerges directly from the domination of man by man ... But it was not until organic community relations ... dissolved into market relationships that the planet itself was reduced to a resource for exploitation. This centuries-long tendency finds its most exacerbating development in modern capitalism. Owing to its inherently competitive nature, bourgeois society not only pits humans against each other, it also pits the mass of humanity against the natural world. Just as men are converted into commodities, so every aspect of nature is converted into a commodity, a resource to be manufactured and merchandised wantonly ... The plundering of the human spirit by the market place is paralleled by the plundering of the earth by capital."* [**Op. Cit.**, p. 24-5]

"Only insofar," Bookchin stresses, *"as the ecology movement **consciously** cultivates an anti-hierarchical and a non-domineering sensibility, structure, and strategy for social change can it retain its very **identity** as the voice for a new balance between humanity and nature and its **goal** for a truly ecological society."* Social ecologists contrast this to what Bookchin labels *"environmentalism"* for while social ecology *"seeks to eliminate the concept of the domination of nature by humanity by eliminating domination of human by human, environmentalism reflects an 'instrumentalist' or technical sensibility in which nature is viewed merely as a passive habit, an agglomeration of external objects and forces, that must be made more 'serviceable' for human use, irrespective of what these uses may be. Environmentalism ... does not bring into question the underlying notions of the present society, notably that man must dominate nature. On the contrary, it seeks to facilitate that domination by developing techniques for diminishing the hazards caused by domination."* [Murray Bookchin, **Towards an Ecological Society**, p. 77]

Social ecology offers the vision of a society in harmony with nature, one which *"involves a fundamental reversal of all the trends that mark the historic development of capitalist technology and bourgeois society – the minute specialisation of machines and labour, the concentration of resources and people in gigantic industrial enterprises and urban entities, the stratification and bureaucratisation of nature and human beings."* Such an ecotopia *"establish entirely new eco-communities that are artistically moulded to the eco-systems in which they are located."* Echoing Kropotkin, Bookchin argues that *"[s]uch an eco-community ... would heal the split between town and country, between mind and body by fusing intellectual with physical work, industry with agricultural in a rotation or diversification of vocational tasks."* This society would be based on the use of appropriate and green technology, a *"new kind of technology – or eco-technology – one composed of flexible, versatile machinery whose productive applications would emphasise durability and quality, not built in obsolescence, and insensate quantitative output of shoddy goods, and a rapid circulation of expendable commodities ... Such an eco-technology would use the inexhaustible energy capacities of nature – the sun and wind, the tides and waterways, the temperature differentials of the earth and the abundance of hydrogen around us as fuels – to provide the eco-community with non-polluting materials or wastes that could be recycled."* [Bookchin, **Op. Cit.**, pp. 68-9]

However, this is not all. As Bookchin stresses an ecological society *"is more than a society that tries to check the mounting disequilibrium that exists between humanity and the natural world. Reduced to simple technical or political issues, this anaemic view of such a society's function degrades the issues raised by an ecological critique and leads them to purely technical and instrumental approaches to ecological problems. Social ecology is, first of all, a **sensibility** that includes not only a critique of hierarchy and domination but a reconstructive outlook ... guided by an ethics that emphasises variety without structuring differences into a hierarchical order ... the precepts for such an ethics ... [are] participation and differentiation."* [**The Modern Crisis**, pp. 24-5]

Therefore social ecologists consider it essential to attack hierarchy and capitalism, not civilisation as such as the root cause of ecological problems. This is one of the key areas in which they disagree with "Primitivist" Anarchist ideas, who tend to be far more critical of **all** aspects of modern life, with some going so far as calling for *"the end of civilisation"* including, apparently, all forms of technology and large scale organisation. We discuss these ideas in section A.3.9.

We must note here that other anarchists, while generally agreeing with its analysis and suggestions, are deeply critical of Social Ecology's support for running candidates in municipal elections. While Social Ecologists see this as a means of creating popular self-managing assemblies and creating a counter power to the state, few anarchists agree. Rather they see it as inherently reformist as well as being hopelessly naive about the possibilities of using elections to bring about social change (see section J.5.14 for a fuller discussion of this). Instead they propose direct action as the means to forward anarchist and ecological ideas, rejecting electioneering as a dead-end which ends up watering down radical ideas and corrupting the people involved (see section J.2 – What is Direct Action?).

Lastly, there is "deep ecology," which, because of its bio-centric nature, many anarchists reject as anti-human. There are few anarchists who think that **people,** as people, are the cause of the ecological crisis, which many deep ecologists seem to suggest. Murray Bookchin, for example, has been particularly outspoken in his criticism of deep ecology and the anti-human ideas that are often associated with it (see **Which Way for the Ecology Movement?**, for example). David Watson has also argued against Deep Ecology (see his **How Deep is Deep Ecology?** written under the name George Bradford). Most anarchists would argue that it is not people but the current system which is the problem, and that only people can change it. In the words of Murray Bookchin:

*"[Deep Ecology's problems] stem from an authoritarian streak in a crude biologism that uses 'natural law' to conceal an ever-diminishing sense of humanity and papers over a profound ignorance of social reality by ignoring the fact it is **capitalism** we are talking about, not an abstraction called 'Humanity' and 'Society.'"* [**The Philosophy of Social Ecology**, p. 160]

Thus, as Morris stresses, *"by focusing entirely on the category of 'humanity' the Deep Ecologists ignore or completely obscure the social origins of ecological problems, or alternatively, biologise what are essentially social problems."* To submerge ecological critique and analysis into a simplistic protest against the human race ignores the real causes and dynamics of ecological destruction and, therefore, ensures an end to this destruction cannot be found. Simply put, it is hardly "people" who are to blame when the vast majority have no real say in the decisions that affect their lives, communities, industries and eco-systems. Rather, it is an economic and social system that places profits and power above people and planet. By focusing on "Humanity" (and so failing to distinguish between rich and poor, men and women, whites and people of colour, exploiters and exploited, oppressors and oppressed) the system we live under is effectively ignored, and so are the institutional causes of ecological problems. This can be *"both reactionary and authoritarian in its implications, and substitutes a naive understanding of 'nature' for a critical study of real social issues and concerns."* [Morris, **Op. Cit.,** p. 135]

Faced with a constant anarchist critique of certain of their spokespersons ideas, many Deep Ecologists have turned away from the anti-human ideas associated with their movement. Deep ecology, particularly the organisation **Earth First!** (EF!), has changed considerably over time, and EF! now has a close working relationship with the **Industrial Workers of the World** (IWW), a syndicalist union. While deep ecology is not a thread of eco-anarchism, it shares many ideas and is becoming more accepted by anarchists as EF! rejects its few misanthropic ideas and starts to see that hierarchy, not the human race, is the problem (for a discussion between Murray Bookchin and leading Earth Firster! Dave Foreman see the book **Defending the Earth**).

A pacifist strand has long existed in anarchism, with Leo Tolstoy being one of its major figures. This strand is usually called **"anarcho-pacifism"** (the term **"non-violent anarchist"** is sometimes used, but this term is unfortunate because it implies the rest of the movement are "violent," which is not the case!). The union of anarchism and pacifism is not surprising given the fundamental ideals and arguments of anarchism. After all, violence, or the threat of violence or harm, is a key means by which individual freedom is destroyed. As Peter Marshall points out, *"[g]iven the anarchist's respect for the sovereignty of the individual, in the long run it is non-violence and not violence which is implied by anarchist values."* [**Demanding the Impossible**, p.637] Malatesta is even more explicit when he wrote that the *"main plank of anarchism is the removal of violence from human relations"* and that anarchists *"are opposed to violence."* [**Errico Malatesta: His Life and Ideas**, p. 53]

However, although many anarchists reject violence and proclaim pacifism; the movement, in general, is not essentially pacifistic (in the sense of opposed all forms of violence at all times). Rather, it is anti-militarist, being against the organised violence of the state but recognising that there are important differences between the violence of the oppressor and the violence of the oppressed. This explains why the anarchist movement has always placed a lot of time and energy in opposing the military machine and capitalist wars while, at the same time, supporting and organising armed resistance against oppression (as in the case of the Makhnovist army during the Russian Revolution which resisted both Red and White armies and the militias the anarchists organised to resist the fascists during the Spanish Revolution – see sections A.5.4 and A.5.6, respectively).

On the question of non-violence, as a rough rule of thumb, the movement divides along Individualist and Social lines. Most Individualist anarchists support purely non-violent tactics of social change, as do the Mutualists. However, Individualist anarchism is not pacifist as such, as many support the idea of violence in self-defence against aggression. Most social anarchists, on the other hand, do support the use of revolutionary violence, holding that physical force will be required to overthrow entrenched power and to resist state and capitalist aggression (although it was an anarcho-syndicalist, Bart de Ligt, who wrote the pacifist classic, **The Conquest of Violence**). As Malatesta put it, violence, while being *"in itself an evil,"* is *"justifiable only when it is necessary to defend oneself and others from violence"* and that a *"slave is always in a state of legitimate defence and consequently, his violence against the boss, against the oppressor, is always morally justifiable."* [**Op. Cit.**, p. 55 and pp. 53-54] Moreover, they stress that, to use the words of Bakunin, since social oppression *"stems far less from individuals than from the organisation of things and from social positions"* anarchists aim to *"ruthlessly destroy positions and things"* rather than people, since the aim of an anarchist revolution is to see the end of privileged classes *"not as individuals, but as* classes." [quoted by Richard B. Saltman, **The Social and Political Thought of Michael Bakunin** p. 121, p. 124 and p. 122]

Indeed, the question of violence is relatively unimportant to most anarchists, as they do not glorify it and think that it should be kept to a minimum during any social struggle or revolution. All anarchists would agree with the Dutch pacifist anarcho-syndicalist Bart de Ligt when he argued that *"the violence and warfare which are characteristic conditions of the capitalist world do not go with the liberation of the individual, which is the historic mission of the exploited classes. The greater the violence, the weaker the revolution, even where violence has deliberately been put at the service of the revolution."* [**The Conquest of Violence**, p. 75]

Similarly, all anarchists would agree with de Ligt on, to use the name of one of his book's chapters, *"the absurdity of bourgeois pacifism."* For de Ligt, and all anarchists, violence is inherent in the capitalist system and any attempt to make capitalism pacifistic is doomed to failure. This is because, on the one hand, war is often just economic competition carried out by other means. Nations often go to war when they face an economic crisis, what they cannot gain in economic struggle they attempt to get by conflict. On the other hand, *"violence is indispensable in modern society … [because] without it the ruling class would be completely unable to maintain its privileged position with regard to the exploited masses in each country. The army is used first and foremost to hold down the workers … when they become discontented."* [Bart de Ligt, **Op. Cit.**, p. 62] As long as the state and capitalism exist, violence is inevitable and so, for anarcho-pacifists, the consistent pacifist must be an anarchist just as the consistent anarchist must be a pacifist.

For those anarchists who are non-pacifists, violence is seen as an unavoidable and unfortunate result of oppression and exploitation as well as the only means by which the privileged classes will renounce their power and wealth. Those in authority rarely give up their power and so must be forced. Hence the need for *"transitional"* violence *"to put an end to the far greater, and permanent, violence which keeps the majority of mankind in servitude."* [Malatesta, **Op. Cit.**, p. 55] To concentrate on the issue of violence versus non-violence is to ignore the real issue, namely how do we change society for the better. As Alexander Berkman pointed out, those anarchists who are pacifists confuse the issue, like those who think *"it's the same as if rolling up your sleeves for work should be considered the work itself."* To the contrary, *"[t]he fighting part of revolution is merely rolling up your sleeves. The real, actual task is ahead."* [**What is Anarchism?**, p. 183] And, indeed, most social struggle and revolutions start relatively peaceful (via strikes, occupations and so on) and only degenerate into violence when those in power try to maintain their position (a classic example of this is in Italy, in 1920, when the occupation of factories by their workers was followed by fascist terror – see section A.5.5).

As noted above, all anarchists are anti-militarists and oppose both the military machine (and so the "defence" industry) as well as statist/capitalist wars (although a few anarchists, like Rudolf Rocker and Sam Dolgoff, supported the anti-fascist capitalist side during the second world war as the lesser evil). The anti-war machine message of anarchists and anarcho-syndicalists was propagated long before the start of the first world war, with syndicalists and anarchists in Britain and North America reprinting a French CGT leaflet urging soldiers not to follow orders and repress their striking fellow workers. Emma Goldman and Alexander Berkman were both arrested and deported from America for organising a **"No-Conscription League"** in 1917 while many anarchists in Europe were jailed for refusing to join the armed forces in the first and second world wars. The anarcho-syndicalist influenced IWW was crushed by a ruthless wave of government repression due to the threat its organising and anti-war message presented to the powerful elites who favoured war. More recently, anarchists, (including people like Noam Chomsky and Paul Goodman) have been active in the peace movement as well as contributing to the resistance to conscription where it still exists. Anarchists took an active part in opposing such wars as the Vietnam War, the Falklands war as well as the Gulf wars of 1991 and 2003 (including, in Italy and Spain, helping to organise strikes in protest against it). And it was during the 1991 Gulf War when many anarchists raised the slogan **"No war but the class war"** which nicely sums up the anarchist opposition to war – namely an evil consequence of any class system, in which the oppressed classes of different countries kill each other for the power and profits of their rulers. Rather than take part in this organised slaughter, anarchists urge working people to fight for their own interests, not those of their masters:

> *"More than ever we must avoid compromise; deepen the chasm between capitalists and wage slaves, between rulers and ruled; preach expropriation of private property and the destruction of states such as the only means of guaranteeing fraternity between peoples and Justice and Liberty for all; and we must prepare to accomplish these things."* [Malatesta, **Op. Cit.**, pp. 250-1]

We must note here that Malatesta's words were written in part against Peter Kropotkin who, for reasons best known to himself, rejected everything he had argued for decades and supported the allies in the First World War as a lesser evil against German authoritarianism and Imperialism. Of course, as Malatesta pointed out, *"all Governments and all capitalist classes"* do *"misdeeds … against the workers and rebels of their own countries."* [**Op. Cit.**, p. 246] He, along with Berkman, Goldman and a host of other anarchists, put their name to International Anarchist Manifesto against the First World War. It expressed the opinion of the bulk of the anarchist movement (at the time and consequently) on war and how to stop it. It is worth quoting from:

> *"The truth is that the cause of wars … rests solely in the existence of the State, which is the form of privilege … Whatever the form it may assume, the State is nothing but organised oppression for the advantage of a privileged minority …*
>
> *"The misfortune of the peoples, who were deeply attached to peace, is that, in order to avoid war, they placed their confidence in the State with its intriguing diplomatists, in democracy, and in political parties … This confidence has been deliberately betrayed, and continues to be so, when governments, with the aid of the whole of the press, persuade their respective people that this war is a war of liberation.*

"We are resolutely against all wars between peoples, and … have been, are, and ever will be most energetically opposed to war.

"The role of the Anarchists … is to continue to proclaim that there is only one war of liberation: that which in all countries is waged by the oppressed against the oppressors, by the exploited against the exploiters. Our part is to summon the slaves to revolt against their masters.

"Anarchist action and propaganda should assiduously and perseveringly aim at weakening and dissolving the various States, at cultivating the spirit of revolt, and arousing discontent in peoples and armies …

"We must take advantage of all the movements of revolt, of all the discontent, in order to foment insurrection, and to organise the revolution which we look to put end to all social wrongs … Social justice realised through the free organisation of producers: war and militarism done away with forever; and complete freedom won, by the abolition of the State and its organs of destruction." ["*International Anarchist Manifesto on the War,*" **Anarchy! An Anthology of Emma Goldman's Mother Earth**, pp. 386-8]

Thus, the attraction of pacifism to anarchists is clear. Violence **is** authoritarian and coercive, and so its use does contradict anarchist principles. That is why anarchists would agree with Malatesta when he argues that *"[w]e are on principle opposed to violence and for this reason wish that the social struggle should be conducted as humanely as possible."* [Malatesta, **Op. Cit.**, p. 57] Most, if not all, anarchists who are not strict pacifists agree with pacifist-anarchists when they argue that violence can often be counterproductive, alienating people and giving the state an excuse to repress both the anarchist movement and popular movements for social change. All anarchists support non-violent direct action and civil disobedience, which often provide better roads to radical change.

So, to sum up, anarchists who are pure pacifists are rare. Most accept the use of violence as a necessary evil and advocate minimising its use. All agree that a revolution which **institutionalises** violence will just recreate the state in a new form. They argue, however, that it is not authoritarian to destroy authority or to use violence to resist violence. Therefore, although most anarchists are not pacifists, most reject violence except in self-defence and even then kept to the minimum.

A.3.5 What is Anarcha-Feminism?

Although opposition to the state and all forms of authority had a strong voice among the early feminists of the 19th century, the more recent feminist movement which began in the 1960's was founded upon anarchist practice. This is where the term anarcha-feminism came from, referring to women anarchists who act within the larger feminist and anarchist movements to remind them of their principles.

The modern anarcha-feminists built upon the feminist ideas of previous anarchists, both male and female. Indeed, anarchism and feminism have always been closely linked. Many outstanding feminists have also been anarchists, including the pioneering Mary Wollstonecraft (author of **A Vindication of the Rights of Woman**), the Communard Louise Michel, and the American anarchists (and tireless champions of women's freedom) Voltairine de Cleyre and Emma Goldman (for the former, see her essays *"Sex Slavery"*, *"Gates of Freedom"*, *"The Case of Woman vs. Orthodoxy"*, *"Those Who Marry Do Ill"*; for the latter see *"The Traffic in Women"*, *"Woman Suffrage"*, *"The Tragedy of Woman's Emancipation"*, *"Marriage and Love"* and *"Victims of Morality"*, for example). **Freedom**, the world's oldest anarchist newspaper, was founded by Charlotte Wilson in 1886. Anarchist women like Virgilia D'Andrea and Rose Pesota played important roles in both the libertarian and labour movements. The **"Mujeres Libres"** (*"Free Women"*) movement in Spain during the Spanish revolution is a classic example of women anarchists organising themselves to defend their basic freedoms and create a society based on women's freedom and equality (see **Free Women of Spain** by Martha Ackelsberg for more details on this important organisation). In addition, all the male major anarchist thinkers (bar Proudhon) were firm supporters of women's equality. For example, Bakunin opposed patriarchy and how the law *"subjects [women] to the absolute domination of the man."* He argued that *"[e]qual rights must belong to men and women"* so that women can *"become independent and be free to forge their own way of life."* He looked forward to the end of *"the authoritarian juridical family"* and *"the full sexual freedom of women."* [**Bakunin on Anarchism**, p. 396 and p. 397]

Thus anarchism has since the 1860s combined a radical critique of capitalism and the state with an equally powerful critique of patriarchy (rule by men). Anarchists, particularly female ones, recognised that modern society was dominated by men. As Ana Maria Mozzoni (an Italian anarchist immigrant in Buenos Aires) put it, women *"will find that the priest who damns you is a man; that the legislator who oppresses you is a man, that the husband who reduces you to an **object** is a man; that the libertine who harasses you is a man; that the capitalist who enriches himself with your ill-paid work and the speculator who calmly pockets the price of your body, are men."* Little has changed since then. Patriarchy still exists and, to quote the anarchist paper **La Questione Sociale**, it is still usually the case that women *"are slaves both in social and private life. If you are a proletarian, you have two tyrants: the man and the boss. If bourgeois, the only sovereignty left to you is that of frivolity and coquetry."* [quoted by Jose Moya, **Italians in Buenos Aires's Anarchist Movement**, pp. 197-8 and p. 200]

Anarchism, therefore, is based on an awareness that fighting patriarchy is as important as fighting against the state or capitalism. For *"[y]ou can have no free, or just, or equal society, nor anything approaching it, so long as womanhood is bought, sold, housed, clothed, fed, and **protected**, as a chattel."* [Voltairine de Cleyre, *"The Gates of Freedom"*, pp. 235-250, Eugenia C. Delamotte, **Gates of Freedom**, p. 242] To quote Louise Michel:

"The first thing that must change is the relationship between the sexes. Humanity has two parts, men and women, and we ought to be walking hand in hand; instead there is antagonism, and it will last as long as the 'stronger' half controls, or think its controls, the 'weaker' half." [**The Red Virgin: Memoirs of Louise Michel**, p. 139]

Thus anarchism, like feminism, fights patriarchy and for women's equality. Both share much common history and a concern about individual freedom, equality and dignity for members of the female sex (although, as we will explain in more depth below, anarchists have always been very critical of mainstream/liberal feminism as not going far enough). Therefore, it is unsurprising that the new wave of feminism of the sixties expressed itself in an anarchistic manner and drew much inspiration from anarchist figures such as Emma Goldman. Cathy Levine points out that, during this time, *"independent groups of women began functioning without the structure, leaders, and other factotums of the male left, creating, independently and simultaneously, organisations similar to those of anarchists of many decades and regions. No accident, either."* [*"The Tyranny of Tyranny,"* **Quiet Rumours: An Anarcha-Feminist Reader**, p. 66] It is no accident because, as feminist scholars have noted, women were among the first victims of hierarchical society, which is thought to have begun with the rise of patriarchy and ideologies of domination during the late Neolithic era. Marilyn French argues (in **Beyond Power**) that the first major social stratification of the human race occurred when men began dominating women, with women becoming in effect a "lower" and "inferior" social class.

The links between anarchism and modern feminism exist in both ideas and action. Leading feminist thinker Carole Pateman notes that her *"discussion [on contract theory and its authoritarian and patriarchal basis] owes something to"* libertarian ideas, that is the *"anarchist wing of the socialist movement."* [**The Sexual Contract**, p. 14] Moreover, she noted in the 1980s how the *"major locus of criticism of authoritarian, hierarchical, undemocratic forms of organisation for the last twenty years has been the women's movement ... After Marx defeated Bakunin in the First International, the prevailing form of organisation in the labour movement, the nationalised industries and in the left sects has mimicked the hierarchy of the state ... The women's movement has rescued and put into practice the long-submerged idea [of anarchists like Bakunin] that movements for, and experiments in, social change must 'prefigure' the future form of social organisation."* [**The Disorder of Women**, p. 201]

Peggy Kornegger has drawn attention to these strong connections between feminism and anarchism, both in theory and practice. *"The radical feminist perspective is almost pure anarchism,"* she writes. *"The basic theory postulates the nuclear family as the basis of all authoritarian systems. The lesson the child learns, from father to teacher to boss to god, is to* **obey** *the great anonymous voice of Authority. To graduate from childhood to adulthood is to become a full-fledged automaton, incapable of questioning or even of thinking clearly."* [*"Anarchism: The Feminist Connection,"* **Quiet Rumours: An Anarcha-Feminist Reader**, p. 26] Similarly, the Zero Collective argues that Anarcha-feminism *"consists in*

recognising the anarchism of feminism and consciously developing it." [*"Anarchism/Feminism,"* pp. 3-7, **The Raven**, no. 21, p. 6] Anarcha-feminists point out that authoritarian traits and values, for example, domination, exploitation, aggressiveness, competitiveness, desensitisation etc., are highly valued in hierarchical civilisations and are traditionally referred to as "masculine." In contrast, non-authoritarian traits and values such as co-operation, sharing, compassion, sensitivity, warmth, etc., are traditionally regarded as "feminine" and are devalued. Feminist scholars have traced this phenomenon back to the growth of patriarchal societies during the early Bronze Age and their conquest of co-operatively based "organic" societies in which "feminine" traits and values were prevalent and respected. Following these conquests, however, such values came to be regarded as "inferior," especially for a man, since men were in charge of domination and exploitation under patriarchy (see, for example, Riane Eisler, **The Chalice and the Blade**; Elise Boulding, **The Underside of History**). Hence anarcha-feminists have referred to the creation of a non-authoritarian, anarchist society based on co-operation, sharing, mutual aid, etc. as the "feminisation of society."

Anarcha-feminists have noted that "feminising" society cannot be achieved without both self-management and decentralisation. This is because the patriarchal-authoritarian values and traditions they wish to overthrow are embodied and reproduced in hierarchies. Thus feminism implies decentralisation, which in turn implies self-management. Many feminists have recognised this, as reflected in their experiments with collective forms of feminist organisations that eliminate hierarchical structure and competitive forms of decision making. Some feminists have even argued that directly democratic organisations are specifically female political forms. (see, for example, Nancy Hartsock *"Feminist Theory and the Development of Revolutionary Strategy"* [Zeila Eisenstein, ed., **Capitalist Patriarchy and the Case for Socialist Feminism**, pp. 56-77]). Like all anarchists, anarcha-feminists recognise that self-liberation is the key to women's equality and thus, freedom. Thus Emma Goldman:

> *"Her development, her freedom, her independence, must come from and through herself. First, by asserting herself as a personality, and not as a sex commodity. Second, by refusing the right of anyone over her body; by refusing to bear children, unless she wants them, by refusing to be a servant to God, the State, society, the husband, the family, etc., by making her life simpler, but deeper and richer. That is, by trying to learn the meaning and substance of life in all its complexities; by freeing herself from the fear of public opinion and public condemnation."*
> [**Anarchism and Other Essays**, p. 211]

Anarcha-feminism tries to keep feminism from becoming influenced and dominated by authoritarian ideologies of either the right or left. It proposes direct action and self-help instead of the mass reformist campaigns favoured by the "official" feminist movement, with its creation of hierarchical and centralist organisations and its illusion that having more women bosses, politicians, and soldiers is a move towards "equality." Anarcha-feminists would point out that the so-called "management science" which women have to learn in order to become mangers in capitalist companies is essentially a set of techniques for controlling and exploiting wage workers in corporate hierarchies, whereas "feminising" society requires the elimination of capitalist wage-slavery and managerial domination altogether. Anarcha-feminists realise that learning how to become an effective exploiter or oppressor is not the path to equality (as one member of the Mujeres Libres put it, *"[w]e did not want to substitute a feminist hierarchy for a masculine one"* [quoted by Martha A. Ackelsberg, **Free Women of Spain**, pp. 22-3] – also see section B.1.4 for a further discussion on patriarchy and hierarchy).

Hence anarchism's traditional hostility to liberal (or mainstream) feminism, while supporting women's liberation and equality. Federica Montseny (a leading figure in the Spanish Anarchist movement) argued that such feminism advocated equality for women, but did not challenge existing institutions. She argued that (mainstream) feminism's only ambition is to give to women of a particular class the opportunity to participate more fully in the existing system of privilege and if these institutions *"are unjust when men take advantage of them, they will still be unjust if women take advantage of them."* [quoted by Martha A. Ackelsberg, **Op. Cit.**, p. 119] Thus, for anarchists, women's freedom did not mean an equal chance to become a boss or a wage slave, a voter or a politician, but rather to be a free and equal individual co-operating as equals in free associations. *"Feminism,"* stressed Peggy Kornegger, *"doesn't mean female corporate power or a woman President; it means no corporate power and no Presidents. The Equal Rights Amendment will not transform society; it only gives women the 'right' to plug into a hierarchical economy. Challenging sexism means challenging all hierarchy – economic, political, and personal. And that means an anarcha-feminist revolution."* [**Op. Cit.**, p. 27]

Anarchism, as can be seen, included a class and economic analysis which is missing from mainstream feminism while, at the same time, showing an awareness to domestic and sex-based power relations which eluded the mainstream socialist movement. This flows from our hatred of hierarchy. As Mozzoni put it, *"Anarchy defends the cause of all the oppressed, and because of this, and in a special way, it defends your [women's] cause, oh! women, doubly oppressed by present society in both the social and private spheres."* [quoted by Moya, **Op. Cit.**, p. 203] This means that, to quote a Chinese anarchist, what anarchists *"mean by equality between the sexes is not just that the men will no longer oppress women. We also want men to no longer to be oppressed by other men, and women no longer to be oppressed by other women."* Thus women should *"completely overthrow rulership, force men to abandon all their special privileges and become equal to women, and make a world with neither the oppression of women nor the oppression of men."* [He Zhen, quoted by Peter Zarrow, **Anarchism and Chinese Political Culture**, p. 147]

So, in the historic anarchist movement, as Martha Ackelsberg notes, liberal/mainstream feminism was considered as being *"too narrowly focused as a strategy for women's emancipation; sexual struggle could not be separated from class struggle or from the anarchist project as a whole."* [**Op. Cit.**, p. 119] Anarcha-feminism continues this tradition by arguing that all forms of hierarchy are wrong, not just patriarchy, and that feminism is in conflict with its own ideals if it desires simply to allow women to have the same chance of being a boss as a man does. They simply state the obvious, namely that they *"do not believe that power in the hands of women could possibly lead to a non-coercive society"* nor do they *"believe that anything good can come out of a mass movement with a leadership elite."* The *"central issues are always power and social hierarchy"* and so people *"are free only when they have power over their own lives."* [Carole Ehrlich, "Socialism, Anarchism and Feminism", **Quiet Rumours: An Anarcha-Feminist Reader**, p. 44] For if, as Louise Michel put it, *"a proletarian is a slave; the wife of a proletarian is even more a slave"* ensuring that the wife experiences an equal level of oppression as the husband misses the point. [**Op. Cit.**, p. 141]

Anarcha-feminists, therefore, like all anarchists oppose capitalism as a denial of liberty. Their critique of hierarchy in the society does not start and end with patriarchy. It is a case of wanting freedom everywhere, of wanting to *"[b]reak up ... every home that rests in slavery! Every marriage that represents the sale and transfer of the individuality of one of its parties to the other! Every institution, social or civil, that stands between man and his right; every tie that renders one a master, another a serf."* [Voltairine de Cleyre, "The Economic Tendency of Freethought", **The Voltairine de Cleyre Reader**, p. 72] The ideal that an "equal opportunity" capitalism would free women ignores the fact that any such system would still see working class women oppressed by bosses (be they male or female). For anarcha-feminists, the struggle for women's liberation cannot be separated from the struggle against hierarchy **as such.** As L. Susan Brown puts it:

> *"Anarchist-feminism, as an expression of the anarchist sensibility applied to feminist concerns, takes the individual as its starting point and, in opposition to relations of domination and subordination, argues for non-instrumental economic forms that preserve individual existential freedom, for both men and women."* [**The Politics of Individualism**, p. 144]

Anarcha-feminists have much to contribute to our understanding of the origins of the ecological crisis in the authoritarian values of hierarchical civilisation. For example, a number of feminist scholars have argued that the domination of nature has paralleled the domination of women, who have been identified with nature throughout history (See, for example, Caroline Merchant, **The Death of Nature**, 1980). Both women and nature are victims of the obsession with control that characterises the authoritarian personality. For this reason, a growing number of both radical ecologists and feminists are recognising that hierarchies must be dismantled in order to achieve their respective goals.

In addition, anarcha-feminism reminds us of the importance of treating women equally with men while, at the same time, respecting women's differences from men. In other words, that recognising and respecting diversity includes women as well as men. Too often many male anarchists assume that, because they are (in theory) opposed to sexism, they are not sexist in practice. Such an assumption is false. Anarcha-feminism brings the question of consistency between theory and practice to the front of social activism and reminds us all that we must fight not only external constraints but also internal ones.

This means that anarcha-feminism urges us to practice what we preach. As Voltairine de Cleyre argued, *"I never expect men to **give** us liberty. No, Women, we are not **worth** it, until we **take** it."* This involves *"insisting on a new code of ethics founded on the law of equal freedom: a code recognising the complete individuality of woman. By making rebels wherever we can. By ourselves **living our beliefs**.... We are revolutionists. And we shall use propaganda by speech, deed, and most of all life – **being** what we teach."* Thus anarcha-feminists, like all anarchists, see the struggle against patriarchy as being a struggle of the oppressed for their own self-liberation, for *"**as a class** I have nothing to hope from men ... No tyrant ever renounced his tyranny until he had to. If history ever teaches us anything it teaches this. Therefore my hope lies in creating rebellion in the breasts of women."* [*"The Gates of Freedom"*, pp. 235-250, Eugenia C. Delamotte, **Gates of Freedom**, p. 249 and p. 239] This was sadly as applicable within the anarchist movement as it was outside it in patriarchal society.

Faced with the sexism of male anarchists who spoke of sexual equality, women anarchists in Spain organised themselves into the **Mujeres Libres** organisation to combat it. They did not believe in leaving their liberation to some day after the revolution. Their liberation was a integral part of that revolution and had to be started today. In this they repeated the conclusions of anarchist women in Illinois Coal towns who grew tried of hearing their male comrades *"shout in favour"* of sexual equality *"in the future society"* while doing nothing about it in the here and now. They used a particularly insulting analogy, comparing their male comrades to priests who *"make false promises to the starving masses ... [that] there will be rewards in paradise."* The argued that mothers should make their daughters *"understand that the difference in sex does not imply inequality in rights"* and that as well as being *"rebels against the social system of today,"* they *"should fight especially against the oppression of men who would like to retain women as their moral and material inferior."* [Ersilia Grandi, quoted by Caroline Waldron Merithew, **Anarchist Motherhood**, p. 227] They formed the **"Luisa Michel"** group to fight against capitalism and patriarchy in the upper Illinois valley coal towns over three decades before their Spanish comrades organised themselves.

For anarcha-feminists, combating sexism is a key aspect of the struggle for freedom. It is not, as many Marxist socialists argued before the rise of feminism, a diversion from the "real" struggle against capitalism which would somehow be automatically solved after the revolution. It is an essential part of the struggle:

> *"We do not need any of your titles ... We want none of them. What we do want is knowledge and education and liberty. We know what our rights are and we demand them. Are we not standing next to you fighting the supreme fight? Are you not strong enough, men, to make part of that supreme fight a struggle for the rights of women? And then men and women together will gain the rights of all humanity."* [Louise Michel, **Op. Cit.**, p. 142]

A key part of this revolutionising modern society is the transformation of the current relationship between the sexes. Marriage is a particular evil for *"the old form of marriage, based on the Bible, 'till death doth part,' ... [is] an institution that stands for the sovereignty of the*

man over the women, of her complete submission to his whims and commands."* Women are reduced *"to the function of man's servant and bearer of his children."* [Goldman, **Op. Cit.**, pp. 220-1] Instead of this, anarchists proposed **"free love,"** that is couples and families based on free agreement between equals rather than one partner being in authority and the other simply obeying. Such unions would be without sanction of church or state for *"two beings who love each other do not need permission from a third to go to bed."* [Mozzoni, quoted by Moya, **Op. Cit.**, p. 200] Equality and freedom apply to more than just relationships. For *"if social progress consists in a constant tendency towards the equalisation of the liberties of social units, then the demands of progress are not satisfied so long as half society, Women, is in subjection. ... Woman ... is beginning to feel her servitude; that there is a requisite acknowledgement to be won from her master before he is put down and she exalted to – Equality. This acknowledgement is, **the freedom to control her own person.** "* [Voltairine de Cleyre, *"The Gates of Freedom"*, **Op. Cit.**, p. 242] Neither men nor state nor church should say what a woman does with her body. A logical extension of this is that women must have control over their own reproductive organs. Thus anarcha-feminists, like anarchists in general, are pro-choice and pro-reproductive rights (i.e. the right of a woman to control her own reproductive decisions). This is a long standing position. Emma Goldman was persecuted and incarcerated because of her public advocacy of birth control methods and the extremist notion that women should decide when they become pregnant (as feminist writer Margaret Anderson put it, *"In 1916, Emma Goldman was sent to prison for advocating that 'women need not always keep their mouth shut and their wombs open.'"*).

Anarcha-feminism does not stop there. Like anarchism in general, it aims at changing **all** aspects of society not just what happens in the home. For, as Goldman asked, *"how much independence is gained if the narrowness and lack of freedom of the home is exchanged for the narrowness and lack of freedom of the factory, sweat-shop, department store, or office?"* Thus women's equality and freedom had to be fought everywhere and defended against all forms of hierarchy. Nor can they be achieved by voting. Real liberation, argue anarcha-feminists, is only possible by direct action and anarcha-feminism is based on women's self-activity and self-liberation for while the *"right to vote, or equal civil rights, may be good demands ... true emancipation begins neither at the polls nor in the courts. It begins in woman's soul ... her freedom will reach as far as her power to achieve freedom reaches."* [Goldman, **Op. Cit.**, p. 216 and p. 224]

The history of the women's movement proves this. Every gain has come from below, by the action of women themselves. As Louise Michel put it, *"[w]e women are not bad revolutionaries. Without begging anyone, we are taking our place in the struggles; otherwise, we could go ahead and pass motions until the world ends and gain nothing."* [**Op. Cit.**, p. 139] If women waited for others to act for them their social position would never have changed. This includes getting the vote in the first place. Faced with the militant suffrage movement for women's votes, British anarchist Rose Witcop recognised that it was *"true that this movement shows us that women who so far have been so submissive to their masters, the men, are beginning to wake up at last to the fact they are not* inferior to those masters." Yet she argued that women would not be freed by votes but *"by their own strength."* [quoted by Sheila Rowbotham, **Hidden from History**, pp. 100-1 and p. 101] The women's movement of the 1960s and 1970s showed the truth of that analysis. In spite of equal voting rights, women's social place had remained unchanged since the 1920s.

Ultimately, as Anarchist Lily Gair Wilkinson stressed, the *"call for 'votes' can never be a call to freedom. For what is it to vote? To vote is to register assent to being ruled by one legislator or another?"* [quoted by Sheila Rowbotham, **Op. Cit.**, p. 102] It does not get to the heart of the problem, namely hierarchy and the authoritarian social relationships it creates of which patriarchy is only a subset of. Only by getting rid of all bosses, political, economic, social and sexual can **genuine** freedom for women be achieved and *"make it possible for women to be human in the truest sense. Everything within her that craves assertion and activity should reach its fullest expression; all artificial barriers should be broken, and the road towards greater freedom cleared of every trace of centuries of submission and slavery."* [Emma Goldman, **Op. Cit.**, p. 214]

A.3.6 What is Cultural Anarchism?

For our purposes, we will define cultural anarchism as the promotion of anti-authoritarian values through those aspects of society traditionally regarded as belonging to the sphere of "culture" rather than "economics" or "politics" – for example, through art, music, drama, literature, education, child-rearing practices, sexual morality, technology, and so forth.

Cultural expressions are anarchistic to the extent that they deliberately attack, weaken, or subvert the tendency of most traditional cultural forms to promote authoritarian values and attitudes, particularly domination and exploitation. Thus a novel that portrays the evils of militarism can be considered as cultural anarchism if it goes beyond the simple "war-is-hell" model and allows the reader to see how militarism is connected with authoritarian institutions (e.g. capitalism and statism) or methods of authoritarian conditioning (e.g. upbringing in the traditional patriarchal family). Or, as John Clark expresses it, cultural anarchism implies *"the development of arts, media, and other symbolic forms that expose various aspects of the system of domination and contrast them with a system of values based on freedom and community."* This *"**cultural** struggle"* would be part of a general struggle *"to combat the material and ideological power of all dominating classes, whether economic, political, racial, religious, or sexual, with a multi-dimensional practice of liberation."* In other words, an *"expanded conception of class analysis"* and *"an amplified practice of class struggle"* which includes, but is not limited to, *"**economic** actions like strikes, boycotts, job actions, occupation, organisations of direct action groups and federations of libertarian workers' groups and development of workers' assemblies, collectives and co-operatives"* and *"**political** activity"* like the *"active interference with implementation of repressive governmental policies,"* the *"non-compliance and resistance against regimentation and bureaucratisation of society"* and *"participation in movements for increasing direct participation in decision-making and local control."* [**The Anarchist Moment**, p. 31]

Cultural anarchism is important – indeed essential – because authoritarian values are embedded in a total system of domination with many aspects besides the political and economic. Hence those values cannot be eradicated even by a combined economic and political revolution if there it is not also accompanied by profound psychological changes in the majority of the population. For mass acquiescence in the current system is rooted in the psychic structure of human beings (their *"character structure,"* to use Wilhelm Reich's expression), which is produced by many forms of conditioning and socialisation that have developed with patriarchal-authoritarian civilisation during the past five or six thousand years.

In other words, even if capitalism and the state were overthrown tomorrow, people would soon create new forms of authority in their place. For authority – a strong leader, a chain of command, someone to give orders and relieve one of the responsibility of thinking for oneself – are what the submissive/authoritarian personality feels most comfortable with. Unfortunately, the majority of human beings fear real freedom, and indeed, do not know what to do with it – as is shown by a long string of failed revolutions and freedom movements in which the revolutionary ideals of freedom, democracy, and equality were betrayed and a new hierarchy and ruling class were quickly created. These failures are generally attributed to the machinations of reactionary politicians and capitalists, and to the perfidy of revolutionary leaders; but reactionary politicians only attract followers because they find a favourable soil for the growth of their authoritarian ideals in the character structure of ordinary people.

Hence the prerequisite of an anarchist revolution is a period of consciousness-raising in which people gradually become aware of submissive/authoritarian traits within themselves, see how those traits are reproduced by conditioning, and understand how they can be mitigated or eliminated through new forms of culture, particularly new child-rearing and educational methods. We will explore this issue more fully in section B.1.5 (What is the mass-psychological basis for authoritarian civilisation?), J.6 (What methods of child rearing do anarchists advocate?), and J.5.13 (What are Modern Schools?)

Cultural anarchist ideas are shared by almost all schools of anarchist thought and consciousness-raising is considered an essential part of any anarchist movement. For anarchists, its important to *"build the new world in the shell of the old"* in all aspects of our lives and creating an anarchist culture is part of that activity. Few anarchists, however, consider consciousness-raising as enough in itself and so combine cultural anarchist activities with organising, using direct action and building libertarian alternatives in capitalist society. The anarchist movement is one that combines practical self-activity with cultural work, with both activities feeding into and supporting the other.

A.3.7 Are there religious anarchists?

Yes, there are. While most anarchists have opposed religion and the idea of God as deeply anti-human and a justification for earthly authority and slavery, a few believers in religion have taken their ideas to anarchist conclusions. Like all anarchists, these religious anarchists have combined an opposition to the state with a critical position with regards to private property and inequality. In other words, anarchism is not necessarily atheistic. Indeed, according to Jacques Ellul, *"biblical thought leads directly to anarchism, and that this is the only 'political anti-political' position in accord with Christian thinkers."* [quoted by Peter Marshall, **Demanding the Impossible**, p. 75]

There are many different types of anarchism inspired by religious ideas. As Peter Marshall notes, the *"first clear expression of an anarchist sensibility may be traced back to the Taoists in ancient China from about the sixth century BC"* and *"Buddhism, particularly in its Zen form, … has … a strong libertarian spirit."* [**Op. Cit.**, p. 53 and p. 65] Some, like the anti-globalisation activist Starhawk, combine their anarchist ideas with Pagan and Spiritualist influences. However, religious anarchism usually takes the form of Christian Anarchism, which we will concentrate on here.

Christian Anarchists take seriously Jesus' words to his followers that *"kings and governors have domination over men; let there be none like that among you."* Similarly, Paul's dictum that there *"is no authority except God"* is taken to its obvious conclusion with the denial of state authority within society. Thus, for a true Christian, the state is usurping God's authority and it is up to each individual to govern themselves and discover that (to use the title of Tolstoy's famous book) **The Kingdom of God is within you**.

Similarly, the voluntary poverty of Jesus, his comments on the corrupting effects of wealth and the Biblical claim that the world was created for humanity to be enjoyed in common have all been taken as the basis of a socialistic critique of private property and capitalism. Indeed, the early Christian church (which could be considered as a liberation movement of slaves, although one that was later co-opted into a state religion) was based upon communistic sharing of material goods, a theme which has continually appeared within radical Christian movements inspired, no doubt, by such comments as *"all that believed were together, and had all things in common, and they sold their possessions and goods, and parted them all, according as every man has need"* and *"the multitude of them that believed were of one heart and of one soul, not one of them said that all of the things which he possessed was his own; but they had all things in common."* (Acts, 2:44,45; 4:32)

Unsurprisingly, the Bible would have been used to express radical libertarian aspirations of the oppressed, which, in later times, would have taken the form of anarchist or Marxist terminology. As Bookchin notes in his discussion of Christianity's contributions to *"the legacy of freedom,"* *"[b]y spawning nonconformity, heretical conventicles, and issues of authority over person and belief, Christianity created not merely a centralised authoritarian Papacy, but also its very antithesis: a quasi-religious anarchism."* Thus *"Christianity's mixed message can be grouped into two broad and highly conflicting systems of belief. On one side there was a radical, activistic, communistic, and libertarian vision of the Christian life"* and *"on the other side there was a conservative, quietistic, materially unwordly, and hierarchical vision."* [**The Ecology of Freedom**, p. 266 and pp. 274-5]

Thus clergyman's John Ball's egalitarian comments (as quoted by Peter Marshall [**Op. Cit.**, p. 89]) during the Peasant Revolt in 1381 in England:

> *"When Adam delved and Eve span,*
> *Who was then a gentleman?"*

The history of Christian anarchism includes the **Heresy of the Free Spirit** in the Middle Ages, numerous Peasant revolts and the **Anabaptists** in the 16th century. The libertarian tradition within Christianity surfaced again in the 18th century in the writings of William Blake and the American Adam Ballou reached anarchist conclusions in his **Practical Christian Socialism** in 1854. However, Christian anarchism became a clearly defined thread of the anarchist movement with the work of the famous Russian author Leo Tolstoy.

Tolstoy took the message of the Bible seriously and came to consider that a true Christian must oppose the state. From his reading of the Bible, Tolstoy drew anarchist conclusions:

> *"ruling means using force, and using force means doing to him whom force is used, what he does not like and what he who uses force would certainly not like done to himself. Consequently ruling means doing to others what we would not they should do unto us, that is, doing wrong."* [**The Kingdom of God is Within You**, p. 242]

Thus a true Christian must refrain from governing others. From this anti-statist position he naturally argued in favour of a society self-organised from below:

> *"Why think that non-official people could not arrange their life for themselves, as well as Government people can arrange it not for themselves but for others?"* [**The Slavery of Our Times**, p. 46]

This meant that *"people can only be freed from slavery by the abolition of Governments."* [**Op. Cit.**, p. 49] Tolstoy urged non-violent action against oppression, seeing a spiritual transformation of individuals as the key to creating an anarchist society. As Max Nettlau argues, the *"great truth stressed by Tolstoy is that the recognition of the power of the good, of goodness, of solidarity – and of all that is called love – lies within **ourselves**, and that it can and must be awakened, developed and exercised **in our own behaviour.**"* [**A Short History of Anarchism**, pp. 251-2] Unsurprisingly, Tolstoy thought the *"anarchists are right in everything … They are mistaken only in thinking that anarchy can be instituted by a revolution."* [quoted by Peter Marshall, **Op. Cit.**, p. 375]

Like all anarchists, Tolstoy was critical of private property and capitalism. He greatly admired and was heavily influenced by Proudhon, considering the latter's *"property is theft"* as *"an absolute truth"* which would *"survive as long as humanity."* [quoted by Jack Hayward, **After the French Revolution**, p. 213] Like Henry George (whose ideas, like those of Proudhon, had a strong impact on him) he opposed private property in land, arguing that *"were it not for the defence of landed property, and its consequent rise in price, people would not be crowded into such narrow spaces, but would scatter over the free land of which there is still so much in the world."* Moreover, *"in this struggle [for landed property] it is not those who work in the land, but always those who take part in government violence, who have the advantage."* Thus Tolstoy recognised that property rights in anything beyond use require state violence to protect them as possession is *"always protected by custom, public opinion, by feelings of justice and reciprocity, and they do not need to be protected by violence."* [**The Slavery of Our Times**, p. 47] Indeed, he argues that:

> *"Tens of thousands of acres of forest lands belonging to one proprietor – while thousands of people close by have no fuel – need protection by violence. So, too, do factories and works where several generations of workmen have been defrauded and are still being defrauded. Yet more do the hundreds of thousands of bushels of grain, belonging to one owner, who has held them back to sell at triple price in time of famine."* [**Op. Cit.**, pp. 47-8]

As with other anarchists, Tolstoy recognised that under capitalism, economic conditions *"compel [the worker] to go into temporary or perpetual slavery to a capitalist"* and so is *"obliged to sell his liberty."* This applied to both rural and urban workers, for the *"slaves of our times are not only all those factory and workshop hands, who must sell themselves completely into the power of the factory and foundry owners in order to exist; but nearly all the agricultural labourers are slaves, working as they do unceasingly to grow another's corn on another's field."* Such a system could only be maintained by violence, for *"first, the fruit of their toil is unjustly and violently taken form the workers, and then the law steps in, and these very articles which have been taken from the workmen – unjustly and by violence – are declared to be the absolute property of those who have stolen them."* [**Op. Cit.**, p. 34, p. 31 and p. 38] Tolstoy argued that capitalism morally and physically ruined individuals and that capitalists were *"slave-drivers."* He considered it impossible for a true Christian to be a capitalist, for a *"manufacturer is a man whose income consists of value squeezed out of the workers, and whose whole occupation is based on forced, unnatural labour"* and therefore, *"he must first give up ruining human lives for his own profit."* [**The Kingdom Of God is Within You**, p. 338 and p. 339] Unsurprisingly, Tolstoy argued that co-operatives were the *"only social activity which a moral, self-respecting person who doesn't want to be a party of violence can take part in."* [quoted by Peter Marshall, **Op. Cit.**, p. 378]

So, for Tolstoy, *"taxes, or land-owning or property in articles of use or in the means of production"* produces *"the slavery of our times."* However, he rejected the state socialist solution to the social problem as political power would create a new form of slavery on the ruins of the old. This was because *"the fundamental cause of slavery is legislation: the fact that there are people who have the power to make laws."* This requires *"organised violence used by people who have power, in order to compel others to obey the laws they (the powerful) have made – in other words, to do their will."* Handing over economic life to the state would simply mean *"there will be people to whom power will be given to regulate all these matters. Some people will decide these questions, and others will obey them."* [Tolstoy, **Op. Cit.**, p. 40, p. 41, p. 43 and p. 25] He correctly prophesised that *"the only thing that will happen"* with the victory of Marxism would be *"that despotism will be passed on. Now the capitalists are ruling, but then the directors of the working class will rule."* [quoted by Marshall, **Op. Cit.**, p. 379]

From his opposition to violence, Tolstoy rejects both state and private property and urged pacifist tactics to end violence within society and create a just society. In Nettlau's words, he *"asserted ... resistance to evil; and to one of the ways of resistance – by active force – he added another way: resistance through disobedience, the passive force."* [**Op. Cit.**, p. 251] In his ideas of a free society, Tolstoy was clearly influenced by rural Russian life and aimed for a society based on peasant farming of communal land, artisans and small-scale co-operatives. He rejected industrialisation as the product of state violence, arguing that *"such division of labour as now exists will ... be impossible in a free society."* [Tolstoy, **Op. Cit.**, p. 26]

Tolstoy's ideas had a strong influence on Gandhi, who inspired his fellow country people to use non-violent resistance to kick Britain out of India. Moreover, Gandhi's vision of a free India as a federation of peasant communes is similar to Tolstoy's anarchist vision of a free society (although we must stress that Gandhi was not an anarchist). The **Catholic Worker Group** in the United States was also heavily influenced by Tolstoy (and Proudhon), as was Dorothy Day a staunch Christian pacifist and anarchist who founded it in 1933. The influence of Tolstoy and religious anarchism in general can also be found in **Liberation Theology** movements in Latin and South America who combine Christian ideas with social activism amongst the working class and peasantry (although we should note that Liberation Theology is more generally inspired by state socialist ideas rather than anarchist ones).

So there is a minority tradition within anarchism which draws anarchist conclusions from religion. However, as we noted in section A.2.20, most anarchists disagree, arguing that anarchism implies atheism and it is no coincidence that biblical thought has, historically, been associated with hierarchy and defence of earthly rulers. Thus the vast majority of anarchists have been and are atheists, for *"to worship or revere any being, natural or supernatural, will always be a form of self-subjugation and servitude that will give rise to social domination. As [Bookchin] writes: 'The moment that human beings fall on their knees before anything that is 'higher' than themselves, hierarchy will have made its first triumph over freedom.'"* [Brian Morris, **Ecology and Anarchism**, p. 137] This means that most anarchists agree with Bakunin that if God existed it would be necessary, for human freedom and dignity, to abolish it. Given what the Bible says, few anarchists think it can be used to justify libertarian ideas rather than support authoritarian ones and are not surprised that the hierarchical side of Christianity has predominated in its long (and generally oppressive) history.

Atheist anarchists point to the fact that the Bible is notorious for advocating all kinds of abuses. How does the Christian anarchist reconcile this? Are they a Christian first, or an anarchist? Equality, or adherence to the Scripture? For a believer, it seems no choice at all. If the Bible is the word of God, how can an anarchist support the more extreme positions it takes while claiming to believe in God, his authority and his laws?

For example, no capitalist nation would implement the no working on the Sabbath law which the Bible expounds. Most Christian bosses have been happy to force their fellow believers to work on the seventh day in spite of the Biblical penalty of being stoned to death (*"Six days shall work be done, but on the seventh day there shall be to you an holy day, a Sabbath of rest to the Lord: whosoever doeth work therein shall be put to death."* Exodus 35:2). Would a Christian anarchist advocate such a punishment for breaking God's law? Equally, a nation which allowed a woman to be stoned to death for not being a virgin on her wedding night would, rightly, be considered utterly evil. Yet this is the fate specified in the "good book" (Deuteronomy 22:13-21). Would premarital sex by women be considered a capital crime by a Christian anarchist? Or, for that matter, should *"a stubborn and rebellious son, which will not obey the voice of his father, or the voice of his mother"* also suffer the fate of having *"all the men of his city ... stone him with stones, that he die"*? (Deuteronomy 21:18-21) Or what of the Bible's treatment of women: *"Wives, submit yourselves unto your own husbands."* (Colossians 3:18) They are also ordered to *"keep silence in the churches."* (I Corinthians 14:34-35). Male rule is explicitly stated: *"I would have you know that the head of every man is Christ; and the head of the woman is the man; and the head of Christ is God."* (I Corinthians 11:3)

Clearly, a Christian anarchist would have to be as highly selective as non-anarchist believers when it comes to applying the teachings of the Bible. The rich rarely proclaim the need for poverty (at least for themselves) and seem happy to forgot (like the churches) the difficulty a rich man apparently has entering heaven, for example. They seem happy to ignore Jesus' admonition that *"If thou wilt be perfect, go and sell that thou hast, and give to the poor, and thou shalt have treasure in heaven: and come and follow me."* (Matthew 19:21). The followers of the Christian right do not apply this to their political leaders, or, for that matter, their spiritual ones. Few apply the maxim to *"Give to every man that asketh of thee; and of him that taketh away thy goods ask them not again."* (Luke 6:30, repeated in Matthew 5:42) Nor do they hold *"all things common"* as practised by the first Christian believers. (Acts 4:32) So if non-anarchist believers are to be considered as ignoring the teachings of the Bible by anarchist ones, the same can be said of them by those they attack.

Moreover idea that Christianity is basically anarchism is hard to reconcile with its history. The Bible has been used to defend injustice far more than it has been to combat it. In countries where Churches hold **de facto** political power, such as in Ireland, in parts of South America, in nineteenth and early twentieth century Spain and so forth, typically anarchists are strongly anti-religious because the Church has the power to suppress dissent and class struggle. Thus the actual role of the Church belies the claim that the Bible is an anarchist text.

In addition, most social anarchists consider Tolstoyian pacifism as dogmatic and extreme, seeing the need (sometimes) for violence to resist greater evils. However, most anarchists would agree with Tolstoyians on the need for individual transformation of values as a key aspect of creating an anarchist society and on the importance of

non-violence as a general tactic (although, we must stress, that few anarchists totally reject the use of violence in self-defence, when no other option is available).

A.3.8 What is "anarchism without adjectives"?

In the words of historian George Richard Esenwein, *"anarchism without adjectives"* in its broadest sense *"referred to an unhyphenated form of anarchism, that is, a doctrine without any qualifying labels such as communist, collectivist, mutualist, or individualist. For others, ... [it] was simply understood as an attitude that tolerated the coexistence of different anarchist schools."* [**Anarchist Ideology and the Working Class Movement in Spain, 1868-1898**, p. 135]

The originator of the expression was Cuban born Fernando Tarrida del Marmol who used it in November, 1889, in Barcelona. He directed his comments towards the communist and collectivist anarchists in Spain who at the time were having an intense debate over the merits of their two theories. "Anarchism without adjectives" was an attempt to show greater tolerance between anarchist tendencies and to be clear that anarchists should not impose a preconceived economic plan on anyone – even in theory. Thus the economic preferences of anarchists should be of *"secondary importance"* to abolishing capitalism and the state, with free experimentation the one rule of a free society.

Thus the theoretical perspective known as *"anarquismo sin adjetives"* ("anarchism without adjectives") was one of the by-products of a intense debate within the movement itself. The roots of the argument can be found in the development of Communist Anarchism after Bakunin's death in 1876. While not entirely dissimilar to Collectivist Anarchism (as can be seen from James Guillaume's famous work *"On Building the New Social Order"* within **Bakunin on Anarchism**, the collectivists did see their economic system evolving into free communism), Communist Anarchists developed, deepened and enriched Bakunin's work just as Bakunin had developed, deepened and enriched Proudhon's. Communist Anarchism was associated with such anarchists as Elisée Reclus, Carlo Cafiero, Errico Malatesta and (most famously) Peter Kropotkin.

Quickly Communist-Anarchist ideas replaced Collectivist Anarchism as the main anarchist tendency in Europe, except in Spain. Here the major issue was not the question of communism (although for Ricardo Mella this played a part) but a question of the modification of strategy and tactics implied by Communist Anarchism. At this time (the 1880s), the Communist Anarchists stressed local (pure) cells of anarchist militants, generally opposed trade unionism (although Kropotkin was not one of these as he saw the importance of militant workers organisations) as well as being somewhat anti-organisation as well. Unsurprisingly, such a change in strategy and tactics came in for a lot of discussion from the Spanish Collectivists who strongly supported working class organisation and struggle.

This conflict soon spread outside of Spain and the discussion found its way into the pages of **La Revolte** in Paris. This provoked many anarchists to agree with Malatesta's argument that *"[i]t is not right* for us, to say the least, to fall into strife over mere hypotheses." [quoted by Max Nettlau, **A Short History of Anarchism**, pp. 198-9] Over time, most anarchists agreed (to use Nettlau's words) that *"we cannot foresee the economic development of the future"* [**Op. Cit.**, p. 201] and so started to stress what they had in common (opposition to capitalism and the state) rather than the different visions of how a free society would operate. As time progressed, most Communist-Anarchists saw that ignoring the labour movement ensured that their ideas did not reach the working class while most Collectivist-Anarchists stressed their commitment to communist ideals and their arrival sooner, rather than later, after a revolution. Thus both groups of anarchists could work together as there was *"no reason for splitting up into small schools, in our eagerness to overemphasise certain features, subject to variation in time and place, of the society of the future, which is too remote from us to permit us to envision all its adjustments and possible combinations."* Moreover, in a free society *"the methods and the individual forms of association and agreements, or the organisation of labour and of social life, will not be uniform and we cannot, at this moment, make and forecasts or determinations concerning them."* [Malatesta, quoted by Nettlau, **Op. Cit.**, p. 173]

Thus, Malatesta continued, *"[e]ven the question as between anarchist-collectivism and anarchist-communism is a matter of qualification, of method and agreement"* as the key is that, no matter the system, *"a new moral conscience will come into being, which will make the wage system repugnant to men [and women] just as legal slavery and compulsion are now repugnant to them."* If this happens then, *"whatever the specific forms of society may turn out to be, the basis of social organisation will be communist."* As long as we *"hold to fundamental principles and … do our utmost to instil them in the masses"* we need not *"quarrel over mere words or trifles but give post-revolutionary society a direction towards justice, equality and liberty."* [quoted by Nettlau, **Op. Cit.**, p. 173 and p. 174]

Similarly, in the United States there was also an intense debate at the same time between Individualist and Communist anarchists. There Benjamin Tucker was arguing that Communist-Anarchists were not anarchists while John Most was saying similar things about Tucker's ideas. Just as people like Mella and Tarrida put forward the idea of tolerance between anarchist groups, so anarchists like Voltairine de Cleyre *"came to label herself simply 'Anarchist,' and called like Malatesta for an 'Anarchism without Adjectives,' since in the absence of government many different experiments would probably be tried in various localities in order to determine the most appropriate form."* [Peter Marshall, **Demanding the Impossible**, p. 393] In her own words, a whole range of economic systems would be *"advantageously tried in different localities. I would see the instincts and habits of the people express themselves in a free choice in every community; and I am sure that distinct environments would call out distinct adaptations."* [*"Anarchism"*, **Exquisite Rebel**, p. 79] Consequently, individualist and communist anarchist *"forms of society, as well as many intermediations, would, in the absence of government, be tried in various localities, according to the instincts and material condition of the people … Liberty and experiment alone can determine the best forms of society. Therefore I no longer label myself otherwise than 'Anarchist' simply."* [*"The Making of An*

Anarchist", **The Voltairine de Cleyre Reader**, pp. 107-8]

These debates had a lasting impact on the anarchist movement, with such noted anarchists as de Cleyre, Malatesta, Nettlau and Reclus adopting the tolerant perspective embodied in the expression "anarchism without adjectives" (see Nettlau's **A Short History of Anarchism**, pages 195 to 201 for an excellent summary of this). It is also, we add, the dominant position within the anarchist movement today with most anarchists recognising the right of other tendencies to the name "anarchist" while, obviously, having their own preferences for specific types of anarchist theory and their own arguments why other types are flawed. However, we must stress that the different forms of anarchism (communism, syndicalism, religious etc) are not mutually exclusive and you do not have to support one and hate the others. This tolerance is reflected in the expression "anarchism without adjectives."

One last point, some "anarcho"-capitalists have attempted to use the tolerance associated with "anarchism without adjectives" to argue that their ideology should be accepted as part of the anarchist movement. After all, they argue, anarchism is just about getting rid of the state, economics is of secondary importance. However, such a use of *"anarchism without adjectives"* is bogus as it was commonly agreed at the time that the types of economics that were being discussed were **anti-capitalist** (i.e. socialist). For Malatesta, for example, there were *"anarchists who foresee and propose other solution, other future forms of social organisation"* than communist anarchism, but they *"desire, just as we do, to destroy political power and private property."* *"Let us do away,"* he argued, *"with all exclusivism of schools of thinking"* and let us *"come to an understanding on ways and means, and go forwards."* [quoted by Nettlau, **Op. Cit.**, p. 175] In other words, it was agreed that capitalism had to be abolished along with the state and once this was the case free experimentation would develop. Thus the struggle against the state was just one part of a wider struggle to end oppression and exploitation and could not be isolated from these wider aims. As "anarcho"-capitalists do not seek the abolition of capitalism along with the state they are not anarchists and so "anarchism without adjectives" does not apply to the so-called "anarchist" capitalists (see section F on why "anarcho"-capitalism is not anarchist).

This is not to say that after a revolution "anarcho"-capitalist communities would not exist. Far from it. If a group of people wanted to form such a system then they could, just as we would expect a community which supported state socialism or theocracy to live under that regime. Such enclaves of hierarchy would exist simply because it is unlikely that everyone on the planet, or even in a given geographical area, will become anarchists all at the same time. The key thing to remember is that no such system would be anarchist and, consequently, is not *"anarchism without adjectives."*

A.3.9 What is anarcho-primitivism?

As discussed in section A.3.3, most anarchists would agree with Situationist Ken Knabb in arguing that *"in a liberated world computers and other modern technologies could be used to eliminate dangerous or boring tasks, freeing everyone to concentrate on more interesting activities."* Obviously *"[c]ertain technologies – nuclear power is the most obvious example – are indeed so insanely dangerous that they will no doubt be brought to a prompt halt. Many other industries which produce absurd, obsolete or superfluous commodities will, of course, cease automatically with the disappearance of their commercial rationales. But many technologies…, however they may presently be misused, have few if any* **inherent** *drawbacks. It's simply a matter of using them more sensibly, bringing them under popular control, introducing a few ecological improvements, and redesigning them for human rather than capitalistic ends."* [**Public Secrets**, p. 79 and p. 80] Thus most eco-anarchists see the use of appropriate technology as the means of creating a society which lives in balance with nature.

However, a small but vocal minority of self-proclaimed Green anarchists disagree. Writers such as John Zerzan, John Moore and David Watson have expounded a vision of anarchism which, they claim, aims to critique every form of power and oppression. This is often called *"anarcho-primitivism,"* which according to Moore, is simply *"a shorthand term for a radical current that critiques the totality of civilisation from an anarchist perspective, and seeks to initiate a comprehensive transformation of human life."* [**Primitivist Primer**]

How this current expresses itself is diverse, with the most extreme elements seeking the end of all forms of technology, division of labour, domestication, "Progress", industrialism, what they call *"mass society"* and, for some, even symbolic culture (i.e. numbers, language, time and art). They tend to call any system which includes these features *"civilisation"* and, consequently, aim for *"the destruction of civilisation"*. How far back they wish to go is a moot point. Some see the technological level that existed before the Industrial Revolution as acceptable, many go further and reject agriculture and all forms of technology beyond the most basic. For them, a return to the wild, to a hunter-gatherer mode of life, is the only way for anarchy is exist and dismiss out of hand the idea that appropriate technology can be used to create an anarchist society based on industrial production which minimises its impact on ecosystems.

Thus we find the primitivist magazine **"Green Anarchy"** arguing that those, like themselves, *"who prioritise the values of personal autonomy or wild existence have reason to oppose and reject all large-scale organisations and societies on the grounds that they necessitate imperialism, slavery and hierarchy, regardless of the purposes they may be designed for."* They oppose capitalism as it is *"civilisation's current dominant manifestation."* However, they stress that it is *"Civilisation, not capitalism per se, was the genesis of systemic authoritarianism, compulsory servitude and social isolation. Hence, an attack upon capitalism that fails to target civilisation can* never abolish the institutionalised coercion that fuels society. To attempt to collectivise industry for the purpose of democratising it is to fail to recognise that all large-scale organisations adopt a direction and form that is independent of its members' intentions."* Thus, they argue, genuine anarchists must oppose industry and technology for *"[h]ierarchical institutions, territorial expansion, and the mechanisation of life are all required for the administration and process of mass production to occur."* For primitivists, *"[o]nly small communities of self-sufficient individuals can coexist with other beings, human or not, without imposing their authority upon them."* Such communities would share essential features with tribal societies, *"[f]or over 99% of human history, humans lived within small and egalitarian extended family arrangements, while drawing their subsistence directly from the land."* [**Against Mass Society**] While such tribal communities, which lived in harmony with nature and had little or no hierarchies, are seen as inspirational, primitivists look (to use the title of a John Zerzan book) forward to seeing the *"Future Primitive."* As John Moore puts it, *"the future envisioned by anarcho-primitivism … is without precedent. Although primitive cultures provide intimations of the future, and that future may well incorporate elements derived from those cultures, an anarcho-primitivist world would likely be quite different from previous forms of anarchy."* [**Op. Cit.**]

For the primitivist, other forms of anarchism are simply self-managed alienation within essentially the same basic system we now endure. Hence Moore's comment that *"classical anarchism"* wants *"to take over civilisation, rework its structures to some degree, and remove its worst abuses and oppressions. However, 99% of life in civilisation remains unchanged in their future scenarios, precisely because the aspects of civilisation they question are minimal … overall life patterns wouldn't change too much."* Thus *"[f]rom the perspective of anarcho-primitivism, all other forms of radicalism appear as reformist, whether or not they regard themselves as revolutionary."* [**Op. Cit.**]

In reply, "classical anarchists" point out three things. Firstly, to claim that the *"worst abuses and oppressions"* account for 1% of capitalist society is simply nonsense and, moreover, something an apologist of that system would happily agree with. Secondly, it is obvious from reading any "classical" anarchist text that Moore's assertions are nonsense. "Classical" anarchism aims to transform society radically from top to bottom, not tinker with minor aspects of it. Do primitivists really think that people who went to the effort to abolish capitalism would simply continue doing 99% of the same things they did before hand? Of course not. In other words, it is not enough to get rid of the boss, although this is a necessary first step! Thirdly, and most importantly, Moore's argument ensures that his new society would be impossible to reach.

So, as can be seen, primitivism has little or no bearing to the traditional anarchist movement and its ideas. The visions of both are simply incompatible, with the ideas of the latter dismissed as authoritarian by the former and anarchists questioning whether primitivism is practical in the short term or even desirable in the long. While supporters of primitivism like to portray it as the most advanced and radical form of anarchism, others are less convinced. They consider it as a confused ideology which draws its followers into absurd positions and, moreover, is utterly impractical. They would agree with Ken Knabb that primitivism is rooted in *"fantasies [which] contain so many obvious self-contradictions that it is hardly necessary to criticise them in any detail. They have questionable relevance to actual past societies and virtually no relevance to present possibilities. Even supposing that life was better in one or another previous era,* **we have to begin from where we are now.** *Modern technology is so interwoven with all aspects of our life that it could not be abruptly discontinued without causing a global chaos that would wipe out billions of people."* [**Op. Cit.**, p. 79]

The reason for this is simply that we live in a highly industrialised and interconnected system in which most people do not have the skills required to live in a hunter-gatherer or even agricultural society. Moreover, it is extremely doubtful that six billion people **could** survive as hunter-gatherers even if they had the necessary skills. As Brian Morris notes, *"[t]he future we are told is 'primitive.' How this is to be achieved in a world that presently sustains almost six billion people (for evidence suggests that the hunter-gatherer lifestyle is only able to support 1 or 2 people per sq. mile)"* primitivists like Zerzan do not tell us. [*"Anthropology and Anarchism,"* pp. 35-41, **Anarchy: A Journal of Desire Armed**, no. 45, p. 38] Most anarchists, therefore, agree with Chomsky's summation that *"I do not think that they are realising that what they are calling for is the mass genocide of millions of people because of the way society is now structured and organised … If you eliminate these structures everybody dies … And, unless one thinks through these things, it's not really serious."* [**Chomsky on Anarchism**, p. 226]

Somewhat ironically, many proponents of primitivsm agree with its critics that the earth would be unable to support six billion living as a hunter-gatherers. This, critics argue, gives primitivism a key problem in that population levels will take time to fall and so any "primitivist" rebellion faces two options. Either it comes about via some kind of collapse of "civilisation" or it involves a lengthy transition period during which "civilisation" and its industrial legacies are decommissioned safely, population levels drop naturally to an appropriate level and people gain the necessary skills required for their new existence.

The problems with the first option should be obvious but, sadly, it is implied by many primitivist writers. Moore, for example, talks about *"when civilisation collapses"* (*"through its own volition, through our efforts, or a combination of the two"*). This implies an extremely speedy process which is confirmed when he talks about the need for *"positive alternatives"* to be built now as *"the social disruption caused by collapse could easily create the psychological insecurity and social vacuum in which fascism and other totalitarian dictatorships could flourish."* [**Op. Cit.**] Social change based on "collapse," "insecurity" and "social disruption" does not sound like a recipe for a successful revolution.

Then there are the anti-organisation dogmas expounded by primitivism. Moore is typical, asserting that *"[o]rganisations, for anarcho-primitivists, are just rackets, gangs for putting a particular ideology in power"* and reiterates the point by saying primitivists stand for *"the abolition of all power relations, including the State … and any kind of party or organisation."* [**Op. Cit.**] Yet without organisation, no modern society could function. There would be a total and instant collapse which would see not only mass starvation but also ecological destruction as nuclear power stations meltdown,

industrial waste seeps into the surrounding environment, cities and towns decay and hordes of starving people fighting over what vegetables, fruits and animals they could find in the countryside. Clearly an anti-organisation dogma can only be reconciled with the idea of a near overnight "collapse" of civilisation, not with a steady progress towards a long term goal. Equally, how many "positive alternatives" could exist without organisation?

Moore dismissed any critique that points out that a collapse would cause mass destruction as *"just smear tactics," "weird fantasies spread by some commentators hostile to anarcho-primitivism who suggest that the population levels envisaged by anarcho-primitivists would have to be achieved by mass die-offs or nazi-style death camps."* The *"commitment of anarcho-primitivists to the abolition of all power relations … means that such orchestrated slaughter remains an impossibility as well as just plain horrendous."* [**Op. Cit.**] Yet no critic is suggesting that primitivists desire such a die-off or seek to organise it. They simply point out that the collapse of civilisation would result in a mass die-off due to the fact that most people do not have the skills necessary to survive it nor could the Earth provide enough food for six billion people trying to live in a primitivist manner. Other primitivists have asserted that it can, stating *"[i]t is not possible for all six billion of the planet's current inhabitants to survive as hunter-gatherers, but it is possible for those who can't to grow their own food in significantly smaller spaces … as has been demonstrated by permaculture, organic gardening, and indigenous horticulture techniques."* [**Against Mass Society**] Unfortunately no evidence was provided to show the truth of this assertion nor that people could develop the necessary skills in time even if it were. It seems a slim hope to place the fate of billions on, so that humanity can be "wild" and free from such tyrannies as hospitals, books and electricity.

Faced with the horrors that such a *"collapse"* would entail, those primitivists who have thought the issue through end up accepting the need for a transition period. John Zerzan, for example, argues that it *"seems evident that industrialisation and the factories could not be gotten rid of instantly, but equally clear that their liquidation must be pursued with all the vigour behind the rush of break-out."* Even the existence of cities is accepted, for *"[c]ultivation within the cities is another aspect of practical transition."* [**On the Transition: Postscript to Future Primitive**]

However, to accept the necessity of a transition period does little more than expose the contradictions within primitivism. Zerzan notes that *"the means of reproducing the prevailing Death Ship (e.g. its technology) cannot be used to fashion a liberated world."* He ponders: *"What would we keep? 'Labour-saving devices?' Unless they involve no division of labour (e.g. a lever or incline), this concept is a fiction; behind the 'saving' is hidden the congealed drudgery of many and the despoliation of the natural world."* How this is compatible with maintaining *"industrialisation and the factories"* for a (non-specified) period is unclear. Similarly, he argues that *"[i]nstead of the coercion of work – and how much of the present could continue without precisely that coercion? – an existence without constraints is an immediate, central objective."* [**Op. Cit.**] How that is compatible with the arguing that industry would be maintained for a time is left unasked, never mind unanswered. And if "work" continues, how is this compatible with the typical primitivist dismissal of "traditional" anarchism, namely that self-management is managing your own alienation and that no one will want to work in a factory or in a mine and, therefore, coercion will have to be used to make them do so? Does working in a self-managed workplace somehow become less alienating and authoritarian during a primitivist transition?

It is an obvious fact that the human population size cannot be reduced significantly by voluntary means in a short period of time. For primitivism to be viable, world population levels need to drop by something like 90%. This implies a drastic reduction of population will take decades, if not centuries, to achieve voluntarily. Given that it is unlikely that (almost) everyone on the planet will decide not to have children, this time scale will almost certainly be centuries and so agriculture and most industries will have to continue (and an exodus from the cities would be impossible immediately). Likewise, reliable contraceptives are a product of modern technology and, consequently, the means of producing them would have to maintained over that time – unless primitivists argue that along with refusing to have children, people will also refuse to have sex.

Then there is the legacy of industrial society, which simply cannot be left to decay on its own. To take just one obvious example, leaving nuclear power plants to melt down would hardly be eco-friendly. Moreover, it is doubtful that the ruling elite will just surrender its power without resistance and, consequently, any social revolution would need to defend itself against attempts to reintroduce hierarchy. Needless to say, a revolution which shunned all organisation and industry as inherently authoritarian would not be able to do this (it would have been impossible to produce the necessary military supplies to fight Franco's fascist forces during the Spanish Revolution if the workers had not converted and used their workplaces to do so, to note another obvious example).

Then there is another, key, contradiction. For if you accept that there is a need for a transition from 'here' to 'there' then primitivism automatically excludes itself from the anarchist tradition. The reason is simple. Moore asserts that *"mass society"* involves *"people working, living in artificial, technologised environments, and [being] subject to forms of coercion and control."* [**Op. Cit.**] So if what primitivists argue about technology, industry and mass society are all true, then any primitivist transition would, by definition, not be libertarian. This is because *"mass society"* will have to remain for some time (at the very least decades, more likely centuries) after a successful revolution and, consequently from a primitivist perspective, be based on *"forms of coercion and control."* There is an ideology which proclaims the need for a transitional system which will be based on coercion, control and hierarchy which will, in time, disappear into a stateless society. It also, like primitivism, stresses that industry and large scale organisation is impossible without hierarchy and authority. That ideology is Marxism. Thus it seems ironic to "classical" anarchists to hear self-proclaimed anarchists repeating Engels arguments against Bakunin as arguments for "anarchy" (see section H.4 for a discussion of Engels claims that industry excludes autonomy).

So if, as seems likely, any transition will take centuries to achieve then the primitivist critique of "traditional" anarchism becomes little more than a joke – and a hindrance to meaningful anarchist practice and social change. It shows the contradiction at the heart

of primitivism. While its advocates attack other anarchists for supporting technology, organisation, self-management of work, industrialisation and so on, they are themselves are dependent on the things they oppose as part of any humane transition to a primitivist society. And given the passion with which they attack other anarchists on these matters, unsurprisingly the whole notion of a primitivist transition period seems impossible to other anarchists. To denounce technology and industrialism as inherently authoritarian and then turn round and advocate their use after a revolution simply does not make sense from a logical or libertarian perspective.

Thus the key problem with primitivism can be seen. It offers no practical means of achieving its goals in a libertarian manner. As Knabb summarises, *"[w]hat begins as a valid questioning of excessive faith in science and technology ends up as a desperate and even less justified faith in the return of a primeval paradise, accompanied by a failure to engage the present system in any but an abstract, apocalyptical way."* To avoid this, it is necessary to take into account where we are now and, consequently, we will have to *"seriously consider how we will deal with all the practical problems that will be posed in the interim."* [**Op. Cit.**, p. 80 and p. 79] Sadly, primitivist ideology excludes this possibility by dismissing the starting point any real revolution would begin from as being inherently authoritarian. Moreover, they are blocking genuine social change by ensuring that no mass movement would ever be revolutionary enough to satisfy their criteria:

> *"Those who proudly proclaim their 'total opposition' to all compromise, all authority, all organisation, all theory, all technology, etc., usually turn out to have no **revolutionary** perspective whatsoever – no practical conception of how the present system might be overthrown or how a post-revolutionary society might work. Some even attempt to justify this lack by declaring that a mere revolution could never be radical enough to satisfy their eternal ontological rebelliousness. Such all-or-nothing bombast may temporarily impress a few spectators, but its ultimate effect is simply to make people blasé."* [Knabb, **Op. Cit.**, pp. 31-32]

Then there is the question of the means suggested for achieving primitivism. Moore argues that the *"kind of world envisaged by anarcho-primitivism is one unprecedented in human experience in terms of the degree and types of freedom anticipated ... so there can't be any limits on the forms of resistance and insurgency that might develop."* [**Op. Cit.**] Non-primitivists reply by saying that this implies primitivists don't know what they want nor how to get there. Equally, they stress that there **must be** limits on what are considered acceptable forms of resistance. This is because means shape the ends created and so authoritarian means will result in authoritarian ends. Tactics are not neutral and support for certain tactics betray an authoritarian perspective.

This can be seen from the UK magazine **"Green Anarchist,"** part of the extreme end of "Primitivism." Due to its inherent unattractiveness for most people, it could never come about by libertarian means (i.e. by the free choice of individuals who create it by their own acts) and so cannot be anarchist as very few people would actually voluntarily embrace such a situation. This led to **"Green Anarchist"** developing a form of eco-vanguardism in order, to use Rousseau's expression, to "force people to be free." This was expressed when the magazine supported the actions and ideas of the (non-anarchist) Unabomber and published an article ("The Irrationalists") by one its editors stating that *"the Oklahoma bombers had the right idea. The pity was that they did not blast any more government offices ... The Tokyo sarin cult had the right idea. The pity was that in testing the gas a year prior to the attack they gave themselves away."* [**Green Anarchist**, no. 51, p. 11] A defence of these remarks was published in the next issue and a subsequent exchange of letters in the US-based **Anarchy: A Journal of Desire Armed** magazine (numbers 48 to 52) saw the other editor justify this sick, authoritarian nonsense as simply examples of *"unmediated resistance"* conducted *"under conditions of extreme repression."* Whatever happened to the anarchist principle that means shape the ends? This means there **are** *"limits"* on tactics, as some tactics are not and can never be libertarian.

However, few primitivists take such an extreme position. Most "primitivist" anarchists rather than being anti-technology and anti-civilisation as such instead (to use David Watson's expression) believe it is a case of the *"affirmation of aboriginal lifeways"* and of taking a far more critical approach to issues such as technology, rationality and progress than that associated with Social Ecology. These eco-anarchists reject *"a dogmatic primitivism which claims we can return in some linear way to our primordial roots"* just as much as the idea of "progress," **"superseding** both Enlightenment and Counter-Enlightenment" ideas and traditions. For them, Primitivism *"reflects not only a glimpse at life before the rise of the state, but also a legitimate response to real conditions of life under civilisation"* and so we should respect and learn from *"palaeolithic and neolithic wisdom traditions"* (such as those associated with Native American tribes and other aboriginal peoples). While we *"cannot, and would not want to abandon secular modes of thinking and experiencing the world ... we cannot reduce the experience of life, and the fundamental, inescapable questions **why** we live, and **how** we live, to secular terms ... Moreover, the boundary between the spiritual and the secular is not so clear. A dialectical understanding that we are our history would affirm an inspirited reason that honours not only atheistic Spanish revolutionaries who died for **el ideal,** but also religious pacifist prisoners of conscience, Lakota ghost dancers, taoist hermits and executed sufi mystics."* [David Watson, **Beyond Bookchin: Preface for a future social ecology**, p. 240, p. 103, p. 240 and pp. 66-67]

Such "primitivist" anarchism is associated with a range of magazines, mostly US-based, like **Fifth Estate**. For example, on the question of technology, they argue that *"[w]hile market capitalism was a spark that set the fire, and remains at the centre of the complex, it is only part of something larger: the forced adaptation of organic human societies to an economic-instrumental civilisation and its mass technics, which are not only hierarchical and external but increasingly 'cellular' and internal. It makes no sense to layer the various elements of this process in a mechanistic hierarchy of first cause and secondary effects."* [Watson, **Op. Cit.**, pp. 127-8] For this reason primitivists are more critical of all aspects of technology, including calls by social ecologists for the use of **appropriate** technology essential in order to liberate humanity and the planet:

> *"To speak of technological society is in fact to refer to **the technics generated within capitalism,** which in turn generate new forms of capital. The notion of a distinct realm of social relations that determine this technology is not only ahistorical and undialectical, it reflects a kind of simplistic base/superstructure schema."* [Watson, **Op. Cit.**, p. 124]

Thus it is not a case of who **uses** technology which determines its effects, rather the effects of technology are determined to a large degree by the society that creates it. In other words, technology is selected which tends to re-enforce hierarchical power as it is those in power who generally select which technology is introduced within society (saying that, oppressed people have this excellent habit of turning technology against the powerful and technological change and social struggle are inter-related – see section D.10). Thus even the use of appropriate technology involves more than selecting from the range of available technology at hand, as these technologies have certain effects regardless of who uses them. Rather it is a question of critically evaluating all aspects of technology and modifying and rejecting it as required to maximise individual freedom, empowerment and happiness. Few Social Ecologists would disagree with this approach, though, and differences are usually a question of emphasis rather than a deep political point.

However, few anarchists are convinced by an ideology which, as Brian Morris notes, dismisses the *"last eight thousand years or so of human history"* as little more than a source *"of tyranny, hierarchical control, mechanised routine devoid of any spontaneity. All those products of the human creative imagination – farming, art, philosophy, technology, science, urban living, symbolic culture – are viewed negatively by Zerzan – in a monolithic sense."* While there is no reason to worship progress, there is just as little need to dismiss all change and development out of hand as oppressive. Nor are they convinced by Zerzan's *"selective culling of the anthropological literature."* [**Op. Cit.**, p. 38] Most anarchists would concurr with Murray Bookchin:

> *"The ecology movement will never gain any real influence or have any significant impact on society if it advances a message of despair rather than hope, of a regressive and impossible return to primordial human cultures, rather than a commitment to human progress and to a unique **human** empathy for life as a whole ... We must recover the utopian impulses, the hopefulness, the appreciation of what is good, what is worth rescuing in human civilisation, as well as what must be rejected, if the ecology movement is to play a transformative and creative role in human affairs. For without changing society, we will not change the diastrous ecological direction in which capitalism is moving."* [**The Ecology of Freedom**, p. 63]

In addition, a position of "turning back the clock" is deeply flawed, for while some aboriginal societies are very anarchistic, not all are. As anarchist anthropologist David Graeber points out, *"we know almost nothing about life in the Palaeolithic, other than the sort of thing that can be gleaned from studying very old skulls ... But what we see in the more recent ethnographic records is endless variety. There were hunter-gatherer societies with nobles and slaves, there are agrarian societies that are fiercely egalitarian. Even in ... Amazonia, one finds some groups who can justly be described as anarchists, like the Piaroa, living alongside others say, the warlike Sherentre, who are clearly anything but.*" [**Fragments of an Anarchist Anthropology**, pp. 53-4] Even if we speculate, like Zerzan, that if we go back far enough we would find all of humanity in anarchistic tribes, the fact remains that certain of these societies did develop into statist, propertarian ones implying that a future anarchist society that is predominantly inspired by and seek to reproduce key elements of prehistoric forms of anarchy is not the answer as "civilisation" may develop again due to the same social or environmental factors.

Primitivism confuses two radically different positions, namely support for a literal return to primitive lifeways and the use of examples from primitive life as a tool for social critique. Few anarchists would disagree with the second position as they recognise that current does not equal better and, consequently, past cultures and societies can have positive (as well as negative) aspects to them which can shed light on what a genuinely human society can be like. Similarly if "primitivism" simply involved questioning technology along with authority, few would disagree. However, this sensible position is, in the main, subsumed within the first one, the idea that an anarchist society would be a literal return to hunter-gatherer society. That this is the case can be seen from primitivist writings (some primitivists say that they are not suggesting the Stone Age as a model for their desired society nor a return to gathering and hunting, yet they seem to exclude any other options by their critique).

So to suggest that primitivism is simply a critique or some sort of *"anarchist speculation"* (to use John Moore's term) seems incredulous. If you demonise technology, organisation, "mass society" and "civilisation" as inherently authoritarian, you cannot turn round and advocate their use in a transition period or even in a free society. As such, the critique points to a mode of action and a vision of a free society and to suggest otherwise is simply incredulous. Equally, if you praise foraging bands and shifting horticultural communities of past and present as examples of anarchy then critics are entitled to conclude that primitivists desire a similar system for the future. This is reinforced by the critiques of industry, technology, "mass society" and agriculture.

Until such time as "primitivists" clearly state which of the two forms of primitivism they subscribe to, other anarchists will not take their ideas that seriously. Given that they fail to answer such basic questions of how they plan to deactivate industry safely and avoid mass starvation without the workers' control, international links and federal organisation they habitually dismiss out of hand as new forms of "governance," other anarchists do not hold much hope that it will happen soon. Ultimately, we are faced with the fact that a revolution will start in society as it is. Anarchism recognises this and suggests a means of transforming it. Primitivism shies away from such minor problems and, consequently, has little to recommend it in most anarchists' eyes.

This is not to suggest, of course, that non-primitivist anarchists think that everyone in a free society must have the same level of technology. Far from it. An anarchist society would be based on free experimentation. Different individuals and groups will pick the way of life that best suits them. Those who seek less technological ways of living will be free to do so as will those who want to apply the benefits of (appropriate) technologies. Similarly, all anarchists support the struggles of those in the developing world against the onslaught of (capitalist) civilisation and the demands of (capitalist) progress.

For more on "primitivist" anarchism see John Zerzan's **Future Primitive** as well as David Watson's **Beyond Bookchin** and **Against the Mega-Machine**. Ken Knabb's essay **The Poverty of Primitivism** is an excellent critique of primitivism as is Brian Oliver Sheppard's **Anarchism vs. Primitivism**.

A.4
Who are the major anarchist thinkers?

Although Gerard Winstanley (**The New Law of Righteousness**, 1649) and William Godwin (**Enquiry Concerning Political Justice**, 1793) had begun to unfold the philosophy of anarchism in the 17th and 18th centuries, it was not until the second half of the 19th century that anarchism emerged as a coherent theory with a systematic, developed programme. This work was mainly started by four people – a German, *Max Stirner* (1806-1856), a Frenchman, *Pierre-Joseph Proudhon* (1809-1865), and two Russians, *Michael Bakunin* (1814-1876) and *Peter Kropotkin* (1842-1921). They took the ideas in common circulation within sections of the working population and expressed them in written form.

Born in the atmosphere of German romantic philosophy, Stirner's anarchism (set forth in **The Ego and Its Own**) was an extreme form of individualism, or **egoism**, which placed the unique individual above all else – state, property, law or duty. His ideas remain a cornerstone of anarchism. Stirner attacked both capitalism and state socialism, laying the foundations of both social and individualist anarchism by his egoist critique of capitalism and the state that supports it. In place of the state and capitalism, Max Stirner urges the *"union of egoists,"* free associations of unique individuals who co-operate as equals in order to maximise their freedom and satisfy their desires (including emotional ones for solidarity, or "intercourse" as Stirner called it). Such a union would be non-hierarchical, for, as Stirner wonders, *"is an association, wherein most members allow themselves to be lulled as regards their most natural and most obvious interests, actually an Egoist's association? Can they really be 'Egoists' who have banded together when one is a slave or a serf of the other?"* [**No Gods, No Masters**, vol. 1, p. 24]

Individualism by definition includes no concrete programme for changing social conditions. This was attempted by Pierre-Joseph Proudhon, the first to describe himself openly as an anarchist. His theories of **mutualism**, **federalism** and workers' **self-management** and **association** had a profound effect on the growth of anarchism as a mass movement and spelled out clearly how an anarchist world could function and be co-ordinated. It would be no exaggeration to state that Proudhon's work defined the fundamental nature of anarchism as both an anti-state and anti-capitalist movement and set of ideas. Bakunin, Kropotkin and Tucker all claimed inspiration from his ideas and they are the immediate source for both social and individualist anarchism, with each thread emphasising different aspects of mutualism (for example, social anarchists stress the associational aspect of them while individualist anarchists the non-capitalist market side). Proudhon's major works include **What is Property**, **System of Economical Contradictions**, **The Principle of Federation** and, and **The Political Capacity of the Working Classes**. His most detailed discussion of what mutualism would look like can be found in his **The General Idea of the Revolution**. His ideas heavily influenced both the French Labour movement and the Paris Commune of 1871.

Proudhon's ideas were built upon by Michael Bakunin, who humbly suggested that his own ideas were simply Proudhon's *"widely developed and pushed right to ... [their] final consequences."* [**Michael Bakunin: Selected Writings**, p. 198] However, he is doing a disservice to his own role in developing anarchism. For Bakunin is the central figure in the development of modern anarchist activism and ideas. He emphasised the importance of **collectivism,** mass insurrection, **revolution** and involvement in the militant **labour movement** as the means of creating a free, classless society. Moreover, he repudiated Proudhon's sexism and added patriarchy to the list of social evils anarchism opposes. Bakunin also emphasised the social nature of humanity and individuality, rejecting the abstract individualism of liberalism as a denial of freedom. His ideas become dominant in the 20th century among large sections of the radical labour movement. Indeed, many of his ideas are almost identical to what would later be called syndicalism or anarcho-syndicalism. Bakunin influenced many union movements – especially in Spain, where a major anarchist social revolution took place in 1936. His works include **Anarchy and Statism** (his only book), **God and the State**, **The Paris Commune and the Idea of the State**, and many others. **Bakunin on Anarchism**, edited by Sam Dolgoff is an excellent collection of his major writings. Brian Morris' **Bakunin: The Philosophy of Freedom** is an excellent introduction to Bakunin's life and ideas.

Peter Kropotkin, a scientist by training, fashioned a sophisticated and detailed anarchist analysis of modern conditions linked to a thorough-going prescription for a future society – **communist-anarchism** – which continues to be the most widely-held theory among anarchists. He identified **mutual aid** as the best means by which individuals can develop and grow, pointing out that competition **within** humanity (and other species) was often not in the best interests of those involved. Like Bakunin, he stressed the importance of direct, economic, class struggle and anarchist participation in any popular movement, particularly in labour unions. Taking Proudhon's and Bakunin's idea of the **commune,** he generalised their insights into a vision of how the social, economic and personal life of a free society would function. He aimed to base anarchism *"on a scientific basis by the study of the tendencies that are apparent now in society and may indicate its further evolution"* towards anarchy while, at the same time, urging anarchists to *"promote their ideas directly amongst the labour organisations and to induce those unions to a direct struggle against capital, without*

placing their faith in parliamentary legislation." [**Anarchism**, p. 298 and p. 287] Like Bakunin, he was a revolutionary and, like Bakunin, his ideas inspired those struggle for freedom across the globe. His major works included **Mutual Aid**, **The Conquest of Bread**, **Field, Factories, and Workshops**, **Modern Science and Anarchism**, **Act for Yourselves**, **The State: Its Historic Role**, **Words of a Rebel**, and many others. A collection of his revolutionary pamphlets is available under the title **Anarchism** and is essential reading for anyone interested in his ideas. In Addition, Graham Purchase's **Evolution and Revolution** and **Kropotkin: The Politics of Community** by Brain Morris are both excellent evaluations of his ideas and how they are still relevant today.

The various theories proposed by these "founding anarchists" are not, however, mutually exclusive: they are interconnected in many ways, and to some extent refer to different levels of social life. Individualism relates closely to the conduct of our private lives: only by recognising the uniqueness and freedom of others and forming unions with them can we protect and maximise our own uniqueness and liberty; mutualism relates to our general relations with others: by mutually working together and co-operating we ensure that we do not work for others. Production under anarchism would be collectivist, with people working together for their own, and the common, good, and in the wider political and social world decisions would be reached communally.

It should also be stressed that anarchist schools of thought are **not** named after individual anarchists. Thus anarchists are **not** *"Bakuninists"*, *"Proudhonists"* or *"Kropotkinists"* (to name three possibilities). Anarchists, to quote Malatesta, *"follow ideas and not men, and rebel against this habit of embodying a principle in a man."* This did not stop him calling Bakunin *"our great master and inspiration."* [**Errico Malatesta: Life and Ideas**, p. 199 and p. 209] Equally, not everything written by a famous anarchist thinker is automatically libertarian. Bakunin, for example, only became an anarchist in the last ten years of his life (this does not stop Marxists using his pre-anarchist days to attack anarchism!). Proudhon turned away from anarchism in the 1850s before returning to a more anarchistic (if not strictly anarchist) position just before his death in 1865. Similarly, Kropotkin's or Tucker's arguments in favour of supporting the Allies during the First World War had nothing to do with anarchism. Thus to say, for example, that anarchism is flawed because Proudhon was a sexist pig simply does not convince anarchists. No one would dismiss democracy, for example, because Rousseau opinions on women were just as sexist as Proudhon's. As with anything, modern anarchists analyse the writings of previous anarchists to draw inspiration, not a dogma. Consequently, we reject the non-libertarian ideas of "famous" anarchists while keeping their positive contributions to the development of anarchist theory. We are sorry to belabour the point, but much of Marxist "criticism" of anarchism basically involves pointing out the negative aspects of dead anarchist thinkers and it is best simply to state clearly the obvious stupidity of such an approach.

Anarchist ideas of course did not stop developing when Kropotkin died. Neither are they the products of just four men. Anarchism is by its very nature an evolving theory, with many different thinkers and activists. When Bakunin and Kropotkin were alive, for example, they drew aspects of their ideas from other libertarian activists.

Bakunin, for example, built upon the practical activity of the followers of Proudhon in the French labour movement in the 1860s. Kropotkin, while the most associated with developing the theory communist-anarchism, was simply the most famous expounder of the ideas that had developed after Bakunin's death in the libertarian wing of the First International and before he became an anarchist. Thus anarchism is the product of tens of thousands of thinkers and activists across the globe, each shaping and developing anarchist theory to meet their needs as part of the general movement for social change. Of the many other anarchists who could be mentioned here, we can mention but a few.

Stirner is not the only famous anarchist to come from Germany. It also produced a number of original anarchist thinkers. Gustav Landauer was expelled from the Marxist Social-Democratic Party for his radical views and soon after identified himself as an anarchist. For him, anarchy was *"the expression of the liberation of man from the idols of state, the church and capital"* and he fought *"**State** socialism, levelling from above, bureaucracy"* in favour of *"free association and union, the absence of authority."* His ideas were a combination of Proudhon's and Kropotkin's and he saw the development of self-managed communities and co-operatives as the means of changing society. He is most famous for his insight that the *"state is a condition, a certain relationship among human beings, a mode of behaviour between them; we destroy it by contracting other relationships, by behaving differently towards one another."* [quoted by Peter Marshall, **Demanding the Impossible**, p. 410 and p. 411] He took a leading part in the Munich revolution of 1919 and was murdered during its crushing by the German state. His book **For Socialism** is an excellent summary of his main ideas.

Other notable German anarchists include Johann Most, originally a Marxist and an elected member of the Reichstag, he saw the futility of voting and became an anarchist after being exiled for writing against the Kaiser and clergy. He played an important role in the American anarchist movement, working for a time with Emma Goldman. More a propagandist than a great thinker, his revolutionary message inspired numerous people to become anarchists. Then there is Rudolf Rocker, a bookbinder by trade who played an important role in the Jewish labour movement in the East End of London (see his autobiography, **The London Years**, for details). He also produced the definitive introduction to **Anarcho-syndicalism** as well as analysing the Russian Revolution in articles like **Anarchism and Sovietism** and defending the Spanish revolution in pamphlets like **The Tragedy of Spain**. His **Nationalism and Culture** is a searching analysis of human culture through the ages, with an analysis of both political thinkers and power politics. He dissects nationalism and explains how the nation is not the cause but the result of the state as well as repudiating race science for the nonsense it is.

In the United States Emma Goldman and Alexander Berkman were two of the leading anarchist thinkers and activists. Goldman united Stirner's egoism with Kropotkin's communism into a passionate and powerful theory which combined the best of both. She also placed anarchism at the centre of feminist theory and activism as well as being an advocate of syndicalism (see her book **Anarchism and Other Essays** and the collection of essays, articles and talks entitled **Red Emma Speaks**). Alexander Berkman, Emma's lifelong companion, produced a classic introduction to anarchist ideas called **What is Anarchism?** (also known as **What is Communist Anarchism?** and the **ABC of Anarchism**). Like Goldman, he supported anarchist involvement in the labour movement was a prolific writer and speaker (the book **Life of An Anarchist** gives an excellent selection of his best articles, books and pamphlets). Both were involved in editing anarchist journals, with Goldman most associated with **Mother Earth** (see **Anarchy! An Anthology of Emma Goldman's Mother Earth** edited by Peter Glassgold) and Berkman **The Blast** (reprinted in full in 2005). Both journals were closed down when the two anarchists were arrested in 1917 for their anti-war activism.

In December 1919, both he and Goldman were expelled by the US government to Russia after the 1917 revolution had radicalised significant parts of the American population, as they were considered too dangerous to be allowed to remain in the land of the free. Exactly two years later, their passports arrived to allow them to leave Russia. The Bolshevik slaughter of the Kronstadt revolt in March 1921 after the civil war ended had finally convinced them that the Bolshevik dictatorship meant the death of the revolution there. The Bolshevik rulers were more than happy to see the back of two genuine revolutionaries who stayed true to their principles. Once outside Russia, Berkman wrote numerous articles on the fate of the revolution (including **The Russian Tragedy** and **The Kronstadt Rebellion**) as well as publishing his diary in book from as **The Bolshevik Myth**. Goldman produced her classic work **My Disillusionment in Russia** as well as publishing her famous autobiography **Living My Life**. She also found time to refute Trotsky's lies about the Kronstadt rebellion in **Trotsky Protests Too Much**.

As well as Berkman and Goldman, the United States also produced other notable activists and thinkers. Voltairine de Cleyre played an important role in the US anarchist movement, enriching both US and international anarchist theory with her articles, poems and speeches. Her work includes such classics as **Anarchism and American Traditions**, **Direct Action**, **Sex Slavery** and **The Dominant Idea**. These are included, along with other articles and some of her famous poems, in **The Voltairine de Cleyre Reader**. These and other important essays are included in **Exquisite Rebel**, another anthology of her writings, while Eugenia C. Delamotte's **Gates of Freedom** provides an excellent overview of her life and ideas as well as selections from her works. In addition, the book **Anarchy! An Anthology of Emma Goldman's Mother Earth** contains a good selection of her writings as well as other anarchists active at the time. Also of interest is the collection of the speeches she made to mark the state murder of the Chicago Martyrs in 1886 (see **the First Mayday: The Haymarket Speeches 1895-1910**). Every November the 11th, except when illness made it impossible, she spoke in their memory. For those interested in the ideas of that previous generation of anarchists which the Chicago Martyrs represented, Albert Parsons' **Anarchism: Its Philosophy and Scientific Basis** is essential reading. His wife, Lucy Parsons, was also an outstanding anarchist activist from the 1870s until her death in 1942 and selections of her writings and speeches can be found in the book **Freedom, Equality & Solidarity** (edited by Gale Ahrens).

Elsewhere in the Americas, Ricardo Flores Magón helped lay the ground for the Mexican revolution of 1910 by founding the (strangely named) **Mexican Liberal Party** in 1905 which organised two unsuccessful uprising against the Diaz dictatorship in 1906 and 1908. Through his paper **Tierra y Libertad** (*"Land and Liberty"*) he influenced the developing labour movement as well as Zapata's peasant army. He continually stressed the need to turn the revolution into a **social** revolution which will *"give the lands to the people"* as well as *"possession of the factories, mines, etc."* Only this would ensure that the people *"will not be deceived."* Talking of the Agrarians (the Zapatista army), Ricardo's brother Enrique he notes that they *"are more or less inclined towards anarchism"* and they can work together because both are *"direct actionists"* and *"they act perfectly revolutionary. They go after the rich, the authorities and the priestcraft"* and have *"burnt to ashes private property deeds as well as all official records"* as well as having *"thrown down the fences that marked private properties."* Thus the anarchists *"propagate our principles"* while the Zapatista's *"put them into practice."* [quoted by David Poole, **Land and Liberty**, p. 17 and p. 25] Ricardo died as a political prisoner in an American jail and is, ironically, considered a hero of the revolution by the Mexican state. A substantial collection of his writings are available in the book **Dreams of Freedom** (which includes an impressive biographical essay which discusses his influence as well as placing his work in historical context).

Italy, with its strong and dynamic anarchist movement, has produced some of the best anarchist writers. Errico Malatesta spent over 50 years fighting for anarchism across the world and his writings are amongst the best in anarchist theory. For those interested in his practical and inspiring ideas then his short pamphlet **Anarchy** cannot be beaten. Collections of his articles can be found in **The Anarchist Revolution** and **Errico Malatesta: His Life and Ideas**, both edited by Vernon Richards. A favourite writing technique was the use of dialogues, such as **At the Cafe: Conversations on Anarchism**. These, using the conversations he had with non-anarchists as their basis, explained anarchist ideas in a clear and down to Earth manner. Another dialogue, **Fra Contadini: A Dialogue on Anarchy**, was translated into many languages, with 100,000 copies printed in Italy in 1920 when the revolution Malatesta had fought for all his life looked likely. At this time Malatesta edited **Umanita Nova** (the first Italian daily anarchist paper, it soon gained a circulation of 50 000) as well as writing the programme for the **Unione Anarchica Italiana**, a national anarchist organisation of some 20 000. For his activities during the factory occupations he was arrested at the age of 67 along with 80 other anarchist activists. Other Italian anarchists of note include Malatesta's friend Luigi Fabbri (sadly little of his work has been translated into English bar **Bourgeois Influences on Anarchism** and **Anarchy and 'Scientific' Communism**) Luigi Galleani produced a very powerful anti-organisational anarchist-communism which proclaimed (in **The End of Anarchism?**) that *"Communism is simply the economic foundation by which the individual has the opportunity to regulate himself and carry out his functions."* Camillo Berneri, before being murdered by the Communists during the Spanish Revolution, continued the fine tradition of critical, practical anarchism associated with Italian anarchism. His study

of Kropotkin's federalist ideas is a classic (**Peter Kropotkin: His Federalist Ideas**). His daughter Marie-Louise Berneri, before her tragic early death, contributed to the British anarchist press (see her **Neither East Nor West: Selected Writings 1939-48** and **Journey Through Utopia**).

In Japan, Hatta Shuzo developed Kropotkin's communist-anarchism in new directions between the world wars. Called "true anarchism," he created an anarchism which was a concrete alternative to the mainly peasant country he and thousands of his comrades were active in. While rejecting certain aspects of syndicalism, they organised workers into unions as well as working with the peasantry for the *"foundation stones on which to build the new society that we long for are none other than the awakening of the tenant farmers"* who *"account for a majority of the population."* Their new society was based on decentralised communes which combined industry and agriculture for, as one of Hatta's comrade's put it, *"the village will cease to be a mere communist agricultural village and become a co-operative society which is a fusion of agriculture and industry."* Hatta rejected the idea that they sought to go back to an ideal past, stating that the anarchists were *"completely opposite to the medievalists. We seek to use machines as means of production and, indeed, hope for the invention of yet more ingenious machines."* [quoted by John Crump, **Hatta Shuzo and Pure Anarchism in Interwar Japan**, p. 122-3, and p. 144]

As far as individualist anarchism goes, the undoubted "pope" was Benjamin Tucker. Tucker, in his **Instead of Book**, used his intellect and wit to attack all who he considered enemies of freedom (mostly capitalists, but also a few social anarchists as well! For example, Tucker excommunicated Kropotkin and the other communist-anarchists from anarchism. Kropotkin did not return the favour). Tucker built on such notable thinkers as Josiah Warren, Lysander Spooner, Stephen Pearl Andrews and William B. Greene, adapting Proudhon's mutualism to the conditions of pre-capitalist America (see Rudolf Rocker's **Pioneers of American Freedom** for details). Defending the worker, artisan and small-scale farmer from a state intent on building capitalism by means of state intervention, Tucker argued that capitalist exploitation would be abolished by creating a totally free non-capitalist market in which the four state monopolies used to create capitalism would be struck down by means of mutual banking and *"occupancy and use"* land and resource rights. Placing himself firmly in the socialist camp, he recognised (like Proudhon) that all non-labour income was theft and so opposed profit, rent and interest. he translated Proudhon's **What is Property** and **System of Economical Contradictions** as well as Bakunin's **God and the State**. Tucker's compatriot, Joseph Labadie was an active trade unionist as well as contributor to Tucker's paper **Liberty**. His son, Lawrence Labadie carried the individualist-anarchist torch after Tucker's death, believing that *"that freedom in every walk of life is the greatest possible means of elevating the human race to happier conditions."*

Undoubtedly the Russian Leo Tolstoy is the most famous writer associated with religious anarchism and has had the greatest impact in spreading the spiritual and pacifistic ideas associated with that tendency. Influencing such notable people as Gandhi and the **Catholic Worker Group** around Dorothy Day, Tolstoy presented a radical interpretation of Christianity which stressed individual responsibility and freedom above the mindless authoritarianism and hierarchy which marks so much of mainstream Christianity. Tolstoy's works, like those of that other radical libertarian Christian William Blake, have inspired many Christians towards a libertarian vision of Jesus' message which has been hidden by the mainstream churches. Thus Christian Anarchism maintains, along with Tolstoy, that *"Christianity in its true sense puts an end to government"* (see, for example, Tolstoy's **The Kingdom of God is within you** and Peter Marshall's **William Blake: Visionary Anarchist**).

More recently, Noam Chomsky (in such works as **Deterring Democracy**, **Necessary Illusions**, **World Orders, Old and New**, **Rogue States**, **Hegemony or Survival** and many others) and Murray Bookchin (**Post-Scarcity Anarchism**, **The Ecology of Freedom**, **Towards an Ecological Society**, and **Remaking Society**, among others) have kept the social anarchist movement at the front of political theory and analysis. Bookchin's work has placed anarchism at the centre of green thought and has been a constant threat to those wishing to mystify or corrupt the movement to create an ecological society. **The Murray Bookchin Reader** contains a representative selection of his writings. Sadly, a few years before his death Bookchin distanced himself from the anarchism he spent nearly four decades advocating (although he remained a libertarian socialist to the end). Chomsky's well documented critiques of U.S. imperialism and how the media operates are his most famous works, but he has also written extensively about the anarchist tradition and its ideas, most famously in his essays *"Notes on Anarchism"* (in **For Reasons of State**) and his defence of the anarchist social revolution against bourgeois historians in *"Objectivity and Liberal Scholarship"* (in **American Power and the New Mandarins**). These and others of his more explicitly anarchist essays and interviews can be found in the collection **Chomsky on Anarchism**. Other good sources for his anarchist ideas are **Radical Priorities**, **Language and Politics** and the pamphlet **Government in the Future**. Both **Understanding Power** and **The Chomsky Reader** are excellent introductions to his thought.

Britain has also seen an important series of anarchist thinkers. Herbert Read (probably the only anarchist to ever accept a knighthood!) wrote several works on anarchist philosophy and theory (see his **Anarchy and Order** compilation of essays). His anarchism flowered directly from his aesthetic concerns and he was a committed pacifist. As well as giving fresh insight and expression to the tradition themes of anarchism, he contributed regularly to the anarchist press (see the collection of articles **A One-Man Manifesto and other writings from Freedom Press**). Another pacifist anarchist was Alex Comfort. As well as writing the **Joy of Sex**, Comfort was an active pacifist and anarchist. He wrote particularly on pacifism, psychiatry and sexual politics from a libertarian perspective. His most famous anarchist book was **Authority and Delinquency** and a collection of his anarchist pamphlets and articles was published under the title **Writings against Power and Death**.

However, the most famous and influential British anarchist must be Colin Ward. He became an anarchist when stationed in Glasgow during the Second World War and came across the local anarchist group there. Once an anarchist, he contributed to the anarchist press extensively. As well as being an editor of **Freedom**, he also edited the influential monthly magazine **Anarchy** during the 1960s (a selection of articles picked by Ward can be found in the book **A Decade of Anarchy**). However, his most famous single book is **Anarchy in Action** where he has updated Kropotkin's **Mutual Aid** by uncovering and documenting the anarchistic nature of everyday life even within capitalism. His extensive writing on housing has emphasised the importance of collective self-help and social management of housing against the twin evils of privatisation and nationalisation (see, for example, his books **Talking Houses** and **Housing: An Anarchist Approach**). He has cast an anarchist eye on numerous other issues, including water use (**Reflected in Water: A Crisis of Social Responsibility**), transport (**Freedom to go: after the motor age**) and the welfare state (**Social Policy: an anarchist response**). His **Anarchism: A Very Short Introduction** is a good starting point for discovering anarchism and his particular perspective on it while **Talking Anarchy** provides an excellent overview of both his ideas and life. Lastly we must mention both Albert Meltzer and Nicolas Walter, both of whom contributed extensively to the anarchist press as well as writing two well known short introductions to anarchism (**Anarchism: Arguments for and against** and **About Anarchism**, respectively).

We could go on; there are many more writers we could mention. But besides these, there are the thousands of "ordinary" anarchist militants who have never written books but whose common sense and activism have encouraged the spirit of revolt within society and helped build the new world in the shell of the old. As Kropotkin put it, *"anarchism was born **among the people**; and it will continue to be full of life and creative power only as long as it remains a thing of the people."* [**Anarchism**, p. 146]

So we hope that this concentration on anarchist thinkers should not be taken to mean that there is some sort of division between activists and intellectuals in the movement. Far from it. Few anarchists are purely thinkers or activists. They are usually both. Kropotkin, for example, was jailed for his activism, as was Malatesta and Goldman. Makhno, most famous as an active participate in the Russian Revolution, also contributed theoretical articles to the anarchist press during and after it. The same can be said of Louise Michel, whose militant activities during the Paris Commune and in building the anarchist movement in France after it did not preclude her writing articles for the libertarian press. We are simply indicating key anarchist thinkers so that those interested can read about their ideas directly.

A.4.1 Are there any thinkers close to anarchism?

Yes. There are numerous thinkers who are close to anarchism. They come from both the liberal and socialist traditions. While this may be considered surprising, it is not. Anarchism has links with both ideologies. Obviously the individualist anarchists are closest to the liberal tradition while social anarchists are closest to the socialist. Indeed, as Nicholas Walter put it, *"Anarchism can be seen as a development from either liberalism or socialism, or from both liberalism and socialism. Like liberals, anarchists want freedom; like* socialists, anarchists want equality." However, "anarchism is not just a mixture of liberalism and socialism ... we differ fundamentally from them." [**About Anarchism**, p. 29 and p. 31] In this he echoes Rocker's comments in **Anarcho-Syndicalism**. And this can be a useful tool for seeing the links between anarchism and other theories however it must be stressed that anarchism offers an *anarchist* critique of both liberalism and socialism and we should not submerge the uniqueness of anarchism into other philosophies.

Section A.4.2 discusses liberal thinkers who are close to anarchism, while section A.4.3 highlights those socialists who are close to anarchism. There are even Marxists who inject libertarian ideas into their politics and these are discussed in section A.4.4. And, of course, there are thinkers who cannot be so easily categorised and will be discussed here.

Economist David Ellerman has produced an impressive body of work arguing for workplace democracy. Explicitly linking his ideas to the early British Ricardian socialists and Proudhon, in such works as **The Democratic Worker-Owned Firm** and **Property and Contract in Economics** he has presented both a rights based and labour-property based defence of self-management against capitalism. He argues that "[t]oday's economic democrats are the *new abolitionists trying to abolish the whole institution of renting people in favour of democratic self-management in the workplace*" for his "*critique is not new; it was developed in the Enlightenment doctrine of inalienable rights. It was applied by abolitionists against the voluntary self-enslavement contract and by political democrats against the voluntary contraction defence of non-democratic government.*" [**The Democratic Worker-Owned Firm**, p. 210] Anyone, like anarchists, interested in producer co-operatives as alternatives to wage slavery will find his work of immense interest.

Ellerman is not the only person to stress the benefits of co-operation. Alfie Kohn's important work on the benefits of co-operation builds upon Kropotkin's studies of mutual aid and is, consequently, of interest to social anarchists. In **No Contest: the case against competition** and **Punished by Rewards**, Kohn discusses (with extensive empirical evidence) the failings and negative impact of competition on those subject to it. He addresses both economic and social issues in his works and shows that competition is not what it is cracked up to be.

Within feminist theory, Carole Pateman is the most obvious libertarian influenced thinker. Independently of Ellerman, Pateman has produced a powerful argument for self-managed association in both the workplace and society as a whole. Building upon a libertarian analysis of Rousseau's arguments, her analysis of contract theory is ground breaking. If a theme has to be ascribed to Pateman's work it could be freedom and what it means to be free. For her, freedom can only be viewed as self-determination and, consequently, the absence of subordination. Consequently, she has advocated a participatory form of democracy from her first major work, **Participation and Democratic Theory** onwards. In that book, a pioneering study of in participatory democracy, she exposed the limitations of liberal democratic theory, analysed the works of Rousseau, Mill and Cole and presented empirical evidence on the benefits of participation on the individuals involved.

In the **Problem of Political Obligation**, Pateman discusses the "liberal" arguments on freedom and finds them wanting. For the liberal, a person must consent to be ruled by another but this opens up the "problem" that they might not consent and, indeed, may never have consented. Thus the liberal state would lack a justification. She deepens her analysis to question why freedom should be equated to consenting to be ruled and proposed a participatory democratic theory in which people collectively make their own decisions (a self-assumed obligation to your fellow citizens rather to a state). In discussing Kropotkin, she showed her awareness of the social anarchist tradition to which her own theory is obviously related.

Pateman builds on this analysis in her **The Sexual Contract**, where she dissects the sexism of classical liberal and democratic theory. She analyses the weakness of what calls 'contractarian' theory (classical liberalism and right-wing "libertarianism") and shows how it leads not to free associations of self-governing individuals but rather social relationships based on authority, hierarchy and power in which a few rule the many. Her analysis of the state, marriage and wage labour are profoundly libertarian, showing that freedom must mean more than consenting to be ruled. This is the paradox of capitalist liberalism, for a person is assumed to be free in order to consent to a contract but once within it they face the reality subordination to another's decisions (see section A.4.2 for further discussion).

Her ideas challenge some of Western culture's core beliefs about individual freedom and her critiques of the major Enlightenment political philosophers are powerful and convincing. Implicit is a critique not just of the conservative and liberal tradition, but of the patriarchy and hierarchy contained within the Left as well. As well as these works, a collection of her essays is available called **The Disorder of Women**.

Within the so-called "anti-globalisation" movement Naomi Klein shows an awareness of libertarian ideas and her own work has a libertarian thrust to it (we call it "so-called" as its members are internationalists, seeking a globalisation from below not one imposed from above by and for a few). She first came to attention as the author of **No Logo**, which charts the growth of consumer capitalism, exposing the dark reality behind the glossy brands of capitalism and, more importantly, highlighting the resistance to it. No distant academic, she is an active participant in the movement she reports on in **Fences and Windows**, a collection of essays on globalisation, its consequences and the wave of protests against it. Klein's articles are well written and engaging, covering the reality of modern capitalism, the gap, as she puts it, "*between rich and power but also between rhetoric and reality, between what is said and what is done. Between the promise of globalisation and its real effects.*" She shows how we live in a world where the market (i.e. capital) is made "freer" while people suffer increased state power and repression. How an unelected Argentine President labels that country's popular assemblies "*antidemocratic.*" How rhetoric about liberty is used as a tool to defend and increase private power (as she reminds us, "*always missing from [the globalisation] discussion is the issue of power. So many of the debates that we have about globalisation theory are actually about power: who holds it, who is exercising it and who is disguising it, pretending it no longer matters*"). [**Fences and Windows**, pp 83-4 and p. 83]

And how people across the world are resisting. As she puts it, "*many [in the movement] are tired of being spoken for and about. They* are demanding a more direct form of political participation." She reports on a movement which she is part of, one which aims for a globalisation from below, one "founded on principles of transparency, accountability and self-determination, one that frees people instead of liberating capital." This means being against a "corporate-driven globalisation ... that is centralising power and wealth into fewer and fewer hands" while presenting an alternative which is about "decentralising power and building community-based decision-making potential – whether through unions, neighbourhoods, farms, villages, anarchist collectives or aboriginal self-government." All strong anarchist principles and, like anarchists, she wants people to manage their own affairs and chronicles attempts around the world to do just that (many of which, as Klein notes, are anarchists or influenced by anarchist ideas, sometimes knowing, sometimes not). [**Op. Cit.**, p. 77, p. 79 and p. 16]

While not an anarchist, she is aware that real change comes from below, by the self-activity of working class people fighting for a better world. Decentralisation of power is a key idea in the book. As she puts it, the "goal" of the social movements she describes is "not to take power for themselves but to challenge power centralisation on principle" and so creating "a new culture of vibrant direct democracy ... one that is fuelled and strengthened by direct participation." She does not urge the movement to invest itself with new leaders and neither does she (like the Left) think that electing a few leaders to make decisions for us equals "democracy" ("the goal is not better faraway rules and rulers but close-up democracy on the ground"). Klein, therefore, gets to the heart of the matter. Real social change is based on empowering the grassroots, "the desire for self-determination, economic sustainability and participatory democracy." Given this, Klein has presented libertarian ideas to a wide audience. [**Op. Cit.**, p. xxvi, p. xxvi-xxvii, p. 245 and p. 233]

Other notable libertarian thinkers include Henry D. Thoreau, Albert Camus, Aldous Huxley, Lewis Mumford, and Oscar Wilde. Thus there are numerous thinkers who approach anarchist conclusions and who discuss subjects of interest to libertarians. As Kropotkin noted a hundred years ago, these kinds of writers "are full of ideas which show how closely anarchism is interwoven with the work that is going on in modern thought in the same direction of enfranchisement of man from the bonds of the state as well as from those of capitalism." [**Anarchism**, p. 300] The only change since then is that more names can be added to the list.

Peter Marshall discusses the ideas of most, but not all, of the non-anarchist libertarians we mention in this and subsequent sections in his book history of anarchism, **Demanding the Impossible**. Clifford Harper's **Anarchy: A Graphic Guide** is also a useful guide for finding out more.

A.4.2 Are there any liberal thinkers close to anarchism?

As noted in the last section, there are thinkers in both the liberal and socialist traditions who approach anarchist theory and ideals. This understandable as anarchism shares certain ideas and ideals with both.

However, as will become clear in sections A.4.3 and A.4.4, anarchism shares most common ground with the socialist tradition it is a part of. This is because classical liberalism is a profoundly elitist tradition. The works of Locke and the tradition he inspired aimed to justify hierarchy, state and private property. As Carole Pateman notes, "Locke's state of nature, with its father-rulers and capitalist economy, would certainly not find favour with anarchists" any more than his vision of the social contract and the liberal state it creates. A state, which as Pateman recounts, in which "only males who own substantial amounts of material property are [the] politically relevant members of society" and exists "precisely to preserve the property relationships of the developing capitalist market economy, not to disturb them." For the majority, the non-propertied, they expressed "tacit consent" to be ruled by the few by "choosing to remain within the one's country of birth when reaching adulthood." [**The Problem of Political Obligation**, p. 141, p. 71, p. 78 and p. 73]

Thus anarchism is at odds with what can be called the pro-capitalist liberal tradition which, flowing from Locke, builds upon his rationales for hierarchy. As David Ellerman notes, "there is a whole liberal tradition of apologising for non-democratic government based on consent – on a voluntary social contract alienating governing rights to a sovereign." In economics, this is reflected in their support for wage labour and the capitalist autocracy it creates for the "employment contract is the modern limited workplace version" of such contracts. [**The Democratic Worker-Owned Firm**, p. 210]

This pro-capitalist liberalism essentially boils down to the liberty to pick a master or, if you are among the lucky few, to become a master yourself. The idea that freedom means self-determination for all at all times is alien to it. Rather it is based on the idea of "self-ownership," that you "own" yourself and your rights. Consequently, you can sell (alienate) your rights and liberty on the market. As we discuss in section B.4, in practice this means that most people are subject to autocratic rule for most of their waking hours (whether in work or in marriage).

The modern equivalent of classical liberalism is the right-wing "libertarian" tradition associated with Milton Friedman, Robert Nozick, von Hayek and so forth. As they aim to reduce the state to simply the defender to private property and enforcer of the hierarchies that social institution creates, they can by no stretch of the imagination be considered near anarchism. What is called "liberalism" in, say, the United States is a more democratic liberal tradition and has, like anarchism, little in common with the shrill pro-capitalist defenders of the minimum state. While they may (sometimes) be happy to denounce the state's attacks on individual liberty, they are more than happy to defend the "freedom" of the property owner to impose exactly the same restrictions on those who use their land or capital.

Given that feudalism combined ownership and rulership, that the governance of people living on land was an attribute of the ownership of that land, it would be no exaggeration to say that the right-wing "libertarian" tradition is simply its modern (voluntary) form. It is no more libertarian than the feudal lords who combated the powers of the King in order to protect their power over their own land and serfs. As Chomsky notes, *"the 'libertarian' doctrines that are fashionable in the US and UK particularly … seem to me to reduce to advocacy of one or another form of illegitimate authority, quite often real tyranny."* [**Marxism, Anarchism, and Alternative Futures**, p. 777] Moreover, as Benjamin Tucker noted with regards their predecessors, while they are happy to attack any state regulation which benefits the many or limits their power, they are silent on the laws (and regulations and "rights") which benefit the few.

However there is another liberal tradition, one which is essentially pre-capitalist which has more in common with the aspirations of anarchism. As Chomsky put it:

> *"These ideas [of anarchism] grow out the Enlightenment; their roots are in Rousseau's **Discourse on Inequality**, Humbolt's **The Limits of State Action**, Kant's insistence, in his defence of the French Revolution, that freedom is the precondition for acquiring the maturity for freedom, not a gift to be granted when such maturity is achieved … With the development of industrial capitalism, a new and unanticipated system of injustice, it is libertarian socialism that has preserved and extended the radical humanist message of the Enlightenment and the classical liberal ideals that were perverted into an ideology to sustain the emerging social order. In fact, on the very same assumptions that led classical liberalism to oppose the intervention of the state in social life, capitalist social relations are also intolerable. This is clear, for example, from the classic work of [Wilhelm von] Humboldt, **The Limits of State Action**, which anticipated and perhaps inspired [John Stuart] Mill … This classic of liberal thought, completed in 1792, is in its essence profoundly, though prematurely, anticapitalist. Its ideas must be attenuated beyond recognition to be transmuted into an ideology of industrial capitalism."* ["Notes on Anarchism", **For Reasons of State**, p. 156]

Chomsky discusses this in more detail in his essay *"Language and Freedom"* (contained in both **Reason of State** and **The Chomsky Reader**). As well as Humbolt and Mill, such "pre-capitalist" liberals would include such radicals as Thomas Paine, who envisioned a society based on artisan and small farmers (i.e. a pre-capitalist economy) with a rough level of social equality and, of course, a minimal government. His ideas inspired working class radicals across the world and, as E.P. Thompson reminds us, Paine's **Rights of Man** was *"a foundation-text of the English [and Scottish] working-class movement."* While his ideas on government are *"close to a theory of anarchism,"* his reform proposals *"set a source towards the social legislation of the twentieth century."* [**The Making of the English Working Class**, p. 99, p. 101 and p. 102] His

combination of concern for liberty and social justice places him close to anarchism.

Then there is Adam Smith. While the right (particularly elements of the "libertarian" right) claim him as a classic liberal, his ideas are more complex than that. For example, as Noam Chomsky points out, Smith advocated the free market because *"it would lead to perfect equality, equality of condition, not just equality of opportunity."* [**Class Warfare**, p. 124] As Smith himself put it, *"in a society where things were left to follow their natural course, where there is perfect liberty"* it would mean that *"advantages would soon return to the level of other employments"* and so *"the different employments of labour and stock must … be either perfectly equal or continually tending to equality."* Nor did he oppose state intervention or state aid for the working classes. For example, he advocated public education to counter the negative effects of the division of labour. Moreover, he was against state intervention because whenever *"a legislature attempts to regulate differences between masters and their workmen, its counsellors are always the masters. When regulation, therefore, is in favour of the workmen, it is always just and equitable; but it is otherwise when in favour of the masters."* He notes how *"the law"* would *"punish"* workers' combinations *"very severely"* while ignoring the masters' combinations (*"if it dealt impartially, it would treat the masters in the same manner"*). [**The Wealth of Nations**, p. 88 and p. 129] Thus state intervention was to be opposed in general because the state was run by the few for the few, which would make state intervention benefit the few, not the many. It is doubtful Smith would have left his ideas on laissez-faire unchanged if he had lived to see the development of corporate capitalism. This critical edge of Smith's work is conveniently ignored by those claiming him for the classical liberal tradition.

Smith, argues Chomsky, was *"a pre-capitalist and anti-capitalist person with roots in the Enlightenment."* Yes, he argues, *"the classical liberals, the [Thomas] Jeffersons and the Smiths, were opposing the concentrations of power that they saw around them … They didn't see other forms of concentration of power which only developed later. When they did see them, they didn't like them. Jefferson was a good example. He was strongly opposed to the concentrations of power that he saw developing, and warned that the banking institutions and the industrial corporations which were barely coming into existence in his day would destroy the achievements of the Revolution."* [**Op. Cit.**, p. 125]

As Murray Bookchin notes, Jefferson *"is most clearly identified in the early history of the United States with the political demands and interests of the independent farmer-proprietor."* [**The Third Revolution**, vol. 1, pp. 188-9] In other words, with pre-capitalist economic forms. We also find Jefferson contrasting the *"aristocrats"* and the *"democrats."* The former are *"those who fear and distrust the people, and wish to draw all powers from them into the hands of the higher classes."* The democrats *"identify with the people, have confidence in them, cherish and consider them as the honest & safe … depository of the public interest,"* if not always *"the most wise."* [quoted by Chomsky, **Powers and Prospects**, p. 88] As Chomsky notes, the *"aristocrats"* were *"the advocates of the rising capitalist state, which Jefferson regarded with dismay, recognising the obvious contradiction between democracy and capitalism."* [**Op. Cit.**, p. 88] Claudio J. Katz's essay on *"Thomas Jefferson's Liberal*

Anticapitalism" usefully explores these issues. [**American Journal of Political Science**, vol. 47, No. 1 (Jan, 2003), pp. 1-17]

Jefferson even went so far as to argue that *"a little rebellion now and then is a good thing … It is a medicine necessary for the sound health of government … The tree of liberty must be refreshed from time to time with the blood of patriots and tyrants."* [quoted by Howard Zinn, **A People's History of the United States**, p. 94] However, his libertarian credentials are damaged by him being both a President of the United States and a slave owner but compared to the other "founding fathers" of the American state, his liberalism is of a democratic form. As Chomsky reminds us, *"all the Founding Fathers hated democracy – Thomas Jefferson was a partial exception, but only partial."* The American state, as a classical liberal state, was designed (to quote James Madison) *"to protect the minority of the opulent from the majority."* Or, to repeat John Jay's principle, the *"people who own the country ought to govern it."* [**Understanding Power**, p. 315] If America is a (formal) democracy rather than an oligarchy, it is in spite of rather than because of classical liberalism.

Then there is John Stuart Mill who recognised the fundamental contradiction in classical liberalism. How can an ideology which proclaims itself for individual liberty support institutions which systematically nullify that liberty in practice? For this reason Mill attacked patriarchal marriage, arguing that marriage must be a voluntary association between equals, with *"sympathy in equality … living together in love, without power on one side or obedience on the other."* Rejecting the idea that there had to be *"an absolute master"* in any association, he pointed out that in *"partnership in business … it is not found or thought necessary to enact that in every partnership, one partner shall have entire control over the concern, and the others shall be bound to obey his rule."* [*"The Subjection of Women,"* quoted by Susan L. Brown, **The Politics of Individualism**, pp. 45-6]

Yet his own example showed the flaw in liberal support for capitalism, for the employee *is* subject to a relationship in which power accrues to one party and obedience to another. Unsurprisingly, therefore, he argued that the *"form of association … which is mankind continue to improve, must be expected in the end to predominate, is not that which can exist between a capitalist as chief, and workpeople without a voice in management, but the association of the labourers themselves on terms of equality, collectively owning the capital … and working under managers elected and removable by themselves."* [**The Principles of Political Economy**, p. 147] Autocratic management during working hours is hardly compatible with Mill's maxim that *"[o]ver himself, over his own body and mind, the individual is sovereign."* Mill's opposition to centralised government and wage slavery brought his ideas closer to anarchism than most liberals, as did his comment that the *"social principle of the future"* was *"how to unite the greatest individual liberty of action with a common ownership in the raw materials of the globe, and equal participation of all in the benefits of combined labour."* [quoted by Peter Marshall, **Demanding the Impossible**, p. 164] His defence of individuality, **On Liberty**, is a classic, if flawed, work and his analysis of socialist tendencies (*"Chapters on Socialism"*) is worth reading for its evaluation of their pros and cons from a (democratic) liberal perspective.

Like Proudhon, Mill was a forerunner of modern-day market socialism and a firm supporter of decentralisation and social participation. This, argues Chomsky, is unsurprising for pre-capitalist classical liberal thought *"is opposed to state intervention in social life, as a consequence of deeper assumptions about the human need for liberty, diversity, and free association. On the same assumptions, capitalist relations of production, wage labour, competitiveness, the ideology of 'possessive individualism' – all must be regarded as fundamentally antihuman. Libertarian socialism is properly to be regarded as the inheritor of the liberal ideals of the Enlightenment."* [*"Notes on Anarchism"*, **Op. Cit.**, p. 157]

Thus anarchism shares commonality with pre-capitalist and democratic liberal forms. The hopes of these liberals were shattered with the development of capitalism. To quote Rudolf Rocker's analysis:

> *"Liberalism and Democracy were pre-eminently political concepts, and since the great majority of the original adherents of both maintained the right of ownership in the old sense, these had to renounce them both when economic development took a course which could not be practically reconciled with the original principles of Democracy, and still less with those of Liberalism. Democracy, with its motto of 'all citizens equal before the law,' and Liberalism with its 'right of man over his own person,' both shipwrecked on the realities of the capitalist economic form. So long as millions of human beings in every country had to sell their labour-power to a small minority of owners, and to sink into the most wretched misery if they could find no buyers, the so-called 'equality before the law' remains merely a pious fraud, since the laws are made by those who find themselves in possession of the social wealth. But in the same way there can also be no talk of a 'right over one's own person,' for that right ends when one is compelled to submit to the economic dictation of another if he does not want to starve."* [**Anarcho-Syndicalism**, p. 10]

A.4.3 Are there any socialist thinkers close to anarchism?

Anarchism developed in response to the development of capitalism and it is in the non-anarchist socialist tradition which anarchism finds most fellow travellers.

The earliest British socialists (the so-called Ricardian Socialists) following in the wake of Robert Owen held ideas which were similar to those of anarchists. For example, Thomas Hodgskin expounded ideas similar to Proudhon's mutualism while William Thompson developed a non-state, communal form of socialism based on *"communities of mutual co-operative"* which had similarities to anarcho-communism (Thompson had been a mutualist before becoming a communist in light of the problems even a non-capitalist market would have). John Francis Bray is also of interest, as is the radical agrarianist Thomas Spence who developed a communal form of land-based socialism which expounded many ideas usually associated with anarchism (see *"The Agrarian Socialism of Thomas Spence"* by Brian Morris in his book **Ecology and Anarchism**). Moreover, the early British trade union movement *"developed, stage by stage, a theory of syndicalism"* 40 years before Bakunin and the libertarian wing of the First International did. [E.P. Thompson, **The Making of the English Working Class**, p. 912] Noel Thompson's **The Real Rights of Man** is a good summary of all these thinkers and movements, as is E.P. Thompson's classic social history of working class life (and politics) of this period, **The Making of the English Working Class**.

Libertarian ideas did not die out in Britain in the 1840s. There was also the quasi-syndicalists of the Guild Socialists of the 1910s and 1920s who advocated a decentralised communal system with workers' control of industry. G.D.H. Cole's **Guild Socialism Restated** is the most famous work of this school, which also included author's S.G. Hobson and A.R. Orage (Geoffrey Osteregaard's **The Tradition of Workers' Control** provides an good summary of the ideas of Guild Socialism). Bertrand Russell, another supporter of Guild Socialism, was attracted to anarchist ideas and wrote an extremely informed and thoughtful discussion of anarchism, syndicalism and Marxism in his classic book **Roads to Freedom**.

While Russell was pessimistic about the possibility of anarchism in the near future, he felt it was *"the ultimate idea to which society should approximate."* As a Guild Socialist, he took it for granted that there could *"be no real freedom or democracy until the men who do the work in a business also control its management."* His vision of a good society is one any anarchist would support: *"a world in which the creative spirit is alive, in which life is an adventure full of joy and hope, based upon the impulse to construct than upon the desire to retain what we possess or to seize what is possessed by others. It must be a world in which affection has free play, in which love is purged of the instinct for domination, in which cruelty and envy have been dispelled by happiness and the unfettered development of all the instincts that build up life and fill it with mental delights."* [quoted by Noam Chomsky, **Problems of Knowledge and Freedom**, pp. 59-60, p. 61 and p. x] An informed and interesting writer on many subjects, his thought and social activism has influenced many other thinkers, including Noam Chomsky (whose **Problems of Knowledge and Freedom** is a wide ranging discussion on some of the topics Russell addressed).

Another important British libertarian socialist thinker and activist was William Morris. Morris, a friend of Kropotkin, was active in the **Socialist League** and led its anti-parliamentarian wing. While stressing he was not an anarchist, there is little real difference between the ideas of Morris and most anarcho-communists (Morris said he was a communist and saw no need to append "anarchist" to it as, for him, communism was democratic and liberatory). A prominent member of the "Arts and Crafts" movement, Morris argued for humanising work and it was, to quot the title of one of his most famous essays, a case of **Useful Work vrs Useless Toil**. His utopia novel **News from Nowhere** paints a compelling vision of a libertarian communist society where industrialisation has been replaced with a communal craft-based economy. It is a utopia which has long appealed to most social anarchists. For a discussion of Morris' ideas, placed in the context of his famous utopia, see

William Morris and News from Nowhere: A Vision for Our Time (Stephen Coleman and Paddy O'Sullivan (eds.))

Also of note is the Greek thinker Cornelius Castoriadis. Originally a Trotskyist, Castoriadis evaluation of Trotsky's deeply flawed analysis of Stalinist Russia as a degenerated workers' state lead him to reject first Leninism and then Marxism itself. This led him to libertarian conclusions, seeing the key issue not who owns the means of production but rather hierarchy. Thus the class struggle was between those with power and those subject to it. This led him to reject Marxist economics as its value analysis abstracted from (i.e. ignored!) the class struggle at the heart of production (Autonomist Marxism rejects this interpretation of Marx, but they are the only Marxists who do). Castoriadis, like social anarchists, saw the future society as one based on radical autonomy, generalised self-management and workers' councils organised from the bottom up. His three volume collected works (**Political and Social Writings**) are essential reading for anyone interested in libertarian socialist politics and a radical critique of Marxism.

Special mention should also be made of Maurice Brinton, who, as well as translating many works by Castoriadis, was a significant libertarian socialist thinker and activist as well. An ex-Trotskyist like Castoriadis, Brinton carved out a political space for a revolutionary libertarian socialism, opposed to the bureaucratic reformism of Labour as well as the police-state "socialism" of Stalinism and the authoritarianism of the Leninism which produced it. He produced numerous key pamphlets which shaped the thinking of a generation of anarchists and other libertarian socialists. These included **Paris: May 1968**, his brilliant eyewitness account of the near-revolution in France, the essential **The Bolsheviks and Workers' Control** in which he exposed Lenin's hostility to workers' self-management, and **The Irrational in Politics**, a restatement and development of the early work of Wilhelm Reich. These and many more articles have been collected in the book **For Workers' Power: The Selected Writings of Maurice Brinton**, edited by David Goodway.

The American radical historian Howard Zinn has sometimes called himself an anarchist and is well informed about the anarchist tradition (he wrote an excellent introductory essay on *"Anarchism"* for a US edition of a Herbert Read book) . As well as his classic **A People's History of the United States**, his writings of civil disobedience and non-violent direct action are essential. An excellent collection of essays by this libertarian socialist scholar has been produced under the title **The Zinn Reader**. Other notable libertarian socialists close to anarchism are Edward Carpenter (see, for example, Sheila Rowbotham's **Edward Carpenter: Prophet of the New Life**) and Simone Weil (**Oppression and Liberty**)

It would also be worthwhile to mention those market socialists who, like anarchists, base their socialism on workers' self-management. Rejecting central planning, they have turned back to the ideas of industrial democracy and market socialism advocated by the likes of Proudhon (although, coming from a Marxist background, they generally fail to mention the link which their central-planning foes stress). Allan Engler (in **Apostles of Greed**) and David Schweickart (in **Against Capitalism** and **After Capitalism**) have provided useful critiques of capitalism and presented a vision of socialism rooted in co-operatively organised workplaces. While retaining an element of government and state in their political ideas, these socialists have placed economic self-management at the heart of their economic vision and, consequently, are closer to anarchism than most socialists.

A.4.4 Are there any Marxist thinkers close to anarchism?

None of the libertarian socialists we highlighted in the last section were Marxists. This is unsurprising as most forms of Marxism are authoritarian. However, this is not the case for all schools of Marxism. There are important sub-branches of Marxism which share the anarchist vision of a self-managed society. These include Council Communism, Situationism and Autonomism. Perhaps significantly, these few Marxist tendencies which are closest to anarchism are, like the branches of anarchism itself, not named after individuals. We will discuss each in turn.

Council Communism was born in the German Revolution of 1919 when Marxists inspired by the example of the Russian soviets and disgusted by the centralism, opportunism and betrayal of the mainstream Marxist social-democrats, drew similar anti-parliamentarian, direct actionist and decentralised conclusions to those held by anarchists since Bakunin. Like Marx's libertarian opponent in the First International, they argued that a federation of workers' councils would form the basis of a socialist society and, consequently, saw the need to build militant workplace organisations to promote their formation. Lenin attacked these movements and their advocates in his diatribe **Left-wing Communism: An Infantile Disorder**, which council communist Herman Gorter demolished in his **An Open Letter to Comrade Lenin**. By 1921, the council communists broke with the Bolshevism that had already effectively expelled them from both the national Communist Parties and the Communist International.

Like the anarchists, they argued that Russia was a state-capitalist party dictatorship and had nothing to do with socialism. And, again like anarchists, the council communists argue that the process of building a new society, like the revolution itself, is either the work of the people themselves or doomed from the start. As with the anarchists, they too saw the Bolshevik take-over of the soviets (like that of the trade unions) as subverting the revolution and beginning the restoration of oppression and exploitation.

To discover more about council communism, the works of Paul Mattick are essential reading. While best known as a writer on Marxist economic theory in such works as **Marx and Keynes**, **Economic Crisis and Crisis Theory** and **Economics, Politics and the Age of Inflation**, Mattick had been a council communist since the German revolution of 1919/1920. His books **Anti-Bolshevik Communism** and **Marxism: The Last Refuge of the Bourgeoisie?** are excellent introductions to his political ideas. Also essential reading are Anton Pannekoek's works. His classic **Workers' Councils** explains council communism from first principles while his **Lenin as Philosopher** dissects Lenin's claims to being a Marxist (Serge Bricianer, **Pannekoek and the Workers' Councils** is the best study of the development of Pannekoek's ideas). In the UK, the militant suffragette Sylvia Pankhurst became a council communist under the impact of the Russian Revolution and, along with anarchists like Guy Aldred, led the opposition to the importation of Leninism into the communist movement there (see Mark Shipway's **Anti-Parliamentary Communism: The Movement for Workers Councils in Britain, 1917-45** for more details of libertarian communism in the UK). Otto Ruhle and Karl Korsch are also important thinkers in this tradition.

Building upon the ideas of council communism, the Situationists developed their ideas in important new directions. Working in the late 1950s and 1960s, they combined council communist ideas with surrealism and other forms of radical art to produce an impressive critique of post-war capitalism. Unlike Castoriadis, whose ideas influenced them, the Situationists continued to view themselves as Marxists, developing Marx's critique of capitalist economy into a critique of capitalist society as alienation had shifted from being located in capitalist production into everyday life. They coined the expression **"The Spectacle"** to describe a social system in which people become alienated from their own lives and played the role of an audience, of spectators. Thus capitalism had turned being into having and now, with the spectacle, it turned having into appearing. They argued that we could not wait for a distant revolution, but rather should liberate ourselves in the here and now, creating events (*"situations"*) which would disrupt the ordinary and normal to jolt people out of their allotted roles within society. A social revolution based on sovereign rank and file assemblies and self-managed councils would be the ultimate "situation" and the aim of all Situationists.

While critical of anarchism, the differences between the two theories are relatively minor and the impact of the Situationists on anarchism cannot be underestimated. Many anarchists embraced their critique of modern capitalist society, their subversion of modern art and culture for revolutionary purposes and call for revolutionising everyday life. Ironically, while Situationism viewed itself as an attempt to transcend traditional forms of Marxism and anarchism, it essentially became subsumed by anarchism. The classic works of Situationism are Guy Debord's **Society of the Spectacle** and Raoul Veneigem's **The Revolution of Everyday Life**. The **Situationist International Anthology** (edited by Ken Knabb) is essential reading for any budding Situationists, as is Knabb's own **Public Secrets**.

Lastly there is Autonomist Marxism. Drawing on the works of council communism, Castoriadis, Situationism and others, it places the class struggle at the heart of its analysis of capitalism. It initially developed in Italy during the 1960s and has many currents, some closer to anarchism than others. While the most famous thinker in the Autonomist tradition is probably Antonio Negri (who coined the wonderful phrase *"money has only one face, that of the boss"* in **Marx Beyond Marx**) his ideas are more traditional Marxist. For an Autonomist whose ideas are closer to anarchism, we need to turn to the US thinker and activist who has written one of the best summaries of Kropotkin's ideas in which he usefully indicates the similarities between anarcho-communism and Autonomist Marxism (*"Kropotkin, Self-valorisation and the Crisis of Marxism,"* **Anarchist Studies**, vol. 2, no. 3). His book **Reading Capital Politically** is an essential text for understanding Autonomism and its history.

For Cleaver, *"autonomist Marxism"* is a generic name for a variety of movements, politics and thinkers who have emphasised the autonomous power of workers – autonomous from capital, obviously, but also from their official organisations (e.g. the trade unions, the political parties) and, moreover, the power of particular groups of working class people to act autonomously from other groups (e.g. women from men). By *"autonomy"* it is meant the ability of working class people to define their own interests and to struggle for them and, critically, to go beyond mere reaction to exploitation and to take the offensive in ways that shape the class struggle and define the future. Thus they place working class power at the centre of their thinking about capitalism, how it develops and its dynamics as well as in the class conflicts within it. This is not limited to just the workplace and just as workers resist the imposition of work inside the factory or office, via slowdowns, strikes and sabotage, so too do the non-waged resist the reduction of their lives to work. For Autonomists, the creation of communism is not something that comes later but is something which is repeatedly created by current developments of new forms of working class self-activity.

The similarities with social anarchism are obvious. Which probably explains why Autonomists spend so much time analysing and quoting Marx to justify their ideas for otherwise other Marxists will follow Lenin's lead on the council communists and label them anarchists and ignore them! For anarchists, all this Marx quoting seems amusing. Ultimately, if Marx really was an Autonomist Marxist then why do Autonomists have to spend so much time re-constructing what Marx "really" meant? Why did he not just say it clearly to begin with? Similarly, why root out (sometimes obscure) quotes and (sometimes passing) comments from Marx to justify your insights? Does something stop being true if Marx did not mention it first? Whatever the insights of Autonomism its Marxism will drag it backwards by rooting its politics in the texts of two long dead Germans. Like the surreal debate between Trotsky and Stalin in the 1920s over *"Socialism in One Country"* conducted by means of Lenin quotes, all that will be proved is not whether a given idea is right but simply that the mutually agreed authority figure (Lenin or Marx) may have held it. Thus anarchists suggest that Autonomists practice some autonomy when it comes to Marx and Engels.

Other libertarian Marxists close to anarchism include Erich Fromm and Wilhelm Reich. Both tried to combine Marx with Freud to produce a radical analysis of capitalism and the personality disorders it causes. Erich Fromm, in such books as **The Fear of Freedom**, **Man for Himself**, **The Sane Society** and **To Have or To Be?** developed a powerful and insightful analysis of capitalism which discussed how it shaped the individual and built psychological barriers to freedom and authentic living. His works discuss many important topics, including ethics, the authoritarian personality (what causes it and how to change it), alienation, freedom, individualism and what a good society would be like.

Fromm's analysis of capitalism and the *"having"* mode of life are incredibly insightful, especially in context with today's consumerism. For Fromm, the way we live, work and organise together influence how we develop, our health (mental and physical) and our happiness, more than we suspect. He questions the sanity of a society which covets property over humanity and adheres to theories of submission and domination rather than self-determination and self-actualisation. His scathing indictment of modern capitalism shows

that it is the main source of the isolation and alienation prevalent today. Alienation, for Fromm, is at the heart of the system (whether private or state capitalism). We are happy to the extent that we realise ourselves and for this to occur our society must value the human over the inanimate (property).

Fromm rooted his ideas in a humanistic interpretation of Marx, rejecting Leninism and Stalinism as an authoritarian corruption of his ideas (*"the destruction of socialism ... began with Lenin."*). Moreover, he stressed the need for a decentralised and libertarian form of socialism, arguing that the anarchists had been right to question Marx's preferences for states and centralisation. As he put it, the *"errors of Marx and Engels ... [and] their centralistic orientation, were due to the fact they were much more rooted in the middle-class tradition of the eighteenth and nineteenth centuries, both psychologically and intellectually, than men like Fourier, Owen, Proudhon and Kropotkin."* As the *"contradiction"* in Marx between *"the principles of centralisation and decentralisation,"* for Fromm *"Marx and Engels were much more 'bourgeois' thinkers than were men like Proudhon, Bakunin, Kropotkin and Landauer. Paradoxical as it sounds, the Leninist development of Socialism represented a regression to the bourgeois concepts of the state and of political power, rather than the new socialist concept as it was expressed so much clearer by Owen, Proudhon and others."* [**The Sane Society**, p. 265, p. 267 and p. 259] Fromm's Marxism, therefore, was fundamentally of a libertarian and humanist type and his insights of profound importance for anyone interested in changing society for the better.

Wilheim Reich, like Fromm, set out to elaborate a social psychology based on both Marxism and psychoanalysis. For Reich, sexual repression led to people amenable to authoritarianism and happy to subject themselves to authoritarian regimes. While he famously analysed Nazism in this way (in **The Mass Psychology of Fascism**, his insights also apply to other societies and movements (it is no co-incidence, for example, that the religious right in America oppose pre-martial sex and use scare tactics to get teenagers to associate it with disease, dirt and guilt).

His argument is that due to sexual repression we develop what he called *"character armour"* which internalises our oppressions and ensures that we can function in a hierarchical society. This social conditioning is produced by the patriarchal family and its net results is a powerful reinforcement and perpetuation of the dominant ideology and the mass production of individuals with obedience built into them, individuals ready to accept the authority of teacher, priest, employer and politician as well as to endorse the prevailing social structure. This explains how individuals and groups can support movements and institutions which exploit or oppress them. In other words, act think, feel and act against themselves and, moreover, can internalise their own oppression to such a degree that they may even seek to defend their subordinate position.

Thus, for Reich, sexual repression produces an individual who is adjusted to the authoritarian order and who will submit to it in spite of all misery and degradation it causes them. The net result is fear of freedom, and a conservative, reactionary mentality. Sexual repression aids political power, not only through the process which makes the mass individual passive and unpolitical, but also by creating in their character structure an interest in actively supporting the authoritarian order.

While his uni-dimensional focus on sex is misplaced, his analysis of how we internalise our oppression in order to survive under hierarchy is important for understanding why so many of the most oppressed people seem to love their social position and those who rule over them. Understanding this collective character structure and how it forms also provides humanity with new means of transcending such obstacles to social change. Only by an awareness of how people's character structure prevents them from becoming aware of their real interests can it be combated and social self-emancipation assured.

Maurice Brinton's **The Irrational in Politics** is an excellent short introduction to Reich's ideas which links their insights to libertarian socialism.

A.5

What are some examples of "Anarchy in Action"?

Anarchism, more than anything else, is about the efforts of millions of revolutionaries changing the world in the last two centuries. Here we will discuss some of the high points of this movement, all of them of a profoundly anti-capitalist nature.

Anarchism **is** about radically changing the world, not just making the present system less inhuman by encouraging the anarchistic tendencies within it to grow and develop. While no purely anarchist revolution has taken place yet, there have been numerous ones with a highly anarchist character and level of participation. And while these have **all** been destroyed, in each case it has been at the hands of outside force brought against them (backed either by Communists or Capitalists), not because of any internal problems in anarchism itself. These revolutions, despite their failure to survive in the face of overwhelming force, have been both an inspiration for anarchists and proof that anarchism is a viable social theory and can be practised on a large scale.

What these revolutions share is the fact they are, to use Proudhon's term, a **"revolution from below"** – they were examples of *"collective activity, of popular spontaneity."* It is only a transformation of society from the bottom up by the action of the oppressed themselves that can create a free society. As Proudhon asked, *"[w]hat serious and lasting Revolution was not made from below, by the people?"* For this reason an anarchist is a *"revolutionary from below."* Thus the social revolutions and mass movements we discuss in this section are examples of popular self-activity and self-liberation (as Proudhon put it in 1848, *"the proletariat must emancipate itself"*). [quoted by George Woodcock, **Pierre-Joseph Proudhon: A Biography**, p. 143 and p. 125] All anarchists echo Proudhon's idea of revolutionary change from below, the creation of a new society by the actions of the oppressed themselves. Bakunin, for example, argued that anarchists are *"foes … of all State organisations as such, and believe that the people can only be happy and free, when, organised from below by means of*

its own autonomous and completely free associations, without the supervision of any guardians, it will create its own life." [**Marxism, Freedom and the State**, p. 63] In section J.7 we discuss what anarchists think a social revolution is and what it involves.

Many of these revolutions and revolutionary movements are relatively unknown to non-anarchists. Most people will have heard of the Russian revolution but few will know of the popular movements which were its life-blood before the Bolsheviks seized power or the role that the anarchists played in it. Few will have heard of the Paris Commune, the Italian factory occupations or the Spanish collectives. This is unsurprising for, as Herbert Read notes, history *"is of two kinds – a record of events that take place publicly, that make the headlines in the newspapers and get embodied in official records – we might call this overground history"* but *"taking place at the same time, preparing for these public events, anticipating them, is another kind of history, that is not embodied in official records, an invisible underground history."* [quoted by William R. McKercher, **Freedom and Authority**, p. 155] Almost by definition, popular movements and revolts are part of *"underground history"*, the social history which gets ignored in favour of elite history, the accounts of the kings, queens, politicians and wealthy whose fame is the product of the crushing of the many.

This means our examples of "anarchy in action" are part of what the Russian anarchist Voline called *"The Unknown Revolution."* Voline used that expression as the title of his classic account of the Russian revolution he was an active participant of. He used it to refer to the rarely acknowledged independent, creative actions of the people themselves. As Voline put it, *"it is not known how to study a revolution"* and most historians *"mistrust and ignore those developments which occur silently in the depths of the revolution … at best, they accord them a few words in passing … [Yet] it is precisely these hidden facts which are important, and which throw a true light on the events under consideration and on the period."* [**The Unknown Revolution**, p. 19] Anarchism, based as it is on revolution from below, has contributed considerably to both the **"underground history"** and the **"unknown revolution"** of the past few centuries and this section of the FAQ will shed some light on its achievements.

It is important to point out that these examples are of wide-scale social experiments and do not imply that we ignore the undercurrent of anarchist practice which exists in everyday life, even under capitalism. Both Peter Kropotkin (in **Mutual Aid**) and Colin Ward (in **Anarchy in Action**) have documented the many ways in which ordinary people, usually unaware of anarchism, have worked together as equals to meet their common interests. As Colin Ward argues, *"an anarchist society, a society which organises itself without authority, is always in existence, like a seed beneath the snow, buried under the weight of the state and its bureaucracy, capitalism and its waste, privilege and its injustices, nationalism and its suicidal loyalties, religious differences and their superstitious separatism."* [**Anarchy in Action**, p. 14]

Anarchism is not only about a future society, it is also about the social struggle happening today. It is not a condition but a process, which we create by our self-activity and self-liberation.

By the 1960's, however, many commentators were writing off the anarchist movement as a thing of the past. Not only had fascism finished off European anarchist movements in the years before and during the war, but in the post-war period these movements were prevented from recovering by the capitalist West on one hand and the Leninist East on the other. Over the same period of time, anarchism had been repressed in the US, Latin America, China, Korea (where a social revolution with anarchist content was put down before the Korean War), and Japan. Even in the one or two countries that escaped the worst of the repression, the combination of the Cold War and international isolation saw libertarian unions like the Swedish SAC become reformist.

But the 60's were a decade of new struggle, and all over the world the 'New Left' looked to anarchism as well as elsewhere for its ideas. Many of the prominent figures of the massive explosion of May 1968 in France considered themselves anarchists. Although these movements themselves degenerated, those coming out of them kept the idea alive and began to construct new movements. The death of Franco in 1975 saw a massive rebirth of anarchism in Spain, with up to 500,000 people attending the CNT's first post-Franco rally. The return to a limited democracy in some South American countries in the late 70's and 80's saw a growth in anarchism there. Finally, in the late 80's it was anarchists who struck the first blows against the Leninist USSR, with the first protest march since 1928 being held in Moscow by anarchists in 1987.

Today the anarchist movement, although still weak, organises tens of thousands of revolutionaries in many countries. Spain, Sweden and Italy all have libertarian union movements organising some 250,000 between them. Most other European countries have several thousand active anarchists. Anarchist groups have appeared for the first time in other countries, including Nigeria and Turkey. In South America the movement has recovered massively. A contact sheet circulated by the Venezuelan anarchist group **Corrio A** lists over 100 organisations in just about every country.

Perhaps the recovery is slowest in North America, but there, too, all the libertarian organisations seem to be undergoing significant growth. As this growth accelerates, many more examples of anarchy in action will be created and more and more people will take part in anarchist organisations and activities, making this part of the FAQ less and less important.

However, it is essential to highlight mass examples of anarchism working on a large scale in order to avoid the specious accusation of "utopianism." As history is written by the winners, these examples of anarchy in action are often hidden from view in obscure books. Rarely are they mentioned in the schools and universities (or if mentioned, they are distorted). Needless to say, the few examples we give are just that, a few.

Anarchism has a long history in many countries, and we cannot attempt to document every example, just those we consider to be important. We are also sorry if the examples seem Eurocentric. We have, due to space and time considerations, had to ignore the syndicalist revolt (1910 to 1914) and the shop steward movement (1917-21) in Britain, Germany (1919-21), Portugal (1974), the Mexican revolution, anarchists in the Cuban revolution, the struggle in Korea against Japanese (then US and Russian) imperialism during and after the Second World War, Hungary (1956), the "the refusal of work" revolt in the late 1960's (particularly in "the hot Autumn" in Italy, 1969), the UK miner's strike (1984-85), the struggle against the Poll Tax in Britain (1988-92), the strikes in France in 1986 and 1995, the Italian COBAS movement in the 80's and 90's, the popular assemblies and self-managed occupied workplaces during the Argentine revolt at the start of the 21st century and numerous other major struggles that have involved anarchist ideas of self-management (ideas that usually develop from the movement themselves, without anarchists necessarily playing a major, or "leading", role).

For anarchists, revolutions and mass struggles are **"festivals of the oppressed,"** when ordinary people start to act for themselves and change both themselves and the world.

A.5.1
The Paris Commune

The Paris Commune of 1871 played an important role in the development of both anarchist ideas and the movement. As Bakunin commented at the time,

> "revolutionary socialism [i.e. anarchism] has just attempted its first striking and practical demonstration in the Paris Commune ... [It] show[ed] to all enslaved peoples (and are there any masses that are not slaves?) the only road to emancipation and health; Paris inflict[ed] a mortal blow upon the political traditions of bourgeois radicalism and [gave] a real basis to revolutionary socialism." [**Bakunin on Anarchism**, pp. 263-4]

The Paris Commune was created after France was defeated by Prussia in the Franco-Prussian war. The French government tried to send in troops to regain the Parisian National Guard's cannon to prevent it from falling into the hands of the population. "Learning that the Versailles soldiers were trying to seize the cannon," recounted participant Louise Michel, "men and women of Montmartre swarmed up the Butte in surprise manoeuvre. Those people who were climbing up the Butte believed they would die, but they were prepared to pay the price." The soldiers refused to fire on the jeering crowd and turned their weapons on their officers. This was March 18th; the Commune had begun and "the people wakened ... The eighteenth of March could have belonged to the allies of kings, or to foreigners, or to the people. It was the people's." [**Red Virgin: Memoirs of Louise Michel**, p. 64]

In the free elections called by the Parisian National Guard, the citizens of Paris elected a council made up of a majority of Jacobins and Republicans and a minority of socialists (mostly Blanquists – authoritarian socialists – and followers of the anarchist Proudhon). This council proclaimed Paris autonomous and desired to recreate France as a confederation of communes (i.e. communities). Within the Commune, the elected council people were recallable and paid an average wage. In addition, they had to report back to the people who had elected them and were subject to recall by electors if they did not carry out their mandates.

Why this development caught the imagination of anarchists is clear – it has strong similarities with anarchist ideas. In fact, the example of the Paris Commune was in many ways similar to how Bakunin had predicted that a revolution would have to occur – a major city declaring itself autonomous, organising itself, leading by example, and urging the rest of the planet to follow it. (See "Letter to Albert Richards" in **Bakunin on Anarchism**). The Paris Commune began the process of creating a new society, one organised from the bottom up. It was "a blow for the decentralisation of political power." [Voltairine de Cleyre, "The Paris Commune," **Anarchy! An Anthology of Emma Goldman's Mother Earth**, p. 67]

Many anarchists played a role within the Commune – for example Louise Michel, the Reclus brothers, and Eugene Varlin (the latter murdered in the repression afterwards). As for the reforms initiated by the Commune, such as the re-opening of workplaces as co-operatives, anarchists can see their ideas of associated labour beginning to be realised. By May, 43 workplaces were co-operatively run and the Louvre Museum was a munitions factory run by a workers' council. Echoing Proudhon, a meeting of the Mechanics Union and the Association of Metal Workers argued that "our economic emancipation ... can only be obtained through the formation of workers' associations, which alone can transform our position from that of wage earners to that of associates." They instructed their delegates to the Commune's Commission on Labour Organisation to support the following objectives:

"The abolition of the exploitation of man by man, the last vestige of slavery;

"The organisation of labour in mutual associations and inalienable capital."

In this way, they hoped to ensure that "equality must not be an empty word" in the Commune. [**The Paris Commune of 1871: The View from the Left**, Eugene Schulkind (ed.), p. 164] The Engineers Union voted at a meeting on 23rd of April that since the aim of the Commune should be "economic emancipation" it should "organise labour through associations in which there would be joint responsibility" in order "to suppress the exploitation of man by man." [quoted by Stewart Edwards, **The Paris Commune 1871**, pp. 263-4]

As well as self-managed workers' associations, the Communards practised direct democracy in a network of popular clubs, popular organisations similar to the directly democratic neighbourhood assemblies ("sections") of the French Revolution. "People, govern yourselves through your public meetings, through your press" proclaimed the newspaper of one Club. The commune was seen as an expression of the assembled people, for (to quote another Club) "Communal power resides in each arrondissement [neighbourhood] wherever men are assembled who have a horror of the yoke and of servitude." Little wonder that Gustave Courbet, artist friend and follower of Proudhon, proclaimed Paris as "a true paradise ... all social groups have established themselves as federations and are masters of their own fate." [quoted by Martin Phillip Johnson, **The Paradise of Association**, p. 5 and p. 6]

In addition the Commune's "Declaration to the French People" echoed many key anarchist ideas. It saw the "political unity" of society as being based on "the voluntary association of all local initiatives, the free and spontaneous concourse of all individual energies for the common aim, the well-being, the liberty and the

security of all." [quoted by Edwards, **Op. Cit.**, p. 218] The new society envisioned by the Communards was one based on the "absolute autonomy of the Commune ... assuring to each its integral rights and to each Frenchman the full exercise of his aptitudes, as a man, a citizen and a labourer. The autonomy of the Commune will have for its limits only the equal autonomy of all other communes adhering to the contract; their association must ensure the liberty of France." ["Declaration to the French People", quoted by George Woodcock, **Pierre-Joseph Proudhon: A Biography**, pp. 276-7] With its vision of a confederation of communes, Bakunin was correct to assert that the Paris Commune was "a bold, clearly formulated negation of the State." [**Bakunin on Anarchism**, p. 264]

Moreover, the Commune's ideas on federation obviously reflected the influence of Proudhon on French radical ideas. Indeed, the Commune's vision of a communal France based on a federation of delegates bound by imperative mandates issued by their electors and subject to recall at any moment echoes Proudhon's ideas (Proudhon had argued in favour of the "implementation of the binding mandate" in 1848 [**No Gods, No Masters**, p. 63] and for federation of communes in his work **The Principle of Federation**).

Thus both economically and politically the Paris Commune was heavily influenced by anarchist ideas. Economically, the theory of associated production expounded by Proudhon and Bakunin became consciously revolutionary practice. Politically, in the Commune's call for federalism and autonomy, anarchists see their "future social organisation ... [being] carried out from the bottom up, by the free association or federation of workers, starting with associations, then going into the communes, the regions, the nations, and, finally, culminating in a great international and universal federation." [Bakunin, **Op. Cit.**, p. 270]

However, for anarchists the Commune did not go far enough. It did not abolish the state within the Commune, as it had abolished it beyond it. The Communards organised themselves "in a Jacobin manner" (to use Bakunin's cutting term). As Peter Kropotkin pointed out, while "proclaiming the free Commune, the people of Paris proclaimed an essential anarchist principle ... they stopped mid-course" and gave "themselves a Communal Council copied from the old municipal councils." Thus the Paris Commune did not "break with the tradition of the State, of representative government, and it did not attempt to achieve within the Commune that organisation from the simple to the complex it inaugurated by proclaiming the independence and free federation of the Communes." This lead to disaster as the Commune council became "immobilised ... by red tape" and lost "the sensitivity that comes from continued contact with the masses ... Paralysed by their distancing from the revolutionary centre – the people – they themselves paralysed the popular initiative." [**Words of a Rebel**, p. 97, p. 93 and p. 97]

In addition, its attempts at economic reform did not go far enough, making no attempt to turn all workplaces into co-operatives (i.e. to expropriate capital) and forming associations of these co-operatives to co-ordinate and support each other's economic activities. Paris, stressed Voltairine de Cleyre, "failed to strike at economic tyranny, and so came of what it could have achieved" which was a "free community whose economic affairs shall be arranged by the groups of actual producers and distributors, eliminating the useless and *harmful element now in possession of the world's capital."* [**Op. Cit.**, p. 67] As the city was under constant siege by the French army, it is understandable that the Communards had other things on their minds. However, for Kropotkin such a position was a disaster:

> *"They treated the economic question as a secondary one, which would be attended to later on, **after** the triumph of the Commune ... But the crushing defeat which soon followed, and the blood-thirsty revenge taken by the middle class, proved once more that the triumph of a popular Commune was materially impossible without a parallel triumph of the people in the economic field."* [**Op. Cit.**, p. 74]

Anarchists drew the obvious conclusions, arguing that *"if no central government was needed to rule the independent Communes, if the national Government is thrown overboard and national unity is obtained by free federation, then a central **municipal** Government becomes equally useless and noxious. The same federative principle would do within the Commune."* [Kropotkin, **Evolution and Environment**, p. 75] Instead of abolishing the state within the commune by organising federations of directly democratic mass assemblies, like the Parisian "sections" of the revolution of 1789-93 (see Kropotkin's **Great French Revolution** for more on these), the Paris Commune kept representative government and suffered for it. *"Instead of acting for themselves ... the people, confiding in their governors, entrusted them the charge of taking the initiative. This was the first consequence of the inevitable result of elections."* The council soon became *"the greatest obstacle to the revolution"* thus proving the *"political axiom that a government cannot be revolutionary."* [**Anarchism**, p. 240, p. 241 and p. 249]

The council become more and more isolated from the people who elected it, and thus more and more irrelevant. And as its irrelevance grew, so did its authoritarian tendencies, with the Jacobin majority creating a *"Committee of Public Safety"* to *"defend"* (by terror) the "revolution." The Committee was opposed by the libertarian socialist minority and was, fortunately, ignored in practice by the people of Paris as they defended their freedom against the French army, which was attacking them in the name of capitalist civilisation and "liberty." On May 21st, government troops entered the city, followed by seven days of bitter street fighting. Squads of soldiers and armed members of the bourgeoisie roamed the streets, killing and maiming at will. Over 25,000 people were killed in the street fighting, many murdered after they had surrendered, and their bodies dumped in mass graves. As a final insult, **Sacré Coeur** was built by the bourgeoisie on the birth place of the Commune, the Butte of Montmartre, to atone for the radical and atheist revolt which had so terrified them.

For anarchists, the lessons of the Paris Commune were threefold. Firstly, a decentralised confederation of communities is the necessary political form of a free society (*"**This was the form that the social revolution must take** – the independent commune."* [Kropotkin, **Op. Cit.**, p. 163]). Secondly, *"there is no more reason for a government inside a Commune than for government above the Commune."* This means that an anarchist community will be based on a confederation of neighbourhood and workplace assemblies freely co-operating together. Thirdly, it is critically important to

unify political and economic revolutions into a **social** revolution. *"They tried to consolidate the Commune first and put off the social revolution until later, whereas the only way to proceed was **to consolidate the Commune by means of the social revolution!**"* [Peter Kropotkin, **Words of a Rebel**, p. 97]

For more anarchist perspectives on the Paris Commune see Kropotkin's essay *"The Paris Commune"* in **Words of a Rebel** (and **The Anarchist Reader**) and Bakunin's *"The Paris Commune and the Idea of the State"* in **Bakunin on Anarchism**.

A.5.2
The Haymarket Martyrs

May 1st is a day of special significance for the labour movement. While it has been hijacked in the past by the Stalinist bureaucracy in the Soviet Union and elsewhere, the labour movement festival of May Day is a day of world-wide solidarity. A time to remember past struggles and demonstrate our hope for a better future. A day to remember that an injury to one is an injury to all.

The history of Mayday is closely linked with the anarchist movement and the struggles of working people for a better world. Indeed, it originated with the execution of four anarchists in Chicago in 1886 for organising workers in the fight for the eight-hour day. Thus May Day is a product of *"**anarchy in action**"* – of the struggle of working people using direct action in labour unions to change the world.

It began in the 1880s in the USA. In 1884, the **Federation of Organised Trades and Labor Unions of the United States and Canada** (created in 1881, it changed its name in 1886 to the **American Federation of Labor**) passed a resolution which asserted that *"eight hours shall constitute a legal day's work from and after May 1, 1886, and that we recommend to labour organisations throughout this district that they so direct their laws as to conform to this resolution."* A call for strikes on May 1st, 1886 was made in support of this demand.

In Chicago the anarchists were the main force in the union movement, and partially as a result of their presence, the unions translated this call into strikes on May 1st. The anarchists thought that the eight hour day could only be won through direct action and solidarity. They considered that struggles for reforms, like the eight hour day, were not enough in themselves. They viewed them as only one battle in an ongoing class war that would only end by social revolution and the creation of a free society. It was with these ideas that they organised and fought.

In Chicago alone, 400 000 workers went out and the threat of strike action ensured that more than 45 000 were granted a shorter working day without striking. On May 3, 1886, police fired into a crowd of pickets at the McCormick Harvester Machine Company, killing at least one striker, seriously wounding five or six others, and injuring an undetermined number. Anarchists called for a mass meeting the next day in Haymarket Square to protest the brutality. According to the Mayor, *"nothing had occurred yet, or looked likely to occur to require interference."* However, as the meeting was breaking up a column of 180 police arrived and ordered the meeting to end. At this moment a bomb was thrown into the police ranks, who opened fire on the crowd. How many civilians were wounded or killed by the police was never exactly ascertained, but 7 policemen eventually died (ironically, only one was the victim of the bomb, the rest were a result of the bullets fired by the police [Paul Avrich, **The Haymarket Tragedy**, p. 208]).

A *"reign of terror"* swept over Chicago, and the *"organised banditti and conscienceless brigands of capital suspended the only papers which would give the side of those whom they crammed into prison cells. They have invaded the homes of everyone who has ever known to have raised a voice or sympathised with those who have aught to say against the present system of robbery and oppression ... they have invaded their homes and subjected them and their families to indignities that must be seen to be believed."* [Lucy Parsons, **Liberty, Equality & Solidarity**, p. 53] Meeting halls, union offices, printing shops and private homes were raided (usually without warrants). Such raids into working-class areas allowed the police to round up all known anarchists and other socialists. Many suspects were beaten up and some bribed. *"Make the raids first and look up the law afterwards"* was the public statement of J. Grinnell, the States Attorney, when a question was raised about search warrants. [*"Editor's Introduction"*, **The Autobiographies of the Haymarket Martyrs**, p. 7]

Eight anarchists were put on trial for accessory to murder. No pretence was made that any of the accused had carried out or even planned the bomb. The judge ruled that it was not necessary for the state to identify the actual perpetrator or prove that he had acted under the influence of the accused. The state did not try to establish that the defendants had in any way approved or abetted the act. In fact, only three were present at the meeting when the bomb exploded and one of those, Albert Parsons, was accompanied by his wife and fellow anarchist Lucy and their two small children to the event.

The reason why these eight were picked was because of their anarchism and union organising, as made clear by that State's Attorney when he told the jury that *"Law is on trial. Anarchy is on trial. These men have been selected, picked out by the Grand Jury, and indicted because they were leaders. They are no more guilty than the thousands who follow them. Gentlemen of the jury; convict these men, make examples of them, hang them and you save our institutions, our society."* The jury was selected by a special bailiff, nominated by the State's Attorney and was explicitly chosen to compose of businessmen and a relative of one of the cops killed. The defence was not allowed to present evidence that the special bailiff had publicly claimed *"I am managing this case and I know what I am about. These fellows are going to be hanged as certain as death."* [**Op. Cit.**, p. 8] Not surprisingly, the accused were convicted. Seven were sentenced to death, one to 15 years' imprisonment.

An international campaign resulted in two of the death sentences being commuted to life, but the world wide protest did not stop the US state. Of the remaining five, one (Louis Lingg) cheated the executioner and killed himself on the eve of the execution. The remaining four (Albert Parsons, August Spies, George Engel and Adolph Fischer) were hanged on November 11th 1887. They are known in Labour history as the Haymarket Martyrs. Between 150,000 and 500,000 lined the route taken by the funeral cortege and between 10,000 to 25,000 were estimated to have watched the burial.

In 1889, the American delegation attending the International Socialist congress in Paris proposed that May 1st be adopted as a workers' holiday. This was to commemorate working class struggle and the *"Martyrdom of the Chicago Eight"*. Since then Mayday has became a day for international solidarity. In 1893, the new Governor of Illinois made official what the working class in Chicago and across the world knew all along and pardoned the Martyrs because of their obvious innocence and because *"the trial was not fair."* To this day, no one knows who threw the bomb – the only definite fact is that it was not any of those who were tried for the act: *"Our comrades were not murdered by the state because they had any connection with the bomb-throwing, but because they had been active in organising the wage-slaves of America."* [Lucy Parsons, **Op. Cit.**, p. 142]

The authorities had believed at the time of the trial that such persecution would break the back of the labour movement. As Lucy Parsons, a participant of the events, noted 20 years later, the Haymarket trial *"was a class trial – relentless, vindictive, savage and bloody. By that prosecution the capitalists sought to break the great strike for the eight-hour day which as being successfully inaugurated in Chicago, this city being the stormcentre of that great movement; and they also intended, by the savage manner in which they conducted the trial of these men, to frighten the working class back to their long hours of toil and low wages from which they were attempting to emerge. The capitalistic class imagined they could carry out their hellish plot by putting to an ignominious death the most progressive leaders among the working class of that day. In executing their bloody deed of judicial murder they succeeded, but in arresting the mighty onward movement of the class struggle they utterly failed."* [Lucy Parsons, **Op. Cit.**, p. 128] In the words of August Spies when he addressed the court after he had been sentenced to die:

> *"If you think that by hanging us you can stamp out the labour movement ... the movement from which the downtrodden millions, the millions who toil in misery and want, expect salvation – if this is your opinion, then hang us! Here you will tread on a spark, but there and there, behind you – and in front of you, and everywhere, flames blaze up. It is a subterranean fire. You cannot put it out."* [quoted by Paul Avrich, **Op. Cit.**, p. 287]

At the time and in the years to come, this defiance of the state and capitalism was to win thousands to anarchism, particularly in the US itself. Since the Haymarket event, anarchists have celebrated May Day (on the 1st of May – the reformist unions and labour parties moved its marches to the first Sunday of the month). We do so to show our solidarity with other working class people across the world, to celebrate past and present struggles, to show our power and remind the ruling class of their vulnerability. As Nestor Makhno put it:

> *"That day those American workers attempted, by organising themselves, to give expression to their protest against the iniquitous order of the State and Capital of the propertied ...*

"The workers of Chicago … had gathered to resolve, in common, the problems of their lives and their struggles …

"Today too … the toilers … regard the first of May as the occasion of a get-together when they will concern themselves with their own affairs and consider the matter of their emancipation." [**The Struggle Against the State and Other Essays**, pp. 59-60]

Anarchists stay true to the origins of May Day and celebrate its birth in the direct action of the oppressed. It is a classic example of anarchist principles of direct action and solidarity, *"an historic event of great importance, inasmuch as it was, in the first place, the first time that workers themselves had attempted to get a shorter work day by united, simultaneous action … this strike was the first in the nature of Direct Action on a large scale, the first in America."* [Lucy Parsons, **Op. Cit.**, pp. 139-40] Oppression and exploitation breed resistance and, for anarchists, May Day is an international symbol of that resistance and power – a power expressed in the last words of August Spies, chiselled in stone on the monument to the Haymarket martyrs in Waldheim Cemetery in Chicago:

"The day will come when our silence will be more powerful than the voices you are throttling today."

To understand why the state and business class were so determined to hang the Chicago Anarchists, it is necessary to realise they were considered the leaders of a massive radical union movement. In 1884, the Chicago Anarchists produced the world's first daily anarchist newspaper, the **Chicagoer Arbeiter-Zeiting**. This was written, read, owned and published by the German immigrant working class movement. The combined circulation of this daily plus a weekly (**Vorbote**) and a Sunday edition (**Fackel**) more than doubled, from 13,000 per issues in 1880 to 26,980 in 1886. Anarchist weekly papers existed for other ethnic groups as well (one English, one Bohemian and one Scandinavian).

Anarchists were very active in the Central Labour Union (which included the eleven largest unions in the city) and aimed to make it, in the words of Albert Parsons (one of the Martyrs), *"the embryonic group of the future 'free society.'"* The anarchists were also part of the **International Working People's Association** (also called the **"Black International"**) which had representatives from 26 cities at its founding convention. The I.W.P.A. soon *"made headway among trade unions, especially in the mid-west"* and its ideas of *"direct action of the rank and file"* and of trade unions *"serv[ing] as the instrument of the working class for the complete destruction of capitalism and the nucleus for the formation of a new society"* became known as the **"Chicago Idea"** (an idea which later inspired the **Industrial Workers of the World** which was founded in Chicago in 1905). [*"Editor's Introduction,"* **The Autobiographies of the Haymarket Martyrs**, p. 4]

This idea was expressed in the manifesto issued at the I.W.P.A.'s Pittsburgh Congress of 1883:

"First – Destruction of the existing class rule, by all means, i.e. by energetic, relentless, revolutionary and international action.

"Second – Establishment of a free society based upon co-operative organisation of production.

"Third – Free exchange of equivalent products by and between the productive organisations without commerce and profit-mongery.

"Fourth – Organisation of education on a secular, scientific and equal basis for both sexes.

"Fifth – Equal rights for all without distinction to sex or race.

"Sixth – Regulation of all public affairs by free contracts between autonomous (independent) communes and associations, resting on a federalistic basis." [**Op. Cit.**, p. 42]

In addition to their union organising, the Chicago anarchist movement also organised social societies, picnics, lectures, dances, libraries and a host of other activities. These all helped to forge a distinctly working-class revolutionary culture in the heart of the *"American Dream."* The threat to the ruling class and their system was too great to allow it to continue (particularly with memories of the vast uprising of labour in 1877 still fresh. As in 1886, that revolt was also meet by state violence – see **Strike!** by J. Brecher for details of this strike movement as well as the Haymarket events). Hence the repression, kangaroo court, and the state murder of those the state and capitalist class considered "leaders" of the movement.

For more on the Haymarket Martyrs, their lives and their ideas, **The Autobiographies of the Haymarket Martyrs** is essential reading. Albert Parsons, the only American born Martyr, produced a book which explained what they stood for called **Anarchism: Its Philosophy and Scientific Basis**. Historian Paul Avrich's **The Haymarket Tragedy** is a useful in depth account of the events.

A.5.3 Building the Syndicalist Unions

Just before the turn of the century in Europe, the anarchist movement began to create one of the most successful attempts to apply anarchist organisational ideas in everyday life. This was the building of mass revolutionary unions (also known as syndicalism or anarcho-syndicalism). The syndicalist movement, in the words of a leading French syndicalist militant, was *"a practical schooling in anarchism"* for it was *"a laboratory of economic struggles"* and organised *"along anarchic lines."* By organising workers into *"libertarian organisations,"* the syndicalist unions were creating the *"free associations of free producers"* within capitalism to combat it and, ultimately, replace it. [Fernand Pelloutier, **No Gods, No Masters**, vol. 2, p. 57, p. 55 and p. 56]

While the details of syndicalist organisation varied from country to country, the main lines were the same. Workers should form themselves into unions (or **syndicates**, the French for union).

While organisation by industry was generally the preferred form, craft and trade organisations were also used. These unions were directly controlled by their members and would federate together on an industrial and geographical basis. Thus a given union would be federated with all the local unions in a given town, region and country as well as with all the unions within its industry into a national union (of, say, miners or metal workers). Each union was autonomous and all officials were part-time (and paid their normal wages if they missed work on union business). The tactics of syndicalism were direct action and solidarity and its aim was to replace capitalism by the unions providing the basic framework of the new, free, society.

Thus, for anarcho-syndicalism, *"the trade union is by no means a mere transitory phenomenon bound up with the duration of capitalist society, it is the germ of the Socialist economy of the future, the elementary school of Socialism in general."* The *"economic fighting organisation of the workers"* gives their members *"every opportunity for direct action in their struggles for daily bread, it also provides them with the necessary preliminaries for carrying through the reorganisation of social life on a [libertarian] Socialist plan by them own strength."* [Rudolf Rocker, **Anarcho-Syndicalism**, p. 59 and p. 62] Anarcho-syndicalism, to use the expression of the I.W.W., aims to build the new world in the shell of the old.

In the period from the 1890's to the outbreak of World War I, anarchists built revolutionary unions in most European countries (particularly in Spain, Italy and France). In addition, anarchists in South and North America were also successful in organising syndicalist unions (particularly Cuba, Argentina, Mexico and Brazil). Almost all industrialised countries had some syndicalist movement, although Europe and South America had the biggest and strongest ones. These unions were organised in a confederal manner, from the bottom up, along anarchist lines. They fought with capitalists on a day-to-day basis around the issue of better wages and working conditions and the state for social reforms, but they also sought to overthrow capitalism through the revolutionary general strike.

Thus hundreds of thousands of workers around the world were applying anarchist ideas in everyday life, proving that anarchy was no utopian dream but a practical method of organising on a wide scale. That anarchist organisational techniques encouraged member participation, empowerment and militancy, and that they also successfully fought for reforms and promoted class consciousness, can be seen in the growth of anarcho-syndicalist unions and their impact on the labour movement. The Industrial Workers of the World, for example, still inspires union activists and has, throughout its long history, provided many union songs and slogans.

However, as a mass movement, syndicalism effectively ended by the 1930s. This was due to two factors. Firstly, most of the syndicalist unions were severely repressed just after World War I. In the immediate post-war years they reached their height. This wave of militancy was known as the "red years" in Italy, where it attained its high point with factory occupations (see section A.5.5). But these years also saw the destruction of these unions in country after county. In the USA, for example, the I.W.W. was crushed by a wave of repression backed whole-heartedly by the media, the state, and the capitalist class. Europe saw capitalism go on the offensive with a new weapon – fascism. Fascism arose (first in Italy

and, most infamously, in Germany) as an attempt by capitalism to physically smash the organisations the working class had built. This was due to radicalism that had spread across Europe in the wake of the war ending, inspired by the example of Russia. Numerous near revolutions had terrified the bourgeoisie, who turned to fascism to save their system.

In country after country, anarchists were forced to flee into exile, vanish from sight, or became victims of assassins or concentration camps after their (often heroic) attempts at fighting fascism failed. In Portugal, for example, the 100,000 strong anarcho-syndicalist CGT union launched numerous revolts in the late 1920s and early 1930s against fascism. In January 1934, the CGT called for a revolutionary general strike which developed into a five day insurrection. A state of siege was declared by the state, which used extensive force to crush the rebellion. The CGT, whose militants had played a prominent and courageous role in the insurrection, was completely smashed and Portugal remained a fascist state for the next 40 years. [Phil Mailer, **Portugal: The Impossible Revolution**, pp. 72-3] In Spain, the CNT (the most famous anarcho-syndicalist union) fought a similar battle. By 1936, it claimed one and a half million members. As in Italy and Portugal, the capitalist class embraced fascism to save their power from the dispossessed, who were becoming confident of their power and their right to manage their own lives (see section A.5.6).

As well as fascism, syndicalism also faced the negative influence of Leninism. The apparent success of the Russian revolution led many activists to turn to authoritarian politics, particularly in English speaking countries and, to a lesser extent, France. Such notable syndicalist activists as Tom Mann in England, William Gallacher in Scotland and William Foster in the USA became Communists (the last two, it should be noted, became Stalinist). Moreover, Communist parties deliberately undermined the libertarian unions, encouraging fights and splits (as, for example, in the I.W.W.). After the end of the Second World War, the Stalinists finished off what fascism had started in Eastern Europe and destroyed the anarchist and syndicalist movements in such places as Bulgaria and Poland. In Cuba, Castro also followed Lenin's example and did what the Batista and Machado dictatorship's could not, namely smash the influential anarchist and syndicalist movements (see Frank Fernandez's **Cuban Anarchism** for a history of this movement from its origins in the 1860s to the 21st century).

So by the start of the second world war, the large and powerful anarchist movements of Italy, Spain, Poland, Bulgaria and Portugal had been crushed by fascism (but not, we must stress, without a fight). When necessary, the capitalists supported authoritarian states in order to crush the labour movement and make their countries safe for capitalism. Only Sweden escaped this trend, where the syndicalist union the SAC is still organising workers. It is, in fact, like many other syndicalist unions active today, growing as workers turn away from bureaucratic unions whose leaders seem more interested in protecting their privileges and cutting deals with management than defending their members. In France, Spain and Italy and elsewhere, syndicalist unions are again on the rise, showing that anarchist ideas are applicable in everyday life.

Finally, it must be stressed that syndicalism has its roots in the ideas of the earliest anarchists and, consequently, was not invented in the

1890s. It is true that development of syndicalism came about, in part, as a reaction to the disastrous "propaganda by deed" period, in which individual anarchists assassinated government leaders in attempts to provoke a popular uprising and in revenge for the mass murders of the Communards and other rebels (see section A.2.18 for details). But in response to this failed and counterproductive campaign, anarchists went back to their roots and to the ideas of Bakunin. Thus, as recognised by the likes of Kropotkin and Malatesta, syndicalism was simply a return to the ideas current in the libertarian wing of the First International.

Thus we find Bakunin arguing that *"it is necessary to organise the power of the proletariat. But this organisation must be the work of the proletariat itself … Organise, constantly organise the international militant solidarity of the workers, in every trade and country, and remember that however weak you are as isolated individuals or districts, you will constitute a tremendous, invincible power by means of universal co-operation."* As one American activist commented, this is *"the same militant spirit that breathes now in the best expressions of the Syndicalist and I.W.W. movements"* both of which express *"a strong world wide revival of the ideas for which Bakunin laboured throughout his life."* [Max Baginski, **Anarchy! An Anthology of Emma Goldman's Mother Earth**, p. 71] As with the syndicalists, Bakunin stressed the *"organisation of trade sections, their federation … bear in themselves the living germs of **the new social order,** which is to replace the bourgeois world. They are creating not only the ideas but also the facts of the future itself."* [quoted by Rudolf Rocker, **Op. Cit.**, p. 50]

Such ideas were repeated by other libertarians. Eugene Varlin, whose role in the Paris Commune ensured his death, advocated a socialism of associations, arguing in 1870 that syndicates were the *"natural elements"* for the rebuilding of society: *"it is they that can easily be transformed into producer associations; it is they that can put into practice the retooling of society and the organisation of production."* [quoted by Martin Phillip Johnson, **The Paradise of Association**, p. 139] As we discussed in section A.5.2, the Chicago Anarchists held similar views, seeing the labour movement as both the means of achieving anarchy and the framework of the free society. As Lucy Parsons (the wife of Albert) put it *"we hold that the granges, trade-unions, Knights of Labour assemblies, etc., are the embryonic groups of the ideal anarchistic society … "* [contained in Albert R. Parsons, **Anarchism: Its Philosophy and Scientific Basis**, p. 110] These ideas fed into the revolutionary unionism of the I.W.W. As one historian notes, the *"proceedings of the I.W.W.'s inaugural convention indicate that the participants were not only aware of the 'Chicago Idea' but were conscious of a continuity between their efforts and the struggles of the Chicago anarchists to initiate industrial unionism."* The Chicago idea represented *"the earliest American expression of syndicalism."* [Salvatore Salerno, **Red November, Black November**, p. 71]

Thus, syndicalism and anarchism are not differing theories but, rather, different interpretations of the same ideas (see for a fuller discussion section H.2.8). While not all syndicalists are anarchists (some Marxists have proclaimed support for syndicalism) and not all anarchists are syndicalists (see section J.3.9 for a discussion why), all social anarchists see the need for taking part in the labour and other popular movements and encouraging libertarian forms of organisation and struggle within them. By doing this, inside and outside of syndicalist unions, anarchists are showing the validity of our ideas. For, as Kropotkin stressed, the *"next revolution must from its inception bring about the seizure of the entire social wealth by the workers in order to transform it into common property. This revolution can succeed only through the workers, only if the urban and rural workers everywhere carry out this objective themselves. To that end, they must initiate their own action in the period **before the revolution**; this can happen only if there is a strong **workers' organisation."*** [**Selected Writings on Anarchism and Revolution**, p. 20] Such popular self-managed organisations cannot be anything but *"anarchy in action."*

A.5.4 Anarchists in the Russian Revolution

The Russian revolution of 1917 saw a huge growth in anarchism in that country and many experiments in anarchist ideas. However, in popular culture the Russian Revolution is seen not as a mass movement by ordinary people struggling towards freedom but as the means by which Lenin imposed his dictatorship on Russia. The truth is radically different. The Russian Revolution was a mass movement from below in which many different currents of ideas existed and in which millions of working people (workers in the cities and towns as well as peasants) tried to transform their world into a better place. Sadly, those hopes and dreams were crushed under the dictatorship of the Bolshevik party – first under Lenin, later under Stalin.

The Russian Revolution, like most history, is a good example of the maxim "history is written by those who win." Most capitalist histories of the period between 1917 and 1921 ignore what the anarchist Voline called *"the unknown revolution"* – the revolution called forth from below by the actions of ordinary people. Leninist accounts, at best, praise this autonomous activity of workers so long as it coincides with their own party line but radically condemn it (and attribute it with the basest motives) as soon as it strays from that line. Thus Leninist accounts will praise the workers when they move ahead of the Bolsheviks (as in the spring and summer of 1917) but will condemn them when they oppose Bolshevik policy once the Bolsheviks are in power. At worse, Leninist accounts portray the movement and struggles of the masses as little more than a backdrop to the activities of the vanguard party.

For anarchists, however, the Russian Revolution is seen as a classic example of a social revolution in which the self-activity of working people played a key role. In their soviets, factory committees and other class organisations, the Russian masses were trying to transform society from a class-ridden, hierarchical statist regime into one based on liberty, equality and solidarity. As such, the initial months of the Revolution seemed to confirm Bakunin's prediction that the *"future social organisation must be made solely from the bottom upwards, by the free associations or federations of workers, firstly in their unions, then in the communes, regions, nations and finally in a great federation, international and universal."* [**Michael Bakunin: Selected Writings**, p. 206] The soviets and factory committees expressed concretely Bakunin's ideas and Anarchists played an important role in the struggle.

The initial overthrow of the Tsar came from the direct action of the masses. In February 1917, the women of Petrograd erupted in bread riots. On February 18th, the workers of the Putilov Works in Petrograd went on strike. By February 22nd, the strike had spread to other factories. Two days later, 200 000 workers were on strike and by February 25th the strike was virtually general. The same day also saw the first bloody clashes between protestors and the army. The turning point came on the 27th, when some troops went over to the revolutionary masses, sweeping along other units. This left the government without its means of coercion, the Tsar abdicated and a provisional government was formed.

So spontaneous was this movement that all the political parties were left behind. This included the Bolsheviks, with the *"Petrograd organisation of the Bolsheviks oppos[ing] the calling of strikes precisely on the eve of the revolution destined to overthrow the Tsar. Fortunately, the workers ignored the Bolshevik 'directives' and went on strike anyway ... Had the workers followed its guidance, it is doubtful that the revolution would have occurred when it did."* [Murray Bookchin, **Post-Scarcity Anarchism**, p. 123]

The revolution carried on in this vein of direct action from below until the new, "socialist" state was powerful enough to stop it.

For the Left, the end of Tsarism was the culmination of years of effort by socialists and anarchists everywhere. It represented the progressive wing of human thought overcoming traditional oppression, and as such was duly praised by leftists around the world. However, **in** Russia things were progressing. In the workplaces and streets and on the land, more and more people became convinced that abolishing feudalism politically was **not** enough. The overthrow of the Tsar made little real difference if feudal exploitation still existed in the economy, so workers started to seize their workplaces and peasants, the land. All across Russia, ordinary people started to build their own organisations, unions, co-operatives, factory committees and councils (or "soviets" in Russian). These organisations were initially organised in anarchist fashion, with recallable delegates and being federated with each other.

Needless to say, all the political parties and organisations played a role in this process. The two wings of the Marxist social-democrats were active (the Mensheviks and the Bolsheviks), as were the Social Revolutionaries (a populist peasant based party) and the anarchists. The anarchists participated in this movement, encouraging all tendencies to self-management and urging the overthrow of the provisional government. They argued that it was necessary to transform the revolution from a purely political one into an economic/social one. Until the return of Lenin from exile, they were the only political tendency who thought along those lines.

Lenin convinced his party to adopt the slogan *"All Power to the Soviets"* and push the revolution forward. This meant a sharp break with previous Marxist positions, leading one ex-Bolshevik turned Menshevik to comment that Lenin had *"made himself a candidate for one European throne that has been vacant for thirty years – the throne of Bakunin!"* [quoted by Alexander Rabinowitch, **Prelude to Revolution**, p. 40] The Bolsheviks now turned to winning mass support, championing direct action and supporting the radical

actions of the masses, policies in the past associated with anarchism (*"the Bolsheviks launched ... slogans which until then had been particularly and insistently been voiced by the Anarchists."* [Voline, **The Unknown Revolution**, p. 210]). Soon they were winning more and more votes in the soviet and factory committee elections. As Alexander Berkman argues, the *"Anarchist mottoes proclaimed by the Bolsheviks did not fail to bring results. The masses relied to their flag."* [**What is Anarchism?**, p. 120]

The anarchists were also influential at this time. Anarchists were particularly active in the movement for workers self-management of production which existed around the factory committees (see M. Brinton, **The Bolsheviks and Workers Control** for details). They were arguing for workers and peasants to expropriate the owning class, abolish all forms of government and re-organise society from the bottom up using their own class organisations – the soviets, the factory committees, co-operatives and so on. They could also influence the direction of struggle. As Alexander Rabinowitch (in his study of the July uprising of 1917) notes:

> *"At the rank-and-file level, particularly within the [Petrograd] garrison and at the Kronstadt naval base, there was in fact very little to distinguish Bolshevik from Anarchist ... The Anarchist-Communists and the Bolsheviks competed for the support of the same uneducated, depressed, and dissatisfied elements of the population, and the fact is that in the summer of 1917, the Anarchist-Communists, with the support they enjoyed in a few important factories and regiments, possessed an undeniable capacity to influence the course of events. Indeed, the Anarchist appeal was great enough in some factories and military units to influence the actions of the Bolsheviks themselves."* [**Op. Cit.**, p. 64]

Indeed, one leading Bolshevik stated in June, 1917 (in response to a rise in anarchist influence), *"[b]y fencing ourselves off from the Anarchists, we may fence ourselves off from the masses."* [quoted by Alexander Rabinowitch, **Op. Cit.**, p. 102]

The anarchists operated with the Bolsheviks during the October Revolution which overthrew the provisional government. But things changed once the authoritarian socialists of the Bolshevik party had seized power. While both anarchists and Bolsheviks used many of the same slogans, there were important differences between the two. As Voline argued, *"[f]rom the lips and pens of the Anarchists, those slogans were sincere and concrete, for they corresponded to their principles and called for action entirely in conformity with such principles. But with the Bolsheviks, the same slogans meant practical solutions totally different from those of the libertarians and did not tally with the ideas which the slogans appeared to express."* [**The Unknown Revolution**, p. 210]

Take, for example, the slogan *"All power to the Soviets."* For anarchists it meant exactly that – organs for the working class to run society directly, based on mandated, recallable delegates. For the Bolsheviks, that slogan was simply the means for a Bolshevik government to be formed over and above the soviets. The difference is important, *"for the Anarchists declared, if 'power' really should belong to the soviets, it could not belong to the Bolshevik party, and if it should belong to that Party, as the Bolsheviks envisaged, it could* not belong to the soviets." [Voline, **Op. Cit.**, p. 213] Reducing the soviets to simply executing the decrees of the central (Bolshevik) government and having their All-Russian Congress be able to recall the government (i.e. those with **real** power) does not equal "all power," quite the reverse.

Similarly with the term *"workers' control of production."* Before the October Revolution Lenin saw *"workers' control"* purely in terms of the *"universal, all-embracing workers' control over the capitalists."* [**Will the Bolsheviks Maintain Power?**, p. 52] He did not see it in terms of workers' management of production itself (i.e. the abolition of wage labour) via federations of factory committees. Anarchists and the workers' factory committees did. As S.A. Smith correctly notes, Lenin used *"the term ['workers' control'] in a very different sense from that of the factory committees."* In fact Lenin's *"proposals … [were] thoroughly statist and centralist in character, whereas the practice of the factory committees was essentially local and autonomous."* [**Red Petrograd**, p. 154] For anarchists, *"if the workers' organisations were capable of exercising effective control [over their bosses], then they also were capable of guaranteeing all production. In such an event, private industry could be eliminated quickly but progressively, and replaced by collective industry. Consequently, the Anarchists rejected the vague nebulous slogan of 'control of production.' They advocated **expropriation – progressive, but immediate – of private industry by the organisations of collective production."*** [Voline, **Op. Cit.**, p. 221]

Once in power, the Bolsheviks systematically undermined the popular meaning of workers' control and replaced it with their own, statist conception. *"On three occasions,"* one historian notes, *"in the first months of Soviet power, the [factory] committee leaders sought to bring their model into being. At each point the party leadership overruled them. The result was to vest both managerial **and** control powers in organs of the state which were subordinate to the central authorities, and formed by them."* [Thomas F. Remington, **Building Socialism in Bolshevik Russia**, p. 38] This process ultimately resulted in Lenin arguing for, and introducing, *"one-man management"* armed with *"dictatorial"* power (with the manager appointed from above by the state) in April 1918. This process is documented in Maurice Brinton's **The Bolsheviks and Workers' Control**, which also indicates the clear links between Bolshevik practice and Bolshevik ideology as well as how both differed from popular activity and ideas.

Hence the comments by Russian Anarchist Peter Arshinov:

> *"Another no less important peculiarity is that [the] October [revolution of 1917] has two meanings – that which the working' masses who participated in the social revolution gave it, and with them the Anarchist-Communists, and that which was given it by the political party [the Marxist-Communists] that captured power from this aspiration to social revolution, and which betrayed and stifled all further development. An enormous gulf exists between these two interpretations of October. The October of the workers and peasants is the suppression of the power of the parasite classes in the name of equality and self-management. The Bolshevik October is the conquest of power by the*

> *party of the revolutionary intelligentsia, the installation of its 'State Socialism' and of its 'socialist' methods of governing the masses."* [**The Two Octobers**]

Initially, anarchists had supported the Bolsheviks, since the Bolshevik leaders had hidden their state-building ideology behind support for the soviets (as socialist historian Samuel Farber notes, the anarchists *"had actually been an unnamed coalition partner of the Bolsheviks in the October Revolution."* [**Before Stalinism**, p. 126]). However, this support quickly "withered away" as the Bolsheviks showed that they were, in fact, not seeking true socialism but were instead securing power for themselves and pushing not for collective ownership of land and productive resources but for government ownership. The Bolsheviks, as noted, systematically undermined the workers' control/self-management movement in favour of capitalist-like forms of workplace management based around *"one-man management"* armed with *"dictatorial powers."*

As regards the soviets, the Bolsheviks were systematically undermining what limited independence and democracy they had. In response to the *"great Bolshevik losses in the soviet elections"* during the spring and summer of 1918 *"Bolshevik armed force usually overthrew the results of these provincial elections."* Also, the *"government continually postponed the new general elections to the Petrograd Soviet, the term of which had ended in March 1918. Apparently, the government feared that the opposition parties would show gains."* [Samuel Farber, **Op. Cit.**, p. 24 and p. 22] In the Petrograd elections, the Bolsheviks *"lost the absolute majority in the soviet they had previously enjoyed"* but remained the largest party. However, the results of the Petrograd soviet elections were irrelevant as a *"Bolshevik victory was assured by the numerically quite significant representation now given to trade unions, district soviets, factory-shop committees, district workers conferences, and Red Army and naval units, in which the Bolsheviks had overwhelming strength."* [Alexander Rabinowitch, *"The Evolution of Local Soviets in Petrograd"*, pp. 20-37, **Slavic Review**, Vol. 36, No. 1, p. 36f] In other words, the Bolsheviks had undermined the democratic nature of the soviet by swamping it by their own delegates. Faced with rejection in the soviets, the Bolsheviks showed that for them "soviet power" equalled party power. To stay in power, the Bolsheviks had to destroy the soviets, which they did. The soviet system remained "soviet" in name only. Indeed, from 1919 onwards Lenin, Trotsky and other leading Bolsheviks were admitting that they had created a party dictatorship and, moreover, that such a dictatorship was essential for any revolution (Trotsky supported party dictatorship even after the rise of Stalinism).

The Red Army, moreover, no longer was a democratic organisation. In March of 1918 Trotsky had abolished the election of officers and soldier committees:

> *"the principle of election is politically purposeless and technically inexpedient, and it has been, in practice, abolished by decree."* [**Work, Discipline, Order**]

As Maurice Brinton correctly summarises:

> *"Trotsky, appointed Commissar of Military Affairs after Brest-Litovsk, had rapidly been reorganising the Red Army. The death penalty for disobedience under fire had been*

restored. So, more gradually, had saluting, special forms of address, separate living quarters and other privileges for officers. Democratic forms of organisation, including the election of officers, had been quickly dispensed with." ["The Bolsheviks and Workers' Control", **For Workers' Power**, pp. 336-7]

Unsurprisingly, Samuel Farber notes that *"there is no evidence indicating that Lenin or any of the mainstream Bolshevik leaders lamented the loss of workers' control or of democracy in the soviets, or at least referred to these losses as a retreat, as Lenin declared with the replacement of War Communism by NEP in 1921."* [**Before Stalinism**, p. 44]

Thus after the October Revolution, anarchists started to denounce the Bolshevik regime and call for a ***"Third Revolution"*** which would finally free the masses from all bosses (capitalist or socialist). They exposed the fundamental difference between the rhetoric of Bolshevism (as expressed, for example, in Lenin's **State and Revolution**) with its reality. Bolshevism in power had proved Bakunin's prediction that the *"dictatorship of the proletariat"* would become the *"dictatorship **over** the proletariat"* by the leaders of the Communist Party.

The influence of the anarchists started to grow. As Jacques Sadoul (a French officer) noted in early 1918:

> *"The anarchist party is the most active, the most militant of the opposition groups and probably the most popular … The Bolsheviks are anxious."* [quoted by Daniel Guérin, **Anarchism**, pp. 95-6]

By April 1918, the Bolsheviks began the physical suppression of their anarchist rivals. On April 12th, 1918, the Cheka (the secret police formed by Lenin in December, 1917) attacked anarchist centres in Moscow. Those in other cities were attacked soon after. As well as repressing their most vocal opponents on the left, the Bolsheviks were restricting the freedom of the masses they claimed to be protecting. Democratic soviets, free speech, opposition political parties and groups, self-management in the workplace and on the land – all were destroyed in the name of "socialism." All this happened, we must stress, **before** the start of the Civil War in late May, 1918, which most supporters of Leninism blame for the Bolsheviks' authoritarianism. During the civil war, this process accelerated, with the Bolsheviks' systematically repressing opposition from all quarters – including the strikes and protests of the very class who they claimed was exercising its "dictatorship" while they were in power!

It is important to stress that this process had started well **before** the start of the civil war, confirming anarchist theory that a "workers' state" is a contraction in terms. For anarchists, the Bolshevik substitution of party power for workers power (and the conflict between the two) did not come as a surprise. The state is the delegation of **power** – as such, it means that the idea of a "workers' state" expressing "workers' power" is a logical impossibility. If workers **are** running society then power rests in their hands. If a state exists then power rests in the hands of the handful of people at the top, **not** in the hands of all. The state was designed for minority rule. No state can be an organ of working class (i.e. majority) self-management due to its basic nature,

structure and design. For this reason anarchists have argued for a bottom-up federation of workers' councils as the agent of revolution and the means of managing society after capitalism and the state have been abolished.

As we discuss in section H, the degeneration of the Bolsheviks from a popular working class party into dictators over the working class did not occur by accident. A combination of political ideas and the realities of state power (and the social relationships it generates) could not help but result in such a degeneration. The political ideas of Bolshevism, with its vanguardism, fear of spontaneity and identification of party power with working class power inevitably meant that the party would clash with those whom it claimed to represent. After all, if the party is the vanguard then, automatically, everyone else is a "backward" element. This meant that if the working class resisted Bolshevik policies or rejected them in soviet elections, then the working class was "wavering" and being influenced by "petty-bourgeois" and "backward" elements. Vanguardism breeds elitism and, when combined with state power, dictatorship.

State power, as anarchists have always stressed, means the delegation of power into the hands of a few. This automatically produces a class division in society – those with power and those without. As such, once in power the Bolsheviks were isolated from the working class. The Russian Revolution confirmed Malatesta's argument that a *"government, that is a group of people entrusted with making laws and empowered to use the collective power to oblige each individual to obey them, is already a privileged class and cut off from the people. As any constituted body would do, it will instinctively seek to extend its powers, to be beyond public control, to impose its own policies and to give priority to its special interests. Having been put in a privileged position, the government is already at odds with the people whose strength it disposes of."* [**Anarchy**, p. 34] A highly centralised state such as the Bolsheviks built would reduce accountability to a minimum while at the same time accelerating the isolation of the rulers from the ruled. The masses were no longer a source of inspiration and power, but rather an alien group whose lack of "discipline" (i.e. ability to follow orders) placed the revolution in danger. As one Russian Anarchist argued,

> *"The proletariat is being gradually enserfed by the state. The people are being transformed into servants over whom there has arisen a new class of administrators – a new class born mainly form the womb of the so-called intelligentsia … We do not mean to say … that the Bolshevik party set out to create a new class system. But we do say that even the best intentions and aspirations must inevitably be smashed against the evils inherent in any system of centralised power. The separation of management from labour, the division between administrators and workers flows logically from centralisation. It cannot be otherwise."* [**The Anarchists in the Russian Revolution**, pp. 123-4]

For this reason anarchists, while agreeing that there is an uneven development of political ideas within the working class, reject the idea that "revolutionaries" should take power on behalf of working people. Only when working people actually run society themselves will a revolution be successful. For anarchists, this meant that "[e]ffective emancipation can be achieved only by the **direct, widespread, and independent action ... of the workers themselves,** grouped ... in their own class organisations ... on the basis of concrete action and self-government, **helped but not governed,** by revolutionaries working in the very midst of, and not above the mass and the professional, technical, defence and other branches." [Voline, **Op. Cit.**, p. 197] By substituting party power for workers power, the Russian Revolution had made its first fatal step. Little wonder that the following prediction (from November 1917) made by anarchists in Russia came true:

> "Once their power is consolidated and 'legalised', the Bolsheviks who are ... men of centralist and authoritarian action will begin to rearrange the life of the country and of the people by governmental and dictatorial methods, imposed by the centre. The[y] ... will dictate the will of the party to all Russia, and command the whole nation. **Your Soviets and your other local organisations will become little by little, simply executive organs of the will of the central government.** In the place of healthy, constructive work by the labouring masses, in place of free unification from the bottom, we will see the installation of an authoritarian and statist apparatus which would act from above and set about wiping out everything that stood in its way with an iron hand." [quoted by Voline, **Op. Cit.**, p. 235]

The so-called "workers' state" could not be participatory or empowering for working class people (as the Marxists claimed) simply because state structures are not designed for that. Created as instruments of minority rule, they cannot be transformed into (nor "new" ones created which are) a means of liberation for the working classes. As Kropotkin put it, Anarchists "maintain that the State organisation, having been the force to which minorities resorted for establishing and organising their power over the masses, cannot be the force which will serve to destroy these privileges." [**Anarchism**, p. 170] In the words of an anarchist pamphlet written in 1918:

> "Bolshevism, day by day and step by step, proves that state power possesses inalienable characteristics; it can change its label, its 'theory', and its servitors, but in essence it merely remains power and despotism in new forms." [quoted by Paul Avrich, "The Anarchists in the Russian Revolution," pp. 341-350, **Russian Review**, vol. 26, issue no. 4, p. 347]

For insiders, the Revolution had died a few months after the Bolsheviks took over. To the outside world, the Bolsheviks and the USSR came to represent "socialism" even as they systematically destroyed the basis of real socialism. By transforming the soviets into state bodies, substituting party power for soviet power, undermining the factory committees, eliminating democracy in the armed forces and workplaces, repressing the political opposition and workers' protests, the Bolsheviks effectively marginalised the working class from its own revolution. Bolshevik ideology and practice were themselves important and sometimes decisive factors in the degeneration of the revolution and the ultimate rise of Stalinism.

As anarchists had predicted for decades previously, in the space of a few months, and before the start of the Civil War, the Bolshevik's "workers' state" had become, like any state, an alien power **over** the working class and an instrument of minority rule (in this case, the rule of the party). The Civil War accelerated this process and soon party dictatorship was introduced (indeed, leading Bolsheviks began arguing that it was essential in any revolution). The Bolsheviks put down the libertarian socialist elements within their country, with the crushing of the uprising at Kronstadt and the Makhnovist movement in the Ukraine being the final nails in the coffin of socialism and the subjugation of the soviets.

The Kronstadt uprising of February, 1921, was, for anarchists, of immense importance (see the appendix "What was the Kronstadt Rebellion?" for a full discussion of this uprising). The uprising started when the sailors of Kronstadt supported the striking workers of Petrograd in February, 1921. They raised a 15 point resolution, the first point of which was a call for soviet democracy. The Bolsheviks slandered the Kronstadt rebels as counter-revolutionaries and crushed the revolt. For anarchists, this was significant as the repression could not be justified in terms of the Civil War (which had ended months before) and because it was a major uprising of ordinary people for **real** socialism. As Voline puts it:

> "Kronstadt was the first entirely independent attempt of the people to liberate themselves of all yokes and carry out the Social Revolution: this attempt was made directly ... by the working masses themselves, without political shepherds, without leaders or tutors. It was the first step towards the third and social revolution." [Voline, **Op. Cit.**, pp. 537-8]

In the Ukraine, anarchist ideas were most successfully applied. In areas under the protection of the Makhnovist movement, working class people organised their own lives directly, based on their own ideas and needs – true social self-determination. Under the leadership of Nestor Makhno, a self-educated peasant, the movement not only fought against both Red and White dictatorships but also resisted the Ukrainian nationalists. In opposition to the call for "national self-determination," i.e. a new Ukrainian state, Makhno called instead for working class self-determination in the Ukraine and across the world. Makhno inspired his fellow peasants and workers to fight for real freedom:

> "Conquer or die – such is the dilemma that faces the Ukrainian peasants and workers at this historic moment ... But we will not conquer in order to repeat the errors of the past years, the error of putting our fate into the hands of new masters; we will conquer in order to take our destinies into our own hands, to conduct our lives according to our own will and our own conception of the truth." [quoted by Peter Arshinov, **History of the Makhnovist Movement**, p. 58]

To ensure this end, the Makhnovists refused to set up governments in the towns and cities they liberated, instead urging the creation of free soviets so that the working people could govern themselves. Taking the example of Aleksandrovsk, once they had liberated the city the Makhnovists "immediately invited the working population to participate in a general conference ... it was proposed that the workers organise the life of the city and the functioning of the factories with their own forces and their own organisations ... The first conference was followed by a second. The problems of organising life according to principles of self-management by workers were examined and discussed with animation by the masses of workers, who all welcomed this ideas with the greatest enthusiasm ... Railroad workers took the first step ... They formed a committee charged with organising the railway network of the region ... From this point, the proletariat of Aleksandrovsk began to turn systematically to the problem of creating organs of self-management." [**Op. Cit.**, p. 149]

The Makhnovists argued that the "freedom of the workers and peasants is their own, and not subject to any restriction. It is up to the workers and peasants themselves to act, to organise themselves, to agree among themselves in all aspects of their lives, as they see fit and desire ... The Makhnovists can do no more than give aid and counsel ... In no circumstances can they, nor do they wish to, govern." [Peter Arshinov, quoted by Guérin, **Op. Cit.**, p. 99] In Alexandrovsk, the Bolsheviks proposed to the Makhnovists spheres of action – their Revkom (Revolutionary Committee) would handle political affairs and the Makhnovists military ones. Makhno advised them "to go and take up some honest trade instead of seeking to impose their will on the workers." [Peter Arshinov in **The Anarchist Reader**, p. 141]

They also organised free agricultural communes which "[a]dmittedly ... were not numerous, and included only a minority of the population ... But what was most precious was that these communes were formed by the poor peasants themselves. The Makhnovists never exerted any pressure on the peasants, confining themselves to propagating the idea of free communes." [Arshinov, **History of the Makhnovist Movement**, p. 87] Makhno played an important role in abolishing the holdings of the landed gentry. The local soviet and their district and regional congresses equalised the use of the land between all sections of the peasant community. [**Op. Cit.**, pp. 53-4]

Moreover, the Makhnovists took the time and energy to involve the whole population in discussing the development of the revolution, the activities of the army and social policy. They organised numerous conferences of workers', soldiers' and peasants' delegates to discuss political and social issues as well as free soviets, unions and communes. They organised a regional congress of peasants and workers when they had liberated Aleksandrovsk. When the Makhnovists tried to convene the third regional congress of peasants, workers and insurgents in April 1919 and an extraordinary congress of several regions in June 1919 the Bolsheviks viewed them as counter-revolutionary, tried to ban them and declared their organisers and delegates outside the law.

The Makhnovists replied by holding the conferences anyway and asking "[c]an there exist laws made by a few people who call themselves revolutionaries, which permit them to outlaw a whole people who are more revolutionary than they are themselves?" and "[w]hose interests should the revolution defend: those of the Party or those of the people who set the revolution in motion with their blood?" Makhno himself stated that he "consider[ed] it an inviolable right of the workers and peasants, a right won by the revolution, to

call conferences on their own account, to discuss their affairs." [**Op. Cit.**, p. 103 and p. 129]

In addition, the Makhnovists "fully applied the revolutionary principles of freedom of speech, of thought, of the press, and of political association. In all cities and towns occupied by the Makhnovists, they began by lifting all the prohibitions and repealing all the restrictions imposed on the press and on political organisations by one or another power." Indeed, the "only restriction that the Makhnovists considered necessary to impose on the Bolsheviks, the left Socialist-Revolutionaries and other statists was a prohibition on the formation of those 'revolutionary committees' which sought to impose a dictatorship over the people." [**Op. Cit.**, p. 153 and p. 154]

The Makhnovists rejected the Bolshevik corruption of the soviets and instead proposed "the free and completely independent soviet system of working people without authorities and their arbitrary laws." Their proclamations stated that the "working people themselves must freely choose their own soviets, which carry out the will and desires of the working people themselves, that is to say. ADMINISTRATIVE, not ruling soviets." Economically, capitalism would be abolished along with the state – the land and workshops "must belong to the working people themselves, to those who work in them, that is to say, they must be socialised." [**Op. Cit.**, p. 271 and p. 273]

The army itself, in stark contrast to the Red Army, was fundamentally democratic (although, of course, the horrific nature of the civil war did result in a few deviations from the ideal – however, compared to the regime imposed on the Red Army by Trotsky, the Makhnovists were much more democratic movement).

The anarchist experiment of self-management in the Ukraine came to a bloody end when the Bolsheviks turned on the Makhnovists (their former allies against the "Whites," or pro-Tsarists) when they were no longer needed. This important movement is fully discussed in the appendix "Why does the Makhnovist movement show there is an alternative to Bolshevism?" of our FAQ. However, we must stress here the one obvious lesson of the Makhnovist movement, namely that the dictatorial policies pursued by the Bolsheviks were not imposed on them by objective circumstances. Rather, the political ideas of Bolshevism had a clear influence in the decisions they made. After all, the Makhnovists were active in the same Civil War and yet did not pursue the same policies of party power as the Bolsheviks did. Rather, they successfully encouraged working class freedom, democracy and power in extremely difficult circumstances (and in the face of strong Bolshevik opposition to those policies). The received wisdom on the left is that there was no alternative open to the Bolsheviks. The experience of the Makhnovists disproves this. What the masses of people, as well as those in power, do and think politically is as much part of the process determining the outcome of history as are the objective obstacles that limit the choices available. Clearly, ideas do matter and, as such, the Makhnovists show that there was (and is) a practical alternative to Bolshevism – anarchism.

The last anarchist march in Moscow until 1987 took place at the funeral of Kropotkin in 1921, when over 10,000 marched behind his coffin. They carried black banners declaring "Where there is authority, there is no freedom" and "The Liberation of the working class is the task of the workers themselves." As the procession passed the Butyrki prison, the inmates sang anarchist songs and shook the bars of their cells.

Anarchist opposition within Russia to the Bolshevik regime started in 1918. They were the first left-wing group to be repressed by the new "revolutionary" regime. Outside of Russia, anarchists continued to support the Bolsheviks until news came from anarchist sources about the repressive nature of the Bolshevik regime (until then, many had discounted negative reports as being from pro-capitalist sources). Once these reliable reports came in, anarchists across the globe rejected Bolshevism and its system of party power and repression. The experience of Bolshevism confirmed Bakunin's prediction that Marxism meant *"the highly despotic government of the masses by a new and very small aristocracy of real or pretended scholars. The people are not learned, so they will be liberated from the cares of government and included in entirety in the governed herd."* [**Statism and Anarchy**, pp. 178-9]

From about 1921 on, anarchists outside of Russia started describing the USSR as *"state-capitalist"* to indicate that although individual bosses might have been eliminated, the Soviet state bureaucracy played the same role as individual bosses do in the West (anarchists **within** Russia had been calling it that since 1918). For anarchists, *"the Russian revolution … is trying to reach … economic equality … this effort has been made in Russia under a strongly centralised party dictatorship … this effort to build a communist republic on the basis of a strongly centralised state communism under the iron law of a party dictatorship is bound to end in failure. We are learning to know in Russia how **not** to introduce communism."* [**Anarchism**, p. 254]

This meant exposing that Berkman called **"The Bolshevik Myth,"** the idea that the Russian Revolution was a success and should be copied by revolutionaries in other countries: *"It is imperative to unmask the great delusion, which otherwise might lead the Western workers to the same abyss as their brothers [and sisters] in Russia. It is incumbent upon those who have seen through the myth to expose its true nature."* [*"The Anti-Climax'"*, **The Bolshevik Myth**, p. 342] Moreover, anarchists felt that it was their revolutionary duty not only present and learn from the facts of the revolution but also show solidarity with those subject to Bolshevik dictatorship. As Emma Goldman argued, she had not *"come to Russia expecting to find Anarchism realised."* Such idealism was alien to her (although that has not stopped Leninists saying the opposite). Rather, she expected to see *"the beginnings of the social changes for which the Revolution had been fought."* She was aware that revolutions were difficult, involving *"destruction"* and *"violence."* That Russia was not perfect was not the source of her vocal opposition to Bolshevism. Rather, it was the fact that *"the Russian people have been **locked out**"* of their own revolution by the Bolshevik state which used *"the sword and the gun to keep the people out."* As a revolutionary she refused *"to side with the master class, which in Russia is called the Communist Party."* [**My Disillusionment in Russia**, p. xlvii and p. xliv]

For more information on the Russian Revolution and the role played by anarchists, see the appendix on "The Russian Revolution" of the FAQ. As well as covering the Kronstadt uprising and the Makhnovists, it discusses why the revolution failed, the role of Bolshevik ideology played in that failure and whether there were any alternatives to Bolshevism.

The following books are also recommended: **The Unknown Revolution** by Voline; **The Guillotine at Work** by G.P. Maximov; **The Bolshevik Myth** and **The Russian Tragedy**, both by Alexander Berkman; **The Bolsheviks and Workers Control** by M. Brinton; **The Kronstadt Uprising** by Ida Mett; **The History of the Makhnovist Movement** by Peter Arshinov; **My Disillusionment in Russia** and **Living My Life** by Emma Goldman; **Nestor Makhno Anarchy's Cossack: The struggle for free soviets in the Ukraine 1917-1921** by Alexandre Skirda.

Many of these books were written by anarchists active during the revolution, many imprisoned by the Bolsheviks and deported to the West due to international pressure exerted by anarcho-syndicalist delegates to Moscow who the Bolsheviks were trying to win over to Leninism. The majority of such delegates stayed true to their libertarian politics and convinced their unions to reject Bolshevism and break with Moscow. By the early 1920's all the anarcho-syndicalist union confederations had joined with the anarchists in rejecting the "socialism" in Russia as state capitalism and party dictatorship.

A.5.5 Anarchists in the Italian Factory Occupations

After the end of the First World War there was a massive radicalisation across Europe and the world. Union membership exploded, with strikes, demonstrations and agitation reaching massive levels. This was partly due to the war, partly to the apparent success of the Russian Revolution. This enthusiasm for the Russian Revolution even reached Individualist Anarchists like Joseph Labadie, who like many other anti-capitalists, saw *"the red in the east [giving] hope of a brighter day"* and the Bolsheviks as making *"laudable efforts to at least try some way out of the hell of industrial slavery."* [quoted by Carlotta R. Anderson, **All-American Anarchist** p. 225 and p. 241]

Across Europe, anarchist ideas became more popular and anarcho-syndicalist unions grew in size. For example, in Britain, the ferment produced the shop stewards' movement and the strikes on Clydeside; Germany saw the rise of IWW inspired industrial unionism and a libertarian form of Marxism called ***"Council Communism"***; Spain saw a massive growth in the anarcho-syndicalist CNT. In addition, it also, unfortunately, saw the rise and growth of both social democratic and communist parties. Italy was no exception.

In Turin, a new rank-and-file movement was developing. This movement was based around the *"internal commissions"* (elected ad hoc grievance committees). These new organisations were based directly on the group of people who worked together in a particular work shop, with a mandated and recallable shop steward elected for each group of 15 to 20 or so workers. The assembly of all the shop stewards in a given plant then elected the "internal commission" for that facility, which was directly and constantly responsible to the body of shop stewards, which was called the *"factory council."*

Between November 1918 and March 1919, the internal commissions had become a national issue within the trade union movement. On February 20, 1919, the Italian Federation of Metal Workers (FIOM) won a contract providing for the election of "internal commissions" in the factories. The workers subsequently tried to transform these organs of workers' representation into factory councils with a managerial function. By May Day 1919, the internal commissions *were becoming the dominant force within the metalworking industry and the unions were in danger of becoming marginal administrative units. Behind these alarming developments, in the eyes of reformists, lay the libertarians.*" [Carl Levy, **Gramsci and the Anarchists**, p. 135] By November 1919 the internal commissions of Turin were transformed into factory councils.

The movement in Turin is usually associated with the weekly **L'Ordine Nuovo** (The New Order), which first appeared on May 1, 1919. As Daniel Guérin summarises, it was *"edited by a left socialist, Antonio Gramsci, assisted by a professor of philosophy at Turin University with anarchist ideas, writing under the pseudonym of Carlo Petri, and also of a whole nucleus of Turin libertarians. In the factories, the Ordine Nuovo group was supported by a number of people, especially the anarcho-syndicalist militants of the metal trades, Pietro Ferrero and Maurizio Garino. The manifesto of **Ordine Nuovo** was signed by socialists and libertarians together, agreeing to regard the factory councils as 'organs suited to future communist management of both the individual factory and the whole society.'"* [**Anarchism**, p. 109]

The developments in Turin should not be taken in isolation. All across Italy, workers and peasants were taking action. In late February 1920, a rash of factory occupations broke out in Liguria, Piedmont and Naples. In Liguria, the workers occupied the metal and shipbuilding plants in Sestri Ponente, Cornigliano and Campi after a breakdown of pay talks. For up to four days, under syndicalist leadership, they ran the plants through factory councils.

During this period the Italian Syndicalist Union (USI) grew in size to around 800 000 members and the influence of the Italian Anarchist Union (UAI) with its 20 000 members and daily paper (**Umanita Nova**) grew correspondingly. As the Welsh Marxist historian Gwyn A. Williams points out *"Anarchists and revolutionary syndicalists were the most consistently and totally revolutionary group on the left ... the most obvious feature of the history of syndicalism and anarchism in 1919-20: rapid and virtually continuous growth ... The syndicalists above all captured militant working-class opinion which the socialist movement was utterly failing to capture."* [**Proletarian Order**, pp. 194-195] In Turin, libertarians *"worked within FIOM"* and had been *"heavily involved in the **Ordine Nuovo** campaign from the beginning."* [**Op. Cit.**, p. 195] Unsurprisingly, **Ordone Nuovo** was denounced as "syndicalist" by other socialists.

It was the anarchists and syndicalists who first raised the idea of occupying workplaces. Malatesta was discussing this idea in **Umanita Nova** in March, 1920. In his words, *"General strikes of protest no longer upset anyone ... One must seek something else. We put forward an idea: take-over of factories ... the method certainly has a future, because it corresponds to the ultimate ends of the workers' movement and constitutes an exercise preparing one for the ultimate act of expropriation."* [**Errico Malatesta: His Life and Ideas**, p. 134] In the same month, during *"a strong syndicalist campaign to establish councils in Mila, Armando Borghi*

[anarchist secretary of the USI] called for mass factory occupations. In Turin, the re-election of workshop commissars was just ending in a two-week orgy of passionate discussion and workers caught the fever. [Factory Council] Commissars began to call for occupations." Indeed, *"the council movement outside Turin was essentially anarcho-syndicalist."* Unsurprisingly, the secretary of the syndicalist metal-workers *"urged support for the Turin councils because they represented anti-bureaucratic direct action, aimed at control of the factory and could be the first cells of syndicalist industrial unions ... The syndicalist congress voted to support the councils. ... Malatesta ... supported them as a form of direct action guaranteed to generate rebelliousness ... **Umanita Nova** and **Guerra di Classe** [paper of the USI] became almost as committed to the councils as **L'Ordine Nuovo** and the Turin edition of **Avanti.**"* [Williams, **Op. Cit.**, p. 200, p. 193 and p. 196]

The upsurge in militancy soon provoked an employer counter-offensive. The bosses organisation denounced the factory councils and called for a mobilisation against them. Workers were rebelling and refusing to follow the bosses orders – "indiscipline" was rising in the factories. They won state support for the enforcement of the existing industrial regulations. The national contract won by the FIOM in 1919 had provided that the internal commissions were banned from the shop floor and restricted to non-working hours. This meant that the activities of the shop stewards' movement in Turin – such as stopping work to hold shop steward elections – were in violation of the contract. The movement was essentially being maintained through mass insubordination. The bosses used this infringement of the agreed contract as the means combating the factory councils in Turin.

The showdown with the employers arrived in April, when a general assembly of shop stewards at Fiat called for sit-in strikes to protest the dismissal of several shop stewards. In response the employers declared a general lockout. The government supported the lockout with a mass show of force and troops occupied the factories and mounted machine gun posts at them. When the shop stewards movement decided to surrender on the immediate issues in dispute after two weeks on strike, the employers responded with demands that the shop stewards councils be limited to non-working hours, in accordance with the FIOM national contract, and that managerial control be re-imposed.

These demands were aimed at the heart of the factory council system and Turin labour movement responded with a massive general strike in defence of it. In Turin, the strike was total and it soon spread throughout the region of Piedmont and involved 500 000 workers at its height. The Turin strikers called for the strike to be extended nationally and, being mostly led by socialists, they turned to the CGL trade union and Socialist Party leaders, who rejected their call.

The only support for the Turin general strike came from unions that were mainly under anarcho-syndicalist influence, such as the independent railway and the maritime workers unions (*"The syndicalists were the only ones to move."*). The railway workers in Pisa and Florence refused to transport troops who were being sent to Turin. There were strikes all around Genoa, among dock workers and in workplaces where the USI was a major influence. So in spite of being *"betrayed and abandoned by the whole socialist* movement," the April movement *"still found popular support"* with *"actions ... either directly led or indirectly inspired by anarcho-syndicalists."* In Turin itself, the anarchists and syndicalists were *"threatening to cut the council movement out from under"* Gramsci and the **Ordine Nuovo** group. [Williams, **Op. Cit.**, p. 207, p. 193 and p. 194]

Eventually the CGL leadership settled the strike on terms that accepted the employers' main demand for limiting the shop stewards' councils to non-working hours. Though the councils were now much reduced in activity and shop floor presence, they would yet see a resurgence of their position during the September factory occupations.

The anarchists *"accused the socialists of betrayal. They criticised what they believed was a false sense of discipline that had bound socialists to their own cowardly leadership. They contrasted the discipline that placed every movement under the 'calculations, fears, mistakes and possible betrayals of the leaders' to the other discipline of the workers of Sestri Ponente who struck in solidarity with Turin, the discipline of the railway workers who refused to transport security forces to Turin and the anarchists and members of the Unione Sindacale who forgot considerations of party and sect to put themselves at the disposition of the Torinesi."* [Carl Levy, **Op. Cit.**, p. 161] Sadly, this top-down "discipline" of the socialists and their unions would be repeated during the factory occupations, with terrible results.

In September, 1920, there were large-scale stay-in strikes in Italy in response to an owner wage cut and lockout. *"Central to the climate of the crisis was the rise of the syndicalists."* In mid-August, the USI metal-workers *"called for both unions to occupy the factories"* and called for *"a preventive occupation"* against lock-outs. The USI saw this as the *"expropriation of the factories by the metal-workers"* (which must *"be defended by all necessary measures"*) and saw the need *"to call the workers of other industries into battle."* [Williams, **Op. Cit.**, p. 236, pp. 238-9] Indeed, *"[i]f the FIOM had not embraced the syndicalist idea of an occupation of factories to counter an employer's lockout, the USI may well have won significant support from the politically active working class of Turin."* [Carl Levy, **Op. Cit.**, p. 129] These strikes began in the engineering factories and soon spread to railways, road transport, and other industries, with peasants seizing land. The strikers, however, did more than just occupy their workplaces, they placed them under workers' self-management. Soon over 500 000 "strikers" were at work, producing for themselves. Errico Malatesta, who took part in these events, writes:

> *"The metal workers started the movement over wage rates. It was a strike of a new kind. Instead of abandoning the factories, the idea was to remain inside without working ... Throughout Italy there was a revolutionary fervour among the workers and soon the demands changed their characters. Workers thought that the moment was ripe to take possession once [and] for all the means of production. They armed for defence ... and began to organise production on their own ... It was the right of property abolished in fact ... ; it was a new regime, a new form of social life that was being ushered*

in. And the government stood by because it felt impotent to offer opposition." [**Errico Malatesta: His Life and Ideas**, p. 134]

Daniel Guérin provides a good summary of the extent of the movement:

> *"The management of the factories ... [was] conducted by technical and administrative workers' committees. Self-management went quite a long way: in the early period assistance was obtained from the banks, but when it was withdrawn the self-management system issued its own money to pay the workers' wages. Very strict self-discipline was required, the use of alcoholic beverages forbidden, and armed patrols were organised for self-defence. Very close solidarity was established between the factories under self-management. Ores and coal were put into a common pool, and shared out equitably."* [**Anarchism**, p. 109]

Italy was *"paralysed, with half a million workers occupying their factories and raising red and black flags over them."* The movement spread throughout Italy, not only in the industrial heartland around Milan, Turin and Genoa, but also in Rome, Florence, Naples and Palermo. The *"militants of the USI were certainly in the forefront of the movement,"* while **Umanita Nova** argued that *"the movement is very serious and we must do everything we can to channel it towards a massive extension."* The persistent call of the USI was for *"an extension of the movement to the whole of industry to institute their 'expropriating general strike.'"* [Williams, **Op. Cit.**, p. 236 and pp. 243-4] Railway workers, influenced by the libertarians, refused to transport troops, workers went on strike against the orders of the reformist unions and peasants occupied the land. The anarchists whole-heartedly supported the movement, unsurprisingly as the *"occupation of the factories and the land suited perfectly our programme of action."* [Malatesta, **Op. Cit.**, p. 135] Luigi Fabbri described the occupations as having *"revealed a power in the proletariat of which it had been unaware hitherto."* [quoted by Paolo Sprinao, **The Occupation of the Factories**, p. 134]

However, after four weeks of occupation, the workers decided to leave the factories. This was because of the actions of the socialist party and the reformist trade unions. They opposed the movement and negotiated with the state for a return to "normality" in exchange for a promise to extend workers' control legally, in association with the bosses. The question of revolution was decided by a vote of the CGL national council in Milan on April 10-11th, without consulting the syndicalist unions, after the Socialist Party leadership refused to decide one way or the other.

Needless to say, this promise of "workers' control" was not kept. The lack of independent inter-factory organisation made workers dependent on trade union bureaucrats for information on what was going on in other cities, and they used that power to isolate factories, cities, and factories from each other. This lead to a return to work, *"in spite of the opposition of individual anarchists dispersed among the factories."* [Malatesta, **Op. Cit.**, p. 136] The local syndicalist union confederations could not provide the necessary framework for a fully co-ordinated occupation movement as the reformist unions refused to work with them; and although the anarchists were a large minority, they were still a minority:

> "At the 'interproletarian' convention held on 12 September (in which the Unione Anarchia, the railwaymen's and maritime workers union participated) the syndicalist union decided that 'we cannot do it ourselves' without the socialist party and the CGL, protested against the 'counter-revolutionary vote' of Milan, declared it minoritarian, arbitrary and null, and ended by launching new, vague, but ardent calls to action." [Paolo Spriano, **Op. Cit.**, p. 94]

Malatesta addressed the workers of one of the factories at Milan. He argued that *"[t]hose who celebrate the agreement signed at Rome [between the Confederazione and the capitalists] as a great victory of yours are deceiving you. The victory in reality belongs to Giolitti, to the government and the bourgeoisie who are saved from the precipice over which they were hanging."* During the occupation the *"bourgeoisie trembled, the government was powerless to face the situation."* Therefore:

> "To speak of victory when the Roman agreement throws you back under bourgeois exploitation which you could have got rid of is a lie. If you give up the factories, do this with the conviction [of] hav[ing] lost a great battle and with the firm intention to resume the struggle on the first occasion and to carry it on in a thorough way ... Nothing is lost if you have no illusion [about] the deceiving character of the victory. The famous decree on the control of factories is a mockery ... because it tends to harmonise your interests and those of the bourgeois which is like harmonising the interests of the wolf and the sheep. Don't believe those of your leaders who make fools of you by adjourning the revolution from day to day. You yourselves must make the revolution when an occasion will offer itself, without waiting for orders which never come, or which come only to enjoin you to abandon action. Have confidence in yourselves, have faith in your future and you will win." [quoted by Max Nettlau, **Errico Malatesta: The Biography of an Anarchist**]

Malatesta was proven correct. With the end of the occupations, the only victors were the bourgeoisie and the government. Soon the workers would face Fascism, but first, in October 1920, *"after the factories were evacuated,"* the government (obviously knowing who the real threat was) *"arrested the entire leadership of the USI and UAI. The socialists did not respond"* and *"more-or-less ignored the persecution of the libertarians until the spring of 1921 when the aged Malatesta and other imprisoned anarchists mounted a hunger strike from their cells in Milan."* [Carl Levy, **Op. Cit.**, pp. 221-2] They were acquitted after a four day trial.

The events of 1920 show four things. Firstly, that workers can manage their own workplaces successfully by themselves, without bosses. Secondly, on the need for anarchists to be involved in the labour movement. Without the support of the USI, the Turin movement would have been even more isolated than it was. Thirdly, anarchists need to be organised to influence the class struggle. The growth of

the UAI and USI in terms of both influence and size indicates the importance of this. Without the anarchists and syndicalists raising the idea of factory occupations and supporting the movement, it is doubtful that it would have been as successful and widespread as it was. Lastly, that socialist organisations, structured in a hierarchical fashion, do not produce a revolutionary membership. By continually looking to leaders, the movement was crippled and could not develop to its full potential.

This period of Italian history explains the growth of Fascism in Italy. As Tobias Abse points out, *"the rise of fascism in Italy cannot be detached from the events of the **biennio rosso**, the two red years of 1919 and 1920, that preceded it. Fascism was a preventive counter-revolution ... launched as a result of the failed revolution"* ["*The Rise of Fascism in an Industrial City*", pp. 52-81, **Rethinking Italian Fascism**, David Forgacs (ed.), p. 54] The term *"preventive counter-revolution"* was originally coined by the leading anarchist Luigi Fabbri, who correctly described fascism as *"the organisation and agent of the violent armed defence of the ruling class against the proletariat, which, to their mind, has become unduly demanding, united and intrusive."* ["*Fascism: The Preventive Counter-Revolution*", pp. 408-416, **Anarchism**, Robert Graham (ed.), p. 410 and p. 409]

The rise of fascism confirmed Malatesta's warning at the time of the factory occupations: *"If we do not carry on to the end, we will pay with tears of blood for the fear we now instill in the bourgeoisie."* [quoted by Tobias Abse, **Op. Cit.**, p. 66] The capitalists and rich landowners backed the fascists in order to teach the working class their place, aided by the state. They ensured *"that it was given every assistance in terms of funding and arms, turning a blind eye to its breaches of the law and, where necessary, covering its back through intervention by armed forces which, on the pretext of restoring order, would rush to the aid of the fascists wherever the latter were beginning to take a beating instead of doling one out."* [Fabbri, **Op. Cit.**, p. 411] To quote Tobias Abse:

> "The aims of the Fascists and their backers amongst the industrialists and agrarians in 1921-22 were simple: to break the power of the organised workers and peasants as completely as possible, to wipe out, with the bullet and the club, not only the gains of the **biennio rosso**, but everything that the lower classes had gained ... between the turn of the century and the outbreak of the First World War." [**Op. Cit.**, p. 54]

The fascist squads attacked and destroyed anarchist and socialist meeting places, social centres, radical presses and Camera del Lavoro (local trade union councils). However, even in the dark days of fascist terror, the anarchists resisted the forces of totalitarianism. *"It is no coincidence that the strongest working-class resistance to Fascism was in ... towns or cities in which there was quite a strong anarchist, syndicalist or anarcho-syndicalist tradition."* [Tobias Abse, **Op. Cit.**, p. 56]

The anarchists participated in, and often organised sections of, the **Arditi del Popolo**, a working-class organisation devoted to the self-defence of workers' interests. The Arditi del Popolo organised and encouraged working-class resistance to fascist squads, often defeating larger fascist forces (for example, *"the total humiliation of* thousands of Italo Balbo's squadristi by a couple of hundred Arditi del Popolo backed by the inhabitants of the working class districts" in the anarchist stronghold of Parma in August 1922 [Tobias Abse, **Op. Cit.**, p. 56]).

The Arditi del Popolo was the closest Italy got to the idea of a united, revolutionary working-class front against fascism, as had been suggested by Malatesta and the UAI. This movement "developed along anti-bourgeois and anti-fascist lines, and was marked by the independence of its local sections." [**Red Years, Black Years: Anarchist Resistance to Fascism in Italy**, p. 2] Rather than being just an "anti-fascist" organisation, the Arditi "were not a movement in defence of 'democracy' in the abstract, but an essentially working-class organisation devoted to the defence of the interests of industrial workers, the dockers and large numbers of artisans and craftsmen." [Tobias Abse, **Op. Cit.**, p. 75] Unsurprisingly, the **Arditi del Popolo** "appear to have been strongest and most successful in areas where traditional working-class political culture was less exclusively socialist and had strong anarchist or syndicalist traditions, for example, Bari, Livorno, Parma and Rome." [Antonio Sonnessa, "Working Class Defence Organisation, Anti-Fascist Resistance and the **Arditi del Popolo** in Turin, 1919-22," pp. 183-218, **European History Quarterly**, vol. 33, no. 2, p. 184]

However, both the socialist and communist parties withdrew from the organisation. The socialists signed a "Pact of Pacification" with the Fascists in August 1921. The communists "preferred to withdraw their members from the Arditi del Popolo rather than let them work with the anarchists." [**Red Years, Black Years**, p. 17] Indeed, "[o]n the same day as the Pact was signed, **Ordine Nuovo** published a PCd'I [Communist Party of Italy] communication warning communists against involvement" in the Arditi del Popolo. Four days later, the Communist leadership "officially abandoned the movement. Severe disciplinary measures were threatened against those communists who continued to participate in, or liase with," the organisation. Thus by "the end of the first week of August 1921 the PSI, CGL and the PCd'I had officially denounced" the organisation. "Only the anarchist leaders, if not always sympathetic to the programme of the [Arditi del Popolo], did not abandon the movement." Indeed, **Umanita Nova** "strongly supported" it "on the grounds it represented a popular expression of anti-fascist resistance and in defence of freedom to organise." [Antonio Sonnessa, **Op. Cit.**, p. 195 and p. 194]

However, in spite of the decisions by their leaders, many rank and file socialists and communists took part in the movement. The latter took part in open "defiance of the PCd'I leadership's growing abandonment" of it. In Turin, for example, communists who took part in the **Arditi del Polopo** did so "less as communists and more as part of a wider, working-class self-identification ... This dynamic was re-enforced by an important socialist and anarchist presence" there. The failure of the Communist leadership to support the movement shows the bankruptcy of Bolshevik organisational forms which were unresponsive to the needs of the popular movement. Indeed, these events show the "libertarian custom of autonomy from, and resistance to, authority was also operated against the leaders of the workers' movement, particularly when they were held to have misunderstood the situation at grass roots level." [Sonnessa, **Op. Cit.**, p. 200, p. 198 and p. 193]

Thus the Communist Party failed to support the popular resistance to fascism. The Communist leader Antonio Gramsci explained why, arguing that "the party leadership's attitude on the question of the Arditi del Popolo ... corresponded to a need to prevent the party members from being controlled by a leadership that was not the party's leadership." Gramsci added that this policy "served to disqualify a mass movement which had started from below and which could instead have been exploited by us politically." [**Selections from Political Writings (1921-1926)**, p. 333] While being less sectarian towards the Arditi del Popolo than other Communist leaders, "[i]n common with all communist leaders, Gramsci awaited the formation of the PCd'I-led military squads." [Sonnessa, **Op. Cit.**, p. 196] In other words, the struggle against fascism was seen by the Communist leadership as a means of gaining more members and, when the opposite was a possibility, they preferred defeat and fascism rather than risk their followers becoming influenced by anarchism.

As Abse notes, "it was the withdrawal of support by the Socialist and Communist parties at the national level that crippled" the Arditi. [**Op. Cit.**, p. 74] Thus "social reformist defeatism and communist sectarianism made impossible an armed opposition that was widespread and therefore effective; and the isolated instances of popular resistance were unable to unite in a successful strategy." And fascism could have been defeated: "Insurrections at Sarzanna, in July 1921, and at Parma, in August 1922, are examples of the correctness of the policies which the anarchists urged in action and propaganda." [**Red Years, Black Years**, p. 3 and p. 2] Historian Tobias Abse confirms this analysis, arguing that "[w]hat happened in Parma in August 1922 ... could have happened elsewhere, if only the leadership of the Socialist and Communist parties thrown their weight behind the call of the anarchist Malatesta for a united revolutionary front against Fascism." [**Op. Cit.**, p. 56]

In the end, fascist violence was successful and capitalist power maintained:

> "The anarchists' will and courage were not enough to counter the fascist gangs, powerfully aided with material and arms, backed by the repressive organs of the state. Anarchists and anarcho-syndicalists were decisive in some areas and in some industries, but only a similar choice of direct action on the parts of the Socialist Party and the General Confederation of Labour [the reformist trade union] could have halted fascism." [**Red Years, Black Years**, pp. 1-2]

After helping to defeat the revolution, the Marxists helped ensure the victory of fascism.

Even after the fascist state was created, anarchists resisted both inside and outside Italy. In America, for example, Italian anarchists played a major role in fighting fascist influence in their communities, none more so that Carlo Tresca, most famous for his role in the 1912 IWW Lawrence strike, who "in the 1920s had no peer among anti-Fascist leaders, a distinction recognised by Mussolini's political police in Rome." [Nunzio Pernicone, **Carlo Tresca: Portrait of a Rebel**, p. 4] Many Italians, both anarchist and non-anarchist, travelled to Spain to resist Franco in 1936 (see Umberto Marzochhi's **Remembering Spain: Italian Anarchist**

Volunteers in the Spanish Civil War for details). During the Second World War, anarchists played a major part in the Italian Partisan movement. It was the fact that the anti-fascist movement was dominated by anti-capitalist elements that led the USA and the UK to place known fascists in governmental positions in the places they "liberated" (often where the town had already been taken by the Partisans, resulting in the Allied troops "liberating" the town from its own inhabitants!).

Given this history of resisting fascism in Italy, it is surprising that some claim Italian fascism was a product or form of syndicalism. This is even claimed by some anarchists. According to Bob Black the *"Italian syndicalists mostly went over to Fascism"* and references David D. Roberts 1979 study **The Syndicalist Tradition and Italian Fascism** to support his claim. [**Anarchy after Leftism**, p. 64] Peter Sabatini in a review in **Social Anarchism** makes a similar statement, saying that syndicalism's *"ultimate failure"* was *"its transformation into a vehicle of fascism."* [**Social Anarchism**, no. 23, p. 99] What is the truth behind these claims?

Looking at Black's reference we discover that, in fact, most of the Italian syndicalists did not go over to fascism, if by syndicalists we mean members of the USI (the Italian Syndicalist Union). Roberts states that:

> *"The vast majority of the organised workers failed to respond to the syndicalists' appeals and continued to oppose [Italian] intervention [in the First World War], shunning what seemed to be a futile capitalist war. The syndicalists failed to convince even a majority within the USI ... the majority opted for the neutralism of Armando Borghi, leader of the anarchists within the USI. Schism followed as De Ambris led the interventionist minority out of the confederation."* [**The Syndicalist Tradition and Italian Fascism**, p. 113]

However, if we take "syndicalist" to mean some of the intellectuals and "leaders" of the pre-war movement, it was a case that the *"leading syndicalists came out for intervention quickly and almost unanimously"* [Roberts, **Op. Cit.**, p. 106] after the First World War started. Many of these pro-war "leading syndicalists" did become fascists. However, to concentrate on a handful of "leaders" (which the majority did not even follow!) and state that this shows that the *"Italian syndicalists mostly went over to Fascism"* staggers belief. What is even worse, as seen above, the Italian anarchists and syndicalists were the most dedicated and successful fighters against fascism. In effect, Black and Sabatini have slandered a whole movement.

What is also interesting is that these "leading syndicalists" were not anarchists and so not anarcho-syndicalists. As Roberts notes *"[i]n Italy, the syndicalist doctrine was more clearly the product of a group of intellectuals, operating within the Socialist party and seeking an alternative to reformism."* They *"explicitly denounced anarchism"* and *"insisted on a variety of Marxist orthodoxy."* The *"syndicalists genuinely desired – and tried – to work within the Marxist tradition."* [**Op. Cit.**, p. 66, p. 72, p. 57 and p. 79] According to Carl Levy, in his account of Italian anarchism, *"[u]nlike other syndicalist movements, the Italian variation coalesced inside a Second International party. Supporters were partially drawn*

from socialist intransigents ... the southern syndicalist intellectuals pronounced republicanism ... Another component ... was the remnant of the Partito Operaio." [*"Italian Anarchism: 1870-1926"* in **For Anarchism: History, Theory, and Practice**, David Goodway (Ed.), p. 51]

In other words, the Italian syndicalists who turned to fascism were, firstly, a small minority of intellectuals who could not convince the majority within the syndicalist union to follow them, and, secondly, Marxists and republicans rather than anarchists, anarcho-syndicalists or even revolutionary syndicalists.

According to Carl Levy, Roberts' book *"concentrates on the syndicalist intelligentsia"* and that *"some syndicalist intellectuals ... helped generate, or sympathetically endorsed, the new Nationalist movement ... which bore similarities to the populist and republican rhetoric of the southern syndicalist intellectuals."* He argues that there *"has been far too much emphasis on syndicalist intellectuals and national organisers"* and that syndicalism *"relied little on its national leadership for its long-term vitality."* [**Op. Cit.**, p. 77, p. 53 and p. 51] If we do look at the membership of the USI, rather than finding a group which *"mostly went over to fascism,"* we discover a group of people who fought fascism tooth and nail and were subject to extensive fascist violence.

To summarise, Italian Fascism had nothing to do with syndicalism and, as seen above, the USI fought the Fascists and was destroyed by them along with the UAI, Socialist Party and other radicals. That a handful of pre-war Marxist-syndicalists later became Fascists and called for a "National-Syndicalism" does not mean that syndicalism and fascism are related (any more than some anarchists later becoming Marxists makes anarchism "a vehicle" for Marxism!).

It is hardly surprising that anarchists were the most consistent and successful opponents of Fascism. The two movements could not be further apart, one standing for total statism in the service of capitalism while the other for a free, non-capitalist society. Neither is it surprising that when their privileges and power were in danger, the capitalists and the landowners turned to fascism to save them. This process is a common feature in history (to list just four examples, Italy, Germany, Spain and Chile).

A.5.6 Anarchism and the Spanish Revolution

As Noam Chomsky notes, *"a good example of a really large-scale anarchist revolution – in fact the best example to my knowledge – is the Spanish revolution in 1936, in which over most of Republican Spain there was a quite inspiring anarchist revolution that involved both industry and agriculture over substantial areas ... And that again was, by both human measures and indeed anyone's economic measures, quite successful. That is, production continued effectively; workers in farms and factories proved quite capable of managing their affairs without coercion from above, contrary to what lots of socialists, communists, liberals and other wanted to believe."* The revolution of 1936 was *"based on three generations of experiment and thought and work which extended anarchist ideas to very large parts of the population."* [**Radical Priorities**, p. 212]

Due to this anarchist organising and agitation, Spain in the 1930's had the largest anarchist movement in the world. At the start of the Spanish "Civil" war, over one and one half million workers and peasants were members of the CNT (the **National Confederation of Labour**), an anarcho-syndicalist union federation, and 30,000 were members of the FAI (the **Anarchist Federation of Iberia**). The total population of Spain at this time was 24 million.

The social revolution which met the Fascist coup on July 18th, 1936, is the greatest experiment in libertarian socialism to date. Here the last mass syndicalist union, the CNT, not only held off the fascist rising but encouraged the widespread take-over of land and factories. Over seven million people, including about two million CNT members, put self-management into practise in the most difficult of circumstances and actually improved both working conditions and output.

In the heady days after the 19th of July, the initiative and power truly rested in the hands of the rank-and-file members of the CNT and FAI. It was ordinary people, undoubtedly under the influence of Faistas (members of the FAI) and CNT militants, who, after defeating the fascist uprising, got production, distribution and consumption started again (under more egalitarian arrangements, of course), as well as organising and volunteering (in their tens of thousands) to join the militias, which were to be sent to free those parts of Spain that were under Franco. In every possible way the working class of Spain were creating by their own actions a new world based on their own ideas of social justice and freedom – ideas inspired, of course, by anarchism and anarchosyndicalism.

George Orwell's eye-witness account of revolutionary Barcelona in late December, 1936, gives a vivid picture of the social transformation that had begun:

> "The Anarchists were still in virtual control of Catalonia and the revolution was still in full swing. To anyone who had been there since the beginning it probably seemed even in December or January that the revolutionary period was ending; but when one came straight from England the aspect of Barcelona was something startling and overwhelming. It was the first time that I had ever been in a town where the working class was in the saddle. Practically every building of any size had been seized by the workers and was draped with red flags or with the red and black flag of the Anarchists; every wall was scrawled with the hammer and sickle and with the initials of the revolutionary parties; almost every church had been gutted and its images burnt. Churches here and there were being systematically demolished by gangs of workman. Every shop and cafe had an inscription saying that it had been collectivised; even the bootblacks had been collectivised and their boxes painted red and black. Waiters and shop-walkers looked you in the face and treated you as an equal. Servile and even ceremonial forms of speech had temporarily disappeared. Nobody said 'Señor' or 'Don' or even 'Usted'; everyone called everyone else 'Comrade' or 'Thou', and said 'Salud!' instead of 'Buenos dias' ... Above all, there was a belief in the revolution and the future, a feeling of having suddenly emerged into an era

> of equality and freedom. Human beings were trying to behave as human beings and not as cogs in the capitalist machine." [**Homage to Catalonia**, pp. 2-3]

The full extent of this historic revolution cannot be covered here. It will be discussed in more detail in Section I.8 of the FAQ. All that can be done is to highlight a few points of special interest in the hope that these will give some indication of the importance of these events and encourage people to find out more about it.

All industry in Catalonia was placed either under workers' self-management **or** workers' control (that is, either totally taking over **all** aspects of management, in the first case, or, in the second, controlling the old management). In some cases, whole town and regional economies were transformed into federations of collectives. The example of the Railway Federation (which was set up to manage the railway lines in Catalonia, Aragon and Valencia) can be given as a typical example. The base of the federation was the local assemblies:

> "All the workers of each locality would meet twice a week to examine all that pertained to the work to be done... The local general assembly named a committee to manage the general activity in each station and its annexes. At [these] meetings, the decisions (direccion) of this committee, whose members continued to work [at their previous jobs], would be subjected to the approval or disapproval of the workers, after giving reports and answering questions."

The delegates on the committee could be removed by an assembly at any time and the highest co-ordinating body of the Railway Federation was the **"Revolutionary Committee,"** whose members were elected by union assemblies in the various divisions. The control over the rail lines, according to Gaston Leval, *"did not operate from above downwards, as in a statist and centralised system. The Revolutionary Committee had no such powers ... The members of the ... committee being content to supervise the general activity and to co-ordinate that of the different routes that made up the network."* [Gaston Leval, **Collectives in the Spanish Revolution**, p. 255]

On the land, tens of thousands of peasants and rural day workers created voluntary, self-managed collectives. The quality of life improved as co-operation allowed the introduction of health care, education, machinery and investment in the social infrastructure. As well as increasing production, the collectives increased freedom. As one member puts it, *"it was marvellous ... to live in a collective, a free society where one could say what one thought, where if the village committee seemed unsatisfactory one could say. The committee took no big decisions without calling the whole village together in a general assembly. All this was wonderful."* [Ronald Fraser, **Blood of Spain**, p. 360]

We discuss the revolution in more detail in section I.8. For example, sections I.8.3 and I.8.4 discuss in more depth the industrial collectives. The rural collectives are discussed in sections I.8.5 and I.8.6. We must stress that these sections are summaries of a vast social movement, and more information can be gathered from such works as Gaston Leval's **Collectives in the Spanish Revolution**, Sam Dolfgoff's **The Anarchist Collectives**, Jose Peirats' **The CNT**

in the Spanish Revolution and a host of other anarchist accounts of the revolution.

On the social front, anarchist organisations created rational schools, a libertarian health service, social centres, and so on. The **Mujeres Libres** (free women) combated the traditional role of women in Spanish society, empowering thousands both inside and outside the anarchist movement (see **The Free Women of Spain** by Martha A. Ackelsberg for more information on this very important organisation). This activity on the social front only built on the work started long before the outbreak of the war; for example, the unions often funded rational schools, workers centres, and so on.

The voluntary militias that went to free the rest of Spain from Franco were organised on anarchist principles and included both men and women. There was no rank, no saluting and no officer class. Everybody was equal. George Orwell, a member of the POUM militia (the POUM was a dissident Marxist party, influenced by Leninism but not, as the Communists asserted, Trotskyist) makes this clear:

> "The essential point of the [militia] system was the social equality between officers and men. Everyone from general to private drew the same pay, ate the same food, wore the same clothes, and mingled on terms of complete equality. If you wanted to slap the general commanding the division on the back and ask him for a cigarette, you could do so, and no one thought it curious. In theory at any rate each militia was a democracy and not a hierarchy. It was understood that orders had to be obeyed, but it was also understood that when you gave an order you gave it as comrade to comrade and not as superior to inferior. There were officers and N.C.O.s, but there was no military rank in the ordinary sense; no titles, no badges, no heel-clicking and saluting. They had attempted to produce within the militias a sort of temporary working model of the classless society. Of course there was not perfect equality, but there was a nearer approach to it than I had ever seen or that I would have though conceivable in time of war ... " [**Op. Cit.**, p. 26]

In Spain, however, as elsewhere, the anarchist movement was smashed between Stalinism (the Communist Party) on the one hand and Capitalism (Franco) on the other. Unfortunately, the anarchists placed anti-fascist unity before the revolution, thus helping their enemies to defeat both them and the revolution. Whether they were forced by circumstances into this position or could have avoided it is still being debated (see section I.8.10 for a discussion of why the CNT-FAI collaborated and section I.8.11 on why this decision was **not** a product of anarchist theory).

Orwell's account of his experiences in the militia's indicates why the Spanish Revolution is so important to anarchists:

> "I had dropped more or less by chance into the only community of any size in Western Europe where political consciousness and disbelief in capitalism were more normal than their opposites. Up here in Aragon one was among tens of thousands of people, mainly though not entirely of working-class origin, all living at the same

level and mingling on terms of equality. In theory it was perfect equality, and even in practice it was not far from it. There is a sense in which it would be true to say that one was experiencing a foretaste of Socialism, by which I mean that the prevailing mental atmosphere was that of Socialism. Many of the normal motives of civilised life – snobbishness, money-grubbing, fear of the boss, etc. – had simply ceased to exist. The ordinary class-division of society had disappeared to an extent that is almost unthinkable in the money-tainted air of England; there was no one there except the peasants and ourselves, and no one owned anyone else as his master ... One had been in a community where hope was more normal than apathy or cynicism, where the word 'comrade' stood for comradeship and not, as in most countries, for humbug. One had breathed the air of equality. I am well aware that it is now the fashion to deny that Socialism has anything to do with equality. In every country in the world a huge tribe of party-hacks and sleek little professors are busy 'proving' that Socialism means no more than a planned state-capitalism with the grab-motive left intact. But fortunately there also exists a vision of Socialism quite different from this. The thing that attracts ordinary men to Socialism and makes them willing to risk their skins for it, the 'mystique' of Socialism, is the idea of equality; to the vast majority of people Socialism means a classless society, or it means nothing at all ... In that community where no one was on the make, where there was a shortage of everything but no boot-licking, one got, perhaps, a crude forecast of what the opening stages of Socialism might be like. And, after all, instead of disillusioning me it deeply attracted me ... " [**Op. Cit.**, pp. 83-84]

For more information on the Spanish Revolution, the following books are recommended: **Lessons of the Spanish Revolution** by Vernon Richards; **Anarchists in the Spanish Revolution** and **The CNT in the Spanish Revolution** by Jose Peirats; **Free Women of Spain** by Martha A. Ackelsberg; **The Anarchist Collectives** edited by Sam Dolgoff; "Objectivity and Liberal Scholarship" by Noam Chomsky (in **The Chomsky Reader**); **The Anarchists of Casas Viejas** by Jerome R. Mintz; and **Homage to Catalonia** by George Orwell.

A.5.7 The May-June Revolt in France, 1968

The May-June events in France placed anarchism back on the radical landscape after a period in which many people had written the movement off as dead. This revolt of ten million people grew from humble beginnings. Expelled by the university authorities of Nanterre in Paris for anti-Vietnam War activity, a group of anarchists (including Daniel Cohn-Bendit) promptly called a protest demonstration. The arrival of 80 police enraged many students, who quit their studies to join the battle and drive the police from the university.

Inspired by this support, the anarchists seized the administration building and held a mass debate. The occupation spread, Nanterre was surrounded by police, and the authorities closed the university down. The next day, the Nanterre students gathered at the Sorbonne University in the centre of Paris. Continual police pressure and the arrest of over 500 people caused anger to erupt into five hours of street fighting. The police even attacked passers-by with clubs and tear gas.

A total ban on demonstrations and the closure of the Sorbonne brought thousands of students out onto the streets. Increasing police violence provoked the building of the first barricades. Jean Jacques Lebel, a reporter, wrote that by 1 a.m., *"[l]iterally thousands helped build barricades … women, workers, bystanders, people in pyjamas, human chains to carry rocks, wood, iron."* An entire night of fighting left 350 police injured. On May 7th, a 50,000-strong protest march against the police was transformed into a day-long battle through the narrow streets of the Latin Quarter. Police tear gas was answered by molotov cocktails and the chant *"Long Live the Paris Commune!"*

By May 10th, continuing massive demonstrations forced the Education Minister to start negotiations. But in the streets, 60 barricades had appeared and young workers were joining the students. The trade unions condemned the police violence. Huge demonstrations throughout France culminated on May 13th with one million people on the streets of Paris.

Faced with this massive protest, the police left the Latin Quarter. Students seized the Sorbonne and created a mass assembly to spread the struggle. Occupations soon spread to every French University. From the Sorbonne came a flood of propaganda, leaflets, proclamations, telegrams, and posters. Slogans such as **"Everything is Possible," "Be Realistic, Demand the Impossible," "Life without Dead Times,"** and **"It is Forbidden to Forbid"** plastered the walls. **"All Power to the Imagination"** was on everyone's lips. As Murray Bookchin pointed out, *"the motive forces of revolution today … are not simply scarcity and material need, but also* **quality of everyday life … the attempt to gain control of one's own destiny***."* [**Post-Scarcity Anarchism**, p. 166]

Many of the most famous slogans of those days originated from the Situationists. The **Situationist International** had been formed in 1957 by a small group of dissident radicals and artists. They had developed a highly sophisticated (if jargon riddled) and coherent analysis of modern capitalist society and how to supersede it with a new, freer one. Modern life, they argued, was mere survival rather than living, dominated by the economy of consumption in which everyone, everything, every emotion and relationship becomes a commodity. People were no longer simply alienated producers, they were also alienated consumers. They defined this kind of society as the **"Spectacle."** Life itself had been stolen and so revolution meant recreating life. The area of revolutionary change was no longer just the workplace, but in everyday existence:

> *"People who talk about revolution and class struggle without referring explicitly to everyday life, without understanding what is subversive about love and what*

is positive in the refusal of constraints, such people have a corpse in their mouth." [quoted by Clifford Harper, **Anarchy: A Graphic Guide**, p. 153]

Like many other groups whose politics influenced the Paris events, the Situationists argued that *"the workers' councils are the only answer. Every other form of revolutionary struggle has ended up with the very opposite of what it was originally looking for."* [quoted by Clifford Harper, **Op. Cit.**, p. 149] These councils would be self-managed and not be the means by which a "revolutionary" party would take power. Like the anarchists of **Noire et Rouge** and the libertarian socialists of **Socialisme ou Barbarie**, their support for a self-managed revolution from below had a massive influence in the May events and the ideas that inspired it.

On May 14th, the Sud-Aviation workers locked the management in its offices and occupied their factory. They were followed by the Cleon-Renault, Lockheed-Beauvais and Mucel-Orleans factories the next day. That night the National Theatre in Paris was seized to become a permanent assembly for mass debate. Next, France's largest factory, Renault-Billancourt, was occupied. Often the decision to go on indefinite strike was taken by the workers without consulting union officials. By May 17th, a hundred Paris Factories were in the hands of their workers. The weekend of the 19th of May saw 122 factories occupied. By May 20th, the strike and occupations were general and involved six million people. Print workers said they did not wish to leave a monopoly of media coverage to TV and radio, and agreed to print newspapers as long as the press *"carries out with objectivity the role of providing information which is its duty."* In some cases print-workers insisted on changes in headlines or articles before they would print the paper. This happened mostly with the right-wing papers such as **'Le Figaro'** or **'La Nation'**.

With the Renault occupation, the Sorbonne occupiers immediately prepared to join the Renault strikers, and led by anarchist black and red banners, 4,000 students headed for the occupied factory. The state, bosses, unions and Communist Party were now faced with their greatest nightmare – a worker-student alliance. Ten thousand police reservists were called up and frantic union officials locked the factory gates. The Communist Party urged their members to crush the revolt. They united with the government and bosses to craft a series of reforms, but once they turned to the factories they were jeered out of them by the workers.

The struggle itself and the activity to spread it was organised by self-governing mass assemblies and co-ordinated by action committees. The strikes were often run by assemblies as well. As Murray Bookchin argues, the *"hope [of the revolt] lay in the extension of self-management in all its forms – the general assemblies and their administrative forms, the action committees, the factory strike committees – to all areas of the economy, indeed to all areas of life itself."* Within the assemblies, *"a fever of life gripped millions, a rewaking of senses that people never thought they possessed."* [**Op. Cit.**, p. 168 and p. 167] It was not a workers' strike or a student strike. It was a **peoples'** strike that cut across almost all class lines.

On May 24th, anarchists organised a demonstration. Thirty thousand marched towards the Palace de la Bastille. The police had the Ministries protected, using the usual devices of tear gas and batons, but the Bourse (Stock Exchange) was left unprotected and a number of demonstrators set fire to it.

It was at this stage that some left-wing groups lost their nerve. The Trotskyist JCR turned people back into the Latin Quarter. Other groups such as UNEF and Parti Socialiste Unife (United Socialist Party) blocked the taking of the Ministries of Finance and Justice. Cohn-Bendit said of this incident *"As for us, we failed to realise how easy it would have been to sweep all these nobodies away…. It is now clear that if, on 25 May, Paris had woken to find the most important Ministries occupied, Gaullism would have caved in at once. … "* Cohn-Bendit was forced into exile later that very night.

As the street demonstrations grew and occupations continued, the state prepared to use overwhelming means to stop the revolt. Secretly, top generals readied 20,000 loyal troops for use on Paris. Police occupied communications centres like TV stations and Post Offices. By Monday, May 27th, the Government had guaranteed an increase of 35% in the industrial minimum wage and an all round-wage increase of 10%. The leaders of the CGT organised a march of 500,000 workers through the streets of Paris two days later. Paris was covered in posters calling for a *"Government of the People."* Unfortunately the majority still thought in terms of changing their rulers rather than taking control for themselves.

By June 5th most of the strikes were over and an air of what passes for normality within capitalism had rolled back over France. Any strikes which continued after this date were crushed in a military-style operation using armoured vehicles and guns. On June 7th, they made an assault on the Flins steelworks which started a four-day running battle which left one worker dead. Three days later, Renault strikers were gunned down by police, killing two. In isolation, those pockets of militancy stood no chance. On June 12th, demonstrations were banned, radical groups outlawed, and their members arrested. Under attack from all sides, with escalating state violence and trade union sell-outs, the General Strike and occupations crumbled.

So why did this revolt fail? Certainly not because "vanguard" Bolshevik parties were missing. It was infested with them. Fortunately, the traditional authoritarian left sects were isolated and outraged. Those involved in the revolt did not require a vanguard to tell them what to do, and the "workers' vanguards" frantically ran after the movement trying to catch up with it and control it.

No, it was the lack of independent, self-managed confederal organisations to co-ordinate struggle which resulted in occupations being isolated from each other. So divided, they fell. In addition, Murray Bookchin argues that *"an awareness among the workers that the factories had to be **worked**, not merely occupied or struck,"* was missing. [**Op. Cit.**, p. 182]

This awareness would have been encouraged by the existence of a strong anarchist movement before the revolt. The anti-authoritarian left, though very active, was too weak among striking workers, and so the idea of self-managed organisations and workers self-management was not widespread. However, the May-June revolt shows that events can change very rapidly. *"Under the influence of the students,"* noted libertarian socialist Maurice Brinton, *"thousands began to query the whole principle of hierarchy … Within a matter of days the tremendous creative potentialities of the people suddenly erupted. The boldest and realistic ideas – and they are usually the same – were advocated, argued, applied. Language, rendered stale by decades of bureaucratic mumbo-jumbo, eviscerated by those who manipulate it for advertising purposes, reappeared as something new and fresh. People re-appropriated it in all its fullness. Magnificently apposite and poetic slogans emerged from the anonymous crowd."* [*"Paris: May 1968"*, **For Workers' Power**, p. 253] The working class, fused by the energy and bravado of the students, raised demands that could not be catered for within the confines of the existing system. The General Strike displays with beautiful clarity the potential power that lies in the hands of the working class. The mass assemblies and occupations give an excellent, if short-lived, example of anarchy in action and how anarchist ideas can quickly spread and be applied in practice.

For more details of these events, see participants Daniel and Gabriel Cohn-Bendit's **Obsolete Communism: The Left-Wing Alternative** or Maurice Brinton's eye-witness account *"Paris: may 1968"* (in his **For Workers' Power**). **Beneath the Paving Stones** edited by Dark Star is a good anthology of Situationist works relating to Paris 68 (it also contains Brinton's essay).

Section B
Why do anarchists oppose the current system?

Section B – Why do anarchists oppose the current system? 120

B.1 Why are anarchists against authority and hierarchy?...................121
B.1.1 What are the effects of authoritarian social relationships?.........................123
B.1.2 Is capitalism hierarchical?..127
B.1.3 What kind of hierarchy of values does capitalism create?............................129
B.1.4 Why do racism, sexism and homophobia exist?..130
B.1.5 How is the mass-psychological basis for authoritarian civilisation created?...............133
B.1.6 Can hierarchy be ended?...136

B.2 Why are anarchists against the state?.............................139
B.2.1 What is main function of the state?..142
B.2.2 Does the state have subsidiary functions?..144
B.2.3 How does the ruling class maintain control of the state?..............................147
B.2.4 How does state centralisation affect freedom?...150
B.2.5 Who benefits from centralisation?..152
B.2.6 Can the state be an independent power within society?...............................155

B.3 Why are anarchists against private property?....................157
B.3.1 What is the difference between private property and possession?................159
B.3.2 What kinds of property does the state protect?...160
B.3.3 Why is property exploitative?...165
B.3.4 Can private property be justified?...166
B.3.5 Is state owned property different from private property?...............................169

B.4 How does capitalism affect liberty?.............................169
B.4.1 Is capitalism based on freedom?..171
B.4.2 Is capitalism based on self-ownership?...173
B.4.3 But no one forces you to work for them!...176
B.4.4 But what about periods of high demand for labour?......................................179
B.4.5 But I want to be "left alone"!...180

B.5 Is capitalism empowering and based on human action?............182

B.6 But won't decisions made by individuals with their own money be the best?...................184

B.7 What classes exist within modern society?............................185
B.7.1 But do classes actually exist?..186
B.7.2 Does social mobility make up for class inequality?.......................................188
B.7.3 Why is the existence of classes denied?..190
B.7.4 What do anarchists mean by "class consciousness"?....................................191

Section B
Why do anarchists oppose the current system?

This section of the FAQ presents an analysis of the basic social relationships of modern society and the structures which create them, particularly those aspects of society that anarchists want to change.

Anarchism is, essentially, a revolt against capitalism. As a political theory it was born at the same time as capitalism and in opposition to it. As a social movement it grew in strength and influence as capitalism colonised more and more parts of society. Rather than simply express opposition to the state, as some so-called experts assert, anarchism has always been opposed to other forms of authority and the oppression they create, in particular capitalism and its particular form of private property. It is no coincidence that Proudhon, the first person to declare themselves an anarchist, did so in a book entitled **What is Property?** (and gave the answer **"It is theft!"**). From Proudhon onwards, anarchism has opposed both the state and capitalism (indeed, it is the one thing such diverse thinkers as Benjamin Tucker and Peter Kropotkin both agreed on). Needless to say, since Proudhon anarchism has extended its critique of authority beyond these two social evils. Other forms of social hierarchy, such as sexism, racism and homophobia, have been rejected as limitations of freedom and equality. So this section of the FAQ summarises the key ideas behind anarchism's rejection of the current system we live under.

This, of course, does not mean that anarchistic ideas have not existed within society before the dawn of capitalism. Far from it. Thinkers whose ideas can be classified as anarchist go back thousands of years and are found in many diverse cultures and places. Indeed, it would be no exaggeration to say that anarchism was born the moment the state and private property were created. However, as Kropotkin noted, while *"from all times there have been Anarchists and Statists"* in our times *"Anarchy was brought forth by the same critical and revolutionary protest that gave rise to Socialism in general."* However, unlike other socialists, anarchists have not stopped at the *"negation of Capitalism and of society based on the subjection of labour to capital"* and went further to *"declare themselves against what constitutes the real strength of Capitalism: the State and its principle supports – centralisation of authority, law, always made by a minority for its own profit, and a form of justice whose chief aim is to protect Authority and Capitalism."* So anarchism was *"not only against Capitalism, but also against these pillars of Capitalism: Law, Authority, and the State."* [**Evolution and Environment**, p. 16 and p. 19]In other words, anarchism as it exists today, as a social movement with a long history of struggle and with a political theory and set of ideas, is the product of the transformation of society which accompanied the creation of the modern (nation-)state and capital and (far more importantly) the reaction, resistance and opposition of those subject to these new social relationships and institutions. As such, the analysis and critique presented in this section of the FAQ will concentrate on modern, capitalist, society.

Anarchists realise that the power of governments and other forms of hierarchy depends upon the agreement of the governed. Fear is not the whole answer, it is far more *"because they [the oppressed] subscribe to the same values as their governors. Rulers and ruled alike believe in the principle of authority, of hierarchy, of power."* [Colin Ward, **Anarchy in Action**, p. 15] With this in mind, we present in this section of the FAQ our arguments to challenge this "consensus," to present the case why we should become anarchists, why authoritarian social relationships and organisations are not in our interests.

Needless to say, this task is not easy. No ruling class could survive unless the institutions which empower it are generally accepted by those subject to them. This is achieved by various means – by propaganda, the so-called education system, by tradition, by the media, by the general cultural assumptions of a society. In this way the dominant ideas in society are those of the dominant elite. This means that any social movement needs to combat these ideas before trying to end them:

> *"People often do not even recognise the existence of systems of oppression and domination. They have to try to struggle to gain their rights within the systems in which they live before they even perceive that there is repression. Take a look at the women's movement. One of the first steps in the development of the women's movement was so-called 'consciousness raising efforts.' Try to get women to perceive that it is not the natural state of the world for them to be dominated and controlled. My grandmother couldn't join the women's movement, since she didn't feel any oppression, in some sense. That's just the way life was, like the sun rises in the morning. Until people can realise that it is not like the sun rising, that it can be changed, that you don't have to follow orders, that you don't have to be beaten, until people can perceive that there is something wrong with that, until that is overcome, you can't go on. And one of the ways to do that is to try to press reforms within the existing systems of repression, and sooner or later you find that you will have to change them."* [Noam Chomsky, **Anarchism Interview**]

This means, as Malatesta stressed, that anarchists *"first task therefore must be to persuade people."* This means that we *"must make people aware of the misfortunes they suffer and of their chances to destroy them … To those who are cold and hungry we will demonstrate how possible and easy it would be to assure everybody their material needs. To those who are oppressed and despised we shall show how it is possible to live happily in a world of people who are free and equal … And when we will have succeeded in arousing the sentiment of rebellion in the minds of men [and women] against the avoidable and unjust evils from which we suffer in society today, and in getting them to understand how they are caused and how it depends on human will to rid ourselves of them"* then we will be able to unite and change them for the better. [**Errico Malatesta: His Life and Ideas**, pp. 185-6]

So we must explain **why** we want to change the system. From this discussion, it will become apparent why anarchists are dissatisfied with the very limited amount of freedom in modern society and why they want to create a truly free society. In the words of Noam Chomsky, the anarchist critique of modern society means:

> "to seek out and identify structures of authority, hierarchy, and domination in every aspect of life, and to challenge them; unless a justification for them can be given, they are illegitimate, and should be dismantled, to increase the scope of human freedom. That includes political power, ownership and management, relations among men and women, parents and children, our control over the fate of future generations (the basic moral imperative behind the environmental movement ...), and much else. Naturally this means a challenge to the huge institutions of coercion and control: the state, the unaccountable private tyrannies that control most of the domestic and international economy [i.e. capitalist corporations and companies], and so on. But not only these." [**Marxism, Anarchism, and Alternative Futures**, p. 775]

This task is made easier by the fact that the "dominating class" has **not** "succeeded in reducing all its subjects to passive and unconscious instruments of its interests." This means that where there is oppression and exploitation there is also resistance – and hope. Even when those oppressed by hierarchical social relations generally accept it, those institutions cannot put out the spark of freedom totally. Indeed, they help produce the spirit of revolt by their very operation as people finally say enough is enough and stand up for their rights. Thus hierarchical societies "contain organic contradictions and [these] are like the germs of death" from which "the possibility of progress" springs. [Malatesta, **Op. Cit.**, pp. 186-7]

Anarchists, therefore, combine their critique of existing society with active participation in the on-going struggles which exist in any hierarchical struggle. As we discuss in section J, we urge people to take **direct action** to fight oppression. Such struggles change those who take part in them, breaking the social conditioning which keeps hierarchical society going and making people aware of other possibilities, aware that other worlds are possible and that we do not have to live like this. Thus struggle is the practical school of anarchism, the means by which the preconditions of an anarchist society are created. Anarchists seek to learn from such struggles while, at the same time, propagating our ideas within them and encouraging them to develop into a general struggle for social liberation and change.

Thus the natural resistance of the oppressed to their oppression encourages this process of justification Chomsky (and anarchism) calls for, this critical evaluation of authority and domination, this undermining of what previously was considered "natural" or "common-sense" **until we started to question it.** As noted above, an essential part of this process is to encourage direct action by the oppressed against their oppressors as well as encouraging the anarchistic tendencies and awareness that exist (to a greater or lesser degree) in any hierarchical society. The task of anarchists is to encourage such struggles and the questioning they produce of society and the way it works. We aim to encourage people to look

at the root causes of the social problems they are fighting, to seek to change the underlying social institutions and relationships which produce them. We seek to create an awareness that oppression can not only be fought, but ended, and that the struggle against an unjust system creates the seeds of the society that will replace it. In other words, we seek to encourage hope and a positive vision of a better world.

However, this section of the FAQ is concerned directly with the critical or "negative" aspect of anarchism, the exposing of the evil inherent in all authority, be it from state, property or whatever and why, consequently, anarchists seek "the destruction of power, property, hierarchy and exploitation." [Murray Bookchin, **Post-Scarcity Anarchism**, p. 11] Later sections will indicate how, after analysing the world, anarchists plan to change it constructively, but some of the constructive core of anarchism will be seen even in this section. After this broad critique of the current system, we move onto more specific areas. Section C explains the anarchist critique of the economics of capitalism. Section D discusses how the social relationships and institutions described in this section impact on society as a whole. Section E discusses the causes (and some suggested solutions) to the ecological problems we face.

B.1
Why are anarchists against authority and hierarchy?

First, it is necessary to indicate what kind of authority anarchism challenges. While it is customary for some opponents of anarchism to assert that anarchists oppose all kinds of authority, the reality of the situation is more complex. While anarchists have, on occasion, stated their opposition to "all authority" a closer reading quickly shows that anarchists reject only one specific form of authority, what we tend to call hierarchy (see section H.4 for more details). This can be seen when Bakunin stated that "the principle of **authority**" was the "eminently theological, metaphysical and political idea that the masses, **always** incapable of governing themselves, must submit at all times to the benevolent yoke of a wisdom and a justice, which in one way or another, is imposed from above." [**Marxism, Freedom and the State**, p. 33]

Other forms of authority are more acceptable to anarchists, it depends whether the authority in question becomes a source of **power** over others or not. That is the key to understanding the anarchist position on authority – if it is **hierarchical** authority, then anarchists are against it. The reason is simple:

> "[n]o one should be entrusted with power, inasmuch as anyone invested with authority must ... became an oppressor and exploiter of society." [Bakunin, **The Political Philosophy of Bakunin**, p. 249]

This distinction between forms of authority is important. As Erich Fromm pointed out, "authority" is "a broad term with two entirely different meanings: it can be either 'rational' or 'irrational' authority. Rational authority is based on competence, and it helps the person who leans on it to grow. Irrational authority is based on power and serves to exploit the person subjected to it." [**To Have or To Be**, pp. 44-45] The same point was made by Bakunin over 100 years earlier when he indicated the difference between authority and *"natural influence."* For Bakunin, individual freedom *"results from th[e] great number of material, intellectual, and moral influences which every individual around him [or her] and which society ... continually exercise ... To abolish this mutual influence would be to die."* Consequently, *"when we reclaim the freedom of the masses, we hardly wish to abolish the effect of any individual's or any group of individual's natural influence upon the masses. What we wish is to abolish artificial, privileged, legal, and official influences."* [**The Basic Bakunin**, p. 140 and p. 141]

It is, in other words, the difference between taking part in a decision and listening to alternative viewpoints and experts (*"natural influence"*) before making your mind up and having a decision **made for you** by a separate group of individuals (who may or may not be elected) because that is their role in an organisation or society. In the former, the individual exercises their judgement and freedom (i.e. is based on rational authority). In the latter, they are subjected to the wills of others, to hierarchical authority (i.e. is based on irrational authority). This is because rational authority *"not only permits but requires constant scrutiny and criticism ... it is always temporary, its acceptance depending on its performance."* The source of irrational authority, on the other hand, *"is always power over people ... Power on the one side, fear on the other, are always the buttresses on which irrational authority is built."* Thus the former is based upon *"equality"* while the latter *"is by its very nature based upon inequality."* [Erich Fromm, **Man for Himself**, pp. 9-10]

This crucial point is expressed in the difference between **having** authority and **being** an authority. Being an authority just means that a given person is generally recognised as competent for a given task, based on his or her individual skills and knowledge. Put differently, it is socially acknowledged expertise. In contrast, having authority is a social relationship based on status and power derived from a hierarchical position, not on individual ability. Obviously this does not mean that competence is not an element for obtaining a hierarchical position; it just means that the real or alleged initial competence is transferred to the title or position of the authority and so becomes independent of individuals, i.e. institutionalised (or what Bakunin termed *"official"*).

This difference is important because the way people behave is more a product of the institutions in which we are raised than of any inherent nature. In other words, social relationships **shape** the individuals involved. This means that the various groups individuals create have traits, behaviours and outcomes that cannot be understood by reducing them to the individuals within them. That is, groups consist not only of individuals, but also relationships between individuals and these relationships will affect those subject to them. For example, obviously *"the exercise of power by some disempowers others"* and so through a *"combination of physical intimidation, economic domination and dependency, and psychological limitations, social institutions and practices affect the way everyone sees the world and her or his place in it."* This, as we discuss in the next section, impacts on those involved in

such authoritarian social relationships as *"the exercise of power in any institutionalised form – whether economic, political or sexual – brutalises both the wielder of power and the one over whom it is exercised."* [Martha A. Ackelsberg, **Free Women of Spain**, p. 41] Authoritarian social relationships means dividing society into (the few) order givers and (the many) order takers, impoverishing the individuals involved (mentally, emotionally and physically) and society as a whole. Human relationships, in all parts of life, are stamped by authority, not liberty. And as freedom can only be created by freedom, authoritarian social relationships (and the obedience they require) do not and cannot educate a person in freedom – only participation (self-management) in all areas of life can do that. *"In a society based on exploitation and servitude,"* in Kropotkin's words, *"human nature itself is degraded"* and it is only *"as servitude disappears"* shall we *"regain our rights."* [**Anarchism**, p. 104]

Of course, it will be pointed out that in any collective undertaking there is a need for co-operation and co-ordination and this need to "subordinate" the individual to group activities is a form of authority. Therefore, it is claimed, a democratically managed group is just as "authoritarian" as one based on hierarchical authority. Anarchists are not impressed by such arguments. Yes, we reply, of course in any group undertaking there is a need make and stick by agreements but anarchists argue that to use the word "authority" to describe two fundamentally different ways of making decisions is playing with words. It obscures the fundamental difference between free association and hierarchical imposition and confuses co-operation with command (as we note in section H.4, Marxists are particularly fond of this fallacy). Simply put, there are two different ways of co-ordinating individual activity within groups – either by authoritarian means or by libertarian means. Proudhon, in relation to workplaces, makes the difference clear:

> *"either the workman ... will be simply the employee of the proprietor-capitalist-promoter; or he will participate ... [and] have a voice in the council, in a word he will become an associate.*
>
> *"In the first case the workman is subordinated, exploited: his permanent condition is one of obedience ... In the second case he resumes his dignity as a man and citizen ... he forms part of the producing organisation, of which he was before but the slave; as, in the town, he forms part of the sovereign power, of which he was before but the subject ... we need not hesitate, for we have no choice ... it is necessary to form an ASSOCIATION among workers ... because without that, they would remain related as subordinates and superiors, and there would ensue two ... castes of masters and wage-workers, which is repugnant to a free and democratic society."* [**General Idea of the Revolution**, pp. 215-216]

In other words, associations can be based upon a form of **rational** authority, based upon **natural influence** and so reflect freedom, the ability of individuals to think, act and feel and manage their own time and activity. Otherwise, we include elements of slavery into our relationships with others, elements that poison the whole and shape us in negative ways (see section B.1.1). Only the reorganisation of society in a libertarian way (and, we may add, the mental transformation such a change requires and would create) will allow the individual to *"achieve more or less complete blossoming, whilst continuing to develop"* and banish *"that spirit of submission that has been artificially thrust upon him [or her]"* [Nestor Makhno, **The Struggle Against the State and Other Essays**, p. 62]

So, anarchists *"ask nothing better than to see [others] ... exercise over us a natural and legitimate influence, freely accepted, and never imposed ... We accept all natural authorities and all influences of fact, but none of right."* [Bakunin, **The Political Philosophy of Bakunin**, p. 255] Anarchist support for free association within directly democratic groups is based upon such organisational forms increasing influence and reducing irrational authority in our lives. Members of such organisations can create and present their own ideas and suggestions, critically evaluate the proposals and suggestions from their fellows, accept those that they agree with or become convinced by and have the option of leaving the association if they are unhappy with its direction. Hence the influence of individuals and their free interaction determine the nature of the decisions reached, and no one has the right to impose their ideas on another. As Bakunin argued, in such organisations *"no function remains fixed and it will not remain permanently and irrevocably attached to one person. Hierarchical order and promotion do not exist ... In such a system, power, properly speaking, no longer exists. Power is diffused to the collectivity and becomes the true expression of the liberty of everyone."* [**Bakunin on Anarchism**, p. 415]

Therefore, anarchists are opposed to **irrational** (e.g., illegitimate) authority, in other words, hierarchy – hierarchy being the institutionalisation of authority within a society. Hierarchical social institutions include the state (see section B.2), private property and the class systems it produces (see section B.3) and, therefore, capitalism (see section B.4). Due to their hierarchical nature, anarchists oppose these with passion. *"Every institution, social or civil,"* argued Voltairine de Cleyre, *"that stands between man [or woman] and his [or her] right; every tie that renders one a master, another a serf; every law, every statue, every be-it-enacted that represents tyranny"* anarchists seek to destroy. However, hierarchy exists beyond these institutions. For example, hierarchical social relationships include sexism, racism and homophobia (see section B.1.4), and anarchists oppose, and fight, them all. Thus, as well as fighting capitalism as being hierarchical (for workers *"slave in a factory,"* albeit *"the slavery ends with the working hours"*) de Cleyre also opposed patriarchal social relationships which produce a *"home that rests on slavery"* because of a *"marriage that represents the sale and transfer of the individuality of one of its parties to the other!"* [**The Voltairine de Cleyre Reader**, p. 72, p. 17 and p. 72]

Needless to say, while we discuss different forms of hierarchy in different sections this does not imply that anarchists think they, and their negative effects, are somehow independent or can be easily compartmentalised. For example, the modern state and capitalism are intimately interrelated and cannot be considered as independent of each other. Similarly, social hierarchies like sexism and racism are used by other hierarchies to maintain themselves (for example,

bosses will use racism to divide and so rule their workers). From this it follows that abolishing one or some of these hierarchies, while desirable, would not be sufficient. Abolishing capitalism while maintaining the state would not lead to a free society (and vice versa) – if it were possible. As Murray Bookchin notes:

> *"there can be a decidedly classless, even a non-exploitative society in the **economic** sense that still preserves hierarchical rule and domination in the **social** sense – whether they take the form of the patriarchal family, domination by age and ethnic groups, bureaucratic institutions, ideological manipulation or a pyramidal division of labour ... classless or not, society would be riddled by domination and, with domination, a general condition of command and obedience, of unfreedom and humiliation, and perhaps most decisively, an abortion of each individual's potentiality for consciousness, reason, selfhood, creativity, and the right to assert full control over her or his daily life."* [**Toward an Ecological Society**, pp. 14-5]

This clearly implies that anarchists *"challenge not only class formations but hierarchies, not only material exploitation but domination in every form."* [Bookchin, **Op. Cit.**, p. 15] Hence the anarchist stress on opposing hierarchy rather than just, say, the state (as some falsely assert) or simply economic class and exploitation (as, say, many Marxists do). As noted earlier (in section A.2.8), anarchists consider all hierarchies to be not only harmful but unnecessary, and think that there are alternative, more egalitarian ways to organise social life. In fact, we argue that hierarchical authority creates the conditions it is presumably designed to combat, and thus tends to be self-perpetuating. Thus hierarchical organisations erode the ability of those at the bottom to manage their own affairs directly so requiring hierarchy and some people in positions to give orders and the rest to follow them. Rather than prevent disorder, governments are among its primary causes while its bureaucracies ostensibly set up to fight poverty wind up perpetuating it, because without poverty, the high-salaried top administrators would be out of work. The same applies to agencies intended to eliminate drug abuse, fight crime, etc. In other words, the power and privileges deriving from top hierarchical positions constitute a strong incentive for those who hold them **not** to solve the problems they are supposed to solve. (For further discussion see Marilyn French, **Beyond Power: On Women, Men, and Morals**, Summit Books, 1985.)

B.1.1 What are the effects of authoritarian social relationships?

Hierarchical authority is inextricably connected with the marginalisation and disempowerment of those without authority. This has negative effects on those over whom authority is exercised, since *"[t]hose who have these symbols of authority and those who benefit from them must dull their subject people's realistic, i.e. critical, thinking and make them believe the fiction [that irrational authority is rational and necessary], ... [so] the mind is lulled into* submission by clichés ... [and] people are made dumb because they become dependent and lose their capacity to trust their eyes and judgement." [Erich Fromm, **To Have or To Be?**, p. 47]

Or, in the words of Bakunin, "*the principle of authority, applied to men who have surpassed or attained their majority, becomes a monstrosity, a source of slavery and intellectual and moral depravity.*" [**God and the State**, p. 41]

This is echoed by the syndicalist miners who wrote the classic **The Miners' Next Step** when they indicate the nature of authoritarian organisations and their effect on those involved. Leadership (i.e. hierarchical authority) "*implies power held by the leader. Without power the leader is inept. The possession of power inevitably leads to corruption ... in spite of ... good intentions ... [Leadership means] power of initiative, this sense of responsibility, the self-respect which comes from expressed manhood [sic!], is taken from the men, and consolidated in the leader. The sum of their initiative, their responsibility, their self-respect becomes his ... [and the] order and system he maintains is based upon the suppression of the men, from being independent thinkers into being 'the men' ... In a word, he is compelled to become an autocrat and a foe to democracy.*" Indeed, for the "*leader,*" such marginalisation can be beneficial, for a leader "*sees no need for any high level of intelligence in the rank and file, except to applaud his actions. Indeed such intelligence from his point of view, by breeding criticism and opposition, is an obstacle and causes confusion.*" [**The Miners' Next Step**, pp. 16-17 and p. 15]

Anarchists argue that hierarchical social relationships will have a negative effect on those subject to them, who can no longer exercise their critical, creative and mental abilities **freely**. As Colin Ward argues, people "*do go from womb to tomb without realising their human potential, precisely because the power to initiate, to participate in innovating, choosing, judging, and deciding is reserved for the top men*" (and it usually **is** men!) [**Anarchy in Action**, p, 42]. Anarchism is based on the insight that there is an interrelationship between the authority structures of institutions and the psychological qualities and attitudes of individuals. Following orders all day hardly builds an independent, empowered, creative personality ("*authority and servility walk ever hand in hand.*" [Peter Kropotkin, **Anarchism**, p. 81]). As Emma Goldman made clear, if a person's "*inclination and judgement are subordinated to the will of a master*" (such as a boss, as most people have to sell their labour under capitalism) then little wonder such an authoritarian relationship "*condemns millions of people to be mere nonentities.*" [**Red Emma Speaks**, p. 50]

As the human brain is a bodily organ, it needs to be used regularly in order to be at its fittest. Authority concentrates decision-making in the hands of those at the top, meaning that most people are turned into executants, following the orders of others. If muscle is not used, it turns to fat; if the brain is not used, creativity, critical thought and mental abilities become blunted and side-tracked onto marginal issues, like sports and fashion. This can only have a negative impact:

> "*Hierarchical institutions foster alienated and exploitative relationships among those who participate in them, disempowering people and distancing them from their*

own reality. Hierarchies make some people dependent on others, blame the dependent for their dependency, and then use that dependency as a justification for further exercise of authority. ... Those in positions of relative dominance tend to define the very characteristics of those subordinate to them ... Anarchists argue that to be always in a position of being acted upon and never to be allowed to act is to be doomed to a state of dependence and resignation. Those who are constantly ordered about and prevented from thinking for themselves soon come to doubt their own capacities ... [and have] difficulty acting on [their] sense of self in opposition to societal norms, standards and expectations.*" [Martha Ackelsberg, **Free Women of Spain**, pp. 40-1]

And so, in the words of Colin Ward, the "*system makes its morons, then despises them for their ineptitude, and rewards its 'gifted few' for their rarity.*" [**Op. Cit.**, p. 43]

This negative impact of hierarchy is, of course, not limited to those subject to it. Those in power are affected by it, but in different ways. As we noted in section A.2.15, power corrupts those who have it as well as those subjected to it. The Spanish Libertarian Youth put it this way in the 1930s:

> "*Against the principle of authority because this implies erosion of the human personality when some men submit to the will of others, arousing in these instincts which predispose them to cruelty and indifference in the face of the suffering of their fellows.*" [quoted by Jose Peirats, **The CNT in the Spanish Revolution**, vol. 2, p. 76]

Hierarchy impoverishes the human spirit. "*A hierarchical mentality,*" notes Bookchin, "*fosters the renunciation of the pleasures of life. It justifies toil, guilt, and sacrifice by the 'inferiors,' and pleasure and the indulgent gratification of virtually every caprice by their 'superiors.' The objective history of the social structure becomes internalised as a subjective history of the psychic structure.*" In other words, being subject to hierarchy fosters the internalisation of oppression – and the denial of individuality necessary to accept it. "*Hierarchy, class, and ultimately the State,*" he stresses, "*penetrate the very integument of the human psyche and establish within it unreflective internal powers of coercion and constraint ... By using guilt and self-blame, the inner State can control behaviour long before fear of the coercive powers of the State have to be invoked.*" [**The Ecology of Freedom**, p. 72 and p. 189]

In a nutshell, "*[h]ierarchies, classes, and states warp the creative powers of humanity.*" However, that is not all. Hierarchy, anarchists argue, also twists our relationships with the environment. Indeed, "*all our notions of dominating nature stem from the very real domination of human by human ... And it is not until we eliminate domination in all its forms ... that we will really create a rational, ecological society.*" For "*the conflicts within a divided humanity, structured around domination, inevitably leads to conflicts with nature. The ecological crisis with its embattled division between humanity and nature stems, above all, from divisions between human and human.*" While the "*rise of capitalism, with a law of life based on competition, capital accumulation, and limitless growth, brought these problems – ecological and social – to an acute point,"* anarchists *"emphasise that major ecological problems have their roots in social problems – problems that go back to the very beginnings of patricentric culture itself."* [Murray Bookchin, **Remaking Society**, p. 72, p. 44, p. 72 and pp. 154-5]

Thus, anarchists argue, hierarchy impacts not only on us but also our surroundings. The environmental crisis we face is a result of the hierarchical power structures at the heart of our society, structures which damage the planet's ecology at least as much as they damage humans. The problems within society, the economic, ethnic, cultural, and gender conflicts, among many others, lie at the core of the most serious ecological dislocations we face. The way human beings deal with each other as social beings is crucial to addressing the ecological crisis. Ultimately, ecological destruction is rooted in the organisation of our society for a degraded humanity can only yield a degraded nature (as capitalism and our hierarchical history have sadly shown).

This is unsurprising as we, as a species, shape our environment and, consequently, whatever shapes us will impact how we do so. This means that the individuals produced by the hierarchy (and the authoritarian mentality it produces) will shape the planet in specific, harmful, ways. This is to be expected as humans act upon their environment deliberately, creating what is most suitable for their mode of existence. If that mode of living is riddled with hierarchies, classes, states and the oppression, exploitation and domination they create then our relations with the natural world will hardly be any better. In other words, social hierarchy and class legitimises our domination of the environment, planting the seeds for the belief that nature exists, like other people, to be dominated and used as required.

Which brings us to another key reason why anarchists reject hierarchy. In addition to these negative psychological effects from the denial of liberty, authoritarian social relationships also produce social inequality. This is because an individual subject to the authority of another has to obey the orders of those above them in the social hierarchy. In capitalism this means that workers have to follow the orders of their boss (see next section), orders that are designed to make the boss richer. And richer they have become, with the Chief Executive Officers (CEOs) of big firms earning 212 times what the average US worker did in 1995 (up from a mere 44 times 30 years earlier). Indeed, from 1994 to 1995 alone, CEO compensation in the USA rose 16 percent, compared to 2.8 percent for workers, which did not even keep pace with inflation, and whose stagnating wages cannot be blamed on corporate profits, which rose a healthy 14.8 percent for that year.

Needless to say, inequality in terms of power will translate itself into inequality in terms of wealth (and vice versa). The effects of such social inequality are wide-reaching. For example, health is affected significantly by inequality. Poor people are more likely to be sick and die at an earlier age, compared to rich people. Simply put, *"the lower the class, the worse the health. Going beyond such static measures, even interruptions in income of the sort caused by unemployment have adverse health effects."* Indeed, the sustained economic hardship associated with a low place in the social hierarchy leads to poorer physical, psychological and cognitive functioning

(*"with consequences that last a decade or more"*). *"Low incomes, unpleasant occupations and sustained discrimination,"* notes Doug Henwood, *"may result in apparently physical symptoms that confuse even sophisticated biomedical scientists … Higher incomes are also associated with lower frequency of psychiatric disorders, as are higher levels of asset ownership."* [**After the New Economy**, pp. 81-2]

Moreover, the **degree** of inequality is important (i.e. the size of the gap between rich and poor). According to an editorial in the **British Medical Journal** *"what matters in determining mortality and health in a society is less the overall wealth of that society and more how evenly wealth is distributed. The more equally wealth is distributed the better the health of that society."* [vol. 312, April 20, 1996, p. 985]

Research in the USA found overwhelming evidence of this. George Kaplan and his colleagues measured inequality in the 50 US states and compared it to the age-adjusted death rate for all causes of death, and a pattern emerged: the more unequal the distribution of income, the greater the death rate. In other words, it is the gap between rich and poor, and not the average income in each state, that best predicts the death rate in each state. [*"Inequality in income and mortality in the United States: analysis of mortality and potential pathways,"* **British Medical Journal**, vol. 312, April 20, 1996, pp. 999-1003]

This measure of income inequality was also tested against other social conditions besides health. States with greater inequality in the distribution of income also had higher rates of unemployment, higher rates of incarceration, a higher percentage of people receiving income assistance and food stamps, a greater percentage of people without medical insurance, greater proportion of babies born with low birth weight, higher murder rates, higher rates of violent crime, higher costs per-person for medical care, and higher costs per person for police protection. Moreover states with greater inequality of income distribution also spent less per person on education, had fewer books per person in the schools, and had poorer educational performance, including worse reading skills, worse mathematics skills, and lower rates of completion of high school.

As the gap grows between rich and poor (indicating an increase in social hierarchy within and outwith of workplaces) the health of a people deteriorates and the social fabric unravels. The psychological hardship of being low down on the social ladder has detrimental effects on people, beyond whatever effects are produced by the substandard housing, nutrition, air quality, recreational opportunities, and medical care enjoyed by the poor (see George Davey Smith, *"Income inequality and mortality: why are they related?"* **British Medical Journal**, Vol. 312, April 20, 1996, pp. 987-988).

So wealth does not determine health. What does is the gap between the rich and the poor. The larger the gap, the sicker the society. Countries with a greater degree of socio-economic inequality show greater inequality in health status; also, that middle-income groups in relatively unequal societies have worse health than comparable, or even poorer, groups in more equal societies. Unsurprisingly, this is also reflected over time. The widening income differentials in both the USA and the UK since 1980 have coincided with a slowing down of improvements in life-expectancy, for example.

Inequality, in short, is bad for our health: the health of a population depends not just on the size of the economic pie, but on how the pie is shared.

This is not all. As well as inequalities in wealth, inequalities in freedom also play a large role in overall human well-being. According to Michael Marmot's **The Status Syndrome: How Social Standing Affects Our Health and Longevity**, as you move up any kind of hierarchy your health status improves. Autonomy and position in a hierarchy are related (i.e. the higher you are in a hierarchy, the more autonomy you have). Thus the implication of this empirical work is that autonomy is a source of good health, that the more control you have over your work environment and your life in general, the less likely you are to suffer the classic stress-related illnesses, such as heart disease. As public-Health scholars Jeffrey Johnson and Ellen Hall have noted, the *"potential to control one's own environment is differentially distributed along class lines."* [quoted by Robert Kuttner, **Everything for Sale**, p. 153]

As would be expected from the very nature of hierarchy, to *"be in a life situation where one experiences relentless demands by others, over which one has relatively little control, is to be at risk of poor health, physically as well as mentally."* Looking at heart disease, the people with greatest risk *"tended to be in occupations with high demands, low control, and low social support. People in demanding positions but with great autonomy were at lower risk."* Under capitalism, *"a relatively small elite demands and gets empowerment, self-actualisation, autonomy, and other work satisfaction that partially compensate for long hours"* while *"epidemiological data confirm that lower-paid, lower-status workers are more likely to experience the most clinically damaging forms of stress, in part because they have less control over their work."* [Kuttner, **Op. Cit.**, p. 153 and p. 154]

In other words, the inequality of autonomy and social participation produced by hierarchy is itself a cause of poor health. There would be positive feedback on the total amount of health – and thus of social welfare – if social inequality was reduced, not only in terms of wealth but also, crucially, in power. This is strong evidence in support of anarchist visions of egalitarianism. Some social structures give more people more autonomy than others and acting to promote social justice along these lines is a key step toward improving our health. This means that promoting libertarian, i.e. self-managed, social organisations would increase not only liberty but also people's health and well-being, both physical and mental. Which is, as we argued above, to be expected as hierarchy, by its very nature, impacts negatively on those subject to it.

This dovetails into anarchist support for workers' control. Industrial psychologists have found that satisfaction in work depends on the "span of autonomy" works have. Unsurprisingly, those workers who are continually making decisions for themselves are happier and live longer. It is the power to control all aspects of your life – work particularly – that wealth and status tend to confer that is the key determinant of health. Men who have low job control face a 50% higher risk of new illness: heart attacks, stroke, diabetes or merely ordinary infections. Women are at slightly lower risk but low job control was still a factor in whether they fell ill or not.

So it is the fact that the boss is a boss that makes the employment relationship so troublesome for health issues (and genuine libertarians). The more bossy the boss, the worse, as a rule is the

job. So part of autonomy is not being bossed around, but that is only part of the story. And, of course, hierarchy (inequality of power) and exploitation (the source of material inequality) are related. As we indicate in the next section, capitalism is based on wage labour. The worker sells their liberty to the boss for a given period of time, i.e. they loose their autonomy. This allows the possibility of exploitation, as the worker can produce more wealth than they receive back in wages. As the boss pockets the difference, lack of autonomy produces increases in social inequality which, in turn, impacts negatively on your well-being.

Then there is the waste associated with hierarchy. While the proponents of authority like to stress its "efficiency," the reality is different. As Colin Ward points out, being in authority *"derives from your rank in some chain of command … But knowledge and wisdom are not distributed in order of rank, and they are no one person's monopoly in any undertaking. The fantastic inefficiency of any hierarchical organisation – any factory, office, university, warehouse or hospital – is the outcome of two almost invariable characteristics. One is that the knowledge and wisdom of the people at the bottom of the pyramid finds no place in the decision-making leadership hierarchy of the institution. Frequently it is devoted to making the institution work in spite of the formal leadership structure, or alternatively to sabotaging the ostensible function of the institution, because it is none of their choosing. The other is that they would rather not be there anyway: they are there through economic necessity rather than through identification with a common task which throws up its own shifting and functional leadership."* [**Op. Cit.**, p. 41]

Hierarchy, in other words, blocks the flow of information and knowledge. Rulers, as Malatesta argued, *"can only make use of the forces that exist in society – except for those great forces"* their action *"paralyses and destroys, and those rebel forces, and all that is wasted through conflicts; inevitable tremendous losses in such an artificial system."* And so as well as individuals being prevented from developing to their fullest, wasting their unfulfilled potentialities, hierarchy also harms society as a whole by reducing efficiency and creativity. This is because input into decisions are limited *"only to those individuals who form the government [of a hierarchical organisation] or who by reason of their position can influence the[ir] policy."* Obviously this means *"that far from resulting in an increase in the productive, organising and protective forces in society,"* hierarchy *"greatly reduce[s] them, limiting initiative to a few, and giving them the right to do everything without, of course, being able to provide them with the gift of being all-knowing."* [**Anarchy**, p. 38 and p. 39]

Large scale hierarchical organisations, like the state, are also marked by bureaucracy. This becomes a necessity in order to gather the necessary information it needs to make decisions (and, obviously, to control those under it). However, soon this bureaucracy becomes the real source of power due to its permanence and control of information and resources. Thus hierarchy cannot *"survive without creating around itself a new privileged class"* as well as being a *"privileged class and cut off from the people"* itself. [Malatesta, **Op. Cit.**, p. 37 and p. 36] This means that those at the top of an institution rarely know the facts on the ground, making decisions in relative ignorance of their impact or the actual needs of the situation or people involved. As economist Joseph Stiglitz concluded from his own experiences in the World Bank, *"immense time and effort are required to effect change even from the inside, in an international bureaucracy. Such organisations are opaque rather than transparent, and not only does far too little information radiate from inside to the outside world, perhaps even less information from outside is able to penetrate the organisation. The opaqueness also means that it is hard for information from the bottom of the organisation to percolate to the top."* [**Globalisation and its Discontents**, p. 33] The same can be said of any hierarchical organisation, whether a nation state or capitalist business.

Moreover, as Ward and Malatesta indicate, hierarchy provokes a struggle between those at the bottom and at the top. This struggle is also a source of waste as it diverts resources and energy from more fruitful activity into fighting it. Ironically, as we discuss in section H.4.4, one weapon forged in that struggle is the **"work to rule,"** namely workers bringing their workplace to a grinding halt by following the dictates of the boss to the letter. This is clear evidence that a workplace only operates because workers exercise their autonomy during working hours, an autonomy which authoritarian structures stifle and waste. A participatory workplace, therefore, would be more efficient and less wasteful than the hierarchical one associated with capitalism. As we discuss in section J.5.12, hierarchy and the struggle it creates always acts as a barrier stopping the increased efficiency associated with workers' participation undermining the autocratic workplace of capitalism.

All this is not to suggest that those at the bottom of hierarchies are victims nor that those at the top of hierarchies only gain benefits – far from it. As Ward and Malatesta indicated, hierarchy by its very nature creates resistance to it from those subjected to it and, in the process, the potential for ending it (see section B.1.6 for more discussion). Conversely, at the summit of the pyramid, we also see the evils of hierarchy.

If we look at those at the top of the system, yes, indeed they often do **very** well in terms of material goods and access to education, leisure, health and so on but they lose their humanity and individuality. As Bakunin pointed out, *"power and authority corrupt those who exercise them as much as those who are compelled to submit to them."* [**The Political Philosophy of Bakunin**, p. 249] Power operates destructively, even on those who have it, reducing their individuality as it *"renders them stupid and brutal, even when they were originally endowed with the best of talents. One who is constantly striving to force everything into a mechanical order at last becomes a machine himself and loses all human feeling."* [Rudolf Rocker, **Anarcho-Syndicalism**, pp. 17-8]

When it boils down to it, hierarchy is self-defeating, for if *"wealth is other people,"* then by treating others as less than yourself, restricting their growth, you lose all the potential insights and abilities these individuals have, so impoverishing your own life and **restricting your own growth.** Unfortunately in these days material wealth (a particularly narrow form of "self-interest") has replaced concern for developing the whole person and leading a fulfilling and creative life (a broad self-interest, which places the individual **within** society, one that recognises that relationships with others shape and develop all individuals). In a hierarchical,

class based society everyone loses to some degree, even those at the "top."

Looking at the environment, the self-defeating nature of hierarchy also becomes clear. The destiny of human life goes hand-in-hand with the destiny of the non-human world. While being rich and powerful may mitigate the impact of the ecological destruction produced by hierarchies and capitalism, it will not stop them and will, eventually, impact on the elite as well as the many.

Little wonder, then, that *"anarchism ... works to destroy authority in all its aspects ... [and] refuses all hierarchical organisation."* [Kropotkin, **Anarchism**, p. 137]

B.1.2 Is capitalism hierarchical?

Yes. Under capitalism workers do not exchange the products of their labour they exchange the labour itself for money. They sell themselves for a given period of time, and in return for wages, promise to obey their paymasters. Those who pay and give the orders – owners and managers – are at the top of the hierarchy, those who obey at the bottom. This means that capitalism, by its very nature, is hierarchical.

As Carole Pateman argues:

> *"Capacities or labour power cannot be used without the worker using his will, his understanding and experience, to put them into effect. The use of labour power requires the presence of its 'owner,' and it remains mere potential until he acts in the manner necessary to put it into use, or agrees or is compelled so to act; that is, the worker must labour. To contract for the use of labour power is a waste of resources unless it can be used in the way in which the new owner requires. The fiction 'labour power' cannot be used; what is required is that the worker labours as demanded. The employment contract must, therefore, create a relationship of command and obedience between employer and worker... In short, the contract in which the worker allegedly sells his labour power is a contract in which, since he cannot be separated from his capacities, he sells command over the use of his body and himself. To obtain the right to use another is to be a (civil) master."* [**The Sexual Contract**, pp. 150-1]

You need only compare this to Proudhon's comments quoted in section B.1 to see that anarchists have long recognised that capitalism is, by its very nature, hierarchical. The worker is subjected to the authority of the boss during working hours (sometimes outside work too). As Noam Chomsky summarises, *"a corporation, factory or business is the economic equivalent of fascism: decisions and control are strictly top-down."* [**Letters from Lexington**, p. 127] The worker's choices are extremely limited, for most people it amount to renting themselves out to a series of different masters (for a lucky few, the option of being a master is available). And master is the right word for, as David Ellerman reminds us, *"[s]ociety seems to have 'covered up' in the popular consciousness the fact* that the traditional name [for employer and employee] is **'master and servant.'"** [**Property and Contract in Economics**, p. 103]

This hierarchical control of wage labour has the effect of alienating workers from their own work, and so from themselves. Workers no longer govern themselves during work hours and so are no longer free. And so, due to capitalism, there is *"an oppression in the land,"* a *"form of slavery"* rooted in current *"property institutions"* which produces *"a social war, inevitable so long as present legal-social conditions endure."* [Voltairine de Cleyre, **Op. Cit.**, pp. 54-5]

Some defenders of capitalism are aware of the contradiction between the rhetoric of the system and its reality for those subject to it. Most utilise the argument that workers consent to this form of hierarchy. Ignoring the economic conditions which force people to sell their liberty on the labour market (see section B.4.3), the issue instantly arises of whether consent is enough in itself to justify the alienation/selling of a person's liberty. For example, there have been arguments for slavery and monarchy (i.e. dictatorship) rooted in consent. Do we really want to say that the only thing wrong with fascism or slavery is that people do not consent to it? Sadly, some right-wing "libertarians" come to that conclusion (see section B.4). Some try to redefine the reality of the command-and-obey of wage labour. *"To speak of managing, directing, or assigning workers to various tasks is a deceptive way of noting that the employer continually is involved in re-negotiation of contracts on terms that must be acceptable to both parties,"* argue two right-wing economists. [Arman Alchian and Harold Demsetz, quoted by Ellerman, **Op. Cit.**, p. 170] So the employer-employee (or, to use the old, more correct, terminology, master-servant) contract is thus a series of unspoken contracts.

However, if an oral contract is not worth the paper it is written on, how valuable is an unspoken one? And what does this *"re-negotiation of contracts"* amount to? The employee decides whether to obey the command or leave and the boss decides whether the employee is obedient and productive enough to remain in under his or her control. Hardly a relationship based on freedom between equal partners! As such, this capitalist defence of wage labour *"is a deceptive way of noting"* that the employee is paid to obey. The contract between them is simply that of obedience on one side and power on the other. That both sides may break the contract does not alter this fact. Thus the capitalist workplace *"is not democratic in spite of the 'consent of the governed' to the employment contract … In the employment contract, the workers alienate and transfer their legal rights to the employer to govern their activities 'within the scope of the employment' to the employer."* [David Ellerman, **The Democratic Worker-Owned Firm**, p. 50]

Ultimately, there is **one** right that cannot be ceded or abandoned, namely the right to personality. If a person gave up their personality they would cease to be a person yet this is what the employment contract imposes. To maintain and develop their personality is a basic right of humanity and it cannot be transferred to another, permanently or temporarily. To argue otherwise would be to admit that under certain circumstances and for certain periods of time a person is not a person but rather a thing to be used by others. Yet this is precisely what capitalism does due to its hierarchical nature. This is not all. Capitalism, by treating labour as analogous to all other commodities denies the key distinction between labour

and other "resources" – that is to say its inseparability from its bearer – labour, unlike other "property," is endowed with will and agency. Thus when one speaks of selling labour there is a necessary subjugation of will (hierarchy). As Karl Polanyi writes:

"Labour is only another name for human activity which goes with life itself, which is in turn not produced for sale but for entirely different reasons, nor can that activity be detached from the rest of life itself, be stored or mobilised … To allow the market mechanism to be sole director of the fate of human beings and their natural environment … would result in the demolition of society. For the alleged commodity 'labour power' cannot be shoved about, used indiscriminately, or even left unused, without affecting also the human individual who happens to be the bearer of this peculiar commodity. In disposing of a man's labour power the system would, incidentally, dispose of the physical, psychological, and moral entity 'man' attached to that tag." [**The Great Transformation**, p. 72]

In other words, labour is much more than the commodity to which capitalism tries to reduce it. Creative, self-managed work is a source of pride and joy and part of what it means to be fully human. Wrenching control of work from the hands of the worker profoundly harms his or her mental and physical health. Indeed, Proudhon went so far as to argue that capitalist companies *"plunder the bodies and souls of the wage-workers"* and were an *"outrage upon human dignity and personality."* [**Op. Cit.**, p. 219] This is because wage labour turns productive activity and the person who does it into a commodity. People *"are not human **beings** so much as human **resources**. To the morally blind corporation, they are tool to generate as much profit as possible. And 'the tool can be treated just like a piece of metal – you use it if you want, you throw it away if you don't want it,' says Noam Chomsky. 'If you can get human beings to become tool like that, it's more efficient by some measure of efficiency … a measure which is based on dehumanisation. You have to dehumanise it. That's part of the system.'"* [Joel Bakan, **The Corporation**, p. 69]

Separating labour from other activities of life and subjecting it to the laws of the market means to annihilate its natural, organic form of existence – a form that evolved with the human race through tens of thousands of years of co-operative economic activity based on sharing and mutual aid – and replacing it with an atomistic and individualistic one based on contract and competition. Unsurprisingly, this relationship is a very recent development and, moreover, the product of substantial state action and coercion (see section F.8 for some discussion of this). Simply put, *"the early labourer … abhorred the factory, where he [or she] felt degraded and tortured."* While the state ensured a steady pool of landless workers by enforcing private property rights, the early manufacturers also utilised the state to ensure low wages, primarily for social reasons – only an overworked and downtrodden labourer with no other options would agree to do whatever their master required of them. *"Legal compulsion and parish serfdom as in England,"* noted Polanyi, *"the rigors of an absolutist labour police as on the Continent, indented labour as in the early Americas were the prerequisites of the 'willing worker.'"* [**Op. Cit.**, pp. 164-5]

Ignoring its origins in state action, the social relationship of wage labour is then claimed by capitalists to be a source of "freedom," whereas in fact it is a form of (in)voluntary servitude (see sections B.4 and A.2.14 for more discussion). Therefore a libertarian who did not support economic liberty (i.e. self-government in industry, libertarian socialism) would be no libertarian at all, and no believer in liberty. Capitalism is based upon hierarchy and the denial of liberty. To present it otherwise denies the nature of wage labour. However, supporters of capitalism try to but – as Karl Polanyi points out – the idea that wage labour is based upon some kind of "natural" liberty is false:

> "To represent this principle [wage labour] as one of non-interference [with freedom], as economic liberals were wont to do, was merely the expression of an ingrained prejudice in favour of a definite kind of interference, namely, such as would destroy non-contractual relations between individuals and prevent their spontaneous re-formation." [**Op. Cit.**, p.163]

As noted above, capitalism itself was created by state violence and the destruction of traditional ways of life and social interaction was part of that task. From the start, bosses spent considerable time and energy combating attempts of working people to join together to resist the hierarchy they were subjected to and reassert human values. Such forms of free association between equals (such as trade unions) were combated, just as attempts to regulate the worse excesses of the system by democratic governments. Indeed, capitalists prefer centralised, elitist and/or authoritarian regimes precisely because they are sure to be outside of popular control (see section B.2.5). They are the only way that contractual relations based on market power could be enforced on an unwilling population. Capitalism was born under such states and as well as backing fascist movements, they made high profits in Nazi Germany and Fascist Italy. Today many corporations *"regularly do business with totalitarian and authoritarian regimes – again, because it is profitable to do so."* Indeed, there is a *"trend by US corporations to invest in"* such countries. [Joel Bakan, **Op. Cit.**, p. 89 and p. 185] Perhaps unsurprisingly, as such regimes are best able to enforce the necessary conditions to commodify labour fully.

B.1.3 What kind of hierarchy of values does capitalism create?

Anarchists argue that capitalism can only have a negative impact on ethical behaviour. This flows from its hierarchical nature. We think that hierarchy must, by its very nature, always impact negatively on morality.

As we argued in section A.2.19, ethics is dependent on both individual liberty and equality between individuals. Hierarchy violates both and so the *"great sources of moral depravity"* are *"capitalism, religion, justice, government."* In *"the domain of economy, coercion has lead us to industrial servitude; in the domain of politics to the State … [where] the nation … becomes nothing but a mass of obedient **subjects** to a central authority."* This has *"contributed*

and powerfully aided to create all the present economic, political, and social evils" and *"has given proof of its absolute impotence to raise the moral level of societies; it has not even been able to maintain it at the level it had already reached."* This is unsurprising, as society developed *"authoritarian prejudices"* and *"men become more and more divided into governors and governed, exploiters and exploited, the moral level fell … and the spirit of the age declined."* By violating equality, by rejecting social co-operation between equals in favour of top-down, authoritarian, social relationships which turn some into the tools of others, capitalism, like the state, could not help but erode ethical standards as the *"moral level"* of society is *"debased by the practice of authority."* [Kropotkin, **Anarchism**, pp. 137-8, p. 106 and p. 139]

However, as well as promoting general unethical behaviour, capitalism produces a specific perverted hierarchy of values – one that places humanity below property. As Erich Fromm argues:

> "The use [i.e. exploitation] of man by man is expressive of the **system of values** underlying the capitalistic system. **Capital, the dead past, employs labour – the living vitality and power of the present.** In the capitalistic hierarchy of values, capital stands higher than labour, amassed things higher than the manifestations of life. Capital employs labour, and not labour capital. The person who owns capital commands the person who 'only' owns his life, human skill, vitality and creative productivity. 'Things' are higher than man. The conflict between capital and labour is much more than the conflict between two classes, more than their fight for a greater share of the social product. It is the conflict between two principles of value: **that between the world of things, and their amassment, and the world of life and its productivity.**" [**The Sane Society**, pp. 94-95]

Capitalism only values a person as representing a certain amount of the commodity called "labour power," in other words, as a **thing**. Instead of being valued as an individual – a unique human being with intrinsic moral and spiritual worth – only one's price tag counts. This replacement of human relationships by economic ones soon results in the replacement of human values by economic ones, giving us an "ethics" of the account book, in which people are valued by how much they earn. It also leads, as Murray Bookchin argues, to a debasement of human values:

> "So deeply rooted is the market economy in our minds that its grubby language has replaced our most hallowed moral and spiritual expressions. We now 'invest' in our children, marriages, and personal relationships, a term that is equated with words like 'love' and 'care.' We live in a world of 'trade-offs' and we ask for the 'bottom line' of any emotional 'transaction.' We use the terminology of contracts rather than that of loyalties and spiritual affinities." [**The Modern Crisis**, p. 79]

With human values replaced by the ethics of calculation, and with only the laws of market and state "binding" people together, social breakdown is inevitable. Little wonder modern capitalism has seen a massive increase in crime and dehumanisation under the freer markets established by "conservative" governments, such as those of Thatcher and Reagan and their transnational corporate masters. We now live in a society where people live in self-constructed fortresses, "free" behind their walls and defences (both emotional and physical).

Of course, some people **like** the "ethics" of mathematics. But this is mostly because – like all gods – it gives the worshipper an easy rule book to follow. "Five is greater than four, therefore five is better" is pretty simple to understand. John Steinbeck noticed this when he wrote:

> "Some of them [the owners] hated the mathematics that drove them [to kick the farmers off their land], and some were afraid, and some worshipped the mathematics because it provided a refuge from thought and from feeling." [**The Grapes of Wrath**, p. 34]

The debasement of the individual in the workplace, where so much time is spent, necessarily affects a person's self-image, which in turn carries over into the way he or she acts in other areas of life. If one is regarded as a commodity at work, one comes to regard oneself and others in that way also. Thus all social relationships – and so, ultimately, **all** individuals – are commodified. In capitalism, literally nothing is sacred – "everything has its price" – be it dignity, self-worth, pride, honour – all become commodities up for grabs. Such debasement produces a number of social pathologies. "Consumerism" is one example which can be traced directly to the commodification of the individual under capitalism. To quote Fromm again, "**Things** have no self, and men who have become things [i.e. commodities on the labour market] can have no self." [**Op. Cit.**, p. 143]

However, people still feel the **need** for selfhood, and so try to fill the emptiness by consuming. The illusion of happiness, that one's life will be complete if one gets a new commodity, drives people to consume. Unfortunately, since commodities are yet more things, they provide no substitute for selfhood, and so the consuming must begin anew. This process is, of course, encouraged by the advertising industry, which tries to convince us to buy what we don't need because it will make us popular/sexy/happy/free/etc. (delete as appropriate!). But consuming cannot really satisfy the needs that the commodities are bought to satisfy. Those needs can only be satisfied by social interaction based on truly human values and by creative, self-directed work.

This does not mean, of course, that anarchists are against higher living standards or material goods. To the contrary, they recognise that liberty and a good life are only possible when one does not have to worry about having enough food, decent housing, and so forth. Freedom and 16 hours of work a day do not go together, nor do equality and poverty or solidarity and hunger. However, anarchists consider consumerism to be a distortion of consumption caused by the alienating and inhuman "account book" ethics of capitalism, which crushes the individual and his or her sense of identity, dignity and selfhood.

B.1.4 Why do racism, sexism and homophobia exist?

Since racism, sexism and homophobia (hatred/fear of homosexuals) are institutionalised throughout society, sexual, racial and gay oppression are commonplace. The primary cause of these three evil attitudes is the need for ideologies that justify domination and exploitation, which are inherent in hierarchy – in other words, "theories" that "justify" and "explain" oppression and injustice. As Tacitus said, *"We hate those whom we injure."* Those who oppress others always find reasons to regard their victims as "inferior" and hence deserving of their fate. Elites need some way to justify their superior social and economic positions. Since the social system is obviously unfair and elitist, attention must be distracted to other, less inconvenient, "facts," such as alleged superiority based on biology or "nature." Therefore, doctrines of sexual, racial, and ethnic superiority are inevitable in hierarchical, class-stratified societies. We will take each form of bigotry in turn.

From an economic standpoint, racism is associated with the exploitation of cheap labour at home and imperialism abroad. Indeed, early capitalist development in both America and Europe was strengthened by the bondage of people, particularly those of African descent. In the Americas, Australia and other parts of the world the slaughter of the original inhabitants and the expropriation of their land was also a key aspect in the growth of capitalism. As the subordination of foreign nations proceeds by force, it appears to the dominant nation that it owes its mastery to its special natural qualities, in other words to its "racial" characteristics. Thus imperialists have frequently appealed to the Darwinian doctrine of "Survival of the Fittest" to give their racism a basis in "nature."

In Europe, one of the first theories of racial superiority was proposed by Gobineau in the 1850s to establish the natural right of the aristocracy to rule over France. He argued that the French aristocracy was originally of Germanic origin while the "masses" were Gallic or Celtic, and that since the Germanic race was "superior", the aristocracy had a natural right to rule. Although the French "masses" didn't find this theory particularly persuasive, it was later taken up by proponents of German expansion and became the origin of German racial ideology, used to justify Nazi oppression of Jews and other "non-Aryan" types. Notions of the "white man's burden" and "Manifest Destiny" developed at about the same time in England and to a lesser extent in America, and were used to rationalise Anglo-Saxon conquest and world domination on a "humanitarian" basis.

Racism and authoritarianism at home and abroad has gone hand in hand. As Rudolf Rocker argued, *"[a]ll advocates of the race doctrine have been and are the associates and defenders of every political and social reaction, advocates of the power principle in its most brutal form … He who thinks that he sees in all political and social antagonisms merely blood-determined manifestations of race, denies all conciliatory influence of ideas, all community of ethical feeling, and must at every crisis take refuge in brute force. In fact, race theory is only the cult of power."* Racism aids the consolidation of elite power by attacking *"all the achievements … in the direction of personal freedom"* and the idea of equality *"[n]o better moral justification could be produced for the industrial bondage which our holders of industrial power keep before them as a picture of the future."* [**Nationalism and Culture**, pp. 337-8]

The idea of racial superiority was also found to have great domestic utility. As Paul Sweezy points out, *"[t]he intensification of social conflict within the advanced capitalist countries ... has to be directed as far as possible into innocuous channels – innocuous, that is to say, from the standpoint of capitalist class rule. The stirring up of antagonisms along racial lines is a convenient method of directing attention away from class struggle,"* which of course is dangerous to ruling-class interests. [**Theory of Capitalist Development**, p. 311] Indeed, employers have often deliberately fostered divisions among workers on racial lines as part of a strategy of "divide and rule" (in other contexts, like Northern Ireland or Scotland, the employers have used religion in the same way instead).

In others, immigrants and native born is the dividing line. The net effect is the same, social oppressions which range from the extreme violence anarchists like Emma Goldman denounced in the American South (*"the atrocities rampant in the South, of negroes lynched, tortured and burned by infuriated crowds without a hand being raised or a word said for their protection"* [**Emma Goldman: A Documentary History of the American Years**, vol. 1, p. 386]) or the pogroms against Jews in Tsarist Russia to discrimination in where people can live, what jobs people can get, less pay and so on.

For those in power, this makes perfect sense as racism (like other forms of bigotry) can be used to split and divide the working class by getting people to blame others of their class for the conditions they all suffer. In this way, the anger people feel about the problems they face are turned away from their real causes onto scapegoats. Thus white workers are subtly (and sometimes not so subtly) encouraged, for example, to blame unemployment, poverty and crime on blacks or Hispanics instead of capitalism and the (white, male) elites who run it and who directly benefit from low wages and high profits. Discrimination against racial minorities and women makes sense for capitalism, for in this way profits are enlarged directly and indirectly. As jobs and investment opportunities are denied to the disadvantaged groups, their wages can be depressed below prevailing levels and profits, correspondingly, increased. Indirectly, discrimination adds capitalist profits and power by increasing unemployment and setting workers against each other. Such factors ensure that capitalism will never "compete" discrimination away as some free-market capitalist economists argue.

In other words, capitalism has benefited and will continue to benefit from its racist heritage. Racism has provided pools of cheap labour for capitalists to draw upon and permitted a section of the population to be subjected to worse treatment, so increasing profits by reducing working conditions and other non-pay related costs. In America, blacks still get paid less than whites for the same work (around 10% less than white workers with the same education, work experience, occupation and other relevant demographic variables). This is transferred into wealth inequalities. In 1998, black incomes were 54% of white incomes while black net worth (including residential) was 12% and non-residential net worth just 3% of white. For Hispanics, the picture was similar with incomes

just 62% of whites, net worth, 4% and non-residential net worth 0%. While just under 15% of white households had zero or negative net worth, 27% of black households and 36% Hispanic were in the same situation. Even at similar levels of income, black households were significantly less wealthy than white ones. [Doug Henwood, **After the New Economy**, p. 99 and pp. 125-6]

All this means that racial minorities are *"subjected to oppression and exploitation on the dual grounds of race and class, and thus have to fight the extra battles against racism and discrimination."* [Lorenzo Kom'boa Ervin, **Anarchism and the Black Revolution**, p. 126]

Sexism only required a "justification" once women started to act for themselves and demand equal rights. Before that point, sexual oppression did not need to be "justified" – it was "natural" (saying that, of course, equality between the sexes was stronger before the rise of Christianity as a state religion and capitalism so the "place" of women in society has fallen over the last few hundred years before rising again thanks to the women's movement).

The nature of sexual oppression can be seen from marriage. Emma Goldman pointed out that marriage *"stands for the sovereignty of the man over the women,"* with her *"complete submission"* to the husbands *"whims and commands."* [**Red Emma Speaks**, p. 164] As Carole Pateman notes, until *"the late nineteenth century the legal and civil position of a wife resembled that of a slave ... A slave had no independent legal existence apart from his master, and husband and wife became 'one person,' the person of the husband."* Indeed, the law *"was based on the assumption that a wife was (like) property"* and only the marriage contract *"includes the explicit commitment to obey."* [**The Sexual Contract**, p. 119, p. 122 and p. 181]

However, when women started to question the assumptions of male domination, numerous theories were developed to explain why women's oppression and domination by men was "natural." Because men enforced their rule over women by force, men's "superiority" was argued to be a "natural" product of their gender, which is associated with greater physical strength (on the premise that "might makes right"). In the 17th century, it was argued that women were more like animals than men, thus "proving" that women had as much right to equality with men as sheep did. More recently, elites have embraced socio-biology in response to the growing women's movement. By "explaining" women's oppression on biological grounds, a social system run by men and for men could be ignored.

Women's subservient role also has economic value for capitalism (we should note that Goldman considered capitalism to be another *"paternal arrangement"* like marriage, both of which robbed people of their *"birthright,"* *"stunts"* their growth, *"poisons"* their bodies and keeps people in *"ignorance, in poverty and dependence."* [**Op. Cit.**, p. 210]). Women often provide necessary (and unpaid) labour which keeps the (usually) male worker in good condition; and it is primarily women who raise the next generation of wage-slaves (again without pay) for capitalist owners to exploit. Moreover, women's subordination gives working-class men someone to look down upon and, sometimes, a convenient target on whom they can take out their frustrations (instead of stirring up trouble at work). As Lucy Parsons pointed out, a working class woman is *"a slave to a slave."*

Sexism, like all forms of bigotry, is reflected in relative incomes and wealth levels. In the US women, on average, were being paid 57% the amount men were in 2001 (an improvement on the 39% 20 years earlier). Part of this is due to fewer women working than men, but for those who do work outside the home their incomes were 66% of men's (up from 47% in 1980 and 38% in 1970). Those who work full time, their incomes 76% of men's, up from the 60% average through most of the 1970s. However, as with the black-white gap, this is due in part to the stagnant income of male workers (in 1998 men's real incomes were just 1% above 1989 levels while women's were 14% above). So rather than the increase in income being purely the result of women entering high-paying and largely male occupations and them closing the gender gap, it has also been the result of the intense attacks on the working class since the 1980s which has de-unionised and de-industrialised America. This has resulted in a lot of high-paying male jobs being lost and more and more women have entered the job market to make sure their families make ends meet. [Henwood, **Op. Cit.**, p. 91-2]

Turning away from averages, we discover that sexism results in women being paid about 12% less than men during the same job, with the same relative variables (like work experience, education and so forth). Needless to say, as with racism, such "relevant variables" are themselves shaped by discrimination. Women, like blacks, are less likely to get job interviews and jobs. Sexism even affects types of jobs, for example, "caring" professions pay less than non-caring ones because they are seen as feminine and involve the kinds of tasks which women do at home without pay. In general, female dominated industries pay less. In 1998, occupations that were over 90% male had a median wage almost 10% above average while those over 90% female, almost 25% below. One study found that a 30% increase in women in an occupation translated into a 10% decline in average pay. Needless to say, having children is bad economic news for most women (women with children earn 10 to 15% less than women without children while for men the opposite is the case). [Henwood, **Op. Cit.**, p. 95-7]

The oppression of lesbians, gays and bisexuals is inextricably linked with sexism. A patriarchal, capitalist society cannot see homosexual practices as the normal human variations they are because they blur that society's rigid gender roles and sexist stereotypes. Most young gay people keep their sexuality to themselves for fear of being kicked out of home and all gays have the fear that some "straights" will try to kick their sexuality out of them if they express their sexuality freely. As with those subject to other forms of bigotry, gays are also discriminated against economically (gay men earning about 4-7% less than the average straight man [Henwood, **Op. Cit.**, p. 100]). Thus the social oppression which result in having an alternative sexuality are experienced on many different levels, from extreme violence to less pay for doing the same work.

Gays are not oppressed on a whim but because of the specific need of capitalism for the nuclear family. The nuclear family, as the primary – and inexpensive – creator of submissive people (growing up within the authoritarian family gets children used to, and "respectful" of, hierarchy and subordination – see section B.1.5) as well as provider and carer for the workforce fulfils an important need for capitalism. Alternative sexualities represent a threat to the family model because they provide a different role model for

people. This means that gays are going to be in the front line of attack whenever capitalism wants to reinforce "family values" (i.e. submission to authority, "tradition", "morality" and so on). The introduction of Clause 28 in Britain is a good example of this, with the government making it illegal for public bodies to promote gay sexuality (i.e. to present it as anything other than a perversion). In American, the right is also seeking to demonise homosexuality as part of their campaign to reinforce the values of the patriarchal family unit and submission to "traditional" authority. Therefore, the oppression of people based on their sexuality is unlikely to end until sexism is eliminated.

This is not all. As well as adversely affecting those subject to them, sexism, racism and homophobia are harmful to those who practice them (and in some way benefit from them) within the working class itself. Why this should be the case is obvious, once you think about it. All three divide the working class, which means that whites, males and heterosexuals hurt themselves by maintaining a pool of low-paid competing labour, ensuring low wages for their own wives, daughters, mothers, relatives and friends. Such divisions create inferior conditions and wages for all as capitalists gain a competitive advantage using this pool of cheap labour, forcing all capitalists to cut conditions and wages to survive in the market (in addition, such social hierarchies, by undermining solidarity against the employer on the job and the state possibly create a group of excluded workers who could become scabs during strikes). Also, "privileged" sections of the working class lose out because their wages and conditions are less than those which unity could have won them. Only the boss really wins.

This can be seen from research into this subject. The researcher Al Szymanski sought to systematically and scientifically test the proposition that white workers gain from racism ["Racial Discrimination and White Gain", in **American Sociological Review**, vol. 41, no. 3, June 1976, pp. 403-414]. He compared the situation of "white" and "non-white" (i.e. black, Native American, Asian and Hispanic) workers in United States and found several key things:

(1) the narrower the gap between white and black wages in an American state, the higher white earnings were relative to white earnings elsewhere. This means that "whites do not benefit economically by economic discrimination. White workers especially appear to benefit economically from the **absence** of economic discrimination ... both in the absolute level of their earnings **and** in relative equality among whites." [p. 413] In other words, the less wage discrimination there was against black workers, the better were the wages that white workers received.

(2) the more "non-white" people in the population of a given American State, the more inequality there was between whites. In other words, the existence of a poor, oppressed group of workers reduced the wages of white workers, although it did not affect the earnings of non-working class whites very much ("the greater the discrimination against [non-white] people, the greater the inequality among whites" [p. 410]). So white workers clearly lost economically from this discrimination.

(3) He also found that "the more intense racial discrimination is, the lower are the white earnings **because** of ... [its effect

on] working-class solidarity." [p. 412] In other words, racism economically disadvantages white workers because it undermines the solidarity between black and white workers and weakens trade union organisation.

So overall, these white workers receive some apparent privileges from racism, but are in fact screwed by it. Thus racism and other forms of hierarchy actually work against the interests of those working class people who practice it – and, by weakening workplace and social unity, benefits the ruling class:

> "As long as discrimination exists and racial or ethnic minorities are oppressed, the entire working class is weakened. This is so because the Capitalist class is able to use racism to drive down the wages of individual segments of the working class by inciting racial antagonism and forcing a fight for jobs and services. This division is a development that ultimately undercuts the living standards of all workers. Moreover, by pitting Whites against Blacks and other oppressed nationalities, the Capitalist class is able to prevent workers from uniting against their common enemy. As long as workers are fighting each other, the Capitalist class is secure."
> [Lorenzo Kom'boa Ervin, **Op. Cit.**, pp. 12-3]

In addition, a wealth of alternative viewpoints, insights, experiences, cultures, thoughts and so on are denied the racist, sexist or homophobe. Their minds are trapped in a cage, stagnating within a mono-culture – and stagnation is death for the personality. Such forms of oppression are dehumanising for those who practice them, for the oppressor lives as a **role**, not as a person, and so are restricted by it and cannot express their individuality **freely** (and so do so in very limited ways). This warps the personality of the oppressor and impoverishes their own life and personality. Homophobia and sexism also limits the flexibility of all people, gay or straight, to choose the sexual expressions and relationships that are right for them. The sexual repression of the sexist and homophobe will hardly be good for their mental health, their relationships or general development.

From the anarchist standpoint, oppression based on race, sex or sexuality will remain forever intractable under capitalism or, indeed, under any economic or political system based on domination and exploitation. While individual members of "minorities" may prosper, racism as a justification for inequality is too useful a tool for elites to discard. By using the results of racism (e.g. poverty) as a justification for racist ideology, criticism of the status quo can, yet again, be replaced by nonsense about "nature" and "biology." Similarly with sexism or discrimination against gays.

The long-term solution is obvious: dismantle capitalism and the hierarchical, economically class-stratified society with which it is bound up. By getting rid of capitalist oppression and exploitation and its consequent imperialism and poverty, we will also eliminate the need for ideologies of racial or sexual superiority used to justify the oppression of one group by another or to divide and weaken the working class. However, struggles against bigotry cannot be left until after a revolution. If they were two things are likely: one, such a revolution would be unlikely to happen and, two, if it were then these problems would more than likely remain in the new society

created by it. Therefore the negative impacts of inequality can and must be fought in the here and now, like any form of hierarchy. Indeed, as we discuss in more detail section B.1.6 by doing so we make life a bit better in the here and now as well as bringing the time when such inequalities are finally ended nearer. Only this can ensure that we can all live as free and equal individuals in a world without the blights of sexism, racism, homophobia or religious hatred.

Needless to say, anarchists totally reject the kind of "equality" that accepts other kinds of hierarchy, that accepts the dominant priorities of capitalism and the state and accedes to the devaluation of relationships and individuality in name of power and wealth. There is a kind of "equality" in having "equal opportunities," in having black, gay or women bosses and politicians, but one that misses the point. Saying "Me too!" instead of "What a mess!" does not suggest real liberation, just different bosses and new forms of oppression. We need to look at the way society is organised, not at the sex, colour, nationality or sexuality of who is giving the orders!

B.1.5 How is the mass-psychological basis for authoritarian civilisation created?

We noted in section A.3.6 that hierarchical, authoritarian institutions tend to be self-perpetuating, because growing up under their influence creates submissive/authoritarian personalities – people who both "respect" authority (based on fear of punishment) and desire to exercise it themselves on subordinates. Individuals with such a character structure do not really want to dismantle hierarchies, because they are afraid of the responsibility entailed by genuine freedom. It seems "natural" and "right" to them that society's institutions, from the authoritarian factory to the patriarchal family, should be pyramidal, with an elite at the top giving orders while those below them merely obey. Thus we have the spectacle of so-called "Libertarians" and "anarcho" capitalists bleating about "liberty" while at the same time advocating factory fascism and privatised states. In short, authoritarian civilisation reproduces itself with each generation because, through an intricate system of conditioning that permeates every aspect of society, it creates masses of people who support the status quo.

Wilhelm Reich has given one of the most thorough analyses of the psychological processes involved in the reproduction of authoritarian civilisation. Reich based his analysis on four of Freud's most solidly grounded discoveries, namely, (1) that there exists an unconscious part of the mind which has a powerful though irrational influence on behaviour; (2) that even the small child develops a lively "genital" sexuality, i.e. a desire for sexual pleasure which has nothing to do with procreation; (3) that childhood sexuality along with the Oedipal conflicts that arise in parent-child relations under monogamy and patriarchy are usually repressed through fear of punishment or disapproval for sexual acts and thoughts; (4) that this blocking of the child's natural sexual activity and extinguishing it from memory does not weaken its force in the unconscious, but actually intensifies it and enables it to manifest itself in various pathological disturbances and anti-social drives; and (5) that, far from being of divine origin, human moral codes are derived from the educational measures used by the parents and parental surrogates in earliest childhood, the most effective of these being the ones opposed to childhood sexuality.

By studying Bronislaw Malinowski's research on the Trobriand Islanders, a woman-centred (matricentric) society in which children's sexual behaviour was not repressed and in which neuroses and perversions as well as authoritarian institutions and values were almost non-existent, Reich came to the conclusion that patriarchy and authoritarianism originally developed when tribal chieftains began to get economic advantages from a certain type of marriage ("cross-cousin marriages") entered into by their sons. In such marriages, the brothers of the son's wife were obliged to pay a dowry to her in the form of continuous tribute, thus enriching her husband's clan (i.e. the chief's). By arranging many such marriages for his sons (which were usually numerous due to the chief's privilege of polygamy), the chief's clan could accumulate wealth. Thus society began to be stratified into ruling and subordinate clans based on wealth.

To secure the permanence of these "good" marriages, strict monogamy was required. However, it was found that monogamy was impossible to maintain without the repression of childhood sexuality, since, as statistics show, children who are allowed free expression of sexuality often do not adapt successfully to life-long monogamy. Therefore, along with class stratification and private property, authoritarian child-rearing methods were developed to inculcate the repressive sexual morality on which the new patriarchal system depended for its reproduction. Thus there is a historical correlation between, on the one hand, pre-patriarchal society, primitive libertarian communism (or *work democracy,*" to use Reich's expression), economic equality, and sexual freedom, and on the other, patriarchal society, a private-property economy, economic class stratification, and sexual repression. As Reich puts it:

"Every tribe that developed from a [matricentric] to a patriarchal organisation had to change the sexual structure of its members to produce a sexuality in keeping with its new form of life. This was a necessary change because the shifting of power and of wealth from the democratic gens [maternal clans] to the authoritarian family of the chief was mainly implemented with the help of the suppression of the sexual strivings of the people. It was in this way that sexual suppression became an essential factor in the division of society into classes.

"Marriage, and the lawful dowry it entailed, became the axis of the transformation of the one organisation into the other. In view of the fact that the marriage tribute of the wife's gens to the man's family strengthened the male's, especially the chief's, position of power, the male members of the higher ranking gens and families developed a keen interest in making the nuptial ties permanent. At this stage, in other words, only the man had an interest in

marriage. In this way natural work-democracy's simple alliance, which could be easily dissolved at any time, was transformed into the permanent and monogamous marital relationship of patriarchy. The permanent monogamous marriage became the basic institution of patriarchal society – which it still is today. To safeguard these marriages, however, it was necessary to impose greater and greater restrictions upon and to depreciate natural genital strivings." [**The Mass Psychology of Fascism**, p. 90]

The suppression of natural sexuality involved in this transformation from matricentric to patriarchal society created various anti-social drives (sadism, destructive impulses, rape fantasies, etc.), which then also had to be suppressed through the imposition of a compulsive morality, which took the place the natural self-regulation that one finds in pre-patriarchal societies. In this way, sex began to be regarded as "dirty," "diabolical," "wicked," etc. – which it had indeed become through the creation of secondary drives. Thus:

"The patriarchal- authoritarian sexual order that resulted from the revolutionary processes of latter-day [matricentrism] (economic independence of the chief's family from the maternal gens, a growing exchange of goods between the tribes, development of the means of production, etc.) becomes the primary basis of authoritarian ideology by depriving the women, children, and adolescents of their sexual freedom, making a commodity of sex and placing sexual interests in the service of economic subjugation. From now on, sexuality is indeed distorted; it becomes diabolical and demonic and has to be curbed." [Reich, **Op. Cit.**, p. 88]

Once the beginnings of patriarchy are in place, the creation of a fully authoritarian society based on the psychological crippling of its members through sexual suppression follows:

*"The moral inhibition of the child's natural sexuality, the last stage of which is the severe impairment of the child's **genital** sexuality, makes the child afraid, shy, fearful of authority, obedient, 'good,' and 'docile' in the authoritarian sense of the words. It has a crippling effect on man's rebellious forces because every vital life-impulse is now burdened with severe fear; and since sex is a forbidden subject, thought in general and man's critical faculty also become inhibited. In short, morality's aim is to produce acquiescent subjects who, despite distress and humiliation, are adjusted to the authoritarian order. Thus, the family is the authoritarian state in miniature, to which the child must learn to adapt himself as a preparation for the general social adjustment required of him later. Man's authoritarian structure – this must be clearly established – is basically produced by the embedding of sexual inhibitions and fear."* [Reich, **Op. Cit.**, p. 30]

In this way, by damaging the individual's power to rebel and think for him/herself, the inhibition of childhood sexuality – and indeed other forms of free, natural expression of bioenergy (e.g. shouting, crying, running, jumping, etc.) – becomes the most important weapon in creating reactionary personalities. This is why every reactionary politician puts such an emphasis on "strengthening the family" and promoting "family values" (i.e. patriarchy, compulsive monogamy, premarital chastity, corporal punishment, etc.). In the words of Reich:

> "Since authoritarian society reproduces itself in the individual structures of the masses with the help of the authoritarian family, it follows that political reaction has to regard and defend the authoritarian family as **the** basis of the 'state, culture, and civilisation....' [It is] **political reaction's germ cell**, the most important centre for the production of reactionary men and women. Originating and developing from definite social processes, it becomes the most essential institution for the preservation of the authoritarian system that shapes it." [**Op. Cit.**, pp. 104-105]

The family is the most essential institution for this purpose because children are most vulnerable to psychological maiming in their first few years, from the time of birth to about six years of age, during which time they are mostly in the charge of their parents. The schools and churches then continue the process of conditioning once the children are old enough to be away from their parents, but they are generally unsuccessful if the proper foundation has not been laid very early in life by the parents. Thus A.S. Neill observes that *"the nursery training is very like the kennel training. The whipped child, like the whipped puppy, grows into an obedient, inferior adult. And as we train our dogs to suit our own purposes, so we train our children. In that kennel, the nursery, the human dogs must be clean; they must feed when we think it convenient for them to feed. I saw a hundred thousand obedient, fawning dogs wag their tails in the Templehof, Berlin, when in 1935, the great trainer Hitler whistled his commands."* [**Summerhill: a Radical Approach to Child Rearing**, p. 100]

The family is also the main agency of repression during adolescence, when sexual energy reaches its peak. This is because the vast majority of parents provide no private space for adolescents to pursue undisturbed sexual relationships with their partners, but in fact actively discourage such behaviour, often (as in fundamentalist Christian families) demanding complete abstinence – at the very time when abstinence is most impossible! Moreover, since teenagers are economically dependent on their parents under capitalism, with no societal provision of housing or dormitories allowing for sexual freedom, young people have no alternative but to submit to irrational parental demands for abstention from premarital sex. This in turn forces them to engage in furtive sex in the back seats of cars or other out-of-the-way places where they cannot relax or obtain full sexual satisfaction. As Reich found, when sexuality is repressed and laden with anxiety, the result is always some degree of what he terms *"orgastic impotence"*: the inability to fully surrender to the flow of energy discharged during orgasm. Hence there is an incomplete release of sexual tension, which results in a state of chronic bioenergetic stasis. Such a condition, Reich found, is the breeding ground for neuroses and reactionary attitudes. (For further details see the section J.6).

In this connection it is interesting to note that "primitive" societies, such as the Trobriand Islanders, prior to their developing patriarchal-authoritarian institutions, provided special community houses where teenagers could go with their partners to enjoy undisturbed sexual relationships – and this with society's full approval. Such an institution would be taken for granted in an anarchist society, as it is implied by the concept of freedom. (For more on adolescent sexual liberation, see section J.6.8.)

Nationalistic feelings can also be traced to the authoritarian family. A child's attachment to its mother is, of course, natural and is the basis of all family ties. Subjectively, the emotional core of the concepts of homeland and nation are mother and family, since the mother is the homeland of the child, just as the family is the "nation in miniature." According to Reich, who carefully studied the mass appeal of Hitler's "National Socialism," nationalistic sentiments are a direct continuation of the family tie and are rooted in a **fixated** tie to the mother. As Reich points out, although infantile attachment to the mother is natural, **fixated** attachment is not, but is a social product. In puberty, the tie to the mother would make room for other attachments, i.e., natural sexual relations, **if** the unnatural sexual restrictions imposed on adolescents did not cause it to be eternalised. It is in the form of this socially conditioned externalisation that fixation on the mother becomes the basis of nationalist feelings in the adult; and it is only at this stage that it becomes a reactionary social force.

Later writers who have followed Reich in analysing the process of creating reactionary character structures have broadened the scope of his analysis to include other important inhibitions, besides sexual ones, that are imposed on children and adolescents. Rianne Eisler, for example, in her book **Sacred Pleasure**, stresses that it is not just a sex-negative attitude but a **pleasure**-negative attitude that creates the kinds of personalities in question. Denial of the value of pleasurable sensations permeates our unconscious, as reflected, for example, in the common idea that to enjoy the pleasures of the body is the "animalistic" (and hence "bad") side of human nature, as contrasted with the "higher" pleasures of the mind and "spirit." By such dualism, which denies a spiritual aspect to the body, people are made to feel guilty about enjoying any pleasurable sensations – a conditioning that does, however, prepare them for lives based on the sacrifice of pleasure (or indeed, even of life itself) under capitalism and statism, with their requirements of mass submission to alienated labour, exploitation, military service to protect ruling-class interests, and so on. And at the same time, authoritarian ideology emphasises the value of suffering, as for example through the glorification of the tough, insensitive warrior hero, who suffers (and inflicts "necessary" suffering on others) for the sake of some pitiless ideal.

Eisler also points out that there is *"ample evidence that people who grow up in families where rigid hierarchies and painful punishments are the norm learn to suppress anger toward their parents. There is also ample evidence that this anger is then often deflected against traditionally disempowered groups (such as minorities, children, and women)."* [**Sacred Pleasure**, p. 187] This repressed anger then becomes fertile ground for reactionary politicians, whose mass appeal usually rests in part on scapegoating minorities for society's problems.

As the psychologist Else Frenkel-Brunswick documents in **The Authoritarian Personality**, people who have been conditioned through childhood abuse to surrender their will to the requirements of feared authoritarian parents, also tend to be very susceptible as adults to surrender their will and minds to authoritarian leaders. *"In other words,"* Frenkel-Brunswick summarises, *"at the same time that they learn to deflect their repressed rage against those they perceive as weak, they also learn to submit to autocratic or 'strong-man' rule. Moreover, having been severely punished for any hint of rebellion (even 'talking back' about being treated unfairly), they gradually also learn to deny to themselves that there was anything wrong with what was done to them as children – and to do it in turn to their own children."* [**The Authoritarian Personality**, p. 187] These are just some of the mechanisms that perpetuate the status quo by creating the kinds of personalities who worship authority and fear freedom. Consequently, anarchists are generally opposed to traditional child-rearing practices, the patriarchal-authoritarian family (and its "values"), the suppression of adolescent sexuality, and the pleasure-denying, pain-affirming attitudes taught by the Church and in most schools. In place of these, anarchists favour non-authoritarian, non-repressive child-rearing practices and educational methods (see sections J.6 and secJ.5.13, respectively) whose purpose is to prevent, or at least minimise, the psychological crippling of individuals, allowing them instead to develop natural self-regulation and self-motivated learning. This, we believe, is the only way to for people to grow up into happy, creative, and truly freedom-loving individuals who will provide the psychological ground where anarchist economic and political institutions can flourish.

B.1.6 Can hierarchy be ended?

Faced with the fact that hierarchy, in its many distinctive forms, has been with us such a long time and so negatively shapes those subject to it, some may conclude that the anarchist hope of ending it, or even reducing it, is little more than a utopian dream. Surely, it will be argued, as anarchists acknowledge that those subject to a hierarchy adapt to it this automatically excludes the creation of people able to free themselves from it?

Anarchists disagree. Hierarchy can be ended, both in specific forms and in general. A quick look at the history of the human species shows that this is the case. People who have been subject to monarchy have ended it, creating republics where before absolutism reigned. Slavery and serfdom have been abolished. Alexander Berkman simply stated the obvious when he pointed out that *"many ideas, once held to be true, have come to be regarded as wrong and evil. Thus the ideas of divine right of kings, of slavery and serfdom. There was a time when the whole world believed those institutions to be right, just, and unchangeable."* However, they became *"discredited and lost their hold upon the people, and finally the institutions that incorporated those ideas were abolished"* as *"they were useful only to the master class"* and *"were done away with by popular uprisings and revolutions."* [**What is Anarchism?**, p. 178] It is unlikely, therefore, that current forms of hierarchy are

exceptions to this process.

Today, we can see that this is the case. Malatesta's comments of over one hundred years ago are still valid: *"the oppressed masses … have never completely resigned themselves to oppression and poverty … [and] show themselves thirsting for justice, freedom and wellbeing."* [**Anarchy**, p. 33] Those at the bottom are constantly resisting both hierarchy and its negative effects and, equally important, creating non-hierarchical ways of living and fighting. This constant process of self-activity and self-liberation can be seen from the labour, women's and other movements – in which, to some degree, people create their own alternatives based upon their own dreams and hopes. Anarchism is based upon, and grew out of, this process of resistance, hope and direct action. In other words, the libertarian elements that the oppressed continually produce in their struggles within and against hierarchical systems are extrapolated and generalised into what is called anarchism. It is these struggles and the anarchistic elements they produce which make the end of all forms of hierarchy not only desirable, but possible.

So while the negative impact of hierarchy is not surprising, neither is the resistance to it. This is because the individual *"is not a blank sheet of paper on which culture can write its text; he [or she] is an entity charged with energy and structured in specific ways, which, while adapting itself, reacts in specific and ascertainable ways to external conditions."* In this *"process of adaptation,"* people develop *"definite mental and emotional reactions which follow from specific properties"* of our nature. [Eric Fromm, **Man for Himself**, p. 23 and p. 22] For example:

> *"Man can adapt himself to slavery, but he reacts to it by lowering his intellectual and moral qualities … Man can adapt himself to cultural conditions which demand the repression of sexual strivings, but in achieving this adaptation he develops … neurotic symptoms. He can adapt to almost any culture pattern, but in so far as these are contradictory to his nature he develops mental and emotional disturbances which force him eventually change these conditions since he cannot change his nature. … If … man could adapt himself to all conditions without fighting those which are against his nature, he would have no history. Human evolution is rooted in man's adaptability and in certain indestructible qualities of his nature which compel him to search for conditions better adjusted to his intrinsic needs."* [**Op. Cit.**, pp. 22-23]

So as well as adaptation to hierarchy, there is resistance. This means that modern society (capitalism), like any hierarchical society, faces a direct contradiction. On the one hand, such systems divide society into a narrow stratum of order givers and the vast majority of the population who are (officially) excluded from decision making, who are reduced to carrying out (executing) the decisions made by the few. As a result, most people suffer feelings of alienation and unhappiness. However, in practice, people try and overcome this position of powerlessness and so hierarchy produces a struggle against itself by those subjected to it. This process goes on all the time, to a greater or lesser degree, and is an essential aspect in creating the possibility of political consciousness, social change and revolution. People refuse to be treated like objects (as required by hierarchical society) and by so doing hierarchy creates the possibility for its own destruction.

For the inequality in wealth and power produced by hierarchies, between the powerful and the powerless, between the rich and the poor, has not been ordained by god, nature or some other superhuman force. It has been created by a specific social system, its institutions and workings – a system based upon authoritarian social relationships which effect us both physically and mentally. So there is hope. Just as authoritarian traits are learned, so can they be **unlearned.** As Carole Pateman summarises, the evidence supports the argument *"that we do learn to participate by participating"* and that a participatory environment *"might also be effective in diminishing tendencies toward non-democratic attitudes in the individual."* [**Participaton and Democratic Theory**, p. 105] So oppression reproduces resistance and the seeds of its own destruction.

It is for this reason anarchists stress the importance of self-liberation (see section A.2.7) and *"support all struggles for partial freedom, because we are convinced that one learns through struggle, and that once one begins to enjoy a little freedom one ends by wanting it all."* [Malatesta, **Errico Malatesta: His Life and Ideas**, p. 195] By means of direct action (see section J.2), people exert themselves and stand up for themselves. This breaks the conditioning of hierarchy, breaks the submissiveness which hierarchical social relationships both need and produce. Thus the daily struggles against oppression *"serve as a training camp to develop"* a person's *"understanding of [their] proper role in life, to cultivate [their] self-reliance and independence, teach him [or her] mutual help and co-operation, and make him [or her] conscious of [their] responsibility. [They] will learn to decide and act on [their] own behalf, not leaving it to leaders or politicians to attend to [their] affairs and look out for [their] welfare. It will be [them] who will determine, together with [their] fellows…, what they want and what methods will best serve their aims."* [Berkman, **Op. Cit.**, p. 206]

In other words, struggle encourages all the traits hierarchy erodes and, consequently, develop the abilities not only to question and resist authority but, ultimately, end it once and for all. This means that any struggle **changes** those who take part in it, politicising them and transforming their personalities by shaking off the servile traits produced and required by hierarchy. As an example, after the sit-down strikes in Flint, Michigan, in 1937 one eye-witness saw how *"the auto worker became a different human being. The women that had participated actively became a different type of women … They carried themselves with a different walk, their heads were high, and they had confidence in themselves."* [Genora (Johnson) Dollinger, contained in **Voices of a People's History of the United States**, Howard Zinn and Anthony Arnove (eds.), p. 349] Such changes happen in all struggles (also see section J.4.2). Anarchists are not surprised for, as discussed in section J.1 and J.2.1, we have long recognised the liberating aspects of social struggle and the key role it plays in creating free people and the other preconditions for needed for an anarchist society (like the initial social structure – see section I.2.3).

Needless to say, a hierarchical system like capitalism cannot survive with a non-submissive working class and the bosses spend a considerable amount of time, energy and resources trying to break the spirits of the working class so they will submit to authority (either unwillingly, by fear of being fired, or willingly, by fooling them into believing that hierarchy is natural or by rewarding subservient behaviour). Unsurprisingly, this never completely succeeds and so capitalism is marked by constant struggles between the oppressed and oppressor. Some of these struggles succeed, some do not. Some are defensive, some are not. Some, like strikes, are visible, other less so (such as working slowly and less efficiently than management desires). And these struggles are waged by both sides of the hierarchical divide. Those subject to hierarchy fight to limit it and increase their autonomy and those who exercise authority fight to increase their power over others. Who wins varies. The 1960s and 1970s saw a marked increase in victories for the oppressed all throughout capitalism but, unfortunately, since the 1980s, as we discuss in section C.8.3, there has been a relentless class war conducted by the powerful which has succeeded in inflicting a series of defeats on working class people. Unsurprisingly, the rich have got richer and more powerful since.

So anarchists take part in the on-going social struggle in society in an attempt to end it in the only way possible, the victory of the oppressed. A key part of this is to fight for partial freedoms, for minor or major reforms, as this strengthens the spirit of revolt and starts the process towards the final end of hierarchy. In such struggles we stress the autonomy of those involved and see them not only as the means of getting more justice and freedom in the current unfree system but also as a means of ending the hierarchies they are fighting once and for all. Thus, for example, in the class struggle we argue for *"[o]rganisation from the bottom up, beginning with the shop and factory, on the foundation of the joint interests of the workers everywhere, irrespective of trade, race, or country."* [Alexander Berkman, **Op. Cit.**, p. 207] Such an organisation, as we discuss in section J.5.2, would be run via workplace assemblies and would be the ideal means of replacing capitalist hierarchy in industry by genuine economic freedom, i.e. worker's self-management of production (see section I.3). Similarly, in the community we argue for popular assemblies (see section J.5.1) as a means of not only combating the power of the state but also replacing it with free, self-managed, communities (see section I.5).

Thus the current struggle itself creates the bridge between what is and what could be:

> *"Assembly and community must arise from within the revolutionary process itself; indeed, the revolutionary process must **be** the formation of assembly and community, and with it, the destruction of power. Assembly and community must become 'fighting words,' not distant panaceas. They must be created as **modes of struggle** against the existing society, not as theoretical or programmatic abstractions."* [Murray Bookchin, **Post-Scarcity Anarchism**, p. 104]

This is not all. As well as fighting the state and capitalism, we also need fight all other forms of oppression. This means that anarchists argue that we need to combat social hierarchies like racism and sexism as well as workplace hierarchy and economic class, that we need to oppose homophobia and religious hatred as well as the political state. Such oppressions and struggles are not diversions from the struggle against class oppression or capitalism but part and parcel of the struggle for human freedom and cannot be ignored without fatally harming it.

As part of that process, anarchists encourage and support all sections of the population to stand up for their humanity and individuality by resisting racist, sexist and anti-gay activity and challenging such views in their everyday lives, everywhere (as Carole Pateman points out, *"sexual domination structures the workplace as well as the conjugal home"* [**The Sexual Contract**, p. 142]). It means a struggle of all working class people against the internal and external tyrannies we face – we must fight against own our prejudices while supporting those in struggle against our common enemies, no matter their sex, skin colour or sexuality. Lorenzo Kom'boa Ervin's words on fighting racism are applicable to all forms of oppression:

> *"Racism must be fought vigorously wherever it is found, even if in our own ranks, and even in ones own breast. Accordingly, we must end the system of white skin privilege which the bosses use to split the class, and subject racially oppressed workers to super-exploitation. White workers, especially those in the Western world, must resist the attempt to use one section of the working class to help them advance, while holding back the gains of another segment based on race or nationality. This kind of class opportunism and capitulationism on the part of white labour must be directly challenged and defeated. There can be no workers unity until the system of super-exploitation and world White Supremacy is brought to an end."* [**Anarchism and the Black Revolution**, p. 128]

Progress towards equality can and has been made. While it is still true that (in the words of Emma Goldman) *"[n]owhere is woman treated according to the merit of her work, but rather as a sex"* [**Red Emma Speaks**, p. 177] and that education is still patriarchal, with young women still often steered away from traditionally "male" courses of study and work (which teaches children that men and women are assigned different roles in society and sets them up to accept these limitations as they grow up) it is also true that the position of women, like that of blacks and gays, **has** improved. This is due to the various self-organised, self-liberation movements that have continually developed throughout history and these are **the** key to fighting oppression in the short term (and creating the potential for the long term solution of dismantling capitalism and the state).

Emma Goldman argued that emancipation begins *"in [a] woman's soul."* Only by a process of internal emancipation, in which the oppressed get to know their own value, respect themselves and their culture, can they be in a position to effectively combat (and overcome) external oppression and attitudes. Only when you respect yourself can you be in a position to get others to respect you. Those men, whites and heterosexuals who are opposed to bigotry, inequality and injustice, must support oppressed groups and refuse to condone racist, sexist or homophobic attitudes and actions by others or themselves. For anarchists, *"not a single member of the Labour movement may with impunity be discriminated against, suppressed or ignored ... Labour [and other] organisations must be built on the principle of equal liberty of all its members. This equality means that only if each worker is a free and independent unit, co-operating with the others from his or her mutual interests, can the whole labour organisation work successfully and become powerful."* [Lorenzo Kom'boa Ervin, **Op. Cit.**, pp. 127-8]

We must all treat people as equals, while at the same time respecting their differences. Diversity is a strength and a source of joy, and anarchists reject the idea that equality means conformity. By these methods, of internal self-liberation and solidarity against external oppression, we can fight against bigotry. Racism, sexism and homophobia can be reduced, perhaps almost eliminated, before a social revolution has occurred by those subject to them organising themselves, fighting back **autonomously** and refusing to be subjected to racial, sexual or anti-gay abuse or to allowing others to get away with it (which plays an essential role in making others aware of their own attitudes and actions, attitudes they may even be blind to!).

The example of the **Mujeres Libres** (Free Women) in Spain during the 1930s shows what is possible. Women anarchists involved in the C.N.T. and F.A.I. organised themselves autonomously to raise the issue of sexism in the wider libertarian movement, to increase women's involvement in libertarian organisations and help the process of women's self-liberation against male oppression. Along the way they also had to combat the (all too common) sexist attitudes of their "revolutionary" male fellow anarchists. Martha A. Ackelsberg's book **Free Women of Spain** is an excellent account of this movement and the issues it raises for all people concerned about freedom. Decades later, the women's movement of the 1960s and 1970s did much the same thing, aiming to challenge the traditional sexism and patriarchy of capitalist society. They, too, formed their own organisations to fight for their own needs as a group. Individuals worked together and drew strength for their own personal battles in the home and in wider society.

Another essential part of this process is for such autonomous groups to actively support others in struggle (including members of the dominant race/sex/sexuality). Such practical solidarity and communication can, when combined with the radicalising effects of the struggle itself on those involved, help break down prejudice and bigotry, undermining the social hierarchies that oppress us all. For example, gay and lesbian groups supporting the 1984/5 UK miners' strike resulted in such groups being given pride of place in many miners' marches. Another example is the great strike by Jewish immigrant workers in 1912 in London which occurred at the same time as a big London Dock Strike. *"The common struggle brought Jewish and non-Jewish workers together. Joint strike meetings were held, and the same speakers spoke at huge joint demonstrations."* The Jewish strike was a success, dealing a *"death-blow to the sweatshop system. The English workers looked at the Jewish workers with quite different eyes after this victory."* Yet the London dock strike continued and many dockers' families were suffering real wants. The successful Jewish strikers started a campaign *"to take some of the dockers' children into their homes."* This practical support *"did a great deal to strengthen the friendship between Jewish and non-Jewish workers."* [Rudolf Rocker, **London Years**, p. 129 and p. 131] This solidarity was repaid in October 1936, when the dockers were at the forefront in stopping Mosley's fascist blackshirts marching through Jewish areas (the famous battle of Cable street).

For whites, males and heterosexuals, the only anarchistic approach is to support others in struggle, refuse to tolerate bigotry in others and to root out their own fears and prejudices (while refusing to be uncritical of self-liberation struggles – solidarity does not imply switching your brain off!). This obviously involves taking the issue of social oppression into all working class organisations and activity, ensuring that no oppressed group is marginalised within them.

Only in this way can the hold of these social diseases be weakened and a better, non-hierarchical system be created. An injury to one is an injury to all.

B.2
Why are anarchists against the state?

As previously noted (see section B.1), anarchists oppose all forms of hierarchical authority. Historically, however, they have spent most of their time and energy opposing two main forms in particular. One is capitalism, the other, the state. These two forms of authority have a symbiotic relationship and cannot be easily separated:

> "[T]he State … and Capitalism are facts and conceptions which we cannot separate from each other. In the course of history these institutions have developed, supporting and reinforcing each other.

> "They are connected with each other – not as mere accidental co-incidences. They are linked together by the links of cause and effect." [Kropotkin, **Evolution and Environment**, p. 94]

In this section, in consequence, as well as explaining why anarchists oppose the state, we will necessarily have to analyse the relationship between it and capitalism.

So what is the state? As Malatesta put it, anarchists "have used the word State, and still do, to mean the sum total of the political, legislative, judiciary, military and financial institutions through which the management of their own affairs, the control over their personal behaviour, the responsibility for their personal safety, are taken away from the people and entrusted to others who, by usurpation or delegation, are vested with the power to make laws for everything and everybody, and to oblige the people to observe them, if need be, by the use of collective force." [**Anarchy**, p. 17] He continues:

> "For us, government [or the state] is made up of all the governors; and the governors … are those who have the power to make **laws** regulating inter-human relations and to see that they are carried out … [and] who have the power, to a greater or lesser degree, to make use of the social power, that is of the physical, intellectual and economic power of the whole community, in order to oblige everybody to carry out their wishes. And this power,

in our opinion, constitutes the principle of government, of authority." [**Op. Cit.**, p. 19]

Kropotkin presented a similar analysis, arguing that the state "not only includes the existence of a power situated above society, but also of a **territorial concentration** as well as the concentration **in the hands of a few of many functions in the life of societies** … A whole mechanism of legislation and of policing has to be developed in order to subject some classes to the domination of others." [**The State: Its Historic Role**, p. 10] For Bakunin, all states "are in essence only machines governing the masses from above, through … a privileged minority, allegedly knowing the genuine interests of the people better than the people themselves." [**The Political Philosophy of Bakunin**, p. 211] On this subject Murray Bookchin writes:

> "Minimally, the State is a professional system of social coercion – not merely a system of social administration as it is still naively regarded by the public and by many political theorists. The word 'professional' should be emphasised as much as the word 'coercion.' … It is only when coercion is institutionalised into a professional, systematic and organised form of social control – that is, when people are plucked out of their everyday lives in a community and expected not only to 'administer' it but to do so with the backing of a monopoly of violence – that we can properly speak of a State." [**Remaking Society**, p. 66]

As Bookchin indicates, anarchists reject the idea that the state is the same as society or that **any** grouping of human beings living and organised together is a state. This confusion, as Kropotkin notes, explains why "anarchists are generally upbraided for wanting to 'destroy society' and of advocating a return to 'the permanent war of each against all.'" Such a position "overlook[s] the fact that Man lived in Societies for thousands of years before the State had been heard of" and that, consequently, the State "is only one of the forms assumed by society in the course of history." [**Op. Cit.**, p. 10]

The state, therefore, is not just federations of individuals or peoples and so, as Malatesta stressed, cannot be used to describe a "human collectively gathered together in a particular territory and making up what is called a social unit irrespective of the way the way said collectivity are grouped or the state of relations between them." It cannot be "used simply as a synonym for society." [**Op. Cit.**, p. 17] The state is a particular form of social organisation based on certain key attributes and so, we argue, "the word 'State' … should be reserved for those societies with the hierarchical system and centralisation." [Peter Kropotkin, **Ethics**, p. 317f] As such, the state "is a historic, transitory institution, a temporary form of society" and one whose "utter extinction" is possible as the "State is not society." [Bakunin, **Michael Bakunin: Selected Writings**, p. 151]

In summary, the state is a specific way in which human affairs are organised in a given area, a way marked by certain institutions which, in turn, have certain characteristics. This does not imply, however, that the state is a monolithic entity that has been the same from its birth to the present day. States vary in many ways, especially in their degree of authoritarianism, in the size and power of their bureaucracy and how they organise themselves. Thus we have monarchies, oligarchies, theocracies, party dictatorships and (more or less) democratic states. We have ancient states, with minimal bureaucracy, and modern ones, with enormous bureaucracy.

Moreover, anarchists argue that *"the **political** regime ... is always an expression of the **economic** regime which exists at the heart of society."* This means that regardless of how the state changes, it *"continues to be shaped by the economic system, of which it is always the expression and, at the same time, the consecration and the sustaining force."* Needless to say, there is not always an exact match and sometimes *"the political regime of a country finds itself lagging behind the economic changes that are taking place, and in that case it will abruptly be set aside and remodelled in a way appropriate to the economic regime that has been established."* [Kropotkin, **Words of a Rebel**, p. 118]

At other times, the state can change its form to protect the economic system it is an expression of. Thus we see democracies turn to dictatorships in the face of popular revolts and movements. The most obvious examples of Pinochet's Chile, Franco's Spain, Mussolini's Italy and Hitler's Germany are all striking confirmations of Bakunin's comment that while *"[n]o government could serve the economic interests of the bourgeoisie better than a republic,"* that class would *"prefer ... military dictatorship"* if needed to crush *"the revolts of the proletariat."* [**Bakunin on Anarchism**, p. 417]

However, as much as the state may change its form it still has certain characteristics which identify a social institution as a state. As such, we can say that, for anarchists, the state is marked by three things:

(1) A ***"monopoly of violence"*** in a given territorial area;

(2) This violence having *"professional,"* institutional nature; and

(3) A hierarchical nature, centralisation of power and initiative into the hands of a few.

Of these three aspects, the last one (its centralised, hierarchical nature) is the most important simply because the concentration of power into the hands of the few ensures a division of society into government and governed (which necessitates the creation of a professional body to enforce that division). Hence we find Bakunin arguing that *"[w]ith the State there must go also ... all organisation of social life from the top downward, via legislation and government."* [**The Political Philosophy of Bakunin**, p. 242] In other words, *"the people was not governing itself."* [Kropotkin, **Op. Cit.**, p. 120]

This aspect implies the rest. In a state, all the people residing in an area are subject to the state, submitting themselves to the individuals who make up the institution of authority ruling that territory. To enforce the will of this few, they must have a monopoly of force within the territory. As the members of the state collectively monopolise political decision making power, they are a privileged body separated by its position and status from the rest of the population as a whole which means they cannot rely on them to enforce its will. This necessities a professional body of some kind to enforce their decisions, a separate police force or army rather than the people armed.

Given this, the division of society into rulers and ruled is the key to what constitutes a state. Without such a division, we would not need a monopoly of violence and so would simply have an association of equals, unmarked by power and hierarchy (such as exists in many stateless "primitive" tribes and will exist in a future anarchist society). And, it must be stressed, such a division exists even in democratic states as *"with the state there is always a hierarchical and status difference between rulers and ruled. Even if it is a democracy, where we suppose those who rule today are not rulers tomorrow, there are still differences in status. In a democratic system, only a tiny minority will ever have the opportunity to rule and these are invariably drawn from the elite."* [Harold Barclay, **The State**, pp. 23-4]

Thus, the *"essence of government"* is that *"it is a thing apart, developing its own interests"* and so is *"an institution existing for its own sake, preying upon the people, and teaching them whatever will tend to keep it secure in its seat."* [Voltairine de Cleyre, **The Voltairine de Cleyre Reader**, p. 27 and p. 26] And so *"despotism resides not so much in the **form** of the State or power as in the very **principle** of the State and political power."* [Bakunin, **Op. Cit.**, p. 211]

As the state is the delegation of power into the hands of the few, it is obviously based on hierarchy. This delegation of power results in the elected people becoming isolated from the mass of people who elected them and outside of their control (see section B.2.4). In addition, as those elected are given power over a host of different issues and told to decide upon them, a bureaucracy soon develops around them to aid in their decision-making and enforce those decisions once they have been reached. However, this bureaucracy, due to its control of information and its permanency, soon has more power than the elected officials. Therefore *"a highly complex state machine ... leads to the formation of a class especially concerned with state management, which, using its acquired experience, begins to deceive the rest for its personal advantage."* [Kropotkin, **Selected Writings on Anarchism and Revolution**, p. 61] This means that those who serve the people's (so-called) servant have more power than those they serve, just as the politician has more power than those who elected him. All forms of state-like (i.e. hierarchical) organisations inevitably spawn a bureaucracy about them. This bureaucracy soon becomes the de facto focal point of power in the structure, regardless of the official rules.

This marginalisation and disempowerment of ordinary people (and so the empowerment of a bureaucracy) is the key reason for anarchist opposition to the state. Such an arrangement ensures that the individual is disempowered, subject to bureaucratic, authoritarian rule which reduces the person to an object or a number, **not** a unique individual with hopes, dreams, thoughts and feelings. As Proudhon forcefully argued:

> *"To be GOVERNED is to be kept in sight, inspected, spied upon, directed, law-driven, numbered, enrolled, indoctrinated, preached at, controlled, estimated, valued, censured, commanded, by creatures who have neither the right, nor the wisdom, nor the virtue to do so ...*
> *To be GOVERNED is to be at every operation, at every transaction, noted, registered, enrolled, taxed, stamped,*

measured, numbered, assessed, licensed, authorised, admonished, forbidden, reformed, corrected, punished. It is, under the pretext of public utility, and in the name of the general interest, to be placed under contribution, trained, ransomed, exploited, monopolised, extorted, squeezed, mystified, robbed; then, at the slightest resistance, the first word of complaint, to be repressed, fined, despised, harassed, tracked, abused, clubbed, disarmed, choked, imprisoned, judged, condemned, shot, deported, sacrificed, sold, betrayed; and, to crown it all, mocked, ridiculed, outraged, dishonoured. That is government; that is its justice; that is its morality." [**General Idea of the Revolution**, p. 294]

Such is the nature of the state that **any** act, no matter how evil, becomes good if it helps forward the interests of the state and the minorities it protects. As Bakunin put it:

*"**The State … is the most flagrant, the most cynical, and the most complete negation of humanity.** It shatters the universal solidarity of all men [and women] on the earth, and brings some of them into association only for the purpose of destroying, conquering, and enslaving all the rest …*

"This flagrant negation of humanity which constitutes the very essence of the State is, from the standpoint of the State, its supreme duty and its greatest virtue … Thus, to offend, to oppress, to despoil, to plunder, to assassinate or enslave one's fellowman [or woman] is ordinarily regarded as a crime. In public life, on the other hand, from the standpoint of patriotism, when these things are done for the greater glory of the State, for the preservation or the extension of its power, it is all transformed into duty and virtue. And this virtue, this duty, are obligatory for each patriotic citizen; everyone is supposed to exercise them not against foreigners only but against one's own fellow citizens … whenever the welfare of the State demands it.

"This explains why, since the birth of the State, the world of politics has always been and continues to be the stage for unlimited rascality and brigandage … This explains why the entire history of ancient and modern states is merely a series of revolting crimes; why kings and ministers, past and present, of all times and all countries – statesmen, diplomats, bureaucrats, and warriors – if judged from the standpoint of simply morality and human justice, have a hundred, a thousand times over earned their sentence to hard labour or to the gallows. There is no horror, no cruelty, sacrilege, or perjury, no imposture, no infamous transaction, no cynical robbery, no bold plunder or shabby betrayal that has not been or is not daily being perpetrated by the representatives of the states, under no other pretext than those elastic words, so convenient and yet so terrible: 'for reasons of state.'" [**Bakunin on Anarchism**, pp. 133-4]

Governments habitually lie to the people they claim to represent in order to justify wars, reductions (if not the destruction) of civil liberties and human rights, policies which benefit the few over the many, and other crimes. And if its subjects protest, the state will happily use whatever force deemed necessary to bring the rebels back in line (labelling such repression "law and order"). Such repression includes the use of death squads, the institutionalisation of torture, collective punishments, indefinite imprisonment, and other horrors at the worse extremes.

Little wonder the state usually spends so much time ensuring the (mis)education of its population – only by obscuring (when not hiding) its actual practises can it ensure the allegiance of those subject to it. The history of the state could be viewed as nothing more than the attempts of its subjects to control it and bind it to the standards people apply to themselves.

Such behaviour is not surprising, given that Anarchists see the state, with its vast scope and control of deadly force, as the "ultimate" hierarchical structure, suffering from all the negative characteristics associated with authority described in the last section. *"Any logical and straightforward theory of the State,"* argued Bakunin, *"is essentially founded upon the principle of **authority**, that is the eminently theological, metaphysical, and political idea that the masses, **always** incapable of governing themselves, must at all times submit to the beneficent yoke of a wisdom and a justice imposed upon them, in some way or other, from above."* [**Bakunin on Anarchism**, p. 142] Such a system of authority cannot help being centralised, hierarchical and bureaucratic in nature. And because of its centralised, hierarchical, and bureaucratic nature, the state becomes a great weight over society, restricting its growth and development and making popular control impossible. As Bakunin put it:

"the so-called general interests of society supposedly represented by the State … [are] in reality … the general and permanent negation of the positive interests of the regions, communes, and associations, and a vast number of individuals subordinated to the State … [in which] all the best aspirations, all the living forces of a country, are sanctimoniously immolated and interred." [**The Political Philosophy of Bakunin**, p. 207]

That is by no means the end of it. As well as its obvious hierarchical form, anarchists object to the state for another, equally important, reason. This is its role as a defender of the economically dominant class in society against the rest of it (i.e. from the working class). This means, under the current system, the capitalists *"need the state to legalise their methods of robbery, to protect the capitalist system."* [Berkman, **What is Anarchism?**, p. 16] The state, as we discuss in section B.2.1, is the defender of private property (see section B.3 for a discussion of what anarchists mean by that term and how it differs from individual possessions).

This means that in capitalist states the mechanisms of state domination are controlled by and for a corporate elite (and hence the large corporations are often considered to belong to a wider *"state-complex"*). Indeed, as we discuss in more depth in section F.8, the *"State has been, and still is, the main pillar and the creator, direct and indirect, of Capitalism and its powers over the masses."*

[Kropotkin, **Evolution and Environment**, p. 97] Section B.2.3 indicates how this domination is achieved in a representative democracy.

However this does not mean anarchists think that the state is purely an instrument of economic class rule. As Malatesta argued, while *"a special class (government) which, provided with the necessary means of repression, exists to legalise and protect the owning class from the demands of the workers ... it uses the powers at its disposal to create privileges for itself and to subject, if it can, the owning class itself as well."* [**Errico Malatesta: His Life and Ideas**, p. 183] Thus the state has interests of its own, distinct from and sometimes in opposition to the economic ruling elite. This means that both state **and** capitalism need to be abolished, for the former is as much a distinct (and oppressive and exploitative) class as the former. This aspects of the state is discussed in section B.2.6.

As part of its role as defender of capitalism, the state is involved in not only in political domination but also in economic domination. This domination can take different forms, varying from simply maintaining capitalist property rights to actually owning workplaces and exploiting labour directly. Thus every state intervenes in the economy in some manner. While this is usually to favour the economically dominant, it can also try and mitigate the anti-social nature of the capitalist market and regulate its worse abuses. We discuss this aspect of the state in section B.2.2.

Needless to say, the characteristics which mark a state did not develop by chance. As we discuss in section H.3.7, anarchists have an evolutionary perspective on the state. This means that it has a hierarchical nature in order to facilitate the execution of its role, its function. As sections B.2.4 and B.2.5 indicate, the centralisation that marks a state is required to secure elite rule and was deliberately and actively created to do so. This means that states, by their very nature, are top-down institutions which centralise power into a few hands and, as a consequence, a state *"with its traditions, its hierarchy, and its narrow nationalism"* can *"not be utilised as an instrument of emancipation."* [Kropotkin, **Evolution and Environment**, p. 78] It is for this reason that anarchists aim to create a new form of social organisation and life, a decentralised one based on decision making from the bottom-up and the elimination of hierarchy.

Finally, we must point out that anarchists, while stressing what states have in common, do recognise that some forms of the state are better than others. Democracies, for example, tend to be less oppressive than dictatorships or monarchies. As such it would be false to conclude that anarchists, *"in criticising the democratic government we thereby show our preference for the monarchy. We are firmly convinced that the most imperfect republic is a thousand times better than the most enlightened monarchy."* [Bakunin, **Bakunin on Anarchism**, p. 144] However, this does not change the nature or role of the state. Indeed, what liberties we have are **not** dependent on the goodwill of the state but rather the result of people standing against it and exercising their autonomy. Left to itself, the state would soon turn the liberties and rights it says it defends into dead-laws – things that look good in print but not practised in real life.

So in the rest of this section we will discuss the state, its role, its

impact on a society's freedom and who benefits from its existence. Kropotkin's classic essay, **The State: It's Historic Role** is recommended for further reading on this subject. Harold Barclay's **The State** is a good overview of the origins of the state, how it has changed over the millenniums and the nature of the modern state.

B.2.1 What is main function of the state?

The main function of the state is to guarantee the existing social relationships and their sources within a given society through centralised power and a monopoly of violence. To use Malatesta's words, the state is basically *"the property owners' **gendarme**."* This is because there are *"two ways of oppressing men [and women]: either directly by brute force, by physical violence; or indirectly by denying them the means of life and thus reducing them to a state of surrender."* The owning class, *"gradually concentrating in their hands the means of production, the real sources of life, agriculture, industry, barter, etc., end up establishing their own power which, by reason of the superiority of its means ... always ends by more or less openly subjecting the political power, which is the government, and making it into its own **gendarme**."* [**Op. Cit.**, p. 23, p. 21 and p. 22]

The state, therefore, is *"the political expression of the economic structure"* of society and, therefore, *"the representative of the people who own or control the wealth of the community and the oppressor of the people who do the work which creates the wealth."* [Nicholas Walter, **About Anarchism**, p. 37] It is therefore no exaggeration to say that the state is the extractive apparatus of society's parasites.

The state ensures the exploitative privileges of its ruling elite by protecting certain economic monopolies from which its members derive their wealth. The nature of these economic privileges varies over time. Under the current system, this means defending capitalist property rights (see section B.3.2). This service is referred to as "protecting private property" and is said to be one of the two main functions of the state, the other being to ensure that individuals are "secure in their persons." However, although this second aim is professed, in reality most state laws and institutions are concerned with the protection of property (for the anarchist definition of "property" see section B.3.1).

From this we may infer that references to the "security of persons," "crime prevention," etc., are mostly rationalisations of the state's existence and smokescreens for its perpetuation of elite power and privileges. This does not mean that the state does not address these issues. Of course it does, but, to quote Kropotkin, any *"laws developed from the nucleus of customs useful to human communities ... have been turned to account by rulers to sanctify their own domination."* of the people, and maintained only by the fear of punishment." [**Anarchism**, p. 215]

Simply put, if the state *"presented nothing but a collection of prescriptions serviceable to rulers, it would find some difficulty in insuring acceptance and obedience"* and so the law reflects customs "essential to the very being of society" but these are *"cleverly* intermingled with usages imposed by the ruling caste and both claim equal respect from the crowd." Thus the state's laws have a "two-fold character." While its "origin is the desire of the ruling class to give permanence to customs imposed by themselves for their own advantage" it also passes into law "customs useful to society, customs which have no need of law to insure respect" – unlike those "other customs useful only to rulers, injurious to the mass of the people, and maintained only by the fear of punishment." [Kropotkin, **Op. Cit.**, pp. 205-6] To use an obvious example, we find the state using the defence of an individual's possessions as the rationale for imposing capitalist private property rights upon the general public and, consequently, defending the elite and the source of its wealth and power against those subject to it.

Moreover, even though the state does take a secondary interest in protecting the security of persons (particularly elite persons), the vast majority of crimes against persons are motivated by poverty and alienation due to state-supported exploitation and also by the desensitisation to violence created by the state's own violent methods of protecting private property. In other words, the state rationalises its existence by pointing to the social evils it itself helps to create (either directly or indirectly). Hence, anarchists maintain that without the state and the crime-engendering conditions to which it gives rise, it would be possible for decentralised, voluntary community associations to deal compassionately (not punitively) with the few incorrigibly violent people who might remain (see section I.5.8).Anarchists think it is pretty clear what the real role of the modern state is. It represents the essential coercive mechanisms by which capitalism and the authority relations associated with private property are sustained. The protection of property is fundamentally the means of assuring the social domination of owners over non-owners, both in society as a whole and in the particular case of a specific boss over a specific group of workers. Class domination is the authority of property owners over those who use that property and it is the primary function of the state to uphold that domination (and the social relationships that generate it). In Kropotkin's words, "the rich perfectly well know that if the machinery of the State ceased to protect them, their power over the labouring classes would be gone immediately." [**Evolution and Environment**, p. 98] Protecting private property and upholding class domination are the same thing.

The historian Charles Beard makes a similar point:

> "Inasmuch as the primary object of a government, beyond mere repression of physical violence, is the making of the rules which determine the property relations of members of society, the dominant classes whose rights are thus to be protected must perforce obtain from the government such rules as are consonant with the larger interests necessary to the continuance of their economic processes, or they must themselves control the organs of government." ["An Economic Interpretation of the Constitution," quoted by Howard Zinn, **Op. Cit.**, p. 89]

This role of the state – to protect capitalism and the property, power and authority of the property owner – was also noticed by Adam Smith:

> "[T]he inequality of fortune … introduces among men a degree of authority and subordination which could not possibly exist before. It thereby introduces some degree of that civil government which is indispensably necessary for its own preservation … [and] to maintain and secure that authority and subordination. The rich, in particular, are necessarily interested to support that order of things which can alone secure them in the possession of their own advantages. Men of inferior wealth combine to defend those of superior wealth in the possession of their property, in order that men of superior wealth may combine to defend them in the possession of theirs … [T]he maintenance of their lesser authority depends upon that of his greater authority, and that upon their subordination to him depends his power of keeping their inferiors in subordination to them. They constitute a sort of little nobility, who feel themselves interested to defend the property and to support the authority of their own little sovereign in order that he may be able to defend their property and to support their authority. Civil government, so far as it is instituted for the security of property, is in reality instituted for the defence of the rich against the poor, or of those who have some property against those who have none at all." [**The Wealth of Nations**, book 5, pp. 412-3]

This is reflected in both the theory and history of the modern state. Theorists of the liberal state like John Locke had no qualms about developing a theory of the state which placed the defence of private property at its heart. This perspective was reflected in the American Revolution. For example, there is the words of John Jay (the first chief justice of the Supreme Court), namely that "the people who own the country ought to govern it." [quoted by Noam Chomsky, **Understanding Power**, p. 315] This was the maxim of the Founding Fathers of American "democracy" and it has continued ever since.

So, in a nutshell, the state is the means by which the ruling class rules. Hence Bakunin:

> "The State is authority, domination, and force, organised by the property-owning and so-called enlightened classes against the masses … the State's domination … [ensures] that of the privileged classes who it solely represents." [**The Basic Bakunin**, p. 140]

Under the current system, this means that the state "constitutes the chief bulwark of capital" because of its "centralisation, law (always written by a minority in the interest of that minority), and courts of justice (established mainly for the defence of authority and capital)." Thus it is "the mission of all governments … is to protect and maintain by force the … privileges of the possessing classes." Consequently, while "[i]n the struggle between the individual and the State, anarchism … takes the side of the individual as against the State, of society against the authority which oppresses it," anarchists are well aware that the state does not exist above society, independent of the classes which make it up. [Kropotkin, **Anarchism**, pp. 149-50, p. 214 and pp. 192-3]

Consequently anarchists reject the idea that the role of the state is simply to represent the interests of the people or "the nation." For *"democracy is an empty pretence to the extent that production, finance and commerce – and along with them, the political processes of the society as well – are under control of 'concentrations of private power.' The 'national interest' as articulated by those who dominate the ... societies will be their special interests. Under these circumstances, talk of 'national interest' can only contribute to mystification and oppression."* [Noam Chomsky, **Radical Priorities**, p. 52] As we discuss in section D.6, nationalism always reflects the interests of the elite, not those who make up a nation and, consequently, anarchists reject the notion as nothing more than a con (i.e. the use of affection of where you live to further ruling class aims and power).

Indeed, part of the state's role as defender of the ruling elite is to do so internationally, defending "national" (i.e. elite) interests against the elites of other nations. Thus we find that at the IMF and World Bank, nations are represented by ministers who are *"closely aligned with particular constituents **within** their countries. The trade ministers reflect the concerns of the business community"* while the *"finance ministers and central bank governors are closely tied to financial community; they come from financial firms, and after their period in service, that is where they return ... These individuals see the world through the eyes of the financial community."* Unsurprisingly, the *"decisions of any institution naturally reflect the perspectives and interests of those who make the decisions"* and so the *"policies of the international economic institutions are all too often closely aligned with the commercial and financial interests of those in the advanced industrial countries."* [Joseph Stiglitz, **Globalisation and its Discontents**, pp. 19-20]

This, it must be stressed, does not change in the so-called democratic state. Here, however, the primary function of the state is disguised by the "democratic" facade of the representative electoral system, through which it is made to appear that the people rule themselves. Thus Bakunin writes that the modern state *"unites in itself the two conditions necessary for the prosperity of the capitalistic economy: State centralisation and the actual subjection of ... the people ... to the minority allegedly representing it but actually governing it."* [**Op. Cit.**, p. 210] How this is achieved is discussed in section B.2.3.

B.2.2 Does the state have subsidiary functions?

Yes, it does. While, as discussed in the last section, the state is an instrument to maintain class rule this does not mean that it is limited to just defending the social relationships in a society and the economic and political sources of those relationships. No state has ever left its activities at that bare minimum. As well as defending the rich, their property and the specific forms of property rights they favoured, the state has numerous other subsidiary functions. What these are has varied considerably over time and space and, consequently, it would be impossible to list them all. However, **why** it does is more straight forward. We can generalise two main

forms of subsidiary functions of the state. The first one is to boost the interests of the ruling elite either nationally or internationally beyond just defending their property. The second is to protect society against the negative effects of the capitalist market. We will discuss each in turn and, for simplicity and relevance, we will concentrate on capitalism (see also section D.1).

The first main subsidiary function of the state is when it intervenes in society to help the capitalist class in some way. This can take obvious forms of intervention, such as subsidies, tax breaks, non-bid government contracts, protective tariffs to old, inefficient, industries, giving actual monopolies to certain firms or individuals, bailouts of corporations judged by state bureaucrats as too important to let fail, and so on. However, the state intervenes far more than that and in more subtle ways. Usually it does so to solve problems that arise in the course of capitalist development and which cannot, in general, be left to the market (at least initially). These are designed to benefit the capitalist class as a whole rather than just specific individuals, companies or sectors.

These interventions have taken different forms in different times and include state funding for industry (e.g. military spending); the creation of social infrastructure too expensive for private capital to provide (railways, motorways); the funding of research that companies cannot afford to undertake; protective tariffs to protect developing industries from more efficient international competition (the key to successful industrialisation as it allows capitalists to rip-off consumers, making them rich and increasing funds available for investment); giving capitalists preferential access to land and other natural resources; providing education to the general public that ensures they have the skills and attitude required by capitalists and the state (it is no accident that a key thing learned in school is how to survive boredom, being in a hierarchy and to do what it orders); imperialist ventures to create colonies or client states (or protect citizen's capital invested abroad) in order to create markets or get access to raw materials and cheap labour; government spending to stimulate consumer demand in the face of recession and stagnation; maintaining a "natural" level of unemployment that can be used to discipline the working class, so ensuring they produce more, for less; manipulating the interest rate in order to try and reduce the effects of the business cycle and undermine workers' gains in the class struggle.

These actions, and others like it, ensure that a key role of the state within capitalism *"is essentially to socialise risk and cost, and to privatise power and profit."* Unsurprisingly, *"with all the talk about minimising the state, in the OECD countries the state continues to grow relative to GNP."* [Noam Chomsky, **Rogue States**, p. 189] Hence David Deleon:

> *"Above all, the state remains an institution for the continuance of dominant socio-economic relations, whether through such agencies as the military, the courts, politics or the police ... Contemporary states have acquired ... less primitive means to reinforce their property systems [than state violence – which is always the means of last, often first, resort]. States can regulate, moderate or resolve tensions in the economy by preventing the bankruptcies of key corporations, manipulating the economy through*

interest rates, supporting hierarchical ideology through tax benefits for churches and schools, and other tactics. In essence, it is not a neutral institution; it is powerfully for the status quo. The capitalist state, for example, is virtually a gyroscope centred in capital, balancing the system. If one sector of the economy earns a level of profit, let us say, that harms the rest of the system – such as oil producers' causing public resentment and increased manufacturing costs – the state may redistribute some of that profit through taxation, or offer encouragement to competitors." ["Anarchism on the origins and functions of the state: some basic notes", **Reinventing Anarchy**, pp. 71-72]

In other words, the state acts to protect the long-term interests of the capitalist class as a whole (and ensure its own survival) by protecting the system. This role can and does clash with the interests of particular capitalists or even whole sections of the ruling class (see section B.2.6). But this conflict does not change the role of the state as the property owners' policeman. Indeed, the state can be considered as a means for settling (in a peaceful and apparently independent manner) upper-class disputes over what to do to keep the system going.

This subsidiary role, it must be stressed, is no accident, It is part and parcel of capitalism. Indeed, *"successful industrial societies have consistently relied on departures from market orthodoxies, while condemning their victims [at home and abroad] to market discipline."* [Noam Chomsky, **World Orders, Old and New**, p. 113] While such state intervention grew greatly after the Second World War, the role of the state as active promoter of the capitalist class rather than just its passive defender as implied in capitalist ideology (i.e. as defender of property) has always been a feature of the system. As Kropotkin put it:

> *"every State reduces the peasants and the industrial workers to a life of misery, by means of taxes, and through the monopolies it creates in favour of the landlords, the cotton lords, the railway magnates, the publicans, and the like … we need only to look round, to see how everywhere in Europe and America the States are constituting monopolies in favour of capitalists at home, and still more in conquered lands [which are part of their empires]."* [**Evolution and Environment**, p. 97]

By *"monopolies,"* it should be noted, Kropotkin meant general privileges and benefits rather than giving a certain firm total control over a market. This continues to this day by such means as, for example, privatising industries but providing them with state subsidies or by (mis-labelled) "free trade" agreements which impose protectionist measures such as intellectual property rights on the world market.

All this means that capitalism has rarely relied on purely economic power to keep the capitalists in their social position of dominance (either nationally, vis-à-vis the working class, or internationally, vis-à-vis competing foreign elites). While a "free market" capitalist regime in which the state reduces its intervention to simply protecting capitalist property rights has been approximated on a few occasions, this is not the standard state of the system – direct force, i.e. state action, almost always supplements it.

This is most obviously the case during the birth of capitalist production. Then the bourgeoisie wants and uses the power of the state to "regulate" wages (i.e. to keep them down to such levels as to maximise profits and force people to attend work regularly), to lengthen the working day and to keep the labourer dependent on wage labour as their own means of income (by such means as enclosing land, enforcing property rights on unoccupied land, and so forth). As capitalism is not and has never been a "natural" development in society, it is not surprising that more and more state intervention is required to keep it going (and if even this was not the case, if force was essential to creating the system in the first place, the fact that it later can survive without further direct intervention does not make the system any less statist). As such, "regulation" and other forms of state intervention continue to be used in order to skew the market in favour of the rich and so force working people to sell their labour on the bosses terms.

This form of state intervention is designed to prevent those greater evils which might threaten the efficiency of a capitalist economy or the social and economic position of the bosses. It is designed not to provide positive benefits for those subject to the elite (although this may be a side-effect). Which brings us to the other kind of state intervention, the attempts by society, by means of the state, to protect itself against the eroding effects of the capitalist market system.

Capitalism is an inherently anti-social system. By trying to treat labour (people) and land (the environment) as commodities, it has to break down communities and weaken eco-systems. This cannot but harm those subject to it and, as a consequence, this leads to pressure on government to intervene to mitigate the most damaging effects of unrestrained capitalism. Therefore, on one side there is the historical movement of the market, a movement that has no inherent limit and that therefore threatens society's very existence. On the other there is society's natural propensity to defend itself, and therefore to create institutions for its protection. Combine this with a desire for justice on behalf of the oppressed along with opposition to the worse inequalities and abuses of power and wealth and we have the potential for the state to act to combat the worse excesses of the system in order to keep the system as a whole going. After all, the government *"cannot want society to break up, for it would mean that it and the dominant class would be deprived of the sources of exploitation."* [Malatesta, **Op. Cit.**, p. 25]

Needless to say, the thrust for any system of social protection usually comes from below, from the people most directly affected by the negative effects of capitalism. In the face of mass protests the state may be used to grant concessions to the working class in cases where not doing so would threaten the integrity of the system as a whole. Thus, social struggle is the dynamic for understanding many, if not all, of the subsidiary functions acquired by the state over the years (this applies to pro-capitalist functions as these are usually driven by the need to bolster the profits and power of capitalists at the expense of the working class).

State legislation to set the length of the working day is an obvious example of this. In the early period of capitalist development, the economic position of the capitalists was secure and, consequently, the state happily ignored the lengthening working day, thus allowing capitalists to appropriate more surplus value from workers and increase the rate of profit without interference. Whatever protests erupted were handled by troops. Later, however, after workers began to organise on a wider and wider scale, reducing the length of the working day became a key demand around which revolutionary socialist fervour was developing. In order to defuse this threat (and socialist revolution is the worst-case scenario for the capitalist), the state passed legislation to reduce the length of the working day.

Initially, the state was functioning purely as the protector of the capitalist class, using its powers simply to defend the property of the few against the many who used it (i.e. repressing the labour movement to allow the capitalists to do as they liked). In the second period, the state was granting concessions to the working class to eliminate a threat to the integrity of the system as a whole. Needless to say, once workers' struggle calmed down and their bargaining position reduced by the normal workings of market (see section B.4.3), the legislation restricting the working day was happily ignored and became "dead laws."

This suggests that there is a continuing tension and conflict between the efforts to establish, maintain, and spread the "free market" and the efforts to protect people and society from the consequences of its workings. Who wins this conflict depends on the relative strength of those involved (as does the actual reforms agreed to). Ultimately, what the state concedes, it can also take back. Thus the rise and fall of the welfare state – granted to stop more revolutionary change (see section D.1.3), it did not fundamentally challenge the existence of wage labour and was useful as a means of regulating capitalism but was "reformed" (i.e. made worse, rather than better) when it conflicted with the needs of the capitalist economy and the ruling elite felt strong enough to do so.

Of course, this form of state intervention does not change the nature nor role of the state as an instrument of minority power. Indeed, that nature cannot help but shape how the state tries to implement social protection and so if the state assumes functions it does so as much in the immediate interest of the capitalist class as in the interest of society in general. Even where it takes action under pressure from the general population or to try and mend the harm done by the capitalist market, its class and hierarchical character twists the results in ways useful primarily to the capitalist class or itself. This can be seen from how labour legislation is applied, for example. Thus even the "good" functions of the state are penetrated with and dominated by the state's hierarchical nature. As Malatesta forcefully put it:

> "The basic function of government ... is always that of oppressing and exploiting the masses, of defending the oppressors and the exploiters ... It is true that to these basic functions ... other functions have been added in the course of history ... hardly ever has a government existed ... which did not combine with its oppressive and plundering activities others which were useful ... to social life. But this does not detract from the fact that government is by nature oppressive ... and that it is in origin and by its attitude, inevitably inclined to defend and strengthen the dominant class; indeed it confirms and aggravates the

> position ... [I]t is enough to understand how and why it carries out these functions to find the practical evidence that whatever governments do is always motivated by the desire to dominate, and is always geared to defending, extending and perpetuating its privileges and those of the class of which it is both the representative and defender." [**Op. Cit.**, pp. 23-4]

This does not mean that these reforms should be abolished (the alternative is often worse, as neo-liberalism shows), it simply recognises that the state is not a neutral body and cannot be expected to act as if it were. Which, ironically, indicates another aspect of social protection reforms within capitalism: they make for good PR. By appearing to care for the interests of those harmed by capitalism, the state can obscure it real nature:

> "A government cannot maintain itself for long without hiding its true nature behind a pretence of general usefulness; it cannot impose respect for the lives of the privileged if it does not appear to demand respect for all human life; it cannot impose acceptance of the privileges of the few if it does not pretend to be the guardian of the rights of all." [Malatesta, **Op. Cit.**, p. 24]

Obviously, being an instrument of the ruling elite, the state can hardly be relied upon to control the system which that elite run. As we discuss in the next section, even in a democracy the state is run and controlled by the wealthy making it unlikely that pro-people legislation will be introduced or enforced without substantial popular pressure. That is why anarchists favour direct action and extra-parliamentary organising (see sections J.2 and J.5 for details). Ultimately, even basic civil liberties and rights are the product of direct action, of *"mass movements among the people"* to *"wrest these rights from the ruling classes, who would never have consented to them voluntarily."* [Rocker, **Anarcho-Syndicalism**, p. 75]

Equally obviously, the ruling elite and its defenders hate any legislation it does not favour – while, of course, remaining silent on its own use of the state. As Benjamin Tucker pointed out about the "free market" capitalist Herbert Spencer, *"amid his multitudinous illustrations ... of the evils of legislation, he in every instance cites some law passed ostensibly at least to protect labour, alleviating suffering, or promote the people's welfare ... But never once does he call attention to the far more deadly and deep-seated evils growing out of the innumerable laws creating privilege and sustaining monopoly."* [**The Individualist Anarchists**, p. 45] Such hypocrisy is staggering, but all too common in the ranks of supporters of "free market" capitalism.

Finally, it must be stressed that none of these subsidiary functions implies that capitalism can be changed through a series of piecemeal reforms into a benevolent system that primarily serves working class interests. To the contrary, these functions grow out of, and supplement, the basic role of the state as the protector of capitalist property and the social relations they generate – i.e. the foundation of the capitalist's ability to exploit. Therefore reforms may modify the functioning of capitalism but they can never threaten its basis. In summary, while the level and nature of statist intervention on behalf of the employing classes may vary, it is always there. No matter what activity it conducts beyond its primary function of protecting private property, what subsidiary functions it takes on, the state always operates as an instrument of the ruling class. This applies even to those subsidiary functions which have been imposed on the state by the general public – even the most popular reform will be twisted to benefit the state or capital, if at all possible. This is not to dismiss all attempts at reform as irrelevant, it simply means recognising that we, the oppressed, need to rely on our own strength and organisations to improve our circumstances.

B.2.3 How does the ruling class maintain control of the state?

In some systems, it is obvious how economic dominant minorities control the state. In feudalism, for example, the land was owned by the feudal lords who exploited the peasantry directly. Economic and political power were merged into the same set of hands, the landlords. Absolutism saw the monarch bring the feudal lords under his power and the relative decentralised nature of feudalism was replaced by a centralised state.

It was this centralised state system which the rising bourgeoisie took as the model for their state. The King was replaced by a Parliament, which was initially elected on a limited suffrage. In this initial form of capitalist state, it is (again) obvious how the elite maintain control of the state machine. As the vote was based on having a minimum amount of property, the poor were effectively barred from having any (official) say in what the government did. This exclusion was theorised by philosophers like John Locke – the working masses were considered to be an object of state policy rather than part of the body of people (property owners) who nominated the government. In this perspective the state was like a joint-stock company. The owning class were the share-holders who nominated the board of directors and the mass of the population were the workers who had no say in determining the management personnel and were expected to follow orders.

As would be expected, this system was mightily disliked by the majority who were subjected to it. Such a "classical liberal" regime was rule by an alien, despotic power, lacking popular legitimacy, and utterly unaccountable to the general population. It is quite evident that a government elected on a limited franchise could not be trusted to treat those who owned no real property with equal consideration. It was predictable that the ruling elite would use the state they controlled to further their own interests and to weaken potential resistance to their social, economic and political power. Which is precisely what they did do, while masking their power under the guise of "good governance" and "liberty." Moreover, limited suffrage, like absolutism, was considered an affront to liberty and individual dignity by many of those subject to it.

Hence the call for universal suffrage and opposition to property qualifications for the franchise. For many radicals (including Marx and Engels) such a system would mean that the working classes would hold "political power" and, consequently, be in a position to end the class system once and for all. Anarchists were not convinced, arguing that "universal suffrage, considered in itself and applied in a society based on economic and social inequality, will be nothing but a swindle and snare for the people" and "the surest way to consolidate under the mantle of liberalism and justice the permanent domination of the people by the owning classes, to the detriment of popular liberty." Consequently, anarchists denied that it "could be used by the people for the conquest of economic and social equality. It must always and necessarily be an instrument hostile to the people, one which supports the **de facto** dictatorship of the bourgeoisie." [Bakunin, **Bakunin on Anarchism**, p. 224]

Due to popular mass movements form below, the vote was won by the male working classes and, at a later stage, women. While the elite fought long and hard to retain their privileged position they were defeated. Sadly, the history of universal suffrage has proven the anarchists right. Even allegedly "democratic" capitalist states are in effect dictatorships of the propertariat. The political history of modern times can be summarised by the rise of capitalist power, the rise, due to popular movements, of (representative) democracy and the continued success of the former to undermine and control the latter.

This is achieved by three main processes which combine to effectively deter democracy. These are the wealth barrier, the bureaucracy barrier and, lastly, the capital barrier. Each will be discussed in turn and all ensure that "representative democracy" remains an "organ of capitalist domination." [Kropotkin, **Words of a Rebel**, p. 127]

The wealth barrier is the most obvious. It takes money to run for office. In 1976, the total spent on the US Presidential election was $66.9 million. In 1984, it was $103.6 million and in 1996 it was $239.9 million. At the dawn of the 21st century, these figures had increased yet again. 2000 saw $343.1 spent and 2004, $717.9 million. Most of this money was spent by the two main candidates. In 2000, Republican George Bush spent a massive $185,921,855 while his Democratic rival Al Gore spent only $120,031,205. Four years later, Bush spent $345,259,155 while John Kerry managed a mere $310,033,347.

Other election campaigns are also enormously expensive. In 2000, the average winning candidate for a seat in the US House of Representatives spent $816,000 while the average winning senator spent $7 million. Even local races require significant amounts of fundraising. One candidate for the Illinois House raised over $650,000 while another candidate for the Illinois Supreme Court raised $737,000. In the UK, similarly prohibitive amounts were spent. In the 2001 general election the Labour Party spent a total of £10,945,119, the Tories £12,751,813 and the Liberal Democrats (who came a distant third) just £1,361,377.

To get this sort of money, wealthy contributors need to be found and wooed, in other words promised that that their interests will be actively looked after. While, in theory, it is possible to raise large sums from small contributions in practice this is difficult. To raise $1 million you need to either convince 50 millionaires to give you $20,000 or 20,000 people to fork out $50. Given that for the elite $20,000 is pocket money, it is hardly surprising that politicians aim for winning over the few, not the many. Similarly with corporations and big business. It is far easier and more efficient in time and energy to concentrate on the wealthy few (whether individuals or companies).

Why do anarchists oppose the current system?

It is obvious: whoever pays the piper calls the tune. And in capitalism, this means the wealthy and business. In the US corporate campaign donations and policy paybacks have reached unprecedented proportions. The vast majority of large campaign donations are, not surprisingly, from corporations. Most of the wealthy individuals who give large donations to the candidates are CEOs and corporate board members. And, just to be sure, many companies give to more than one party.

Unsurprisingly, corporations and the rich expect their investments to get a return. This can be seen from George W. Bush's administration. His election campaigns were beholden to the energy industry (which has backed him since the beginning of his career as Governor of Texas). The disgraced corporation Enron (and its CEO Kenneth Lay) were among Bush's largest contributors in 2000. Once in power, Bush backed numerous policies favourable to that industry (such as rolling back environmental regulation on a national level as he had done in Texas). His supporters in Wall Street were not surprised that Bush tried to privatise Social Security. Nor were the credit card companies when the Republicans tighten the noose on bankrupt people in 2005. By funding Bush, these corporations ensured that the government furthered their interests rather than the people who voted in the election.

This means that as a *"consequence of the distribution of resources and decision-making power in the society at large ... the political class and the cultural managers typically associate themselves with the sectors that dominate the private economy; they are either drawn directly from those sectors or expect to join them."* [Chomsky, **Necessary Illusions**, p. 23] This can be seen from George W. Bush's quip at an elite fund-raising gala during the 2000 Presidential election: *"This is an impressive crowd – the haves and the have-mores. Some people call you the elites; I call you my base."* Unsurprisingly:

> *"In the real world, state policy is largely determined by those groups that command resources, ultimately by virtue of their ownership and management of the private economy or their status as wealthy professionals. The major decision-making positions in the Executive branch of the government are typically filled by representatives of major corporations, banks and investment firms, a few law firms that cater primarily to corporate interests and thus represent the broad interests of owners and managers rather than some parochial interest ... The Legislative branch is more varied, but overwhelmingly, it is drawn from the business and professional classes."*
> [Chomsky, **On Power and Ideology**, pp. 116-7]

That is not the only tie between politics and business. Many politicians also have directorships in companies, interests in companies, shares, land and other forms of property income and so forth. Thus they are less like the majority of constituents they claim to represent and more like the wealthy few. Combine these outside earnings with a high salary (in the UK, MP's are paid more than twice the national average) and politicians can be among the richest 1% of the population. Thus not only do we have a sharing of common interests the elite, the politicians are part of it. As such, they can hardly be said to be representative of the general public

and are in a position of having a vested interest in legislation on property being voted on.

Some defend these second jobs and outside investments by saying that it keeps them in touch with the outside world and, consequently, makes them better politicians. That such an argument is spurious can be seen from the fact that such outside interests never involve working in McDonald's flipping burgers or working on an assembly line. For some reason, no politician seeks to get a feeling for what life is like for the average person. Yet, in a sense, this argument **does** have a point. Such jobs and income do keep politicians in touch with the world of the elite rather than that of the masses and, as the task of the state is to protect elite interests, it cannot be denied that this sharing of interests and income with the elite can only aid that task!

Then there is the sad process by which politicians, once they leave politics, get jobs in the corporate hierarchy (particularly with the very companies they had previously claimed to regulate on behalf of the public). This was termed "the revolving door." Incredibly, this has changed for the worse. Now the highest of government officials arrive directly from the executive offices of powerful corporations. Lobbyists are appointed to the jobs whose occupants they once vied to influence. Those who regulate and those supposed to be regulated have become almost indistinguishable.

Thus politicians and capitalists go hand in hand. Wealth selects them, funds them and gives them jobs and income when in office. Finally, once they finally leave politics, they are often given directorships and other jobs in the business world. Little wonder, then, that the capitalist class maintains control of the state.

That is not all. The wealth barrier operates indirectly too. This takes many forms. The most obvious is in the ability of corporations and the elite to lobby politicians. In the US, there is the pervasive power of Washington's army of 24,000 registered lobbyists – and the influence of the corporate interests they represent. These lobbyists, whose job it is to convince politicians to vote in certain ways to further the interests of their corporate clients help shape the political agenda even further toward business interests than it already is. This Lobby industry is immense – and exclusively for big business and the elite. Wealth ensures that the equal opportunity to garner resources to share a perspective and influence the political progress is monopolised by the few: *"where are the desperately needed countervailing lobbies to represent the interests of average citizens? Where are the millions of dollars acting in **their** interests? Alas, they are notably absent."* [Joel Bakan, **The Corporation**, p. 107]

However, it cannot be denied that it is up to the general population to vote for politicians. This is when the indirect impact of wealth kicks in, namely the role of the media and the Public Relations (PR) industry. As we discuss in section D.3, the modern media is dominated by big business and, unsurprisingly, reflects their interests. This means that the media has an important impact on how voters see parties and specific politicians and candidates. A radical party will, at best, be ignored by the capitalist press or, at worse, subject to smears and attacks. This will have a corresponding negative impact on their election prospects and will involve the affected party having to invest substantially more time, energy and resources in countering the negative media coverage. The PR industry has a similar effect, although that has the advantage of not having to bother with appearing to look factual or unbiased. Add to this the impact of elite and corporation funded *"think tanks"* and the political system is fatally skewed in favour of the capitalist class (also see section D.2).

In a nutshell:

> *"The business class dominates government through its ability to fund political campaigns, purchase high priced lobbyists and reward former officials with lucrative jobs ... [Politicians] have become wholly dependent upon the same corporate dollars to pay for a new professional class of PR consultants, marketeers and social scientists who manage and promote causes and candidates in essentially the same manner that advertising campaigns sell cars, fashions, drugs and other wares."* [John Stauber and Sheldon Rampton, **Toxic Sludge is Good for You**, p. 78]

That is the first barrier, the direct and indirect impact of wealth. This, in itself, is a powerful barrier to deter democracy and, as a consequence, it is usually sufficient in itself. Yet sometimes people see through the media distortions and vote for reformist, even radical, candidates. As we discuss in section J.2.6, anarchists argue that the net effect of running for office is a general **de**-radicalising of the party involved. Revolutionary parties become reformist, reformist parties end up maintaining capitalism and introducing policies the opposite of which they had promised. So while it is unlikely that a radical party could get elected and remain radical in the process, it is possible. If such a party did get into office, the remaining two barriers kick in: the bureaucracy barrier and the capital barrier.

The existence of a state bureaucracy is a key feature in ensuring that the state remains the ruling class's *"policeman"* and will be discussed in greater detail in section J.2.2 (Why do anarchists reject voting as a means for change?). Suffice to say, the politicians who are elected to office are at a disadvantage as regards the state bureaucracy. The latter is a permanent concentration of power while the former come and go. Consequently, they are in a position to tame any rebel government by means of bureaucratic inertia, distorting and hiding necessary information and pushing its own agenda onto the politicians who are in theory their bosses but in reality dependent on the bureaucracy. And, needless to say, if all else fails the state bureaucracy can play its final hand: the military coup.

This threat has been applied in many countries, most obviously in the developing world (with the aid of Western, usually US, imperialism). The coups in Iran (1953) and Chile (1973) are just two examples of this process. Yet the so-called developed world is not immune to it. The rise of fascism in Italy, Germany, Portugal and Spain can be considered as variations of a military coup (particularly the last one where fascism was imposed by the military). Wealthy business men funded para-military forces to break the back of the labour movement, forces formed by ex-military people. Even the New Deal in America was threatened by such a coup. [Joel Bakan, **Op. Cit.**, pp. 86-95] While such regimes do protect the interests of capital and are, consequently, backed by it, they do hold problems for

capitalism. This is because, as with the Absolutism which fostered capitalism in the first place, this kind of government can get ideas above its station This means that a military coup will only be used when the last barrier, the capital barrier, is used and fails.

The capital barrier is obviously related to the wealth barrier insofar as it relates to the power that great wealth produces. However, it is different in how it is applied. The wealth barrier restricts who gets into office, the capital barrier controls whoever does so. The capital barrier, in other words, are the economic forces that can be brought to bear on any government which is acting in ways disliked of by the capitalist class.

We see their power implied when the news report that changes in government, policies and law have been *"welcomed by the markets."* As the richest 1% of households in America (about 2 million adults) owned 35% of the stock owned by individuals in 1992 – with the top 10% owning over 81% – we can see that the *"opinion"* of the markets actually means the power of the richest 1-5% of a country's population (and their finance experts), power derived from their control over investment and production. Given that the bottom 90% of the US population has a smaller share (23%) of all kinds of investable capital that the richest 1/2% (who own 29%), with stock ownership being even more concentrated (the top 5% holding 95% of all shares), its obvious why Doug Henwood argues that stock markets are *"a way for the very rich as a class to own an economy's productive capital stock as a whole,"* are a source of *"political power"* and a way to have influence over government policy. [**Wall Street: Class Racket**]

The mechanism is simple enough. The ability of capital to disinvest (capital flight) and otherwise adversely impact the economy is a powerful weapon to keep the state as its servant. The companies and the elite can invest at home or abroad, speculate in currency markets and so forth. If a significant number of investors or corporations lose confidence in a government they will simply stop investing at home and move their funds abroad. At home, the general population feel the results as demand drops, layoffs increase and recession kicks in. As Noam Chomsky notes:

> *"In capitalist democracy, the interests that must be satisfied are those of capitalists; otherwise, there is no investment, no production, no work, no resources to be devoted, however marginally, to the needs of the general population."* [**Turning the Tide**, p. 233]

This ensures the elite control of government as government policies which private power finds unwelcome will quickly be reversed. The power which "business confidence" has over the political system ensures that democracy is subservient to big business. As summarised by Malatesta:

> *"Even with universal suffrage – we could well say even more so with universal suffrage – the government remained the bourgeoisie's servant and **gendarme**. For were it to be otherwise with the government hinting that it might take up a hostile attitude, or that democracy could ever be anything but a pretence to deceive the people, the bourgeoisie, feeling its interests threatened, would by quick to react, and would use all the influence*

*and force at its disposal, by reason of its wealth, to recall the government to its proper place as the bourgeoisie's **gendarme**."* [**Anarchy**, p. 23]

It is due to these barriers that the state remains an instrument of the capitalist class while being, in theory, a democracy. Thus the state machine remains a tool by which the few can enrich themselves at the expense of the many. This does not mean, of course, that the state is immune to popular pressure. Far from it. As indicated in the last section, direct action by the oppressed can and has forced the state to implement significant reforms. Similarly, the need to defend society against the negative effects of unregulated capitalism can also force through populist measures (particularly when the alternative may be worse than the allowing the reforms, i.e. revolution). The key is that such changes are **not** the natural function of the state.

So due to their economic assets, the elites whose incomes are derived from them – namely, finance capitalists, industrial capitalists, and landlords – are able to accumulate vast wealth from those whom they exploit. This stratifies society into a hierarchy of economic classes, with a huge disparity of wealth between the small property-owning elite at the top and the non-property-owning majority at the bottom. Then, because it takes enormous wealth to win elections and lobby or bribe legislators, the propertied elite are able to control the political process – and hence the state – through the *"power of the purse."* In summary:

> *"No democracy has freed itself from the rule by the well-to-do anymore than it has freed itself from the division between the ruler and the ruled ... at the very least, no democracy has jeopardised the role of business enterprise. Only the wealthy and well off can afford to launch viable campaigns for public office and to assume such positions. Change in government in a democracy is a circulation from one elite group to another."* [Harold Barclay, **Op. Cit.**, p. 47]

In other words, elite control of politics through huge wealth disparities insures the continuation of such disparities and thus the continuation of elite control. In this way the crucial political decisions of those at the top are insulated from significant influence by those at the bottom. Finally, it should be noted that these barriers do not arise accidentally. They flow from the way the state is structured. By effectively disempowering the masses and centralising power into the hands of the few which make up the government, the very nature of the state ensures that it remains under elite control. This is why, from the start, the capitalist class has favoured centralisation. We discuss this in the next two sections.

(For more on the ruling elite and its relation to the state, see C. Wright Mills, **The Power Elite** [Oxford, 1956]; cf. Ralph Miliband, **The State in Capitalist Society** [Basic Books, 1969] and **Divided Societies** [Oxford, 1989]; G. William Domhoff, **Who Rules America?** [Prentice Hall, 1967]; and **Who Rules America Now? A View for the '80s** [Touchstone, 1983]).

It is a common idea that voting every four or so years to elect the public face of a highly centralised and bureaucratic machine means that ordinary people control the state and, as a consequence, are free. In reality, this is a false idea. In any system of centralised power the general population have little say in what affects them and, as a result, their freedom is extremely limited.

Obviously, to say that this idea is false does not imply that there is no difference between a liberal republic and a fascistic or monarchical state. Far from it. The vote is an important victory wrested from the powers that be. That, of course, is not to suggest that anarchists think that libertarian socialism is only possible after universal suffrage has been won or that it is achievable via it. Far from it. It is simply to point out that being able to pick your ruler is a step forward from having one imposed upon you. Moreover, those considered able to pick their ruler is, logically, also able to do without one.

However, while the people are proclaimed to be sovereign in a democratic state, in reality they alienate their power and hand over control of their affairs to a small minority. Liberty, in other words, is reduced to merely the possibility *"to pick rulers"* every four or five years and whose mandate (sic!) is *"to legislate on any subject, and his decision will become law."* [Kropotkin, **Words of a Rebel**, p. 122 and p. 123]

In other words, representative democracy is not "liberty" nor "self-government." It is about alienating power to a few people who then (mis)rule in your name. To imply it is anything else is nonsense. So while we get to pick a politician to govern in our name it does not follow that they represent those who voted for them in any meaningful sense. As shown time and time again, "representative" governments can happily ignore the opinions of the majority while, at the same time, verbally praising the "democracy" it is abusing (New Labour in the UK during the run up to the invasion of Iraq was a classic example of this). Given that politicians can do what they like for four or five years once elected, it is clear that popular control via the ballot box is hardly effective or even meaningful.

Indeed, such "democracy" almost always means electing politicians who say one thing in opposition and do the opposite once in office. Politicians who, at best, ignore their election manifesto when it suits them or, at worse, introduce the exact opposite. It is the kind of "democracy" in which people can protest in their hundreds of thousands against a policy only to see their "representative" government simply ignore them (while, at the same time, seeing their representatives bend over backward ensuring corporate profits and power while speaking platitudes to the electorate and their need to tighten their belts). At best it can be said that democratic governments tend to be less oppressive than others but it does not follow that this equates to liberty.

State centralisation is the means to ensure this situation and the debasement of freedom it implies.

All forms of hierarchy, even those in which the top officers are elected are marked by authoritarianism and centralism. Power is concentrated in the centre (or at the top), which means that society becomes *"a heap of dust animated from without by a subordinating, centralist idea."* [P. J. Proudhon, quoted by Martin Buber, **Paths in Utopia**, p. 29] For, once elected, top officers can do as they please, and, as in all bureaucracies, many important decisions are made by non-elected staff. This means that the democratic state is a contradiction in terms:

> *"In the democratic state the election of rulers by alleged majority vote is a subterfuge which helps individuals to believe that they control the situation. They are selecting persons to do a task for them and they have no guarantee that it will be carried out as they desired. They are abdicating to these persons, granting them the right to impose their own wills by the threat of force. Electing individuals to public office is like being given a limited choice of your oppressors ... Parliamentary democracies are essentially oligarchies in which the populace is led to believe that it delegates all its authority to members of parliament to do as they think best."* [Harold Barclay, **Op. Cit.**, pp. 46-7]

The nature of centralisation places power into the hands of the few. Representative democracy is based on this delegation of power, with voters electing others to govern them. This cannot help but create a situation in which freedom is endangered – universal suffrage *"does not prevent the formation of a body of politicians, privileged in fact though not in law, who, devoting themselves exclusively to the administration of the nation's public affairs, end by becoming a sort of political aristocracy or oligarchy."* [Bakunin, **The Political Philosophy of Bakunin**, p. 240]

This should not come as a surprise, for to *"create a state is to institutionalise power in a form of machine that exists **apart** from the people. It is to professionalise rule and policy making, to create a distinct interest (be it of bureaucrats, deputies, commissars, legislators, the military, the police, ad nauseam) that, however weak or however well-intentioned it may be at first, eventually takes on a corruptive power of its own."* [Murray Bookchin, *"The Ecological Crisis, Socialism, and the need to remake society,"* pp. 1-10, **Society and Nature**, vol. 2, no. 3, p. 7]

Centralism makes democracy meaningless, as political decision-making is given over to professional politicians in remote capitals. Lacking local autonomy, people are isolated from each other (atomised) by having no political forum where they can come together to discuss, debate, and decide among themselves the issues they consider important. Elections are not based on natural, decentralised groupings and thus cease to be relevant. The individual is just another "voter" in the mass, a political "constituent" and nothing more. The amorphous basis of modern, statist elections *"aims at nothing less than to abolish political life in towns, communes and departments, and through this destruction of all municipal and regional autonomy to arrest the development of universal suffrage."* [Proudhon, quoted by Martin Buber, **Op. Cit.**, p. 29]

Thus people are disempowered by the very structures that claim to allow them to express themselves. To quote Proudhon again, in the centralised state *"the citizen divests himself of sovereignty,*

the town and the Department and province above it, absorbed by central authority, are no longer anything but agencies under direct ministerial control."* He continues:

> *"The Consequences soon make themselves felt: the citizen and the town are deprived of all dignity, the state's depredations multiply, and the burden on the taxpayer increases in proportion. It is no longer the government that is made for the people; it is the people who are made for the government. Power invades everything, dominates everything, absorbs everything."* [**The Principle of Federation**, p. 59]

As intended, as isolated people are no threat to the powers that be. This process of marginalisation can be seen from American history, for example, when town meetings were replaced by elected bodies, with the citizens being placed in passive, spectator roles as mere "voters" (see next section). Being an atomised voter is hardly an ideal notion of "freedom," despite the rhetoric of politicians about the virtues of a "free society" and "The Free World" – as if voting once every four or five years could ever be classed as "liberty" or even "democracy."

Marginalisation of the people is the key control mechanism in the state and authoritarian organisations in general. Considering the European Community (EC), for example, we find that the *"mechanism for decision-making between EC states leaves power in the hands of officials (from Interior ministries, police, immigration, customs and security services) through a myriad of working groups. Senior officials ... play a critical role in ensuring agreements between the different state officials. The EC Summit meetings, comprising the 12 Prime Ministers, simply rubber-stamp the conclusions agreed by the Interior and Justice Ministers. It is only then, in this intergovernmental process, that parliaments and people are informed (and them only with the barest details)."* [Tony Bunyon, **Statewatching the New Europe**, p. 39]

As well as economic pressures from elites, governments also face pressures within the state itself due to the bureaucracy that comes with centralism. There is a difference between the state and government. The state is the permanent collection of institutions that have entrenched power structures and interests. The government is made up of various politicians. It's the institutions that have power in the state due to their permanence, not the representatives who come and go. As Clive Ponting (an ex-civil servant himself) indicates, *"the function of a political system in any country ... is to regulate, but not to alter radically, the existing economic structure and its linked power relationships. The great illusion of politics is that politicians have the ability to make whatever changes they like."* [quoted in **Alternatives**, no.5, p. 19]

Therefore, as well as marginalising the people, the state also ends up marginalising "our" representatives. As power rests not in the elected bodies, but in a bureaucracy, popular control becomes increasingly meaningless. As Bakunin pointed out, *"liberty can be valid only when ... [popular] control [of the state] is valid. On the contrary, where such control is fictitious, this freedom of the people likewise becomes a mere fiction."* [**Op. Cit.**, p. 212] State centralisation ensures that popular control is meaningless.

This means that state centralism can become a serious source of danger to the liberty and well-being of most of the people under it. *"The bourgeois republicans,"* argued Bakunin, *"do not yet grasp this simple truth, demonstrated by the experience of all times and in all lands, that every organised power standing above and over the people necessarily excludes the freedom of peoples. The political state has no other purpose than to protect and perpetuate the exploitation of the labour of the proletariat by the economically dominant classes, and in so doing the state places itself against the freedom of the people."* [**Bakunin on Anarchism**, p. 416]

Unsurprisingly, therefore, *"whatever progress that has been made … on various issues, whatever things have been done for people, whatever human rights have been gained, have not been gained through the calm deliberations of Congress or the wisdom of presidents or the ingenious decisions of the Supreme Court. Whatever progress has been made … has come because of the actions of ordinary people, of citizens, of social movements. Not from the Constitution."* That document has been happily ignored by the official of the state when it suits them. An obvious example is the 14th Amendment of the US Constitution, which *"didn't have any meaning until black people rose up in the 1950s and 1960s in the South in mass movements … They made whatever words there were in the Constitution and the 14th Amendment have some meaning for the first time."* [Howard Zinn, **Failure to Quit**, p. 69 and p. 73]

This is because the *"fact that you have got a constitutional right doesn't mean you're going to get that right. Who has the power on the spot? The policeman on the street. The principal in the school. The employer on job. The Constitution does not cover private employment. In other words, the Constitution does not cover most of reality."* Thus our liberty is not determined by the laws of the state. Rather *"the source and solution of our civil liberties problems are in the situations of every day … Our actual freedom is determined not by the Constitution or the Court, but by the power the policeman has over us on the street or that of the local judge behind him; by the authority of our employers; … by the welfare bureaucrats if we are poor; … by landlords if we are tenants."* Thus freedom and justice *"are determined by power and money"* rather than laws. This points to the importance of popular participation, of social movements, for what those do are *"to create a countervailing power to the policeman with a club and a gun. That's essentially what movements do: They create countervailing powers to counter the power which is much more important than what is written down in the Constitution or the laws."* [Zinn, **Op. Cit.**, pp. 84-5, pp. 54-5 and p. 79]

It is precisely this kind of mass participation that centralisation kills. Under centralism, social concern and power are taken away from ordinary citizens and centralised in the hands of the few. This results in any formally guaranteed liberties being effectively ignored when people want to use them, if the powers at be so decide. Ultimately, isolated individuals facing the might of a centralised state machine are in a weak position. Which is way the state does what it can to undermine such popular movements and organisations (going so far as to violate its own laws to do so).

As should be obvious, by centralisation anarchists do not mean simply a territorial centralisation of power in a specific central location (such as in a nation state where power rests in a central government located in a specific place). We also mean the centralisation of **power** into a few hands. Thus we can have a system like feudalism which is territorially decentralised (i.e. made up on numerous feudal lords without a strong central state) while having power centralised in a few hands locally (i.e. power rests in the hands of the feudal lords, not in the general population). Or, to use another example, we can have a laissez-faire capitalist system which has a weak central authority but is made up of a multitude of autocratic workplaces. As such, getting rid of the central power (say the central state in capitalism or the monarch in absolutism) while retaining the local authoritarian institutions (say capitalist firms and feudal landlords) would not ensure freedom. Equally, the abolition of local authorities may simply result in the strengthening of central power and a corresponding weakening of freedom.

B.2.5 Who benefits from centralisation?

No social system would exist unless it benefited someone or some group. Centralisation, be it in the state or the company, is no different. In all cases, centralisation directly benefits those at the top, because it shelters them from those who are below, allowing the latter to be controlled and governed more effectively. Therefore, it is in the direct interests of bureaucrats and politicians to support centralism.

Under capitalism, however, various sections of the business class also support state centralism. This is the symbiotic relationship between capital and the state. As will be discussed later (in section F.8), the state played an important role in "nationalising" the market, i.e. forcing the "free market" onto society. By centralising power in the hands of representatives and so creating a state bureaucracy, ordinary people were disempowered and thus became less likely to interfere with the interests of the wealthy. *"In a republic,"* writes Bakunin, *"the so-called people, the legal people, allegedly represented by the State, stifle and will keep on stifling the actual and living people"* by *"the bureaucratic world"* for *"the greater benefit of the privileged propertied classes as well as for its own benefit."* [**Op. Cit.**, p. 211]

Examples of increased political centralisation being promoted by wealthy business interests by can be seen throughout the history of capitalism. *"In revolutionary America, 'the nature of city government came in for heated discussion,' observes Merril Jensen … Town meetings … 'had been a focal point of revolutionary activity'. The anti-democratic reaction that set in after the American revolution was marked by efforts to do away with town meeting government … Attempts by conservative elements were made to establish a 'corporate form (of municipal government) whereby the towns would be governed by mayors and councils' elected from urban wards … [T]he merchants 'backed incorporation consistently in their efforts to escape town meetings.'"* [Murray Bookchin, **Towards an Ecological Society**, p. 182]

Here we see local policy making being taken out of the hands of the many and centralised in the hands of the few (who are always the wealthy). France provides another example:

"The Government found ... the folkmotes [of all households] 'too noisy', too disobedient, and in 1787, elected councils, composed of a mayor and three to six syndics, chosen among the wealthier peasants, were introduced instead." [Peter Kropotkin, **Mutual Aid**, pp. 185-186]

This was part of a general movement to disempower the working class by centralising decision making power into the hands of the few (as in the American revolution). Kropotkin indicates the process at work:

"[T]he middle classes, who had until then had sought the support of the people, in order to obtain constitutional laws and to dominate the higher nobility, were going, now that they had seen and felt the strength of the people, to do all they could to dominate the people, to disarm them and to drive them back into subjection.

[...]

*"[T]hey made haste to legislate in such a way that the political power which was slipping out of the hand of the Court should not fall into the hands of the people. Thus ... [it was] proposed ... to divide the French into two classes, of which one only, the **active** citizens, should take part in the government, whilst the other, comprising the great mass of the people under the name of **passive** citizens, should be deprived of all political rights ... [T]he [National] Assembly divided France into departments ... always maintaining the principle of excluding the poorer classes from the Government ... [T]hey excluded from the primary assemblies the mass of the people ... who could no longer take part in the primary assemblies, and accordingly had no right to nominate the electors [who chose representatives to the National Assembly], or the municipality, or any of the local authorities ...*

*"And finally, the **permanence** of the electoral assemblies was interdicted. Once the middle-class governors were appointed, these assemblies were not to meet again. Once the middle-class governors were appointed, they must not be controlled too strictly. Soon the right even of petitioning and of passing resolutions was taken away – 'Vote and hold your tongue!'*

*"As to the villages ... the general assembly of the inhabitants ... [to which] belonged the administration of the affairs of the commune ... were forbidden by the ... law. Henceforth only the well-to-do peasants, the **active** citizens, had the right to meet, **once a year**, to nominate the mayor and the municipality, composed of three or four middle-class men of the village.*

"A similar municipal organisation was given to the towns ... "[Thus] the middle classes surrounded themselves with every precaution in order to keep the municipal power in the hands of the well-to-do members of the community." [**The Great French Revolution**, vol. 1, pp. 179-186]

Thus centralisation aimed to take power away from the mass of the people and give it to the wealthy. The power of the people rested in popular assemblies, such as the *"Sections"* and *"Districts"* of Paris (expressing, in Kropotkin's words, *"the principles of anarchism"* and *"practising ... Direct Self-Government"* [**Op. Cit.**, p. 204 and p. 203]) and village assemblies. However, the National Assembly *"tried all it could to lessen the power of the districts ... [and] put an end to those hotbeds of Revolution ... [by allowing] **active** citizens only ... to take part in the electoral and administrative assemblies."* [**Op. Cit.**, p. 211] Thus the *"central government was steadily endeavouring to subject the sections to its authority"* with the state *"seeking to centralise everything in its own hands ... [I]ts depriving the popular organisations ... all ... administrative functions ... and its subjecting them to its bureaucracy in police matters, meant the death of the sections."* [**Op. Cit.**, vol. 2, p. 549 and p. 552]

As can be seen, both the French and American revolutions saw a similar process by which the wealthy centralised power into their own hands (volume one of Murray Bookchin's **The Third Revolution** discusses the French and American revolutions in some detail). This ensured that working class people (i.e. the majority) were excluded from the decision making process and subject to the laws and power of a few. Which, of course, benefits the minority class whose representatives have that power. This was the rationale for the centralisation of power in every revolution. Whether it was the American, French or Russian, the centralisation of power was the means to exclude the many from participating in the decisions that affected them and their communities.

For example, the founding fathers of the American State were quite explicit on the need for centralisation for precisely this reason. For James Madison the key worry was when the *"majority"* gained control of *"popular government"* and was in a position to *"sacrifice to its ruling passion or interest both the public good and the rights of other citizens."* Thus the *"public good"* escaped the *"majority"* nor was it, as you would think, what the public thought of as good (for some reason left unexplained, Madison considered the majority able to pick those who **could** identify the public good). To safeguard against this, he advocated a republic rather than a democracy in which the citizens *"assemble and administer the government in person ... have ever been found incompatible with personal security or the rights of property."* He, of course, took it for granted that *"[t]hose who hold and those who are without property have ever formed distinct interests in society."* His schema was to ensure that private property was defended and, as a consequence, the interests of those who held protected. Hence the need for *"the delegation of the government ... to a small number of citizens elected by the rest."* This centralisation of power into a few hands locally was matched by a territorial centralisation for the same reason. Madison favoured *"a large over a small republic"* as a *"rage for paper money, for an abolition of debts, for an equal division of property, or for any other improper or wicked project, will be less apt to pervade the whole body of the Union than a particular member of it."* [contained in **Voices of a People's History of the United States**, Howard Zinn and Anthony Arnove (eds.), pp. 109-113] This desire to have a formal democracy, where the masses are mere spectators of events rather than participants, is a recurring theme in capitalism (see the chapter *"Force and Opinion"* in Noam Chomsky's **Deterring**

Democracy for a good overview).

On the federal and state levels in the US after the Revolution, centralisation of power was encouraged, since *"most of the makers of the Constitution had some direct economic interest in establishing a strong federal government."* Needless to say, while the rich elite were well represented in formulating the principles of the new order, four groups were not: *"slaves, indentured servants, women, men without property."* Needless to say, the new state and its constitution did not reflect their interests. Given that these were the vast majority, *"there was not only a positive need for strong central government to protect the large economic interests, but also immediate fear of rebellion by discontented farmers."* [Howard Zinn, **A People's History of the United States**, p. 90] The chief event was Shay's Rebellion in western Massachusetts. There the new Constitution had raised property qualifications for voting and, therefore, no one could hold state office without being wealthy. The new state was formed to combat such rebellions, to protect the wealthy few against the many.

Moreover, state centralisation, the exclusion of popular participation, was essential to mould US society into one dominated by capitalism:

> *"In the thirty years leading up to the Civil War, the law was increasingly interpreted in the courts to suit capitalist development. Studying this, Morton Horwitz (**The Transformation of American Law**) points out that the English common-law was no longer holy when it stood in the way of business growth ... Judgements for damages against businessmen were taken out of the hands of juries, which were unpredictable, and given to judges ... The ancient idea of a fair price for goods gave way in the courts to the idea of caveat emptor (let the buyer beware) ... contract law was intended to discriminate against working people and for business ... The pretence of the law was that a worker and a railroad made a contract with equal bargaining power ... 'The circle was completed; the law had come simply to ratify those forms of inequality that the market system had produced.'"* [Zinn, **Op. Cit.**, p. 234]

The US state was created on elitist liberal doctrine and actively aimed to reduce democratic tendencies (in the name of "individual liberty"). What happened in practice (unsurprisingly enough) was that the wealthy elite used the state to undermine popular culture and common right in favour of protecting and extending their own interests and power. In the process, US society was reformed in their own image:

> *"By the middle of the nineteenth century the legal system had been reshaped to the advantage of men of commerce and industry at the expense of farmers, workers, consumers, and other less powerful groups in society ... it actively promoted a legal distribution of wealth against the weakest groups in society."* [Morton Horwitz, quoted by Zinn, **Op. Cit.**, p. 235]

In more modern times, state centralisation and expansion has gone hand in glove with rapid industrialisation and the growth of business. As Edward Herman points out, *"[t]o a great extent, it was the growth in business size and power that elicited the countervailing emergence of unions and the growth of government. Bigness **beyond** business was to a large extent a response to bigness **in** business."* [**Corporate Control, Corporate Power**, p. 188 – see also, Stephen Skowronek, **Building A New American State: The Expansion of National Administrative Capacities, 1877-1920**] State centralisation was required to produce bigger, well-defined markets and was supported by business when it acted in their interests (i.e. as markets expanded, so did the state in order to standardise and enforce property laws and so on). On the other hand, this development towards "big government" created an environment in which big business could grow (often encouraged by the state by subsidies and protectionism – as would be expected when the state is run by the wealthy) as well as further removing state power from influence by the masses and placing it more firmly in the hands of the wealthy. It is little wonder we see such developments, for *"[s]tructures of governance tend to coalesce around domestic power, in the last few centuries, economic power."* [Noam Chomsky, **World Orders, Old and New**, p. 178]

State centralisation makes it easier for business to control government, ensuring that it remains their puppet and to influence the political process. For example, the European Round Table (ERT) *"an elite lobby group of ... chairmen or chief executives of large multi-nationals based mainly in the EU ... [with] 11 of the 20 largest European companies [with] combined sales [in 1991] ... exceeding $500 billion, ... approximately 60 per cent of EU industrial production,"* makes much use of the EU. As two researchers who have studied this body note, the ERT *"is adept at lobbying ... so that many ERT proposals and 'visions' are mysteriously regurgitated in Commission summit documents."* The ERT *"claims that the labour market should be more 'flexible,' arguing for more flexible hours, seasonal contracts, job sharing and part time work. In December 1993, seven years after the ERT made its suggestions [and after most states had agreed to the Maastricht Treaty and its "social chapter"], the European Commission published a white paper ... [proposing] making labour markets in Europe more flexible."* [Doherty and Hoedeman, *"Knights of the Road,"* **New Statesman**, 4/11/94, p. 27]

The current talk of globalisation, NAFTA, and the Single European Market indicates an underlying transformation in which state growth follows the path cut by economic growth. Simply put, with the growth of transnational corporations and global finance markets, the bounds of the nation-state have been made economically redundant. As companies have expanded into multi-nationals, so the pressure has mounted for states to follow suit and rationalise their markets across *"nations"* by creating multi-state agreements and unions.

As Noam Chomsky notes, G7, the IMF, the World Bank and so forth are a *"de facto world government,"* and *"the institutions of the transnational state largely serve other masters [than the people], as state power typically does; in this case the rising transnational corporations in the domains of finance and other services, manufacturing, media and communications."* [**Op. Cit.**, p. 179]

As multi-nationals grow and develop, breaking through national boundaries, a corresponding growth in statism is required.

Moreover, a *"particularly valuable feature of the rising de facto governing institutions is their immunity from popular influence, even awareness. They operate in secret, creating a world subordinated to the needs of investors, with the public 'put in its place', the threat of democracy reduced"* [Chomsky, **Op. Cit.**, p. 178].

This does not mean that capitalists desire state centralisation for everything. Often, particularly for social issues, relative decentralisation is often preferred (i.e. power is given to local bureaucrats) in order to increase business control over them. By devolving control to local areas, the power which large corporations, investment firms and the like have over the local government increases proportionally. In addition, even middle-sized enterprise can join in and influence, constrain or directly control local policies and set one workforce against another. Private power can ensure that *"freedom"* is safe, **their** freedom.

No matter which set of bureaucrats are selected, the need to centralise social power, thus marginalising the population, is of prime importance to the business class. It is also important to remember that capitalist opposition to *"big government"* is often financial, as the state feeds off the available social surplus, so reducing the amount left for the market to distribute to the various capitals in competition.

In reality, what capitalists object to about "big government" is its spending on social programs designed to benefit the poor and working class, an "illegitimate" function which "wastes" part of the surplus that might go to capital (and also makes people less desperate and so less willing to work cheaply). Hence the constant push to reduce the state to its "classical" role as protector of private property and the system, and little else. Other than their specious quarrel with the welfare state, capitalists are the staunchest supporters of government (and the "correct" form of state intervention, such as defence spending), as evidenced by the fact that funds can always be found to build more prisons and send troops abroad to advance ruling-class interests, even as politicians are crying that there is "no money" in the treasury for scholarships, national health care, or welfare for the poor.

State centralisation ensures that *"as much as the equalitarian principles have been embodied in its political constitutions, it is the bourgeoisie that governs, and it is the people, the workers, peasants included, who obey the laws made by the bourgeoisie"* who *"has in fact if not by right the exclusive privilege of governing."* This means that *"political equality … is only a puerile fiction, an utter lie."* It takes a great deal of faith to assume that the rich, *"being so far removed from the people by the conditions of its economic and social existence"* can *"give expression in the government and in the laws, to the feelings, the ideas, and the will of the people."* Unsurprisingly, we find that *"in legislation as well as in carrying on the government, the bourgeoisie is guided by its own interests and its own instincts without concerning itself much with the interests of the people."* So while *"on election days even the proudest bourgeois who have any political ambitions are forced to court … The Sovereign People."* But on the *"day after the elections every one goes back to their daily business"* and the politicians are given carte blanche to rule in the name of the people they claim to represent." [Bakunin, **The Political Philosophy of Bakunin**, p. 218 and p. 219]

Yes it can. Given the power of the state machine, it would be hard to believe that it could always be simply a tool for the economically dominant minority in a society. Given its structure and powers, it can use them to further its own interests. Indeed, in some circumstances it can be the ruling class itself.

However, in normal times the state is, as we discussed in section B.2.1, a tool of the capitalist class. This, it must be stressed, does not mean that they always see *"eye to eye."* Top politicians, for example, are part of the ruling elite, but they are in competition with other parts of it. In addition, different sectors of the capitalist class are competing against each other for profits, political influence, privileges, etc. The bourgeoisie, argued Malatesta, *"are always at war among themselves … Thus the games of the swings, the manoeuvres, the concessions and withdrawals, the attempts to find allies among the people against the conservatives, and among the conservatives against the people."* [**Anarchy**, p. 25] This means that different sections of the ruling class will cluster around different parties, depending on their interests, and these parties will seek to gain power to further those interests. This may bring them into conflict with other sections of the capitalist class. The state is the means by which these conflicts can be resolved.

Given that the role of the state is to ensure the best conditions for capital **as a whole,** this means that, when necessary, it can and does work against the interests of certain parts of the capitalist class. To carry out this function the state needs to be above individual capitalists or companies. This is what can give the state the appearance of being a neutral social institution and can fool people into thinking that it represents the interests of society as a whole. Yet this sometime neutrality with regards to individual capitalist companies exists only as an expression of its role as an instrument of capital in general. Moreover, without the tax money from successful businesses the state would be weakened and so the state is in competition with capitalists for the surplus value produced by the working class. Hence the anti-state rhetoric of big business which can fool those unaware of the hand-in-glove nature of modern capitalism to the state.

As Chomsky notes:

> *"There has always been a kind of love-hate relationship between business interests and the capitalist state. On the one hand, business wants a powerful state to regulate disorderly markets, provide services and subsidies to business, enhance and protect access to foreign markets and resources, and so on. On the other hand, business does not want a powerful competitor, in particular, one that might respond to different interests, popular interests, and conduct policies with a redistributive effect, with regard to income or power."* [**Turning the Tide**, p. 211]

As such, the state is often in conflict with sections of the capitalist class, just as sections of that class use the state to advance their own interests within the general framework of protecting the capitalist system (i.e. the interests of the ruling class **as a class**). The state's role is to resolve such disputes within that class peacefully. Under modern capitalism, this is usually done via the *"democratic"* process (within which we get the chance of picking the representatives of the elite who will oppress us least).

Such conflicts sometimes give the impression of the state being a "neutral" body, but this is an illusion – it exists to defend class power and privilege – but exactly which class it defends can change. While recognising that the state protects the power and position of the economically dominant class within a society anarchists also argue that the state has, due to its hierarchical nature, interests of its own. Thus it cannot be considered as simply the tool of the economically dominant class in society. States have their own dynamics, due to their structure, which generate their own classes and class interests and privileges (and which allows them to escape from the control of the economic ruling class and pursue their own interests, to a greater or lesser degree). As Malatesta put it *"the government, though springing from the bourgeoisie and its servant and protector, tends, as with every servant and every protector, to achieve its own emancipation and to dominate whoever it protects."* [**Op. Cit.**, p. 25]

Thus, even in a class system like capitalism, the state can act independently of the ruling elite and, potentially, act against their interests. As part of its role is to mediate between individual capitalists/corporations, it needs sufficient power to tame them and this requires the state to have some independence from the class whose interests it, in general, defends. And such independence can be used to further its own interests, even to the detriment of the capitalist class, if the circumstances allow. If the capitalist class is weak or divided then the state can be in a position to exercise its autonomy vis-à-vis the economically dominant elite, using against the capitalists as a whole the tools it usually applies to them individually to further its own interests and powers.

This means that the state it not just *"the guardian of capital"* for it *"has a vitality of its own and constitutes … a veritable social class apart from other classes … ; and this class has its own particular parasitical and usurious interests, in conflict with those of the rest of the collectivity which the State itself claims to represent … The State, being the depository of society's greatest physical and material force, has too much power in its hands to resign itself to being no more than the capitalists' guard dog."* [Luigi Fabbri, quoted by David Berry, **A History of the French Anarchist Movement, 1917-1945**, p. 39]

Therefore the state machine (and structure), while its modern form is intrinsically linked to capitalism, cannot be seen as being a tool usable by the majority. This is because the *"State, any State – even when it dresses-up in the most liberal and democratic form – is essentially based on domination, and upon violence, that is upon despotism – a concealed but no less dangerous despotism."* The State *"denotes power, authority, domination; it presupposes inequality in fact."* [**The Political Philosophy of Michael Bakunin**, p. 211 and p. 240] The state, therefore, has its own specific logic, its own priorities and its own momentum. It constitutes its own locus of power which is not merely a derivative of economic class power. Consequently, the state can be beyond the control of the economically dominant class and it need not reflect economic relations.

This is due to its hierarchical and centralised nature, which empowers the few who control the state machine – *"[e]very state power, every government, by its nature places itself outside and over the people and inevitably subordinates them to an organisation and to aims which are foreign to and opposed to the real needs and aspirations of the people."* If *"the whole proletariat … [are] members of the government … there will be no government, no state, but, if there is to be a state there will be those who are ruled and those who are slaves."* [**Bakunin on Anarchism**, p. 328 and p. 330]

In other words, the state bureaucracy is itself directly an oppressor and can exist independently of an economically dominant class. In Bakunin's prophetic words:

> *"What have we seen throughout history? The State has always been the patrimony of some privileged class: the sacerdotal class, the nobility, the bourgeoisie – and finally, when all other classes have exhausted themselves, the class of the bureaucracy enters the stage and then the State falls, or rises, if you please, to the position of a machine."* [**The Political Philosophy of Michael Bakunin**, p. 208]

This is unsurprising. For anarchists, *"the State organisation … [is] the force to which minorities resorted for establishing and organising their power over the masses."* It does not imply that these minorities need to be the economically dominant class in a society. The state is *"a superstructure built to the advantage of Landlordism, Capitalism, and Officialism."* [**Evolution and Environment**, p. 82 and p. 105] Consequently, we cannot assume that abolishing one or even two of this unholy trinity will result in freedom nor that all three share exactly the same interests or power in relation to the others. Thus, in some situations, the landlord class can promote its interests over those of the capitalist class (and vice versa) while the state bureaucracy can grow at the expense of both.

As such, it is important to stress that the minority whose interests the state defends need not be an economically dominant one (although it usually is). Under some circumstances a priesthood can be a ruling class, as can a military group or a bureaucracy. This means that the state can also effectively **replace** the economically dominant elite as the exploiting class. This is because anarchists view the state as having (class) interests of its own.

As we discuss in more detail in section H.3.9, the state cannot be considered as merely an instrument of (economic) class rule. History has shown numerous societies where the state **itself** was the ruling class and where no other dominant economic class existed. The experience of Soviet Russia indicates the validity of this analysis. The reality of the Russian Revolution contrasted starkly with the Marxist claim that a state was simply an instrument of class rule and, consequently, the working class needed to build its own state within which to rule society. Rather than being an instrument by which working class people could run and transform society in their own interests, the new state created by the Russian Revolution soon became a power over the class it claimed to represent (see section H.6 for more on this). The working class was exploited and dominated by the new state and its bureaucracy rather than by the capitalist class as previously. This did not happen by chance. As we discuss in section H.3.7, the state has evolved certain characteristics (such as centralisation, delegated power and so on) which ensure its task as enforcer of minority rule is achieved. Keeping those characteristics will inevitably mean keeping the task they were created to serve.

Thus, to summarise, the state's role is to repress the individual and the working class as a whole in the interests of economically dominant minorities/classes and in its own interests. It is *a society for mutual insurance between the landlord, the military commander, the judge, the priest, and later on the capitalist, in order to support such other's authority over the people, and for exploiting the poverty of the masses and getting rich themselves."* Such was the *"origin of the State; such was its history; and such is its present essence."* [Kropotkin, **Evolution and Environment**, p. 94]

So while the state is an instrument of class rule it does **not** automatically mean that it does not clash with sections of the class it represents nor that it has to be the tool of an economically dominant class. One thing is sure, however. The state is not a suitable tool for securing the emancipation of the oppressed.

B.3

Why are anarchists against private property?

Private property is one of the three things all anarchists oppose, along side hierarchical authority and the state. Today, the dominant system of private property is capitalist in nature and, as such, anarchists tend to concentrate on this system and its property rights regime. We will be reflecting this here but do not, because of this, assume that anarchists consider other forms of private property regime (such as, say, feudalism) as acceptable. This is not the case – anarchists are against every form of property rights regime which results in the many working for the few.

Anarchist opposition to private property rests on two, related, arguments. These were summed up by Proudhon's maxims (from What is Property? that *"property is theft"* and *"property is despotism."* In his words, *"Property … violates equality by the rights of exclusion and increase, and freedom by despotism … [and has] perfect identity with robbery."* [Proudhon, What is Property, p. 251] Anarchists, therefore, oppose private property (i.e. capitalism) because it is a source of coercive, hierarchical authority as well as exploitation and, consequently, elite privilege and inequality. It is based on and produces inequality, in terms of both wealth and power.

We will summarise each argument in turn.

The statement *"property is theft"* is one of anarchism's most famous sayings. Indeed, it is no exaggeration to say that anyone who rejects this statement is not an anarchist. This maxim works in two related ways. Firstly, it recognises the fact that the earth and its resources, the common inheritance of all, have been monopolised by a few. Secondly, it argues that, as a consequence of this, those who own property exploit those who do not. This is because those who do not

own have to pay or sell their labour to those who do own in order to get access to the resources they need to live and work (such as workplaces, machinery, land, credit, housing, products under patents, and such like – see section B.3.2 for more discussion).

As we discuss in section B.3.3, this exploitation (theft) flows from the fact that workers do not own or control the means of production they use and, as a consequence, are controlled by those who do during work hours. This alienation of control over labour to the boss places the employer in a position to exploit that labour – to get the worker to produce more than they get paid in wages. That is precisely **why** the boss employs the worker. Combine this with rent, interest and intellectual property rights and we find the secret to maintaining the capitalist system as all allow enormous inequalities of wealth to continue and keep the resources of the world in the hands of a few.

Yet labour cannot be alienated. Therefore when you sell your labour you sell yourself, your liberty, for the time in question. This brings us to the second reason why anarchists oppose private property, the fact it produces authoritarian social relationships. For all true anarchists, property is opposed as a source of authority, indeed despotism. To quote Proudhon on this subject:

> *"The proprietor, the robber, the hero, the sovereign – for all these titles are synonymous – imposes his will as law, and suffers neither contradiction nor control; that is, he pretends to be the legislative and the executive power at once … [and so] property engenders despotism … That is so clearly the essence of property that, to be convinced of it, one need but remember what it is, and observe what happens around him. Property is the right to **use** and **abuse** … if goods are property, why should not the proprietors be kings, and despotic kings – kings in proportion to their **facultes bonitaires**? And if each proprietor is sovereign lord within the sphere of his property, absolute king throughout his own domain, how could a government of proprietors be any thing but chaos and confusion?"* [**Op. Cit.**, pp. 266-7]

In other words, private property is the state writ small, with the property owner acting as the *"sovereign lord"* over their property, and so the absolute king of those who use it. As in any monarchy, the worker is the subject of the capitalist, having to follow their orders, laws and decisions while on their property. This, obviously, is the total denial of liberty (and dignity, we may note, as it is degrading to have to follow orders). And so private property (capitalism) necessarily excludes participation, influence, and control by those who use, but do not own, the means of life.

It is, of course, true that private property provides a sphere of decision-making free from outside interference – but only for the property's owners. But for those who are not property owners the situation if radically different. In a system of exclusively private property does not guarantee them any such sphere of freedom. They have only the freedom to sell their liberty to those who **do** own private property. If I am evicted from one piece of private property, where can I go? Nowhere, unless another owner agrees to allow me access to their piece of private property. This means that everywhere I can stand is a place where I have no right to stand without permission and, as a consequence, I exist only by the sufferance of the property owning elite. Hence Proudhon:

> "Just as the commoner once held his land by the munificence and condescension of the lord, so to-day the working-man holds his labour by the condescension and necessities of the master and proprietor." [Proudhon, **Op. Cit.**, p. 128]

This means that far from providing a sphere of independence, a society in which all property is private thus renders the property-less completely dependent on those who own property. This ensures that the exploitation of another's labour occurs and that some are subjected to the will of others, in direct contradiction to what the defenders of property promise. This is unsurprising given the nature of the property they are defending:

> "Our opponents … are in the habit of justifying the right to private property by stating that property is the condition and guarantee of liberty.
>
> "And we agree with them. Do we not say repeatedly that poverty is slavery?
>
> "But then why do we oppose them?
>
> "The reason is clear: in reality the property that they defend is capitalist property, namely property that allows its owners to live from the work of others and which therefore depends on the existence of a class of the disinherited and dispossessed, forced to sell their labour to the property owners for a wage below its real value … This means that workers are subjected to a kind of slavery, which, though it may vary in degree of harshness, always means social inferiority, material penury and moral degradation, and is the primary cause of all the ills that beset today's social order." [Malatesta, **The Anarchist Revolution**, p. 113]

It will, of course, be objected that no one forces a worker to work for a given boss. However, as we discuss in section B.4.3, this assertion (while true) misses the point. While workers are not forced to work for a **specific** boss, they inevitably have to work for a boss. This is because there is literally no other way to survive – all other economic options have been taken from them by state coercion. The net effect is that the working class has little choice but to hire themselves out to those with property and, as a consequence, the labourer "has sold and surrendered his liberty" to the boss. [Proudhon, **Op. Cit.**, p. 130]

Private property, therefore, produces a very specific form of authority structure within society, a structure in which a few govern the many during working hours. These relations of production are inherently authoritarian and embody and perpetuate the capitalist class system. The moment you enter the factory gate or the office door, you lose all your basic rights as a human being. You have no freedom of speech nor association and no right of assembly. If you were asked to ignore your values, your priorities, your judgement, and your dignity, and leave them at the door when you enter your home, you would rightly consider that tyranny yet that is exactly what you do during working hours if you are a worker. You have no say in what goes on. You may as well be a horse (to use John Locke's analogy – see section B.4.2) or a piece of machinery.

Little wonder, then, that anarchists oppose private property as Anarchy is "the absence of a master, of a sovereign" [Proudhon, **Op. Cit.**, p. 264] and call capitalism for what it is, namely **wage slavery**!

For these reasons, anarchists agree with Rousseau when he stated:

> "The first man who, having fenced off a plot of land, thought of saying, 'This is mine' and found people simple enough to believe him was the real founder of civil society. How many crimes, wars, murders, how many miseries and horrors might the human race had been spared by the one who, upon pulling up the stakes or filling in the ditch, had shouted to his fellow men: 'Beware of listening to this impostor; you are lost if you forget the fruits of the earth belong to all and that the earth belongs to no one.'" ["Discourse on Inequality," **The Social Contract and Discourses**, p. 84]

This explains anarchist opposition to capitalism. It is marked by two main features, "private property" (or in some cases, state-owned property – see section B.3.5) and, consequently, wage labour and exploitation and authority. Moreover, such a system requires a state to maintain itself for as "long as within society a possessing and non-possessing group of human beings face one another in enmity, the state will be indispensable to the possessing minority for the protection for its privileges." [Rudolf Rocker, Anarcho-Syndicalism, p. 11] Thus private ownership of the means of production is only possible if there is a state, meaning mechanisms of organised coercion at the disposal of the propertied class (see section B.2).

Also, it ought to be easy to see that capitalism, by giving rise to an ideologically inalienable "right" to private property, will also quickly give rise to inequalities in the distribution of external resources, and that this inequality in resource distribution will give rise to a further inequality in the relative bargaining positions of the propertied and the property less. While apologists for capitalism usually attempt to justify private property by claiming that "self-ownership" is a "universal right" (see section B.4.2 – "Is capitalism based on self-ownership?"), it is clear that capitalism actually makes universal autonomy implied by the flawed concept of self-ownership (for the appeal of the notion of self-ownership rests on the ideal that people are not used as a means but only as an end in themselves). The capitalist system, however, has undermined autonomy and individual freedom, and ironically, has used the term "self-ownership" as the basis for doing so. Under capitalism, as will be seen in section B.4, most people are usually left in a situation where their best option is to allow themselves to be used in just those ways that are logically incompatible with genuine self-ownership, i.e. the autonomy which makes it initially an appealing concept.

Only libertarian socialism can continue to affirm the meaningful autonomy and individual freedom which self-ownership promises whilst building the conditions that guarantee it. Only by abolishing private property can there be access to the means of life for all, so making the autonomy which self-ownership promises but cannot deliver a reality by universalising self-management in all aspects of life.

Before discussing the anti-libertarian aspects of capitalism, it will be necessary to define *"private property"* as distinct from *"personal possessions"* and show in more detail why the former requires state protection and is exploitative.

B.3.1 What is the difference between private property and possession?

Anarchists define *"private property"* (or just *"property,"* for short) as state-protected monopolies of certain objects or privileges which are used to control and exploit others. *"Possession,"* on the other hand, is ownership of things that are not used to exploit others (e.g. a car, a refrigerator, a toothbrush, etc.). Thus many things can be considered as either property or possessions depending on how they are used.

To summarise, anarchists are in favour of the kind of property which *"cannot be used to exploit another – those kinds of personal possessions which we accumulate from childhood and which become part of our lives."* We are opposed to the kind of property *"which can be used only to exploit people – land and buildings, instruments of production and distribution, raw materials and manufactured articles, money and capital."* [Nicholas Walter, **About Anarchism**, p. 40] As a rule of thumb, anarchists oppose those forms of property which are owned by a few people but which are used by others. This leads to the former controlling the latter and using them to produce a surplus for them (either directly, as in the case of a employee, or indirectly, in the case of a tenant).

The key is that *"possession"* is rooted in the concept of *"use rights"* or *"usufruct"* while *"private property"* is rooted in a divorce between the users and ownership. For example, a house that one lives in is a possession, whereas if one rents it to someone else at a profit it becomes property. Similarly, if one uses a saw to make a living as a self-employed carpenter, the saw is a possession; whereas if one employs others at wages to use the saw for one's own profit, it is property. Needless to say, a capitalist workplace, where the workers are ordered about by a boss, is an example of *"property"* while a co-operative, where the workers manage their own work, is an example of *"possession."* To quote Proudhon:

> *"The proprietor is a man who, having absolute control of an instrument of production, claims the right to enjoy the product of the instrument without using it himself. To this end he lends it."* [**Op. Cit.**, p. 293]

While it may initially be confusing to make this distinction, it is very useful to understand the nature of capitalist society. Capitalists tend to use the word *"property"* to mean anything from a toothbrush to a transnational corporation – two very different things, with very different impacts upon society. Hence Proudhon:

> *"Originally the word **property** was synonymous with **proper** or **individual possession.** It designated each individual's special right to the use of a thing. But when*

this right of use … became active and paramount – that is, when the usufructuary converted his right to personally use the thing into the right to use it by his neighbour's labour – then property changed its nature and this idea became complex." [**Op. Cit.**, pp. 395-6]

Proudhon graphically illustrated the distinction by comparing a lover as a possessor, and a husband as a proprietor! As he stressed, the *"double definition of property – domain and possession – is of highest importance; and must be clearly understood, in order to comprehend"* what anarchism is really about. So while some may question why we make this distinction, the reason is clear. As Proudhon argued, *"it is proper to call different things by different names, if we keep the name 'property' for the former [possession], we must call the latter [the domain of property] robbery, repine, brigandage. If, on the contrary, we reserve the name 'property' for the latter, we must designate the former by the term **possession** or some other equivalent; otherwise we should be troubled with an unpleasant synonym."* [**Op. Cit.**, p. 65 and p. 373]

The difference between property and possession can be seen from the types of authority relations each generates. Taking the example of a capitalist workplace, its clear that those who own the workplace determine how it is used, not those who do the actual work. This leads to an almost totalitarian system. As Noam Chomsky points out, *"the term 'totalitarian' is quite accurate. There is no human institution that approaches totalitarianism as closely as a business corporation. I mean, power is completely top-down. You can be inside it somewhere and you take orders from above and hand 'em down. Ultimately, it's in the hands of owners and investors."* Thus the actual producer does not control their own activity, the product of their labour nor the means of production they use. In modern class societies, the producer is in a position of subordination to those who actually do own or manage the productive process.

In an anarchist society, as noted, actual use is considered the only title. This means that a workplace is organised and run by those who work within it, thus reducing hierarchy and increasing freedom and equality within society. Hence anarchist opposition to private property and capitalism flows naturally from anarchism's basic principles and ideas. Hence all anarchists agree with Proudhon:

> *"Possession is a right; property is against right. Suppress property while maintaining possession."* [**Op. Cit.**, p. 271]

As Alexander Berkman frames this distinction, anarchism *"abolishes private ownership of the means of production and distribution, and with it goes capitalistic business. Personal possession remains only in the things you use. Thus, your watch is your own, but the watch factory belongs to the people. Land, machinery, and all other public utilities will be collective property, neither to be bought nor sold. Actual use will be considered the only title – not to ownership but to possession."* [**What is Anarchism?**, p. 217]

This analysis of different forms of property is at the heart of both social and individualist anarchism. This means that all anarchists seek to change people's opinions on what is to be considered as valid forms of property, aiming to see that *"the Anarchistic view that occupancy and use should condition and limit landholding becomes the prevailing view"* and so ensure that *"individuals should no longer be protected by their fellows in anything but personal occupation and cultivation [i.e. use] of land."* [Benjamin Tucker, **The Individualist Anarchists**, p. 159 and p. 85] The key differences, as we noted in section A.3.1, is how they apply this principle.

This anarchist support for possession does not imply the break up of large scale organisations such as factories or other workplaces which require large numbers of people to operate. Far from it. Anarchists argue for association as the complement of possession. This means applying *"occupancy and use"* to property which is worked by more than one person results in associated labour, i.e. those who collectively work together (i.e. use a given property) manage it and their own labour as a self-governing, directly democratic, association of equals (usually called *"self-management"* for short). This logically flows from the theory of possession, of *"occupancy and use."* For if production is carried on in groups who is the legal occupier of the land? The employer or their manager? Obviously not, as they are by definition occupying more than they can use by themselves. Clearly, the association of those engaged in the work can be the only rational answer. Hence Proudhon's comment that *"all accumulated capital being social property, no one can be its exclusive proprietor." "In order to destroy despotism and inequality of conditions, men must ... become associates"* and this implies workers' self-management – *"leaders, instructors, superintendents ... must be chosen from the labourers by the labourers themselves."* [Proudhon, **Op. Cit.**, p. 130, p. 372 and p. 137]

In this way, anarchists seek, in Proudhon's words, *"abolition of the proletariat"* and consider a key idea of our ideas that *"Industrial Democracy must ... succeed Industrial Feudalism."* [Proudhon, **Selected Writings of Pierre-Joseph Proudhon**, p. 179 and p. 167] Thus an anarchist society would be based on possession, with workers' self-management being practised at all levels from the smallest one person workplace or farm to large scale industry (see section I.3 for more discussion).

Clearly, then, all anarchists seek to transform and limit property rights. Capitalist property rights would be ended and a new system introduced rooted in the concept of possession and use. While the exact nature of that new system differs between schools of anarchist thought, the basic principles are the same as they flow from the same anarchist theory of property to be found in Proudhon's, What is Property?.

Significantly, William Godwin in his Enquiry Concerning Political Justice makes the same point concerning the difference between property and possession (although not in the same language) fifty years before Proudhon, which indicates its central place in anarchist thought. For Godwin, there were different kinds of property. One kind was *"the empire to which every [person] is entitled over the produce of his [or her] own industry."* However, another kind was *"a system, in whatever manner established, by which one man enters into the faculty of disposing of the produce of another man's industry."* This *"species of property is in direct contradiction"* to the former kind (he similarities with subsequent anarchist ideas is striking). For Godwin, inequality produces a *"servile"* spirit in the poor and, moreover, a person who *"is born to poverty, may be said, under a another name, to be born a slave."* [**The Anarchist Writings of William Godwin**, p. 133, p. 134, p. 125 and p. 126]

Needless to say, anarchists have not be totally consistent in using this terminology. Some, for example, have referred to the capitalist and landlord classes as being the *"possessing classes."* Others prefer to use the term *"personal property"* rather than *"possession"* or *"capital"* rather than *"private property."* Some, like many individualist anarchists, use the term *"property"* in a general sense and qualify it with *"occupancy and use"* in the case of land, housing and workplaces. However, no matter the specific words used, the key idea is the same.

B.3.2 What kinds of property does the state protect?

Kropotkin argued that the state was *"the instrument for establishing monopolies in favour of the ruling minorities."* [**Anarchism**, p. 286] In every system of class exploitation, a ruling class controls access to the means of production in order to extract tribute from labour. Capitalism is no exception. In this system the state maintains various kinds of *"class monopolies"* (to use Tucker's phrase) to ensure that workers do not receive their *"natural wage,"* the full product of their labour. While some of these monopolies are obvious (such as tariffs, state granted market monopolies and so on), most are *"behind the scenes"* and work to ensure that capitalist domination does not need extensive force to maintain.

Under capitalism, there are four major kinds of property, or exploitative monopolies, that the state protects:

(1) the power to issue credit and currency, the basis of capitalist banking;

(2) land and buildings, the basis of landlordism;

(3) productive tools and equipment, the basis of industrial capitalism;

(4) ideas and inventions, the basis of copyright and patent (*"intellectual property"*) royalties.

By enforcing these forms of property, the state ensures that the objective conditions within the economy favour the capitalist, with the worker free only to accept oppressive and exploitative contracts within which they forfeit their autonomy and promise obedience or face misery and poverty. Due to these *"initiations of force"* conducted **previously** to any specific contract being signed, capitalists enrich themselves at our expense because we *"are compelled to pay a heavy tribute to property holders for the right of cultivating land or putting machinery into action."* [Kropotkin, **The Conquest of Bread**, p. 103] These conditions obviously also make a mockery of free agreement (see section B.4).

These various forms of state intervention are considered so normal many people do not even think of them as such. Thus we find defenders of "free market" capitalism thundering against forms of "state intervention" which are designed to aid the poor while seeing nothing wrong in defending intellectual property rights, corporations, absentee landlords and the other multitude of laws and taxes capitalists and their politicians have placed and kept upon the statute-books to skew the labour market in favour of themselves (see section F.8 on the state's role in developing capitalism in the first place).

Needless to say, despite the supposedly subtle role of such *"objective"* pressures in controlling the working class, working class resistance has been such that capital has never been able to dispense with the powers of the state, both direct and indirect. When *"objective"* means of control fail, the capitalists will always turn to the use of state repression to restore the *"natural"* order. Then the *"invisible"* hand of the market is replaced by the visible fist of the state and the indirect means of securing ruling class profits and power are supplemented by more direct forms by the state. As we indicate in section D.1, state intervention beyond enforcing these forms of private property is the norm of capitalism, not the exception, and is done so to secure the power and profits of the capitalist class.

To indicate the importance of these state backed monopolies, we shall sketch their impact.

The credit monopoly, by which the state controls who can and cannot issue or loan money, reduces the ability of working class people to create their own alternatives to capitalism. By charging high amounts of interest on loans (which is only possible because competition is restricted) few people can afford to create co-operatives or one-person firms. In addition, having to repay loans at high interest to capitalist banks ensures that co-operatives often have to undermine their own principles by having to employ wage labour to make ends meet (see section J.5.11). It is unsurprising, therefore, that the very successful Mondragon co-operatives in the Basque Country created their own credit union which is largely responsible for the experiment's success.

Just as increasing wages is an important struggle within capitalism, so is the question of credit. Proudhon and his followers supported the idea of a **People's Bank.** If the working class could take over and control increasing amounts of money it could undercut capitalist power while building its own alternative social order (for money is ultimately the means of buying labour power, and so authority over the labourer – which is the key to surplus value production). Proudhon hoped that by credit being reduced to cost (namely administration charges) workers would be able to buy the means of production they needed. While most anarchists would argue that increased working class access to credit would no more bring down capitalism than increased wages, all anarchists recognise how more cheap credit, like more wages, can make life easier for working people and how the struggle for such credit, like the struggle for wages, might play a useful role in the development of the power of the working class within capitalism. Obvious cases that spring to mind are those where money has been used by workers to finance their struggles against capital, from strike funds and weapons to the periodical avoidance of work made possible by sufficiently high money income. Increased access to cheap credit would give working class people slightly more options than selling their liberty or facing misery (just as increased wages and unemployment benefit also gives us more options).

Therefore, the credit monopoly reduces competition to capitalism from co-operatives (which are generally more productive than capitalist firms) while at the same time forcing down wages for all workers as the demand for labour is lower than it would otherwise be. This, in turn, allows capitalists to use the fear of the sack to extract higher levels of surplus value from employees, so consolidating capitalist power (within and outwith the workplace)

and expansion (increasing set-up costs and so creating oligarchic markets dominated by a few firms). In addition, high interest rates transfer income directly from producers to banks. Credit and money are both used as weapons in the class struggle. This is why, again and again, we see the ruling class call for centralised banking and use state action (from the direct regulation of money itself, to the attempted management of its flows by the manipulation of the interest) in the face of repeated threats to the nature (and role) of money within capitalism.

The credit monopoly has other advantages for the elite. The 1980s were marked by a rising debt burden on households as well as the increased concentration of wealth in the US. The two are linked. Due to *"the decline in real hourly wages, and the stagnation in household incomes, the middle and lower classes have borrowed more to stay in place"* and they have *"borrowed from the very rich who have [become] richer."* By 1997, US households spent $1 trillion (or 17% of the after-tax incomes) on debt service. *"This represents a massive upward redistribution of income."* And why did they borrow? The bottom 40% of the income distribution *"borrowed to compensate for stagnant or falling incomes"* while the upper 20% borrowed *"mainly to invest."* Thus *"consumer credit can be thought of as a way to sustain mass consumption in the face of stagnant or falling wages. But there's an additional social and political bonus, from the point of view of the creditor class: it reduces pressure for higher wages by allowing people to buy goods they couldn't otherwise afford. It helps to nourish both the appearance and reality of a middle-class standard of living in a time of polarisation. And debt can be a great conservatising force; with a large monthly mortgage and/or MasterCard bill, strikes and other forms of troublemaking look less appealing than they would other wise."* [Doug Henwood, **Wall Street**, pp. 64-6]

Thus credit *"is an important form of social coercion; mortgaged workers are more pliable."* [Henwood, **Op. Cit.**, p. 232] Money is power and any means which lessens that power by increasing the options of workers is considered a threat by the capitalist class – whether it is tight labour markets, state provided unemployment benefit, or cheap, self-organised, credit – will be resisted. The credit monopoly can, therefore, only be fought as part of a broader attack on all forms of capitalist social power.

In summary, the credit monopoly, by artificially restricting the option to work for ourselves, ensures we work for a boss while also enriching the few at the expense of the many.

The land monopoly consists of enforcement by government of land titles which do not rest upon personal occupancy and use. It also includes making the squatting of abandoned housing and other forms of property illegal. This leads to ground-rent, by which landlords get payment for letting others use the land they own but do not actually cultivate or use. It also allows the ownership and control of natural resources like oil, gas, coal and timber. This monopoly is particularly exploitative as the owner cannot claim to have created the land or its resources. It was available to all until the landlord claimed it by fencing it off and barring others from using it.

Until the nineteenth century, the control of land was probably the single most important form of privilege by which working people were forced to accept less than its product as a wage. While this monopoly is less important in a modern capitalist society (as few people know how to farm), it still plays a role (particularly in terms of ownership of natural resources). At a minimum, every home and workplace needs land on which to be built. Thus while cultivation of land has become less important, the use of land remains crucial. The land monopoly, therefore, ensures that working people find no land to cultivate, no space to set up shop and no place to sleep without first having to pay a landlord a sum for the privilege of setting foot on the land they own but neither created nor use. At best, the worker has mortgaged their life for decades to get their wee bit of soil or, at worse, paid their rent and remained as property-less as before. Either way, the landlords are richer for the exchange.

Moreover, the land monopoly did play an important role in **creating** capitalism (also see section F.8.3). This took two main forms. Firstly, the state enforced the ownership of large estates in the hands of a single family. Taking the best land by force, these landlords turned vast tracks of land into parks and hunting grounds so forcing the peasants little option but to huddle together on what remained. Access to superior land was therefore only possible by paying a rent for the privilege, if at all. Thus an elite claimed ownership of vacant lands, and by controlling access to it (without themselves ever directly occupying or working it) they controlled the labouring classes of the time. Secondly, the ruling elite also simply stole land which had traditionally been owned by the community. This was called enclosure, the process by which common land was turned into private property. Economist William Lazonick summaries this process:

> "The reorganisation of agricultural land [the enclosure movement] ... inevitably undermined the viability of traditional peasant agriculture ... [it] created a sizeable labour force of disinherited peasants with only tenuous attachments to the land. To earn a living, many of these peasants turned to 'domestic industry' – the production of goods in their cottages ... It was the eighteenth century expansion of domestic industry ... that laid the basis for the British Industrial Revolution. The emergence of labour-saving machine technology transformed ... textile manufacture ... and the factory replaced the family home as the predominant site of production." [**Business Organisation and the Myth of the Market Economy**, pp. 3-4]

By being able to *"legally"* bar people from *"their"* property, the landlord class used the land monopoly to ensure the creation of a class of people with nothing to sell but their labour (i.e. liberty). Land was taken from those who traditionally used it, violating common rights, and it was used by the landlord to produce for their own profit (more recently, a similar process has been going on in the Third World as well). Personal occupancy was replaced by landlordism and agricultural wage slavery, and so *"the Enclosure Acts ... reduced the agricultural population to misery, placed them at the mercy of the landowners, and forced a great number of them to migrate to the towns where, as proletarians, they were delivered to the mercy of the middle-class manufacturers."* [Peter Kropotkin, **The Great French Revolution**, vol. 1, pp. 117-8]

A variation of this process took place in countries like America, where the state took over ownership of vast tracks of land and then sold it to farmers. As Howard Zinn notes, the Homestead Act *"gave 160 acres of western land, unoccupied and publicly owned, to anyone who would cultivate it for fives years. Anyone willing to pay $1.25 an acre could buy a homestead. Few ordinary people had the $200 necessary to do this; speculators moved in and bought up much of the land."* [**A People's History of the United States**, p. 233] Those farmers who did pay the money often had to go into debt to do so, placing an extra burden on their labour. Vast tracks of land were also given to railroad and other companies either directly (by gift or by selling cheap) or by lease (in the form of privileged access to state owned land for the purpose of extracting raw materials like lumber and oil). Either way, access to land was restricted and those who actually did work it ended up paying a tribute to the landlord in one form or another (either directly in rent or indirectly by repaying a loan).

This was the land monopoly in action (also see sections F.8.3, F.8.4 and F.8.5 for more details) and from it sprang the tools and equipment monopoly as domestic industry could not survive in the face of industrial capitalism. Confronted with competition from industrial production growing rich on the profits produced from cheap labour, the ability of workers to own their own means of production decreased over time. From a situation where most workers owned their own tools and, consequently, worked for themselves, we now face an economic regime were the tools and equipment needed for work are owned by a capitalists and, consequently, workers now work for a boss.

The tools and equipment monopoly is similar to the land monopoly as it is based upon the capitalist denying workers access to their capital unless the worker pays tribute to the owner for using it. While capital is *"simply stored-up labour which has already received its pay in full"* and so *"the lender of capital is entitled to its return intact, and nothing more"* (to use Tucker's words), due to legal privilege the capitalist is in a position to charge a *"fee"* for its use. This is because, with the working class legally barred from both the land and available capital (the means of life), members of that class have little option but to agree to wage contracts which let capitalists extract a *"fee"* for the use of their equipment (see section B.3.3).

Thus the capital-monopoly is, like the land monopoly, enforced by the state and its laws. This is most clearly seen if you look at the main form in which such capital is held today, the corporation. This is nothing more than a legal construct. *"Over the last 150 years,"* notes Joel Bakan, *"the corporation has risen from relative obscurity to becomes the world's dominant economic institution."* The law has been changed to give corporations *"limited liability"* and other perks in order *"to attract valuable incorporation business ... by jettisoning unpopular [to capitalists] restrictions from ... corporate laws."* Finally, the courts *"fully transformed the corporation onto a 'person,' with its own identity ... and empowered, like a real person, to conduct business in its own name, acquire assets, employ workers, pay taxes, and go to court to assert its rights and defend its actions."* In America, this was achieved using the 14th Amendment (which was passed to protect freed slaves!). In summary, the corporation *"is not an independent 'person' with its own rights, needs, and desires ... It is a state-created tool for advancing social and economic policy."* [**The Corporation**, p. 5, p. 13, p. 16 and p. 158]

Nor can it be said that this monopoly is the product of hard work and saving. The capital-monopoly is a recent development and how this situation developed is usually ignored. If not glossed over as irrelevant, some fairy tale is spun in which a few bright people saved and worked hard to accumulate capital and the lazy majority flocked to be employed by these (almost superhuman) geniuses. In reality, the initial capital for investing in industry came from wealth plundered from overseas or from the proceeds of feudal and landlord exploitation. In addition, as we discuss in section F.8, extensive state intervention was required to create a class of wage workers and ensure that capital was in the best position to exploit them. This explicit state intervention was scaled down once the capital-monopoly found its own feet.

Once this was achieved, state action became less explicit and becomes focused around defending the capitalists' property rights. This is because the *"fee"* charged to workers was partly reinvested into capital, which reduced the prices of goods, ruining domestic industry and so narrowing the options available to workers in the economy. In addition, investment also increased the set-up costs of potential competitors, which continued the dispossession of the working class from the means of production as these *"natural"* barriers to entry into markets ensured few members of that class had the necessary funds to create co-operative workplaces of appropriate size. So while the land monopoly was essential to create capitalism, the *"tools and equipment"* monopoly that sprang from it soon became the mainspring of the system.

In this way usury became self-perpetuating, with apparently *"free exchanges"* being the means by which capitalist domination survives. In other words, "past initiations of force" combined with the current state protection of property ensure that capitalist domination of society continues with only the use of *"defensive"* force (i.e. violence used to protect the power of property owners against unions, strikes, occupations, etc.). The *"fees"* extracted from previous generations of workers has ensured that the current one is in no position to re-unite itself with the means of life by *"free competition"* (in other words, the paying of usury ensures that usury continues). Needless to say, the surplus produced by this generation will be used to increase the capital stock and so ensure the dispossession of future generations and so usury becomes self-perpetuating. And, of course, state protection of *"property"* against *"theft"* by working people ensures that property remains theft and the **real** thieves keep their plunder.

As far as the *"ideas"* monopoly is concerned, this has been used to enrich capitalist corporations at the expense of the general public and the inventor. Patents make an astronomical price difference. Until the early 1970s, for example, Italy did not recognise drug patents. As a result, Roche Products charged the British National Health Service over 40 times more for patented components of Librium and Valium than charged by competitors in Italy. As Tucker argued, the patent monopoly *"consists in protecting investors and authors against competition for a period long enough to enable them to extort from the people a reward enormously in excess of the labour measure of their services, – in other words, in giving certain people a right of property for a term of years and facts of nature, and the power to extract tribute from others for the use of this natural wealth which should be open to all."* [**The Individualist Anarchists**, p. 86]

The net effect of this can be terrible. The Uruguay Round of global trade negotiations *"strengthen intellectual property rights. American and other Western drug companies could now stop drug companies in India and Brazil from 'stealing' their intellectual property. But these drug companies in the developing world were making these life-saving drugs available to their citizens at a fraction of the price at which the drugs were sold by the Western drug companies … Profits of the Western drug companies would go up … but the increases profits from sales in the developing world were small, since few could afford the drugs … [and so] thousands were effectively condemned to death, becomes governments and individuals in developing countries could no longer pay the high prices demanded."* [Joseph Stiglitz, **Globalisation and its discontents**, pp. 7-8] While international outrage over AIDS drugs eventually forced the drug companies to sell the drugs at cost price in late 2001, the underlying intellectual property rights regime was still in place.

The irony that this regime was created in a process allegedly about trade liberalisation should not go unnoticed. *"Intellectual property rights,"* as Noam Chomsky correctly points out, *"are a protectionist measure, they have nothing to do with free trade – in fact, they're the exact **opposite** of free trade."* [**Understanding Power**, p. 282] The fundamental injustice of the *"ideas monopoly"* is exacerbated by the fact that many of these patented products are the result of government funding of research and development, with private industry simply reaping monopoly profits from technology it did not spend a penny to develop. In fact, extending government aid for research and development is considered an important and acceptable area of state intervention by governments and companies verbally committed to the neo-liberal agenda.

The *"ideas monopoly"* actually works against its own rationale. Patents suppress innovation as much as they encourage it. The research scientists who actually do the work of inventing are required to sign over patent rights as a condition of employment, while patents and industrial security programs used to bolster competitive advantage on the market actually prevent the sharing of information, so reducing innovation (this evil is being particularly felt in universities as the new *"intellectual property rights"* regime is spreading there). Further research stalls as the incremental innovation based on others' patents is hindered while the patent holder can rest on their laurels as they have no fear of a competitor improving the invention. They also hamper technical progress because, by their very nature, preclude the possibility of independent discovery. Also, of course, some companies own a patent explicitly not to use it but simply to prevent someone else from so doing.

As Noam Chomsky notes, today trade agreements like GATT and NAFTA *"impose a mixture of liberalisation and protection, going far beyond trade, designed to keep wealth and power firmly in the hands of the masters."* Thus *"investor rights are to be protected and enhanced"* and a key demand *"is increased protection for 'intellectual property,' including software and patents, with patent rights extending to process as well as product"* in order to *"ensure that US-based corporations control the technology of the future"* and so *"locking the poor majority into dependence on high-priced products of Western agribusiness, biotechnology, the pharmaceutical* industry and so on." [**World Orders, Old and New**, p. 183, p. 181 and pp. 182-3] This means that if a company discovers a new, more efficient, way of producing a drug then the *"ideas monopoly"* will stop them and so *"these are not only highly protectionist measures ... they're a blow **against** economic efficiency and technological process – that just shows you how much 'free trade' really is involved in all of this."* [Chomsky, **Understanding Power**, p. 282]

All of which means that the corporations (and their governments) in the developed world are trying to prevent emergence of competition by controlling the flow of technology to others. The "free trade" agreements are being used to create monopolies for their products and this will either block or slow down the rise of competition. While corporate propagandists piously denounce "anti-globalisation" activists as enemies of the developing world, seeking to use trade barriers to maintain their (Western) lifestyles at the expense of the poor nations, the reality is different. The *"ideas monopoly"* is being aggressively used to either suppress or control the developing world's economic activity in order to keep the South as, effectively, one big sweatshop. As well as reaping monopoly profits directly, the threat of "low-wage" competition from the developing world can be used to keep the wage slaves of the developed world in check and so maintain profit levels at home.

This is not all. Like other forms of private property, the usury produced by it helps ensure it becomes self-perpetuating. By creating "legal" absolute monopolies and reaping the excess profits these create, capitalists not only enrich themselves at the expense of others, they also ensure their dominance in the market. Some of the excess profits reaped due to patents and copyrights are invested back into the company, securing advantages by creating various "natural" barriers to entry for potential competitors. Thus patents impact on business structure, encouraging the formation and dominance of big business.

Looking at the end of the nineteenth century, the ideas monopoly played a key role in promoting cartels and, as a result, laid the foundation for what was to become corporate capitalism in the twentieth century. Patents were used on a massive scale to promote concentration of capital, erect barriers to entry, and maintain a monopoly of advanced technology in the hands of western corporations. The exchange or pooling of patents between competitors, historically, has been a key method for the creation of cartels in industry. This was true especially of the electrical appliance, communications, and chemical industries. For example, by the 1890s, two large companies, General Electric and Westinghouse, *"monopolised a substantial part of the American electrical manufacturing industry, and their success had been in large measure the result of patent control."* The two competitors simply pooled their patents and *"yet another means of patent and market control had developed: corporate patent-pooling agreements. Designed to minimise the expense and uncertainties of conflict between the giants, they greatly reinforced the position of each vis-à-vis lesser competitors and new entrants into the field."* [David Noble, **American By Design**, p. 10]

While the patent system is, in theory, promoted to defend the small scale inventor, in reality it is corporate interests that benefit. As David Noble points out, the *"inventor, the original focus of the patent system, tended to increasingly to 'abandon' his patent in*

exchange for corporate security; he either sold or licensed his patent rights to industrial corporations or assigned them to the company of which he became an employee, bartering his genius for a salary. In addition, by means of patent control gained through purchase, consolidation, patent pools, and cross-licensing agreements, as well as by regulated patent production through systematic industrial research, the corporations steadily expanded their 'monopoly of monopolies.'"* As well as this, corporations used *"patents to circumvent anti-trust laws."* This reaping of monopoly profits at the expense of the customer made such *"tremendous strides"* between 1900 and 1929 and *"were of such proportions as to render subsequent judicial and legislative effects to check corporate monopoly through patent control too little too late."* [**Op. Cit.**, p. 87, p. 84 and p. 88]

Things have changed little since Edwin Prindle, a corporate patent lawyer, wrote in 1906 that:

> *"Patents are the best and most effective means of controlling competition. They occasionally give absolute command of the market, enabling their owner to name the price without regard to the cost of production ... Patents are the only legal form of absolute monopoly ... The power which a patentee has to dictate the conditions under which his monopoly may be exercised had been used to form trade agreements throughout practically entire industries."* [quoted by Noble, **Op. Cit.**, p. 89]

Thus, the ruling class, by means of the state, is continually trying to develop new forms of private property by creating artificial scarcities and monopolies, e.g. by requiring expensive licenses to engage in particular types of activities, such as broadcasting or producing certain kinds of medicines or products. In the *"Information Age,"* usury (use fees) from intellectual property are becoming a much more important source of income for elites, as reflected in the attention paid to strengthening mechanisms for enforcing copyright and patents in the recent GATT agreements, or in US pressure on foreign countries (like China) to respect such laws.

This allows corporations to destroy potential competitors and ensure that their prices can be set as high as possible (and monopoly profits maintained indefinitely). It also allows them to enclose ever more of the common inheritance of humanity, place it under private ownership and charge the previous users money to gain access to it. As Chomsky notes, *"U.S. corporations must control seeds, plant varieties, drugs, and the means of life generally."* [**World Orders, Old and New**, p. 183] This has been termed *"bio-piracy"* (a better term may be the new enclosures) and it is a process by which *"international companies [are] patenting traditional medicines or foods."* They *"seek to make money from 'resources' and knowledge that rightfully belongs to the developing countries"* and *"in so doing, they squelch domestic firms that have long provided the products. While it is not clear whether these patents would hold up in court if they were effectively challenged, it is clear that the less developed countries many not have the legal and financial resources required to challenge the patent."* [Joseph Stiglitz, **Op. Cit.**, p. 246] They may also not withstand the economic pressures they may experience if the international markets conclude that such acts indicate a regime that is less that business friendly. That the people who were dependent on the generic drugs or plants can no longer afford them is as irrelevant as the impediments to scientific and technological advance they create.

In other words, capitalists desire to skew the *"free market"* in their favour by ensuring that the law reflects and protects their interests, namely their *"property rights."* By this process they ensure that co-operative tendencies within society are crushed by state-supported "market forces." As Noam Chomsky puts it, modern capitalism is *"state protection and public subsidy for the rich, market discipline for the poor."* [*"Rollback, Part I"*, **Z Magazine**] Self-proclaimed defenders of "free market" capitalism are usually nothing of the kind, while the few who actually support it only object to the *"public subsidy"* aspect of modern capitalism and happily support state protection for property rights.

All these monopolies seek to enrich the capitalist (and increase their capital stock) at the expense of working people, to restrict their ability to undermine the ruling elites power and wealth. All aim to ensure that any option we have to work for ourselves (either individually or collectively) is restricted by tilting the playing field against us, making sure that we have little option but to sell our labour on the *"free market"* and be exploited. In other words, the various monopolies make sure that "natural" barriers to entry (see section C.4) are created, leaving the heights of the economy in the control of big business while alternatives to capitalism are marginalised at its fringes.

So it is these kinds of property and the authoritarian social relationships that they create which the state exists to protect. It should be noted that converting private to state ownership (i.e. nationalisation) does not fundamentally change the nature of property relationships; it just removes private capitalists and replaces them with bureaucrats (as we discuss in section B.3.5).

B.3.3 Why is property exploitative?

To answer this question, consider the monopoly of productive *"tools and equipment."* This monopoly, obtained by the class of industrial capitalists, allows this class in effect to charge workers a *"fee"* for the privilege of using the monopolised tools and equipment.

This occurs because property, in Proudhon words, *"excommunicates"* the working class. This means that private property creates a class of people who have no choice but to work for a boss in order to pay the landlord rent or buy the goods they, as a class, produce but do not own. The state enforces property rights in land, workplaces and so on, meaning that the owner can bar others from using them and enforce **their** rules on those they do let use *"their"* property. So the boss *"gives you a job; that is, permission to work in the factory or mill which was not built by him but by other workers like yourself. And for that permission you help to support him for ... as long as you work for him."* [Alexander Berkman, **What is Anarchism?**, p. 14] This is called wage labour and is, for anarchists, the defining characteristic of capitalism.

This class of people who are dependent on wages to survive was sometimes called the *"proletariat"* by nineteenth century anarchists. Today most anarchists usually call it the *"working class"* as most workers in modern capitalist nations are wage workers rather than peasants or artisans (i.e. self-employed workers who are also exploited by the private property system, but in different ways). It should also be noted that property used in this way (i.e. to employ and exploit other people's labour) is also called **"capital"** by anarchists and other socialists. Thus, for anarchists, private property generates a class system, a regime in which the few, due to their ownership of wealth and the means of producing it, rule over the many who own very little (see section B.7 for more discussion of classes).

This ensures that the few can profit from the work of others:

> *"In the capitalist system the working man cannot [in general] work for himself ... So ... you must find an employer. You work for him ... In the capitalist system the whole working class sells its labour power to the employing class. The workers build factories, make machinery and tools, and produce goods. The employers keep the factories, the machinery, the tools and the goods for themselves as **their profit**. The workers only get their wages ... Though the workers, as a class, have built the factories, a slice of their daily labour is taken from them for the privilege of **using** those factories ... Though the workers have made the tools and the machinery, another slice of their daily labour is taken from them for the privilege of **using** those tools and machinery ...*
>
> *"Can you guess now why the wisdom of Proudhon said that **the possessions of the rich are stolen property**? Stolen from the producer, the worker."* [Berkman, **Op. Cit.**, pp. 7-8]

Thus the daily theft/exploitation associated with capitalism is dependent on the distribution of wealth and private property (i.e. the initial theft of the means of life, the land, workplaces and housing by the owning class). Due to the dispossession of the vast majority of the population from the means of life, capitalists are in an ideal position to charge a *"use-fee"* for the capital they own, but neither produced nor use. Having little option, workers agree to contracts within which they forfeit their autonomy during work and the product of that work. This results in capitalists having access to a *"commodity"* (labour) that can potentially produce more value than it gets paid for in wages.

For this situation to arise, for wage labour to exist, workers must not own or control the means of production they use. As a consequence, they are controlled by those who do own the means of production they use during work hours. As their labour is owned by their boss and as labour cannot be separated from the person who does it, the boss effectively owns the worker for the duration of the working day and, as a consequence, exploitation becomes possible. This is because during working hours, the owner can dictate (within certain limits determined by worker resistance and solidarity as well as objective conditions, such as the level of unemployment within an industry or country) the organisation, level, duration, conditions, pace and intensity of work, and so the amount of output (which the owner has sole rights over even though they did not produce it).

Thus the *"fee"* (or *"surplus value"*) is created by owners paying workers less than the full value added by their labour to the products or services they create for the firm. The capitalist's profit is thus the difference between this *"surplus value,"* created by and appropriated from labour, minus the firm's overhead and cost of raw materials (See also section C.2 – *"Where do profits come from?"*).

So property is exploitative because it allows a surplus to be monopolised by the owners. Property creates hierarchical relationships within the workplace (the *"tools and equipment monopoly"* might better be called the *"power monopoly"*) and as in any hierarchical system, those with the power use it to protect and further their own interests at the expense of others. Within the workplace there is resistance by workers to this oppression and exploitation, which the *"hierarchical … relations of the capitalist enterprise are designed to resolve this conflict in favour of the representatives of capital."* [William Lazonick, **Op. Cit.**, p. 184]

Needless to say, the state is always on hand to protect the rights of property and management against the actions of the dispossessed. When it boils down to it, it is the existence of the state as protector of the *"power monopoly"* that allows it to exist at all.

So, capitalists are able to appropriate this surplus value from workers solely because they own the means of production, not because they earn it by doing productive work themselves. Of course some capitalists **may** also contribute to production, in which case they are in fairness entitled to the amount of value added to the firm's output by their own labour; but owners typically pay themselves much more than this, and are able to do so because the state guarantees them that right as property owners (which is unsurprising, as they alone have knowledge of the firms inputs and outputs and, like all people in unaccountable positions, abuse that power – which is partly why anarchists support direct democracy as the essential counterpart of free agreement, for no one in power can be trusted not to prefer their own interests over those subject to their decisions). And of course many capitalists hire managers to run their businesses for them, thus collecting income for doing nothing except owning.

Capitalists' profits, then, are a form of state-supported exploitation. This is equally true of the interest collected by bankers and rents collected by landlords. Without some form of state, these forms of exploitation would be impossible, as the monopolies on which they depend could not be maintained. For instance, in the absence of state troops and police, workers would simply take over and operate factories for themselves, thus preventing capitalists from appropriating an unjust share of the surplus they create.

B.3.4 Can private property be justified?

No. Even though a few supporters of capitalism recognise that private property, particularly in land, was created by the use of force, most maintain that private property is just. One common defence of private property is found in the work of Robert Nozick (a supporter of *"free market"* capitalism). For Nozick, the use of force makes acquisition illegitimate and so any current title to the property is illegitimate (in other words, theft and trading in stolen goods does not make ownership of these goods legal). So, if the initial acquisition of land was illegitimate then all current titles are also illegitimate. And since private ownership of land is the basis of capitalism, capitalism itself would be rendered illegal.

To get round this problem, Nozick utilises the work of Locke (*"The Lockean Proviso"*) which can be summarised as:

(1) People own themselves and, consequently, their labour.

(2) The world is initially owned in common (or unowned in Nozick's case.)

(3) By working on common (or unowned) resources, people turn it into their own property because they own their own labour.

(4) You can acquire absolute rights over a larger than average share in the world, if you do not worsen the condition of others.

(5) Once people have appropriated private property, a free market in capital and labour is morally required.

However, there are numerous flaws in this theory. Most obvious is why does the mixing of something you own (labour) with something owned by all (or unowned) turn it in your property? Surely it would be as likely to simply mean that you have lost the labour you have expended (for example, few would argue that you owned a river simply because you swam or fished in it). Even if we assume the validity of the argument and acknowledge that by working on a piece of land creates ownership, why assume that this ownership must be based on **capitalist** property rights? Many cultures have recognised no such *"absolute"* forms of property, admitted the right of property in what is produced but not the land itself.

As such, the assumption that expending labour turns the soil into private property does not automatically hold. You could equally argue the opposite, namely that labour, while producing ownership of the goods created, does not produce property in land, only possession. In the words of Proudhon:

> *"I maintain that the possessor is paid for his trouble and industry … but that he acquires no right to the land. 'Let the labourer have the fruits of his labour.' Very good; but I do not understand that property in products carries with it property in raw material. Does the skill of the fisherman, who on the same coast can catch more fish than his fellows, make him proprietor of the fishing-grounds? Can the expertness of a hunter ever be regarded as a property-title to a game-forest? The analogy is perfect, –*

the industrious cultivator finds the reward of his industry in the abundancy and superiority of his crop. If he has made improvements in the soil, he has the possessor's right of preference. Never, under any circumstances, can he be allowed to claim a property-title to the soil which he cultivates, on the ground of his skill as a cultivator.

"To change possession into property, something is needed besides labour, without which a man would cease to be proprietor as soon as he ceased to be a labourer. Now, the law bases property upon immemorial, unquestionable possession; that is, prescription. Labour is only the sensible sign, the physical act, by which occupation is manifested. If, then, the cultivator remains proprietor after he has ceased to labour and produce; if his possession, first conceded, then tolerated, finally becomes inalienable, – it happens by permission of the civil law, and by virtue of the principle of occupancy. So true is this, that there is not a bill of sale, not a farm lease, not an annuity, but implies it …

"Man has created every thing – every thing save the material itself. Now, I maintain that this material he can only possess and use, on condition of permanent labour, – granting, for the time being, his right of property in things which he has produced.

*"This, then, is the first point settled: property in product, if we grant so much, does not carry with it property in the means of production; that seems to me to need no further demonstration. There is no difference between the soldier who possesses his arms, the mason who possesses the materials committed to his care, the fisherman who possesses the water, the hunter who possesses the fields and forests, and the cultivator who possesses the lands: all, if you say so, are proprietors of their products – not one is proprietor of the means of production. The right to product is exclusive – **jus in re**; the right to means is common – **jus ad rem**."* [**What is Property?**, pp. 120-1]

Proudhon's argument has far more historical validity than Nozick's. Common ownership of land combined with personal use has been the dominant form of property rights for tens of thousands of years while Nozick's *"natural law"* theory dates back to Locke's work in the seventeenth century (itself an attempt to defend the encroachment of capitalist norms of ownership over previous common law ones). Nozick's theory only appears valid because we live in a society where the dominant form of property rights are capitalist. As such, Nozick is begging the question – he is assuming the thing he is trying to prove. Ignoring these obvious issues, what of Nozick's actual argument?

The first thing to note is that it is a fairy tale, it is a myth. The current property system and its distribution of resources and ownership rights is a product of thousands of years of conflict, coercion and violence. As such, given Nozick's arguments, it is illegitimate and the current owners have no right to deprive others of access to them

or to object to taxation or expropriation. However, it is precisely this conclusion which Nozick seeks to eliminate by means of his story. By presenting an ahistoric thought experiment, he hopes to convince the reader to ignore the actual history of property in order to defend the current owners of property from redistribution. Nozick's theory is only taken seriously because, firstly, it assumes the very thing it is trying to justify (i.e. capitalist property rights) and, as such, has a superficial coherence as a result and, secondly, it has obvious political utility for the rich.

The second thing to note is that the argument itself is deeply flawed. To see why, take (as an example) two individuals who share land in common. Nozick allows for one individual to claim the land as their own as long as the *"process normally giving rise to a permanent bequeathable property right in a previously unowned thing will not do so if the position of others no longer at liberty to use the thing is therefore worsened."* [**Anarchy, State and Utopia**, p. 178] Given this, one of our two land sharers can appropriate the land as long as they can provide the other with a wage greater than what they were originally producing. If this situation is achieved then, according to Nozick, the initial appropriation was just and so are all subsequent market exchanges. In this way, the unowned world becomes owned and a market system based on capitalist property rights in productive resources (the land) and labour develop.

Interestingly, for an ideology that calls itself "libertarian" Nozick's theory defines *"worse off"* in terms purely of material welfare, compared to the conditions that existed within the society based upon common use. However, the fact is if one person appropriated the land that the other cannot live off the remaining land then we have a problem. The other person has no choice but to agree to become employed by the landowner. The fact that the new land owner offers the other a wage to work their land that exceeds what the new wage slave originally produced may meet the *"Lockean Proviso"* misses the point. The important issue is that the new wage slave has no option but to work for another and, as a consequence, becomes subject to that person's authority. In other words, being *"worse off"* in terms of liberty (i.e. autonomy or self-government) is irrelevant for Nozick, a **very** telling position to take.

Nozick claims to place emphasis on self-ownership in his ideology because we are separate individuals, each with our own life to lead. It is strange, therefore, to see that Nozick does not emphasise people's ability to act on their own conception of themselves in his account of appropriation. Indeed, there is no objection to an appropriation that puts someone in an unnecessary and undesirable position of subordination and dependence on the will of others.

Notice that the fact that individuals are now subject to the decisions of other individuals is not considered by Nozick in assessing the fairness of the appropriation. The fact that the creation of private property results in the denial of important freedoms for wage slaves (namely, the wage slave has no say over the status of the land they had been utilising and no say over how their labour is used). Before the creation of private property, all managed their own work, had self-government in all aspects of their lives. After the appropriation, the new wage slave has no such liberty and indeed must accept the conditions of employment within which they relinquish control over how they spend much of their time. That this is issue is irrelevant for the Lockean Proviso shows how concerned about liberty capitalism actually is. Considering Nozick's many claims in favour of self-ownership and why it is important, you would think that the autonomy of the newly dispossessed wage slaves would be important to him. However, no such concern is to be found – the autonomy of wage slaves is treated as if it were irrelevant. Nozick claims that a concern for people's freedom to lead their own lives underlies his theory of unrestricted property-rights, but, this apparently does not apply to wage slaves. His justification for the creation of private property treats only the autonomy of the land owner as relevant. However, as Proudhon rightly argues:

> *"if the liberty of man is sacred, it is equally sacred in all individuals; that, if it needs property for its objective action, that is, for its life, the appropriation of material is equally necessary for all … Does it not follow that if one individual cannot prevent another … from appropriating an amount of material equal to his own, no more can he prevent individuals to come."* [**Op. Cit.**, pp. 84-85]

The implications of Nozick's argument become clear once we move beyond the initial acts of appropriation to the situation of a developed capitalist economy. In such a situation, **all** of the available useful land has been appropriated. There is massive differences in who owns what and these differences are passed on to the next generation. Thus we have a (minority) class of people who own the world and a class of people (the majority) who can only gain access to the means of life on terms acceptable to the former. How can the majority really be said to own themselves if they may do nothing without the permission of others (the owning minority).

Under capitalism people are claimed to own themselves, but this is purely formal as most people do not have independent access to resources. And as they have to use other peoples' resources, they become under the control of those who own the resources. In other words, private property reduces the autonomy of the majority of the population and creates a regime of authority which has many similarities to enslavement. As John Stuart Mill put it:

> *"No longer enslaved or made dependent by force of law, the great majority are so by force of property; they are still chained to a place, to an occupation, and to conformity with the will of an employer, and debarred by the accident of birth to both the enjoyments, and from the mental and moral advantages, which others inherit without exertion and independently of desert. That this is an evil equal to almost any of those against which mankind have hitherto struggles, the poor are not wrong in believing."* ["Chapters on Socialism", **Principles of Political Economy**, pp. 377-8]

Capitalism, even though claiming formal self-ownership, in fact not only restricts the self-determination of working class people, it also makes them a resource for others. Those who enter the market after others have appropriated all the available property are limited to charity or working for others. The latter, as we discuss in section C, results in exploitation as the worker's labour is used to enrich others. Working people are compelled to co-operate with the current scheme of property and are forced to benefit others. This means that self-determination requires resources as well as rights over one's physical and mental being. Concern for self-determination (i.e. meaningful self-ownership) leads us to common property plus workers' control of production and so some form of libertarian socialism – **not** private property and capitalism.

And, of course, the appropriation of the land requires a state to defend it against the dispossessed as well as continuous interference in people's lives. Left to their own devices, people would freely use the resources around them which they considered unjustly appropriated by others and it is only continuous state intervention that prevents then from violating Nozick's principles of justice (to use Nozick's own terminology, the *"Lockean Proviso"* is a patterned theory, his claims otherwise not withstanding).

In addition, we should note that private ownership by one person presupposes non-ownership by others (*"we who belong to the proletaire class, property excommunicates us!"* [Proudhon, **Op. Cit.**, p. 105]) and so the *"free market"* restricts as well as creates liberties just as any other economic system. Hence the claim that capitalism constitutes *"economic liberty"* is obviously false. In fact, it is **based** upon denying liberty for the vast majority during work hours (as well as having serious impacts on liberty outwith work hours due to the effects of concentrations of wealth upon society).

Perhaps Nozick can claim that the increased material benefits of private property makes the acquisition justified. However, it seems strange that a theory supporting "liberty" should consider well off slaves to be better than poor free men and women. As Nozick claims that the wage slaves consent is not required for the initial acquisition, so perhaps he can claim that the gain in material welfare outweighs the loss of autonomy and so allows the initial act as an act of paternalism. But as Nozick opposes paternalism when it restricts private property rights he can hardly invoke it when it is required to generate these rights. And if we exclude paternalism and emphasise autonomy (as Nozick claims he does elsewhere in his theory), then justifying the initial creation of private property becomes much more difficult, if not impossible.

And if each owner's title to their property includes the historical shadow of the Lockean Proviso on appropriation, then such titles are invalid. Any title people have over unequal resources will be qualified by the facts that *"property is theft"* and that *"property is despotism."* The claim that private property is economic liberty is obviously untrue, as is the claim that private property can be justified in terms of anything except *"might is right."*

In summary, *"[i]f the right of life is equal, the right of labour is equal, and so is the right of occupancy."* This means that *"those who do not possess today are proprietors by the same title as those who do possess; but instead of inferring therefrom that property should be shared by all, I demand, in the name of general security, its entire abolition."* [Proudhon, **Op. Cit.**, p. 77 and p. 66] Simply put, if it is right for the initial appropriation of resources to be made then, by that very same reason, it is right for others in the same and subsequent generations to abolish private property in favour of a system which respects the liberty of all rather than a few.

For more anarchist analysis on private property and why it cannot be justified (be it by occupancy, labour, natural right, or whatever) consult Proudhon's classic work What is Property?. For further discussion on capitalist property rights see section F.4.

B.3.5 Is state owned property different from private property?

No, far from it.

State ownership should not be confused with the common or public ownership implied by the concept of *"use rights."* The state is a hierarchical instrument of coercion and, as we discussed in section B.2, is marked by power being concentrated in a few hands. As the general populace is, by design, excluded from decision making within it this means that the state apparatus has control over the property in question. As the general public and those who use a piece of property are excluded from controlling it, state property is identical to private property. Instead of capitalists owning it, the state bureaucracy does.

This can easily be seen from the example of such so-called *"socialist"* states as the Soviet Union or China. To show why, we need only quote a market socialist who claims that China is not capitalist. According to David Schweickart a society is capitalist if, *"[i]n order to gain access to means of production (without which no one can work), most people must contract with people who own (or represent the owners of) such means. In exchange for a wage of a salary, they agree to supply the owners with a certain quantity and quality of labour. It is a crucial characteristic of the institution of wage labour that the goods or services produced do not belong to the workers who produce them but to those who supply the workers with the means of production."* Anarchists agree with Schweickart's definition of capitalism. As such, he is right to argue that a *"society of small farmers and artisans … is not a capitalist society, since wage labour is largely absent."* He is, however, wrong to assert that a *"society in which most of [the] means of production are owned by the central government or by local communities – contemporary China, for example – is not a capitalist society, since private ownership of the means of production is not dominant."* [**After Capitalism**, p. 23]

The reason is apparent. As Emma Goldman said (pointing out the obvious), if property is nationalised *"it belongs to the state; this is, the government has control of it and can dispose of it according to its wishes and views … Such a condition of affairs may be called state capitalism, but it would be fantastic to consider it in any sense Communistic"* (as that needs the *"socialisation of the land and of the machinery of production and distribution"* which *"belong[s] to the people, to be settled and used by individuals or groups according to their needs"* based on *"free access"*). [**Red Emma Speaks**, pp. 406-7]

Thus, by Schweickart's own definition, a system based on state ownership **is** capitalist as the workers clearly do not own the own means of production they use, the state does. Neither do they own the goods or services they produce, the state which supplies the workers with the means of production does. The difference is that rather than being a number of different capitalists there is only one, the state. It is, as Kropotkin warned, the *"mere substitution … of the State as the universal capitalist for the present capitalists."* [**Evolution and Environment**, p. 106] This is why anarchists have tended to call such regimes *"state capitalist"* as the state basically replaces the capitalist as boss.

While this is most clear for regimes like China's which are dictatorships, the logic also applies to democratic states. No matter if a state is democratic, state ownership is a form of exclusive property ownership which implies a social relationship which is totally different from genuine forms of socialism. Common ownership and use rights produce social relationships based on liberty and equality. State ownership, however, presupposes the existence of a government machine, a centralised bureaucracy, which stands above the members of society, both as individuals and as a group, and has the power to coerce and dominate them. In other words, when a state owns the means of life, the members of society remain proletarians, non-owners, excluded from control. Both legally and in reality, the means of life belong not to them, but to the state. As the state is not an abstraction floating above society but rather a social institution made up of a specific group of human beings, this means that this group controls and so effectively owns the property in question, not society as a whole nor those who actually use it. Just as the owning class excludes the majority, so does the state bureaucracy which means it owns the means of production, whether or not this is formally and legally recognised.

This explains why libertarian socialists have consistently stressed workers' self-management of production as the basis of any real form of socialism. To concentrate on ownership, as both Leninism and social democracy have done, misses the point. Needless to say, those regimes which have replaced capitalist ownership with state property have shown the validity of the anarchist analysis in these matters (*"all-powerful, centralised Government with State Capitalism as its economic expression,"* to quote Emma Goldman's summation of Lenin's Russia [**Op. Cit.**, p. 388]). State property is in no way fundamentally different from private property – all that changes is who exploits and oppresses the workers.

For more discussion see section H.3.13 – *"Why is state socialism just state capitalism?"*

B.4

How does capitalism affect liberty?

Private property is in many ways like a private form of state. The owner determines what goes on within the area he or she "owns," and therefore exercises a monopoly of power over it. When power is exercised over one's self, it is a source of freedom, but under capitalism it is a source of coercive authority. As Bob Black points out in **The Abolition of Work**:

> *"The liberals and conservatives and Libertarians who lament totalitarianism are phoneys and hypocrites … You find the same sort of hierarchy and discipline in an office or factory as you do in a prison or a monastery … A worker is a part-time slave. The boss says when to show up, when to leave, and what to do in the meantime. He tells you how much work to do and how fast. He is free to carry his control to humiliating extremes, regulating,*

if he feels like it, the clothes you wear or how often you go to the bathroom. With a few exceptions he can fire you for any reason, or no reason. He has you spied on by snitches and supervisors, he amasses a dossier on every employee. Talking back is called 'insubordination,' just as if a worker is a naughty child, and it not only gets you fired, it disqualifies you for unemployment compensation ... The demeaning system of domination I've described rules over half the waking hours of a majority of women and the vast majority of men for decades, for most of their lifespans. For certain purposes it's not too misleading to call our system democracy or capitalism or – better still – industrialism, but its real names are factory fascism and office oligarchy. Anybody who says these people are 'free' is lying or stupid." [**The Abolition of Work and other essays**, p. 21]

In response to this, defenders of capitalism usually say something along the lines of *"It's a free market and if you don't like it, find another job."* Of course, there are a number of problems with this response. Most obviously is the fact that capitalism is not and has never been a "free market." As we noted in section B.2, a key role of the state has been to protect the interests of the capitalist class and, as a consequence of this, it has intervened time and time again to skew the market in favour of the bosses. As such, to inform us that capitalism is something it has never been in order to defend it from criticism is hardly convincing.

However, there is another more fundamental issue with the response, namely the assumption that tyranny is an acceptable form of human interaction. To say that your option is either tolerate this boss or seek out another (hopefully more liberal) one suggests an utter lack of understanding what freedom is. Freedom is not the opportunity to pick a master, it is to be have autonomy over yourself. What capitalist ideology has achieved is to confuse having the ability to pick a master with freedom, that consent equates to liberty – regardless of the objective circumstances shaping the choices being made or the nature of the social relationships such choices produce.

While we return to this argument in section B.4.3, a few words seem appropriate now. To see why the capitalist response misses the point, we need only transfer the argument from the economic regime to the political. Let us assume a system of dictatorial states on an island. Each regime is a monarchy (i.e. a dictatorship). The King of each land decrees what his subjects do, who they associate with and, moreover, appropriates the fruit of their labour in exchange for food, clothing and shelter for however many hours a day he wants (the King is generous and allows his subjects some time to themselves in the evening and weekends). Some of the Kings even decree what their subjects will wear and how they will greet their fellow subjects. Few people would say that those subject to such arrangements are free.

Now, if we add the condition that any subject is free to leave a Kingdom but only if another King will let them join his regime, does that make it any more free? Slightly, but not by much. The subjects how have a limited choice in who can govern them but the **nature** of the regime they are subjected to does not change. What we

would expect to see happen is that those subjects whose skills are in demand will get better, more liberal, conditions than the others (as long as they are in demand). For the majority the conditions they are forced to accept will be as bad as before as they are easily replaceable. Both sets of subjects, however, are still under the autocratic rule of the monarchs. Neither are free but the members of one set have a more liberal regime than the others, dependent on the whims of the autocrats and their need for labour.

That this thought experiment reflects the way capitalism operates is clear. Little wonder anarchists have echoed Proudhon's complaint that *"our large capitalist associations [are] organised in the spirit of commercial and industrial feudalism."* [**Selected Writings of Pierre-Joseph Proudhon**, p. 72] Ironically, rather than deny the anarchist claim, defenders of capitalism have tried to convince us that such a regime is liberty incarnate. Yet the statist nature of private property can be seen in (right-wing) "Libertarian" (i.e. "classical" liberal) works representing the extremes of laissez-faire capitalism:

> *"[I]f one starts a private town, on land whose acquisition did not and does not violate the Lockean proviso [of non-aggression], persons who chose to move there or later remain there would have no* **right** *to a say in how the town was run, unless it was granted to them by the decision procedures for the town which the owner had established."* [Robert Nozick, **Anarchy, State and Utopia**, p. 270]

This is voluntary feudalism, nothing more. And, indeed, it was. Such private towns have existed, most notably the infamous company towns of US history. Howard Zinn summarises the conditions of such "private towns" in the Colorado mine fields:

> *"Each mining camp was a feudal dominion, with the company acting as lord and master. Every camp had a marshal, a law enforcement officer paid by the company. The 'laws' were the company's rules. Curfews were imposed, 'suspicious' strangers were not allowed to visit the homes, the company store had a monopoly on goods sold in the camp. The doctor was a company doctor, the schoolteachers hired by the company ... Political power in Colorado rested in the hands of those who held economic power. This meant that the authority of Colorado Fuel & Iron and other mine operators was virtually supreme ... Company officials were appointed as election judges. Company-dominated coroners and judges prevented injured employees from collecting damages."* [**The Colorado Coal Strike, 1913-14**, pp. 9-11]

Unsurprisingly, when the workers rebelled against this tyranny, they were evicted from their homes and the private law enforcement agents were extremely efficient in repressing the strikers: *"By the end of the strike, most of the dead and injured were miners and their families."* The strike soon took on the features of a war, with battles between strikers and their supporters and the company thugs. Ironically, when the National Guard was sent in to "restore order" the *"miners, having faced in the first five weeks of the strike what they considered a reign of terror at the hands of the private* guards, … looked forward" to their arrival. They "did not know that the governor was sending these troops under pressure from the mine operators." Indeed, the banks and corporations lent the state funds to pay for the militia. It was these company thugs, dressed in the uniform of the state militia, who murdered woman and children in the infamous Ludlow Massacre of April 20th, 1914. [**Op. Cit.**, p. 22, p. 25, p. 35]

Without irony the **New York Times** editorialised that the "militia was as impersonal and impartial as the law." The corporation itself hired Ivy Lee ("the father of public relations in the United States") to change public opinion after the slaughter. Significantly, Lee produced a series of tracts labelled "Facts Concerning the Struggle in Colorado for Industrial Freedom." The head of the corporation (Rockefeller) portrayed his repression of the strikers as blow for workers' freedom, to "defend the workers' right to work." [quoted by Zinn, **Op. Cit.**, p. 44, p. 51 and p. 50] So much for the capitalism being the embodiment of liberty.

Of course, it can be claimed that "market forces" will result in the most liberal owners being the most successful, but a nice master is still a master (and, of course, capitalism then was more "free market" than today, suggesting that this is simply wishful thinking). To paraphrase Tolstoy, "the liberal capitalist is like a kind donkey owner. He will do everything for the donkey – care for it, feed it, wash it. Everything except get off its back!" And as Bob Black notes, "Some people giving orders and others obeying them: this is the essence of servitude. … But freedom means more than the right to change masters." [The Libertarian as Conservative, **The Abolition of Work and other essays**, p. 147] That supporters of capitalism often claim that this "right" to change masters **is** the essence of "freedom" is a telling indictment of the capitalist notion of "liberty."

Needless to say, the authoritarianism of capitalism is not limited to the workplace. Capitalists seek to bolster their power within society as a whole, via the state. Capitalists call upon and support the state when it acts in **their** interests and when it supports **their** authority and power. Any apparent "conflict" between state and capital is like two gangsters fighting over the proceeds of a robbery: they will squabble over the loot and who has more power in the gang, but they need each other to appropriate the goods and defend their "property" against those from whom they stole it.

Unlike a company, however, the democratic state can be influenced by its citizens, who are able to act in ways that limit (to some extent) the power of the ruling elite to be "left alone" to enjoy their power. As a result, the wealthy hate the democratic aspects of the state, and its ordinary citizens, as potential threats to their power. This "problem" was noted by Alexis de Tocqueville in early 19th-century America:

> "It is easy to perceive that the wealthy members of the community entertain a hearty distaste to the democratic institutions of their country. The populace is at once the object of their scorn and their fears."

These fears have not changed, nor has the contempt for democratic ideas. To quote one US Corporate Executive, "one man, one vote will result in the eventual failure of democracy as we know it." [L. Silk and D. Vogel, **Ethics and Profits: The Crisis of Confidence in American Business**, pp. 189f]

This contempt for democracy does not mean that capitalists are **anti**-state. Far from it. As previously noted, capitalists depend on the state. This is because "[classical] Liberalism, is in theory a kind of anarchy without socialism, and therefore is simply a lie, for freedom is not possible without equality … The criticism liberals direct at government consists only of wanting to deprive it some of its functions and to call upon the capitalists to fight it out amongst themselves, but it cannot attack the repressive functions which are of its essence: for without the **gendarme** the property owner could not exist." [Errico Malatesta, **Anarchy**, p. 47]

We have discussed the state and how the ruling elite control in section B.2 and will not do so here. Nor we will discuss the ways in which the elite use that state to enforce private property (see section B.3) or use the state to intervene in society (see section D.1). Rather, the rest of this section will discuss how capitalism impacts on freedom and autonomy and why the standard apologetics by defenders of capitalism fail.

B.4.1 Is capitalism based on freedom?

For anarchists, freedom means both "freedom from" and "freedom to." "Freedom from" signifies not being subject to domination, exploitation, coercive authority, repression, or other forms of degradation and humiliation. "Freedom to" means being able to develop and express one's abilities, talents, and potentials to the fullest possible extent compatible with the maximum freedom of others. Both kinds of freedom imply the need for self-management, responsibility, and independence, which basically means that people have a say in the decisions that affect their lives. And since individuals do not exist in a social vacuum, it also means that freedom **must** take on a collective aspect, with the associations that individuals form with each other (e.g. communities, work groups, social groups) being run in a manner which allows the individual to participate in the decisions that the group makes. Thus freedom for anarchists requires participatory democracy, which means face-to-face discussion and voting on issues by the people affected by them.

Are these conditions of freedom met in the capitalist system? Obviously not. Despite all their rhetoric about "democracy," most of the "advanced" capitalist states remain only superficially democratic – and this because the majority of their citizens are employees who spend about half their waking hours under the thumb of capitalist dictators (bosses) who allow them no voice in the crucial economic decisions that affect their lives most profoundly and require them to work under conditions inimical to independent thinking. If the most basic freedom, namely freedom to think for oneself, is denied, then freedom itself is denied.

The capitalist workplace is profoundly undemocratic. Indeed, as Noam Chomsky points out, the oppressive authority relations in the typical corporate hierarchy would be called fascist or totalitarian if we were referring to a political system. In his words :

Why do anarchists oppose the current system?

"There's nothing individualistic about corporations. These are big conglomerate institutions, essentially totalitarian in character, but hardly individualistic. There are few institutions in human society that have such strict hierarchy and top-down control as a business organisation. Nothing there about 'don't tread on me`. You're being tread on all the time." [**Keeping the Rabble in Line**, p. 280]

Far from being "based on freedom," then, capitalism actually destroys freedom. In this regard, Robert E. Wood, the chief executive officer of Sears, spoke plainly when he said *"[w]e stress the advantages of the free enterprise system, we complain about the totalitarian state, but... we have created more or less of a totalitarian system in industry, particularly in large industry."* [quoted by Allan Engler, **Apostles of Greed**, p. 68]Or, as Chomsky puts it, supporters of capitalism do not understand *"the **fundamental** doctrine, that you should be free from domination and control, including the control of the manager and the owner"* [Feb. 14th, 1992 appearance on **Pozner/Donahue**].

Under corporate authoritarianism, the psychological traits deemed most desirable for average citizens to possess are efficiency, conformity, emotional detachment, insensitivity, and unquestioning obedience to authority – traits that allow people to survive and even prosper as employees in the company hierarchy. And of course, for "non-average" citizens, i.e., bosses, managers, administrators, etc., **authoritarian** traits are needed, the most important being the ability and willingness to dominate others.

But all such master/slave traits are inimical to the functioning of real (i.e. participatory/libertarian) democracy, which requires that citizens have qualities like flexibility, creativity, sensitivity, understanding, emotional honesty, directness, warmth, realism, and the ability to mediate, communicate, negotiate, integrate and co-operate. Therefore, capitalism is not only **un**democratic, it is **anti**-democratic, because it promotes the development of traits that make real democracy (and so a libertarian society) impossible.

Many capitalist apologists have attempted to show that capitalist authority structures are "voluntary" and are, therefore, somehow not a denial of individual and social freedom. Milton Friedman (a leading free market capitalist economist) has attempted to do just this. Like most apologists for capitalism he ignores the authoritarian relations explicit within wage labour (within the workplace, "co-ordination" is based upon top-down command, **not** horizontal co-operation). Instead he concentrates on the decision of a worker to sell their labour to a **specific** boss and so ignores the lack of freedom within such contracts. He argues that *"individuals are effectively free to enter or not enter into any particular exchange, so every transaction is strictly voluntary … The employee is protected from coercion by the employer because of other employers for whom he can work."* [**Capitalism and Freedom**, pp. 14-15]

Friedman, to prove the free nature of capitalism, compares capitalism with a simple exchange economy based upon independent producers. He states that in such a simple economy each household *"has the alternative of producing directly for itself, [and so] it need not enter into any exchange unless it benefits from it. Hence no exchange will take place unless both parties do benefit from it. Co-operation is thereby achieved without coercion."* Under capitalism

(or the *"complex"* economy) Friedman states that *"individuals are effectively free to enter or not to enter into any particular exchange, so that every transaction is strictly voluntary."* [**Op. Cit.**, p. 13 and p. 14]

A moments thought, however, shows that capitalism is not based on *"strictly voluntary"* transactions as Friedman claims. This is because the proviso that is required to make every transaction *"strictly voluntary"* is **not** freedom not to enter any **particular** exchange, but freedom not to enter into any exchange **at all.**

This, and only this, was the proviso that proved the simple model Friedman presents (the one based upon artisan production) to be voluntary and non-coercive; and nothing less than this would prove the complex model (i.e. capitalism) is voluntary and non-coercive. But Friedman is clearly claiming above that freedom not to enter into any **particular** exchange is enough and so, **only by changing his own requirements**, can he claim that capitalism is based upon freedom.

It is easy to see what Friedman has done, but it is less easy to excuse it (particularly as it is so commonplace in capitalist apologetics). He moved from the simple economy of exchange between independent producers to the capitalist economy without mentioning the most important thing that distinguishes them – namely the separation of labour from the means of production. In the society of independent producers, the worker had the choice of working for themselves – under capitalism this is not the case. For capitalist economists like Friedman, workers choose whether to work or not. The bosses must pay a wage to cover the "disutility" of labour. In reality, of course, most workers face the choice of working or starvation/poverty. Capitalism is based upon the existence of a labour force without access to capital or land, and therefore without a choice as to whether to put its labour in the market or not. Friedman would, hopefully, agree that where there is no choice there is coercion. His attempted demonstration that capitalism co-ordinates without coercion therefore fails.

Capitalist apologists are able to convince some people that capitalism is "based on freedom" only because the system has certain superficial **appearances** of freedom. On closer analysis these appearances turn out to be deceptions. For example, it is claimed that the employees of capitalist firms have freedom because they can always quit. To requote Bob Black:

"Some people giving orders and others obeying them: this is the essence of servitude. Of course, as [right-Libertarians] smugly [observe], 'one can at least change jobs,' but you can't avoid having a job – just as under statism one can at least change nationalities but you can't avoid subjection to one nation-state or another. But freedom means more than the right to change masters." [*"The Libertarian as Conservative"*, **The Abolition of Work and other essays**, p. 147]

Under capitalism, workers have only the Hobson's choice of being governed/exploited or living on the street.

Anarchists point out that for choice to be real, free agreements and associations must be based on the social equality of those who enter into them, and both sides must receive roughly equivalent benefit. But social relations between capitalists and employees can never be equal, because private ownership of the means of production gives rise to social hierarchy and relations of coercive authority and subordination, as was recognised even by Adam Smith (see below).

The picture painted by Walter Reuther (one time head of the US autoworkers' union) of working life in America before the Wagner act is a commentary on class inequality : *"Injustice was as common as streetcars. When men walked into their jobs, they left their dignity, their citizenship and their humanity outside. They were required to report for duty whether there was work or not. While they waited on the convenience of supervisors and foremen they were unpaid. They could be fired without a pretext. They were subjected to arbitrary, senseless rules ... Men were tortured by regulations that made difficult even going to the toilet. Despite grandiloquent statements from the presidents of huge corporations that their door was open to any worker with a complaint, there was no one and no agency to which a worker could appeal if he were wronged. The very idea that a worker could be wronged seemed absurd to the employer."* Much of this indignity remains, and with the globalisation of capital, the bargaining position of workers is further deteriorating, so that the gains of a century of class struggle are in danger of being lost.

A quick look at the enormous disparity of power and wealth between the capitalist class and the working class shows that the benefits of the "agreements" entered into between the two sides are far from equal. Walter Block, a leading ideologue of the Canadian right-libertarian "think-tank" the Fraser Institute, makes clear the differences in power and benefits when discussing sexual harassment in the workplace:

> *"Consider the sexual harassment which continually occurs between a secretary and a boss ... while objectionable to many women, [it] is not a coercive action. It is rather part of a package deal in which the secretary agrees to **all** aspects of the job when she agrees to accept the job, and especially when she agrees to **keep** the job. The office is, after all, private property. The secretary does not have to remain if the 'coercion' is objectionable."* [quoted by Engler, **Op. Cit.**, p. 101]

The primary goal of the Fraser Institute is to convince people that all other rights must be subordinated to the right to enjoy wealth. In this case, Block makes clear that under private property, only bosses have "freedom to," and most also desire to ensure they have "freedom from" interference with this right.

So, when capitalists gush about the "liberty" available under capitalism, what they are really thinking of is their state-protected freedom to exploit and oppress workers through the ownership of property, a freedom that allows them to continue amassing huge disparities of wealth, which in turn insures their continued power and privileges. That the capitalist class in liberal-democratic states **gives** workers the right to change masters (though this is not true under state capitalism) is far from showing that capitalism is based on freedom, For as Peter Kropotkin rightly points out, *"freedoms are not given, they are taken."* [Peter Kropotkin, **Words of a Rebel**, p. 43] In capitalism, you are "free" to do anything you are permitted to do by your masters, which amounts to "freedom" with a collar and leash.

B.4.2 Is capitalism based on self-ownership?

Murray Rothbard, a leading "libertarian" capitalist, claims that capitalism is based on the *"basic axiom"* of *"the right to self-ownership."* This *"axiom"* is defined as *"the absolute right of each man [sic] ... to control [his or her] body free of coercive interference. Since each individual must think, learn, value, and choose his or her ends and means in order to survive and flourish, the right to self-ownership gives man [sic] the right to perform these vital activities without being hampered by coercive molestation."* [**For a New Liberty**, pp. 26-27]

At first sight, this appears to sound reasonable. That we "own" ourselves and, consequently, we decide what we do with ourselves has an intuitive appeal. Surely this is liberty? Thus, in this perspective, liberty *"is a condition in which a person's ownership rights in his own body and his legitimate material property are **not** invaded, are not aggressed against."* It also lends itself to contrasts with slavery, where one individual owns another and *"the slave has little or no right to self-ownership; his person and his produce are systematically expropriated by his master by the use of violence."* [Rothbard, **Op. Cit.**, p. 41] This means that "self-ownership" can be portrayed as the opposite of slavery: we have the dominion over ourselves that a slaveholder has over their slave. This means that slavery is wrong because the slave owner has stolen the rightful property of the slave, namely their body (and its related abilities). This concept is sometimes expressed as people having a "natural" or "inalienable" right to own their own body and the product of their own labour.

Anarchists, while understanding the appeal of the idea, are not convinced. That "self-ownership," like slavery, places issues of freedom and individuality within the context of private property – as such it shares the most important claim of slavery, namely that people can be objects of the rules of private property. It suggests an alienated perspective and, moreover, a fatal flaw in the dogma. This can be seen from how the axiom is used in practice. In as much as the term "self-ownership" is used simply as an synonym for "individual autonomy" anarchists do not have an issue with it. However, the "basic axiom" is not used in this way by the theorists of capitalism. Liberty in the sense of individual autonomy is not what "self-ownership" aims to justify. Rather, it aims to justify the denial of liberty, not its exercise. It aims to portray social relationships, primarily wage labour, in which one person commands another as examples of liberty rather than what they are, examples of domination and oppression. In other words, "self-ownership" becomes the means by which the autonomy of individuals is limited, if not destroyed, in the name of freedom and liberty.

This is exposed in the right-libertarian slogan *"human rights are property rights."* Assuming this is true, it means that you can alienate your rights, rent them or sell them like any other kind of property. Moreover, if you have no property, you have no human rights as you have no place to exercise them. As Ayn Rand, another ideologue for "free market" capitalism stated, *"there can be no such thing as the right to unrestricted freedom of speech (or of action)* on someone else's property." [**Capitalism: The Unknown Ideal**, p. 258] If you are in someone else's property (say at work) you have no basic rights at all, beyond the right not to be harmed (a right bosses habitually violate anyway by ignoring health and safety issues).

Self-ownership justifies this. You have rented out the property in your person (labour services) and, consequently, another person can tell you what to do, when to do and how to do it. Thus property comes into conflict with liberty. If you argue that *"human rights are property rights"* you automatically ensure that human rights are continually violated in practice simply because there is a conflict between property and liberty. This is not surprising, as the "property rights" theory of liberty was created to justify the denial of other people's liberty and the appropriation of their labour.

Clearly, then, we reach a problem with "self-ownership" (or property in the person) once we take into account private property and its distribution. In a nutshell, capitalists don't pay their employees to perform the other *"vital activities"* listed by Rothbard (learning, valuing, choosing ends and means) – unless, of course, the firm requires that workers undertake such activities in the interests of company profits. Otherwise, workers can rest assured that any efforts to engage in such *"vital activities"* on company time **will** be *"hampered"* by *"coercive molestation."* Therefore wage labour (the basis of capitalism) in practice **denies** the rights associated with "self-ownership," thus alienating the individual from his or her basic rights. Or as Michael Bakunin expressed it, *"the worker sells his person and his liberty for a given time"* under capitalism. [**The Political Philosophy of Bakunin**, p. 187]

In a society of relative equals, "property" would not be a source of power as use would co-incidence with occupancy (i.e. private property would be replaced by possession). For example, you would still be able to fling a drunk out of your home. But in a system based on wage labour (i.e. capitalism), property is a different thing altogether, becoming a source of **institutionalised** power and coercive authority through hierarchy. As Noam Chomsky writes, capitalism is based on *"a **particular form** of authoritarian control. Namely, the kind that comes through private ownership and control, which is an **extremely** rigid system of domination."* When "property" is purely what you, as an individual, use (i.e. **possession**) it is not a source of power. In capitalism, however, "property" rights no longer coincide with **use** rights, and so they become a **denial** of freedom and a source of authority and power over the individual.

As we've seen in the discussion of hierarchy (sections A.2.8 and B.1), all forms of authoritarian control depend on *"coercive molestation"* – i.e. the use or threat of sanctions. This is definitely the case in company hierarchies under capitalism. Bob Black describes the authoritarian nature of capitalism as follows:

> *"[T]he place where [adults] pass the most time and submit to the closest control is at work. Thus … it's apparent that the source of the greatest direct duress experienced by the ordinary adult is **not** the state but rather the business that employs him. Your foreman or supervisor gives you more or-else orders in a week than the police*

do in a decade." [*"The Libertarian as Conservative"*, **The Abolition of Work and other essays**, p. 145]

In developing nations, this control can easily been seen to be an utter affront to human dignity and liberty. There a workplace is often *"surrounded by barbed wire. Behind its locked doors … workers are supervised by guards who beat and humiliate them on the slightest pretext … Each worker repeats the same action – sewing on a belt loop, stitching a sleeve – maybe two thousand times a day. They work under painfully bright lights, for twelve- to fourteen-hour shifts, in overheated factories, with too few bathroom breaks, and restricted access to water (to reduce the need for more bathroom breaks), which is often foul and unfit for human consumption in any event."* The purpose is *"to maximise the amount of profit that could be wrung out"* of the workers, with the *"time allocated to each task"* being calculated in *"units of ten thousands of a second."* [Joel Bakan, **The Corporation**, pp. 66-7] While in the developed world the forms of control are, in general, nowhere as extreme (in thanks due to hard won labour organising and struggle) the basic principle is the same. Only a sophist would argue that the workers "owned" themselves and abilities for the period in question – yet this is what the advocates of "self-ownership" do argue.

So if by the term "self-ownership" it is meant "individual autonomy" then, no, capitalism is not based on it. Ironically, the theory of "self-ownership" is used to undercut and destroy genuine self-ownership during working hours (and, potentially, elsewhere). The logic is simple. As I own myself I am, therefore, able to sell myself as well, although few advocates of "self-ownership" are as blunt as this (as we discuss in section F.2.2 right-libertarian Robert Nozick accepts that voluntary slavery flows from this principle). Instead they stress that we "own" our labour and we contract them to others to use. Yet, unlike other forms of property, labour cannot be alienated. Therefore when you sell your labour you sell yourself, your liberty, for the time in question. By alienating your labour power, you alienate the substance of your being, your personality, for the time in question.

As such, "self-ownership" ironically becomes the means of justifying authoritarian social relationships which deny the autonomy it claims to defend. Indeed, these relationships have similarities with slavery, the very thing which its advocates like to contrast "self-ownership" to. While modern defenders of capitalism deny this, classical economist James Mill let the cat out of the bag by directly comparing the two. It is worthwhile to quote him at length:

> *"The great capitalist, the owner of a manufactory, if he operated with slaves instead of free labourers, like the West India planter, would be regarded as owner both of the capital, and of the labour. He would be owner, in short, of both instruments of production: and the whole of the produce, without participation, would be his own.*
>
> *"What is the difference, in the case of the man, who operates by means of labourers receiving wages? The labourer, who receives wages, sells his labour for a day, a week, a month, or a year, as the case may be. The manufacturer, who pays these wages, buys the labour, for the day, the year, or whatever period it may be.*

He is equally therefore the owner of the labour, with the manufacturer who operates with slaves. The only difference is, in the mode of purchasing. The owner of the slave purchases, at once, the whole of the labour, which the man can ever perform: he, who pays wages, purchases only so much of a man's labour as he can perform in a day, or any other stipulated time. Being equally, however, the owner of the labour, so purchased, as the owner of the slave is of that of the slave, the produce, which is the result of this labour, combined with his capital, is all equally his own. In the state of society, in which we at present exist, it is in these circumstances that almost all production is effected: the capitalist is the owner of both instruments of production: and the whole of the produce is his." [*"Elements of Political Economy"* quoted by David Ellerman, **Property and Contract in Economics**, pp. 53-4

Thus the only *"difference"* between slavery and capitalist labour is the *"mode of purchasing."* The labour itself and its product in both cases is owned by the *"great capitalist."* Clearly this is a case of, to use Rothbard's words, during working hours the worker *"has little or no right to self-ownership; his person and his produce are systematically expropriated by his master."* Little wonder anarchists have tended to call wage labour by the more accurate term **"wage slavery."** For the duration of the working day the boss owns the labour power of the worker. As this cannot be alienated from its "owner" this means that the boss effectively owns the worker – and keeps the product of their labour for the privilege of so doing!

There are key differences of course. At the time, slavery was not a voluntary decision and the slaves could not change their master (although in some cultures, such as Ancient Rome, people over the could sell themselves in slavery while *"voluntary slavery is sanctioned in the Bible."* [Ellerman, **Op. Cit.**, p. 115 and p. 114]). Yet the fact that under wage slavery people are not forced to take a specific job and can change masters does not change the relations of authority created between the two parties. As we note in the next section, the objection that people can leave their jobs just amounts to saying "love it or leave it!" and does not address the issue at hand. The vast majority of the population cannot avoid wage labour and remain wage workers for most of their adult lives. It is virtually impossible to distinguish being able to sell your liberty/labour piecemeal over a lifetime from alienating your whole lifetime's labour at one go. Changing who you alienate your labour/liberty to does not change the act and experience of alienation.

Thus the paradox of self-ownership. It presupposes autonomy only in order to deny it. In order to enter a contract, the worker exercises autonomy in deciding whether it is advantageous to rent or sell his or her property (their labour power) for use by another (and given that the alternative is, at best, poverty unsurprisingly people do consider it "advantageous" to "consent" to the contract). Yet what is rented or sold is **not** a piece of property but rather a self-governing individual. Once the contract is made and the property rights are transferred, they no longer have autonomy and are treated like any other factor of production or commodity.

In the "self-ownership" thesis this is acceptable due to its assumption that people and their labour power are property. Yet the worker cannot send along their labour by itself to an employer. By its very nature, the worker has to be present in the workplace if this "property" is to be put to use by the person who has bought it. The consequence of contracting out your labour (your property in the person) is that your autonomy (liberty) is restricted, if not destroyed, depending on the circumstances of the particular contract signed. This is because employers hire people, not a piece of property.

So far from being based on the "right to self-ownership," then, capitalism effectively denies it, alienating the individual from such basic rights as free speech, independent thought, and self-management of one's own activity, which individuals have to **give up** when they are employed. But since these rights, according to Rothbard, are the products of humans **as** humans, wage labour alienates them from themselves, exactly as it does the individual's labour power and creativity. For you do not sell your skills, as these skills are **part** of you. Instead, what you have to sell is your **time**, your labour power, and so **yourself.** Thus under wage labour, rights of "self-ownership" are always placed below property rights, the only "right" being left to you is that of finding another job (although even this right is denied in some countries if the employee owes the company money).

It should be stressed that this is **not** a strange paradox of the "self-ownership" axiom. Far from it. The doctrine was most famously expounded by John Locke, who argued that *"every Man has a **Property** in his own **Person**. This no Body has any Right to but himself."* However, a person can sell, *"for a certain time, the Service he undertakes to do, in exchange for Wages he is to receive."* The buyer of the labour then owns both it and its product. *"Thus the Grass my Horse has bit; the Turfs my Servant has cut; and the Ore I have digg'd in any place where I have a right to them in common with others, becomes my **Property,** without the assignation or consent of any body. The **labour** that was mine ... hath **fixed** my **Property** in them."* [**Second Treatise on Government**, Section 27, Section 85 and Section 28]

Thus a person (the servant) becomes the equivalent of an animal (the horse) once they have sold their labour to the boss. Wage labour denies the basic humanity and autonomy of the worker. Rather than being equals, private property produces relations of domination and alienation. Proudhon compared this to an association in which, *"while the partnership lasts, the profits and losses are divided between them; since each produces, not for himself, but for the society; when the time of distribution arrives it is not the producer who is considered, but the associated. That is why the slave, to whom the planter gives straw and rice; and the civilised labour, to whom the capitalist pays a salary which is always too small, – not being associated with their employers, although producing with them, – are disregarded when the product is divided. Thus the horse who draws our coaches ... produce with us, but are not associated with us; we take their product but do not share it with them. The animals and labourers whom we employ hold the same relation to us."* [**What is Property?**, p. 226]

So while the capitalist Locke sees nothing wrong in comparing a person to an animal, the anarchist Proudhon objects to the fundamental injustice of a system which turns a person into a resource for another to use. And we do mean resource, as the self-ownership thesis is also the means by which the poor become little more than spare parts for the wealthy. After all, the poor own their bodies and, consequently, can sell all or part of it to a willing party. This means that someone in dire economic necessity can sell parts of their body to the rich. Ultimately, *"[t]o tell a poor man that he* **has** *property because he* **has** *arms and legs – that the hunger from which he suffers, and his power to sleep in the open air are his property, – is to play upon words, and to add insult to injury."* [Proudhon, **Op. Cit.**, p. 80]

Obviously the ability to labour is **not** the property of a person – it is their possession. Use and ownership are fused and cannot be separated out. As such, anarchists argue that the history of capitalism shows that there is a considerable difference whether one said (like the defenders of capitalism) that slavery is wrong because every person has a natural right to the property of their own body, or because every person has a natural right freely to determine their own destiny (like the anarchists). The first kind of right is alienable and in the context of a capitalist regime ensures that the many labour for those who own the means of life. The second kind of right is inalienable as long as a person remained a person and, therefore, liberty or self-determination is not a claim to ownership which might be both acquired and surrendered, but an inextricable aspect of the activity of being human.

The anarchist position on the inalienable nature of human liberty also forms the basis for the excluded to demand access to the means necessary to labour. *"From the distinction between possession and property,"* argued Proudhon, *"arise two sorts of rights: the* **jus in re**, *the right* **in** *a thing, the right by which I may reclaim the property which I have acquired, in whatever hands I find it; and* **jus ad rem**, *the right* **to** *a thing, which gives me a claim to become a proprietor … In the first, possession and property are united; the second includes only naked property. With me who, as a labourer, have a right to the possession of the products of Nature and my own industry – and who, as a proletaire, enjoy none of them – it is by virtue of the* **jus de rem** *that I demand admittance to the* **jus in re**.*"* [**Op. Cit.**, p. 65] Thus to make the self-ownership of labour and its products a reality for those who do the actual work in society rather than a farce, property must be abolished – both in terms of the means of life and also in defining liberty and what it means to be free.

So, contrary to Rothbard's claim, capitalism in practice uses the rhetoric of self-ownership to alienate the right to genuine self-ownership because of the authoritarian structure of the workplace, which derives from private property. If we desire real self-ownership, we cannot renounce it for most of our adult lives by becoming wage slaves. Only workers' self-management of production, not capitalism, can make self-ownership a reality:

> *"They speak of 'inherent rights', 'inalienable rights', 'natural rights,' etc … Unless the material conditions for equality exist, it is worse than mockery to pronounce men equal. And unless there is equality (and by equality I mean equal chances for every one to make the most of himself [or herself]) unless, I say, these equal changes exist, freedom, either of though, speech, or action, is*

> *equally a mockery … As long as the working-people … tramp the streets, whose stones they lay, whose filth they clean, whose sewers they dig, yet upon which they must not stand too long lest the policeman bid them 'move on'; as long as they go from factory to factory, begging for the opportunity to be a slave, receiving the insults of bosses and foreman, getting the old 'no,' the old shake of the head, in these factories they built, whose machines they wrought; so long as they consent to be herd like cattle, in the cities, driven year after year, more and more, off the mortgaged land, the land they cleared, fertilised, cultivated, rendered of value … so long as they continue to do these things vaguely relying upon some power outside themselves, be it god, or priest, or politician, or employer, or charitable society, to remedy matters, so long deliverance will be delayed. When they conceive the possibility of a complete international federation of labour, whose constituent groups shall take possession of land, mines, factories, all the instruments of production…, in short, conduct their own industry without regulative interference from law-makers or employers, then we may hope for the only help which counts for aught – Self-Help; the only condition which can guarantee free speech [along with their other rights] (and no paper guarantee needed)."* [Voltairine de Cleyre, **The Voltairine de Cleyre Reader**, pp. 4-6]

To conclude, the idea that capitalism is based on self-ownership is radically at odds with reality if, by self-ownership, it is meant self-determination or individual autonomy. However, this is not surprising given that the rationale behind the self-ownership thesis is precisely to justify capitalist hierarchy and its resulting restrictions on liberty. Rather than being a defence of liberty, self-ownership is designed to facilitate its erosion. In order to make the promise of autonomy implied by the concept of "self-ownership" a reality, private property will need to be abolished.

For more discussion of the limitations, contradictions and fallacies of defining liberty in terms of self-ownership and property rights, see section F.2.

B.4.3 But no one forces you to work for them!

Of course it is claimed that entering wage labour is a "voluntary" undertaking, from which both sides allegedly benefit. However, due to **past** initiations of force (e.g. the seizure of land by conquest), the control of the state by the capitalist class plus the tendency for capital to concentrate, a relative handful of people now control vast wealth, depriving all others access to the means of life. Thus denial of free access to the means of life is based ultimately on the principle of "might makes right." And as Murray Bookchin so rightly points out, *"the means of life must be taken for what they literally are: the means without which life is impossible. To deny them to people is more than 'theft' … it is outright homicide."* [**Remaking Society**, p. 187]

David Ellerman has also noted that the past use of force has resulted in the majority being limited to those options allowed to them by the powers that be:

"It is a veritable mainstay of capitalist thought ... that the moral flaws of chattel slavery have not survived in capitalism since the workers, unlike the slaves, are free people making voluntary wage contracts. But it is only that, in the case of capitalism, the denial of natural rights is less complete so that the worker has a residual legal personality as a free 'commodity owner.' He is thus allowed to voluntarily put his own working life to traffic. When a robber denies another person's right to make an infinite number of other choices besides losing his money or his life and the denial is backed up by a gun, then this is clearly robbery even though it might be said that the victim making a 'voluntary choice' between his remaining options. When the legal system itself denies the natural rights of working people in the name of the prerogatives of capital, and this denial is sanctioned by the legal violence of the state, then the theorists of 'libertarian' capitalism do not proclaim institutional robbery, but rather they celebrate the 'natural liberty' of working people to choose between the remaining options of selling their labour as a commodity and being unemployed." [quoted by Noam Chomsky, **The Chomsky Reader**, p. 186]

Therefore the existence of the labour market depends on the worker being separated from the means of production. The natural basis of capitalism is wage labour, wherein the majority have little option but to sell their skills, labour and time to those who **do** own the means of production. In advanced capitalist countries, less than 10% of the working population are self-employed (in 1990, 7.6% in the UK, 8% in the USA and Canada – however, this figure includes **employers** as well, meaning that the number of self-employed **workers** is even smaller!). Hence for the vast majority, the labour market is their only option.

Michael Bakunin notes that these facts put the worker in the position of a serf with regard to the capitalist, even though the worker is formally "free" and "equal" under the law:

*"Juridically they are both equal; but economically the worker is the serf of the capitalist ... thereby the worker sells his person and his liberty for a given time. The worker is in the position of a serf because this terrible threat of starvation which daily hangs over his head and over his family, will force him to accept any conditions imposed by the gainful calculations of the capitalist, the industrialist, the employer.... The worker always has the **right** to leave his employer, but has he the means to do so? No, he does it in order to sell himself to another employer. He is driven to it by the same hunger which forces him to sell himself to the first employer. Thus the worker's liberty ... is only a theoretical freedom, lacking any means for its possible realisation, and consequently it is only a fictitious liberty, an utter falsehood. The truth is that the whole life of the worker is simply a continuous and dismaying succession*

of terms of serfdom – voluntary from the juridical point of view but compulsory from an economic sense – broken up by momentarily brief interludes of freedom accompanied by starvation; in other words, it is real slavery." [**The Political Philosophy of Bakunin**, pp. 187-8]

Obviously, a company cannot **force** you to work for them but, in general, you have to work for **someone**. How this situation developed is, of course, usually ignored. If not glossed over as irrelevant, some fairy tale is spun in which a few bright people saved and worked hard to accumulate capital and the lazy majority flocked to be employed by these (almost superhuman) geniuses. In the words of one right-wing economist (talking specifically of the industrial revolution but whose argument is utilised today):

"The factory owners did not have the power to compel anybody to take a factory job. They could only hire people who were ready to work for the wages offered to them. Low as these wage rates were, they were nonetheless much more than these paupers could earn in any other field open to them." [Ludwig von Mises, **Human Action**, pp. 619-20]

Notice the assumptions. The workers just happen have such a terrible set of options – the employing classes have absolutely nothing to do with it. And these owners just happen to have all these means of production on their hands while the working class just happen to be without property and, as a consequence, forced to sell their labour on the owners' terms. That the state enforces capitalist property rights and acts to defend the power of the owning class is just another co-incidence among many. The possibility that the employing classes might be directly implicated in state policies that reduced the available options of workers is too ludicrous even to mention.

Yet in the real world, the power of coincidence to explain all is less compelling. Here things are more grim as the owning class clearly benefited from numerous acts of state violence and a general legal framework which restricted the options available for the workers. Apparently we are meant to believe that it is purely by strange co-incidence the state was run by the wealthy and owning classes, not the working class, and that a whole host of anti-labour laws and practices were implemented by random chance.

It should be stressed that this nonsense, with its underlying assumptions and inventions, is still being peddled today. It is being repeated to combat the protests that "multinational corporations exploit people in poor countries." Yes, it will be readily admitted, multinationals **do** pay lower wages in developing countries than in rich ones: that is why they go there. However, it is argued, this represents economic advancement compared to what the other options available are. As the corporations do not force them to work for them and they would have stayed with what they were doing previously the charge of exploitation is wrong. Would you, it is stressed, leave your job for one with less pay and worse conditions? In fact, the bosses are doing them a favour in paying such low wages for the products the companies charge such high prices in the developed world for.

And so, by the same strange co-incidence that marked the

industrial revolution, capitalists today (in the form of multinational corporations) gravitate toward states with terrible human rights records. States where, at worse, death squads torture and "disappear" union and peasant co-operative organisers or where, at best, attempts to organise a union can get you arrested or fired and blacklisted. States where peasants are being forced off their land as a result of government policies which favour the big landlords. By an equally strange coincidence, the foreign policy of the American and European governments is devoted to making sure such anti-labour regimes stay in power. It is a co-incidence, of course, that such regimes are favoured by the multinationals and that these states spend so much effort in providing a "market friendly" climate to tempt the corporations to set up their sweatshops there. It is also, apparently, just a co-incidence that these states are controlled by the local wealthy owning classes and subject to economic pressure by the transnationals which invest and wish to invest there.

It is clear that when a person who is mugged hands over their money to the mugger they do so because they prefer it to the "next best alternative." As such, it is correct that people agree to sell their liberty to a boss because their "next best alternative" is worse (utter poverty or starvation are not found that appealing for some reason). But so what? As anarchists have been pointing out for over a century, the capitalists have systematically used the state to limit options for the many, to create a buyers' market for labour by skewing the conditions under which workers can sell their labour in the bosses favour. To then merrily answer all criticisms of this set-up with the response that the workers "voluntarily agreed" to work on those terms is just hypocrisy. Does it really change things if the mugger (the state) is only the agent (hired thug) of another criminal (the owning class)?

As such, hymns to the "free market" seem somewhat false when the reality of the situation is such that workers do not need to be forced at gun point to enter a specific workplace because of **past** (and more often than not, current) "initiation of force" by the capitalist class and the state which have created the objective conditions within which we make our employment decisions. Before any **specific** labour market contract occurs, the separation of workers from the means of production is an established fact (and the resulting "labour" market usually gives the advantage to the capitalists as a class). So while we can usually pick which capitalist to work for, we, in general, cannot choose to work for ourselves (the self-employed sector of the economy is tiny, which indicates well how spurious capitalist liberty actually is). Of course, the ability to leave employment and seek it elsewhere is an important freedom. However, this freedom, like most freedoms under capitalism, is of limited use and hides a deeper anti-individual reality.

As Karl Polanyi puts it:

> "In human terms such a postulate [of a labour market] implied for the worker extreme instability of earnings, utter absence of professional standards, abject readiness to be shoved and pushed about indiscriminately, complete dependence on the whims of the market. [Ludwig Von] Mises justly argued that if workers 'did not act as trade unionists, but reduced their demands and changed their locations and occupations according to the labour market,

> they would eventually find work.' This sums up the position under a system based on the postulate of the commodity character of labour. It is not for the commodity to decide where it should be offered for sale, to what purpose it should be used, at what price it should be allowed to change hands, and in what manner it should be consumed or destroyed." [**The Great Transformation**, p. 176]

(Although we should point out that von Mises argument that workers will "eventually" find work as well as being nice and vague – how long is "eventually"?, for example – is contradicted by actual experience. As the Keynesian economist Michael Stewart notes, in the nineteenth century workers *"who lost their jobs had to redeploy fast or starve (and even this feature of the nineteenth century economy … did not prevent prolonged recessions)"* [**Keynes in the 1990s**, p. 31] Workers "reducing their demands" may actually worsen an economic slump, causing more unemployment in the short run and lengthening the length of the crisis. We address the issue of unemployment and workers "reducing their demands" in more detail in section C.9).

It is sometimes argued that capital needs labour, so both have an equal say in the terms offered, and hence the labour market is based on "liberty." But for capitalism to be based on real freedom or on true free agreement, both sides of the capital/labour divide must be equal in bargaining power, otherwise any agreement would favour the most powerful at the expense of the other party. However, due to the existence of private property and the states needed to protect it, this equality is de facto impossible, regardless of the theory. This is because. in general, capitalists have three advantages on the "free" labour market – the law and state placing the rights of property above those of labour, the existence of unemployment over most of the business cycle and capitalists having more resources to fall back on. We will discuss each in turn.

The first advantage, namely property owners having the backing of the law and state, ensures that when workers go on strike or use other forms of direct action (or even when they try to form a union) the capitalist has the full backing of the state to employ scabs, break picket lines or fire "the ring-leaders." This obviously gives employers greater power in their bargaining position, placing workers in a weak position (a position that may make them, the workers, think twice before standing up for their rights).

The existence of unemployment over most of the business cycle ensures that *"employers have a structural advantage in the labour market, because there are typically more candidates … than jobs for them to fill."* This means that *"[c]ompetition in labour markets us typically skewed in favour of employers: it is a buyers market. And in a buyer's market, it is the sellers who compromise. Competition for labour is not strong enough to ensure that workers' desires are always satisfied."* [Juliet B. Schor, **The Overworked American**, p. 71, p. 129] If the labour market generally favours the employer, then this obviously places working people at a disadvantage as the threat of unemployment and the hardships associated with it encourages workers to take any job and submit to their bosses demands and power while employed. Unemployment, in other words, serves to discipline labour. The higher the prevailing unemployment rate, the harder it is to find a new job, which raises the cost of job loss and makes it less likely for workers to strike, join unions, or to resist employer demands, and so on.

As Bakunin argued, *"the property owners... are **likewise** forced to seek out and purchase labour... **but not in the same measure** ... [there is no] equality between those who offer their labour and those who purchase it."* [**Op. Cit.**, p. 183] This ensures that any "free agreements" made benefit the capitalists more than the workers (see the next section on periods of full employment, when conditions tilt in favour of working people).

Lastly, there is the issue of inequalities in wealth and so resources. The capitalist generally has more resources to fall back on during strikes and while waiting to find employees (for example, large companies with many factories can swap production to their other factories if one goes on strike). And by having more resources to fall back on, the capitalist can hold out longer than the worker, so placing the employer in a stronger bargaining position and so ensuring labour contracts favour them. This was recognised by Adam Smith:

> *"It is not difficult to foresee which of the two parties [workers and capitalists] must, upon all ordinary occasions... force the other into a compliance with their terms... In all such disputes the masters can hold out much longer... though they did not employ a single workman [the masters] could generally live a year or two upon the stocks which they already acquired. Many workmen could not subsist a week, few could subsist a month, and scare any a year without employment. In the long-run the workman may be as necessary to his master as his master is to him; but the necessity is not so immediate ... [I]n disputes with their workmen, masters must generally have the advantage."* [**Wealth of Nations**, pp. 59-60]

How little things have changed.

So, while it is definitely the case that no one forces you to work for them, the capitalist system is such that you have little choice but to sell your liberty and labour on the "free market." Not only this, but the labour market (which is what makes capitalism capitalism) is (usually) skewed in favour of the employer, so ensuring that any "free agreements" made on it favour the boss and result in the workers submitting to domination and exploitation. This is why anarchists support collective organisation (such as unions) and resistance (such as strikes), direct action and solidarity to make us as, if not more, powerful than our exploiters and win important reforms and improvements (and, ultimately, change society), even when faced with the disadvantages on the labour market we have indicated. The despotism associated with property (to use Proudhon's expression) is resisted by those subject to it and, needless to say, the boss does not always win.

B.4.4 But what about periods of high demand for labour?

Of course there are periods when the demand for labour exceeds supply, but these periods hold the seeds of depression for capitalism, as workers are in an excellent position to challenge, both individually and collectively, their allotted role as commodities. This point is discussed in more detail in section C.7 (What causes the capitalist business cycle?) and so we will not do so here. For now it's enough to point out that during normal times (i.e. over most of the business cycle), capitalists often enjoy extensive authority over workers, an authority deriving from the unequal bargaining power between capital and labour, as noted by Adam Smith and many others.

However, this changes during times of high demand for labour. To illustrate, let us assume that supply and demand approximate each other. It is clear that such a situation is only good for the worker. Bosses cannot easily fire a worker as there is no one to replace them and the workers, either collectively by solidarity or individually by "exit" (i.e. quitting and moving to a new job), can ensure a boss respects their interests and, indeed, can push these interests to the full. The boss finds it hard to keep their authority intact or from stopping wages rising and causing a profits squeeze. In other words, as unemployment drops, workers power increases.

Looking at it another way, giving someone the right to hire and fire an input into a production process vests that individual with considerable power over that input unless it is costless for that input to move; that is unless the input is perfectly mobile. This is only approximated in real life for labour during periods of full employment, and so perfect mobility of **labour** costs problems for a capitalist firm because under such conditions workers are not dependent on a particular capitalist and so the level of worker effort is determined far more by the decisions of workers (either collectively or individually) than by managerial authority. The threat of firing cannot be used as a threat to increase effort, and hence production, and so full employment increases workers power.

With the capitalist firm being a fixed commitment of resources, this situation is intolerable. Such times are bad for business and so occur rarely with free market capitalism (we must point out that in neo-classical economics, it is assumed that all inputs – including capital – are perfectly mobile and so the theory ignores reality and assumes away **capitalist production** itself!).

During the last period of capitalist boom, the post-war period, we can see the breakdown of capitalist authority and the fear this held for the ruling elite. The Trilateral Commission's 1975 report, which attempted to "understand" the growing discontent among the general population, makes our point well. In periods of full employment, according to the report, there is *"an excess of democracy."* In other words, due to the increased bargaining power workers gained during a period of high demand for labour, people started thinking about and acting upon their needs as **humans,** not as commodities embodying labour power. This naturally had devastating effects on capitalist and statist authority: *"People no longer felt the same compulsion to obey those whom they had previously considered superior to themselves in age, rank, status, expertise, character, or talent".*

This loosening of the bonds of compulsion and obedience led to "previously passive or unorganised groups in the population, blacks, Indians, Chicanos, white ethnic groups, students and women... embark[ing] on concerted efforts to establish their claims to opportunities, rewards, and privileges, which they had not considered themselves entitled to before."

Such an "excess" of participation in politics of course posed a serious threat to the status quo, since for the elites who authored the report, it was considered axiomatic that "the effective operation of a democratic political system usually requires some measure of apathy and non-involvement on the part of some individuals and groups. ... In itself, this marginality on the part of some groups is inherently undemocratic, but it is also one of the factors which has enabled democracy to function effectively." Such a statement reveals the hollowness of the establishment's concept of 'democracy,' which in order to function effectively (i.e. to serve elite interests) must be "inherently undemocratic."

Any period where people feel empowered allows them to communicate with their fellows, identify their needs and desires, and resist those forces that deny their freedom to manage their own lives. Such resistance strikes a deadly blow at the capitalist need to treat people as commodities, since (to re-quote Polanyi) people no longer feel that it "is not for the commodity to decide where it should be offered for sale, to what purpose it should be used, at what price it should be allowed to change hands, and in what manner it should be consumed or destroyed." Instead, as thinking and feeling people, they act to reclaim their freedom and humanity.

As noted at the beginning of this section, the economic effects of such periods of empowerment and revolt are discussed in section C.7. We will end by quoting the Polish economist Michal Kalecki, who noted that a continuous capitalist boom would **not** be in the interests of the ruling class. In 1943, in response to the more optimistic Keynesians, he noted that "to maintain the high level of employment ... in the subsequent boom, a strong opposition of 'business leaders' is likely to be encountered ... lasting full employment is not at all to their liking. The workers would 'get out of hand' and the 'captains of industry' would be anxious 'to teach them a lesson'" because "under a regime of permanent full employment, 'the sack' would cease to play its role as a disciplinary measure. The social position of the boss would be undermined and the self assurance and class consciousness of the working class would grow. Strikes for wage increases and improvements in conditions of work would create political tension ... 'discipline in the factories' and 'political stability' are more appreciated by business leaders than profits. Their class interest tells them that lasting full employment is unsound from their point of view and that unemployment is an integral part of the normal capitalist system." [quoted by Malcolm C. Sawyer, **The Economics of Michal Kalecki,** p. 139 and p. 138]

Therefore, periods when the demand for labour outstrips supply are not healthy for capitalism, as they allow people to assert their freedom and humanity – both fatal to the system. This is why news of large numbers of new jobs sends the stock market plunging and why capitalists are so keen these days to maintain a "natural" rate of unemployment (that it has to be maintained indicates that it is **not** "natural"). Kalecki, we must point out, also correctly predicted

the rise of "a powerful bloc" between "big business and the rentier interests" against full employment and that "they would probably find more than one economist to declare that the situation was manifestly unsound." The resulting "pressure of all these forces, and in particular big business" would "induce the Government to return to ... orthodox policy." [Kalecki, quoted by Sawyer, **Op. Cit.**, p. 140] This is exactly what happened in the 1970s, with the monetarists and other sections of the "free market" right providing the ideological support for the business lead class war, and whose "theories" (when applied) promptly generated massive unemployment, thus teaching the working class the required lesson.

So, although detrimental to profit-making, periods of recession and high unemployment are not only unavoidable but are necessary to capitalism in order to "discipline" workers and "teach them a lesson." And in all, it is little wonder that capitalism rarely produces periods approximating full employment – they are **not** in its interests (see also section C.9). The dynamics of capitalism makes recession and unemployment inevitable, just as it makes class struggle (which creates these dynamics) inevitable.

B.4.5 But I want to be "left alone"!

It is ironic that supporters of laissez-faire capitalism, such as "Libertarians" and "anarcho"-capitalists, should claim that they want to be "left alone," since capitalism **never** allows this. As Max Stirner expressed it:

> "Restless acquisition does not let us take breath, take a calm **enjoyment**. We do not get the comfort of our possessions ... " [Max Stirner **The Ego and Its Own**, p. 268]

Capitalism cannot let us "take breath" simply because it needs to grow or die, which puts constant pressure on both workers and capitalists (see section D.4.1). Workers can never relax or be free of anxiety about losing their jobs, because if they do not work, they do not eat, nor can they ensure that their children will get a better life. Within the workplace, they are not "left alone" by their bosses in order to manage their own activities. Instead, they are told what to do, when to do it and how to do it. Indeed, the history of experiments in workers' control and self-management within capitalist companies confirms our claims that, for the worker, capitalism is incompatible with the desire to be "left alone." As an illustration we will use the **"Pilot Program"** conducted by General Electric between 1968 and 1972.

General Electric proposed the "Pilot Program" as a means of overcoming the problems they faced with introducing Numeric Control (N/C) machinery into its plant at Lynn River Works, Massachusetts. Faced with rising tensions on the shop floor, bottlenecks in production and low-quality products, GE management tried a scheme of "job enrichment" based on workers' control of production in one area of the plant. By June 1970 the workers' involved were "on their own" (as one manager put it) and "[i]n terms of group job enlargement this was when the Pilot Project really began, with immediate results in increased output and machine utilisation, and a reduction on manufacturing losses. As one union official remarked two years later, 'The fact that we broke down a traditional policy of GE [that the union could never have a hand in managing the business] was in itself satisfying, especially when we could throw success up to them to boot.'" [David Noble, **Forces of Production**, p. 295]

The project, after some initial scepticism, proved to be a great success with the workers involved. Indeed, other workers in the factory desired to be included and the union soon tried to get it spread throughout the plant and into other GE locations. The success of the scheme was that it was based on workers' managing their own affairs rather than being told what to do by their bosses – "We are human beings," said one worker, "and want to be treated as such." [quoted by Noble, **Op. Cit.**, p. 292] To be fully human means to be free to govern oneself in all aspects of life, including production.

However, just after a year of the workers being given control over their working lives, management stopped the project. Why? "In the eyes of some management supporters of the 'experiment,' the Pilot Program was terminated because management as a whole refused to give up any of its traditional authority … [t]he Pilot Program foundered on the basic contradiction of capitalist production: Who's running the shop?" [Noble, **Op. Cit.**, p. 318]

Noble goes on to argue that to GE's top management, "the union's desire to extend the program appeared as a step toward greater workers control over production and, as such, a threat to the traditional authority rooted in private ownership of the means of production. Thus the decision to terminate represented a defence not only of the prerogatives of production supervisors and plant managers but also of the power vested in property ownership." He notes that this result was not an isolated case and that the "demise of the GE Pilot Program followed the typical pattern for such 'job enrichment experiments'" [**Op. Cit.**, p. 318 and p. 320] Even though "[s]everal dozen well-documented experiments show that productivity increases and social problems decrease when workers participate in the work decisions affecting their lives" [Department of Health, Education and Welfare study quoted by Noble, **Op. Cit.**, p. 322] such schemes are ended by bosses seeking to preserve their own power, the power that flows from private property.

As one worker in the GE Pilot Program stated, "[w]e just want to be left alone." They were not – capitalist social relations prohibit such a possibility (as Noble correctly notes, "the 'way of life' for the management meant controlling the lives of others" [**Op. Cit.**, p. 294 and p. 300]). In spite of improved productivity, projects in workers' control are scrapped because they undermined both the power of the capitalists – and by undermining their power, you potentially undermine their profits too ("If we're all one, for manufacturing reasons, we must share in the fruits equitably, just like a co-op business." [GE Pilot Program worker, quoted by Noble, **Op. Cit.**, p. 295]).

As we argue in more detail in section J.5.12, profit maximisation can work against efficiency, meaning that capitalism can harm the overall economy by promoting less efficient production techniques (i.e. hierarchical ones against egalitarian ones) because it is in the interests of capitalists to do so and the capitalist market rewards that behaviour. This is because, ultimately, profits are unpaid labour. If you empower labour, give workers' control over their work then they will increase efficiency and productivity (they know how to do their job the best) but you also erode authority structures within the workplace. Workers' will seek more and more control (freedom naturally tries to grow) and this, as the Pilot Program worker clearly saw, implies a co-operative workplace in which workers', **not** managers, decide what to do with the surplus produced. By threatening power, you threaten profits (or, more correctly, who controls the profit and where it goes). With the control over production **and** who gets to control any surplus in danger, it is unsurprising that companies soon abandon such schemes and return to the old, less efficient, hierarchical schemes based on "Do what you are told, for as long as you are told." Such a regime is hardly fit for free people and, as Noble notes, the regime that replaced the GE Pilot Program was "designed to 'break' the pilots of their new found 'habits' of self-reliance, self-discipline, and self-respect." [**Op. Cit.**, p. 307]

Thus the experience of workers' control project within capitalist firms indicates well that capitalism cannot "leave you alone" if you are a wage slave.

Moreover, capitalists themselves cannot relax because they must ensure their workers' productivity rises faster than their workers' wages, otherwise their business will fail (see sections C.2 and C.3). This means that every company has to innovate or be left behind, to be put out of business or work. Hence the boss is not "left alone" – their decisions are made under the duress of market forces, of the necessities imposed by competition on individual capitalists. Restless acquisition – in this context, the necessity to accumulate capital in order to survive in the market – always haunts the capitalist. And since unpaid labour is the key to capitalist expansion, work must continue to exist and grow – necessitating the boss to control the working hours of the worker to ensure that they produce more goods than they receive in wages. The boss is not "left alone" nor do they leave the worker alone.

These facts, based upon the authority relations associated with private property and relentless competition, ensure that the desire to be "left alone" cannot be satisfied under capitalism.

As Murray Bookchin observes:

> "Despite their assertions of autonomy and distrust of state authority … classical liberal thinkers did not in the last instance hold to the notion that the individual is completely free from lawful guidance. Indeed, their interpretation of autonomy actually presupposed quite definite arrangements beyond the individual – notably, the laws of the marketplace. Individual autonomy to the contrary, these laws constitute a social organising system in which all 'collections of individuals' are held under the sway of the famous 'invisible hand' of competition. Paradoxically, the laws of the marketplace override the exercise of 'free will' by the same sovereign individuals who otherwise constitute the "collection of individuals." ["Communalism: The Democratic Dimension of Anarchism", pp. 1-17, **Democracy and Nature** no. 8, p. 4]

Human interaction is an essential part of life. Anarchism proposes to eliminate only undesired social interactions and authoritarian impositions, which are inherent in capitalism and indeed in any hierarchical form of socio-economic organisation (e.g. state socialism). Hermits soon become less than human, as social interaction enriches and develops individuality. Capitalism may attempt to reduce us to hermits, only "connected" by the market, but such a denial of our humanity and individuality inevitably feeds the spirit of revolt. In practice the "laws" of the market and the hierarchy of capital will never "leave one alone," but instead, crush one's individuality and freedom. Yet this aspect of capitalism conflicts with the human "instinct for freedom," as Noam Chomsky describes it, and hence there arises a counter-tendency toward radicalisation and rebellion among any oppressed people (see section J).

One last point. The desire to "be left alone" often expresses two drastically different ideas – the wish to be your own master and manage your own affairs and the desire by bosses and landlords to have more power over their property. However, the authority exercised by such owners over their property is also exercised over **those who use that property.** Therefore, the notion of "being left alone" contains two contradictory aspects within a class ridden and hierarchical society. Obviously anarchists are sympathetic to the first, inherently libertarian, aspect – the desire to manage your own life, in your own way – but we reject the second aspect and any implication that it is in the interests of the governed to leave those in power alone. Rather, it is in the interest of the governed to subject those with authority over them to as much control as possible – for obvious reasons.

Therefore, working people are more or less free to the extent that they **restrict** the ability of their bosses to be "left alone." One of the aims of anarchists within a capitalist society is **ensure** that those in power are **not** "left alone" to exercise their authority over those subject to it. We see solidarity, direct action and workplace and community organisation as a means of interfering with the authority of the state, capitalists and property owners until such time as we can destroy such authoritarian social relationships once and for all.

Hence anarchist dislike of the term "laissez-faire" – within a class society it can only mean protecting the powerful against the working class (under the banner of "neutrally" enforcing property rights and so **the power derived from them**). However, we are well aware of the other, libertarian, vision expressed in the desire to be "left alone." That is the reason we have discussed why capitalist society can never actually achieve that desire – it is handicapped by its hierarchical and competitive nature – and how such a desire can be twisted into a means of enhancing the power of the few over the many.

B.5

Is capitalism empowering and based on human action?

A key element of the social vision propounded by capitalism, particularly "libertarian" capitalism, is that of "voting" by the "customer," which is compared to political voting by the "citizen." According to Milton Friedman, *"when you vote in the supermarket, you get precisely what you voted for and so does everyone else."* Such "voting" with one's pocket is then claimed to be an example of the wonderful "freedom" people enjoy under capitalism (as opposed to "socialism," always equated by right-wingers with **state** socialism, which will be discussed in section H). However, in evaluating this claim, the difference between customers and citizens is critical.

The customer chooses between products on the shelf that have been designed and built by others for the purpose of profit. The consumer is the end-user, essentially a spectator rather than an actor, merely choosing between options created elsewhere by others. Market decision making is therefore fundamentally **passive** and **reactionary,** i.e. based on reacting to developments initiated by others. In contrast, the "citizen" is actively involved, at least ideally, in all stages of the decision making process, either directly or through elected delegates. Therefore, given decentralised and participatory-democratic organisations, decision making by citizens can be **pro-active,** based on human **action** in which one takes the initiative and sets the agenda oneself. Indeed, most supporters of the "citizen" model support it precisely **because** it actively involves individuals in participating in social decision making, so creating an educational aspect to the process and developing the abilities and powers of those involved.

In addition, the power of the consumer is not evenly distributed across society. Thus the expression "voting" when used in a market context expresses a radically different idea than the one usually associated with it. In political voting everyone gets one vote, in the market it is one vote per dollar. What sort of "democracy" is it that gives one person more votes than tens of thousands of others combined?

Therefore the "consumer" idea fails to take into account the differences in power that exist on the market as well as assigning an essentially passive role to the individual. At best they can act on the market as isolated individuals through their purchasing power. However, such a position is part of the problem for, as E. F. Schumacher argues, the *"buyer is essentially a bargain hunter; he is not concerned with the origin of the goods or the conditions under which they have been produced. His sole concern is to obtain the best value for money."* He goes on to note that the market *"therefore respects only the surface of society and its significance relates to the momentary situation as it exists there and then. There is no probing into the depths of things, into the natural or social facts that lie behind them."* [**Small is Beautiful**, p. 29]

Indeed, the "customer" model actually works **against** any attempt to "probe" the facts of things. Firstly, consumers rarely know the significance or implications of the goods they are offered because the price mechanism withholds such information from them. Secondly, because the atomistic nature of the market makes discussion about the "why" and "how" of production difficult – we get to choose between various "whats". Instead of critically evaluating the pros and cons of certain economic practices, all we are offered is the option of choosing between things already produced. We can only **re**-act when the damage is already done by picking the option which does least damage (often we do not have even that choice). And to discover a given products social and ecological impact we have to take a pro-active role by joining groups which provide this sort of information (information which, while essential for a rational decision, the market does not and cannot provide).

Moreover, the "consumer" model fails to recognise that the decisions we make on the market to satisfy our "wants" are determined by social and market forces. What we are capable of wanting is relative to the forms of social organisation we live in. For example, people choose to buy cars because General Motors bought up and destroyed the tram network in the 1930s and people buy "fast food" because they have no time to cook because of increasing working hours. This means that our decisions within the market are often restricted by economic pressures. For example, the market forces firms, on pain of bankruptcy, to do whatever possible to be cost-effective. Firms that pollute, have bad working conditions and so on often gain competitive advantage in so doing and other firms either have to follow suit or go out of business. A "race to the bottom" ensures, with individuals making "decisions of desperation" just to survive. Individual commitments to certain values, in other words, may become irrelevant simply because the countervailing economic pressures are simply too intense (little wonder Robert Owen argued that the profit motive was *a principle entirely unfavourable to individual and public happiness*").

And, of course, the market also does not, and cannot, come up with goods that we do not want in our capacity as consumers but desire to protect for future generations or because of ecological reasons. By making the protection of the planet, eco-systems and other such "goods" dependent on the market, capitalism ensures that unless we put our money where our mouth is we can have no say in the protection of such goods as eco-systems, historical sites, and so on. The need to protect such "resources" in the long term is ignored in favour of short-termism – indeed, if we do not "consume" such products today they will not be there tomorrow. Placed within a society that the vast majority of people often face difficulties making ends meet, this means that capitalism can never provide us with goods which we would like to see available as **people** (either for others or for future generations or just to protect the planet) but cannot afford or desire as **consumers.**

It is clearly a sign of the increasing dominance of capitalist ideology that the "customer" model is being transferred to the political arena. This reflects the fact that the increasing scale of political institutions has reinforced the tendency noted earlier for voters to become passive spectators, placing their "support" behind one or another "product" (i.e. party or leader). As Murray Bookchin comments, *"educated, knowledgeable citizens become reduced to mere taxpayers who exchange money for 'services.'"* [**Remaking Society**, p. 71] In practice, due to state centralism, this turns the political process into an extension of the market, with "citizens"

being reduced to "consumers." Or, in Erich Fromm's apt analysis, *"The functioning of the political machinery in a democratic country is not essentially different from the procedure on the commodity market. The political parties are not too different from big commercial enterprises, and the professional politicians try to sell their wares to the public."* [**The Sane Society**, pp. 186-187]

But does it matter? Friedman suggests that being a customer is **better** than being a citizen as you get "precisely" what you, and everyone else, wants.

The key questions here are whether people always get what they want when they shop. Do consumers who buy bleached newsprint and toilet paper **really** want tons of dioxins and other organochlorides in rivers, lakes and coastal waters? Do customers who buy cars **really** want traffic jams, air pollution, motorways carving up the landscape and the greenhouse effect? And what of those who do not buy these things? They are also affected by the decisions of others. The notion that only the consumer is affected by his or her decision is nonsense – as is the childish desire to get "precisely" what you want, regardless of the social impact.

Perhaps Friedman could claim that when we consume we also approve of its impact. But when we "vote" on the market we cannot say that we approved of the resulting pollution (or distribution of income or power) because that was not a choice on offer. Such changes are **pre-defined** or an aggregate outcome and can only be chosen by a collective decision. In this way we can modify outcomes we could bring about individually but which harm us collectively. And unlike the market, in politics we can **change our minds** and revert back to a former state, undoing the mistakes made. No such option is available on the market.

So Friedman's claims that in elections *"you end up with something different from what you voted for"* is equally applicable to the market place.

These considerations indicate that the "consumer" model of human action is somewhat limited (to say the least!). Instead we need to recognise the importance of the "citizen" model, which we should point out includes the "consumer" model within it. Taking part as an active member of the community does not imply that we stop making individual consumption choices between those available, all it does is potentially enrich our available options by removing lousy choices (such as ecology or profit, cheap goods or labour rights, family or career).

In addition we must stress its role in developing those who practice the "citizen" model and how it can enrich our social and personal life. Being active within participatory institutions fosters and develops an active, "public-spirited" type of character. Citizens, because they are making **collective** decisions have to weight other interests **as well as** their own and so consider the impact on themselves, others, society and the environment of possible decisions. It is, by its very nature, an educative process by which all benefit by developing their critical abilities and expanding their definition of self-interest to take into account themselves as part of a society and eco-system **as well as** as an individual. The "consumer" model, with its passive and exclusively private/money orientation develops few of people's faculties and narrows their self-interest to such a degree that their "rational" actions can actually (indirectly) harm them.

As Noam Chomsky argues, it is *"now widely realised that the economists 'externalities' can no longer be consigned to footnotes. No one who gives a moment's thought to the problems of contemporary society can fail to be aware of the social costs of consumption and production, the progressive destruction of the environment, the utter irrationality of the utilisation of contemporary technology, the inability of a system based on profit or growth maximisation to deal with needs that can only be expressed collectively, and the enormous bias this system imposes towards maximisation of commodities for personal use in place of the general improvement of the quality of life."* [**Radical Priorities**, pp. 190-1]

The "citizen" model takes on board the fact that the sum of rational individual decisions may not yield a rational collective outcome (which, we must add, harms the individuals involved and so works against their self-interest). Social standards, created and enriched by a process of discussion and dialogue can be effective in realms where the atomised "consumer" model is essentially powerless to achieve constructive social change, never mind protect the individual from "agreeing" to "decisions of desperation" that leave them and society as a whole worse off (see also sections E.3 and E.5).

This is **not** to suggest that anarchists desire to eliminate individual decision making, far from it. An anarchist society will be based upon individuals making decisions on what they want to consume, where they want to work, what kind of work they want to do and so on. So the aim of the "citizen" model is not to "replace" the "consumer" model, but only to improve the social environment within which we make our individual consumption decisions. What the "citizen" model of human action desires is to place such decisions within a social framework, one that allows each individual to take an active part in improving the quality of life for us all by removing "Hobson choices" as far as possible.

B.6

But won't decisions made by individuals with their own money be the best?

This question refers to an argument commonly used by capitalists to justify the fact that investment decisions are removed from public control under capitalism, with private investors making all the decisions. Clearly the assumption behind this argument is that individuals suddenly lose their intelligence when they get together and discuss their common interests. But surely, through debate, we can enrich our ideas by social interaction. In the marketplace we do not discuss but instead act as atomised individuals.

This issue involves the *"Isolation Paradox,"* according to which the very logic of individual decision-making is different from that of collective decision-making. An example is the *"tyranny of small decisions."* Let us assume that in the soft drink industry some companies start to produce (cheaper) non-returnable bottles. The end result of this is that most, if not all, the companies making returnable bottles lose business and switch to non-returnables. Result? Increased waste and environmental destruction.

This is because market price fails to take into account social costs

and benefits, indeed it **mis**-estimates them for both buyer/seller and to others not involved in the transaction. This is because, as Schumacher points out, the *"strength of the idea of private enterprise lies in its terrifying simplicity. It suggests that the totality of life can be reduced to one aspect – profits..."* [**Small is Beautiful**, p. 215] But life cannot be reduced to one aspect without impoverishing it and so capitalism *"knows the price of everything but the value of nothing."*

Therefore the market promotes "the tyranny of small decisions" and this can have negative outcomes for those involved. The capitalist "solution" to this problem is no solution, namely to act after the event. Only after the decisions have been made and their effects felt can action be taken. But by then the damage has been done. Can suing a company **really** replace a fragile eco-system? In addition, the economic context has been significantly altered, because investment decisions are often difficult to unmake.

In other words, the operations of the market provide an unending source of examples for the argument that the aggregate results of the pursuit of private interest may well be collectively damaging. And as collectives are made up of individuals, that means damaging to the individuals involved. The remarkable ideological success of "free market" capitalism is to identify the anti-social choice with self-interest, so that any choice in the favour of the interests which we share collectively is treated as a piece of self-sacrifice. However, by atomising decision making, the market often actively works against the self-interest of the individuals that make it up.

Game theory is aware that the sum of rational choices do not automatically yield a rational group outcome. Indeed, it terms such situations as "collective action" problems. By not agreeing common standards, a "race to the bottom" can ensue in which a given society reaps choices that we as individuals really don't want. The rational pursuit of individual self-interest leaves the group, and so most individuals, worse off. The problem is not bad individual judgement (far from it, the individual is the only person able to know what is best for them in a given situation). It is the absence of social discussion and remedies that compels people to make unbearable choices because the available menu presents no good options.

By **not** discussing the impact of their decisions with everyone who will be affected, the individuals in question have not made a better decision. Of course, under our present highly centralised statist and capitalist system, such a discussion would be impossible to implement, and its closest approximation – the election process – is too vast, bureaucratic and dominated by wealth to do much beyond passing a few toothless laws which are generally ignored when they hinder profits.

However, let's consider what the situation would be like under libertarian socialism, where the local community assemblies discuss the question of returnable bottles along with the workforce. Here the function of specific interest groups (such as consumer co-operatives, ecology groups, workplace Research and Development action committees and so on) would play a critical role in producing information. Knowledge, as Bakunin, Kropotkin, etc. knew, is widely dispersed throughout society and the role of interested parties is essential in making it available to others. Based upon this information and the debate it provokes, the collective decision reached would most probably favour returnables over waste. This would be a better decision from a social and ecological point of view, and one that would benefit the individuals who discussed and agreed upon its effects on themselves and their society.

In other words, anarchists think we have to take an active part in creating the menu as well as picking options from it which reflect our individual tastes and interests.

It needs to be emphasised that such a system does not involve discussing and voting on everything under the sun, which would paralyse all activity. To the contrary, most decisions would be left to those interested (e.g. workers decide on administration and day-to-day decisions within the factory), the community decides upon policy (e.g. returnables over waste). Neither is it a case of electing people to decide for us, as the decentralised nature of the confederation of communities ensures that power lies in the hands of local people.

This process in no way implies that "society" decides what an individual is to consume. That, like all decisions affecting the individual only, is left entirely up to the person involved. Communal decision-making is for decisions that impact both the individual and society, allowing those affected by it to discuss it among themselves as equals, thus creating a rich social context within which individuals can act. This is an obvious improvement over the current system, where decisions that often profoundly alter people's lives are left to the discretion of an elite class of managers and owners, who are supposed to "know best."

There is, of course, the danger of "tyranny of the majority" in any democratic system, but in a direct libertarian democracy, this danger would be greatly reduced, for reasons discussed in section I.5.6 (Won't there be a danger of a "tyranny of the majority" under libertarian socialism?).

B.7

What classes exist within modern society?

For anarchists, class analysis is an important means of understanding the world and what is going on in it. While recognition of the fact that classes actually exist is less prevalent now than it once was, this does not mean that classes have ceased to exist. Quite the contrary. As we'll see, it means only that the ruling class has been more successful than before in obscuring the existence of class.

Class can be objectively defined: the relationship between an individual and the sources of power within society determines his or her class. We live in a class society in which a few people possess far more political and economic power than the majority, who usually work for the minority that controls them and the decisions that affect them. This means that class is based both on exploitation **and** oppression, with some controlling the labour of others for their own gain. The means of oppression have been indicated in earlier parts of section B, while section C (What are the myths of capitalist economics?) indicates exactly how exploitation occurs within a society apparently based on free and equal exchange. In addition, it also highlights the effects on the economic system itself of this

exploitation. The social and political impact of the system and the classes and hierarchies it creates is discussed in depth in section D (How do statism and capitalism affect society?).

We must emphasise at the outset that the idea of the "working class" as composed of nothing but industrial workers is simply false. It is **not** applicable today, if it ever was. Power, in terms of hire/ fire and investment decisions, is the important thing. Ownership of capital as a means of determining a person's class, while still important, does not tell the whole story. An obvious example is that of the higher layers of management within corporations. They have massive power within the company, basically taking over the role held by the actual capitalist in smaller firms. While they may technically be "salary slaves" their power and position in the social hierarchy indicate that they are members of the ruling class in practice (and, consequently, their income is best thought of as a share of profits rather than a wage). Much the same can be said of politicians and state bureaucrats whose power and influence does not derive from the ownership of the means of production but rather then control over the means of coercion. Moreover, many large companies are owned by other large companies, through pension funds, multinationals, etc. (in 1945, 93% of shares were owned by individuals; by 1997, this had fallen to 43%). Needless to say, if working-class people own shares that does not make them capitalists as the dividends are **not** enough to live on nor do they give them any say in how a company is run).

For most anarchists, there are two main classes:

(1) **Working class** – those who have to work for a living but have no real control over that work or other major decisions that affect them, i.e. order-takers. This class also includes the unemployed, pensioners, etc., who have to survive on handouts from the state. They have little wealth and little (official) power. This class includes the growing service worker sector, most (if not the vast majority) of "white collar" workers as well as traditional "blue collar" workers. Most self-employed people would be included in this class, as would the bulk of peasants and artisans (where applicable). In a nutshell, the producing classes and those who either were producers or will be producers. This group makes up the vast majority of the population.

(2) **Ruling class** – those who control investment decisions, determine high level policy, set the agenda for capital and state. This is the elite at the top, owners or top managers of large companies, multinationals and banks (i.e., the capitalists), owners of large amounts of land (i.e. landlords or the aristocracy, if applicable), top-level state officials, politicians, and so forth. They have real power within the economy and/or state, and so control society. In a nutshell, the owners of power (whether political, social or economic) or the master class. This group consists of around the top 5-15% of the population.

Obviously there are "grey" areas in any society, individuals and groups who do not fit exactly into either the working or ruling class. Such people include those who work but have some control over other people, e.g. power of hire/fire. These are the people who make the minor, day-to-day decisions concerning the running of capital or state. This area includes lower to middle management, professionals, and small capitalists.

There is some argument within the anarchist movement whether this "grey" area constitutes another ("middle") class or not. Most anarchists say no, most of this "grey" area are working class, others (such as the British **Class War Federation**) argue it is a different class. One thing is sure, all anarchists agree that most people in this "grey" area have an interest in getting rid of the current system just as much as the working class (we should point out here that what is usually called "middle class" in the USA and elsewhere is nothing of the kind, and usually refers to working class people with decent jobs, homes, etc. As class is considered a rude word in polite society in the USA, such mystification is to be expected).

So, there will be exceptions to this classification scheme. However, most of society share common interests, as they face the economic uncertainties and hierarchical nature of capitalism.

We do not aim to fit all of reality into this class scheme, but only to develop it as reality indicates, based on our own experiences of the changing patterns of modern society. Nor is this scheme intended to suggest that all members of a class have identical interests or that competition does not exist between members of the same class, as it does between the classes. Capitalism, by its very nature, is a competitive system. As Malatesta pointed out, *"one must bear in mind that on the one hand the bourgeoisie (the property owners) are always at war amongst themselves ... and that on the other hand the government, though springing from the bourgeoisie and its servant and protector, tends, as every servant and every protector, to achieve its own emancipation and to dominate whoever it protects. Thus the game of the swings, the manoeuvres, the concessions and the withdrawals, the attempts to find allies among the people and against the conservatives, and among conservatives against the people, which is the science of the governors, and which blinds the ingenuous and phlegmatic who always wait for salvation to come down to them from above."* [**Anarchy**, p. 25]

However, no matter how much inter-elite rivalry goes on, at the slightest threat to the system from which they benefit, the ruling class will unite to defend their common interests. Once the threat passes, they will return to competing among themselves for power, market share and wealth. Unfortunately, the working class rarely unites as a class, mainly due to its chronic economic and social position. At best, certain sections unite and experience the benefits and pleasure of co-operation. Anarchists, by their ideas and action try to change this situation and encourage solidarity within the working class in order to resist, and ultimately get rid of, capitalism. However, their activity is helped by the fact that those in struggle often realise that *"solidarity is strength"* and so start to work together and unite their struggles against their common enemy. Indeed, history is full of such developments.

B.7.1 But do classes actually exist?

So do classes actually exist, or are anarchists making them up? The fact that we even need to consider this question points to the pervasive propaganda efforts by the ruling class to suppress class consciousness, which will be discussed further on. First, however, let's examine some statistics, taking the USA as an example. We have done so because the States has the reputation of being a land of opportunity and capitalism. Moreover, class is seldom talked about there (although its business class is **very** class conscious). Moreover, when countries have followed the US model of freer capitalism (for example, the UK), a similar explosion of inequality develops along side increased poverty rates and concentration of wealth into fewer and fewer hands.

There are two ways of looking into class, by income and by wealth. Of the two, the distribution of wealth is the most important to understanding the class structure as this represents your assets, what you own rather than what you earn in a year. Given that wealth is the source of income, this represents the impact and power of private property and the class system it represents. After all, while all employed workers have an income (i.e. a wage), their actual wealth usually amounts to their personal items and their house (if they are lucky). As such, their wealth generates little or no income, unlike the owners of resources like companies, land and patents. Unsurprisingly, wealth insulates its holders from personal economic crises, like unemployment and sickness, as well as gives its holders social and political power. It, and its perks, can also be passed down the generations. Equally unsurprisingly, the distribution of wealth is much more unequal than the distribution of income.

At the start of the 1990s, the share of total US income was as follows: one third went to the top 10% of the population, the next 30% gets another third and the bottom 60% gets the last third. Dividing the wealth into thirds, we find that the top 1% owns a third, the next 9% owns a third, and bottom 90% owns the rest. [David Schweickart, **After Capitalism**, p. 92] Over the 1990s, the inequalities in US society have continued to increase. In 1980, the richest fifth of Americans had incomes about ten times those of the poorest fifth. A decade later, they has twelve times. By 2001, they had incomes over fourteen times greater. [Doug Henwood, **After the New Economy**, p. 79] Looking at the figures for private family wealth, we find that in 1976 the wealthiest one percent of Americans owned 19% of it, the next 9% owned 30% and the bottom 90% of the population owned 51%. By 1995 the top 1% owned 40%, more than owned by the bottom 92% of the US population combined – the next 9% had 31% while the bottom 90% had only 29% of total (see Edward N. Wolff, **Top Heavy: A Study of Increasing Inequality in America** for details).

So in terms of wealth ownership, we see a system in which a very small minority own the means of life. In 1992 the richest 1% of households – about 2 million adults – owned 39% of the stock owned by individuals. The top 10%, owned over 81%. In other words, the bottom 90% of the population had a smaller share (23%) of investable capital of all kinds than the richest 1/2% (29%). Stock ownership was even more densely concentrated, with the richest 5% holding 95% of all shares. [Doug Henwood, **Wall Street: Class racket**] Three years later, *"the richest 1% of households ... owned 42% of the stock owned by individuals, and 56% of the bonds ... the top 10% together owned nearly 90% of both."* Given that around 50% of all corporate stock is owned by households, this means that 1% of the population *"owns a quarter of the productive capital and future profits of corporate America; the top 10% nearly half."* [Doug Henwood, **Wall Street**, pp. 66-7] Unsurprisingly, the Congressional Budget Office estimates that more than half of corporate profits ultimately accrue to the wealthiest 1 percent of taxpayers, while only about 8 percent go to the bottom 60 percent.

Henwood summarises the situation by noting that *"the richest tenth of the population has a bit over three-quarters of all the wealth in this society, and the bottom half has almost none – but it has lots of debt."* Most middle-income people have most of their (limited) wealth in their homes and if we look at non-residential wealth we find a *"very, very concentrated"* situation. The *"bottom half of the population claimed about 20% of all income in 2001 – but only 2% of non-residential wealth. The richest 5% of the population claimed about 23% of income, a bit more than the entire bottom half. But it owned almost two-thirds – 65% – of the wealth."* [**After the New Economy**, p. 122]

In terms of income, the period since 1970 has also been marked by increasing inequalities and concentration:

> *"According to estimates by the economists Thomas Piketty and Emmanuel Saez – confirmed by data from the Congressional Budget Office – between 1973 and 2000 the average real income of the bottom 90 percent of American taxpayers actually fell by 7 percent. Meanwhile, the income of the top 1 percent rose by 148 percent, the income of the top 0.1 percent rose by 343 percent and the income of the top 0.01 percent rose 599 percent."* [Paul Krugman, *"The Death of Horatio Alger"*, **The Nation**, January 5, 2004]

Doug Henwood provides some more details on income [**Op. Cit.**, p. 90]:

Changes in income, 1977-1999

	real income growth	Share of total income		
	1977-99	1977	1999	Change
poorest 20%	-9%	5.7%	4.2%	-1.5%
second 20%	+1	11.5	9.7	-1.8
middle 20%	+8	16.4	14.7	-1.7
fourth 20%	+14	22.8	21.3	-1.5
top 20%	+43	44.2	50.4	+6.2
top 1%	+115	7.3	12.9	+5.6

By far the biggest gainers from the wealth concentration since the 1980s have been the super-rich. The closer you get to the top, the bigger the gains. In other words, it is not simply that the top 20 percent of families have had bigger percentage gains than the rest. Rather, the top 5 percent have done better than the next 15, the top 1 percent better than the next 4 per cent, and so on.

As such, if someone argues that while the share of national income going to the top 10 percent of earners has increased that it does not matter because anyone with an income over $81,000 is in that top 10 percent they are missing the point. The lower end of the top ten per cent were not the big winners over the last 30 years. Most of the gains in the share in that top ten percent went to the top 1 percent (who earn at least $230,000). Of these gains, 60 percent went to the top 0.1 percent (who earn more than $790,000). And of these gains, almost half went to the top 0.01 percent (a mere 13,000 people who had an income of at least $3.6 million and an average income of $17 million). [Paul Krugman, *"For Richer"*, **New York Times**, 20/10/02]

All this proves that classes do in fact exist, with wealth and power concentrating at the top of society, in the hands of the few.

To put this inequality of income into some perspective, the average full-time Wal-Mart employee was paid only about $17,000 a year in 2004. Benefits are few, with less than half the company's workers covered by its health care plan. In the same year Wal-Mart's chief executive, Scott Lee Jr., was paid $17.5 million. In other words, every two weeks he was paid about as much as his average employee would earn after a lifetime working for him.

Since the 1970s, most Americans have had only modest salary increases (if that). The average annual salary in America, expressed in 1998 dollars (i.e., adjusted for inflation) went from $32,522 in 1970 to $35,864 in 1999. That is a mere 10 percent increase over nearly 30 years. Over the same period, however, according to Fortune magazine, the average real annual compensation of the top 100 C.E.O.'s went from $1.3 million – 39 times the pay of an average worker – to $37.5 million, more than 1,000 times the pay of ordinary workers.

Yet even here, we are likely to miss the real picture. The average salary is misleading as this does not reflect the distribution of wealth. For example, in the UK in the early 1990s, two-thirds of workers earned the average wage or below and only a third above. To talk about the "average" income, therefore, is to disguise remarkable variation. In the US, adjusting for inflation, average family income – total income divided by the number of families – grew 28% between 1979 and 1997. The median family income – the income of a family in the middle (i.e. the income where half of families earn more and half less) grew by only 10%. The median is a better indicator of how typical American families are doing as the distribution of income is so top heavy in the USA (i.e. the average income is considerably higher than the median). It should also be noted that the incomes of the bottom fifth of families actually fell slightly. In other words, the benefits of economic growth over nearly two decades have **not** trickled down to ordinary families. Median family income has risen only about 0.5% per year. Even worse, *"just about all of that increase was due to wives working longer hours, with little or no gain in real wages."* [Paul Krugman, *"For Richer"*, **Op. Cit.**]

So if America does have higher average or per capita income than other advanced countries, it is simply because the rich are richer. This means that a high average income level can be misleading if a large amount of national income is concentrated in relatively few hands. This means that large numbers of Americans are worse off economically than their counterparts in other advanced countries. Thus Europeans have, in general, shorter working weeks and longer holidays than Americans. They may have a lower average income than the United States but they do not have the same inequalities. This means that the median European family has a standard of living roughly comparable with that of the median U.S. family – wages may even be higher.

As Doug Henwood notes, *"[i]nternational measures put the United States in a disgraceful light ... The soundbite version of the LIS [Luxembourg Income Study] data is this: for a country th[at] rich, [it] ha[s] a lot of poor people."* Henwood looked at both relative and absolute measures of income and poverty using the cross-border comparisons of income distribution provided by the LIS and discovered that *"[f]or a country that thinks itself universally middle class [i.e. middle income], the United States has the second-smallest middle class of the nineteen countries for which good LIS data exists."* Only Russia, a country in near-total collapse was worse (40.9% of the population were middle income compared to 46.2% in the USA. Households were classed as poor if their incomes were under 50 percent of the national medium; near-poor, between 50 and 62.5 percent; middle, between 62.5 and 150 percent; and well-to-do, over 150 percent. The USA rates for poor (19.1%), near-poor (8.1%) and middle (46.2%) were worse than European countries like Germany (11.1%, 6.5% and 64%), France (13%, 7.2% and 60.4%) and Belgium (5.5%, 8.0% and 72.4%) as well as Canada (11.6%, 8.2% and 60%) and Australia (14.8%, 10% and 52.5%).

The reasons for this? Henwood states that the *"reasons are clear – weak unions and a weak welfare state. The social-democratic states – the ones that interfere most with market incomes – have the largest [middles classes]. The US poverty rate is nearly twice the average of the other eighteen."* Needless to say, "middle class" as defined by income is a very blunt term (as Henwood states). It says nothing about property ownership or social power, for example, but income is often taken in the capitalist press as the defining aspect of "class" and so is useful to analyse in order to refute the claims that the free-market promotes general well-being (i.e. a larger "middle class"). That the most free-market nation has the worse poverty rates **and** the smallest "middle class" indicates well the anarchist claim that capitalism, left to its own devices, will benefit the strong (the ruling class) over the weak (the working class) via "free exchanges" on the "free" market (as we argue in section C.7, only during periods of full employment – and/or wide scale working class solidarity and militancy – does the balance of forces change in favour of working class people. Little wonder, then, that periods of full employment also see falling inequality – see James K. Galbraith's **Created Unequal** for more details on the correlation of unemployment and inequality).

Of course, it could be objected that this relative measure of poverty and income ignores the fact that US incomes are among the highest in the world, meaning that the US poor may be pretty well off by foreign standards. Henwood refutes this claim, noting that *"even on absolute measures, the US performance is embarrassing. LIS researcher Lane Kenworthy estimated poverty rates for fifteen countries using the US poverty line as the benchmark ... Though the United States has the highest average income, it's far from having the lowest poverty rate."* Only Italy, Britain and Australia had higher levels of absolute poverty (and Australia exceeded the US value by 0.2%, 11.9% compared to 11.7%). Thus, in both absolute **and**

relative terms, the USA compares badly with European countries. [Doug Henwood, *"Booming, Borrowing, and Consuming: The US Economy in 1999"*, pp.120-33, **Monthly Review**, vol. 51, no. 3, pp. 129-31]

In summary, therefore, taking the USA as being the most capitalist nation in the developed world, we discover a class system in which a very small minority own the bulk of the means of life and get most of the income. Compared to other Western countries, the class inequalities are greater and the society is more polarised. Moreover, over the last 20-30 years those inequalities have increased spectacularly. The ruling elite have become richer and wealth has flooded upwards rather than trickled down.

The cause of the increase in wealth and income polarisation is not hard to find. It is due to the increased economic and political power of the capitalist class and the weakened position of working class people. As anarchists have long argued, any "free contract" between the powerful and the powerless will benefit the former far more than the latter. This means that if the working class's economic and social power is weakened then we will be in a bad position to retain a given share of the wealth we produce but is owned by our bosses and accumulates in the hands of the few.

Unsurprisingly, therefore, there has been an increase in the share of total income going to capital (i.e., interest, dividends, and rent) and a decrease in the amount going to labour (wages, salaries, and benefits). Moreover, an increasing part of the share to labour is accruing to high-level management (in electronics, for example, top executives used to pay themselves 42 times the average worker in 1991, a mere 5 years later it was 220 times as much).

Since the start of the 1980s, unemployment and globalisation has weakened the economic and social power of the working class. Due to the decline in the unions and general labour militancy, wages at the bottom have stagnated (real pay for most US workers is lower in 2005 than it was in 1973!). This, combined with "trickle-down" economic policies of tax cuts for the wealthy, tax raises for the working classes, the maintaining of a "natural" law of unemployment (which weakens unions and workers power) and cutbacks in social programs, has seriously eroded living standards for all but the upper strata – a process that is clearly leading toward social breakdown, with effects that will be discussed later (see section D.9).

Little wonder Proudhon argued that the law of supply and demand was a *"deceitful law ... suitable only for assuring the victory of the strong over the weak, of those who own property over those who own nothing."* [quoted by Alan Ritter, **The Political Thought of Pierre-Joseph Proudhon**, p. 121]

B.7.2 Does social mobility make up for class inequality?

Faced with the massive differences between classes under capitalism we highlighted in the last section, many supporters of capitalism still deny the obvious. They do so by confusing a **caste** system with a **class** system. In a caste system, those born into it stay in it all their lives. In a class system, the membership of classes can and does change over time.

Therefore, it is claimed, what is important is not the existence of classes but of social mobility (usually reflected in income mobility). According to this argument, if there is a high level of social/income mobility then the degree of inequality in any given year is unimportant. This is because the redistribution of income over a person's life time would be very even. Thus the inequalities of income and wealth of capitalism does not matter as capitalism has high social mobility.

Milton Friedman puts the argument in this way:

> "Consider two societies that have the same distribution of annual income. In one there is a great mobility and change so that the position of particular families in the income hierarchy varies widely from year to year. In the other, there is great rigidity so that each family stays in the same position. Clearly, in any meaningful sense, the second would be the more unequal society. The one kind of inequality is a sign of dynamic change, social mobility, equality of opportunity; the other of a status society. The confusion behind these two kinds of inequality is particularly important, precisely because competitive free-enterprise capitalism tends to substitute the one for the other." [**Capitalism and Freedom**, p. 171]

As with so many things, Friedman is wrong in his assertion (and that is all it is, no evidence is provided). The more free market capitalist regimes have **less** social mobility than those, like Western Europe, which have extensive social intervention in the economy. As an added irony, the facts suggest that implementing Friedman's suggested policies in favour of his beloved "competitive free-enterprise capitalism" has made social mobility less, not greater. In effect, as with so many things, Friedman ensured the refutation of his own dogmas.

Taking the USA as an example (usually considered one of the most capitalist countries in the world) there is income mobility, but not enough to make income inequality irrelevant. Census data show that 81.6 percent of those families who were in the bottom quintile of the income distribution in 1985 were still there in the next year; for the top quintile, it was 76.3 percent.

Over longer time periods, there is more mixing but still not that much and those who do slip into different quintiles are typically at the borders of their category (e.g. those dropping out of the top quintile are typically at the bottom of that group). Only around 5% of families rise from bottom to top, or fall from top to bottom. In other words, the class structure of a modern capitalist society is pretty solid and "much of the movement up and down represents fluctuations around a fairly fixed long term distribution." [Paul Krugman, **Peddling Prosperity**, p. 143]

Perhaps under a "pure" capitalist system things would be different? Ronald Reagan helped make capitalism more "free market" in the 1980s, but there is no indication that income mobility increased significantly during that time. In fact, according to one study by Greg Duncan of the University of Michigan, the middle class shrank during the 1980s, with fewer poor families moving up or rich families moving down. Duncan compared two periods. During the first period (1975 to 1980) incomes were more equal than they are today. In the second (1981 to 1985) income inequality began

soaring. In this period there was a reduction in income mobility upward from low to medium incomes of over 10%.

Here are the exact figures [cited by Paul Krugman, "The Rich, the Right, and the Facts," **The American Prospect** no. 11, Fall 1992, pp. 19-31]:

Percentages of families making transitions to and from middle class (5-year period before and after 1980)

Transition	Before 1980	After 1980
Middle income to low income	8.5	9.8
Middle income to high income	5.8	6.8
Low income to middle income	35.1	24.6
High income to middle income	30.8	27.6

Writing in 2004, Krugman returned to this subject. The intervening twelve years had made things worse. America, he notes, is "more of a caste society than we like to think. And the caste lines have lately become a lot more rigid." Before the rise of neo-liberalism in the 1980s, America had more intergenerational mobility. "A classic 1978 survey found that among adult men whose fathers were in the bottom 25 percent of the population as ranked by social and economic status, 23 percent had made it into the top 25 percent. In other words, during the first thirty years or so after World War II, the American dream of upward mobility was a real experience for many people." However, a new survey of today's adult men "finds that this number has dropped to only 10 percent. That is, over the past generation upward mobility has fallen drastically. Very few children of the lower class are making their way to even moderate affluence. This goes along with other studies indicating that rags-to-riches stories have become vanishingly rare, and that the correlation between fathers' and sons' incomes has risen in recent decades. In modern America, it seems, you're quite likely to stay in the social and economic class into which you were born." [Paul Krugman, "The Death of Horatio Alger", **The Nation**, January 5, 2004]

British Keynesian economist Will Hutton quotes US data from 2000-1 which "compare[s] the mobility of workers in America with the four biggest European economies and three Nordic economies." The US "has the lowest share of workers moving from the bottom fifth of workers into the second fifth, the lowest share moving into the top 60 per cent and the highest share unable to sustain full-time employment." He cites an OECD study which "confirms the poor rates of relative upward mobility for very low-paid American workers; it also found that full-time workers in Britain, Italy and Germany enjoy much more rapid growth in their earnings than those in the US ... However, downward mobility was more marked in the US; American workers are more likely to suffer a reduction in their real earnings than workers in Europe." Thus even the OECD (the "high priest of deregulation") was "forced to conclude that countries with more deregulated labour and product markets (pre-eminently the US) do not appear to have higher relative mobility, nor do low-paid workers in these economies experience more upward mobility. The OECD is pulling its punches. The US experience is worse than Europe's." Numerous studies have shown that "either there is no difference" in income mobility between the USA and Europe "or that there is less mobility in the US." [**The World We're In**, pp. 166-7]

Little wonder, then, that Doug Henwood argues that *"the final appeal of apologists of the American way is an appeal to our legendary mobility"* fails. In fact, *"people generally don't move far from the income class they are born into, and there is little difference between US and European mobility patterns. In fact, the United States has the largest share of what the OECD called 'low-wage' workers, and the poorest performance on the emergence from the wage cellar of any country it studied."* [**Op. Cit.**, p. 130]

Indeed, *"both the US and British poor were more likely to stay poor for a long period of time: almost half of all people who were poor for one year stayed poor for five or more years, compared with 30% in Canada and 36% in Germany. And, despite claims of great upward mobility in the US, 45% of the poor rose out of poverty in a given year, compared with 45% in the UK, 53% in Germany, and 56% in Canada. And of those who did exit poverty, 15% of Americans were likely to make a round trip back under the poverty line, compared with 16% in Germany, 10% in the UK, and 7% in Canada."* [Doug Henwood, **After the New Economy**, pp. 136-7]

A 2005 study of income mobility by researchers at the London School of Economics (on behalf of the educational charity the Sutton Trust) confirms that the more free market a country, the worse is its levels of social mobility. [Jo Blanden, Paul Gregg and Stephen Machin, **Intergenerational Mobility in Europe and North America**, April, 2005] They found that Britain has one of the worst records for social mobility in the developed world, beaten only by the USA out of eight European and North American countries. Norway was the best followed by Denmark, Sweden, Finland, Germany and Canada.

This means that children born to poor families in Britain and the USA are less likely to fulfil their full potential than in other countries and are less likely to break free of their backgrounds than in the past. In other words, we find it harder to earn more money and get better jobs than our parents. Moreover, not only is social mobility in Britain much lower than in other advanced countries, it is actually declining and has fallen markedly over time. The findings were based on studies of two groups of children, one set born in the 1950s and the other in the 1970s. In the UK, while 17 per cent of the former made it from the bottom quarter income group to the top, only 11 per cent of the latter did so. Mobility in the Nordic countries was twice that of the UK. While only the US did worse than the UK in social mobility

The puzzle of why, given that there is no evidence of American exceptionalism or higher social mobility, the myth persists has an easy solution. It has utility for the ruling class in maintaining the system. By promoting the myth that people can find the path to the top easy then the institutions of power will not be questioned, just the moral character of the many who do not.

Needless to say, income mobility does not tell the whole story. Increases in income do not automatically reflect changes in class, far from it. A better paid worker is still working class and, consequently, still subject to oppression and exploitation during working hours. As such, income mobility, while important, does not address inequalities in power. Similarly, income mobility does not make up for a class system and its resulting authoritarian social relationships and inequalities in terms of liberty, health and social influence. And the facts suggest that the capitalist dogma of

"meritocracy" that attempts to justify this system has little basis in reality. Capitalism is a class ridden system and while there is some changes in the make-up of each class they are remarkably fixed, particularly once you get to the top 5-10% of the population (i.e. the ruling class).

Logically, this is not surprising. There is no reason to think that more unequal societies should be more mobile. The greater the inequality, the more economic power those at the top will have and, consequently, the harder it will be those at the bottom to climb upwards. To suggest otherwise is to argue that it is easier to climb a mountain than a hill! Unsurprisingly the facts support the common sense analysis that the higher the inequality of incomes and wealth, the lower the equality of opportunity and, consequently, the lower the social mobility.

Finally, we should point out even if income mobility was higher it does not cancel out the fact that a class system is marked by differences in **power** which accompany the differences in income. In other words, because it is possible (in theory) for everyone to become a boss this does not make the power and authority that bosses have over their workers (or the impact of their wealth on society) any more legitimate (just because everyone – in theory – can become a member of the government does not make government any less authoritarian). Because the membership of the boss class can change does not negate the fact that such a class exists.

Ultimately, using (usually highly inflated) notions of social mobility to defend a class system is unconvincing. After all, in most slave societies slaves could buy their freedom and free people could sell themselves into slavery (to pay off debts). If someone tried to defend slavery with the reference to this fact of social mobility they would be dismissed as mad. The evil of slavery is not mitigated by the fact that a few slaves could stop being slaves if they worked hard enough.

B.7.3 Why is the existence of classes denied?

It is clear, then, that classes do exist, and equally clear that individuals can rise and fall within the class structure – though, of course, it's easier to become rich if you're born in a rich family than a poor one. Thus James W. Loewen reports that *"ninety-five percent of the executives and financiers in America around the turn of the century came from upper-class or upper-middle-class backgrounds. Fewer than 3 percent started as poor immigrants or farm children. Throughout the nineteenth century, just 2 percent of American industrialists came from working-class origins"* [in *"Lies My Teacher Told Me"* citing William Miller, *"American Historians and the Business Elite,"* in **Men in Business**, pp. 326-28; cf. David Montgomery, **Beyond Equality**, pg. 15] And this was at the height of USA "free market" capitalism. According to a survey done by C. Wright Mills and reported in his book **The Power Elite**, about 65% of the highest-earning CEOs in American corporations come from wealthy families. Meritocracy, after all, does not imply a "classless" society, only that some mobility exists between classes. Yet we continually hear that class is an outmoded concept; that classes don't exist any more, just atomised individuals who all enjoy "equal opportunity," "equality before the law," and so forth. So what's going on?

The fact that the capitalist media are the biggest promoters of the "end-of-class" idea should make us wonder exactly **why** they do it. Whose interest is being served by denying the existence of classes? Clearly it is those who run the class system, who gain the most from it, who want everyone to think we are all "equal." Those who control the major media don't want the idea of class to spread because they themselves are members of the ruling class, with all the privileges that implies. Hence they use the media as propaganda organs to mould public opinion and distract the middle and working classes from the crucial issue, i.e., their own subordinate status. This is why the mainstream news sources give us nothing but superficial analyses, biased and selective reporting, outright lies, and an endless barrage of yellow journalism, titillation, and "entertainment," rather than talking about the class nature of capitalist society (see section D.3 – "How does wealth influence the mass media?")

The universities, think tanks, and private research foundations are also important propaganda tools of the ruling class. This is why it is virtually taboo in mainstream academic circles to suggest that anything like a ruling class even exists in the United States. Students are instead indoctrinated with the myth of a "pluralist" and "democratic" society – a Never-Never Land where all laws and public policies supposedly get determined only by the amount of "public support" they have – certainly not by any small faction wielding power in disproportion to its size.

To deny the existence of class is a powerful tool in the hands of the powerful. As Alexander Berkman points out, "[o]ur social institutions are founded on certain ideas; so long as the latter are generally believed, the institutions built on them are safe. Government remains strong because people think political authority and legal compulsion necessary. Capitalism will continue as long as such an economic system is considered adequate and just. The weakening of the ideas which support the evil and oppressive present day conditions means the ultimate breakdown of government and capitalism." ["Author's Foreword," **What is Anarchism?**, p. xii]

Unsurprisingly, to deny the existence of classes is an important means of bolstering capitalism, to undercut social criticism of inequality and oppression. It presents a picture of a system in which only individuals exist, ignoring the differences between one set of people (the ruling class) and the others (the working class) in terms of social position, power and interests. This obviously helps those in power maintain it by focusing analysis away from that power and its sources (wealth, hierarchy, etc.).

It also helps maintain the class system by undermining collective struggle. To admit class exists means to admit that working people share common interests due to their common position in the social hierarchy. And common interests can lead to common action to change that position. Isolated consumers, however, are in no position to act for themselves. One individual standing alone is easily defeated, whereas a **union** of individuals supporting each other is not. Throughout the history of capitalism there have been attempts by the ruling class – often successful – to destroy working class organisations. Why? Because in union there is power – power which can destroy the class system as well as the state and create a new world.

That's why the very existence of class is denied by the elite. It's part of their strategy for winning the battle of ideas and ensuring that people remain as atomised individuals. By "manufacturing consent" (to use Walter Lipman's expression for the function of the media), force need not be used. By limiting the public's sources of information to propaganda organs controlled by state and corporate elites, all debate can be confined within a narrow conceptual framework of capitalist terminology and assumptions, and anything premised on a different conceptual framework can be marginalised. Thus the average person is brought to accept current society as "fair" and "just," or at least as "the best available," because no alternatives are ever allowed to be discussed.

B.7.4 What do anarchists mean by "class consciousness"?

Given that the existence of classes is often ignored or considered unimportant ("boss and worker have common interests") in mainstream culture, its important to continually point out the facts of the situation: that a wealthy elite run the world and the vast majority are subjected to hierarchy and work to enrich this elite. To be class conscious means that we are aware of the objective facts and act appropriately to change them.

This is why anarchists stress the need for **"class consciousness,"** for recognising that classes exist and that their interests are in **conflict.** The reason why this is the case is obvious enough. As Alexander Berkman argues, "the interests of capital and labour are not the same. No greater lie was ever invented than the so-called 'identity of interests' [between capital and labour] ... labour produces all the wealth of the world ... [and] capital is owned by the masters is stolen property, stolen products of labour. Capitalist industry is the process of continuing to appropriate the products of labour for the benefit of the master class ... It is clear that your interests as a worker are **different** from the interests of your capitalistic masters. More than different: they are entirely opposite; in fact, contrary, antagonistic to each other. The better wages the boss pays you, the less profit he makes out of you. It does not require great philosophy to understand that." [**What is Anarchism?**, pp. 75-6]

That classes are in conflict can be seen from the post-war period in most developed countries. Taking the example of the USA, the immediate post-war period (the 1950s to the 1970s) were marked by social conflict, strikes and so forth. From the 1980s onwards, there was a period of relative social peace because the bosses managed to inflict a series of defeats on the working class. Workers became less militant, the trade unions went into a period of decline and the success of capitalism was proclaimed. If the interests of both classes were the same we would expect that all sections of society would have benefited more in the 1980s onwards than between the 1950s to 1970s. This is **not** the case. While income grew steadily across the board between 1950 and 1980s, since then wealth has flooded up to the top while those at the bottom found it harder to make ends meet.

Why do anarchists oppose the current system?

A similar process occurred in the 1920s when Alexander Berkman stated the obvious:

> "The masters have found a very effective way to paralyse the strength of organised labour. They have persuaded the workers that they have the same interests as the employers ... that what is good for the employer is good for his employees ... [that] the workers will not think of fighting their masters for better conditions, but they will be patient and wait till the employer can 'share his prosperity' with them. They will also consider the interests of 'their' country and they will not 'disturb industry' and the 'orderly life of the community' by strikes and stoppage of work. If you listen to your exploiters and their mouthpieces you will be 'good' and consider only the interests of your masters, of your city and country – but no one cares about **your** interests and those of your family, the interests of your union and of your fellow workers of the labouring class. 'Don't be selfish,' they admonish you, while the boss is getting rich by your being good and unselfish. And they laugh in their sleeves and thank the Lord that you are such an idiot." [**Op. Cit.**, pp. 74-5]

So, in a nutshell, class consciousness is to look after your own interest as a member of the working class. To be aware that there is inequality in society and that you cannot expect the wealthy and powerful to be concerned about anyone's interest except their own. That only by struggle can you gain respect and an increased slice of the wealth you produce but do not own. And that there is *"an irreconcilable antagonism"* between the ruling class and working class *"which results inevitably from their respective stations in life."* The riches of the former are *"based on the exploitation and subjugation of the latter's labour"* which means *"war between"* the two *"is unavoidable."* For the working class desires *"only equality"* while the ruling elite *"exist[s] only through inequality."* For the latter, *"as a separate class, equality is death"* while for the former *"the least inequality is slavery."* [Bakunin, **The Basic Bakunin**, p. 97 and pp. 91-2]

Although class analysis may at first appear to be a novel idea, the conflicting interests of the classes is **well** recognised on the other side of the class divide. For example, James Madison in the **Federalist Paper** #10 states that *"those who hold and those who are without have ever formed distinct interests in society."* For anarchists, class consciousness means to recognise what the bosses already know: the importance of solidarity with others in the same class position as oneself and of acting together as equals to attain common goals. The difference is that the ruling class wants to keep the class system going while anarchists seek to end it once and for all.

It could therefore be argued that anarchists actually want an **"anti-class"** consciousness to develop – that is, for people to recognise that classes exist, to understand **why** they exist, and act to abolish the root causes for their continued existence (*"class consciousness,"* argues Vernon Richards, *"but not in the sense of wanting to perpetuate classes, but the consciousness of their existence, an understanding of why they exist, and a determination, informed by knowledge and militancy, to abolish them."* [**The Impossibilities of Social Democracy**, p. 133]). In short, anarchists want to eliminate classes, not universalise the class of "wage worker" (which would presuppose the continued existence of capitalism).

More importantly, class consciousness does not involve "worker worship." To the contrary, as Murray Bookchin points out, *"[t]he worker begins to become a revolutionary when he undoes his [or her] 'workerness', when he [or she] comes to detest his class status here and now, when he begins to shed ... his work ethic, his character-structure derived from industrial discipline, his respect for hierarchy, his obedience to leaders, his consumerism, his vestiges of puritanism."* [**Post-Scarcity Anarchism**, p. 119] For, in the end, anarchists *"cannot build until the working class gets rid of its illusions, its acceptance of bosses and faith in leaders."* [Marie-Louise Berneri, **Neither East Nor West**, p. 19]

It may be objected that there are only individuals and anarchists are trying to throw a lot of people in a box and put a label like "working class" on them. In reply, anarchists agree, yes, there are "only" individuals but some of them are bosses, most of them are working class. This is an objective division within society which the ruling class does its best to hide but which comes out during social struggle. And such struggle is part of the process by which more and more oppressed people subjectively recognise the objective facts. And by more and more people recognising the facts of capitalist reality, more and more people will want to change them.

Currently there are working class people who want an anarchist society and there are others who just want to climb up the hierarchy to get to a position where they can impose their will to others. But that does not change the fact that their current position is that they are subjected to the authority of hierarchy and so can come into conflict with it. And by so doing, they must practise self-activity and this struggle can change their minds, what they think, and so they become radicalised. This, the radicalising effects of self-activity and social struggle, is a key factor in why anarchists are involved in it. It is an important means of creating more anarchists and getting more and more people aware of anarchism as a viable alternative to capitalism.

Ultimately, it does not matter what class you are, it's what you **believe in** that matters. And what you **do.** Hence we see anarchists like Bakunin and Kropotkin, former members of the Russian ruling class, or like Malatesta, born into an Italian middle class family, rejecting their backgrounds and its privileges and becoming supporters of working class self-liberation. But anarchists base their activity primarily on the working class (including peasants, self-employed artisans and so on) because the working class is subject to hierarchy and so have a real need to resist to exist. This process of resisting the powers that be can and does have a radicalising effect on those involved and so what they believe in and what they do **changes.** Being subject to hierarchy, oppression and exploitation means that it is in the working class people's *"own interest to abolish them. It has been truly said that 'the emancipation of the workers must be accomplished by the workers themselves,' for no social class will do it for them ... It is ... **the interest** of the proletariat to emancipate itself from bondage ... It is only by growing to a true realisation of their present position, by visualising their possibilities and powers, by learning unity and co-operation, and practising* *them, that the masses can attain freedom."* [Alexander Berkman, **Op. Cit.**, pp. 187-8]

We recognise, therefore, that only those at the bottom of society have a **self**-interest in freeing themselves from the burden of those at the top, and so we see the importance of class consciousness in the struggle of oppressed people for self-liberation. Thus, *"[f]ar from believing in the messianic role of the working class, the anarchists' aim is to **abolish** the working class in so far as this term refers to the underprivileged majority in all existing societies … What we do say is that no revolution can succeed without the active participation of the working, producing, section of the population … The power of the State, the values of authoritarian society can only be challenged and destroyed by a greater power and new values."* [Vernon Richards, **The Raven**, no. 14, pp. 183-4] Anarchists also argue that one of the effects of direct action to resist oppression and exploitation of working class people would be the **creation** of such a power and new values, values based on respect for individual freedom and solidarity (see sections J.2 and J.4 on direct action and its liberating potential).

As such, class consciousness also means recognising that working class people not only have an interest in ending its oppression but that we also have the power to do so. *"This power, the people's power,"* notes Berkman, *"is **actual**: it cannot be taken away, as the power of the ruler, of the politician, or of the capitalist can be. It cannot be taken away because it does not consist of possessions but in ability. It is the ability to create, to produce; the power that feeds and clothes the world, that gives us life, health and comfort, joy and pleasure."* The power of government and capital *"disappear when the people refuse to acknowledge them as masters, refuse to let them lord it over them."* This is *"the all-important **economic power**"* of the working class. [**Op. Cit.**, p. 87, p. 86 and p. 88]

This potential power of the oppressed, anarchists argue, shows that not only are classes wasteful and harmful, but that they can be ended once those at the bottom seek to do so and reorganise society appropriately. This means that we have the power to transform the economic system into a non-exploitative and classless one as *"only a productive class may be libertarian in nature, because it does not need to exploit."* [Albert Meltzer, **Anarchism: Arguments For and Against**, p. 23]

Finally, it is important to stress that anarchists think that class consciousness **must** also mean to be aware of **all** forms of hierarchical power, not just economic oppression. As such, class consciousness and class conflict is not simply about inequalities of wealth or income but rather questioning all forms of domination, oppression and exploitation.

For anarchists, *"[t]he class struggle does not centre around material exploitation alone but also around spiritual exploitation, … [as well as] psychological and environmental oppression."* [Bookchin, **Op. Cit.**, p. 151] This means that we do not consider economic oppression to be the only important thing, ignoring struggles and forms of oppression outside the workplace. To the contrary, workers are human beings, not the economically driven robots of capitalist and Leninist mythology. They are concerned about everything that affects them – their parents, their children, their friends, their neighbours, their planet and, very often, total strangers.

Section C
What are the myths of capitalist economics?

Section C – What are the myths of capitalist economics? 196

C.1 What is wrong with economics? 199
C.1.1 Is economics really value free? 204
C.1.2 Is economics a science? 209
C.1.3 Can you have an economics based on individualism? 212
C.1.4 What is wrong with equilibrium analysis? 215
C.1.5 Does economics really reflect the reality of capitalism? .. 218
C.1.6 Is it possible to have a non-equilibrium based capitalist economics? 223

C.2 Why is capitalism exploitative? 227
C.2.1 What is "surplus value"? 229
C.2.2 How does exploitation happen? 231
C.2.3 Is owning capital sufficient reason to justify profits? 234
C.2.4 Is profit the reward for the productivity of capital? 236
C.2.5 Do profits represent the contribution of capital to production? .. 239
C.2.6 Does interest represent the "time value" of money? 242
C.2.7 Are interest and profit not the reward for waiting? 247
C.2.8 Are profits the result of entrepreneurial activity and innovation? 251
C.2.9 Do profits reflect a reward for risk? 256

C.3 What determines the distribution between labour and capital? 259

C.4 Why does the market become dominated by Big Business? 262
C.4.1 How extensive is Big Business? 264
C.4.2 What are the effects of Big Business on society? 266
C.4.3 What does the existence of Big Business mean for economic theory and wage labour? 267

C.5 Why does Big Business get a bigger slice of profits? 270
C.5.1 Aren't the super-profits of Big Business due to its higher efficiency? 272

C.6 Can market dominance by Big Business change? 274

C.7 What causes the capitalist business cycle? 275
C.7.1 What role does class struggle play in the business cycle? .. 277
C.7.2 What role does the market play in the business cycle? ... 280
C.7.3 What role does investment play in the business cycle? ... 283

C.8 Is state control of money the cause of the business cycle? 286
C.8.1 Does this mean that Keynesianism works? 292
C.8.2 What happened to Keynesianism in the 1970s? 295
C.8.3 How did capitalism adjust to the crisis in Keynesianism? .. 297

C.9 Would laissez-faire capitalism reduce unemployment? 302
C.9.1 Would cutting wages reduce unemployment? 307
C.9.2 Is unemployment caused by wages being too high? 313
C.9.3 Are "flexible" labour markets the answer to unemployment? .. 317
C.9.4 Is unemployment voluntary? 323

C.10 Is "free market" capitalism the best way to reduce poverty? 324
C.10.1 Hasn't neo-liberalism benefited the world's poor? 328
C.10.2 Does "free trade" benefit everyone? 332
C.10.3 Does "free market" capitalism benefit everyone, *especially* working class people? .. 335
C.10.4 Does growth automatically mean people are better off? .. 338

C.11 Doesn't neo-liberalism in Chile prove that the free market benefits everyone? 342
C.11.1 Who benefited from Chile's "economic miracle"? 346
C.11.2 What about Chile's economic growth and low inflation? .. 349
C.11.3 Did neo-liberal Chile confirm capitalist economics? 350

C.12 Doesn't Hong Kong show the potentials of "free market" capitalism? 353

Section C
What are the myths of capitalist economics?

Within capitalism, economics plays an important ideological role. Economics has been used to construct a theory from which exploitation and oppression are excluded, by definition. We will attempt here to explain why capitalism is deeply exploitative. Elsewhere, in section B, we have indicated why capitalism is oppressive and will not repeat ourselves here.

In many ways economics plays the role within capitalism that religion played in the Middle Ages, namely to provide justification for the dominant social system and hierarchies. *"The priest keeps you docile and subjected,"* argued Malatesta, *"telling you everything is God's will; the economist says it's the law of nature."* They *"end up saying that no one is responsible for poverty, so there's no point rebelling against it."* [**Fra Contadini**, p. 21] Even worse, they usually argue that collective action by working class people is counterproductive and, like the priest, urge us to tolerate current oppression and exploitation with promises of a better future (in heaven for the priest, for the economist it is an unspecified "long run"). It would be no generalisation to state that if you want to find someone to rationalise and justify an obvious injustice or form of oppression then you should turn to an economist (preferably a "free market" one).

That is not the only similarity between the "science" of economics and religion. Like religion, its basis in science is usually lacking and its theories more based upon "leaps of faith" than empirical fact. Indeed, it is hard to find a "science" more unconcerned about empirical evidence or building realistic models than economics. Just looking at the assumptions made in "perfect competition" shows that (see section C.1 for details). This means that economics is immune to such trivialities as evidence and fact, although that does not stop economics being used to rationalise and justify certain of these facts (such as exploitation and inequality). A classic example is the various ways economists have sought to explain what anarchists and other socialists have tended to call **"surplus value"** (i.e. profits, interest and rent). Rather than seek to explain its origin by an empirical study of the society it exists in (capitalism), economists have preferred to invent "just-so" stories, little a-historic parables about a past which never existed, used to illustrate (and so defend) a present class system and its inequalities and injustices. The lessons of a fairy tale about a society that has never existed are used as a guide for one which does and, by some strange co-incidence, they happen to justify the existing class system and its distribution of income. Hence the love of Robinson Crusoe in economics.

Ironically, this favouring of theory (ideology would be a better term) is selective as their exposure as fundamentally flawed does not stop them being repeated. As we discuss in section C.2, the neoclassical theory of capital was proven to be incorrect by left-wing economists. This was admitted by their opponents: *"The question that confronts us is not whether the Cambridge Criticism is theoretically valid. It is. Rather the question is an empirical or econometric one: is there sufficient substitutability within the system to establish neo-classical results?"* Yet this did not stop this theory being taught to this day and the successful critique forgotten. Nor has econometrics successfully refuted the analysis, as capital specified in terms of money cannot reflect a theoretical substance (neo-classical "capital") which could not exist in reality. However, that is unimportant for *"[u]ntil the econometricians have the answer for us, placing reliance upon neo-classical economic theory is a matter of faith,"* which, of course, he had [C. E. Ferguson, **The Neo-classical Theory of Production and Distribution**, p. 266 and p. xvii]

Little wonder that Joan Robinson, one of the left-wing economists who helped expose the bankruptcy of the neo-classical theory of capital, stated that economics was *"back where it was, a branch of theology."* [**Collected Economic Papers**, Vol. 4, p. 127] It remains there more than thirty years later:

> *"Economics is not a science. Many economists – particularly those who believe that decisions on whether to get married can be reduced to an equation – see the world as a complex organism that can be understood using the right differential calculus. Yet everything we know about economics suggests that it is a branch and not a particularly advanced one, of witchcraft."* [Larry Elliot and Dan Atkinson, **The Age of Insecurity**, p. 226]

The weakness of economics is even acknowledged by some within the profession itself. According to Paul Ormerod, *"orthodox economics is in many ways an empty box. Its understanding of the world is similar to that of the physical sciences in the Middle Ages. A few insights have been obtained which stand the test of time, but they are very few indeed, and the whole basis of conventional economics is deeply flawed."* Moreover, he notes the *"overwhelming empirical evidence against the validity of its theories."* It is rare to see an economist be so honest. The majority of economists seem happy to go on with their theories, trying to squeeze life into the Procrustean bed of their models. And, like the priests of old, make it hard for non-academics to question their dogmas as *"economics is often intimidating. Its practitioners … have erected around the discipline a barrier of jargon and mathematics which makes the subject difficult to penetrate for the non-initiated."* [**The Death of Economics**, p. ix, p. 67 and p. ix]

So in this section of our FAQ, we will try to get to the heart of modern capitalism, cutting through the ideological myths that supporters of the system have created around it. This will be a difficult task, as the divergence of the reality of capitalism and the economics that is used to explain (justify, more correctly) it is large. For example, the preferred model used in neo-classical economics is that of "perfect competition" which is based on a multitude of small firms producing homogenous products in a market which none of them are big enough to influence (i.e. have no market power). This theory was developed in the late 19th century when the real economy was marked by the rise of big business, a dominance which continues to this day. Nor can it be said that even small firms produce identical products – product differentiation and brand loyalty are key factors for any business. In other words, the model reflected (and still reflects) the exact opposite of reality.

In spite of the theoretical models of economics having little or no relation to reality, they are used to both explain and justify the current system. As for the former, the truly staggering aspect of economics for those who value the scientific method is the immunity of its doctrines to empirical refutation (and, in some cases, theoretical refutation). The latter is the key to not only understanding why economics is in such a bad state but also why it stays like that. While economists like to portray themselves as objective scientists, merely analysing the system, the development of their "science" has always been marked with apologetics, with rationalising the injustices of the existing system. This can be seen best in attempts by economists to show that Chief Executive Officers (CEOs) of firms, capitalists and landlords all deserve their riches while workers should be grateful for what they get. As such, economics has never been value free simply because what it says affects people and society. This produces a market for economic ideology in which those economists who supply the demand will prosper. Thus we find many *"fields of economics and economic policy where the responses of important economic professionals and the publicity given economic findings are correlated with the increased market demand for specific conclusions and a particular ideology."* [Edward S. Herman, *"The Selling of Market Economics,"* pp. 173-199, **New Ways of Knowing**, Marcus G. Raskin and Herbert J. Bernstein (eds.), p.192]

Even if we assume the impossible, namely that economists and their ideology can truly be objective in the face of market demand for their services, there is a root problem with capitalist economics. This is that it the specific social relations and classes produced by capitalism have become embedded into the theory. Thus, as an example, the concepts of the marginal productivity of land and capital are assumed to universal in spite the fact that neither makes any sense outside an economy where one class of people owns the means of life while another sells their labour to them. Thus in an artisan/peasant society or one based around co-operatives, there would be no need for such concepts for in such societies, the distinction between wages and profits has no meaning and, as a result, there is no income to the owners of machinery and land and no need to explain it in terms of the "marginal productivity" of either. Thus mainstream economics takes the class structure of capitalism as a natural, eternal, fact and builds up from there. Anarchists, like other socialists, stress the opposite, namely that capitalism is a specific historical phase and, consequently, there are no universal economic laws and if you change the system the laws of economics change. Unless you are a capitalist economist, of course, when the same laws apply no matter what.

In our discussion, it is important to remember that capitalist economics is **not** the same as the capitalist economy. The latter exists quite independently of the former (and, ironically, usually flourishes best when the policy makers ignore it). Dissident economist Steve Keen provides a telling analogy between economics and meteorology. Just as *"the climate would exist even if there were no intellectual discipline of meteorology, the economy itself would exist whether or not the intellectual pursuit of economics existed."* Both share *"a fundamental raison d'etre,"* namely *"that of attempting to understand a complex system."* However, there are differences. Like weather forecasters, *"economists frequently get their forecasts of the economic future wrong. But in fact, though weather forecasts are sometimes incorrect, overall meteorologists have an enviable record of accurate prediction – whereas the economic record is tragically bad."* This means it is impossible to ignore economics (*"to treat it and its practitioners as we these days treat astrologers"*) as it is a social discipline and so what we *"believe about economics therefore has an impact upon human society and the way we relate to one another."* Despite *"the abysmal predictive record of their discipline,"* economists *"are forever recommending ways in which the institutional environment should be altered to make the economy work better."* By that they mean make the real economy more like their models, as *"the hypothetical pure market performs better than the mixed economy in which we live."* [**Debunking Economics**, pp. 6-8] Whether this actually makes the world a better place is irrelevant (indeed, economics has been so developed as to make such questions irrelevant as what happens on the market is, by definition, for the best).

Here we expose the apologetics for what they are, expose the ideological role of economics as a means to justify, indeed ignore, exploitation and oppression. In the process of our discussion we will often expose the ideological apologetics that capitalist economics create to defend the status quo and the system of oppression and exploitation it produces. We will also attempt to show the deep flaws in the internal inconsistencies of mainstream economics. In addition, we will show how important reality is when evaluating the claims of economics.

That this needs to be done can be seen by comparing the promise of economics with its actual results when applied in reality. Mainstream economics argues that it is based on the idea of "utility" in consumption, i.e. the subjective pleasure of individuals. Thus production is, it is claimed, aimed at meeting the demands of consumers. Yet for a system supposedly based on maximising individual happiness ("utility"), capitalism produces a hell of a lot of unhappy people. Some radical economists have tried to indicate this and have created an all-embracing measure of well-being called the Index of Sustainable Economic Welfare (ISEW). Their conclusions, as summarised by Elliot and Atkinson, are significant:

> *"In the 1950s and 1960s the ISEW rose in tandem with per capita GDP. It was a time not just of rising incomes, but of greater social equity, low crime, full employment and expanding welfare states. But from the mid-1970s onwards the two measures started to move apart. GDP per head continued its inexorable rise, but the ISEW started to decline as a result of lengthening dole queues, social exclusion, the explosion in crime, habitat loss, environmental degradation and the growth of environment- and stress-related illness. By the start of the 1990s, the ISEW was almost back to the levels at which it started in the early 1950s."* [Larry Elliot and Dan Atkinson, **Op. Cit.**, p. 248]

So while capitalism continues to produce more and more goods and, presumably, maximises more and more individual utility, actual real people are being "irrational" and not realising they are, in fact, better off and happier. Ironically, when such unhappiness is pointed out most defenders of capitalism dismiss people's expressed woe's as irrelevant. Apparently **some** subjective evaluations are considered more important than others!

Given that the mid-1970s marked the start of neo-liberalism, the promotion of the market and the reduction of government interference in the economy, this is surely significant. After all, the *"global economy of the early 21st century looks a lot more like the economic textbook ideal than did the world of the 1950s ... All these changes have followed the advance of economists that the unfettered market is the best way to allocate resources, and that well-intentioned interventions which oppose market forces will actually do more harm than good."* As such, *"[w]ith the market so much more in control of the global economy now than fifty years ago, then if economists are right, the world **should be** a manifestly better place: it should be growing faster, with more stability, and income should go to those who deserve it."* However, *"[u]nfortunately, the world refuses to dance the expected tune. In particularly, the final ten years of the 20th century were marked, not by tranquil growth, but by crises."* [Steve Keen, **Op. Cit.**, p. 2] These problems and the general unhappiness with the way society is going is related to various factors, most of which are impossible to reflect in mainstream economic analysis. They flow from the fact that capitalism is a system marked by inequalities of wealth and power and so how it develops is based on them, not the subjective evaluations of atomised individuals that economics starts with. This in itself is enough to suggest that capitalist economics is deeply flawed and presents a distinctly flawed picture of capitalism and how it actually works.

Anarchists argue that this is unsurprising as economics, rather than being a science is, in fact, little more than an ideology whose main aim is to justify and rationalise the existing system. We agree with libertarian Marxist Paul Mattick's summation that economics is *"actually no more than a sophisticated apology for the social and economic **status quo**"* and hence the *"growing discrepancy between [its] theories and reality."* [**Economics, Politics and the Age of Inflation**, p. vii] Anarchists, unsurprisingly, see capitalism as a fundamentally exploitative system rooted in inequalities of power and wealth dominated by hierarchical structures (capitalist firms). In the sections that follow, the exploitative nature of capitalism is explained in greater detail. We would like to point out that for anarchists, exploitation is not more important than domination. Anarchists are opposed to both equally and consider them to be two sides of the same coin. You cannot have domination without exploitation nor exploitation without domination. As Emma Goldman pointed out, under capitalism:

> *"wealth means power; the power to subdue, to crush, to exploit, the power to enslave, to outrage, to degrade ... Nor is this the only crime ... Still more fatal is the crime of turning the producer into a mere particle of a machine, with less will and decision than his master of steel and iron. Man is being robbed not merely of the products of his labour, but of the power of free initiative, of originality, and the interest in, or desire for, the things he is making."*
> [**Red Emma Speaks**, pp. 66-7]

Needless to say, it would be impossible to discuss or refute **every** issue covered in a standard economics book or every school of economics. As economist Nicholas Kaldor notes, *"[e]ach year new fashions sweep the 'politico-economic complex' only to disappear again with equal suddenness ... These sudden bursts of fashion are a sure sign of the 'pre-scientific' stage [economics is in], where any crazy idea can get a hearing simply because nothing is known with sufficient confidence to rule it out."* [**The Essential Kaldor**, p. 377] We will have to concentrate on key issues like the flaws in mainstream economics, why capitalism is exploitative, the existence and role of economic power, the business cycle, unemployment and inequality.

Nor do we wish to suggest that all forms of economics are useless or equally bad. Our critique of capitalist economics does not suggest that no economist has contributed worthwhile and important work to social knowledge or our understanding of the economy. Far from it. As Bakunin put it, property *"is a god"* and has *"its metaphysics. It is the science of the bourgeois economists. Like any metaphysics it is a sort of twilight, a compromise between truth and falsehood, with the latter benefiting from it. It seeks to give falsehood the appearance of truth and leads truth to falsehood."* [**The Political Philosophy of Bakunin**, p. 179] How far this is true varies form school to school, economist to economist. Some have a better understanding of certain aspects of capitalism than others. Some are more prone to apologetics than others. Some are aware of the problems of modern economics and *"some of the most committed economists have concluded that, if economics is to become less of a religion and more of a science, then the foundations of economics should be torn down and replaced"* (although, *"left to [their] own devices"*, economists *"would continue to build an apparently grand edifice upon rotten foundations."*). [Keen, **Op. Cit.**, p. 19]

As a rule of thumb, the more free market a particular economist or school of economics is, the more likely they will be prone to apologetics and unrealistic assumptions and models. Nor are we suggesting that if someone has made a positive contribution in one or more areas of economic analysis that their opinions on other subjects are correct or compatible with anarchist ideas. It is possible to present a correct analysis of capitalism or capitalist economics while, at the same time, being blind to the problems of Keynesian economics or the horrors of Stalinism. As such, our quoting of certain critical economists does not imply agreement with their political opinions or policy suggestions.

Then there is the issue of what do we mean by the term "capitalist economics"? Basically, any form of economic theory which seeks to rationalise and defend capitalism. This can go from the extreme of free market capitalist economics (such as the so-called "Austrian" school and Monetarists) to those who advocate state intervention to keep capitalism going (Keynesian economists). We will not be discussing those economists who advocate state capitalism. As a default, we will take "capitalist economics" to refer to the mainstream "neoclassical" school as this is the dominant form of the ideology and many of its key features are accepted by the others. This seems applicable, given that the current version of capitalism being promoted is neo-liberalism where state intervention is minimised and, when it does happen, directed towards benefiting the ruling elite.

Lastly, one of the constant refrains of economists is the notion that the public is ignorant of economics. The implicit assumption behind this bemoaning of ignorance by economists is that the world should be run either by economists or on their recommendations. In section C.11 we present a case study of a nation, Chile, unlucky enough to have that fate subjected upon it. Unsurprisingly, this rule by economists could only be imposed as a result of a military coup and subsequent dictatorship. As would be expected, given the biases of economics, the wealthy did very well, workers less so (to put it mildly), in this experiment. Equally unsurprising, the system was proclaimed an economic miracle – before it promptly collapsed.

So this section of the FAQ is our modest contribution to making economists happier by making working class people less ignorant of their subject. As Joan Robinson put it:

> "In short, no economic theory gives us ready-made answers. Any theory that we follow blindly will lead us astray. To make good use of an economic theory, we must first sort out the relations of the propagandist and the scientific elements in it, then by checking with experience, see how far the scientific element appears convincing, and finally recombine it with our own political views. The purpose of studying economics is not to acquire a set of ready-made answers to economic questions, but to learn how to avoid being deceived by economists."
> [**Contributions to Modern Economics**, p. 75]

C.1
What is wrong with economics?

In a nutshell, a lot. While economists like to portray their discipline as "scientific" and "value free", the reality is very different. It is, in fact, very far from a science and hardly "value free." Instead it is, to a large degree, deeply ideological and its conclusions almost always (by a strange co-incidence) what the wealthy, landlords, bosses and managers of capital want to hear. The words of Kropotkin still ring true today:

> "Political Economy has always confined itself to stating facts occurring in society, and justifying them in the interest of the dominant class ... Having found [something] profitable to capitalists, it has set it up as a **principle**."
> [**The Conquest of Bread**, p. 181]

This is at its best, of course. At its worse economics does not even bother with the facts and simply makes the most appropriate assumptions necessary to justify the particular beliefs of the economists and, usually, the interests of the ruling class. This is the key problem with economics: it is **not** a science. It is **not** independent of the class nature of society, either in the theoretical models it builds or in the questions it raises and tries to answer. This is due, in part, to the pressures of the market, in part due to the assumptions and methodology of the dominant forms of economics. It is a mishmash of ideology and genuine science, with the former (unfortunately) being the bulk of it.

The argument that economics, in the main, is not a science is not

one restricted to anarchists or other critics of capitalism. Some economists are well aware of the limitations of their profession. For example, Steve Keen lists many of the flaws of mainstream (neoclassical) economics in his excellent book **Debunking Economics**, noting that (for example) it is based on a *"dynamically irrelevant and factually incorrect instantaneous static snap-shot"* of the real capitalist economy. [**Debunking Economics**, p. 197] The late Joan Robinson argued forcefully that the neoclassical economist *"sets up a 'model' on arbitrarily constructed assumptions, and then applies 'results' from it to current affairs, without even trying to pretend that the assumptions conform to reality."* [**Collected Economic Papers**, vol. 4, p. 25] More recently, economist Mark Blaug has summarised many of the problems he sees with the current state of economics:

> "Economics has increasing become an intellectual game played for its own sake and not for its practical consequences. Economists have gradually converted the subject into a sort of social mathematics in which analytical rigor as understood in math departments is everything and empirical relevance (as understood in physics departments) is nothing ... general equilibrium theory ... using economic terms like 'prices', 'quantities', 'factors of production,' and so on, but that nevertheless is clearly and even scandalously unrepresentative of any recognisable economic system ...
>
> "Perfect competition never did exist and never could exist because, even when firms are small, they do not just take the price but strive to make the price. All the current textbooks say as much, but then immediately go on to say that the 'cloud-cuckoo' fantasyland of perfect competition is the benchmark against which we may say something significant about real-world competition ... But how can an idealised state of perfection be a benchmark when we are never told how to measure the gap between it and real-world competition? It is implied that all real-world competition is 'approximately' like perfect competition, but the degree of the approximation is never specified, even vaguely ...
>
> "Think of the following typical assumptions: perfectly infallible, utterly omniscient, infinitely long-lived identical consumers; zero transaction costs; complete markets for all time-stated claims for all conceivable events, no trading of any kind at disequilibrium prices; infinitely rapid velocities of prices and quantities; no radical, incalculable uncertainty in real time but only probabilistically calculable risk in logical time; only linearly homogeneous production functions; no technical progress requiring embodied capital investment, and so on, and so on – all these are not just unrealistic but also unrobust assumptions. And yet they figure critically in leading economic theories."
> [*"Disturbing Currents in Modern Economics"*, **Challenge!**, Vol. 41, No. 3, May-June, 1998]

So neoclassical ideology is based upon special, virtually ad hoc, assumptions. Many of the assumptions are impossible, such as the popular assertion that individuals can accurately predict the future (as required by "rational expectations" and general equilibrium theory), that there are a infinite number of small firms in every market or that time is an unimportant concept which can be abstracted from. Even when we ignore those assumptions which are obviously nonsense, the remaining ones are hardly much better. Here we have a collection of apparently valid positions which, in fact, rarely have any basis in reality. As we discuss in section C.1.2, an essential one, without which neoclassical economics simply disintegrates, has very little basis in the real world (in fact, it was invented simply to ensure the theory worked as desired). Similarly, markets often adjust in terms of quantities rather than price, a fact overlooked in general equilibrium theory. Some of the assumptions are mutually exclusive. For example, the neo-classical theory of the supply curve is based on the assumption that some factor of production cannot be changed in the short run. This is essential to get the concept of diminishing marginal productivity which, in turn, generates a rising marginal cost and so a rising supply curve. This means that firms **within** an industry cannot change their capital equipment. However, the theory of perfect competition requires that in the short period there are no barriers to entry, i.e. that anyone **outside** the industry can create capital equipment and move into the market. These two positions are logically inconsistent.

In other words, although the symbols used in mainstream may have economic sounding names, the theory has no point of contact with empirical reality (or, at times, basic logic):

> "Nothing in these abstract economic models actually **works** in the real world. It doesn't matter how many footnotes they put in, or how many ways they tinker around the edges. The whole enterprise is totally rotten at the core: it has no relation to reality." [Noam Chomsky, **Understanding Power**, pp. 254-5]

As we will indicate, while its theoretical underpinnings are claimed to be universal, they are specific to capitalism and, ironically, they fail to even provide an accurate model of that system as it ignores most of the real features of an actual capitalist economy. So if an economist does not say that mainstream economics has no bearing to reality, you can be sure that what he or she tells you will be more likely ideology than anything else. "Economic reality" is not about facts; it's about faith in capitalism. Even worse, it is about blind faith in what the economic ideologues say about capitalism. The key to understanding economists is that they believe that if it is in an economic textbook, then it must be true – particularly if it confirms any initial prejudices. The opposite is usually the case.

The obvious fact that the real world is not like that described by economic text books can have some funny results, particularly when events in the real world contradict the textbooks. For most economists, or those who consider themselves as such, the textbook is usually preferred. As such, much of capitalist apologetics is faith-driven. Reality has to be adjusted accordingly.

A classic example was the changing positions of pundits and "experts" on the East Asian economic miracle. As these economies grew spectacularly during the 1970s and 1980s, the experts universally applauded them as examples of the power of free markets. In 1995, for example, the right-wing Heritage Foundation's index of economic freedom had four Asian countries in its top seven countries. The **Economist** explained at the start of 1990s that Taiwan and South Korea had among the least price-distorting regimes in the world. Both the Word Bank and IMF agreed, downplaying the presence of industrial policy in the region. This was unsurprising. After all, their ideology said that free markets would produce high growth and stability and so, logically, the presence of both in East Asia must be driven by the free market. This meant that, for the true believers, these nations were paradigms of the free market, reality not withstanding. The markets agreed, putting billions into Asian equity markets while foreign banks loaned similar vast amounts.

In 1997, however, all this changed when all the Asian countries previously qualified as "free" saw their economies collapse. Overnight the same experts who had praised these economies as paradigms of the free market found the cause of the problem – extensive state intervention. The free market paradise had become transformed into a state regulated hell! Why? Because of ideology – the free market is stable and produces high growth and, consequently, it was impossible for any economy facing crisis to be a free market one! Hence the need to disown what was previously praised, without (of course) mentioning the very obvious contradiction.

In reality, these economies had always been far from the free market. The role of the state in these "free market" miracles was extensive and well documented. So while East Asia *"had not only grown faster and done better at reducing poverty than any other region of the world … it had also been more stable,"* these countries *"had been successful not only in spite of the fact that they had not followed most of the dictates of the Washington Consensus [i.e. neo-liberalism], but **because** they had not."* The government had played *"important roles … far from the minimalist [ones] beloved"* of neo-liberalism. During the 1990s, things had changed as the IMF had urged a *"excessively rapid financial and capital market liberalisation"* for these countries as sound economic policies. This *"was probably the single most important cause of the [1997] crisis"* which saw these economies suffer meltdown, *"the greatest economic crisis since the Great Depression"* (a meltdown worsened by IMF aid and its underlying dogmas). Even worse for the believers in market fundamentalism, those nations (like Malaysia) that refused IMF suggestions and used state intervention has a *"shorter and shallower"* downturn than those who did not. [Joseph Stiglitz, **Globalisation and its Discontents**, p. 89, p. 90, p. 91 and p. 93] Even worse, the obvious conclusion from these events is more than just the ideological perspective of economists, it is that "the market" is not all-knowing as investors (like the experts) failed to see the statist policies so bemoaned by the ideologues of capitalism **after** 1997.

This is not to say that the models produced by neoclassical economists are not wonders of mathematics or logic. Few people would deny that a lot of very intelligent people have spent a lot of time producing some quite impressive mathematical models in economics. It is a shame that they are utterly irrelevant to reality. Ironically, for a theory that claims to be so concerned about allocating scarce resources efficiently, economics has used a lot of time and energy refining the analyses of economies which have not, do not, and will not ever exist. In other words, scare resources have been inefficiently allocated to produce waste.

Why? Perhaps because there is a demand for such nonsense? Some economists are extremely keen to apply their methodology in all sorts of areas outside the economy. No matter how inappropriate, they seek to colonise every aspect of life. One area, however, seems immune to such analysis. This is the market for economic theory. If, as economists stress, every human activity can be analysed by economics then why not the demand and supply of economics itself? Perhaps because if that was done some uncomfortable truths would be discovered?

Basic supply and demand theory would indicate that those economic theories which have utility to others would be provided by economists. In a system with inequalities of wealth, effective demand is skewed in favour of the wealthy. Given these basic assumptions, we would predict that only these forms of economists which favour the requirements of the wealthy would gain dominance as these meet the (effective) demand. By a strange co-incidence, this is **precisely** what has happened. This did and does not stop economists complaining that dissidents and radicals were and are biased. As Edward Herman points out:

> "Back in 1849, the British economist Nassau Senior chided those defending trade unions and minimum wage regulations for expounding an 'economics of the poor.' The idea that he and his establishment confreres were putting forth an 'economics of the rich' never occurred to him; he thought of himself as a scientist and spokesperson of true principles. This self-deception pervaded mainstream economics up to the time of the Keynesian Revolution of the 1930s. Keynesian economics, though quickly tamed into an instrument of service to the capitalist state, was disturbing in its stress on the inherent instability of capitalism, the tendency toward chronic unemployment, and the need for substantial government intervention to maintain viability. With the resurgent capitalism of the past 50 years, Keynesian ideas, and their implicit call for intervention, have been under incessant attack, and, in the intellectual counterrevolution led by the Chicago School, the traditional laissez-faire ('let-the-fur-fly') economics of the rich has been re-established as the core of mainstream economics."
> [**The Economics of the Rich**]

Herman goes on to ask "[w]hy do the economists serve the rich?" and argues that "[f]or one thing, the leading economists are among the rich, and others seek advancement to similar heights. Chicago School economist Gary Becker was on to something when he argued that economic motives explain a lot of actions frequently attributed to other forces. He of course never applied this idea to economics as a profession." There are a great many well paying think tanks, research posts, consultancies and so on that create an "'effective demand' that should elicit an appropriate supply resource."

Elsewhere, Herman notes the "class links of these professionals to the business community were strong and the ideological element was realised in the neoclassical competitive model ... Spin-off negative effects on the lower classes were part of the 'price of

progress.' It was the elite orientation of these questions [asked by economics], premises, and the central paradigm [of economic theory] that caused matters like unemployment, mass poverty, and work hazards to escape the net of mainstream economist interest until well into the twentieth century." Moreover, "the economics profession in the years 1880-1930 was by and large strongly conservative, reflecting in its core paradigm its class links and sympathy with the dominant business community, fundamentally anti-union and suspicious of government, and tending to view competition as the true and durable state of nature." [Edward S. Herman, "The Selling of Market Economics," pp. 173-199, **New Ways of Knowing**, Marcus G. Raskin and Herbert J. Bernstein (eds.),p. 179-80 and p. 180]

Rather than scientific analysis, economics has always been driven by the demands of the wealthy ("How did [economics] get instituted? As a weapon of class warfare." [Chomsky, **Op. Cit.**, p. 252]). This works on numerous levels. The most obvious is that most economists take the current class system and wealth/income distribution as granted and generate general "laws" of economics from a specific historical society. As we discuss in the next section, this inevitably skews the "science" into ideology and apologetics. The analysis is also (almost inevitably) based on individualistic assumptions, ignoring or downplaying the key issues of groups, organisations, class and the economic and social power they generate. Then there are the assumptions used and questions raised. As Herman argues, this has hardly been a neutral process:

> "the theorists explicating these systems, such as Carl Menger, Leon Walras, and Alfred Marshall, were knowingly assuming away formulations that raised disturbing questions (income distribution, class and market power, instability, and unemployment) and creating theoretical models compatible with their own policy biases of status quo or modest reformism ... Given the choice of 'problem,' ideology and other sources of bias may still enter economic analysis if the answer is predetermined by the structure of the theory or premises, or if the facts are selected or bent to prove the desired answer." [**Op. Cit.**, p. 176]

Needless to say, economics is a "science" with deep ramifications within society. As a result, it comes under pressure from outside influences and vested interests far more than, say, anthropology or physics. This has meant that the wealthy have always taken a keen interest that the "science" teaches the appropriate lessons. This has resulted in a demand for a "science" which reflects the interests of the few, not the many. Is it **really** just a co-incidence that the lessons of economics are just what the bosses and the wealthy would like to hear? As non-neoclassical economist John Kenneth Galbraith noted in 1972:

> "Economic instruction in the United States is about a hundred years old. In its first half century economists were subject to censorship by outsiders. Businessmen and their political and ideological acolytes kept watch on departments of economics and reacted promptly to heresy, the latter being anything that seemed to threaten the sanctity of property, profits, a proper tariff policy and a balanced budget, or that suggested sympathy for unions,

public ownership, public regulation or, in any organised way, for the poor." [**The Essential Galbraith**, p. 135]

Is it **really** surprising that having the wealthy fund (and so control) the development of a "science" has produced a body of theory which so benefits their interests? Or that they would be keen to educate the masses in the lessons of said "science", lessons which happen to conclude that the best thing workers should do is obey the dictates of the bosses, sorry, the market? It is really just a co-incidence that the repeated use of economics is to spread the message that strikes, unions, resistance and so forth are counter-productive and that the best thing worker can do is simply wait patiently for wealth to trickle down?

This co-incidence has been a feature of the "science" from the start. The French Second Empire in the 1850s and 60s saw *"numerous private individuals and organisation, municipalities, and the central government encouraged and founded institutions to instruct workers in economic principles."* The aim was to *"impress upon [workers] the salutary lessons of economics."* Significantly, the *"weightiest motive"* for so doing *"was fear that the influence of socialist ideas upon the working class threatened the social order."* The revolution of 1848 *"convinced many of the upper classes that the must prove to workers that attacks upon the economic order were both unjustified and futile."* Another reason was the recognition of the right to strike in 1864 and so workers *"had to be warned against abuse of the new weapon."* The instruction *"was always with the aim of refuting socialist doctrines and exposing popular misconceptions. As one economist stated, it was not the purpose of a certain course to initiate workers into the complexities of economic science, but to define principles useful for 'our conduct in the social order.'"* The interest in such classes was related to the level of *"worker discontent and agitation."* The impact was less than desired: *"The future Communard Lefrancais referred mockingly to the economists ... and the 'banality' and 'platitudes' of the doctrine they taught. A newspaper account of the reception given to the economist Joseph Garnier states that Garnier was greeted with shouts of: 'He is an economist' ... It took courage, said the article, to admit that one was an economist before a public meeting."* [David I. Kulstein, "Economics Instruction for Workers during the Second Empire," pp. 225-234, **French Historical Studies**, vol. 1, no. 2, p. 225, p. 226, p. 227 and p. 233]

This process is still at work, with corporations and the wealthy funding university departments and posts as well as their own *"think tanks"* and paid PR economists. The control of funds for research and teaching plays it part in keeping economics the *"economics of the rich."* Analysing the situation in the 1970s, Herman notes that the *"enlarged private demand for the services of economists by the business community ... met a warm supply response."* He stressed that *"if the demand in the market is for specific policy conclusions and particular viewpoints that will serve such conclusions, the market will accommodate this demand."* Hence *"blatantly ideological models ... are being spewed forth on a large scale, approved and often funded by large vested interests"* which helps *"shift the balance between ideology and science even more firmly toward the former."* [**Op. Cit.**, p. 184, p. 185 and p. 179] The idea that "experts" funded and approved by the wealthy would

be objective scientists is hardly worth considering. Unfortunately, many people fail to exercise sufficient scepticism about economists and the economics they support. As with most experts, there are two obvious questions with which any analysis of economics should begin: *"Who is funding it?"* and *"Who benefits from it?"*

However, there are other factors as well, namely the hierarchical organisation of the university system. The heads of economics departments have the power to ensure the continuation of their ideological position due to the position as hirer and promoter of staff. As economics *"has mixed its ideology into the subject so well that the ideologically unconventional usually appear to appointment committees to be scientifically incompetent."* [Benjamin Ward, **What's Wrong with Economics?**, p. 250] Galbraith termed this *"a new despotism,"* which consisted of *"defining scientific excellence in economics not as what is true but as whatever is closest to belief and method to the scholarly tendency of the people who already have tenure in the subject. This is a pervasive test, not the less oppressive for being, in the frequent case, both self-righteous and unconscious. It helps ensure, needless to say, the perpetuation of the neoclassical orthodoxy."* [**Op. Cit.**, p. 135] This plays a key role in keeping economics an ideology rather than a science:

> *"The power inherent in this system of quality control within the economics profession is obviously very great. The discipline's censors occupy leading posts in economics departments at the major institutions ... Any economist with serious hopes of obtaining a tenured position in one of these departments will soon be made aware of the criteria by which he is to be judged ... the entire academic program ... consists of indoctrination in the ideas and techniques of the science."* [Ward, **Op. Cit.**, pp. 29-30]

All this has meant that the "science" of economics has hardly changed in its basics in over one hundred years. Even notions which have been debunked (and have been acknowledged as such) continue to be taught:

> *"The so-called mainline teaching of economic theory has a curious self-sealing capacity. Every breach that is made in it by criticism is somehow filled up by admitting the point but refusing to draw any consequence from it, so that the old doctrines can be repeated as before. Thus the Keynesian revolution was absorbed into the doctrine that, 'in the long run,' there is a natural tendency for a market economy to achieve full employment of available labour and full utilisation of equipment; that the rate of accumulation is determined by household saving; and that the rate of interest is identical with the rate of profit on capital. Similarly, Piero Sraffa's demolition of the neoclassical production function in labour and 'capital' was admitted to be unanswerable, but it has not been allowed to affect the propagation of the 'marginal productivity' theory of wages and profits.*
>
> *"The most sophisticated practitioners of orthodoxy maintain that the whole structure is an exercise in pure logic which has no application to real life at all. All the same they give their pupils the impression that they are*

being provided with an instrument which is valuable, indeed necessary, for the analysis of actual problems." [Joan Robinson, **Op. Cit.**, vol. 5, p. 222]

The social role of economics explains this process, for *"orthodox traditional economics ... was a plan for explaining to the privileged class that their position was morally right and was necessary for the welfare of society. Even the poor were better off under the existing system that they would be under any other ... the doctrine [argued] that increased wealth of the propertied class brings about an automatic increase of income to the poor, so that, if the rich were made poorer, the poor would necessarily become poorer too."* [Robinson, **Op. Cit.**, vol. 4, p. 242]

In such a situation, debunked theories would continue to be taught simply because what they say has a utility to certain sections of society:

> *"Few issues provide better examples of the negative impact of economic theory on society than the distribution of income. Economists are forever opposing 'market interventions' which might raise the wages of the poor, while defending astronomical salary levels for top executives on the basis that if the market is willing to pay them so much, they must be worth it. In fact, the inequality which is so much a characteristic of modern society reflects power rather than justice. This is one of the many instances where unsound economic theory makes economists the champions of policies which, is anything, undermine the economic foundations of modern society."* [Keen, **Op. Cit.**, p. 126]

This argument is based on the notion that wages equal the marginal productivity of labour. This is supposed to mean that as the output of workers increase, their wages rise. However, as we note in section C.1.5, this law of economics has been violated for the last thirty-odd years in the US. Has this resulted in a change in the theory? Of course not. Not that the theory is actually correct. As we discuss in section C.2.5, marginal productivity theory has been exposed as nonsense (and acknowledged as flawed by leading neo-classical economists) since the early 1960s. However, its utility in defending inequality is such that its continued use does not really come as a surprise.

This is not to suggest that mainstream economics is monolithic. Far from it. It is riddled with argument and competing policy recommendations. Some theories rise to prominence, simply to disappear again (*"See, the 'science' happens to be a very flexible one: you can change it to do whatever you feel like, it's that kind of 'science.'"* [Chomsky, **Op. Cit.**, p. 253]). Given our analysis that economics is a commodity and subject to demand, this comes as no surprise. Given that the capitalist class is always in competition within itself and different sections have different needs at different times, we would expect a diversity of economics beliefs within the "science" which rise and fall depending on the needs and relative strengths of different sections of capital. While, overall, the "science" will support basic things (such as profits, interest and rent are **not** the result of exploitation) but the actual policy recommendations will vary. This is not to say that certain individuals or schools will

not have their own particular dogmas or that individuals rise above such influences and act as real scientists, of course, just that (in general) supply is not independent of demand or class influence.

Nor should we dismiss the role of popular dissent in shaping the "science." The class struggle has resulted in a few changes to economics, if only in terms of the apologetics used to justify non-labour income. Popular struggles and organisation play their role as the success of, say, union organising to reduce the working day obviously refutes the claims made against such movements by economists. Similarly, the need for economics to justify reforms can become a pressing issue when the alternative (revolution) is a possibility. As Chomsky notes, during the 19th century (as today) popular struggle played as much of a role as the needs of the ruling class in the development of the "science":

> *"[Economics] changed for a number of reasons. For one thing, these guys had won, so they didn't need it so much as an ideological weapon anymore. For another, they recognised that they themselves needed a powerful interventionist state to defend industry form the hardships of competition in the open market – as they had always **had** in fact. And beyond that, eliminating people's 'right to live' was starting to have some negative side-effects. First of all, it was causing riots all over the place ... Then something even worse happened – the population started to organise: you got the beginning of an organised labour movement ... then a socialist movement developed. And at that point, the elites ... recognised that the game had to be called off, else they **really** would be in trouble ... it wasn't until recent years that laissez-faire ideology was revived again – and again, it was a weapon of class warfare ... And it doesn't have any more validity than it had in the early nineteenth century – in fact it has even **less**. At least in the early nineteenth century ... [the] assumptions had **some** relation to reality. Today those assumptions have **no** relation to reality."* [**Op. Cit.**, pp. 253-4]

Whether the *"economics of the rich"* or the *"economics of the poor"* win out in academia is driven far more by the state of the class war than by abstract debating about unreal models. Thus the rise of monetarism came about due to its utility to the dominant sections of the ruling class rather than it winning any intellectual battles (it was decisively refuted by leading Keynesians like Nicholas Kaldor who saw their predicted fears become true when it was applied – see section C.8). Hopefully by analysing the myths of capitalist economics we will aid those fighting for a better world by giving them the means of counteracting those who claim the mantle of "science" to foster the *"economics of the rich"* onto society.

To conclude, neo-classical economics shows the viability of an unreal system and this is translated into assertions about the world that we live in. Rather than analyse reality, economics evades it and asserts that the economy works *"as if"* it matched the unreal assumptions of neoclassical economics. No other science would take such an approach seriously. In biology, for example, the notion that the world can be analysed *"as if"* God created it is called Creationism and rightly dismissed. In economics, such people are generally awarded professorships or even the (so-called) Nobel prize in economics (Keen critiques the *as if"* methodology of economics in chapter 7 of his **Debunking Economics**). Moreover, and even worse, policy decisions will be enacted based on a model which has no bearing in reality – with disastrous results (for example, the rise and fall of Monetarism).

Its net effect to justify the current class system and diverts serious attention from critical questions facing working class people (for example, inequality and market power, what goes on in production, how authority relations impact on society and in the workplace). Rather than looking to how things are produced, the conflicts generated in the production process and the generation as well as division of products/surplus, economics takes what was produced as given, as well as the capitalist workplace, the division of labour and authority relations and so on. The individualistic neoclassical analysis by definition ignores such key issues as economic power, the possibility of a structural imbalance in the way economic growth is distributed, organisation structure, and so on.

Given its social role, it comes as no surprise that economics is not a genuine science. For most economists, the *"scientific method (the inductive method of natural sciences) [is] utterly unknown to them."* [Kropotkin, **Anarchism**, p. 179] The argument that most economics is not a science is not limited to just anarchists or other critics of capitalism. Many dissident economics recognise this fact as well, arguing that the profession needs to get its act together if it is to be taken seriously. Whether it could retain its position as defender of capitalism if this happens is a moot point as many of the theorems developed were done so explicitly as part of this role (particularly to defend non-labour income – see section C.2). That economics can become much broader and more relevant is always a possibility, but to do so would mean to take into account an unpleasant reality marked by class, hierarchy and inequality rather than logic deductions derived from Robinson Crusoe. While the latter can produce mathematical models to reach the conclusions that the market is already doing a good job (or, at best, there are some imperfections which can be counterbalanced by the state), the former cannot.

Anarchists, unsurprisingly, take a different approach to economics. As Kropotkin put it, *"we think that to become a science, Political Economy has to be built up in a different way. It must be treated as a natural science, and use the methods used in all exact, empirical sciences."* [**Evolution and Environment**, p. 93] This means that we must start with the world as it is, not as economics would like it to be. It must be placed in historical context and key facts of capitalism, like wage labour, not taken for granted. It must not abstract from such key facts of life as economic and social power. In a word, economics must reject those features which turn it into a sophisticated defence of the status quo. Given its social role within capitalism (and the history and evolution of economic thought), it is doubtful it will ever become a real science simply because it it did it would hardly be used to defend that system.

C.1.1 Is economics really value free?

Modern economists try and portray economics as a "value-free science." Of course, it rarely dawns on them that they are usually just taking existing social structures for granted and building economic dogmas around them, so justifying them. At best, as Kropotkin pointed out:

> *"[A]ll the so-called laws and theories of political economy are in reality no more than statements of the following nature: 'Granting that there are always in a country a considerable number of people who cannot subsist a month, or even a fortnight, without earning a salary and accepting for that purpose the conditions of work imposed upon them by the State, or offered to them by those whom the State recognises as owners of land, factories, railways, etc., then the results will be so and so.'*
>
> *"So far academic political economy has been only an enumeration of what happens under these conditions – without distinctly stating the conditions themselves. And then, having described **the facts** which arise in our society under these conditions, they represent to us these **facts** as rigid, **inevitable economic laws.**"* [**Anarchism**, p. 179]

In other words, economists usually take the political and economic aspects of capitalist society (such as property rights, inequality and so on) as given and construct their theories around it. At best. At worse, economics is simply speculation based on the necessary assumptions required to prove the desired end. By some strange coincidence these ends usually bolster the power and profits of the few and show that the free market is the best of all possible worlds. Alfred Marshall, one of the founders of neoclassical economics, once noted the usefulness of economics to the elite:

> *"From Metaphysics I went to Ethics, and found that the justification of the existing conditions of society was not easy. A friend, who had read a great deal of what are called the Moral Sciences, constantly said: 'Ah! if you understood Political Economy you would not say that'"* [quoted by Joan Robinson, **Collected Economic Papers**, vol. 4, p. 129]

Joan Robinson added that *"[n]owadays, of course, no one would put it so crudely. Nowadays, the hidden persuaders are concealed behind scientific objectivity, carefully avoiding value judgements; they are persuading all the better so."* [**Op. Cit.**, p. 129] The way which economic theory systematically says what bosses and the wealthy want to hear is just one of those strange co-incidences of life, one which seems to befall economics with alarming regularity. How does economics achieve this strange co-incidence, how does the "value free" "science" end up being wedded to producing apologetics for the current system? A key reason is the lack of concern about history, about how the current distribution of income and wealth was created. Instead, the current distribution of wealth and income is taken for granted.

This flows, in part, from the static nature of neoclassical economics. If your economic analysis starts and ends with a snapshot of time, with a given set of commodities, then how those commodities get into a specific set of hands can be considered irrelevant – particularly when you modify your theory to exclude the possibility of proving income redistribution will increase overall utility (see section C.1.3). It also flows from the social role of economics as defender of capitalism. By taking the current distribution of income and wealth as given, then many awkward questions can be automatically excluded from the "science."

This can be seen from the rise of neoclassical economics in the 1870s and 1880s. The break between classical political economy and economics was marked by a change in the kind of questions being asked. In the former, the central focus was on distribution, growth, production and the relations between social classes. The exact determination of individual prices was of little concern, particularly in the short run. For the new economics, the focus became developing a rigorous theory of price determination. This meant abstracting from production and looking at the amount of goods available at any given moment of time. Thus economics avoided questions about class relations by asking questions about individual utility, so narrowing the field of analysis by asking politically harmless questions based on unrealistic models (for all its talk of rigour, the new economics did not provide an answer to how real prices were determined any more than classical economics had simply because its abstract models had no relation to reality).

It did, however, provide a naturalistic justification for capitalist social relations by arguing that profit, interest and rent are the result of individual decisions rather than the product of a specific social system. In other words, economics took the classes of capitalism, internalised them within itself, gave them universal application and, by taking for granted the existing distribution of wealth, justified the class structure and differences in market power this produces. It does not ask (or investigate) **why** some people own all the land and capital while the vast majority have to sell their labour on the market to survive. As such, it internalises the class structure of capitalism. Taking this class structure as a given, economics simply asks the question how much does each "factor" (labour, land, capital) contribute to the production of goods.

Alfred Marshall justified this perspective as follows:

> "In the long run the earnings of each agent (of production) are, as a rule, sufficient only to recompense the sum total of the efforts and sacrifices required to produce them … with a partial exception in the case of land … especially much land in old countries, if we could trace its record back to their earliest origins. But the attempt would raise controversial questions in history and ethics as well as in economics; and the aims of our present inquiry are prospective rather than retrospective." [**Principles of Economics**, p. 832]

Which is wonderfully handy for those who benefited from the theft of the common heritage of humanity. Particularly as Marshall himself notes the dire consequences for those without access to the means of life on the market:

> "When a workman is in fear of hunger, his need of money is very great; and, if at starting he gets the worst of the bargaining, it remains great … That is all the more probably because, while the advantage in bargaining is likely to be pretty well distributed between the two sides of a market for commodities, it is more often on the side of the buyers than on that of the sellers in a market for labour." [**Op. Cit.**, pp. 335-6]

Given that market exchanges will benefit the stronger of the parties involved, this means that inequalities become stronger and more secure over time. Taking the current distribution of property as a given (and, moreover, something that must not be changed) then the market does not correct this sort of injustice. In fact, it perpetuates it and, moreover, it has no way of compensating the victims as there is no mechanism for ensuring reparations. So the impact of previous acts of aggression has an impact on how a specific society developed and the current state of the world. To dismiss "retrospective" analysis as it raises "controversial questions" and "ethics" is not value-free or objective science, it is pure ideology and skews any "prospective" enquiry into apologetics.

This can be seen when Marshall noted that labour "is often sold under special disadvantages, arising from the closely connected group of facts that labour power is 'perishable,' that the sellers of it are commonly poor and have no reserve fund, and that they cannot easily withhold it from the market." Moreover, the "disadvantage, wherever it exists, is likely to be cumulative in its effects." Yet, for some reason, he still maintains that "wages of every class of labour tend to be equal to the net product due to the additional labourer of this class." [**Op. Cit.**, p. 567, p. 569 and p. 518] Why should it, given the noted fact that workers are at a disadvantage in the market place? Hence Malatesta:

> "Landlords, capitalists have robbed the people, with violence and dishonesty, of the land and all the means of production, and in consequence of this initial theft can each day take away from workers the product of their labour." [**Errico Malatesta: His Life and Ideas**, p. 168]

As such, how could it possibly be considered "scientific" or "value-free" to ignore history? It is hardly "retrospective" to analyse the roots of the current disadvantage working class people have in the current and "prospective" labour market, particularly given that Marshall himself notes their results. This is a striking example of what Kropotkin deplored in economics, namely that in the rare situations when social conditions were "mentioned, they were forgotten immediately, to be spoken of no more." Thus reality is mentioned, but any impact this may have on the distribution of income is forgotten for otherwise you would have to conclude, with the anarchists, that the "appropriation of the produce of human labour by the owners of capital [and land] exists only because millions of men [and women] have literally nothing to live upon, unless they sell their labour force and their intelligence at a price that will make the net profit of the capitalist and 'surplus value' possible." [**Evolution and Environment**, p. 92 and p. 106]

This is important, for respecting property rights is easy to talk about but it only faintly holds some water if the existing property ownership distribution is legitimate. If it is illegitimate, if the current property titles were the result of theft, corruption, colonial conquest, state intervention, and other forms of coercion then things are obviously different. That is why economics rarely, if ever, discusses this. This does not, of course, stop economists arguing against current interventions in the market (particularly those associated with the welfare state). In effect, they are arguing that it is okay to reap the benefits of past initiations of force but it is wrong to try and rectify them. It is as if someone walks into a room of people, robs them at gun point and then asks that they should respect each others property rights from now on and only engage in voluntary exchanges with what they had left. Any attempt to establish a moral case for the "free market" in such circumstances would be unlikely to succeed. This is free market capitalist economics in a nutshell: never mind past injustices, let us all do the best we can given the current allocations of resources.

Many economists go one better. Not content in ignoring history, they create little fictional stories in order to justify their theories or the current distribution of wealth and income. Usually, they start from isolated individuals or a community of approximately equal individuals (a community usually without any communal institutions). For example, the "waiting" theories of profit and interest (see section C.2.7) requires such a fiction to be remotely convincing. It needs to assume a community marked by basic equality of wealth and income yet divided into two groups of people, one of which was industrious and farsighted who abstained from directly consuming the products created by their **own** labour while the other was lazy and consumed their income without thought of the future. Over time, the descendants of the diligent came to own the means of life while the descendants of the lazy and the prodigal have, to quote Marx, *"nothing to sell but themselves."* In that way, modern day profits and interest can be justified by appealing to such *"insipid childishness."* [**Capital**, vol. 1, p. 873] The real history of the rise of capitalism is, as we discuss in section F.8, grim.

Of course, it may be argued that this is just a model and an abstraction and, consequently, valid to illustrate a point. Anarchists disagree. Yes, there is often the need for abstraction in studying an economy or any other complex system, but this is not an abstraction, it is propaganda and a historical invention used not to illustrate an abstract point but rather a specific system of power and class. That these little parables and stories have all the necessary assumptions and abstractions required to reach the desired conclusions is just one of those co-incidences which seem to regularly befall economics.

The strange thing about these fictional stories is that they are given much more credence than real history within economics. Almost always, fictional "history" will always top actual history in economics. If the actual history of capitalism is mentioned, then the defenders of capitalism will simply say that we should not penalise current holders of capital for actions in the dim and distant past (that current and future generations of workers are penalised goes unmentioned). However, the fictional "history" of capitalism suffers from no such dismissal, for invented actions in the dim and distant past justify the current owners holdings of wealth and the income that generates. In other words, heads I win, tails you loose.

Needless to say, this (selective) myopia is not restricted to just

history. It is applied to current situations as well. Thus we find economists defending current economic systems as "free market" regimes in spite of obvious forms of state intervention. As Chomsky notes:

> *"when people talk about … free-market 'trade forces' inevitably kicking all these people out of work and driving the whole world towards a kind of a Third World-type polarisation of wealth … that's true if you take a narrow enough perspective on it. But if you look into the factors that **made** things the way they are, it doesn't even come **close** to being true, it's not remotely in touch with reality. But when you're studying economics in the ideological institutions, that's all irrelevant and you're not supposed to ask questions like these."* [**Understanding Power**, p. 260]

To ignore all that and simply take the current distribution of wealth and income as given and then argue that the "free market" produces the best allocation of resources is staggering. Particularly as the claim of *"efficient allocation"* does not address the obvious question: "efficient" for whose benefit? For the idealisation of freedom in and through the market ignores the fact that this freedom is very limited in scope to great numbers of people as well as the consequences to the individuals concerned by the distribution of purchasing power amongst them that the market throws up (rooted, of course in the original endowments). Which, of course, explains why, even **if** these parables of economics were true, anarchists would still oppose capitalism. We extend Thomas Jefferson's comment that the *"earth belongs always to the living generation"* to economic institutions as well as political – the past should not dominate the present and the future (Jefferson: *"Can one generation bind another and all others in succession forever? I think not. The Creator has made the earth for the living, not for the dead. Rights and powers can only belong to persons, not to things, not to mere matter unendowed with will"*). For, as Malatesta argued, people should *"not have the right … to subject people to their rule and even less of bequeathing to the countless successions of their descendants the right to dominate and exploit future generations."* [**At the Cafe**, p. 48]

Then there is the strange co-incidence that "value free" economics generally ends up blaming all the problems of capitalism on workers. Unemployment? Recession? Low growth? Wages are too high! Proudhon summed up capitalist economic theory well when he stated that *"Political economy – that is, proprietary despotism – can never be in the wrong: it must be the proletariat."* [**System of Economical Contradictions**, p. 187] And little has changed since 1846 (or 1776!) when it comes to economics "explaining" capitalism's problems (such as the business cycle or unemployment).

As such, it is hard to consider economics as "value free" when economists regularly attack unions while being silent or supportive of big business. According to neo-classical economic theory, both are meant to be equally bad for the economy but you would be hard pressed to find many economists who would urge the breaking up of corporations into a multitude of small firms as their theory demands, the number who will thunder against "monopolistic" labour is substantially higher (ironically, as we note in section C.1.4, their own theory shows that they must urge the break up of corporations or support unions for, otherwise, unorganised labour **is** exploited). Apparently arguing that high wages are always bad but high profits are always good is value free.

So while big business is generally ignored (in favour of arguments that the economy works *"as if"* it did not exist), unions are rarely given such favours. Unlike, say, transnational corporations, unions are considered monopolistic. Thus we see the strange situation of economists (or economics influenced ideologies like right-wing "libertarians") enthusiastically defending companies that raise their prices in the wake of, say, a natural disaster and making windfall profits while, at the same time, attacking workers who decide to raise their wages by striking for being selfish. It is, of course, unlikely that they would let similar charges against bosses pass without comment. But what can you expect from an ideology which presents unemployment as a good thing (namely, increased leisure – see section C.1.5) and being rich as, essentially, a **disutility** (the pain of abstaining from present consumption falls heaviest on those with wealth – see section C.2.7).

Ultimately, only economists would argue, with a straight face, that the billionaire owner of a transnational corporation is exploited when the workers in his sweatshops successfully form a union (usually in the face of the economic and political power wielded by their boss). Yet that is what many economists argue: the transnational corporation is not a monopoly but the union is and monopolies exploit others! Of course, they rarely state it as bluntly as that. Instead they suggest that unions get higher wages for their members by forcing other workers to take less pay (i.e. by exploiting them). So when bosses break unions they are doing this **not** to defend their profits and power but really to raise the standard of other, less fortunate, workers? Hardly. In reality, of course, the reason why unions are so disliked by economics is that bosses, in general, hate them. Under capitalism, labour is a cost and higher wages means less profits (all things being equal). Hence the need to demonise unions, for one of the less understood facts is that while unions increase wages for members, they also increase wages for non-union workers. This should not be surprising as non-union companies have to raise wages to stop their workers unionising and to compete for the best workers who will be drawn to the better pay and conditions of union shops (as we discuss in section C.9, the neoclassical model of the labour market is seriously flawed).

Which brings us to another key problem with the claim that economics is "value free," namely the fact that it takes the current class system of capitalism and its distribution of wealth as not only a fact but as an ideal. This is because economics is based on the need to be able to differentiate between each factor of production in order to determine if it is being used optimally. In other words, the given class structure of capitalism is required to show that an economy uses the available resources efficiently or not. It claims to be "value free" simply because it embeds the economic relationships of capitalist society into its assumptions about nature.

Yet it is impossible to define profit, rent and interest independently of the class structure of any given society. Therefore, this *"type of distribution is the peculiarity of capitalism. Under feudalism the surplus was extracted as land rent. In an artisan economy each commodity is produced by a men with his own tools; the distinction between wages and profits has no meaning there."* This means

that *"the very essence of the theory is bound up with a particular institution – wage labour. The central doctrine is that 'wages tend to equal marginal product of labour.' Obviously this has no meaning for a peasant household where all share the work and the income of their holding according to the rules of family life; nor does it apply in a [co-operative] where, the workers' council has to decide what part of net proceeds to allot to investment, what part to a welfare fund and what part to distribute as wage."* [Joan Robinson, **Collected Economic Papers**, p. 26 and p. 130] This means that the "universal" principles of economics end up by making any economy which does **not** share the core social relations of capitalism inherently "inefficient." If, for example, workers own all three "factors of production" (labour, land and capital) then the "value-free" laws of economics concludes that this will be inefficient. As there is only "income", it is impossible to say which part of it is attributable to labour, land or machinery and, consequently, if these factors are being efficiently used. This means that the "science" of economics is bound up with the current system and its specific class structure and, therefore, as a *"ruling class paradigm, the competitive model"* has the *"substantial"* merit that *"it can be used to rule off the agenda any proposals for substantial reform or intervention detrimental to large economic interests … as the model allows (on its assumptions) a formal demonstration that these would reduce efficiency."* [Edward S. Herman, *"The Selling of Market Economics,"* pp. 173-199, **New Ways of Knowing**, Marcus G. Raskin and Herbert J. Bernstein (eds.), p. 178]

Then there are the methodological assumptions based on individualism. By concentrating on individual choices, economics abstracts from the social system within which such choices are made and what influences them. Thus, for example, the analysis of the causes of poverty is turned towards the failings of individuals rather than the system as a whole (to be poor becomes a personal stigma). That the reality on the ground bears little resemblance to the myth matters little – when people with two jobs still fail to earn enough to feed their families, it seems ridiculous to call them lazy or selfish. It suggests a failure in the system, not in the poor themselves. An individualistic analysis is guaranteed to exclude, by definition, the impact of class, inequality, social hierarchies and economic/social power and any analysis of any inherent biases in a given economic system, its distribution of wealth and, consequently, its distribution of income between classes.

This abstracting of individuals from their social surroundings results in the generating economic "laws" which are applicable for all individuals, in all societies, for all times. This results in all concrete instances, no matter how historically different, being treated as expressions of the same universal concept. In this way the uniqueness of contemporary society, namely its basis in wage labour, is ignored (*"The period through which we are passing … is distinguished by a special characteristic – WAGES."* [Proudhon, **Op. Cit.**, p. 199]). Such a perspective cannot help being ideological rather than scientific. By trying to create a theory applicable for all time (and so, apparently, value free) they just hide the fact their theory assumes and justifies the inequalities of capitalism (for example, the assumption of given needs and distribution of wealth and income secretly introduces the social relations of the current society back into the model, something which the model had supposedly abstracted from). By stressing individualism, scarcity and competition, in reality economic analysis reflects nothing more than the dominant ideological conceptions found in capitalist society. Very few economic systems or societies in the history of humanity have actually reflected these aspects of capitalism (indeed, a lot of state violence has been used to create these conditions by breaking up traditional forms of society, property rights and customs in favour of those desired by the current ruling elite).

The very general nature of the various theories of profit, interest and rent should send alarm bells ringing. Their authors construct these theories based on the deductive method and stress how they are applicable in **every** social and economic system. In other words, the theories are just that, theories derived independently of the facts of the society they are in. It seems somewhat strange, to say the least, to develop a theory of, say, interest independently of the class system within which it is charged but this is precisely what these "scientists" do. It is understandable why. By ignoring the current system and its classes and hierarchies, the economic aspects of this system can be justified in terms of appeals to universal human existence. This will raise less objections than saying, for example, that interest exists because the rich will only part with their money if they get more in return and the poor will pay for this because they have little choice due to their socio-economic situation. Far better to talk about "time preference" rather than the reality of class society (see section C.2.6).

Neoclassical economics, in effect, took the "political" out of "political economy" by taking capitalist society for granted along with its class system, its hierarchies and its inequalities. This is reflected in the terminology used. These days even the term capitalism has gone out of fashion, replaced with the approved terms *"market system,"* the *"free market"* or *"free enterprise."* Yet, as Chomsky noted, terms such as *"free enterprise"* are used *"to designate a system of autocratic governance of the economy in which neither the community nor the workforce has any role (a system we would call 'fascist' if translated to the political sphere)."* [**Language and Politics**, p. 175] As such, it seems hardly "value-free" to proclaim a system free when, in reality, most people are distinctly not free for most of their waking hours and whose choices outside production are influenced by the inequality of wealth and power which that system of production create.

This shift in terminology reflects a political necessity. It effectively removes the role of wealth (capital) from the economy. Instead of the owners and manager of capital being in control or, at the very least, having significant impact on social events, we have the impersonal activity of *"the markets"* or *"market forces."* That such a change in terminology is the interest of those whose money accords them power and influence goes without saying. By focusing on the market, economics helps hide the real sources of power in an economy and attention is drawn away from such a key questions of how money (wealth) produces power and how it skews the "free market" in its favour. All in all, as dissident economist John Kenneth Galbraith once put it, *"[w]hat economists believe and teach is rarely hostile to the institutions that reflect the dominant economic power. Not to notice this takes effort, although many succeed."* [**The Essential Galbraith**, p. 180]

This becomes obvious when we look at the advice economics gives to working class people. In theory, economics is based on individualism and competition yet when it comes to what workers should do, the "laws" of economics suddenly switch. The economist will now deny that competition is a good idea and instead urge that the workers co-operate (i.e. obey) their boss rather than compete (i.e. struggle over the division of output and authority in the workplace). They will argue that there is *"harmony of interests"* between worker and boss, that it is in the **self**-interest of workers **not** to be selfish but rather to do whatever the boss asks to further **the bosses** interests (i.e. profits).

That this perspective implicitly recognises the **dependent** position of workers, goes without saying. So while the sale of labour is portrayed as a market exchange between equals, it is in fact an authority relation between servant and master. The conclusions of economics is simply implicitly acknowledging that authoritarian relationship by identifying with the authority figure in the relationship and urging obedience to them. It simply suggests workers make the best of it by refusing to be independent individuals who need freedom to flourish (at least during working hours, outside they can express their individuality by shopping).

This should come as no surprise, for, as Chomsky notes, economics is rooted in the notion that *"you only harm the poor by making them believe that they have rights other than what they can win on the market, like a basic right to live, because that kind of right interferes with the market, and with efficiency, and with growth and so on – so ultimately people will just be worse off if you try to recognise them."* [**Op. Cit.**, p. 251] Economics teaches that you must accept change without regard to whether it is appropriate it not. It teaches that you must not struggle, you must not fight. You must simply accept whatever change happens. Worse, it teaches that resisting and fighting back are utterly counter-productive. In other words, it teaches a servile mentality to those subject to authority. For business, economics is ideal for getting their employees to change their attitudes rather than collectively change how their bosses treat them, structure their jobs or how they are paid – or, of course, change the system.

Of course, the economist who says that they are conducting "value free" analysis are indifferent to the kinds of relationships within society is being less than honest. Capitalist economic theory is rooted in very specific assumptions and concepts such as "economic man" and "perfect competition." It claims to be "value-free" yet its preferred terminology is riddled with value connotations. For example, the behaviour of "economic man" (i.e., people who are self-interested utility maximisation machines) is described as *"rational."* By implication, then, the behaviour of real people is *"irrational"* whenever they depart from this severely truncated account of human nature and society. Our lives consist of much more than buying and selling. We have goals and concerns which cannot be bought or sold in markets. In other words, humanity and liberty transcend the limits of property and, as a result, economics. This, unsurprisingly, affects those who study the "science" as well:

> *"Studying economics also seems to make you a nastier person. Psychological studies have shown that economics graduate students are more likely to 'free ride' – shirk contributions to an experimental 'public goods' account*

in the pursuit of higher private returns – than the general public. Economists also are less generous than other academics in charitable giving. Undergraduate economics majors are more likely to defect in the classic prisoner's dilemma game that are other majors. And on other tests, students grow less honest – expressing less of a tendency, for example, to return found money – after studying economics, but not studying a control subject like astronomy.

"This is no surprise, really. Mainstream economics is built entirely on a notion of self-interested individuals, rational self-maximisers who can order their wants and spend accordingly. There's little room for sentiment, uncertainty, selflessness, and social institutions. Whether this is an accurate picture of the average human is open to question, but there's no question that capitalism as a system and economics as a discipline both reward people who conform to the model." [Doug Henwood, **Wall Street**, p, 143]

So is economics "value free"? Far from it. Given its social role, it would be surprising that it were. That it tends to produce policy recommendations that benefit the capitalist class is not an accident. It is rooted in the fibre of the "science" as it reflects the assumptions of capitalist society and its class structure. Not only does it take the power and class structures of capitalism for granted, it also makes them the ideal for any and every economy. Given this, it should come as no surprise that economists will tend to support policies which will make the real world conform more closely to the standard (usually neoclassical) economic model. Thus the models of economics become more than a set of abstract assumptions, used simply as a tool in theoretical analysis of the casual relations of facts. Rather they become political goals, an ideal towards which reality should be forced to travel.

This means that economics has a dual character. On the one hand, it attempts to prove that certain things (for example, that free market capitalism produces an optimum allocation of resources or that, given free competition, price formation will ensure that each person's income corresponds to their productive contribution). On the other, economists stress that economic "science" has nothing to do with the question of the justice of existing institutions, class structures or the current economic system. And some people seem surprised that this results in policy recommendations which consistently and systematically favour the ruling class.

C.1.2 Is economics a science?

In a word, no. If by "scientific" it is meant in the usual sense of being based on empirical observation and on developing an analysis that was consistent with and made sense of the data, then most forms of economics are not a science.

Rather than base itself on a study of reality and the generalisation of theory based on the data gathered, economics has almost always been based on generating theories rooted on whatever assumptions were required to make the theory work. Empirical confirmation, if it happens at all, is usually done decades later and if the facts contradict the economics, so much the worse for the facts.

A classic example of this is the neo-classical theory of production. As noted previously, neoclassical economics is focused on individual evaluations of existing products and, unsurprisingly, economics is indelibly marked by *"the dominance of a theoretical vision that treats the inner workings of the production process as a 'black box.'"* This means that the *"neoclassical theory of the 'capitalist' economy makes no qualitative distinction between the corporate enterprise that employs tens of thousands of people and the small family undertaking that does no employ any wage labour at all. As far as theory is concerned, it is technology and market forces, not structures of social power, that govern the activities of corporate capitalists and petty proprietors alike."* [William Lazonick, **Competitive Advantage on the Shop Floor**, p. 34 and pp. 33-4] Production in this schema just happens – inputs go in, outputs go out – and what happens inside is considered irrelevant, a technical issue independent of the social relationships those who do the actual production form between themselves – and the conflicts that ensure.

The theory does have a few key assumptions associated with it, however. First, there are diminishing returns. This plays a central role. In mainstream diminishing returns are required to produce a downward sloping demand curve for a given factor. Second, there is a rising supply curve based on rising marginal costs produced by diminishing returns. The average variable cost curve for a firm is assumed to be U-shaped, the result of first increasing and then diminishing returns. These are logically necessary for the neo-classical theory to work.

Non-economists would, of course, think that these assumptions are generalisations based on empirical evidence. However, they are not. Take the U-shaped average cost curve. This was simply invented by A. C. Pigou, *"a loyal disciple of [leading neo-classical Alfred] Marshall and quite innocent of any knowledge of industry. He therefore constructed a U-shaped average cost curve for a firm, showing economies of scale up to a certain size and rising costs beyond it."* [Joan Robinson, **Collected Economic Papers**, vol. 5, p. 11] The invention was driven by need of the theory, not the facts. With increasing returns to scale, then large firms would have cost advantages against small ones and would drive them out of business in competition. This would destroy the concept of perfect competition. However, the invention of the average cost curve allowed the theory to work as "proved" that a competitive market could **not** become dominated by a few large firms, as feared.

The model, in other words, was adjusted to ensure that it produced the desired result rather than reflect reality. The theory was required to prove that markets remained competitive and the existence of diminishing marginal returns to scale of production **did** tend by itself to limit the size of individual firms. That markets did become dominated by a few large firms was neither here nor there. It did not happen in theory and, consequently, that was the important thing and so *"when the great concentrations of power in the multinational corporations are bringing the age of national employment policy to an end, the text books are still illustrated by U-shaped curves showing the limitation on the size of firms in a perfectly competitive market."* [Joan Robinson, **Contributions to Modern Economics**, p. 5]

To be good, a theory must have two attributes: They accurately describe the phenomena in question and they make accurate predictions. Neither holds for Pigou's invention: reality keeps getting in the way. Not only did the rise of a few large firms dominating markets indirectly show that the theory was nonsense, when empirical testing was finally done decades after the theory was proposed it showed that in most cases the opposite is the case: that there were constant or even falling costs in production. Just as the theories of marginality and diminishing marginal returns taking over economics, the real world was showing how wrong it was with the rise of corporations across the world.

So the reason why the market become dominated by a few firms should be obvious enough: actual corporate price is utterly different from the economic theory. This was discovered when researchers did what the original theorists did not think was relevant: they actually asked firms what they did and the researchers consistently found that, for the vast majority of manufacturing firms their average costs of production declined as output rose, their marginal costs were always well below their average costs, and substantially smaller than 'marginal revenue', and the concept of a 'demand curve' (and therefore its derivative 'marginal revenue') was simply irrelevant.

Unsurprisingly, real firms set their prices prior to sales, based on a mark-up on costs at a target rate of output. In other words, they did not passively react to the market. These prices are an essential feature of capitalism as prices are set to maintain the long-term viability of the firm. This, and the underlying reality that per-unit costs fell as output levels rose, resulted in far more stable prices than were predicted by traditional economic theory. One researcher concluded that administered prices *"differ so sharply from the behaviour to be expected from"* the theory *"as to challenge the basic conclusions"* of it. He warned that until such time as *"economic theory can explain and take into account the implications"* of this empirical data, *"it provides a poor basis for public policy."* Needless to say, this did not disturb neo-classical economists or stop them providing public policy recommendations. [Gardiner C. Means, *"The Administered-Price Thesis Reconfirmed"*, **The American Economic Review**, pp. 292-306, Vol. 62, No. 3, p. 304]

One study in 1952 showed firms a range of hypothetical cost curves, and asked firms which ones most closely approximated their own costs. Over 90% of firms chose a graph with a declining average cost rather than one showing the conventional economic theory of rising marginal costs. These firms faced declining average cost, and their marginal revenues were much greater than marginal cost at all levels of output. Unsurprisingly, the study's authors concluded if this sample was typical then it was *"obvious that short-run marginal price theory should be revised in the light of reality."* We are still waiting. [Eiteman and Guthrie, *"The Shape of the Average Cost Curve"*, **The American Economic Review**, pp. 832-8, Vol. 42, No. 5, p. 838]

A more recent study of the empirical data came to the same conclusions, arguing that it is *"overwhelming bad news … for economic theory."* While economists treat rising marginal cost as the rule, 89% of firms in the study reported marginal costs which were either constant or declined with output. As for price elasticity, it is not a vital operational concept for corporations. In other words, the *"firms that sell 40 percent of GDP believe their demand is totally insensitive to price"* while *"only about one-sixth of GDP is sold under conditions of elastic demand."* [A.S. Blinder, E. Cabetti, D. Lebow and J. Rudd, **Asking About Prices**, p. 102 and p. 101]

Thus empirical research has concluded that actual price setting has nothing to do with clearing the market by equating market supply to market demand (i.e. what economic theory sees as the role of prices). Rather, prices are set to enable the firm to continue as a going concern and equating supply and demand in any arbitrary period of time is irrelevant to a firm which hopes to exist for the indefinite future. As Lee put it, basing himself on extensive use of empirical research, *"market prices are not market-clearing or profit-maximising prices, but rather are enterprise-, and hence transaction-reproducing prices."* Rather than a non-existent equilibrium or profit maximisation at a given moment determining prices, the market price is *"set and the market managed for the purpose of ensuring continual transactions for those enterprises in the market, that is for the benefit of the business leaders and their enterprises."* A significant proportion of goods have prices based on mark-up, normal cost and target rate of return pricing procedures and are relatively stable over time. Thus *"the existence of stable, administered market prices implies that the markets in which they exist are not organised like auction markets or like the early retail markets and oriental bazaars"* as imagined in mainstream economic ideology. [Frederic S. Lee, **Post Keynesian Price Theory**, p. 228 and p. 212]

Unsurprisingly, most of these researchers were highly critical the conventional economic theory of markets and price setting. One viewed the economists' concepts of perfect competition and monopoly as virtual nonsense and *"the product of the itching imaginations of uninformed and inexperienced armchair theorisers."* [Tucker, quoted by Lee, **Op. Cit.**, p. 73f] Which **was** exactly how it was produced.

No other science would think it appropriate to develop theory utterly independently of phenomenon under analysis. No other science would wait decades before testing a theory against reality. No other science would then simply ignore the facts which utterly contradicted the theory and continue to teach that theory as if it were a valid generalisation of the facts. But, then, economics is not a science.

This strange perspective makes sense once it is realised how key the notion of diminishing costs is to economics. In fact, if the assumption of increasing marginal costs is abandoned then so is perfect competition and *"the basis of which economic laws can be constructed ... is shorn away,"* causing the *"wreckage of the greater part of general equilibrium theory."* This will have *"a very destructive consequence for economic theory,"* in the words of one leading neo-classical economist. [John Hicks, **Value and Capital**, pp. 83-4] As Steve Keen notes, this is extremely significant:

> *"Strange as it may seem ... this is a very big deal. If marginal returns are constant rather than falling, then the neo-classical explanation of everything collapses. Not only can economic theory no longer explain how much a firm produces, it can explain nothing else.*
>
> *"Take, for example, the economic theory of employment and wage determination ... The theory asserts that the real wage is equivalent to the marginal product of labour ... An employer will employ an additional worker if the amount the worker adds to output – the worker's marginal product – exceeds the real wage ... [This] explains the economic predilection for blaming everything on wages being too high – neo-classical economics can be summed up, as [John Kenneth] Galbraith once remarked, in the twin propositions that the poor don't work hard enough because they're paid too much, and the rich don't work hard enough because they're not paid enough ...*
>
> *"If in fact the output to employment relationship is relatively constant, then the neo-classical explanation for employment and output determination collapses. With a flat production function, the marginal product of labour will be constant, and it will **never** intersect the real wage. The output of the form then can't be explained by the cost of employing labour ... [This means that] neo-classical economics simply cannot explain anything: neither the level of employment, nor output, nor, ultimately, what determines the real wage ... the entire edifice of economics collapses."* [**Debunking Economics**, pp. 76-7]

It should be noted that the empirical research simply confirmed an earlier critique of neo-classical economics presented by Piero Sraffa in 1926. He argued that while the neo-classical model of production works in theory only if we accept its assumptions. If those assumptions do not apply in practice, then it is irrelevant. He therefore *"focussed upon the economic assumptions that there were 'factors of production' which were fixed in the short run, and that supply and demand were independent of each other. He argued that these two assumptions could be fulfilled simultaneously. In circumstances where it was valid to say some factor of production was fixed in the short term, supply and demand could not independent, so that every point on the supply curve would be associated with a different demand curve. On the other hand, in circumstances where supply and demand could justifiably be treated as independent, then it would be impossible for any factor of production to be fixed. Hence the marginal costs of production would be constant."* He stressed firms would have to be irrational to act otherwise, foregoing the chance to make profits simply to allow

economists to build their models of how they should act. [Keen, **Op. Cit.**, pp. 66-72]

Another key problem in economics is that of time. This has been known, and admitted, by economists for some time. Marshall, for example, stated that *"the element of **time**"* was *"the source of many of the greatest difficulties of economics."* [**Principles of Economics**, p. 109] The founder of general equilibrium theory, Walras, recognised that the passage of time wrecked his whole model and stated that we *"shall resolve the ... difficulty purely and simply by ignoring the time element at this point."* This was due, in part, because production *"requires a certain lapse of time."* [**Elements of Pure Economics**, p. 242] This was generalised by Gerard Debreu (in his Nobel Prize for economics winning **Theory of Value**) who postulated that everyone makes their sales and purchases for all time in one instant.

Thus the cutting edge of neo-classical economics, general equilibrium ignores both time **and** production. It is based on making time stop, looking at finished goods, getting individuals to bid for them and, once all goods are at equilibrium, allowing the transactions to take place. For Walras, this was for a certain moment of time and was repeated, for his followers it happened once for all eternity. This is obviously not the way markets work in the real world and, consequently, the dominant branch of economics is hardly scientific. Sadly, the notion of individuals having full knowledge of both now and the future crops up with alarming regularly in the "science" of economics.

Even if we ignore such minor issues as empirical evidence and time, economics has problems even with its favoured tool, mathematics. As Steve Keen has indicated, economists have *"obscured reality using mathematics because they have practised mathematics badly, and because they have not realised the limits of mathematics."* indeed, there are *"numerous theorems in economics that reply upon mathematically fallacious propositions."* [**Op. Cit.**, p. 258 and p. 259] For a theory born from the desire to apply calculus to economics, this is deeply ironic. As an example, Keen points to the theory of perfect competition which assumes that while the demand curve for the market as a whole is downward sloping, an individual firm in perfect competition is so small that it cannot affect the market price and, consequently, faces a horizontal demand curve. Which is utterly impossible. In other words, economics breaks the laws of mathematics.

These are just two examples, there are many, many more. However, these two are pretty fundamental to the whole edifice of modern economic theory. Much, if not most, of mainstream economics is based upon theories which have little or no relation to reality. Kropotkin's dismissal of *"the metaphysical definitions of the academical economists"* is as applicable today. [**Evolution and Environment**, p. 92] Little wonder dissident economist Nicholas Kaldor argued that:

> *"The Walrasian [i.e. general] equilibrium theory is a highly developed intellectual system, much refined and elaborated by mathematical economists since World War II – an intellectual experiment ... But it does not constitute a scientific hypothesis, like Einstein's theory of relativity or Newton's law of gravitation, in that its basic assumptions*

are axiomatic and not empirical, and no specific methods have been put forward by which the validity or relevance of its results could be tested. The assumptions make assertions about reality in their implications, but these are not founded on direct observation, and, in the opinion of practitioners of the theory at any rate, they cannot be contradicted by observation or experiment." [**The Essential Kaldor**, p. 416]

C.1.3 Can you have an economics based on individualism?

In a word, no. No economic system is simply the sum of its parts. The idea that capitalism is based on the subjective evaluations of individuals for goods flies in the face of both logic and the way capitalism works. In other words, modern economics is based on a fallacy. While it would be expected for critics of capitalism to conclude this, the ironic thing is that economists themselves have proven this to be the case.

Neoclassical theory argues that marginal utility determines demand and price, i.e. the price of a good is dependent on the intensity of demand for the marginal unit consumed. This was in contrast to classic economics, which argued that price (exchange value) was regulated by the cost of production, ultimately the amount of labour used to create it. While realistic, this had the political drawback of implying that profit, rent and interest were the product of unpaid labour and so capitalism was exploitative. This conclusion was quickly seized upon by numerous critics of capitalism, including Proudhon and Marx. The rise of marginal utility theory meant that such critiques could be ignored.

However, this change was not unproblematic. The most obvious problem with it is that it leads to circular reasoning. Prices are supposed to measure the "marginal utility" of the commodity, yet consumers need to know the price **first** in order to evaluate how best to maximise their satisfaction. Hence it *"obviously rest[s] on circular reasoning. Although it tries to explain prices, prices [are] necessary to explain marginal utility."* [Paul Mattick, **Economics, Politics and the Age of Inflation**, p.58] In the end, as Jevons (one of the founders of the new economics) acknowledged, the price of a commodity is the only test we have of the utility of the commodity to the producer. Given that marginality utility was meant to explain those prices, the failure of the theory could not be more striking.

However, this is the least of its problems. At first, the neoclassical economists used cardinal utility as their analysis tool. Cardinal utility meant that it was measurable between individuals, i.e. that the utility of a given good was the same for all. While this allowed prices to be determined, it caused obvious political problems as it obviously justified the taxation of the wealthy. As cardinal utility implied that the "utility" of an extra dollar to a poor person was clearly greater than the loss of one dollar to a rich man, it was appropriated by reformists precisely to justify social reforms and taxation.

Capitalist economists had, yet again, created a theory that could be used to attack capitalism and the income and wealth hierarchy it produces. As with classical economics, socialists and other social reformists used the new theories to do precisely that, appropriating it to justify the redistribution of income and wealth downward (i.e. back into the hands of the class who had created it in the first place). Combine this with the high levels of class conflict at the time and it should come as no surprise that the "science" of economics was suitably revised.

There was, of course, a suitable "scientific" rationale for this revision. It was noted that as individual evaluations are inherently subjective, it is obvious that cardinal utility was impossible in practice. Of course, cardinality was not totally rejected. Neoclassical economics retained the idea that capitalists maximise profits, which is a cardinal quantity. However for demand utility became "ordinal," that is utility was considered an individual thing and so could not be measured. This resulted in the conclusion that there was no way of making interpersonal comparisons between individuals and, consequently, no basis for saying a pound in the hands of a poor person had more utility than if it had remained in the pocket of a billionaire. The economic case for taxation was now, apparently, closed. While you may think that income redistribution was a good idea, it was now proven by "science" that this little more than a belief as all interpersonal comparisons were now impossible. That this was music to the ears of the wealthy was, of course, just one of those strange co-incidences which always seems to plague economic "science."

The next stage of the process was to abandon then ordinal utility in favour of "indifference curves" (the continued discussion of "utility" in economics textbooks is primarily heuristic). In this theory consumers are supposed to maximise their utility by working out which bundle of goods gives them the highest level of satisfaction based on the twin constraints of income and given prices (let us forget, for the moment, that marginal utility was meant to determines prices in the first place). To do this, it is assumed that incomes and tastes are independent and that consumers have pre-existing preferences for all possible bundles.

This produces a graph that shows different quantities of two different goods, with the "indifference curves" showing the combinations of goods which give the consumer the same level of satisfaction (hence the name, as the consumer is "indifferent" to any combination along the curve). There is also a straight line representing relative prices and the consumer's income and this budget line shows the uppermost curve the consumer can afford to reach. That these indifference curves could not be observed was not an issue although leading neo-classical economist Paul Samuelson provided an apparent means see these curves by his concept of *"revealed preference"* (a basic tautology). There is a reason why "indifference curves" cannot be observed. They are literally impossible for human beings to calculate once you move beyond a trivially small set of alternatives and it is impossible for actual people to act as economists argue they do. Ignoring this slight problem, the "indifference curve" approach to demand can be faulted for another, even more basic, reason. It does not prove what it seeks to show:

> *"Though mainstream economics began by assuming that this hedonistic, individualist approach to analysing*

consumer demand was intellectually sound, **it ended up proving that it was not.** The critics were right: society is more than the sum of its individual members." [Steve Keen, **Debunking Economics**, p. 23]

As noted above, to fight the conclusion that redistributing wealth would result in a different level of social well-being, economists had to show that *"altering the distribution of income did not alter social welfare. They worked out that two conditions were necessary for this to be true: (a) that all people have the same tastes; (b) that each person's tastes remain the same as her income changes, so that every additional dollar of income was spent exactly the same way as all previous dollars."* The former assumption *"in fact amounts to assuming that there is only one person in society"* or that *"society consists of a multitude of identical drones"* or clones. The latter assumption *"amounts to assuming that there is only one commodity – since otherwise spending patterns would necessary change as income rose."* [Keen, **Op. Cit.**, p. 24] This is the real meaning of the assumption that all goods and consumers can be considered *"representative."* Sadly, such individuals and goods do not exist. Thus:

> *"Economics can prove that 'the demand curve slows downward in price' for a single individual and a single commodity. But in a society consisting of many different individuals with many different commodities, the 'market demand curve' is more probably jagged, and slopes every which way. One essential building block of the economic analysis of markets, the demand curve, therefore does not have the characteristics needed for economic theory to be internally consistent … most mainstream academic economists are aware of this problem, but they pretend that the failure can be managed with a couple of assumptions. Yet the assumptions themselves are so absurd that only someone with a grossly distorted sense of logic could accept them. That grossly distorted sense of logic is acquired in the course of a standard education in economics."* [**Op. Cit.**, pp. 25-7]

Rather than produce a *"social indifference map which had the same properties as the individual indifference maps"* by adding up all the individual maps, economics *"proved that this consistent summation from individual to society could **not** be achieved."* Any sane person would have rejected the theory at this stage, but not economists. Keen states the obvious: *"That economists, in general, failed to draw this inference speaks volumes for the unscientific nature of economic theory."* They simply invented *"some fudge to disguise the gapping hole they have uncovered in the theory."* [**Op. Cit.**, p. 40 and p. 48] Ironically, it took over one hundred years and advanced mathematical logic to reach the same conclusion that the classical economists took for granted, namely that individual utility could not be measured and compared. However, instead of seeking exchange value (price) in the process of production, neoclassical economists simply that made a few absurd assumptions and continued on its way as if nothing was wrong.

This is important because *"economists are trying to prove that a market economy necessarily maximises social welfare. If they can't prove that the market demand curve falls smoothly as price rises, they can't prove that the market maximises social welfare."* In addition, *"the concept of a social indifference curve is crucial to many of the key notions of economics: the argument that free trade is necessarily superior to regulated trade, for example, is first constructed using a social indifference curve. Therefore, if the concept of a social indifference curve itself is invalid, then so too are many of the most treasured notions of economics."* [Keen, **Op. Cit.**, p. 50] This means much of economic theory is invalidated and with it the policy recommendations based on it.

This elimination of individual differences in favour of a society of clones by marginalism is not restricted to demand. Take the concept of the *"representative firm"* used to explain supply. Rather than a theoretical device to deal with variety, it ignores diversity. It is a heuristic concept which deals with a varied collection of firms by identifying a single set of distinct characteristics which are deemed to represent the essential qualities of the industry as a whole. It is **not** a single firm or even a typical or average firm. It is an imaginary firm which exhibits the "representative" features of the entire industry, i.e. it treats an industry as if it were just one firm. Moreover, it should be stressed that this concept is driven by the needs to prove the model, not by any concern over reality. The *"real weakness"* of the *"representative firm"* in neo-classical economics is that it is *"no more than a firm which answers the requirements expected from it by the supply curve"* and because it is *"nothing more than a small-scale replica of the industry's supply curve that it is unsuitable for the purpose it has been called into being."* [Kaldor, **The Essential Kaldor**, p. 50]

Then there is neoclassical analysis of the finance market. According to the Efficient Market Hypothesis, information is disseminated equally among all market participants, they all hold similar interpretations of that information and all can get access to all the credit they need at any time at the same rate. In other words, everyone is considered to be identical in terms of what they know, what they can get and what they do with that knowledge and cash. This results in a theory which argues that stock markets accurately price stocks on the basis of their unknown future earnings, i.e. that these identical expectations by identical investors are correct. In other words, investors are able to correctly predict the future and act in the same way to the same information. Yet if everyone held identical opinions then there would be no trading of shares as trading obviously implies **different** opinions on how a stock will perform. Similarly, in reality investors are credit rationed, the rate of borrowing tends to rise as the amount borrowed increases and the borrowing rate normally exceeds the leading rate. The developer of the theory was honest enough to state that the *"consequence of accommodating such aspects of reality are likely to be disastrous in terms of the usefulness of the resulting theory … The theory is in a shambles."* [W.F Sharpe, quoted by Keen, **Op. Cit.**, p. 233]

Thus the world was turned into a single person simply to provide a theory which showed that stock markets were "efficient" (i.e. accurately reflect unknown future earnings). In spite of these slight problems, the theory was accepted in the mainstream as an accurate reflection of finance markets. Why? Well, the implications of this theory are deeply political as it suggests that finance markets will never experience bubbles and deep slumps. That this contradicts the well-known history of the stock market was considered unimportant.

Unsurprisingly, *"as time went on, more and more data turned up which was not consistent with"* the theory. This is because the model's world *"is clearly not our world."* The theory *"cannot apply in a world in which investors differ in their expectations, in which the future is uncertain, and in which borrowing is rationed."* It *"should never have been given any credibility – yet instead it became an article of faith for academics in finance, and a common belief in the commercial world of finance."* [Keen, **Op. Cit.**, p. 246 and p. 234] This theory is at the root of the argument that finance markets should be deregulated and as many funds as possible invested in them. While the theory may benefit the minority of share holders who own the bulk of shares and help them pressurise government policy, it is hard to see how it benefits the rest of society. Alternative, more realistic theories, argue that finance markets show endogenous instability, result in bad investment as well as reducing the overall level of investment as investors will not fund investments which are not predicted to have a sufficiently high rate of return. All of which has a large and negative impact on the real economy. Instead, the economic profession embraced a highly unreal economic theory which has encouraged the world to indulge in stock market speculation as it argues that they do not have bubbles, booms or bursts (that the 1990s stock market bubble finally burst like many previous ones is unlikely to stop this). Perhaps this has to do the implications for economic theory for this farcical analysis of the stock market? As two mainstream economists put it:

> *"To reject the Efficient Market Hypothesis for the whole stock market ... implies broadly that production decisions based on stock prices will lead to inefficient capital allocations. More generally, if the application of rational expectations theory to the virtually 'idea' conditions provided by the stock market fails, then what confidence can economists have in its application to other areas of economics...?"* [Marsh and Merton, quoted by Doug Henwood, **Wall Street**, p. 161]

Ultimately, neoclassical economics, by means of the concept of "representative" agent, has proved that subjective evaluations could not be aggregated and, as a result, a market supply and demand curves cannot be produced. In other words, neoclassical economics has shown that if society were comprised of one individual, buying one good produced by one factory then it could accurately reflect what happened in it. *"It is stating the obvious,"* states Keen, *"to call the representative agent an 'ad hoc' assumption, made simply so that economists can pretend to have a sound basis for their analysis, when in reality they have no grounding whatsoever."* [**Op. Cit.**, p. 188]

There is a certain irony about the change from cardinal to ordinal utility and finally the rise of the impossible nonsense which are "indifference curves." While these changes were driven by the need to deny the advocates of redistributive taxation policies the mantel of economic science to justify their schemes, the fact is by rejecting cardinal utility, it becomes impossible to say whether state action like taxes decreases utility at all. With ordinal utility and its related concepts, you cannot actually show that government intervention actually harms "social utility." All you can say is that they are indeterminate. While the rich may lose income and the poor gain,

it is impossible to say anything about social utility without making an interpersonal (cardinal) utility comparison. Thus, ironically, ordinal utility based economics provides a much weaker defence of free market capitalism by removing the economist of the ability to call any act of government "inefficient" and they would have to be evaluated in, horror of horrors, non-economic terms. As Keen notes, it is *"ironic that this ancient defence of inequality ultimately backfires on economics, by making its impossible to construct a market demand curve which is independent on the distribution of income ... economics cannot defend any one distribution of income over any other. A redistribution of income that favours the poor over the rich cannot be formally opposed by economic theory."* [**Op. Cit.**, p. 51]

Neoclassical economics has also confirmed that the classical perspective of analysing society in terms of classes is also more valid than the individualistic approach it values. As one leading neo-classical economist has noted, if economics is *"to progress further we may well be forced to theorise in terms of groups who have collectively coherent behaviour."* Moreover, the classical economists would not be surprised by the admission that *"the addition of production **can** help"* economic analysis nor the conclusion that the *"idea that we should start at the level of the isolated individual is one which we may well have to abandon ... If we aggregate over several individuals, such a model is unjustified."* [Alan Kirman, "The Intrinsic Limits of Modern Economy Theory", pp. 126-139, The Economic Journal, Vol. 99, No. 395, p. 138, p. 136 and p. 138]

So why all the bother? Why spend over 100 years driving economics into a dead-end? Simply because of political reasons. The advantage of the neoclassical approach was that it abstracted away from production (where power relations are clear) and concentrated on exchange (where power works indirectly). As libertarian Marxist Paul Mattick notes, the *"problems of bourgeois economics seemed to disappear as soon as one ignored production and attended only to the market ... Viewed apart from production, the price problem can be dealt with purely in terms of the market."* [**Economic Crisis and Crisis Theory**, p. 9] By ignoring production, the obvious inequalities of power produced by the dominant social relations within capitalism could be ignored in favour of looking at abstract individuals as buyers and sellers. That this meant ignoring such key concepts as time by forcing economics into a static, freeze frame, model of the economy was a price worth paying as it allowed capitalism to be justified as the best of all possible worlds:

> *"On the one hand, it was thought essential to represent the winning of profit, interest, and rent as participation in the creation of wealth. On the other, it was thought desirable to found the authority of economics on the procedures of natural science. This second desire prompted a search for general economic laws independent of time and circumstances. If such laws could be proven, the existing society would thereby be legitimated and every idea of changing it refuted. Subjective value theory promised to accomplish both tasks at once. Disregarding the exchange relationship peculiar to capitalism – that between the sellers and buyers of labour power – it could explain the division of the social product, under whatever forms, as*

resulting from the needs of the exchangers themselves." [Mattick, **Op. Cit.**, p. 11]

The attempt to ignore production implied in capitalist economics comes from a desire to hide the exploitative and class nature of capitalism. By concentrating upon the "subjective" evaluations of individuals, those individuals are abstracted away from real economic activity (i.e. production) so the source of profits and power in the economy can be ignored (section C.2 indicates why exploitation of labour in production is the source of profit, interest and rent and **not** exchanges in the market).

Hence the flight from classical economics to the static, timeless world of individuals exchanging pre-existing goods on the market. The evolution of capitalist economics has always been towards removing any theory which could be used to attack capitalism. Thus classical economics was rejected in favour of utility theory once socialists and anarchists used it to show that capitalism was exploitative. Then this utility theory was modified over time in order to purge it of undesirable political consequences. In so doing, they ended up not only proving that an economics based on individualism was impossible but also that it cannot be used to oppose redistribution policies after all.

C.1.4 What is wrong with equilibrium analysis?

The dominant form of economic analysis since the 1880s has been equilibrium analysis. While equilibrium had been used by classical economics to explain what regulated market prices, it did not consider it as reflecting any real economy. This was because classical economics analysed capitalism as a mode of production rather than as a mode of exchange, as a mode of circulation, as neo-classical economics does. It looked at the process of creating products while neo-classical economics looked at the price ratios between already existing goods (this explains why neo-classical economists have such a hard time understanding classical or Marxist economics, the schools are talking about different things and why they tend to call any market system "capitalism" regardless of whether wage labour predominates of not). The classical school is based on an analysis of markets based on production of commodities through time. The neo-classical school is based on an analysis of markets based on the exchange of the goods which exist at any moment of time.

This indicates what is wrong with equilibrium analysis, it is essentially a static tool used to analyse a dynamic system. It assumes stability where none exists. Capitalism is always unstable, always out of equilibrium, since *"growing out of capitalist competition, to heighten exploitation, ... the relations of production ... [are] in a state of perpetual transformation, which manifests itself in changing relative prices of goods on the market. Therefore the market is continuously in disequilibrium, although with different degrees of severity, thus giving rise, by its occasional approach to an equilibrium state, to the illusion of a tendency toward equilibrium."* [Mattick, **Op. Cit.**, p. 51] Given this obvious fact of the real economy, it comes as no surprise that dissident economists consider equilibrium analysis as *"a major*

*obstacle to the development of economics as a **science** – meaning by the term 'science' a body of theorems based on assumptions that are **empirically** derived (from observations) and which embody hypotheses that are capable of verification both in regard to the assumptions and the predictions."* [Kaldor, **The Essential Kaldor**, p. 373]

Thus the whole concept is an unreal rather than valid abstraction of reality. Sadly, the notions of "perfect competition" and (Walrasian) "general equilibrium" are part and parcel of neoclassical economics. It attempts to show, in the words of Paul Ormerod, *"that under certain assumptions the free market system would lead to an allocation of a given set of resources which was in a very particular and restricted sense optimal from the point of view of every individual and company in the economy."* [**The Death of Economics**, p. 45] This was what Walrasian general equilibrium proved. However, the assumptions required prove to be somewhat unrealistic (to understate the point). As Ormerod points out:

> *"[i]t cannot be emphasised too strongly that ... the competitive model is far removed from being a reasonable representation of Western economies in practice ... [It is] a travesty of reality. The world does not consist, for example, of an enormous number of small firms, none of which has any degree of control over the market ... The theory introduced by the marginal revolution was based upon a series of postulates about human behaviour and the workings of the economy. It was very much an experiment in pure thought, with little empirical rationalisation of the assumptions."* [**Op. Cit.**, p. 48]

Indeed, *"the weight of evidence"* is *"against the validity of the model of competitive general equilibrium as a plausible representation of reality."* [**Op. Cit.**, p. 62] For example, to this day, economists still start with the assumption of a multitude of firms, even worse, a "continuum" of them exist in **every** market. How many markets are there in which there is an infinite number of traders? This means that from the start the issues and problems associated with oligopoly and imperfect competition have been abstracted from. This means the theory does not allow one to answer interesting questions which turn on the asymmetry of information and bargaining power among economic agents, whether due to size, or organisation, or social stigmas, or whatever else. In the real world, oligopoly is common place and asymmetry of information and bargaining power the norm. To abstract from these means to present an economic vision at odds with the reality people face and, therefore, can only propose solutions which harm those with weaker bargaining positions and without information.

General equilibrium is an entirely static concept, a market marked by perfect knowledge and so inhabited by people who are under no inducement or need to act. It is also timeless, a world without a future and so with no uncertainty (any attempt to include time, and so uncertainty, ensures that the model ceases to be of value). At best, economists include "time" by means of comparing one static state to another, i.e. *"the features of one non-existent equilibrium were compared with those of a later non-existent equilibrium."* [Mattick, **Op. Cit.**, p. 22] How the economy actually changed from one stable state to another is left to the imagination. Indeed, the idea of any long-run equilibrium is rendered irrelevant by the movement towards it as the equilibrium also moves. Unsurprisingly, therefore, to construct an equilibrium path through time requires all prices for all periods to be determined at the start and that everyone foresees future prices correctly for eternity – including for goods not invented yet. Thus the model cannot easily or usefully account for the reality that economic agents do not actually know such things as future prices, future availability of goods, changes in production techniques or in markets to occur in the future, etc. Instead, to achieve its results – proofs about equilibrium conditions – the model assumes that actors have perfect knowledge at least of the probabilities of all possible outcomes for the economy. The opposite is obviously the case in reality:

> "Yet the main lessons of these increasingly abstract and unreal theoretical constructions are also increasingly taken on trust ... It is generally taken for granted by the great majority of academic economists that the economy always approaches, or is near to, a state of 'equilibrium' ... all propositions which the **pure** mathematical economist has shown to be valid only on assumptions that are manifestly unreal – that is to say, directly contrary to experience and not just 'abstract.' In fact, equilibrium theory has reached the stage where the pure theorist has successfully (though perhaps inadvertently) demonstrated that the main implications of this theory cannot possibly hold in reality, but has not yet managed to pass his message down the line to the textbook writer and to the classroom." [Kaldor, **Op. Cit.**, pp. 376-7]

In this timeless, perfect world, "free market" capitalism will prove itself an efficient method of allocating resources and all markets will clear. In part at least, General Equilibrium Theory is an abstract answer to an abstract and important question: Can an economy relying only on price signals for market information be orderly? The answer of general equilibrium is clear and definitive – one can describe such an economy with these properties. However, no actual economy has been described and, given the assumptions involved, none could ever exist. A theoretical question has been answered involving some amount of intellectual achievement, but it is a answer which has no bearing to reality. And this is often termed the "high theory" of equilibrium. Obviously most economists must treat the real world as a special case.

Little wonder, then, that Kaldor argued that his "basic objection to the theory of general equilibrium is not that it is abstract – all theory is abstract and must necessarily be so since there can be no analysis without abstraction – but that it starts from the wrong kind of abstraction, and therefore gives a misleading 'paradigm' ... of the world as it is; it gives a misleading impression of the nature and the manner of operation of economic forces." Moreover, belief that equilibrium theory is the only starting point for economic analysis has survived "despite the increasing (**not** diminishing) arbitrariness of its based assumptions – which was forced upon its practitioners by the ever more precise cognition of the needs of logical consistency. In terms of gradually converting an 'intellectual experiment' ... into a scientific theory – in other words, a set of theorems directly related to observable phenomena – the development of theoretical economics was one of continual **de**gress, not **pro**gress ... The process ... of **relaxing** the unreal basis assumptions ... has not yet started. Indeed, [they get] ... thicker and more impenetrable with every successive reformation of the theory." [**Op. Cit.**, p. 399 and pp. 375-6]

Thus General Equilibrium theory analyses an economic state which there is no reason to suppose will ever, or has ever, come about. It is, therefore, an abstraction which has no discernible applicability or relevance to the world as it is. To argue that it can give insights into the real world is ridiculous. While it is true that there are certain imaginary intellectual problems for which the general equilibrium model is well designed to provide precise answers (if anything really could), in practice this means the same as saying that if one insists on analysing a problem which has no real world equivalent or solution, it may be appropriate to use a model which has no real-world application. Models derived to provide answers to imaginary problems will be unsuitable for resolving practical, real-world economic problems or even providing a useful insight into how capitalism works and develops.

This can have devastating real world impact, as can be seen from the results of neoclassical advice to Eastern Europe and other countries in their transition from state capitalism (Stalinism) to private capitalism. As Joseph Stiglitz documents it was a disaster for all but the elite due to the "market fundamentalism preached" by economists It resulted in "a marked deterioration" in most peoples "basic standard of living, reflected in a host of social indicators" and well as large drops in GDP. [**Globalisation and its discontents**, p. 138 and p. 152] Thus real people can be harmed by unreal theory. That the advice of neoclassical economists has made millions of people look back at Stalinism as "the good old days" should be enough to show its intellectual and moral bankruptcy.

What can you expect? Mainstream economic theory begins with axioms and assumptions and uses a deductive methodology to arrive at conclusions, its usefulness in discovering how the world works is limited. The deductive method is **pre-scientific** in nature. The axioms and assumptions can be considered fictitious (as they have negligible empirical relevance) and the conclusions of deductive models can only really have relevance to the structure of those models as the models themselves bear no relation to economic reality:

> "Some theorists, even among those who reject general equilibrium as useless, praise its logical elegance and completeness ... But if any proposition drawn from it is applied to an economy inhabited by human beings, it immediately becomes self-contradictory. Human life does not exist outside history and no one had correct foresight of his own future behaviour, let alone of the behaviour of all the other individuals which will impinge upon his. I do not think that it is right to praise the logical elegance of a system which becomes self-contradictory when it is applied to the question that it was designed to answer." [Joan Robinson, **Contributions to Modern Economics**, pp. 127-8]

Not that this deductive model is internally sound. For example, the assumptions required for perfect competition are mutually exclusive. In order for the market reach equilibrium, economic actors need to able to affect it. So, for example, if there is an excess supply some companies must lower their prices. However, such acts contradict the basic assumption of "perfect competition," namely that the number of buyers and sellers is so huge that no one individual actor (a firm or a consumer) can determine the market price by their actions. In other words, economists assume that the impact of each firm is zero but yet when these zeroes are summed up over the whole market the total is greater than zero. This is impossible. Moreover, the *"requirements of equilibrium are carefully examined in the Walrasian argument but there is no way of demonstrating that a market which starts in an out-of-equilibrium position will tend to get into equilibrium, except by putting further very severe restrictions on the already highly abstract argument."* [Joan Robinson, **Collected Economic Papers**, vol. 5, p. 154] Nor does the stable unique equilibrium actually exist for, ironically, *"mathematicians have shown that, under fairly general conditions, general equilibrium is unstable."* [Keen, **Debunking Economics**, p. 173]

Another major problem with equilibrium theory is the fact that it does not, in fact, describe a capitalist economy. It should go without saying that models which focus purely on exchange cannot, by definition, offer a realistic analysis, never mind description, of the capitalism or the generation of income in an industrialised economy. As Joan Robinson summarises:

> *"The neo-classical theory ... pretends to derive a system of prices from the relative scarcity of commodities in relation to the demand for them. I say **pretend** because this system cannot be applied to capitalist production.*
>
> *"The Walrasian conception of equilibrium arrived at by higgling and haggling in a market illuminates the account of prisoners of war swapping the contents of their Red Cross parcels.*
>
> *"It makes sense also, with some modifications, in an economy of artisans and small traders ...*
>
> *"Two essential characteristics of industrial capitalism are absent in these economic systems – the distinction between income from work and income from property and the nature of investments made in the light of uncertain expectations about a long future."* [**Collected Economic Papers**, vol. 5, p. 34]

Even such basic things as profits and money have a hard time fitting into general equilibrium theory. In a perfectly competitive equilibrium, super-normal profit is zero so profit fails to appear. Normal profit is assumed to be the contribution capital makes to output and is treated as a cost of production and notionally set as the zero mark. A capitalism without profit? Or growth, *"since there is no profit or any other sort of surplus in the neoclassical equilibrium, there can be no expanded reproduction of the system."* [Mattick, **Op. Cit.**, p. 22] It also treats capitalism as little more than a barter economy. The concept of general equilibrium is incompatible with the actual role of money in a capitalist economy.

The assumption of *"perfect knowledge"* makes the keeping of cash reserves as a precaution against unexpected developments would not be necessary as the future is already known. In a world where there was absolute certainty about the present and future there would be no need for a medium of exchange like money at all. In the real world, money has a real effect on production an economic stability. It is, in other words, not neutral (although, conveniently, in a fictional world with neutral money *"crises **do not occur**"* and it *"assumed away the very matter under investigation,"* namely depressions. [Keynes, quoted by Doug Henwood, **Wall Street**, p. 199]).

Given that general equilibrium theory does not satisfactorily encompass such things as profit, money, growth, instability or even firms, how it can be considered as even an adequate representation of any real capitalist economy is hard to understand. Yet, sadly, this perspective has dominated economics for over 100 years. There is almost no discussion of how scarce means are organised to yield outputs, the whole emphasis is on exchanges of ready made goods. This is unsurprising, as this allows economics to abstract from such key concepts as power, class and hierarchy. It shows the *"the bankruptcy of academic economic teaching. The structure of thought which it expounds was long ago proven to be hollow. It consisted of a set of propositions which bore hardly any relation to the structure and evolution of the economy that they were supposed to depict."* [Joan Robinson, **Op. Cit.**, p. 90]

Ultimately, equilibrium analysis simply presents an unreal picture of the real world. Economics treat a dynamic system as a static one, building models rooted in the concept of equilibrium when a non-equilibrium analysis makes obvious sense. As Steven Keen notes, it is not only the real world that has suffered, so has economics:

> *"This obsession with equilibrium has imposed enormous costs on economics ... unreal assumptions are needed to maintain conditions under which there will be a unique, 'optimal' equilibrium ... If you believe you can use unreality to model reality, then eventually your grip on reality itself can become tenuous."* [**Op. Cit.**, p. 177]

Ironically, given economists usual role in society as defenders of big business and the elite in general, there is one conclusion of general equilibrium theory which does have some relevance to the real world. In 1956, two economists *"demonstrated that serious problems exist for the model of competitive equilibrium if any of its assumptions are breached."* They were *"not dealing with the fundamental problem of whether a competitive equilibrium exists,"* rather they wanted to know what happens if the assumptions of the model were violated. Assuming that two violations existed, they worked out what would happen if only one of them were removed. The answer was a shock for economists – *"If just one of many, or even just one of two [violations] is removed, it is not possible to prejudge the outcome. The economy as a whole can theoretically be worse off if just one violation exists than it is when two such violations exist."* In other words, any single move towards the economists' ideal market may make the world worse off. [Ormerod, **Op. Cit.**, pp. 82-4]

What Kelvin Lancaster and Richard Lipsey had shown in their paper *"The General Theory of the Second Best"* [**Review of Economic**

Studies, December 1956] has one obvious implication, namely that neoclassical economics itself has shown that trade unions were essential to stop workers being exploited under capitalism. This is because the neoclassical model requires there to be a multitude of small firms and no unions. In the real world, most markets are dominated by a few big firms. Getting rid of unions in such a less than competitive market would result in the wage being less than the price for which the marginal worker's output can be sold, i.e. workers are exploited by capital. In other words, economics has **itself** disproved the neoclassical case against trade unions. Not that you would know that from neoclassical economists, of course. In spite of knowing that, in their own terms, breaking union power while retaining big business would result, in the exploitation of labour, neoclassical economists lead the attack on "union power" in the 1970s and 1980s. The subsequent explosion in inequality as wealth flooded upwards provided empirical confirmation of this analysis.

Strangely, though, most neoclassical economists are still as anti-union as ever – in spite of both their own ideology and the empirical evidence. That the anti-union message is just what the bosses want to hear can just be marked up as yet another one of those strange co-incidences which the value-free science of economics is so prone to. Suffice to say, if the economics profession ever questions general equilibrium theory it will be due to conclusions like this becoming better known in the general population.

C.1.5 Does economics really reflect the reality of capitalism?

As we discussed in section C.1.2, mainstream economics is rooted in capitalism and capitalist social relations. It takes the current division of society into classes as both given **as well as** producing the highest form of efficiency. In other words, mainstream economics is rooted in capitalist assumptions and, unsurprisingly, its conclusions are, almost always, beneficial to capitalists, managers, landlords, lenders and the rich rather than workers, tenants, borrowers and the poor.

However, on another level mainstream capitalist economics simply does **not** reflect capitalism at all. While this may seem paradoxical, it is not. Neoclassical economics has always been marked by apologetics. Consequently, it must abstract or ignore from the more unpleasant and awkward aspects of capitalism in order to present it in the best possible light.

Take, for example, the labour market. Anarchists, like other socialists, have always stressed that under capitalism workers have the choice between selling their liberty/labour to a boss or starving to death (or extreme poverty, assuming some kind of welfare state). This is because they do not have access to the means of life (land and workplaces) unless they sell their labour to those who own them. In such circumstances, it makes little sense to talk of liberty as the only real liberty working people have is, if they are lucky, agreeing to be exploited by one boss rather than another. How much an person works, like their wages, will be based on the

relative balance of power between the working and capitalist classes in a given situation.

Unsurprisingly, neoclassical economics does not portray the choice facing working class people in such a realistic light. Rather, it argues that the amount of hours an individual works is based on their preference for income and leisure time. Thus the standard model of the labour market is somewhat paradoxical in that there is no actual labour in it. There is only income, leisure and the preference of the individual for more of one or the other. It is leisure that is assumed to be a "normal good" and labour is just what is left over after the individual "consumes" all the leisure they want. This means that working resolves itself into the vacuous double negative of not-not-working and the notion that all unemployment is voluntary.

That this is nonsense should be obvious. How much "leisure" can someone indulge in without an income? How can an economic theory be considered remotely valid when it presents unemployment (i.e. no income) as the ultimate utility in an economy where everything is (or should be) subject to a price? Income, then, has an overwhelming impact upon the marginal utility of leisure time. Equally, this perspective cannot explain why the prospect of job loss is seen with such fear by most workers. If the neoclassical (non-)analysis of the labour market were true, workers would be happy to be made unemployed. In reality, fear of the sack is a major disciplining tool within capitalism. That free market capitalist economists have succeeded in making unemployment appear as a desirable situation suggests that its grip on the reality of capitalism is slim to say the least (here, as in many other areas, Keynes is more realistic although most of his followers have capitulated faced with neoclassical criticism that standard Keynesian theory had bad micro-economic foundations rather than admit that later was nonsense and the former *"an emasculated version of Keynes"* inflicted on the world by J.R. Hicks. [Keen, **Op. Cit.**, p. 211]).

However, this picture of the "labour" market does hide the reality of working class dependency and, consequently, the power of the capitalist class. To admit that workers do not exercise any free choice over whether they work or not and, once in work, have to accept the work hours set by their employers makes capitalism seem less wonderful than its supporters claim. Ultimately, this fiction of the labour market being driven by the workers' desire for "leisure" and that all unemployment is "voluntary" is rooted in the need to obscure the fact that unemployment is an essential feature of capitalism and, consequently, is endemic to it. This is because it is the fundamental disciplinary mechanism of the system (*"it is a whip in [the bosses'] hands, constantly held over you, so you will slave hard for him and 'behave' yourself,"* to quote Alexander Berkman). As we argued in section B.4.3, capitalism **must** have unemployment in order to ensure that workers will obey their bosses and not demand better pay and conditions (or, even worse, question why they have bosses in the first place). It is, in other words, *"inherent in the wage system"* and *"the fundamental condition of successful capitalist production."* While it is *"dangerous and degrading"* to the worker, it is *"very advantageous to the boss"* and so capitalism *"can't exist without it."* [Berkman, **What is Anarchism?**, p. 26] The experience of state managed full employment between (approximately) 1950 and 1970 confirms this analysis, as does the subsequent period (see section C.7.1).

For the choice of leisure and labour to be a reality, then workers need an independent source of income. The model, in other words, assumes that workers need to be enticed by the given wage and this is only the case when workers have the option of working for themselves, i.e. that they own their own means of production. If this were the case, then it would not be capitalism. In other words, the vision of the labour market in capitalist economics assumes a non-capitalist economy of artisans and peasant farmers – precisely the kind of economy capitalism destroyed (with the help of the state). An additional irony of this neoclassical analysis is that those who subscribe to it most are also those who attack the notion of a generous welfare state (or oppose the idea of welfare state in all forms). Their compliant is that with a welfare state, the labour market becomes "inefficient" as people can claim benefits and so need not seek work. Yet, logically, they should support a generous welfare state as it gives working people a genuine choice between labour and leisure. That bosses find it hard to hire people should be seen as a good thing as work is obviously being evaluated as a "disutility" rather than as a necessity. As an added irony, as we discuss in section C.9, the capitalist analysis of the labour market is **not** based on any firm empirical evidence nor does it have any real logical basis (it is just an assumption). In fact, the evidence we do have points against it and in favour of the socialist analysis of unemployment and the labour market.

One of the reasons why neoclassical economics is so blasé about unemployment is because it argues that it should never happen. That capitalism has always been marked by unemployment and that this rises and falls as part of the business cycle is a inconvenient fact which neoclassical economics avoided seriously analysing until the 1930s. This flows from Say's law, the argument that supply creates its own demand. This theory, and its more formally put Walras' Law, is the basis on which the idea that capitalism could never face a general economic crisis is rooted in. That capitalism has **always** been marked by boom and bust has never put Say's Law into question except during the 1930s and even then it was quickly put back into the centre of economic ideology.

For Say, "every producer asks for money in exchange for his products only for the purpose of employing that money again immediately in the purchase of another product." However, this is not the case in a capitalist economy as capitalists seek to accumulate wealth and this involves creating a difference between the value of commodities someone desired to sell and buy on the market. While Say asserts that people simply want to consume commodities, capitalism is marked by the desire (the need) to accumulate. The ultimate aim is **not** consumption, as Say asserted (and today's economists repeat), but rather to make as much profit as possible. To ignore this is to ignore the essence of capitalism and while it may allow the economist to reason away the contradictions of that system, the reality of the business cycle cannot be ignored.

Say's law, in other words, assumes a world without **capital**:

> "what is a given stock of capital? In this context, clearly, it is the actual equipment and stocks of commodities that happen to be in existence today, the result of recent or remote past history, together with the know-how, skill of labour, etc., that makes up the state of technology.

> Equipment ... is designed for a particular range of uses, to be operated by a particular labour force. There is not a great deal of play in it. The description of the stock of equipment in existence at any moment as 'scare means with alternative uses' is rather exaggerated. The uses in fact are fairly specific, though they may be changed over time. But they **can** be utilised, at any moment, by offering less or more employment to labour. This is a characteristic of the wage economy. In an artisan economy, where each producer owns his own equipment, each produces what he can and sells it for what it will fetch. Say's law, that goods are the demand for goods, was ceasing to be true at the time he formulated it." [Joan Robinson, **Collected Economic Papers**, vol. 4, p. 133]

As Keen notes, Say's law "envisage[s] an exchange-only economy: an economy in which goods exist at the outset, but where no production takes place. The market simply enables the exchange of pre-existing goods." However, once we had capital to the economy, things change as capitalists wish "to supply more than they demand, and to accumulate the difference as profit which adds to their wealth." This results in an excess demand and, consequently, the possibility of a crisis. Thus mainstream capitalist economics "is best suited to the economic irrelevance of an exchange-only economy, or a production economy in which growth does not occur. If production and growth do occur, then they take place outside the market, when ironically the market is the main intellectual focus of neoclassical economics. Conventional economics is this a theory which suits a state economy ... when what is needed are theories to analyse dynamic economies." [**Debunking Economics**, p. 194, p. 195 and p. 197]

Ultimately, capital assets are not produced for their own sake but in expectation of profits. This obvious fact is ignored by Say's law, but was recognised by Marx (and subsequently acknowledged by Keynes as being correct). As Keen notes, unlike Say and his followers, "Marx's perspective thus integrates production, exchange and credit as holistic aspects of a capitalist economy, and therefore as essential elements of any theory of capitalism. Conventional economics, in contrast, can only analyse an exchange economy in which money is simply a means to make barter easier." [**Op. Cit.**, pp. 195-6]

Rejecting Say's Law as being applicable to capitalism means recognising that the capitalist economy is not stable, that it can experience booms and slumps. That this reflects the reality of that economy should go without saying. It also involves recognising that it can take time for unemployed workers to find new employment, that unemployment can by involuntary and that bosses can gain advantages from the fear of unemployment by workers.

That last fact, the fear of unemployment is used by bosses to get workers to accept reductions in wages, hours and benefits, is key factor facing workers in any real economy. Yet, according to the economic textbooks, workers should have been falling over themselves to maximise the utility of leisure and minimise the disutility of work. Similarly, workers should not fear being made unemployed by globalisation as the export of any jobs would simply have generated more economic activity and so the displaced workers would immediately be re-employed (albeit at a lower wage, perhaps). Again, according to the economic textbooks, these lower wages would generate even more economic activity and thus lead, in the long run, to higher wages. If only workers had only listened to the economists then they would realise that that not only did they actually gain (in the long run) by their wages, hours and benefits being cut, many of them also gained (in the short term) increased utility by not having to go to work. That is, assuming the economists know what they are talking about.

Then there is the question of income. For most capitalist economics, a given wage is supposed to be equal to the *"marginal contribution"* that an individual makes to a given company. Are we **really** expected to believe this? Common sense (and empirical evidence) suggests otherwise. Consider Mr. Rand Araskog, the CEO of ITT in 1990, who in that year was paid a salary of $7 million. Is it conceivable that an ITT accountant calculated that, all else being the same, the company's $20.4 billion in revenues that year would have been $7 million less without Mr. Araskog – hence determining his marginal contribution to be $7 million? This seems highly unlikely.

Which feeds into the question of exploding CEO pay. While this has affected most countries, the US has seen the largest increases (followed by the UK). In 1979 the CEO of a UK company earned slightly less than 10 times as much as the average worker on the shop floor. By 2002 a boss of a FTSE 100 company could expect to make 54 times as much as the typical worker. This means that while the wages for those on the shopfloor went up a little, once inflation is taken into account, the bosses wages arose from £200,000 per year to around £1.4m a year. In America, the increase was even worse. In 1980, the ratio of CEO to worker pay 50 to 1. Twenty years later it was 525 to 1, before falling back to 281 to 1 in 2002 following the collapse of the share price bubble. [Larry Elliott, *"Nice work if you can get it: chief executives quietly enrich themselves for mediocrity,"* **The Guardian**, 23 January, 2006]

The notion of marginal productivity is used to justify many things on the market. For example, the widening gap between high-paid and low-paid Americans (it is argued) simply reflects a labour market efficiently rewarding more productive people. Thus the compensation for corporate chief executives climbs so sharply because it reflects their marginal productivity. The strange thing about this kind of argument is that, as we indicate in section C.2.5, the problem of defining and measuring capital wrecked the entire neoclassical theory of marginal factor productivity and with it the associated marginal productivity theory of income back in the 1960s – and was admitted as the leading neo-classical economists of the time. That marginal productivity theory is still invoked to justify capitalist inequalities shows not only how economics ignores the reality of capitalism but also the intellectual bankruptcy of the "science" and whose interests it, ultimately, serves.

In spite of this awkward little fact, what of the claims made based on it? Is this pay **really** the result of any increased productivity on the part of CEOs? The evidence points the other way. This can be seen from the performance of the economies and companies in question. In Britain trend growth was a bit more than 2% in 1980 and is still a bit more than 2% a quarter of a century later. A study of corporate performance in Britain and the United States looked at the companies that make up the FTSE 100 index in Britain and

the S&P 500 in the US and found that executive income is rarely justified by improved performance. [Julie Froud, Sukhdev Johal, Adam Leaver and Karel Williams, **Financialisation and Strategy: Narrative and Number**] Rising stock prices in the 1990s, for example, were the product of one of the financial market's irrational bubbles over which the CEO's had no control or role in creating.

During the same period as soaring CEO pay, workers' real wages remained flat. Are we to believe that since the 1980s, the marginal contribution of CEOs has increased massively whereas workers' marginal contributions remained stagnant? According to economists, in a free market wages should increase until they reach their marginal productivity. In the US, however, during the 1960s *"pay and productivity grew in tandem, but they separated in the 1970s. In the 1990s boom, pay growth lagged behind productivity by almost 30%."* Looking purely at direct pay, *"overall productivity rose four times as fast as the average real hourly wage – and twenty times as fast in manufacturing."* Pay did catch up a bit in the late 1990s, but after 2000 *"pay returned to its lagging position."* [Doug Henwood, **After the New Economy**, pp. 45-6] In other words, over two decades of free market reforms has produced a situation which has refuted the idea that a workers wage equals their marginal productivity.

The standard response by economists would be to state that the US economy is not a free market. Yet the 1970s, after all, saw the start of reforms based on the recommendations of free market capitalist economists. The 1980s and 1990s saw even more. Regulation was reduced, if not effectively eliminated, the welfare state rolled back and unions marginalised. So it staggers belief to state that the US was **more** free market in the 1950s and 1960s than in the 1980s and 1990s but, logically, this is what economists suggest. Moreover, this explanation sits ill at ease with the multitude of economists who justified growing inequality and skyrocketing CEO pay and company profits during this period in terms of free market economics. What is it to be? If the US is not a free market, then the incomes of companies and the wealth are **not** the result of their marginal contribution but rather are gained at the expense of the working class. If the US is a free market, then the rich are justified (in terms of economic theory) in their income but workers' wages do not equal their marginal productivity. Unsurprisingly, most economists do not raise the question, never mind answer it.

So what is the reason for this extreme wage difference? Simply put, it's due to the totalitarian nature of capitalist firms (see section B.4). Those at the bottom of the company have no say in what happens within it; so as long as the share-owners are happy, wage differentials will rise and rise (particularly when top management own large amounts of shares!). It is capitalist property relations that allow this monopolisation of wealth by the few who own (or boss) but do not produce. The workers do not get the full value of what they produce, nor do they have a say in how the surplus value produced by their labour gets used (e.g. investment decisions). Others have monopolised both the wealth produced by workers and the decision-making power within the company (see section C.2 for more discussion). This is a private form of taxation without representation, just as the company is a private form of statism. Unlike the typical economist, most people would not consider it too strange a coincidence that the people with power in a company, when working out who contributes most to a product, decide it's themselves!

Whether workers will tolerate stagnating wages depends, of course, on the general economic climate. High unemployment and job insecurity help make workers obedient and grateful for any job and this has been the case for most of the 1980s and 1990s in both America and the UK. So a key reason for the exploding pay is to be found in the successful class struggle the ruling class has been waging since the 1970s. There has *"been a real shift in focus, so that the beneficiaries of corporate success (such as it is) are no longer the workers and the general public as a whole but shareholders. And given that there is evidence that only households in the top half of the income distribution in the UK and the US hold shares, this represents a significant redistribution of money and power."* [Larry Elliott, **Op. Cit.**] That economics ignores the social context of rising CEO pay says a lot about the limitations of modern economics and how it can be used to justify the current system.

Then there is the trivial little thing of production. Economics used to be called "political economy" and was production orientated. This was replaced by an economics based on marginalism and subjective evaluations of a given supply of goods is fixed. For classical economics, to focus on an instant of time was meaningless as time does not stop. To exclude production meant to exclude time, which as we noted in section C.1.2 this is precisely and knowingly what marginalist economics did do. This means modern economics simply ignores production as well as time and given that profit making is a key concern for any firm in the real world, such a position shows how irrelevant neoclassical economics really is.

Indeed, the neo-classical theory falls flat on its face. Basing itself, in effect, on a snapshot of time its principles for the rational firm are, likewise, based on time standing still. It argues that profit is maximised where marginal cost equals marginal revenue yet this is only applicable when you hold time constant. However, a real firm will not maximise profit with respect to quantity but also in respect to time. The neoclassical rule about how to maximise profit *"is therefore correct if the quantity produced never changes"* and *"by ignoring time in its analysis of the firm, economic theory ignores some of the most important issues facing a firm."* Neo-classical economics exposes its essentially static nature again. It *"ignores time, and is therefore only relevant in a world in which time does no matter."* [Keen, **Op. Cit.**, pp. 80-1]

Then there is the issue of consumption. While capitalist apologists go on about *"consumer sovereignty"* and the market as a *"consumers democracy,"* the reality is somewhat different. Firstly, and most obviously, big business spends a lot of money trying to shape and influence demand by means of advertising. Not for them the neoclassical assumption of "given" needs, determined outside the system. So the reality of capitalism is one where the "sovereign" is manipulated by others. Secondly, there is the distribution of resources within society.

Market demand is usually discussed in terms of tastes, not in the distribution of purchasing power required to satisfy those tastes. Income distribution is taken as given, which is very handy for those with the most wealth. Needless to say, those who have a lot of money will be able to maximise their satisfactions far easier than those who have little. Also, of course, they can out-bid those with

less money. If capitalism is a "consumers" democracy then it is a strange one, based on *"one dollar, one vote."* It should be obvious whose values are going to be reflected most strongly in the market. If we start with the orthodox economics (convenient) assumption of a *"given distribution of income"* then any attempt to determine the best allocation of resources is flawed to start with as money replaces utility from the start. To claim after that the market based distribution is the best one is question begging in the extreme.

In other words, under capitalism, it is not individual need or "utility" as such that is maximised, rather it is **effective** utility (usually called "effective demand") – namely utility that is backed up with money. This is the reality behind all the appeals to the marvels of the market. As right-wing guru von Hayek put, the *"[s]pontaneous order produced by the market does not ensure that what general opinion regards as more important needs are always met before the less important ones."* [*"Competition as a discovery process"*, **The Essence of Hayek**, p. 258] Which is just a polite way of referring to the process by which millionaires build a new mansion while thousands are homeless or live in slums or feed luxury food to their pets while humans go hungry. It is, in effect, to dismiss the needs of, for example, the 37 million Americans who lived below the poverty line in 2005 (12.7% of the population, the highest percentage in the developed world and is based on the American state's absolute definition of poverty, looking at relative levels, the figures are worse). Similarly, the 46 million Americans without health insurance may, of course, think that their need to live should be considered as *"more important"* than, say, allowing Paris Hilton to buy a new designer outfit. Or, at the most extreme, when agribusiness grow cash crops for foreign markets while the landless starve to death. As E.P. Thompson argues, Hayek's answer:

> *"promote[s] the notion that high prices were a (painful) remedy for dearth, in drawing supplies to the afflicted region of scarcity. But what draws supply are not high prices but sufficient money in their purses to pay high prices. A characteristic phenomenon in times of dearth is that it generates unemployment and empty pursues; in purchasing necessities at inflated prices people cease to be able to buy inessentials [causing unemployment] … Hence the number of those able to pay the inflated prices declines in the afflicted regions, and food may be exported to neighbouring, less afflicted, regions where employment is holding up and consumers still have money with which to pay. In this sequence, high prices can actually withdraw supply from the most afflicted area."* [**Customs in Common**, pp. 283-4]

Therefore *"the law of supply and demand"* may not be the "most efficient" means of distribution in a society based on inequality. This is clearly reflected in the "rationing" by purse which this system is based on. While in the economics books, price is the means by which scare resources are "rationed" in reality this creates many errors. As Thompson notes, *"[h]owever persuasive the metaphor, there is an elision of the real Relationships assigned by price, which suggests … ideological sleight-of-mind. Rationing by price does not allocate resources equally among those in need; it reserves the*

What are the myths of capitalist economics?

supply to those who can pay the price and excludes those who can't.... The raising of prices during dearth could 'ration' them [the poor] out of the market altogether." [**Op. Cit.**, p. 285] Which is precisely what does happen. As economist (and famine expert) Amartya Sen notes:

> "Take a theory of entitlements based on a set of rights of 'ownership, transfer and rectification.' In this system a set of holdings of different people are judged to be just (or unjust) by looking at past history, and not by checking the consequences of that set of holdings. But what if the consequences are recognisably terrible? ... [R]efer[ing] to some empirical findings in a work on famines ... evidence [is presented] to indicate that in many large famines in the recent past, in which millions of people have died, there was no over-all decline in food availability at all, and the famines occurred precisely because of shifts in entitlement resulting from exercises of rights that are perfectly legitimate. ... [Can] famines ... occur with a system of rights of the kind morally defended in various ethical theories, including Nozick's. I believe the answer is straightforwardly yes, since for many people the only resource that they legitimately possess, viz. their labour-power, may well turn out to be unsaleable in the market, giving the person no command over food ... [i]f results such as starvations and famines were to occur, would the distribution of holdings still be morally acceptable despite their disastrous consequences? There is something deeply implausible in the affirmative answer." [**Resources, Values and Development**, pp. 311-2]

Recurring famines were a constant problem during the laissez-faire period of the British Empire. While the Irish Potato famine is probably the best known, the fact is that millions died due to starvation mostly due to a firm belief in the power of the market. In British India, according to the most reliable estimates, the deaths from the 1876-1878 famine were in the range of 6-8 million and between 1896 and 1900, were between 17 to 20 million. According to a British statistician who analysed Indian food security measures in the two millennia prior to 1800, there was one major famine a century in India. Under British rule there was one every four years. Over all, the late 1870s and the late 1890s saw somewhere between 30 to 60 million people die in famines in India, China and Brazil (not including the many more who died elsewhere). While bad weather started the problem by placing the price of food above the reach of the poorest, the market and political decisions based on profound belief in it made the famine worse. Simply put, had the authorities distributed what food existed, most of the victims would have survived yet they did not as this would have, they argued, broke the laws of the market and produced a culture of dependency. [Mike Davis, **Late Victorian Holocausts**] This pattern, incidentally, has been repeated in third world countries to this day with famine countries exporting food as the there is no "demand" for it at home.

All of which puts Hayek's glib comments about *"spontaneous order"* into a more realistic context. As Kropotkin put it:

> "The very essence of the present economic system is that the worker can never enjoy the well-being he [or she] has produced ... Inevitably, industry is directed ... not towards what is needed to satisfy the needs of all, but towards that which, at a given moment, brings in the greatest profit for a few. Of necessity, the abundance of some will be based on the poverty of others, and the straitened circumstances of the greater number will have to be maintained at all costs, that there may be hands to sell themselves for a part only of what which they are capable of producing; without which private accumulation of capital is impossible." [**Anarchism**, p. 128]

In other words, the market cannot be isolated and abstracted from the network of political, social and legal relations within which it is situated. This means that all that "supply and demand" tells us is that those with money can demand more, and be supplied with more, than those without. Whether this is the "most efficient" result for society cannot be determined (unless, of course, you assume that rich people are more valuable than working class ones **because** they are rich). This has an obvious effect on production, with "effective demand" twisting economic activity and so, under capitalism, meeting needs is secondary as the *"only aim is to increase the profits of the capitalist."* [Kropotkin, **Op. Cit.**, p. 55]). George Barrett brings home of evil effects of such a system:

> "To-day the scramble is to compete for the greatest profits. If there is more profit to be made in satisfying my lady's passing whim than there is in feeding hungry children, then competition brings us in feverish haste to supply the former, whilst cold charity or the poor law can supply the latter, or leave it unsupplied, just as it feels disposed. That is how it works out." [**Objections to Anarchism**, p. 347]

Therefore, as far as consumption is concerned, anarchists are well aware of the need to create and distribute necessary goods to those who require them. This, however, cannot be achieved under capitalism and for all its talk of "utility," "demand", "consumer sovereignty" and so forth the real facts are those with most money determine what is an "efficient" allocation of resources. This is directly, in terms of their control over the means of life as well as indirectly, by means of skewing market demand. For if financial profit is the sole consideration for resource allocation, then the wealthy can outbid the poor and ensure the highest returns. The less wealthy can do without.

All in all, the world assumed by neo-classical economics is not the one we actually live in, and so applying that theory is both misleading and (usually) disastrous (at least to the "have-nots"). While this may seen surprisingly, it is not once we take into account its role as apologist and defender of capitalism. Once that is recognised, any apparent contradiction falls away.

C.1.6 Is it possible to have a non-equilibrium based capitalist economics?

Yes, it is but it would be unlikely to be free-market based as the reality of capitalism would get the better of its apologetics. This can be seen from the two current schools of economics which, rightly, reject the notion of equilibrium – the post-Keynesian school and the so-called Austrian school.

The former has few illusions in the nature of capitalism. At its best, this school combines the valid insights of classical economics, Marx and Keynes to produce a robust radical (even socialist) critique of both capitalism and capitalist economics. At its worse, it argues for state intervention to save capitalism from itself and, politically, aligns itself with social democratic (*"liberal"*, in the USA) movements and parties. If economics does become a science, then this school of economics will play a key role in its development. Economists of this school include Joan Robinson, Nicholas Kaldor, John Kenneth Galbraith, Paul Davidson and Steven Keen. Due to its non-apologetic nature, we will not discuss it here.

The Austrian school has a radically different perspective. This school, so named because its founders were Austrian, is passionately pro-capitalist and argues against **any** form of state intervention (bar, of course, the definition and defence of capitalist property rights and the power that these create). Economists of this school include Eugen von Böhm-Bawerk, Ludwig von Mises, Murray Rothbard, Israel Kirzner and Friedrich Hayek (the latter is often attacked by other Austrian economists as not being sufficiently robust in his opposition to state intervention). It is very much a minority school.

As it shares many of the same founding fathers as neoclassical economics and is rooted in marginalism, the Austrian school is close to neoclassical economics in many ways. The key difference is that it rejects the notion that the economy is in equilibrium and embraces a more dynamic model of capitalism. It is rooted in the notion of entrepreneurial activity, the idea that entrepreneurs act on information and disequilibrium to make super profits and bring the system closer to equilibrium. Thus, to use their expression, their focus is on the market process rather than a non-existent end state. As such, it defends capitalism in terms of how it reacts to **dis**-equilibrium and presents a theory of the market process that brings the economy closer to equilibrium. And fails.

The claim that markets tend continually towards equilibrium, as the consequence of entrepreneurial actions, is hard to justify in terms of its own assumptions. While the adjustments of a firm may bring the specific market it operates in more towards equilibrium, their ramifications may take other markets away from it and so any action will have stabilising and destabilising aspects to it. It strains belief to assume that entrepreneurial activity will only push an economy more towards equilibrium as any change in the supply and demand for any specific good leads to changes in the markets for other goods (including money). That these adjustments will all (mostly) tend towards equilibrium is little more than wishful thinking.

While being more realistic than mainstream neo-classical theory, this method abandons the possibility of demonstrating that the market outcome is in any sense a realisation of the individual preferences of whose interaction it is an expression. It has no way of establishing the supposedly stabilising character of entrepreneurial activity or its alleged socially beneficial character as the dynamic process could lead to a divergence rather than a convergence of behaviour. A dynamic system need not be self-correcting, particularly in the labour market, nor show any sign of self-equilibrium (i.e. it will be subject to the business cycle).

Given that the Austrian theory is, in part, based on Say's Law the critique we presented in the last section also applies here. However, there is another reason to think the Austrian self-adjusting perspective on capitalism is flawed and this is rooted in their own analysis. Ironically enough, economists of this school often maintain that while equilibrium does not exist their analysis is rooted on two key markets being in such a state: the labour market and the market for credit. The reason for these strange exceptions to their general assumption is, fundamentally, political. The former is required to deflect claims that "pure" capitalism would result in the exploitation of the working class, the latter is required to show that such a system would be stable.

Looking at the labour market, the Austrians argue that free market capitalism would experience full employment. That this condition is one of equilibrium does not seem to cause them much concern. Thus we find von Hayek, for example, arguing that the *"cause of unemployment … is a deviation of prices and wages from their equilibrium position which would establish itself with a free market and stable money. But we can never know at what system of relative prices and wages such an equilibrium would establish itself."* Therefore, *"the deviation of existing prices from that equilibrium position … is the cause of the impossibility of selling part of the labour supply."* [**New Studies**, p. 201] Therefore, we see the usual embrace of equilibrium theory to defend capitalism against the evils it creates even by those who claim to know better.

Of course, the need to argue that there would be full employment under "pure" capitalism is required to maintain the fiction that everyone will be better off under it. It is hard to say that working class people will benefit if they are subject to high levels of unemployment and the resulting fear and insecurity that produces. As would be expected, the Austrian school shares the same perspective on unemployment as the neoclassical school, arguing that it is *"voluntary"* and the result of the price of labour being too high (who knew that depressions were so beneficial to workers, what with some having more leisure to enjoy and the others having higher than normal wages?). The reality of capitalism is very different than this abstract model.

Anarchists have long realised that the capitalist market is based upon inequalities and changes in power. Proudhon argued that *"[t]he manufacturer says to the labourer, 'You are as free to go elsewhere with your services as I am to receive them. I offer you so much.' The merchant says to the customer, 'Take it or leave it; you are master of your money, as I am of my goods. I want so much.' Who will yield? The weaker."* He, like all anarchists, saw that domination, oppression and exploitation flow from inequalities of market/economic power and that the *"power of invasion lies in superior strength."* [**What is Property?**, p. 216 and p. 215] This is particularly the case in the labour market, as we argued in section B.4.3.

As such, it is unlikely that "pure" capitalism would experience full employment for under such conditions the employers loose the upper hand. To permanently experience a condition which, as we indicate in section C.7, causes "actually existing" capitalism so many problems seems more like wishful thinking than a serious analysis. If unemployment is included in the Austrian model (as it should) then the bargaining position of labour is obviously weakened and, as a consequence, capital will take advantage and gather profits at the expense of labour. Conversely, if labour is empowered by full employment then they can use their position to erode the profits and managerial powers of their bosses. Logically, therefore, we would expect less than full unemployment and job insecurity to be the normal state of the economy with short periods of full unemployment before a slump. Given this, we would expect "pure" capitalism to be unstable, just as the approximations to it in history have always been. Austrian economics gives no reason to believe that would change in the slightest. Indeed, given their obvious hatred of trade unions and the welfare state, the bargaining power of labour would be weakened further during most of the business cycle and, contra Hayek, unemployment would remain and its level would fluctuate significantly throughout the business cycle.

Which brings us to the next atypical market in Austrian theory, namely the credit market. According to the Austrian school, "pure" capitalism would not suffer from a business cycle (or, at worse, a very mild one). This is due to the lack of equilibrium in the credit market due to state intervention (or, more correctly, state non-intervention). Austrian economist W. Duncan Reekie provides a summary:

> "The business cycle is generated by monetary expansion and contraction ... When new money is printed it appears as if the supply of savings has increased. Interest rates fall and businessmen are misled into borrowing additional founds to finance extra investment activity ... This would be of no consequence if it had been the outcome of [genuine saving] ... – but the change was government induced. The new money reaches factor owners in the form of wages, rent and interest ... the factor owners will then spend the higher money incomes in their existing consumption:investment proportions ... Capital goods industries will find their expansion has been in error and malinvestments have been incurred." [**Markets, Entrepreneurs and Liberty**, pp. 68-9]

This analysis is based on their notion that the interest rate reflects the "time preference" of individuals between present and future goods (see section C.2.6 for more details). The argument is that banks or governments manipulate the money supply or interest rates, making the actual interest rate different from the "real" interest rate which equates savings and loans. Of course, that analysis is dependent on the interest rate equating savings and loans which is, of course, an equilibrium position. If we assume that the market for credit shows the same disequilibrium tendencies as other markets, then the possibility for malinvestment is extremely likely as banks and other businesses extend credit based on inaccurate assumptions

about present conditions and uncertain future developments in order to secure greater profits. Unsurprisingly, the Austrians (like most economists) expect the working class to bear the price for any recession in terms of real wage cuts in spite of their theory indicating that its roots lie in capitalists and bankers seeking more profits and, consequently, the former demanding and the latter supplying more credit than the "natural" interest rate would supply.

Ironically, therefore, the Austrian business cycle is rooted in the concept of **dis**-equilibrium in the credit market, the condition it argues is the standard situation in all other markets. In effect, they think that the money supply and interest rates are determined exogenously (i.e. outside the economy) by the state. However, this is unlikely as the evidence points the other way, i.e. to the endogenous nature of the money supply itself. This account of money (proposed strongly by, among others, the post-Keynesian school) argues that the money supply is a function of the demand for credit, which itself is a function of the level of economic activity. In other words, the banking system creates as much money as people need and any attempt to control that creation will cause economic problems and, perhaps, crisis. Money, in other words, emerges from **within** the system and so the Austrian attempt to "blame the state" is simply wrong. As we discuss in section C.8, attempts by the state to control the money during the Monetarist disasters of the early 1980s failed and it is unlikely that this would change in a "pure" capitalism marked by a totally privatised banking system.

It should also be noted that in the 1930s, the Austrian theory of the business cycle lost the theoretical battle with the Keynesian one (not to be confused with the neoclassical-Keynesian synthesis of the post-war years). This was for three reasons. Firstly, it was irrelevant (its conclusion was do nothing). Secondly, it was arrogant (it essentially argued that the slump would not have happened if people had listened to them and the pain of depression was fully deserved for not doing so). Thirdly, and most importantly, the leading Austrian theorist on the business cycle was completely refuted by Piero Sraffa and Nicholas Kaldor (Hayek's own follower who turned Keynesian) both of whom exposed the internal contradictions of his analysis.

The empirical record backs our critique of the Austrian claims on the stability of capitalism and unemployment. Throughout the nineteenth century there were a continual economic booms and slumps. This was the case in the USA, often pointed to as an approximately laissez-faire economy, where the last third of the 19th century (often considered as a heyday of private enterprise) was a period of profound instability and anxiety. Between 1867 and 1900 there were 8 complete business cycles. Over these 396 months, the economy expanded during 199 months and contracted during 197. Hardly a sign of great stability (since the end of world war II, only about a fifth of the time has spent in periods of recession or depression, by way of comparison). Overall, the economy went into a slump, panic or crisis in 1807, 1817, 1828, 1834, 1837, 1854, 1857, 1873, 1882, and 1893 (in addition, 1903 and 1907 were also crisis years). Full employment, needless to say, was not the normal situation (during the 1890s, for example, the unemployment rate exceeded 10% for 6 consecutive years, reaching a peak of 18.4% in 1894, and was under 4% for just one, 1892). So much for temporary and mild slumps, prices adjusting fast and markets clearing quickly in pre-Keynesian economies!

Luckily, though, the Austrian school's methodology allows it to ignore such irritating constrictions as facts, statistics, data, history or experimental confirmation. While neoclassical economics at least **pretends** to be scientific, the Austrian school displays its deductive (i.e. pre-scientific) methodology as a badge of pride along side its fanatical love of free market capitalism. For the Austrians, in the words of von Mises, economic theory *"is not derived from experience; it is prior to experience"* and *"no kind of experience can ever force us to discard or modify **a priori** theorems; they are logically prior to it and cannot be either proved by corroborative experience or disproved by experience to the contrary."* And if this does not do justice to a full exposition of the phantasmagoria of von Mises' **a priorism**, the reader may take some joy (or horror) from the following statement:

> *"If a contradiction appears between a theory and experience, **we must always assume** that a condition pre-supposed by the theory was not present, or else there is some error in our observation. The disagreement between the theory and the facts of experience frequently forces us to think through the problems of the theory again. **But so long as a rethinking of the theory uncovers no errors in our thinking, we are not entitled to doubt its truth"*** [emphasis added, quoted by Homa Katouzian, **Ideology and Method in Economics**, pp. 39-40]

In other words, if reality is in conflict with your ideas, do not adjust your views because reality must be at fault! The scientific method would be to revise the theory in light of the facts. It is not scientific to reject the facts in light of the theory! Without experience, any theory is just a flight of fantasy. For the higher a deductive edifice is built, the more likely it is that errors will creep in and these can only be corrected by checking the analysis against reality. Starting assumptions and trains of logic may contain inaccuracies so small as to be undetectable, yet will yield entirely false conclusions. Similarly, trains of logic may miss things which are only brought to light by actual experiences or be correct, but incomplete or concentrate on or stress inappropriate factors. To ignore actual experience is to loose that input when evaluating a theory.

Ignoring the obvious problems of the empirical record, as any consistent Austrian would, the question does arise why does the Austrian school make exceptions to its disequilibrium analysis for these two markets. Perhaps this is a case of political expediency, allowing the ideological supporters of free market capitalism to attack the notion of equilibrium when it clearly clashes with reality but being able to return to it when attacking, say, trade unions, welfare programmes and other schemes which aim to aid working class people against the ravages of the capitalist market? Given the self-appointed role of Austrian economics as the defender of "pure" (and, illogically, not so pure) capitalism that conclusion is not hard to deny.

Rejecting equilibrium is not as straightforward as the Austrians hope, both in terms of logic and in justifying capitalism. Equilibrium plays a role in neo-classical economics for a reason. A disequilibrium trade means that people on the winning side of the bargain will gain real income at the expense of the losers. In other words, Austrian economics is rooted (in most markets, at least) in the idea that trading benefits one side more than the other which flies in the face of the repeated dogma that trade benefits both parties. Moreover, rejecting the idea of equilibrium means rejecting any attempt to claim that workers' wages equal their just contribution to production and so to society. If equilibrium does not exist or is never actually reached then the various economic laws which "prove" that workers are not exploited under capitalism do not apply. This also applies to accepting that any real market is unlike the ideal market of perfect competition. In other words, by recognising and taking into account reality capitalist economics cannot show that capitalism is stable, non-exploitative or that it meets the needs of all.

Given that they reject the notion of equilibrium as well as the concept of empirical testing of their theories and the economy, their defence of capitalism rests on two things: "freedom" and anything else would be worse. Neither are particularly convincing.

Taking the first option, this superficially appears appealing, particularly to anarchists. However this stress on "freedom" – the freedom of individuals to make their own decisions – flounders on the rocks of capitalist reality. Who can deny that individuals, when free to choose, will pick the option they consider best for themselves? However, what this praise for individual freedom ignores is that capitalism often reduces choice to picking the lesser of two (or more) evils due to the inequalities it creates (hence our reference to the **quality** of the decisions available to us). The worker who agrees to work in a sweatshop does "maximise" her "utility" by so doing – after all, this option is better than starving to death – but only an ideologue blinded by capitalist economics will think that she is free or that her decision is not made under (economic) compulsion.

The Austrian school is so in love with markets they even see them where they do not exist, namely inside capitalist firms. There, hierarchy reigns and so for all their talk of "liberty" the Austrian school at best ignores, at worse exalts, factory fascism (see section F.2.1) For them, management is there to manage and workers are there to obey. Ironically, the Austrian (like the neo-liberal) ethic of "freedom" is based on an utterly credulous faith in authority in the workplace. Thus we have the defenders of "freedom" defending the hierarchical and autocratic capitalist managerial structure, i.e. "free" workers subject to a relationship distinctly **lacking** freedom. If your personal life were as closely monitored and regulated as your work life, you would rightly consider it oppression.

In other words, this idealisation of freedom through the market completely ignores the fact that this freedom can be, to a large number of people, very limited in scope. Moreover, the freedom associated with capitalism, as far as the labour market goes, becomes little more than the freedom to pick your master. All in all, this defence of capitalism ignores the existence of economic inequality (and so power) which infringes the freedom and opportunities of others. Social inequalities can ensure that people end up *"wanting what they get"* rather than *"getting what they want"* simply because they have to adjust their expectations and behaviour to fit into the patterns determined by concentrations of economic power. This is particularly the case within the labour market, where sellers of labour power are usually at a disadvantage when compared to buyers due to the existence of unemployment as we have discussed.

As such, their claims to be defenders of "liberty" ring hollow in anarchist ears. This can be seen from the 1920s. For all their talk of "freedom", when push came to shove, they end up defending authoritarian regimes in order to save capitalism when the working classes rebel against the "natural" order. Thus we find von Mises, for example, arguing in the 1920s that it *"cannot be denied that Fascism and similar movements aiming at the establishment of dictatorships are full of the best intentions and that their intervention has, for the moment, saved European civilisation. The merit that Fascism has thereby won for itself will live eternally in history."* [**Liberalism**, p. 51] Faced with the Nazis in the 1930s, von Mises changed his tune somewhat as, being Jewish, he faced the same state repression he was happy to see inflicted upon rebellious workers the previous decade. Unsurprisingly, he started to stress that Nazi was short for "National Socialism" and so the horrors of fascism could be blamed on "socialism" rather than the capitalists who funded the fascist parties and made extensive profits under them once the labour, anarchist and socialist movements had been crushed.

Similarly, when right-wing governments influenced by the Austrian school were elected in various countries in the 1980s, those countries saw an increase in state authoritarianism and centralisation. In the UK, for example, Thatcher's government strengthened the state and used it to break the labour movement (in order to ensure management authority over their workers). In other words, instead of regulating capital and the people, the state just regulates the people. The general public will have the freedom of doing what the market dictates and if they object to the market's "invisible hand", then the very visible fist of the state (or private defence companies) will ensure they do. We can be sure if a large anarchist movement developed the Austrian economists will, like von Mises in the 1920s, back whatever state violence was required to defend "civilisation" against it. All in the name of "freedom," of course.

Then there is the idea that anything else than "pure" capitalism would be worse. Given their ideological embrace of the free market, the Austrians attack those economists (like Keynes) who tried to save capitalism from itself. For the Austrian school, there is only capitalism or "socialism" (i.e. state intervention) and they cannot be combined. Any attempt to do so would, as Hayek put it in his book **The Road to Serfdom**, inevitably lead to totalitarianism. Hence the Austrians are at the forefront in attacking the welfare state as not only counterproductive but inherently leading to fascism or, even worse, some form of state socialism. Needless to say, the state's role in creating capitalism in the first place is skilfully ignored in favour of endless praise for the "natural" system of capitalism. Nor do they realise that the victory of state intervention they so bemoan is, in part, necessary to keep capitalism going and, in part, a consequence of attempts to approximate their utopia (see section D.1 for a discussion).

Not that Hayek's thesis has any empirical grounding. No state has ever become fascist due to intervening in the economy (unless a right-wing coup happens, as in Chile, but that was not his argument). Rather, dictatorial states have implemented planning rather than democratic states becoming dictatorial after intervening in the economy. Moreover, looking at the Western welfare states, the key

compliant by the capitalist class in the 1960s and 1970s was not a lack of general freedom but rather too much. Workers and other previously oppressed but obedient sections of society were standing up for themselves and fighting the traditional hierarchies within society. This hardly fits in with serfdom, although the industrial relations which emerged in Pinochet's Chile, Thatcher's Britain and Reagan's America does. The call was for the state to defend the *"management's right to manage"* against rebellious wage slaves by breaking their spirit and organisation while, at the same time, intervening to bolster capitalist authority in the workplace. That this required an increase in state power and centralisation would only come as a surprise to those who confuse the rhetoric of capitalism with its reality.

Similarly, it goes without saying Hayek's thesis was extremely selectively applied. It is strange to see, for example, Conservative politicians clutching Hayek's **Road to Serfdom** with one hand and using it to defend cutting the welfare state while, with the other, implementing policies which give billions to the Military Industrial Complex. Apparently "planning" is only dangerous to liberty when it is in the interests of the many. Luckily, defence spending (for example) has no such problems. As Chomsky stresses, *"the 'free market' ideology is very* **useful** *– it's a weapon against the general population … because it's an argument against social spending, and it's a weapon against poor people abroad … But nobody [in the ruling class] really pays attention to this stuff when it comes to actual planning – and no one ever has."* [**Understanding Power**, p. 256] That is why anarchists stress the importance of reforms from **below** rather than from above – as long as we have a state, any reforms should be directed first and foremost to the (much more generous) welfare state for the rich rather than the general population (the experience of the 1980s onwards shows what happens when reforms are left to the capitalist class).

This is not to say that Hayek's attack upon those who refer to totalitarian serfdom as a "new freedom" was not fully justified. Nor is his critique of central planning and state "socialism" without merit. Far from it. Anarchists would agree that any valid economic system must be based on freedom and decentralisation in order to be dynamic and meet needs, they simply apply such a critique to capitalism **as well as** state socialism. The ironic thing about Hayek's argument is that he did not see how his theory of tacit knowledge, used to such good effect against state socialist ideas of central planning, were just as applicable to critiquing the highly centralised and top-down capitalist company and economy. Nor, ironically enough, that it was just as applicable to the price mechanism he defended so vigorously (as we note in section I.1.2, the price system hides as much, if not more, necessary information than it provides). As such, his defence of capitalism can be turned against it and the centralised, autocratic structures it is based on.

To conclude, while its open and extreme support for free market capitalism and its inequalities is, to say the least, refreshing, it is not remotely convincing or scientific. In fact, it amounts to little more than a vigorous defence of business power hidden behind a thin rhetoric of "free markets." As it preaches the infallibility of capitalism, this requires a nearly unyielding defence of corporations, economic and social power and workplace hierarchy. It must dismiss the obvious fact that allowing big business to flourish into oligopoly and monopoly (as it does, see section C.4) reduces the possibility of competition solving the problem of unethical business practices and worker exploitation, as they claim. This is unsurprising, as the Austrian school (like economics in general) identifies "freedom" with the "freedom" of private enterprise, i.e. the lack of accountability of the economically privileged and powerful. This simply becomes a defence of the economically powerful to do what they want (within the laws specified by their peers in government).

Ironically, the Austrian defence of capitalism is dependent on the belief that it will remain close to equilibrium. However, as seems likely, capitalism is endogenously unstable, then any real "pure" capitalism will be distant from equilibrium and, as a result, marked by unemployment and, of course, booms and slumps. So it is possible to have a capitalist economics based on non-equilibrium, but it is unlikely to convince anyone that does not already believe that capitalism is the best system ever unless they are unconcerned about unemployment (and so worker exploitation) and instability. As Steve Keen notes, it is *"an alternative way to ideologically support a capitalist economy ... If neoclassical economics becomes untenable for any reason, the Austrians are well placed to provide an alternative religion for believers in the primacy of the market over all other forms of social organisation."* [Keen, **Debunking Economics**, p. 304]

Those who seek freedom for all and want to base themselves on more than faith in an economic system marked by hierarchy, inequality and oppression would be better seeking a more realistic and less apologetic economic theory.

C.2

Why is capitalism exploitative?

For anarchists, capitalism is marked by the exploitation of labour by capital. While this is most famously expressed by Proudhon's **"property is theft,"** this perspective can be found in all forms of anarchism. For Bakunin, capitalism was marked by an *"economic relationship between the exploiter and exploited"* as it meant the few have *"the power and right to live by exploiting the labour of someone else, the right to exploit the labour of those who possess neither property nor capital and who thus are forced to sell their productive power to the lucky owners of both."* [**The Political Philosophy of Bakunin**, p. 183] This means that when a worker *"sells his labour to an employee ... some part of the value of his produce will be unjustly taken by the employer."* [Kropotkin, **Anarchism and Anarchist-Communism**, p. 52]

At the root this criticism is based, ironically enough, on the **capitalist** defence of private property as the product of labour. As noted in section B.4.2, Locke defended private property in terms of labour yet allowed that labour to be sold to others. This allowed the buyers of labour (capitalists and landlords) to appropriate the product of other people's labour (wage workers and tenants) and so, in the words of dissident economist David Ellerman, *"capitalist production, i.e. production based on the employment contract*

denies workers the right to the (positive and negative) fruit of their labour. Yet people's right to the fruits of their labour has always been the natural basis for private property appropriation. Thus capitalist production, far from being founded on private property, in fact denies the natural basis for private property appropriation." [**The Democratic worker-owned firm**, p. 59] This was expressed by Proudhon in the following way:

> *"Whoever labours becomes a proprietor – this is an inevitable deduction from the principles of political economy and jurisprudence. And when I say proprietor, I do not mean simply (as do our hypocritical economists) proprietor of his allowance, his salary, his wages, – I mean proprietor of the value his creates, and by which the master alone profits ... **The labourer retains, even after he has received his wages, a natural right in the thing he was produced.**"* [**What is Property?**, pp. 123-4]

In other words, taking the moral justification for capitalism, anarchists argue that it fails to meet its own criteria (*"With me who, as a labourer, have a right to the possession of the products of Nature and my own industry – and who, as a proletaire [wage labourer], enjoy none of them."* [Proudhon, **Op. Cit.**, p. 65]). Whether this principle should be applied in a free society is a moot point within anarchism. Individualist and mutualist anarchists argue it should be and, therefore, say that individual workers should receive the product of their toil (and so argue for distribution according to deed). Communist-anarchists argue that *"social ownership and sharing according to need ... would be the best and most just economic arrangement."* This is for two reasons. Firstly, because *"in modern industry"* there is *"no such thing"* as an individual product as *"all labour and the products of labour are social."* [Berkman, **What is Anarchism?**, pp. 169-70] Secondly, in terms of simple justice need is not related to the ability to work and, of course, it would be wrong to penalise those who cannot work (i.e. the sick, the young and the old). Yet, while anarchists disagree over exactly how this should be most justly realised, they all agree that labour should control **all** that it produces (either individually or collectively) and, consequently, non-labour income is exploitation (it should be stressed that as both schemes are voluntary, there is no real contradiction between them). Anarchists tend to call non-labour income "surplus-value" or "usury" and these terms are used to group together profits, rent and interest (see section C.2.1 for details).

That this critique is a problem for capitalism can be seen from the many varied and wonderful defences created by economists to justify non-labour income. Economists, at least in the past, saw the problem clear enough. John Stuart Mill, the final great economist of the classical school, presented the typical moral justification of capitalism, along with the problems it causes. As he explains in his classic introduction to economics, the *"institution of property, when limited to its essential elements, consists in the recognition, in each person, of a right to the exclusive disposal of what he or she have produced by their own exertions ... The foundation of the whole is, the right of producers to what they themselves have produced."* He then notes the obvious contradiction – workers do

not receive what they have produced. Thus it *"may be objected"* that capitalist society *"recognises rights of property in individuals over which they have not produced,"* for example *"the operatives in a manufactory create, by their labour and skill, the whole produce; yet, instead of it belonging to them, the law gives them only their stipulated hire [wages], and transfers the produce to someone who has merely supplied the funds, without perhaps contributing to the work itself."* [**Principles of Political Economy**, p. 25] With the rise of neoclassical economics, the problem remained and so the need to justify capitalism continued to drive economics. J. B. Clark, for example, knew what was at stake and, like Mill, expressed it:

> *"When a workman leaves the mill, carrying his pay in his pocket, the civil law guarantees to him what he thus takes away; but before he leaves the mill he is the rightful owner of a part of the wealth that the day's industry has brought forth. Does the economic law which, in some way that he does not understand, determines what his pay shall be, make it to correspond with the amount of his portion of the day's product, or does it force him to leave some of his rightful share behind him? A plan of living that should force men to leave in their employer's hands anything that by right of creation is theirs, would be an institutional robbery – a legally established violation of the principle on which property is supposed to rest."* [**The Distribution of Wealth**, pp. 8-9]

Why should the owners of land, money and machinery get an income in the first place? Capitalist economics argues that everything involves a cost and, as such, people should be rewarded for the sacrifices they suffer when they contribute to production. Labour, in this schema, is considered a cost to those who labour and, consequently, they should be rewarded for it. Labour is thought of a disutility, i.e. something people do not want, rather than something with utility, i.e. something people do want. Under capitalism (like any class system), this perspective makes some sense as workers are bossed about and often subject to long and difficult labour. Most people will happily agree that labour is an obvious cost and should be rewarded.

Economists, unsurprisingly, have tended to justify surplus value by arguing that it involves as much cost and sacrifice as labour. For Mill, labour *"cannot be carried on without materials and machinery … All these things are the fruits of previous production. If the labourers possessed of them, they would not need to divide the produce with any one; but while they have them not, an equivalent must be given to those who have."* [**Op. Cit.**, p. 25] This rationale for profits is called the "abstinence" or "waiting" theory. Clark, like Mill, expressed a defence of non-labour income in the face of socialist and anarchist criticism, namely the idea of marginal productivity to explain and justify non-labour income. Other theories have been developed as the weaknesses of previous ones have been exposed and we will discuss some of them in subsequent sections.

The ironic thing is that, well over 200 years after it came of age with Adam Smith's **Wealth of Nations**, economics has no agreed explanation for the source of surplus value. As dissident economists Michele I. Naples and Nahid Aslanbeigui show, introductory economics texts provide *"no consistent, widely accepted theory"* on the profit rate. Looking at the top three introductions to economics, they discovered that there was a *"strange amalgam"* of theories which is *"often confusing, incomplete and inconsistent."* Given that internal consistency is usually heralded as one of the hallmarks of neoclassical theory, *"the theory must be questioned."* This *"failure … to provide a coherent theory of the rate of profit in the short run or long run"* is damning, as the *"absence of a coherent explanation for the profit rate represents a fundamental failure for the neoclassical model."* [*"What **does** determine the profit rate? The neoclassical theories present in introductory textbooks,"* pp. 53-71, **Cambridge Journal of Economics**, vol. 20, p. 53, p. 54, p. 69 and p. 70]

As will become clear, anarchists consider defences of *"surplus value"* to be essentially ideological and without an empirical base. As we will attempt to indicate, capitalists are not justified in appropriating surplus value from workers for no matter how this appropriation is explained by capitalist economics, we find that inequality in wealth and power are the real reasons for this appropriation rather than some actual productive act on the part of capitalists, investors or landlords. Mainstream economic theories generally seek to justify the distribution of income and wealth rather than to understand it. They are parables about what should be rather than what is. We argue that any scientific analysis of the source of *"surplus value"* cannot help conclude that it is due, primarily, to inequalities of wealth and, consequently, inequalities of power on the market. In other words, that Rousseau was right:

> *"The terms of social compact between these two estates of men may be summed up in a few words: 'You have need of me, because I am rich and you are poor. We will therefore come to an agreement. I will permit you to have the honour of serving me, on condition that you bestow on me that little you have left, in return for the pains I shall take to command you.'"* [**The Social Contract and Discourses**, p. 162]

This is the analysis of exploitation we present in more detail in section C.2.2. To summarise it, labour faces social inequality when it passes from the market to production. In the workplace, capitalists exercise social power over how labour is used and this allows them to produce more value from the productive efforts of workers than they pay for in wages. This social power is rooted in social dependence, namely the fact that workers have little choice but to sell their liberty to those who own the means of life. To ensure the creation and appropriation of surplus-value, capitalists must not only own the production process and the product of the workers' labour, they must own the labour of the workers itself. In other words, they must control the workers. Hence capitalist production must be, to use Proudhon's term, *"despotism."* How much surplus-value can be produced depends on the relative economic power between bosses and workers as this determines the duration of work and the intensity of labour, however its roots are the same – the hierarchical and class nature of capitalist society.

C.2.1 What is "surplus value"?

Before discussing how surplus-value exists and the flaws in capitalist defences of it, we need to be specific about what we mean by the term *"surplus value."* To do this we must revisit the difference between possession and private property we discussed in section B.3. For anarchists, private property (or capital) is *"the power to produce without labour."* [Proudhon, **What is Property?**, p. 161] As such, surplus value is created when the owners of property let others use them and receive an income from so doing. Therefore something only becomes capital, producing surplus value, under specific social relationships.

Surplus value is *"the difference between the value produced by the workers and the wages they receive"* and is *"appropriated by the landlord and capitalist class ... absorbed by the non-producing classes as profits, interest, rent, etc."* [Charlotte Wilson, **Anarchist Essays**, pp. 46-7] It basically refers to any non-labour income (some anarchists, particularly individualist anarchists, have tended to call *"surplus value"* usury). As Proudhon noted, it *"receives different names according to the thing by which it is yielded: if by land, **ground-rent**; if by houses and furniture, **rent**; if by life-investments, **revenue**; if by money, **interest**; if by exchange, **advantage**, **gain**, **profit** (three things which must not be confounded with the wages of legitimate price of labour)."* [**Op. Cit.**, p. 159]

For simplicity, we will consider *"surplus value"* to have three component parts: profits, interest and rent. All are based on payment for letting someone else use your property. Rent is what we pay to be allowed to exist on part of the earth (or some other piece of property). Interest is what we pay for the use of money. Profit is what we pay to be allowed to work a farm or use a piece of machinery. Rent and interest are easy to define, they are obviously the payment for using someone else's property and have existed long before capitalism appeared. Profit is a somewhat more complex economic category although, ultimately, is still a payment for using someone else's property.

The term "profit" is often used simply, but incorrectly, to mean an excess over costs. However, this ignores the key issue, namely how a workplace is organised. In a co-operative, for example, while there is a surplus over costs, *"there is no profit, only income to be divided among members. Without employees the labour-managed firm does not have a wage bill, and labour costs are not counted among the expenses to be extracted from profit, as they are in the capitalist firm."* This means that the *"**economic category of profit does not exist in the labour-managed firm,** as it does in the capitalist firm where wages are a cost to be subtracted from gross income before a residual profit is determined ... Income shared among all producers is net income generated by the firm: the total of value added by human labour applied to the means of production, less payment of all costs of production and any reserves for depreciation of plant and equipment."* [Christopher Eaton Gunn, **Workers' Self-Management in the United States**, p. 41 and p. 45] Gunn, it should be noted, follows both Proudhon and Marx

in his analysis (*"Let us suppose the workers are themselves in possession of their respective means of production and exchange their commodities with one another. These commodities would not be products of capital."* [Marx, **Capital**, vol. 3, p. 276]).

In other words, by profits we mean income that flows to the owner of a workplace or land who hires others to do the work. As such returns to capital are as unique to capitalism as unemployment is. This means that a farmer who works their own land receives a labour income when they sell the crop while one who hires labourers to work the land will receives a non-labour income, profit. Hence the difference between **possession** and **private property** (or **capital**) and anarchist opposition to *"capitalist property, that is, property which allows some to live by the work of others and which therefore presupposes a class of ... people, obliged to sell their labour power to the property-owners for less than its value."* [Malatesta, **Errico Malatesta: His Life and Ideas**, p. 102]

Another complication arises due to the fact that the owners of private property sometimes do work on them (i.e. be a boss) or hire others to do boss-like work on their behalf (i.e. executives and other managerial staff). It could be argued that bosses and executives are also *"workers"* and so contribute to the value of the commodities produced. However, this is not the case. Exploitation does not just happen, it needs to be organised and managed. In other words, exploitation requires labour (*"There is work and there is work,"* as Bakunin noted, *"There is productive labour and there is the labour of exploitation."* [**The Political Philosophy of Bakunin**, p. 180]). The key is that while a workplace would grind to a halt without workers, the workers could happily do without a boss by organising themselves into an association to manage their own work. As such, while bosses may work, they are not taking part in productive activity but rather exploitative activity.

Much the same can be said of executives and managers. Though they may not own the instruments of production, they are certainly buyers and controllers of labour power, and under their auspices production is still **capitalist** production. The creation of a "salary-slave" strata of managers does not alter the capitalist relations of production. In effect, the management strata are **de facto** capitalists and they are like "working capitalist" and, consequently, their "wages" come from the surplus value appropriated from workers and realised on the market. Thus the exploitative role of managers, even if they can be fired, is no different from capitalists. Moreover, *"shareholders and managers/technocrats share common motives: to make profits and to reproduce hierarchy relations that exclude most of the employees from effective decision making"* [Takis Fotopoulos, "The Economic Foundations of an Ecological Society", pp. 1-40, **Society and Nature**, No.3, p. 16] In other words, the high pay of the higher levels of management is a share of profits **not** a labour income based on their contribution to production but rather due to their position in the economic hierarchy and the power that gives them.

So management is paid well because they monopolise power in the company and can get away with it. As Bakunin argued, within the capitalist workplace *"administrative work ... [is] monopolised ... if I concentrate in my hands the administrative power, it is not because the interests of production demand it, but in order to serve my own ends, the ends of exploitation. As absolute boss of my establishment*

I get for my labours [many] … times more than my workers get for theirs." [**Op. Cit.**, p. 186] Given this, it is irrelevant whether those in the hierarchy simply control (in the case of managers) or actually own the means of production. What counts is that those who do the actual work are excluded from the decision making process.

This is not to say that 100 percent of what managers do is exploitative. The case is complicated by the fact that there is a legitimate need for co-ordination between various aspects of complex production processes – a need that would remain under libertarian socialism and would be filled by elected and recallable (and in some cases rotating) managers (see section I.3). But under capitalism, managers become parasitic in proportion to their proximity to the top of the pyramid. In fact, the further the distance from the production process, the higher the salary; whereas the closer the distance, the more likely that a "manager" is a worker with a little more power than average. In capitalist organisations, the less you do, the more you get. In practice, executives typically call upon subordinates to perform managerial (i.e. co-ordinating) functions and restrict themselves to broader policy-making decisions. As their decision-making power comes from the hierarchical nature of the firm, they could be easily replaced if policy making was in the hands of those who are affected by it. As such, their role as managers do not require them to make vast sums. They are paid that well currently because they monopolise power in the company and can, consequently, get away with deciding that they, unsurprisingly, contribute most to the production of useful goods rather than those who do the actual work.

Nor are we talking, as such, of profits generated by buying cheap and selling dear. We are discussing the situation at the level of the economy as a whole, **not** individual transactions. The reason is obvious. If profits could just be explained in terms of buying cheap in order to sell dear then, over all, such transactions would cancel each other out when we look at the market as a whole as any profit will cancel any loss. For example if someone buys a product at £20 and sells it at £25 then there would be no surplus overall as someone else will have to pay £20 for something which cost £25. In other words, what one person gains as a seller, someone else will lose as a buyer and no net surplus has been created. Capitalists, in other words, do not simply profit at each other's expense. There is a creation of surplus rather than mere redistribution of a given product. This means that we are explaining why production results in a aggregate surplus and why it gets distributed between social classes under capitalism.

This means that capitalism is based on the creation of surplus rather than mere redistribution of a given sum of products. If this were not the case then the amount of goods in the economy would not increase, growth would not exist and all that would happen is that the distribution of goods would change, depending on the transactions made. Such a world would be one without production and, consequently, not realistic. Unsurprisingly, as we noted in section C.1, this is the world of neoclassical economics. This shows the weakness of attempts to explain the source of profits in terms of the market rather than production. While the market can explain how, perhaps, a specific set of goods and surplus is distributed, it cannot explain how a surplus is generated in the first place. To understand how a surplus is created we need to look at the process

of value creation. For this, it is necessary to look at production to see if there is something which produces more than it gets paid for. Anarchists, like other socialists, argue that this is labour and, consequently, that capitalism is an exploitative system. We discuss why in the next section.

Obviously, pro-capitalist economics argues against this theory of how a surplus arises and the conclusion that capitalism is exploitative. We will discuss the more common arguments below. However, one example will suffice here to see why labour is the source of a surplus, rather than (say) "waiting", risk or the productivity of capital (to list some of the more common explanations for capitalist appropriation of surplus value). This is a card game. A good poker-player uses equipment (capital), takes risks, delays gratification, engages in strategic behaviour, tries new tricks (innovates), not to mention cheats, and can make large winnings. However, no surplus product results from such behaviour; the gambler's winnings are simply redistributions from others with no new production occurring. For one to win, the rest must lose. Thus risk-taking, abstinence, entrepreneurship, and so on might be necessary for an individual to receive profits but they are far from sufficient for them not to be the result of a pure redistribution from others.

In short, our discussion of exploitation under capitalism is first and foremost an economy-wide one. We are concentrating on how value (goods and services) and surplus value (profits, rent and interest) are produced rather than how they are distributed. The distribution of goods between people and the division of income into wages and surplus value between classes is a secondary concern as this can only occur under capitalism if workers produce goods and services to sell (this is the direct opposite of mainstream economics which assumes a static economy with almost no discussion of how scarce means are organised to yield outputs, the whole emphasis is on exchanges of ready made goods).

Nor is this distribution somehow fixed. As we discuss in section C.3, how the amount of value produced by workers is divided between wages and surplus value is source of much conflict and struggle, the outcome of which depends on the balance of power between and within classes. The same can be said of surplus value. This is divided between profits, interest and rent – capitalists, financiers and landlords. This does not imply that these sections of the exploiting class see eye to eye or that there is not competition between them. Struggle goes on within classes as well as between classes and this applies at the top of the economic hierarchy as at the bottom. The different sections of the ruling elite fight over their share of surplus value. This can involve fighting over control of the state to ensure that their interests are favoured over others. For example, the Keynesian post-war period can be considered a period when industrial capitalists shaped state policy while the period after 1973 represents a shift in power towards finance capital.

We must stress, therefore, that the exploitation of workers is not defined as payment less than competitive ("free market") for their labour. Rather, exploitation occurs even if they are paid the market wage. This is because workers are paid for their ability to labour (their *"labour-power,"* to use Marx's term) rather the labour itself. This means that for a given hour's work (labour), the capitalist expects the worker to produce more than their wage (labour power). How much more is dependent on the class struggle and the objective circumstances each side faces. Indeed, a rebellious workforce willing to take direct action in defence of their interests will not allow subjection or its resulting exploitation.

Similarly, it would be wrong to confuse exploitation with low wages. Yes, exploitation is often associated with paying low wages but it is more than possible for real wages to go up while the rate of exploitation falls or rises. While some anarchists in the nineteenth century did argue that capitalism was marked by falling real wages, this was more a product of the time they were living through rather than an universal law. Most anarchists today argue that whether wages rise or fall depends on the social and economic power of working people and the historic context of a given society. This means, in other words, that labour is exploited not because workers have a low standard of living (although they can) but because labour produces the whole of the value created in any process of production or creation of a service but gets only part of it back.

As such, it does not matter **if** real wages do go up or not. Due to the accumulation of capital, the social and economic power of the capitalists and their ability to extract surplus-value can go up at a higher rate than real wages. The key issue is one of freedom rather than the possibility of consuming more. Bosses are in a position, due to the hierarchical nature of the capitalist workplace, to make workers produce more than they pay them in wages. The absolute level of those wages is irrelevant to the creation and appropriation of value and surplus-value as this happens at all times within capitalism.

As an example, since the 1970s American workers have seen their wages stagnate and have placed themselves into more and more debt to maintain an expected standard of living. During this time, productivity has increased and so they have been increasingly exploited. However, between 1950s and 1970s wages did increase along with productivity. Strong unions and a willingness to strike mitigated exploitation and increased living standards but exploitation continued. As Doug Henwood notes, while *"average incomes have risen considerably"* since 1945, *"the amount of work necessary to earn those incomes has risen with equal relentlessness ... So, despite the fact that productivity overall is up more than threefold"* over this time *"the average worker would have to toil six months longer to make the average family income."* [**After the New Economy**, pp. 39-40] In other words, rising exploitation **can** go hand in hand with rising wages.

Finally, we must stress that we are critiquing economics mostly in its own terms. On average workers sell their labour-power at a "fair" market price and still exploitation occurs. As sellers of a commodity (labour-power) they do not receive its full worth (i.e. what they actually produce). Even if they did, almost all anarchists would still be against the system as it is based on the worker becoming a wage-slave and subject to hierarchy. In other words, they are not free during production and, consequently, they are still being robbed, although this time it is as human beings rather than a factor of production (i.e. they are oppressed rather than exploited). As Bookchin put it:

> *"To the modern mind, labour is viewed as a rarefied, abstract activity, a process extrinsic to human notions of genuine self-actualisation. One usually 'goes to work' the*

way a condemned person 'goes' to a place of confinement: the workplace is little more than a penal institution in which mere existence must pay a penalty in the form of mindless labour ... We 'measure' labour in hours, products, and efficiency, but rarely do we understand it as a concrete human activity. Aside from the earnings it generates, labour is normally alien to human fulfilment ... [as] the rewards one acquires by submitting to a work discipline. By definition, these rewards are viewed as incentives for submission, rather than for the freedom that should accompany creativity and self-fulfilment. We commonly are 'paid' for supinely working on our knees, not for heroically standing on our feet." [**The Ecology of Freedom**, p. 308]

Almost all anarchists seek to change this, combat oppression and alienation as well as exploitation (some individualist anarchists are the exception on this issue). Needless to say, the idea that we could be subject to oppression during working hours and ***not*** be exploited is one most anarchists would dismiss as a bad joke and, as a result, follow Proudhon and demand the abolition of wage labour (most take it further and advocate the abolition of the wages system as well, i.e. support libertarian communism).

C.2.2 How does exploitation happen?

In order to make more money, money must be transformed into capital, i.e., workplaces, machinery and other *"capital goods."* By itself, however, capital (like money) produces nothing. While a few even talk about *"making money work for you"* (as if pieces of paper can actually do any form of work!) obviously this is not the case – human beings have to do the actual work. As Kropotkin put it, *"if [the capitalist] locks [his money] up, it will not increase, because [it] does not grow like seed, and after a lapse of a twelve month he will not find £110 in his drawer if he only put £100 into it.* [**The Place of Anarchism in Socialistic Evolution**, p. 4] Capital only becomes productive in the labour process when workers use it:

> *"Values created by net product are classed as savings and capitalised in the most highly exchangeable form, the form which is freest and least susceptible of depreciation, – in a word, the form of specie, the only constituted value. Now, if capital leaves this state of freedom and **engages itself**, – that is, takes the form of machines, buildings, etc., – it will still be susceptible of exchange, but much more exposed than before to the oscillations of supply and demand. Once engaged, it cannot be **disengaged** without difficulty; and the sole resource of its owner will be exploitation. Exploitation alone is capable of maintaining engaged capital at its nominal value."* [**System of Economical Contradictions**, p. 291]

Under capitalism, workers not only create sufficient value (i.e. produced commodities) to maintain existing capital and their own existence, they also produce a surplus. This surplus expresses itself as a surplus of goods and services, i.e. an excess of commodities compared to the number a workers' wages could buy back. The wealth of the capitalists, in other words, is due to them *"accumulating the product of the labour of others."* [Kropotkin, **Op. Cit.**, p. 3] Thus Proudhon:

> *"The working man cannot … repurchase that which he has produced for his master. It is thus with all trades whatsoever … since, producing for a master who in one form or another makes a profit, they are obliged to pay more for their own labour than they get for it."* [**What is Property**, p. 189]

In other words, the price of all produced goods is greater than the money value represented by the workers' wages (plus raw materials and overheads such as wear and tear on machinery) when those goods were produced. The labour contained in these "surplus-products" is the source of profit, which has to be realised on the market (in practice, of course, the value represented by these surplus-products is distributed throughout all the commodities produced in the form of profit – the difference between the cost price and the market price). In summary, surplus value is unpaid labour and hence capitalism is based on exploitation. As Proudhon noted, *"**Products,** say economists, **are only bought by products**. This maxim is property's condemnation. The proprietor producing neither by his own labour nor by his implement, and receiving products in exchange for nothing, is either a parasite or a thief."* [**Op. Cit.**, p. 170]

It is this appropriation of wealth from the worker by the owner which differentiates capitalism from the simple commodity production of artisan and peasant economies. All anarchists agree with Bakunin when he stated that:

> *"**what is property, what is capital in their present form?** For the capitalist and the property owner they mean the power and the right, guaranteed by the State, to live without working … [and so] the power and right to live by exploiting the work of someone else … those … [who are] forced to sell their productive power to the lucky owners of both."* [**The Political Philosophy of Bakunin**, p. 180]

It is the nature of capitalism for the monopolisation of the worker's product by others to exist. This is because of private property in the means of production and so in *"consequence of [which] … [the] worker, when he is able to work, finds no acre to till, no machine to set in motion, unless he agrees to sell his labour for a sum inferior to its real value."* [Peter Kropotkin, **Anarchism**, p. 55] Therefore workers have to sell their labour on the market. However, as this "commodity" *"cannot be separated from the person of the worker like pieces of property. The worker's capacities are developed over time and they form an integral part of his self and self-identity; capacities are internally not externally related to the person. Moreover, capacities or labour power cannot be used without the worker using his will, his understanding and experience, to put them into effect. The use of labour power requires the presence of its 'owner' … To contract for the use of labour power is a waste of resources unless it can be used in the way in which the new*

owner requires … The employment contract must, therefore, create a relationship of command and obedience between employer and worker." So, "the contract in which the worker allegedly sells his labour power is a contract in which, since he cannot be separated from his capacities, he sells command over the use of his body and himself … The characteristics of this condition are captured in the term **wage slave.**"* [Carole Pateman, **The Sexual Contract**, pp. 150-1]

Or, to use Bakunin's words, *"the worker sells his person and his liberty for a given time"* and so *"concluded for a term only and reserving to the worker the right to quit his employer, this contract constitutes a sort of **voluntary** and **transitory** serfdom."* [**The Political Philosophy of Bakunin**, p. 187] This domination is the source of the surplus, for *"wage slavery is not a consequence of exploitation – exploitation is a consequence of the fact that the sale of labour power entails the worker's subordination. The employment contract creates the capitalist as master; he has the political right to determine how the labour of the worker will be used, and – consequently – can engage in exploitation."* [Pateman, **Op. Cit.**, p. 149]

So profits exist because the worker sells themselves to the capitalist, who then owns their activity and, therefore, controls them (or, more accurately, **tries** to control them) like a machine. Benjamin Tucker's comments with regard to the claim that capital is entitled to a reward are of use here. He notes that some *"combat … the doctrine that surplus value – oftener called profits – belong to the labourer because he creates it, by arguing that the horse … is rightly entitled to the surplus value which he creates for his owner. So he will be when he has the sense to claim and the power to take it…. Th[is] argument … is based upon the assumption that certain men are born owned by other men, just as horses are. Thus its **reductio ad absurdum** turns upon itself."* [**Instead of a Book**, pp. 495-6] In other words, to argue that capital should be rewarded is to implicitly assume that workers are just like machinery, another "factor of production" rather than human beings and the creator of things of value. So profit exists because during the working day the capitalist controls the activity and output of the worker (i.e. owns them during working hours as activity cannot be separated from the body and *"[t]here is an integral relationship between the body and self. The body and self are not identical, but selves are inseparable from bodies."* [Carole Pateman, **Op. Cit.**, p. 206]).

Considered purely in terms of output, this results in, as Proudhon noted, workers working *"for an entrepreneur who pays them and keeps their products."* [quoted by Martin Buber, **Paths in Utopia**, p. 29] The ability of capitalists to maintain this kind of monopolisation of another's time and output is enshrined in *"property rights"* enforced by either public or private states. In short, therefore, property *"is the right to enjoy and dispose at will of another's goods – the fruit of an other's industry and labour."* [P-J Proudhon, **What is Property**, p. 171] And because of this "right," a worker's wage will always be less than the wealth that he or she produces.

The surplus value produced by labour is divided between profits, interest and rent (or, more correctly, between the owners of the various factors of production other than labour). In practice, this surplus is used by the owners of capital for: (a) investment (b) to pay themselves dividends on their stock, if any; (c) to pay for rent and interest payments; and (d) to pay their executives and managers (who are sometimes identical with the owners themselves) much higher salaries than workers. As the surplus is being divided between different groups of capitalists, this means that there can be clashes of interest between (say) industrial capitalists and finance capitalists. For example, a rise in interest rates can squeeze industrial capitalists by directing more of the surplus from them into the hands of rentiers. Such a rise could cause business failures and so a slump (indeed, rising interest rates is a key way of regulating working class power by generating unemployment to discipline workers by fear of the sack). The surplus, like the labour used to reproduce existing capital, is embodied in the finished commodity and is realised once it is sold. This means that workers do not receive the full value of their labour, since the surplus appropriated by owners for investment, etc. represents value added to commodities by workers – value for which they are not paid nor control.

The size of this surplus, the amount of unpaid labour, can be changed by changing the duration and intensity of work (i.e. by making workers labour longer and harder). If the duration of work is increased, the amount of surplus value is increased absolutely. If the intensity is increased, e.g. by innovation in the production process, then the amount of surplus value increases relatively (i.e. workers produce the equivalent of their wage sooner during their working day resulting in more unpaid labour for their boss). Introducing new machinery, for example, increases surplus-value by reducing the amount of work required per unit of output. In the words of economist William Lazonick:

> "As a general rule, all market prices, including wages, are given to the particular capitalist. Moreover, in a competitive world a particular capitalist cannot retain privileged access to process or product innovations for any appreciable period of time. But the capitalist does have privileged access to, and control over, the workers that he employs. Precisely because the work is not perfectly mobile but is dependent on the capitalist to gain a living, the capitalist is not subject to the dictates of market forces in dealing with the worker in the production process. The more dependent the worker is on his or her particular employer, the more power the capitalist has to demand longer and harder work in return for a day's pay. The resultant unremunerated increase in the productivity of the worker per unit of time is the source of surplus-value.
>
> "The measure of surplus-value is the difference between the value-added by and the value paid to the worker. As owner of the means of production, the industrial capitalist has a legal right to keep the surplus-value for himself." [**Competitive Advantage on the Shop Floor**, p. 54]

Such surplus indicates that labour, like any other commodity, has a use value and an exchange value. Labour's exchange value is a worker's wages, its use value their ability to work, to do what the capitalist who buys it wants. Thus the existence of "surplus products" indicates that there is a difference between the exchange value of labour and its use value, that labour can **potentially** create

more value than it receives back in wages. We stress potentially, because the extraction of use value from labour is not a simple operation like the extraction of so many joules of energy from a ton of coal. Labour power cannot be used without subjecting the labourer to the will of the capitalist – unlike other commodities, labour power remains inseparably embodied in human beings. Both the extraction of use value and the determination of exchange value for labour depends upon – and are profoundly modified by – the actions of workers. Neither the effort provided during an hours work, nor the time spent in work, nor the wage received in exchange for it, can be determined without taking into account the worker's resistance to being turned into a commodity, into an order taker. In other words, the amount of "surplus products" extracted from a worker is dependent upon the resistance to dehumanisation within the workplace, to the attempts by workers to resist the destruction of liberty during work hours.

Thus unpaid labour, the consequence of the authority relations explicit in private property, is the source of profits. Part of this surplus is used to enrich capitalists and another to increase capital, which in turn is used to increase profits, in an endless cycle (a cycle, however, which is not a steady increase but is subject to periodic disruption by recessions or depressions – "The business cycle." The basic causes for such crises will be discussed later, in sections C.7 and C.8).

It should be noted that few economists deny that the "value added" by workers in production must exceed the wages paid. It has to, if a profit is to be made. As Adam Smith put it:

> "As soon as stock has accumulated in the hands of particular persons, some of them will naturally employ it in setting to work industrious people, whom they will supply with materials and subsistence, in order to make a profit by the sale of their work, or by what their labour adds to the value of the materials … The value which the workmen add to the materials, therefore, resolves itself in this case into two parts, of which one pays their wages, the other the profits of their employer upon the whole stock of materials and wages which he advanced. He could have no interest to employ them, unless he expected from the sale of their work something more than what was sufficient to replace his stock to him." [**The Wealth of Nations**, p. 42]

That surplus value consists of unpaid labour is a simple fact. The difference is that non-socialist economists refuse to explain this in terms of exploitation. Like Smith, David Ricardo argued in a similar manner and justified surplus value appropriation in spite of this analysis. Faced with the obvious interpretation of non-labour income as exploitation which could easily be derived from classical economics, subsequent economists have sought to obscure this fact and have produced a series of rationales to justify the appropriation of workers labour by capitalists. In other words, to explain and justify the fact that capitalism is not based on its own principle that labour creates and justifies property. These rationales have developed over time, usually in response to socialist and anarchist criticism of capitalism and its economics (starting in response to the so-called Ricardian Socialists who predated Proudhon and Marx and who first made such an analysis commonplace). These have been based on many factors, such as the abstinence or waiting by the capitalist, the productivity of capital, "time-preference," entrepreneurialism and so forth. We discuss most rationales and indicate their weaknesses in subsequent sections.

C.2.3 Is owning capital sufficient reason to justify profits?

No, it is not. To understand why, we must first explain the logic behind this claim. It is rooted in what is termed "marginal productivity" theory. In the words of one of its developers:

> "If each productive function is paid for according to the amount of its product, then each man get what he himself produces. If he works, he gets what he creates by working; if he provides capital, he gets what his capital produces; and if, further, he renders service by co-ordinating labour and capital, he gets the product that can be separately traced to that function. Only in one of these ways can a man produce anything. If he receives all that he brings into existence through any one of these three functions, he receives all that he creates at all." [John Bates Clark, **The Distribution of Wealth**, p.7]

Needless to say, this analysis was based on the need to justify the existing system, for it was "the purpose of this work to show that the distribution of income to society is controlled by a natural law, and that this law, if it worked without friction, would give to every agent of production the amount of wealth which that agent creates." In other words, "what a social class gets is, under natural law, what it contributes to the general output of industry." [Clark, **Op. Cit.**, p. v and p. 313] And only mad people can reject a "natural law" like gravity – or capitalism!

Most schools of capitalist economics, when they bother to try and justify non-labour income, hold to this theory of productivity. Unsurprisingly, as it proves what right-wing economist Milton Friedman called the "capitalist ethic": "To each according to what he and the instruments he owns produces." [**Capitalism and Freedom**, pp. 161-162] As such, this is one of the key defences of capitalism, based as it is on the productive contribution of each factor (labour, land and capital). Anarchists are unconvinced.

Unsurprisingly, this theory took some time to develop given the theoretical difficulties involved. After all, you need all three factors to produce a commodity, say a bushel of wheat. How can we determine what percentage of the price is due to the land, what percentage to labour and what percentage to capital? You cannot simply say that the "contribution" of each factor just happens to be identical to its cost (i.e. the contribution of land is what the market rent is) as this is circular reasoning. So how is it possible to specify contribution of each factor of production independently of the market mechanism in such a way as to show, firstly, that the contributions add up to 100 percent and, secondly, that the free market will in fact return to each factor its respective contribution?

This is where marginal productivity theory comes in. In neo-classical theory, the contribution of a specific factor is defined as the marginal product of that factor when the other factors are left constant. Take, as an example, a hundred bushels of wheat produced by X acres of land being worked by Y workers using £Z worth of capital. The contribution of land can then be defined as the increase in wheat that an extra acre of land would produce (X+1) if the same number of workers employed the same capital worked it. Similarly, the contribution of a worker would be the increase that would result if an additional worker was hired (Y + 1) to work the same land (X) with the same capital (£Z). The contribution of capital, obviously, would be the increase in wheat produced by the same number of workers (X) working the same amount of land (Y) using one more unit of capital (£Z+1). Then mathematics kicks in. If enough assumptions are made in terms of the substitutability of factors, diminishing returns, and so forth, then a mathematical theorem (Euler's Theorem) can be used to show that the sum of these marginal contributions would be a hundred bushels. Applying yet more assumptions to ensure "perfect competition" it can be mathematically proven that the rent per acre set by this perfect market will be precisely the contribution of the land, that the market wage will be the contribution of the worker, and the market interest rate will be the contribution of capital. In addition, it can be shown that any monopoly power will enable a factor owner to receive more than it contributes, so exploiting the others.

While this is impressive, the problems are obvious. As we discuss in section C.2.5, this model does not (indeed, cannot) describe any actual real economy. However, there is a more fundamental issue than mere practicality or realism, namely that it confuses a **moral** principle (that factors should receive in accordance with their productive contributions) with an ownership issue. This is because even if we want to say that land and capital "contribute" to the final product, we cannot say the same for the landowner or the capitalist. Using our example above, it should be noted that neither the capitalist nor the landowner actually engages in anything that might be called a productive activity. Their roles are purely passive, they simply allow what they own to be used by the people who do the actual work, the labourers.

Marginal productivity theory shows that with declining marginal productivity, the contribution of labour is less than the total product. The difference is claimed to be precisely the contribution of capital and land. But what is this "contribution" of capital and land? Without any labourers there would be no output. In addition, in physical terms, the marginal product of, say, capital is simply the amount by which production would decline if one piece of capital were taken out of production. It does not reflect any productive activity whatsoever on the part of the owner of said capital. **It does not, therefore, measure his or her productive contribution.** In other words, capitalist economics tries to confuse the owners of capital with the machinery they own. Unlike labour, whose "ownership" cannot be separated from the productive activities being done, capital and land can be rewarded without their owners actually doing anything productive at all.

For all its amazing mathematics, the neo-classical solution fails simply because it is not only irrelevant to reality, it is not relevant ethically.

To see why, let us consider the case of land and labour (capital is more complex and will be discussed in the next two sections). Marginal productivity theory can show, given enough assumptions, that five acres of land can produce 100 bushels of wheat with the labour of ten men and that the contribution of land and labour are, respectively, 40 and 60 bushels each. In other words, that each worker receives a wage representing 6 bushels of wheat while the landlord receives an income of 40 bushels. As socialist David Schweickart notes, *"we have derived both the contribution of labour and the contribution of land from purely technical considerations. We have made no assumptions about ownership, competition, or any other social or political relationship. No covert assumptions about capitalism have been smuggled into the analysis."* [**After Capitalism**, p. 29]

Surely this means that economics has produced a defence of non-labour income? Not so, as it ignores the key issue of what represents a valid contribution. The conclusion that the landlord (or capitalist) is entitled to their income *"in no way follows from the technical premises of the argument. Suppose our ten workers had cultivated the five acres **as a worker collective.** In this, they would receive the entire product, all one hundred bushels, instead of sixty. Is this unfair? To whom should the other forty bushels go? To the land, for its 'contribution'? Should the collective perhaps burn forty bushels as an offering to the Land-God? (Is the Land-Lord the representative on Earth of this Land-God?)."* [**Op. Cit.**, p. 30] It should be noted that Schweickart is echoing the words of Proudhon:

> *"How much does the proprietor increase the utility of his tenant's products? Has he ploughed, sowed, reaped, mowed, winnowed, weeded? … I admit that the land is an implement; but who made it? Did the proprietor? Did he – by the efficacious virtue of the right of property, by this **moral quality** infused into the soil – endow it with vigour and fertility? Exactly there lies the monopoly of the proprietor, though he did not make the implement, he asks pay for its use. When the Creator shall present himself and claim farm-rent, we will consider the matter with him; or even when the proprietor – his pretended representative – shall exhibit his power of attorney."*
> [**What is Property?**, pp. 166-7]

In other words, granting permission cannot be considered as a "contribution" or a "productive" act:

> *"We can see that a moral sleight-of-hand has been performed. A technical demonstration has passed itself off as a moral argument by its choice of terminology, namely, by calling a marginal product a 'contribution.' The 'contribution = ethical entitlement' of the landowner has been identified with the 'contribution = marginal product' of the land … What is the nature of the landowner's 'contribution' here? We can say that the landlord **contributed the land** to the workers, but notice the qualitative difference between his 'contribution' and the contribution of his workforce. He 'contributes' his land – but the land remains intact and remains his at the end of the harvest, whereas the labour contributed by each labourer is gone. If the labourers do not expend **more***

labour next harvest, they will get nothing more, whereas the landowner can continue to 'contribute' year after year (lifting not a finger), and be rewarded year after year for doing so." [Schweickart, **Op. Cit.**, p. 30]

As the examples of the capitalist and co-operative farms shows, the "contribution" of land and capital can be rewarded without their owners doing anything at all. So what does it mean, "capital's share"? After all, no one has ever given money to a machine or land. That money goes to the owner, not the technology or resource used. When "land" gets its "reward" it involves money going to the landowner **not** fertiliser being spread on the land. Equally, if the land and the capital were owned by the labourers then "capital" and "land" would receive nothing despite both being used in the productive process and, consequently, having "aided" production. Which shows the fallacy of the idea that profits, interest and rent represent a form of "contribution" to the productive process by land and capital which needs rewarded. They only get a "reward" when they hire labour to work them, i.e. they give permission for others to use the property in question in return for telling them what to do and keeping the product of their labour.

As Proudhon put it, *"[w]ho is entitled to the rent of the land? The producer of the land, without doubt. Who made the land? God. Then, proprietor, retire!"* [**Op. Cit.**, p. 104] Much the same can be said of "capital" (workplaces, machinery, etc.) as well. The capitalist, argued Berkman, *"gives you a job; that is permission to work in the factory or mill which was not built by him but by other workers like yourself. And for that permission you help to support him for the rest of your life or as long as you work for him."* [**What is Anarchism?**, p. 14]

So non-labour income exists **not** because of the owners of capital and land "contribute" to production but because they, as a class, **own** the means of life and workers have to sell their labour and liberty to them to gain access:

> *"We cry shame on the feudal baron who forbade the peasant to turn a clod of earth unless he surrendered to his lord a fourth of his crop. We called those the barbarous times, But if the forms have changed, the relations have remained the same, and the worker is forced, under the name of free contract, to accept feudal obligations."*
> [Kropotkin, **The Conquest of Bread**, pp. 31-2]

It is capitalist property relations that allow this monopolisation of wealth by those who own (or boss) but do not produce. The workers do not get the full value of what they produce, nor do they have a say in how the surplus value produced by their labour gets used (e.g. investment decisions). Others have monopolised both the wealth produced by workers and the decision-making power within the company. This is a private form of taxation without representation, just as the company is a private form of statism.

Therefore, providing capital is **not** a productive act, and keeping the profits that are produced by those who actually do use capital is an act of theft. This does not mean, of course, that creating capital goods is not creative nor that it does not aid production. Far from it! But owning the outcome of such activity and renting it does not justify capitalism or profits. In other words, while we need machinery, workplaces, houses and raw materials to produce goods we do **not** need landlords and capitalists.

The problem with the capitalists' "contribution to production" argument is that one must either assume (a) a strict definition of who is the producer of something, in which case one must credit only the worker(s), or (b) a looser definition based on which individuals have contributed to the circumstances that made the productive work possible. Since the worker's productivity was made possible in part by the use of property supplied by the capitalist, one can thus credit the capitalist with "contributing to production" and so claim that he or she is entitled to a reward, i.e. profit.

However, if one assumes (b), one must then explain why the chain of credit should stop with the capitalist. Since all human activity takes place within a complex social network, many factors might be cited as contributing to the circumstances that allowed workers to produce – e.g. their upbringing and education, the contribution of other workers in providing essential products, services and infrastructure that permits their place of employment to operate, and so on (even the government, which funds infrastructure and education). Certainly the property of the capitalist contributed in this sense. But his contribution was less important than the work of, say, the worker's mother. Yet no capitalist, so far as we know, has proposed compensating workers' mothers with any share of the firm's revenues, and particularly not with a **greater** share than that received by capitalists! Plainly, however, if they followed their own logic consistently, capitalists would have to agree that such compensation would be fair.

In summary, while some may consider that profit is the capitalist's "contribution" to the value of a commodity, the reality is that it is nothing more than the reward for owning capital and giving permission for **others** to produce using it. As David Schweickart puts it, "'providing capital' means nothing more than 'allowing it to be used.' But an act of granting permission, in and of itself, is not a productive activity. If labourers cease to labour, production ceases in any society. But if owners cease to grant permission, production is affected only if their **authority** over the means of production is respected." [**Against Capitalism**, p. 11]

This authority, as discussed earlier, derives from the coercive mechanisms of the state, whose primary purpose is to ensure that capitalists have this ability to grant or deny workers access to the means of production. Therefore, not only is "providing capital" not a productive activity, it depends on a system of organised coercion which requires the appropriation of a considerable portion of the value produced by labour, through taxes, and hence is actually parasitic. Needless to say, rent can also be considered as "profit", being based purely on "granting permission" and so not a productive activity. The same can be said of interest, although the arguments are somewhat different (see section C.2.6).

So, even if we assume that capital and land **are** productive, it does not follow that owning those resources entitles the owner to an income. However, this analysis is giving too much credit to capitalist ideology. The simple fact is that capital is **not** productive at all. Rather, "capital" only contributes to production when used by labour (land does produce use values, of course, but these only become available once labour is used to pick the fruit, reap the corn or dig the coal). As such, profit is not the reward for the productivity

of capital. Rather **labour** produces the marginal productivity of capital. This is discussed in the next section.

C.2.4 Is profit the reward for the productivity of capital?

In a word, no. As Proudhon pointed out, *"Capital, tools, and machinery are likewise unproductive ... The proprietor who asks to be rewarded for the use of a tool or for the productive power of his land, takes for granted, then, that which is radically false; namely, that capital produces by its own effort – and, in taking pay for this imaginary product, he literally receives something for nothing."* [**What is Property?**, p. 169] In other words, only labour is productive and profit is not the reward for the productivity of capital.

Needless to say, capitalist economists disagree. *"Here again the philosophy of the economists is wanting. To defend usury they have pretended that capital was productive, and they have changed a metaphor into a reality,"* argued Proudhon. The socialists had *"no difficulty in overturning their sophistry; and through this controversy the theory of capital has fallen into such disfavour that today, in the minds of the people, **capitalist** and **idler** are synonymous terms."* [**System of Economical Contradictions**, p. 290]

Sadly, since Proudhon's time, the metaphor has regained its hold, thanks in part to neo-classical economics and the "marginal productivity" theory. We explained this theory in the last section as part of our discussion on why, even if we assume that land and capital **are** productive this does not, in itself, justify capitalist profit. Rather, profits accrue to the capitalist simply because he or she gave their permission for others to use their property. However, the notion that profits represent that "productivity" of capital is deeply flawed for other reasons. The key one is that, by themselves, capital and land produce nothing. As Bakunin put it, *"neither property nor capital produces anything when not fertilised by labour."* [**The Political Philosophy of Bakunin**, p. 183]

In other words, capital is "productive" simply because people use it. This is hardly a surprising conclusion. Mainstream economics recognises it in its own way (the standard economic terminology for this is that *"factors usually do not work alone"*). Needless to say, the conclusions anarchists and defenders of capitalism draw from this obvious fact are radically different.

The standard defence of class inequalities under capitalism is that people get rich by producing what other people want. That, however, is hardly ever true. Under capitalism, people get rich by hiring other people to produce what other people want or by providing land, money or machinery to those who do the hiring. The number of people who have became rich purely by their own labour, without employing others, is tiny. When pressed, defenders of capitalism will admit the basic point and argue that, in a free market, everyone gets in income what their contribution in producing these goods indicates. Each factor of production (land, capital and labour) is treated in the same way and their marginal productivity indicates what their contribution to a finished product is and so their income. Thus wages represent the marginal productivity of labour, profit the marginal productivity of capital and rent the marginal productivity of land. As we have used land and labour in the previous section, we will concentrate on land and "capital" here. We must note, however, that marginal productivity theory has immense difficulties with capital and has been proven to be internally incoherent on this matter (see next section). However, as mainstream economics ignores this, so will we for the time being.

So what of the argument that profits represent the contribution of capital? The reason why anarchists are not impressed becomes clear when we consider ten men digging a hole with spades. Holding labour constant means that we add spades to the mix. Each new spade increases productivity by the same amount (because we assume that labour is homogenous) until we reach the eleventh spade. At that point, the extra spade lies unused and so the marginal contribution of the spade ("capital") is zero. This suggests that the socialists are correct, capital **is** unproductive and, consequently, does not deserve any reward for its use.

Of course, it will be pointed out that the eleventh spade cost money and, as a result, the capitalist would have stopped at ten spades and the marginal contribution of capital equals the amount the tenth spade added. Yet the only reason that spade added anything to production was because there was a worker to use it. In other words, as economist David Ellerman stresses, the *"point is that capital itself does not 'produce' at all; capital is used by Labour to produce the outputs ... Labour produces the marginal product of capital."* [**Property and Contract in Economics**, p. 204] As such, to talk of the "marginal product" of capital is meaningless as holding labour constant is meaningless:

> *"Consider, for example, the 'marginal product of a shovel' in a simple production process wherein three workers use two shovels and a wheelbarrow to dig out a cellar. Two of the workers use two shovels to fill the wheelbarrow which the third worker pushes a certain distance to dump the dirt. The marginal productivity of a shovel is defined as the extra product produced when an extra shovel is added and the other factors, such as labour, are held constant. The labour is the human activity of carrying out this production process. If labour was held 'constant' is the sense of carrying out the same human activity, then any third shovel would just lie unused and the extra product would be identically zero.*
>
> *"'Holding labour constant' really means reorganising the human activity in a more capital intensive way so that the extra shovel will be optimally utilised. For instance, all three workers could use the three shovels to fill the wheelbarrow and then they could take turns emptying the wheelbarrow. In this manner, the workers would use the extra shovel and by so doing they would produce some extra product (additional earth moved during the same time period). This extra product would be called the 'marginal product of the shovel, but in fact it is produced by the workers who are also using the additional shovel ... [Capital] does not 'produce' its marginal product. Capital does not 'produce' at all. Capital is used by Labour to*

produce the output. When capital is increased, Labour produces extra output by using up the extra capital ... In short, **Labour produced the marginal product of capital** (and used up the extra capital services)." [**Op. Cit.**, pp. 207-9]

Therefore, the idea that profits equals the marginal productivity of capital is hard to believe. Capital, in this perspective, is not only a tree which bears fruit even if its owner leaves it uncultivated, it is a tree which also picks its own fruit, prepares it and serves it for dinner! Little wonder the classical economists (Smith, Ricardo, John Stuart Mill) considered capital to be unproductive and explained profits and interest in other, less obviously false, means.

Perhaps the "marginal productivity" of capital is simply what is left over once workers have been paid their "share" of production, i.e. once the marginal productivity of labour has been rewarded. Obviously the marginal product of labour and capital are related. In a production process, the contribution of capital will (by definition) be equal to total price minus the contribution of labour. You define the marginal product of labour, it is necessary to keep something else constant. This means either the physical inputs other than labour are kept constant, or the rate of profit on capital is kept constant. As economist Joan Robinson noted:

> *"I found this satisfactory, for it destroys the doctrine that wages are regulated by marginal productivity. In a short-period case, where equipment is given, at full-capacity operation the marginal physical product of labour is indeterminate. When nine men with nine spades are digging a hole, to add a tenth man could increase output only to the extent that nine dig better if they have a rest from time to time. On the other hand, to subtract the ninth man would reduce output by more or less the average amount. The wage must lie somewhere between the average value of output per head and zero, so that marginal product is greater or much less than the wage according as equipment is being worked below or above its designed capacity."* [**Contributions to Modern Economics**, p. 104]

If wages are not regulated by marginal productivity theory, then neither is capital (or land). Subtracting labour while keeping capital constant simply results in unused equipment and unused equipment, by definition, produces nothing. What the "contribution" of capital is dependent, therefore, on the economic power the owning class has in a given market situation (as we discuss in section C.3). As William Lazonick notes, the neo-classical theory of marginal productivity has two key problems which flow from its flawed metaphor that capital is "productive":

> *"The first flaw is the assumption that, at any point in time, the productivity of a technology is given to the firm, irrespective of the social context in which the firm attempts to utilise the technology ... this assumption, typically implicit in mainstream economic analysis and [is] derived from an ignorance of the nature of the production process as much as everything else ... "*

"The second flaw in the neo-classical theoretical structure is the assumption that factor prices are independent of factor productivities. On the basis of this assumption, factor productivities arising from different combinations of capital and labour can be taken as given to the firm; hence the choice of technique depends only on variations in relative factor prices. It is, however, increasingly recognised by economists who speak of 'efficiency wages' that factor prices and factor productivities may be linked, particularly for labour inputs ... the productivity of a technology depends on the amount of effort that workers choose to supply." [**Competitive Advantage on the Shop Floor**, p. 130 and pp. 133-4]

In other words, neo-classical economics forgets that technology has to be used by workers and so its "productivity" depends on how it is applied. If profit did flow as a result of some property of machinery then bosses could do without autocratic workplace management to ensure profits. They would have no need to supervise workers to ensure that adequate amounts of work are done in excess of what they pay in wages. This means the idea (so beloved by pro-capitalist economics) that a worker's wage **is** the equivalent of what she produces is one violated everyday within reality:

"Managers of a capitalist enterprise are not content simply to respond to the dictates of the market by equating the wage to the value of the marginal product of labour. Once the worker has entered the production process, the forces of the market have, for a time at least, been superseded. The effort-pay relation will depend not only on market relations of exchange but also ... on the hierarchical relations of production – on the relative power of managers and workers within the enterprise." [William Lazonick, **Business Organisation and the Myth of the Market Economy**, pp. 184-5]

But, then again, capitalist economics is more concerned with justifying the status quo than being in touch with the real world. To claim that a workers wage represents her contribution and profit capital's is simply false. Capital cannot produce anything (never mind a surplus) unless used by labour and so profits do not represent the productivity of capital. In and of themselves, fixed costs do not create value. Whether value is created depends on how investments are developed and used once in place. Which brings us back to labour (and the social relationships which exist within an economy) as the fundamental source of surplus value.

Then there is the concept of profit sharing, whereby workers are get a share of the profits made by the company. Yet profits are the return to capital. This shatters the notion that profits represent the contribution of capital. **If** profits were the contribution of the productivity of equipment, then sharing profits would mean that capital was not receiving its full *"contribution"* to production (and so was being exploited by labour!). It is unlikely that bosses would implement such a scheme unless they knew they would get more profits out of it. As such, profit sharing is usually used as a technique to **increase** productivity and profits. Yet in neo-classical economics, it seems strange that such a technique would be required if profits, in

fact, **did** represent capital's "contribution." After all, the machinery which the workers are using is the same as before profit sharing was introduced – how could this unchanged capital stock produce an increased "contribution"? It could only do so if, in fact, capital was unproductive and it was the unpaid efforts, skills and energy of workers' that actually was the source of profits. Thus the claim that profit equals capital's "contribution" has little basis in fact.

As capital is not autonomously productive and goods are the product of human (mental and physical) labour, Proudhon was right to argue that *"Capital, tools, and machinery are likewise unproductive ... The proprietor who asks to be rewarded for the use of a tool or for the productive power of his land, takes for granted, then, that which is radically false; namely, that capital produces by its own effort – and, in taking pay for this imaginary product, he literally receives something for nothing."* [**What is Property?**, p. 169]

It will be objected that while capital is not productive in itself, its use does make labour more productive. As such, surely its owner is entitled to some share of the larger output produced by its aid. Surely this means that the owners of capital deserve a reward? Is this difference not the "contribution" of capital? Anarchists are not convinced. Ultimately, this argument boils down to the notion that giving permission to use something is a productive act, a perspective we rejected in the last section. In addition, providing capital is unlike normal commodity production. This is because capitalists, unlike workers, get paid multiple times for one piece of work (which, in all likelihood, they paid others to do) and **keep** the result of that labour. As Proudhon argued:

*"He [the worker] who manufactures or repairs the farmer's tools receives the price **once**, either at the time of delivery, or in several payments; and when this price is once paid to the manufacturer, the tools which he has delivered belong to him no more. Never can he claim double payment for the same tool, or the same job of repairs. If he annually shares in the products of the farmer, it is owing to the fact that he annually does something for the farmer.*

"The proprietor, on the contrary, does not yield his implement; eternally he is paid for it, eternally he keeps it." [**Op. Cit.**, pp. 169-170]

While the capitalist, in general, gets their investment back plus something extra, the workers can never get their time back. That time has gone, forever, in return for a wage which allows them to survive in order to sell their time and labour (i.e. liberty) again. Meanwhile, the masters have accumulated more capital and their the social and economic power and, consequently, their ability to extract surplus value goes up at a higher rate than the wages they have to pay (as we discuss in section C.7, this process is not without problems and regularly causes economic crisis to break out).

Without labour nothing would have been produced and so, in terms of justice, **at best** it could be claimed that the owners of capital deserve to be paid only for what has been used of their capital (i.e. wear and tear and damages). While it is true that the value invested in fixed capital is in the course of time transferred to the commodities produced by it and through their sale transformed into money, this does not represent any actual labour by the owners of capital. Anarchists reject the ideological sleight-of-hand that suggests otherwise and recognise that (mental and physical) labour is the **only** form of contribution that can be made by humans to a productive process. Without labour, nothing can be produced nor the value contained in fixed capital transferred to goods. As Charles A. Dana pointed out in his popular introduction to Proudhon's ideas, *"[t]he labourer without capital would soon supply his wants by its production ... but capital with no labourers to consume it can only lie useless and rot."* [**Proudhon and his "Bank of the People"**, p. 31] If workers do not control the full value of their contributions to the output they produce then they are exploited and so, as indicated, capitalism is based upon exploitation.

Of course, as long as "capital" **is** owned by a different class than as those who use it, this is extremely unlikely that the owners of capital will simply accept a "reward" of damages. This is due to the hierarchical organisation of production of capitalism. In the words of the early English socialist Thomas Hodgskin *"capital does not derive its utility from previous, but present labour; and does not bring its owner a profit because it has been stored up, but because it is a means of obtaining a command over labour."* [**Labour Defended against the Claims of Capital**] It is more than a strange coincidence that the people with power in a company, when working out who contributes most to a product, decide it is themselves!

This means that the notion that labour gets its "share" of the products created is radically false for, as *"a description of **property rights**, the distributive shares picture is quite misleading and false. The simple fact is that one legal party owns all the product. For example, General Motors doesn't just own 'Capital's share' of the GM cars produced; it owns all of them."* [Ellerman, **Op. Cit.**, p. 27] Or as Proudhon put it, *"Property is the right to enjoy and dispose of another's goods, – the fruit of another's industry and labour."* The only way to finally abolish exploitation is for workers to manage their own work and the machinery and tools they use. This is implied, of course, in the argument that labour is the source of property for *"if labour is the sole basis of property, I cease to be a proprietor of my field as soon as I receive rent for it from another ... It is the same with all capital."* Thus, *"all production being necessarily collective"* and *"all accumulated capital being social property, no one can be its exclusive proprietor."* [**What is Property?**, p. 171, p. 133 and p. 130]

The reason why capital gets a "reward" is simply due to the current system which gives the capitalist class an advantage which allows them to refuse access to their property except under the condition that they command the workers to make more than they have to pay in wages and keep their capital at the end of the production process to be used afresh the next. So while capital is not productive and owning capital is not a productive act, under capitalism it is an enriching one and will continue to be so until such time as that system is abolished. In other words, profits, interest and rent are not founded upon any permanent principle of economic or social life but arise from a specific social system which produce specific social relationships. Abolish wage labour by co-operatives, for example, and the issue of the "productivity" of "capital" disappears as "capital" no longer exists (a machine is a machine, it only becomes capital when it is used by wage labour).

So rather than the demand for labour being determined by the technical considerations of production, it is determined by the need of the capitalist to make a profit. This is something the neo-classical theory implicitly admits, as the marginal productivity of labour is just a roundabout way of saying that labour-power will be bought as long as the wage is not higher than the profits that the workers produce. In other words, wages do not rise above the level at which the capitalist will be able to produce and realise surplus-value. To state that workers will be hired as long as the marginal productivity of their labour exceeds the wage is another way of saying that workers are exploited by their boss. So even if we do ignore reality for the moment, this defence of profits does **not** prove what it seeks to – it shows that labour **is** exploited under capitalism.

However, as we discuss in the next section, this whole discussion is somewhat beside the point. This is because marginal productivity theory has been conclusively proven to be flawed by dissident economics and has been acknowledged as such by leading neo-classical economists.

C.2.5 Do profits represent the contribution of capital to production?

In a word, no. While we have assumed the validity of "marginal productivity" theory in relation to capital in the previous two sections, the fact is that the theory is deeply flawed. This is on two levels. Firstly, it does not reflect reality in any way. Secondly, it is logically flawed and, even worse, this has been known to economists for decades. While the first objection will hardly bother most neo-classical economists (what part of that dogma **does** reflect reality?), the second should as intellectual coherence is what replaces reality in economics. However, in spite of "marginal productivity" theory being proven to be nonsense and admitted as such by leading neo-classical economists, it is still taught in economic classes and discussed in text books as if it were valid.

We will discuss each issue in turn.

The theory is based on a high level of abstraction and the assumptions used to allow the mathematics to work are so extreme that no real world example could possibly meet them. The first problem is determining the level at which the theory should be applied. Does it apply to individuals, groups, industries or the whole economy? For depending on the level at which it is applied, there are different problems associated with it and different conclusions to be drawn from it. Similarly, the time period over which it is to be applied has an impact. As such, the theory is so vague that it would be impossible to test as its supporters would simply deny the results as being inapplicable to **their** particular version of the model.

Then there are problems with the model itself. While it has to assume that factors are identical in order to invoke the necessary mathematical theory, none of the factors used are homogenous in the real world. Similarly, for Euler's theory to be applied, there must be constant returns to scale and this does not apply either (it would be fair to say that the assumption of constant returns to scale was postulated to allow the theorem to be invoked in the first place rather than as a result of a scientific analysis of real industrial conditions). Also, the model assumes an ideal market which cannot be realised and any real world imperfections make it redundant. In the model, such features of the real world as oligopolistic markets (i.e. markets dominated by a few firms), disequilibrium states, market power, informational imperfections of markets, and so forth do not exist. Including any of these real features invalidates the model and no "factor" gets its just rewards.

Moreover, like neo-classical economics in general, this theory just assumes the original distribution of ownership. As such, it is a boon for those who have benefited from previous acts of coercion – their ill-gotten gains can now be used to generate income for them!

Finally, "marginal productivity" theory ignores the fact that most production is collective in nature and, as a consequence, the idea of subtracting a single worker makes little or no sense. As soon as there is *"a division of labour and an interdependence of different jobs, as is the case generally in modern industry,"* its *"absurdity can immediately be shown."* For example, *"[i]f, in a coal-fired locomotive, the train's engineer is eliminated, one does not 'reduce a little' of the product (transportation), one eliminates it completely; and the same is true if one eliminates the fireman. The 'product' of this indivisible team of engineer and fireman obeys a law of all or nothing, and there is no 'marginal product' of the one that can be separated from the other. The same thing goes on the shop floor, and ultimately for the modern factory as a whole, where jobs are closely interdependent."* [Cornelius Castoriadis, **Political and Social Writings**, vol. 3, p. 213] Kropotkin made the same point, arguing it *"is utterly impossible to draw a distinction between the work"* of the individuals collectively producing a product as all *"contribute … in proportion to their strength, their energy, their knowledge, their intelligence, and their skill."* [**The Conquest of Bread**, p. 170 and p. 169]

This suggests another explanation for the existence of profits than the "marginal productivity" of capital. Let us assume, as argued in marginal productivity theory, that a worker receives exactly what she has produced because if she ceases to work, the total product will decline by precisely the value of her wage. However, this argument has a flaw in it. This is because the total product will decline by more than that value if two or more workers leave. This is because the wage each worker receives under conditions of perfect competition is assumed to be the product of the **last** labourer in neo-classical theory. The neo-classical argument presumes a "declining marginal productivity," i.e. the marginal product of the last worker is assumed to be less than the second last and so on. In other words, in neo-classical economics, all workers bar the mythical "last worker" do not receive the full product of their labour. They only receive what the **last** worker is claimed to produce and so everyone **bar** the last worker does not receive exactly what he or she produces. In other words, all the workers are exploited bar the last one.

However, this argument forgets that co-operation leads to increased productivity which the capitalists appropriate for themselves. This is because, as Proudhon argued, *"the capitalist has paid as many times one day's wages"* rather than the workers collectively and, as such, *"he has paid nothing for that immense power which results from the union and harmony of labourers, and the convergence and simultaneousness of their efforts. Two hundred grenadiers*

stood the obelisk of Luxor upon its base in a few hours; do you suppose that one man could have accomplished the same task in two hundred days? Nevertheless, on the books of the capitalist, the amount of wages would have been the same." Therefore, the capitalist has *"paid all the individual forces"* but *"the collective force still remains to be paid. Consequently, there remains a right of collective property"* which the capitalist *"enjoy[s] unjustly."* [**What is Property?**, p. 127 and p. 130]

As usual, therefore, we must distinguish between the ideology and reality of capitalism. As we indicated in section C.1, the model of perfect competition has no relationship with the real world. Unsurprisingly, marginal productivity theory is likewise unrelated to reality. This means that the assumptions required to make "marginal productivity" theory work are so unreal that these, in themselves, should have made any genuine scientist reject the idea out of hand. Note, we are **not** opposing abstract theory, **every** theory abstracts from reality is some way. We are arguing that, to be valid, a theory has to reflect the real situation it is seeking to explain in some meaningful way. Any abstractions or assumptions used must be relatively trivial and, when relaxed, not result in the theory collapsing. This is not the case with marginal productivity theory. It is important to recognise that there are degrees of abstraction. There are *"negligibility assumptions"* which state that some aspect of reality has little or no effect on what is being analysed. Sadly for marginal productivity theory, its assumptions are not of this kind. Rather, they are *"domain assumptions"* which specify *"the conditions under which a particular theory will apply. If those conditions do not apply, then neither does the theory."* [Steve Keen, **Debunking Economics**, p. 151] This is the case here.

However, most economists will happily ignore this critique for, as noted repeatedly, basing economic theory on reality or realistic models is not considered a major concern by neoclassical economists. However, "marginal productivity" theory applied to capital is riddled with logical inconsistencies which show that it is simply wrong. In the words of the noted left-wing economist Joan Robinson:

> *"The neo-classicals evidently had not been told that the neo-classical theory did not contain a solution of the problems of profits or of the value of capital. They have erected a towering structure of mathematical theorems on a foundation that does not exist. Recently [in the 1960s, leading neo-classical economist] Paul Samuelson was sufficiently candid to admit that the basis of his system does not hold, but the theorems go on pouring out just the same."* [**Contributions to Modern Economics**, p. 186]

If profits **are** the result of private property and the inequality it produces, then it is unsurprising that neoclassical theory would be as foundationless as Robinson argues. After all, this is a **political** question and neo-classical economics was developed to ignore such questions. Marginal productivity theory has been subject to intense controversy, precisely because it claims to show that labour is not exploited under capitalism (i.e. that each factor gets what it contributes to production). We will now summarise this successful criticism.

The first major theoretical problem is obvious: how do you measure capital? In neoclassical economics, capital is referred to as machinery of all sorts as well as the workplaces that house them. Each of these items is, in turn, made up of a multitude of other commodities and many of these are assemblies of other commodities. So what does it mean to say, as in marginal productivity theory, that "capital" is varied by one unit? The only thing these products have in common is a price and that is precisely what economists **do** use to aggregate capital. Sadly, though, shows *"that there is no meaning to be given to a 'quantity of capital' apart from the rate of profit, so that the contention that the 'marginal product of capital' determines the rate of profit is meaningless."* [Robinson, **Op. Cit.**, p. 103] This is because argument is based on circular reasoning:

> *"For long-period problems we have to consider the meaning of the rate of profit on capital … the value of capital equipment, reckoned as its future earnings discounted at a rate of interest equal to the rate of profit, is equal to its initial cost, which involves prices including profit at the same rate on the value of the capital involved in producing it, allowing for depreciation at the appropriate rate over its life up to date.*
>
> *"The value of a stock of capital equipment, therefore, involves the rate of profit. There is no meaning in a 'quantity of capital' apart from the rate of profit."* [**Collected Economic Papers**, vol. 4, p. 125]

Looking at it another way, neo-classical economics seeks to simultaneously solve the problems of production and income distribution. It attempts to show how the level of employment of capital and labour is determined as well as how national income is divided between the two. The latter is done by multiplying the quantities of labour and capital by the equilibrium wage and interest rate, respectively. In the long term, equilibrium conditions are governed by the net marginal productivity of each factor, with each supplied until its net marginal revenue is zero. This is why the market rate of interest is used as capital is assumed to have marginal productivity and the existing market interest reflects that.

Yet in what sense can we say that capital has marginal productivity? How is the stock of capital to be measured? One measure is to take the present value of the income stream expected to accrue to capital owners. However, where does this discount rate and net income stream come from? To find a value for these, it is necessary to estimate a national income and the division of income between labour and capital but that is what the analysis was meant to produce. In other words, the neo-classical theory requires assumptions which are, in fact, the solution. This means that value of capital is dependent on the distribution of income. As there is no rationale offered for choosing one income distribution over another, the neo-classical theory does not solve the problem it set out to investigate but rather simply assumes it away. It is a tautology. It asks how the rate of profit is determined and answers by referencing the quantity of capital and its marginal revenue product. When asked how these are determined, the reply is based on assuming a division of future income and the discounting of the returns of capital with the market rate of interest. That is, it simply

says that the market rate of interest is a function of the market rate of interest (and an assumed distribution of income).

In other words, according to neoclassical theory, the rate of profit and interest depends on the amount of capital, and the amount of capital depends on the rate of profit and interest. One has to assume a rate of profit in order to demonstrate the equilibrium rate of return is determined. This issue is avoided in neo-classical economics simply by ignoring it (it must be noted that the same can be said of the "Austrian" concept of *"roundaboutness"* as *"it is impossible to define one way of producing a commodity as 'more roundabout' than another independently of the rate of profit … Therefore the Austrian notion of roundaboutness is as internally inconsistent as the neoclassical concept of the marginal productivity of capital."* [Steve Keen, **Debunking Economics**, p. 302]).

The next problem with the theory is that "capital" is treated as something utterly unreal. Take, for example, leading neoclassical Dennis Robertson's 1931 attempt to explain the marginal productivity of labour when holding "capital" constant:

> *"If ten men are to be set out to dig a hole instead of nine, they will be furnished with ten cheaper spades instead of nine more expensive ones; or perhaps if there is no room for him to dig comfortably, the tenth man will be furnished with a bucket and sent to fetch beer for the other nine."* [*"Wage-grumbles"*, **Economic Fragments**, p. 226]

So to work out the marginal productivity of the factors involved, *"ten cheaper spades"* somehow equals nine more expensive spades? How is this keeping capital constant? And how does this reflect reality? Surely, any real world example would involve sending the tenth digger to get another spade? And how do nine expensive spades become ten cheaper ones? In the real world, this is impossible but in neoclassical economics this is not only possible but required for the theory to work. As Robinson argued, in neo-classical theory the *"concept of capital all the man-made factors are boiled into one, which we may call **leets** … [which], though all made up of one physical substance, is endowed with the capacity to embody various techniques of production … and a change of technique can be made simply by squeezing up or spreading out leets, instantaneously and without cost."* [**Contributions to Modern Economics**, p. 106] This allows economics to avoid the obvious aggregation problems with "capital", make sense of the concept of adding an extra unit of capital to discover its "marginal productivity" and allows capital to be held "constant" so that the "marginal productivity" of labour can be found. For when *"the stock of means of production in existence can be represented as a quantity of ectoplasm, we can say, appealing to Euler's theorem, that the rent per unit of ectoplasm is equal to the marginal product of the given quantity of ectoplasm when it is fully utilised. This does not seem to add anything of interest to the argument."* [**Op. Cit.**, p. 99] This ensures reality has to be ignored and so economic theory need not discuss any practical questions:

> *"When equipment is made of leets, there is no distinction between long and short-period problems … Nine spades are lumps of leets; when the tenth man turns up it is squeezed out to provide him with a share of equipment*

nine-tenths of what each man had before ... There is no room for imperfect competition. There is no possibility of disappointed expectations ... There is no problem of unemployment ... Unemployed workers would bid down wages and the pre-existing quantity of leets would be spread out to accommodate them." [**Op. Cit.**, p. 107]

The concept that capital goods are made of ectoplasm and can be remoulded into the profit maximising form from day to day was invented in order to prove that labour and capital both receive their contribution to society, to show that labour is not exploited. It is not meant to be taken literally, it is only a parable, but without it the whole argument (and defence of capitalism) collapses. Once capital equipment is admitted to being actual, specific objects that cannot be squeezed, without cost, into new objects to accommodate more or less workers, such comforting notions that profits equal the (marginal) contribution of "capital" or that unemployment is caused by wages being too high have to be discarded for the wishful thinking they most surely are.

The last problem arises when we ignore these issues and assume that marginal productivity theory is correct. Consider the notion of the short run, where at least one factor of production cannot be varied. To determine its marginal productivity then capital has to be the factor which is varied. However, common sense suggests that capital is the least flexible factor and if that can be varied then every other one can be as well? As dissident economist Piero Sraffa argued, when a market is defined broadly enough, then the key neoclassical assumption that the demand and supply of a commodity are independent breaks down. This was applied by another economist, Amit Bhaduri, to the "capital market" (which is, by nature, a broadly defined industry). Steve Keen usually summarises these arguments, noting that *"at the aggregate level [of the economy as a whole], the desired relationship – the rate of profit equals the marginal productivity of capital – will not hold true"* as it only applies *"when the capital to labour ratio is the same in all industries – which is effectively the same as saying there is only one industry."* This *"proves Sraffa's assertion that, when a broadly defined industry is considered, changes in its conditions of supply and demand will affect the distribution of income."* This means that a *"change in the capital input will change output, but it also changes the wage, and the rate of profit ... As a result, the distribution of income is neither meritocratic nor determined by the market. The distribution of income is to some significant degree determined independently of marginal productivity and the impartial blades of supply and demand ... To be able to work out prices, it is first necessary to know the distribution of income ... There is therefore nothing sacrosanct about the prices that apply in the economy, and equally nothing sacrosanct about the distribution of income. It reflects the relative power of different groups in society."* [**Op. Cit.**, p. 136]

It should be noted that this critique bases itself on the neoclassical assumption that it is possible to define a factor of production called capital. In other words, even if we assume that neo-classical economics theory of capital is not circular reasoning, it's theory of distribution is still logically wrong.

So mainstream economics is based on a theory of distribution which

is utterly irrelevant to the real world and is incoherent when applied to capital. This would not be important except that it is used to justify the distribution of income in the real world. For example, the widening gap between rich and poor (it is argued) simply reflects a market efficiently rewarding more productive people. Thus the compensation for corporate chief executives climbs so sharply because it reflects their marginal productivity. Except, of course, the theory supports no such thing – except in a make believe world which cannot exist (laissez fairy land, anyone?).

It must be noted that this successful critique of neoclassical economics by dissident economists was first raised by Joan Robinson in the 1950s (it usually called the Cambridge Capital Controversy). It is rarely mentioned these days. While most economic textbooks simply repeat the standard theory, the fact is that this theory has been successfully debunked by dissident economists over four decades go. As Steve Keen notes, while leading neoclassical economists admitted that the critique was correct in the 1960s, today *"economic theory continues to use exactly the same concepts which Sraffa's critique showed to be completely invalid"* in spite the *"definitive capitulation by as significant an economist as Paul Samuelson."* As he concludes: *"There is no better sign of the intellectual bankruptcy of economics than this."* [**Op. Cit.**, p. 146, p. 129 and p. 147]

Why? Simply because the Cambridge Capital Controversy would expose the student of economics to some serious problems with neo-classical economics and they may start questioning the internal consistency of its claims. They would also be exposed to alternative economic theories and start to question whether profits **are** the result of exploitation. As this would put into jeopardy the role of economists as, to quote Marx, the *"hired prize-fighters"* for capital who replace *"genuine scientific research"* with *"the bad conscience and evil intent of apologetics."* Unsurprisingly, he characterised this as *"vulgar economics."* [**Capital**, vol. 1, p. 97]

C.2.6 Does interest represent the "time value" of money?

One defence of interest is the notion of the "time value" of money, that individuals have different "time preferences." Most individuals prefer, it is claimed, to consume now rather than later while a few prefer to save now on the condition that they can consume more later. Interest, therefore, is the payment that encourages people to defer consumption and so is dependent upon the subjective evaluations of individuals. It is, in effect, an exchange over time and so surplus value is generated by the exchange of present goods for future goods.

Based on this argument, many supporters of capitalism claim that it is legitimate for the person who provided the capital to get back **more** than they put in, because of the "time value of money." This is because investment requires savings and the person who provides those had to postpone a certain amount of current consumption and only agree to do this only if they get an increased amount later (i.e. a portion, over time, of the increased output that their saving makes possible). This plays a key role in the economy as it provide the funds from which investment can take place and the economy grow.

In this theory, interest rates are based upon this "time value" of money and the argument is rooted in the idea that individuals have different "time preferences." Some economic schools, like the Austrian school, argue that the actions by banks and states to artificially lower interest rates (by, for example, creating credit or printing money) create the business cycle as this distorts the information about people's willingness to consume now rather than later leading to over investment and so to a slump.

That the idea of doing nothing (i.e. not consuming) can be considered as productive says a lot about capitalist theory. However, this is beside the point as the argument is riddled with assumptions and, moreover, ignores key problems with the notion that savings always lead to investment.

The fundamental weakness of the theory of time preference must be that it is simply an unrealistic theory and does not reflect where the supply of capital does come from. It **may** be appropriate to the decisions of households between saving and consumption, but the main source of new capital is previous profit under capitalism. The motivation of making profits is not the provision of future means of consumption, it is profits for their own sake. The nature of capitalism requires profits to be accumulated into capital for if capitalists **did** only consume the system would break down. While from the point of view of mainstream economics such profit-making for its own sake is irrational, in reality it is imposed on the capitalist by capitalist competition. Only by constantly investing, by introducing new technology, work practices and products, can the capitalists keep their capital (and income) intact. Thus the motivation of capitalists to invest is imposed on them by the capitalist system, not by subjective evaluations between consuming more later rather than now.

Ignoring this issue and looking at the household savings, the theory still raises questions. The most obvious problem is that an individual's psychology is conditioned by the social situation they find themselves in. Ones "time preference" is determined by ones social position. If one has more than enough money for current needs, one can more easily "discount" the future (for example, workers will value the future product of their labour less than their current wages simply because without those wages there will be no future). We will discuss this issue in more detail later and will not do so here (see section C.2.7).

The second thing to ask is why should the supply price of waiting be assumed to be positive? If the interest rate simply reflects the subjective evaluations of individuals then, surely, it could be negative or zero. Deferred gratification is as plausible a psychological phenomenon as the overvaluation of present satisfactions, while uncertainty is as likely to produce immediate consumption as it is to produce provision for the future (saving). Thus Joan Robinson:

> "The rate of interest (excess of repayment over original loan) would settle at the level which equated supply and demand for loans. Whether it was positive or negative would depend upon whether spendthrifts or prudent family men happened to predominate in the community. There is no **a priori** presumption in favour of a positive

rate. Thus, the rate of interest cannot be accounted for as the 'cost of waiting.'

> "The reason why there is always a demand for loans at a positive rate of interest, in an economy where there is property in the means of production and means of production are scarce, is that finance expended now can be used to employ labour in productive processes which will yield a surplus in the future over costs of production. Interest is positive because profits are positive (though at the same time the cost and difficulty of obtaining finance play a part in keeping productive equipment scarce, and so contribute to maintaining the level of profits)."
> [**Contributions to Modern Economics**, p. 83]

It is only because money provides the authority to allocate resources and exploit wage labour that money now is more valuable ("we know that mere saving itself brings in nothing, so long as the pence saved are not used to exploit." [Kropotkin, **The Conquest of Bread**, p. 59]). The capitalist does not supply "time" (as the "time value" theory argues), the loan provides authority/power and so the interest rate does not reflect "time preference" but rather the utility of the loan to capitalists, i.e. whether it can be used to successfully exploit labour. If the expectations of profits by capitalists are low (as in, say, during a depression), loans would not be desired no matter how low the interest rate became. As such, the interest rate is shaped by the general profit level and so be independent of the "time preference" of individuals.

Then there is the problem of circularity. In any real economy, interest rates obviously shape people's saving decisions. This means that an individual's "time preference" is shaped by the thing it is meant to explain:

> "But there may be some savers who have the psychology required by the text books and weigh a preference for present spending against an increment of income (interest, dividends and capital gains) to be had from an increment of wealth. But what then? Each individual goes on saving or dis-saving till the point where his individual subjective rate of discount is equal to the market rate of interest. There has to be a market rate of interest for him to compare his rate of discount to." [Joan Robinson, **Op. Cit.**, pp. 11-12]

Looking at the individuals whose subjective evaluations allegedly determine the interest rate, there is the critical question of motivation. Looking at lenders, do they **really** charge interest because they would rather spend more money later than now? Hardly, their motivation is far more complicated than that. It is doubtful that many people actually sit down and work out how much their money is going to be "worth" to them a year or more from now. Even if they did, the fact is that they really have no idea how much it will be worth. The future is unknown and uncertain and, consequently, it is implausible that "time preference" plays the determining role in the decision making process.

In most economies, particularly capitalism, the saver and lender are rarely the same person. People save and the banks use it to loan it to others. The banks do not do this because they have a low "time preference" but because they want to make profits. They are a business and make their money by charging more interest on loans than they give on savings. Time preference does not enter into it, particularly as, to maximise profits, banks loan out more (on credit) than they have in savings and, consequently, make the actual interest rate totally independent of the rate "time preference" would (in theory) produce.

Given that it would be extremely difficult, indeed impossible, to stop banks acting in this way, we can conclude that even if "time preference" were true, it would be of little use in the real world. This, ironically, is recognised by the same free market capitalist economists who advocate a "time preference" perspective on interest. Usually associated with the "Austrian" school, they argue that banks should have 100% reserves (i.e. they loan out only what they have in savings, backed by gold). This implicitly admits that the interest rate does not reflect "time preference" but rather the activities (such as credit creation) of banks (not to mention other companies who extend business credit to consumers). As we discuss in section C.8, this is not due to state meddling with the money supply or the rate of interest but rather the way capitalism works.

Moreover, as the banking industry is marked, like any industry, by oligopolistic competition, the big banks will be able to add a mark up on services, so distorting any interest rates set even further from any abstract "time preference" that exists. Therefore, the structure of that market will have a significant effect on the interest rate. Someone in the same circumstances with the same "time preference" will get radically different interest rates depending on the "degree of monopoly" of the banking sector (see section C.5 for "degree of monopoly"). An economy with a multitude of small banks, implying low barriers of entry, will have different interest rates than one with a few big firms implying high barriers (if banks are forced to have 100% gold reserves, as desired by many "free market" capitalists, then these barriers may be even higher). As such, it is highly unlikely that "time preference" rather than market power is a more significant factor in determining interest rates in any **real** economy. Unless, of course, the rather implausible claim is made that the interest rate would be the same no matter how competitive the banking market was – which, of course, is what the "time preference" argument does imply.

Nor is "time preference" that useful when we look at the saver. People save money for a variety of motives, few (if any) of which have anything to do with "time preference." A common motive is, unsurprisingly, uncertainty about the future. Thus people put money into savings accounts to cover possible mishaps and unexpected developments (as in *"saving for a rainy day"*). Indeed, in an uncertain world future money may be its own reward for immediate consumption is often a risky thing to do as it reduces the ability to consume in the future (for example, workers facing unemployment in the future could value the same amount of money more then than now). Given that the future is uncertain, many save precisely for precautionary reasons and increasing current consumption is viewed as a disutility as it is risky behaviour. Another common reason would be to save because they do not have enough money to buy what they want now. This is particularly the case with working class families who face stagnating or falling income or face financial

difficulties.[Henwood, **Wall Street**, p. 65] Again, "time preference" does not come into it as economic necessity forces the borrowers to consume more now in order to be around in the future.

Therefore, money lending is, for the poor person, not a choice between more consumption now/less later and less consumption now/more later. If there is no consumption now, there will not be any later. So not everybody saves money because they want to be able to spend more at a future date. As for borrowing, the real reason for it is necessity produced by the circumstances people find themselves in. As for the lender, their role is based on generating a current and future income stream, like any business. So if "time preference" seems unlikely for the lender, it seems even more unlikely for the borrower or saver. Thus, while there is an element of time involved in decisions to save, lend and borrow, it would be wrong to see interest as the consequence of "time preference." Most people do not think in terms of it and, therefore, predicting their behaviour using it would be silly.

At the root of the matter is that for the vast majority of cases in a capitalist economy, an individual's "time preference" is determined by their social circumstances, the institutions which exist, uncertainty and a host of other factors. As inequality drives "time preference," there is no reason to explain interest rates by the latter rather than the former. Unless, of course, you are seeking to rationalise and justify the rich getting richer. Ultimately, interest is an expression of inequality, **not** exchange:

> "If there is chicanery afoot in calling 'money now' a different good than 'money later,' it is by no means harmless, for the intended effect is to subsume money lending under the normative rubric of exchange ... [but] there are obvious differences ... [for in normal commodity exchange] both parties have something [while in loaning] he has something you don't ... [so] inequality dominates the relationship. He has more than you have now, and he will get back more than he gives." [Schweickart, **Against Capitalism**, p. 23]

While the theory is less than ideal, the practice is little better. Interest rates have numerous perverse influences in any real economy. In neo-classical and related economics, saving does not have a negative impact on the economy as it is argued that non-consumed income must be invested. While this could be the case when capitalism was young, when the owners of firms ploughed their profits back into them, as financial institutions grew this became less so. Saving and investment became different activities, governed by the rate of interest. If the supply of savings increased, the interest rate would drop and capitalists would invest more. If the demand for loans increased, then the interest rate would rise, causing more savings to occur.

While the model is simple and elegant, it does have its flaws. These were first analysed by Keynes during the Great Depression of the 1930s, a depression which the neo-classical model said was impossible.

For example, rather than bring investment into line with savings, a higher interest can cause savings to fall as *"[h]ousehold saving, of course, is mainly saving up to spend later, and ... it is likely to respond the wrong way. A higher rate of return means that 'less'* saving is necessary to get a given pension or whatever." [Robinson, **Op. Cit.**, p. 11] Similarly, higher interest rates need not lead to higher investment as higher interest payments can dampen profits as both consumers and industrial capitalists have to divert more of their finances away from real spending and towards debt services. The former causes a drop in demand for products while the latter leaves less for investing.

As argued by Keynes, the impact of saving is not as positive as some like to claim. Any economy is a network, where decisions affect everyone. In a nutshell, the standard model fails to take into account changes of income that result from decisions to invest and save (see Michael Stewart's **Keynes and After** for a good, if basic, introduction). This meant that if some people do not consume now, demand falls for certain goods, production is turned away from consumption goods, and this has an effect on all. Some firms will find their sales failing and may go under, causing rising unemployment. Or, to put it slightly differently, aggregate demand – and so aggregate supply – is changed when some people postpone consumption, and this affects others. The decrease in the demand for consumer goods affects the producers of these goods. With less income, the producers would reduce their expenditure and this would have repercussions on other people's incomes. In such circumstances, it is unlikely that capitalists would be seeking to invest and so rising savings would result in falling investment in spite of falling interest rates. In an uncertain world, investment will only be done if capitalists think that they will end up with more money than they started with and this is unlikely to happen when faced with falling demand.

Whether rising interest rates do cause a crisis is dependent on the strength of the economy. During a strong expansion, a modest rise in interest rates may be outweighed by rising wages and profits. During a crisis, falling rates will not counteract the general economic despair. Keynes aimed to save capitalism from itself and urged state intervention to counteract the problems associated with free market capitalism. As we discuss in section C.8.1, this ultimately failed partly due to the mainstream economics gutting Keynes' work of key concepts which were incompatible with it, partly due to Keynes' own incomplete escape from neoclassical economics, partly due the unwillingness of rentiers to agree to their own euthanasia but mostly because capitalism is inherently unstable due to the hierarchical (and so oppressive and exploitative) organisation of production.

Which raises the question of whether someone who saves deserve a reward for so doing? Simply put, no. Why? Because the act of saving is no more an act of production than is purchasing a commodity (most investment comes from retained profits and so the analogy is valid). Clearly the reward for purchasing a commodity is that commodity. By analogy, the reward for saving should be not interest but one's savings – the ability to consume at a later stage. Particularly as the effects of interest rates and savings can have such negative impacts on the rest of the economy. It seems strange, to say the least, to reward people for helping do so. Why should someone be rewarded for a decision which may cause companies to go bust, so **reducing** the available means of production as reduced demand results in job loses and idle factories? Moreover, this problem *"becomes ever more acute the richer or more inegalitarian the society becomes, since*

wealthy people tend to save more than poor people." [Schweickart, **After Capitalism**, p. 43]

Supporters of capitalists assume that people will not save unless promised the ability to consume **more** at a later stage, yet close examination of this argument reveals its absurdity. People in many different economic systems save in order to consume later, but only in capitalism is it assumed that they need a reward for it beyond the reward of having those savings available for consumption later. The peasant farmer "defers consumption" in order to have grain to plant next year, even the squirrel "defers consumption" of nuts in order to have a stock through winter. Neither expects to see their stores increase in size over time. Therefore, saving is rewarded by saving, as consuming is rewarded by consuming. In fact, the capitalist "explanation" for interest has all the hallmarks of apologetics. It is merely an attempt to justify an activity without careful analysing it.

To be sure, there is an economic truth underlying this argument for justifying interest, but the formulation by supporters of capitalism is inaccurate and unfortunate. There is a sense in which 'waiting' is a condition for capital **increase**, though not for capital per se. Any society which wishes to increase its stock of capital goods may have to postpone some gratification. Workplaces and resources turned over to producing capital goods cannot be used to produce consumer items, after all. How that is organised differs from society to society. So, like most capitalist economics there is a grain of truth in it but this grain of truth is used to grow a forest of half-truths and confusion.

As such, this notion of "waiting" only makes sense in a 'Robinson Crusoe' style situation, **not** in any form of real economy. In a real economy, we do not need to "wait" for our consumption of goods until investment is complete since the division of labour/work has replaced the succession in time by a succession in place. We are dealing with an already well developed system of **social** production and an economy based on a social distribution of labour in which there are available all the various stages of the production process. As such, the notion that "waiting" is required makes little sense. This can be seen from the fact that it is not the capitalist who grants an advance to the worker. In almost all cases the worker is paid by their boss **after** they have completed their work. That is, it is the worker who makes an advance of their labour power to the capitalist. This waiting is only possible because *"no species of labourer depends on any previously prepared stock, for in fact no such stock exists; but every species of labourer does constantly, and at all times, depend for his supplies on the co-existing labour of some other labourers."* [Thomas Hodgskin, **Labour Defended Against the Claims of Capital**] This means that the workers, as a class, creates the fund of goods out of which the capitalists pay them.

Ultimately, selling the use of money (paid for by interest) is not the same as selling a commodity. The seller of the commodity does not receive the commodity back as well as its price, unlike the typical lender of money. In effect, as with rent and profits, interest is payment for permission to use something and, therefore, not a productive act which should be rewarded. It is **not** the same as other forms of exchange. Proudhon pointed out the difference:

*"Comparing a loan to a **sale**, you say: Your argument is as valid against the latter as against the former, for the hatter who sells hats does not **deprive** himself.*

*"No, for he receives for his hats – at least he is reputed to receive for them – their exact value immediately, neither **more** nor **less**. But the capitalist lender not only is not deprived, since he recovers his capital intact, but he receives more than his capital, more than he contributes to the exchange; he receives in addition to his capital an interest which represents no positive product on his part. Now, a service which costs no labour to him who renders it is a service which may become gratuitous."* [**Interest and Principal: The Circulation of Capital, Not Capital Itself, Gives Birth to Progress**]

The reason why interest rates do not fall to zero is due to the class nature of capitalism, **not** "time preference." That it is ultimately rooted in social institutions can be seen from Böhm-Bawerk's acknowledgement that monopoly can result in exploitation by increasing the rate of interest above the rate specified by "time preference" (i.e. the market):

"Now, of course, the circumstances unfavourable to buyers may be corrected by active competition among sellers ... But, every now and then, something will suspend the capitalists' competition, and then those unfortunates, whom fate has thrown on a local market ruled by monopoly, are delivered over to the discretion of the adversary. Hence direct usury, of which the poor borrower is only too often the victim; and hence the low wages forcibly exploited from the workers ...

"It is not my business to put excesses like these, where there actually is exploitation, under the aegis of that favourable opinion I pronounced above as to the essence of interest. But, on the other hand, I must say with all emphasis, that what we might stigmatise as 'usury' does not consist in the obtaining of a gain out of a loan, or out of the buying of labour, but in the immoderate extent of that gain ... Some gain or profit on capital there would be if there were no compulsion on the poor, and no monopolising of property; and some gain there must be. It is only the height of this gain where, in particular cases, it reaches an excess, that is open to criticism, and, of course, the very unequal conditions of wealth in our modern communities bring us unpleasantly near the danger of exploitation and of usurious rates of interest."
[**The Positive Theory of Capital**, p. 361]

Little wonder, then, that Proudhon continually stressed the need for working people to organise themselves and credit (which, of course, they would have done naturally, if it were not for the state intervening to protect the interests, income and power of the ruling class, i.e. of itself and the economically dominant class). If, as Böhm-Bawerk admitted, interest rates could be high due to institutional factors then, surely, they do not reflect the "time preferences" of individuals. This means that they could be lower (effectively zero)

if society organised itself in the appropriate manner. The need for savings could be replaced by, for example, co-operation and credit (as already exists, in part, in any developed economy). Organising these could ensure a positive cycle of investment, growth and savings (Keynes, it should be noted, praised Proudhon's follower Silvio Gesell in **The General Theory**. For a useful discussion see Dudley Dillard's essay *"Keynes and Proudhon"* [**The Journal of Economic History**, vol. 2, No. 1, pp. 63-76]).

Thus the key flaw in the theory is that of capitalist economics in general. By concentrating on the decisions of individuals, it ignores the social conditions in which these decisions are made. By taking the social inequalities and insecurities of capitalism as a given, the theory ignores the obvious fact that an individual's "time preference" will be highly shaped by their circumstances. Change those circumstances and their "time preference" will also change. In other words, working people have a different "time preference" to the rich because they are poorer. Similarly, by focusing on individuals, the "time preference" theory fails to take into account the institutions of a given society. If working class people have access to credit in other forms than those supplied by capitalists then their "time preference" will differ radically. As an example, we need only look at credit unions. In communities with credit unions the poor are less likely to agree to get into an agreement from a loan shark. It seems unlikely, to say the least, that the "time preference" of those involved has changed. They are subject to the same income inequalities and pressures as before, but by uniting with their fellows they give themselves better alternatives.

As such, "time preference" is clearly not an independent factor. This means that it cannot be used to justify capitalism or the charging of interest. It simply says, in effect, that in a society marked by inequality the rich will charge the poor as much interest as they can get away with. This is hardly a sound basis to argue that charging interest is a just or a universal fact. It reflects social inequality, the way a given society is organised and the institutions it creates. Put another way, there is no "natural" rate of interest which reflects the subjective "time preferences" of abstract individuals whose decisions are made without any social influence. Rather, the interest rate depends on the conditions and institutions within the economy as a whole. The rate of interest is positive under capitalism because it is a class society, marked by inequality and power, **not** because of the "time preference" of abstract individuals.

In summary, providing capital and charging interest are not productive acts. As Proudhon argued, *"all rent received (nominally as damages, but really as payment for a loan) is an act of property – of robbery."* [**What is Property**, p. 171]

C.2.7 Are interest and profit not the reward for waiting?

Another defence of surplus value by capitalist economics is also based on time. This argument is related to the "time preference" one we have discussed in the last section and is, likewise, rooted in the idea that money now is different than money later and, as a consequence, surplus value represents (in effect) an exchange of present goods for future ones. This argument has two main forms, depending on whether it is interest or profits which are being defended, but both are based on this perspective. We will discuss each in turn.

One of the oldest defences of interest is the "abstinence" theory first postulated by Nassau Senior in 1836. For Senior, abstinence is a sacrifice of present enjoyment for the purpose achieving some distant result. This demands the same heavy sacrifice as does labour, for to *"abstain from the enjoyment which is in our power, or to seek distant rather than immediate results, are among the most painful exertions of the human will."* Thus wages and interest/ profit *"are to be considered as the rewards of peculiar sacrifices, the former the remuneration for labour, and the latter for abstinence from immediate enjoyment."* [**An Outline of the Science of Political Economy**, p. 60 and p. 91]

Today, the idea that interest is the reward for "abstinence" on the part of savers is still a common one in capitalist economics. However, by the end of the nineteenth century, Senior's argument had become known as the "waiting" theory while still playing the same role in justifying non-labour income. One of the leading neo-classical economists of his day, Alfred Marshall, argued that *"[i]f we admit [a commodity] is the product of labour alone, and not of labour and waiting, we can no doubt be compelled by an inexorable logic to admit that there is no justification of interest, the reward for waiting."* [**Principles of Economics**, p. 587] While implicitly recognising that labour is the source of all value in capitalism (and that abstinence is not the **source** of profits), it is claimed that interest is a justifiable claim on the surplus value produced by a worker.

Why is this the case? Capitalist economics claims that by "deferring consumption," the capitalist allows new means of production to be developed and so should be rewarded for this sacrifice. In other words, in order to have capital available as an input – i.e. to bear costs now for returns in the future – someone has to be willing to postpone his or her consumption. That is a real cost, and one that people will pay only if rewarded for it:

> *"human nature being what it is, we are justified in speaking of the interest on capital as the reward of the sacrifice involved in waiting for the enjoyment of material resources, because few people would save much without reward; just as we speak of wages as the reward of labour, because few people would work hard without reward."* [**Op. Cit.**, p. 232]

The interest rate is, in neo-classical economic theory, set when the demand for loans meets the supply of savings. The interest rate stems from the fact that people prefer present spending over future spending. If someone borrows £200 for one year at 5%, this is basically the same as saying that they would rather have £200 now than £210 a year from now. Thus interest is the cost of providing a service, namely time. People are able to acquire today what they would otherwise not have until sometime in the future. With a loan, interest is the price of the advantage obtained from having money immediately rather than having to wait for.

This, on first appearance, seems plausible. If you accept the logic of capitalist economics and look purely at individuals and their preferences independently of their social circumstances then it can make sense. However, once you look wider you start to see this argument start to fall apart. Why is it that the wealthy are willing to save and provide funds while it is the working class who do not save and get into debt? Surely a person's "time preference" is dependent on their socio-economic position? As we argued in the last section, this means that any subjective evaluation of the present and future is dependent on, not independent of, the structure of market prices and income distribution. It varies with the income of individual and their class position, since the latter will condition the degree or urgency of present wants and needs.

So this theory appears ludicrous to a critic of capitalism – simply put, does the mine owner really sacrifice more than a miner, a rich stockholder more than an autoworker working in their car plant, a millionaire investor more than a call centre worker? As such, the notion that "waiting" explains interest is question begging in the extreme as it utterly ignores inequality within a society. After all, it is far easier for a rich person to "defer consumption" than for someone on an average income. This is borne out by statistics, for as Simon Kuznets has noted, *"only the upper income groups save; the total savings of groups below the top decile are fairly close to zero."* [**Economic Growth and Structure**, p. 263] Obviously, therefore, in modern society it is the capitalist class, the rich, who refrain from expending their income on immediate consumption and *"abstain."* Astonishingly, working class people show no such desire to abstain from spending their wages on immediate consumption. It does not take a genius to work out why, although many economists have followed Senior in placing the blame for working class lack of abstinence on poor education rather than, say, the class system they live in (for Senior, *"the worse educated"* classes *"are always the most improvident, and consequently the least abstinent."* [**Op. Cit.**, p. 60]).

Therefore, the plausibility of interest as payment for the pain of deferring consumption rests on the premise that the typical saving unit is a small or medium-income household. But in contemporary capitalist societies, this is not the case. Such households are not the source of most savings; the bulk of interest payments do not go to them. As such, interest is the dependent factor and so "waiting" cannot explain interest. Rather, interest is product of social inequality and the social relationships produced by an economy. Lenders lend because they have the funds to do so while borrowers borrow because without money now they may not be around later. As those with funds are hardly going without by lending, it does not make much sense to argue that they would spend even more today without the temptation of more income later.

To put this point differently, the capitalist proponents of interest only consider "postponing consumption" as an abstraction, without making it concrete. For example, a capitalist may "postpone consumption" of his 10th Rolls Royce because he needs the money to upgrade some machinery in his factory; whereas a single mother may have to "postpone consumption" of food or adequate housing in order to attempt to better take care of her children. The two situations are vastly different, yet the capitalist equates them. This equation implies that "not being able to buy anything you want" is the same as "not being able to buy things you need", and is thus skewing the obvious difference in costs of such postponement of consumption!Thus Proudhon's comments that the loaning of capital *"does not involve an actual sacrifice on the part of the capitalist"* and so *"does not deprive himself … of the capital which be lends. He lends it, on the contrary, precisely because the loan is not a deprivation to him; he lends it because he has no use for it himself, being sufficiently provided with capital without it; he lends it, finally, because he neither intends nor is able to make it valuable to him personally, – because, if he should keep it in his own hands, this capital, sterile by nature, would remain sterile, whereas, by its loan and the resulting interest, it yields a profit which enables the capitalist to live without working. Now, to live without working is, in political as well as moral economy, a contradictory proposition, an impossible thing."* [**Interest and Principal: A Loan is a Service**] In other words, contra Marshall, saving is **not** a sacrifice for the wealthy and, as such, not deserving a reward. Proudhon goes on:

> *"The proprietor who possesses two estates, one at Tours, and the other at Orleans, and who is obliged to fix his residence on the one which he uses, and consequently to abandon his residence on the other, can this proprietor claim that he deprives himself of anything, because he is not, like God, ubiquitous in action and presence? As well say that we who live in Paris are deprived of a residence in New York! Confess, then, that the privation of the capitalist is akin to that of the master who has lost his slave, to that of the prince expelled by his subjects, to that of the robber who, wishing to break into a house, finds the dogs on the watch and the inmates at the windows."*

Given how much income this "abstinence" or "waiting" results in, we can only conclude that it is the most painful of decisions possible for a multi-millionaire to decide **not** to buy that fifth house and instead save the money. The effort to restrain themselves from squandering their entire fortunes all at once must be staggering. In the capitalist's world, an industrialist who decides not to consume a part of their riches "suffers" a cost equivalent to that of someone who postpones consumption of their meagre income to save enough to get something they need. Similarly, if the industrialist "earns" a hundred times more in interest than the wage of the worker who toils in their workplace, the industrialist "suffers" hundred times more discomfort living in his palace than, say, the coal miner does working at the coal face in dangerous conditions or the worker stuck in a boring McJob they hate. The "disutility" of postponing consumption while living in luxury is obviously 100 times greater than the "disutility" of, say, working for a living and so should be rewarded appropriately.

As there is no direct relationship between interest received and the "sacrifice" involved (if anything, it is an **inverse** relationship), the idea that interest is the reward for waiting is simply nonsense. You need be no anarchist to come to this obvious conclusion. It was admitted as much by a leading capitalist economist and his argument simply echoes Proudhon's earlier critique:

> *"the existence and height of interest by no means invariably correspond with the existence and the height of a 'sacrifice of abstinence.' Interest, in exceptional cases, is received where there has been no individual sacrifice of abstinence. High interest is often got where the sacrifice of the abstinence is very trifling – as in the case of [a] millionaire – and 'low interest' is often got where the sacrifice entailed by the abstinence is very great. The hardly saved sovereign which the domestic servant puts in the savings bank bears, absolutely and relatively, less interest than the lightly spared thousands which the millionaire puts to fructify in debenture and mortgage funds. These phenomena fit badly into a theory which explains interest quite universally as a 'wage of abstinence.'"* [Eugen von Böhm-Bawerk, **Capital and Interest**, p. 277]

All in all, as Joan Robinson pointed out, *"that the rate of interest is the 'reward for waiting' but 'waiting' only means owning wealth … In short, a man who refrains from blowing his capital in orgies and feasts can continue to get interest on it. This seems perfectly correct, but as a theory of distribution it is only a circular argument."* [**Contributions to Modern Economics**, p. 11] Interest is not the reward for "waiting," rather it is one of the (many) rewards for being rich. This was admitted as much by Marshall himself, who noted that the *"power to save depends on an excess of income over necessary expenditure; and this is greatest among the wealthy."* [**Op. Cit.**, p. 229]

Little wonder, then, that neo-classical economists introduced the term **waiting** as an "explanation" for returns to capital (such as interest). Before this change in the jargon of economics, mainstream economists used the notion of "abstinence" (the term used by Nassau Senior) to account for (and so justify) interest. Just as Senior's "theory" was seized upon to defend returns to capital, so was the term "waiting" after it was introduced in the 1880s. Interestingly, while describing **exactly** the same thing, "waiting" became the preferred term simply because it had a less apologetic ring to it. Both describe the *"sacrifice of present pleasure for the sake of future"* yet, according to Marshall, the term *"abstinence"* was *"liable to be misunderstood"* because there were just too many wealthy people around who received interest and dividends without ever having abstained from anything. As he admitted, the *"greatest accumulators of wealth are very rich persons, some [!] of whom live in luxury, and certainly do not practise abstinence in that sense of the term in which it is convertible with abstemiousness."* So he opted for the term "waiting" because there was *"advantage"* in its use to describe *"the accumulation of wealth"* as the *"result of a postponement of enjoyment."* [**Op. Cit.**, pp. 232-3] This is particularly the case as socialists had long been pointing out the obvious fact that capitalists do not *"abstain"* from anything.

The lesson is obvious, in mainstream economics if reality conflicts with your theory, do not reconsider the theory, change its name!

The problems of "waiting" and "abstinence" as the source of interest becomes even clearer when we look at inherited wealth. Talking about "abstinence" or "waiting" when discussing a capitalist inheriting a company worth millions is silly. Senior recognised this, arguing that income in this case is not profit, but rather *"has all the attributes of rent."* [**Op. Cit.**, p. 129] That such a huge portion of capitalist revenue would not be considered profit shows the bankruptcy of any theory which sees profit as the reward for "waiting." However, Senior's argument does show that interest payments need not reflect any positive contribution to production by those who receive it. Like the landlord receiving payment for owning a gift of nature, the capitalist receives income for simply monopolising the work of previous generations and, as Smith put it, the *"rent of land, considered as the price paid for the use of land, is naturally a monopoly price."* [**The Wealth of Nations**, p. 131]

Even capitalist economists, while seeking to justify interest, admit that it *"arises independently of any personal act of the capitalist. It accrues to him even though he has not moved any finger in creating it … And it flows without ever exhausting that capital from which it arises, and therefore without any necessary limit to its continuance. It is, if one may use such an expression in mundane matters, capable of everlasting life."* [Böhm-Bawerk, **Op. Cit.**, p. 1] Little wonder we argued in section C.2.3 that simply owning property does not justify non-labour income.

In other words, due to **one** decision not to do anything (i.e. **not** to consume), a person (and his or her heirs) may receive **forever** a reward that is not tied to any productive activity. Unlike the people actually doing the work (who only get a reward every time they "contribute" to creating a commodity), the capitalist will get rewarded for just **one** act of abstention. This is hardly a just arrangement. As David Schweickart has pointed out, *"Capitalism does reward some individuals perpetually. This, if it is to be justified by the canon of contribution, one must defend the claim that some contributions are indeed eternal."* [**Against Capitalism**, p. 17] As we noted in section C.1.1, current and future generations should not be dominated by the actions of the long dead.

The "waiting" theory, of course, simply seeks to justify interest rather than explain its origin. If the capitalist really **did** deserve an income as a reward for their abstinence, where does it come from? It cannot be created passively, merely by the decision to save, so interest exists because the exploitation of labour exists. As Joan Robinson summarised:

> *"Obviously, the reward of saving is owning some more wealth. One of the advantages, though by no means the only one, of owning wealth is the possibility of getting interest on it.*

> *"But why is it possible to get interest? Because businesses make profits and are willing to borrow."* [**Collected Economic Papers**, vol. 5, p. 36]

This is the key. If ones ability and willingness to "wait" is dependent on social facts (such as available resources, ones class, etc.), then interest cannot be based upon subjective evaluations, as these are not the independent factor. In other words, saving does not express "waiting", it simply expresses the extent of inequality and interest expresses the fact that workers have to sell their labour to others in order to survive:

> *"The notion that human beings discount the future certainly seems to correspond to everyone's subjective experience, but the conclusion drawn from it is a **non sequitor**, for most people have enough sense to want to be able to exercise consuming power as long as fate permits, and many people are in the situation of having a higher income in the present than they expect in the future (salary earners will have to retire, business may be better now than it seems likely to be later, etc.) and many look beyond their own lifetime and wish to leave consuming power to their heirs. Thus a great many … are eagerly looking for a reliable vehicle to carry purchasing power into the future … It is impossible to say what price would rule if there were a market for present **versus** future purchasing power, unaffected by any other influence except the desires of individuals about the time-pattern of their consumption. It might will be such a market would normally yield a negative rate of discount …*

> *"The rate of interest is normally positive for a quite different reason. Present purchasing power is valuable partly because, under the capitalist rules of the game, it permits its owner … to employ labour and undertake production which will yield a surplus of receipts over costs. In an economy in which the rate of profit is expected to be positive, the rate of interest is positive … [and so] the present value of purchasing power exceeds its future value to the corresponding extent … This is nothing whatever to do with the subjective **rate of discount of the future** of the individual concerned … "* [**The Accumulation of Capital**, p. 395]

So, interest has little to do with "waiting" and a lot more to do with the inequalities associated with the capitalist system. In effect, the "waiting" theory assumes what it is trying to prove. Interest is positive simply because capitalists can appropriate surplus value from workers and so current money is more valuable than future money because of this fact. Ironically, therefore, the pro-capitalist theories of who abstains are wrong, *"since saving is mainly out of profits, and real wages tend to be lower the higher the rate of profit, the abstinence associated with saving is mainly done by the workers, who do not receive any share in the 'reward.'"* [Robinson, **Op. Cit.**, p. 393]

In other words, "waiting" does not produce a surplus, labour does. As such, to *"say that those who hold financial instruments can lay claim to a portion of the social product by abstaining or waiting provides no explanation of what makes the production process profitable, and hence to what extent interest claims or dividends can be paid. Reliance on a waiting theory of the return to capital represented nothing less than a reluctance of economists to confront the sources of value creation and analyse the process of economic development."* [William Lazonick, **Competitive Advantage on the**

Shop Floor, p. 267] This would involve having to analyse the social relations between workers and managers/bosses on the shop floor, which would be to bring into question the whole nature of capitalism and any claims it was based upon freedom.

To summarise, the idea that interest is the "reward" for waiting simply ignores the reality of class society and, in effect, rewards the wealthy for being wealthy. Neo-classical economics implies that being rich is the ultimate disutility. The hardships ("sacrifices") of having to decide to consume or invest their riches weighs as heavily on the elite as they do on the scales of utility. Compared to, say, working in a sweatshop, fearing unemployment (sorry, maximising "leisure") or not having to worry about saving (as your income just covers your out-goings) it is clear which are the greatest sacrifices and which are rewarded accordingly under capitalism.

Much the same argument can be applied to "time-preference" theories of profit. These argue that profits are the result of individuals preferring present goods to future ones. Capitalists pay workers wages, allowing them to consume now rather than later. This is the providing of time and this is rewarded by profits. This principle was first stated clearly by Eugen von Böhm-Bawerk and has been taken as the basis of the "Austrian" school of capitalist economics (see section C.1.6). After rejecting past theories of interest (including, as noted above, "abstinence" theories, which he concluded the socialists were right to mock), Böhm-Bawerk argued that profits could only be explained by means of time preference:

> "**The loan is a real exchange of present goods against future goods** … present goods invariably possess a greater value than future goods of the same number and kind, and therefore a definite sum of present goods can, as a rule, only be purchased by a larger sum of future goods. Present goods possess an agio in future goods. **This agio is interest.** It is not a separate equivalent for a separate and durable use of the loaned goods, for that is inconceivable; it is a part equivalent of the loaned sum, kept separate for practical reasons. The replacement of the capital + the interest constitutes the full equivalent." [**Capital and Interest**, p. 259]

For him, time preference alone is the reason for profit/interest due to the relative low value of future goods, compared to present goods. Capital goods, although already present in their physical state, are really **future** goods in their "economic nature" as is labour. This means that workers are paid the amount their labour creates in terms of **future** goods, not **current** goods. This difference between the high value of current goods and low value of future goods is the source of surplus value:

> "This, and nothing else, is the foundation of the so-called 'cheap' buying of production instruments, and especially of labour, which the Socialists rightly explain as the source of profit on capital, but wrongly interpret … as the result of a robbery or exploitation of the working classes by the propertied classes." [**The Positive Theory of Capital**, p. 301]

The capitalists are justified in keeping this surplus value because they provided the time required for the production process to occur.

Thus surplus value is the product of an exchange, the exchange of present goods for future ones. The capitalist bought labour at its full present value (i.e. the value of its future product) and so there is no exploitation as the future goods are slowly maturing during the process of production and can then be sold at its full value as a present commodity. Profit, like interest, is seen as resulting from varying estimates of the present and future needs.

As should be obvious, our criticisms of the "waiting" theory of interest apply to this justification of profits. Money in itself does not produce profit any more than interest. It can only do that when invested in **actual** means of production which are put to work by actual people. As such, "time preference" only makes sense in an economy where there is a class of property-less people who are unable to "wait" for future goods as they would have died of starvation long before they arrived.

So it is the **class** position of workers which explains their time preferences, as Böhm-Bawerk **himself** acknowledged. Thus capitalism was marked by an "*enormous number of wage-earners who cannot employ their labour remuneratively by working on their own account, and are accordingly, as a body, inclined and ready to sell the future product of their labour for a considerably less amount of present goods.*" So, being poor, meant that they lacked the resources to "wait" for "future" goods and so became dependent (as a class) on those who do. This was, in his opinion the "*sole ground of that much-talked-of and much-deplored dependence of labourer on capitalist.*" It is "*only because the labourers cannot wait till the roundabout process … delivers up its products ready for consumption, that they become economically dependent on the capitalists who already hold in their possession what we have called 'intermediate products.'*" [**Op. Cit.**, p. 330 and p. 83]

Böhm-Bawerk, ironically, simply repeats (although in different words) **and agrees** with the socialist critique of capitalism which, as we discussed in section C.2.2, is also rooted in the class dependence of workers to capitalists (Bakunin, for example, argued that the capitalists were "*profiting by the economic dependence of the worker*" in order to exploit them by "*turn[ing] the worker into a subordinate.*" [**The Political Philosophy of Bakunin**, p. 188]). The difference is that Böhm-Bawerk thinks that the capitalists deserve their income from wealth while anarchists, like other socialists, argue they do not as they simply are being rewarded for being wealthy. Böhm-Bawerk simply cannot bring himself to acknowledge that an individual's psychology, their subjective evaluations, are conditioned by their social circumstances and so cannot comprehend the **class** character of capitalism and profit. After all, a landless worker will, of course, estimate the "sacrifice" or "disutility" of selling their labour to a master as much less than the peasant farmer or artisan who possesses their own land or tools. The same can be said of workers organised into a union.

As such, Böhm-Bawerk ignores the obvious, that the source of non-labour income is not in individual subjective evaluations but rather the **social** system within which people live. The worker does not sell her labour power because she "underestimates" the value of future goods but because she lacks the means of obtaining any sort of goods at all except by the selling of her labour power. There is no real choice between producing for herself or working for a boss – she has no real opportunity of doing the former at all and so **has** to do the latter. This means that workers sells their labour (future goods) "voluntarily" for an amount less than its value (present goods) because their class position ensures that they cannot "wait." So, if profit is the price of time, then it is a monopoly price produced by the class monopoly of wealth ownership under capitalism. Needless to say, as capital is accumulated from surplus value, the dependence of the working class on the capitalists will tend to grow over time as the "waiting" required to go into business will tend to increase also.

An additional irony of Böhm-Bawerk's argument is that is very similar to the "abstinence" theory he so rightly mocked and which he admitted the socialists were right to reject. This can be seen from one of his followers, right-"libertarian" Murray Rothbard:

> "What has been the contribution of these product-owners, or 'capitalists', to the production process? It is this: the saving and restriction of consumption, instead of being done by the owners of land and labour, has been done by the **capitalists.** The capitalists originally saved, say, 95 ounces of gold which they could have then spent on consumers' goods. They refrained from doing so, however, and, instead, **advanced** the money to the original owners of the factors. They **paid** the latter for their services while they were working, thus advancing them money before the product was actually produced and sold to the consumers. The capitalists, therefore, made an essential contribution to production. They relieved the owners of the original factors from the necessity of sacrificing present goods and waiting for future goods." [**Man, Economy, and State**, pp. 294-95]

This meant that without risk, "[e]ven if financial returns and consumer demand are certain, **the capitalists are still providing present goods to the owners of labour and land** and thus relieving them of the burden of waiting until the future goods are produced and finally transformed into consumers' goods." [**Op. Cit.**, p. 298] Capitalists pay out, say, £100,000 this year in wages and reap £200,000 next year not because of exploitation but because both parties prefer this amount of money this year rather than next year. Capitalists, in other words, pay out wages in advance and then wait for a sale. They will only do so if compensated by profit.

Rothbard's argument simply assumes a **class** system in which there is a minority of rich and a majority of property-less workers. The reason why workers cannot "wait" is because if they did they would starve to death. Unsurprisingly, then, they prefer their wages now rather than next year. Similarly, the reason why they do not save and form their own co-operatives is that they simply cannot "wait" until their workplace is ready and their products are sold before eating and paying rent. In other words, their decisions are rooted in their class position while the capitalists (the rich) have shouldered the "burden" of abstinence so that they can be rewarded with even more money in the future. Clearly, the time preference position and the "waiting" or "abstinence" perspective are basically the same (Rothbard even echoes Senior's lament about the improvident working class, arguing that *the major problem with the lower-class poor is irresponsible present-mindedness."* [**For a New Liberty**, p. 154]). As such, it is subject to the same critique (as can be found

in, say, the works of a certain Eugen von Böhm-Bawerk).

In other words, profit has a **social** basis, rooted in the different economic situation of classes within capitalism. It is not the fact of "waiting" which causes profits but rather the monopoly of the means of life by the capitalist class which is the basis of *"economic dependence."* Any economic theory which fails to acknowledge and analyse this social inequality is doomed to failure from the start.

To conclude, the arguments that "waiting" or "time preference" explain or justify surplus value are deeply flawed simply because they ignore the reality of class society. By focusing on individual subjective evaluations, they ignore the social context in which these decisions are made and, as a result, fail to take into account the class character of interest and profit. In effect, they argue that the wealthy deserve a reward for being wealthy. Whether it is to justify profits or interest, the arguments used simply show that we have an economic system that works only by bribing the rich!

C.2.8 Are profits the result of entrepreneurial activity and innovation?

One of the more common arguments in favour of profits is the notion that they are the result of innovation or entrepreneurial activity, that the creative spirit of the capitalist innovates profits into existence. This perspective is usually associated with the so-called "Austrian" school of capitalist economics but has become more common in the mainstream of economics, particularly since the 1970s.

There are two related themes in this defence of profits – innovation and entrepreneurial activity. While related, they differ in one key way. The former (associated with Joseph Schumpeter) is rooted in production while the former seeks to be of more general application. Both are based on the idea of "discovery", the subjective process by which people use their knowledge to identify gaps in the market, new products or services or new means of producing existing goods. When entrepreneurs discover, for example, a use of resources, they bring these resources into a new (economic) existence. Accordingly, they have created something **ex nihilo** (out of nothing) and therefore are entitled to the associated profit on generally accepted moral principle of *"finders keepers."*

Anarchists, needless to say, have some issues with such an analysis. The most obvious objection is that while *"finders keepers"* may be an acceptable ethical position on the playground, it is hardly a firm basis to justify an economic system marked by inequalities of liberty and wealth. Moreover, discovering something does **not** entitle you to an income from it. Take, for example, someone who discovers a flower in a wood. That, in itself, will generate no income of any kind. Unless the flower is picked and taken to a market, the discoverer cannot "profit" from discovering it. If the flower is left untouched then it is available for others to appropriate unless some means are used to stop them (such as guarding the flower). This means, of course, limiting the discovery potential of others, like the state enforcing copyright stops the independent discovery of the same idea, process or product.

As such, "discovery" is not sufficient to justify non-labour income as an idea remains an idea unless someone applies it. To generate an income (profit) from a discovery you need to somehow take it to the market and, under capitalism, this means getting funds to invest in machinery and workplaces. However, these in themselves do nothing and, consequently, workers need to be employed to produce the goods in question. If the costs of producing these goods is less than the market price, then a profit is made. Does this profit represent the initial "discovery"? Hardly for without funds the idea would have remained just that. Does the profit represent the contribution of "capital"? Hardly, for without the labour of the workers the workplace would have remained still and the product would have remained an idea.

Which brings us to the next obvious problem, namely that "entrepreneurial" activity becomes meaningless when divorced from owning capital. This is because any action which is taken to benefit an individual and involves "discovery" is considered entrepreneurial. Successfully looking for a better job? Your new wages are entrepreneurial profit. Indeed, successfully finding **any** job makes the wages entrepreneurial profit. Workers successfully organising and striking to improve their pay and conditions? An entrepreneurial act whose higher wages are, in fact, entrepreneurial profit. Selling your shares in one company and buying others? Any higher dividends are entrepreneurial profit. Not selling your shares? Likewise. What income flow could **not** be explained by "entrepreneurial" activity if we try hard enough?

In other words, the term becomes meaningless unless it is linked to owning capital and so any non-trivial notion of entrepreneurial activity requires private property, i.e. property which functions as capital. This can be seen from an analysis of whether entrepreneurship which is **not** linked to owning capital or land creates surplus value (profits) or not. It is possible, for example, that an entrepreneur can make a profit by buying cheap in one market and selling dear in another. However, this simply redistributes existing products and surplus value, it does not **create** them. This means that the entrepreneur does not create something from nothing, he takes something created by others and sells it at a higher price and so gains a slice of the surplus value created by others. If buying high and selling low **was** the cause of surplus value, then profits overall would be null as any gainer would be matched by a loser. Ironically, for all its talk of being concerned about process, this defence of entrepreneurial profits rests on the same a **static** vision of capitalism as does neo-classical economics.

Thus entrepreneurship is inherently related to inequalities in economic power, with those at the top of the market hierarchy having more ability to gain benefits of it than those at the bottom. Entrepreneurship, in other words, rather than an independent factor is rooted in social inequality. The larger one's property, the more able they are to gather and act on information advantages, i.e. act in as an entrepreneur. Moreover the ability to exercise the entrepreneurial spirit or innovate is restricted by the class system of capitalism. To implement a new idea, you need money. As it is extremely difficult for entrepreneurs to act on the opportunities they have observed without the ownership of property, so profit due to innovation simply becomes yet another reward for already being wealthy or, at best, being able to convince the wealthy to loan you money in the expectation of a return. Given that credit is unlikely to be forthcoming to those without collateral (and most working class people are asset-poor), entrepreneurs are almost always capitalists because of social inequality. Entrepreneurial opportunities are, therefore, not available to everyone and so it is inherently linked to private property (i.e. capital).

So while entrepreneurship in the abstract may help explain the distribution of income, it neither explains why surplus value exists in the first place nor does it justify the entrepreneur's appropriation of part of that surplus. To explain why surplus value exists and why capitalists may be justified in keeping it, we need to look at the other aspect of entrepreneurship, innovation as this is rooted in the actual production process.

Innovation occurs in order to expand profits and so survive competition from other companies. While profits can be redistributed in circulation (for example by oligopolistic competition or inflation) this can only occur at the expense of other people or capitals (see sections C.5 and C.7). Innovation, however, allows the generation of profits directly from the new or increased productivity (i.e. exploitation) of labour it allows. This is because it is in production that commodities, and so profits, are created and innovation results in new products and/or new production methods. New products mean that the company can reap excess profits until competitors enter the new market and force the market price down by competition. New production methods allow the intensity of labour to be increased, meaning that workers do more work relative to their wages (in other words, the cost of production falls relative to the market price, meaning extra profits).

So while competition ensures that capitalist firms innovate, innovation is the means by which companies can get an edge in the market. This is because innovation means that *"capitalist excess profits come from the production process ... when there is an above-average rise in labour productivity; the reduced costs then enable firms to earn higher than average profits in their products. But this form of excess profits is only temporary and disappears again when improved production methods become more general."* [Paul Mattick, **Economics, Politics and the Age of Inflation**, p. 38] Capitalists, of course, use a number of techniques to stop the spread of new products or production methods in order to maintain their position, such as state enforced intellectual property rights.

Innovation as the source of profits is usually associated with economist Joseph Schumpeter who described and praised capitalism's genius for *"creative destruction"* caused by capitalists who innovate, i.e. introduce new goods and means of production. Schumpeter's analysis of capitalism is more realistic than the standard neo-classical perspective. He recognised that capitalism was marked by a business cycle which he argued flowed from cycles of innovation conducted by capitalists. He also rejected the neo-classical assumption of perfect competition, arguing that the *"introduction of new methods of production and new commodities is hardly compatible with perfect and perfectly prompt competition from the start ... As a matter of fact, perfect competition has always been temporarily stemmed whenever anything new is being introduced."* [**Capitalism, Socialism and Democracy**, p. 104] This analysis presents a picture of capitalism more like it actually is rather than what economics would like it to be. However, this does not mean that its justification for profits is correct, far from it. Anarchists do agree that it is true that individuals do see new potential and act in innovative ways to create new products or processes. However, this is not the source of surplus value. This is because an innovation only becomes a source of profits once it actually produced, i.e. once workers have toiled to create it (in the case of new goods) or used it (in the case of new production techniques). An idea in and of itself produces nothing unless it is applied. The reason why profits result from innovation is due to the way the capitalist firm is organised rather than any inherent aspect of innovation.

Ultimately, entrepreneurialism is just a fancy name for decision making and, as such, it is a **labour** income (labour refers to physical **and** mental activities). However, as noted above, there are two types of labour under capitalism, the labour of production and the labour of exploitation. Looking at entrepreneurialism in a workplace situation, it is obvious that it is **not** independent of owning or managing capital and so it is impossible to distinguish profits produced by "entrepreneurial" activity and profits resulting from a return on property (and so the labour of others). In other words, it is the labour of exploitation and any income from it is simply monopoly profit. This is because the capitalist or manager has a monopoly of power within the workplace and, consequently, can reap the benefits this privileged position ensures. The workers have their opportunities for entrepreneurialism restricted and monopolised by the few in power who, when deciding who contributes most to production, strangely enough decide it is themselves.

This can be seen from the fact that innovation in terms of new technology is used to help win the class war at the point of production for the capitalists. As the aim of capitalist production is to maximise the profits available for capitalists and management to control, it follows that capitalism will introduce technology that will allow more surplus value to be extracted from workers. As Cornelius Castoriadis argues, capitalism *does not utilise a socially neutral technology for capitalist ends. Capitalism has created capitalist technology, which is by no means neutral. The real essence of capitalist technology is not to develop production for production's sake: It is to subordinate and dominate the producers."* [**Political and Social Writings**, vol. 2, p. 104] Therefore, "innovation" (technological improvement) can be used to increase the power of capital over the workforce, to ensure that workers will do as they are told. In this way innovation can maximise surplus value production by trying to increase domination during working hours as well as by increasing productivity by new processes.

These attempts to increase profits by using innovation is the key to capitalist expansion and accumulation. As such innovation plays a key role within the capitalist system. However, the source of profits does not change and remains in the labour, skills and creativity of workers in the workplace. As such, innovation results in profits because labour is exploited in the production process, **not** due to some magical property of innovation.

The question now arises whether profits are justified as a reward for those who made the decision to innovate in the first place. This, however, fails for the obvious reason that capitalism is marked by a hierarchical organisation of production. It is designed so that a few make all the decisions while the majority are excluded from power. As such, to say that capitalists or managers deserve their profits due to innovation is begging the question. Profits which are claimed to flow from innovation are, in fact, the reward for having a monopoly, namely the monopoly of decision making within the workplace, rather than some actual contribution to production. The only thing management does is decide which innovations to pursue and to reap the benefits they create. In other words, they gain a reward simply due to their monopoly of decision making power within a firm. Yet this hierarchy only exists because of capitalism and so can hardly be used to defend that system and the appropriation of surplus value by capitalists.

Thus, if entrepreneurial spirit is the source of profit then we can reply that under capitalism the means of exercising that spirit is monopolised by certain classes and structures. The monopoly of decision making power in the hands of managers and bosses in a capitalist firm ensure that they also monopolise the rewards of the entrepreneurialism their workforce produce. This, in turn, reduces the scope for innovation as this division of society into people who do mental and physical labour *destroy[s] the love of work and the capacity for invention"* and under such a system, the worker *"lose[s] his intelligence and his spirit of invention."* [Kropotkin, **The Conquest of Bread**, p. 183 and p. 181]

These issues should be a key concern **if** entrepreneurialism **really** were considered as the unique source of profit. However, such issues as management power are rarely, if ever, discussed by the Austrian school. While they thunder against state restrictions on entrepreneurial activity, boss and management restrictions are always defended (if mentioned at all). Similarly, they argue that state intervention (say, anti-monopoly laws) can only harm consumers as it tends to discourage entrepreneurial activity yet ignore the restrictions to entrepreneurship imposed by inequality, the hierarchical structure of the capitalist workplace and negative effects both have on individuals and their development (as discussed in section B.1.1).

This, we must stress, is the key problem with the idea that innovation is the root of surplus value. It focuses attention to the top of the capitalist hierarchy, to business leaders. This implies that they, the bosses, create "wealth" and without them nothing would be done. For example, leading "Austrian" economist Israel Kirzner talks of *"the necessarily indivisible entrepreneur"* who *"is responsible for the entire product, The contributions of the factor inputs, being without an entrepreneurial component, are irrelevant for the ethical position being taken."* ["Producer, Entrepreneur, and the Right to Property," pp. 185-199, **Perception, Opportunity, and Profit**, p. 195] The workforce is part of the *"factor inputs"* who are considered *"irrelevant."* He quotes economist Frank Knight to bolster this analysis that the entrepreneur solely creates wealth and, consequently, deserves his profits:

> *"Under the enterprise system, a special social class, the businessman, direct economic activity:* ***they are in the strict sense the producers, while the great mass of the population merely furnishes them with productive services, placing their persons and their property at the disposal of this class."*** [quoted by Kirzner, **Op. Cit.**, p. 189]

If, as Chomsky stresses, the capitalist firm is organised in a fascist way, the "entrepreneurial" defence of profits is its ideology, its **"Führerprinzip"** (the German for *leader principle*). This ideology sees each organisation as a hierarchy of leaders, where every leader (Führer, in German) has absolute responsibility in his own area, demands absolute obedience from those below him and answers only to his superiors. This ideology was most infamously applied by fascism but its roots lie in military organisations which continue to use a similar authority structure today.

Usually defenders of capitalism contrast the joys of "individualism" with the evils of "collectivism" in which the individual is sub-merged into the group or collective and is made to work for the benefit of the group. Yet when it comes to capitalist industry, they stress the abilities of the people at the top of the company, the owner, the entrepreneur, and treat as unpeople those who do the actual work (and ignore the very real subordination of those lower down the hierarchy). The entrepreneur is considered the driving force of the market process and the organisations and people they govern are ignored, leading to the impression that the accomplishments of a firm are the personal triumphs of the capitalists, as though their subordinates are merely tools not unlike the machines on which they labour.

The ironic thing about this argument is that if it were true, then the economy would grind to a halt (we discuss this more fully in our critique of Engels's diatribe against anarchism *On Authority* in section H.4.4). It exposes a distinct contradiction within capitalism. While the advocates of entrepreneurialism assert that the entrepreneur is the only real producer of wealth in society, the fact is that the entrepreneurialism of the workforce industry is required to implement the decisions made by the bosses. Without this unacknowledged input, the entrepreneur would be impotent. Kropotkin recognised this fact when he talked of the workers *"who have added to the original invention"* little additions and contributions *"without which the most fertile idea would remain fruitless."* Nor does the idea itself develop out of nothing as *"every invention is a synthesis, the resultant of innumerable inventions which have preceded it."* [**Op. Cit.**, p. 30] Thus Cornelius Castoriadis:

> *"The capitalist organisation of production is profoundly contradictory…. It claims to reduce the worker to a limited and determined set of tasks, but it is obliged at the same time to rely upon the universal capacities he develops both as a function of and in opposition to the situation in which he is placed…. Production can be carried out only insofar as the worker himself organises his work and goes beyond his theoretical role of pure and simply executant,"*
> [**Political and Social Writings**, vol. 2, p. 181]

Moreover, such a hierarchical organisation cannot help but generate wasted potential. Most innovation is the cumulative effect of lots of incremental process improvements and the people most qualified to identify opportunities for such improvements are, obviously, those involved in the process. In the hierarchical capitalist firm, those most aware of what would improve efficiency have the least power to do anything about it. They also have the least incentive as well, as any productivity increases resulting from their improvements will almost always enrich their bosses and investors, not them. Indeed,

any gains may be translated into layoffs, soaring stock prices, and senior management awarding itself a huge bonus for "cutting costs." What worker in his right mind would do something to help their worst enemy? As such, capitalism hinders innovation:

> *"capitalism divides society into a narrow stratum of directors (whose function is to decide and organise everything) and the vast majority of the population, who are reduced to carrying out (executing) the decisions made by these directors. As a result of this very fact, most people experience their own lives as something alien to them…. It is nonsensical to seek to organise people … as if they were mere objects…. In real life, capitalism is obliged to base itself on people's capacity for self-organisation, on the individual and collective creativity of the producers. Without making use of these abilities the system would not survive a day. But the whole 'official' organisation of modern society both ignores and seeks to suppress these abilities to the utmost. The result is not only an enormous waste due to untapped capacity. The system does more: It **necessarily** engenders opposition, a struggle against it by those upon whom it seeks to impose itself…. The net result is not only waste but perpetual conflict."*
> [Castoriadis, **Op. Cit.**, p. 93]

While workers make the product and make entrepreneurial decisions every day, in the face of opposition of the company hierarchy, the benefits of those decisions are monopolised by the few who take all the glory for themselves. The question now becomes, why should capitalists and managers have a monopoly of power and profits when, in practice, they do not and cannot have a monopoly of entrepreneurialism within a workplace? If the output of a workplace is the result of the combined mental and physical activity (entrepreneurialism) of all workers, there is no justification either for the product or "innovation" (i.e. decision making power) to be monopolised by the few.

We must also stress that innovation itself is a form of labour – mental labour. Indeed, many companies have Research and Development groups in which workers are paid to generate new and innovative ideas for their employers. This means that innovation is not related to property ownership at all. In most modern industries, as Schumpeter himself acknowledged, innovation and technical progress is conducted by *"teams of trained specialists, who turn out what is required and make it work in predictable ways"* and so *"[b]ureau and committee work tends to replace individual action."* This meant that *"the leading man … is becoming just another office worker – and one who is not always difficult to replace."* [**Op. Cit.**, p. 133] And we must also point out that many new innovations come from individuals who combine mental and physical labour outside of capitalist companies. Given this, it is difficult to argue that profits are the result of innovation of a few exceptional people rather than by workers when the innovations, as well as being worked or produced by workers are themselves are created by teams of workers.

As such, "innovation" and "entrepreneurialism" is not limited to a few great people but rather exists in all of us. While the few may currently monopolise "entrepreneurialism" for their own benefit, an economy does not need to work this way. Decision making need **not** be centralised in a few hands. Ordinary workers can manage their own productive activity, innovate and make decisions to meet social and individual needs (i.e. practice "entrepreneurialism"). This can be seen from various experiments in workers' control where increased equality within the workplace actually increases productivity and innovation. As these experiments show workers, when given the chance, can develop numerous "good ideas" **and**, equally as important, produce them. A capitalist with a "good idea," on the other hand, would be powerless to produce it without workers and it is this fact that shows that innovation, in and of itself, is not the source of surplus value.

So, contrary to much capitalist apologetics, innovation is not the monopoly of an elite class of humans. It is part of all of us, although the necessary social environment needed to nurture and develop it in all is crushed by the authoritarian workplaces of capitalism and the effects of inequalities of wealth and power within society as a whole. If workers were truly incapable of innovation, any shift toward greater control of production by workers should result in decreased productivity. What one actually finds, however, is just the opposite: productivity increased dramatically as ordinary people were given the chance, usually denied them, to apply their skills and talents. They show the kind of ingenuity and creativity people naturally bring to a challenging situation – if they are allowed to, if they are participants rather than servants or subordinates.

In fact, there is *"a growing body of empirical literature that is generally supportive of claims for the economic efficiency of the labour-managed firm. Much of this literature focuses on productivity, frequently finding it to be positively correlated with increasing levels of participation … Studies that encompass a range of issues broader than the purely economic also tend to support claims for the efficiency of labour managed and worker-controlled firms … In addition, studies that compare the economic preference of groups of traditionally and worker-controlled forms point to the stronger performance of the latter."* [Christopher Eaton Gunn, **Workers' Self-Management in the United States**, pp. 42-3] This is confirmed by David Noble, who points out that *"the self-serving claim"* that *"centralised management authority is the key to productivity"* is *"belied by nearly every sociological study of work."* [**Progress without People**, p. 65]

During the Spanish Revolution of 1936-39, workers self-managed many factories following the principles of participatory democracy. Productivity and innovation in the Spanish collectives was exceptionally high (particularly given the difficult economic and political situation they faced). As Jose Peirats notes, industry was *"transformed from top to bottom … there were achieved feats pregnant with significance for people who had always striven to deny the reality of the wealth of popular initiatives unveiled by revolutions."* Workers made suggestions and presented new inventions, *"offering the product of their discoveries, genius or imaginings."* [**The CNT in the Spanish Revolution**, vol. 2, p. 86] The metal-working industry is a good example. As Augustine Souchy observes, at the outbreak of the Civil War, the metal industry in Catalonia was *"very poorly developed."* Yet within months, the Catalonian metal workers had rebuilt the industry from scratch, converting factories to the production of war materials for the anti-fascist troops. A few days after the July 19th revolution, the Hispano-Suiza Automobile Company was already converted to the manufacture of armoured cars, ambulances, weapons, and munitions for the fighting front. *"Experts were truly astounded,"* Souchy writes, *"at the expertise of the workers in building new machinery for the manufacture of arms and munitions. Very few machines were imported. In a short time, two hundred different hydraulic presses of up to 250 tons pressure, one hundred seventy-eight revolving lathes, and hundreds of milling machines and boring machines were built."* [**The Anarchist Collectives: Workers' Self-management in the Spanish Revolution, 1936-1939**, Sam Dolgoff (ed.), p. 96]

Similarly, there was virtually no optical industry in Spain before the July revolution, only some scattered workshops. After the revolution, the small workshops were voluntarily converted into a production collective. *"The greatest innovation,"* according to Souchy, *"was the construction of a new factory for optical apparatuses and instruments. The whole operation was financed by the voluntary contributions of the workers. In a short time the factory turned out opera glasses, telemeters, binoculars, surveying instruments, industrial glassware in different colours, and certain scientific instruments. It also manufactured and repaired optical equipment for the fighting fronts … What private capitalists failed to do was accomplished by the creative capacity of the members of the Optical Workers' Union of the CNT."* [**Op. Cit.**, pp. 98-99]

More recently, the positive impact of workers' control has been strikingly confirmed in studies of the Mondragon co-operatives in Spain, where workers are democratically involved in production decisions and encouraged to innovate. As George Bennello notes, *"Mondragon productivity is very high – higher than in its capitalist counterparts. Efficiency, measured as the ratio of utilised resources – capital and labour – to output, is far higher than in comparable capitalist factories."* [*"The Challenge of Mondragon"*, **Reinventing Anarchy, Again**, p. 216]

The example of Lucas Aerospace during the 1970s, indicates well the creative potential waiting to be utilised and wasted due to capitalism. Faced with massive job cuts and restructuring, the workers and their Shop Stewards SSCC in 1976 proposed an alternative Corporate Plan to Lucas's management. This was the product of two years planning and debate among Lucas workers. Everyone from unionised engineers, to technicians to production workers and secretaries was involved in drawing it up. It was based on detailed information on the machinery and equipment that all Lucas sites had, as well as the type of skills that were in the company. The workers designed the products themselves, using their own experiences of work and life. While its central aim was to head off Lucas's planned job cuts, it presented a vision of a better world by arguing that the concentration on military goods and markets was neither the best use of resources nor in itself desirable. It argued that if Lucas was to look away from military production it could expand into markets for socially useful goods (such as medical equipment) where it already had some expertise and sales. The management were not interested, it was their 'right' to "manage" Lucas and to decide where its resources would be used, including the 18,000 people working there. Management were more than happy to exclude the workforce from any say in such fundamental matters as implementing the workers' ideas would have shown how unnecessary they, the bosses, actually were.

Another example of wasted worker innovation is provided by the US car industry. In the 1960s, Walter Reuther, president of the United Auto Workers (UAW) had proposed to the Johnson Whitehouse that the government help the US car companies to produce small cars, competing with Volkswagen which had enjoyed phenomenal success in the U.S. market. The project, unsurprisingly, fell through as the executives of the car companies were uninterested. In the 1970s, higher petrol prices saw US buyers opt for smaller cars and the big US manufacturers were caught unprepared. This allowed Toyota, Honda and other Asian car companies to gain a crucial foothold in the American market. Unsurprisingly, resistance by the union and workforce were blamed for the industry's problems when, in fact, it was the bosses, not the unions, who were blind to a potential market niche and the industry's competitive challenges.

Therefore, far from being a threat to innovation, workers' self-management would increase it and, more importantly, direct it towards improving the quality of life for all as opposed to increasing the profits of the few (this aspect of an anarchist society will be discussed in more detail in section I). This should be unsurprising, as vesting a minority with managerial authority and deciding that the others should be cogs results in a massive loss of social initiative and drive. In addition, see sections J.5.10, J.5.11 and J.5.12 for more on why anarchists support self-management and why, in spite of its higher efficiency and productivity, the capitalist market will select against it.To conclude, capitalist workplace hierarchy actually hinders innovation and efficiency rather than fosters it. To defend profits by appealing to innovation is, in such circumstances, deeply ironic. Not only does it end up simply justifying profits in terms of monopoly power (i.e. hierarchical decision making rewarding itself), that power also wastes a huge amount of potential innovation in society – namely the ideas and experience of the workforce excluded from the decision making process. Given that power produces resistance, capitalism ensures that the *"creative faculties [the workers] are not allowed to exercise on behalf of a social order that rejects them (and which they reject) are now utilised against that social order"* and so *"work under capitalism"* is *"a perpetual waste of creative capacity, and a constant struggle between the worker and his own activity."* [Castoriadis, **Op. Cit.**, p. 93 and p. 94]

Therefore, rather than being a defence of capitalist profit taking (and the inequality it generates) innovation backfires against capitalism. Innovation flourishes best under freedom and this points towards libertarian socialism and workers' self-management. Given the chance, workers can manage their own work and this results in increased innovation and productivity, so showing that capitalist monopoly of decision making power hinders both. This is unsurprising, for only equality can maximise liberty and so workers' control (rather than capitalist power) is the key to innovation. Only those who confuse freedom with the oppression of wage labour would be surprised by this.

C.2.9 Do profits reflect a reward for risk?

Another common justification of surplus value is that of "risk taking", namely the notion that non-labour income is justified because its owners took a risk in providing money and deserve a reward for so doing.

Before discussing why anarchists reject this argument, it must be noted that in the mainstream neo-classical model, risk and uncertainty plays no role in generating profits. According to general equilibrium theory, there is no uncertainty (the present and future are known) and so there is no role for risk. As such, the concept of profits being related to risk is more realistic than the standard model. However, as we will argue, such an argument is unrealistic in many other ways, particularly in relation to modern-day corporate capitalism.

It is fair to say that the appeal of risk to explain and justify profits lies almost entirely in the example of the small investor who gambles their savings (for example, by opening a bar) and face a major risk if the investment does not succeed. However, in spite of the emotional appeal of such examples, anarchists argue that they are hardly typical of investment decisions and rewards within capitalism. In fact, such examples are used precisely to draw attention away from the way the system works rather than provide an insight into it. That is, the higher apparent realism of the argument hides an equally unreal model of capitalism as the more obviously unrealistic theories which seek to rationalise non-labour income.

So does "risk" explain or justify non-labour income? No, anarchists argue. This is for five reasons. Firstly, the returns on property income are utterly independent on the amount of risk involved. Secondly, all human acts involve risk of some kind and so why should property owners gain exclusively from it? Thirdly, risk as such it not rewarded, only **successful** risks are and what constitutes success is dependent on production, i.e. exploiting labour. Fourthly, most "risk" related non-labour income today plays **no** part in aiding production and, indeed, is simply not that risky due to state intervention. Fifthly, risk in this context is not independent of owning capital and, consequently, the arguments against "waiting" and innovation apply equally to this rationale. In other words, "risk" is simply yet another excuse to reward the rich for being wealthy.

The first objection is the most obvious. It is a joke to suggest that capitalism rewards in proportion to risk. There is little or no relationship between income and the risk that person faces. Indeed, it would be fairer to say that return is **inversely** proportional to the amount of risk a person faces. The most obvious example is that of a worker who wants to be their own boss and sets up their own business. That is a genuine risk, as they are risking their savings and are willing to go into debt. Compare this to a billionaire investor with millions of shares in hundreds of companies. While the former struggles to make a living, the latter gets a large regular flow of income without raising a finger. In terms of risk, the investor is wealthy enough to have spread their money so far that, in practical terms, there is none. Who has the larger income?

As such, the risk people face is dependent on their existing wealth and so it is impossible to determine any relationship between it and the income it is claimed to generate. Given that risk is inherently subjective, there is no way of discovering its laws of operation except by begging the question and using the actual rate of profits to measure the cost of risk-bearing.

The second objection is equally as obvious. The suggestion that risk taking is the source and justification for profits ignores the fact that virtually all human activity involves risk. To claim that capitalists should be paid for the risks associated with investment is to implicitly state that money is more valuable that human life. After all, workers risk their health and often their lives in work and often the most dangerous workplaces are those associated with the lowest pay. Moreover, providing safe working conditions can eat into profits and by cutting health and safety costs, profits can rise. This means that to reward capitalist "risk", the risk workers face may actually increase. In the inverted world of capitalist ethics, it is usually cheaper (or more "efficient") to replace an individual worker than a capital investment. Unlike investors, bosses and the corporate elite, workers **do** face risk to life or limb daily as part of their work. Life is risky and no life is more risky that that of a worker who may be ruined by the "risky" decisions of management, capitalists and investors seeking to make their next million. While it is possible to diversify the risk in holding a stock portfolio that is not possible with a job. A job cannot be spread across a wide array of companies diversifying risk.

In other words, workers face much greater risks than their employers and, moreover, they have no say in what risks will be taken with their lives and livelihoods. It is workers who pay the lion's share of the costs of failure, not management and stockholders. When firms are in difficulty, it is the workers who are asked to pay for the failures of management though pay cuts and the elimination of health and other benefits. Management rarely get pay cuts, indeed they often get bonuses and "incentive" schemes to get them to do the work they were (over) paid to do in the first. When a corporate manager makes a mistake and their business actually fails, his workers will suffer far more serious consequences than him. In most cases, the manager will still live comfortably (indeed, many will receive extremely generous severance packages) while workers will face the fear, insecurity and hardship of having to find a new job. Indeed, as we argued in section C.2.1, it is the risk of unemployment that is a key factor in ensuring the exploitation of labour in the first place.

As production is inherently collective under capitalism, so must be the risk. As Proudhon put it, it may be argued that the capitalist *"alone runs the risk of the enterprise"* but this ignores the fact that capitalist cannot *"alone work a mine or run a railroad"* nor *"alone carry on a factory, sail a ship, play a tragedy, build the Pantheon."* He asked: *"Can anybody do such things as these, even if he has all the capital necessary?"* And so *"association"* becomes *"absolutely necessary and right"* as the *"work to be accomplished"* is *"the common and undivided property of all those who take part therein."* If not, shareholders would *"plunder the bodies and souls of the wage-workers"* and it would be *"an outrage upon human dignity and personality."* [**The General Idea of the Revolution**, p. 219] In other words, as production is collective, so is the risk faced and, consequently, risk cannot be used to justify excluding people from

controlling their own working lives or the fruit of their labour.

This brings us to the third reason, namely how "risk" contributes to production. The idea that "risk" is a contribution to production is equally flawed. Obviously, no one argues that **failed** investments should result in investors being rewarded for the risks they took. This means that **successful** risks are what counts and this means that the company has produced a desired good or service. In other words, the argument for risk is dependent on the investor providing capital which the workers of the company used productivity to create a commodity. However, as we discussed in section C.2.4 capital is **not** productive and, as a result, an investor may expect the return of their initial investment but no more. At best, the investor has allowed others to use their money but, as section C.2.3 indicated, giving permission to use something is not a productive act.

However, there is another sense in which risk does not, in general, contribute to production within capitalism, namely finance markets. This bring us to our fourth objection, namely that most kinds of "risks" within capitalism do **not** contribute to production and, thanks to state aid, not that risky.

Looking at the typical "risk" associated with capitalism, namely putting money into the stock market and buying shares, the idea that "risk" contributes to production is seriously flawed. As David Schweickart points out, *"[i]n the vast majority of cases, when you buy stock, you give your money not to the company but to another private individual. You buy your share of stock from someone who is cashing in his share. Not a nickel of your money goes to the company itself. The company's profits would have been exactly the same, with or without your stock purchase."* [**After Capitalism**, p. 37] In fact between 1952 and 1997, about 92% of investment was paid for by firms' own internal funds and so *"the stock market contributes virtually nothing to the financing of outside investment."* Even new stock offerings only accounted for 4% of non-financial corporations capital expenditures. [Doug Henwood, **Wall Street**, p. 72] *"In spite of the stock market's large symbolic value, it is notorious that it has relatively little to do with the production of goods and services,"* notes David Ellerman, *"The overwhelming bulk of stock transactions are in second-hand shares so the capital paid for shares usually goes to other stock traders, not to productive enterprises issuing new shares."* [**The Democratic worker-owned firm**, p. 199]

In other words, most investment is simply the "risk" associated with buying a potential income stream in an uncertain world. The buyer's action has not contributed to producing that income stream in any way whatsoever yet it results in a claim on the labour of others. At best, it could be said that a previous owner of the shares at some time in the past has *"contributed"* to production by providing money but this does not justify non-labour income. As such, investing in shares may rearrange existing wealth (often to the great advantage of the rearrangers) but it does not produce anything. New wealth flows from production, the use of labour on existing wealth to create new wealth.

Ironically, the stock market (and the risk it is based on) harms this process. The notion that dividends represent the return for "risk" may be faulted by looking at how the markets operate in reality, rather than in theory. Stock markets react to recent movements in the price of stock markets, causing price movements to build upon price movements. According to academic finance economist

Bob Haugen, this results in finance markets having endogenous instability, with such price-driven volatility accounting for over three-quarters of all volatility in finance markets. This leads to the market directing investments very badly as some investment is wasted in over-valued companies and under-valued firms cannot get finance to produce useful goods. The market's endogenous volatility reduces the overall level of investment as investors will only fund projects which return a sufficiently high level of return. This results in a serious drag on economic growth. As such, "risk" has a large and negative impact on the real economy and it seems ironic to reward such behaviour. Particularly as the high rate of return is meant to compensate for the risk of investing in the stock market, but in fact most of this risk results from the endogenous stability of the market itself. [Steve Keen, **Debunking Economics**, pp. 249-50]

Appeals to "risk" to justify capitalism are somewhat ironic, given the dominant organisational form within capitalism – the corporation. These firms are based on *"limited liability"* which was designed explicitly to reduce the risk faced by investors. As Joel Bakan notes, before this "no matter how much, or how little, a person had invested in a company, he or she was **personally** liable, without limit, for the company's debts. Investors' homes, savings, and other personal assess would be exposed to claims by creditors if a company failed, meaning that a person risked financial ruin simply by owning shares in a company. Stockholding could not becomes a truly attractive option … until that risk was removed, which it soon was. By the middle of the nineteenth century, business leaders and politicians broadly advocated changing the law to limit the liability of shareholders to the amounts they had invested in a company. If a person bought $100 worth of shares, they reasoned, he or she should be immune to liability for anything beyond that, regardless of what happened to the company." Limited liability's *"sole purpose … is to shield them from legal responsibility for corporations' actions"* as well as reducing the risks of investing (unlike for small businesses). [**The Corporation**, p. 11 and p. 79]

This means that stock holders (investors) in a corporation hold no liability for the corporation's debts and obligations. As a result of this state granted privilege, potential losses cannot exceed the amount which they paid for their shares. The rationale used to justify this is the argument that without limited liability, a creditor would not likely allow any share to be sold to a buyer of at least equivalent creditworthiness as the seller. This means that limited liability allows corporations to raise funds for riskier enterprises by reducing risks and costs from the owners and shifting them onto other members of society (i.e. an externality). It is, in effect, a state granted privilege to trade with a limited chance of loss but with an unlimited chance of gain.

This is an interesting double-standard. It suggests that corporations are not, in fact, owned by shareholders at all since they take on none of the responsibility of ownership, especially the responsibility to pay back debts. Why should they have the privilege of getting profit during good times when they take none of the responsibility during bad times? Corporations are creatures of government, created with the social privileges of limited financial liability of shareholders. Since their debts are ultimately public, why should their profits be private?

Needless to say, this reducing of risk is not limited to within a state, it is applied internationally as well. Big banks and corporations lend money to developing nations but *"the people who borrowed the money [i.e. the local elite] aren't held responsible for it. It's the people … who have to pay [the debts] off … The lenders are protected from risk. That's one of the main functions of the IMF, to provide risk free insurance to people who lend and invest in risky loans. They earn high yields because there's a lot of risk, but they don't have to take the risk, because it's socialised. It's transferred in various ways to Northern taxpayers through the IMP and other devices … The whole system is one in which the borrowers are released from the responsibility. That's transferred to the impoverished mass of the population in their own countries. And the lenders are protected from risk."* [Noam Chomsky, **Propaganda and the Public Mind**, p. 125]

Capitalism, ironically enough, has developed precisely by externalising risk and placing the burden onto other parties – suppliers, creditors, workers and, ultimately, society as a whole. *"Costs and risks are socialised,"* in other words, *"and the profit is privatised."* [Noam Chomsky, **Op. Cit.**, p. 185] To then turn round and justify corporate profits in terms of risk seems to be hypocritical in the extreme, particularly by appealing to examples of small business people whom usually face the burdens caused by corporate externalising of risk! Doug Henwood states the obvious when he writes shareholder *"liabilities are limited by definition to what they paid for the shares"* and *"they can always sell their shares in a troubled firm, and if they have diversified portfolios, they can handle an occasional wipe-out with hardly a stumble. Employees, and often customers and suppliers, are rarely so well-insulated."* Given that the *"signals emitted by the stock market are either irrelevant or harmful to real economic activity, and that the stock market itself counts for little or nothing as a source of finance"* and the argument for risk as a defence of profits is extremely weak. [**Op. Cit.**, p. 293 and p. 292]

Lastly, the risk theory of profit fails to take into account the different risk-taking abilities of that derive from the unequal distribution of society's wealth. As James Meade puts it, while *"property owners can spread their risks by putting small bits of their property into a large number of concerns, a worker cannot easily put small bits of his effort into a large number of different jobs. This presumably is the main reason we find risk-bearing capital hiring labour"* and not vice versa. [quoted by David Schweickart, **Against Capitalism**, pp. 129-130]

It should be noted that until the early nineteenth century, self-employment was the normal state of affairs and it has declined steadily to reach, at best, around 10% of the working population in Western countries today. It would be inaccurate, to say the least, to explain this decline in terms of increased unwillingness to face potential risks on the part of working people. Rather, it is a product of increased costs to set up and run businesses which acts as a very effect **natural** barrier to competition (see section C.4). With limited resources available, most working people simply **cannot** face the risk as they do not have sufficient funds in the first place and, moreover, if such funds are found the market is hardly a level playing field.

This means that going into business for yourself is always a possibility, but that option is very difficult without sufficient assets. Moreover, even if sufficient funds are found (either by savings or a loan), the risk is extremely high due to the inability to diversify investments and the constant possibility that larger firms will set-up shop in your area (for example, Wal-Mart driving out small businesses or chain pubs, cafes and bars destroying local family businesses). So it is true that there is a small flow of workers into self-employment (sometimes called the petit bourgeoisie) and that, of these, a small amount become full-scale capitalists. However, these are the exceptions that prove the rule – there is a greater return into wage slavery as enterprises fail.

Simply put, the distribution of wealth (and so ability to take risks) is so skewed that such possibilities are small and, in spite being highly risky, do not provide sufficient returns to make most of them a success. That many people **do** risk their savings and put themselves through stress, insecurity and hardship in this way is, ironically, hardly a defence of capitalism as it suggests that wage labour is so bad that many people will chance everything to escape it. Sadly, this natural desire to be your own boss generally becomes, if successful, being someone else's boss! Which means, in almost all cases, it shows that to become rich you need to exploit other people's labour.

So, as with "waiting" (see section C.2.7), taking a risk is much easier if you are wealthy and so risk is simply another means for rewarding the wealthy for being wealthy. In other words, risk aversion is the dependent, not the independent, factor. The distribution of wealth determines the risks people willing to face and so cannot explain or justify that wealth. Rather than individual evaluations determining "risk", these evaluations will be dependent on the class position of the individuals involved. As Schweickart notes, *"large numbers of people simply do not have any discretionary funds to invest. They can't play at all … among those who can play, some are better situated than others. Wealth gives access to information, expert advice, and opportunities for diversification that the small investor often lacks."* [**After Capitalism**, p. 34] As such, profits do not reflect the real cost of risk but rather the scarcity of people with anything to risk (i.e. inequality of wealth).

Similarly, given that the capitalists (or their hired managers) have a monopoly of decision making power within a firm, any risks made by a company reflects that hierarchy. As such, risk and the ability to take risks are monopolised in a few hands. If profit **is** the product of risk then, ultimately, it is the product of a hierarchical company structure and, consequently, capitalists are simply rewarding themselves because they have power within the workplace. As with "innovation" and "entrepreneurialism" (see section C.2.8), this rationale for surplus value depends on ignoring how the workplace is structured. In other words, because managers monopolise decision making ("risk") they also monopolise the surplus value produced by workers. However, the former in no way justifies this appropriation nor does it create it.

Risk is not an independent factor and so cannot be the source of profit. Indeed other activities can involve far more risk and be rewarded less. Needless to say, the most serious consequences of "risk" are usually suffered by working people who can lose their jobs, health and even lives all depending on how the risks of the wealthy turn out in an uncertain world. As such, it is one thing to gamble your own income on a risky decision but quite another when that decision can ruin the lives of others. If quoting Keynes is not too out of place: *"Speculators may do no harm as bubbles on a steady stream of enterprise. But the position is serious when enterprise becomes the bubble on a whirlpool of speculation. When the capital development of a country becomes a by-product of the activities of a casino, the job is likely to be ill-done."* [**The General Theory of Employment, Interest and Money**, p. 159]

Appeals of risk to justify capitalism simply exposes that system as little more than a massive casino. In order for such a system to be fair, the participants must have approximately equal chances of winning. However, with massive inequality the wealthy face little chance of loosing. For example, if a millionaire and a pauper both repeatedly bet a pound on the outcome of a coin toss, the millionaire will always win as the pauper has so little reserve money that even a minor run of bad luck will bankrupt him.

Ultimately, *"the capitalist investment game (as a whole and usually in its various parts) is a positive sum. In most years more money is made in the financial markets than is lost. How is this possible? It is possible only because those who engage in real productive activity receive less than that to which they would be entitled were they fully compensated for what they produce. The reward, allegedly for risk, derives from this discrepancy."* [David Schweickart, **Op. Cit.**, p. 38] In other words, people would not risk their money unless they could make a profit and the willingness to risk is dependent on current and expected profit levels and so cannot explain them. To focus on risk simply obscures the influence that property has upon the ability to enter a given industry (i.e. to take a risk in the first place) and so distracts attention away from the essential aspects of how profits are actually generated (i.e. away from production and its hierarchical organisation under capitalism).

So risk does not explain how surplus value is generated nor is it it's origin. Moreover, as the risk people face and the return they get is dependent on the wealth they have, it cannot be used to justify this distribution. Quite the opposite, as return and risk are usually inversely related. If risk was the source of surplus value or justified it, the riskiest investment and poorest investor would receive the highest returns and this is not the case. In summary, the "risk" defence of capitalism does not convince.

C.3
What determines the distribution between labour and capital?

In short, class struggle determines the distribution of income between classes (As Proudhon put it, the expression *"the relations of profits to wages"* means *"the war between labour and capital."* [**System of Economical Contradictions**, p. 130]). This, in turn, is dependent on the balance of power within any given economy at any given time.

Given our analysis of the source of surplus value in section C.2.2, this should come as no surprise. Given the central role of labour in creating both goods (things with value) and surplus value, production prices determine market prices. This means that market prices are governed, however indirectly, by what goes on in production. In any company, wages determine a large percentage of the production costs. Looking at other costs (such as raw materials), again wages play a large role in determining their price. Obviously the division of a commodity's price into costs and profits is not a fixed ratio, which mean that prices are the result of complex interactions of wage levels and productivity. Within the limits of a given situation, the class struggle between employers and employees over wages, working conditions and benefits determines the degree of exploitation within a society and so the distribution of income, i.e. the relative amount of money which goes to labour (i.e. wages) and capital (surplus value).

To quote libertarian socialist Cornelius Castoriadis:

"Far from being completely dominated by the will of the capitalist and forced to increase indefinitely the yield of labour, production is determined just as much by the workers' individual and collective resistance to such increases. The extraction of 'use value from labour power' is not a technical operation; it is a process of bitter struggle in which half the time, so to speak, the capitalists turn out to be losers.

"The same thing holds true for living standards, i.e., real wage levels. From its beginnings, the working class has fought to reduce the length of the workday and to raise wage levels. It is this struggle that has determined how these levels have risen and fallen over the years …

"Neither the actual labour rendered during an hour of labour time nor the wage received in exchange for this work can be determined by any kind of 'objective' law, norm, or calculation … What we are saying does not mean that specifically economic or even 'objective' factors play no real in determining wage levels. Quite the contrary. At any given instant, the class struggle comes into play only within a given economic – and, more generally, objective – framework, and it acts not only directly but also through the intermediary of a series of partial 'economic mechanisms.' To give only one example among thousands, an economic victory for workers in one sector has a ripple effect on overall wage levels, not only because it can encourage other workers to be more combative, but also because sectors with lower wage levels will experience greater difficulties recruiting manpower. None of these mechanisms, however, can effectively act on its own and have its own significance if taken separately from the class struggle. And the economic context itself is always gradually affected one way or another by this struggle."
[**Political and Social Writings**, vol. 2, p. 248]

The essential point is that the extraction of surplus value from workers is not a simple technical operation, as implied by the neo-classical perspective (and, ironically, classical Marxism as Castoriadis explains in his classic work *"Modern Capitalism and Revolution"*

[**Op. Cit.**, pp. 226-343]). As noted previously, unlike the extraction of so many joules from a ton of coal, extracting surplus value ("use value") from labour power involves conflict between people, between classes. Labour power is unlike all other commodities – it is and remains inseparably embodied in human beings. This means that the division of profits and wages in a company and in the economy as a whole is dependent upon and modified by the actions of workers (and capitalists), both as individuals and as a class. It is this struggle which, ultimately, drives the capitalist economy, it is this conflict between the human and commodity aspects of labour power that ultimately brings capitalism into repeated crisis (see section C.7).

From this perspective, the neo-classical argument that a factor in production (labour, capital or land) receives an income share that indicates its productive power "at the margin" is false. Rather, it is a question of power – and the willingness to use it. As Christopher Eaton Gunn points out, the neo-classical argument *"take[s] no account of power – of politics, conflict, and bargaining – as more likely indicators of relative shares of income in the real world."* [**Workers' Self-Management in the United States**, p. 185] Ultimately, working class struggle is an *"indispensable means of raising their standard of living or defending their attained advantages against the concerted measures of the employers."* It is *"not only a means for the defence of immediate economic interests, it is also a continuous schooling for their powers of resistance, showing them every day that every last right has to be won by unceasing struggle against the existing system."* [Rocker, **Anarcho-Syndicalism**, p. 78]

If the power of labour is increasing, its share in income will tend to increase and, obviously, if the power of labour decreased it would fall. And the history of the post-war economy supports such an analysis, with labour in the advanced countries share of income falling from 68% in the 1970s to 65.1% in 1995 (in the EU, it fell from 69.2% to 62%). In the USA, labour's share of income in the manufacturing sector fell from 74.8% to 70.6% over the 1979-89 period, reversing the rise in labour's share that occurred over the 1950s, 1960s and 1970s. The reversal in labour's share occurred at the same time as labour's power was undercut by right-wing governments who have pursued business friendly "free market" policies to combat "inflation" (an euphemism for working class militancy and resistance) by undermining working class power and organisation by generating high unemployment.

Thus, for many anarchists, the relative power between labour and capital determines the distribution of income between them. In periods of full employment or growing workplace organisation and solidarity, workers wages will tend to rise faster. In periods where there is high unemployment and weaker unions and less direct action, labour's share will fall. From this analysis anarchists support collective organisation and action in order to increase the power of labour and ensure we receive more of the value we produce.

The neo-classical notion that rising productivity allows for increasing wages is one that has suffered numerous shocks since the early 1970s. Usually wage increases lag behind productivity. For example, during Thatcher's reign of freer markets, productivity rose by 4.2%, 1.4% higher than the increase in real earnings between 1980-88. Under Reagan, productivity increased by 3.3%, accompanied by a fall of 0.8% in real earnings. Remember, though, these are averages and hide the actual increases in pay differentials between workers and managers. To take one example, the real wages for employed single men between 1978 and 1984 in the UK rose by 1.8% for the bottom 10% of that group, for the highest 10%, it was a massive 18.4%. The average rise (10.1%) hides the vast differences between top and bottom. In addition, these figures ignore the starting point of these rises – the often massive differences in wages between employees (compare the earnings of the CEO of McDonalds and one of its cleaners). In other words, 2.8% of nearly nothing is still nearly nothing!

Looking at the USA again, we find that workers who are paid by the hour (the majority of employees) saw their average pay peak in 1973. Since then, it had declined substantially and stood at its mid-1960s level in 1992. For over 80 per cent of the US workforce (production and non-supervisory workers), real wages have fallen by 19.2 per cent for weekly earnings and 13.4 per cent for hourly earnings between 1973 and 1994. Productivity had risen by 23.2 per cent. Combined with this drop in real wages in the USA, we have seen an increase in hours worked. In order to maintain their current standard of living, working class people have turned to both debt and longer working hours. Since 1979, the annual hours worked by middle-income families rose from 3 020 to 3 206 in 1989, 3 287 in 1996 and 3 335 in 1997. In Mexico we find a similar process. Between 1980 and 1992, productivity rose by 48 per cent while salaries (adjusted for inflation) fell by 21 per cent.

Between 1989 to 1997, productivity increased by 9.7% in the USA while median compensation decreased by 4.2%. In addition, median family working hours grew by 4% (or three weeks of full-time work) while its income increased by only 0.6 % (in other words, increases in working hours helped to create this slight growth). If the wages of workers were related to their productivity, as argued by neo-classical economics, you would expect wages to increase as productivity rose, rather than fall. However, if wages are related to economic power, then this fall is to be expected. This explains the desire for "flexible" labour markets, where workers' bargaining power is eroded and so more income can go to profits rather than wages.

It is amazing how far the US in 2005, the paradigm for neo-liberalism, is from the predictions of neo-classical economic textbooks. Since the 1970s, there has only been one period of sustained good times for working people, the late 1990s. Before and after this period, there has been wage stagnation (between 2000 and 2004, for example, the real median family income **fell** by 3%). While the real income of households in the lowest fifth grew by 6.1% between 1979 and 2000, the top fifth saw an increase of 70% and the average income of the top 1% grew by 184%. This rising inequality was fuelled by the expansion of income from capital and an increased concentration of capital income in the top 1% (who received 57.5% of all capital income in 2003, compared to 37.8% in 1979). This reflected the increased share of income flowing to corporate profits (profits rates in 2005 were the highest in 36 years). If the pre-tax return to capital had remained at its 1979 level, then hourly compensation would have been 5% higher. In 2005 dollars, this represents an annual transfer of $235 billion from labour to capital. [Lawrence Mishel, Jered Bernstein, and Sylvia Allegretto,

The State of Working America 2006/7, pp. 2-3]

Labour's share of income in the corporate sector fell from 82.1% in 179 to 81.1% in 1989, and then to 79.1% in 2005. However, this fall is even worse for labour as labour income *"includes the pay of Chief Executive Officers (CEOs), thereby overstating the income share going to 'workers' and understating 'profits,' since the bonuses and stock options given CEOs are more akin to profits than wages"* and so *"some of the profits are showing up in CEO paychecks and are counted as worker pay."* [**Op. Cit.**, p. 83 and p. 84]

Unsurprisingly, there has been a *"stunning disconnect between the rapid productivity growth and pay growth,"* along with a *"tremendous widening of the wage gap between those at the top of the wage scale, particularly corporate chief executive officers [CEO], and other wage earners."* Between 1979 and 1995, wages *"were stagnant or fell for the bottom 60% of wage earners"* and grew by 5% for the 80th percentile. Between 1992 and 2005, saw median CEO pay rise by 186.2% while the media worker saw only a 7.2% rise in their wages. Wealth inequality was even worse, with the wealth share of the bottom 80% shrinking by 3.8 percentage points (which was gained by the top 5% of households). Using the official standard of poverty, 11.3% of Americans were in poverty in 2000, rising to 12.7% in 2004 (*"This is the first time that poverty rose through each of the first three years of a recovery"*). However, the official poverty line is hopelessly out of date (for a family of four it was 48% of median family income in 1960, in 2006 it is 29%). Using a threshold of twice the official value sees an increase in poverty from 29.3% to 31.2% [**Op. Cit.**, p. 4, p. 5, p. 7, p. 9 and p. 11]

Of course, it will be argued that only in a perfectly competitive market (or, more realistically, a truly "free" one) will wages increase in-line with productivity. However, you would expect that a regime of **freer** markets would make things better, not worse. This has not happened. The neo-classical argument that unions, struggling over wages and working conditions will harm workers in the "long run" has been dramatically refuted since the 1970s – the decline of the labour movement in the USA has been marked by falling wages, not rising ones, for example. Despite of rising productivity, wealth has **not** "trickled down" – rather it has flooded up (a situation only surprising to those who believe economic textbooks or what politicians say). In fact, between 1947 and 1973, the median family income rose by 103.9% while productivity rose by 103.7% and so wages and productivity went hand-in-hand. Since the mid-1970s this close mapping broke down. From 1973 to 2005, productivity rose by 75.5% while income increased by a mere 21.8%, less than one-third the rate of productivity (from 2000 to 2004, productivity rose by 14% while family income fell by 2.9%). This wedge is the source of rising inequality, with the upper classes claiming most of the income growth. [**Op. Cit.**, p. 46]

All of which refutes those apologists for capitalism who cite the empirical fact that, in a modern capitalist economy, a large majority of all income goes to "labour," with profit, interest and rent adding up to something under twenty percent of the total. Of course, even if surplus value were less than 20% of a workers' output, this does not change its exploitative nature (just as, for the capitalist apologist, taxation does not stop being "theft" just because it is around 10% of all income). However, this value for profit, interest and rent is based on a statistical sleight-of-hand, as "worker" is defined as including everyone who has a salary in a company, including managers and CEOs. The large incomes which many managers and all CEOs receive would, of course, ensure that a large majority of all income does go to "labour." Thus this "fact" ignores the role of most managers as de facto capitalists and their income represents a slice of surplus value rather than wages. This sleight-of-hand also obscures the results of this distribution for while the 70% of "labour" income goes into many hands, the 20% representing surplus value goes into the hands of a few. So even if we ignore the issue of CEO "wages", the fact is that a substantial amount of money is going into the hands of a small minority which will, obviously, skew income, wealth and economic power away from the vast majority.

To get a better picture of the nature of exploitation within modern capitalism we have to compare workers wages to their productivity. According to the World Bank, in 1966, US manufacturing wages were equal to 46% of the value-added in production (value-added is the difference between selling price and the costs of raw materials and other inputs to the production process). In 1990, that figure had fallen to 36% and by 1993, to 35%. Figures from the 1992 Economic Census of the US Census Bureau indicate it had reached 19.76% (39.24% if we take the **total** payroll which includes managers and so on). In the US construction industry, wages were 35.4% of value added in 1992 (with total payroll, 50.18%). Therefore the argument that because a large percentage of income goes to "labour" capitalism is fine hides the realities of that system and the exploitation its hierarchical nature creates.

Overall, since the 1970s working class America has seen stagnating income, rising working hours and falling social (i.e. income-class) mobility while, at the same time, productivity has been rising and inequality soaring. While this may come as a surprise (or be considered a paradox by capitalist economics, a paradox usually to be justified and rationalised if acknowledged at all) anarchists consider this to be a striking confirmation of their analysis. Unsurprisingly, in a hierarchical system those at the top do better than those at the bottom. The system is set up so that the majority enrich the minority. That is why anarchists argue that workplace organisation and resistance is essential to maintain – and even increase – labour's income. For if the share of income between labour and capital depends on their relative power – and it does – then only the actions of workers themselves can improve their situation and determine the distribution of the value they create.

This analysis obviously applied **within** classes as well. At any time, there is a given amount of unpaid labour in circulation in the form of goods or services representing more added value than workers were paid for. This given sum of unpaid labour (surplus value) represents a total over which the different capitalists, landlords and bankers fight over. Each company tries to maximise its share of that total, and if a company does realise an above-average share, it means that some other companies receive less than average.

The key to distribution within the capitalist class is, as between that class and the working class, power. Looking at what is normally, although somewhat inaccurately, called monopoly this is obvious. The larger the company with respect to its market, the more likely it is to obtain a larger share of the available surplus, for reasons

discussed later (see section C.5). While this represents a distribution of surplus value **between** capitalists based on market power, the important thing to note here is that while companies compete on the market to realise their share of the total surplus (unpaid labour) the **source** of these profits does not lie in the market, but in production. One cannot buy what does not exist and if one gains, another loses.

Market power also plays a key role in producing inflation, which has its roots in the ability of firms to pass cost increases to consumers in the form of higher prices. This represents a distribution of income from lenders to borrowers, i.e. from finance capital to industrial capital and labour to capital (as capital "borrows" labour, i.e. the workers are paid **after** they have produced goods for their bosses). How able capitalists are to pass on costs to the general population depends on how able they are to withstand competition from other companies, i.e. how much they dominate their market and can act as a price setter. Of course, inflation is not the only possible outcome of rising costs (such as wage rises). It is always possible to reduce profits or increase the productivity of labour (i.e. increase the rate of exploitation). The former is rarely raised as a possibility, as the underlying assumption seems to be that profits are sacrosanct, and the latter is dependent, of course, on the balance of forces within the economy.

In the next section, we discuss why capitalism is marked by big business and what this concentrated market power means to the capitalist economy.

C.4
Why does the market become dominated by Big Business?

As noted in section C.1.4, the standard capitalist economic model assumes an economy made up of a large number of small firms, none of which can have any impact on the market. Such a model has no bearing to reality:

> "The facts show ... that capitalist economies tend over time and with some interruptions to become more and more heavily concentrated." [M.A. Utton, **The Political Economy of Big Business**, p. 186]

As Bakunin argued, capitalist production *"must ceaselessly expand at the expense of the smaller speculative and productive enterprises devouring them."* Thus *"[c]ompetition in the economic field destroys and swallows up the small and even medium-sized enterprises, factories, land estates, and commercial houses for the benefit of huge capital holdings."* [**The Political Philosophy of Bakunin**, p. 182] The history of capitalism has proven him right. while the small and medium firm has not disappeared, economic life under capitalism is dominated by a few big firms.

This growth of business is rooted in the capitalist system itself. The dynamic of the "free" market is that it tends to becomes dominated by a few firms (on a national, and increasingly, international, level), resulting in oligopolistic competition and higher profits for the companies in question (see next section for details and evidence). This occurs because only established firms can afford the large capital investments needed to compete, thus reducing the number of competitors who can enter or survive in a given the market. Thus, in Proudhon's words, *"competition kills competition."* [**System of Economical Contradictions**, p. 242] In other words, capitalist markets evolve toward oligopolistic concentration.

This *"does not mean that new, powerful brands have not emerged [after the rise of Big Business in the USA after the 1880s]; they have, but in such markets ... which were either small or non-existent in the early years of this century."* The dynamic of capitalism is such that the *"competitive advantage [associated with the size and market power of Big Business], once created, prove[s] to be enduring."* [Paul Ormerod, **The Death of Economics**, p. 55]

For people with little or no capital, entering competition is limited to new markets with low start-up costs (*"In general, the industries which are generally associated with small scale production ... have low levels of concentration"* [Malcolm C. Sawyer, **The Economics of Industries and Firms**, p. 35]). Sadly, however, due to the dynamics of competition, these markets usually in turn become dominated by a few big firms, as weaker firms fail, successful ones grow and capital costs increase (*"Each time capital completes its cycle, the individual grows smaller in proportion to it."* [Josephine Guerts, **Anarchy: A Journal of Desire Armed** no. 41, p. 48]).

For example, between 1869 and 1955 *"there was a marked growth in capital per person and per number of the labour force. Net capital per head rose ... to about four times its initial level ... at a rate of about 17% per decade."* The annual rate of gross capital formation rose *"from $3.5 billion in 1869-1888 to $19 billion in 1929-1955, and to $30 billion in 1946-1955. This long term rise over some three quarters of a century was thus about nine times the original level"* (in constant, 1929, dollars). [Simon Kuznets, **Capital in the American Economy**, p. 33 and p. 394] To take the steel industry as an illustration: in 1869 the average cost of steel works in the USA was $156,000, but by 1899 it was $967,000 – a 520% increase. From 1901 to 1950, gross fixed assets increased from $740,201 to $2,829,186 in the steel industry as a whole, with the assets of Bethlehem Steel increasing by 4,386.5% from 1905 ($29,294) to 1950 ($1,314,267). These increasing assets are reflected both in the size of workplaces and in the administration levels in the company as a whole (i.e. **between** individual workplaces).

The reason for the rise in capital investment is rooted in the need for capitalist firms to gain a competitive edge on their rivals. As noted in section C.2, the source of profit is the unpaid labour of workers and this can be increased by one of two means. The first is by making workers work longer for less on the same machinery (the generation of absolute surplus value, to use Marx's term). The second is to make labour more productive by investing in new machinery (the generation of relative surplus value, again using Marx's terminology). The use of technology drives up the output per worker relative to their wages and so the workforce is exploited at a higher rate (how long before workers force their bosses to raise their wages depends on the balance of class forces as we noted in the last section). This means that capitalists are driven by the market to accumulate capital. The first firm to introduce new techniques reduces their costs relative to the market price,

so allowing them to gain a surplus profit by having a competitive advantage (this addition profit disappears as the new techniques are generalised and competition invests in them).

As well as increasing the rate of exploitation, this process has an impact on the structure of the economy. With the increasing ratio of capital to worker, the cost of starting a rival firm in a given, well-developed, market prohibits all but other large firms from doing so (and here we ignore advertising and other distribution expenses, which increase start-up costs even more – *"advertising raises the capital requirements for entry into the industry"* [Sawyer, **Op. Cit.**, p. 108]). J. S. Bain (in **Barriers in New Competition**) identified three main sources of entry barrier: economies of scale (i.e. increased capital costs and their more productive nature); product differentiation (i.e. advertising); and a more general category he called *"absolute cost advantage."*

This last barrier means that larger companies are able to outbid smaller companies for resources, ideas, etc. and put more money into Research and Development and buying patents. Therefore they can have a technological and material advantage over the small company. They can charge "uneconomic" prices for a time (and still survive due to their resources) – an activity called *"predatory pricing"* – and/or mount lavish promotional campaigns to gain larger market share or drive competitors out of the market. In addition, it is easier for large companies to raise external capital, and risk is generally less.

In addition, large firms can have a major impact on innovation and the development of technology – they can simply absorb newer, smaller, enterprises by way of their economic power, buying out (and thus controlling) new ideas, much the way oil companies hold patents on a variety of alternative energy source technologies, which they then fail to develop in order to reduce competition for their product (of course, at some future date they may develop them when it becomes profitable for them to do so). Also, when control of a market is secure, oligopolies will usually delay innovation to maximise their use of existing plant and equipment or introduce spurious innovations to maximise product differentiation. If their control of a market is challenged (usually by other big firms, such as the increased competition Western oligopolies faced from Japanese ones in the 1970s and 1980s), they can speed up the introduction of more advanced technology and usually remain competitive (due, mainly, to the size of the resources they have available).

These barriers work on two levels – **absolute** (entry) barriers and **relative** (movement) barriers. As business grows in size, the amount of capital required to invest in order to start a business also increases. This restricts entry of new capital into the market (and limits it to firms with substantial financial and/or political backing behind them):

> *"Once dominant organisations have come to characterise the structure of an industry, immense barriers to entry face potential competitors. Huge investments in plant, equipment, and personnel are needed ... [T]he development and utilisation of productive resources **within** the organisation takes considerable time, particularly in the face of formidable incumbents ... It is therefore one thing for a few business organisations to*

emerge in an industry that has been characterised by ... highly competitive conditions. It is quite another to break into an industry ... [marked by] oligopolistic market power." [William Lazonick, **Business Organisation and the Myth of the Market Economy**, pp. 86-87]

Moreover, **within** the oligopolistic industry, the large size and market power of the dominant firms mean that smaller firms face expansion disadvantages which reduce competition. The dominant firms have many advantages over their smaller rivals – significant purchasing power (which gains better service and lower prices from suppliers as well as better access to resources), privileged access to financial resources, larger amounts of retained earnings to fund investment, economies of scale both within and **between** workplaces, the undercutting of prices to "uneconomical" levels and so on (and, of course, they can **buy** the smaller company – IBM paid $3.5 billion for Lotus in 1995. That is about equal to the entire annual output of Nepal, which has a population of 20 million). The large firm or firms can also rely on its established relationships with customers or suppliers to limit the activities of smaller firms which are trying to expand (for example, using their clout to stop their contacts purchasing the smaller firms products).

Little wonder Proudhon argued that *"[i]n competition ... victory is assured to the heaviest battalions."* [**Op. Cit.**, p. 260]

As a result of these entry/movement barriers, we see the market being divided into two main sectors – an oligopolistic sector and a more competitive one. These sectors work on two levels – within markets (with a few firms in a given market having very large market shares, power and excess profits) and within the economy itself (some markets being highly concentrated and dominated by a few firms, other markets being more competitive). This results in smaller firms in oligopolistic markets being squeezed by big business along side firms in more competitive markets. Being protected from competitive forces means that the market price of oligopolistic markets is **not** forced down to the average production price by the market, but instead it tends to stabilise around the production price of the smaller firms in the industry (which do not have access to the benefits associated with dominant position in a market). This means that the dominant firms get super-profits while new capital is not tempted into the market as returns would not make the move worthwhile for any but the biggest companies, who usually get comparable returns in their own oligopolised markets (and due to the existence of market power in a few hands, entry can potentially be disastrous for small firms if the dominant firms perceive expansion as a threat).

Thus whatever super-profits Big Business reap are maintained due to the advantages it has in terms of concentration, market power and size which reduce competition (see section C.5 for details).

And, we must note, that the processes that saw the rise of national Big Business is also at work on the global market. Just as Big Business arose from a desire to maximise profits and survive on the market, so *"[t]ransnationals arise because they are a means of consolidating or increasing profits in an oligopoly world."* [Keith Cowling and Roger Sugden, **Transnational Monopoly Capitalism**, p. 20] So while a strictly national picture will show a market dominated by, say, four firms, a global view shows us twelve firms

instead and market power looks much less worrisome. But just as the national market saw a increased concentration of firms over time, so will global markets. Over time a well-evolved structure of global oligopoly will appear, with a handful of firms dominating most global markets (with turnovers larger than most countries GDP – which is the case even now. For example, in 1993 Shell had assets of US$ 100.8 billion, which is more than double the GDP of New Zealand and three times that of Nigeria, and total sales of US$ 95.2 billion).

Thus the very dynamic of capitalism, the requirements for survival on the market, results in the market becoming dominated by Big Business (*"the more competition develops, the more it tends to reduce the number of competitors."* [P-J Proudhon, **Op. Cit.**, p. 243]). The irony that competition results in its destruction and the replacement of market co-ordination with planned allocation of resources is one usually lost on supporters of capitalism.

C.4.1 How extensive is Big Business?

The effects of Big Business on assets, sales and profit distribution are clear. In the USA, in 1985, there were 14,600 commercial banks. The 50 largest owned 45.7 of all assets, the 100 largest held 57.4%. In 1984 there were 272,037 active corporations in the manufacturing sector, 710 of them (one-fourth of 1 percent) held 80.2 percent of total assets. In the service sector (usually held to be the home of small business), 95 firms of the total of 899,369 owned 28 percent of the sector's assets. In 1986 in agriculture, 29,000 large farms (only 1.3% of all farms) accounted for one-third of total farm sales and 46% of farm profits. In 1987, the top 50 firms accounted for 54.4% of the total sales of the **Fortune** 500 largest industrial companies. [Richard B. Du Boff, **Accumulation and Power**, p. 171] Between 1982 and 1992, the top two hundred corporations increased their share of global Gross Domestic Product from 24.2% to 26.8%, *"with the leading ten taking almost half the profits of the top two hundred."* This underestimates economic concentration as it *"does not take account of privately owned giants."* [Chomsky, **World Orders, Old and New**, p. 181]

The process of market domination is reflected by the increasing market share of the big companies. In Britain, the top 100 manufacturing companies saw their market share rise from 16% in 1909, to 27% in 1949, to 32% in 1958 and to 42% by 1975. In terms of net assets, the top 100 industrial and commercial companies saw their share of net assets rise from 47% in 1948 to 64% in 1968 to 80% in 1976 [R.C.O. Matthews (ed.), **Economy and Democracy**, p. 239]. Looking wider afield, we find that in 1995 about 50 firms produce about 15 percent of the manufactured goods in the industrialised world. There are about 150 firms in the world-wide motor vehicle industry. But the two largest firms, General Motors and Ford, together produce almost one-third of all vehicles. The five largest firms produce half of all output and the ten largest firms produce three-quarters. Four appliance firms manufacture 98 percent of the washing machines made in the United States. In the U. S. meatpacking industry, four firms account for over 85 percent of the output of beef, while the other 1,245 firms have less than 15 percent of the market.

While the concentration of economic power is most apparent in the manufacturing sector, it is not limited to that sector. We are seeing increasing concentration in the service sector – airlines, fast-food chains ,and the entertainment industry are just a few examples. In America Coke, Pepsi, and Cadbury-Schweppes dominate soft drinks while Budweiser, Miller, and Coors share the beer market. Nabisco, Keebler and Pepperidge Farms dominate the cookie industry. Expansions and mergers play their role in securing economic power and dominance. In 1996 the number three company in the US cookie industry was acquired by Keebler, which (in turn) was acquired by Kellogg in 2000. Nabisco is a division of Kraft/Philip Morris and Pepperidge Farm is owned by relatively minor player Campbell. Looking at the US airline industry, considered the great hope for deregulation in 1978, it has seen the six largest companies control of the market rise from 73% in 1978 to 85% in 1987 (and increasing fares across the board). ["*Unexpected Result of Airline Decontrol is Return to Monopolies*," **Wall Street Journal**, 20/07/1987] By 1998, the top six's share had increased by 1% but control was effectively higher with three code-sharing alliances now linking all six in pairs.[Amy Taub, "*Oligopoly!*" **Multinational Monitor**, November 1998, p. 9]

This process of concentration is happening in industries historically considered arenas of small companies. In the UK, a few big supermarkets are driving out small corner shops (the four-firm concentration ratio of the supermarket industry is over 70%) while the British brewing industry has a staggering 85% ratio. In American, the book industry is being dominated by a few big companies, both in production and distribution. A few large conglomerates publish most leading titles while a few big chains (Barnes & Nobles and Borders) have the majority of retail sales. On the internet, Amazon dominates the field in competition with the online versions of the larger bookshops. This process occurs in market after market. As such, it should be stressed that increasing concentration afflicts most, if not all sectors of the economy. There are exceptions, of course, and small businesses never disappear totally but even in many relatively de-centralised and apparently small-scale businesses, the trend to consolidation has unmistakable:

> "The latest data available show that in the manufacturing sector the four largest companies in a given industry controlled an average of 40 percent of the industry's output in 1992, and the top eight had 52 percent. These shares were practically unchanged from 1972, but they are two percentage points higher than in 1982. Retail trade (department stores, food stores, apparel, furniture, building materials and home supplies, eating and drinking places, and other retail industries) also showed a jump in market concentration since the early 1980s. The top four firms accounted for an average of 16 percent of the retail industry's sales in 1982 and 20 percent in 1992; for the eight largest, the average industry share rose from 22 to 28 percent. Some figures now available for 1997 suggest that concentration continued to increase during the 1990s; of total sales receipts in the overall economy, companies with 2,500 employees or more took in 47 percent in 1997, compared with 42 percent in 1992.

> "In the financial sector, the number of commercial banks fell 30 percent between 1990 and 1999, while the ten largest were increasing their share of loans and other industry assets from 26 to 45 percent. It is well established that other sectors, including agriculture and telecommunications, have also become more concentrated in the 1980s and 1990s. The overall rise in concentration has not been great-although the new wave may yet make a major mark-but the upward drift has taken place from a starting point of highly concentrated economic power across the economy." [Richard B. Du Boff and Edward S. Herman, "*Mergers, Concentration, and the Erosion of Democracy*", **Monthly Review**, May 2001]

So, looking at the **Fortune** 500, even the 500th firm is massive (with sales of around $3 billion). The top 100 firms usually have sales significantly larger than bottom 400 put together. Thus the capitalist economy is marked by a small number of extremely large firms, which are large in both absolute terms and in terms of the firms immediately below them. This pattern repeats itself for the next group and so on, until we reach the very small firms (where the majority of firms are).

The other effect of Big Business is that large companies tend to become more diversified as the concentration levels in individual industries increase. This is because as a given market becomes dominated by larger companies, these companies expand into other markets (using their larger resources to do so) in order to strengthen their position in the economy and reduce risks. This can be seen in the rise of "subsidiaries" of parent companies in many different markets, with some products apparently competing against each other actually owned by the same company!

Tobacco companies are masters of this diversification strategy; most people support their toxic industry without even knowing it! Don't believe it? Well, if are an American and you ate any Jell-O products, drank Kool-Aid, used Log Cabin syrup, munched Minute Rice, quaffed Miller beer, gobbled Oreos, smeared Velveeta on Ritz crackers, and washed it all down with Maxwell House coffee, you supported the tobacco industry, all without taking a puff on a cigarette! Similarly, in other countries. Simply put, most people have no idea which products and companies are owned by which corporations, which goods apparently in competition with others in fact bolster the profits of the same transnational company.

Ironically, the reason why the economy becomes dominated by Big Business has to do with the nature of competition itself. In order to survive (by maximising profits) in a competitive market, firms have to invest in capital, advertising, and so on. This survival process results in barriers to potential competitors being created, which results in more and more markets being dominated by a few big firms. This oligopolisation process becomes self-supporting as oligopolies (due to their size) have access to more resources than smaller firms. Thus the dynamic of competitive capitalism is to negate itself in the form of oligopoly.

C.4.2 What are the effects of Big Business on society?

Unsurprisingly many pro-capitalist economists and supporters of capitalism try to downplay the extensive evidence on the size and dominance of Big Business in capitalism.

Some deny that Big Business is a problem – if the market results in a few companies dominating it, then so be it (the "Chicago" and "Austrian" schools are at the forefront of this kind of position – although it does seem somewhat ironic that "market advocates" should be, at best, indifferent, at worse, celebrate the suppression of market co-ordination by **planned** co-ordination within the economy that the increased size of Big Business marks). According to this perspective, oligopolies and cartels usually do not survive very long, unless they are doing a good job of serving the customer.

We agree – it is oligopolistic **competition** we are discussing here. Big Business has to be responsive to demand (when not manipulating/creating it by advertising, of course), otherwise they lose market share to their rivals (usually other dominant firms in the same market, or big firms from other countries). However, the response to demand can be skewed by economic power and, while responsive to some degree, an economy dominated by big business can see super-profits being generated by externalising costs onto suppliers and consumers (in terms of higher prices). As such, the idea that the market will solve all problems is simply assuming that an oligopolistic market will respond "as if" it were made up of thousands and thousands of firms with little market power. An assumption belied by the reality of capitalism since its birth.

Moreover, the "free market" response to the reality of oligopoly ignores the fact that we are more than just consumers and that economic activity and the results of market events impact on many different aspects of life. Thus our argument is not focused on the fact we pay more for some products than we would in a more competitive market – it is the **wider** results of oligopoly we should be concerned with, not just higher prices, lower "efficiency" and other economic criteria. If a few companies receive excess profits just because their size limits competition the effects of this will be felt **everywhere.**

For a start, these "excessive" profits will tend to end up in few hands, so skewing the income distribution (and so power and influence) within society. The available evidence suggests that *"more concentrated industries generate a lower wage share for workers"* in a firm's value-added. [Keith Cowling, **Monopoly Capitalism**, p. 106] The largest firms retain only 52% of their profits, the rest is paid out as dividends, compared to 79% for the smallest ones and *"what might be called rentiers share of the corporate surplus – dividends plus interest as a percentage of pretax profits and interest – has risen sharply, from 20-30% in the 1950s to 60-70% in the early 1990s."* The top 10% of the US population own well over 80% of stock and bonds owned by individuals while the top 5% of stockowners own 94.5% of all stock held by individuals. Little wonder wealth has become so concentrated since the 1970s [Doug Henwood, **Wall Street**, p. 75, p. 73 and pp. 66-67]. At its most basic, this skewing of income provides the capitalist class with more

resources to fight the class war but its impact goes much wider than this.

Moreover, the *"level of aggregate concentration helps to indicate the degree of centralisation of decision-making in the economy and the economic power of large firms."* [Malcolm C. Sawyer, **Op. Cit.**, p. 261] Thus oligopoly increases and centralises economic power over investment decisions and location decisions which can be used to play one region/country and/or workforce against another to lower wages and conditions for all (or, equally likely, investment will be moved away from countries with rebellious work forces or radical governments, the resulting slump teaching them a lesson on whose interests count). As the size of business increases, the power of capital over labour and society also increases with the threat of relocation being enough to make workforces accept pay cuts, worsening conditions, "down-sizing" and so on and communities increased pollution, the passing of pro-capital laws with respect to strikes, union rights, etc. (and increased corporate control over politics due to the mobility of capital).

Also, of course, oligopoly results in political power as their economic importance and resources gives them the ability to influence government to introduce favourable policies – either directly, by funding political parties or lobbying politicians, or indirectly by investment decisions (i.e. by pressuring governments by means of capital flight – see section D.2). Thus concentrated economic power is in an ideal position to influence (if not control) political power and ensure state aid (both direct and indirect) to bolster the position of the corporation and allow it to expand further and faster than otherwise. More money can also be ploughed into influencing the media and funding political think-tanks to skew the political climate in their favour. Economic power also extends into the labour market, where restricted labour opportunities as well as negative effects on the work process itself may result. All of which shapes the society we live in; the laws we are subject to; the "evenness" and "levelness" of the "playing field" we face in the market and the ideas dominant in society (see section D.3).

So, with increasing size, comes the increasing power, the power of oligopolies to *"influence the terms under which they choose to operate. Not only do they **react** to the level of wages and the pace of work, they also **act** to determine them … The credible threat of the shift of production and investment will serve to hold down wages and raise the level of effort [required from workers] … [and] may also be able to gain the co-operation of the state in securing the appropriate environment … [for] a redistribution towards profits"* in value/added and national income. [Keith Cowling and Roger Sugden, **Transnational Monopoly Capitalism**, p. 99]

Since the market price of commodities produced by oligopolies is determined by a mark-up over costs, this means that they contribute to inflation as they adapt to increasing costs or falls in their rate of profit by increasing prices. However, this does not mean that oligopolistic capitalism is not subject to slumps. Far from it. Class struggle will influence the share of wages (and so profit share) as wage increases will not be fully offset by price increases – higher prices mean lower demand and there is always the threat of competition from other oligopolies. In addition, class struggle will also have an impact on productivity and the amount of surplus value in the economy as a whole, which places major limitations on the stability of the system. Thus oligopolistic capitalism still has to contend with the effects of social resistance to hierarchy, exploitation and oppression that afflicted the more competitive capitalism of the past.

The distributive effects of oligopoly skews income, thus the degree of monopoly has a major impact on the degree of inequality in household distribution. The flow of wealth to the top helps to skew production away from working class needs (by outbidding others for resources and having firms produce goods for elite markets while others go without). The empirical evidence presented by Keith Cowling *"points to the conclusion that a redistribution from wages to profits will have a depressive impact on consumption"* which may cause depression. [**Op. Cit.**, p. 51] High profits also means that more can be retained by the firm to fund investment (or pay high level managers more salaries or increase dividends, of course). When capital expands faster than labour income over-investment is an increasing problem and aggregate demand cannot keep up to counteract falling profit shares (see section C.7 on more about the business cycle). Moreover, as the capital stock is larger, oligopoly will also have a tendency to deepen the eventual slump, making it last long and harder to recover from.

Looking at oligopoly from an efficiency angle, the existence of super profits from oligopolies means that the higher price within a market allows inefficient firms to continue production. Smaller firms can make average (non-oligopolistic) profits **in spite** of having higher costs, sub-optimal plant and so on. This results in inefficient use of resources as market forces cannot work to eliminate firms which have higher costs than average (one of the key features of capitalism according to its supporters). And, of course, oligopolistic profits skew allocative efficiency as a handful of firms can out-bid all the rest, meaning that resources do not go where they are most needed but where the largest effective demand lies. This impacts on incomes as well, for market power can be used to bolster CEO salaries and perks and so drive up elite income and so skew resources to meeting their demand for luxuries rather than the needs of the general population. Equally, they also allow income to become unrelated to actual work, as can be seen from the sight of CEO's getting massive wages while their corporation's performance falls.

Such large resources available to oligopolistic companies also allows inefficient firms to survive on the market even in the face of competition from other oligopolistic firms. As Richard B. Du Boff points out, efficiency can also be *"impaired when market power so reduces competitive pressures that administrative reforms can be dispensed with. One notorious case was … U.S. Steel [formed in 1901]. Nevertheless, the company was hardly a commercial failure, effective market control endured for decades, and above normal returns were made on the watered stock … Another such case was Ford. The company survived the 1930s only because of cash reserves stocked away in its glory days. 'Ford provides an excellent illustration of the fact that a really large business organisation can withstand a surprising amount of mismanagement.'"* [**Accumulation and Power**, p. 174]

This means that the market power which bigness generates can counteract the costs of size, in terms of the bureaucratic administration it generates and the usual wastes associated with centralised, top-down hierarchical organisation. The local and practical knowledge so necessary to make sensible decision cannot be captured by capitalist hierarchies and, as a result, as bigness increases, so does the inefficiencies in terms of human activity, resource use and information. However, this waste that workplace bureaucracy creates can be hidden in the super-profits which big business generates which means, by confusing profits with efficiency, capitalism helps misallocate resources. This means, as price-setters rather than price-takers, big business can make high profits even when they are inefficient. Profits, in other words, do not reflect "efficiency" but rather how effectively they have secured market power. In other words, the capitalist economy is dominated by a few big firms and so profits, far from being a signal about the appropriate uses of resources, simply indicate the degree of economic power a company has in its industry or market.

Thus Big Business reduces efficiency within an economy on many levels as well as having significant and lasting impact on society's social, economic and political structure.

The effects of the concentration of capital and wealth on society are very important, which is why we are discussing capitalism's tendency to result in big business. The impact of the wealth of the few on the lives of the many is indicated in section D of the FAQ. As shown there, in addition to involving direct authority over employees, capitalism also involves indirect control over communities through the power that stems from wealth.

Thus capitalism is not the free market described by such people as Adam Smith – the level of capital concentration has made a mockery of the ideas of free competition.

C.4.3 What does the existence of Big Business mean for economic theory and wage labour?

Here we indicate the impact of Big Business on economic theory itself and wage labour. In the words of Michal Kalecki, perfect competition is "a most unrealistic assumption" and *"when its actual status of a handy model is forgotten becomes a dangerous myth."* [quoted by Malcolm C. Sawyer, **The Economics of Michal Kalecki**, p. 8] Unfortunately mainstream capitalist economics is **built** on this myth. Ironically, it was against a *"background [of rising Big Business in the 1890s] that the grip of marginal economics, an imaginary world of many small firms … was consolidated in the economics profession."* Thus, *"[a]lmost from its conception, the theoretical postulates of marginal economics concerning the nature of companies [and of markets, we must add] have been a travesty of reality."* [Paul Ormerod, **Op. Cit.**, pp. 55-56]

This can be seen from the fact that mainstream economics has, for most of its history, effectively ignored the fact of oligopoly for most of its history. Instead, economics has refined the model of "perfect competition" (which cannot exist and is rarely, if ever, approximated) and developed an analysis of monopoly (which is also rare). Significantly, an economist could still note in 1984 that *"traditional economy theory … offers very little indeed by way of explanation of oligopolistic behaviour"* in spite (or, perhaps, **because**) it was "the most important market situation today" (as "instances of monopoly" are "as difficult to find as perfect competition."). In other words, capitalist economics does "not know how to explain the most important part of a modern industrial economy." [Peter Donaldson, **Economics of the Real World** p. 141, p. 140 and p. 142]

Over two decades later, the situation had not changed. For example, one leading introduction to economics notes "the prevalence of oligopoly" and admits it "is far more common than either perfect competition or monopoly." However, "the analysis of oligopoly turns out to present some puzzles for which they is no easy solution" as "the analysis of oligopoly is far more difficult and messy than that of perfect competition." Why? "When we try to analyse oligopoly, the economists usual way of thinking – asking how self-interested individuals would behave, then analysing their interaction – does not work as well as we might hope." Rest assured, though, there is no need to reconsider the "usual way" of economic analysis to allow it to analyse something as marginal as the most common market form for, by luck, "the industry behaves 'almost' as if it were perfectly competitive." [Paul Krugman and Robin Wells, **Economics**, p. 383, p. 365 and p. 383] Which is handy, to say the least.

Given that oligopoly has marked capitalist economics since, at least, the 1880s it shows how little concerned with reality mainstream economics is. In other words, neoclassicalism was redundant when it was first formulated (if four or five large firms are responsible for most of the output of an industry, avoidance of price competition becomes almost automatic and the notion that all firms are price takers is an obvious falsehood). That mainstream economists were not interested in including such facts into their models shows the ideological nature of the "science" (see section C.1 for more discussion of the non-scientific nature of mainstream economics).

This does not mean that reality has been totally forgotten. Some work was conducted on "imperfect competition" in the 1930s independently by two economists (Edward Chamberlin and Joan Robinson) but these were exceptions to the rule and even these models were very much in the traditional analytical framework, i.e. were still rooted in the assumptions and static world of neo-classical economics. These models assume that there are many producers and many consumers in a given market and that there are no barriers to entry and exit, that is, the characteristics of a monopolistically competitive market are almost exactly the same as in perfect competition, with the exception of heterogeneous products. This meant that monopolistic competition involves a great deal of non-price competition. This caused Robinson to later distance herself from her own work and look for more accurate (non-neoclassical) ways to analyse an economy.

As noted, neo-classical economics **does** have a theory on "monopoly," a situation (like perfect competition) which rarely exists. Ignoring that minor point, it is as deeply flawed as the rest of that ideology. It argues that "monopoly" is bad because it produces a lower output for a higher price. Unlike perfect competition, a monopolist can set a price above marginal cost and so exploit consumers by over pricing. In contrast, perfectly competitive markets force their members to set price to be equal to marginal cost. As it is rooted in the assumptions we exposed as nonsense as section C.1, this neo-classical theory on free competition and monopoly is similarly invalid. As Steve Keen notes, there is "no substance" to the neo-classical "critique of monopolies" as it "erroneously assumes that the perfectly competitive firm faces a horizontal demand curve," which is impossible given a downward sloping market demand curve. This means that "the individual firm and the market level aspects of perfect competition are inconsistent" and the apparent benefits of competition in the model are derived from "a mathematical error of confusing a very small quantity with zero." While "there are plenty of good reasons to be wary of monopolies … economic theory does not provide any of them." [**Debunking Economics**, p. 108, p. 101, p. 99, p. 98 and p. 107]

This is not to say that economists have ignored oligopoly. Some have busied themselves providing rationales by which to defend it, rooted in the assumption that "the market can do it all, and that regulation and antitrust actions are misconceived. First, theorists showed that efficiency gains from mergers might reduce prices even more than monopoly power would cause them to rise. Economists also stressed 'entry,' claiming that if mergers did not improve efficiency any price increases would be wiped out eventually by new companies entering the industry. Entry is also the heart of the theory of 'contestable markets,' developed by economic consultants to AT&T, who argued that the ease of entry in cases where resources (trucks, aircraft) can be shifted quickly at low cost, makes for effective competition." By pure co-incidence, AT&T had hired economic consultants as part of their hundreds of millions of dollars antitrust defences, in fact some 30 economists from five leading economics departments during the 1970s and early 1980s. [Edward S. Herman, "The Threat From Mergers: Can Antitrust Make a Difference?", **Dollars and Sense**, no. 217, May/June 1998]

Needless to say, these new "theories" are rooted in the same assumptions of neo-classical economists and, as such, are based on notions we have already debunked. As Herman notes, they "suffer from over-simplification, a strong infusion of ideology, and lack of empirical support." He notes that mergers "often are motivated by factors other than enhancing efficiency – such as the desire for monopoly power, empire building, cutting taxes, improving stock values, and even as a cover for poor management (such as when the badly-run U.S. Steel bought control of Marathon Oil)." The conclusion of these models is usually, by way of co-incidence, that an oligopolistic market acts "as if" it were a perfectly competitive one and so we need not be concerned by rising market dominance by a few firms. Much work by the ideological supporters of "free market" capitalism is based on this premise, namely that reality works "as if" it reflected the model (rather than vice versa, in a real science) and, consequently, market power is nothing to be concerned about (that many of these "think tanks" and university places happen to be funded by the super-profits generated by big business is, of course, purely a co-incidence as these "scientists" act "as if" they were neutrally funded). In Herman's words: "Despite their inadequacies, the new apologetic theories have profoundly affected policy, because they provide an intellectual rationale for the agenda of the powerful." [**Op. Cit.**]

It may be argued (and it has) that the lack of interest in analysing a real economy by economists is because oligopolistic competition is hard to model mathematically. Perhaps, but this simply shows the limitations of neo-classical economics and if the tool used for a task are unsuitable, surely you should change the tool rather than (effectively) ignore the work that needs to be done. Sadly, most economists have favoured producing mathematical models which can say a lot about theory but very little about reality. That economics can become much broader and more relevant is always a possibility, but to do so would mean to take into account an unpleasant reality marked by market power, class, hierarchy and inequality rather than logical deductions derived from Robinson Crusoe. While the latter can produce mathematical models to reach the conclusions that the market is already doing a good job (or, at best, there are some imperfections which can be fixed by minor state interventions), the former cannot. Which, of course, is makes it hardly a surprise that neo-classical economists favour it so (particularly given the origins, history and role of that particular branch of economics).

This means that economics is based on a model which assumes that firms have no impact on the markets they operate it. This assumption is violated in most real markets and so the neo-classical conclusions regarding the outcomes of competition cannot be supported. That the assumptions of economic ideology so contradicts reality also has important considerations on the "voluntary" nature of wage labour. If the competitive model assumed by neo-classical economics held we would see a wide range of ownership types (including co-operatives, extensive self-employment and workers hiring capital) as there would be no "barriers of entry" associated with firm control. This is not the case – workers hiring capital is non-existent and self-employment and co-operatives are marginal. The dominant control form is capital hiring labour (wage slavery).

With a model based upon "perfect competition," supporters of capitalism could build a case that wage labour is a voluntary choice – after all, workers (in such a market) could hire capital or form co-operatives relatively easily. But the **reality** of the "free" market is such that this model does not exist – and as an assumption, it is seriously misleading. If we take into account the actuality of the capitalist economy, we soon have to realise that oligopoly is the dominant form of market and that the capitalist economy, by its very nature, restricts the options available to workers – which makes the notion that wage labour is a "voluntary" choice untenable.

If the economy is so structured as to make entry into markets difficult and survival dependent on accumulating capital, then these barriers are just as effective as government decrees. If small businesses are squeezed by oligopolies then chances of failure are increased (and so off-putting to workers with few resources) and if income inequality is large, then workers will find it very hard to find the collateral required to borrow capital and start their own co-operatives. Thus, looking at the **reality** of capitalism (as opposed to the textbooks) it is clear that the existence of oligopoly helps to maintain wage labour by restricting the options available on the "free market" for working people. Chomsky states the obvious:

> "If you had equality of power, you could talk about freedom, but when all the power is concentrated in one place, then freedom's a joke. People talk about a 'free market.' Sure. You and I are perfectly free to set up an automobile company and compete with General Motors. Nobody's stopping us. That freedom is meaningless … It's just that power happens to be organised so that only

certain options are available. Within that limited range of options, those who have the power say, 'Let's have freedom.' That's a very skewed form of freedom. The principle is right. How freedom works depends on what the social structures are. If the freedoms are such that the only choices you have objectively are to conform to one or another system of power, there's no freedom."
[**Language and Politics**, pp. 641-2]

As we noted in section C.4, those with little capital are reduced to markets with low set-up costs and low concentration. Thus, claim the supporters of capitalism, workers still have a choice. However, this choice is (as we have indicated) somewhat limited by the existence of oligopolistic markets – so limited, in fact, that less than 10% of the working population are self-employed workers. Moreover, it is claimed, technological forces may work to increase the number of markets that require low set-up costs (the computing market is often pointed to as an example). However, similar predictions were made over 100 years ago when the electric motor began to replace the steam engine in factories. "The new technologies [of the 1870s] may have been compatible with small production units and decentralised operations … That … expectation was not fulfilled." [Richard B. Du Boff, **Op. Cit.**, p. 65] From the history of capitalism, we imagine that markets associated with new technologies will go the same way (and the evidence seems to support this).

The reality of capitalist development is that even **if** workers invested in new markets, one that require low set-up costs, the dynamic of the system is such that over time these markets will also become dominated by a few big firms. Moreover, to survive in an oligopolised economy small co-operatives will be under pressure to hire wage labour and otherwise act as capitalist concerns. Therefore, even if we ignore the massive state intervention which created capitalism in the first place (see section F.8), the dynamics of the system are such that relations of domination and oppression will always be associated with it – they cannot be "competed" away as the actions of competition creates and re-enforces them (also see sections J.5.11 and J.5.12 on the barriers capitalism places on co-operatives and self-management even though they are more efficient).

So the effects of the concentration of capital on the options open to us are great and very important. The existence of Big Business has a direct impact on the "voluntary" nature of wage labour as it produces very effective "barriers of entry" for alternative modes of production. The resultant pressures big business place on small firms also reduces the viability of co-operatives and self-employment to survive **as** co-operatives and non-employers of wage labour, effectively marginalising them as true alternatives. Moreover, even in new markets the dynamics of capitalism are such that **new** barriers are created all the time, again reducing our options.

Overall, the **reality** of capitalism is such that the equality of opportunity implied in models of "perfect competition" is lacking. And without such equality, wage labour cannot be said to be a "voluntary" choice between available options – the options available have been skewed so far in one direction that the other alternatives have been marginalised.

C.5
Why does Big Business get a bigger slice of profits?

As described in the last section, due to the nature of the capitalist market, large firms soon come to dominate. Once a few large companies dominate a particular market, they form an oligopoly from which a large number of competitors have effectively been excluded, thus reducing competitive pressures. In this situation there is a tendency for prices to rise above what would be the "market" level, as the oligopolistic producers do not face the potential of new capital entering "their" market (due to the relatively high capital costs and other entry/movement barriers).

The domination of a market by a few big firms results in exploitation, but of a different kind than that rooted in production. Capitalism is based on the extraction of surplus value of workers in the production process. When a market is marked by oligopoly, this exploitation is supplemented by the exploitation of **consumers** who are charged higher prices than would be the case in a more competitive market. This form of competition results in Big Business having an "unfair" slice of available profits as oligopolistic profits are *"created at the expense of individual capitals still caught up in competition."* [Paul Mattick, **Economics, Politics, and the Age of Inflation**, p. 38]

To understand why big business gets a bigger slice of the economic pie, we need to look at what neo-classical economics tries to avoid, namely production and market power. Mainstream economics views capitalism as a mode of distribution (the market), not a mode of production. Rather than a world of free and equal exchanges, capitalism is marked by hierarchy, inequality and power. This reality explains what regulates market prices and the impact of big business. In the long term, market price cannot be viewed independently of production. As David Ricardo put it:

> *"It is the cost of production which must ultimately regulate the price of commodities, and not, as has been often said, the proportion between the supply and demand: the proportion between supply and demand may, indeed, for a time, affect the market value of a commodity, until it is supplied in greater or less abundance, according as the demand may have increased or diminished; but this effect will be only of temporary duration."* [**The Principles of Political Economy and Taxation**, p. 260]

Market prices, in this (classical) analysis, are the prices that prevail at any given time on the market (and change due to transient and random variations). Natural prices are the cost of production and act as centres of gravitational attraction for market prices. Over time, market prices tend towards natural prices but are considered unlikely to exactly meet them. Natural prices can only change due to changes in the productive process (for example, by introducing new, more productive, machinery and/or by decreasing the wages of the workforce relative to its output). Surplus value (the difference between market and natural prices) are the key to understanding how supply changes to meet demand. This produces the dynamic of market forces:

> *"Let us suppose that all commodities are at their natural price, and consequently that the profits of capital in all employments are exactly at the same rate … Suppose now that a change of fashion should increase the demand for silks, and lessen that for woollens; their natural price, the quantity of labour necessary to their production, would continue unaltered, but the market price of silks would rise, and that of woollens would fall; and consequently the profits of the silk manufacturer would be above, whilst those of the woollen manufacturer would be below, the general and adjusted rate of profits … This increased demand for silks would however soon be supplied, by the transference of capital and labour from the woollen to the silk manufacture; when the market prices of silks and woollens would again approach their natural prices, and then the usual profits would be obtained by the respective manufacturers of those commodities. It is then the desire, which every capitalist has, of diverting his funds from a less to a more profitable employment, that prevents the market price of commodities from continuing for any length of time either much above, or much below their natural price."* [**Op. Cit.**, p. 50]

This means that *"capital moves from relatively stagnating into rapidly developing industries … The extra profit, in excess of the average profit, won at a given price level disappears again, however, with the influx of capital from profit-poor into profit-rich industries,"* so increasing supply and reducing prices, and thus profits. In other words, *"market relations are governed by the production relations."* [Paul Mattick, **Economic Crisis and Crisis Theory**, p. 49 and p. 51]

In a developed capitalist economy it is not as simple as this – there are various "average" profits depending on what Michal Kalecki termed the ***"degree of monopoly"*** within a market. This theory *"indicates that profits arise from monopoly power, and hence profits accrue to firms with more monopoly power … A rise in the degree of monopoly caused by the growth of large firms would result in the shift of profits from small business to big business."* [Malcolm C. Sawyer, **The Economics of Michal Kalecki**, p. 36] This means that a market with a high "degree of monopoly" will have a few firms in it with higher than average profit levels (or rate of return) compared to the smaller firms in the sector or to those in more competitive markets.

The "degree of monopoly" reflects such factors as level of market concentration and power, market share, extent of advertising, barriers to entry/movement, collusion and so on. The higher these factors, the higher the degree of monopoly and the higher the mark-up of prices over costs (and so the share of profits in value added). Our approach to this issue is similar to Kalecki's in many ways although we stress that the degree of monopoly affects how profits are distributed **between** firms, **not** how they are created in the first place (which come, as argued in section C.2, from the *"unpaid labour of the poor"* – to use Kropotkin's words).

There is substantial evidence to support such a theory. J.S Bain in **Barriers in New Competition** noted that in industries where the level of seller concentration was very high and where entry barriers were also substantial, profit rates were higher than average. Research has tended to confirm Bain's findings. Keith Cowling summarises this later evidence:

> "[A]s far as the USA is concerned ... there are grounds for believing that a significant, but not very strong, relationship exists between profitability and concentration ... [along with] a significant relationship between advertising and profitability [an important factor in a market's "degree of monopoly"] ... [Moreover w]here the estimation is restricted to an appropriate cross-section [of industry] ... both concentration and advertising appeared significant [for the UK]. By focusing on the impact of changes in concentration overtime ... [we are] able to circumvent the major problems posed by the lack of appropriate estimates of price elasticities of demand ... [to find] a significant and positive concentration effect ... It seems reasonable to conclude on the basis of evidence for both the USA and UK that there is a significant relationship between concentration and price-cost margins." [**Monopoly Capitalism**, pp. 109-110]

We must note that the price-cost margin variable typically used in these studies subtracts the wage and **salary** bill from the value added in production. This would have a tendency to reduce the margin as it does not take into account that most management salaries (particularly those at the top of the hierarchy) are more akin to profits than costs (and so should **not** be subtracted from value added). Also, as many markets are regionalised (particularly in the USA) nation-wide analysis may downplay the level of concentration existing in a given market.

The argument is not that big business charges "high prices" in respect to smaller competitors but rather they charge high prices in comparison to their costs. This means that a corporation can sell at the standard market price (or even undercut the prices of small business) and still make higher profits than average. In other words, market power ensures that prices do not fall to cost. Moreover, market power ensures that "costs" are often inflicted on others as big business uses its economic clout to externalise costs onto suppliers and its workers. For example, this means that farmers and other small producers will agree to lower prices for goods when supplying large supermarkets while the employees have to put up with lower wages and benefits (which extend through the market, creating lower wages and fewer jobs for retail workers in the surrounding area). Possibly, lower prices can be attributed to lower quality products (which workers are forced to buy in order to make their lower wages go further).

This means that large firms can maintain their prices and profits above "normal" (competitive) levels without the assistance of government simply due to their size and market power (and let us not forget the important fact that Big Business rose during the period in which capitalism was closest to "laissez faire" and the size and activity of the state was small). As much of mainstream economics is based on the idea of "perfect competition" (and the related concept that the free market is an efficient allocater of resources when it approximates this condition) it is clear that such a finding cuts to the heart of claims that capitalism is a system based upon equal opportunity, freedom and justice. The existence of Big Business and the impact it has on the rest of the economy and society at large exposes capitalist economics as a house built on sand.

Another side effect of oligopoly is that the number of mergers will tend to increase in the run up to a slump. Just as credit is expanded in an attempt to hold off the crisis (see section C.8), so firms will merge in an attempt to increase their market power and so improve their profit margins by increasing their mark-up over costs. As the rate of profit levels off and falls, mergers are an attempt to raise profits by increasing the degree of monopoly in the market/economy. However, this is a short term solution and can only postpone, but not stop, the crisis as its roots lie in production, **not** the market (see section C.7) – there is only so much surplus value around and the capital stock cannot be wished away. Once the slump occurs, a period of cut-throat competition will start and then, slowly, the process of concentration will start again (as weak firms go under, successful firms increase their market share and capital stock and so on).

The development of oligopolies within capitalism thus causes a redistribution of profits away from small capitalists to Big Business (i.e. small businesses are squeezed by big ones due to the latter's market power and size). Moreover, the existence of oligopoly can and does result in increased costs faced by Big Business being passed on in the form of price increases, which can force other companies, in unrelated markets, to raise **their** prices in order to realise sufficient profits. Therefore, oligopoly has a tendency to create price increases across the market as a whole and can thus be inflationary.

For these (and other) reasons many small businessmen and members of the middle-class wind up hating Big Business (while trying to replace them!) and embracing ideologies which promise to wipe them out. Hence we see that both ideologies of the "radical" middle-class – Libertarianism and fascism – attack Big Business, either as "the socialism of Big Business" targeted by Libertarianism or the "International Plutocracy" by Fascism. As Peter Sabatini notes:

> "At the turn of the century, local entrepreneurial (proprietorship/partnership) business [in the USA] was overshadowed in short order by transnational corporate capitalism. ... The various strata comprising the capitalist class responded differentially to these transpiring events as a function of their respective position of benefit. Small business that remained as such came to greatly resent the economic advantage corporate capitalism secured to itself, and the sweeping changes the latter imposed on the presumed ground rules of bourgeois competition. Nevertheless, because capitalism is liberalism's raison d'etre, small business operators had little choice but to blame the state for their financial woes, otherwise they moved themselves to another ideological camp (anti-capitalism). Hence, the enlarged state was imputed as the primary cause for capitalism's 'aberration' into its monopoly form, and thus it became the scapegoat for small business complaint." [**Libertarianism: Bogus Anarchy**]

However, despite the complaints of small capitalists, the tendency of markets to become dominated by a few big firms is an obvious side-effect of capitalism itself. *"If the home of 'Big Business' was once the public utilities and manufacturing it now seems to be equally comfortable in any environment."* [M.A. Utton, **Op. Cit.**, p. 29] This is because in their drive to expand (which they must do in order to survive), capitalists invest in new machinery and plants in order to reduce production costs and so increase profits. Hence a successful capitalist firm will grow in size over time in order to squeeze out competitors and, in so doing, it naturally creates formidable natural barriers to competition – excluding all but other large firms from undermining its market position.

C.5.1 Aren't the super-profits of Big Business due to its higher efficiency?

Obviously the analysis of Big Business profitability presented in section C.5 is denied by supporters of capitalism. H. Demsetz of the pro-"free" market "Chicago School" of economists (which echoes the "Austrian" school's position that whatever happens on a free market is for the best) argues that **efficiency** (not degree of monopoly) is the cause of the super-profits for Big Business. His argument is that if oligopolistic profits are due to high levels of concentration, then the big firms in an industry will not be able to stop smaller ones reaping the benefits of this in the form of higher profits. So if concentration leads to high profits (due, mostly, to collusion between the dominant firms) then smaller firms in the same industry should benefit too.

However, his argument is flawed as it is not the case that oligopolies practice overt collusion. The barriers to entry/mobility are such that the dominant firms in a oligopolistic market do not have to compete by price and their market power allows a mark-up over costs which market forces cannot undermine. As their only possible competitors are similarly large firms, collusion is not required as these firms have no interest in reducing the mark-up they share and so they "compete" over market share by non-price methods such as advertising (advertising, as well as being a barrier to entry, reduces price competition and increases mark-up).

In his study, Demsetz notes that while there is a positive correlation between profit rate and market concentration, smaller firms in the oligarchic market are **not** more profitable than their counterparts in other markets. [M.A. Utton, **The Political Economy of Big Business**, p. 98] From this Demsetz concludes that oligopoly is irrelevant and that the efficiency of increased size is the source of excess profits. But this misses the point – smaller firms in concentrated industries will have a similar profitability to firms of similar size in less concentrated markets, **not** higher profitability. The existence of super profits across **all** the firms in a given industry would attract firms to that market, so reducing profits. However, because profitability is associated with the large firms in the market the barriers of entry/movement associated with Big Business stops this process happening. **If** small firms were as profitable, then entry would be easier and so the "degree of monopoly" would be low and

we would see an influx of smaller firms.

While it is true that bigger firms may gain advantages associated with economies of scale the question surely is, what stops the smaller firms investing and increasing the size of their companies in order to reap economies of scale within and between workplaces? What is stopping market forces eroding super-profits by capital moving into the industry and increasing the number of firms, and so increasing supply? If barriers exist to stop this process occurring, then concentration, market power and other barriers to entry/ movement (not efficiency) is the issue. Competition is a **process,** not a state, and this indicates that "efficiency" is not the source of oligopolistic profits (indeed, what creates the apparent "efficiency" of big firms is likely to be the barriers to market forces which add to the mark-up!).

It is important to recognise what is "small" and "big" is dependent on the industry in question and so size advantages obviously differ from industry to industry. The optimum size of plant may be large in some sectors but relatively small in others (some workplaces have to be of a certain size in order to be technically efficient in a given market). However, this relates to technical efficiency, rather than overall "efficiency" associated with a firm. This means that technological issues cannot, by themselves, explain the size of modern corporations. Technology may, at best, explain the increase in size of the factory, but it does not explain why the modern large firm comprises multiple factories. In other words, the company, the **administrative** unit, is usually much larger than the workplace, the **production** unit. The reasons for this lie in the way in which production technologies interacted with economic institutions and market power.

It seems likely that large firms gather "economies of scale" due to the size of the firm, not plant, as well as from the level of concentration within an industry: *"Considerable evidence indicates that economies of scale [at plant level] ... do not account for the high concentration levels in U.S. industry"* [Richard B. Du Boff, **Accumulation and Power**, p. 174] Further, *"the explanation for the enormous growth in aggregate concentration must be found in factors other than economies of scale at plant level."* [M.A. Utton, **Op. Cit.**, p. 44] Co-ordination of individual plants by the visible hand of management seems to play a key role in creating and maintaining dominant positions within a market. And, of course, these structures are costly to create and maintain as well as taking time to build up. Thus the size of the firm, with the economies of scale **beyond** the workplace associated with the economic power this produces within the market creates formidable barriers to entry/movement.

So an important factor influencing the profitability of Big Business is the clout that market power provides. This comes in two main forms – horizontal and vertical controls:

> *"Horizontal controls allow oligopolies to control necessary steps in an economic process from material supplies to processing, manufacturing, transportation and distribution. Oligopolies ... [control] more of the highest quality and most accessible supplies than they intend to market immediately ... competitors are left with lower quality or more expensive supplies ... [It is also] based*

on exclusive possession of technologies, patents and franchises as well as on excess productive capacity ...

"Vertical controls substitute administrative command for exchange between steps of economic processes. The largest oligopolies procure materials from their own subsidiaries, process and manufacture these in their own refineries, mills and factories, transport their own goods and then market these through their own distribution and sales network." [Allan Engler, **Apostles of Greed**, p. 51]

Moreover, large firms reduce their costs due to their privileged access to credit and resources. Both credit and advertising show economies of scale, meaning that as the size of loans and advertising increase, costs go down. In the case of finance, interest rates are usually cheaper for big firms than small ones and while *"firms of all sizes find most [about 70% between 1970 and 1984] of their investments without having to resort to [financial] markets or banks"* size does have an impact on the *"importance of banks as a source of finance"*: *"Firms with assets under $100 million relied on banks for around 70% of their long-term debt ... those with assets from $250 million to $1 billion, 41%; and those with over $1 billion in assets, 15%."* [Doug Henwood, **Wall Street**, p. 75] Also dominant firms can get better deals with independent suppliers and distributors due to their market clout and their large demand for goods/inputs, also reducing their costs.

This means that oligopolies are more "efficient" (i.e. have higher profits) than smaller firms due to the benefits associated with their market power rather than vice versa. Concentration (and firm size) leads to "economies of scale" which smaller firms in the same market cannot gain access to. Hence the claim that any positive association between concentration and profit rates is simply recording the fact that the largest firms tend to be most efficient, and hence more profitable, is wrong. In addition, *"Demsetz's findings have been questioned by non-Chicago [school] critics"* due to the inappropriateness of the evidence used as well as some of his analysis techniques. Overall, *"the empirical work gives limited support"* to this "free-market" explanation of oligopolistic profits and instead suggest market power plays the key role. [William L. Baldwin, **Market Power, Competition and Anti-Trust Policy**, p. 310, p. 315]

Unsurprisingly we find that the *"bigger the corporation in size of assets or the larger its market share, the higher its rate of profit: these findings confirm the advantages of market power ... Furthermore, 'large firms in concentrated industries earn systematically higher profits than do all other firms, about 30 percent more ... on average,' and there is less variation in profit rates too."* Thus, concentration, not efficiency, is the key to profitability, with those factors what create "efficiency" themselves being very effective barriers to entry which helps maintain the "degree of monopoly" (and so mark-up and profits for the dominant firms) in a market. Oligopolies have varying degrees of administrative efficiency and market power, all of which consolidate its position. Thus the *"barriers to entry posed by decreasing unit costs of production and distribution and by national organisations of managers, buyers, salesmen, and service personnel made oligopoly advantages cumulative – and were as global in their implications as they were national."* [Richard B. Du Boff, **Accumulation and Power**, p. 175 and p. 150]

This explains why capitalists always seek to acquire monopoly power, to destroy the assumptions of neo-classical economics, so they can influence the price, quantity and quality of the product. It also ensures that in the real world there are, unlike the models of mainstream economics, entrenched economic forces and why there is little equal opportunity. Why, in other words, the market in most sectors is an oligopoly.

This recent research confirms Kropotkin's analysis of capitalism found in his classic work **Fields, Factories and Workshops**. Kropotkin, after extensive investigation of the actual situation within the economy, argued that *"it is not the superiority of the **technical** organisation of the trade in a factory, nor the economies realised on the prime-mover, which militate against the small industry ... but the more advantageous conditions for **selling** the produce and for **buying** the raw produce which are at the disposal of big concerns."* Since the *"manufacture being a strictly private enterprise, its owners find it advantageous to have all the branches of a given industry under their own management: they thus cumulate the profits of the successful transformations of the raw material ... [and soon] the owner finds his advantage in being able to hold the command of the market. But from a **technical** point of view the advantages of such an accumulation are trifling and often doubtful."* He sums up by stating that *"[t]his is why the 'concentration' so much spoken of is often nothing but an amalgamation of capitalists for the purpose of **dominating the market,** not for cheapening the technical process."* [**Fields, Factories and Workshops Tomorrow**, p. 147, p. 153 and p. 154]

It should be stressed that Kropotkin, like other anarchists, recognised that technical efficiencies differed from industry to industry and so the optimum size of plant may be large in some sectors but relatively small in others. As such, he did not fetishise "smallness" as some Marxists assert (see section H.2.3). Rather, Kropotkin was keenly aware that capitalism operated on principles which submerged technical efficiency by the price mechanism which, in turn, was submerged by economic power. While not denying that "economies of scale" existed, Kropotkin recognised that what counts as "efficient" under capitalism is specific to that system. Thus whatever increases profits is "efficient" under capitalism, whether it is using market power to drive down costs (credit, raw materials or labour) or internalising profits by building suppliers. Under capitalism profit is used as a (misleading) alternative for efficiency (influenced, as it is, by market power) and this distorts the size of firms/workplaces. In a sane society, one based on economic freedom, workplaces would be re-organised to take into account technical efficiency and the needs of the people who used them rather than what maximises the profits and power of the few.

All this means is that the "degree of monopoly" within an industry helps determine the distribution of profits within an economy, with some of the surplus value "created" by other companies being realised by Big Business. Hence, the oligopolies reduce the pool of profits available to other companies in more competitive markets by charging consumers higher prices than a more competitive market would. As high capital costs reduce mobility within and exclude most competitors from entering the oligopolistic market, it means that only if the oligopolies raise their prices **too** high can real competition become possible (i.e. profitable) again and so *"it should not be concluded that oligopolies can set prices as high as they like. If prices are set too high, dominant firms from other industries would be tempted to move in and gain a share of the exceptional returns. Small producers – using more expensive materials or out-dated technologies – would be able to increase their share of the market and make the competitive rate of profit or better."* [Allan Engler, **Op. Cit.**, p. 53]

Big Business, therefore, receives a larger share of the available surplus value in the economy, due to its size advantage and market power, not due to "higher efficiency".

C.6
Can market dominance by Big Business change?

Capital concentration, of course, does not mean that in a given market, dominance will continue forever by the same firms, no matter what. However, the fact that the companies that dominate a market can change over time is no great cause for joy (no matter what supporters of free market capitalism claim). This is because when market dominance changes between companies all it means is that **old** Big Business is replaced by **new** Big Business:

> *"Once oligopoly emerges in an industry, one should not assume that sustained competitive advantage will be maintained forever … once achieved in any given product market, oligopoly creates barriers to entry that can be overcome only by the development of even more powerful forms of business organisation that can plan and co-ordinate even more complex specialised divisions of labour."* [William Lazonick, **Business Organisation and the Myth of the Market Economy**, p. 173]

The assumption that the "degree of monopoly" will rise over time is an obvious one to make and, in general, the history of capitalism has tended to support doing so. While periods of rising concentration will be interspersed with periods of constant or falling levels, the general trend will be upwards (we would expect the degree of monopoly to remain the same or fall during booms and rise to new levels in slumps). Yet even if the "degree of monopoly" falls or new competitors replace old ones, it is hardly a great improvement as changing the company hardly changes the impact of capital concentration or Big Business on the economy. While the faces may change, the system itself remains the same. As such, it makes little real difference if, for a time, a market is dominated by 6 large firms rather than, say, 4. While the **relative** level of barriers may fall, the **absolute** level may increase and so restrict competition to established big business (either national or foreign) and it is the absolute level which maintains the class monopoly of capital over labour.

Nor should we expect the "degree of monopoly" to constantly increase, there will be cycles of expansion and contraction in line with the age of the market and the business cycle. It is obvious that at the start of a specific market, there will be a relative high "degree of monopoly" as a few pioneering create a new industry. Then the level of concentration will fall as competitors entry the market. Over time, the numbers of firms will drop due to failure and mergers. This process is accelerated during booms and slumps. In the boom, more companies feel able to try setting up or expanding in a specific market, so driving the "degree of monopoly" down. However, in the slump the level of concentration will rise as more and more firms go to the wall or try merge to survive (for example, there were 100 car producers in the USA in 1929, ten years later there were only three). So our basic point is **not** dependent on any specific tendency of the degree of monopoly. It can fall somewhat as, say, five large firms come to dominate a market rather than, say, three over a period of a few years. The fact remains that barriers to competition remain strong and deny any claims that any real economy reflects the "perfect competition" of the textbooks.

So even in a in a well-developed market, one with a high degree of monopoly (i.e. high market concentration and capital costs that create barriers to entry into it), there can be decreases as well as increases in the level of concentration. However, how this happens is significant. New companies can usually only enter under four conditions:

(1)   They have enough capital available to them to pay for set-up costs and any initial losses. This can come from two main sources, from other parts of their company (e.g. Virgin going into the cola business) or large firms from other areas/nations enter the market. The former is part of the diversification process associated with Big Business and the second is the globalisation of markets resulting from pressures on national oligopolies (see section C.4). Both of which increases competition within a given market for a period as the number of firms in its oligopolistic sector has increased. Over time, however, market forces will result in mergers and growth, increasing the degree of monopoly again.

(2)   They get state aid to protect them against foreign competition until such time as they can compete with established firms and, critically, expand into foreign markets: *"Historically,"* notes Lazonick, *"political strategies to develop national economies have provided critical protection and support to overcome … barriers to entry."* [**Op. Cit.**, p. 87] An obvious example of this process is, say, the 19th century US economy or, more recently the South East Asian "Tiger" economies (these having *"an intense and almost unequivocal commitment on the part of government to build up the international competitiveness of domestic industry"* by creating *"policies and organisations for governing the market."* [Robert Wade, **Governing the Market**, p. 7]).

(3)   Demand exceeds supply, resulting in a profit level which tempts other big companies into the market or gives smaller firms already there excess profits, allowing them to expand. Demand still plays a limiting role in even the most oligopolistic market (but this process hardly decreases barriers to entry/ mobility or oligopolistic tendencies in the long run).

(4)   The dominant companies raise their prices too high or become complacent and make mistakes, so allowing other big

firms to undermine their position in a market (and, sometimes, allow smaller companies to expand and do the same). For example, many large US oligopolies in the 1970s came under pressure from Japanese oligopolies because of this. However, as noted in section C.4.2, these declining oligopolies can see their market control last for decades and the resulting market will still be dominated by oligopolies (as big firms are generally replaced by similar sized, or bigger, ones).

Usually some or all of these processes are at work at once and some can have contradictory results. Take, for example, the rise of "globalisation" and its impact on the "degree of monopoly" in a given national market. On the national level, "degree of monopoly" may fall as foreign companies invade a given market, particularly one where the national producers are in decline (which has happened to a small degree in UK manufacturing in the 1990s, for example). However, on the international level the degree of concentration may well have risen as only a few companies can actually compete on a global level. Similarly, while the "degree of monopoly" within a specific national market may fall, the balance of (economic) power within the economy may shift towards capital and so place labour in a weaker position to advance its claims (this has, undoubtedly, been the case with "globalisation" – see section D.5.3).

Let us consider the US steel industry as an example. The 1980s saw the rise of the so-called "mini-mills" with lower capital costs. The mini-mills, a new industry segment, developed only after the US steel industry had gone into decline due to Japanese competition. The creation of Nippon Steel, matching the size of US steel companies, was a key factor in the rise of the Japanese steel industry, which invested heavily in modern technology to increase steel output by 2,216% in 30 years (5.3 million tons in 1950 to 122.8 million by 1980). By the mid 1980s, the mini-mills and imports each had a quarter of the US market, with many previously steel-based companies diversifying into new markets.

Only by investing $9 billion to increase technological competitiveness, cutting workers wages to increase labour productivity, getting relief from stringent pollution control laws and (very importantly) the US government restricting imports to a quarter of the total home market could the US steel industry survive. The fall in the value of the dollar also helped by making imports more expensive. In addition, US steel firms became increasingly linked with their Japanese "rivals," resulting in increased centralisation (and so concentration) of capital.

Therefore, only because competition from foreign capital created space in a previously dominated market, driving established capital out, combined with state intervention to protect and aid home producers, was a new segment of the industry able to get a foothold in the local market. With many established companies closing down and moving to other markets, and once the value of the dollar fell which forced import prices up and state intervention reduced foreign competition, the mini-mills were in an excellent position to increase US market share. It should also be noted that this period in the US steel industry was marked by increased "co-operation" between US and Japanese companies, with larger companies the outcome. This meant, in the case of the mini-mills, that the cycle of capital formation and concentration would start again, with bigger companies driving out the smaller ones through competition.

Nor should we assume that an oligopolistic markets mean the end of all small businesses. Far from it. Not only do small firms continue to exist, big business itself may generate same scale industry around it (in the form of suppliers or as providers of services to its workers). We are not arguing that small businesses do not exist, but rather than their impact is limited compared to the giants of the business world. In fact, within an oligopolistic market, existing small firms always present a problem as some might try to grow beyond their established niches. However, the dominant firms will often simply purchase the smaller one firm, use its established relationships with customers or suppliers to limit its activities or stand temporary losses and so cut its prices below the cost of production until it runs competitors out of business or establishes its price leadership, before raising prices again.

As such, our basic point is **not** dependent on any specific tendency of the degree of monopoly. It can fall somewhat as, say, six large firms come to dominate a market rather than, say, four. The fact remains that barriers to competition remain strong and deny any claims that any real economy reflects the "perfect competition" of the textbooks. So, while the actual companies involved may change over time, the economy as a whole will always be marked by Big Business due to the nature of capitalism. That's the way capitalism works – profits for the few at the expense of the many.

C.7

What causes the capitalist business cycle?

The business cycle is the term used to describe the boom and slump nature of capitalism. Sometimes there is full employment, with workplaces producing more and more goods and services, the economy grows and along with it wages. However, as Proudhon argued, this happy situation does not last:

> "But industry, under the influence of property, does not proceed with such regularity ... As soon as a demand begins to be felt, the factories fill up, and everybody goes to work. Then business is lively ... Under the rule of property, the flowers of industry are woven into none but funeral wreaths. The labourer digs his own grave ... [the capitalist] tries ... to continue production by lessening expenses. Then comes the lowering of wages; the introduction of machinery; the employment of women and children ... the decreased cost creates a larger market ... [but] the productive power tends to more than ever outstrip consumption ... To-day the factory is closed. Tomorrow the people starve in the streets ... In consequence of the cessation of business and the extreme cheapness of merchandise ... frightened creditors hasten to withdraw their funds [and] Production is suspended, and labour comes to a standstill." [**What is Property**, pp. 191-192]

Why does this happen? For anarchists, as Proudhon noted, it's to do with the nature of capitalist production and the social relationships it creates (*"the rule of property"*). The key to understanding the business cycle is to understand that, to use Proudhon's words, *"Property sells products to the labourer for more than it pays him for them; therefore it is impossible."* [**Op. Cit.**, p. 194] In other words, the need for the capitalist to make a profit from the workers they employ is the underlying cause of the business cycle. If the capitalist class cannot make enough surplus value (profit, interest, rent) then it will stop production, sack people, ruin lives and communities until such time as enough can once again be extracted from working class people. As Proudhon put it (using the term *"interest"* to cover all forms of surplus value):

> *"The primary cause of commercial and industrial stagnations is, then, interest on capital, – that interest which the ancients with one accord branded with the name of usury, whenever it was paid for the use of money, but which they did not dare to condemn in the forms of house-rent, farm-rent, or profit: as if the nature of the thing lent could ever warrant a charge for the lending; that is, robbery."* [**Op. Cit.**, p. 193]

So what influences the level of surplus value? There are two main classes of pressure on surplus value production, what we will call the **"subjective"** and **"objective"** (we will use the term profits to cover surplus value from now on as this is less cumbersome and other forms of surplus value depend on the amount extracted from workers on the shopfloor). The "subjective" pressures are to do with the nature of the social relationships created by capitalism, the relations of domination and subjection which are the root of exploitation and the resistance to them. In other words the subjective pressures are the result of the fact that *"property is despotism"* (to use Proudhon's expression) and are a product of the class struggle. This will be discussed in section C.7.1. The objective pressures are related to how capitalism works and fall into two processes. The first is the way in which markets do not provide enough information to producers to avoid disproportionalities within the market. In other words, that the market regularly produces situations where there is too much produced for specific markets leading to slumps The second objective factor is related to the process by which *"productive power tends more and more to outstrip consumption"* (to use Proudhon's words), i.e. over-investment or over-accumulation. These are discussed in sections C.7.2 and C.7.3, respectively.

Before continuing, we would like to stress here that all three factors operate together in a real economy and we have divided them purely to help explain the issues involved in each one. The class struggle, market "communication" creating disproportionalities and over-investment all interact. Due to the needs of the internal (class struggle) and external (inter-company) competition, capitalists have to invest in new means of production. As workers' power increases during a boom, capitalists innovate and invest in order to try and counter it. Similarly, to get market advantage (and so increased profits) over their competitors, a company invests in new machinery. While this helps increase profits for individual companies in the short term, it leads to collective over-investment and falling profits in the long term. Moreover, due to lack of effective communication within the market caused by the price mechanism firms rush to produce

more goods and services in specific boom markets, so leading to over-production and the resulting gluts result in slumps. This process is accelerated by the incomplete information provided by the interest rate, which results in investment becoming concentrated in certain parts of the economy. Relative over-investment can occur, increasing and compounding any existing tendencies for over-production and so creating the possibility of crisis. In addition, the boom encourages new companies and foreign competitors to try and get market share, so decreasing the *"degree of monopoly"* in an industry, and so reducing the mark-up and profits of big business (which, in turn, can cause an increase in mergers and take-overs towards the end of the boom).

Meanwhile, as unemployment falls workers' power, confidence and willingness to stand up for their rights increases, causing profit margins to be eroded at the point of production. This has the impact of reducing tendencies to over-invest as workers resist the introduction of new technology and techniques. The higher wages also maintain and even increase demand for the finished goods and services produced, allowing firms to realise the potential profits their workers have created. Rising wages, therefore, harms the potential for **producing** profits by increasing costs yet it increases the possibility for **realising** profits on the market as firms cannot make profits if there is no demand for their goods and their inventories of unsold goods pile up. In other words, wages are costs for any specific firm but the wages other companies pay are a key factor in the demand for what it produces. This contradictory effect of class struggle matches the contradictory effect of investment. Just as investment causes crisis because it is useful, the class struggle both hinders over-accumulation of capital and maintains aggregate demand (so postponing the crisis) while at the same time eroding capitalist power and so profit margins at the point of production (so accelerating it).

And we should note that these factors work in reverse during a slump, creating the potential for a new boom. In terms of workers, rising unemployment empowers the capitalists who take advantage of the weakened position of their employees to drive through wage cuts or increase productivity in order to improve the profitability of their companies (i.e. increase surplus value). Labour will, usually, accept the increased rate of exploitation this implies to remain in work. This results in wages falling and so, potentially, allows profit margins to rise. However, wage cuts result in falling demand for goods and services and so, overall, the net effect of cutting wages may be an overall **drop** in demand which would make the slump worse. There is a contradictory aspect to the objective pressures as well during a slump. The price mechanism hinders the spread of knowledge required for production and investment decisions to be made. While collectively it makes sense for firms to start producing and investing more, individual firms are isolated from each other. Their expectations are negative, they expect the slump to continue and so will be unwilling to start investing again. In the slump, many firms go out of business so reducing the amount of fixed capital in the economy and so over-investment is reduced. As overall investment falls, so the average rate of profit in the economy can increase. Yet falling investment means that firms in that sector of the economy will face stagnant demand and in the face of an uncertain future will be a drag on other sectors. In addition, as firms go under the *"degree of monopoly"* of each industry increases which increases the mark-up and profits of big business yet the overall market situation is such that their goods cannot be sold.

Eventually, however, the slump will end (few anarchists accept the notion that capitalism will self-destruct due to internal economic processes). The increased surplus value production made possible by high unemployment is enough relative to the (reduced) fixed capital stock to increase the rate of profit. This encourages capitalists to start investing again and a boom begins (a boom which contains the seeds of its own end). How long this process takes cannot be predicted in advance (which is why Keynes stressed that in the long run we are all dead). It depends on objective circumstances, how excessive the preceding boom was, government policy and how willing working class people are to pay the costs for the capitalist crisis.

Thus subjective and objective factors interact and counteract with each other, but in the end a crisis will result simply because the system is based upon wage labour and the producers are not producing for themselves. Ultimately, a crisis is caused because capitalism is production for profit and when the capitalist class does not (collectively) get a sufficient rate of profit for whatever reason then a slump is the result. If workers produced for themselves, this decisive factor would not be an issue as no capitalist class would exist. Until that happens the business cycle will continue, driven by "subjective" and "objective" pressures – pressures that are related directly to the nature of capitalist production and the wage labour on which it is based. Which pressure will predominate in any given period will be dependent on the relative power of classes. One way to look at it is that slumps can be caused when working class people are "too strong" or "too weak." The former means that we are able to reduce the rate of exploitation, squeezing the profit rate by keeping an increased share of the surplus value we produce. The later means we are too weak to stop income distribution being shifted in favour of the capitalist class, which results in over-accumulation and rendering the economy prone to a failure in aggregate demand. The 1960s and 1970s are the classic example of what happens when "subjective" pressures predominate while the 1920s and 1930s show the "objective" ones at work.

Finally, it must be stressed that this analysis does **not** imply that anarchists think that capitalism will self-destruct. In spite of crises being inevitable and occurring frequently, revolution is not. Capitalism will only be eliminated by working class revolution, when people see the need for social transformation and not imposed on people as the by-product of an economic collapse.

C.7.1 What role does class struggle play in the business cycle?

At its most basic, the class struggle (the resistance to hierarchy in all its forms) is the main cause of the business cycle. As we argued in sections B.1.2 and C.2, capitalists in order to exploit a worker must first oppress them. But where there is oppression, there is resistance; where there is authority, there is the will to freedom. Hence capitalism is marked by a continuous struggle between worker and boss at the point of production as well as struggle outside of the workplace against other forms of hierarchy.

This class struggle reflects a conflict between workers attempts at liberation and self-empowerment and capital's attempts to turn the individual worker into a small cog in a big machine. It reflects the attempts of the oppressed to try to live a fully human life, when the *"worker claims his share in the riches he produces; he claims his share in the management of production; and he claims not only some additional well-being, but also his full rights in the higher enjoyment of science and art."* [Peter Kropotkin, **Anarchism**, pp. 48-49] As Errico Malatesta argued:

> *"If [workers] succeed in getting what they demand, they will be better off: they will earn more, work fewer hours and will have more time and energy to reflect on things that matter to them, and will immediately make greater demands and have greater needs … [T]here exists no natural law (law of wages) which determines what part of a worker's labour should go to him [or her] … Wages, hours and other conditions of employment are the result of the struggle between bosses and workers. The former try and give the workers as little as possible; the latter try, or should try to work as little, and earn as much, as possible. Where workers accept any conditions, or even being discontented, do not know how to put up effective resistance to the bosses demands, they are soon reduced to bestial conditions of life. Where, instead, they have ideas of how human beings should live and know how to join forces, and through refusal to work or the latent and open threat of rebellion, to win bosses respect, in such cases, they are treated in a relatively decent way … Through struggle, by resistance against the bosses, therefore, workers can, up to a certain point, prevent a worsening of their conditions as well as obtaining real improvement."* [**Errico Malatesta: His Life and Ideas**, pp. 191-2]

It is this struggle that determines wages and indirect income such as welfare, education grants and so forth. This struggle also influences the concentration of capital, as capital attempts to use technology to get an advantage against their competitors by driving down prices by increasing the productivity of labour (i.e., to extract the maximum surplus value possible from employees). And, as will be discussed in section D.10, increased capital investment also reflects an attempt to increase the control of the worker by capital (or to replace them with machinery that cannot say "no") **plus** the transformation of the individual into "the mass worker" who can be fired and replaced with little or no hassle. For example, Proudhon quotes an *"English Manufacturer"* who states that he invested in machinery precisely to replace humans by machines because machines are easier to control:

> *"The insubordination of our workforce has given us the idea of dispensing with them. We have made and stimulated every imaginable effort of the mind to replace the service of men by tools more docile, and we have achieved our object. Machinery has delivered capital from*

the oppression of labour." [quoted by Proudhon, **System of Economical Contradictions**, p. 189]

(To which Proudhon replied *"[w]hat a misfortunate that machinery cannot also deliver capital from the oppression of consumers!"* The over-production and reductions in demand caused by machinery replacing people soon destroys these illusions of automatic production by a slump – see section C.7.3).

Therefore, class struggle influences both wages and capital investment, and so the prices of commodities in the market. It also, more importantly, determines profit levels and it is the rise and fall of profit levels that are the ultimate cause of the business cycle. This is because, under capitalism, production's *"only aim is to increase the profits of the capitalist. And we have, therefore, – the continuous fluctuations of industry, the crisis coming periodically."* [Kropotkin, **Op. Cit.**, p. 55]

A common capitalist myth, derived from neo-classical (and related) ideology, is that free-market capitalism will result in a continuous boom. Since the cause of slumps is allegedly state interference in the market (particularly in credit and money), eliminating such meddling will obviously bring reality into line with the textbooks and, consequently, eliminate such negative features of "actually existing" capitalism as the business cycle. Let us assume, for a moment, that this is the case (as will be discussed in section C.8, this is **not** the case). In the "boom economy" of capitalist dreams there will be full employment yet while this helps *"increase total demand, its fatal characteristic from the business view is that it keeps the reserve army of the unemployed low, thereby protecting wage levels and strengthening labour's bargaining power."* [Edward S. Herman, **Beyond Hypocrisy**, p. 93] This leads to the undermining of full employment as profit margins are placed under pressure (which explains why bosses have lead the fight against government full employment policies).

The process should be obvious enough. Full employment results in a situation where workers are in a very strong position, a strength which can undermine the system. This is because capitalism always proceeds along a tightrope. If a boom is to continue smoothly, real wages must develop within a certain band. If their growth is too low then capitalists will find it difficult to sell the products their workers have produced and so, because of this, face what is often called a *"realisation crisis"* (i.e. the fact that capitalists cannot make a profit if they cannot sell their products). If real wage growth is too high then the conditions for producing profits are undermined as labour gets more of the value it produces. This means that in periods of boom, when unemployment is falling, the conditions for realisation improve as demand for consumer goods increase, thus expanding markets and encouraging capitalists to invest. However, such an increase in investment (and so employment) has an adverse effect on the conditions for **producing** surplus value as labour can assert itself at the point of production, increase its resistance to the demands of management and, far more importantly, make its own.

If an industry or country experiences high unemployment, workers will put up with longer hours, stagnating wages, worse conditions and new technology in order to remain in work. This allows capital to extract a higher level of profit from those workers, which in turn signals other capitalists to invest in that area. As investment increases, unemployment falls. As the pool of available labour runs dry, then wages will rise as employers bid for scare resources and workers feel their power. As workers are in a better position they can go from resisting capital's agenda to proposing their own (e.g. demands for higher wages, better working conditions and even for workers' control). As workers' power increases, the share of income going to capital falls, as do profit rates, and capital experiences a profits squeeze and so cuts down on investment and employment and/or wages. The cut in investment increases unemployment in the capital goods sector of the economy, which in turn reduces demand for consumption goods as jobless workers can no longer afford to buy as much as before. This process accelerates as bosses fire workers or cut their wages and the slump deepens and so unemployment increases, which begins the cycle again. This can be called "subjective" pressure on profit rates.

This interplay of profits and wages can be seen in most business cycles. As an example, let us consider the crisis which ended post-war Keynesianism in the early 1970's and paved the way for the neo-liberal reforms of Thatcher and Reagan. This crisis, which started in 1973, had its roots in the 1960s boom and the profits squeeze it produced. If we look at the USA we find that it experienced continuous growth between 1961 and 1969 (the longest in its history until then). From 1961 onwards, unemployment steadily fell, effectively creating full employment. From 1963, the number of strikes and total working time lost steadily increased (the number of strikes doubled from 1963 to 1970, with the number of wildcat strike rising from 22% of all strikes in 1960 to 36.5% in 1966). By 1965 both the business profit shares and business profit rates peaked. The fall in profit share and rate of profit continued until 1970 (when unemployment started to increase), where it rose slightly until the 1973 slump occurred. In addition, after 1965, inflation started to accelerate as capitalist firms tried to maintain their profit margins by passing cost increases to consumers (as we discuss section C.8.2, inflation has far more to do with capitalist profits than it has with money supply or wages). This helped to reduce real wage gains and maintain profitability over the 1968 to 1973 period above what it otherwise would have been, which helped postpone, but not stop, a slump.

Looking at the wider picture, we find that for the advanced capital countries as a whole, the product wage rose steadily between 1962 and 1971 while productivity fell. The growth of the product wage (the real cost to the employer of hiring workers) exceeded that of productivity growth in the late 1960s, slightly after the year in which profit share in national income and the rate of profit peaked. From then on, productivity continued to fall while the product wage continued to rise. This process, the result of falling unemployment and rising workers' power (expressed, in part, by an explosion in the number of strikes across Europe and elsewhere), helped to ensure that workers keep an increasing share of the value they produced. The actual post-tax real wages and productivity in the advanced capitalist countries increased at about the same rate from 1960 to 1968 but between 1968 and 1973 the former increased at a larger rate than the latter (hence the profits squeeze). Moreover, increased international competition meant that many domestic companies where limited in their responses to the profits squeeze as well as facing a global decrease in demand for their products. This resulted in profit shares and rates declining to around 80% of their previous peak levels across the advanced capitalist nations. [Philip Armstrong, Andrew Glyn and John Harrison, **Capitalism Since 1945**, pp. 178-80, pp. 182-4 and pp. 192-3]

It must be stressed that social struggle was not limited to the workplace. In the 1960s a *"series of strong liberation movements emerged among women, students and ethnic minorities. A crisis of social institutions was in progress, and large social groups were questioning the very foundations of the modern, hierarchical society: the patriarchal family, the authoritarian school and university, the hierarchical workplace or office, the bureaucratic trade union or party."* [Takis Fotopoulos, *"The Nation-state and the Market,"* pp. 37-80, **Society and Nature**, Vol. 2, No. 2, p. 58] In stark contrast to the predictions of the right, state intervention within capitalism to maintain full employment and provide social services like health care had **not** resulted in a *"Road to Serfdom."* The opposite occurred, with previously marginalised sectors of the population resisting their oppression and exploitation by questioning authority in more and more areas of life – including, it must be stressed, within our own organisations as well (for example, the rank and file of trade unions had to rebel just as much against their own officials as they had against the bureaucracy of the capitalist firm).

These social struggles resulted in an economic crisis as capital could no longer oppress and exploit working class people sufficiently in order to maintain a suitable profit rate. This crisis was then used to discipline the working class and restore capitalist authority within and outside the workplace (see section C.8.2). We should also note that this process of social revolt in spite, or perhaps because of, the increase of material wealth was predicted by Malatesta. In 1922 he argued that:

> *"The fundamental error of the reformists is that of dreaming of solidarity, a sincere collaboration, between masters and servants, between proprietors and workers ...*

> *"Those who envisage a society of well stuffed pigs which waddle contentedly under the ferule of a small number of swineherd; who do not take into account the need for freedom and the sentiment of human dignity ... can also imagine and aspire to a technical organisation of production which assures abundance for all and at the same time materially advantageous both to bosses and the workers. But in reality 'social peace' based on abundance for all will remain a dream, so long as society is divided into antagonistic classes, that is employers and employees. And there will be neither peace nor abundance.*

> *"The antagonism is spiritual rather than material. There will never be a sincere understanding between bosses and workers for the better exploitation [sic!] of the forces of nature in the interests of mankind, because the bosses above all want to remain bosses and secure always more power at the expense of the workers, as well as by competition with other bosses, whereas the workers have had their fill of bosses and don't want more!"* [**Op. Cit.**, pp. 78-79]

The experience of the post-war compromise and social democratic reform shows that, ultimately, the social question is not poverty but rather freedom. However, to return to the impact of class struggle on capitalism.

It is the awareness that full employment is bad for business which is the basis of the so-called *"Non-Accelerating Inflation Rate of Unemployment"* (NAIRU). As we will discuss in more detail in section C.9, the NAIRU is the rate of unemployment for an economy under which inflation, it is claimed, starts to accelerate. While the basis of this "theory" is slim (the NAIRU is an invisible, mobile rate and so the "theory" can explain every historical event simply because you can prove anything when your datum cannot be seen by mere mortals) it is very useful for justifying policies which aim at attacking working people, their organisations and their activities. The NAIRU is concerned with a *"wage-price"* spiral caused by falling unemployment and rising workers' rights and power. Of course, you never hear of an *"interest-price"* spiral or a *"rent-price"* spiral or a *"profits-price"* spiral even though these are also part of any price. It is always a *"wage-price"* spiral, simply because interest, rent and profits are income to capital and so, by definition, above reproach. By accepting the logic of NAIRU, the capitalist system implicitly acknowledges that it and full employment are incompatible and so with it any claim that it allocates resources efficiently or labour contracts benefit both parties equally.

For these reasons, anarchists argue that a continual "boom" economy is an impossibility simply because capitalism is driven by profit considerations, which, combined with the subjective pressure on profits due to the class struggle between workers and capitalists, **necessarily** produces a continuous boom-and-bust cycle. When it boils down to it, this is unsurprising, as *"industry is directed, and will have to be directed, not towards what is needed to satisfy the needs of all, but towards that which, at a given moment, brings in the greatest temporary profit to a few. Of necessity, the abundance of some will be based upon the poverty of others, and the straitened circumstances of the greater number will have to be maintained at all costs, that there may be hands to sell themselves for a part only of that which they are capable of producing, without which private accumulation of capital is impossible!"* [Kropotkin, **Op. Cit.**, p. 128]

Of course, when such "subjective" pressures are felt on the system, when private accumulation of capital is threatened by improved circumstances for the many, the ruling class denounces working class "greed" and "selfishness." When this occurs we should remember what Adam Smith had to say on this subject:

> *"In reality high profits tend much more to raise the price of work than high wages.... That part of the price of the commodity that resolved itself into wages would ... rise only in arithmetical proportion to the rise in wages. But if profits of all the different employers of those working people should be raised five per cent., that price of the commodity which resolved itself into profit would ... rise in geometrical proportion to this rise in profit ... Our merchants and master manufacturers complain of the bad effects of high wages in raising the price and thereby lessening the sale of their goods at home and*

abroad. They say nothing concerning the bad effects of high profits. They are silent with regard to the pernicious effects of their own gains. They complain only of those of other people." [**The Wealth of Nations**, pp. 87-88]

As an aside, we must note that these days we would have to add economists to Smith's *"merchants and master manufacturers."* Not that this is surprising, given that economic theory has progressed (or degenerated) from Smith's disinterested analysis into apologetics for any action of the boss (a classic example, we must add, of supply and demand, with the marketplace of ideas responding to a demand for such work from *"our merchants and master manufacturers"*). Any "theory" which blames capitalism's problems on "greedy" workers will always be favoured over one that correctly places them in the contradictions created by wage slavery. Ultimately, capitalist economics blame every problem of capitalism on the working class refusing to kow-tow to the bosses (for example, unemployment is caused by wages being too high rather than bosses needing unemployment to maintain their power and profits – see section C.9.2 on empirical evidence that indicates that the first explanation is wrong).

Before concluding, one last point. While it may appear that our analysis of the "subjective" pressures on capitalism is similar to that of mainstream economics, this is not the case. This is because our analysis recognises that such pressures are inherent in the system, have contradictory effects (and so cannot be easily solved without making things worse before they get better) and hold the potential for creating a free society. Our analysis recognises that workers' power and resistance **is** bad for capitalism (as for any hierarchical system), but it also indicates that there is nothing capitalism can do about it without creating authoritarian regimes (such as Nazi Germany) or by generating massive amounts of unemployment (as was the case in the early 1980s in both the USA and the UK, when right-wing governments mismanaged the economy into deep recessions) and even this is no guarantee of eliminating working class struggle as can be seen, for example, from 1930s America.

This means that our analysis shows the limitations and contradictions of the system as well as its need for workers to be in a weak bargaining position in order for it to "work" (which explodes the myth that capitalism is a free society). Moreover, rather than portray working people as victims of the system (as is the case in many Marxist analyses of capitalism) our analysis recognises that we, both individually and collectively, have the power to influence and **change** that system by our activity. We should be proud of the fact that working people refuse to negate themselves or submit their interests to that of others or play the role of order-takers required by the system. Such expressions of the human spirit, of the struggle of freedom against authority, should not be ignored or down-played, rather they should be celebrated. That the struggle against authority causes the system so much trouble is not an argument against social struggle, it is an argument against a system based on hierarchy, oppression, exploitation and the denial of freedom.

To sum up, in many ways, social struggle is the inner dynamic of the system, and its most basic contradiction: while capitalism tries to turn the majority of people into commodities (namely, bearers of

labour power), it also has to deal with the human responses to this process of objectification (namely, the class struggle). However, it does not follow that cutting wages will solve a crisis – far from it, for, as we argue in section C.9.1, cutting wages will deepen any crisis, making things worse before they get better. Nor does it follow that, if social struggle were eliminated, capitalism would work fine. After all, if we assume that labour power is a commodity like any other, its price will rise as demand increases relative to supply (which will either produce inflation or a profits squeeze, probably both). Therefore, even without the social struggle which accompanies the fact that labour power cannot be separated from the individuals who sell it, capitalism would still be faced with the fact that only surplus labour (unemployment) ensures the creation of adequate amounts of surplus value.

Moreover, even assuming that individuals can be totally happy in a capitalist economy, willing to sell their freedom and creativity for a little more money, putting up, unquestioningly, with every demand and whim of their bosses (and so negating their own personality and individuality in the process), capitalism does have "objective" pressures limiting its development. So while social struggle, as argued above, can have a decisive effect on the health of the capitalist economy, it is not the only problem the system faces. This is because there are objective pressures within the system beyond and above the authoritarian social relations it produces and the resistance to them. These pressures are discussed next, in sections C.7.2 and C.7.3.

C.7.2 What role does the market play in the business cycle?

A major problem with capitalism is the working of the capitalist market itself. For the supporters of "free market" capitalism, the market provides all the necessary information required to make investment and production decisions. This means that a rise or fall in the price of a commodity acts as a signal to everyone in the market, who then respond to that signal. These responses will be co-ordinated by the market, resulting in a healthy economy.

This perspective is expressed well by right-liberal, Frederick von Hayek in his *"The Uses of Knowledge in Society"* (reprinted in **Individualism and Economic Order**). Using the example of the tin market, he defends capitalism against central planning on its ability to handle the division of knowledge within society and its dynamic use of this dispersed knowledge when demand or supply changes. *"Assume,"* he argues, *"that somewhere in the world a new opportunity for the use of some raw material, say tin, has arisen, or that one of the sources of supply of tin has been eliminated. It does not matter for our purpose and it is very significant that it does not matter which of these two causes has made tin more scarce. All that the users of tin need to know is that some of the tin they used to consume is now more profitably employed elsewhere, and that in consequence they must economise tin. There is no need for the great majority of them even to know where the more urgent need has arisen, or in favour of what other uses they ought to husband the supply."* The subsequent rise in its price will result in reduced consumption as many users will economise on its use and so the information that tin has become (relatively) scarcer spreads throughout the economy and influences not only tin users, but also its substitutes and the substitutes of these substitutes and so on. This will move the economy towards equilibrium without the people informed knowing anything about the original causes for these changes. *"The whole acts as one market, not because any of its members survey the whole field, but because their limited individual fields of vision sufficiently overlap so that through many intermediaries the relevant information is communicated to all."* ("The use of knowledge in society," pp. 519-30, **American Economic Review**, Vol. 35, No. 4, , p. 526)

While it can be granted that this account of the market is not without foundation, it is also clear that the price mechanism does not communicate all the relevant information needed by companies or individuals. This means that capitalism does not work in the way suggested in the economic textbooks. It is the workings of the price mechanism itself which leads to booms and slumps in economic activity and the resulting human and social costs they entail. This can be seen if we investigate the actual processes hidden behind the workings of the price mechanism.

The key problem with Hayek's account is that he does not discuss the **collective** results of the individual decisions he highlights. It is true that faced with a rise in the price of tin, individual firms will cut back on its use. Yet there is no reason to suppose that the net result of these actions will bring the demand and supply of tin back to equilibrium. In fact, it is just as likely that the reduction in demand for tin is such that its producers face falling sales and so cut back production even more. Similarly, a rising demand for tin could easily result in all tin producers increasing supply so much as to produce a glut on the market. Proudhon described this process well in the 1840s:

> *"A peasant who has harvested twenty sacks of wheat, which he with his family proposes to consume, deems himself twice as rich as if he had harvested only ten; likewise a housewife who has spun fifty yards of linen believes that she is twice as rich as if she had spun but twenty-five. Relatively to the household, both are right; looked at in their external relations, they may be utterly mistaken. If the crop of wheat is double throughout the whole country, twenty sacks will sell for less than ten would have sold for if it had been but half as great; so, under similar circumstances, fifty yards of linen will be worth less than twenty-five: so that value decreases as the production of utility increases, and a producer may arrive at poverty by continually enriching himself."* [**The System of Economical Contradictions**, pp. 77-78]

He argued that this occurred due to the *"contradiction"* of *"the double character of value"* (i.e. between value in use and value in exchange). [**Op. Cit.**, p. 78]

As John O'Neill argues (basing himself on Marx rather than Proudhon), when producers *"make plans concerning future production, they are planning not with respect of demand at the present moment ... but with respect to expected demand at some future moment ... when their products reach the market."* The price mechanism provides information that indicates the relationship between supply and demand **now** and while this information **is** relevant to producers plans, it is not **all** the information that is relevant or is required by those involved. It cannot provide information which will allow producers to predict demand later. *"A major component of the information required for such a prediction is that of the plans of other producers which respond to that demand. This is information that the market, as a competitive system, fails to distribute."* It is this *"informational restriction"* which is one of the sources of why there is a business cycle. This is because each producer *"responds to the same signal the change in price. However, each agent acts independently of the response of other producers and consumers."* The result is *"an overproduction of goods in relation to effective demand for them. Goods cannot be sold. There is a realisation crisis: producers cannot realise the value of their products. Given this overproduction, demand falls against supply. There is a slump. This eventually leads to a rise in demand against supply, production expends leading to another boom, and so on."* [**The Market**, pp. 134-5]

This information cannot be supplied due to competition. Simply put, if A and B are in competition, if A informs B of her activities and B does not reciprocate, then B is in a position to compete more effectively than A. Hence communication within the market is discouraged and each production unit is isolated from the rest. In other words, each person or company responds to the same signal (the change in price) but each acts independently of the response of other producers and consumers. The result is often a slump in the market, causing unemployment and economic disruption. Thus the market *"blocks the communication of information and fails to co-ordinate plans for economic action."* [**Op. Cit.**, p. 137]

This, it should be noted, is not a problem of people making a series of unrelated mistakes. *"Rather, it is that the market imparts the same information to affected agents, and this information is such that the rational strategy for all agents is to expand production or contract consumption, while it is not rational for all agents to act in this manner collectively."* In other words, the information the market provides is not sufficient for rational decision making and naturally results in disproportionalities in the market. Thus the price mechanism actively encourages *"the suppression of the mutual exchange of information concerning planned responses"* to current prices and this *"leads to over production."* So it is **not** a question of inaccurate prediction (although given that the future is unknowable and unpredictable this is a factor). Instead, it is *"one of individually rational responses to the same signal resulting in collectively irrational responses."* [**Op. Cit.**, p. 135 and p. 197]

This means that prices in themselves do not provide adequate knowledge for rational decision making as they are not at their long-run equilibrium levels. This causes a problem for Hayek's account of the market process as he stresses that actual prices never are at this (purely theoretical) price. As we discuss in section C.8, Hayek's own theory of the business cycle shows the negative impact which the 'misinformation' conveyed by disequilibrium prices can cause on the economy. In that analysis, the disequilibrium price that leads to very substantial macroeconomic distortions is the rate of interest but, obviously, the same argument applies for commodity prices as well. This means that the market process, based on the reactions of profit-maximising firms to the same (unsustainable) prices for a commodity can generating mal-investment and subsequent market distributions on a wide level. Simply put, the price mechanism may carry information regarding the terms on which various commodities may currently be exchanged but it does not follow that a knowledge of these exchange ratios enable agents to calculate the future profitability of their production decisions (social usefulness is, of course, of no concern).

It is this irrationality and lack of information which feed into the business cycle. *"These local booms and slumps in production ... are then amplified into general crises precisely through the interconnections in the market that Hayek highlights in his example of the production and consumption of tin."* [O'Neill, **Op. Cit.**, p. 136] The negative effects of over-production in one market will be passed on to those which supply it with goods in the shape of decreased demand. These firms will now experience relative over-production which, in turn, will affect their suppliers. Whatever benefits may accrue to consumers of these goods in the shape of lower prices will be reduced as demand for their products drops as more and more workers are made unemployed or their wages are cut (which means that **real** wages remain constant as prices are falling alongside money wages – see section C.9.1 for details). Firms will also seek to hoard money, leading to yet more falling demand for goods and so unemployed labour is joined by under-utilisation of capacity.

Which brings us to the issue of money and its role in the business cycle. "Free market" capitalist economics is based on Say's Law. This is the notion that supply creates its own demand and so general gluts of goods and mass unemployment are impossible. As we noted in section C.1.5, this vision of economic activity is only suited to precapitalist economies or ones without money for money is considered as nothing more than an aid to barter, a medium of exchange only. It ignores the fact that money is a store of value and, as such, can be held onto precisely for that reason. This means that Say's Law is invalid as its unity between sale and purchase can be disturbed so causing the chain of contractual relationships to be broken. Simply put, someone who sells a product need not spend their income on another product at the same time. Unlike barter, the sale of one commodity is an act distinct from the purchase of another. Money, in other words, *"brings in time"* into the market process and *"the possibility of hoarding."* Time *"because a good is usually sold some time after it is made, running the risk that its sale price could fall below the cost of production, wiping out the capitalist's expected profit."* Hoarding *"because income need not be spent but may merely be kept idle."* [Doug Henwood, **Wall Street**, p. 232]

This means that over-production becomes possible and bankruptcies and unemployment can become widespread and so a slump can start. *"As any Marxian or Keynesian crisis theorist can tell you,"* Henwood summarises, *"the separation of purchase and sale is one of the great flashpoints of capitalism; an expected sale that goes unmade can drive a capitalist under, and can unravel a chain of financial commitments. Multiply that by a thousand or two and you have great potential mischief."* Thus *"the presence of money as a store of value, the possibility of keeping wealth in financial form rather than spending it promptly on commodities, always introduces*

the possibility of crisis." That is, the possibility *"of an excess of capital lacking a profitable investment outlet, and an excess of goods that couldn't be sold profitably on the open market."* [**Op. Cit.**, pp. 93-4 and p. 94]

So when the market prices of goods fall far below their cost prices then production and investment stagnate. This is because profits can only be transformed into capital at a loss and so it lies idle in banks. Thus unemployed labour is associated with unemployed capital, i.e. excess money. This desire for capitalists to increase their demand for storing their wealth in money rather than investing it is driven by the rate of profit in the economy. Bad times result in increased hoarding and so a general fall in aggregate demand. Lowering interest rates will not provoke a demand for such money hoards, as claimed in "free market" capitalist theory, as few capitalists will seek to invest in a recession as expected profits will be lower than the interest rate.

However, it should be stressed that disproportionalities of production between industries and the separation of production and sale do not **per se** result in a general crisis. If that were the case the capitalism would be in a constant state of crisis as markets are rarely in a state of equilibrium and sales do not instantly result in purchases. This means that market dislocations need not automatically produce a general crisis in the economy as the problems associated with localised slumps can be handled when the overall conditions within an economy are good. It simply provides the **potential** for crisis and a means of transmitting and generalising local slumps when the overall economic situation is weak. In other words, it is an accumulative process in which small changes can build up on each other until the pressures they exert become unstoppable. The key thing to remember is that capitalism is an inherently dynamic system which consists of different aspects which develop unevenly (i.e., disproportionately). Production, credit, finance markets, circulation of money and goods, investment, wages, profits as well as specific markets get out of step. An economic crisis occurs when this process gets too far out of line.

This process also applies to investment as well. So far, we have assumed that firms adjust to price changes without seeking new investment. This is, of course, unlikely to always be the case. As we discuss in section C.8, this analysis of the market providing incomplete information also applies to the market for credit and other forms of external financing. This results in a situation where the problems associated with over-production can be amplified by over-investment. This means that the problems associated with markets creating disproportionalities are combined with the problems resulting from increased productivity and capital investment which are discussed in the next section.

C.7.3 What role does investment play in the business cycle?

Other problems for capitalism arise due to the increases in productivity which occur as a result of capital investment or new working practices which aim to increase short term profits for the company. The need to maximise profits results in more and more investment in order to improve the productivity of the workforce (i.e. to increase the amount of surplus value produced). A rise in productivity, however, means that whatever profit is produced is spread over an increasing number of commodities. This profit still needs to be realised on the market but this may prove difficult as capitalists produce not for existing markets but for expected ones. As individual firms cannot predict what their competitors will do, it is rational for them to try to maximise their market share by increasing production (by increasing investment). As the market does not provide the necessary information to co-ordinate their actions, this leads to supply exceeding demand and difficulties realising sufficient profits. In other words, a period of over-production occurs due to the over-accumulation of capital.

Due to the increased investment in the means of production, variable capital (labour) uses a larger and larger constant capital (the means of production). As labour is the source of surplus value, this means that in the short term profits may be increased by the new investment, i.e. workers must produce more, in relative terms, than before so reducing a firms production costs for the commodities or services it produces. This allows increased profits to be realised at the current market price (which reflects the old costs of production). Exploitation of labour must increase in order for the return on total (i.e. constant **and** variable) capital to increase or, at worse, remain constant. However, while this is rational for one company, it is not rational when all firms do it (which they must in order to remain in business). As investment increases, the surplus value workers have to produce must increase faster. As long as the rate of exploitation produced by the new investments is high enough to counteract the increase in constant capital and keep the profit rate from falling, then the boom will continue. If, however, the mass of possible profits in the economy is too small compared to the total capital invested (both in means of production, fixed, and labour, variable) then the possibility exists for a general fall in the rate of profit (the ratio of profit to investment in capital and labour). Unless exploitation increases sufficiently, already produced surplus value earmarked for the expansion of capital may not be realised on the market (i.e. goods may not be sold). If this happens, then the surplus value will remain in its money form, thus failing to act as capital. In other words, accumulation will grind to a halt and a slump will start.

When this happens, over-investment has occurred. No new investments are made, goods cannot be sold resulting in a general reduction of production and so increased unemployment as companies fire workers or go out of business. This removes more and more constant capital from the economy, increasing unemployment which forces those with jobs to work harder, for longer so allowing the mass of profits produced to be increased, resulting (eventually) in an increase in the rate of profit. Once profit rates are high enough, capitalists have the incentive to make new investments and slump turns to boom. As we discuss in section C.8, the notion that investment will be helped by lowing interest rates in a slump fails to understand that *"the rate of investment decisions is an increasing function of the difference between the prospective rate of profit and the rate of interest."* [Michal Kalecki, quoted by Malcolm Sawyer, **The Economics of Michal Kalecki**, p. 98] If profit rates are depressed due to over-investment then even the lowest interest rates will have little effect. In other words, expectations of capitalists and investors are a key issue and these are shaped by the general state of the economy.

It could be argued that such an analysis is flawed as no company would invest in machinery if it would reduce its rate of profit. But such an objection is flawed, simply because (as we noted) such investment is perfectly sensible (indeed, a necessity) for a specific firm. By investing they gain (potentially) an edge in the market and so increased profits for a period. This forces their competitors to act likewise and **they** invest in new technology. Unfortunately, while this is individually sensible, collectively it is not as the net result of these individual acts is over-investment in the economy as a whole. Moreover, unlike the model of perfect competition, in a real economy capitalists have no way of knowing the future, and so the results of their own actions never mind the actions of their competitors. Thus over-accumulation of capital is the natural result of competition simply because even if we assume that the bosses of the firms are individually rational they are driven to make decisions which are collectively irrational to remain in business. The future is unknowable and so the capitalist has no idea what the net result of their decisions will be nor the state of the economy when their investment decisions are finally active. Both of these factors ensure that firms act as they do, investing in machinery which, in the end, will result in a crisis of over-accumulation.

The logic is simple and is rooted in the concept of *"the fallacy of composition."* To use an analogy, if you attend a rock concert and take a box to stand on then you will get a better view. If others do the same, you will be in exactly the same position as before. Worse, even, as it may be easier to loose your balance and come crashing down in a heap (and, perhaps, bringing others with you). This analogy shows why introducing new machinery, which is profitable for an individual company, has such a potentially negative effect on the economy as a whole. While it is profitable for an individual company in the short term, its overall effect means that it is **not** profitable for all in the long run. As Kalecki put it, the *"tragedy of investment is that it causes crisis because it is useful. Doubtless many people will consider this theory paradoxical. But it is not the theory which is paradoxical, but its subject – the capitalist economy."* [quoted by Sawyer **Op. Cit.**, p. 156] This paradox applies to the issue of wages as well:

> *"What a system is that which leads a business man to think with delight that society will soon be able to dispense with men!* **Machinery has delivered capital from the oppression of labour!** *... Fool! though the workmen cost you something, they are your customers: what will you do with your products, when, driven away by you, they*

shall consume them no longer? Thus machinery, after crushing the workmen, is not slow in dealing employers a counter-blow; for, if production excludes consumption, it is soon obliged to stop itself.

[...]

"These failures were caused by over-production, – that is, by an inadequate market, or the distress of the people. What a pity that machinery cannot also deliver capital from the oppression of consumers! What a misfortune that machines do not buy the fabrics which they weave! The ideal society will be reached when commerce, agriculture, and manufactures can proceed without a man upon earth!" [Proudhon, **System of Economical Contradictions**, pp. 189-90]

So, if the profit rate falls to a level that does not allow capital formation to continue, a slump sets in. This general slump means that the rate of profit over the whole economy falls due to excessive investment. When one industry over-invests and over-produces, it cuts back production, introduces cost-cutting measures, fires workers and so on in order to try and realise more profits. These may spread if the overall economic is fragile as the reduced demand for industries that supplied the affected industry impacts on the **general** demand (via a fall in inputs as well as rising unemployment). The related industries now face over-production themselves and the natural response to the information supplied by the market is for individual companies to reduce production, fire workers, etc., which again leads to declining demand. This makes it even harder to realise profit on the market and leads to more cost cutting, deepening the crisis. While individually this is rational, collectively it is not and so soon all industries face the same problem. A local slump is propagated through the economy.

Cycles of prosperity, followed by over-production and then depression are the natural result of capitalism. Over-production is the result of over-accumulation, and over-accumulation occurs because of the need to maximise short-term profits in order to stay in business. So while the crisis appears as a glut of commodities on the market, as there are more commodities in circulation that can be purchased by the aggregate demand (*"Property sells products to the labourer for more than it pays him for them,"* to use Proudhon's words), its roots are deeper. It lies in the nature of capitalist production itself.

"Over-production," we should point out, exists only from the viewpoint of capital, **not** of the working class:

"What economists call over-production is but a production that is above the purchasing power of the worker ... this sort of over-production remains fatally characteristic of the present capitalist production, because workers cannot buy with their salaries what they have produced and at the same time copiously nourish the swarm of idlers who live upon their work." [Kropotkin, **Op. Cit.**, pp. 127-128]

In other words, over-production and under-consumption reciprocally imply each other. There is no over production except in regard to a given level of solvent demand. There is no deficiency in demand except in relation to a given level of production. The goods "over-produced" may be required by consumers, but the market price is too low to generate a profit and so existing goods must be destroyed and production must be reduced in order to artificially increase it. So, for example, the sight of food and other products being destroyed while people are in need of them is a common one in depression years.

So, while the crisis appears on the market as a *"commodity glut"* (i.e. as a reduction in effective demand) and is propagated through the economy by the price mechanism, its roots lie in production. Until such time as profit levels stabilise at an acceptable level, thus allowing renewed capital expansion, the slump will continue. The social costs of the wage cutting this requires is yet another "externality," to be bothered with only if they threaten capitalist power and wealth.

There are means, of course, by which capitalism can postpone (but not stop) a general crisis developing. The extension of credit by banks to both investors and consumers is the traditional, and most common, way. Imperialism, by which markets are increased and profits are extracted from less developed countries and used to boost the imperialist countries profits, is another method (*"The workman being unable to purchase with their wages the riches they are producing, industry must search for markets elsewhere."* [Kropotkin, **Op. Cit.**, p. 55]). Another is state intervention in the economy (such as minimum wages, the incorporation of trades unions into the system, arms production, manipulating interest rates to maintain a *"natural"* rate of unemployment to keep workers on their toes, etc.). Another is state spending to increase aggregate demand, which can increase consumption and so lessen the dangers of over-production. However, these have (objective and subjective) limits and can never succeed in stopping depressions from occurring as they ultimately flow from capitalist production and the need to make profits.

A classic example of these "objective" pressures on capitalism is the "Roaring Twenties" that preceded the Great Depression of the 1930s. After the 1921 slump, there was a rapid rise in investment in the USA with investment nearly doubling between 1919 and 1927. Because of this investment in capital equipment, manufacturing production grew by 8.0% per annum between 1919 and 1929 and labour productivity grew by an annual rate of 5.6% (this is including the slump of 1921-22). With costs falling and prices comparatively stable, profits increased which in turn lead to high levels of capital investment (the production of capital goods increased at an average annual rate of 6.4%). [William Lazonick, **Competitive Advantage on the Shop Floor**, p. 241] The optimism felt by business as a result of higher profits was reflected in the wealthy sections of America. In the 1920s prosperity was concentrated at the top. One-tenth of the top 1% of families received as much income as the bottom 42% and only 2.3% of the population enjoyed incomes over $100,00 (60% of families made less than $2,000 a year, 42% less than $1,000). While the richest 1% owned 40% of the nation's wealth by 1929 (and the number of people claiming half-million dollar incomes rose from 156 in 1920 to 1,489 in 1929) the bottom 93% of the population experienced a 4% drop in real disposable per-capita income between 1923 and 1929. However, in spite (or, perhaps, because) of this, US capitalism was booming and belief in capitalism was at its peak.

But by 1929 all this had changed with the stock market crash – followed by a deep depression. What was its cause? Given our analysis presented in section C.7.1, it may have been expected to have been caused by the "boom" decreasing unemployment, so increased working class power and leading to a profits squeeze but this was not the case. This slump was **not** the result of working class resistance, indeed the 1920s were marked by a labour market which was continuously favourable to employers. This was for two reasons. Firstly, the "Palmer Raids" at the end of the 1910s saw the state root out radicals in the US labour movement and wider society. Secondly, the deep depression of 1920-21 (during which national unemployment rates averaged over 9%, the highest level over any two-year period since the 1890s) changed the labour market from a seller's to a buyer's market. This allowed the bosses to apply what became to be known as *"the American Plan,"* namely firing workers who belonged to a union and forcing them to sign *"yellow-dog"* contracts (promises not to join a union) to gain or keep their jobs. Reinforcing this was the use of legal injunctions by employers against work protests and the use of industrial spies to identify and sack union members. This class war from above made labour weak, which is reflected in the influence and size of unions falling across the country. As union membership declined, the number of strikes reached their lowest level since the early 1880s, falling to just over 700 per year between 1927 to 1930 (compared to 3,500 per year between 1916 and 1921). [Lazonick, **Op. Cit.**, pp. 249-251] The key thing to remember is that the impact of unemployment is not limited to the current year's figures. High unemployment rates have a sustained impact on the organisations, morale, and bargaining power of workers even if unemployment rates fall afterwards. This was the situation in the 1920s, with workers remembering the two years of record unemployment rates of 1921 and 1922 (in fact, the unemployment rate for manufacturing workers was close to the overall rate in 1933).

During the post-1922 boom, this position did not change. The national 3.3% unemployment rate hid the fact that non-farm unemployment averaged 5.5% between 1923 and 1929. Across all industries, the growth of manufacturing output did not increase the demand for labour. Between 1919 and 1929, employment of production workers fell by 1% and non-production employment fell by about 6% (during the 1923 to 29 boom, production employment only increased by 2%, and non-production employment remained constant). This was due to the introduction of labour saving machinery and the rise in the capital stock. In addition, the numbers seeking work were boosted by new immigrants and the unwillingness of existing ones to return home due to difficulties returning to America. Lastly, the greatest source of industrial labour supply came from the American farm – there was a flood of rural workers into the urban labour market over the 1920s. [Lazonick, **Op. Cit.**, pp. 252-5] It is interesting to note that even **with** a labour market favourable to employers for over 5 years, unemployment was still high. This suggests that the neo-classical "argument" (assertion would be more correct) that unemployment within capitalism is caused by strong unions or high real wages is somewhat flawed to say the least (see section C.9).

Facing high unemployment, workers' quit rates fell due to fear of loosing jobs (particularly those workers with relatively higher wages). This, combined with the steady decline of the unions and the very low number of strikes, indicates that labour was weak. This is reflected in the share of total manufacturing income going to wages fell from 57.5% in 1923-24 to 52.6% in 1928/29 (between 1920 and 1929, it fell by 5.7%). Productivity increased from an annual rate of 1.2% between 1909 and 1919 to 5.6% between 1919 and 1929. This increase in productivity was reflected in the fact that over the post-1922 boom, the share of manufacturing income paid in salaries rose from 17% to 18.3% and the share to capital rose from 25.5% to 29.1%. Managerial salaries rose by 21.9% and firm surplus by 62.6% between 1920 and 1929. [Lazonick, **Op. Cit.**, pp. 241-2] Any notion that the 1929 crash was the result of a rebellious working class is not applicable.

The key to understanding what happened lies in the contradictory nature of capitalist production. The "boom" conditions were the result of capital investment, which increased productivity thereby reducing costs and increasing profits. The large and increasing investment in capital goods was the principal device by which profits were spent. In addition, those sectors of the economy marked by big business (i.e. oligopoly, a market dominated by a few firms) placed pressures upon the more competitive ones. As big business, as usual, received a higher share of profits due to their market position (see section C.5), this lead to many firms in the more competitive sectors of the economy facing a profitability crisis during the 1920s.

The increase in investment, while directly squeezing profits in the more competitive sectors of the economy, also eventually caused the rate of profit to stagnate, and then fall, over the economy as a whole. While the mass of available profits in the economy grew, it eventually became too small compared to the total capital invested. Moreover, with the fall in the share of income going to labour and the rise of inequality, aggregate demand for goods could not keep up with production leading to unsold goods (which is another way of expressing the process of over-investment leading to over-production, as over-production implies under-consumption and vice versa). As expected returns (profitability) on investments hesitated, a decline in investment demand occurred and so a slump began (rising predominantly from the capital stock rising faster than profits). Investment flattened out in 1928 and turned down in 1929. With the stagnation in investment, a great speculative orgy occurred in 1928 and 1929 in an attempt to enhance profitability. This unsurprisingly failed and in October 1929 the stock market crashed, paving the way for the Great Depression of the 1930s.

This process of over-investment relative to consumption is based on rising labour productivity combined with stagnant wages or relative slow wage growth. This implies inadequate workers' consumption but rising profit rates. This is possible as long as aggregate demand remains sufficient, which it can as long as high profit rates stimulate investment (i.e., money is not saved or sufficient credit is generated to ensure that investment spending does not lag consumption). Investment creates new capacity and that implies the need for further increases in investment, capitalist luxury consumption, and credit-based consumption to maintain aggregate demand. This profit-led growth is hard to sustain as high profits rates are difficult to maintain due to low working class income as both investment and capitalist luxury consumption are more unstable. Investment is more volatile than consumption, so the average degree of instability increases which, in turn, means that the probability of a slump rises. Further, this type of growth creates imbalances between sectors of the economy as firms rush to invest in profitable sections leading to relative over-production and over-investment in those areas (see last section). With the rise in unstable forms of demand, an economy becomes increasingly fragile and so increasingly vulnerable to "shocks." The stock market crash of 1929 was such a shock and the resulting panic and reduced demand for luxury goods and investment that it produced exposed the underlying weakness of the economy. After the Crash, restrictive fiscal and monetary policies and falling demand interacted to break this unstable prosperity and to accelerate the slump. This was reinforced by wage-cut induced under-consumption as well as debt deflation making over-investment worse in relation to over demand within the economy. So US prosperity was fragile long before late 1929, due to the process of over-investment relative to demand which lead the economy to be reliant on unstable forms of demand such as luxury consumption and investment.

The crash of 1929 indicates the "objective" limits of capitalism. Even with a very weak position of labour crisis still occurred and prosperity turned to "hard times." In contradiction to neo-classical economic theory, the events of the 1920s indicate that even if the capitalist assumption that labour is a commodity like all others **is** approximated in real life, capitalism is still subject to crisis (ironically, a militant union movement in the 1920s would have postponed crisis by shifting income from capital to labour, increasing aggregate demand, reducing investment and supporting the more competitive sectors of the economy!). Therefore, any neo-classical "blame labour" arguments for crisis (which were so popular in the 1930s and 1970s) only tells half the story (if that). Even if workers **do** act in a servile way to capitalist authority, capitalism will still be marked by boom and bust (as shown by the 1920s and 1980/90s).

To conclude, capitalism will suffer from a boom-and-bust cycle due to the above-mentioned objective pressures on profit production, even if we ignore the subjective revolt against authority by workers, explained earlier. In other words, even if the capitalist assumption that workers are not human beings but only "variable capital" **were** true, it would not mean that capitalism would be a crisis free system. However, for most anarchists, such a discussion is somewhat academic for human beings are not commodities, the labour "market" is not like the iron market, and the subjective revolt against capitalist domination will exist as long as capitalism does.

C.8

Is state control of money the cause of the business cycle?

As explained in the last section, capitalism will suffer from a boom-and-bust cycle due to objective pressures on profit production even if we ignore the subjective revolt against authority by working class people. It is this two-way pressure on profit rates, the subjective and objective, which causes the business cycle and such economic problems as *"stagflation."* However, for supporters of the free market, this conclusion is unacceptable and so they usually try to explain the business cycle in terms of **external** influences rather than those generated by the way capitalism works. Most pro-"free market" capitalists blame government intervention in the market, particularly state control over money, as the source of the business cycle. This analysis is defective, as will be shown below.

First it should be noted that many supporters of capitalism ignore the "subjective" pressures on capitalism that we discussed in section C.7.1. In addition, the problems associated with rising capital investment (as highlighted in section C.7.3) are also usually ignored, because they usually consider capital to be "productive" and so cannot see how its use could result in crises. This leaves them with the problems associated with the price mechanism, as discussed in section C.7.2. It is here, in the market for credit and money, that the role of the state comes into play, distorting the natural workings of the market and causing the ups and downs of business.

In pre-Keynesian bourgeois economics, the reason why Say's Law is applicable in a money economy is the interest rate. As we discussed in section C.2.6, this is claimed to reflect the *"time preference"* of individuals. While it is possible for sales not to be turned into purchases in the market, the money involved is not withdrawn from the economy. Rather, it is saved and made available to investors. The interest rate is the means by which savings and investment come into line. This means that Say's Law is maintained as savings are used to purchase capital goods and so demand and supply match. As long as interest rates are working as they should, the possibility of a general crisis is impossible. The problem is that the credit system does not work exactly as it claimed and this lies with the banks who introduce fractional reserve banking. This allows them to loan out more money than they have in savings in order to increase their profits. This lowers the rate of interest below its *"natural"* (or equilibrium) rate and thus firms get price signals which do not reflect the wishes of consumers for future goods rather than current ones. This causes over-investment and, ultimately, a crisis. This is because, eventually, interest rates must rise and projects which were profitable at the lower rate of interest will no longer be so. The moral of the theory is that if the actual rate of interest equalled the *"natural"* rate then a situation of *"neutral"* money would be achieved and so misdirections of production would be avoided, so ending the business cycle.

As far as capitalist economics had a theory of the business cycle, this was it and it was the dominant ideological position within the profession until publication of Keynes' **The General Theory of Employment, Interest and Money** in 1936. Politically, it was very useful as it recommended that the state should do nothing during the crisis and this was the preferred position of right-wing governments in America and Britain. It was forcefully argued by "Austrian" economist Frederick von Hayek during the early 1930s, who was repeating the earlier arguments of his mentor Ludwig von Mises and has been repeated by their followers ever since. Yet, for some strange reason, they almost always fail to mention that Hayek was roundly defeated in the theoretical battles of the time by Keynesians. In fact, his former students (including John Hicks and Nicholas Kaldor) showed how Hayek's theory was flawed and he gave up business cycle research in the early 1940s for other work. Kaldor's first critique (*"Capital Intensity and the Trade Cycle"*), for example, resulted in Hayek completely rewriting his theory while Kaldor's second article (*"Professor Hayek and the Concertina-effect"*) showed that Hayek's Ricardo Effect was only possible under some very special circumstances and so highly unlikely. [Kaldor, **Essays on Economic Stability and Growth**, pp. 120-147 and pp. 148-176]

Kaldor's critique was combined with an earlier critique by Piero Sraffa who noted that Hayek's desire for *"neutral"* money was simply impossible in any real capitalist economy for *"a state of things in which money is 'neutral' is identical with a state in which there is no money at all."* Hayek *"completely ignored"* the fact that *"money is not only the medium of exchange, but also a store of value"* which *"amounts to assuming away the very object of the inquiry."* Sraffa also noted that the starting point of Hayek's theory was flawed: *"An essential confusion ... is the belief that the divergence of rates is a characteristic of a money economy ... If money did not exist, and loans were made in terms of all sorts of commodities, there would be a single rate which satisfies the conditions of equilibrium, but there might be at any moment as many 'natural' rates of interest as there are commodities, though they would not be 'equilibrium' rates. The 'arbitrary' action of the banks is by no means a necessary condition for the divergence; if loans were made in wheat and farmers (or for that matter the weather) 'arbitrarily changed' the quantity of wheat produced, the actual rate of interest on loans in terms of wheat would diverge from the rate on other commodities and there would be no single equilibrium rate."* [*"Dr. Hayek on Money and Capital,"* pp. 42-53, **The Economic Journal**, vol. 42, no. 165, p. 42, pp. 43-4 and p. 49] Hayek admitted that this was a possibility, to which Sraffa replied:

> *"only under conditions of equilibrium would there be a single rate, and that when saving was in progress there would be at any one moment be many 'natural' rates, possibly as many as there are commodities; so that it would be not merely difficult in practice, but altogether inconceivable, that the money rate would be equal to 'the' natural rate ... Dr. Hayek now acknowledges the multiplicity of the 'natural' rates, but he has nothing more to say on this specific point than that they 'all would be equilibrium rates.' The only meaning (if it be a meaning) I can attach to this is that his maxim of policy now requires that the money rate should be equal to all these divergent*

natural rates." [*"A Rejoinder,"* pp. 249-251, **Op. Cit.**, Vol. 42, No. 166, p. 251]

Then there was the practical suggestions that flowed from the analysis, namely do nothing. It also implied that the best thing to do in a recession or depression is not to spend, but rather to save as this will bring the savings and loans back into the equilibrium position. Economist R. F. Kahn recounted when Hayek presented his theory at a seminar in Cambridge University. His presentation was followed by silence. Then Kahn asked the obvious question: *"Is it your view that if I went out tomorrow and bought a new overcoat, that would increase unemployment?"* All that Hayek could offer in reply was the unconvincing claim that to show why would require a complicated mathematical argument. The notion that reducing consumption in a depression was the best thing to do convinced few people and the impact of such saving should be obvious, namely a collapse in demand for goods and services. Any savings would, in the circumstances of a recession, be unlikely to be used for investing. After all, which company would start increasing its capital stock facing a fall in demand and which capitalist would venture to create a new company during a depression? Unsurprisingly, few economists thought that advocating a deflationary policy in the midst of the most severe economic crisis in history made much sense. It may have been economic orthodoxy but making the depression worse in order to make things better would have ensured either the victory of fascism or some-sort of socialist revolution.

Given these practical considerations and the devastating critiques inflicted upon it, Keynesian theory became the dominant theme in economics (particularly once it had been lobotomised of any ideas which threatened neo-classical supremacy – see section C.8.1). This has not, as noted, stopped Hayek's followers repeating his theory to this day (nor has its roots in equilibrium theory bothered them – see section C.1.6). Bearing this in mind, it is useful to discuss this theory because it reflects the pre-Keynesian orthodoxy although we must stress that our discussion of "Austrian" economics here should not be taken as suggesting that they are a significant school of thought or that their influence is large. Far from it – they still remain on the sidelines of economics where they were pushed after von Hayek's defeat in the 1930s. We use them simply because they are the only school of thought which still subscribes fully to the pre-Keynesian position. Most modern neo-classical economists pay at least lip-service to Keynes.

Take, for example, "Austrian" economist W. Duncan Reekie's argument that the business cycle *"is generated by monetary expansion and contraction ... When new money is printed it appears as if the supply of savings has increased. Interest rates fall and businessmen are misled into borrowing additional funds to finance extra investment activity."* This would be of *"no consequence"* if it had been the outcome of genuine saving *"but the change was government induced ... Capital goods industries will find their expansion has been in error and malinvestments have been incurred"* and so there has been *"wasteful mis-investment due to government interference with the market."* [**Markets, Entrepreneurs and Liberty**, pp. 68-9]

Yet the government does **not** force banks to make excessive loans and this is the first, and most obvious, fallacy of argument. After all, what Reekie is actually complaining about when he argues that "state action" creates the business cycle by creating excess money is that the state **allows** bankers to meet the demand for credit by creating it. This makes sense, for how could the state force bankers to expand credit by loaning more money than they have savings? This is implicitly admitted when Reekie argues that "[o]nce fractional reserve banking is introduced, however, the supply of money substitutes will include fiduciary media. The ingenuity of bankers, other financial intermediaries and the endorsement and **guaranteeing of their activities by governments and central banks** has ensured that the quantity of fiat money is immense." [**Op. Cit.**, p. 73] As we will discuss in detail below what is termed "credit money" (created by banks) is an essential part of capitalism and would exist without a system of central banks. This is because money is created from within the system, in response to the needs of capitalists. In a word, the money supply is endogenous.

The second fallacy of this theory of the business cycle lies with the assumption that the information provided by the interest rate itself is sufficient in itself to ensure rational investment decisions, it that provides companies and individuals with accurate information about how price changes will affect future trends in production. Specifically, the claim is that changes in interest rates (i.e. changes in the demand and supply of credit) indirectly inform companies of the responses of their competitors. As John O'Neill argues, the argument assumes "that information about the planned responses of producers in competition is indirectly distributed by changes in interest rates: the planned increase in production by separate producers is reflected in an increased demand for credit, and hence a rise in interest rates." [**The Market**, p. 135]

For example, if the price of tin rises, this will lead to an expansion in investment in the tin industry to reap the higher profits this implies. This would lead to a rise in interest rates as more credit is demanded. This rise in interest rates lowers anticipated profits and dampens the expansion. The expansion of credit stops this process by distorting the interest rate and so stops it performing its economic function. This results in overproduction as interest rates do not reflect **real** savings and so capitalists over-invest in new capital, capital which appears profitable only because the interest rate is artificially low. When the rate inevitably adjusts upwards towards its "natural" value, the invested capital becomes unprofitable and so over-investment appears. Hence, according to the argument, by eliminating state control of money these negative effects of capitalism would disappear as the credit system, if working correctly, will communicate all the relevant information required by capitalists.

"However," argues O'Neil, "this argument is flawed. It is not clear that the relevant information is communicated by changes in interest rates." This is because interest rates reflect the general aggregate demand for credit in an economy. However, the information which a **specific** company requires "if the over-expansion in the production of some good is to be avoided is not the general level of demand for credit, but the level of demand amongst competitors." It does not provide the relative demands in different industries (the parallels with Sraffa's critique should be obvious). "An increase in the planned production of some good by a group of competitors will be reflected in a proportional change in interest rates only if it is

assumed that the change in demand for credit by that group is identical with that found in the economy as a whole, i.e. if rates of change in the demand for credit are even throughout an economy. However, there is no reason to suppose such an assumption is true, given the different production cycles of different industries." This will produce differing needs for credit (in both terms of amount and of intensity). "Assuming uneven changes in the demand for credit" between industries reflecting uneven changes in their requirements it is quite possible for over-investment (and so over-production) to occur "even if the credit system is working 'satisfactorily'" (i.e., as it should in theory). The credit system, therefore, "does not communicate the relevant information" and for this reason "it is not the case that we must look to a departure from an ideal credit system to explain the business cycle." [**Op. Cit.**, pp. 135-6]

Another underlying assumption in this argument is that the economy is close to equilibrium (a concept which "Austrian" economists claim to reject). After all, rising interest rates will cause debt-servicing to become harder even if it reflects the "natural" rate. Equally, it also suggests that both banks and firms are capable of seeing into the future. For even **if** the credit market is working as postulated in the theory it does not mean that firms and banks do not make mistakes nor experience unexpected market situations. In such circumstances, firms may find it impossible to repay loans, credit chains may start to break as more and more firms find themselves in economic difficulties. Just because actual interest rates somehow equal the natural rate does not make the future any more certain nor does it ensure that credit is invested wisely. Crucially, it does not ensure that credit is not used to inflate a bubble or add to over-investment in a specific sector of the economy. To assume otherwise suggests the firms and banks rarely make mistakes and that the accumulative impact of all decisions move an economy always towards, and never away from, equilibrium. As Post-Keynesian Paul Davidson dryly noted, "Austrian subjectivists cannot have it both ways – they cannot argue for the importance of time, uncertainty, and money, and simultaneously presume that plan or pattern co-ordination must exist and is waiting to be discovered." ["The economics of ignorance or the ignorance of economics?", pp. 467-87, **Critical Review**, vol. 3, no. 3-4, p. 468]

In other words, the notion that if the actual interest rate somehow equalled the "natural" one is not only rooted in equilibrium but also the neo-classical notion of perfect knowledge of current and future events – all of which "Austrian" economists are meant to reject. This can be seen when Murray Rothbard states that entrepreneurs "are trained to forecast the market correctly; they only make mass errors when governmental or bank intervention distorts the 'signals' of the market." He even attacks Joseph Schumpeter's crisis theory because, in effect, Schumpeter does not show how entrepreneurs cannot predict the future ("There is no explanation offered on the lack of accurate forecasting … why were not the difficulties expected and discounted?"). [**America's Great Depression**, p. 48 and p. 70] Rothbard does not ponder why bankers, who are surely entrepreneurs as well, make **their** errors nor why the foresight of business people in an uncertain and complex economy seems to fail them in the face of repeated actions of banks (which they could, surely, have "expected and discounted"). This means that the argument concerning distortions of the interest rate does not, as such, explain the occurrence of over-investment (and so the business cycle). Therefore, it cannot be claimed that removing state interference in the market for money will also remove the business-cycle.

However, these arguments do have an element of truth in them. Expansion of credit above the *"natural"* level which equates it with savings can and does allow capital to expand further than it otherwise would and so **encourages** over-investment (i.e. it builds upon trends already present rather than **creating** them). While we have ignored the role of credit expansion in our comments above to stress that credit is not fundamental to the business cycle, it is useful to discuss this as it is an essential factor in real capitalist economies. Indeed, without it capitalist economies would not have grown as fast as they have. Credit is fundamental to capitalism and this is the last fallacy in the pre-Keynesian argument. In a real economy, it is the most important. Even assuming that the actual rate of interest **could** always equal the equilibrium rate and that it reflected the natural rate of all commodities and all industries, it would not matter as banks would always seek to make profits by extending credit and so artificially lower the actual interest rate during booms. To understand why, we need to explain the flaws in the main laissez-faire approaches to money.

There are three main approaches to the question of eliminating state control of money in "free market" capitalist economics – Monetarism, the 100% gold reserve limit for banks and what is often called "free banking." All three are associated with the right and all three are wrong. The first two are easy to dismiss. Monetarism has been tried and has failed spectacularly in the early 1980s. As it was a key aspect of the neo-liberal war on working class people at this time we will discuss its limitations as part of our account of this period in section C.8.3.

The second option, namely imposing a 100% gold reserve limit for banks is highly interventionist and so not remotely laissez-faire (why should the banking industry be subject to state regulation unlike the rest?). Its logic is simple, namely to ensure that banks do not make loans unless they have sufficient savings to cover them all. In other words, it seeks to abolish the credit cycle by abolishing credit by making banks keep 100% gold reserves against notes. This, in effect, abolishes banking as an industry. Simply put (and it seems strange to have to point this out to supporters of capitalism) banks seek to make a profit and do so by providing credit. This means that any capitalist system will be, fundamentally, one with credit money as banks will always seek to make a profit on the spread between loan and deposit rates. It is a necessity for the banking system and so non-fractional banking is simply not possible. The requirement that banks have enough cash on hand to meet all depositors demand amounts to the assertion that banks do not lend any money. A 100% reserve system is not a reformed or true banking system. It is the abolition of the banking system. Without fractional reserves, banks cannot make any loans of any kind as they would not be in a position to give their clients their savings if they have made loans. Only someone completely ignorant of a real capitalist economy could make such a suggestion and, unsurprisingly, this position is held by members of the "Austrian" school (particularly its minimum state wing).

This leaves "free banking." This school of thought is, again, associated with the "Austrian" school of economics and right-wing "libertarians" in general. It is advocated by those who seek to eliminate fractional reserve banking but balk by the regulations required by a 100% gold standard (Rothbard gets round this by arguing this standard *"would be part and parcel of the general libertarian legal prohibition against fraud."* [**Op. Cit.**, p. 32]). It is based on totally privatising the banking system and creating a system in which banks and other private companies compete on the market to get their coins and notes accepted by the general population. This position, it must be stressed, is not the same as anarchist mutual banking as it is seen not as a way of reducing usury to zero but rather as a means of ensuring that interest rates work as they are claimed to do in capitalist theory.

The "free banking" school argues that under competitive pressures, banks would maintain a 100% ratio between the credit they provide and the money they issue with the reserves they actually have. They argue that under the present system, banks can create more credit than they have funds/reserves available as the state exists as lender of last resort and so banks will count on it to bail them out in bad times. Market forces would ensure the end of fractional reserve banking and stop them pushing the rate of interest below its "natural rate." So if banks were subject to market forces, it is argued, then they would not generate credit money, interest rates would reflect the real rate and so over-investment, and so crisis, would be a thing of the past. Knowing that the state would not step in to save them will also force banks to be prudent in their activities.

This analysis, however, is flawed. We have noted one flaw above, namely the problem that interest rates do not provide sufficient or correct information for investment decisions. Thus relative over-investment could still occur. Another problem is the endogenous nature of money and credit and the pressures this puts on banks. As Steve Keen notes, Austrian economists think that *"the current system of State money means that the money supply is entirely exogenous and under the control of the State authorities. They then attribute much of the cyclical behaviour of the economy to government meddling with the money supply and the rate of interest."* In contrast, Post-Keynesian economists argue that *"though it may appear that the State controls the money supply, the complex chain of causation in the finance sector actually works backwards"* with *"private banks and other credit-generating institutions largely forc[ing] the State's hand. Thus the money supply is largely endogenously determined by the market economy, rather than imposed upon it exogenously by the State."* He notes that the *"empirical record certainly supports Post-Keynesians rather than Austrians on this point. Statistical evidence about the leads and lags between the State-determined component of money supply and broad credit show that the latter 'leads' the former."* [**Debunking Economics**, p. 303] Moreover, as our discussion of the failure of Monetarism will show, central banks could **not** control the money supply when they tried.

To understand why, we need to turn to the ideas of the noted Post-Keynesian economist Hyman Minsky. He created an analysis of the finance and credit markets which gives an insight into why it is doubtful that even a "free banking" system would resist the temptation to create credit money (i.e. loaning more money than available savings). This model is usually called *"The Financial Instability Hypothesis."*

Let us assume that the economy is going into the recovery period after a crash. Initially firms would be conservative in their investment while banks would lend within their savings limit and to low-risk investments. In this way the banks do ensure that the interest rate reflects the "natural" rate. However, this combination of a growing economy and conservatively financed investment means that most projects succeed and this gradually becomes clear to managers/capitalists and bankers. As a result, both managers and bankers come to regard the present risk premium as excessive. New investment projects are evaluated using less conservative estimates of future cash flows. This is the foundation of the new boom and its eventual bust. In Minsky's words, *"stability is destabilising."*

As the economy starts to grow, companies increasingly turn to external finance and these funds are forthcoming because the banking sector shares the increased optimism of investors. Let us not forget that banks are private companies too and so seek profits as well. As Minsky argues, *"bankers live in the same expectational climate as businessmen"* and so *"profit-seeking bankers will find ways of accommodating their customers … Banks and bankers are not passive managers of money to lend or to invest; they are in business to maximise profits."* [quoted by L. Randall Wray, **Money and Credit in Capitalist Economies**, p. 85] Providing credit is the key way of doing this and so credit expansion occurs. If they did not, the boom would soon turn into slump as investors would have no funds available for them and interest rates would increase, thus forcing firms to pay more in debt repayment, an increase which many firms may not be able to do or find difficult. This in turn would suppress investment and so production, generating unemployment (as companies cannot "fire" investments as easily as they can fire workers), so reducing consumption demand along with investment demand, so deepening the slump.

To avoid this and to take advantage of the rising economy, bankers accommodate their customers and generate credit rather than rise interest rates. In this way they accept liability structures both for themselves and for their customers *"that, in a more sober expectational climate, they would have rejected."* [Minsky, **Inflation, Recession and Economic Policy**, p. 123] The banks innovate their financial products, in other words, in line with demand. Firms increase their indebtedness and banks are more than willing to allow this due to the few signs of financial strain in the economy. The individual firms and banks increase their financial liability, and so the whole economy moves up the liability structure. Like other businesses, banks operate in an uncertain environment and have no way of knowing whether their actions will increase the fragility within the economy or push it into crisis.

The central banks, meanwhile, accommodate the banks activity. They do not and cannot force them to create credit. Alan Holmes, a senior vice president at the New York Federal Reserve, put the process this way:

> *"In the real world, banks extend credit, creating deposits in the process, and look for the reserves later. The question then becomes one of whether and how the Federal Reserve will accommodate the demand for*

> *reserves. In the very short run, the Federal Reserve has little or no choice about accommodating that demand, over time, its influence can obviously be felt."* [quoted by Doug Henwood, **Wall Street**, p. 220]

As long as profits exceed debt servicing requirements, the system will continue to work. Eventually, though, interest rates rise as the existing extension of credit appears too high to the banks or the central bank. This affects all firms, from the most conservatively financed to the most speculative, and "pushes" them up even higher up the liability structure. Refinancing existing debts is made at the higher rate of interest, increasing cash outflows and reducing demand for investment as the debt burden increases. Conservatively financed firms can no longer can repay their debts easily, less conservative ones fail to pay them and so on. The margin of error narrows and firms and banks become more vulnerable to unexpected developments, such a new competitors, strikes, investments which do not generate the expected rate of return, credit becoming hard to get, interest rates increase and so on. In the end, the boom turns to slump and firms and banks fail. The state then intervenes to try and stop the slump getting worse (with varying degrees of success and failure).

Thus the generation of credit is a spontaneous process rooted in the nature of capitalism and is fundamentally endogenous in nature. This means that the business cycle is an inherent part of capitalism even if we assume that it is caused purely by disequilibrium in the credit market. In other words, it is more than likely that the credit market will be in disequilibrium like every other market in any real capitalist economy – and for the same reasons. As such, the natural rate of interest relies on concepts of equilibrium that are not only inconsistent with reality but also with the broader principles of "Austrian" economic ideology.

The "free banking" school reject this claim and argue that private banks in competition would **not** do this as this would make them appear less competitive on the market and so customers would frequent other banks (this is the same process by which inflation would be solved). However, it is **because** the banks are competing that they innovate – if they do not, another bank or company would in order to get more profits. Keynesian economist Charles P. Kindleburger comments:

> *"As a historical generalisation, it can be said that every time the authorities stabilise or control some quantity of money … in moments of euphoria more will be produced. Or if the definition of money is fixed in terms of particular assets, and the euphoria happens to 'monetise' credit in new ways that are excluded from the definition, the amount of money defined in the old way will not grow, but its velocity will increase … fix any [definition of money] and the market will create new forms of money in periods of boom to get round the limit."* [**Manias, Panics and Crashes**, p. 48]

This can be seen from the fact that *"[b]ank notes … and bills of exchange … were initially developed because of an inelastic supply of coin."* Thus monetary expansion *"is systematic and endogenous rather than random and exogenous."* [Kindleburger, **Op. Cit.**, p. 51 and p. 150] This means that *"any shortage of commonly-used types* *[of money]* is bound to lead to the emergence of new types; indeed, this is how, historically, first bank notes and the chequing account emerged." If the state tries to regulate one form of money, *"lending and borrowing is diverted to other sources."* [Nicholas Kaldor, *"The New Monetarism"*, **The Essential Kaldor**, p. 481 and p. 482] This means that the notion that abolishing central banking will result in the use of gold and 100% reverses and so eliminate the business cycle is misplaced:

> *"This view overlooks the fact that the **emergence** of money-substitutes – whether in the form of bank notes, bank accounts, or credit cards – was a spontaneous process, not planned or regulated 'from above' by some central authority, and for that reason alone it is impossible to treat some arbitrary definition of money (which included specific forms of such money-substitutes in the definition of money) as an exogenous variable. The emergence of surrogate money was a spontaneous process resulting from the development of the banking system; this development brought a steady increase in the ratio of money substitutes of 'real' money."* [Nicholas Kaldor, **The Scourge of Monetarism**, p. 44f]

This process can be seen at work in Adam Smith's time. Then Scotland was based on a competitive banking system in which banking firms issued their own money and maintained their own reserve of gold. Yet, as Smith notes, they issued more money than was available in the banks coffers:

> *"Though some of those notes [the banks issued] are continually coming back for payment, part of them continue to circulate for months and years together. Though he [the banker] has generally in circulation, therefore, notes to the extent of a hundred thousand pounds, twenty thousand pounds in gold and silver may frequently be a sufficient provision for answering occasional demands."* [**The Wealth of Nations**, pp. 257-8]

In other words, the competitive banking system did not, in fact, eliminate fractional reserve banking. Ironically enough, Smith noted that *"the Bank of England paid very dearly, not only for its own imprudence, but for the much greater imprudence of almost all of the Scotch [sic!] banks."* Thus the central bank was more conservative in its money and credit generation than the banks under competitive pressures! Indeed, Smith argues that the banking companies did not, in fact, act in line with their interests as assumed by the "free banking" school for *"had every particular banking company always understood and attended to its own particular interest, the circulation never could have been overstocked with paper money. But every particular baking company has not always understood and attended to its own particular interest, and the circulation has frequently been overstocked with paper money."* Thus we have reserve banking plus bankers acting in ways opposed to their *"particular interest"* (i.e. what economists consider to be their actual self-interest rather than what the bankers actually thought was their self-interest!) in a system of competitive banking. Why could this be the case? Smith mentions, in passing, a possible reason. He notes that *"the high profits of trade afforded a great temptation to over-trading"* and

that while a *"multiplication of banking companies ... increases the security of the public"* by forcing them *"to be more circumspect in their conduct"* it also *"obliges all bankers to be more liberal in their dealings with their customers, lest their rivals should carry them away."* [**Op. Cit.**, p. 269, p. 267, p. 274 and p. 294]

Thus the banks were pulled in two directions at once, to accommodate their loan customers and make more profits while being circumspect in their activities to maintain sufficient reserves for the demands of their savers. Which factor prevails would depend on the state of the economy, with up-swings provoking liberal lending (as described by Minsky). Moreover, given that credit generation is meant to produce the business cycle, it is clear from the case of Scotland that competitive banking would not, in fact, stop either. This also was the case with 19th century America, which did not have a central bank for most of that period and that *"left the volatile US financial system without any kind of lender of last resort, but in booms all kinds of funny money passed."* This lead to *"thousands of decentralised banks ... hoarding reserves"* and so *"starving the system of liquidity precisely at the moment it was most badly needed"* while *"the up cycles were also extraordinary, powered by loose credit and kinky currencies (like privately issued banknotes)."* [Doug Henwood, **Op. Cit.**, p. 93 and p. 94]

As Nicholas Kaldor argued, *"the essential function of banks in the creation of 'finance' (or credit) was well understood by Adam Smith, who ... regarded branch-banking as a most important invention for the enrichment of society. He described how, as a result of the finance banks were able to place at the disposal of producers, the real income of Scotland doubled or trebled in a remarkably short time. Expressed in Keynesian terms, the 'finance' provided by banks made it possible to increase investments ahead of income or savings, and to provide the savings counterpart of the investment out of the additional income generated through a multiplier process by the additional spending."* This process, however, was unstable which naturally lead to the rise of central banks. *"Since the notes issued by some banks were found more acceptable than those of others, giving rise to periodic payments crises and uncertainty, it was sooner or later everywhere found necessary to concentrate the right of issuing bank notes in the hands of a single institution."* [*"How Monetarism Failed,"* **Further Essays on Economic Theory and Policy**, p. 181] In addition, from an anarchist perspective, no ruling class wants economic instability to undermine its wealth and income generating ability (Doug Henwood provides a useful summary of this process, and the arguments used to justify it within the American ruling class, for the creation of the US Federal Reserve at the start of the 20th century. [**Wall Street**, pp. 92-5]). Nor would any ruling class want too easy credit undermining its power over the working class by holding down unemployment too long (or allowing working class people to create their own financial institutions).

Thus the over supply of credit, rather than being the **cause** of the crisis is actually a symptom. Competitive investment drives the business cycle expansion, which is allowed and encouraged by the competition among banks in supplying credit. Such expansion complements – and thus amplifies – other objective tendencies towards crisis, such as over-investment and disproportionalities. In other words, a pure "free market" capitalism would still have a business cycle as this cycle is caused by the nature of capitalism, not by state intervention. In reality (i.e. in "actually existing" capitalism), state manipulation of money (via interest rates) is essential for the capitalist class as it allows indirect profit-generating activity, such as ensuring a "natural" level of unemployment to keep profits up, an acceptable level of inflation to ensure increased profits, and so forth, as well as providing a means of tempering the business cycle, organising bailouts and injecting money into the economy during panics. Ultimately, if state manipulation of money caused the problems of capitalism, we would not have seen the economic successes of the post-war Keynesian experiment or the business cycle in pre-Keynesian days and in countries which had a more free banking system (for example, nearly half of the late 19th century in the US was spent in periods of recession and depression, compared to a fifth since the end of World War II).

It is true that all crises have been preceded by a speculatively-enhanced expansion of production and credit. This does not mean, however, that crisis **results** from speculation and the expansion of credit. The connection is not causal in free market capitalism. The expansion and contraction of credit is a mere symptom of the periodic changes in the business cycle, as the decline of profitability contracts credit just as an increase enlarges it. So while there are some similarities in the pre-Keynesian/"Austrian" theory and the radical one outlined here, the key differences are two-fold. Firstly, the pro-capitalist theory argues that it is possible for capitalist banks **not** to act, well, like capitalists if subject to competition (or regulated enough). This seems highly unlikely and fits as badly into their general theories as the notion that disequilibrium in the credit market is the root of the business cycle. Secondly, the radical position stresses that the role of credit reflect deeper causes. Paul Mattick gives the correct analysis:

> "[M]oney and credit policies can themselves change nothing with regard to profitability or insufficient profits. Profits come only from production, from the surplus value produced by workers…. The expansion of credit has always been taken as a sign of a coming crisis, in the sense that it reflected the attempt of individual capital entities to expand despite sharpening competition, and hence survive the crisis…. Although the expansion of credit has staved off crisis for a short time, it has never prevented it, since ultimately it is the real relationship between total profits and the needs of social capital to expand in value which is the decisive factor, and that cannot be altered by credit." [**Economics, Politics and the Age of Inflation**, pp. 17-18]

In short, the apologists of capitalism confuse the symptoms for the disease.

The cyclical movements on the real side of the economy will be enhanced (both upwards and downwards) by events in its financial side and this may result in greater amplitudes in the cycle but the latter does not create the former. Where there *is no profit to be had, credit will not be sought."* While extension of the credit system *"can be a factor deferring crisis, the actual outbreak of crisis makes it into an aggravating factor because of the larger amount of capital that must be devalued."* [Paul Mattick, **Economic Crisis and Crisis**

Theory, p. 138] But this is also a problem facing competing private companies using the gold standard. The money supply reflects the economic activity within a country and if that supply cannot adjust, interest rates rise and provoke a crisis. Thus the need for a flexible money supply (as desired, for example, by Mutualists and the US Individualist Anarchists).

It must always be remembered that a loan is not like other commodities. Its exchange value is set by its use value. As its use value lies in investing and so generating a stream of income, the market rate of interest is governed by the average expectations of profits for the capitalist class. Thus credit is driven by its **perceived** use-value rather than its cost of production or the amount of money a bank has. Its possible use value reflects the prospective exchange-values (prices and profits) it can help produce. This means that uncertainty and expectations play a key role in the credit and financial markets and these impact on the real economy. This means that money can **never** be neutral and so capitalism will be subject to the business cycle and so unemployment will remain a constant threat over the heads of working class people. In such circumstances, the notion that capitalism results in a level playing field for classes is simply not possible and so, except in boom times, working class will be at a disadvantage on the labour market.

To sum up, *"[i]t is not credit but only the increase in production made possible by it that increases surplus value. It is then the rate of exploitation which determines credit expansion."* [Paul Mattick, **Economics, Politics and the Age of Inflation**, p. 18] Hence credit money would increase and decrease in line with capitalist profitability, as predicted in capitalist economic theory. But this could not affect the business cycle, which has its roots in production for capital (i.e. profit) and capitalist authority relations, to which the credit supply would obviously reflect, and not vice versa.

C.8.1 Does this mean that Keynesianism works?

If state interference in credit generation does not cause the business cycle, does that mean Keynesianism capitalism can work? Keynesian economics, as opposed to free market capitalism, maintains that the state can and should intervene in the economy in order to stop economic crises from occurring. Can it work? To begin to answer that question, we must first quickly define what is meant by Keynesianism as there are different kinds of Keynesianist policies and economics.

As far as economics goes, Keynes' co-worker Joan Robinson coined the phrase *"Bastard Keynesianism"* to describe the vulgarisation of his economics and its stripping of all aspects which were incompatible with the assumptions of neo-classical economics. Thus the key notion of uncertainty was eliminated and his analysis of the labour market reduced to the position he explicitly rejected, namely that unemployment was caused by price rigidities. This process was aided by the fact that Keynes retained significant parts of the neo-classical position in his analysis and argued that the role of the state was limited to creating the overall conditions necessary to allow the neo-classical system to come *"into its own again"* and allow capitalism *"to realise the full potentialities of production."* [**The General Theory**, pp. 378-9] Unlike many of his more radical followers, Keynes was blind to real nature of capitalism as a class based system and so failed to understand the functional role that unemployment plays within it (see section C.1.5).

However, the context in which Keynes worked explains much. Faced with the dire situation capitalism faced during the 1930s, he presented a new theoretical analysis of capitalism that both explained the crisis and suggested policies that would, without interfering with its general principles, end it. Keynes' work was aided both by the practical failure of traditional solutions and growing fear of revolution and so even the most died-in-the-wool neo-classical economists could not keep his theory from being tried. When it appeared to work that, on one level, ended the argument. However, at a deeper level, at the level of theory, the struggle was just beginning. As the neo-classical (and Austrian) tradition is axiom-led rather than empirically-led (otherwise their axioms would have been abandoned long ago), the mere fact that capitalism was in crisis and that Keynes had presented a theory more in line with the reality was not enough to change mainstream economics. From the start, neo-classical economists began their counter-attack. Led by Paul Samuelson in the US and John Hicks in the UK, they set about making Keynes' theories safe for neo-classical economics. They did this by using mathematics on a part of his theory, leaving out all those bits that were inconsistent with neo-classical axioms. This bowdlerised version of Keynes soon became the standard in undergraduate courses.

The fate of Keynes reinforces the comment of French revolutionary Louis de Saint-Just that *"those who make revolution half way only dig their own graves."* Keynes ideas were only a partial break with the neo-classical orthodoxy and, as such, allowed the basis for the neo-classical-Keynesian synthesis which dominated post-war economics until the mid-1970s as well as giving the Monetarist counter-revolution space to grow. Perhaps this partial break is understandable, given the dominance of neo-classical ideas in the economics profession it may have been too much to expect them to renounce all their dogmas yet it ensured that any developments towards an economics based on science rather than ideology would be resigned to the sidelines.

It is important to stress that Keynes was, first and foremost, a supporter of capitalism. He aimed to save it, not to end it. As he put it the *"**class war** will find me on the side of the educated bourgeoisie."* [quoted by Henwood, **Wall Street**, p. 212] That he presented a more accurate picture of capitalism and exposed some of the contradictions within neo-classical economics is part of the reason he was and is so hated by many on the right, although his argument that the state should limit some of the power of individual firms and capitalists and redistribute some income and wealth was a far more important source of that hatred. That he helped save capitalism from itself (and secure their fortunes) did not seem to concern his wealthy detractors. They failed to understand Keynes often sounded more radical than he actually was. Doug Henwood gives a good overview of Keynes' ideas (and limitations) in chapter 5 of his book **Wall Street**.

What of Keynesian policies? The *"Bastard Keynesianism"* of the post-war period (for all its limitations) did seem to have some impact on capitalism. This can be seen from comparing Keynesianism with what came before. The more laissez-faire period was nowhere near as stable as modern day supporters of free(r) market capitalists like to suggest. There were continual economic booms and slumps. The last third of the 19th century (often considered as the heyday of private enterprise) was a period of profound instability and anxiety as it *"was characterised by violent booms and busts, in nearly equal measure, since almost half the period was one of panic and depression."* America spent nearly half of the late 19th century in periods of recession and depression. By way of comparison, since the end of world war II, only about a fifth of the time has been. [Doug Henwood, **Wall Street**, p. 94 and p. 54] Between 1867 and 1900 there were 8 complete business cycles. Over these 396 months, the economy expanded during 199 months and contracted during 197. Hardly a sign of great stability. Overall, the economy went into a slump, panic or crisis in 1807, 1817, 1828, 1834, 1837, 1854, 1857, 1873, 1882, and 1893 (in addition, 1903 and 1907 were also crisis years).

Then there is what is often called the *"Golden Age of Capitalism,"* the boom years of (approximately) 1945 to 1975. This post-war boom presents compelling evidence that Keynesianism can effect the business cycle for the better by reducing its tendency to develop into a full depression. By intervening in the economy, the state would reduce uncertainty for capitalists by maintaining overall demand which will, in turn, ensure conditions where they will invest their money rather than holding onto it (what Keynes termed *"liquidity-preference"*). In other words, to create conditions where capitalists will desire to invest and ensure the willingness on the part of capitalists to act as capitalists.

This period of social Keynesianism after the war was marked by reduced inequality, increased rights for working class people, less unemployment, a welfare state you could actually use and so on. Compared to present-day capitalism, it had much going for it. However, Keynesian capitalism is still capitalism and so is still based upon oppression and exploitation. It was, in fact, a more refined form of capitalism, within which the state intervention was used to protect capitalism from itself while trying to ensure that working class struggle against it was directed, via productivity deals, into keeping the system going. For the population at large, the general idea was that the welfare state (especially in Europe) was a way for society to get a grip on capitalism by putting some humanity into it. In a confused way, the welfare state was promoted as an attempt to create a society in which the economy existed for people, not people for the economy.

While the state has always had a share in the total surplus value produced by the working class, only under Keynesianism is this share increased and used actively to manage the economy. Traditionally, placing checks on state appropriation of surplus value had been one of the aims of classical capitalist thought (simply put, cheap government means more surplus value available for capitalists to compete for). But as capital has accumulated, so has the state increased and its share in social surplus (for control over the domestic enemy has to be expanded and society protected from the destruction caused by free market capitalism). It must be stressed that state intervention was not **totally** new for *"[f]rom its origins, the United States had relied heavily on state intervention* and protection for the development of industry and agriculture, from the textile industry in the early nineteenth century, through the steel industry at the end of the century, to computers, electronics, and biotechnology today. Furthermore, the same has been true of every other successful industrial society." [Noam Chomsky, **World Orders, Old and New**, p. 101] The difference was that such state action was directed to social goals as well as bolstering capitalist profits (much to the hatred of the right).

The roots of the new policy of higher levels and different forms of state intervention lie in two related factors. The Great Depression of the 1930s had lead to the realisation that attempts to enforce widespread reductions in money wages and costs (the traditional means to overcome depression) simply did not work. As Keynes stressed, cutting wages reduced prices and so left real wages unaffected. Worse, it reduced aggregate demand and lead to a deepening of the slump (see section C.9.1 for details). This meant that leaving the market to solve its own problems would make things a lot worse before they became better. Such a policy would, moreover, be impossible because the social and economic costs would have been too expensive. Working class people simply would not tolerate more austerity imposed on them and increasingly took direct action to solve their problems. For example, America saw a militant strike wave involving a half million workers in 1934, with factory occupations and other forms of militant direct action commonplace. It was only a matter of time before capitalism was either ended by revolution or saved by fascism, with neither prospect appealing to large sections of the ruling class.

So instead of attempting the usual class war (which may have had revolutionary results), sections of the capitalist class thought a new approach was required. This involved using the state to manipulate demand in order to increase the funds available for capital. By means of demand bolstered by state borrowing and investment, aggregate demand could be increased and the slump ended. In effect, the state acts to encourage capitalists to act like capitalists by creating an environment when they think it is wise to invest again. As Paul Mattick points out, the *"additional production made possible by deficit financing does appear as additional demand, but as demand unaccompanied by a corresponding increase in total profits … [this] functions immediately as an increase in demand that stimulates the economy as a whole and can become the point for a new prosperity"* if objective conditions allow it. [**Economic Crisis and Crisis Theory**, p. 143]

State intervention can, in the short term, postpone crises by stimulating production. This can be seen from the in 1930s New Deal period under Roosevelt when the economy grew five years out of seven compared to it shrinking every year under the pro-laissez-faire Republican President Herbert Hoover (under Hoover, the GNP shrank an average of -8.4 percent a year, under Roosevelt it grew by 6.4 percent). The 1938 slump after 3 years of growth under Roosevelt was due to a decrease in state intervention:

> *"The forces of recovery operating within the depression, as well as the decrease in unemployment via public expenditures, increased production up to the output level of 1929. This was sufficient for the Roosevelt administration to drastically reduce public works … in*

a new effort to balance the budget in response to the demands of the business world … The recovery proved to be short-lived. At the end of 1937 the Business Index fell from 110 to 85, bringing the economy back to the state in which it had found itself in 1935 … Millions of workers lost their jobs once again." [Paul Mattick, **Economics, Politics and the Age of Inflation**, p. 138]

The rush to war made Keynesian policies permanent. With the success of state intervention during the second world war, Keynesianism was seen as a way of ensuring capitalist survival. The resulting boom is well known, with state intervention being seen as the way of ensuring prosperity for all sections of society. It had not fully recovered from the Great Depression and the boom economy during the war had obviously contrasted deeply with the stagnation of the 1930s. Plus, of course, a militant working class, which had put up with years of denial in the struggle against fascist-capitalism would not have taken lightly to a return to mass unemployment and poverty. Capitalism had to turn to continued state intervention as it is not a viable system. So, politically and economically a change was required. This change was provided by the ideas of Keynes, a change which occurred under working class pressure but in the interests of the ruling class.

So there is no denying that for a considerable time, capitalism has been able to prevent the rise of depressions which so plagued the pre-war world and that this was accomplished by government interventions. This is because Keynesianism can serve to initiate a new prosperity and postpone crisis by state intervention to bolster demand and encourage profit investment. This can mitigate the conditions of crisis, since one of its short-term effects is that it offers private capital a wider range of action and an improved basis for its own efforts to escape the shortage of profits for accumulation. In addition, Keynesianism can fund Research and Development in new technologies and working methods (such as automation) which can increase profits, guarantee markets for goods as well as transferring wealth from the working class to capital via indirect taxation and inflation. In the long run, however, Keynesian *"management of the economy by means of monetary and credit policies and by means of state-induced production must eventually find its end in the contradictions of the accumulation process."* [Paul Mattick, **Op. Cit.**, p. 18] This is because it cannot stop the tendency to (relative) over-investment, disproportionalities and profits squeeze we outlined in section C.7. In fact, due to its maintenance of full employment it increases the possibility of a crisis arising due to increased workers' power at the point of production.

So, these interventions did not actually set aside the underlying causes of economic and social crisis. The modifications of the capitalist system could not totally countermand the subjective and objective limitations of a system based upon wage slavery and social hierarchy. This can be seen when the rosy picture of post-war prosperity changed drastically in the 1970s when economic crisis returned with a vengeance, with high unemployment occurring along with high inflation. This soon lead to a return to a more "free market" capitalism with, in Chomsky's words, *"state protection and public subsidy for the rich, market discipline for the poor."* This process and its aftermath are discussed in the next section.

C.8.2 What happened to Keynesianism in the 1970s?

Basically, the subjective and objective limitations to Keynesianism we highlighted in the last section were finally reached in the early 1970s. It, in effect, came into conflict with the reality of capitalism as a class and hierarchical system. It faced either revolution to increase popular participation in social, political and economic life (and so eliminate capitalist power), an increase in social democratic tendencies (and so become some kind of democratic state capitalist regime) or a return to free(r) market capitalist principles by increasing unemployment and so placing a rebellious people in its place. Under the name of fighting inflation, the ruling class unsurprisingly picked the latter option.

The 1970s are a key time in modern capitalism. In comparison to the two previous decades, it suffered from high unemployment and high inflation rates (the term stagflation is usually used to describe this). This crisis was reflected in mass strikes and protests across the world. Economic crisis returned, with the state interventions that for so long kept capitalism healthy either being ineffective or making the crisis worse. In other words, a combination of social struggle and a lack of surplus value available to capital resulted in the breakdown of the successful post-war consensus. Both subjected the *"Bastard Keynesianism"* of the post-war period to serious political and ideological challenges. This lead to a rise in neo-classical economic ideology and the advocating of free(r) market capitalism as the solution to capitalism's problems. This challenge took, in the main, the form of Milton Friedman's Monetarism.

The roots and legacy of this breakdown in Keynesianism are informative and worth analysing. The post-war period marked a distinct change for capitalism, with new, higher levels of state intervention. The mix of intervention obviously differed from country to country, based upon the needs and ideologies of the ruling parties and social elites as well as the impact of social movements and protests. In Europe, nationalisation was widespread as inefficient capital was taken over by the state and reinvigorated by state funding while social spending was more important as Social Democratic parties attempted to introduce reforms. Chomsky describes the process in the USA:

> "Business leaders recognised that social spending could stimulate the economy, but much preferred the military Keynesian alternative – for reasons having to do with privilege and power, not 'economic rationality.' This approach was adopted at once, the Cold War serving as the justification. ... The Pentagon system was considered ideal for these purposes. It extends well beyond the military establishment, incorporating also the Department of Energy ... and the space agency NASA, converted by the Kennedy administration to a significant component of the state-directed public subsidy to advanced industry. These arrangements impose on the public a large burden of the costs of industry (research and development, R&D) and provide a guaranteed market for excess production, a useful cushion for management decisions. Furthermore,

> this form of industrial policy does not have the undesirable side-effects of social spending directed to human needs. Apart from unwelcome redistributive effects, the latter policies tend to interfere with managerial prerogatives; useful production may undercut private gain, while state-subsidised waste production ... is a gift to the owner and manager, to whom any marketable spin-offs will be promptly delivered. Social spending may also arouse public interest and participation, thus enhancing the threat of democracy ... The defects of social spending do not taint the military Keynesian alternative. For such reasons, **Business Week** explained, 'there's a tremendous social and economic difference between welfare pump-priming and military pump-priming,' the latter being far preferable." [**World Orders, Old and New**, pp. 100-1]

Over time, social Keynesianism took increasing hold even in the USA, partly in response to working class struggle, partly due to the need for popular support at elections and partly due to *"[p]opular opposition to the Vietnam war [which] prevented Washington from carrying out a national mobilisation ... which might have made it possible to complete the conquest without harm to the domestic economy. Washington was forced to fight a 'guns-and-butter' war to placate the population, at considerable economic cost."* [Chomsky, **Op. Cit.**, pp. 157-8]

Social Keynesianism directs part of the total surplus value to workers and unemployed while military Keynesianism transfers surplus value from the general population to capital and from capital to capital. This allows R&D and capital to be publicly subsidised, as well as essential but unprofitable capital to survive. As long as real wages did not exceed a rise in productivity, Keynesianism would continue. However, both functions have objective limits as the transfer of profits from successful capital to essential, but less successful, or long term investment can cause a crisis is there is not enough profit available to the system as a whole. The surplus value producing capital, in this case, would be handicapped due to the transfers and cannot respond to economic problems as freely as before. This was compounded by the world becoming economically "tripolar," with a revitalised Europe and a Japan-based Asian region emerging as major economic forces. This placed the USA under increased pressure, as did the Vietnam War. Increased international competition meant the firms were limited in how they could adjust to the increased pressures they faced in the class struggle.

This factor, class struggle, cannot be underestimated. In fact, the main reason for the 1970s breakdown was social struggle by working people. The only limit to the rate of growth required by Keynesianism to function is the degree to which final output consists of consumption goods for the presently employed population instead of investment. As long as wages rise in line with productivity, capitalism does well and firms invest (indeed, investment is the most basic means by which work, i.e. capitalist domination, is imposed). However, faced with a workforce which is able to increase its wages and resist the introduction of new technologies then capitalism will face a crisis. The net effect of full employment was the increased rebellious of the working class (both inside and outside the workplace). This struggle was directed against hierarchy in general, with workers, students, women, ethnic groups, anti-war protesters and the unemployed all organising successful struggles against authority. This struggle attacked the hierarchical core of capitalism as well as increasing the amount of income going to labour, resulting in a profit squeeze (see section C.7). By the 1970s, capitalism and the state could no longer ensure that working class struggles could be contained within the system.

This profits squeeze reflected the rise in inflation. While it has become commonplace to argue that Keynesianism did not predict the possibility of exploding inflation, this is not entirely true. While Keynes and the mainstream Keynesians failed to take into account the impact of full employment on class relations and power, his left-wing followers did not. Influenced by Michal Kalecki, they argued that full employment would impact on power at the point of production and, consequently, prices. To quote Joan Robinson from 1943:

> "The first function of unemployment (which has always existed in open or disguised forms) is that it maintains the authority of master over man. The master has normally been in a position to say: 'If you don't want the job, there are plenty of others who do.' When the man can say: 'If you don't want to employ me, there are plenty of others who will', the situation is radically altered. One effect of such a change might be to remove a number of abuses to which the workers have been compelled to submit in the past ... [Another is that] the absence of fear of unemployment might go further and have a disruptive effect upon factory discipline ... [He may] us[e] his newly-found freedom from fear to snatch every advantage that he can ...

> "The change in the workers' bargaining position which would follow from the abolition of unemployment would show itself in another and more subtle way. Unemployment ... has not only the function of preserving discipline in industry, but also indirectly the function of preserving the value of money ... there would be a constant upward pressure upon money wage-rates ... the vicious spiral of wages and prices might become chronic ... if it moved too fast, it might precipitate a violent inflation." [**Collected Economic Papers**, vol. 1, pp. 84-5]

Thus left-wing Keynesians (who later founded the Post-Keynesian school of economics) recognised that capitalists *"could recoup themselves for rising costs by raising prices."* [**Op. Cit.**, p. 85] This perspective was reflected in a watered-down fashion in mainstream economics by means of the Philips Curve. When first suggested in the 1958, this was taken to indicate a stable relationship between unemployment and inflation. As unemployment fell, inflation rose. This relationship fell apart in the 1970s, as inflation rose as unemployment rose.

Neo-classical (and other pro-"free market" capitalist) economics usually argues that inflation is purely a monetary phenomenon, the result of there being more money in circulation than is needed for the sale of the various commodities on the market. This was the position of Milton Friedman and his Monetarist school during the

1960s and 1970s. However, this is not true. In general, there is no relationship between the money supply and inflation. The amount of money can increase while the rate of inflation falls, for example (as we will discuss in the next section, Monetarism itself ironically proved there is no relationship). Inflation has other roots, namely it is *"an expression of inadequate profits that must be offset by price and money policies ... Under any circumstances, inflation spells the need for higher profits."* [Paul Mattick, **Economics, Politics and the Age of Inflation**, p. 19] Inflation leads to higher profits by making labour cheaper. That is, it reduces *"the real wages of workers ... [which] directly benefits employers ... [as] prices rise faster than wages, income that would have gone to workers goes to business instead."* [J. Brecher and T. Costello, **Common Sense for Hard Times**, p. 120]

Inflation, in other words, is a symptom of an on-going struggle over income distribution between classes. It is caused when capitalist profit margins are reduced (for whatever reason, subjective or objective) and the bosses try to maintain them by increasing prices, i.e. by passing costs onto consumers. This means that it would be wrong to conclude that wage increases "cause" inflation as such. To do so ignores the fact that workers do not set prices, capitalists do. Any increase in costs could, after all, be absorbed by lowering profits. Instead working class people get denounced for being "greedy" and are subjected to calls for "restraint" – in order for their bosses to make sufficient profits! As Joan Robinson put it, while capitalist economics denies it (unlike, significantly, Adam Smith) there is an *"inflationary pressure that arises from an increase in the share of gross profits in gross income. How are workers to be asked to accept 'wage restraint' unless there is a restraint on profits? ... unemployment is the problem. If it could be relived by tax cuts, generating purchasing power, would not a general cut in profit margins be still more effective? These are the questions that all the rigmarole about marginal productivity is designed to prevent us from discussing."* [**Collected Economic Papers**, vol. 4, p. 134]

Inflation and the response by the capitalist class to it, in their own ways, shows the hypocrisy of capitalism. After all, wages are increasing due to "natural" market forces of supply and demand. It is the **capitalists** who are trying to buck the market by refusing to accept lower profits caused by conditions on it. Obviously, to use Benjamin Tucker's expression, under capitalism market forces are good for the goose (labour) but bad for the gander (capital). The so-called "wages explosion" of the late 1960s was a symptom of this shift in class power away from capital and to labour which full employment had created. The growing expectations and aspirations of working class people led them not only to demand more of the goods they produced, it had start many questioning why social hierarchies were needed in the first place. Rather than accept this as a natural outcome of the eternal laws of supply and demand, the boss class used the state to create a more favourable labour market environment (as, it should be stressed, it has always done).

This does not mean that inflation suits all capitalists equally (nor, obviously, does it suit those social layers who live on fixed incomes and who thus suffer when prices increase but such people are irrelevant in the eyes of capital). Far from it – during periods of inflation, lenders tend to lose and borrowers tend to gain. The opposition to high levels of inflation by many supporters of capitalism is based upon this fact and the division within the capitalist class it indicates. There are two main groups of capitalists, finance capitalists and industrial capitalists. The latter can and do benefit from inflation (as indicated above) but the former sees high inflation as a threat. When inflation is accelerating it can push the real interest rate into negative territory and this is a horrifying prospect to those for whom interest income is fundamental (i.e. finance capital). In addition, high levels of inflation can also fuel social struggle, as workers and other sections of society try to keep their income at a steady level. As social struggle has a politicising effect on those involved, a condition of high inflation could have serious impacts on the political stability of capitalism and so cause problems for the ruling class.

How inflation is viewed in the media and by governments is an expression of the relative strengths of the two sections of the capitalist class and of the level of class struggle within society. For example, in the 1970s, with the increased international mobility of capital, the balance of power came to rest with finance capital and inflation became the source of all evil. This shift of influence to finance capital can be seen from the rise of rentier income. The distribution of US manufacturing profits indicate this process – comparing the periods 1965-73 to 1990-96, we find that interest payments rose from 11% to 24%, dividend payments rose from 26% to 36% while retained earnings fell from 65% to 40%. Given that retained earnings are the most important source of investment funds, the rise of finance capital helps explain why, in contradiction to the claims of the right-wing, economic growth has become steadily worse as markets have been liberalised – funds that could have been resulted in real investment have ended up in the finance machine. In addition, the waves of strikes and protests that inflation produced had worrying implications for the ruling class as they showed a working class able and willing to contest their power and, perhaps, start questioning **why** economic and social decisions were being made by a few rather than by those affected by them. However, as the underlying reasons for inflation remained (namely to increase profits) inflation itself was only reduced to acceptable levels, levels that ensured a positive real interest rate and acceptable profits.

Thus, Keynesianism sowed the seeds of its own destruction. Full employment had altered the balance of power in the workplace and economy from capital to labour. The prediction of socialist economist Michal Kalecki that full employment would erode social discipline had become true (see section B.4.4). Faced with rising direct and indirect costs due to this, firms passed them on to consumers. Yet consumers are also, usually, working class and this provoked more direct action to increase real wages in the face of inflation. Within the capitalist class, finance capital was increasing in strength at the expense of industrial capital. Facing the erosion of their loan income, states were subject to economic pressures to place fighting inflation above maintaining full employment. While Keynes had hoped that *"the rentier aspect of capitalism [was] a transitional phase"* and his ideas would lead to *"the euthanasia of the rentier,"* finance capital was not so willing to see this happen. [**The General Theory**, p. 376] The 1970s saw the influence of an increasingly assertive finance capital rise at a time when significant numbers within ranks of industrial capitalists were sick of full employment

and wanted compliant workers again. The resulting recessions may have harmed individual capitalists (particularly smaller ones) but the capitalist class as a whole did very well of them (and, as we noted in section B.2, one of the roles of the state is to manage the system in the interests of the capitalist class **as a whole** and this can lead it into conflict with **some** members of that class). Thus the maintenance of sufficiently high unemployment under the mantra of fighting inflation as the de facto state policy from the 1980s onwards (see section C.9). While industrial capital might want a slightly stronger economy and a slightly lower rate of unemployment than finance capital, the differences are not significant enough to inspire major conflict. After all, bosses in any industry *"like slack in the labour market"* as it *"makes for a pliant workforce"* and, of course, *"many non-financial corporations have heavy financial interests."* [Doug Henwood, **Wall Street**, pp. 123-4 and p. 135]

It was these processes and pressures which came to a head in the 1970s. In other words, post-war Keynesianism failed simply because it could not, in the long term, stop the subjective and objective pressures which capitalism always faces. In the 1970s, it was the subjective pressure which played the key role, namely social struggle was the fundamental factor in economic developments. The system could not handle the struggle of human beings against the oppression, exploitation, hierarchy and alienation they are subject to under capitalism.

C.8.3 How did capitalism adjust to the crisis in Keynesianism?

Basically by using, and then managing, the 1970s crisis to discipline the working class in order to reap increased profits and secure and extend the ruling classes' power. It did this using a combination of crisis, free(r) markets and adjusted Keynesianism as part of a ruling elite lead class war against labour.

In the face of crisis in the 1970s, Keynesianist redirection of profits between capitals and classes had become a burden to capital as a whole and had increased the expectations and militancy of working people to dangerous levels. The crisis of the 1970s and early 1980s helped control working class power and unemployment was utilised as a means of saving capitalism and imposing the costs of free(r) markets onto society as whole. The policies implemented were ostensibly to combat high inflation. However, as left-wing economist Nicholas Kaldor summarised, inflation may have dropped but this lay *"in their success in transforming the labour market from a twentieth-century sellers' market to a nineteenth-century buyers' market, with wholesome effects on factory discipline, wage claims, and proneness to strike."* [**The Scourge of Monetarism**, p. xxiii] Another British economist described this policy memorably as *"deliberately setting out to base the viability of the capitalist system on the maintenance of a large 'industrial reserve army' [of the unemployed] … [it is] the incomes policy of Karl Marx."* [Thomas Balogh, **The Irrelevance of Conventional Economics**, pp. 177-8]

The aim, in summary, was to swing the balance of social, economic and political power back to capital and ensure the road to (private) serfdom was followed. The rationale was fighting inflation.

Initially the crisis was used to justify attacks on working class people in the name of the free market. And, indeed, capitalism was made more market based, although with a "safety net" and "welfare state" for the wealthy. We have seen a partial return to *"what economists have called freedom of industry and commerce, but which really meant the relieving of industry from the harassing and repressive supervision of the State, and the giving to it full liberty to exploit the worker, whom was still to be deprived of his freedom."* The *"crisis of democracy"* which so haunted the ruling class in the 1960s and 1970s was overcome and replaced with, to use Kropotkin's words, the *"liberty to exploit human labour without any safeguard for the victims of such exploitation and the political power organised as to assure freedom of exploitation to the middle-class."* [Kropotkin, **The Great French Revolution**, vol.1, p. 28 and p. 30]

Fighting inflation, in other words, was simply code used by the ruling class for fighting the class war and putting the working class back in its place in the social hierarchy. *"Behind the economic concept of inflation was a fear among elites that they were losing control"* as the *"sting of unemployment was lessened and workers became progressively less docile."* [Doug Henwood, **After the New Economy**, p. 204] Milton Friedman's Monetarism was the means by which this was achieved. While (deservedly) mostly forgotten now, Monetarism was very popular in the 1970s and was the economic ideology of choice of both Reagan and Thatcher. This was the economic justification for the restructuring of capitalism and the end of social Keynesianism. Its legacy remains to some degree in the overriding concern over inflation which haunts the world's central banks and other financial institutions, but its specific policy recommendations have been dropped in practice after failing spectacularly when applied (a fact which, strangely, was not mentioned in the eulogies from the right that marked Friedman's death).

According to Monetarism, the problem with capitalism was money related, namely that the state and its central bank printed too much money and, therefore, its issue should be controlled. Friedman stressed, like most capitalist economists, that monetary factors are **the** most important feature in explaining such problems of capitalism as the business cycle, inflation and so on. This is unsurprising, as it has the useful ideological effect of acquitting the inner-workings of capitalism of any involvement in such developments. Slumps, for example, may occur, but they are the fault of the state interfering in the economy. Inflation was a purely monetary phenomenon caused by the state printing more money than required by the growth of economic activity (for example, if the economy grew by 2% but the money supply increased by 5%, inflation would rise by 3%). This analysis of inflation is deeply flawed, as we will see. This was how Friedman explained the Great Depression of the 1930s in the USA, for example (see, for example, his *"The Role of Monetary Policy"* [**American Economic Review**, Vol. 68, No. 1, pp. 1-17]).

Thus Monetarists argued for controlling the money supply, of placing the state under a *"monetary constitution"* which ensured that the central banks be required by law to increase the quantity of money at a constant rate of 3-5% a year. This would ensure that inflation would be banished, the economy would adjust to its natural equilibrium, the business cycle would become mild (if not disappear)

and capitalism would finally work as predicted in the economics textbooks. With the *"monetary constitution"* money would become *"depoliticised"* and state influence and control over money would be eliminated. Money would go back to being what it is in neo-classical theory, essentially neutral, a link between production and consumption and capable of no mischief on its own. Hence the need for a *"legislated rule"* which would control *"the behaviour of the stock of money"* by *"instructing the monetary authority to achieve a specified rate of growth in the stock of money."* [**Capitalism and Freedom**, p. 54]

Unfortunately for Monetarism, its analysis was simply wrong. It cannot be stressed enough how deeply flawed and ideological Friedman's arguments were. As one critique noted, his assumptions have *"been shown to be fallacious and the empirical evidence questionable if not totally misinterpreted."* Moreover, *"none of the assumptions which Friedman made to reach his extraordinary conclusions bears any relation to reality. They were chosen precisely because they led to the desired conclusion, that inflation is a purely monetary phenomenon, originating solely in excess monetary demand."* [Thomas Balogh, **Op. Cit.**, p. 165 and p. 167] For Kaldor, Friedman's claims that empirical evidence supported his ideology were false. *"Friedman's assertions lack[ed] any factual foundation whatsoever."* He stressed, *"They ha[d] no basis in fact, and he seems to me have invented them on the spur of the moment."* [**Op. Cit.**, p. 26] There was no relationship between the money supply and income.

Even more unfortunately for both the theory and (far more importantly) vast numbers of working class people, it was proven wrong not only theoretically but also empirically. Monetarism was imposed on both the USA and the UK in the early 1980s, with disastrous results. As the Thatcher government in 1979 applied Monetarist dogma the most whole-heartedly we will concentrate on that regime (the same basic things occurred under Reagan as well but he embraced military Keynesianism sooner and so mitigated its worse effects. [Michael Stewart, **Keynes and After**, p. 181] This did not stop the right proclaiming the Reagan boom as validation of "free market" economics!).

Firstly, the attempt to control the money supply failed, as predicted by Nicholas Kaldor (see his 1970 essay *"The New Monetarism"*). This is because the money supply, rather than being set by the central bank or the state (as Friedman claimed), is a function of the demand for credit, which is itself a function of economic activity. To use economic terminology, Friedman had assumed that the money supply was "exogenous" and so determined outside the economy by the state when, in fact, it is "endogenous" in nature (i.e. comes from **within** the economy). [**The Essential Kaldor**, p. 483] This means that any attempt by the central bank to control the money supply, as desired by Friedman, will fail.

The experience of the Thatcher and Reagan regimes indicates this well. The Thatcher government could not meet the money controls it set. It took until 1986 before the Tory government stopped announcing monetary targets, persuaded no doubt by the embarrassment caused by its inability to hit them. In addition, the variations in the money supply showed that Friedman's argument on what caused inflation was also wrong. According to his theory, inflation was caused by the money supply increasing faster than the economy, yet inflation **fell** as the money supply increased. Between 1979 and 1981-2, its growth rose and was still higher in 1982-3 than it had been in 1978-9 yet inflation was down to 4.6% in 1983. As the moderate conservative MP Ian Gilmore pointed out, *"[h]ad Friedmanite monetarism … been right, inflation would have been about 16 per cent in 1982-3, 11 per cent in 1983-4, and 8 per cent in 1984-5. In fact … in the relevant years it never approached the levels infallibly predicted by monetarist doctrine."* [Ian Gilmore, **Dancing With Dogma**, p. 57 and pp. 62-3] So, as Henwood summarises, *"even the periods of recession and recovery disprove monetarist dogma."* [**Wall Street**, p. 202]

However, the failed attempt to control the money supply had other, more important effects, namely exploding interest and unemployment rates. Being unable to control the supply of money, the government did the next best thing: it tried to control the demand for money by raising interest rates. Unfortunately for the Tories their preferred measure for the money supply included interest-bearing bank deposits. This meant, as the government raised interest rates in its attempts to control the money supply, it was profitable for people to put more money on deposit. Thus the rise in interest rates promoted people to put money in the bank, so increasing the particular measure of the money supply the government sought to control which, in turn, lead them to increase interest rates. [Michael Stewart, **Keynes in the 1990s**, p. 50]

The exploding interest rates used in a vain attempt to control the money supply was the last thing Britain needed in the early 1980s. The economy was already sliding into recession and government attempts to control the money supply deepened it. While Milton Friedman predicted *"only a modest reduction in output and employment"* as a *"side effect of reducing inflation to single figures by 1982,"* in fact Britain experienced its deepest recession since the 1930s. [quoted by Michael Stewart, **Keynes and After**, p. 179] As Michael Stewart dryly notes, it *"would be difficult to find an economic prediction that that proved more comprehensively inaccurate."* Unemployment rose from around 5% in 1979 to 13% in the middle of 1985 (and would have been even higher but for a change in the method used for measuring it, a change implemented to knock numbers off of this disgraceful figure). In 1984 manufacturing output was still 10% lower than it had been in 1979. [**Op. Cit.**, p. 180] Little wonder Kaldor stated that Monetarism was *"a terrible curse, a visitation of evil spirits, with particularly unfortunate, one could almost say devastating, effects on"* Britain. [*"The Origins of the New Monetarism,"* pp. 160-177, **Further Essays on Economic Theory and Policy**, p. 160]

Eventually, inflation did fall. From an anarchist perspective, however, this fall in inflation was the result of the high unemployment of this period as it weakened labour, so allowing profits to be made in production rather than in circulation (see last section for this aspect of inflation). With no need for capitalists to maintain their profits via price increases, inflation would naturally decrease as labour's bargaining position was weakened by the fear mass unemployment produced in the workforce. Rather than being a purely monetary phenomena as Friedman claimed, inflation was a product of the profit needs of capital and the state of the class struggle. The net effect of the deep recession of the early 1980s and mass unemployment during the 1980s (and 1990s) was to control working class people by

putting the fear of being fired back. The money supply had nothing to do with it and attempts to control it would, of necessity, fail and the only tool available to governments would be raising interest rates. This would reduce inflation only by depressing investment, generating unemployment, and so (eventually) slowing the growth in wages as workers bear the brunt of the recessions by lowering their real income (i.e., paying higher prices on the same wages). Which is what happened in the 1980s.

It is also of interest to note that even in Friedman's own test case of his basic contention, the Great Depression of 1929-33, he got it wrong. For Friedman, the *"fact is that the Great Depression, like most other periods of severe unemployment, was produced by government mismanagement rather than by any inherent instability of the private economy."* [**Op. Cit.**, p. 54] Kaldor pointed out that *"[a]ccording to Friedman's own figures, the amount of 'high-powered money' … in the US increased, not decreased, throughout the Great Contraction: in July 1932, it was more than 10 per cent higher than in July, 1929 … The Great Contraction of the money supply … occurred **despite** this increase in the monetary base."* [*"The New Monetarism"*, **The Essential Kaldor**, pp. 487-8] Other economists also investigated Friedman's claims, with similar result. Peter Temin, for example, critiqued them from a Keynesian point of view, asking whether the decline in spending resulted from a decline in the money supply or the other way round. He noted that while the Monetarist *"narrative is long and complex"* it *"offers far less support for [its] assertions than appears at first. In fact, it assumes the conclusion and describes the Depression in terms of it; it does not test or prove it at all."* He examined the changes in the real money balances and found that they increased between 1929 and 1931 from between 1 and 18% (depending on choice of money aggregate used and how it was deflated). Overall, the money supply not only did not decline but actually increased 5% between August 1929 and August 1931. Temin concluded that there is no evidence that money caused the depression after the stock market crash. [**Did Monetary Forces Cause the Great Depression?**, pp. 15-6 and p. 141]

There is, of course, a slight irony about Friedman's account of the Great Depression. Friedman suggested that the Federal Reserve actually caused the Great Depression, that it was in some sense a demonstration of the evils of government intervention. In his view, the US monetary authorities followed highly deflationary policies and so the money supply fell because they forced or permitted a sharp reduction in the monetary base. In other words, because they failed to exercise the responsibilities assigned to them. This is the core of his argument. Yet it is important to stress that by this he did not, in fact, mean that it happened because the government had intervened in the market. Ironically, Friedman argued it happened because the government did **not** intervene fast or far enough thus making a bad situation much worse. In other words, it was not interventionist enough!

This self-contradictory argument arises because Friedman was an ideologue for capitalism and so sought to show that it was a stable system, to exempt capitalism from any systemic responsibility for recessions. That he ended up arguing that the state caused the Great Depression by doing nothing (which, ironically, was what Friedman usually argued it should do) just shows the power of ideology over logic or facts. Its fleeting popularity was due to its utility in the class war for the ruling class at that time. Given the absolute failure of Monetarism, in both theory and practice, it is little talked about now. That in the 1970s it was the leading economic dogma of the right explains why this is the case. Given that the right usually likes to portray itself as being strong on the economy it is useful to indicate that this is **not** the case – unless you think causing the deepest recessions since the 1930s in order to create conditions where working class people are put in their place so the rich get richer is your definition of sound economic policy. As Doug Henwood summarises, there *"can be no doubt that monetarism ... throughout the world from the Chilean coup onward, has been an important part of a conscious policy to crush labour and redistribute income and power toward capital."* [**Wall Street**, pp. 201-2]

For more on Monetarism, the work of its greatest critic, Nicholas Kaldor, is essential reading (see for example, *"Origins of the new Monetarism"* and *"How Monetarism Failed"* in **Further Essays on Economic Theory and Policy**, *"The New Monetarism"* in **The Essential Kaldor** and **The Scourge of Monetarism**).

So under the rhetoric of "free market" capitalism, Keynesianism was used to manage the crisis as it had previously managed the prosperity. "Supply Side" economics (combined with neo-classical dogma) was used to undercut working class power and consumption and so allow capital to reap more profits off working class people by a combination of reduced regulation for the capitalist class and state intervention to control the working class. Unemployment was used to discipline a militant workforce and as a means of getting workers to struggle **for** work instead of **against** wage labour. With the fear of job loss hanging over their heads, workers put up with speedups, longer hours, worse conditions and lower wages and this increased the profits that could be extracted directly from workers as well as reducing business costs by allowing employers to reduce on-job safety and protection and so on. The labour "market" was fragmented to a large degree into powerless, atomised units with unions fighting a losing battle in the face of a recession made much worse by government policy (and justified by economic ideology). In this way capitalism could successfully change the composition of demand from the working class to capital.

Needless to say, we still living under the legacy of this process. As we indicated in section C.3, there has been a significant shift in income from labour to capital in the USA. The same holds true in the UK, as does rising inequality and higher rates of poverty. While the economy is doing well for the few, the many are finding it harder to make ends meet and, as a result, are working harder for longer and getting into debt to maintain their income levels (in a sense, it could be argued that aggregate demand management has been partially privatised as so many working class people are in debt). Unsurprisingly 70% of the recent gain in per capita income in the Reagan-Bush years went to the top 1% of income earners (while the bottom lost absolutely). Income inequality increased, with the income of the bottom fifth of the US population falling by 18% while that of the richest fifth rose by 8%. [Noam Chomsky, **World Orders, Old and New**, p. 141] Combined with bubbles in stocks and housing, the illusion of a good economy is maintained while only those at the top are doing well (see section B.7 on rising inequality). This disciplining of the working class has been successful, resulting

in the benefits of rising productivity and growth going to the elite. Unemployment and underemployment are still widespread, with most newly created jobs being part-time and insecure.

Indirect means of increasing capital's share in the social income were also used, such as reducing environment regulations, so externalising pollution costs onto current and future generations. In Britain, state owned monopolies were privatised at knock-down prices allowing private capital to increase its resources at a fraction of the real cost. Indeed, some nationalised industries were privatised **as monopolies** for a period allowing monopoly profits to be extracted from consumers before the state allowed competition in those markets. Indirect taxation also increased, reducing working class consumption by getting us to foot the bill for capitalist restructuring as well as military-style Keynesianism. Internationally, the exploitation of under-developed nations increased with $418 billion being transferred to the developed world between 1982 and 1990 [Chomsky, **Op. Cit.**, p. 130] Capital also became increasingly international in scope, as it used advances in technology to move capital to third world countries where state repression ensured a less militant working class. This transfer had the advantage of increasing unemployment in the developed world, so placing more pressures upon working class resistance.

This policy of capital-led class war, a response to the successful working class struggles of the 1960s and 1970s, obviously reaped the benefits it was intended to for capital. Income going to capital has increased and that going to labour has declined and the "labour market" has been disciplined to a large degree (but not totally we must add). Working people have been turned, to a large degree, from participants into spectators, as required for any hierarchical system. The human impact of these policies cannot be calculated. Little wonder, then, the utility of neo-classical dogma to the elite – it could be used by rich, powerful people to justify the fact that they are pursuing social policies that create poverty and force children to die. As Chomsky argues, *"one aspect of the internationalisation of the economy is the extension of the two-tiered Third World mode to the core countries. Market doctrine thus becomes an essential ideological weapon at home as well, its highly selective application safely obscured by the doctrinal system. Wealth and power are increasingly concentrated. Service for the general public – education, health, transportation, libraries, etc. – become as superfluous as those they serve, and can therefore be limited or dispensed with entirely."* [**Year 501**, p. 109]

The state managed recession has had its successes. Company profits are up as the *"competitive cost"* of workers is reduced due to fear of job losses. The Wall Street Journal's review of economic performance for the last quarter of 1995 is headlined *"Companies' Profits Surged 61% on Higher Prices, Cost Cuts."* After-tax profits rose 62% from 1993, up from 34% for the third quarter. While working America faces stagnant wages, Corporate America posted record profits in 1994. **Business Week** estimated 1994 profits to be up *"an enormous 41% over [1993],"* despite a bare 9% increase in sales, a *"colossal success,"* resulting in large part from a *"sharp"* drop in the *"share going to labour,"* though *"economists say labour will benefit – eventually."* [quoted by Noam Chomsky, *"Rollback III"*, **Z Magazine**, April 1995] Labour was still waiting over a decade later.

Moreover, for capital, Keynesianism still goes on as before, combined (as usual) with praises to market miracles. For example, Michael Borrus, co-director of the Berkeley Roundtable on the International Economy (a corporate-funded trade and technology research institute), cites a 1988 Department of Commerce study that states that *"five of the top six fastest growing U.S. industries from 1972 to 1988 were sponsored or sustained, directly or indirectly, by federal investment."* He goes on to state that the *"winners [in earlier years were] computers, biotechnology, jet engines, and airframes"* all *"the by-product of public spending."* [quoted by Chomsky, **World Orders, Old and New**, p. 109] As James Midgley points out, *"the aggregate size of the public sector did not decrease during the 1980s and instead, budgetary policy resulted in a significant shift in existing allocations from social to military and law enforcement."* [*"The radical right, politics and society"*, **The Radical Right and the Welfare State**, Howard Glennerster and James Midgley (eds.), p. 11] Indeed, the US state funds one third of all civil R&D projects, and the UK state provides a similar subsidy. [Chomsky, **Op. Cit.**, p. 107] And, of course, the state remains waiting to save the elite from their own market follies (for example, after the widespread collapse of Savings and Loans Associations in deregulated corruption and speculation, the 1980s pro-"free market" Republican administration happily bailed them out, showing that market forces were only for one class).

The corporate owned media attacks social Keynesianism, while remaining silent or justifying pro-business state intervention. Combined with extensive corporate funding of right-wing "think-tanks" which explain why (the wrong sort of) social programmes are counter-productive, the corporate state system tries to fool the population into thinking that there is no alternative to the rule by the market while the elite enrich themselves at the public's expense. This means that state intervention has not ended as such. We are still in the age of Keynes, but social Keynesianism has been replaced by military Keynesianism cloaked beneath the rhetoric of "free market" dogma. This is a mix of free(r) markets (for the many) and varying degrees of state intervention (for the select few), while the state has become stronger and more centralised (*"prisons also offer a Keynesian stimulus to the economy, both to the construction business and white collar employment; the fastest growing profession is reported to be security personnel."* [Chomsky, **Year 501**, p. 110]). In other words, pretty much the same situation that has existed since the dawn of capitalism (see section D.1) – free(r) markets supported by ready use of state power as and when required.

The continued role of the state means that it is unlikely that a repeat of the Great Depression is possible. The large size of state consumption means that it stabilises aggregate demand to a degree unknown in 1929 or in the 19th century period of free(r) market capitalism. This is **not** to suggest that deep recessions will not happen (they have and will). It is simply to suggest that they will **not** turn into a deep depression. Unless, of course, ideologues who believe the "just-so" stories of economic textbooks and the gurus of capitalism gain political office and start to dismantle too much of the modern state. As Thatcher showed in 1979, it is possible to deepen recessions considerably if you subscribe to flawed economic theory (ideology would be a better word) and do not care about the

impact it is having on the general public – and, more importantly, if the general public cannot stop you.

However, as we discuss in section C.10 the net effect of this one-sided class war has not been as good as has been suggested by the ideologues of capitalism and the media. Faced with the re-imposition of hierarchy, the quality of life for the majority has fallen (consumption, i.e. the quantity of life, may not but that is due to a combination of debt, increased hours at work and more family members taking jobs to make ends meet). This, in turn, has lead to a fetish over economic growth. As Joan Robinson put it in the 1970s when this process started the *"economists have relapsed into the slogans of laisser faire – what is profitable promotes growth; what is most profitable is best. But people have began to notice that the growth of statistical GNP is not the same thing as an increase in welfare."* [**Collected Economic Papers**, vol. 4, p. 128] Yet even here, the post-1970s experience is not great. A quarter century of top heavy growth in which the vast majority of economic gains have gone to the richest 10% of the population has not produced the rate of GDP growth promised for it. In fact, the key stimulus for growth in the 1990s and 2000s was bubbles, first in the stock market and then in the housing market. Moreover, rising personal debt has bolstered the economy in a manner which are as unsustainable as the stock and housing bubbles which, in part, supported it. How long the system will stagger on depends, ultimately, on how long working class people will put up with it and having to pay the costs inflicted onto society and the environment in the pursuit of increasing the wealth of the few.

While working class resistance continues, it is largely defensive, but, as in the past, this can and will change. Even the darkest night ends with the dawn and the lights of working class resistance can be seen across the globe. For example, the anti-Poll Tax struggle in Britain against the Thatcher Government was successful as have been many anti-cuts struggles across the USA and Western Europe, the Zapatista uprising in Mexico was inspiring as was the Argentine revolt against neo-liberalism and its wave of popular assemblies and occupied workplaces. In France, the anti-CPE protests showed a new generation of working class people know not only how to protest but also nonsense when they hear it. In general, there has been continual strikes and protests across the world. Even in the face of state repression and managed economic recession, working class people are still fighting back. The job for anarchists to is encourage these sparks of liberty and help them win.

C.9

Would laissez-faire capitalism reduce unemployment?

In order to answer this question, we must first have to point out that "actually existing capitalism" tries to manage unemployment to ensure a compliant and servile working class. This is done under the name of fighting "inflation" but, in reality, it is about controlling wages and maintaining high profit rates for the capitalist class. Market discipline for the working class, state protection for the ruling class, in other words. As Edward Herman points out:

> "Conservative economists have even developed a concept of a 'natural rate of unemployment,' a metaphysical notion and throwback to an eighteenth century vision of a 'natural order,' but with a modern apologetic twist. The natural rate is defined as the minimum unemployment level consistent with price level stability, but, as it is based on a highly abstract model that is not directly testable, the natural rate can only be inferred from the price level itself. That is, if prices are going up, unemployment is below the 'natural rate' and too low, whether the actual rate is 4, 8, or 10 percent. In this world of conservative economics, anybody is 'voluntarily' unemployed. Unemployment is a matter of rational choice: some people prefer 'leisure' over the real wage available at going (or still lower) wage rates …

> "Apart from the grossness of this kind of metaphysical legerdemain, the very concept of a natural rate of unemployment has a huge built-in bias. It takes as granted all the other institutional factors that influence the price level-unemployment trade-off (market structures and independent pricing power, business investment policies at home and abroad, the distribution of income, the fiscal and monetary mix, etc.) and focuses solely on the tightness of the labour market as the controllable variable. Inflation is the main threat, the labour market (i.e. wage rates and unemployment levels) is the locus of the solution to the problem." [**Beyond Hypocrisy**, p. 94]

Unsurprisingly, Herman defines this "natural" rate as *"the rate of unemployment preferred by the propertied classes."* [**Op. Cit.**, p. 156] The theory behind this is usually called the ***"Non-Accelerating Inflation Rate of Unemployment"*** (or NAIRU). Like many of the worse aspects of modern economics, the concept was raised Milton Friedman in the late 1960s. At around the same time, Edmund Phelps independently developed the theory (and gained the "Nobel Prize" in economics for so doing in 2006). Both are similar and both simply repeat, in neo-classical jargon, the insight which critics of capitalism had argued for over a century: unemployment is a necessary aspect of capitalism for it is essential to maintaining the power of the boss over the worker. Ironically, therefore, modern neo-classical economics is based on a notion which it denied for

over a century (this change may be, in part, because the ruling elite thinks it has won the class war and has, currently, no major political and social movements it has to refute by presenting a rosy picture of the system).

Friedman raised his notion of a *"Natural Rate of Unemployment"* in 1968. He rooted it in the neo-classical perspective of individual expectations rather than, say, the more realistic notion of class conflict. His argument was simple. There exists in the economy some *"natural"* rate associated with the real wage an ideal economy would produce (this is *"the level that would be ground out by the Walrasian system of general equilibrium equations,"* to quote him). Attempts by the government to reduce actual unemployment below this level would result in rising inflation. This is because there would be divergence between the actual rate of inflation and its expected rate. By lowering unemployment, bosses have to raise wages and this draws unemployed people into work (note the assumption that unemployment is voluntary). However, rising wages were passed on by bosses in rising prices and so the **real** wage remains the same. This eventually leads to people leaving the workforce as the real wage has fallen back to the previous, undesired, levels. However, while the unemployment level rises back to its *"natural"* level, inflation does not. This is because workers are interested in real wages and, so if inflation is at, say, 2% then they will demand wage increases that take this into account. If they expect inflation to increase again then workers will demand **more** wages to make up for it, which in turn will cause prices to rise (although Friedman downplayed that this was because **bosses** were increasing their prices to maintain profit levels). This will lead to rising inflation **and** rising unemployment. Thus the expectations of individuals are the key.

For many economists, this process predicted the rise of stagflation in the 1970s and gave Friedman's Monetarist dogmas credence. However, this was because the *"Bastard Keynesianism"* of the post-war period was rooted in the same neo-classical assumptions used by Friedman. Moreover, they had forgotten the warnings of left-wing Keynesians in the 1940s that full unemployment would cause inflation as bosses would pass on wage rises onto consumers. This class based analysis, obviously, did not fit in well with the panglossian assumptions of neo-classical economics. Yet basing an analysis on individual expectations does not answer the question whether these expectations are meet. With strong organisation and a willingness to act, workers can increase their wages to counteract inflation. This means that there are two main options within capitalism. The first option is to use price controls to stop capitalists increasing their prices. However, this contradicts the sacred laws of supply and demand and violates private property. Which brings us to the second option, namely to break unions and raise unemployment to such levels that workers think twice about standing up for themselves. In this case, workers cannot increase their money wages and so their real wages drop.

Guess which option the capitalist state went for? As Friedman made clear when he introduced the concept there was really nothing *"natural"* about the natural rate theory as it was determined by state policy:

"I do not mean to suggest that it is immutable and unchangeable. On the contrary, many of the market characteristics that determine its level are man-made and policy-made. In the United States, for example, legal minimum wage rates ... and the strength of labour unions all make the natural rate of unemployment higher than it would otherwise be." ["*The Role of Monetary Policy,*" pp. 1-17, **American Economic Review**, Vol. 68, No. 1, p. 9]

Thus the "natural" rate is really a social and political phenomenon which, in effect, measures the bargaining strength of working people. This suggests that inflation will fall when working class people are in no position to recoup rising prices in the form of rising wages. The "Natural Rate" is, in other words, about class conflict.

This can be seen when the other (independent) inventor of the "natural" rate theory won the Nobel Prize in 2006. Unsurprisingly, the **Economist** magazine was cock-a-hoop. ["*A natural choice: Edmund Phelps earns the economics profession's highest accolade*", Oct 12th 2006] The reasons why became clear. According to the magazine, *"Phelps won his laurels in part for kicking the feet from under his intellectual forerunners"* by presenting a (neo-classical) explanation for the breakdown of the so-called *"Phillips curve."* This presented a statistical trade-off between inflation and unemployment (*"unemployment was low in Britain when wage inflation was high, and high when inflation was low"*). The problem was that economists *"were quick – too quick – to conclude that policymakers therefore faced a grand, macroeconomic trade-off"* in which, due to *"such a tight labour market, companies appease workers by offering higher wages. They then pass on the cost in the form of dearer prices, cheating workers of a higher real wage. Thus policy makers can engineer lower unemployment only through deception."* Phelps innovation was to argue that *"[e]ventually workers will cotton on, demanding still higher wages to offset the rising cost of living. They can be duped for as long as inflation stays one step ahead of their rising expectations of what it will be."* The similarities with Friedman's idea are obvious. This meant that the *"stable trade-off depicted by the Phillips curve is thus a dangerous mirage"* which broke down in the 1970s with the rise of stagflation.

Phelps argued that there was a *"natural"* rate of unemployment, where *"workers' expectations are fulfilled, prices turn out as anticipated, and they no longer sell their labour under false pretences."* This *"equilibrium does not, sadly, imply full employment"* and so capitalism required *"leaving some workers mouldering on the shelf. Given economists' almost theological commitment to the notion that markets clear, the presence of unemployment in the world requires a theodicy to explain it."* The religious metaphor does seem appropriate as most economists (and **The Economist**) do treat the market like a god (a theodicy is a specific branch of theology and philosophy that attempts to reconcile the existence of evil in the world with the assumption of a benevolent God). And, as with all gods, sacrifices are required and Phelps' theory is the means by which this is achieved. As the magazine noted: *"in much of his work he contends that unemployment is necessary to cow workers, ensuring their loyalty to the company and their diligence on the job, at a wage the company can afford to pay"* (i.e., one

which would ensure a profit).

It is this theory which has governed state policy since the 1980s. In other words, government's around the world have been trying to *"cow workers"* in order to ensure their obedience (*"loyalty to the company"*). Unsurprisingly, attempts to lower the *"natural rate"* have all involved using the state to break the economic power of working class people (attacking unions, increasing interest rates to increase unemployment in order to temporarily *"cow"* workers and so on). All so that profits can be keep high in the face of the rising wages caused by the natural actions of the market!

Yet it must be stressed that Friedman's and Phelps' conclusions are hardly new. Anarchists and other socialists had been arguing since the 1840s that capitalism had no tendency to full employment either in theory or in practice. They have also noted how periods of full employment bolstered working class power and harmed profits. It is, as we stressed in section C.1.5, the fundamental disciplinary mechanism of the system. Somewhat ironically, then, Phelps got bourgeois economics highest prize for restating, in neo-classical jargon, the model of the labour market expounded by, say, Marx:

> *"If [capital's] accumulation on the one hand increases the demand for labour, it increases on the other the supply of workers by 'setting them free', while at the same time the pressure of the unemployed compels those that are employed to furnish more labour, and therefore makes the supply of labour to a certain extent independent of the supply of labourers. The movement of the law of supply and demand of labour on this basis completes the despotism of capital. Thus as soon as the workers learn the secret of why it happens that the more they work, the more alien wealth they produce ... as soon as, by setting up trade unions, etc., they try to organise a planned co-operation between employed and unemployed in order to obviate or to weaken the ruinous effects of this natural law of capitalistic production on their class, so soon capital and its sycophant, political economy, cry out at the infringement of the 'eternal' and so to speak 'sacred' law of supply and demand. Every combination of employed and unemployed disturbs the 'pure' action of this law. But on the other hand, as soon as ... adverse circumstances prevent the creation of an industrial reserve army and, with it, the absolute dependence of the working-class upon the capitalist class, capital, along with its platitudinous Sancho Panza, rebels against the 'sacred' law of supply and demand, and tries to check its inadequacies by forcible means."* [**Capital**, Vol. 1, pp. 793-4]

That the **Economist** and Phelps are simply echoing, and confirming, Marx is obvious. Modern economics, while disparaging Marx, has integrated this idea into its macro-economic policy recommendations by urging the state to manipulate the economy to ensure that "inflation" (i.e. wage rises) are under control. Economics has played its role of platitudinous sycophant well while Phelps' theory has informed state interference (*"forcible means"*) in the economy since the 1980s, with the expected result that wages have failed to keep up with rising productivity and so capital as enriched itself at the expense of labour (see section C.3 for details). The use of Phelps' theory by capital in the class war is equally obvious – as was so blatantly stated by **The Economist** and the head of the American Federal Reserve during this period:

> "there's supporting testimony from Alan Greenspan. Several times during the late 1990s, Greenspan worried publicly that, as unemployment drifted steadily lower the 'pool of available workers' was running dry. The dryer it ran, the greater risk of 'wage inflation,' meaning anything more than minimal increases. Productivity gains took some of the edge of this potentially dire threat, said Greenspan, and so did 'residual fear of job skill obsolescence, which has induced a preference for job security over wage gains' ... Workers were nervous and acting as if the unemployment rate were higher than the 4% it reached in the boom. Still, Greenspan was a bit worried, because ... if the pool stayed dry, 'Significant increases in wages, in excess of productivity growth, [would] inevitably emerge, absent the unlikely repeal of the law of supply and demand.' Which is why Greenspan & Co. raised short-term interest rates by about two points during 1999 and the first half of 2000. There was no threat of inflation ... nor were there any signs of rising worker militancy. But wages were creeping higher, and the threat of the sack was losing some of its bite." [Doug Henwood, **After the New Economy**, pp. 206-7]

Which is quite ironic, given that Greenspan's role in the economy was, precisely, to *"repeal"* the *"law of supply and demand."* As one left-wing economist puts it (in a chapter correctly entitled *"The Workers Are Getting Uppity: Call In the Fed!"*), the Federal Reserve (like all Central Banks since the 1980s) *"worries that if too many people have jobs, or if it is too easy for workers to find jobs, there will be upward pressure on wages. More rapid wage growth can get translated into more rapidly rising prices – in other words, inflation. So the Fed often decides to raise interest rates to slow the economy and keep people out of work in order to keep inflation from increasing and eventually getting out of control."* However, *"[m]ost people probably do not realise that the Federal Reserve Board, an agency of the government, intervenes in the economy to prevent it from creating too many jobs. But there is even more to the story. When the Fed hits the brakes to slow job growth, it is not doctors, lawyers, and CEOs who end up without jobs. The people who lose are those in the middle and the bottom – sales clerks, factory workers, custodians, and dishwashers. These are the workers who don't get hired or get laid off when the economy slows or goes into a recession."* [**The Conservative Nanny State**, p. 31] Thus the state pushes up unemployment rates to slow wage growth, and thereby relieve inflationary pressure. The reason should be obvious:

> "In periods of low unemployment, workers don't only gain from higher wages. Employers must make efforts to accommodate workers' various needs, such as child care or flexible work schedules, because they know that workers have other employment options. The Fed is well aware of the difficulties that employers face in periods of

low unemployment. It compiles a regular survey, called the 'Beige Book,' of attitudes from around the country about the state of the economy. Most of the people interviewed for the Beige Book are employers.

> "From 1997 to 2000, when the unemployment rate was at its lowest levels in 30 years, the Beige Book was filled with complaints that some companies were pulling workers from other companies with offers of higher wages and better benefits. Some Beige Books reported that firms had to offer such non-wage benefits as flexible work hours, child care, or training in order to retain workers. The Beige Books give accounts of firms having to send buses into inner cities to bring workers out to the suburbs to work in hotels and restaurants. It even reported that some employers were forced to hire workers with handicaps in order to meet their needs for labour.

> "From the standpoint of employers, life is much easier when the workers are lined up at the door clamouring for jobs than when workers have the option to shop around for better opportunities. Employers can count on a sympathetic ear from the Fed. When the Fed perceives too much upward wage pressure, it slams on the brakes and brings the party to an end. The Fed justifies limiting job growth and raising the unemployment rate because of its concern that inflation may get out of control, but this does not change the fact that it is preventing workers, and specifically less-skilled workers, from getting jobs, and clamping down on their wage growth." [**Op. Cit.**, pp. 32-3]

This has not happened by accident. Lobbying by business, as another left-wing economist stresses, *"is directed toward increasing their economic power"* and business *"has been a supporter of macroeconomic policies that have operated the economy with higher rates of unemployment. The stated justification is that this lowers inflation, but it also weakens workers' bargaining power."* Unsurprisingly, *"the economic consequence of the shift in the balance of power in favour of business ... has served to redistribute income towards profits at the expense of wages, thereby lowering demand and raising unemployment."* In effect, the Federal Reserve *"has been using monetary policy as a form of surrogate incomes policy, and this surrogate policy has been tilted against wages in favour of profits"* and so is regulating the economy *"in a manner favourable to business."* [Thomas I. Palley, **Plenty of Nothing**, p. 77, p. 111 and pp. 112-3] That this is done under the name of fighting inflation should not fool us:

> "Mild inflation is often an indication that workers have some bargaining strength and may even have the upper hand. Yet, it is at exactly this stage that the Fed now intervenes owning to its anti-inflation commitment, and this intervention raises interest rates and unemployment. Thus, far from being neutral, the Fed's anti-inflation policy implies siding with business in the ever-present conflict between labour and capital over distribution of the fruits

of economic activity ... natural-rate theory serves as the perfect cloak for a pro-business policy stance." [**Op. Cit.**, p. 110]

In a sense, it is understandable that the ruling class within capitalism desires to manipulate unemployment in this way and deflect questions about their profit, property and power onto the state of the labour market. High prices can, therefore, be blamed on high wages rather than high profits, rents and interest while, at the same time, workers will put up with lower hours and work harder and be too busy surviving to find the time or the energy to question the boss's authority either in theory or in practice. So managing the economy by manipulating interest rates to increase unemployment levels when required allows greater profits to be extracted from workers as management hierarchy is more secure. People will put up with a lot in the face of job insecurity. As left-wing economist Thomas Balogh put it, full employment *"generally removes the need for servility, and thus alters the way of life, the relationship between classes ... weakening the dominance of men over men, dissolving the master-servant relation. It is the greatest engine for the attainment by all of human dignity and greater equality."* [**The Irrelevance of Conventional Economics**, p. 47]

Which explains, in part, why the 1960s and 1970s were marked by mass social protest against authority rather than von Hayek's *"Road to Serfdom."* It also explains why the NAIRU was so enthusiastically embraced and applied by the ruling class. When times are hard, workers with jobs think twice before standing up to their bosses and so work harder, for longer and in worse conditions. This ensures that surplus value is increased relative to wages (indeed, in the USA, real wages have stagnated since 1973 while profits have grown massively). In addition, such a policy ensures that political discussion about investment, profits, power and so on (*"the other institutional factors"*) are reduced and diverted because working class people are too busy trying to make ends meet. Thus the state intervenes in the economy to **stop** full employment developing to combat inflation and instability on behalf of the capitalist class.

That this state manipulation is considered consistent with the "free market" says a lot about the bankruptcy of the capitalist system and its defenders. But, then, for most defenders of the system state intervention on behalf of capital is part of the natural order, unlike state intervention (at least in rhetoric) on behalf of the working class (and shows that Kropotkin was right to stress that the state **never** practices "laissez-faire" with regard to the working class – see section D.1). Thus neo-liberal capitalism is based on monetary policy that explicitly tries to weaken working class resistance by means of unemployment. If "inflation" (i.e. labour income) starts to increase, interest rates are raised so causing unemployment and, it is hoped, putting the plebes back in their place. In other words, the road to private serfdom has been cleared of any barriers imposed on it by the rise of the working class movement and the policies of social democracy implemented after the Second World War to stop social revolution. This is the agenda pursued so strongly in America and Britain, imposed on the developing nations and urged upon Continental Europe.

Although the aims and results of the NAIRU should be enough to condemn it out of hand, it can be dismissed for other reasons. First

and foremost, this "natural" rate is both invisible and can move. This means trying to find it is impossible (although it does not stop economists trying, and then trying again when rate inflation and unemployment rates refute the first attempt, and then trying again and again). In addition, it is a fundamentally a meaningless concept – you can prove anything with an invisible, mobile value – it is an non-refutable concept and so, fundamentally, non-scientific. Close inspection reveals natural rate theory to be akin to a religious doctrine. This is because it is not possible to conceive of a test that could possibly falsify the theory. When predictions of the natural rate turn out wrong (as they repeatedly have), proponents can simply assert that the natural rate has changed. That has led to the most recent incarnation of the theory in which the natural rate is basically the trend rate of unemployment. Whatever trend is observed is natural – case closed.

Since natural rate theory cannot be tested, a sensible thing would be to examine its assumptions for plausibility and reasonableness. However, Milton Friedman's early work on economic methodology blocks this route as he asserted that realism and plausibility of assumptions have no place in economics. With most economists blindly accepting this position, the result is a church in which entry is conditional on accepting particular assumptions about the working of markets. The net effect is to produce an ideology, an ideology which survives due to its utility to certain sections of society.

If this is the case, and it is, then any attempts to maintain the "natural" rate are also meaningless as the only way to discover it is to watch **actual** inflation levels and raising interest rates appropriately. Which means that people are being made unemployed on the off-chance that the unemployment level will drop below the (invisible and mobile) "natural" rate and harm the interests of the ruling class (high inflation rates harms interest incomes and full employment squeezes profits by increasing workers' power). This does not seem to bother most economists, for whom empirical evidence at the best of times is of little consequence. This is doubly true with the NAIRU, for with an invisible, mobile value, the theory is always true after the fact – if inflation rises as unemployment rises, then the natural rate has increased; if inflation falls as unemployment rises, it has fallen! As post-Keynesian economist James K. Galbraith noted in his useful critique of the NAIRU, *"as the real unemployment rate moves, the apparent NAIRU moves in its shadow"* and its *"estimates and re-estimates seem largely a response to predictive failure. We still have no theory, and no external evidence, governing the fall of the estimated NAIRU. The literature simply observes that inflation hasn't occurred and so the previous estimate must have been too high."* He stresses, economists have held *"to a concept in the face of twenty years of unexplained variation, predictive failure, and failure of the profession to coalesce on procedural issues."* [**Created Unequal**, p. 180] Given that most mainstream economists subscribe to this fallacy, it just shows how the "science" accommodates itself to the needs of the powerful and how the powerful will turn to any old nonsense if it suits their purpose. A better example of supply and demand for ideology could not be found.

So, supporters of "free market" capitalism do have a point, "actually existing capitalism" has created high levels of unemployment. What **is** significant is that most supporters of capitalism consider that this is a laissez-faire policy! Sadly, the ideological supporters of pure capitalism rarely mention this state intervention on behalf of the capitalist class, preferring to attack trade unions, minimum wages, welfare and numerous other "imperfections" of the labour market which, strangely, are designed (at least in rhetoric) to benefit working class people. Ignoring that issue, however, the question now arises, would a "purer" capitalism create full employment?

First, we should point out that some supporters of "free market" capitalism (most notably, the "Austrian" school) claim that real markets are not in equilibrium at all, i.e. that the nature state of the economy is one of disequilibrium. As we noted in section C.1.6, this means full employment is impossible as this is an equilibrium position but few explicitly state this obvious conclusion of their own theories and claim against logic that full employment can occur (full employment, it should be stressed, has never meant 100% employment as they will always be some people looking for a job and so by that term we mean close to 100% employment). Anarchists agree: full employment can occur in "free market" capitalism but not for ever nor even for long periods. As the Polish socialist economist Michal Kalecki pointed out in regards to pre-Keynesian capitalism, *"[n]ot only is there mass unemployment in the slump, but average employment throughout the cycle is considerably below the peak reached in the boom. The reserve of capital equipment and the reserve army of unemployed are typical features of capitalist economy at least throughout a considerable part of the [business] cycle."* [quoted by Malcolm C. Sawyer, **The Economics of Michal Kalecki**, pp. 115-6]

It is doubtful that "pure" capitalism will be any different. This is due to the nature of the system. What is missing from the orthodox analysis is an explicit discussion of class and class struggle (implicitly, they are there and almost always favour the bosses). Once this is included, the functional reason for unemployment becomes clear. It serves to discipline the workforce, who will tolerate being bossed about much more with the fear that unemployment brings. This holds down wages as the threat of unemployment decreases the bargaining power of workers. This means that unemployment is not only a natural product of capitalism, it is an essential part of it.

So cycles of short periods approaching full employment and followed by longer periods of high unemployment are actually a more likely outcome of pure capitalism than continued full employment. As we argued in sections C.1.5 and C.7.1 capitalism needs unemployment to function successfully and so "free market" capitalism will experience periods of boom and slump, with unemployment increasing and decreasing over time (as can be seen from 19th century capitalism). So as Juliet Schor, a labour economist, put it, usually *"employers have a structural advantage in the labour market, because there are typically more candidates ready and willing to endure this work marathon [of long hours] than jobs for them to fill."* Under conditions of full-employment *"employers are in danger of losing the upper hand"* and hiring new workers *"suddenly becomes much more difficult. They are harder to find, cost more, and are less experienced."* These considerations *"help explain why full employment has been rare."* Thus competition in the labour market is *"typically skewed in favour of employers: it is a buyers market. And in a buyer's market, it is the sellers who compromise."* In the end, workers adapt to this inequality of power and instead of getting what they want, they want what they get (to use Schor's

expression). Under full employment this changes. In such a situation it is the bosses who have to start compromising. And they do not like it. As Schor notes, America *"has never experienced a sustained period of full employment. The closest we have gotten is the late 1960s, when the overall unemployment rate was under 4 percent for four years. But that experience does more to prove the point than any other example. The trauma caused to business by those years of a tight labour market was considerable. Since then, there has been a powerful consensus that the nation cannot withstand such a low rate of unemployment."* Hence the support for the NAIRU to ensure that *"forced idleness of some helps perpetuate the forced overwork of others."* [**The Overworked American**, p. 71, p. 75, p. 129, pp. 75-76 and p. 76]

So, full employment under capitalism is unlikely to last long (nor would full employment booms fill a major part of the business cycle). In addition, it should be stressed that the notion that capitalism naturally stays at equilibrium or that unemployment is temporary adjustments is false, even given the logic of capitalist economics. As Proudhon argued:

> *"The economists admit it [that machinery causes unemployment]: but here they repeat their eternal refrain that, after a lapse of time, the demand for the product having increased in proportion to the reduction in price [caused by the investment], labour in turn will come finally to be in greater demand than ever. Undoubtedly, with time, the equilibrium will be restored; but I must add again, the equilibrium will be no sooner restored at this point than it will be disturbed at another, because the spirit of invention never stops."* [**System of Economical Contradictions**, pp. 200-1]

That capitalism creates permanent unemployment and, indeed, needs it to function is a conclusion that few, if any, pro-"free market" capitalists subscribe to. Faced with the empirical evidence that full employment is rare in capitalism, they argue that reality is not close enough to their theories and must be changed (usually by weakening the power of labour by welfare "reform" and reducing "union power"). Thus reality is at fault, not the theory (to re-quote Proudhon, *"Political economy – that is, proprietary despotism – can never be in the wrong: it must be the proletariat."* [**Op. Cit.** p. 187]) So if unemployment exists, then its because real wages are too high, not because capitalists need unemployment to discipline labour (see section C.9.2 for evidence that this argument is false). Or if real wages are falling as unemployment is rising, it can only mean that the real wage is not falling fast enough – empirical evidence is never enough to falsify logical deductions from assumptions!

(As an aside, it is one of amazing aspects of the "science" of economics that empirical evidence is never enough to refute its claims. As the Post-Keynesian economist Nicholas Kaldor once pointed out, *"[b]ut unlike any scientific theory, where the basic assumptions are chosen on the basis of direct observation of the phenomena the behaviour of which forms the subject-matter of the theory, the basic assumptions of economic theory are either of a kind that are unverifiable ... or of a kind which are directly contradicted by observation."* [**Further Essays on Applied Economics**, pp. 177-8])

Of course, reality often has the last laugh on any ideology. For example, since the late 1970s and early 1980s right-wing capitalist parties have taken power in many countries across the world. These regimes made many pro-free market reforms, arguing that a dose of market forces would lower unemployment, increase growth and so on. The reality proved somewhat different. For example, in the UK, by the time the Labour Party under Tony Blair come back to office in 1997, unemployment (while falling) was still higher than it had been when the last Labour government left office in 1979 (this in spite of repeated redefinitions of unemployment by the Tories in the 1980s to artificially reduce the figures). 18 years of labour market reform had **not** reduced unemployment even under the new definitions. This outcome was identical to New Zealand's neo-liberal experiment, were its overall effect was unimpressive, to say the least: lower growth, lower productivity and feeble real wage increases combined with rising inequality and unemployment. Like the UK, unemployment was still higher in 1997 than it had been in 1979. Over a decade of "flexible" labour markets had increased unemployment (more than doubling it, in fact, at one point as in the UK under Thatcher). It is no understatement to argue, in the words of two critics of neo-liberalism, that the *"performance of the world economy since capital was liberalised has been worse than when it was tightly controlled"* and that *"[t]hus far, [the] actual performance [of liberalised capitalism] has not lived up to the propaganda."* [Larry Elliot and Dan Atkinson, **The Age of Insecurity**, p. 274 and p. 223] In fact, as Palley notes, *"wage and income growth that would have been deemed totally unsatisfactory a decade ago are now embraced as outstanding economic performance."* [**Op. Cit.**, p. 202]

Lastly, it is apparent merely from a glance at the history of capitalism during its laissez-faire heyday in the 19th century that "free" competition among workers for jobs does not lead to full employment. Between 1870 and 1913, unemployment was at an average of 5.7% in the 16 more advanced capitalist countries. This compares to an average of 7.3% in 1913-50 and 3.1% in 1950-70. [Takis Fotopoulos, *"The Nation-State and the Market"*, pp. 37-80, **Society and Nature**, Vol. 2, No. 2, p. 61] If laissez-faire did lead to full employment, these figures would, surely, be reversed.

As discussed above, full employment **cannot** be a fixed feature of capitalism due to its authoritarian nature and the requirements of production for profit. To summarise, unemployment has more to do with private property than the wages of our fellow workers or any social safety nets working class movements have managed to pressure the ruling class to accept. However, it is worthwhile to discuss why the "free market" capitalist is wrong to claim that unemployment within their system will not exist for long periods of time. In addition, to do so will also indicate the poverty of their theory of, and "solution" to, unemployment and the human misery they would cause. We do this in the next section.

C.9.1 Would cutting wages reduce unemployment?

The "free market" capitalist (i.e., neo-classical, neo-liberal or "Austrian") argument is that unemployment is caused by the real wage of labour being higher than the market clearing level. The basic argument is that the market for labour is like any other market and as the price of a commodity increases, the demand for it falls. In terms of labour, high prices (wages) causes lower demand (unemployment). Workers, it is claimed, are more interested in money wages than real wages (which is the amount of goods they can buy with their money wages). This leads them to resist wage cuts even when prices are falling, leading to a rise in their real wages and so they price themselves out of work without realising it. From this analysis comes the argument that if workers were allowed to compete 'freely' among themselves for jobs, real wages would decrease and so unemployment would fall. State intervention (e.g. unemployment benefit, social welfare programmes, legal rights to organise, minimum wage laws, etc.) and labour union activity are, according to this theory, the cause of unemployment, as such intervention and activity forces wages above their market level and so force employers to "let people go." The key to ending unemployment is simple: cut wages.

This position was brazenly put by "Austrian" economist Murray Rothbard. He opposed any suggestion that wages should **not** be cut as the notion that *"the first shock of the depression must fall on profits and not on wages."* This was *"precisely the reverse of sound policy since profits provide the motive power for business activity."* [**America's Great Depression**, p. 188] Rothbard's analysis of the Great Depression is so extreme it almost reads like a satirical attack on the laissez-faire position as his hysterical anti-unionism makes him blame unions for the depression for, apparently, merely existing (even in an extremely weakened state) for their influence was such as to lead economists and the President to recommend to numerous leading corporate business men **not** to cut wages to end the depression (wages were cut, but not sufficiently as prices also dropped as we will discuss in the next section). It should be noted that Rothbard takes his position on wage cutting despite of an account of the business cycle rooted in bankers lowering interest rates and bosses over-investing as a result (see section C.8). So despite not setting interest rates nor making investment decisions, he expected working class people to pay for the actions of bankers and capitalists by accepting lower wages! Thus working class people must pay the price of the profit seeking activities of their economic masters who not only profited in good times, but can expect others to pay the price in bad ones. Clearly, Rothbard took the first rule of economics to heart: the boss is always right.

The chain of logic in this explanation for unemployment is rooted in many of the key assumptions of neo-classical and other marginalist economics. A firm's demand for labour (in this schema) is the marginal physical product of labour multiplied by the price of the output and so it is dependent on marginal productivity theory. It is assumed that there are diminishing returns and marginal productivity as only this produces a downward-sloping labour demand curve. For labour, it is assumed that its supply curve is upwards slopping. So it must be stressed that marginal productivity theory lies at the core of "free market" capitalist theories of output and distribution and so unemployment as the marginal product of labour is interpreted as the labour demand curve. This enforces the viewpoint that unemployment is caused by wages being too high as firms adjust production to bring the marginal cost of their products (the cost of producing one more item) into equality with the product's market-determined price. So a drop in labour costs theoretically leads to an expansion in production, producing jobs for the "temporarily" unemployed and moving the economy toward full-employment. So, in this theory, unemployment can only be reduced by lowering the real wages of workers currently employed. Thus the unfettered free market would ensure that all those who want to work at the equilibrium real wage will do so. By definition, any people who were idle in such a pure capitalism would be voluntarily enjoying leisure and **not** unemployed. At worse, mass unemployment would be a transitory disturbance which will quickly disappear if the market is flexible enough and there are no imperfections in it (such as trade unions, workers' rights, minimum wages, and so on).

Sadly for these arguments, the assumptions required to reach it are absurd as the conclusions (namely, that there is no involuntary unemployment as markets are fully efficient). More perniciously, when confronted with the reality of unemployment, most supporters of this view argue that it arises only because of government-imposed rigidities and trade unions. In their "ideal" world without either, there would, they claim, be no unemployment. Of course, it is much easier to demand that nothing should be done to alleviate unemployment and that workers' real wages be reduced when you are sitting in a tenured post in academia safe from the labour market forces you wish others to be subjected to (in their own interests).

This perspective suffered during the Great Depression and the threat of revolution produced by persistent mass unemployment meant that dissident economists had space to question the orthodoxy. At the head of this re-evaluation was Keynes who presented an alternative analysis and solution to the problem of unemployment in his 1936 book **The General Theory of Employment, Interest and Money** (it should be noted that the Polish socialist economist Michal Kalecki independently developed a similar theory a few years before Keynes but without the neo-classical baggage Keynes brought into his work).

Somewhat ironically, given the abuse he has suffered at the hands of the right (and some of his self-proclaimed followers), Keynes took the assumptions of neo-classical economics on the labour market as the starting point of his analysis. As such, critics of Keynes's analysis generally misrepresent it. For example, right-liberal von Hayek asserted that Keynes *"started from the correct insight that the regular cause of extensive unemployment is real wages that are too high. The next step consisted in the proposition that a direct lowering of money wages could be brought about only by a struggle so painful and prolonged that it could not be contemplated. Hence he concluded that real wages must be lowered by the process of lowering the value of money,"* i.e. by inflation. Thus *"the supply of money must be so increased as to raise prices to a level where the real value of the prevailing money wage is no longer greater than the productivity of the workers seeking employment."* [**The**

Constitution of Liberty, p. 280] This is echoed by libertarian Marxist Paul Mattick who presented an identical argument, stressing that for Keynes *"wages were less flexible than had been generally assumed"* and lowering real wages by inflation *"allowed for more subtle ways of wage-cutting than those traditionally employed."* [**Marx and Keynes**, p. 7]

Both are wrong. These arguments are a serious distortion of Keynes's argument. While he did start by assuming the neo-classical position that unemployment was caused by wages being too high, he was at pains to stress that even with ideally flexible labour markets cutting real wages would **not** reduce unemployment. As such, Keynes argued that unemployment was **not** caused by labour resisting wage cuts or by "sticky" wages. Indeed, any "Keynesian" economist who does argue that "sticky" wages are responsible for unemployment shows that he or she has not read Keynes – Chapter two of the **General Theory** critiques precisely this argument. Taking neo-classical economics at its word, Keynes analyses what would happen **if** the labour market were perfect and so he assumes the same model as his neo-classical opponents, namely that unemployment is caused by wages being too high and there is flexibility in both commodity and labour markets. As he stressed, his *"criticism of the accepted [neo-]classical theory of economics has consisted not so much in finding logical flaws in its analysis as in pointing out that its tacit assumptions are seldom or never satisfied, with the result that it cannot solve the economic problems of the actual world."* [**The General Theory**, p. 378]

What Keynes did was to consider the **overall** effect of cutting wages on the economy as a whole. Given that wages make up a significant part of the costs of a commodity, *"if money-wages change, one would have expected the [neo-]classical school to argue that prices would change in almost the same proportion, leaving the real wage and the level of unemployment practically the same as before."* However, this was not the case, causing Keynes to point out that they *"do not seem to have realised that … their supply curve for labour will shift bodily with every movement of prices."* This was because labour cannot determine its own real wage as prices are controlled by bosses. Once this is recognised, it becomes obvious that workers do not control the cost of living (i.e., the real wage). Therefore trade unions *"do not raise the obstacle to any increase in aggregate employment which is attributed to them by the [neo-]classical school."* So while workers could, in theory, control their wages by asking for less pay (or, more realistically, accepting any wage cuts imposed by their bosses as the alternative is unemployment) they do not have any control over the prices of the goods they produce. This means that they have **no** control over their real wages and so **cannot** reduce unemployment by pricing themselves into work by accepting lower wages. Given these obvious facts, Keynes concluded that there was *"no ground for the belief that a flexible wage policy is capable of continuous full employment … The economic system cannot be made self-adjusting along these lines."* [**Op. Cit.**, p. 12, pp. 8-9, p. 15 and p. 267] As he summarised:

> *"the contention that the unemployment which characterises a depression is due to a refusal by labour to accept a reduction of money-wages is not clearly supported by the facts. It is not very plausible to assert*

that unemployment in the United States in 1932 was due either to labour obstinately refusing to accept a reduction of money-wages or to its demanding a real wage beyond what the productivity of the economic machine was capable of furnishing ... Labour is not more truculent in the depression than in the boom – far from it. Nor is its physical productivity less. These facts from experience are a **prima facie** *ground for questioning the adequacy of the [neo-]classical analysis."* [**Op. Cit.**, p. 9]

This means that the standard neo-classical argument was flawed. While cutting wages may make sense for one firm, it would not have this effect throughout the economy as is required to reduce unemployment as a whole. This is another example of the fallacy of composition. What may work with an individual worker or firm will not have the same effect on the economy as a whole for cutting wages for all workers would have a massive effect on the aggregate demand for their firms products.

For Keynes and Kalecki, there were two possibilities if wages were cut. One possibility, which Keynes considered the most likely, would be that a cut in money wages across the whole economy would see a similar cut in prices. The net effect of this would be to leave real wages unchanged. The other assumes that as wages are cut, prices remain unchanged or only fall by a small amount (i.e. if wealth was redistributed from workers to their employers). This is the underlying assumption of "free market" argument that cutting wages would end the slump. In this theory, cutting real wages would increase profits and investment and this would make up for any decline in working class consumption and so its supporters reject the claim that cutting real wages would merely decrease the demand for consumer goods without automatically increasing investment sufficiently to compensate for this.

However, in order make this claim, the theory depends on three critical assumptions, namely that firms can expand production, that they will expand production, and that, if they do, they can sell their expanded production. This theory and its assumptions can be questioned. To do so we will draw upon David Schweickart's excellent summary. [**Against Capitalism**, pp. 105-7]

The first assumption states that it is always possible for a company to take on new workers. Yet increasing production requires more than just labour. Tools, raw materials and work space are all required in addition to new workers. If production goods and facilities are not available, employment will not be increased. Therefore the assumption that labour can always be added to the existing stock to increase output is plainly unrealistic, particularly if we assume with neo-classical economics that all resources are fully utilised (for an economy operating at less than full capacity, the assumption is somewhat less inappropriate).

Next, will firms expand production when labour costs decline? Hardly. Increasing production will increase supply and eat into the excess profits resulting from the fall in wages (assuming, of course, that demand holds up in the face of falling wages). If unemployment did result in a lowering of the general market wage, companies might use the opportunity to replace their current workers or force them to take a pay cut. If this happened, neither production nor employment would increase. However, it could be argued that the

excess profits would increase capital investment in the economy (a key assumption of neo-liberalism). The reply is obvious: perhaps, perhaps not. A slumping economy might well induce financial caution and so capitalists could stall investment until they are convinced the sustained higher profitability will last.

This feeds directly into the last assumption, namely that the produced goods will be sold. Assuming that money wages are cut, but prices remain the same then this would be a cut in real wages. But when wages decline, so does worker purchasing power, and if this is not offset by an increase in spending elsewhere, then total demand will decline. However, it can be argued that not everyone's real income would fall: incomes from profits would increase. But redistributing income from workers to capitalists, a group who tend to spend a smaller portion of their income on consumption than do workers, could reduce effective demand and increase unemployment. Moreover, business does not (cannot) instantaneously make use of the enlarged funds resulting from the shift of wages to profit for investment (either because of financial caution or lack of existing facilities). In addition, which sane company would increase investment in the face of falling demand for its products? So when wages decline, so does workers' purchasing power and this is unlikely to be offset by an increase in spending elsewhere. This will lead to a reduction in aggregate demand as profits are accumulated but unused, so leading to stocks of unsold goods and renewed price reductions. This means that the cut in real wages will be cancelled out by price cuts to sell unsold stock and unemployment remains. In other words, contrary to neo-classical economics, a fall in wages may result in the same or even more unemployment as aggregate demand drops and companies cannot find a market for their goods. And so, *"[i]f prices do not fall, it is still worse, for then real wages are reduced and unemployment is increased directly by the fall in the purchase of consumption goods."* [Joan Robinson, **Further Contributions to Economics**, p. 34]

The "Pigou" (or *"real balance"*) effect is another neo-classical argument that aims to prove that (in the end) capitalism will pass from slump to boom quickly. This theory argues that when unemployment is sufficiently high, it will lead to the price level falling which would lead to a rise in the real value of the money supply and so increase the real value of savings. People with such assets will have become richer and this increase in wealth will enable people to buy more goods and so investment will begin again. In this way, slump passes to boom naturally.

However, this argument is flawed in many ways. In reply, Michal Kalecki argued that, firstly, Pigou had *"assumed that the banking system would maintain the stock of money constant in the face of declining incomes, although there was no particular reason why they should."* If the money stock changes, the value of money will also change. Secondly, that *"the gain in money holders when prices fall is exactly offset by the loss to money providers. Thus, whilst the real value of a deposit in bank account rises for the depositor when prices fell, the liability represented by that deposit for the bank also rises in size."* And, thirdly, *"that falling prices and wages would mean that the real value of outstanding debts would be increased, which borrowers would find it increasingly difficult to repay as their real income fails to keep pace with the rising real value of debt. Indeed, when the falling prices and wages are generated by low levels of* demand, the aggregate real income will be low. Bankruptcies follow, debts cannot be repaid, and a confidence crisis was likely to follow." In other words, debtors may cut back on spending more than creditors would increase it and so the depression would continue as demand did not rise. [Malcolm C. Sawyer, **The Economics of Michal Kalecki**, p. 90]So, the traditional neo-classical reply that investment spending will increase because lower costs will mean greater profits, leading to greater savings, and ultimately, to greater investment is weak. Lower costs will mean greater profits only if the products are sold, which they might not be if demand is adversely affected. In other words, a higher profit margins do not result in higher profits due to fall in consumption caused by the reduction of workers purchasing power. And, as Michal Kalecki argued, wage cuts in combating a slump may be ineffective because gains in profits are not applied immediately to increase investment and the reduced purchasing power caused by the wage cuts causes a fall in sales, meaning that higher profit margins do not result in higher profits. Moreover, as Keynes pointed out long ago, the forces and motivations governing saving are quite distinct from those governing investment. Hence there is no necessity for the two quantities always to coincide. So firms that have reduced wages may not be able to sell as much as before, let alone more. In that case they will cut production, add to unemployment and further reduce demand. This can set off a vicious downward spiral of falling demand and plummeting production leading to depression, a process described by Kropotkin (nearly 40 years before Keynes made the same point in **The General Theory**):

> "Profits being the basis of capitalist industry, low profits explain all ulterior consequences.
>
> "Low profits induce the employers to reduce the wages, or the number of workers, or the number of days of employment during the week.... As Adam Smith said, low profits ultimately mean a reduction of wages, and low wages mean a reduced consumption by the worker. Low profits mean also a somewhat reduced consumption by the employer; and both together mean lower profits and reduced consumption with that immense class of middlemen which has grown up in manufacturing countries, and that, again, means a further reduction of profits for the employers." [**Fields, Factories and Workshops Tomorrow**, p. 33]

So, as is often the case, Keynes was simply including into mainstream economics perspectives which had long been held by critics of capitalism and dismissed by the orthodoxy. Keynes' critique of Say's Law essentially repeated Marx's while Proudhon pointed out in 1846 that *"if the producer earns less, he will buy less"* and this will *"engender … over-production and destitution."* This was because *"though the workmen cost [the capitalist] something, they are [his] customers: what will you do with your products, when driven away by [him], they shall consume no longer?"* This means that cutting wages and employment would not work for they are *"not slow in dealing employers a counter-blow; for if production excludes consumption, it is soon obliged to stop itself."* [**System of Economical Contradictions**, p. 204 and p. 190] Significantly,

Keynes praised Proudhon's follower Silvio Gesell for getting part of the answer and for producing *"an anti-Marxian socialism"* which the *"future will learn more from"* than Marx. [**Op. Cit.**, p. 355]

So far our critique of the "free market" position has, like Keynes's, been within the assumptions of that theory itself. More has to be said, though, as its assumptions are deeply flawed and unrealistic. It should be stressed that while Keynes's acceptance of much of the orthodoxy ensured that at least some of his ideas become part of the mainstream, Post-Keynesians like Joan Robinson would latter bemoan the fact that he sought a compromise rather than clean break with the orthodoxy. This lead to the rise of the post-war neo-classical synthesis, the so-called "Keynesian" argument that unemployment was caused by wages being "sticky" and the means by which the right could undermine social Keynesianism and ensure a return to neo-classical orthodoxy.

Given the absurd assumptions underlying the "free market" argument, a wider critique is possible as it reflects reality no more than any other part of the pro-capitalist ideology which passes for mainstream economics.

As noted above, the argument that unemployment is caused by wages being too high is part of the wider marginalist perspective. Flaws in that will mean that its explanation of unemployment is equally flawed. So it must be stressed that the marginalist theory of distribution lies at the core of its theories of both output and unemployment. In that theory, the marginal product of labour is interpreted as the labour demand curve as the firm's demand for labour is the marginal physical product of labour multiplied by the price of the output and this produces the viewpoint that unemployment is caused by wages being too high. So given the central role which marginal productivity theory plays in the mainstream argument, it is useful to start our deeper critique by re-iterating that, as indicated in section C.2, Joan Robinson and Piero Sraffa had successfully debunked this theory in the 1950s. *"Yet for psychological and political reasons,"* notes James K. Galbraith, *"rather than for logical and mathematical ones, the capital critique has not penetrated mainstream economics. It likely never will. Today only a handful of economists seem aware of it."* ["The distribution of income", pp. 32-41, Richard P. F. Holt and Steven Pressman (eds.), **A New Guide to Post Keynesian Economics**, p. 34] Given that this underlies the argument that high wages cause high unemployment, it means that the mainstream argument for cutting wages has no firm theoretical basis.

It should also be noted that the assumption that adding more labour to capital is always possible flows from the assumption of marginal productivity theory which treats "capital" like an ectoplasm and can be moulded into whatever form is required by the labour available (see section C.2.5 for more discussion). Hence Joan Robinson's dismissal of this assumption, for *"the difference between the future and the past is eliminated by making capital 'malleable' so that mistakes can always be undone and equilibrium is always guaranteed … with 'malleable' capital the demand for labour depends on the level of wages."* [**Contributions to Modern Economics**, p. 6] Moreover, *"labour and capital are not often as smoothly substitutable for each other as the [neo-classical] model requires … You can't use one without the other. You can't measure the marginal productivity of one without the other."* Demand for capital and labour is, sometimes, a **joint** demand and so it is often to adjust wages to a worker's marginal productivity independent of the cost of capital. [Hugh Stretton, **Economics: A New Introduction**, p. 401]

Then there is the role of diminishing returns. The assumption that the demand curve for labour is always downward sloping with respect to aggregate employment is rooted in the notion that industry operates, at least in the short run, under conditions of diminishing returns. However, diminishing returns are **not** a feature of industries in the real world. Thus the assumption that the downward slopping marginal product of labour curve is identical to the aggregate demand curve for labour is not true as it is inconsistent with empirical evidence. *"In a system at increasing returns,"* noted one economist, *"the direct relation between real wages and employment tends to render the ordinary mechanism of wage adjustment ineffective and unstable."* [Ferdinando Targetti, **Nicholas Kaldor**, p. 344] In fact, as discussed in section C.1.2, without this assumption mainstream economics cannot show that unemployment is, in fact, caused by real wages being too high (along with many other things).

Thus, if we accept reality, we must end up *"denying the inevitability of a negative relationship between real wages and employment."* Post-Keynesian economists have not found any empirical links between the growth of unemployment since the early in 1970s and changes in the relationship between productivity and wages and so there is *"no theoretical reason to expect a negative relationship between employment and the real wage, even at the level of the individual firm."* Even the beloved marginal analysis cannot be used in the labour market, as *"[m]ost jobs are offered on a take-it-or-leave-it basis. Workers have little or no scope to vary hours of work, thereby making marginal trade-offs between income and leisure. There is thus no worker sovereignty corresponding to the (very controversial) notion of consumer sovereignty."* Over all, *"if a relationship exists between aggregate employment and the real wage, it is employment that determines wages. Employment and unemployment are product market variables, not labour market variables. Thus attempts to restore full employment by cutting wages are fundamentally misguided."* [John E. King, *"Labor and Unemployment,"* pp. 65-78, Holt and Pressman (eds.), **Op. Cit.**, p. 68, pp. 67-8, p. 72, p. 68 and p. 72] In addition:

> *"Neo-classical theorists themselves have conceded that a negative relationship between the real wage and the level of employment can be established only in a one-commodity model; in a multi-commodity framework no such generalisation is possible. This confines neo-classical theory to an economy without money and makes it inapplicable to a capitalist or entrepreneurial economy."* [**Op. Cit.**, p. 71]

And, of course, the whole analysis is rooted in the notion of perfect competition. As Nicholas Kaldor mildly put it:

> *"If economics had been a 'science' in the strict sense of the word, the empirical observation that most firms operate in imperfect markets would have forced economists to scrap their existing theories and to start thinking on entirely new lines ... unfortunately economists do not*

feel under the same compulsion to maintain a close correspondence between theoretical hypotheses and the facts of experience."* [**Further Essays on Economic Theory ad Policy**, p. 19]

Any real economy is significantly different from the impossible notion of perfect competition and *"if there exists even one monopoly anywhere in the system ... it follows that others must be averaging less than the marginal value of their output. So to concede the existence of monopoly requires that one either drop the competitive model entirely or construct an elaborate new theory ... that divides the world into monopolistic, competitive, and subcompetitive ('exploited') sectors."* [James K. Galbraith, **Created Unequal**, p. 52] As noted in section C.4.3, mainstream economists have admitted that monopolistic competition (i.e., oligopoly) is the dominant market form but they cannot model it due to the limitations of the individualistic assumptions of bourgeois economics. Meanwhile, while thundering against unions the mainstream economics profession remains strangely silent on the impact of big business and pro-capitalist monopolies like patents and copyrights on distribution and so the impact of real wages on unemployment.

All this means that *"neither the demand for labour nor the supply of labour depends on the real wage. It follows from this that the labour market is not a true market, for the price associated with it, the wage rate, is incapable of performing any market-clearing function, and thus variations in the wage rate cannot eliminate unemployment."* [King, **Op. Cit.**, p. 65] As such, the *"conventional economic analysis of markets ... is unlikely to apply"* to the labour market and as a result *"wages are highly unlikely to reflect workers' contributions to production."* This is because economists treat labour as no different from other commodities yet *"economic theory supports no such conclusion."* At its most basic, labour is **not** produced for profit and the *"supply curve for labour can 'slope backward' – so that a fall in wages can cause an increase in the supply of workers."* In fact, the idea of a backward sloping supply curve for labour is just as easy to derive from the assumptions used by economists to derive their standard one. This is because workers may prefer to work less as the wage rate rises as they will be better off even if they do not work more. Conversely, very low wage rates are likely to produce a very high supply of labour as workers need to work more to meet their basic needs. In addition, as noted at the end of section C.1.4, economic theory itself shows that workers will not get a fair wage when they face very powerful employers unless they organise unions. [Steve Keen, **Debunking Economics**, pp. 111-2 and pp. 119-23]

Strong evidence for this model of the labour market can be found from the history of capitalism. Continually we see capitalists turn to the state to ensure low wages in order to ensure a steady supply of labour (this was a key aim of state intervention during the rise of capitalism, incidentally). For example, in central and southern Africa mining companies tried to get locals to labour. They had little need for money, so they worked a day or two then disappeared for the rest of the week. To avoid simply introducing slavery, some colonial administrators introduced and enforced a poll-tax. To earn enough to pay it, workers had to work a full week. [Hugh Stretton, **Op. Cit.**,

p. 403] Much the same was imposed on British workers at the dawn of capitalism. As Stephen Marglin points out, the *"indiscipline of the labouring classes, or more bluntly, their laziness, was widely noted by eighteenth century observers."* By laziness or indiscipline, these members of the ruling class meant the situation where *"as wages rose, workers chose to work less."* In economic terms, *"a backward bending labour supply curve is a most natural phenomenon as long as the individual worker controls the supply of labour."* However, *"the fact that higher wages led workers to choose more leisure ... was disastrous"* for the capitalists. Unsurprisingly, the bosses did not meekly accept the workings of the invisible hand. Their *"first recourse was to the law"* and they *"utilised the legislative, police and judicial powers of the state"* to ensure that working class people had to supply as many hours as the bosses demanded. [*"What do Bosses do?"*, pp. 60-112, **Review of Radical Political Economy**, Vol. 6, No. 2, pp. 91-4]

This means that the market supply curve *"could have any shape at all"* and so economic theory *"fails to prove that employment is determined by supply and demand, and reinforces the real world observation that involuntary unemployment can exist"* as reducing the wage need not bring the demand and supply of labour into alignment. While the possibility of backward-bending labour supply curves is sometimes pointed out in textbooks, the assumption of an upward sloping supply curve is taken as the normal situation but *"there is no theoretical – or empirical – justification for this."* Sadly for the world, this assumption is used to draw very strong conclusions by economists. The standard arguments against minimum wage legislation, trade unions and demand management by government are all based on it. Yet, as Keen notes, such important policy positions *"should be based upon robust intellectual or empirical foundations, rather than the flimsy substrate of mere fancy. Economists are quite prone to dismiss alternative perspectives on labour market policy on this very basis – that they lack any theoretical or empirical foundations. Yet their own policy positions are based as much on wishful thinking as on wisdom."* [**Op. Cit.**, pp. 121-2 and p. 123]

Within a capitalist economy the opposite assumption to that taken by economics is far more likely, namely that there **is** a backward sloping labour supply curve. This is because the decision to work is **not** one based on the choice between wages and leisure made by the individual worker. Most workers do **not** choose whether they work or not, and the hours spent working, by comparing their (given) preferences and the level of real wages. They do **not** practice voluntary leisure waiting for the real wage to exceed their so-called *"reservation"* wage (i.e. the wage which will tempt them to forsake a life of leisure for the disutility of work). Rather, most workers have to take a job because they do not have a choice as the alternative is poverty (at best) or starvation and homelessness (at worst). The real wage influences the decision on how much labour to supply rather than the decision to work or not. This is because as workers and their families have a certain basic living standard to maintain and essential bills which need to be paid. As earnings increase, basic costs are covered and so people are more able to work less and so the supply of labour tends to fall. Conversely, if real earnings fall because the real wage is less then the supply of labour may **increase** as people work more hours and/or more family members start working to make enough to cover the bills (this is because,

once in work, most people are obliged to accept the hours set by their bosses). This is the opposite of what happens in "normal" markets, where lower prices are meant to produce a **decrease** in the amount of the commodity supplied. In other words, the labour market is not a market, i.e. it reacts in different ways than other markets (Stretton provides a good summary of this argument [**Op. Cit.**, pp. 403-4 and p. 491]).

So, as radical economists have correctly observed, such considerations undercut the "free market" capitalist contention that labour unions and state intervention are responsible for unemployment (or that depressions will easily or naturally end by the workings of the market). To the contrary, insofar as labour unions and various welfare provisions prevent demand from falling as low as it might otherwise go during a slump, they apply a brake to the downward spiral. Far from being responsible for unemployment, they actually mitigate it. For example, unions, by putting purchasing power in the hands of workers, stimulate demand and keep employment higher than the level it would have been. Moreover, wages are generally spent immediately and completely whilst profits are not. A shift from profits to wages may stimulate the economy since more money is spent but there will be a delayed cut in consumption out of profits. [Malcolm Sawyer, **The Economics of Michal Kalecki**, p. 118] All this should be obvious, as wages (and benefits) may be costs for some firms but they are revenue for even more. Moreover, labour is not like other commodities and reacts to changes in price in different ways.

Given the dynamics of the labour "market" (if such a term makes much sense given its atypical nature), any policies based on applying "economics 101" to it will be doomed to failure. As such, any book entitled **Economics in One Lesson** must be viewed with suspicion unless it admits that what it expounds has little or no bearing to reality and urges the reader to take at least the second lesson. Of course, a few people actually do accept the simplistic arguments that reside in such basic economics texts and think that they explain the world (these people usually become right-"libertarians" and spend the rest of their lives ignoring their own experience and reality in favour of a few simple axioms). The wage-cutting argument (like most of economics) asserts that any problems are due to people not listening to economists and that there is no economic power, there are no "special interests" – it is just that people are stupid. Of course, it is irrelevant that it is much easier to demand that workers' real wages be reduced when you are sitting in a tenured post in academia. True to their ideals and "science", it is refreshing to see how many of these "free market" economists renounce tenure so that their wages can adjust automatically as the market demand for their ideologically charged comments changes.

So when economic theories extol suffering for future benefits, it is always worth asking who suffers, and who benefits. Needless to say, the labour market flexibility agenda is anti-union, anti-minimum wage, and anti-worker protection. This agenda emerges from theoretical claims that price flexibility can restore full employment and it rests on dubious logic, absurd assumptions and a false analogy, comparing the labour market with the market for peanuts. Which, ironically, is appropriate as the logic of the model is that workers will end up working for peanuts! As such, the "labour market" model has a certain utility as it removes the problem of institutions and, above all, power from the perspective of the economist. In fact, institutions such as unions can only be considered as a problem in this model rather than a natural response to the unique nature of the labour "market" which, despite the obvious differences, most economists treat like any other.

To conclude, a cut in wages may deepen any slump, making it deeper and longer than it otherwise would be. Rather than being the solution to unemployment, cutting wages will make it worse (we will address the question of whether wages being too high actually causes unemployment in the first place, in the next section). Given that, as we argued in section C.8.2, inflation is caused by insufficient profits for capitalists (they try to maintain their profit margins by price increases) this spiralling effect of cutting wages helps to explain what economists term *"stagflation"* – rising unemployment combined with rising inflation (as seen in the 1970s). As workers are made unemployed, aggregate demand falls, cutting profit margins even more and in response capitalists raise prices in an attempt to recoup their losses. Only a very deep recession can break this cycle (along with labour militancy and more than a few workers and their families).

Thus the capitalist solution to crisis is based on working class people paying for capitalism's contradictions. For, according to the mainstream theory, when the production capacity of a good exceeds any reasonable demand for it, the workers must be laid off and/or have their wages cut to make the company profitable again. Meanwhile the company executives – the people responsible for the bad decisions to build lots of factories – continue to collect their fat salaries, bonuses and pensions, and get to stay on to help manage the company through its problems. For, after all, who better, to return a company to profitability than those who in their wisdom ran it into bankruptcy? Strange, though, no matter how high their salaries and bonuses get, managers and executives **never** price **themselves** out of work.

All this means that working class people have two options in a slump – accept a deeper depression in order to start the boom-bust cycle again or get rid of capitalism and with it the contradictory nature of capitalist production which produces the business cycle in the first place (not to mention other blights such as hierarchy and inequality). In the end, the only solution to unemployment is to get rid of the system which created it by workers seizing their means of production and abolishing the state. When this happens, then production for the profit of the few will be ended and so, too, the contradictions this generates.

C.9.2 Is unemployment caused by wages being too high?

As we noted in the last section, most capitalist economic theories argue that unemployment is caused by wages being too high. Any economics student will tell you that labour is like any other commodity and so if its price is too high then there will be less demand for it, so producing an excess supply of it on the market. Thus high wages will reduce the quantity of labour demanded and so create unemployment – a simple case of "supply and demand."

From this theory we would expect that areas and periods with high wages will also have high levels of unemployment. Unfortunately for the theory, this does not seem to be the case. Even worse for it, high wages are generally associated with booms rather than slumps and this has been known to mainstream economics since at least 1939 when in March of that year **The Economic Journal** printed an article by Keynes about the movement of real wages during a boom in which he evaluated the empirical analysis of two labour economists (entitled *"Relative Movements of Real Wages and Output"* this is contained as an Appendix of most modern editions of **The General Theory**).

These studies showed that *"when money wages are rising, real wages have usually risen too; whilst, when money wages are falling, real wages are no more likely to rise than to fall."* Keynes admitted that in **The General Theory** he was *"accepting, without taking care to check the facts"*, a *"widely held"* belief. He discussed where this belief came from, namely leading 19th century British economist Alfred Marshall who had produced a *"generalisation"* from a six year period between 1880-86 which was not true for the subsequent business cycles of 1886 to 1914. He also quotes another leading economist, Arthur Pigou, from 1927 on how *"the upper halves of trade cycles have, on the whole, been associated with higher rates of real wages than the lower halves"* and indicates that he provided evidence on this from 1850 to 1910 (although this did not stop Pigou reverting to the *"Marshallian tradition"* during the Great Depression and blaming high unemployment on high wages). [**The General Theory**, p. 394, p. 398 and p. 399] Keynes conceded the point, arguing that he had tried to minimise differences between his analysis and the standard perspective. He stressed that while he assumed countercyclical real wages his argument did not depend on it and given the empirical evidence provided by labour economists he accepted that real wages were pro-cyclical in nature.

The reason why this is the case is obvious given the analysis in the last section. Labour does not control prices and so cannot control its own real wage. Looking at the Great Depression, it seems difficult to blame it on workers refusing to take pay cuts when by 1933 *"wages and salaries in U.S. manufacturing were less than half their 1929 levels and, in automobiles and steel, were under 40 percent of the 1929 levels."* In Detroit, there had been 475,000 auto-workers. By 1931 *"almost half has been laid off."* [William Lazonick, **Competitive Advantage on the Shop Floor**, p. 271] The notion of all powerful unions or workers' resistance to wage cuts causing high unemployment hardly fits these facts. Peter Temin provides information on real wages in manufacturing during the depression years. Using 1929 as the base year, weekly average real wages (i.e., earnings divided by the consumer price index) fell each year to reach a low of 85.5% by 1932. Hourly real wages remained approximately constant (rising to 100.1% in 1930 and then 102.6% in 1931 before falling to 99% in 1932). The larger fall in weekly wages was due to workers having a shorter working week. The *"effect of shorter hours and lower wages was to decrease the income of employed workers."* Thus the notion that lowering wages will increase employment seems as hard to support as the notion that wages being too high caused the depression in the first place. Temin argues, *"no part of the [neo-]classical story is accurate."* [**Did Monetary Forces Cause the Great Depression?**, pp. 139-40]

It should be noted that the consensus of economists is that during this period the evidence seems to suggest that real wages **did** rise overall. This was because the prices of commodities fell faster than did the wages paid to workers. Which confirms Keynes, as he had argued that workers cannot price themselves into work as they have no control over prices. However, there is no reason to think that high real wages caused the high unemployment as the slump itself forced producers to cut prices (not to mention wages). Rather, the slump caused the increase in real wages.

Since then, economists have generally confirmed that real wage are procyclical. In fact, *"a great deal of empirical research has been conducted in this area – research which mostly contradicts the neo-classical assumption of an inverse relation between real wages and employment."* [Ferdinando Targetti, **Nicholas Kaldor**, p. 50] Nicholas Kaldor, one of the first Keynesians, also stressed that the notion that there is an inverse relationship between real wages and employment is *"contradicted by numerous empirical studies which show that, in the short period, changes in real wages are positively correlated with changes in employment and not negatively."* [**Further Essays on Economic Theory and Policy**, p. 114fn] As Hugh Stretton summarises in his excellent introductory text on economics:

> *"In defiance of market theory, the demand for labour tends strongly to vary **with** its price, not inversely to it. Wages are high when there is full employment. Wages – especially for the least-skilled and lowest paid – are lowest when there is least employment. The causes chiefly run from the employment to the wages, rather than the other way. Unemployment weakens the bargaining power, worsens the job security and working conditions, and lowers the pay of those still in jobs.*
>
> *"The lower wages do not induce employers to create more jobs … most business firms have no reason to take on more hands if wages decline. Only empty warehouses, or the prospect of more sales can get them to do that, and these conditions rarely coincide with falling employment and wages. The causes tend to work the other way: unemployment lowers wages, and the lower wages do not restore the lost employment."* [**Economics: A New Introduction**, pp. 401-2]

Will Hutton, the British neo-Keynesian economist, summarises research by two other economists that suggests high wages do not cause unemployment:

> *"the British economists David Blanchflower and Andrew Oswald [examined] … the data in twelve countries about the actual relation between wages and unemployment – and what they have discovered is another major challenge to the free market account of the labour market. Free market theory would predict that low wages would be correlated with low local unemployment; and high wages with high local unemployment.*
>
> *"Blanchflower and Oswald have found precisely the opposite relationship. The higher the wages, the lower*

the local unemployment – and the lower the wages, the higher the local unemployment. As they say, this is not a conclusion that can be squared with free market text-book theories of how a competitive labour market should work." [**The State We're In**, p. 102]

Unemployment was highest where real wages were lowest and nowhere had falling wages being followed by rising employment or falling unemployment. Blanchflower and Oswald stated that their conclusion is that employees *"who work in areas of high unemployment earn less, other things constant, than those who are surrounded by low unemployment."* [**The Wage Curve**, p. 360] This relationship, the exact opposite of that predicted by "free market" capitalist economics, was found in many different countries and time periods, with the curve being similar for different countries. Thus, the evidence suggests that high unemployment is associated with low earnings, not high, and vice versa.

Looking at less extensive evidence, if minimum wages and unions cause unemployment, why did the South-eastern states of the USA (with a **lower** minimum wage and weaker unions) have a **higher** unemployment rate than North-western states during the 1960s and 1970s? Or why, when the (relative) minimum wage declined under Reagan and Bush in the 1980s, did chronic unemployment accompany it? [Allan Engler, **The Apostles of Greed**, p. 107] Or the **Low Pay Network** report *"Priced Into Poverty"* which discovered that in the 18 months before they were abolished, the British Wages Councils (which set minimum wages for various industries) saw a rise of 18,200 in full-time equivalent jobs compared to a net loss of 39,300 full-time equivalent jobs in the 18 months afterwards. Given that nearly half the vacancies in former Wages Council sectors paid less than the rate which it is estimated Wages Councils would now pay, and nearly 15% paid less than the rate at abolition, there should (by the "free market" argument) have been rises in employment in these sectors as pay fell. The opposite happened. This research shows that the falls in pay associated with Wages Council abolition had not created more employment. Indeed, employment growth was more buoyant prior to abolition than subsequently. So whilst Wages Council abolition did not result in more employment, the erosion of pay rates caused by their abolition resulted in more families having to endure poverty pay. Significantly, the introduction of a national minimum wage by the first New Labour government did not have the dire impact "free market" capitalist economists and politicians predicted.

It should also be noted that an extensive analysis of the impact of minimum wage increases at the state level in America by economists David Card and Alan Kreuger found the facts contradicted the standard theory, with rises in the minimum wage having a small positive impact on both employment and wages for all workers. [**Myth and Measurement: The New Economics of the Minimum Wage**] While their work was attacked by business leaders and economists from think-tanks funded by them, Card and Kreuger's findings that raising the lowest wages had no effect on unemployment or decreased it proved to be robust. In particular, when replying to criticism of their work by other economists who based their work, in part, on data supplied by a business funded think-tank Card and Krueger discovered that not only was that work consistent with their original findings but that the *"only data set that indicates a significant decline in employment"* was by some amazing coincidence *"the small set of restaurants collected by"* the think tank. [*"Minimum Wages and Employment: A Case Study of the Fast-Food Industry in New Jersey and Pennsylvania: Reply"*, pp. 1397-1420, **The American Economic Review**, Vol. 90, No. 5, p. 1419] For a good overview of *"how the fast food industry and its conservative allies sought to discredit two distinguished economists, and how the attack backfired"* when *"the two experts used by the fast food industry to impeach Card and Krueger, effectively ratified them"* see John Schmitt's *"Behind the Numbers: Cooked to Order."* [**The American Prospect**, May-June 1996, pp. 82-85]

(This does not mean that anarchists support the imposition of a legal minimum wage. Most anarchists do not because it takes the responsibility for wages from unions and other working class organisations, where it belongs, and places it in the hands of the state. We mention these examples in order to highlight that the "free market" capitalist argument has serious flaws with it.)

Empirical evidence does not support the argument the "free market" capitalist argument that unemployment is caused by real wages being too high. The phenomenon that real wages tend to increase during the upward swing of the business cycle (as unemployment falls) and fall during recessions (when unemployment increases) renders the standard interpretation that real wages govern employment difficult to maintain (real wages are *"pro-cyclical,"* to use economic terminology). This evidence makes it harder for economists to justify policies based on a direct attack on real wages as the means to cure unemployment.

While this evidence may come as a shock to those who subscribe to the arguments put forward by those who think capitalist economics reflect the reality of that system, it fits well with the anarchist and other socialist analysis. For anarchists, unemployment is a means of disciplining labour and maintaining a suitable rate of profit (i.e. unemployment is a key means of ensuring that workers are exploited). As full employment is approached, labour's power increases, so reducing the rate of exploitation and so increasing labour's share of the value it produces (and so higher wages). Thus, from an anarchist point of view, the fact that wages are higher in areas of low unemployment is not a surprise, nor is the phenomenon of pro-cyclical real wages. After all, as we noted in section C.3, the ratio between wages and profits are, to a large degree, a product of bargaining power and so we would expect real wages to grow in the upswing of the business cycle, fall in the slump and be high in areas of low unemployment.

The evidence therefore suggests that the "free market" capitalist claim that unemployment is caused by unions, "too high" wages, and so on, is false. Indeed, by stopping capitalists appropriating more of the income created by workers, high wages maintain aggregate demand and contribute to higher employment (although, of course, high employment cannot be maintained indefinitely under wage slavery due to the rise in workers' power this implies). Rather, unemployment is a key aspect of the capitalist system and cannot be got rid of within it. The "free market" capitalist "blame the workers" approach fails to understand the nature and dynamic of the system (given its ideological role, this is unsurprising). So high real wages for workers increases aggregate demand and

reduces unemployment from the level it would be if the wage rate was cut. This is supported by most of the research into wage dynamics during the business cycle and by the *"wage curve"* of numerous countries. This suggests that the demand for labour is independent of the real wages and so the price of labour (wages) is incapable of performing any market clearing function. The supply and demand for labour are determined by two different sets of factors. The relationship between wages and unemployment flows from the latter to the former rather than the reverse: the wage is influenced by the level of unemployment. Thus wages are not the product of a labour market which does not really exist but rather is the product of *"institutions, customs, privilege, social relations, history, law, and above all power, with an admixture of ingenuity and luck. But of course power, and particularly market or monopoly power, changes with the general of demand, the rate of growth, and the rate of unemployment. In periods of high employment, the weak gain on the strong; in periods of high unemployment, the strong gain on the weak."* [Galbraith, **Created Unequal**, p. 266]

This should be obvious enough. It is difficult for workers to resist wage cuts and speeds-up when faced with the fear of mass unemployment. As such, higher rates of unemployment *"reduce labour's bargaining power vis-à-vis business, and this helps explain why wages have declined and workers have not received their share of productivity growth"* (between 1970 and 1993, only the top 20% of the US population increased its share of national income). [Thomas I. Palley, **Plenty of Nothing**, p. 55 and p. 58] Strangely, though, this obvious fact seems lost on most economists. In fact, if you took their arguments seriously then you would have to conclude that depressions and recessions are the periods during which working class people do the best! This is on two levels. First, in neo-classical economics work is considered a disutility and workers decide not to work at the market-clearing real wage because they prefer leisure to working. Leisure is assumed to be intrinsically good and the wage the means by which workers are encouraged to sacrifice it. Thus high unemployment must be a good thing as it gives many more people leisure time. Second, for those in work their real wages are higher than before, so their income has risen. Alfred Marshall, for example, argued that in depressions money wages fell but not as fast as prices. A *"powerful friction"* stopped this, which *"establish[ed] a higher standard of living among the working classes"* and a *"diminish[ing of] the inequalities of wealth."* When asked whether during a period of depression the employed working classes got more than they did before, he replied *"[m]ore than they did before, on the average."* [quoted by Keynes, **Op. Cit.**, p. 396]

Thus, apparently, working class people do worse in booms than in slumps and, moreover, they can resist wage cuts more in the face of mass unemployment than in periods approaching full employment. That the theory which produced these conclusions could be taken remotely seriously shows the dangers of deducing an economic ideology from a few simple axioms rather than trusting in empirical evidence and common sense derived from experience. Nor should it come as too great a surprise, as "free market" capitalist economics tends to ignore (or dismiss) the importance of economic power and the social context within which individuals make their choices. As Bob Black acidly put it with regards to the 1980s, it *"wasn't the*

workers *who took these gains [of increased productivity], not in higher wages, not in safer working conditions, and not in shorter hours – hours of work have* **increased** *... It must be, then, that in the 80s and after workers have 'chosen' lower wages, longer hours* **and** *greater danger on the job. Yeah, sure."* ["Smokestack Lightning," pp. 43-62, **Friendly Fire**, p. 61]

In the real world, workers have little choice but to accept a job as they have no independent means to exist in a pure capitalist system and so no wages means no money for buying such trivialities as food and shelter. The decision to take a job is, for most workers, a non-decision – paid work is undertaken out of economic necessity and so we are not in a position to refuse work because real wages are too low to be worth the effort (the welfare state reduces this pressure, which is why the right and bosses are trying to destroy it). With high unemployment, pay and conditions will worsen while hours and intensity of labour will increase as the fear of the sack will result in increased job insecurity and so workers will be more willing to placate their bosses by obeying and not complaining. Needless to say, empirical evidence shows that *"when unemployment is high, inequality rises. And when unemployment is low, inequality tends to fall."* [James K. Galbraith, **Op. Cit.**, p. 148] This is unsurprising as the *"wage curve"* suggests that it is unemployment which drives wage levels, not the other way round. This is important as higher unemployment would therefore create higher inequality as workers are in no position to claim back productivity increases and so wealth would flood upwards. Then there is the issue of the backward-bending supply curve of labour we discussed at the end of the last section. As the "labour market" is not really a market, cutting real wages will have the opposite effect on the supply of labour than its supporters claim. It is commonly found that as real wages fall, hours at work become longer and the number of workers in a family increases. This is because the labour supply curve is negatively sloped as families need to work more (i.e., provide more labour) to make ends meet. This means that a fall in real wages may **increase** the supply of labour as workers are forced to work longer hours or take second jobs simply to survive. The net effect of increasing supply would be to **decrease** real wages even more and so, potentially, start a vicious circle and make the recession deeper. Looking at the US, we find evidence that supports this analysis. As the wages for the bottom 80% of the population fell in real terms under Reagan and Bush in the 1980s, the number of people with multiple jobs increased as did the number of mothers who entered the labour market. In fact, *"the only reason that family income was maintained is the massive increase in labour force participation of married women ... Put simply, jobs paying family wages have been disappearing, and sustaining a family now requires that both adults work ... The result has been a squeeze on the amount of time that people have for themselves ... there is a loss of life quality associated with the decline in time for family ... they have also been forced to work longer ... Americans are working longer just to maintain their current position, and the quality of family life is likely declining. A time squeeze has therefore accompanied the wage squeeze."* [Palley, **Op. Cit.**, pp. 63-4] That is, the supply of labour **increased** as its price fell (Reagan's turn to military Keynesianism and incomplete nature of the "reforms" ensured that a deep spiral was avoided).

To understand why this is the case, it is necessary to think about the impact eliminating the minimum wage and trade unions would actually have. First, of course, there would be a drop in the wages of the poorest workers as the assertion is that the minimum wage increases unemployment by forcing wages up. The assertion is that the bosses would then employ more workers as a result. However, this assumes that extra workers could easily be added to the existing capital stock which may not be the case. Assuming this is the case (and it **is** a big assumption), what happens to the workers who have had their pay cut? Obviously, they still need to pay their bills which means they either cut back on consumption and/or seek more work (assuming that prices have not fallen, as this would leave the real wage unchanged). If the former happens, then firms may find that they face reduced demand for their products and, consequently, have no need for the extra employees predicted by the theory. If the latter happens, then the ranks of those seeking work will increase as people look for extra jobs or people outside the labour market (like mothers and children) are forced into the job market. As the supply of workers increase, wages **must** drop according to the logic of the "free market" position. This does not mean that a recovery is impossible, just that in the short and medium terms cutting wages will make a recession worse and be unlikely to **reduce** unemployment for some time..

This suggests that a "free market" capitalism, marked by a fully competitive labour market, no welfare programmes nor unemployment benefits, and extensive business power to break unions and strikes would see aggregate demand constantly rise and fall, in line with the business cycle, and unemployment and inequality would follow suit. Moreover, unemployment would be higher over most of the business cycle (and particularly at the bottom of the slump) than under a capitalism with social programmes, militant unions and legal rights to organise because the real wage would not be able to stay at levels that could support aggregate demand nor could the unemployed use their benefits to stimulate the production of consumer goods. This suggests that a fully competitive labour market, as in the 19th century, would increase the instability of the system – an analysis which was confirmed in the 1980s (*"the relationship between measured inequality and economic stability ... was weak but if anything it suggests that the more egalitarian countries showed a more stable pattern of growth after 1979."* [Dan Corry and Andrew Glyn, *"The Macroeconomics of equality, stability and growth"*, **Paying for Inequality**, Andrew Glyn and David Miliband (eds.) pp. 212-213]).

So, in summary, the available evidence suggests that **high** wages are associated with **low** levels of unemployment. While this should be the expected result from any realistic analysis of the economic power which marks capitalist economies, it does not provide much support for claims that only by cutting real wages can unemployment be reduced. The "free market" capitalist position and one based on reality have radically different conclusions as well as political implications. Ultimately, most laissez-faire economic analysis is unpersuasive both in terms of the facts and their logic. While economics may be marked by axiomatic reasoning which renders everything the markets does as optimal, the problem is precisely that it is pure axiomatic reasoning with little or no regard for the real world. Moreover, by some strange coincidence, they usually involve policy implications which generally make the rich richer by weakening the working class. Unsurprisingly, decades of empirical evidence have not shifted the faith of those who think that the simple axioms of economics take precedence over the real world nor has this faith lost its utility to the economically powerful.

C.9.3 Are "flexible" labour markets the answer to unemployment?

The usual "free market" capitalist (or neo-liberal) argument is that labour markets must become more "flexible" to solve the problem of unemployment. This is done by weakening unions, reducing (or abolishing) the welfare state, and so on. In defence of these policies, their proponents point to the low unemployment rates of the USA and UK and contrast them to the claimed economic woes of Europe (particularly France and Germany). As we will indicate in this section, this stance has more to do a touching faith that deregulating the labour market brings the economy as a whole closer to the ideal of "perfect competition" than a balanced analysis and assessment of the available evidence. Moreover, it is always important to remember, as tenured economists (talking of protective labour market institutions!) seem to forget, that deregulation can and does have high economic (and not to mention individual and social) costs too.

The underlying argument for flexible labour markets is the notion that unemployment is cased by wages being too high and due to market imperfections wages are sticky downwards. While both claims, as we have seen above, are dubious both factually and logically this has not stopped this position becoming the reigning orthodoxy in elite circles. By market imperfections it is meant trade unions, laws which protect labour, unemployment benefit and other forms of social welfare provision (and definitely **not** big business, patent and copyright laws, or any other pro-business state interventions). All these ensure that wages for those employed are inflexible downwards and the living standards of those unemployed are too high to induce them to seek work. This means that orthodox economics is based on (to use John Kenneth Galbraith's justly famous quip) the assumption that the rich do not work because they are paid too little, while the poor do not work because they are paid too much.

We should first point out that attacks on social welfare have a long pedigree and have been conducted with much the same rationale – it made people lazy and gave them flexibility when seeking work. For example, the British **Poor Law Report** of the 1830s *"built its case against relief on the damage done by poor relief to personal morality and labour discipline (much the same thing in the eyes of the commissioners)."* [David McNally, **Against the Market**, p. 101] The report itself stated that *"the greatest evil"* of the system was *"the spirit of laziness and insubordination that it creates."* [quoted by McNally, **Op. Cit.**, p. 101]

While the rhetoric used to justify attacks on welfare has changed somewhat since then, the logic and rationale have not. They have as their root the need to eliminate anything which provided working class people any means for independence from the labour market.

It has always aimed to ensure that the fear of the sack remains a powerful tool in the bosses arsenal and to ensure that their authority is not undermined. Ironically, therefore, its underlying aims are to **decrease** the options available to working class people, i.e. to reduce **our** flexibility within the labour market by limiting our options to finding a job fast or face dire poverty (or worse).

Secondly, there is a unspoken paradox to this whole process. If we look at the stated, public, rationale behind "flexibility" we find a strange fact. While the labour market is to be made more "flexible" and in line with ideal of "perfect competition", on the capitalist side no attempt is being made to bring **it** into line with that model. Let us not forget that perfect competition (the theoretical condition in which all resources, including labour, will be efficiently utilised) states that there must be a large number of buyers and sellers. This is the case on the sellers side of the "flexible" labour market, but this is **not** the case on the buyers (where, as indicated in section C.4, oligopoly reigns). Most who favour labour market "flexibility" are also those most against the breaking up of big business and oligopolistic markets or are against attempts to stop mergers between dominant companies in and across markets. Yet the model requires **both** sides to be made up of numerous small firms without market influence or power. So why expect making one side more "flexible" will have a positive effect on the whole?

There is no logical reason for this to be the case and as we noted in section C.1.4, neo-classical economics agrees – in an economy with both unions and big business, removing the former while retaining the latter will **not** bring it closer to the ideal of perfect competition. With the resulting shift in power on the labour market things will get worse as income is distributed from labour to capital. Which is, we must stress, precisely what **has** happened since the 1980s and the much lauded "reforms" of the labour market. It is a bit like expecting peace to occur between two warring factions by disarming one side and arguing that because the number of guns have been halved peacefulness has doubled! Of course, the only "peace" that would result would be the peace of the graveyard or a conquered people – subservience can pass for peace, if you do not look too close. In the end, calls for the "flexibility" of labour indicate the truism that, under capitalism, labour exists to meet the requirements of capital (or living labour exists to meet the needs of dead labour, a truly insane way to organise a society).

Then there is the key question of comparing reality with the rhetoric. As economist Andrew Glyn points out, the neo-liberal orthodoxy on this issue *"has been strenuously promoted despite weak evidence for the magnitude of its benefits and in almost total neglect of its costs."* In fact, *"there is no evidence that the countries which carried out more reforms secured significant falls in unemployment."* This is perhaps unsurprising as *"there is plenty of support for such deregulation from business even without strong evidence that unemployment would be reduced."* As far as welfare goes, the relationship between unemployment and benefits is, if anything, in the 'wrong' direction (higher benefits go along with lower unemployment). Of course there are a host of other influences on unemployment but *"if benefits were very important we might expect **some** degree of correlation in the 'right' (positive) direction … such a lack of simple relation with unemployment applies to other likely suspects such as employment protection and* union membership." [**Capitalism Unleashed**, p. 48, p. 121, p. 48 and p. 47]

Nor is it mentioned that the history of labour market flexibility is somewhat at odds with the theory. It is useful to remember that American unemployment was far worse than Europe's during the 1950s, 60s and 70s. In fact, it did not get better than the European average until the second half of the 1980s. [David R. Howell, *"Introduction"*, pp. 3-34, **Fighting Unemployment**, David R. Howell (ed.), pp. 10-11] To summarise:

"it appears to be only relatively recently that the maintained greater flexibility of US labour markets has apparently led to a superior performance in terms of lower unemployment, despite the fact this flexibility is no new phenomenon. Comparing, for example, the United States with the United Kingdom, in the 1960s the United States averaged 4.8 per cent, with the United Kingdom at 1.9 per cent; in the 1970s the United States rate rose to 6.1 per cent, with the United Kingdom rising to 4.3 per cent, and it was only in the 1980s that the ranking was reversed with the United States at 7.2 per cent and the United Kingdom at 10 per cent … Notice that this reversal of rankings in the 1980s took place despite all the best efforts of Mrs Thatcher to create labour market flexibility … [I]f labour market flexibility is important in explaining the level of unemployment … why does the level of unemployment remain so persistently high in a country, Britain, where active measures have been taken to create flexibility?" [Keith Cowling and Roger Sugden, **Beyond Capitalism**, p. 9]

If we look at the fraction of the labour force without a job in America, we find that in 1969 it was 3.4% (7.3% including the underemployed) and **rose** to 6.1% in 1987 (16.8% including the underemployed). Using more recent data, we find that, on average, the unemployment rate was 6.2% in 1990-97 compared to 5.0% in the period 1950-65. In other words, labour market "flexibility" has not reduced unemployment levels, in fact "flexible" labour markets have been associated with higher levels of unemployment. Of course, we are comparing different time periods. A lot changed between the 1960s and the 1990s and so comparing these periods cannot be the whole answer. However, it does seem strange that the period with stronger unions, higher minimum wages and more generous welfare state should be associated with **lower** unemployment than the subsequent "flexible" period. It is possible that the rise in flexibility and the increase in unemployment may be unrelated. If we look at different countries over the same time period we can see if "flexibility" actually reduces unemployment. As one British economist notes, this may not be the case:

"Open unemployment is, of course, lower in the US. But once we allow for all forms of non-employment [such as underemployment, jobless workers who are not officially registered as such and so on], there is little difference between Europe and the US: between 1988 and 1994, 11 per cent of men aged 25-55 were not in work in France, compared with 13 per cent in the UK, 14 per cent in the

US and 15 per cent in Germany." [Richard Layard, quoted by John Gray, **False Dawn**, p. 113]

Also when evaluating the unemployment records of a country, other factors than the "official" rate given by the government must taken into account. Firstly, different governments have different definitions of what counts as unemployment. As an example, the USA has a more restrictive definition of who is unemployed than Germany. For example, in 2005 Germany's unemployment rate was officially 11.2%. However, using the US definition it was only around 9% (7% in what was formerly West Germany). The official figure was higher as it included people, such as those involuntarily working part-time, as being unemployed who are counted as being employed in the USA. America, in the same year, had an unemployment rate of around 5%. So comparing unadjusted unemployment figures will give a radically different picture of the problem than using standardised ones. Sadly far too often business reporting in newspapers fail to do this.

In addition, all estimates of America's unemployment record must take into account its incarceration rates. The prison population is not counted as part of the labour force and so is excluded when calculating unemployment figures. This is particularly significant as those in prison are disproportionately from demographic groups with very high unemployment rates and so it is likely that a substantial portion of these people would be unemployed if they were not in jail. If America and the UK did not have the huge surge in prison population since the 1980s neo-liberal reforms, the unemployment rate in both countries would be significantly higher. In the late 1990s, for example, more than a million extra people would have been seeking work if the US penal policies resembled those of any other Western nation. [John Gray, **Op. Cit.**, p. 113] England and Wales, unsurprisingly, tops the prison league table for Western Europe. In 2005, 145 per 100,000 of their population was incarcerated. In comparison, France had a rate of 88 while Germany had one of 97. This would, obviously, reduce the numbers of those seeking work on the labour market and, consequently, reduce the unemployment statistics.

While the UK is praised for its "flexible" labour market in the 2000s, many forget the price which was paid to achieve it and even more fail to realise that the figures hide a somewhat different reality. It is therefore essential to remember Britain's actual economic performance during Thatcher's rule rather than the "economically correct" narrative we have inherited from the media and economic "experts." When Thatcher came to office in 1979 she did so promising to end the mass unemployment experienced under Labour (which had doubled between 1974 and 1979). Unemployment then tripled in her first term, rising to over 3 million in 1982 (for the first time since the 1930s, representing 1 in 8 people). This was due in large part to the application of Monetarist dogma making the recession far worse than it had to be. Unemployment remained at record levels throughout the 1980s, only dropping to below its 1979 level in 1997 when New Labour took office. It gets worse. Faced with unemployment rising to well over 10%, Thatcher's regime did what any respectable government would – it cooked the books. It changed how unemployment was recorded in order to artificially lower the official unemployment records. It also should be stressed that the UK unemployment figures do not take into account the Thatcherite policy of shunting as many people as possible off the unemployment roles and onto sickness and incapacity benefits during the 1980s and 1990s ("*In some countries, like the UK and the Netherlands, many [of the unemployed] found their way onto sickness benefit ... Across the UK, for example, there was a strong positive correlation between numbers on sickness benefits and the local unemployment rate.*" [Glyn, **Op. Cit.**, p. 107]). Once these "hidden" people are included the unemployment figures of Britain are similar to those countries, such as France and Germany, who are more honest in recording who is and is not unemployed.

Eighteen years of high unemployment and a massive explosion in those on incapacity benefits is hardly an advert for the benefits of "flexible" labour market. However, a very deep recession, double-figure unemployment for most of the decade, defeats for key strikes and unions plus continued high unemployment for nearly two decades had an impact on the labour movement. It made people willing to put up with anything in order to remain in work. Hence Thatcher's "economic miracle" – the working class finally knew its place in the social hierarchy.

Thus, if a politician is elected who is hailed by the right as a "new Thatcher", i.e., seeking to "reform" the economy (which is "economically correct" speak for using the state to break working class militancy) then there are some preconditions required before they force their populations down the road to (private) serfdom. They will have to triple unemployment in under three years and have such record levels last over a decade, provoke the deepest recession since the 1930s, oversee the destruction of the manufacturing sector and use the powers of the state to break the mass protests and strikes their policies will provoke. Whether they are successful depends on the willingness of working class people to stand up for their liberties and rights and so impose, from the streets, the changes that are really needed – changes that politicians will not, indeed cannot, achieve.

Nor should it be forgotten that here are many European countries with around the same, or lower, official unemployment rates as the UK with much less "flexible" labour markets. Taking the period 1983 to 1995, we find that around 30 per cent of the population of OECD Europe lived in countries with average unemployment rates lower than the USA and around 70 per cent in countries with lower unemployment than Canada (whose wages are only slightly less flexible than the USA). Furthermore, the European countries with the lowest unemployment rates were not noted for their labour market flexibility (Austria 3.7%, Norway 4.1%, Portugal 6.4%, Sweden 3.9% and Switzerland 1.7%). Britain, which probably had the most flexible labour market had an average unemployment rate higher than half of Europe. And the unemployment rate of Germany is heavily influenced by areas which were formally in East Germany. Looking at the former West German regions only, unemployment between 1983 and 1995 was 6.3%, compared to 6.6% in the USA (and 9.8% in the UK). This did not change subsequently. There are many regulated European countries with lower unemployment than the USA (in 2002, 10 of 18 European countries had lower unemployment rates). Thus:

"*Often overlooked in the 1990s in the rush to embrace market fundamentalism and to applaud the American model was the fact that several European countries with strong welfare states consistently reported unemployment rates well below that of the United States ... At the same time, other European welfare sates, characterised by some of the lowest levels of wage inequality and the highest levels of social protection in the developed world, experienced substantial declines in unemployment over the 1990s, reaching levels that are now below that of the United States.*" [David R. Howell, "*Conclusion*", pp. 310-43, **Op. Cit.**, p. 310]

As such, it is important to remember that "*the empirical basis*" of the neo-liberal OECD-IMF orthodoxy is "*limited.*" [Howell, **Op. Cit.**, p. 337] In fact, the whole "Europe is in a state of decline" narrative which is used to justify the imposition of neo-liberal reforms there is better understood as the corporate media's clever ploy to push Europe into the hands of the self-destructing neo-liberalism that is slowly taking its toll on Britain and America rather than a serious analysis of the real situation there.

Take, for example, the issue of high youth unemployment in many European countries which reached international awareness during the French anti-CPE protests in 2006. In fact, the percentage of prime-age workers (25-54) in employment is pretty similar in "regulated" France, Germany and Sweden as in "flexible" America and Britain (it is much higher for women in Sweden). However, there are significant differences in youth employment rates and this suggests where the apparent unemployment problem lies in Europe. This problem is due to the statistical method used to determine the unemployment figures. The standard measure of unemployment divides the number unemployed by the numbers unemployed plus employed. The flaw in this should be obvious. For example, assume that 90% of French youths are in education and of the remaining 10%, 5% are in work and 5% are unemployed. This last 10% are the "labour force" and so we would get a massive 50% unemployment rate but this is due to the low (5%) employment rate. Looking at the youth population as a whole, only 5% are actually unemployed. [David R. Howell, "*Introduction*", pp. 3-34, **Op. Cit.**, pp. 13-14] By the standard measure, French males age 15-24 had an unemployment rate of 20.8% in 2007, as compared to 11.8% in America. Yet this difference is mainly because, in France (as in the rest of Europe), there are many more young males not in the labour force (more are in school and fewer work part time while studying). As those who are not in the labour market are not counted in the standard measure, this gives an inflated value for youth unemployment. A far better comparison would be to compare the number of unemployed divided by the population of those in the same age group. This results in the USA having a rate of 8.3% and France 8.6%.

Another source of the "decline" of Europe is usually linked to lower GDP growth over the past few years compared to countries like Britain and the USA. Yet this perspective fails to take into account internal income distribution. Both the USA and UK are marked by large (and increasing) inequality and that GDP growth is just as unequally distributed. In America, for example, most of GDP growth since the 1980s has been captured by the top 5% of the population while median wages have been (at best) flat. Ignoring the enrichment of the elite in the USA and UK would mean that GDP growth would be, at least for the bulk of the population, better in Europe. This means that while Europe may have grown more slowly, it benefits more than just the ruling class. Then there are such factors as poverty and social mobility. Rates of poverty are much worse in the neo-liberal countries, while social mobility has fallen in the US and UK since the 1980s. There are less poor people in Europe and they stay in poverty for shorter periods of time compared to America and Britain.

Moreover, comparing Europe's income or GDP per person to the U.S. fails to take into account the fact that Europeans work far less than Americans or British people. So while France may have lagged America in per capita income in 2007 ($30,693 to $43,144), it cannot be said that working class people are automatically worse off as French workers have a significantly shorter working week and substantially more holidays. Less hours at work and longer holidays may impact negatively on GDP but only an idiot would say that this means the economy is worse, never mind the quality of life. Economists, it should be remembered, cannot say that one person is worse off than another if she has less income due to working fewer hours. So GDP per capita may be higher in the US, but only because American workers work more hours and **not** because they are more productive. Like other Europeans, the French have decided to work less and enjoy it more. So it is important to remember that GDP is not synonymous with well-being and that inequality can produce misleading per capita income comparisons.

A far better indicator of economic welfare is productivity. It is understandable that this is not used as a measure when comparing America to Europe as it is as high, or higher, in France and other Western European countries as it is in the US (and much higher than in the UK where low wages and long hours boost the figure). And it should be remembered that rising productivity in the US has not been reflecting in rising wages since 1980. The gains of productivity, in other words, have been accumulated by the boss class and not by the hard working American people (whose working week has steadily increased during that period). Moreover, France created more private sector jobs (+10% between 1996 and 2002, according to the OECD) than the UK (+6%) or the US (+5%). Ironically, given the praise it receives for being a neo-liberal model, the UK economy barely created any net employment in the private sector between 2002 and 2007 (unemployment **had** dropped, but that was due to increased state spending which led to a large rise in public sector jobs).

Then there is the fact that some European countries **have** listened to the neo-liberal orthodoxy and reformed their markets but to little success. So it should be noted that *"there has in fact already been a very considerable liberalisation and reform in Europe,"* both in product and labour markets. In fact, during the 1990s Germany and Italy reformed their labour markets *"roughly ten times"* as much as the USA. The *"point is that reforms should have boosted productivity growth in Europe,"* but they did not. If regulation *"was the fundamental problem, some positive impact on labour productivity growth should have come already from the very substantial deregulation already undertaken. Deregulation should*

have contributed to an acceleration in productivity growth in Europe whereas actually productivity growth declines. It is hard to see how regulation, which was declining, could be the source of Europe's slowdown." [Glyn, **Op. Cit.**, p. 144]

So, perhaps, "flexibility" is not the solution to unemployment some claim it is (after all, the lack of a welfare state in the 19th century did not stop mass unemployment nor long depressions occurring). Indeed, a strong case can be made (and has been by left-wing economists) that the higher open unemployment in Europe has a lot less to do with "rigid" structures and "pampered" citizens than it does with the fiscal and monetary austerity produced by the excessively tight monetary policies of the European Central Bank plus the requirements of the Maastricht Treaty and the *"Growth and Stability pact"* which aims to reduce demand expansion (i.e. wage rises) under the name of price stability (i.e., the usual mantra of fighting inflation by lowering wage increases). So, *"[i]n the face of tight monetary policy imposed first by the [German] Bundesbank and then by the European Central Bank … it has been essential to keep wages moderate and budget deficits limited. With domestic demand severely constrained, many European countries experienced particularly poor employment growth in the mid-1990s."* [David R. Howell, *"Conclusion"*, **Op. Cit.**, p. 337] This has been essentially imposed by the EU bureaucrats onto the European population and as these policies, like the EU itself, has the support of most of Europe's ruling class such an explanation is off the political agenda.

So if "flexibility" does not result in lower unemployment, just what is it good for? The net results of American labour market "flexibility" were summarised by head the US Federal Reserve Alan Greenspan in 1997. He was discussing the late 1990s boom (which was, in fact, the product of the dot.com bubble rather than the dawn of a new era so many claimed at the time). He explained why unemployment managed to fall below the standard NAIRU rate without inflation increasing. In his words:

> *"Increases in hourly compensation … have continued to fall far short of what they would have been had historical relationships between compensation gains and the degree of labour market tightness held … As I see it, heightened job insecurity explains a significant part of the restraint on compensation and the consequent muted price inflation … The continued reluctance of workers to leave their jobs to seek other employment as the labour market has tightened provides further evidence of such concern, as does the tendency toward longer labour union contracts … The low level of work stoppages of recent years also attests to concern about job security … The continued decline in the share of the private workforce in labour unions has likely made wages more responsive to market forces … Owing in part to the subdued behaviour of wages, profits and rates of return on capital have risen to high levels."* [quoted by Jim Stanford, *"Testing the Flexibility Paradigm: Canadian Labor Market Performance in International Context,"* pp. 119-155, **Fighting Unemployment**, David R. Howell (ed.), pp. 139-40]

Under such circumstances, it is obvious why unemployment could drop and inflation remain steady. Yet there is a massive contradiction in Greenspan's account. As well as showing how keenly the Federal Reserve investigates the state of the class struggle, ready to intervene when the workers may be winning, it also suggests that flexibility works just one way:

> *"Some of the features highlighted by Greenspan reflect precisely a **lack** of flexibility in the labour market: a lack of response of compensation to tight labour markets, a reluctance of workers to leave their jobs, and the prevalence of long-term contracts that lock employment arrangements for six or more years at a time. And so Greenspan's portrayal of the unique features of the US model suggests that something more than flexibility is the key ingredient at work – or at least that 'flexibility' is being interpreted once again from an unbalanced and one-sided perspective. It is, rather, a high degree of labour market **discipline** that seems to be the operative force. US workers remain insecure despite a relatively low unemployment rate, and hence compensation gains … were muted. This implies a consequent redistribution of income from labour to capital … Greenspan's story is more about **fear** than it is about flexibility – and hence this famous testimony has come to be known as Greenspan's 'fear factor' hypothesis, in which he concisely described the importance of labour market discipline for his conduct of monetary policy."* [Jim Stanford, **Op. Cit.**, p. 140]

So while this attack on the wages, working conditions and social welfare is conducted under the pre-Keynesian notion of wages being *"sticky"* downwards, the underlying desire is to impose a "flexibility" which ensures that wages are *"sticky"* **upwards.** This suggests a certain one-sidedness to the "flexibility" of modern labour markets: employers enjoy the ability to practice flexploitation but the flexibility of workers to resist is reduced.

Rather than lack of "flexibility," the key factor in explaining high unemployment in Europe is the anti-inflationary policies of its central banks, which pursue high interest rates in order to "control" inflation (i.e. wages). In contrast, America has more flexibility simply due to the state of the working class there. With labour so effectively crushed in America, with so many workers feeling they cannot change things or buying into the individualistic premises of capitalism thanks to constant propaganda by business funded think-tanks, the US central bank can rely on job insecurity and ideology to keep workers in their place in spite of relatively lower official unemployment. Meanwhile, as the rich get richer many working class people spend their time making ends meet and blaming everyone and everything but their ruling class for their situation (*"US families must work even more hours to achieve the standard of living their predecessors achieved 30 years ago."* [David R. Howell, *"Conclusion"*, **Op. Cit.**, p. 338]).

All this is unsurprising for anarchists as we recognise that "flexibility" just means weakening the bargaining power of labour in order to increase the power and profits of the rich (hence the expression **"flexploitation"**!). Increased "flexibility" has been associated with **higher,** not lower unemployment. This, again, is unsurprising, as a "flexible" labour market basically means one in which workers are glad to have any job and face increased insecurity at work (actually,

"insecurity" would be a more honest word to use to describe the ideal of a competitive labour market rather than *"flexibility"* but such honesty would let the cat out of the bag). In such an environment, workers' power is reduced meaning that capital gets a larger share of the national income than labour and workers are less inclined to stand up for their rights. This contributes to a fall in aggregate demand, so increasing unemployment. In addition, we should note that "flexibility" may have little effect on unemployment (although not on profits) as a reduction of labour's bargaining power may result in **more** rather than less unemployment. This is because firms can fire "excess" workers at will, increase the hours of those who remain and stagnating or falling wages reduces aggregate demand. Thus the paradox of increased "flexibility" resulting in higher unemployment is only a paradox in the neo-classical framework. From an anarchist perspective, it is just the way the system works as is the paradox of overwork and unemployment occurring at the same time.

So while "free market" economics portrays unions as a form of market failure, an interference with the natural workings of the market system and recommends that the state should eliminate them or ensure that they are basically powerless to act, this simply does not reflect the real world. Any real economy is marked by the economic power of big business (in itself, according to neo-classical economics, a distortion of the market). Unless workers organise then they are in a weak position and will be even more exploited by their economic masters. Left-wing economist Thomas I. Palley presents the correct analysis of working class organisation when he wrote:

> *"The reality is that unions are a correction of market failure, namely the massive imbalance of power that exists between individual workers and corporate capital. The importance of labour market bargaining power for the distribution of income, means that unions are a fundamental prop for widespread prosperity. Weakening unions does not create a 'natural' market: it just creates a market in which business has the power to dominate labour.*
>
> *"The notion of perfect natural markets is built on the assumption that market participants have no power. In reality, the process of labour exchange is characterised not only by the presence of power, but also by gross inequality of power. An individual worker is at a great disadvantage in dealing with large corporations that have access to massive pools of capital and can organise in a fashion that renders every individual dispensable … Unions help rectify the imbalance of power in labour markets, and they therefore correct market failure rather than causing it."* [**Op. Cit.**, pp. 36-7]

The welfare state also increases the bargaining power of workers against their firms and limits the ability of firms to replace striking workers with scabs. Given this, it is understandable why bosses hate unions and any state aid which undermines their economic power. Thus the *"hallmark"* of the neo-liberal age *"is an economic environment that pits citizen against citizen for the benefit of those who own and manage"* a country. [**Op. Cit.**, p. 203]

And we must add that whenever governments have attempted to make the labour market *"fully competitive"* it has either been the product of dictatorship (e.g. Chile under Pinochet) or occurred at the same time as increased centralisation of state power and increased powers for the police and employers (e.g. Britain under Thatcher, Reagan in the USA). This is the agenda which is proscribed for Western Europe. In 2006, when successful street protests stopped a proposed labour market reform in France (the CPE), one American journalist, Elaine Sciolino, complained that *"the government seems to fear its people; the people seem to fear change."* [**New York Times**, March 17 2006] Such are the contradictions of neo-liberalism. While proclaiming the need to reduce state intervention, it requires increased state power to impose its agenda. It needs to make people fear their government and fear for their jobs. Once that has been achieved, then people will accept "change" (i.e. the decisions of their economic, social and political bosses) without question. That the French people do not want a British or American style labour market, full of low-wage toilers who serve at the boss's pleasure should not come as a surprise. Nor should the notion that elected officials in a supposed democracy are meant to reflect the feelings of the sovereign people be considered as unusual or irrational.

The anti-democratic nature of capitalist "flexiblity" applies across the world. Latin American Presidents trying to introduce neo-liberalism into their countries have had to follow suit and *"ride roughshod over democratic institutions, using the traditional Latin American technique of governing by decree in order to bypass congressional opposition … Civil rights have also taken a battering. In Bolivia, the government attempted to defuse union opposition … by declaring a state of siege and imprisoning 143 strike leaders … In Colombia, the government used anti-terrorist legislation in 1993 to try 15 trade union leaders opposing the privatisation of the state telecommunications company. In the most extreme example, Peru's Alberto Fujimori dealt with a troublesome Congress by simply dissolving it … and seizing emergency powers."* [Duncan Green, **The Silent Revolution**, p. 157]

This is unsurprising. People, when left alone, will create communities, organise together to collectively pursue their own happiness, protect their communities and environment. In other words, they will form groups, associations and unions to control and influence the decisions that affect them. In order to create a "fully competitive" labour market, individuals must be atomised and unions, communities and associations weakened, if not destroyed, in order to fully privatise life. State power must be used to disempower the mass of the population, restrict their liberty, control popular organisations and social protest and so ensure that the free market can function without opposition to the human suffering, misery and pain it would cause. People, to use Rousseau's evil term, *"must be forced to be free."* And, unfortunately for neo-liberalism, the countries that tried to reform their labour market still suffered from high unemployment, plus increased social inequality and poverty and where still subject to the booms and slumps of the business cycle.

Of course, bosses and the elite are hardly going to present their desire for higher profits and more power in those terms. Hence the need to appear concerned about the fate of the unemployed. As such, it is significant, of course, that right-wing economists only seem to become concerned over unemployment when trade unions are organising or politicians are thinking of introducing or raising the minimum wage. Then they will talk about how these will raise unemployment and harm workers, particularly those from ethnic minorities. Given that bosses always oppose such policies, we must conclude that they are, in fact, seeking a situation where there is full employment and finding willing workers is hard to do. This seems, to say the least, an unlikely situation. If bosses were convinced that, for example, raising the minimum wage would increase unemployment rather than their wages bill they would be supporting it wholeheartedly as it would allow them to pressurise their workers into labouring longer and harder to remain in employment. Suffice to say, bosses are in no hurry to see their pool of wage slaves drained and so their opposition to trade unions and minimum wages are the product of need for profits rather than some concern for the unemployed.

This applies to family issues as well. In its support for "free markets" you can get a taste of the schizophrenic nature of the conservative right's approach to family values. On the one hand, they complain that families do not spend enough time together as they are under financial pressure and this results both parents going out to work and working longer hours. Families will also suffer because businesses do not have to offer paid maternity leave, paid time off, flexitime, paid holidays, or other things that benefit them. However, the right cannot bring themselves to advocate unions and strike action by workers (or state intervention) to achieve this. Ironically, their support for "free market" capitalism and "individualism" undermines their support for "family values." Ultimately, that is because profits will always come before parents.

All this is unsurprising as, ultimately, the only real solution to unemployment and overwork is to end wage labour and the liberation of humanity from the needs of capital. Anarchists argue that an economy should exist to serve people rather than people existing to serve the economy as under capitalism. This explains why capitalism has always been marked by a focus on "what the economy wants" or "what is best for the economy" as having a capitalist economy always results in profit being placed over people. Thus we have the paradoxical situation, as under neo-liberalism, where an economy is doing well while the bulk of the population are not.

Finally, we must clarify the anarchist position on state welfare (we support working class organisations, although we are critical of unions with bureaucratic and top-down structures). As far as state welfare goes, anarchists do not place it high on the list of things we are struggling against (once the welfare state for the rich has been abolished, then, perhaps, we will reconsider that). As we will discuss in section D.1.5, anarchists are well aware that the current neo-liberal rhetoric of "minimising" the state is self-serving and hides an attack on the living standards of working class people. As such, we do not join in such attacks regardless of how critical we may be of aspects of the welfare state for we seek genuine reform from below by those who use it rather than "reform" from above by politicians and bureaucrats in the interests of state and capital. We also seek to promote alternative social institutions which, unlike the welfare state, are under working class control and so cannot be cut by decree from above. For further discussion, see sections J.5.15 and J.5.16.

C.9.4 Is unemployment voluntary?

Here we point out another aspect of the free market capitalist "blame the workers" argument, of which the diatribes against unions and workers' rights highlighted above is only a part. This is the assumption that unemployment is not involuntary but is freely chosen by workers. As Nicholas Kaldor put it, for "free market" economists involuntary unemployment *"cannot exist because it is excluded by the assumptions."* [**Further Essays on Applied Economics**, p. x] Many neo-classical economists claim that unemployed workers calculate that their time is better spent searching for more highly paid employment (or living on welfare than working) and so desire to be jobless. That this argument is taken seriously says a lot about the state of modern capitalist economic theory, but as it is popular in many right-wing circles, we should discuss it.

David Schweickart notes, these kinds of arguments ignore *"two well-established facts: First, when unemployment rises, it is layoffs, not [voluntary] quits, that are rising. Second, unemployed workers normally accept their first job offer. Neither of these facts fits well with the hypothesis that most unemployment is a free choice of leisure."* [**Against Capitalism**, p. 108] When a company fires a number of its workers, it can hardly be said that the sacked workers have calculated that their time is better spent looking for a new job. They have no option. Of course, there are numerous jobs advertised in the media. Does this not prove that capitalism always provides jobs for those who want them? Hardly, as the number of jobs advertised must have some correspondence to the number of unemployed and the required skills and those available. If 100 jobs are advertised in an areas reporting 1,000 unemployed, it can scarcely be claimed that capitalism tends to full employment. This hardly gives much support to the right-wing claim that unemployment is "voluntary" and gives an obvious answer to right-wing economist Robert Lucas's quest *"to explain why people allocate time to ... unemployment, we need to know why they prefer it to all other activities."* [quoted by Schweickart, **Op. Cit.**, p. 108] A puzzle indeed! Perhaps this unworldly perspective explains why there has been no real effort to verify the assertion that unemployment is "voluntary leisure."

Somewhat ironically, given the desire for many on the right to deny the possibility of involuntary unemployment this perspective became increasingly influential at precisely the same time as the various theories of the so-called "natural rate" of unemployment did (see section C.9). Thus, at the same time as unemployment was proclaimed as being a "voluntary" choice economics was also implicitly arguing that this was nonsense, that unemployment **is** an essential disciplinary tool within capitalism to keep workers in their place (sorry, to fight inflation).

In addition, it is worthwhile to note that the right-wing assumption that higher unemployment benefits and a healthy welfare state promote unemployment is not supported by the evidence. As

a moderate member of the British Conservative Party notes, the *"OECD studied seventeen industrial countries and found no connect between a country's unemployment rate and the level of its social-security payments."* [**Dancing with Dogma**, p. 118] Moreover, the economists David Blanchflower and Andrew Oswald *"Wage Curve"* for many different countries is approximately the same for each of the fifteen countries they looked at. This also suggests that labour market unemployment is independent of social-security conditions as their "wage curve" can be considered as a measure of wage flexibility. Both of these facts suggest that unemployment is involuntary in nature and cutting social-security will **not** affect unemployment.

Another factor in considering the nature of unemployment is the effect of decades of "reform" of the welfare state conducted in both the USA and UK since 1980. During the 1960s the welfare state was far more generous than it was in the 1990s and unemployment was lower. If unemployment was "voluntary" and due to social-security being high, we would expect a decrease in unemployment as welfare was cut (this was, after all, the rationale for cutting it in the first place). In fact, the reverse occurred, with unemployment rising as the welfare state was cut. Lower social-security payments did not lead to lower unemployment, quite the reverse in fact.

Faced with these facts, some may conclude that as unemployment is independent of social security payments then the welfare state can be cut. However, this is not the case as the size of the welfare state does affect the poverty rates and how long people remain in poverty. In the USA, the poverty rate was 11.7% in 1979 and rose to 13% in 1988, and continued to rise to 15.1% in 1993. The net effect of cutting the welfare state was to help **increase** poverty. Similarly, in the UK during the same period, to quote the ex-Thatcherite John Gray, there *"was the growth of an underclass. The percentage of British (non-pensioner) households that are wholly workless – that is, none of whose members is active in the productive economy – increased from 6.5 per cent in 1975 to 16.4 per cent in 1985 and 19.1 per cent in 1994 ... Between 1992 and 1997 there was a 15 per cent increase in unemployed lone parents ... This dramatic growth of an underclass occurred as a direct consequence of neo-liberal welfare reforms, particularly as they affected housing."* [**False Dawn**, p. 30] This is the opposite of the predictions of right-wing theories and rhetoric.

As Gray correctly argues, the *"message of the American [and other] New Right has always been that poverty and the under class are products of the disincentive effects of welfare, not the free market."* He goes on to note that it *"has never squared with the experience of the countries of continental Europe where levels of welfare provision are far more comprehensive than those of the United States have long co-existed with the absence of anything resembling an American-style underclass. It does not touch at virtually any point the experience of other Anglo-Saxon countries."* He points to the example of New Zealand where *"the theories of the American New Right achieved a rare and curious feat – self-refutation by their practical application. Contrary to the New Right's claims, the abolition of nearly all universal social services and the stratification of income groups for the purpose of targeting welfare benefits selectively created a neo-liberal poverty trap."* [**Op. Cit.**, p. 42]

So while the level of unemployment benefits and the welfare state may have little impact on the level of unemployment (which is to be expected if the nature of unemployment is essentially involuntary), it **does** have an effect on the nature, length and persistency of poverty. Cutting the welfare state increases poverty and the time spent in poverty (and by cutting redistribution, it also increases inequality).

If we look at the relative size of a nation's social security transfers as a percentage of Gross Domestic Product and its relative poverty rate we find a correlation. Those nations with a high level of spending have lower rates of poverty. In addition, there is a correlation between the spending level and the number of persistent poor. Those nations with high spending levels have more of their citizens escape poverty. For example, Sweden has a single-year poverty rate of 3% and a poverty escape rate of 45% and Germany has figures of 8% and 24% (and a persistent poverty rate of 2%). In contrast, the USA has figures of 20% and 15% (and a persistent poverty rate of 42%).

Given that a strong welfare state acts as a kind of floor under the wage and working conditions of labour, it is easy to see why capitalists and the supporters of "free market" capitalism seek to undermine it. By undermining the welfare state, by making labour "flexible," profits and power can be protected from working people standing up for their rights and interests. Little wonder the claimed benefits of "flexibility" have proved to be so elusive for the vast majority while inequality has exploded. The welfare state, in other words, reduces the attempts of the capitalist system to commodify labour and increases the options available to working class people. While it did not reduce the need to get a job, the welfare state did undermine dependence on any particular employee and so increased workers' independence and power. It is no coincidence that the attacks on unions and the welfare state was and is framed in the rhetoric of protecting the *"right of management to manage"* and of driving people back into wage slavery. In other words, an attempt to increase the commodification of labour by making work so insecure that workers will not stand up for their rights.

Unemployment has tremendous social costs, with the unemployed facing financial insecurity and the possibility of indebtedness and poverty. Many studies have found that unemployment results in family distribution, ill health (both physical and mental), suicide, drug addition, homelessness, malnutrition, racial tensions and a host of other, negative, impacts. Given all this, given the dire impact of joblessness, it strains belief that people would **choose** to put themselves through it. The human costs of unemployment are well documented. There is a stable correlation between rates of unemployment and the rates of mental-hospital admissions. There is a connection between unemployment and juvenile and young-adult crime. The effects on an individual's self-respect and the wider implications for their community and society are massive. As David Schweickart concludes the *"costs of unemployment, whether measured in terms of the cold cash of lost production and lost taxes or in the hotter units of alienation, violence, and despair, are likely to be large under Laissez Faire."* [**Op. Cit.**, p. 109]

Of course, it could be argued that the unemployed should look for work and leave their families, home towns, and communities in order to find it. However, this argument merely states that people should change their whole lives as required by "market forces" (and the wishes – *"animal spirits,"* to use Keynes' term – of those who own capital). In other words, it just acknowledges that capitalism results in people losing their ability to plan ahead and organise their lives (and that, in addition, it can deprive them of their sense of identity, dignity and self-respect as well), portraying this as somehow a requirement of life (or even, in some cases, noble).

It seems that capitalism is logically committed to viciously contravening the very values upon which it claims it be built, namely the respect for the innate worth and separateness of individuals. This is hardly surprising, as capitalism is based on reducing individuals to the level of another commodity (called "labour"). To requote Karl Polanyi:

> *"In human terms such a postulate [of a labour market] implied for the worker extreme instability of earnings, utter absence of professional standards, abject readiness to be shoved and pushed about indiscriminately, complete dependence on the whims of the market. [Ludwig Von] Mises justly argued that if workers 'did not act as trade unionists, but reduced their demands and changed their locations and occupations according to the labour market, they would eventually find work.' This sums up the position under a system based on the postulate of the commodity character of labour. It is not for the commodity to decide where it should be offered for sale, to what purpose it should be used, at what price it should be allowed to change hands, and in what manner it should be consumed or destroyed."* [**The Great Transformation**, p. 176]

However, people are **not** commodities but living, thinking, feeling individuals. The "labour market" is more a social institution than an economic one and people and work more than mere commodities. If we reject the neo-liberals' assumptions for the nonsense they are, their case fails. Capitalism, ultimately, cannot provide full employment simply because labour is **not** a commodity (and as we discussed in section C.7, this revolt against commodification is a key part of understanding the business cycle and so unemployment).

C.10
Is "free market" capitalism the best way to reduce poverty?

It is far to say that supporters of "free-market" capitalism make the claim that their system not only benefits everyone, but especially working class people (indeed, the very poorest sectors of society). This was the position during the so-called "anti-globalisation" protests at the turn of the 21st century, when the issue of global inequality and poverty was forced to the front of politics (for a time). In response, the likes of the Economist portrayed itself and the big businesses seeking lower costs and higher profits as the real champions of the poor (particularly in the third world).

In this perspective growth is the key to reducing (absolute) poverty rather than, say, redistribution, struggle for reforms by means of direct action and popular self-organisation or (heaven forbid!) social revolution. The logic is simple. Economic growth of 1% per year will double an economy in 70 years, while 3% does so in just over 23 years and 5% growth takes a mere 15 years. Thus the standard right-wing argument is that we should promote "free market" capitalism as this is a growth machine par excellence. In fact, any form of redistribution or social struggle is considered counter-productive in this viewpoint as it is harms overall growth by either scaring away capital from a country or blunts the incentives of the elite to strive to "produce" more wealth. Over time, wealth will (to coin a well-worn phrase) "trickle down" from the wealthy to the many.

What to make of this claim? Again, it does contain an element of truth. As capitalism is a "grow or die" economy (see section D.4), obviously the amount of wealth available to society increases for **all** as the economy expands. So the poor will, in general, be better off **absolutely** in any growing economy (at least in economic terms). This was the case under Soviet state capitalism as well: the poorest worker in the 1980s was obviously far better off economically than one in the 1920s. As such, what counts is **relative** differences between classes and periods within a growth economy. Given the thesis that free-market capitalism will benefit the poor **especially,** we have to ask: is this actually true and, of so, can the other classes benefit equally well? This means we need to ask whether the assumption to concentrate on **absolute** poverty or inequality rather that **relative** values makes more sense. Similarly, we need to question the assumption that "free market" capitalism is the growth machine its supporters assert and whether the benefits of the growth it produces does, in fact, "trickle down." Questioning these assumptions is essential.

The key problem with evaluating such claims is, of course, the fact that an economy, like a society, is a very complex system which evolves through time. There are few opportunities for "controlled experiments" with which to test differing analyses and theories. This means that any attempt to analyse these claims must be based on looking at different countries and time periods in order to contrast them. Thus we will look at the same countries at different periods (the more social democratic post-war period to the more neo-liberal post-1980s and more neo-liberal countries with those in which free-market "reforms" have not been pushed as far). As we will show, the track record of "free(r) market" capitalism has been, at best, distinctly unimpressive and, at worse, significantly poorer.

However, this appeal to reality will not convince many supporters of capitalism. For the true believer in the capitalist market, this kind of evidence does not create doubt in their ideas, only the conviction that the experiments did not go far enough. Thus, for the ideologue, freer market capitalism handily tells us nothing about free market capitalism – unless, of course, they can be portrayed as an "economic miracle" (regardless of the facts). For "advocates of the market," the sanctity of private property and private contracts is held as an inalienable natural right. To refute charges that this will simply benefit the already wealthy they spend much time arguing that unfettered capitalism is also the only economic system which will produce the greatest benefit for the greatest number. In other words, that absolute capitalist markets and private property

rights coincide **exactly** with personal interest. A clearer example of wishful thinking could hardly be asked for. Yet it is not hard to see what function this plays. Few people will be persuaded by their assumptions on property and markets, given the common sense objection that free exchange between the weak and the strong will, obviously, benefit the latter more. Yet more people may be convinced to go along with "free market" proposals by considerations of economic efficiency and the hope that the poor will see their living standards improve over time (particularly if "experts" with economics degrees are involved as people often assume they know what they are talking about).

Now, the empirical track-record of what is called capitalism is decidedly mixed. There are three courses of action open to the market advocate. The first is to embrace the property-rights argument wholeheartedly, and say that we should adopt pure capitalism even if it hurts a large percentage of the population because it is the right thing to do. This would be unconvincing for most people as economic austerity and serf-like working conditions in return for protecting the power and property rights of the few who actually own the wealth would find few (sane or disinterested) supporters. Then it could be argued that the empirical track-record of "actually existing" capitalism should be ignored in favour of economic ideology as reality is simply not pure enough. That, again, would be unconvincing for the obvious reason that we would be being asked to have faith in the validity of economics (as we have noted before, this would not be wise given its surreal assumptions and non-scientific nature). This would have one positive side-effect, as doing this would mean that that "market advocates" would have to stop claiming that all the good things we have are due to something (capitalism) that does not exist. So that option is unlikely to have many supporters or convince many. Finally, it could be argued that contrary to appearances capitalism really **does** benefit everyone. While this option is not compatible with intellectual honesty, it is by the far the most popular within the ranks of "market advocates." This is undoubtedly because the wealthy and corporations are always willing to pay well for people happy to defend their power and profits against the reality they produce.

So what of the claim that capitalism is the best way to help the poor, that capitalism will especially benefit working class people? To make sense (i.e. to be more than simply a rhetoric assertion), it must rest on two basic notions. Firstly, that "free market" capitalism will have a higher growth rate than alternative forms of that system (such as state capitalism or regulated capitalism). Secondly, that inequality will be less and share of wages in the national income more in a "free market" than in other systems (this must be the case, otherwise "free market" reforms do not **especially** help working class people). We will discuss the first claim here, before discussing the track record of neo-liberalism in the next section followed by a discussion of the history of capitalism and free trade in section C.10.2. We then analyse the failings of the equality defence in section C.10.3 before ending with a discussion on the limitations of looking at income and growth in evaluating how capitalism benefits the working class (section C.10.4). As we show, there is substantial evidence to suggest that the standard defences of "free market" capitalism are not up to much. Let us be clear and state there is generally a positive correlation between economic growth and the income of the poor. We are not attacking economic growth as such but rather asking whether neo-liberalism's own defence actually stands up.

Looking at the historical picture, then, yes, capitalism does produce much more economic growth than previous social systems such as slavery and feudalism. However, defending capitalism on the basis that it better than a slave based economy is hardly a strong foundation (particularly when capitalists are happy to locate to dictatorships which have slave-like labour conditions). The more substantive argument is based on the assumption that "free market" capitalism produces faster economic growth than other forms of that system and that growth of the economic pie is more important than how it is distributed. In other words, the same (or even smaller) share of a bigger pie in the future is better than a bigger share of the existing pie. This means we need to look at the economic performance of capitalist economies, comparing the neo-liberal ones to regulated social democratic ones. We would expect the former to be performing significantly better than the latter in addition to being more dynamic **after** reforms than before. The reality hardly matches the claims.

The attempt to compare and contrast economies can be found in, say, the works of Milton Friedman to show the superiority of his beloved "free market" capitalism. However, as economist Thomas Balogh notes, to prove that *"socialistic policies"* had crippled Britain's economic growth since 1945 Friedman began *"by misrepresenting the size of the public sector ... he chooses a ratio which, though irrelevant, gives spurious support to his thesis."* Equally, Friedman compares post-war Britain to post-war Japan and West Germany, conveniently failing to note that both hardly had minimal states (for example, West Germany had approximately the same level of state spending as the UK and Japan had the social planning of its Ministry of Industry and Trade). As Balogh notes, the *"consequences of socialism are then illustrated by reference to the weak economic performance of Britain in comparison with Japan and Germany since 1945. This is an odd comparison to choose when judging the impact of 'socialism' on Britain. Surely what we need is to compare the British performance during a period of sustained boom under 'Friedmanism', e.g. in the period 1900-13, with the record under 'socialism,' say 1945-75."* However, to do that would mean noting that the average annual rate of growth per head of GNP between 1900 and 1913 was a mere 0.2%, compared to 2.2% between 1948 and 1975. Even taking other starting dates (such as the slump year 1893) produces a smaller rate of growth that the post-war period. [**The Irrelevance of Conventional Economics**, p. 181]

Nor do things get better when we look at the Friedman influenced Thatcher government which turned the UK into a poster-child for neo-liberalism. Here, yet again, the facts do not really support the claims in favour of "free(r) markets". As Ian Gilmore, a moderate conservative MP at the time, points out *"[d]uring the Thatcher years growth was lower than in any period of similar length since the war."* He notes *"the vast discrepancy between what the Thatcherites claimed for their policies and what actually happened."* Unsurprisingly, there was an *"unparalleled rise in poverty,"* as *"relative poverty grew significantly during the 1980s,"* from a nearly a tenth in 1979 to nearly a fifth in 1987. In 1979, the poorest fifth had just under 10% of post-tax income and the richest fifth had

37%. Ten years later, this had fallen to 7% and risen to 43% (*"The rich got rich, and the poor got poorer"*). *"Not only did the poor not share in the limited growth that took place between 1979 and 1990, the poor were relatively poorer than they had been in 1979."* [**Dancing with Dogma**, pp. 83-4, p. 87, p. 142, p. 138 and p. 172] we will return to this issue in section C.10.3.

Things did not get any better in the 1990s. Growth in GDP per capita was steadily decreased in the UK, from 2.3% per annum between 1950 and 1970, to 2.1% between 1970 and 1979 and to 1.9% between 1979 and 1997. For the US, a similar process was at work (from 2.0%, to 2.3% to 1.5%). At best, it can be said that the growth rates of Germany and France between 1979 and 1997 were worse (at 1.7% and 1.4%, respectively). However, before 1979 their growth was much higher (at 5.1%/4.5% between 1950 and 1970 and 2.8%/3.3% between 1970 and 1979, respectively). Growth in labour productivity per hour worked is hardly impressive, being 2.3% between 1979 and 1997 compared to 0.8% for the US, 2.4% for France and 2.2% for Germany. This is well below the 1950-1970 figure of 3.0% and only slightly better than 2.1% during the strike bound 1970s. In 1979, the UK was 9th of 15 EU members in OECD measures of prosperity. By 1995, it was 11th before rising back to 10th in 1999. In summary, *"the idea that Britain has a clearly superior economy to the continent is a delusion."* [Adair Turner, **Just Capital: The Liberal Economy**, p. 200, pp. 199-200 and p. 196]

The best that can be said of Thatcherism is that during the 1980s, *"Britain put an end to three decades of relative decline and caught up some lost ground versus continental leaders ... But Britain's absolute productivity and prosperity performance is still below the European average and its pace of catch-up has been slow."* Combine this with longer working hours compared to the rest of Europe, we have a situation in the UK where *"too many companies relying on low wages and a flexible labour market to remain competitive, rather than on investment in capital equipment and technique."* Looking at the historical picture, it should be stressed that the UK has been in decline since the 1880s, when it remained the only developed nation to embrace free trade and that between the 1950s and 1970s, the *"absolute growth rates per capita ... compared well with the inter-war years and with the period of British leadership in the nineteenth century."* This lack of success for neo-liberal reforms can also be seen in New Zealand. The economic results of its liberalisation project were just as poor. Between 1984-98 per capita income grew only about 5.4%, or 0.4% per annum, well below the EU average and one of the lowest rates of increase among the OECD countries. [Turner, **Op. Cit.**, p. 196, p. 212, p. 199 and p. 240fn] Needless to say, because the rich got richer and rebellious workers were controlled, both the UK and New Zealand were proclaimed "economic miracles."

This lack of dynamism is not limited just to the UK or New Zealand. As left-wing economist Andrew Glyn notes, the *"fact that there was no general improvement in growth in the 1980s could be explained away by the fact that the ... policies ... were only picking up steam. But the real puzzle is the 15 years since 1990. Why [have these free market policies] ... failed to bring an increase in the growth rate."* In fact, growth per year has steadily fallen since 1973 with 1990-2004 the lowest rate yet for the USA, Europe and Japan. This applies to other economic indicators as well. *"The fact that output per head has been growing more slowly since 1990 than it did in the turbulent period 1973-9, never mind the Golden Age, must be a severe disappointment to those who believed that unleashing the free market would restore rapid growth."* He summarises the evidence by pointing out that *"economic performance overall has been unspectacular."* [**Capitalism Unleashed**, pp. 130-1 and p. 151]

As Chomsky summarises, *"neoliberal-style programs began to take shape in the 1970s"* and since then real wages *"for the majority have largely stagnated or declined ... the relatively weak benefits system has declined as well. Incomes are maintained only by extending working hours well beyond those in similar societies, while inequality has soared"* (as has personal debt). Moreover, *"this is a vast change from the preceding quarter century, when economic growth was the highest on record for a protracted period and also egalitarian. Social indicators, which closely tracked economic growth until the mid-1970s, then diverged, declining to the level of 1960 by the year 2000."* [**Failed States**, p. 211]

The assumption is that producing free(r) markets and a pure(r) capitalism will result in higher growth and so rising living standards. *"So far,"* note two experts, *"the promises have not been realised. As trade and financial markets have been flung open, incomes have risen not faster, but slower. Equality among nations has not improved, with many of the poorest nations suffering an absolute decline in incomes. Within nations, inequality seems to have worsened ... the trend to towards more inequality."* In the two decades after 1980, *"overall income growth slowed dramatically."* For example, the rich countries saw annual per capita income growth fall from 4.8% (1965-80) to 1.4% (1980-95). Medium countries saw a fall from 3.8% to 3.1% (excluding China, this was 3.2% to 0.6% as China rose from 4.1% to 8.6%). For the poorest nations, there was a rise from 1.4% to 2.0% but this becomes 1.2% to 0.1% when India is excluded (India saw a rise from 1.5% to 3.2%). In fact, income dropped by -0.4% a year between 1980 and 1995 for the least developed countries (it had risen 0.4% a year between 1965 and 1980). *"In more advanced countries ... income growth was lower in the 1990s than in the 1980s. Over the entire post-1980 period, it was substantially below that of the 1960s and 1970s."* In America, for example, annual growth of per capita income has dropped from 2.3% between 1960-79, to 1.5% between 1979 and 1989 and 1.0% between 1989 and 1996 (per capita income growth up to 1998 was 1.4% per year, still less than the 1.6% per cent between 1973 and 1980 and 1980s and about half the growth over the 1960 to 1973 period). Given that income equality improved during the 1960s and 1970s, before worsening after 1980 for most countries, particularly the USA, this means that even these most increases flowed overwhelming to those at the top of the income hierarchy. In America, the working hours for a middle-class family has increased by 10.4% between 1979 and 1997. In other words, working class people are working more for less. In most advanced nations, there has *"not been a sizeable increase in poverty,"* the *"exceptions [being] the USA and the United Kingdom, where poverty grew, respectively, by 2.4 and 5.4 percentage points between 1979 and 1991."* [Jeff Faux and Larry Mishel, *"Inequality and the Global Economy"*, pp. 93-111, Will Hutton and Anthony

Giddens (eds.), **On The Edge**, pp. 93-4, p. 96, p. 97, p. 98, p. 101, p. 102 and p. 100]

This lack of rise in growth is a definite feature of neo-liberalism. The promises of the "free market" capitalism have not borne fruit:

"Growth did not accelerate. It slowed down. During the 1960s, the average rate of growth of world GDP per capita was 3.5% per annum ... The average rate of growth of world GDP per capital was 2.1% per annum during the 1970s, 1.3% per annum during the 1980s and 1% per annum during the 1990s. This growth was more volatile compared with the past, particularly in the developing world. the growth was also unevenly distributed across countries ...

"Economic inequalities have increased in the late twentieth century as the income gap between rich and poor countries, between rich and the poor in the world's population, as also between rich and poor people within countries, has widened. The ratio of GDP per capital in the richest country to GDP per capita in the poorest country of the world rose from 35:1 in 1950 to 42:1 in 1970 and 62:1 in 1990. The ratio of GDP per capita in the 20 richest countries to GDP per capita in the poorest 20 countries of the world rose from 54:1 during 1960-62 to 121:1 during 2000-2002. The income gap between people has also widened over time. The ratio of the average GNP per capita in the richest quintile of the world's population to the poorest quintile in the world's population rose from 31:1 in 1965 to 60:1 in 1990 and 74:1 in 1997 ... Income distribution within countries also worsened ... Between 1975 and 2000, the share of the richest 1% in gross income rose from 8% to 17% in the US, from 8.8% to 13.3% in Canada and from 6.1% to 13% in the UK." [Deepak Nayyar, *"Globalisation, history and development: a tale of two centuries,"* pp. 137-159, **Cambridge Journal of Economics**, Vol. 30, No. 1, pp. 153-4 and p. 154]

In fact, between 1950 and 1973 there was a vastly superior economic performance compared to what came before and what came after. If laissez-faire capitalism would benefit "everyone" more than "really existing capitalism," the growth rate would be **higher** during the later period, which more closely approximated laissez faire. It is not. As such, we should always remember that if anything is proclaimed an "economic miracle" it is unlikely to actually be so, at least for the working class. Looking at the American triumphantism of the late 1990s, it was easy to forget that in the 1980s and early 1990s, despair at the US economy was commonplace. Then people looked to Japan, just as they had looked to Europe in the 1960s.

We must also note that there is a standard response by believers in "laissez-faire" capitalism when inconvenient facts are presented to them, namely to stress that we have not reached the market utopia yet and more reforms are required (*"a feature of hard-line free-market analysis [is] that when liberalisation does not work the reason is always timidity and the solution is obvious. Complete the job."* [Glyn, **Op. Cit.**, p. 143]). Another possible defence would be to stress that the results would have been worse if the reforms had not been implemented. These are, of course, possibilities but given the rhetoric used by the defenders of capitalism on the wonders and efficiency of free markets, it seems strange that making them freer would have such negative effects.

Looking at the history of capitalism, it appears that social-democratic capitalism, with strong unions and a welfare state, produces not only more growth but also more equitable growth (as one expert notes, *"[i]f the 'welfare state' were abolished and taxes reduced accordingly, society would become a great deal more unequal."* [John Hills, **Inequality and the State**, p. 195]). Movement to more laissez-faire capitalism has resulted not only in lower growth but also growth which accumulates in fewer hands (which makes sense considering the basic anarchist insight that a free exchange benefits the stronger of the two parties). As such, based on its own criteria (namely economic growth), then neo-liberalism has to be judged a failure. Do not get us wrong. It is possible to still advocate laissez-faire capitalism on ethical grounds (if that is the right word). It is simply doubtful that it will produce the boost in economic growth (or employment) that its advocates suggest. It may do, of course, as "actually existing" capitalism is still far from the pure system of the textbooks but it is significant that movements towards the ideal have produced **less** growth along with greater inequality and relative poverty.

This is **not** to suggest that anarchists support social-democratic capitalism rather than more laissez-faire forms. Far from it – we seek to end all forms of that system. However, it is significant that the more equal forms of capitalism based on strong and militant unions produced better results than "free(r) market" forms. This suggests that the standard right-wing arguments that collective organising and fighting to keep an increased share of the wealth we produce harms the overall economy and so is harmful in the long run are deeply flawed. Instead, it is the **lack** of any struggle for equality and freedom that is correlated with bad overall economic performance. Of course, such struggles are a pain for the capitalist class. Rather than produce a *"road to serfdom,"* social-democracy created the full employment environment which produced a rebellious population. The move towards "free(r) markets" was a response to this social struggle, an attempt to enserf the population which has proven to be somewhat successful. As such, Kalecki's 1940s prediction we quoted in section B.4.4 has been proven correct: the ruling class would prefer social peace (i.e. obedience) rather than higher growth (particularly if they get to monopolise most of the gains of that lower growth).

Finally, we should note that there is a slight irony to see right-wingers saying that "pure(r)" capitalism would benefit the poor especially. This is because they usually reject the idea that aggregate economic statistics are a meaningful concept or that the government should collate such data (this is a particular feature of the "Austrian" school of economics). As such, it would be near impossible to determine if living standards had improved any faster than under the current system. Given the history of "actually existing" capitalism, it is probably wise that many "market advocates" do so. Moreover, any subjective evaluation, such as asking people, which resulted in a negative response would be dismissed out of hand as "envy." Ironically, for an ideology which says it bases itself on "subjective"

evaluations, economists are always ready to ignore any which conflict with their ideas. Needless to say, even if it could be proven beyond doubt that "pure(r)" capitalism did **not** help the poor but rather enriched the wealthy then almost all "free market" capitalists would **not** change their ideas. This is because, for them, the outcomes of the market are hallowed and if they result in increased poverty then so be it. It just shows that the poor are lazy and not worth higher incomes. That they sometimes utilise the rhetoric of social concern simply shows that most people still have concern and solidarity for their fellows, a concern which capitalism has not managed to totally remove (much to the chagrin of the likes of von Hayek – see chapter 11 of Alan Haworth's **Anti-Libertarianism** for a short but relevant discussion of this).

C.10.1 Hasn't neo-liberalism benefited the world's poor?

Until the wave of so-called "anti-globalisation" protests (a more accurate term would be "global justice" protests) erupted in the late 1990s, there was no real need for the neo-liberal agenda to justify its performance. When opposition could not be ignored, then it had to be undermined. This lead to a host of articles and books justifying neo-liberalism in terms of it helping the world's poorest peoples. This has meant denying the reality of 30 years of neo-liberal reforms in favour of concentrating on absolute poverty figures.

This is understandable. As we discuss in the section C.10.4, absolute inequality and poverty is a good means of making discussion of the real issues meaningless. Moreover, as noted above, as capitalism must grow to survive wealth will tend to increase for all members of society over time. The real question is whether "free(r) markets increase or reduce growth rates and how they impact on relative levels of poverty and inequality. Given that the last few decades indicate how free(r) markets result in increased inequality, it is obvious why defenders of capitalism would seek to focus attention on absolute income. While denied by some, inequality has risen under globalisation. Those who deny it usually do so because the doctrines of the powerful are at stake. Some, in spite of the evidence, are that world-wide economic inequality has fallen thanks to global capitalism.

At the forefront of such claims is the **Economist** magazine, which played its usual role of ideological cheerleader for the ruling class. Discussing *"Global economic inequality"*, the magazine argued that the claim that inequality has risen is false. Ironically, their own article refutes its own conclusions as it presented a graph which showed an upward relationship between economic growth from 1980 to 2000 and original income level for a large group of countries. This means that global economic inequality **has** increased – as they admit, this means *"that the poor are falling behind, and that cross-country inequality is getting worse."* [*"More or less equal?"*, the **Economist**, 11th March, 2004]

However, this conclusion is ideologically incorrect and so something must be done to achieve the correct position in order to defend capitalism against the anti-capitalist bias of reality. They did this by adding another chart which weights each point by population. This showed that two of the largest countries of their group, China and India, grew among the fastest. Using this data they make the claim that inequality has, in fact, fallen under neo-liberalism. Once you look at individuals rather than countries then the claim can be made that world-wide inequality has been falling under "free(r) market" capitalism. While an impressive piece of ideological obfuscation, the argument ignores changes **within** countries. The article states that *"average incomes in India and China are going up extremely rapidly"* but not every person receives the average. The average hides a lot. For example, 9 homeless people have an average income of £0 but add a multi-millionaire and the average income of the ten people is in the millions. On average, at the end of a game of poker everyone has the same amount of money they started with. As such, to ignore the fact that inequality increased dramatically in both countries during the 1990s is disgraceful when trying to evaluate whether poverty has actually decreased or not. And it should be obvious that if inequality is increasing **within** a country then it must also be increasing internationally as well.

Significantly, *"where governments adopted the [neo-liberal] Washington Consensus, the poor have benefited less from growth."* [Joseph E. Stiglitz, **Globalization and its Discontents**, p. 79] The mantra that economic growth is so wonderful is hard to justify when the benefits of that growth are being enjoyed by a small proportion of the people and the burdens of growth (such as rising job insecurity, loss of benefits, wage stagnation and decline for the majority of workers, declining public services, loss of local communities and so forth) are being borne by so many. Which does seem to be the case under neo-liberalism (which, undoubtedly, explains why it is portrayed so positively in the business press).

To be fair, the article does note the slow and declining incomes in the past 20 years in sub-Saharan Africa but rest assured, the magazine stresses, this area *"suffers not from globalisation, but from lack of it."* This means that this area can be ignored when evaluating the results of neo-liberalism. Yet this is unconvincing as these nations are hardly isolated from the rest of the world. As they are suffering from debt and western imposed structural adjustment programs it seems illogical to ignore them – unless it is a way to improve neo-liberalism's outcomes by evading its greatest failures.

Then there is the comparison being made. The Economist looks solely at the years 1980-2000 yet surely the right comparison would be between this period and the twenty years before 1980? Once that is done, it becomes clear why the magazine failed to do so for *"economic growth and almost all of the other indicators, the last 20 years have shown a very clear decline in progress as compared with the previous two decades."* While it is *"commonly believed that the shift towards globalisation has been a success, at least regarding growth,"* in fact *"the progress achieved in the two decades of globalisation has been considerably less than the progress in the period from 1960 to 1980."* For low and middle-income countries, performance is *"much worse ... than the period from 1960 to 1980."* *"Summing up the evidence on per capita income growth, countries at every level of per capita GDP performed worse on average in the period of globalisation than in the period from 1960 to 1980."* [Mark Weisbrot, Dean Baker, Egor Kraev and Judy Chen, **The Scorecard on Globalization 1980-2000: Twenty Years of Diminished Progress**] In fact:

> *"The poorest group went from a per capita GDP growth rate of 1.9 percent annually in 1960-80, to a decline of 0.5 percent per year (1980-2000). For the middle group (which includes mostly poor countries), there was a sharp decline from an annual per capita growth rate of 3.6 percent to just less than 1 percent. Over a 20-year period, this represents the difference between doubling income per person, versus increasing it by just 21 percent."* [**Op. Cit.**]

Nor should we forget that there is a *"gallery of nations whose economies soured shortly after their leaders were lauded by the global policy elite for pursuing sound economic fundamentals."* [Jeff Faux and Larry Mishel, **Op. Cit.**, p. 94] This process of proclaiming the success of neo-liberalism before it implodes started with the original neo-liberal experiment, namely Pinochet's Chile whose economy imploded just after Milton Friedman proclaimed it an "economic miracle" (see section C.11).

Latin America has suffered the most attention from neo-liberalism and its institutions so it would be useful to look there for evaluating the claims of its supporters (*"the IMF talks with pride about the progress that Latin America made in market reforms"* [Stiglitz, **Op. Cit.**, p. 79]). Rather than success story, there has been *"a long period of economic failure: for the prior 20 years, 1980-1999, the region grew by only 11 percent (in per capita terms) over the whole period. This is the worst 20-year growth performance for more than a century, even including the years of the Great Depression."* By comparison, *"for the two decades from 1960-1979, Latin America experienced per capita GDP growth of 80 percent."* In fact, *"using the 1960-1979 period as a baseline, the quarter century for 1980-2004 is dismal. Annual growth in GDP per capita registers a mere 0.5 percent, as opposed to 3.0 percent over the previous period. Countries that are now considered relatively successful are not doing very well compared to past performance. For example, Mexico registers 0.8 percent annual per capita growth for 1980-2004, as compared with 3.3 percent for 1960-79. For Brazil, which one had one of the fastest growing economies in the world, per capita growth is only 0.8 percent annually for 1980-2004, as compared with 4.9 percent for 1960-79."* For Latin America as a whole, real per-capita growth was 3.0% in the 1960s, 2.9% in the 1970s, -0.3% in the 1980s and 1.4% in the 1990s. This means that for 1980-1999, *"the region's per capita GDP grew at an annual rate of only 0.5 percent, a cumulative total of 11 percent for the two decades."* By comparison, *"from 1960-1979, per capita growth was 3.0 percent, or 80 percent for these two decades."* [Mark Weisbrot and David Rosnick, **Another Lost Decade?: Latin America's Growth Failure Continues into the 21st Century**] Looking at Mexico, for example, since NAFTA per capita GDP growth in Mexico has averaged less than 1.0% annually. This is an extremely poor growth record for a developing country. Successful developing countries, such as South Korea and Taiwan have managed to sustain per capita GDP growth rates that have averaged more than 4.0% since the sixties. In fact, Mexico managed to sustain a per capita GDP growth rate of more than 4.0% in the period from 1960 to 1980, when it was following a path of import substitution. But, then, neither South Korea nor Taiwan followed the dictates of neo-liberalism.

Over all it is important to stress that neo-liberalism has failed its own test:

> *"Economic growth over the last twenty years, the period during which [neo-liberalism] policies ... have been put into place, has been dramatically reduced ... to assume that the World Bank and the IMF have brought 'growth-enhancing policies' to their client countries goes against the overwhelming weight of the evidence over the last two decades ... In short, there is no region of the world that the Bank or Fund can point to as having succeeded through adopting the policies that they promote – or in many cases, impose – upon borrowing countries."* [Mark Weisbrot, Dean Baker, Robert Naiman, and Gila Neta, **Growth May Be Good for the Poor – But are IMF and World Bank Policies Good for Growth?**]

As Chomsky summarises, the periods of fastest and prolonged growth have not coincided with phases of extensive liberalisation. In fact, neoliberal reforms have *"been accompanied by much slower rates of growth and reduced progress on social indicators ... There are exceptions to the general tendency: high growth rates were recorded among those who ignored the rules (and with tremendous inequality and other severe side effects in China and India)."* Growth rates in fact fell, by *"over half"* compared to the preceding period of statist policies (particularly when measured per capita). [**Op. Cit.**, pp. 216-7] For most countries, growth was higher in the 1950s, 1960s and even the 1970s. This suggests that neo-liberalism fails even its own tests as noted by one economist who compared the reality of successful development to the neo-liberal myth:

> *"the poor growth records of developing countries over the last two decades suggest this line of defence [i.e. it brings higher growth] is simply untenable ... The plain fact is that the Neo-Liberal 'policy reforms' have not been able to deliver their central promise – namely, economic growth."* [Ha-Joon Chang, **Kicking Away the Ladder**, p. 128]

Then there is the issue of what the magazine fails to mention. For a start, it excludes the ex-Stalinist regimes in Eastern Europe. This is understandable for obvious reasons. If these nations were included, then their rising inequality and poverty since they became part of the global market would have to be mentioned and this would make its defence of neo-liberalism much harder (as would the fact life expectancies fell to Third World levels). As economist Joseph Stiglitz points out, the neo-liberal reforms brought the ex-Stalinist countries *"unprecedented poverty."* In 1989, only 2% of Russians lived in poverty, by the late 1998 that number had soared to 23.8%, using the $2 a day standard. More than 40% had less that $4 a day. Other post-Stalinist countries *"have seen comparable, if not worse, increases in poverty."* Overall, this reform package has *"entailed one of the largest increases in poverty in history."* [**Globalization and its Discontents**, p. 6, p. 153 and p. 182]

The GDP in the former Stalinist states fell between 20% and 40% in the decade after 1989, an economic contraction which can only be compared to the Great Depression of the 1930s. Of the 19 ex-Stalinist economies, only Poland's GDP exceeded that of 1989, the year transition began. In only 5 was GDP per capita more than 80% of the 1989 level. [Chang, **Op. Cit.**, p. 129] Only a small minority saw their real wages rise; the vast majority experienced a spectacular fall in living standards. It took the Czech Republic, for example eight years until average real wages reached their 1989 level. Unemployment became widespread. In 2005, Slovakia had 27% of its under-25s are unemployed while in Poland 39% of under-25s were without a job (the highest figure in Europe) and 17% of the population were below the poverty line.

Overall, between 1985 and 2000, growth in GDP per capita was negative in 17 transition countries while the *"incidence of poverty increased in most countries of Latin America, the Caribbean and Sub-Saharan Africa during the 1980s and the 1990s. Much of Eastern Europe and Central Asia experiences a sharp rise in poverty during the 1990s."* East, Southwest and South Asia did experience a steady decline in the incidence of poverty, but *"most of this improvement is accounted for by changes in just two countries, with large populations, China and India."* [Deepak Nayyar, **Op. Cit.**, p. 154, pp. 154-5 and p. 155] Hardly an inspiring result.

And what of the actual economic regimes in China and India? One left-wing economist notes that *"in the early stages of China's high growth period there was an expansion of state employment, including in the dynamic and crucial manufacturing sector ... in its most recent phase, private capital accumulation dominates the growth process in China, although the state still strongly influences the pattern of investment through its control of the credit system and its policy of creating 'national champions' in sectors such as cars and steel."* Not to mention, of course, its role in the labour market. There is no freedom to organise – the country is, in effect, one big workplace and the state bosses do not tolerate freedom of association, assembly and speech any more than any other company. Unsurprisingly, labour discipline *"is very harsh"* and workers may find it difficult to change jobs and migrate to urban areas. [Andrew Glyn, **Op. Cit.**, p. 87 and p. 94]

As one expert notes, in the case of both India and China *"the main trade reforms took place **after** the onset of high growth. Moreover, these countries' trade restrictions remain among the highest in the world."* In India, its *"trend growth rate increased substantially in the early 1980s"* while *"serious trade reform did not start until 1991-93 ... tariffs were actually higher in the rising growth period of the 1980s than in the low-growth 1970s."* Thus claims of *"the beneficial effects of trade liberalisation on poverty have to be seen as statements based on faith rather than evidence."* [Dani Rodrik, **Comments on 'Trade, Growth, and Poverty by D. Dollar and A. Kraay**] As Chomsky notes, there is a deliberate policy which *"muddles export orientation with neo-liberalism, so that if a billion Chinese experience high growth under export-orientated policies that radically violate neo-liberal principles, the increase in average global growth rates can be hailed as a triumph of the principles that are violated."* [**Op. Cit.**, p. 217] It should also be mentioned that both these states avoided the 1980s debt crisis by avoiding Western banks in the 1970s. They also maintain capital controls, so that hot money cannot flow freely in and out, and have large state sectors. At least the **Economist** itself notes that *"[n]either country is an exemplar of free market capitalism – far from it."* That says it all about the defenders of free market capitalism; they defend their ideas by pointing to countries which do not apply them!

It should be stressed that this praise for the "free market" using regimes which hardly meet the criteria has a long history. This has included both Japan and the East Asian Tigers in the 1970s and 1980s as *"the spectacular growth of these countries ... is fundamentally due to activist industrial, trade and technology policies (ITT) by the state."* [Chang, **Op. Cit.**, p. 49] As an expert on these economies notes, *"the legend is not fully consistent with the way the governments have in practice behaved,"* namely adopting *"over a long period of time a much more aggressive, dirigistic set of industrial policies than free-trading principles would justify."* In fact, their *"governments were deeply committed to increasing and sustaining high levels of investment and to steering its composition."* He bemoans the *"assumption that only those features of economic policy consistent with neoclassical principles could have contributed to good economic performance"* and so explanations for such *"accordingly ignore non-neoclassical features."* [Robert Wade, *"What can Economics Learn from East Asian Success?"*, pp. 68-79, **Annals of the American Academy of Political and Social Science**, vol. 505, pp. 70-1, p. 72 and p. 68]

This analysis was proved right when, ironically, the praise turned to attack when the 1997 crisis erupted and all the features previously ignored or denied were brought onto the central stage to explain the slump (*"When their bubbles imploded, the same countries were denounced by the policy elites for something called 'crony capitalism' – a year earlier, the term had been 'business-friendly environment.'"* [Jeff Faux and Larry Mishel, **Op. Cit.**, p. 94]). As Robert Wade noted, *"the perception shifted from 'miracle Asia' to 'Asian crony state capitalism' almost over night,"* a term used *"to convey a told-you-so moral about the dangers of government intervention."* [*"From 'miracle' to 'cronyism': explaining the Great Asian Slump"*, pp. 673-706, **Cambridge Journal of Economics**, Vol. 22, No. 6, p. 699 and p. 700] Ironically, Japan's 1990s woes and the 1997 crisis both occurred **after** those states liberalised their economies (as recommended by, of course, economists and the IMF). Unsurprisingly, we discover Milton Friedman pointing (in 2002!) to the *"dramatic success of the market-orientated policies of the East Asian tigers"* as if they gave support to his ideological position of laissez-faire capitalism. [**Op. Cit.**, p. ix]

Then there is the issue of "economic liberty" as such. Milton Friedman stated in 2002 that the *"limited increase in economic freedom has changed the face of China, strikingly confirming our faith in the power of free markets."* [**Op. Cit.**, pp. viii-ix] Faith is the right word, as only the faithful could fail to note that there is no free market in China as it does not have basic freedoms for labour. How much "economic freedom" is there for workers under a brutal dictatorship? How can it be claimed, with a straight face, that there is an *"increase in economic freedom"* in such regimes? It seems, therefore, that for right-wing economists that their *"faith"* in "free markets" is *"confirmed"* by an authoritarian system that obviously and constantly violates the freedom of labour. But then again, workers have never been considered highly by the profession. What has always counted is the freedom of the boss and, consequently, a regime that secures that is always praised (and we discuss in section C.11, Friedman has a track record in this).

The selectively of the supporters of "free market" capitalists is truly staggering. Take, as an example, globalisation and anti-globalisation protests. Supports of the trade deals accused critics as being against "free trade" and, by implication, against freedom. Yet the deals they supported were based on accepting the current labour standards across the world. This means accepting the labour conditions of states, usually dictatorships, which habitually deny a free market (even a capitalist one) to its workers – all in the name of the free market! Which makes the "free market" supporters of neo-liberalism utter hypocrites. They are happy to accept a "free market" in which the denial of freedom of workers to form unions is an intrinsic part. It also suggests that the much attacked critics of "trade" deals who demand that basic standards of freedom for workers be incorporated into them are those who truly support "free trade" and the "free market." Those who advocate unrestricted trade with dictatorial regimes (where workers are thrown in prison, at best, or assassinated, at worse, if they organise or talk about unions and protests) are engaging in the worse form of doublethink when they appropriate the term "freedom" for their position.

It is easy to understand why supporters of capitalism do so. In such regimes, capital is free and the many abuses of freedom are directed towards the working class. These suppress wages and the resulting competition can be used to undermine workers wages, conditions and freedoms back home. This is why neo-liberals and such like agree to a range of global policies that give substantial freedoms to capitalists to operate unhindered around the world while, at the same time, fiercely resistant to any demands that the freedom of workers be given equal concern (this is why Chomsky talks about the *"international global justice movement, ludicrously called 'anti-globalisation' because they favour globalisation that privileges the interests of people, not investors and financial institutions."* [**Op. Cit.**, p. 259]). In other words, free markets are fine for capitalists, but not for workers. And if anyone disagrees, they turn round and accuse their critics of being opposed to "freedom"! As such, anti-globalisation protesters are right. People in such regimes are not free and it is meaningless to talk of the benefits of "free markets" when a free market in labour does not exist. It does, of course, show how genuine the defenders of capitalism are about freedom.

So has global poverty fallen since the rise of neo-liberalism in 1970s? Perhaps it has, but only if you apply the World Bank measure (i.e. a living standard of less than a dollar a day). If that is done then the number of individuals in dire poverty is (probably) falling (although Joseph Stiglitz states that *"the actual number of people living in poverty ... actually increased by almost 100 million"* in the 1990s and he argues that globalisation as practised *"has not succeeded in reducing poverty."* [**Op. Cit.**, p. 5 and p. 6]). However, the vast bulk of those who have risen out of dire poverty are in China and India, that is in the two countries which do not follow the neo-liberal dogma. In those that did follow the recommendations of neo-liberalism, in Africa, Latin America and Eastern Europe, poverty and growth rates are much worse. Chang states the obvious:

> *"So we have an apparent 'paradox' here – at least if you are a Neo-Liberal economist. All countries, but especially developing countries, grew much faster when they used 'bad' policies during the 1960-1980 period than when*

*they used 'good' ones during the following two decades …
Now, the interesting thing is that these 'bad' policies are
basically those that the NDCs [Now Developed Countries]
had pursued when they were developing countries
themselves. Given this, we can only conclude that, in
recommending the allegedly 'good' policies, the NDCs are
in effect 'kicking away the ladder' by which they have
climbed to the top."* [**Op. Cit.**, p. 129]

Hardly a glowing recommendation for the prescriptions favoured by
the **Economist** and other supporters of free market capitalism. Nor
very convincing support for solving the problems of neo-liberalism
with yet more globalisation (of the same, neo-liberal, kind). One
thing is true, though. The accepted wisdom of the age is that
the road to prosperity and international acceptance is "economic
liberalisation" or some other euphemism for opening economies
to foreign investment. What this really means is that authoritarian
regimes that allow their subjects to be exploited by international
capital rather than state bureaucracies will find apologists among
those who profit from such transactions or get paid by them. That
this involves violation of the freedom of working class people
and the labour "market" does not seem to bother them for, they
stress, the long term material benefits this will create outweigh
such restrictions on the eternal and sacred laws of economics. That
"freedom" is used to justify this just shows how debased that concept
has become under capitalism and within capitalist ideology.

C.10.2 Does "free trade" benefit everyone?

As we discussed in the last section, the post-1980 era of neo-liberal
globalisation and "free(r) markets" has not been as beneficial to
the developing world as the defenders of neo-liberalism suggest. In
fact, these economies have done worse under neo-liberalism than
they did under state-aided forms of development between 1950 and
1980. The only exceptions post-1980 have been those states which
have rejected the dogmas of neo-liberalism and used the state to
foster economic development rather than rely on "free trade."

It would, of course, be churlish to note that this is a common
feature of capitalist development. Industrialisation has always been
associated with violations of the sacred laws of economics and
freedom for workers. In fact, the central conceit of neo-liberalism
is that it ignores the evidence of history but this is unsurprising
(as noted in section C.1.2, economics has a distinct bias against
empirical evidence). This applies to the notion of free trade as well
as industrialisation, both of which show the economists lack of
concern with reality.

Most economists are firm supporters of free trade, arguing that
it benefits all countries who apply it. The reason why was first
explained by David Ricardo, one of the founding fathers of the
discipline. Using the example of England and Portugal and wine
and cloth, he argued that international trade would benefit both
countries even if one country (Portugal) produced both goods
more cheaply than the other because it was relative costs which

counted. This theory, called comparative advantage, meant that it
would be mutually beneficial for both countries to specialise in the
goods they had a relative advantage in and trade. So while it is
cheaper to produce cloth in Portugal than England, it is cheaper
still for Portugal to produce excess wine, and trade that for English
cloth. Conversely, England benefits from this trade because its cost
for producing cloth has not changed but it can now get wine at
closer to the cost of cloth. By each country specialising in producing
one good, the sum total of goods internationally increases and,
consequently, everyone is better off when these goods are traded.
[**The Principles of Political Economy and Taxation**, pp. 81-3]
This argument is still considered as the bed-rock of the economics
of international trade and is used to refute arguments in favour
of policies like protectionism. Strangely, though, economists have
rarely compared the outcome of these policies. Perhaps because
as Chomsky notes, *"if you want to know how well those theorems
actually work, just compare Portugal and England after a hundred
years of development."* [**Understanding Power**, p. 254] One
economist who did was the German Friedrich List who, in 1837,
urged people *"to turn his attention to Portugal and to England and
to compare the economies of these two countries. I am sure that
he can have no doubts as to which country is prosperous and which
has lost its economic independence, is dead from an intellectual,
commercial and industrial point of view, and is decadent, poverty
stricken and weak."* [**The Natural System of Political Economy**,
pp. 169-70] Unsurprisingly, List used this example to bolster his
case for protectionism. Little has changed. Allan Engler notes
that *"[a]fter nearly 200 years, comparative advantage had given
Portugal no noticeable advantage."* While the UK became the leading
industrial power, Portugal remained a poor agricultural economy:
*"Britain's manufacturing industries were the most efficient in the
world, Portugal had little choice but to be an exporter of agricultural
products and raw materials."* In 1988, Portugal's per capita GDP
was less than one third that of the UK. When "Purchasing power
parity" is factored in, Portugal's per capita GDP was barely more
than half of the UK. [**Apostles of Greed**, p. 132]

Nor should we forget that free trade takes the economic agent as
the country. Unlike an individual, a nation is divided by classes
and marked by inequalities of wealth, power and influence. Thus
while free trade may increase the sum-total of wealth in a specific
country, it does not guarantee that its benefits or losses will be
distributed equally between social classes, never mind individuals.
Thus capitalists may favour free trade at specific times because it
weakens the bargaining power of labour, so allowing them to reap
more income at the workers' expense (as producers and consumers).
Taking the example of the so-called "free trade" agreements of the
1990s, there was no reason to believe that benefits of such trade
may accrue to all within a given state nor that the costs will be
afflicted on all classes. Subsequent developments confirmed such a
perspective, with the working class suffering the costs of corporate-
led "globalisation" while the ruling class gained the benefits. Not
that such developments bothered most economists too much, of
course. Equally, while the total amount of goods may be increased
by countries pursuing their comparative advantage it does not
automatically follow that trade between them will distribute the
benefits equally either between the countries or within them.

As with exchange between classes, trade between countries is subject to economic power and so free trade can easily lead to the enrichment of one at the expense of the other. This means that the economically powerful will tend to support free trade as they will reap more from it.

Therefore the argument for free trade cannot be abstracted from its impact or the interests it serves, as Joan Robinson pointed out:

> "When Ricardo set out the case against protection he was supporting British economic interests. Free trade ruined Portuguese industry. Free trade for **others** is in the interests of the strongest competitor in world markets, and a sufficiently strong competitor has no need for protection at home. Free trade doctrine, in practice, is a more subtle form of Mercantilism. When Britain was the workshop of the world, universal free trade suited her interests. When (with the aid of protection) rival industries developed in Germany and the United States, she was still able to preserve free trade for her own exports in the Empire."
> [**Collected Economic Papers**, vol. 5, p. 28]

This echoes the analysis of List who said that the British advocacy of free trade was primarily political in nature and not to mention hypocritical. Its political aim was to destroy potential competitors by flooding their markets with goods, so ruining their industrial base and making them exporters of raw materials for British industry rather than producers of finished goods. He argued that a *"study of the true consequences"* of free trade *"provide the key to England's commercial policy from that day to this. The English have always been cosmopolitans and philanthropists in theory but always monopolists in practice."* [**Op. Cit.**, p. 167] Moreover, such a position was hypocritical because Britain industrialised by means of state intervention and now sought to deny that option to other nations.

List advocated that the state should protect infant industries until such time as they could survive international competition. Once industrialised, the state could then withdraw. He did not deny that free trade may benefit agricultural exporters, but only at the expense of industrial development and spill-over benefits it generates for the economy as a whole. In other words, free trade harmed the less-developed nation in terms of its economic prosperity and independence in the long run. Protectionism allowed the development of local industrial capitalism while free trade bolstered the fortunes of foreign capitalist nations (a Hobson's choice, really, from an anarchist perspective). This was the situation with British capitalism, as *"Britain had very high tariffs on manufacturing products as late as the 1820s, some two generations after the start of its Industrial Revolution ... Measures other than tariff protection were also deployed"* (such as banning imports from competitors). [Chang, **Op. Cit.**, p. 22] Needless to say, trade unions were illegal during this period of industrialisation and troops were regularly deployed to crush strikes, riots and rebellions. Economist Thomas Balogh confirms this analysis:

> "The fact is that Britain's economic growth forged ahead of its European competitors while it was exploiting an effective monopoly of the steam engine, from 1780 to 1840. Through most of that period the nation had a high and complicated tariff..., massive public investment and spending ... and an extensive public welfare system with wage supplements and welfare allowances indexed to basic costs of living ... There followed a long period, from about 1840 to 1931, when Britain did indeed have the freest trade and relatively speaking the cheapest government and (until 1914) the smallest public sector among the industrially developing nations, Yet, for competitiveness, that century saw the relative decline of the country. Numerous competing countries, led by the US and Germany, emerged and overtook and passed Britain in output and income per head. Every one of them had protective tariffs, and a bigger (relative) public sector than the British." [**Op. Cit.**, p. 180]

Significantly, and highly embarrassingly for neo-classical economists, the one nation which embraced free trade ideology most, namely the UK in the latter half of the 19th century, suffered economic decline in comparison to its competitors who embraced protectionist and other statist economic policies. It would be churlish to note that this is the exact opposite of what the theory predicts.

In historical terms, List has been proven correct numerous times. If the arguments for free trade were correct, then the United States and Germany (plus Japan, South Korea, etc., more recently), would be economic backwaters while Portugal would have flourished. The opposite happened. By the 1900s, Britain was overtaken economically by America and Germany, both of whom industrialised by means of protectionism and other forms of state intervention. As such, we should not forget that Adam Smith confidently predicted that protectionism in America would *"would retard instead of accelerating the further increase in the value of their annual progress, and would obstruct instead of promoting the progress of their country towards real wealth and greatness."* He considered it best that capital be *"employed in agriculture"* rather than manufacturing. [**The Wealth of Nations**, p. 328 and p. 327]). The historical record hardly supports Smith's predictions as *"throughout the nineteenth century and up to the 1920s, the USA was the fastest growing economy in the world, despite being the most protectionist during almost all of this period ... Most interestingly, the two best 20-year GDP per capita growth performances during the 1830-1910 period were 1870-1890 (2.1 per cent) and 1890-1910 (two per cent) – both period of particularly high protectionism. It is hard to believe that this association between the degree of protectionism and overall growth is purely coincidental."* [**Op. Cit.**, p. 30]

As with the UK, America *"remained the most ardent practitioner of infant industry protection until the First World War, and even until the Second."* Like UK, the state played its role in repressing labour, for while unions were usually not technically illegal, they were subject to anti-trust laws (at state and then federal level) as well as force during strikes from troops and private police forces. It was *"only after the Second World War that the USA – with its industrial supremacy unchallenged – finally liberalised its trade and started championing the cause of free trade."* [Chang, **Op. Cit.**, p. 28 and p. 29] Unsurprisingly, faced with growing international competition it practised protectionism and state aid while keeping the rhetoric of free trade to ensure that any potential competitor had its industries ruined by being forced to follow policies the US never applied in the same situation. Chomsky summarises:

> "So take a look at one of the things you don't say if you're an economist within one of the ideological institutions, although surely every economist has to know it. Take the fact that there is not a single case on record in history of any country that has developed successfully through adherence to 'free market' principles: none." [**Op. Cit.**, p. 255]

Not that this has disabused most economists from repeating Ricardo's theory as if it told the full story of international trade or has been empirically verified. As Chang puts it, his approach of studying the actual history of specific countries and generalising conclusions *"is concrete and inductive"* and *"contrasts strongly with the currently dominant Neoclassical approach based on abstract and deductive methods."* This has meant that *"contemporary discussion on economic development policy-making has been peculiarly ahistoric."* [**Op. Cit.**, p. 6] This is unsurprising, as there is a distinct tendency within mainstream economics not to check to see if whether the theory conforms to reality. It is as if we **know** that capitalist economics is true, so why bother to consider the evidence. So no matter how implausible a given theory is, capitalist economics simply asks us to take them on trust. Perhaps this is because they are nothing more than logical deductions from various assumptions and comparing them to reality would expose not only the bankruptcy of the theory but also the bogus claims that economics relates to reality or is a science?

That these theories survive at all is due to their utility to vested interests and, of course, their slightly complicated logical beauty. It should be noted, in passing, that the free trade argument is based on **reducing** international competition. It recommends that different countries specialise in different industries. That this would make sense for, say, a country with industry (marked by increasing returns to scale and significant spill-over effects into other areas of the economy) rather than one based on agriculture (marked by decreasing returns to scale) goes without saying. That the policy would turn the world into a provider of raw materials and markets rather than a source of competitors for the most advanced nation is just one of these co-incidences capitalist economics suffers from.

As such, it is not a coincidence that both the classic "free trade" and current neo-liberal position does allow a nation to secure its dominance in the market by forcing the ruling elites in **other** nations to subscribe to rules which hinder their freedom to develop in their own way. As we discuss in section D.5, the rise of neo-liberalism can be viewed as the latest in a long series of imperialist agendas designed to secure benefits of trade to the West as well as reducing the number of rivals on the international market. As Chang notes, Britain's move to free trade after 1846 *"was based on its then unchallenged economic superiority and was intricately linked with its imperial policy."* The stated aim was to halt the move to industrialisation in Europe by promoting agricultural markets. Outside of the West, *"most of the rest of the world was forced to practice free trade through colonialism and ... unequal treaties."* These days, this policy is implemented via international organisations which impose Western-dominated rules. As Chang notes, the *"developed*

countries did not get where they are now through policies and the institutions that they recommend to developing countries today. Most of them actively used 'bad' trade and industrial policies ... practices that these days are frowned upon, if not actively banned, by the WTO." [**Op. Cit.**, p. 16, p. 23, p. 16 and p. 2]

In other words, the developed countries are making it difficult for the developing countries to use policies and institutions which they themselves so successfully used previously. This, as with the "free trade" arguments of the 19th century, is simply a means of controlling economic development in other countries to reduce the number of potential competitors and to secure markets in other countries. In addition, we must also stress that the threat of capital flight within western countries also raises competitive pressures for labour and so has the added benefit of helping tame rebellious workers in the imperialist nations themselves. These factors help explain the continued support for free trade theory in economic circles in spite of the lack of empirical evidence in its favour. But then again, given that most economists cannot understand how one class exploits another by means of exchange within a national market due to its economic power, it would be surprising if they could see it within international markets.

To generalise, it appears that under capitalism there are two main options for a country. Either it submits itself to the dictates of global finance, embracing neo-liberal reforms and seeing its growth fall and inequality rise or (like every other successful industrialiser) it violates the eternal laws of economics by using the state to protect and govern its home market and see growth rise along with inequality. As Chang notes, looking at the historical record a *"consistent pattern emerges, in which all the catching-up economies use activist industrial, trade and technology (ITT) policies ... to promote economic development."* He stresses *"it was the UK and the USA, the supposed homes of free trade policy, which used tariff protection most aggressively."* The former *"implemented the kinds of ITT policies that became famous for their use in ... Japan, Korea and Taiwan."* [**Op. Cit.**, pp. 125-6, p. 59 and pp. 60-1] In addition, another aspect of this process involves repressing the working class so that **we** pay the costs for industrialising. Unions were illegal when Britain used its ITT policies while the *"labour market in Taiwan and Korea, for example, has been about as close to a free market as it is possible to get, due in part to government repression of unions."* [*"What can Economics Learn from East Asian Success?"*, **Op. Cit.**, p. 70] Given that unions are anathema to neo-classical and Austrian economics, it is understandable why their repression should be considered relatively unproblematic (in fact, according to economic ideology repressing unions can be considered to be in the interests of the working class as, it is claimed, unions harm non-unionised workers – who knew that bosses and their states were such philanthropists?).

Neither option has much to recommend it from an anarchist perspective. As such, our stating of facts associated with the history of "actually existing" capitalism should not be construed to imply that anarchists support state-run development. Far from it. We are simply noting that the conclusion of history seems to be that countries industrialise and grow faster when the state governs the market in significant ways while, at the same time, repressing the labour movement. This is unsurprising, for as we discuss in section

D.1, this process of state intervention is part and parcel of capitalism and, as noted in section F.8, has always been a feature of its rise in the first place (to use Marx's expression, a process of *"primitive accumulation"* has always been required to create capitalism). This does not mean, just to state the obvious, that anarchists support protectionism against "free trade." In a class system, the former will tend to benefit local capitalists while the latter will benefit foreign ones. Then there is the social context. In a predominantly rural economy, protectionism is a key way to create capitalism. For example, this was the case in 19th century America and it should be noted that the Southern slave states were opposed to protectionism, as were the individualist anarchists. In other words, protectionism was a capitalist measure which pre-capitalists and anti-capitalists opposed as against their interests. Conversely, in a developed capitalist economy "free trade" (usually very selectively applied) can be a useful way to undermine workers wages and working conditions as well as foreign capitalist competitors (it may also change agriculture itself in developing countries, displacing small peasant farmers from the land and promoting capitalist agriculture, i.e. one based on large estates and wage labour).

For the anarchist, while it is true that in the long run option two does raise the standard of living faster than option one, it should always be remembered that we are talking about a **class** system and so the costs and benefits will be determined by those in power, not the general population. Moreover, it cannot be assumed that people in developing countries actually want a Western lifestyle (although the elites who run those countries certainly do, as can be seen from the policies they are imposing). As Bookchin once noted, *"[a]s Westerners, 'we' tend to assume out of hand that 'they' want or need the same kind of technologies and commodities that capitalism produced in America and Europe … With the removal of imperialism's mailed fist, a new perspective could open for the Third World."* [**Post-Scarcity Anarchism**, pp. 156-7]

Suffice to say, there are other means to achieve development (assuming that is desired) based on working class control of industry. Given this, the only genuine solution for developing countries would be to get rid of their class systems and create a society where working people take control of their own fates, i.e. anarchism. Hence we find Proudhon, for example, stating he *"oppose[d] the free traders because they favour interest, while they demand the abolition of tariffs."* He advocated the opposite, supporting free trade *"as a consequence of the abolition of interest"* (i.e. capitalism). Thus the issue of free trade cannot be separated from the kind of society practising it nor from the creation of a free society. Abolishing capitalism in one country, he argued, would lead to other nations reforming themselves, which would *"emancipate their lower classes; in a word, to bring about revolution. Free trade would then become equal exchange."* [**The General Idea of the Revolution**, pp. 235-8] Unless that happens, then no matter whether protectionism or free trade is applied, working class people will suffer its costs and will have to fight for any benefits it may bring.

C.10.3 Does "free market" capitalism benefit everyone, *especially* working class people?

One defence of capitalism is that, appearances and popular opinion to the contrary, it benefits working class people **more** than the ruling class.

This argument can be found in right-liberal economist Milton Friedman's defence of capitalism in which he addresses the claim that *"the extension and development of capitalism has meant increased inequality."* Not so, he states. *"Among the Western countries alone,"* he argues, *"inequality appears to be less, in any meaningful sense, the more highly capitalist the country is … With respect to changes over time, the economic progress achieved in the capitalist countries has been accompanied by a drastic diminution in inequality."* In fact, *"a free society [i.e. capitalism] in fact tends towards greater material equality than any other yet tried."* Thus, according to Friedman, a *"striking fact, contrary to popular conception, is that capitalism leads to less inequality than alternative systems of organisation and that the development of capitalism has greatly lessened the extent of inequality. Comparisons over space and time alike confirm this."* [**Capitalism and Freedom**, p. 168, pp. 169-70, p. 195 and p. 169]

Friedman makes other claims to the superiority of capitalism. Thus he states that not only do non-capitalist societies *"tend to have wider inequality than capitalist, even as measured by annual income"* in such systems inequality *"tends to be permanent, whereas capitalism undermines status and introduces social mobility."* Like most right-wingers, he stresses the importance of social mobility and argues that a society with little change in position *"would be the more unequal society."* Finally, he states that *"[o]ne of the most striking facts which run counter to people's expectations has to do with the source of income. The more capitalistic a country is, the smaller the fraction of income for the use of what is generally regarded as capital, and the larger the fraction paid for human services."* [**Op. Cit.**, pp. 171-2, p. 171 and pp. 168-9]

Friedman, as he regularly did, failed to present any evidence to support his claims or any of his *"striking fact[s]"* so it is hard to evaluate the truthfulness of any of this specific assertions. One possible way of doing so would be to consider the actual performance of specific countries before and after 1980. That year is significant as this marked the assumption of office of Thatcher in the UK and Reagan in the US, both of whom were heavily influenced by Friedman and other supporters of "free market" capitalism. If his claims were true, then we would expect **decreases** in equality, social mobility and the share of *"human services"* before 1980 (the period of social Keynesian policies) and **increases** in all three after. Sadly for Friedman (and us!), the facts are counter to his assertions – equality, mobility and share of income for *"human services"* all decreased post-1980.

As we showed in section B.7, inequality rose **and** social mobility fell since 1980 in the USA and the UK (social democratic nations have a better record on both). As far as the share of income goes, that too has failed to support his assertions. Even in 1962, the facts did not support his assertion as regards the USA. According to figures from the U.S. Department of Commerce the share of labour in 1929 was 58.2% and this rose to 69.5% by 1959. Even looking at just private employees, this was a rise from 52.5% to 58% (income for government employees, including the military went from 5.7% to 12.2%). In addition, "proprietor's income" (which represents income to the owner of a business which combines work effort and ownership, for example a farmer or some other self-employed worker) fell, with farm income going from 6.8% to 3.0%, while other such income dropped from 10.1% to 8.7%. [Walter S. Measday, *"Labor's Share in the National Income,"* **The Quarterly Review of Economics & Business**, Vol. 2, No. 3, August 1962] Unless Friedman would argue that 1929 America was more statist than 1959, it seems that his assertion was false even when it was first made. How did his comment fare after he made it? Looking at the period after 1959 there was continuing increase in labour share in the national income, peaking in the 1970s before steadily dropping over the following decades (it dropped to below 1948 levels in 1983 and stayed there). [Alan B. Krueger, *"Measuring Labor's Share"*, **The American Economic Review**, vol. 89, No.2, May 1999] Since then the downward trend has continued.

It would be churlish to note that the 1970s saw the rise of influence of Friedman's ideas in both countries and that they were applied in the early 1980s.

There are problems with using labour share. For example it moves with the business cycle (rising in recessions and falling in booms). In addition, there can be other forms of labour compensation as well as wages. Looking at total compensation to labour, this amounts to around 70% of total US income between 1950 and 2000 (although this, too, peaked in the 1970s before falling [Krueger, **Op. Cit.**]). However, this "labour" income can be problematic. For example, employer provided health care is considered as non-wage compensation so it is possible for rising health care costs to be reflected in rising labour compensation yet this hardly amounts to a rising labour share as the net gain would be zero. Then there is the question of government employees and welfare benefits which, of course, are considered labour income. Unfortunately, Friedman provides no clue as to which statistics he is referring to, so we do not know whether to include total compensation or not in evaluating his claims.

One group of economists have taken the issue of government transfers into account. Since 1979, there has been an *"increased share of capital income (such as rent, dividends, interest payments, and capital gains) and a corresponding smaller share earned as wages and salaries."* Most families receive little or no capital income, but it is *"a very important source of income to the top 1% and especially the top 0.1% (who receive more than a third of all capital income)."* In 1959, total labour income was 73.5% while capital income was 13.3% of market-based income (personal income less government transfers). By 1979, these were 75.8% and 15.1%, respectively. The increases for both are due to a fall in "proprietor's income" from 13.3% to 9.1%. By 2000, capital income had risen to 19.1% while labour's share had fallen to 71.8% (proprietor's income remained the same). This *"shift away from labour income and toward capital income is unique in the post-war period and is partly responsible for the ongoing growth of inequality since 1979."*

[Lawrence Mishel, Jered Bernstein, and Sylvia Allegretto, **The State of Working America 2006/7**, p. 76 and p. 79]

It should be noted that Friedman repeated the standard economist (and right-wing) argument that a better way to increase wages than unions or struggle is to make workers more productive. That lifts everyone's standard of living. At least it used to. Between 1945 and 1980, worker wages did, indeed, track productivity increases. This was also the high period of union density in America. After 1980, that link was broken. By a strange co-incidence, this was when the Friedman-inspired Reagan effectively legalised and encouraged union busting. Since then, productivity increases are going almost entirely to the top tenth of the population, while median incomes have stagnated. Without unions and robust worker bargaining power, productivity increases have not been doing much for workers. Not that people like Friedman actually mentioned that rather significant fact.

Then there is the issue of *"human services"* itself. This is **not** the same as labour income at all as it includes, for example, management pay. As we indicated in section C.3, this "labour" income is better thought of as **capital** income as that specific labour is rooted in the control of capital. That this is the case can be seen by the numerous defences of exploding CEO pay by right-wing think tanks, journals and economists as well as the lack of concern about the inflationary nature of such massive "pay" rises (particularly when contrasted to the response over very slight increases in workers' pay). This means that "labour" income could remain constant while CEO salaries explode and worker wages stagnate or even fall, as is the case in both the US (and UK) since 1980. In such circumstances, looking at "human services" becomes misleading as returns to capital are listed as "labour" simply because they are in the form of bosses pay. Equally, CEO perks and bonuses would be included as "labour" non-wage compensation.

To see what this means we must use an example. Take a country with 100 people with a combined income of £10,000. The average income would be £100 each. Taking a labour/capital split of 70/30, we get an income to labour of £7000 and an income to capital of £3000. Assuming that 5% of the population own the capital stock, that is an average income of £600 each while labour gets an average of £73.68. However, 10% of the population are managers and assuming another 70/30 split between management and worker income this means that management gets £2100 in total (an average of £210) while workers get £4900 (an average of £57.65). This means that the owners of capital get 6 times the national average income, managers just over twice that amount and workers just over half the average. In other words, a national statistic of 70% labour income hides the reality that workers, who make up 85% of the population, actually get less than half the income (49%). Capital income, although less, is distributed to fewer people and so causes massive inequality (15% of the population get an average income of £340, nearly 6 times more than the average for the remaining 85% while the upper 5% get over 10 times). If the share of management in labour income rises to 35%, then workers wages fall and inequality rises while labour income remains constant at 70% (management's average income rises to £363.33 while workers' falls to £53.53). It should be stressed this example **underestimates** inequality in capitalist economies, particularly ones which had the misfortunate to apply Friedman's ideas.

Looking further afield, this pattern has been repeated everywhere "free(r) market" capitalism has been imposed. In Chile equality and labour's share increased during the 1960s and early 1970s, only for both to plummet under Pinochet's Friedman-inspired neo-liberal regime (see section C.11 for the grim details of *"economic liberty"* there). In Thatcher's Britain, inequality rose while labour share and social mobility fell. Between 1978 and 1990, the share of wages and salaries in household income in the UK fell from 65.8% to 57.4%. The share for capital income (rent, interest and dividends) more than doubled (from 4.9% to 10.0%).Unsurprisingly, this rise *"directly contributed to the increase in overall inequality"* (48% of all investment income went to the richest tenth of households). [John Hill, **Inequality and the State**, p. 88]

Looking at how increases in income and wealth were distributed, we find that gains since 1979 went predominantly to the rich. Before that, the income of all sections of society grew at roughly the same level between 1961 and 1979. Most of the increase was near the mean, the one exception was the lowest tenth whose incomes rose significantly higher than the rest. This meant that *"over the 1960s and 1970s as a whole all income groups benefited from rising incomes, the lowest rising fastest."* After 1978 *"the pattern broke down"* and incomes for the highest tenth rose by 60-68 percent while at the medium it grew by about 30% between 1979 and 1994/5. The lower down the income distribution, the lower the growth (in fact, after housing costs the income of bottom 10% was 8% lower in 1994/5 than in 1979). As in America during the same period a fence turned into stairs as the nearer to the bottom the slower income grew, the nearer the top the faster income grew (i.e. roughly equal growth turned into growth which increased as income increased – see section B.7.1). Between 1979 and 1990/91, the bottom 70% saw their income share fall. During the Major years, from 1992 to 1997, inequality stopped growing simply because hardly anyone's income grew. Over all, between 1979 and 2002/3, the share of all incomes received by the bottom half fell from 22% to 37%. This is more than the whole of the bottom half combined. The bottom 10% saw their share of income fall from 4.3% to 3% (after housing costs, this was 4.0% to 2.0%). Only the top tenth saw their income increase (from 20.6% to 28%). About 40% of the total increase in real net incomes went to the top tenth between 1979 and 2002-3. 17% of the increase in after-tax incomes went to the top 1%, about 13% went to the top 0.5% (*"Wealth is much more unequally distributed than incomes."*). [John Hills, **Op. Cit.**, p. 20, p. 21, p. 23 and p. 37]

Unsurprisingly, income inequality widened considerably (which more than reversed all the moves towards equality of income that had taken place since 1945) and Britain went from being one of the more equal countries in the industrialised countries to being one of the most unequal. The numbers below half the median income rose. In the 1960s, this was roughly 10%, before falling to 6% in 1977. It then *"rose sharply"* and peaked at 21% in 1991/92 before stabilising at 18-19%. After housing costs, this meant a rise from 7% to 25% below half the average income, falling to 23%. It should be noted that the pre-Thatcher period gives *"the lie to the notion that 'relative' poverty can never be reduced."* In summary, by the early 1990s *"relative poverty was twice the level it had been in*

the 1960s, and three times what it had been in the late 1970s." It seems needless to add that social mobility fell. [John Hills, **Op. Cit.**, p. 48, p. 263 and pp. 120-1]

The same can be said of Eastern Europe. This is particularly significant, for if Friedman's assertions were right then we would expect that the end of Stalinism in Eastern Europe would have seen a decrease in inequality. As in Chile, Britain, New Zealand and America, the opposite occurred – inequality exploded. By the start of the 21st century Eastern Europe was challenging neo-liberal Britain at the top of the European income inequality tables.

The historical record does not give much support to claims that free(r) market capitalism is best for working class people. Real wage growth rose to around 5% per year in the early 1970s, before falling substantially to under 2% from the 1980s onwards for 13 OECD countries. In fact, *"real wage have growth very slowly in OECD countries since 1979, an extraordinary turn-round from the 3-5% growth rates of the 1960s."* In the US, the median wage was actually less in 2003 than in 1979. Average wages actually declined until 1995, then they increased somewhat so that the average growth rate for the 1990s was less than 0.5% a year. Europe and Japan have done only a little better, with growth of around 1% per year. This is unsurprising, given the rise in returns to capital after 1979 for *"real wages do not automatically grow as fast as labour productivity. The general increase in the share of profits ... pulls real wage growth behind productivity growth."* Within the labour force, inequality has risen. Wage differentials *"are considerably higher in the UK/US group than in Europe"* and have grown faster. Real wages for the top 10% grew by 27.2% between 1979 and 2003, compared to 10.2% in the middle (real wages for the bottom 10% did not grow). In Europe, *"real wages grew at the bottom at a similar rate to the average."* The top 1% of wage-earners in the USA doubled their total wage share between 1979 and 1998 from 6.2% to 10.9%, whilst the top 0.1% nearly tripled their share to 4.1%. Almost all of the increase in the top 10% went to the top 5%, and about two-thirds to the top 1%. In France, the share of the top 1% remained the same. Overall, *"labour's position tended to be more eroded in the more free market economies like the USA and UK than in European economies where social protection [including trade unionism] was already stronger."* [Andrew Glyn, **Op. Cit.**, p. 6 p. 116, p. 117, p. 118 and p. 127]

Looking at inequality and poverty, the conclusion is that liberalisation of markets *"tend to bring greater inequality."* In fact, the rise in the UK was strongest in the 1980s, the Thatcher period while New Zealand *"saw as big an increase in inequality as the UK."* The USA *"maintained its position as the most unequal country with inequality increasing in both decades."* In summary, *"the increase in inequality has been noticeably greater in the inegalitarian liberal economies than in Northern Europe."* Moreover, *"liberal countries have larger proportions of their populations in poverty"* than European ones. Unsurprisingly, New Zealand and the UK (both poster-childs for neo-liberalism) *"had the biggest increases in numbers in poverty between the mid-1980s and 2000."* In the mid-1990s, 20-25% of workers in the UK, Canada and USA were earning less than 65% of median earnings, compared to 5-8% in Scandinavia and Belgium. This rise income inequality *"tend to reproduce themselves through the generations."* There *"is far **less** social mobility in the USA"* than in Scandinavia, Germany and Canada and there has been a *"severe decline in social mobility"* in the UK after the Friedman-inspired Thatcherism of the 1980s and 1990s. Unsurprisingly, there has been *"a rise in the importance of property incomes."*, with the ratio of property income to labour income rising from 15% in the USA in 1979 to 18% in 2002. In France it went from 7% to 12% and is around 8% in Norway and Finland. [**Op. Cit.**, p. 167, p. 168, p. 169, p. 171, p. 169, p. 173, p. 174 and p. 170]

Needless to say, given the lack of evidence presented when Friedman first published his book in 1962, the 40th anniversary edition was equally fact free. 40 years is more than enough time to evaluate his claims particularly given that approximately half-way through this period, Friedman's ideas became increasingly influential and applied, in varying degrees in many countries (particularly in the UK under Thatcher and the US under Reagan). Friedman does not mention the developments in equality, mobility or labour share in 2002, simply making the general statement that he was *"enormously gratified by how well the book has withstood time."* Except, of course, where reality utterly contradicted it! This applies not only to his claims on equality, income shares and poverty, but also the fundamental basis of his Monetarist dogma, namely the aim to control the *"behaviour of the stock of money"* by means of *"a legislated rule instructing the monetary authority to achieve a specified rates of growth in the stock of money."* [**Op. Cit.**, p. ix and p. 54] As we indicated in section C.8, the devastating results of applying this centre-piece of his ideology means that it hardly *"withstood time"* by any stretch of the imagination! In other words, we have a case of self-refutation that has few equals.To conclude, as defences of capitalism based on equality are unlikely to survive contact with reality, the notion that this system is really the best friend of the working person and the poor needs to be defended by other means. This is where the growth argument we debunked in the last two sections comes in. Neither has much basis in reality.

Of course, the usual excuse should be noted. It could be argued that the reason for this lack of correlation of reality with ideology is that capitalism is not "pure" enough. That, of course, is a valid argument (as Friedman notes, Thatcher and Reagan *"were able to curb leviathan, through not to cut it down."* [**Op. Cit.**, p. vii]). State intervention has hardly disappeared since 1980 but given the lush praise given to the "magic" of the market you would expect **some** improvement. When Friedman died in 2006, the praise from the right-wing and business press was extensive, listing him as one of the most, if not **the** most, influential economist of the late 20th century. It seems strange, then, to suggest that the market is now **less** free than at the height of the post-war Keynesian period. To do so would suggest that Reagan, Thatcher and Pinochet had little or no impact on the economy (or that they made it worse in terms of state intervention). In other words, that Friedman was, in fact, the **least** influential economist of the late 20th century (as opposed to one of the worst, if we compare his assertions to reality before and after the policies they inspired were implemented). However, he helped make the rich richer, so the actual impact of what he actually suggested for the bulk of the population can be cheerfully ignored.

C.10.4 Does growth automatically mean people are better off?

In the above sections we have discussed the effects of neo-liberal reforms purely in terms of economic statistics such as growth rates and so on. This means we have critiqued capitalism in its own terms, in terms of its supporters own arguments in its favour. As shown, in terms of equality, social mobility and growth the rise of "free(r) market" capitalism has not been all its supporters have asserted. Rather than produce more equality, less poverty and increased growth, the opposite has occurred. Where some progress on these areas have occurred, such as in Asia, the countries have **not** embraced the neo-liberal model.

However, there is a deeper critique to be made of the notion that capitalism benefits everyone, especially the poor. This relates to the **quality** of life, rather than the quantity of money available. This is an extremely important aspect to the question of whether "free market" capitalism will result in everyone being "better off." The typical capitalist tendency is to consider quantitative values as being the most important consideration. Hence the concern over economic growth, profit levels, and so on, which dominate discussions on modern life. However, as E.P. Thompson makes clear, this ignores important aspects of human life:

"simple points must be made. It is quite possible for statistical averages and human experiences to run in opposite directions. A per capita increase in quantitative factors may take place at the same time as a great qualitative disturbance in people's way of life, traditional relationships, and sanctions. People may consume more goods and become less happy or less free at the same time … [For example] real wages [may have] advanced … but at the cost of longer hours and greater intensity of labour…. In statistical terms, this reveals an upward curve. To the families concerned it might feel like immiseration.

"Thus it is perfectly possible … [to have an] improvement in average material standards … [at the same time as] intensified exploitation, greater insecurity, and increasing human misery … most people [can be] 'better off' than their forerunners had been fifty years before, but they had suffered and continued to suffer this … improvement as a catastrophic experience." [**The Making of the English Working Class**, p. 231]

Thompson was specifically referring to the experience of the British industrial revolution on the working class but his analysis is of general note (its relevance goes far beyond evaluating past or current industrialisation processes). This means that concentrating on, say, absolute poverty or income growth (as defenders of neo-liberalism do) means to ignore the quality of life which this increased income is associated with. For example, a peasant farmer who has to leave his farm for employment in a factory may consider having bosses dictating his every move, an increased working day and intensity of work more significant than, say, a net increase in his income.

That this farmer may have been driven off his farm as a result of neo-liberal or other "reforms" is another factor which has to be taken into account. If, to suggest another possibility, Health and Safety regulations reduce work speeds, then national output will be reduced just as unions will stop firms making their workers labour more intensely for longer. However, increased output at the expense of those who do the work is not unproblematic (i.e. real wages may increase but at the cost of longer hours, less safety and greater intensity of labour). Another obvious example would be the family where the husband gets "downsized" from a good manufacturing job. He may get a lower paying service industry job, which forces his wife (and perhaps children) to get a job in order to make ends meet. Family income may increase slightly as a result, but at a heavy cost to the family and their way of life. Therefore the standard of living in the abstract may have increased, but, for the people in question, they would feel that it had deteriorated considerably. As such, economic growth need not imply rising standards of living in terms if the **quality** of life decreases as incomes rise.

This is, in part, because if the economy worked as neoclassical theory demanded, then people would go to work not knowing how much they would be paid, how long they would be employed for or, indeed, whether they had a job at all when they got there. If they rented their home, they would not even know whether they had a home to come back to. This is because every price would have to be subject to constant change in order to adjust to equilibrium. Insecurity, in other words, is at the heart of the economy and this is hardly productive of community or "family" values (and other expressions used in the rhetoric of the right while they promote an economic system which, in practice, undermines them in the name of profit). In other words, while a society may become materially better off over time, it becomes worse off in terms of **real** wealth, that is those things which make life worth living. Thus capitalism has a corrosive effect on human relationships, the pleasure of productive activity (work), genuine freedom for the many, how we treat each other and so on. The corrosive effects of economics are not limited simply to the workplace but seep into all other aspects of your life.

Even assuming that free market capitalism could generate high growth rates (and that assumption is not borne out in the real world), this is not the end of the matter. How the growth is distributed is also important. The benefits of growth may accumulate to the few rather than the many. Per capita and average increases may hide a less pleasant reality for those at the bottom of the social hierarchy. An obvious example would be a society in which there is massive inequality, where a few are extremely rich and the vast majority are struggling to make ends meet. Such a society could have decent growth rates and per capita and average income may grow. However, if such growth is concentrated at the top, in the hands of the already wealthy, the reality is that economic growth does not benefit the many as the statistics suggest. As such, it is important to stress that average growth may not result in a bettering for all sections of a society. In fact, *"there are plenty of instances in which the poor, and the majority of the population. have been left behind in the era of globalisation – even where per capita income has grown."* This is not limited to just developing countries. Two episodes like this occurred in the United States, with data showing

that *"the per capita income of the poor falling from 1979-84, and 1989-94, while per capita income rose."* Overall, the US has seen its median wage and real wages for the bottom 20th of its populations fall between 1973 and 1997 while *"per capita income in the US has risen by 70 percent. For the median wage and bottom-quintile wage to actually **fall** during this same period is an economic change of momentous proportions, from the point of view of the majority of Americans."* [Mark Weisbrot, Dean Baker, Robert Naiman, and Gila Neta, **Growth May Be Good for the Poor – But are IMF and World Bank Policies Good for Growth?**] This is a classic example of society with substantial inequality seeing the benefits of growth accrue to the already rich. To state the obvious, **how** the benefits of growth are distributed cannot be ignored.

In addition, consumerism may not lead to the happiness or the "better society" which many economists imply to be its results. If consumerism is an attempt to fill an empty life, it is clearly doomed to failure. If capitalism results in an alienated, isolated existence, consuming more will hardly change that. The problem lies within the individual and the society within which they live. Hence, quantitative increases in goods and services may not lead to anyone "benefiting" in any meaningful way. Similarly, there is the issue of the quality of the production and consumption produced by economic growth. Values like GDP do not tell us much in terms of what was produced and its social and environmental impact. Thus high growth rates could be achieved by the state expanding its armed forces and weaponry (i.e. throwing money to arms corporations) while letting society go to rot (as under Reagan). Then there is awkward fact that negative social developments, such as pollution and rising crime, can contribute to a rising value for GDP). This happens because the costs of cleaning up, say, an oil spill involves market transactions and so gets added to the GDP for an economy.

As such, the notion that growth **as such** is good should be rejected in favour of a critical approach to the issue which asks growth for what and for whom. As Chomsky puts it, *"[m]any indigenous people apparently do not see any reason why their lives, societies, and cultures should be disrupted or destroyed so that New Yorkers can sit in SUVs in traffic gridlock."* [**Failed States**, p. 259] Under capitalism, much "productivity" is accounted for by economic activity that is best described as wasteful: military spending; expanding police and prison bureaucracies; the spiralling cost of (privatised) healthcare; suburban sprawl; the fast-food industry and its inevitable ill effects on health; cleaning up pollution; specifying and defending intellectual and other property rights; treating the illnesses caused by over-work, insecurity and stress; and so on. As Alexander Berkman once noted, capitalism spawns many forms of "work" and "productive" activity which only make sense within that system and could *"be automatically done away with"* in a sane society. [**What is Anarchism?**, pp. 223-5] Equally, "productivity" and living standards can stand at odds with each other. For example, if a country has a lower working week and take longer holidays, these would clearly depress GDP. This is the case with America and France, with approximately equal productivity the latter spends less time in work and more time off. Yet it takes a capitalist ideologue to say that such a country is worse off as a nation for all that time people spend enjoying themselves.

These issues are important to remember when listening to "free market" gurus discussing economic growth from their "gated communities," insulated from the surrounding deterioration of society and nature caused by the workings of capitalism. In other words, quality is often more important than quantity. This leads to the important idea that some (even many) of the requirements for a truly human life cannot be found on any market, no matter how "free" it may be. Equally, a "free" market can lead to unfree people as they are driven to submit themselves to the authority of bosses due to economic pressures and the threat of unemployment.

So it can be said that laissez-faire capitalism will benefit all, **especially** the poor, only in the sense that all can potentially benefit as an economy increases in size. Of course, the mantra that economic growth is so wonderful is hard to justify when the benefits of that growth are being enjoyed by a small proportion of the people and the burdens of growth (such as rising job insecurity, loss of benefits, wage stagnation and decline for the majority of workers, declining public services, loss of local communities and so forth) are being borne by so many (as is the case with the more to freer markets from the 1980s). If we look at actually existing capitalism, we can start to draw some conclusions about whether a pure laissez-faire capitalism will actually benefit working people. The United States has a small public sector by international standards and in many ways it is the closest large industrial nation to the unknown ideal of pure capitalism. It is also interesting to note that it is also number one, or close to it, in the following areas [Richard Du Boff, **Accumulation and Power**, pp. 183-4]:

> Lowest level of job security for workers, with greatest chance of being dismissed without notice or reason.
> Greatest chance for a worker to become unemployed without adequate unemployment and medical insurance.
> Less leisure time for workers, such as holiday time.
> One of the most lopsided income distribution profiles.
> Lowest ratio of female to male earnings, in 1987 64% of the male wage.
> Highest incidence of poverty in the industrial world.
> Among the worse rankings of all advanced industrial nations for pollutant emissions into the air.
> Highest murder rates.
> Worse ranking for life expectancy and infant morality.

It seems strange that the more laissez-faire system has the worse job security, least leisure time, highest poverty and inequality if laissez-faire will **especially** benefit the poor or working people. In fact, we find the more free market the regime, the worse it is for the workers. Americans have longer hours and shorter holidays than Western Europeans and more people live in poverty. 22% of American children grow up in poverty, which means that it ranks 22nd out of the 23 industrialised nations, ahead of only Mexico and behind all 15 of the pre-2004 EU countries.

According to a 2007 United Nations report, the worse places to be a child are in neo-liberal societies such as the UK and USA (the UK was bottom, at number 21 one below the US). The UNICEF report dealt with the condition of children in advanced capitalist countries and found that both the UK and US are way down the list on education, health, poverty, and well-being. While UNICEF

preferred to state that this is because of a "dog eat dog society", it is hardly a coincidence that these two societies have most embraced the principles of neo-liberalism and have repeatedly attacked the labour movement, civil society in general as well as the welfare state in the interests of capital. In contrast, the social democratic northern European countries have the best results. One could also point out, for example, that Europeans enjoy more leisure time, better health, less poverty, less inequality and thus more economic security, greater intergenerational economic mobility, better access to high-quality social services like health care and education, and manage to do it all in a far more environmentally sustainable way (Europe generates about half the CO2 emissions for the same level of GDP) compared to the US or the UK.

A definite case of what is good for the economy (profits) is bad for people. To state the obvious, an economy and the people in that economy are not identical. The former can be doing well, but not the latter – particularly if inequality is skewing distribution of any rising incomes. So while the economy may be doing well, its (median) participant (and below) may see very little of it.

Of course, defenders of laissez-faire capitalism will point out that the United States, like the UK and any other real country, is far from being laissez-faire. This is true, yet it seems strange that the further an economy moves from that "ideal" the better conditions get for those who, it is claimed, will especially benefit from it. As such, non-believers in pure capitalism have cause for dissent although for the typical "market advocate" such comparisons tell us little – unless they happen to bolster their case then "actually existing" capitalism can be used as an example.

Ultimately, the real issue is to do with quality of life and relative changes. Yet the argument that capitalism helps the poorest most via high economic growth is rooted in comparing "free market" capitalism with historical example, i.e. in the notion of **absolute** inequality rather than **relative** inequality and poverty. Thus poverty (economic, cultural and social) in, say, America can be dismissed simply on the grounds that poor people in 2005 have more and better goods than those in 1905. The logic of an absolute position (as intended, undoubtedly) is such as to make even discussing poverty and inequality pointless as it is easy to say that there are **no** poor people in the West as no one lives in a cave. But, then again, using absolute values it is easy to prove that there were no poor people in Medieval Europe, either, as they did not live in caves and, compared to hunter gatherers or the slaves of antiquity, they had much better living standards. As such, any regime would be praiseworthy, by the absolute standard as even slavery would have absolutely better living standards than, say, the earliest humans.

In this respect, the words of Adam Smith are as relevant as ever. In **The Wealth of Nations** Smith states the following:

> "By necessaries I understand not only the commodities which are indispensably necessary for the support of life, but whatever the custom of the country renders it indecent for creditable people, even of the lowest order, to be without. A linen shirt, for example, is, strictly speaking, not a necessary of life. The Greeks and Romans lived, I suppose, very comfortably though they had no linen. But in the present times, through the greater part of Europe,

a creditable day-labourer would be ashamed to appear in public without a linen shirt, the want of which would be supposed to denote that disgraceful degree of poverty which, it is presumed, nobody can well fall into without extreme bad conduct ... Under necessaries, therefore, I comprehend not only those things which nature, but those things which the established rules of decency have rendered necessary to the lowest rank of people." (Book Five, Chapter II, Article IV)

As usual, Adam Smith is right while his erstwhile ideological followers are wrong. They may object, noting that strictly speaking Smith was talking of *"necessaries"* rather than poverty. However, his concept of necessaries implies a definition of poverty and this is obviously based not on some unchanging biological concept of subsistence but on whatever *"the custom of the country"* or *"the established rules of decency"* consider necessary. Marx made the same point in his later works, when he distanced himself from his earlier notion that capitalism resulted in **absolute** impoverishment. As he put it in volume 1 of **Capital**, *"the number and extent of [the worker's] so-called necessary requirements, as also the manner and extent they are satisfied, are themselves products of history, and depend therefore to a great extent on the level of civilisation attained by a country ... In contrast, therefore, with the case of other commodities, the determination of the value of labour-power contains a historical and moral element."* [p. 275]

It is ironic that those today who most aggressively identify themselves as disciples of Smith are also the people who are most opposed to definitions of poverty that are consistent with this definition of "necessaries" (this is unsurprising, as those who invoke his name most usually do so in pursuit of ideas alien to his work). This is done for the usual self-interested motives. For example, Thatcher's government originally had little problem with the concept of relative poverty and *"[o]nly when its policies had led to a conspicuous growth of relative poverty was the idea denounced, and the decision taken by the government ... that absolute poverty (undefined and unqualified) was the only reality."* [Ian Gilmore, **Op. Cit.**, p. 136] Smith's perspective, significantly, is that followed by most poverty researchers, who use a relative measure in evaluating poverty rates. The reason is unsurprising as poor is relative to the living standards and customs of a time and place. Some sceptic might regurgitate the unoriginal response that the poor in the West are rich compared to people in developing countries, but they do not live in those countries. True, living standards have improved considerably over time but comparing the poor of today with those of centuries past is also meaningless. The poor today are poor relative to what it takes to live and develop their individual potentials in their own societies, not in (for example) 18th century Scotland or half-way across the globe (even Milton Friedman had to grudgingly admit that *"poverty is in part a relative matter."* [**Op. Cit.**, p. 191]). Considering the harmful effects of relative inequality we indicated in section B.1, this position is perfectly justified.

The notion of absolute poverty being the key dates back to at least Locke who argued in his **Second Treatise** on government that in America *"a King of a large and fruitful Territory there feeds, lodges, and is clad worse than a day Labourer in England."* (section 41)

Ignoring the dubious anthropological assertions, his claim was made as part of a general defence of enclosing common land and turning independent workers into dependent wage slaves. The key to his argument is that the accumulation of property and land beyond that useable by an individual along with the elimination of customary rights for poor individuals was justified because owners of the enclosed land would hire workers and increase the overall wealth available. This meant that the dispossessed workers (and particularly their descendants) would be better off materially (see C.B MacPherson's **The Political Theory of Possessive Individualism: From Hobbes to Locke** for an excellent discussion of this). The links with the current debate on globalisation are clear, with so-called "market advocates" and "individualists" providing extensive apologetics for capital moving to authoritarian regimes which systematically violate individual rights and the principles of the "free" market precisely in terms of the increased material wealth this (eventually) produces. But then it is easy for bosses, tenured professors and well paid think-tank experts to pontificate that such sacrifices (for others, of course) are worth it in the long run.

This apparently strange transformation of "individualists" into "collectivists" (justifying the violation of individual rights in terms of the greater good) has a long precedent. Indeed, it can only be considered strange if you are ignorant of the nature and history of capitalism as well as the contortions its defenders have inflicted on themselves (and by yet another of these strange co-incidences that so regularly afflicts capitalism and its supporters, the individuals whose liberty and rights are considered expendable are always members of the working class). So the notion of absolute poverty has always been associated with defending inequalities of wealth and power as well as providing justification in terms of long term benefit for the violation of the "freedom" and "individual rights" they claim to defend. Significantly, the contemporary representatives of the landlords who imposed enclosures framed their arguments precisely in terms of restricting the independence (i.e. freedom) of the working population. As Marxist David McNally summarises after providing extensive quotes, it was *"precisely these elements of material and spiritual independence that many of the most outspoken advocates of enclosure sought to destroy."* They *"were remarkably forthright in this respect. Common rights and access to common lands, they argued, allowed a degree of social and economic independence, and thereby produced a lazy, dissolute mass of rural poor ... Denying such people common lands and common rights would force them to conform to the harsh discipline imposed by the market in labour."* [**Against the Market**, p. 19] This would only be considered paradoxical if you equate freedom with capitalism.

The underlying assumption under all this is that liberty (at least for working class people) is less important than material wealth, a vision rightly attacked when Stalinism seemed to be out-performing the West in terms of growth before the 1970s. Yet the question, surely, is would individuals freely agree to be subjected to the dictates of a boss for 10-12 hours a day if other alternatives had not been closed off by state intervention? As we discuss in section F.8, the answer has always been no. This is the case today. For example, Naomi Klein interviews one boss of a third-world sweatshop who explained that *"for the lowly province worker, working inside an enclosed factory is better than being outside."* One of his workers rebutted this, stating *"Our rights are being trampled"* and that the boss said that *"because he has not experienced working in a factory and the conditions inside."* Another noted that *"of course he would say that we prefer this work – it is beneficial to him, but not to us."* Another states the obvious: *"But we are landless, so we have no choice but to work in the economic zone even though it is very hard and the situation is unfair."* [quoted by Klein, **No Logo**, p. 220 and p. 221] It should noted that the boss has, of course, the backing of a great many economists (including many moderately left-wing ones) who argue that sweatshops are better than no jobs and that these countries cannot afford basic workers' rights (as these are class societies, it means that their ruling class cannot afford to give their workers the beneficial aspects of a free market, namely the right to organise and associate freely). It is amazing how quickly an economist or right-liberal will proclaim that a society cannot expect the luxury of a free market, at least for the working class, and how these "individualists" will proclaim that the little people must suffer in order for the greater good to be achieved.

As for the regimes within these factories, Klein notes that they are extremely authoritarian. The largest free-trade zone in the Philippines is *"a miniature military state inside a democracy"* and the *"management is military-style, the supervisors often abusive."* As would be expected, *"no questioning of authority is expected or permitted"* and in some *"strikes are officially illegal"* (rather than unofficially banned). [**Op. Cit.**, p. 204, p. 205 and p. 214] As with the original industrial revolution, capitalism takes advantages of other forms of social hierarchy in developing countries. As Stephen A. Marglin noted, the women and children, *"who by all accounts constituted the overwhelming majority of factory workers in the early days, were there not because they choose to be but because their husbands and fathers told them to be. The application of revealed preference to their presence in the factory requires a rather elastic view of the concept of individual choice."* [*"What do Bosses do?"*, pp. 60-112, **The Review of Radical Political Economics**, vol. 6, No. 2, p. 98] In other words, while the workers **may** be better off in terms of wages they are not better off in terms of liberty, equality and dignity. Luckily there are economists around to explain, on their behalf, that these workers cannot afford such luxuries.

Looking beyond the empirical investigation, we should point out the slave mentality behind these arguments. After all, what does this argument actually imply? Simply that economic growth is the only way for working people to get ahead. If working people put up with exploitative working environments, in the long run capitalists will invest some of their profits and so increase the economic cake for all. So, like religion, "free market" economics argue that we must sacrifice in the short term so that (perhaps) in the future our living standards will increase (*"you'll get pie in the sky when you die"* as Joe Hill said about religion). Moreover, any attempt to change the "laws of the market" (i.e. the decisions of the rich) by collective action will only harm the working class. If the defenders of capitalism were genuinely interested in individual freedom they would be urging the oppressed masses to revolt rather than defending the investing of capital in oppressive regimes in terms of the freedom they are so willing to sacrifice when it comes to workers. But, of course, these defenders of "freedom" will be the first to point out that such revolts make for a bad investment climate – capital will be frightened away

to countries with a more "realistic" and "flexible" workforce (usually made so by state repression).

In other words, capitalist economics praises servitude over independence, kow-towing over defiance and altruism over egoism. The "rational" person of neo-classical economics does not confront authority, rather he accommodates himself to it. For, in the long run, such self-negation will pay off with a bigger cake with (it is claimed) correspondingly bigger crumbs "trickling" downwards. In other words, in the short-term, the gains may flow to the elite but in the future we will all gain as some of it will trickle (back) down to the working people who created them in the first place. But, unfortunately, in the real world uncertainty is the rule and the future is unknown. The history of capitalism shows that economic growth is quite compatible with stagnating wages, increasing poverty and insecurity for workers and their families, rising inequality and wealth accumulating in fewer and fewer hands (the examples of the USA and Chile from the 1970s to 1990s spring to mind). And, of course, even **if** workers kow-tow to bosses, the bosses may just move production elsewhere anyway (as tens of thousands of "down-sized" workers across the West can testify). For more details of this process in the USA see Edward S. Herman's article *"Immiserating Growth: The First World"* in Z Magazine, July 1994.

For anarchists it seems strange to wait for a bigger cake when we can have the whole bakery. If control of investment was in the hands of those it directly effects (working people) then it could be directed into socially and ecologically constructive projects rather than being used as a tool in the class war and to make the rich richer. The arguments against "rocking the boat" are self-serving (it is obviously in the interests the rich and powerful to defend a given income and property distribution) and, ultimately, self-defeating for those working people who accept them. In the end, even the most self-negating working class will suffer from the negative effects of treating society as a resource for the economy, the higher mobility of capital that accompanies growth and effects of periodic economic and long term ecological crisis. When it boils down to it, we all have two options – you can do what is right or you can do what you are told. "Free market" capitalist economics opts for the latter.

C.11

Doesn't neo-liberalism in Chile prove that the free market benefits everyone?

Chile is considered by some to be one of the economic success stories of the modern world. It can be considered as the first laboratory for neo-liberal economic dogma, first under Pinochet's dictatorship and later when his regime had been replaced by a more democratic one. It can be considered as the template for the economic vision later applied by Reagan and Thatcher in the West. What happened in Chile was repeated (to some degree) wherever neo-liberal policies were implemented. As such, it makes a good case study to evaluate the benefits of free(r) market capitalism and the claims of capitalist economics.

For the right, Chile was pointed to as a casebook in sound economics and is held up as an example of the benefits of capitalism. Milton Friedman, for example, stated in 1982 that the Military Junta *"has supported a fully free-market economy as a matter of principle. Chile is an economic miracle."* [quoted by Elton Rayack, **Not so Free to Choose**, p. 37] Then US President George Bush praised the Chilean economic record in December 1990 when he visited that country, stating Chile deserved its *"reputation as an economic model"* for others to follow.

However, the reality of the situation is radically different. As Chilean expert Peter Winn argues, *"[w]e question whether Chile's neoliberal boom ... should be regarded as a miracle. When confronted by such a claim, scholars and students should always ask: a miracle for **whom** – and at what cost?"* [*"Introduction"*, Peter Winn (ed.), **Victims of the Chilean Miracle**, p. 12] As we will prove, Chile's "economic miracle" is **very** class dependent. For its working class, the neo-liberal reforms of the Pinochet regime have resulted in a worsening of their lives; if you are a capitalist then it has been a miracle. That the likes of Friedman claim the experiment as a "miracle" shows where their sympathies lie – and how firm a grasp they have of reality.

The reason why the Chilean people become the first test case for neo-liberalism is significant. They did not have a choice. General Pinochet was the figure-head of a military coup in 1973 against the democratically elected left-wing government led by President Allende. This coup was the culmination of years of US interference by the US in Chilean politics and was desired by the US **before** Allende took office in November 1970 (*"It is the firm and continuing policy that Allende be overthrown by a coup,"* as one CIA memo put it in October of that year [quoted by Gregory Palast, *"A Marxist threat to cola sales? Pepsi demands a US coup. Goodbye Allende. Hello Pinochet"*, **The Observer**, 8/11/1998]). Then American president Richard Nixon imposed an embargo on Chile and began a covert plan to overturn the Allende government. In the words of the US ambassador to Chile, the Americans *"will do all in our power to condemn Chileans to utmost poverty."* [quoted by Noam Chomsky, **Deterring Democracy**, p. 395]

According to notes taken by CIA director Richard Helms at a 1970 meeting in the Oval Office, his orders were to *"make the economy scream."* This was called Project FUBELT and its aims were clear: *"The Director [of the CIA] told the group that President Nixon had decided that an Allende regime in Chile was not acceptable to the United States. The President asked the Agency to prevent Allende from coming to power or to unseat him."* [*"Genesis of Project FUBELT"* document dated September 16, 1970] Not all aid was cut. During 1972 and 1973 the US increased aid to the military and increased training Chilean military personnel in the United States and Panama. In other words, the coup was helped by the US state and various US corporations both directly and indirectly, by undermining the Chilean economy.

Thousands of people were murdered by the forces of "law and order" and Pinochet's forces *"are conservatively estimated to have killed over 11,000 people in his first year in power."* [P. Gunson, A. Thompson, G. Chamberlain, **The Dictionary of Contemporary Politics of South America**, p. 228] Military units embarked on an operation called the Caravan of Death to hunt down those they considered subversives (i.e. anyone suspected or accused of holding left-wing views or sympathies). Torture and rape were used extensively and when people did not just disappear, their mutilated bodies were dumped in plain view as a warning to others. While the Chilean government's official truth and reconciliation committee places the number of disappeared at roughly 3,000, church and human rights groups estimate the number is far higher, at over 10,000. Hundreds of thousands fled into exile. Thus ended Allende's "democratic road to Socialism." The terror did not end after the coup and dictatorship's record on human rights was rightly denounced as barbaric.

Friedman, of course, stressed his *"disagreement with the authoritarian political system of Chile."* [quoted by Rayack, **Op. Cit.**, p. 61] For the time being we will ignore the obvious contradiction in this "economic miracle", i.e. why it almost always takes authoritarian/fascistic states to introduce "economic liberty." Rather we will take the right at its word and concentrate on the economic facts of the free-market capitalism imposed on the Chilean people. They claim it was a free market and given that, for example, Friedman was a leading ideologue for capitalism we can assume that the regime approximated the workings of such a system. We will discuss the illogical nature and utter hypocrisy of the right's position in section D.11, where we also discuss the limited nature of the democratic regime which replaced Pinochet and the real relationship between economic and political liberty.

Faced with an economic crisis, in 1975 Pinochet turned to the ideas of Milton Friedman and a group of Chilean economist who had been taught by him at the University in Chicago. A short meeting between Friedman and Pinochet convinced the dictator to hand economic policy making to Friedman's acolytes (who became known as "the Chicago Boys" for obvious reasons). These were free-market economists, working on a belief in the efficiency and fairness of the free market and who desired to put the laws of supply and demand back to work. They set out to reduce the role of the state in terms of regulation and social welfare as these, they argued, had restricted Chile's growth by reducing competition, lowering growth, artificially increasing wages, and leading to inflation. The ultimate goal, Pinochet once said, was to make Chile *"not a nation of proletarians, but a nation of entrepreneurs."* [quoted by Thomas E. Skidmore and Peter H. Smith, **Modern Latin America**, p. 137]

The role of the Chicago Boys cannot be understated. They had a close relationship with the military from 1972, and according to one expert had a key role in the coup:

> *"In August of 1972 a group of ten economists under the leadership of de Castro began to work on the formulation of an economic programme that would replace [Allende's one].... In fact, the existence of the plan was essential to any attempt on the part of the armed forces to overthrow Allende as the Chilean armed forces did not have any economic plan of their own."* [Silvia Borzutzky, *"The Chicago Boys, social security and welfare in Chile"*, **The Radical Right and the Welfare State**, Howard Glennerster and James Midgley (eds.), p. 88]

This plan also had the backing of certain business interests. Unsurprisingly, immediately after the coup, many of its authors entered key Economic Ministries as advisers. [Rayack, **Op. Cit.**, p. 52] It is also interesting to note that *"[a]ccording to the report of the United States Senate on covert actions in Chile, the activities of these economists were financed by the Central Intelligence Agency (CIA)."* [Borzutzky, **Op. Cit.**, p. 89] Obviously some forms of state intervention were more acceptable than others.

April 1975 saw the Chicago Boys assume *"what was in effect dictatorial control over economic policy … The monetarists were now in a commanding position to put in place Friedman's recommendations, and they didn't hesitate."* The actual results of the free market policies introduced by the dictatorship were far less than the "miracle" claimed by Friedman and a host of other right-wingers. The initial effects of introducing free market policies was a shock-induced depression which resulted in GDP dropping by 12.9% the year "shock treatment" was imposed (Latin America saw a 3.8% rise), real wages falling to 64.9% of their 1970 level and unemployment rising to 20 percent. Even Pinochet *"had to concede that the social cost of the shock treatment was greater than he expected."* [Rayack, **Op. Cit.**, p. 56, p. 41 and p. 57] For Friedman, his *"only concern"* with the plan was *"whether it would be pushed long enough and hard enough."* [quoted by Joseph Collins and John Lear, **Chile's Free-Market Miracle: A Second Look**, p. 29] Unsurprisingly, the *"rigorous imposition of the neoliberal economic model after 1975 soon threatened [workers] job security too"* and they *"bore the brunt"* of the changes in terms of *"lost jobs and raised work norms."* [Winn, *"No Miracle for Us,"* Peter Winn (ed.), **Op. Cit.**, p. 131]After the depression of 1975, the economy started to grow again. This is the source of claim of an "economic miracle." Friedman, for example, used 1976 as his base-line, so excluding the depression year of 1975 which his recommended shock treatment deepened. This is dishonest as it fails to take into account not only the impact of neo-liberal policies but also that a deep recession often produces a vigorous upsurge:

> *"By taking 1975, a recession year in which the Chilean economy declined by 13 percent, as the starting point of their analysis, the Chicago Boys obscured the fact that their 'boom' was more a recovery from the deep recession than a new economic expansion. From 1974 to 1981, the Chilean economy grew at a modest 1.4 percent a year on average. Even at the height of the 'boom' in 1980, effective unemployment was so high – 17 percent – that 5 percent of the workforce were in government make-work programs, a confession of failure for neoliberals who believe in the market as self-correcting and who abhor government welfare programs. Nor did the Chicago Boys call attention to the extreme concentration of capital, precipitous fall in real wages and negative redistribution of income that their policies promoted, or their disincentives to productive investment."* [Peter Winn, *"The Pinochet Era"*, **Op. Cit.**, pp. 28-9]

Between 1975 and 1982, the regime implemented numerous economic reforms based on the suggestions of the Chicago Boys and their intellectual gurus Friedman and von Hayek. They privatised numerous state owned industries and resources and, as would be expected, the privatisations were carried out in such a

way as to profit the wealthy. *"The denationalisation process,"* notes Rayack, *"was carried out under conditions that were extremely advantageous for the new owners … the enterprises were sold at sharply undervalued prices."* Only large conglomerates could afford them, so capital became even more concentrated. [**Op. Cit.**, p. 67] When it privatised its interests in the forestry processing plants in the country the government followed the privatisation of other areas of the economy and they *"were sold at a discount, according to one estimate, at least 20 per cent below their value."* Thus *"the privatisations were bargain sell-offs of public assets,"* which amounted to a *"subsidy from the national treasury to the buyers of 27 to 69 percent"* and so *"[c]ontrol of the common wealth of the entire nation passed to a handful of national and foreign interests that captured most of the subsidy implicit in the rock bottom prices."* [Joseph Collins and John Lear, **Chile's Free-Market Miracle: A Second Look**, p. 206, p. 54 and p. 59]

By 1978, the Chicago Boys *"were pressing for new laws that would bring labour relations in line with the neoliberal economic model in which the market, not the state, would regulate factors of production."* [Winn, *"The Pinochet Era"*, Winn (ed.), **Op. Cit.**, p. 31] According to Pinochet's Minister of Labour (1978-81), the Labour relations had been *"modernised"* and that *"politicised"* labour leaders and their *"privileged fiefdoms"* had been eliminated, with workers no longer having *"monopolies"* on job positions. Rather than government intervention, negotiation between capital and labour was now left to *"individual responsibility and the discipline of the market."* The stated aim was to *"introduce democracy into the world of Chilean unions and resolve problems that for decades had been obstacles for the progress of workers."* [quoted by Joseph Collins and John Lear, *"Working in Chile's Free Market"*, pp. 10-29, **Latin American Perspectives**, vol. 22, No. 1, pp. 10-11 and p. 16] The hypocrisy of a technocratic bureaucrat appointed by a military dictatorship talking about introducing democracy into unions is obvious. The price of labour, it was claimed, now found its correct level as set by the "free" market.

All of which explains Friedman's 1991 comment that the *"real miracle of Chile"* was that Pinochet *"support[ed] a free market regime designed by principled believers in a free market."* [**Economic Freedom, Human Freedom, Political Freedom**] As to be expected with Friedman, the actual experience of implementing his dogmas refuted both them and his assertions on capitalism. Moreover, the working class paid the price.

The advent of the "free market" led to reduced barriers to imports *"on the ground the quotas and tariffs protected inefficient industries and kept prices artificially high. The result was that many local firms lost out to multinational corporations. The Chilean business community, which strongly supported the coup in 1973, was badly affected."* [Skidmore and Smith, **Op. Cit.**, p. 138] The decline of domestic industry cost thousands of better-paying jobs. Looking at the textile sector, firms survived because of *"lowered labour costs and increased productivity."* The sector has *"low real wages, which dramatically altered"* its international competitiveness. In other words, the Chilean textile industry *"had restructured itself on the back of its workers."* [Peter Winn, *"No Miracle for Us"*, Winn (ed.), **Op. Cit.**, p. 130] The mines were *"enormously profitable after 1973 because of increased labour discipline, the reduction in costs due to* *the contraction of real wages, and an increase in production based on expansion programs initiated during the late 1960s."* [Thomas Miller Klubock, *"Class, Community, and Neoliberalism in Chile"*, **Op. Cit.**, p. 241] This was the **real** basis of the 1976 to 1981 "economic miracle" Friedman praised in 1982.

As with most neo-liberal experiments, the post-1975 "miracle" was built on sand. It was *"a speculative bubble that was hailed as an 'economic miracle' until it burst in the 1981-82 bank crash that brought the deregulated Chilean economy down in its wake."* It was *"largely short-term speculative capital ... producing a bubble in stock market and real estate values"* and *"by 1982 the economy was in shambles and Chile in the throes of its worse economic crisis since the depression of the 1930s. A year later, massive social protests defied Pinochet's security forces."* [Winn, **Op. Cit.**, p. 38] Thus *"the bottom fell out of the economy"* and Chile's GDP fell 14% in one year. In the textile industry alone, an estimated 35 to 45% of companies failed. [Collins and Lear, **Op. Cit.**, p. 15]

So after 7 years of free(r) market capitalism, Chile faced yet another economic crisis which, in terms of unemployment and falling GDP was even greater than that experienced during the terrible shock treatment of 1975. Real wages dropped sharply, falling in 1983 to 14% below what they had been in 1970. Bankruptcies skyrocketed, as did foreign debt and unemployment. [Rayack, **Op. Cit.**, p. 69] Chile's GNP *"fell by more than 15 percent, while its real disposable GNP declined by 19 percent. The industrial sector contracted by more than 21 percent and construction by more than 23 percent. Bankruptcies tripled ... It was a crisis comparable to the Great Depression of the 1930s, which affected Chile more severely than any other country in the world."* The same can be said of this crisis, for while GNP in Chile feel 14% during 1982-3, the rest of Latin America experienced 3.5% drop as whole. [Winn, **Op. Cit.**, p. 41 and p. 66] By 1983, the Chilean economy was devastated and it was only by the end of 1986 that Gross Domestic Product per capita (barely) equalled that of 1970. Unemployment (including those on government make-work programmes) had risen to a third of the labour force by mid-1983. By 1986, per capita consumption was actually 11% lower than the 1970 level. [Skidmore and Smith, **Op. Cit.**, p. 138]

Faced with this massive economic collapse (a collapse that somehow slipped Friedman's mind when he was evaluating the Chilean experiment in 1991), the regime organised a massive bailout. The "Chicago Boys" resisted this measure, arguing with dogmatic arrogance that there was no need for government intervention or policy changes because they believed in the self-correcting mechanisms of the market would resolve any economic problem. However, they were applying a simplistic textbook version of the economy to a complex reality which was spectacularly different from their assumptions. When that reality refused to respond in the way predicted by their ideological musing, the state stepped in simply because the situation had become so critical it could not avoid it.

The regime did do some things to help the unemployed, with 14% of the labour force enrolled in two government make-work programs that paid less than the minimum wage by October 1983. However, aid for the capitalist class was far more substantial. The IMF offered loans to Chile to help it out of the mess its economic policies had helped create, but under strict conditions (such as making the Chilean public responsible for paying the billions in foreign loans contracted by **private** banks and firms). The total bailout cost 3% of Chile's GNP for three years, a cost which was passed on to the population (this *"socialisation of private debts were both striking and unequal"*). This follows the usual pattern of "free market" capitalism – market discipline for the working class, state aid for the elite. During the "miracle," the economic gains had been privatised; during the crash the burden for repayment was socialised. In fact, the regime's intervention into the economy was so extensive that, *"[w]ith understandable irony, critics lampooned the 'Chicago road to socialism.'"* [Winn, **Op. Cit.**, p. 66 and p. 40]

Significantly, of the 19 banks that the government had privatised, all but five failed. These along with the other bankrupt firms fell back into government hands, a fact the regime sought to downplay by failing to classify them as public companies. Once the debts had been *"assumed by the public,"* their *"assets were sold to private interests."* Significantly, the *"one bank that had not been privatised and the other publicly owned companies survived the crisis in relatively good shape"* and almost all of them were *"turning a profit, generating for the government in profits and taxes 25 percent of its total revenues ... Thus the public companies that had escaped the Chicago Boy's privatisations ... enabled a financially strapped government to resuscitate the failed private banks and companies."* [Collins and Lear, **Chile's Free-Market Miracle: A Second Look**, pp. 51-2] Needless to say, the recovery (like the illusionary boom) was paid for by the working class. The 1982 crash meant that *"something had to give, and the Chicago Boys decided that it would be wages. Wages, they explained, should be allowed to find their natural level."* An 1982 decree *"transferred much of the burden of recovery and profitability to workers and became central to Chile's economic recovery throughout the rest of the decade."* [Collins and Lear, **Op. Cit.**, p. 20 and p. 19] For the miners, between late 1973 and May 1983, real average wages dropped by 32.6% and workers' benefits were reduced (for example, the free medical attention and health care that had been won in the 1920s were dropped). [Thomas Miller Klubock, *"Class, Community, and Neoliberalism in Chile,"* Winn (ed.), **Op. Cit.**, p. 217] As Peter Winn summarises:

> *"Chile's workers, who had paid the social costs of the illusory neoliberal 'miracle,' now paid as well the highest price for the errors of their nation's military rulers and Chicago Boy technocrats and the imprudence of their country's capitalists. Plant closing and layoffs drove the effective unemployment rate above 30 percent, while real wages for those lucky enough to retain their jobs fell by nearly 11 percent in 1979-82 and by some 20 percent during the 1980s. In addition, inflation jumped to over 20 percent in both 1982 and 1983, and the budget surplus gave way to a deficit equal to 3 percent of the GNP by 1983. By then, Chile's foreign debt was 13 percent higher than its GNP ... Chile's economy contracted 400 percent more in 1982-83 than the rest of Latin America."* ["The Pinochet Era", Winn (ed.), **Op. Cit.**, pp. 41-2]

Unsurprisingly, for the capitalist class things were somewhat different. Private banks *"were bailed out by the government, which* spent *$6 billion in subsidies during 1983-85 (equal to 30 percent of the GNP!) but were made subject to strict government regulation designed to assure their solvency. Controls were also placed on flows of foreign capital.*" [Winn, **Op. Cit.**, p. 42] The government also raised tariffs from 10% to between 20 and 35% and the peso was drastically devalued. [Collins and Lear, **Op. Cit.**, p. 15] Pinochet's state took a more active role in promoting economic activity. For example, it developed new export industries which "*benefited from a series of subsidies, privatisations, and deregulations that allowed for unrestricted exploitation of natural resources of limited renewability. Equally important were low wages, great flexibility of employers vis-à-vis workers, and high levels of unemployment.*" [Collins and Lear, **Op. Cit.**, p. 20] The forestry sector was marked by government hand-outs to the already rich. Joseph Collins and John Lear argue that the neoliberals' "*stated goals were to curtail sharply the direct role of government in forestry and to let market mechanisms determine the prices and direct the use of resources. Yet government intervention and subsidies were in fact central to reorienting the benefits of forestry production away from the rural population towards a handful of national and foreign companies.*" [**Op. Cit.**, p. 205]

By 1986, the economy had stabilised and the crisis was over. However, the recovery was paid for by the working class as "*wages stayed low*" even as the economy began to recover. Low wages were key to the celebrated 'miracle' recovery. From 1984 to 1989 the gross national product grew an average of 6 percent annually. By 1987 Chile had recovered the production levels of 1981, and by 1989 production levels exceeded 1981 levels by 10 percent. The average wage, by contrast, was 5 percent lower at the end of the decade than it had been in 1981 – almost 10 percent lower than the average 1970 wage. The drop in the minimum wage "*was even more drastic.*" Public unrest during the economic crisis made it politically difficult to eliminate, so it "*was allowed to erode steadily in the face of inflation. By 1988, it was 40 percent lower in real terms than it had been in 1981 … In that year 32 percent of the workers in Santiago earned the minimum wage or less.*" Thus, "*recovery and expansion after 1985 depended on two ingredients that are unsustainable over the long term and in a democratic society,*" namely "*an intensified exploitation of the labour force*" and "*the unregulated exploitation of nonrenewable natural resources such as native forests and fishing areas, which amounted to a one-time subsidy to domestic conglomerates and multinationals.*" [Collins and Lear, **Op. Cit.**, **Op. Cit.**, p. 83, p. 84 and p. 35]

In summary, "*the experiment has been an economic disaster.*" [Rayack, **Op. Cit.**, p. 72]

C.11.1 Who benefited from Chile's "economic miracle"?

Given that Chile was hardly an "economic miracle," the question arises why it was termed so by people like Friedman. To answer that question, we need to ask who actually benefited from the neo-liberalism Pinochet imposed. To do this we need to recognise that capitalism is a class system and these classes have different interests. We would expect any policies which benefit the ruling elite to be classed as an "economic miracle" regardless of how adversely they affect the general population (and vice versa). In the case of Chile, this is precisely what happened.

Rather than benefit everyone, neo-liberalism harmed the majority. Overall, by far the hardest group hit was the working class, particularly the urban working class. By 1976, the third year of Junta rule, real wages had fallen to 35% below their 1970 level. It was only by 1981 that they has risen to 97.3% of the 1970 level, only to fall again to 86.7% by 1983. Unemployment, excluding those on state make-work programmes, was 14.8% in 1976, falling to 11.8% by 1980 (this is still double the average 1960s level) only to rise to 20.3% by 1982. [Rayack, **Op. Cit.**, p. 65] Between 1980 and 1988, the real value of wages grew only 1.2 percent while the real value of the minimum wage declined by 28.5 percent. During this period, urban unemployment averaged 15.3 percent per year. [Silvia Borzutzky, **Op. Cit.**, p. 96] Even by 1989 the unemployment rate was still at 10% (the rate in 1970 was 5.7%) and the real wage was still 8% lower than in 1970. Between 1975 and 1989, unemployment averaged 16.7%. In other words, after nearly 15 years of free market capitalism, real wages had still not exceeded their 1970 levels and unemployment was still higher. As would be expected in such circumstances the share of wages in national income fell from 42.7% in 1970 to 33.9% in 1993. Given that high unemployment is often attributed by the right to strong unions and other labour market "imperfections," these figures are doubly significant as the Chilean regime, as noted above, reformed the labour market to improve its "competitiveness."

After 1982, "*stagnant wages and the unequal distribution of income severely curtailed buying power for most Chileans, who would not recover 1970 consumption levels until 1989.*" [Collins and Lear, **Op. Cit.**, p. 25] By 1988, "*the average real wage had returned to 1980 levels, but it was still well below 1970 levels. Moreover, in 1986, some 37 percent of the labour force worked in the informal sector, where wages were lower and benefits often non-existent. Many worked for minimum wage which in 1988 provided only half of what an average family required to live decently – and a fifth of the workers didn't even earn that. A survey … concluded that nearly half of Chileans lived in poverty.*" [Winn, "*The Pinochet Era*", **Op. Cit.**, p. 48] This was far more in absolute and relative terms than at any time in the in the preceding three decades. [Collins and Lear, "*Working in Chile's Free Market*", **Op. Cit.**, p. 26]

Per capita consumption fell by 23% from 1972-87. The proportion of the population below the poverty line (the minimum income required for basic food and housing) increased from 20% to 44.4% between 1970 and 1987. Per capita health care spending was more than halved from 1973 to 1985, setting off explosive growth in poverty-related diseases such as typhoid, diabetes and viral hepatitis. On the other hand, while consumption for the poorest 20% of the population of Santiago dropped by 30%, it rose by 15% for the richest 20%. [Noam Chomsky, **Year 501**, pp. 190-191] The percentage of Chileans without adequate housing increased from 27 to 40 percent between 1972 and 1988, despite the claims of the government that it would solve homelessness via market friendly policies.

So after two decades of Neoliberalism, the Chilean worker can look forward to *"a job that offers little stability and low wages, usually a temporary one or one in the informal economy ... Much of the growth in jobs after the 1982-1983 crash came in economic sectors characterised by seasonal employment ... [and are] notorious for their low pay, long hours, and high turnover."* In 1989, over 30% of jobs were in the formal sector in the Santiago metropolitan area with incomes less than half the average of those in the formal sector. For those with jobs, *"the work pace intensified and the work day lengthened ... Many Chileans worked far longer than the legal maximum work week of 48 hours without being paid for the extra hours. Even free-market celebrants ... admit that extra unpaid hours remain a serious problem"* in 1989. In fact, it is *"commonly assumed that employees work overtime without pay or else"* and, unsurprisingly, the *"pattern resembles the European production systems of the mid-19th century."* [Collins and Lear, **Op. Cit.**, p. 22 pp. 22-3, p. 23, p. 24 and p. 25] Unsurprisingly, as in neo-liberal America, wages have become divorced from productivity growth. Even in the 1990s, *"there is evidence that productivity growth outpaced real wage growth by as much as a ratio 3:1 in 1993 and 5:1 in 1997."* [Volker Frank, *"Politics without Policy"*, **Op. Cit.**, p. 73]

Similar comments are possible in regards to the privatised pension system, regarded by many right-wingers as a success and a model for other countries. However, on closer inspection this system shows its weaknesses – indeed, it can be argued that the system is only a success for those companies making extensive profits from it (administration costs of the Chilean system are almost 30% of revenues, compared to 1% for the U.S. Social Security system [Doug Henwood, **Wall Street**, p. 305]). For working people, it is a disaster. According to SAFP, the government agency which regulates the system, 96% of the known workforce were enrolled in February 1995, but 43.4% of these were not adding to their funds. Perhaps as many as 60% do not contribute regularly (given the nature of the labour market, this is unsurprising). Unfortunately, regular contributions are required to receive full benefits. Critics argue that only 20% of contributors will actually receive good pensions.

Workers need to find money for health care as their *"remuneration has been reduced to the wage, ending most benefits that workers had gained over the years [before the coup]. Moreover, the privatisation of such social services as health care and retirement security ... [has meant] the costs were now taken entirely from employee earnings."* Unsurprisingly, *"[l]onger work days and a stepped-up pace of work increased the likelihood of accidents and illness. From 1982 to 1985 the number of reported workplace accidents almost doubled. Public health experts estimate, however, that over three-quarters of workplace accidents went unreported,*

in part because over half of the workforce is without any kind of accident insurance." [Collins and Lear, **Op. Cit.**, p. 20 and p. 25]

It is interesting to note that when this programme was introduced, the armed forces and police were allowed to keep their own generous public plans. If the plans **were** are as good as their supporters claim, you would think that those introducing them would have joined them. Obviously what was good enough for the masses were not suitable for the rulers and the holders of the guns they depended upon. Given the subsequent fate of that scheme, it is understandable that the ruling elite and its minions did not want middle-men to make money off their savings and did not trust their pensions to the fluctuations of the stock market. Their subjects, however, were less lucky. All in all, Chile's privatised social security system *"transferred worker savings in the form of social security contributions from the public to the private sector, making them available to the country's economic groups for investment. Given the oligopic concentration of wealth and corporate control under Pinochet, this meant handing the forced savings of workers over to Chile's most powerful capitalists."* That is, *"to shore up capital markets through its transfer of worker savings to Chile's business elites."* [Winn, *"The Pinochet Era"*, **Op. Cit.**, p. 64 and p. 31]

The same applies to the health system, with the armed forces and national police and their dependants having their own public health care system. This means that they avoid the privatised health system which the wealthy use and the run-down public system which the majority have access to. The market ensures that for most people, *"the actual determining factor is not 'choice,' but one's ability to pay."* By 1990, only 15% of Chileans were in the private system (of these, nearly 75% are form the top 30% of the population by income). This means that there are three medical systems in Chile. The well-funded public one for armed forces and police, a good to excellent private system for the elite few and a *"grossly under-funded, rundown, over-burdened"* one *"for some 70% of Chileans."* Most *"pay more and receive less."* [Collins and Lear, **Op. Cit.**, p. 99 and p. 246]

The impact on individuals extended beyond purely financial considerations, with the Chilean labour force *"once accustomed to secure, unionised jobs [before Pinochet] ... [being turned] into a nation of anxious individualists ... [with] over half of all visits to Chile's public health system involv[ing] psychological ailments, mainly depression. 'The repression isn't physical any more, it's economic – feeding your family, educating your child,' says Maria Pena, who works in a fishmeal factory in Concepcion. 'I feel real anxiety about the future', she adds, 'They can chuck us out at any time. You can't think five years ahead. If you've got money you can get an education and health care; money is everything here now.'"* Little wonder, then, that *"adjustment has created an atomised society, where increased stress and individualism have damaged its traditionally strong and caring community life ... suicides have increased threefold between 1970 and 1991 and the number of alcoholics has quadrupled in the last 30 years ... [and] family breakdowns are increasing, while opinion polls show the current crime wave to be the most widely condemned aspect of life in the new Chile. 'Relationships are changing,' says Betty Bizamar, a 26-year-old trade union leader. 'People use each other, spend less time with their family. All they talk about is money, things. True friendship is difficult now.'"* [Duncan Green, **Op. Cit.**, p. 96 and p. 166]

The experiment with free market capitalism also had serious impacts for Chile's environment. The capital city of Santiago became one of the most polluted cities in the world due the free reign of market forces. With no environmental regulation there is general environmental ruin and water supplies have severe pollution problems. [Noam Chomsky, **Year 501**, p. 190] With the bulk of the country's experts being based on the extraction and low processing of natural resources, eco-systems and the environment have been plundered in the name of profit and property. The depletion of natural resources, particularly in forestry and fishing, is accelerating due to the self-interested behaviour of a few large firms looking for short term profit.

So, in summary, Chile's workers *"were central target's of [Pinochet's] political repression and suffered greatly from his state terror. They also paid a disproportionate share of the costs of his regime's regressive social policies. Workers and their organisations were also the primary targets of Pinochet's labour laws and among the biggest losers from his policies of privatisation and deindustrialisation."* [Winn, *"Introduction"*, **Op. Cit.**, p. 10]

Given that the majority of Chile's people where harmed by the economic policies of the regime, how can it be termed a "miracle"? The answer can be found in another consequence of Pinochet's neo-classical monetarist policies, namely *"a contraction of demand, since workers and their families could afford to purchase fewer goods. The reduction in the market further threatened the business community, which started producing more goods for export and less for local consumption. This posed yet another obstacle to economic growth and led to increased concentration of income and wealth in the hands of a small elite."* [Skidmore and Smith, **Op. Cit.**, p. 138]

It is the increased wealth of the elite that we see the true "miracle" of Chile. When the leader of the Christian Democratic Party returned from exile in 1989 he said that economic growth that benefited the top 10% of the population had been achieved (Pinochet's official institutions agreed). [Noam Chomsky, **Deterring Democracy**, p. 231] This is more than confirmed by other sources. According to one expert in the Latin American neo-liberal revolutions, the elite *"had become massively wealthy under Pinochet."* [Duncan Green, **The Silent Revolution**, p. 216] In 1980, the richest 10% of the population took 36.5% of the national income. By 1989, this had risen to 46.8%. By contrast, the bottom 50% of income earners saw their share fall from 20.4% to 16.8% over the same period. Household consumption followed the same pattern. In 1970, the top 20% of households had 44.5% of consumption. This rose to 51% in 1980 and to 54.6% in 1989. Between 1970 and 1989, the share going to the other 80% fell. The poorest 20% of households saw their share fall from 7.6% in 1970 to 4.4% in 1989. The next 20% saw their share fall from 11.8% to 8.2%, and middle 20% share fell from 15.6% to 12.7%. The next 20% saw their share of consumption fall from 20.5% to 20.1%. In other words, *"at least 60 percent of the population was relatively, if not absolutely, worse off."* [James Petras and Fernando Ignacio Leiva, **Democracy and Poverty in Chile**, p. 39 and p. 34]

In summary, *"the distribution of income in Chile in 1988, after a*

decade of free-market policies, was markedly regressive. Between 1978 and 1988 the richest 10 percent of Chileans increased their share of national income from 37 to 47 percent, while the next 30 percent saw their share shrink from 23 to 18%. The income share of the poorest fifth of the population dropped from 5 to 4 percent." [Collins and Lear, **Op. Cit.**, p. 26] In the last years of Pinochet's dictatorship, the richest 10% of the rural population saw their income rise by 90% between 1987 and 1990. The share of the poorest 25% fell from 11% to 7%. The legacy of Pinochet's social inequality could still be found in 1993, with a two-tier health care system within which infant mortality is 7 per 1000 births for the richest fifth of the population and 40 per 1000 for the poorest fifth. [Duncan Green, **Op. Cit.**, p. 108 and p. 101] Between 1970 and 1989, labour's share of the national income fell from 52.3% to 30.7% (it was 62.8% in 1972). Real wages in 1987 were still 81.2% of their 1980-1 level. [Petras and Leiva, **Op. Cit.**, p. 34, p. 25 and p. 170]

Thus Chile has been a "miracle" for the capitalist class, with its successes being *"enjoyed primarily (and in many areas, exclusively) by the economic and political elites. In any society shot through with enormous inequalities in wealth and income, the market ... works to concentrate wealth and income."* There has been *"a clear trend toward more concentrated control over economic resources ... Economic concentration is now greater than at any other time in Chile's history"* with multinational corporations reaping *"rich rewards from Chile's free-market policies"* (*"not surprisingly, they enthusiastically applaud the model and push to implant it everywhere"*). Ultimately, it is *"unconscionable to consider any economic and social project successful when the percentage of those impoverished ... more than doubled."* [Collins and Lear, **Chile's Free-Market Miracle: A Second Look**, p. 252 and p. 253]

Thus the wealth created by the Chilean economy during the Pinochet years did **not** "trickle down" to the working class (as claimed would happen by "free market" capitalist dogma) but instead accumulated in the hands of the rich. As in the UK and the USA, with the application of "trickle down economics" there was a vast skewing of income distribution in favour of the already-rich. That is, there has been a 'trickle-up' (or rather, a **flood** upwards). Which is hardly surprising, as exchanges between the strong and weak will favour the former (which is why anarchists support working class organisation and collective action to make us stronger than the capitalists and why Pinochet repressed them).

Overall, *"in 1972, Chile was the second most equal country in Latin America; by 2002 it was the second most **un**equal country in the region."* [Winn, *"The Pinochet Era"*, **Op. Cit.**, p. 56] Significantly, this refutes Friedman's 1962 assertion that *"capitalism leads to less inequality ... inequality appears to be less ... the more highly capitalist the country is."* [**Capitalism and Freedom**, p. 169] As with other countries which applied Friedman's ideas (such as the UK and US), inequality soared in Chile. Ironically, in this as in so many cases, implementing his ideas refuted his own assertions.

There are two conclusions which could be drawn. Firstly, that Chile is now **less** capitalist after applying Friedman's dogmas. Secondly, that Friedman did not know what he was talking about. The second option seems the most likely, although for some defenders of the faith Chile's neo-liberal experiment may not have been "pure" enough. However, this kind of assertion will only convince the true believer.

C.11.2 What about Chile's economic growth and low inflation?

Given the actual results of the experiment, there are only two areas left to claim an "economic miracle." These are combating inflation and increasing economic growth. Neither can be said to be "miraculous."

As far as inflation goes, the Pinochet regime **did** reduce it, eventually. At the time of the CIA-backed coup it was around 500% (given that the US undermined the Chilean economy – *"make the economy scream"*, Richard Helms, the director of the CIA – high inflation would be expected). By 1982 it was 10% and between 1983 to 1987, it fluctuated between 20 and 31%. It took eight years for the Chicago Boys to control inflation and, significantly, this involved *"the failure of several stabilisation programmes at an elevated social cost … In other words, the stabilisation programs they prescribed not only were not miraculous – they were not successful."* [Winn, *"The Pinochet Era"*, **Op. Cit.**, p. 63] In reality, inflation was not controlled by means of Friedman's Monetarism but rather by state repression as left-wing Keynesian Nicholas Kaldor points out:

> *"The rate of growth of the money supply was reduced from 570 per cent in 1973 … to 130 per cent in 1977. But this did not succeed in moderating the growth of the money GNP or of the rise in prices, because – lo and behold! – no sooner did they succeed in moderating the growth of the money supply down, than the velocity of circulation shot up, and inflation was greater with a lower rate of growth of the money supply … they have managed to bring down the rate of growth of prices … And how? By the method well tried by Fascist dictatorships. It is a kind of incomes policy. It is a prohibition of wage increases with concentration camps for those who disobey and, of course, the prohibition of trade union activity and so on. And so it was not monetarism that brought the Chilean inflation down … [It was based on] methods which by-passed the price mechanism."* [**The Economic Consequences of Mrs Thatcher**, p. 45]

Inflation was controlled by means of state repression and high unemployment, a combination of the incomes policy of Hitler and Mussolini and Karl Marx (i.e., Friedman's "natural rate of unemployment" we debunked in section C.9). In other words, Monetarism and "free market" capitalism did not reduce inflation (as was the case with Thatcher and Reagan was well).

Which leaves growth, the only line of defence possible for the claim of a Chilean "Miracle." As we discussed in section C.10, the right argue that relative shares of wealth are not important, it is the absolute level which counts. While the share of the economic pie may have dropped for most Chileans, the right argue that the high economic growth of the economy meant that they were receiving a smaller share of a bigger pie. We will ignore the well documented facts that the **level** of inequality, rather than absolute levels of standards of living, has most effect on the health of a population and that ill-health is inversely correlated with income (i.e. the poor have worse health that the rich). We will also ignore other issues related to the distribution of wealth, and so power, in a society (such as the free market re-enforcing and increasing inequalities via "free exchange" between strong and weak parties, as the terms of any exchange will be skewed in favour of the stronger party, an analysis which the Chilean experience provides extensive evidence for with its "competitive" and "flexible" labour market). In other words, growth without equality can have damaging effects which are not, and cannot be, indicated in growth figures.

So we will consider the claim that the Pinochet regime's record on growth makes it a "miracle" (as nothing else could). However, when we look at the regime's growth record we find that it is hardly a "miracle" at all – the celebrated economic growth of the 1980s must be viewed in the light of the two catastrophic recessions which Chile suffered in 1975 and 1982. As Edward Herman points out, this growth was *"regularly exaggerated by measurements from inappropriate bases (like the 1982 trough)."* [**The Economics of the Rich**]

This point is essential to understand the actual nature of Chile's "miracle" growth. For example, supporters of the "miracle" pointed to the period 1978 to 1981 (when the economy grew at 6.6 percent a year) or the post 1982-84 recession up-swing. However, this is a case of "lies, damn lies, and statistics" as it does not take into account the catching up an economy goes through as it leaves a recession. During a recovery, laid-off workers go back to work and the economy experiences an increase in growth due to this. This means that the deeper the recession, the higher the subsequent growth in the up-turn. So to see if Chile's economic growth was a miracle and worth the decrease in income for the many, we need to look at whole business cycle, rather than for the upturn. If we do this we find that Chile had the second worse rate of growth in Latin America between 1975 and 1980. The average growth in GDP was 1.5% per year between 1974 and 1982, which was lower than the average Latin American growth rate of 4.3% and lower than the 4.5% of Chile in the 1960's. [Rayack, **Op. Cit.**, p. 64]

This meant that, in per capita terms, Chile's GDP only increased by 1.5% per year between 1974-80. This was considerably less than the 2.3% achieved in the 1960's. The average growth in GDP was 1.5% per year between 1974 and 1982, which was lower than the average Latin American growth rate of 4.3% and lower than the 4.5% of Chile in the 1960s. Between 1970 and 1980, per capita GDP grew by only 8%, while for Latin America as a whole, it increased by 40%. Between the years 1980 and 1982 during which all of Latin America was adversely affected by depression conditions, per capita GDP fell by 12.9 percent, compared to a fall of 4.3 percent for Latin America as a whole. [Rayack, **Op. Cit.**, p. 57 and p. 64]

Thus, between 1970 and 1989, Chile's GDP *"grew at a slow pace (relative to the 1960s and to other Latin American countries over the same period) with an average rate of 1.8-2.0 per cent. On a per capita basis … GDP [grew] at a rate (0.1-0.2 per cent) well below the Latin American average … [B]y 1989 the GDP was still 6.1 per cent below the 1981 level, not having recovered the level reached in 1970. For the entire period of military rule (1974-1989) only five Latin American countries had a worse record. Some miracle!"* [Petras and Leiva, **Op. Cit.**, p. 32]

Thus the growth "miracles" refer to recoveries from depression-like collapses, collapses that can be attributed in large part to the free-market policies imposed on Chile! Overall, the growth "miracle" under Pinochet turns out to be non-existent. The full time frame illustrates Chile's lack of significant economic and social process between 1975 and 1989. Indeed, the economy was characterised by instability rather than real growth. The high levels of growth during the boom periods (pointed to by the right as evidence of the "miracle") barely made up for the losses during the bust periods.

All in all, the experience of Chile under Pinochet and its "economic miracle" indicates that the costs involved in creating a free market capitalist regime are heavy, at least for the majority. Rather than being transitional, these problems have proven to be structural and enduring in nature, as the social, environmental, economic and political costs become embedded into society. The murky side of the Chilean "miracle" is simply not reflected in the impressive macroeconomic indictors used to market "free market" capitalism, indicators themselves subject to manipulation as we have seen.

C.11.3 Did neo-liberal Chile confirm capitalist economics?

No. Despite claims by the likes of Friedman, Chile's neo-liberal experiment was no "economic miracle" and, in fact, refuted many of the key dogmas of capitalist economics. We can show this by comparing the actual performance of "economic liberty" with Friedman's predictions about it.

The first thing to note is that neo-liberal Chile hardly supports the claim that the free market is stable. In fact, it was marked by deep recessions followed by periods of high growth as the economic recovered. This resulted in overall (at best) mediocre growth rates (see last section).

Then there is the fact that the Chilean experiment refutes key neo-classical dogmas about the labour market. In **Capitalism and Freedom**, Friedman was at pains to attack trade unions and the idea that they defended the worker from coercion by the boss. Nonsense, he asserted, the *"employee is protected from coercion by the employer because of other employers for whom he can work."* [pp. 14-5] Thus collective action in the form of, say, unions is both unnecessary and, in fact, harmful. The ability of workers to change jobs is sufficient and the desire of capitalist economists is always to make the real labour market become more like the ideal market of perfect competition – lots of atomised individuals who are price takers, not price setters. While big business gets ignored, unions are demonised.

The problem is that such "perfect" labour markets are hard to create outside of dictatorships. Pinochet's reign of terror created such a market. Faced with the possibility of death and torture if they stood up for their rights, the only **real** alternative most workers had was that of finding a new job. So while the labour market was far from being an expression of "economic liberty," Chile's dictatorship **did**

produce a labour market which almost perfectly reflected the neo-classical (and Austrian) ideal. Workers become atomised individuals as state terror forced them to eschew acting as trade unionists and seeking collective solutions to their (individual and collective) problems. Workers had no choice **but** to seek a new employer if they felt they were being mistreated or under-valued. Terror created the preconditions for the workings of an ideal capitalist labour market. Friedman's talk of "economic liberty" in Chile suggests that Friedman thought that a "free market" in labour would work "as if" it were subject to death squads. In other words, that capitalism needs an atomised workforce which is too scared to stand up for themselves. Undoubtedly, he would prefer such fear to be imposed by purely "economic" means (unemployment playing its usual role) but as his work on the "natural rate of unemployment" suggests, he is not above appealing to the state to maintain it.

Unfortunately for capitalist ideology, Chile refuted that notion, with its workers subject to the autocratic power of the boss and having to give concession after concession simply to remain in work. Thus the *"total overhaul of the labour law system [which] took place between 1979 and 1981 … aimed at creating a perfect labour market, eliminating collective bargaining, allowing massive dismissal of workers, increasing the daily working hours up to twelve hours and eliminating the labour courts."* [Silvia Borzutzky, **Op. Cit.**, p. 91] In reality, the Labour code simply reflected the power property owners have over their wage slaves and *"was solidly probusiness. It was intended to maximise the flexibility of management's use of labour and to keep any eventual elected government from intervening on behalf of labour in negotiations between employers and workers."* This was hidden, of course, by *"populist rhetoric."* [Collins and Lear, **Op. Cit.**, p. 16] In fact, the Plan Laboral *"was intended to definitely shift the balance of power in labour relations in favour of business and to weaken the workers and unions that formed the central political base of the Left."* [Winn, *"The Pinochet Era"*, **Op. Cit.**, p. 31]

Unsurprisingly, *"workers … have not received a fair share of the benefits from the economic growth and productivity increases that their labour has produced and that they have had to bear a disproportionate share of the costs of this restructuring in their wages, working conditions, job quality, and labour relations."* [Winn, *"Introduction"*, **Op. Cit.**, p. 10]

Chile, yet again, refuted another of Friedman's assertions about capitalism. In 1975, he wrongly predicted that the unemployed caused by the Monetarist recession would quickly find work, telling a Santiago audience that they would *"be surprised how fast people would be absorbed by a growing private-sector economy."* [quoted by Rayack, **Op. Cit.**, p. 57] Unemployment reached record levels for decades, as the free market regime *"has been slow to create jobs. During the 1960s unemployment hovered around 6 percent; by contrast, the unemployment level for the years 1974 to 1987 averaged 20 percent of the workforce. Even in the best years of the boom (1980-1981) it stayed as high as 18 percent. In the years immediately following the 1982 crash, unemployment – including government emergency work programs – peaked at 35 percent of the workforce."* Unsurprisingly, the *"most important rationalisation"* made by Chilean industry *"was the lowering of labour costs. This was accomplished through massive layoffs, intensifying the work* of remaining workers, and pushing wage levels well below historic levels." This was aided by unemployment levels which "officially averaged 20 percent from 1974 to 1987. Chronic high levels of unemployment afforded employers considerable leverage in setting working conditions and wage levels ... Not surprisingly, workers who managed to hold onto their jobs were willing to make repeated concessions to employers, and in order to get jobs employees often submitted to onerous terms." Between 1979 and 1982, more than a fifth of manufacturing companies failed and employment in the sector fell by over a quarter. In the decade before 1981, out of every 26 workers, 13 became unemployed, 5 joined the urban informal sector and 8 were on a government emergency employment program. It should be stressed that official statistics "underestimate the real level of unemployment" as they exclude people who worked just one day in the previous week. A respected church-sponsored institute on employment found that in 1988, unemployment in Santiago was as high as 21%. [Lear and Collins, **Op. Cit.**, p. 22, p. 15, p. 16, p. 15 and p. 22]

The standard free-market argument is that unemployment is solved by subjecting the wage level to the rigours of the market. While wages will be lower, more people will be employed. As we discussed in section C.9, the logic and evidence for such claims is spurious. Needless to say, Friedman never revised his claims in the light of the empirical evidence produced by the application of his ideas.

Given the fact that "labour" (i.e., an individual) is not produced for the market in the first place, you can expect it to react differently from other "commodities." For example, a cut in its price will generally increase supply, not decrease it, simply because people have to eat, pay the rent and so forth. Cutting wages will see partners and children sent to work, plus the acceptance of longer hours by those who remain in work. As such, the idea that unemployment is caused by wages being too high has always been a specious and self-serving argument, one refuted not only by logic but that bane of economics, empirical evidence. This was the case with Chile's "economic miracle," where declining wages forced families to seek multiple incomes in order to survive: "The single salary that could support a family was beyond the reach of most workers; the norm, in fact, was for spouses and children to take on temporary and informal jobs ... Even with multiple incomes, many families were hard-pressed to survive." [Lear and Collins, **Op. Cit.**, p. 23] Which, of course, refutes "free market" capitalist claim that the labour market is like any other market. In reality, it is not and so it is hardly surprising that a drop in the price of labour **increased** supply nor that the demand for labour did not increase to in response to the drop in its real wage.

Lastly, there is the notion that collective action in the market by the state or trade unions harms the general population, particularly the poor. For neo-classical and Austrian economists, labour is the source of all of capitalism's problems (and any government silly enough to pander to the economically illiterate masses). Pinochet's regime allowed them to prove this was the case. Again Chile refuted them.

The "Chicago Boys" had no illusions that fascism was required to create free market capitalism. According to Sergio de Castro, the architect of the economic programme Pinochet imposed, fascism was required to introduce "economic liberty" because "it provided

a lasting regime; it gave the authorities a degree of efficiency that it was not possible to obtain in a democratic regime; and it made possible the application of a model developed by experts and that did not depend upon the social reactions produced by its implementation." [quoted by Silvia Borzutzky, "The Chicago Boys, social security and welfare in Chile", **The Radical Right and the Welfare State**, Howard Glennerster and James Midgley (eds.), p. 90] They affirmed that "in a democracy we could not have done one-fifth of what we did." [quoted by Winn, "The Pinochet Era", Winn (ed.), **Op. Cit.**, p. 28]

Given the individualistic assumptions of neo-classical and Austrian economics, it is not hard to conclude that creating a police state in order to control industrial disputes, social protest, unions, political associations, and so on, is what is required to introduce the ground rules the capitalist market requires for its operation. As socialist Brian Barry argues in relation to the Thatcher regime in Britain which was also heavily influenced by the ideas of "free market" capitalists like Milton Friedman and Frederick von Hayek:

> "Some observers claim to have found something paradoxical in the fact that the Thatcher regime combines liberal individualist rhetoric with authoritarian action. But there is no paradox at all. Even under the most repressive conditions ... people seek to act collectively in order to improve things for themselves, and it requires an enormous exercise of brutal power to fragment these efforts at organisation and to force people to pursue their interests individually ... left to themselves, people will inevitably tend to pursue their interests through collective action – in trade unions, tenants' associations, community organisations and local government. Only the pretty ruthless exercise of central power can defeat these tendencies: hence the common association between individualism and authoritarianism, well exemplified in the fact that the countries held up as models by the free-marketers are, without exception, authoritarian regimes." ["The Continuing Relevance of Socialism", Robert Skidelsky (ed.), **Thatcherism**, p. 146]

Little wonder, then, that Pinochet's regime was marked by authoritarianism, terror and rule by savants. Indeed, "[t]he Chicago-trained economists emphasised the scientific nature of their programme and the need to replace politics by economics and the politicians by economists. Thus, the decisions made were not the result of the will of the authority, but they were determined by their scientific knowledge. The use of the scientific knowledge, in turn, would reduce the power of government since decisions will be made by technocrats and by the individuals in the private sector." [Silvia Borzutzky, **Op. Cit.**, p. 90] However, as Winn points out:

> "Although the Chicago Boys justified their policies with a discourse of liberty, they were not troubled by the contradiction of basing the economic freedom they promoted on the most dictatorial regime in Chilean history – or in denying workers the freedom to strike or bargain collectively. At bottom, the only freedom that they cared about was the economic liberty of those Chileans and foreigners with capital to invest and consume, and that

'freedom,' de Castro believed, was best assured by an authoritarian government and a passive labour force. In short, their notions of freedom were both selective and self-serving." [**Op. Cit.**, p. 28]

Of course, turning authority over to technocrats and private power does not change its nature – only who has it. Pinochet's regime saw a marked shift of governmental power away from protection of individual rights to a protection of capital and property rather than an abolition of that power altogether. As would be expected, only the wealthy benefited. The working class were subjected to attempts to create a "perfect labour market" – and only terror can turn people into the atomised commodities such a market requires. Perhaps when looking over the nightmare of Pinochet's regime we should ponder these words of Bakunin in which he indicates the negative effects of running society by means of science books and "experts":

"human science is always and necessarily imperfect … were we to force the practical life of men – collective as well as individual – into rigorous and exclusive conformity with the latest data of science, we would thus condemn society as well as individuals to suffer martyrdom on a Procrustean bed, which would soon dislocate and stifle them, since life is always an infinitely greater thing than science." [**The Political Philosophy of Bakunin**, p. 79]

The Chilean experience of rule by free market ideologues prove Bakunin's points beyond doubt. Chilean society was forced onto the Procrustean bed by the use of terror and life was forced to conform to the assumptions found in economics textbooks. And as we proved above, only those with power or wealth did well out of the experiment. From an anarchist perspective, the results were all too sadly predictable. The only surprising thing is that the right point to the experiment as a success story.

Since Chile has become (mostly) a democracy (with the armed forces still holding considerable influence) the post-Pinochet governments have made minor reforms. For example, *"tax increases targeted for social spending for the poor"* allowed them to *"halve the 1988 45 percent poverty rate bequeathed by Pinochet."* In fact, the *"bulk of this spending"* was aimed at *"the poorest of the poor, the 25 percent of the population classified as destitute in 1988."* [Winn, *"The Pinochet Era,"* **Op. Cit.**, p. 50, p. 52 and p. 55]

However, while this *"curtailed absolute poverty, they did not reduce inequality … From 1990 to 1996 the share of the national income of the poorest 20 percent of the population stagnated beneath 4 percent, while that of the richest 20 percent inched up from 56 percent to 57 percent … the distribution of income was one of the most unequal in the world. In Latin America, only Brazil was worse."* [Paul W Drake, *"Foreword"*, Winn (ed.), **Op. Cit.**, p. xi] The new government raised the minimum wage in 1990 by 17% in real terms, with another rise of approximately 15% two years later. This had a significant effect on income as *"a substantial number of the Chilean labour force receives wages and salaries that are only slightly above the minimum wage."* [Volker Frank, *"Politics without Policy"*, Winn (ed.), **Op. Cit.**, p. 73 and p. 76] In stark contrast to the claims of neo-classical economics, the rise in the minimum wage did not increase unemployment. In fact, it **dropped** to 4.4%, in 1992, the lowest since the early 1970s.

Overall, increased social spending on health, education and poverty relief has occurred since the end of the dictatorship and has lifted over a million Chileans out of poverty between 1987 and 1992 (the poverty rate has dropped from 44.6% in 1987 to 23.2% in 1996, although this is still higher than in 1970). However, inequality is still a major problem as are other legacies from the Pinochet era, such as the nature of the labour market, income insecurity, family separations, alcoholism, and so on. Yet while *"both unemployment and poverty decreased, in part because of programs targeted at the poorest sectors of the population by centre-left governments with greater social concern than the Pinochet dictatorship,"* many problems remain such as *"a work week that was among the longest in the world."* [Winn, *"Introduction"*, **Op. Cit.**, p. 4]

Chile has moved away from Pinochet's "free-market" model in other ways too. In 1991, Chile introduced a range of controls over capital, including a provision for 30% of all non-equity capital entering Chile to be deposited without interest at the central bank for one year. This reserve requirement – known locally as the encaje – amounts to a tax on capital flows that is higher the shorter the term of the loan. As William Greider points out, Chile *"has managed in the last decade to achieve rapid economic growth by abandoning the pure free-market theory taught by American economists and emulating major elements of the Asian strategy, including forced savings and the purposeful control of capital. The Chilean government tells foreign investors where they may invest, keeps them out of certain financial assets and prohibits them from withdrawing their capital rapidly."* [**One World, Ready or Not**, p. 280]

Needless to say, while state aid to the working class has increased somewhat, state welfare for business is still the norm. After the 1982 crash, the Chilean Economic Development Agency (CORFO) reverted to its old role in developing Chilean industry (after the coup, it did little more than just selling off state property at discount prices to the wealthy). In other words, the post-recession "miracle" of the 1980s was due, in part, to a state organisation whose remit was promoting economic development, supporting business with new technology as well as technical and financial assistance. It, in effect, promoted joint public-private sectors initiatives. One key example was its role in funding and development of new resource-sector firms, such as the forestry sector and the fishing industry. While free-marketeers have portrayed the boom in natural-resource extraction as the result of the "free market," in reality private capital lacked the initiative and foresight to develop these industries and CORFO provided aid as well as credits and subsidies to encourage it. [James M. Cypher, *"Is Chile a Neoliberal Success?"*, **Dollars & Sense**, September/October 2004] Then there is the role of Fundación Chile, a public-private agency designed to develop firms in new areas where private capital will not invest. This pays for research and development before selling its stake to the private sector once a project becomes commercially viable. [Jon Jeter, *"A Smoother Road To Free Markets,"* **Washington Post**, 21/01/2004] In other words, a similar system of state intervention promoted by the East-Asian Tigers (and in a similar fashion, ignored by the ideologues of "free market" capitalism – but, then, state action for capitalists never seems to count as interfering in the market).

Thus the Chilean state has violated its "free market" credentials, in many ways, very successfully too. While it started in the 1980s, post-Pinochet it has extended this to include aid to the working class. Thus the claims of free-market advocates that Chile's rapid growth in the 1990s is evidence for their model are false (just as their claims concerning South-East Asia also proved false, claims conveniently forgotten when those economies went into crisis). Needless to say, Chile is under pressure to change its ways and conform to the dictates of global finance. In 1998, Chile eased its controls, following heavy speculative pressure on its currency, the peso. That year economic growth halved and contracted 1.1% in 1999.

So even the neo-liberal jaguar has had to move away from a purely free market approach on social issues and the Chilean government has had to intervene into the economy in order to start putting back together the society ripped apart by market forces and authoritarian government. However, fear of the military has ensured that reforms have been minor and, consequently, Chile cannot be considered a genuine democracy. In other words, "economic liberty" has not produced genuine "political liberty" as Friedman (and others) claim (see section D.11). Ultimately, for all but the tiny elite at the top, the Pinochet regime of "economic liberty" was a nightmare. Economic "liberty" only seemed to benefit one group in society, an obvious "miracle." For the vast majority, the "miracle" of economic "liberty" resulted, as it usually does, in increased inequality, exploitation, poverty, pollution, crime and social alienation. The irony is that many right-wing free-marketers point to it as a model of the benefits of capitalism.

C.12

Doesn't Hong Kong show the potentials of "free market" capitalism?

Given the general lack of laissez-faire capitalism in the world, examples to show its benefits are few and far between. Rather than admit that the ideal is simply impossible, conservative and right-"libertarian" ideologues scour the world and history for examples. Rarely do they let facts get in the way of their searching – until the example expresses some negative features such as economic crisis (repression of working class people or rising inequality and poverty are of little consequence). Once that happens, then all the statist features of those economies previously ignored or downplayed will be stressed in order to protect the ideal from reality.

One such example is Hong Kong, which is often pointed to by right-wingers as an example of the power of capitalism and how a "pure" capitalism will benefit all. It has regularly been ranked as first in the "Index of Economic Freedom" produced by the Heritage Foundation, a US-based conservative think tank ("economic freedom" reflecting what you expect a right-winger would consider important). Milton Friedman played a leading role in this idealisation of the former UK colony. In his words:

"Take the fifty-year experiment in economic policy provided by Hong Kong between the end of World War II and ... when Hong Kong reverted to China.

"In this experiment, Hong Kong represents the experimental treatment ... I take Britain as one control because Britain, a benevolent dictator, imposed different policies on Hong Kong from the ones it pursued at home ...

"Nonetheless, there are some statistics, and in 1960, the earliest date for which I have been able to get them, the average per capita income in Hong Kong was 28 percent of that in Great Britain; by 1996, it had risen to 137 percent of that in Britain. In short, from 1960 to 1996, Hong Kong's per capita income rose from about one-quarter of Britain's to more than a third larger than Britain's ... I believe that the only plausible explanation for the different rates of growth is socialism in Britain, free enterprise and free markets in Hong Kong. Has anybody got a better explanation? I'd be grateful for any suggestions." [**The Hong Kong Experiment**]

It should be stressed that by "socialism" Friedman meant state spending, particularly that associated with welfare ("Direct government spending is less than 15 percent of national income in Hong Kong, more than 40 percent in the United States." [**Op. Cit.**]). What to make of his claims?

It is undeniable that the figures for Hong Kong's economy are impressive. Per-capita GDP by end 1996 should reach US$ 25,300, one of the highest in Asia and higher than many western nations. Enviable tax rates – 16.5% corporate profits tax, 15% salaries tax. In the first 5 years of the 1990's Hong Kong's economy grew at a tremendous rate – nominal per capita income and GDP levels (where inflation is not factored in) almost doubled. Even accounting for inflation, growth was brisk. The average annual growth rate in real terms of total GDP in the 10 years to 1995 was six per cent, growing by 4.6 per cent in 1995. However, looking more closely, we find a somewhat different picture than that painted by those who claim Hong Kong as an example of the wonders of free market capitalism. Once these basic (and well known) facts are known, it is hard to take Friedman's claims seriously. Of course, there are aspects of laissez-faire to the system (it does not subsidise sunset industries, for example) however, there is much more to Hong Kong that these features. Ultimately, laissez-faire capitalism is more than just low taxes.

The most obvious starting place is the fact that the government owns all the land. To state the obvious, land nationalisation is hardly capitalistic. It is one of the reasons why its direct taxation levels are so low. As one resident points out:

"The main explanation for low tax rates ... is not low social spending. One important factor is that Hong Kong does not have to support a defence industry ... The most crucial explanation ... lies in the fact that less than half of the government's revenue comes from direct taxation.

"The Hong Kong government actually derives much of its revenue from land transactions. The territory's land is technically owned by the government, and the government fills its coffers by selling fifty-year leases to developers (the fact that there are no absolute private property rights to land will come as another surprise to boosters of 'Hong Kong-style' libertarianism) ... The government has an interest in maintaining high property values ... if it is to maintain its policy of low taxation. It does this by carefully controlling the amount of land that is released for sale ... It is, of course, those buying new homes and renting from the private sector who pay the price for this policy. Many Hong Kongers live in third world conditions, and the need to pay astronomical residential property prices is widely viewed as an indirect form of taxation." [Daniel A. Bell, *"Hong Kong's Transition to Capitalism"*, pp. 15-23, **Dissent**, Winter 1998, pp. 15-6]

The ownership of land and the state's role as landlord partly explains the low apparent ratio of state spending to GDP. If the cost of the subsidised housing land were accounted for at market prices in the government budget, the ratio would be significantly higher. As noted, Hong Kong had no need to pay for defence as this cost was borne by the UK taxpayer. Include these government-provided services at their market prices and the famously low share of government spending in GDP climbs sharply.

Luckily for many inhabitants of Hong Kong, the state provides a range of social welfare services in housing, education, health care and social security. The government has a very basic, but comprehensive social welfare system. This started in the 1950s, when the government launched one of the largest public housing schemes in history to house the influx of about 2 million people fleeing Communist China. Hong Kong's social welfare system really started in 1973, when the newly appointed governor *"announced that public housing, education, medical, and social welfare services would be treated as the four pillars of a fair and caring society."* He launched a public housing program and by 1998, 52 percent of the population *"live in subsidised housing, most of whom rent flats from the Housing Authority with rents set at one-fifth the market level (the rest have bought subsidised flats under various home-ownership schemes, with prices discounted 50 percent from those in the private sector)."* Beyond public housing, Hong Kong *"also has most of the standard features of welfare states in Western Europe. There is an excellent public health care system: private hospitals are actually going out of business because clean and efficient public hospitals are well subsidised (the government pays 97 percent of the costs)."* Fortunately for the state, the territory initially had a relatively youthful population compared with western countries which meant it had less need for spending on pensions and help for the aged (this advantage is declining as the population ages). In addition, the *"large majority of primary schools and secondary schools are either free of heavily subsidised, and the territory's tertiary institutions all receive most of their funds from the public coffers."* [Bell, **Op. Cit.**, pp. 16-7 and p. 17] We can be sure that when conservatives and right-"libertarians" use Hong Kong as a model, they are **not** referring to these aspects of the regime.

Given this, Hong Kong has *"deviated from the myth of a laissez-faire economy with the government limiting itself to the role of the 'night watchman'"* as it *"is a welfare state."* In 1995-6, it spent 47 percent of its public expenditure on social services (*"only slightly less than the United Kingdom"*). Between 1992 and 1998, welfare spending increased at a real rate of at least 10 percent annually. [Bell, **Op. Cit.**, p. 16] *"Without doubt,"* two experts note, *"the development of public housing in Hong Kong has contributed greatly to the social well-being of the Territory."* Overall, social welfare *"is the third largest [state] expenditure ... after education and health."* [Simon X. B. Zhao and I. Zhand, *"Economic Growth and Income Inequality in Hong Kong: Trends and Explanations,"* pp. 74-103, **China: An International Journal**, Vol. 3, No. 1, p. 95 and p. 97] Hong Kong spent 11.6% of its GDP on welfare spending in 2004, for example. Moreover, this state intervention is not limited to just social welfare provision. Hong Kong has an affordable public transport system in which the government has substantial equity in most transport systems and grants franchises and monopolised routes. So as well as being the monopoly owner of land and the largest landlord, the state imposes rent controls, operates three railways and regulates transport services and public utilities as monopoly franchises. It subsidises education, health care, welfare and charity. It also took over the ownership and management of several banks in the 1980s to prevent a general bank run. Overall, since the 1960s *"the Hong Kong government's involvement in everyday life has increased steadily and now reaches into many vital areas of socio-economic development."* [Ming K Chan, *"The Legacy of the British Administration of Hong Kong: A View from Hong Kong,"* pp. 567-582, **The China Quarterly**, no. 151, p. 575 and p. 574] It also intervened massively in the stock market during the 1997 Asian crisis. Strangely, Friedman failed to note any of these developments nor point to the lack of competition in many areas of the domestic economy and the high returns given to competition-free utility companies.

The state did not agree to these welfare measures by choice, as they were originally forced upon it by fears of social unrest, first by waves of migrants fleeing from China and then by the need to portray itself as something more than an uncaring colonial regime. However, the other form of intervention it pursued **was** by choice, namely the collusion between the state and business elites. As one expert notes, the *"executive-led 'administrative non-party' state was heavily influenced by the business community"* with *"the composition of various government advisory boards, committees and the three councils"* reflecting this as *"business interests had an overwhelming voice in the consultation machinery (about 70% of the total membership)."* This is accurately described as a *"bureaucratic-cum-corporatist state"* with *"the interests of government and the private sector dominating those of the community."* Overall, *"the government and private sector share common interests and have close links."* [Mae Kam Ng, *"Political Economy and Urban Planning,"* **Progress in Planning**, P. Diamond and B. H. Massan (eds.), vol. 51, Part 1, p. 11 and p. 84] Sizeable fortunes will be made when there are interlocking arrangements between the local oligarchies and the state.

Another commentator notes that the myth of Hong Kong's laissez-faire regime *"has been disproved in academic debates more than a* decade ago" and points to "the hypocrisy of laissez-faire colonialism" which is marked by "a government which is actively involved, fully engaged and often interventionist, whether by design or necessity." He notes that "the most damaging legacy [of colonial rule] was the blatantly pro-business bias in the government's decision-making." There has been "collusion between the colonial officialdom and the British economic elites." Indeed, "the colonial regime has been at fault for its subservience to business interests as manifested in its unwillingness until very recently, not because of laissez-faire but from its pro-business bias, to legislate against cartels and monopolies and to regulate economic activities in the interests of labour, consumers and the environment ... In other words, free trade and free enterprise with an open market ... did not always mean fair trade and equal opportunity: the regime intervened to favour British and big business interests at the expense of both fair play and of a level playing field for all economic players regardless of class or race." [Ming K Chan, "The Legacy of the British Administration of Hong Kong: A View from Hong Kong," pp. 567-582, **The China Quarterly**, no. 151, p. 577, p. 576, p. 575 and pp. 575-6] Bell notes that a British corporation "held the local telephone monopoly until 1995" while another "holds all the landing rights at Hong Kong airport." [**Op. Cit.**, p. 21]

Unsurprisingly, as it owns all the land, the government has "a strong position in commanding resources to direct spatial development in the territory." There is a "three-tiered system of land-use plans." The top-level, for example, "maps out the overall land development strategy to meet the long-term socio-economic needs of Hong Kong" and it is "prepared and reviewed by the administration and there is no public input to it." This planning system is, as noted, heavily influenced by the business sector and its "committees operate largely behind closed doors and policy formulation could be likened to a black-box operation." "Traditionally," Ng notes, "the closed door and Hong Kong centred urban planning system had served to maintain economic dynamism in the colony. With democratisation introduced in the 1980s, the planning system is forced to be more open and to serve not just economic interests." [Mae Kam Ng, **Op. Cit.**, p. 11, p. 39, p. 37 and p. 13] As Chan stresses, "the colonial government has continuously played a direct and crucial role as a very significant economic participant. Besides its control of valuable resources, the regime's command of the relevant legal, political and social institutions and processes also indirectly shapes economic behaviour and societal development." [**Op. Cit.**, p. 574]

Overall, as Bell notes, "one cannot help but notice the large gap between this reality and the myth of an open and competitive market where only talent and luck determine the economic winners." [**Op. Cit.**, p. 16] As an expert in the Asian Tiger economies summarises:

> "to conclude ... that Hong Kong is close to a free market economy is misleading ... Not only is the economy managed from outside the formal institutions of government by the informal coalition of peak private economic organisations, but government itself also has available some unusual instruments for influencing industrial activity. It owns all the land ... It controls rents in part of the public housing market and supplies subsidised public housing to roughly

half the population, thereby helping to keep down the cost of labour. And its ability to increase or decrease the flow of immigrants from China also gives it a way of affecting labour costs." [Robert Wade, **Governing the Market**, p. 332]

This means that the Hong Kong system of "laissez-faire" is marked by the state having close ties with the major banks and trading companies, which, in turn, are closely linked to the life-time expatriates who largely run the government. This provides a "point of concentration" to conduct negotiations in line with an implicit development strategy. Therefore it is pretty clear that Hong Kong does not really show the benefits of "free market" capitalism. Wade indicates that we can consider Hong Kong as a "special case or as a less successful variant of the authoritarian-capitalist state." [**Op. Cit.**, p. 333]

There are other explanations for Hong Kong's high growth rates than simply "capitalism." Firstly, Hong Kong is a city state and cities have a higher economic growth rate than regions (which are held back by large rural areas). This is because the agricultural sector rarely achieves high economic growth rates and so in its absence a high growth rate is easier to achieve. Secondly, there is Hong Kong's location and its corresponding role as an entrepôt economy. Wade notes that "its economic growth is a function of its service role in a wider regional economy, as entrepôt trader, regional headquarters for multinational companies, and refuge for nervous money." [**Op. Cit.**, p. 331] Being between China and the rest of the world means its traders could act as a middleman, earning income from the mark-up they could impose on goods going through the territory. This is why Hong Kong is often referred to as an entrepôt economy, a place that imports, stores, and re-exports goods. In other words, Hong Kong made a lot of its money because many Chinese exports and imports went through it and its traders marked-up the prices. It should be obvious if most of Western Europe's goods went through, say, Liverpool, that city would have a very good economic performance regardless of other factors. This option is hardly available to most cities, never mind countries.

Then there is the issue of state ownership of land. As Mae Kam Ng reports, monopoly ownership of all land by the state sets the context for super-profits by government and finance capital generally. [**Op. Cit.**, p. 13] Unsurprisingly, most government land "is sold to just three real-estate developers" who "sit on huge tracts of land, drop-feeding apartments onto the market so as to maintain high property prices." Between 1992 and 1996, for example, prices increased fourfold and profits doubled. The heads of two of the property firms were on the list of the world's ten richest men in 1998. "Meanwhile, potential new entrants to the market are restricted by the huge cost of paying land-conversion premiums that are the bedrock of government revenues." This is a "cosy arrangement between the government and major developers." [Daniel A. Bell, **Op. Cit.**, p. 16]

The role as headquarters for companies and as a financial centre also plays a part. It means an essential part of its success is that it gets surplus value produced elsewhere in the world. Handling other people's money is a sure-fire way of getting rich and this will have a nice impact on per-capita income figures (as will selling goods produced in sweat-shops in dictatorships like China). There has been a gradual shift in economic direction to a more service-oriented economy which has stamped Hong Kong as one of the world's foremost financial centres. This highly developed sector is served by some 565 banks and deposit-taking companies from over 40 countries, including 85 of the world's top 100 in terms of assets. In addition, it is the 8th largest stock market in the world (in terms of capitalisation) and the 2nd largest in Asia. By 1995, Hong Kong was the world's 10th largest exporter of services with the industry embracing everything from accounting and legal services, insurance and maritime to telecommunications and media. The contribution of the services sectors as a whole to GDP increased from 60 per cent in 1970 to 83 per cent in 1994.

Meanwhile, manufacturing industry has moved to low wage countries such as southern China (by the end of the 1970's, Hong Kong's manufacturing base was less competitive, facing increasing costs in land and labour – in other words, workers were starting to benefit from economic growth and so capital moved elsewhere). The economic reforms introduced by Deng Xiaoping in southern China in 1978 were important, as this allowed capital access to labour living under a dictatorship (just as American capitalists invested heavily in Nazi Germany – labour rights were null, profits were high). It is estimated about 42,000 enterprises in the province have Hong Kong participation and 4,000,000 workers (nine times larger than the territory's own manufacturing workforce) are now directly or indirectly employed by Hong Kong companies. In the late 1980's Hong Kong trading and manufacturing companies began to expand further a field than just southern China. By the mid 1990's they were operating across Asia, in Eastern Europe and Central America. This shift, incidentally, has resulted in deindustrialisation and a *"decrease in real income among manual workers"* as they moved to the lower end service sector. [Simon X. B. Zhao and I. Zhand, **Op. Cit.**, p. 88]Then there is the criteria Friedman uses, namely per-capita GDP. As we have repeatedly stressed, averages hide a lot of important and relevant information when evaluating a society. So it must be stressed that Friedman's criteria of per capita income is an average and, as such, hides the effect of inequality. This means that a society with huge numbers of poor people and a handful of ultra-rich individuals may have a higher average income than a more equal society. This is the case of, say, America compared to Sweden. Unsurprisingly, Hong Kong is a very unequal society and this inequality is growing (so his claim that Hong Kong is capitalist refutes his 1962 assertion that the more capitalist economies are more equal). *"Behind the impressive GDP figures,"* indicates Chan, *"is a widening income gap between the super-rich and the grassroots, with 650,000 people reportedly living below the poverty line."* [**Op. Cit.**, p. 576] As Bell points out, 13% lived below the poverty line in 1999, compared to 8% in 1971. This is partly explained by *"the rising proportion of elderly people and single-parent families."* However, economic integration with China has played a role as Hong Kong's manufacturing sector *"has been almost entirely transferred to the southern province of Guangdong (where labour is cheaper and workers' rights are practically non-existent), with the consequence that Hong Kong's industrial workers now find it much harder to find decent jobs in Hong Kong. Most end up working in low-paying service jobs without much hope of upward mobility."* [**Op. Cit.**, pp. 21-2]

As other experts note, while Hong Kong may have a GDP-per-capita of a developed nation, its distribution of household income was similar to that of Guatemala. Looking at the 1960s onwards, income distribution only improved between 1966 and 1971, after this period the share of the bottom 30% of the population went down continuously while the top 20% saw an increase in their share of total income. In fact, from the 1980s, *"the top 20% of households managed to account for over 50 per cent of the total income."* In fact, the bottom 60% of the population saw a decline in their share of income between 1971 and 1996. Overall, *"high-income households increased their wealth progressively faster than low-income households."* This polarisation, they argue, will continue as the economy de-industrialises: *"in the absence of proper social policies, it will generate a small, extremely wealthy class of the 'new rich' and simultaneously a large population of the 'working poor.'"* [Simon X. B. Zhao and L. Zhand, **Op. Cit.**, p. 85, p. 80, p. 82, p. 84 and p. 102]

Given that everywhere cannot be such a service provider, it does not provide much of an indication of how "free market" capitalism would work in, say, the United States. And as there is in fact extensive (if informal) economic management and that the state owns all the land and subsidies rent and health care, how can it be even considered an example of "free market" capitalism in action? Unless, of course, you consider that "economic freedom" best flourishes under a dictatorship which owns all the land, which has close links to business interests, provides a comprehensive, if basic, welfare state and is dependent on another country to provide its defence needs and the head of its executive. While most American's would be envious of Hong Kong's welfare state, it is doubtful that many would consider its other features as desirable. How many would be happy with being under a *"benevolent dictator"* (perhaps being turned into a colony of Britain again?) whose appointed government works closely with the local business elite? Having a political regime in which the wealthy can influence the government without the need for elections may be considered too a high price to pay just to get subsidised housing, health care and education. Given a choice between freedom and a high rate of growth, how many would pick the latter over the former?

It is no coincidence that like most examples of the wonders of the free market, Hong Kong was not a democracy. It was a relatively liberal colonial dictatorship. But political liberty does not rate highly with many supporters of laissez-faire capitalism (such as right-"libertarians", for example). However, the two are linked. Which explains why we have spent so much time debunking the "free market" capitalism claims over Hong Kong. It is more than simply a concern over basic facts and correcting inaccurate assertions. Rather it is a concern over the meaning of freedom and the dubious assumption that freedom can be compartmentalised. While Hong Kong may be a more appealing example that Pinochet's Chile, it still rests on the assumption that the masses should be excluded from having a say over their communities (in their own interests, of course, and **never,** of course, in the interests of those who do the excluding) and that freedom is simply the ability to change bosses (or become one yourself). Ultimately, there is a big difference between "free" and "business-friendly." Hong Kong is the latter simply because it is not the former. Its success is testament that dictatorships can be more reliable defenders of class privilege than democracies.

This can be seen from the attitude of Hong Kong's business elite to the democratic reforms introduced in the 1990s and integration with China. Significantly, *"the nominally socialist Chinese government consistently opposed the introduction of further social welfare programs in Hong Kong."* This is because *"it has chosen to enter into a strategic alliance with Hong Kong's business class"* (*"To earn support of corporate bosses, the Chinese government organised timely interventions on behalf of Hong Kong companies"*). Unsurprisingly, the first Beijing-appointed executive was made up of successful business men and one of its first acts was to suspend pro-labour laws passed by the out-going legislature. [Bell, **Op. Cit.**, p. 17, p. 18 and pp. 19-20] The Chinese government opposed attempts to extend democracy, imposing a complex electoral system which, in the words of the **Asian Wall Street Journal**, was a *"means of reducing public participation in the political process while stacking the next legislature with people who depend on favours from the regime in Hong Kong or Beijing and answer to narrow special interests, particularly the business elite."* [quoted by Bell, **Op. Cit.**, pp. 18-9]

This reflects the fact that business tycoons are worried that democracy would lead to increased welfare spending with one, for example, predicting that the *"under-educated, and those who did not pay tax would elect candidates who stood for more social spending, which would turn Hong Kong into a 'welfare state' … If we had a 100-per-cent directly elected LegCo, only social welfare-oriented candidates will be elected. Hong Kong is a business city and we [sic!] do not want to end up being a social welfare state."* [*"Tycoon warns on protests,"* **The Standard**, 29 April 2004] Such a government can ignore public opinion and the electorate more than in an independent democracy and, of course, can be more influenced by business (as the history of Hong Kong testifies).

Overall, it is fair to say that Friedman only saw what he wanted to see and contrasted his idealised vision with Britain and explained the divergent economic performances of both countries to a conflict between "socialism" and "capitalism." How he failed to notice that the reality of Hong Kong was one marked by collusion between big business and the state and that in key areas the regime was much more "socialist" than its British counterpart is difficult to understand given his willingness to use it as an example. It seems intellectually dishonest to fail to mention that the state owned all the land and was the biggest landlord with at least 50% of the population living in subsidised housing. Then there are the facts of almost free medical treatment at government clinics and hospitals and an education system almost entirely funded by the government. These are all massive interventions in the marketplace, interventions Friedman spent many decades fighting in the USA. He did, however, contribute to the myth that the British were benign imperialists and the "free market" they introduced into Hong Kong was in the interests of all rather than for those who exercised the dictatorship.

Section D
How do statism and capitalism affect society?

Section D – How do statism and capitalism affect society? 360

D.1 Why does state intervention occur? 361
D.1.1 Does state intervention cause the problems to begin with? 364
D.1.2 Is state intervention the result of democracy? 366
D.1.3 Is state intervention socialistic? 369
D.1.4 Is laissez-faire capitalism actually without state intervention? 371
D.1.5 Do anarchists support state intervention? 372

D.2 What influence does wealth have over politics? 375
D.2.1 Is capital flight really that powerful? 377
D.2.2 How extensive is business propaganda? 378

D.3 How does wealth influence the mass media? 380
D.3.1 How does the structure of the media affect its content? 381
D.3.2 What is the effect of advertising on the mass media? 382
D.3.3 Why do the media rely on government and business "experts" for information? 382
D.3.4 How is "flak" used as a means of disciplining the media? 383
D.3.5 Why is "anticommunism" used as control mechanism? 384
D.3.6 Isn't the "propaganda model" a conspiracy theory? 385
D.3.7 Isn't the model contradicted by the media reporting government and business failures? 385

D.4 What is the relationship between capitalism and the ecological crisis? 386

D.5 What causes imperialism? 388
D.5.1 How has imperialism changed over time? 391
D.5.2 Is imperialism just a product of private capitalism? 395
D.5.3 Does globalisation mean the end of imperialism? 398
D.5.4 What is the relationship between imperialism and the social classes within capitalism? 401

D.6 Are anarchists against Nationalism? 403

D.7 Are anarchists opposed to National Liberation struggles? 405

D.8 What causes militarism and what are its effects? 408

D.9 Why does political power become concentrated under capitalism? 411
D.9.1 What is the relationship between wealth polarisation and authoritarian government? 414
D.9.2 Why is government surveillance of citizens on the increase? 416
D.9.3 What causes justifications for racism to appear? 417

D.10 How does capitalism affect technology? 419

D.11 Can politics and economics be separated from each other? 424
D.11.1 What does Chile tell us about the right and its vision of liberty? 426
D.11.2 But surely Chile proves that "economic freedom" creates political freedom? 428

Section D
How does statism and capitalism affect society?

This section of the FAQ indicates how both statism and capitalism affect the society they exist in. It is a continuation of sections B (Why do anarchists oppose the current system?) and C (What are the myths of capitalist economics?) and it discusses the impact of the underlying social and power relationships within the current system on society.

This section is important because the institutions and social relationships capitalism and statism spawn do not exist in a social vacuum, they have deep impacts on our everyday lives. These effects go beyond us as individuals (for example, the negative effects of hierarchy on our individuality) and have an effect on how the political institutions in our society work, how technology develops, how the media operates and so on. As such, it is worthwhile to point out how (and why) statism and capitalism affect society as a whole outwith the narrow bounds of politics and economics.

So here we sketch some of the impact concentrations of political and economic power have upon society. While many people attack the *results* of these processes (like specific forms of state intervention, ecological destruction, imperialism, etc.) they usually ignore their *causes.* This means that the struggle against social evils will be never-ending, like a doctor fighting the symptoms of a disease without treating the disease itself or the conditions which create it in the first place. We have indicated the roots of the problems we face in earlier sections; now we discuss how these impact on other aspects of our society. This section of the FAQ explores the interactions of the causes and results and draws out how the authoritarian and exploitative nature of capitalism and the state affects the world we live in.

It is important to remember that most supporters of capitalism refuse to do this. Yes, some of them point out **some** flaws and problems within society but they never relate them to the system as such. As Noam Chomsky points out, they *"ignor[e] the catastrophes of capitalism or, on the rare occasions when some problem is noticed, attribut[e] them to any cause **other** than the system that consistently brings them about."* [**Deterring Democracy**, p. 232] Thus we have people, say, attacking imperialist adventures while, at the same time, supporting the capitalist system which drives it. Or opposing state intervention in the name of "freedom" while supporting an economic system which by its working forces the state to intervene simply to keep it going and society together. The contradictions multiply, simply because the symptoms are addressed, never the roots of the problems.

That the system and its effects are interwoven can best be seen from the fact that while right-wing parties have been elected to office promising to reduce the role of the state in society, the actual size and activity of the state has not been reduced, indeed it has usually increased in scope (both in size and in terms of power and centralisation). This is unsurprising, as "free market" implies a strong (and centralised) state – the "freedom" of management to

manage means that the freedom of workers to resist authoritarian management structures must be weakened by state action. Thus, ironically, state intervention within society will continue to be needed in order to ensure that society survives the rigours of market forces and that elite power and privilege are protected from the masses.

The thing to remember is that the political and economic spheres are not independent. They interact in many ways, with economic forces prompting political reactions and changes, and vice versa. Overall, as Kropotkin stressed, there are *"intimate links ... between the political regime and the economic regime."* [**Words of a Rebel**, p. 118]

These means that it is impossible to talk of, say, capitalism as if it could exist without shaping and being shaped by the state and society. Equally, to think that the state could intervene as it pleased in the economy fails to take into account the influence economic institutions and forces have on it. This has always been the case, as the state *"is a hybridisation of political and social institutions, of coercive with distributive functions, of highly punitive with regulatory procedures, and finally of class with administrative needs – this melding process has produced very real ideological and practical paradoxes that persist as major issues today."* [Bookchin, **The Ecology of Freedom**, p. 196] These paradoxes can only be solved, anarchists argue, by abolishing the state and the social hierarchies it either creates (the state bureaucracy) or defends (the economically dominant class). Until then, reforms of the system will be incomplete, be subject to reversals and have unintended consequences.

These links and interaction between statism and capitalism are to be expected due to their similar nature. As anarchists have long argued, at root they are based on the same hierarchical principle. Proudhon, for example, regarded *"the capitalist principle"* and *"the governmental principle"* as *"one and the same principle ... abolition of the exploitation of man by man and the abolition of the government of man by man, are one and the same formula."* [quoted by Wayne Thorpe, **"The Workers Themselves"**, p. 279] This means that anarchists reject the notion that political reforms are enough in themselves and instead stress that they must be linked to (or, at least, take into account) economic change. This means, for example, while we oppose specific imperialist wars and occupation, we recognise that they will reoccur until such time as the economic forces which generate them are abolished. Similarly, we do not automatically think all attempts to reduce state intervention should be supported simply because they appear to reduce the state. Instead, we consider who is introducing the reforms, why they are doing so and what the results will be. If the "reforms" are simply a case of politicians redirecting state intervention away from the welfare state to bolster capitalist power and profits, we would not support the change. Anarchist opposition to neo-liberalism flows from our awareness of the existence of economic and social power and inequality and its impact on society and the political structure.

In some ways, this section discusses class struggle **from above**, i.e. the attacks on the working class conducted by the ruling class by means of its state. While it appears that every generation has someone insisting that the "class war" is dead and/or obsolete (Tony Blair did just that in the late 1990s), what they mean is that class struggle **from below** is dead (or, at least, they wish it so). What is ignored is that the class struggle from above continues even if class struggle from below appears to have disappeared (until it reappears in yet another form). This should be unsurprising as any ruling class will be seeking to extend its profits, powers and privileges, a task aided immensely by the reduced pressure from below associated with periods of apparent social calm (Blair's activities in office being a striking confirmation of this). Ultimately, while you may seek to ignore capitalism and the state, neither will ignore you. That this produces resistance should be obvious, as is the fact that demise of struggle from below have always been proven wrong.

By necessity, this section will not (indeed, cannot) cover all aspects of how statism and capitalism interact to shape both the society we live in and ourselves as individuals. We will simply sketch the forces at work in certain important aspects of the current system and how anarchists view them. Thus our discussion of imperialism, for example, will not get into the details of specific wars and interventions but rather give a broad picture of why they happen and why they have changed over the years. However, we hope to present enough detail for further investigation as well as an understanding of how anarchists analyse the current system based on our anti-authoritarian principles and how the political and economic aspects of capitalism interact.

D.1

Why does state intervention occur?

The most obvious interaction between statism and capitalism is when the state intervenes in the economy. Indeed, the full range of capitalist politics is expressed in how much someone thinks this should happen. At one extreme, there are the right-wing liberals (sometimes mistakenly called "libertarians") who seek to reduce the state to a defender of private property rights. At the other, there are those who seek the state to assume full ownership and control of the economy (i.e. state capitalists who are usually mistakenly called "socialists"). In practice, the level of state intervention lies between these two extremes, moving back and forth along the spectrum as necessity requires.

For anarchists, capitalism as an economy requires state intervention. There is, and cannot be, a capitalist economy which does not exhibit some form of state action within it. The state is forced to intervene in society for three reasons:

(1) To bolster the power of capital as a whole within society.

(2) To benefit certain sections of the capitalist class against others.

(3) To counteract the anti-social effects of capitalism.

From our discussion of the state and its role in section B.2, the first two reasons are unexpected and straight forward. The state is an instrument of class rule and, as such, acts to favour the continuation of the system as a whole. The state, therefore, has always intervened in the capitalist economy, usually to distort the market in favour of the capitalist class within its borders as against

the working class and foreign competitors. This is done by means of taxes, tariffs, subsidies and so forth.

State intervention has been a feature of capitalism from the start. As Kropotkin argued, *"nowhere has the system of 'non-intervention of the State' ever existed. Everywhere the State has been, and still is, the main pillar and the creator, direct and indirect, of Capitalism and its powers over the masses. Nowhere, since States have grown up, have the masses had the freedom of resisting the oppression by capitalists ... The state has **always** interfered in the economic life in favour of the capitalist exploiter. It has always granted him protection in robbery, given aid and support for further enrichment. **And it could not be otherwise.** To do so was one of the functions – the chief mission – of the State."* [**Evolution and Environment**, pp. 97-8]

In addition to this role, the state has also regulated certain industries and, at times, directly involved itself in employing wage labour to product goods and services. The classic example of the latter is the construction and maintenance of a transport network in order to facilitate the physical circulation of goods. As Colin Ward noted, transport *"is an activity heavily regulated by government. This regulation was introduced, not in the interests of the commercial transport operators, but in the face of their intense opposition, as well as that of the ideologists of 'free' enterprise."* He gives the example of the railways, which were *"built at a time when it was believed that market forces would reward the good and useful and eliminate the bad or socially useless."* However, *"it was found necessary as early as 1840 for the government's Board of Trade to regulate and supervise them, simply for the protection of the public."* [**Freedom to Go**, p. 7 and pp. 7-8]

This sort of intervention was to ensure that no one capitalist or group of capitalists had a virtual monopoly over the others which would allow them to charge excessive prices. Thus the need to bolster capital as a whole may involve regulating or expropriating certain capitalists and sections of that class. Also, state ownership was and is a key means of rationalising production methods, either directly by state ownership or indirectly by paying for Research and Development. That certain sections of the ruling class may seek advantages over others by control of the state is, likewise, a truism.

All in all, the idea that capitalism is a system without state intervention is a myth. The rich use the state to bolster their wealth and power, as would be expected. Yet even if such a thing as a truly "laissez-faire" capitalist state were possible, it would still be protecting capitalist property rights and the hierarchical social relations these produce against those subject to them. This means, as Kropotkin stressed, it *"has never practised"* the idea of laissez faire. In fact, *"while all Governments have given the capitalists and monopolists full liberty to enrich themselves with the underpaid labour of working men [and women] ... they have **never, nowhere** given the working [people] the liberty of opposing that exploitation. Never has any Government applied the 'leave things alone' principle to the exploited masses. It reserved it for the exploiters only."* [**Op. Cit.**, p. 96] As such, under pure "free market" capitalism state intervention would still exist but it would be limited to repressing the working class (see section D.1.4 for more discussion).

Then there is the last reason, namely counteracting the destructive effects of capitalism itself. As Chomsky puts it, *"in a predatory capitalist economy, state intervention would be an absolute necessity to preserve human existence and to prevent the destruction of the physical environment – I speak optimistically … social protection … [is] therefore a minimal necessity to constrain the irrational and destructive workings of the classical free market."* [**Chomsky on Anarchism**, p. 111] This kind of intervention is required simply because *"government cannot want society to break up, for it would mean that it and the dominant class would be deprived of sources of exploitation; nor can it leave society to maintain itself without official intervention, for then people would soon realise that government serves only to defend property owners … and they would hasten to rid themselves of both."* [Malatesta, **Anarchy**, p. 25]

So while many ideologues of capitalism thunder against state intervention (for the benefit of the masses), the fact is that capitalism itself produces the need for such intervention. The abstractly individualistic theory on which capitalism is based ("everyone for themselves") results in a high degree of statism since the economic system itself contains no means to combat its own socially destructive workings. The state must also intervene in the economy, not only to protect the interests of the ruling class but also to protect society from the atomising and destructive impact of capitalism. Moreover, capitalism has an inherent tendency toward periodic recessions or depressions, and the attempt to prevent them has become part of the state's function. However, since preventing them is impossible (they are built into the system – see section C.7), in practice the state can only try to postpone them and ameliorate their severity. Let's begin with the need for social intervention.

Capitalism is based on turning both labour and land into commodities. As socialist Karl Polanyi points out, however, *"labour and land are no other than the human beings themselves of which every society consists and the natural surroundings in which it exists; to include labour and land in the market mechanism means to subordinate the substance of society itself to the laws of the market."* And this means that *"human society has become an accessory to the economic system,"* with humanity placing itself fully in the hands of supply and demand. But such a situation *"could not exist for any length of time without annihilating the human and natural substance of society; it would have physically destroyed man and transformed his surroundings into a wilderness."* This, inevitably, provokes a reaction in order to defend the basis of society and the environment that capitalism needs, but ruthlessly exploits. As Polanyi summarises, *"the countermove against economic liberalism and laissez-faire possessed all the unmistakable characteristics of a spontaneous reaction … [A] closely similar change from laissez-faire to 'collectivism' took place in various countries at a definite stage of their industrial development, pointing to the depth and independence of the underlying causes of the process."* [**The Great Transformation**, p. 71, pp. 41-42 and pp. 149-150]

To expect that a community would remain indifferent to the scourge of unemployment, dangerous working conditions, 16-hour working days, the shifting of industries and occupations, and the moral and psychological disruption accompanying them – merely because economic effects, in the long run, might be better – is an absurdity. Similarly, for workers to remain indifferent to, for example, poor working conditions, peacefully waiting for a new boss to offer them

better conditions, or for citizens to wait passively for capitalists to start voluntarily acting responsibly toward the environment, is to assume a servile and apathetic role for humanity. Luckily, labour refuses to be a commodity and citizens refuse to stand idly by while the planet's ecosystems are destroyed.

In other words, the state and many of its various policies are not imposed from outside of the capitalist system. It is not some alien body but rather has evolved in response to clear failings within capitalism itself (either from the perspective of the ruling elite or from the general population). It contrast, as the likes of von Hayek did, to the "spontaneous" order of the market versus a "designed" order associated with state fails to understand that the latter can come about in response to the former. In other words, as Polanyi noted, state intervention can be a *"spontaneous reaction"* and so be a product of social evolution itself. While the notion of a spontaneous order may be useful to attack undesired forms of state intervention (usually social welfare, in the case of von Hayek), it fails to note this process at work nor the fact that the state itself played a key role in the creation of capitalism in the first place as well as specifying the rules for the operation and so evolution of the market itself.

Therefore state intervention occurs as a form of protection against the workings of the market. As capitalism is based on atomising society in the name of "freedom" on the competitive market, it is hardly surprising that defence against the anti-social workings of the market should take statist forms – there being few other structures capable of providing such defence (as such social institutions have been undermined, if not crushed, by the rise of capitalism in the first place). Thus, ironically, "individualism" produces a "collectivist" tendency within society as capitalism destroys communal forms of social organisation in favour of ones based on abstract individualism, authority, and hierarchy – all qualities embodied in the state, the sole remaining agent of collective action in the capitalist worldview. Strangely, conservatives and other right-wingers fail to see this, instead spouting on about "traditional values" while, at the same time, glorifying the "free market." This is one of the (many) ironic aspects of free market dogma, namely that it is often supported by people who are at the forefront of attacking the **effects** of it. Thus we see conservatives bemoaning the breakdown of traditional values while, at the same time, advocating the economic system whose operation weakens family life, breaks up communities, undermines social bonds and places individual gain above all else, particularly "traditional values" and "community." They seem blissfully unaware that capitalism destroys the traditions they claim to support and recognises only monetary values.

In addition to social protection, state intervention is required to protect a country's economy (and so the economic interests of the ruling class). As Noam Chomsky points out, even the USA, home of "free enterprise," was marked by *"large-scale intervention in the economy after independence, and conquest of resources and markets … [while] a centralised developmental state [was constructed] committed to [the] creation and entrenchment of domestic manufacture and commerce, subsidising local production and barring cheaper British imports, constructing a legal basis for private corporate power, and in numerous other ways providing an escape from the stranglehold of comparative advantage."* [**World Orders, Old and New**, p. 114] State intervention is as natural to capitalism as wage labour.

In the case of Britain and a host of other countries (and more recently in the cases of Japan and the Newly Industrialising Countries of the Far East, like Korea) state intervention was the key to development and success in the "free market." (see, for example, Robert Wade's **Governing the Market**). In other "developing" countries which have had the misfortune to be subjected to "free-market reforms" (e.g. neo-liberal Structural Adjustment Programs) rather than following the interventionist Japanese and Korean models, the results have been devastating for the vast majority, with drastic increases in poverty, homelessness, malnutrition, etc. (for the elite, the results are somewhat different of course). In the nineteenth century, states only turned to laissez-faire once they could benefit from it and had a strong enough economy to survive it: *"Only in the mid-nineteenth century, when it had become powerful enough to overcome any competition, did England [sic!] embrace free trade."* [Chomsky, **Op. Cit.**, p. 115] Before this, protectionism and other methods were used to nurture economic development. And once laissez-faire started to undermine a country's economy, it was quickly revoked. For example, protectionism is often used to protect a fragile economy and militarism has always been a favourite way for the ruling elite to help the economy, as is still the case, for example, in the "Pentagon System" in the USA (see section D.8). Therefore, contrary to conventional wisdom, state intervention will always be associated with capitalism due to: (1) its authoritarian nature; (2) its inability to prevent the anti-social results of the competitive market; (3) its fallacious assumption that society should be *"an accessory to the economic system"*; (4) the class interests of the ruling elite; and (5) the need to impose its authoritarian social relationships upon an unwilling population in the first place. Thus the contradictions of capitalism necessitate government intervention. The more the economy grows, the greater become the contradictions and the greater the contradictions, the greater the need for state intervention. The development of capitalism as a system provides amble empirical support for this theoretical assessment.

Part of the problem is that the assumption that "pure" capitalism does not need the state is shared by both Marxists and supporters of capitalism. *"So long as capital is still weak,"* Marx wrote, *"it supports itself by leaning on the crutches of past, or disappearing, modes of production. As soon as it begins to feel itself strong, it throws away these crutches and moves about in accordance with its own laws of motion. But as soon as it begins to feel itself as a hindrance to further development and is recognised as such, it adapts forms of behaviour through the harnessing of competition which seemingly indicate its absolute rule but actually point to its decay and dissolution."* [quoted by Paul Mattick, **Marx and Keynes**, p. 96] Council Communist Paul Mattick comments that a *"healthy"* capitalism *"is a strictly competitive capitalism, and the imperfections of competition in the early and late stages of its development must be regarded as the ailments of an infantile and of a senile capitalism. For a capitalism which restricts competition cannot find its indirect 'regulation' in the price and market movements which derive from the value relations in the production process."* [**Op. Cit.**, p. 97] However, this gives capitalism far too much credit – as well as ignoring how far the reality of that system

is from the theory. State intervention has always been a constant aspect of economic life under capitalism. Its limited attempts at laissez-faire have always been failures, resulting in a return to its statist roots. The process of selective laissez-faire and collectivism has been as much a feature of capitalism in the past as it is now. Indeed, as Noam Chomsky argues, *"[w]hat is called 'capitalism' is basically a system of corporate mercantilism, with huge and largely unaccountable private tyrannies exercising vast control over the economy, political systems, and social and cultural life, operating in close co-operation with powerful states that intervene massively in the domestic economy and international society. That is dramatically true of the United States, contrary to much illusion. The rich and privileged are no more willing to face market discipline than they have been in the past, though they consider it just fine for the general population."* [**Marxism, Anarchism, and Alternative Futures**, p. 784] As Kropotkin put it:

> *"What, then is the use of talking, with Marx, about the 'primitive accumulation' – as if this 'push' given to capitalists were a thing of the past? ... In short, nowhere has the system of 'non-intervention of the State' ever existed ... Nowhere, since States have grown up, have the masses had the freedom of resisting the oppression by capitalists. The few rights they have now they have gained only by determination and endless sacrifice.*
>
> *"To speak therefore of 'non-intervention of the State' may be all right for middle-class economists, who try to persuade the workers that their misery is 'a law of Nature.' But – how can Socialists use such language?"* [**Op. Cit.**, pp. 97-8]

In other words, while Marx was right to note that the *"silent compulsion of economic relations sets the seal on the domination of the capitalist over the worker"* he was wrong to state that *"[d]irect extra-economic force is still of course used, but only in exceptional cases."* The ruling class rarely lives up to its own rhetoric and while *"rely[ing] on his [the workers'] dependence on capital"* it always supplements that with state intervention. As such, Marx was wrong to state it was *"otherwise during the historical genesis of capitalist production."* It is not only the *"rising bourgeoisie"* which *"needs the power of the state"* nor is it just *"an essential aspect of so-called primitive accumulation."* [**Capital**, vol. 1, pp. 899-900]

The enthusiasm for the "free market" since the 1970s is in fact the product of the extended boom, which in turn was a product of a state co-ordinated war economy and highly interventionist Keynesian economics (a boom that the apologists of capitalism use, ironically, as "evidence" that "capitalism" works) plus an unhealthy dose of nostalgia for a past that never existed. It's strange how a system that has never existed has produced so much! When the Keynesian system went into crisis, the ideologues of "free market" capitalism seized their chance and found many in the ruling class willing to utilise their rhetoric to reduce or end those aspects of state intervention which benefited the many or inconvenienced themselves. However, state intervention, while reduced, did not end. It simply became more focused in the interests of the elite (i.e. the natural order). As Chomsky stresses, the "minimal state" rhetoric of the capitalists is a lie, for they will *"never get rid of the state because they need it for their own purposes, but they love to use this as an ideological weapon against everyone else."* They are *"not going to survive without a massive state subsidy, so they want a powerful state."* [**Chomsky on Anarchism**, p. 215]

And neither should it be forgotten that state intervention was required to create the "free" market in the first place. To quote Polanyi again, *"[f]or as long as [the market] system is not established, economic liberals must and will unhesitatingly call for the intervention of the state in order to establish it, and once established, in order to maintain it."* [**Op. Cit.**, p. 149] Protectionism and subsidy (mercantilism) – along with the liberal use of state violence against the working class – was required to create and protect capitalism and industry in the first place (see section F.8 for details).

In short, although laissez-faire may be the ideological basis of capitalism – the religion that justifies the system – it has rarely if ever been actually practised. So, while the ideologues are praising "free enterprise" as the fountainhead of modern prosperity, the corporations and companies are gorging at the table of the State. As such, it would be wrong to suggest that anarchists are somehow "in favour" of state intervention. This is not true. We are "in favour" of reality, not ideology. The reality of capitalism is that it needs state intervention to be created and needs state intervention to continue (both to secure the exploitation of labour and to protect society from the effects of the market system). That we have no truck with the myths of "free market" economics does not mean we "support" state intervention beyond recognising it as a fact of a system we want to end and that some forms of state intervention are better than others.

D.1.1 Does state intervention cause the problems to begin with?

It depends. In the case of state intervention on behalf of the ruling class, the answer is always yes! However, in terms of social intervention the answer is usually no.

However, for classical liberals (or, as we would call them today, neo-liberals, right-wing "libertarians" or "conservatives"), state intervention is the root of all evil. It is difficult for anarchists to take such argument that seriously. Firstly, it is easily concluded from their arguments that they are only opposed to state intervention on behalf of the working class (i.e. the welfare state or legal support for trade unionism). They either ignore or downplay state intervention on behalf of the ruling class (a few **do** consistently oppose all state intervention beyond that required to defend private property, but these unsurprisingly have little influence beyond appropriation of some rhetoric and arguments by those seeking to bolster the ruling elite). So most of the right attack the social or regulatory activities of the government, but fail to attack those bureaucratic activities (like defence, protection of property) which they agree with. As such, their arguments are so selective as to be little more than self-serving special pleading. Secondly, it does appear that their concern for social problems is limited simply to their utility for attacking those aspects of state intervention which claim to

help those most harmed by the current system. They usually show greater compassion for the welfare of the elite and industry than for the working class. For the former, they are in favour of state aid, for the latter the benefits of economic growth is all that counts.

So what to make of claims that it is precisely the state's interference with the market which causes the problems that society blames on the market? For anarchists, such a position is illogical, for *"whoever says regulation says limitation: now, how to conceive of limiting privilege before it existed?"* It *"would be an effect without a cause"* and so *"regulation was a corrective to privilege"* and not vice versa. *"In logic as well as in history, everything is appropriated and monopolised when laws and regulations arrive."* [Proudhon, **System of Economic Contradictions**, p. 371] As economist Edward Herman notes:

> *"The growth of government has closely followed perceived failings of the private market system, especially in terms of market instability, income insecurity, and the proliferation of negative externalities. Some of these deficiencies of the market can be attributed to its very success, which have generated more threatening externalities and created demands for things the market is not well suited to provide. It may also be true that the growth of the government further weakens the market. This does not alter the fact that powerful underlying forces – not power hungry bureaucrats or frustrated intellectuals – are determining the main drift."* [Edward Herman, **Corporate Control, Corporate Power**, pp. 300-1]

In other words, state intervention is the result of the problems caused by capitalism rather than their cause. To say otherwise is like arguing that murder is the result of passing laws against it.

As Polanyi explains, the neo-liberal premise is false, because state intervention always *"dealt with some problem arising out of modern industrial conditions or, at any rate, in the market method of dealing with them."* In fact, most of these "collectivist" measures were carried out by *"convinced supporters of laissez-faire … [and who] were as a rule uncompromising opponents of [state] socialism or any other form of collectivism."* [**Op. Cit.**, p. 146] Sometimes such measures were introduced to undermine support for socialist ideas caused by the excesses of "free market" capitalism but usually there were introduced due to a pressing social need or problem which capitalism created but could not meet or solve. This means that key to understanding state intervention, therefore, is to recognise that politics is a **not** a matter of free will on behalf of politicians or the electorate. Rather they are the outcome of the development of capitalism itself and result from social, economic or environmental pressures which the state has to acknowledge and act upon as they were harming the viability of the system as a whole.

Thus state intervention did not spring out of thin air, but occurred in response to pressing social and economic needs. This can be observed in the mid 19th century, which saw the closest approximation to laissez-faire in the history of capitalism. As Takis Fotopoulos argues, *"the attempt to establish pure economic liberalism, in the sense of free trade, a competitive labour market and the Gold Standard, did not last more than 40 years, and by the 1870s and 1880s protectionist legislation was back … It was also significant … [that all* major capitalist powers] passed through a period of free trade and laissez-faire, followed by a period of anti-liberal legislation." ["The Nation-state and the Market", pp. 37-80, **Society and Nature**, Vol. 2, No. 2, p. 48]

For example, the reason for the return of protectionist legislation was the Depression of 1873-86, which marked the end of the first experiment with pure economic liberalism. Paradoxically, then, the attempt to liberalise the markets led to more regulation. In light of our previous analysis, this is not surprising. Neither the owners of the country nor the politicians desired to see society destroyed, the result to which unhindered laissez-faire leads. Apologists of capitalism overlook the fact that "[a]t the beginning of the Depression, Europe had been in the heyday of free trade." [Polanyi, **Op. Cit.**, p. 216] State intervention came about in response to the social disruptions resulting from laissez-faire. It did not cause them.

Similarly, it is a fallacy to state, as Ludwig von Mises did, that "as long as unemployment benefit is paid, unemployment must exist." [quoted by Polanyi, **Op. Cit.**, p. 283] This statement is not only ahistoric but ignores the existence of the **involuntary** unemployment (the purer capitalism of the nineteenth century regularly experienced periods of economic crisis and mass unemployment). Even such a die-hard exponent of the minimal state as Milton Friedman recognised involuntary unemployment existed:

> "The growth of government transfer payments in the form of unemployment insurance, food stamps, welfare, social security, and so on, has reduced drastically the suffering associated with involuntary unemployment ... most laid-off workers ... may enjoy nearly as high an income when unemployed as when employed ... At the very least, he need not be so desperate to find another job as his counterpart in the 1930's. He can afford to be choosy and to wait until he is either recalled or a more attractive job turns up." [quoted by Elton Rayack, **Not so Free to Choose**, p. 130]

Which, ironically, contradicts Friedman's own claims as regards the welfare state. In an attempt to show that being unemployed is not as bad as people believe Friedman "glaringly contradicts two of his main theses, (1) that the worker is free to choose and (2) that no government social programs have achieved the results promised by its proponents." As Rayack notes, by "admitting the existence of involuntary unemployment, Friedman is, in essence, denying that ... the market protects the worker's freedom to choose ... In addition, since those social programs have made it possible for the worker to be 'choosy; in seeking employment, to that extent the welfare state has increased his freedom." [**Op. Cit.**, p. 130] But, of course, the likes of von Mises will dismiss Friedman as a "socialist" and no further thought is required.

That governments started to pay out unemployment benefit is not surprising, given that mass unemployment can produce mass discontent. This caused the state to start paying out a dole in order eliminate the possibility of crime as well as working class self-help, which could conceivably have undermined the status quo. The elite was well aware of the danger in workers organising for their own benefit and tried to counter-act it. What the likes of von Mises forget is that the state has to consider the long term viability of the system

rather than the ideologically correct position produced by logically deducting abstract principles.

Sadly, in pursuing of ideologically correct answers, capitalist apologists often ignore common sense. If one believes people exist for the economy and not the economy for people, one becomes willing to sacrifice people and their society today for the supposed economic benefit of future generations (in reality, current profits). If one accepts the ethics of mathematics, a future increase in the size of the economy is more important than current social disruption. Thus Polanyi again: "a social calamity is primarily a cultural not an economic phenomenon that can be measured by income figures." [**Op. Cit.**, p. 157] And it is the nature of capitalism to ignore or despise what cannot be measured.

This does not mean that state intervention cannot have bad effects on the economy or society. Given the state's centralised, bureaucratic nature, it would be impossible for it **not** to have some bad effects. State intervention can and does make bad situations worse in some cases. It also has a tendency for self-perpetuation. As Elisée Reclus put it:

> "As soon as an institution is established, even if it should be only to combat flagrant abuses, it creates them anew through its very existence. It has to adapt to its bad environment, and in order to function, it must do so in a pathological way. Whereas the creators of the institution follow only noble ideals, the employees that they appoint must consider above all their remuneration and the continuation of their employment." ["The Modern State", pp. 201-15, John P. Clark and Camille Martin (eds.), **Anarchy, Geography, Modernity**, p. 207]

As such, welfare within a bureaucratic system will have problems but getting rid of it will hardly **reduce** inequality (as proven by the onslaught on it by Thatcher and Reagan). This is unsurprising, for while the state bureaucracy can never eliminate poverty, it can and does reduce it – if only to keep the bureaucrats secure in employment by showing some results.

Moreover, as Malatesta notes, "the practical evidence [is] that whatever governments do is always motivated by the desire to dominate, and is always geared to defending, extending and perpetuating its privileges and those of the class of which it is both the representative and defender." [**Anarchy**, p. 24] In such circumstances, it would be amazing that state intervention did not have negative effects. However, to criticise those negative effects while ignoring or downplaying the far worse social problems which produced the intervention in the first place is both staggeringly illogical and deeply hypocritical. As we discuss later, in section D.1.5, the anarchist approach to reforms and state intervention is based on this awareness.

D.1.2 Is state intervention the result of democracy?

No. Social and economic intervention by the modern state began long before universal suffrage became widespread. While this intervention was usually in the interests of the capitalist class, it was sometimes done explicitly in the name of the general welfare and the public interest. Needless to say, while the former usually goes unmentioned by defenders of capitalism, the latter is denounced and attacked as violations of the natural order (often in terms of the sinister sounding "collectivist" measures).

That democracy is not the root cause for the state's interference in the market is easily seen from the fact that non-democratic capitalist states presided over by defenders of "free market" capitalism have done so. For example, in Britain, acts of state intervention were introduced when property and sexual restrictions on voting rights still existed. More recently, taking Pinochet's neo-liberal dictatorship in Chile, we find that the state, as would be expected, *"often intervened on behalf of private and foreign business interests."* Given the history of capitalism, this is to be expected. However, the state also practised social intervention at times, partly to diffuse popular disaffection with the economic realities the system generated (disaffection that state oppression could not control) and partly to counter-act the negative effects of its own dogmas. As such, *"[f]ree-market ideologues are reluctant to acknowledge that even the Pinochet government intervened in many cases in the market-place in last-minute attempts to offset the havoc wrecked by its free-market policies (low-income housing, air quality, public health, etc.)"* [Joseph Collins and John Lear, **Chile's Free-Market Miracle: A Second Look**, p. 254]

The notion that it is "democracy" which causes politicians to promise the electorate state action in return for office is based on a naive viewpoint of representative democracy. The centralist and hierarchical nature of "representative" democracy means that the population at large has little real control over politicians, who are far more influenced by big business, business lobby groups, and the state bureaucracy. This means that truly popular and democratic pressures are limited within the capitalist state and the interests of elites are far more decisive in explaining state actions.

Obviously anarchists are well aware that the state does say it intervenes to protect the interests of the general public, not the elite. While much of this is often rhetoric to hide policies which (in reality) benefit corporate interests far more than the general public, it cannot be denied that such intervention does exist, to some degree. However, even here the evidence supports the anarchist claim that the state is an instrument of class rule, not a representative of the general interest. This is because such reforms have, in general, been few and far between compared to those laws which benefit the few.

Moreover, historically when politicians have made legal changes favouring the general public rather than the elite they have done so only after intense social pressure from below. For examples, the state only passed pro-union laws only when the alternative was disruptive industrial conflict. In the US, the federal government, at best, ignored or, at worse, actively suppressed labour unions during the 19th century. It was only when mineworkers were able to shut down the anthracite coal fields for months in 1902, threatening disruption of heating supplies around the country, that Teddy Roosevelt supported union demands for binding arbitration to raise wages. He was the first President in American history to intervene in a strike in a positive manner on behalf of workers.

This can be seen from the "New Deal" and related measures of limited state intervention to stimulate economic recovery during the Great Depression. These were motivated by more material reasons than democracy. Thus Takis Fotopoulos argues that *"[t]he fact ... that 'business confidence' was at its lowest could go a long way in explaining the much more tolerant attitude of those controlling production towards measures encroaching on their economic power and profits. In fact, it was only when – and as long as – state interventionism had the approval of those actually controlling production that it was successful."* [*"The Nation-state and the Market"*, **Op. Cit.**, p. 55] As anarchist Sam Dolgoff notes, the New Deal in America (and similar policies elsewhere) was introduced, in part, because the *"whole system of human exploitation was threatened. The political state saved itself, and all that was essential to capitalism, doing what 'private enterprise' could not do. Concessions were made to the workers, the farmers, the middle-class, while the private capitalists were deprived of some of their power."* [**The American Labor Movement**, pp. 25-6] Much the same can be said of the post-war Keynesianism consensus, which combined state aid to the capitalist class with social reforms. These reforms were rarely the result of generous politicians but rather the product of social pressures from below and the needs of the system as a whole. For example, the extensive reforms made by the 1945 Labour Government in the UK was the direct result of ruling class fear, not socialism. As Quentin Hogg, a Conservative M.P., put it in the House of Commons in 1943: *"If you do not give the people social reforms, they are going to give you revolution."* Memories of the near revolutions across Europe after the First World War were obviously in many minds, on both sides.

Needless to say, when the ruling class considered a specific reform to be against its interests, it will be abolished or restricted. An example of this can be seen in the 1934 Wagner Act in the USA, which gave US labour its first and last political victory. The Act was passed due to the upsurge in wildcat strikes, factory occupations and successful union organising drives which were spreading throughout the country. Its purpose was specifically to calm this struggle in order to preserve "labour peace." The act made it legal for unions to organise, but this placed labour struggles within the boundaries of legal procedures and so meant that they could be more easily controlled. In addition, this concession was a form of appeasement whose effect was to make those involved in union actions less likely to start questioning the fundamental bases of the capitalist system. Once the fear of a militant labour movement had passed, the Wagner Act was undermined and made powerless by new laws, laws which made illegal the tactics which forced the politicians to pass the law in the first place and increased the powers of bosses over workers. The same can be said of other countries.

The pattern is clear. It is always the case that things need to change on the ground first and then the law acknowledges the changes.

Any state intervention on behalf of the general public or workers have all followed people and workers organising and fighting for their rights. If labour or social "peace" exists because of too little organising and protesting or because of lack of strength in the workplace by unions, politicians will feel no real pressure to change the law and, consequently, refuse to. As Malatesta put it, the *"only limit to the oppression of government is that power with which the people show themselves capable of opposing it … When the people meekly submit to the law, or their protests are feeble and confined to words, the government studies its own interests and ignores the needs of the people; when the protests are lively, insistent, threatening, the government … gives way or resorts to repression."* [**Errico Malatesta: His Life and Ideas**, p. 196]

Needless to say, the implication of classical liberal ideology that popular democracy is a threat to capitalism is the root of the fallacy that democracy leads to state intervention. The notion that by limiting the franchise the rich will make laws which benefit all says more about the classical liberals' touching faith in the altruism of the rich than it does about their understanding of human nature, the realities of both state and capitalism and their grasp of history. The fact that they can join with John Locke and claim with a straight face that all must abide by the rules that only the elite make says a lot about their concept of "freedom."

Some of the more modern classical liberals (for example, many right-wing "libertarians") advocate a "democratic" state which cannot intervene in economic matters. This is no solution, however, as it only gets rid of the statist response to real and pressing social problems caused by capitalism without supplying anything better in its place. This is a form of paternalism, as the elite determines what is, and is not, intervention and what the masses should, and should not, be able to do (in their interests, of course). Then there is the obvious conclusion that any such regime would have to exclude change. After all, if people can change the regime they are under they may change it in ways that the right does not support. The provision for ending economic and other reforms would effectively ban most opposition parties as, by definition, they could do nothing once in power. How this differs from a dictatorship would be hard to say – after all, most dictatorships have parliamentary bodies which have no power but which can talk a lot.

Needless to say, the right often justify this position by appealing to the likes of Adam Smith but this, fails to appreciate the changing political and economic situation since those days. As market socialist Allan Engler argues:

> "In Smith's day government was openly and unashamedly an instrument of wealth owners. Less than 10 per cent of British men – and no women at all – had the right to vote. When Smith opposed government interference in the economy, he was opposing the imposition of wealth owners' interests on everybody else. Today, when neoconservatives oppose state interference, their aim to the opposite: to stop the representatives of the people from interfering with the interests of wealth owners." [**Apostles of Greed**, p. 104]

As well as the changing political situation, Smith's society was without the concentrations of economic power that marks

capitalism as a developed system. Whether Smith would have been happy to see his name appropriated to defend corporate power is, obviously, a moot point. However, he had no illusions that the state of his time interfered to bolster the elite, not the many (for example: *"Whenever the law has attempted to regulate the wages of workmen, it has always been rather to lower them than to raise them."* [**The Wealth of Nations**, p. 119]). As such, it is doubtful he would have agreed with those who involve his name to defend corporate power and trusts while advocating the restriction of trade unions as is the case with modern day neo-liberalism:

> "Whenever the legislature attempts to regulate the differences between masters and their workmen, its counsellors are always masters. When the regulation, therefore, is in favour of the workmen, it is always just and equitable … When masters combine together in order to reduce the wages of their workmen, they commonly enter into a private bond or agreement … Were the workmen to enter into a contrary combination of the same kind. not to accept of a certain wage under a certain penalty, the law would punish them very severely; and if dealt impartially, it would treat the masters in the same way." [**Op. Cit.**, p. 129]

The interest of merchants and master manufacturers, Smith stressed, *"is always in some respects different from, and even opposite to, that of the public … The proposal of any new law or regulation of commerce which comes from this order ought always to be listened to with great precaution, and ought never to be adopted till after having been long and carefully examined, not only with the most scrupulous, but with the most suspicious attention. It comes from an order of men whose interest is never exactly the same with that of the public, who have generally an interest to deceive and even to oppress the public, and who accordingly have, upon many occasions, both deceived and oppressed it."* [**Op. Cit.**, pp. 231-2] These days Smith would have likely argued that this position applies equally to attempts by big business to **revoke** laws and regulations!

To view the state intervention as simply implementing the wishes of the majority is to assume that classes and other social hierarchies do not exist, that one class does not oppress and exploit another and that they share common interests. It means ignoring the realities of the current political system as well as economic, for political parties will need to seek funds to campaign and that means private cash. Unsurprisingly, they will do what their backers demands and this dependence the wealthy changes the laws all obey. This means that any government will tend to favour business and the wealthy as the parties are funded by them and so they get some say over what is done. Only those parties which internalise the values and interests of their donors will prosper and so the wealthy acquire an unspoken veto power over government policy. In other words, parties need to beg the rich for election funds. Some parties do, of course, have trade union funding, but this is easily counteracted by pressure from big business (i.e., that useful euphemism, *"the markets"*) and the state bureaucracy. This explains why the unions in, say, Britain spend a large part of their time under Labour governments trying to influence it by means of strikes and lobbying.

The defenders of "free market" capitalism appear oblivious as to the reasons **why** the state has approved regulations and nationalisations as well as **why** trade unions, (libertarian and statist) socialist and populist movements came about in the first place. Writing all these off as the products of ideology and/or economic ignorance is far too facile an explanation, as is the idea of power hungry bureaucrats seeking to extend their reach. The truth is much more simple and lies at the heart of the current system. The reasons why various "anti-capitalist" social movements and state interventions arise with such regular periodicity is because of the effects of an economic system which is inherently unstable and exploitative. For example, social movements arose in the 19th century because workers, artisans and farmers were suffering the effects of a state busy creating the necessary conditions for capitalism. They were losing their independence and had become, or were being turned, into wage slaves and, naturally, hated it. They saw the negative effects of capitalism on their lives and communities and tried to stop it.

In terms of social regulation, the fact is that they were often the result of pressing needs. Epidemics, for example, do not respect property rights and the periodic deep recessions that marked 19th century capitalism made the desire to avoid them an understandable one on the part of the ruling elite. Unlike their ideological followers in the latter part of the century and onwards, the political economists of the first half of the nineteenth century were too intelligent and too well informed to advocate out-and-out laissez-faire. They grasped the realities of the economic system in which they worked and thought and, as a result, were aware of clash between the logic of pure abstract theory and the demands of social life and morality. While they stressed the pure theory, the usually did so in order to justify the need for state intervention in some particular aspect of social or economic life. John Stuart Mill's famous chapter on *"the grounds and limits of the laissez-faire and non-interference principle"* in his **Principles of Political Economy** is, perhaps, the most obvious example of this dichotomy (unsurprisingly, von Mises dismissed Mill as a "socialist" – recognising the problems which capitalism itself generates will make you ideologically suspect to the true believer).

To abolish these reforms without first abolishing capitalism is to return to the social conditions which produced the social movements in the first place. In other words, to return to the horrors of the 19th century. We can see this in the USA today, where this process of turning back the clock is most advanced: mass criminality, lower life expectancy, gated communities, increased work hours, and a fortune spent on security. However, this should not blind us to the limitations of these movements and reforms which, while coming about as a means to overcome the negative effects of corporate capitalism upon the population, **preserved** that system. In terms of successful popular reform movements, the policies they lead to were (usually) the minimum standard agreed upon by the capitalists themselves to offset social unrest.

Unsurprisingly, most opponents of state intervention are equally opposed to popular movements and the pressures they subject the state to. However trying to weaken (or even get rid of) the social movements which have helped reform capitalism ironically helps bolster the power and centralisation of the state. This is because to get rid of working class organisations means eliminating a key

counter-balance to the might of the state. Atomised individuals not only cannot fight capitalist exploitation and oppression, they also cannot fight and restrict the might of the state nor attempt to influence it even a fraction of what the wealthy elite can via the stock market and management investment decisions. As such, von Hayek's assertion that *"it is inexcusable to pretend that … the pressure which can be brought by the large firms or corporation is comparable to that of the organisation of labour"* is right, but in the exact opposite way he intended. [**Law, Legislation and Liberty**, vol. III, p. 89] Outside the imagination of conservatives and right-wing liberals, big business has much greater influence than trade unions on government policy (see section D.2 for some details). While trade union and other forms of popular action are more visible than elite pressures, it does not mean that the form does not exist or less influential. Quite the reverse. The latter may be more noticeable, true, but is only because it has to be in order to be effective and because the former is so prevalent.

The reality of the situation can be seen from looking at the US, a political system where union influence is minimal while business influence and lobbying is large scale (and has been since the 1980s). A poll of popular attitudes about the 2005 US budget *"revealed that popular attitudes are virtually the inverse of policy."* In general, there is a *"dramatic divide between public opinion and public policy,"* but public opinion has little impact on state officials. Unsurprisingly, the general population *"do not feel that the government is responsive to the public will."* The key to evaluating whether a state is a functioning democracy is dependent on *"what public opinion is on major issues"* and *"how it relates to public policy."* In the case of the US, business interests are supreme and, as such, *"[n]ot only does the US government stand apart from the rest of the world on many crucial issues, but even from its own population."* The state *"pursues the strategic and economic interests of dominant sectors of the domestic population,"* unless forced otherwise by the people (for *"rights are not likely to be granted by benevolent authorities"* but rather by *"education and organising"*). In summary, governments implement policies which benefit *"the short-term interests of narrow sectors of power and wealth … It takes wilful blindness not to see how these commitments guide … policy."* [Chomsky, **Failed States**, p. 234, p. 235, p. 228, p. 229, p. 262, p. 263 and p. 211] A clearer example of how capitalist "democracy" works can hardly be found.

Von Hayek showed his grasp of reality by stating that the real problem is *"not the selfish action of individual firms but the selfishness of organised groups"* and so *"the real exploiters in our present society are not egotistic capitalists … but organisations which derive their power from the moral support of collective action and the feeling of group loyalty."* [**Op. Cit.**, p. 96] So (autocratic) firms and (state privileged) corporations are part of the natural order, but (self-organised and, at worse, relatively democratic) unions are not. Ignoring the factual issues of the power and influence of wealth and business, the logical problem with this opinion is clear. Companies are, of course, *"organised groups"* and based around *"collective action"*. The difference is that the actions and groups are dictated by the few individuals at the top. As would be expected, the application of his ideas by the Thatcher government not only bolstered capitalist power and resulted in increased inequality and exploitation (see section J.4.2) but also a strengthening and centralisation of state power. One aspect of this the introduction of government regulation of unions as well as new legislation which increase police powers to restrict the right to strike and protest (both of which were, in part, due opposition to free market policies by the population).

Anarchists may agree that the state, due to its centralisation and bureaucracy, crushes the spontaneous nature of society and is a handicap to social progress and evolution. However, leaving the market alone to work its course fallaciously assumes that people will happily sit back and let market forces rip apart their communities and environment. Getting rid of state intervention without getting rid of capitalism and creating a free society would mean that the need for social self-protection would still exist but that there would be even less means of achieving it than now. The results of such a policy, as history shows, would be a catastrophe for the working class (and the environment, we must add) and beneficial only for the elite (as intended, of course).

Ultimately, the implication of the false premise that democracy leads to state intervention is that the state exists for the benefit of the majority, which uses the state to exploit the elite! Amazingly, many capitalist apologists accept this as a valid inference from their premise, even though it's obviously a **reductio ad absurdum** of that premise as well as going against the facts of history. That the ruling elite is sometimes forced to accept state intervention outside its preferred area of aid for itself simply means that, firstly, capitalism is an unstable system which undermines its own social and ecological basis and, secondly, that they recognise that reform is preferable to revolution (unlike their cheerleaders).

D.1.3 Is state intervention socialistic?

No. Libertarian socialism is about self-liberation and self-management of one's activities. Getting the state to act for us is the opposite of these ideals. In addition, the question implies that socialism is connected with its nemesis, statism, and that socialism means even more bureaucratic control and centralisation ("socialism is the contrary of governmentalism." [Proudhon, **No Gods, No Masters**, vol. 1, p. 63]). As Kropotkin stressed: "State bureaucracy and centralisation are as irreconcilable with socialism as was autocracy with capitalist rule." [**Evolution and Environment**, p. 185] The history of both social democracy and state socialism proved this, with the former merely reforming some aspects of capitalism while keeping the system intact while the latter created an even worse form of class system.

The identification of socialism with the state is something that social democrats, Stalinists and capitalist apologists **all** agree upon. However, as we'll see in section H.3.13, "state socialism" is in reality just state capitalism – the turning of the world into "one office and one factory" (to use Lenin's expression). Little wonder that most sane people join with anarchists in rejecting it. Who wants to work under a system in which, if one does not like the boss (i.e. the state), one cannot even quit?

The theory that state intervention is "creeping socialism" takes the laissez-faire ideology of capitalism at its face value, not realising that it is ideology rather than reality. Capitalism is a dynamic system and evolves over time, but this does not mean that by moving away from its theoretical starting point it is negating its essential nature and becoming socialistic. Capitalism was born from state intervention, and except for a very short period of laissez-faire which ended in depression has always depended on state intervention for its existence. As such, while there "may be a residual sense to the notion that the state serves as an equaliser, in that without its intervention the destructive powers of capitalism would demolish social existence and the physical environment, a fact that has been well understood by the masters of the private economy who have regularly called upon the state to restrain and organise these forces. But the common idea that the government acts as a social equaliser can hardly be put forth as a general principle." [Noam Chomsky, **The Chomsky Reader**, p. 185]

The list of state aid to business is lengthy and can hardly be considered as socialistic or egalitarian is aim (regardless of its supporters saying it is about creating "jobs" rather than securing profits, the reality of the situation). Government subsidies to arms companies and agribusiness, its subsidy of research and development work undertaken by government-supported universities, its spending to ensure a favourable international climate for business operations, its defence of intellectual property rights, its tort reform (i.e. the business agenda of limiting citizen power to sue corporations), its manipulation of unemployment rates, and so forth, are all examples of state intervention which can, by no stretch of the imagination be considered as "socialistic." As left-liberal economist Dean Baker notes:

> "The key flaw in the stance that most progressives have taken on economic issues is that they have accepted a framing whereby conservatives are assumed to support market outcomes, while progressives want to rely on the government … The reality is that conservatives have been quite actively using the power of the government to shape market outcomes in ways that redistribute income upward. However, conservatives have been clever enough to not own up to their role in this process, pretending all along that everything is just the natural working of the market. And, progressives have been foolish enough to go along with this view." [**The Conservative Nanny State: How the Wealthy Use the Government to Stay Rich and Get Richer**, p. v]

He stresses, that "both conservatives and liberals want government intervention. The difference between them is the goal of government intervention, and the fact that conservatives are smart enough to conceal their dependence on the government." They "want to use the government to distribute income upward to higher paid workers, business owners, and investors. They support the establishment of rules and structures that have this effect." Dean discusses numerous examples of right-wing forms of state action, and notes that "[i]n these areas of public policy … conservatives are enthusiastic promoters of big government. They are happy to have the government intervene into the inner workings of the economy to make sure that money flows in the direction they like – upward. It is accurate to say that conservatives don't like big government social programs, but not because they don't like big government. The problem with big government social programs is that they tend to distribute money downward, or provide benefits to large numbers of people." It seems redundant to note that "conservatives don't own up to the fact that the policies they favour are forms of government intervention. Conservatives do their best to portray the forms of government intervention that they favour, for example, patent and copyright protection, as simply part of the natural order of things." [**Op. Cit.**, p. 1 and p. 2]

This, it should be stressed, is unexpected. As we explained in section B.2, the state is an instrument of minority rule. As such, it strains belief that state intervention would be socialist in nature. After all, if the state is an agent of a self-interesting ruling class, then its laws are inevitably biased in its favour. The ultimate purpose of the state and its laws are the protection of private property and so the form of law is a class weapon while its content is the protection of class interests. They are inseparable.

So the state and its institutions can "challenge the use of authority by other institutions, such as cruel parents, greedy landlords, brutal bosses, violent criminals" as well as "promot[ing] desirable social activities, such as public works, disaster relief, communications and transport systems, poor relief, education and broadcasting." Anarchists argue, though, the state remains "primarily ... oppressive" and its "main function is in fact to hold down the people, to limit freedom" and that "all the benevolent functions of the state can be exercised and often have been exercised by voluntary associations." Moreover, "the essential function of the state is to maintain the existing inequality" and so "cannot redistribute wealth fairly because it is the main agency of the unfair distribution." This is because it is "the political expression of the economic structure, that it is the representative of the people who own or control the wealth of the community and the oppressor of the people who do the work which creates wealth." [Walters, **About Anarchism**, p. 36 and p. 37]

The claim that state intervention is "socialist" also ignores the realities of power concentration under capitalism. Real socialism equalises power by redistributing it to the people, but, as Noam Chomsky points out, "[i]n a highly inegalitarian society, it is most unlikely that government programs will be equalisers. Rather, it is to be expected that they will be designed and manipulated by private power for their own benefits; and to a significant degree the expectation is fulfilled. It is not very likely that matters could be otherwise in the absence of mass popular organisations that are prepared to struggle for their rights and interests." [**Op. Cit.**, p. 184] The notion that "welfare equals socialism" is nonsense, although it can reduce poverty and economic inequality somewhat. As Colin Ward notes, "when socialists have achieved power" they have produced nothing more than "[m]onopoly capitalism with a veneer of social welfare as a substitute for social justice." [**Anarchy in Action**, p. 18]

This analysis applies to state ownership and control of industry. Britain, for example, saw the nationalisation of roughly 20% of the economy by the 1945 Labour Government. These were the most unprofitable sections of the economy but, at the time, essential for the economy as a whole. By taking it into state ownership, these sections could be rationalised and developed at public expense. Rather than nationalisation being feared as "socialism,"

the capitalist class had no real issue with it. As anarchists at the time noted, "the real opinions of capitalists can be seen from Stock Exchange conditions and statements of industrialists [rather] than the Tory Front bench ... [and from these we] see that the owning class is not at all displeased with the record and tendency of the Labour Party." [Vernon Richards (ed.), **Neither Nationalisation nor Privatisation – Selections from Freedom 1945-1950**, p. 9]

Moreover, the example of nationalised industries is a good indicator of the non-socialist nature of state intervention. Nationalisation meant replacing the capitalist bureaucrat with a state one, with little real improvement for those subjected to the "new" regime. At the height of the British Labour Party's post-war nationalisations, anarchists were pointing out its anti-socialist nature. Nationalisation was "really consolidating the old individual capitalist class into a new and efficient class of managers to run ... state capitalism" by "installing the really creative industrialists in dictatorial managerial positions." [Vernon Richards (ed.), **Op. Cit.**, p. 10] Thus, in practice, the real examples of nationalisation confirmed Kropotkin's prediction that it would be "an exchange of present capitalism for state-capitalism" and simply be "nothing but a new, perhaps improved, but still undesirable form of the wage system." [**Evolution and Environment**, p. 193 and p. 171] The nationalised industries were expected, of course, to make a profit, partly for "repaying the generous compensation plus interest to the former owners of the mainly bankrupt industries that the Labour government had taken over." [Richards, **Op. Cit.**, p. 7]

Ultimately, state ownership at local or national level is hardly socialistic in principle or in practice. As Kropotkin stressed, "no reasonable man [or woman] will expect that Municipal Socialism, any more than Co-operation, could solve to any extent the Social problem." This was because it was "self-evident that [the capitalists] will not let themselves be expropriated without opposing resistance. They may favour municipal [or state] enterprise for a time; but the moment they see that it really begins to reduce the number of paupers ... or gives them regular employment, and consequently threatens to reduce the profits of the exploiters, they will soon put an end to it." [**Act for Yourselves**, p. 94 and p. 95] The rise of Monetarism in the 1970s and the subsequent enthronement of the "Natural Rate" of unemployment thesis proves this argument.

While state intervention is hardly socialistic, what can be said is that "the positive feature of welfare legislation is that, contrary to the capitalist ethic, it is a testament to human solidarity. The negative feature is precisely that it is an arm of the state." [Colin Ward, **Talking Anarchy**, p. 79] For anarchists, while "we are certainly in full sympathy with all that is being done to widen the attributes of city life and to introduce communistic conceptions into it. But it is only through a Social Revolution, made by the workers themselves, that the present exploitation of Labour by Capital can be altered." [Kropotkin, **Op. Cit.**, pp. 95-6] As British anarchists stressed during the first post-war Labour Government:

> "The fact that the alternative, under capitalism, is destitution and the sharper anomalies of poverty, does not make the Liberal-Socialistic alternative a sound proposition."

"The only rational insurance against the evils of poverty and industrialism and old age under the wages system is the abolition of poverty and the wages system, and the transformation of industrialism to serve human ends instead of grinding up human beings." [Vernon Richards (ed.), **World War – Cold War**, p. 347]

In reality, rather than genuine socialism we had reformists *"operating capitalism while trying to give it a socialist gloss."* [**Op. Cit.**, p. 353] The fact is that the ruling class oppose those forms of state intervention which aim, at least in rhetoric, to help working class people. This does not make such reforms socialistic. The much more substantial state intervention for the elite and business are simply part of the natural order and go unmentioned. That this amounts to a welfare state for the wealthy or socialism for the rich is, of course, one of the great unspeakable truths of capitalism.

D.1.4 Is laissez-faire capitalism actually without state intervention?

The underlying assumption in the neo-liberal and conservative attacks against state intervention is the assumption that their minimal state is without it. The reality of the situation is, of course, different. Even the minimal state of the ideologues dreams intervenes on behalf of the ruling class in order to defend capitalist power and the property and property rights this flows from.

This means that the laissez-faire position is a form of state intervention as well. State "neutrality" considered as simply enforcing property rights (the "minimal state") instantly raises the question of **whose** conception of property rights, popular ones or capitalist ones? Unsurprisingly, the capitalist state enforces capitalist notions of property. In other words, it sanctions and supports economic inequality and the privileges and power of those who own property and, of course, the social relationships such a system generates. Yet by defending capitalist property, the state can hardly remain "neutral" with regards to ownership and the power it generates. In other words, the "neutral" state **has** to intervene to defend the authority of the boss or landlord over the workers they exploit and oppress. It is not a "public body" defending some mythical "public interest" but rather a defender of class society and the socio-economic relationships such a system creates. Political power, therefore, reflects and defends economic and social power.

As Kropotkin argued, the *"major portion"* of laws have *"but one object – to protect private property, i.e. wealth acquired by the exploitation of man by man. Their aim is to open to capital fresh fields for exploitation, and to sanction the new forms which that exploitation continually assumes, as capital swallows up another branch of human activity … They exist to keep up the machinery of government which serves to secure to capital the exploitation and monopoly of wealth produced."* This means that all modern states *"all serve one God – capital; all have but one object – to facilitate the exploitation of the worker by the capitalist."* [**Anarchism**, p. 210]

Given that the capitalist market is marked by inequalities of power, any legal framework will defend that power. The state simply allows the interaction between parties to determine the norms of conduct in any contract. This ensures that the more powerful party to impose its desires on the weaker one as the market, by definition, does not and cannot have any protections against the imposition of private power. The state (or legal code) by enforcing the norms agreed to by the exchange is just as much a form of state intervention as more obvious forms of state action. In other words, the state's monopoly of power and coercion is used to enforce the contracts reached between the powerful and powerless. As such contracts will hardly be neutral, the state cannot be a neutral arbiter when presiding over capitalism. The net result is simply that the state allows the more powerful party to an exchange to have authority over the weaker party – all under the fiction of equality and freedom. And, as Malatesta stressed, state power and centralisation will have to increase:

"liberalism, is in theory a kind of anarchy without socialism, and therefore is simply a lie, for freedom is not possible without equality, and real anarchy cannot exist without solidarity, without socialism. The criticism liberals direct at government consists of wanting to deprive it of some of its functions and to call upon the capitalists to fight it out among themselves, but it cannot attack the repressive functions which are of its essence: for with the **gendarme** *the property owner could not exist, indeed the government's powers of repression must perforce increase as free competition results in more discord and inequality."* [**Anarchy**, p. 46]

His comments were more than confirmed by the rise of neo-liberalism nearly a century later which combined the "free(r) market" with a strong state marked by more extensive centralisation and police powers.

This is unsurprising, as laissez-faire capitalism being *"unable to solve its celebrated problem of the harmony of interests, [is forced] to impose laws, if only provisional ones, and abdicates in its turn before this new authority that is incompatible with the practice of liberty."* [Proudhon, quoted by Alan Ritter, **The Political Thought of Pierre-Joseph Proudhon**, p. 122] Thus capitalism always has to rely on the state, on political coercion, if only the minimal state, to assure its survival. The capitalist market has to, in other words, resort to the coercion it claims to avoid once people start to question its shortcomings. Of course, this coercion need not be monopolised in the form of state police and armed forces. It has been enforced successfully by private police forces and security guards, but it does not change the fact that force is required to maintain capitalist property, power and property rights.

In summary, **all** forms of capitalism rest on the superior force of economic elites who have the backing of the state to defend the sources of that power as well as any contracts it has agreed to. In other words, "laissez-faire" capitalism does not end state intervention, it simply creates a situation where the state leaves the market process to the domination of those who occupy superior market positions. As Kropotkin put it, capitalism *"is called the* *freedom of transactions but it is more truly called the freedom of exploitation."* [**Words of a Rebel**, p. 119]

Given this, it may be objected that in this case there is no reason for the ruling class to interfere with the economy. If economic coercion is sufficient, then the elite has no need to turn to the state for aid. This objection, however, fails to appreciate that the state **has** to interfere to counteract the negative impacts of capitalism. Moreover, as we discussed in section C.7, economic coercion becomes less pressing during periods of low unemployment and these tend to provoke a slump. It is in the interests of the ruling elite to use state action to reduce the power of the working classes in society. Thus we find the Federal Reserve in the USA studying economic statistics to see if workers are increasing their bargaining power on the labour market (i.e. are in a position to demand more wages or better conditions). If so, then interest rates are increased and the resulting unemployment and job insecurity make workers more likely to put up with low pay and do what their bosses demand. As Doug Henwood notes, *"policy makers are exceedingly obsessed with wage increases and the state of labour militancy. They're not only concerned with the state of the macroeconomy, conventionally defined, they're also concerned with the state of the class struggle, to use the old-fashioned language."* [**Wall Street**, p. 219] Little wonder the ruling class and its high priests within the "science" of economics have embraced the concept of a "natural rate" of unemployment (see section C.9 on this and as we indicated in section C.6, this has been **very** enriching for the ruling class since 1980).

Ultimately, the business class wants the state to intervene in the economy beyond the minimum desired by a few ideologues of capitalism simply to ensure it gets even more wealth and power – and to ensure that the system does not implode. Ironically, to get capitalism to work as some of its defenders want it to would require a revolution in itself – against the capitalists! Yet if we go to the trouble of fighting public tyranny (the state), why should we stop there? Why should private tyranny (capitalism, its autocratic structures and hierarchical social relationships) remain untouched? Particularly, as Chomsky notes, under capitalism *"minimising the state means strengthening the private sectors. It narrows the domain within which public influence can be expressed. That's not an anarchist goal ... It's minimising the state and increasing an even worse power,"* namely capitalist firms and corporations which are *"private totalitarian organisations."* [**Chomsky on Anarchism**, p. 214 and p. 213] In other words, if a government "privatises" some government function, it is not substituting a market for a bureaucracy. It is substituting a private bureaucracy for a public one, usually at rock-bottom prices, so that some more capitalists can make a profit. All the economic mumbo-jumbo is just a smokescreen for this fact.

D.1.5 Do anarchists support state intervention?

So where do anarchists stand on state intervention? This question does not present a short answer simply because it is a complex issue. On the one hand, as Proudhon stressed, the state exists to *"maintain **order** in society, by consecrating and sanctifying obedience of the citizens to the State, subordination of the poor to the rich, of the common people to the upper class, of the worker to the idler."* [**The General Idea of the Revolution**, p. 243] In such circumstances, appealing to the state makes little sense. On the other hand, the modern state does do some good things (to varying degrees). As a result of past popular struggles, there is a basic welfare system in some countries which does help the poorest sections of society. That aspect of state intervention is what is under attack by the right under the slogan of "minimising the state."

In the long term, of course, the real solution is to abolish capitalism *"and both citizens and communities will have no need of the intervention of the State."* [Proudhon, **Op. Cit.**, p. 268] In a free society, social self-defence would not be statist but would be similar in nature to trade unionism, co-operatives and pressure groups – individuals working together in voluntary associations to ensure a free and just society – within the context of an egalitarian, decentralised and participatory system which eliminates or reduces the problems in the first place (see section I).

However, that does not answer the question of what we do in the here and now when faced with demands that the welfare state (for the working class, **not** corporate welfare) and other reforms be rolled back. This attack has been on going since the 1970s, accelerating since 1980. We should be clear that claims to be minimising the state should be taken with a massive pitch of salt as the likes of Reagan were *"elected to office promising to downsize government and to 'get the government off the people's back,' even though what he meant was to deregulate big business, and make them free to exploit the workers and make larger profits."* [Lorenzo Kom'boa Ervin, **Anarchism and the Black Revolution**, p. 100] As such, it would be a big mistake to confuse anarchist hostility to the state with the rhetoric of right-wing politicians seeking to reduce social spending (Brian Oliver Sheppard discusses this issue well in his article *"Anarchism vs. Right-Wing 'Anti-Statism'"* [**Anarcho-Syndicalist Review**, no. 31, Spring 2001]). Chomsky puts it well:

> *"State authority is now under severe attack in the more democratic societies, but not because it conflicts with the libertarian vision. Rather the opposite: because it offers (weak) protection to some aspects of that vision. Governments have a fatal flaw: unlike the private tyrannies, the institutions of state power and authority offer to the despised public an opportunity to play some role, however limited, in managing their own affairs. That defect is intolerable to the masters ... the goals of a committed anarchist should be to defend some state institutions from the attack against them, while trying at the same time to pry them open to more meaningful public*

participation – and, ultimately, to dismantle them in a much more free society, of the appropriate circumstances can be achieved." [**Chomsky on Anarchism**, p. 193 and p. 194]

There is, of course, a tension in this position. The state may be influenced by popular struggle but it remains an instrument of **capitalist** rule. It may intervene in society as a result of people power and by the necessity to keep the system as a whole going, but it is bureaucratic and influenced by the wealthy and big business. Indeed, the onslaught on the welfare state by both Thatcher and Reagan was conducted under a "democratic" mandate although, in fact, these governments took advantage of the lack of real accountability between elections. They took advantage of an aspect of the state which anarchists had been warning of for decades, being *"well aware that [the politician] can now commit crimes with immunity, [and so] the elected official finds himself immediately exposed to all sorts of seductions on behalf of the ruling classes"* and so implemented policies *"solicited by big industry, high officials, and above all, by international finance."* [Elisée Reclus, **The Modern State**, p. 208 and pp. 208-9]

As such, while anarchists are against the state, our position on state intervention depends on the specific issue at hand. Most of us think state health care services and unemployment benefits (for example) are more socially useful than arms production, and in lieu of more anarchistic solutions, better than the alternative of "free market" capitalism. This does not mean we are happy with state intervention, which in practice undermines working class self-help, mutual aid and autonomy. Also, state intervention of the "social" nature is often paternalistic, run by and for the "middle classes" (i.e. professional/managerial types and other self-proclaimed "experts"). However, until such time as a viable anarchist counterculture is created, we have little option but to "support" the lesser evil (and make no mistake, it **is** an evil).

Taking the issue of privatisation of state owned and run industry, the anarchist position is opposition to both. As we noted in section D.1.3, the anarchist prediction that if you substitute government ownership for private ownership, *"nothing is changed but the stockholders and the management; beyond that, there is not the least difference in the position of the workers."* [Proudhon, quoted by Ritter, **Op. Cit.**, pp. 167-8] However, privatisation is a rip-off of the general public for the benefit of the wealthy:

> *"Privatisation of public services – whether it is through the direct sale of utilities or through indirect methods such as PFI and PPP – involves a massive transfer of wealth from taxpayers to the pockets of private business interests. It negates the concept of there being such a thing as 'public service' and subjects everything to the bottom line of profit. In other words it seeks to maximise the profits of a few at the expense of wages and social obligations. Furthermore, privatisation inevitably leads to an attack on wages and working conditions – conditions which have been fought for through years of trade union agitation are done away with at the scratch of a pen."* [Gregor Kerr, *"Privatisation: the rip-off of public resources"*, pp. 14-18, **Black and Red Revolution**, no. 11, p. 16]

In response to such "reforms", anarchists propose an alternatives to both options. Anarchists aim not at state ownership but to *"transfer all that is needed for production … from the hands of the individual capitalists into those of the communities of producers and consumers."* [Kropotkin, **Environment and Evolution**, pp. 169-70] In other words, while *"[i]n today's world 'public sector' has come to mean 'government.' It is only if 'public sector' can be made to mean 'people's ownership' in a real sense that the call for public ownership can be a truly radical one."* [Kerr, **Op. Cit.**, p. 18] This is based on a common-sense conclusion from the analysis of the state as an instrument of the ruling class:

> *"While anarchists oppose the privatisation of state assets and services for the reasons discussed above, we do not call – as some on the left do – for the 'nationalisation' of services as a solution to problems … We'd be expecting the same politicians who are busily implementing the neo-liberal agenda to now take on the role of workers' protectors … it is important to point out that the 'nationalise it' or 'take it into public ownership' slogan is far too often spun out by people on the left without their taking into account that there is a massive difference between state control/ownership and workers' control/ ownership … we all know that even if the revenues … were still in state ownership, spending it on housing the homeless or reducing hospital waiting lists would not top the agenda of the government.*
>
> *"Put simply, state ownership does not equal workers' ownership … we are sold the lie that the resource … is 'public property.' The reality however is that far from being in the ownership of 'the public,' ordinary people have no direct say in the allocation of these resources. Just as working class people are consistently alienated from the product of their labour, this selling of the idea of 'public ownership' over which the public have no real say leads to an increase in apathy and a sense of helplessness among ordinary people. It is much more likely that the political establishment who control the purse strings supposedly 'in the public interest' will actually spend revenues generated from these 'public assets' on measures that will have the long-term effect of re-enforcing rather than alleviating social division. Public policy consistently results in an increase in the gap between the well-off and the poor."* [Kerr, **Opt. Cit.**, pp. 16-7 and p. 17]

Thus an anarchist approach to this issue would be to reject both privatisation **and** nationalisation in favour of socialisation, i.e. placing nationalised firms under workers' self-management. In the terms of public utilities, such as water and power suppliers, they could be self-managed by their workers in association with municipal co-operatives – based on one member, one vote – which would be a much better alternative than privatising what is obviously a natural monopoly (which, as experience shows, simply facilitates the fleecing of the public for massive private profit). Christie and Meltzer state the obvious:

*"It is true that government takes over the control of certain necessary social functions. It does not follow that **only** the state could assume such control. The postmen are 'civil servants' only because the State makes them such. The railways were not always run by the state, They belonged to the capitalists [and do once more, at least in the UK], and could as easily have been run by the railway workers.*

"The opponents of anarchism assure us that if we put government under a ban, there would be no education, for the state controls the schools. There would be no hospitals – where would the money come from? Nobody would work – who would pay their wages? ... But in reality, not ... the state, but the people provide what the people have. If the people do not provide for themselves, the state cannot help them. It only appears to do so because it is in control. Those who have power may apportion work or regulate the standard of living, but this is part of the attack upon the people, not something undertaken on their behalf." [**The Floodgates of Anarchy**, pp. 148-149]

Much the same can be said of other aspects of state intervention. For example, if we look at state education or welfare an anarchist solution could be to press for *"workers' control by all the people involved"* in an institution, in other words *"the extension of the principle of freedom from the economic to the political side of the health [and education] system[s]."* [Nicholas Walters, **About Anarchism**, p. 76] The aim is to create *"new forms of organisation for the social functions that the state fulfils through the bureaucracy."* [Colin Ward, **Anarchy in Action**, p. 19] This means that anarchists, as part of the wider socialist, labour and social movements seek *"to counterbalance as much as we [can] the centralistic, bureaucratic ambitions of Social Democracy."* [Kropotkin, **Act for Yourselves**, p. 120] This applies both to the organisation and tactics of popular movements as well as the proposed reforms and how they are implemented.

In terms of social reforms, anarchists stress that it cannot be left in the hands of politicians (i.e. the agents of the ruling class). It should be obvious that if you let the ruling class decide (on the basis of their own needs and priorities) which reforms to introduce you can guess which ones will be implemented. If the state establishes what is and is not a "reform", then it will implement those which it favours in a manner which benefits itself and the capitalist class. Such top-down "liberalisation" will only increase the power and freedom of the capitalist class and make capitalist and statist exploitation more efficient. It will not undermine the restrictions on liberty for the many which ensure the profits, property and power of the few in the first place. That is, there will be minor changes around the edges of the state system in order to give more "freedom" to landlords and employers to lord it over their tenants and workers. This can be seen from the experience of neo-liberalism across the world.

This means that the decision of what aspects of statism to dismantle first should **never** be handed over to politicians and bureaucrats who are inevitably agents of the capitalist class. It should be

decided from below and guided by an overall strategy of dismantling capitalism **as a system.** That means that any reforms should be aimed at those forms of state intervention which bolster the profits and power of the ruling class and long before addressing those laws which are aimed at making exploitation and oppression tolerable for the working class. If this is not done, then any "reforms" will be directed by the representatives of the business class and, consequently, aim to cut social programmes people actually need while leaving welfare for the rich in place. As such, anarchists argue that pressure from below is required to prioritise reforms based on genuine need rather than the interests of capital. For example, in the UK this would involve, say, urging the privatisation of the Royal Family before even thinking about "reforming" the National Health Service or fighting for the state to "get off the backs" of the unions trying to deregulate business. The key is that people reject a *"naive appeal to the legislators and high officials, waiting for salvation through their deliberations and decrees."* In reality *"freedom does not come begging, but rather must be conquered."* [Reclus, **Op. Cit.**, p. 210] This is not done, then the results will simply confirm Voltairine de Cleyre's insight:

"Nearly all laws which were originally framed with the intention of benefiting workers, have either turned into weapons in their enemies' hands, or become dead letters unless the workers through their organisations have directly enforced their observance. So that in the end, it is direct action that has to be relied on anyway." [**The Voltairine de Cleyre Reader**, p. 59]

A classic example of the former are the anti-trust laws in America, originally aimed at breaking the power of capitalist monopoly but that were soon turned against labour unions and strikers. De Cleyre's second point is a truism and, obviously, means that anarchists aim to strengthen popular organisations and create mass movements which use direct action to defend their rights. Just because there are laws protecting workers, for example, there is no guarantee that they will be enforced – unless workers themselves are strong enough to make sure the bosses comply with the law.

Anarchists are in favour of self-directed activity and direct action to get improvements and defend reforms in the here and now. By organising strikes and protests ourselves, we can improve our lives. This does not mean that using direct action to get favourable laws passed or less-favourable ones revoked is a waste of time. Far from it. However, unless ordinary people use their own strength and grassroots organisations to enforce the law, the state and employers will honour any disliked law purely in the breach. By trusting the state, social self-protection against the market and power concentrations becomes hollow. In the end, what the state gives (or, more correctly, is pressurised into giving), it can take away but what we create and run ourselves is always responsive to **our** desires and interests. We have seen how vulnerable state welfare is to pressures from the capitalist class to see that this is a truism.

This is not to deny that in many ways such state "support" can be used as a means of regaining some of the power and labour stolen from us by capitalists in the first place. State intervention **can** give working people more options than they otherwise would have. If state action could not be used in this way, it is doubtful that capitalists and their hired "experts" would spend so much time trying to undermine and limit it. As the capitalist class happily uses the state to enforce its power and property rights, working people making whatever use they can of it is to be expected. Be that as it may, this does not blind anarchists to the negative aspects of the welfare state and other forms of state intervention (see section J.5.15 for anarchist perspectives on the welfare state).

One problem with state intervention, as Kropotkin saw, is that the state's absorption of social functions *"necessarily favoured the development of an unbridled, narrow-minded individualism. In proportion as the obligations towards the State grew in numbers, the citizens were evidently relieved from their obligations towards each other."* [**Mutual Aid**, p. 183] In the case of state "social functions," such as the British National Health Service, although they were created as a **result** of the social atomisation caused by capitalism, they have tended to **reinforce** the individualism and lack of personal and social responsibility that produced the need for such action in the first place. The pressing need, therefore, is for working class people need *"independent control … of their own welfare programs. Mutual aid and welfare arrangements are necessary."* [Sam Dolgoff, **The American Labour Movement**, p. 26] Specific forms of community and social self-help and their historical precedents are discussed in section J.5.16.

This means that the anarchist task is building popular resistance to the state and capitalism and that may, at time, involves resisting attempts to impose "reforms" which harm the working class and enrich and empower the ruling class. As such, few anarchists subscribe to the notion that we should support capitalism inspired "minimising" of the state in the believe that this will increase poverty and inequality and so speed up the arrival of a social revolution. However, such a position fails to appreciate that social change is only possible when the hope for a better future has not been completely destroyed:

> *"Like many others I have believed in my youth that as social conditions became worse, those who suffered so much would come to realise the deeper causes of their poverty and suffering. I have since been convinced that such a belief is a dangerous illusion … There is a pitch of material and spiritual degradation from which a man can no longer rise. Those who have been born into misery and never knew a better state are rarely able to resist and revolt … Certainly the old slogan, 'The worse the better', was based on an erroneous assumption. Like that other slogan, 'All or nothing', which made many radical oppose any improvement in the lot of the workers, even when the workers demanded it, on the ground that it would distract the mind of the proletariat, and turn it away from the road which leads to social emancipation. It is contrary to all the experience of history and of psychology; people who are not prepared to fight for the betterment of their living conditions are not likely to fight for social emancipation. Slogans of this kind are like a cancer in the revolutionary movement."* [Rudolf Rocker, **London Years**, pp. 25-6]

The anarchist position is, therefore, a practical one based on the specific situation rather than a simplistic application of what is ideologically correct. Rolling back the state in the abstract is not without problems in a class and hierarchy ridden system where opportunities in life are immensely unequal. As such, any *"effort to develop and implement government programs that really were equalisers would lead to a form of class war, and in the present state of popular organisations and distribution of effective power, there can hardly be much doubt as to who would win."* [Chomsky, **The Chomsky Reader**, p. 184] Anarchists seek to build the grassroots resistance, for politicians like Reagan, Bush Snr and JR, Thatcher and so on do not get elected without some serious institutional forces at work. It would be insane to think that once a particularly right-wing politician leaves office those forces will go away or stop trying to influence the political decision making process.

The task of anarchists therefore is not to abstractly oppose state intervention but rather to contribute to popular self-organisation and struggle, creating pressures from the streets and workplaces that governments cannot ignore or defy. This means supporting direct action rather than electioneering (see section J.2) for the *"make-up of the government, the names, persons and political tendencies which rubbed shoulders in it, were incapable of effecting the slightest amendment to the enduring quintessence of the state organism … And the price of entering the of strengthening the state is always unfailingly paid in the currency of a weakening of the forces offering it their assistance. For every reinforcement of state power there is always … a corresponding debilitation of grassroots elements. Men may come and go, but the state remains."* [Jose Peirats, **The CNT in the Spanish Revolution**, vol. 2, p. 150]

D.2
What influence does wealth have over politics?

The short answer is: a great deal of influence, directly and indirectly. We have already touched on this in section B.2.3. Here we will expand on those remarks.

State policy in a capitalist democracy is usually well-insulated from popular influence but very open to elite influence and money interests. Let's consider the possibility of direct influence first. It's obvious that elections cost money and that only the rich and corporations can realistically afford to take part in a major way. Even union donations to political parties cannot effectively compete with those from the business classes. For example, in the 1972 US presidential elections, of the $500 million spent, only about $13 million came from trade unions. The vast majority of the rest undoubtedly came from Big Business and wealthy individuals. For the 1956 elections, the last year for which direct union-business comparisons are possible, the contributions of 742 businessmen matched those of unions representing 17 million workers. This, it should be stressed was at a time when unions had large memberships and before the decline of organised labour in America. Thus the evidence shows that it is *"irrefutable"* that *"businessmen contribute* vastly greater sums of money to political campaigns than do other groups [in society]. Moreover, they have special ease of access to government officials, and they are disproportionately represented at all upper levels of government." [David Schweickart, **Against Capitalism**, pp. 210-1]

Therefore, logically, politics will be dominated by the rich and powerful – in fact if not in theory – since, in general, only the rich can afford to run and only parties supported by the wealthy will gain enough funds and favourable press coverage to have a chance (see section D.3 for the wealthy's control of the mass media). Of course, there are many countries which do have labour-based parties, often allied with union movements, as is the case in Western Europe, for example. Yet even here, the funds available for labour parties are always less than those of capitalist supported parties, meaning that the ability of the former to compete in "fair" elections is hindered. In addition, the political agenda is dominated by the media and as the media are owned by and dependent upon advertising from business, it is hardly surprising that independent labour-based political agendas are difficult to follow or be taken seriously. Unsurprisingly, many of these so-called labour or social-democratic parties have moved to the right (particularly since the 1980s). In Britain, for example, the New Labour government which was elected in 1997 simply, in the main, followed the policies of the previous Conservative Governments and saw its main funding switch from unions to wealthy business men (sometimes in the form of "loans" which could be hidden from the accounts). Significantly, New Labour's success was in part dependent on support from the right-wing media empire of Rupert Murdoch (Blair even consulted with him on policy, indicating his hold over the government).

Then there are the barriers involved once a party has gained office. Just because a party has become the government, it does not mean that they can simply implement their election promises. There are also significant pressures on politicians from the state bureaucracy itself. The state structure is designed to ensure that real power lies not in the hands of elected representatives but rather in the hands of officials, of the state bureaucracy which ensures that any pro-labour political agenda will be watered down and made harmless to the interests of the ruling class. We discuss this in section J.2.2 and will not do so here.

To this it must be added that wealth has a massive **indirect** influence over politics (and so over society and the law). We have noted above that wealth controls the media and its content. However, beyond this there is what can be called "Investor Confidence," which is another important source of influence. This is *the key to capitalist stability,"* notes market socialist David Schweickart. *"If a government initiates policies that capitalists perceive to be opposed to their interests, they may, with neither organisation nor even spitefulness, become reluctant to invest [or actually dis-invest] in the offending country (or region or community), not if 'the climate for business is bad.' The outcome of such isolated acts is an economic downturn, and hence political instability. So a government … has no real choice but to regard the interests of business as privileged. In a very real sense, what is good for business really is good for the country. If business suffers, so will everyone else."* [**Op. Cit.**, pp. 214-5]

Hence Chomsky's comment that when *"popular reform candidates … get elected … you get [a] capital strike – investment capital*

flows out of the country, there's a lowering of investment, and the economy grinds to a halt … The reason is quite simple. In our society, real power does not happen to lie in the political system, it lies in the private economy; that's were the decisions are made about what's produced, how much is produced, what's consumed, where investment takes place, who has jobs, who controls the resources, and so on and so forth. And as long as that remains the case, changes inside the political system can make **some** difference – I don't want to say it's zero – but the differences are going to be very slight."* This means that government policy is forced to make *"the rich folk happy"* otherwise *"everything's going to grind to a halt."* [**Understanding Power**, pp. 62-3] As we discuss in the next section, this is precisely what **has** happened.

David Noble provides a good summary of the effects of such indirect pressures when he writes firms *"have the ability to transfer production from one country to another, to close a plant in one and reopen it elsewhere, to direct and redirect investment wherever the 'climate' is most favourable [to business]…. [I]t has enabled the corporation to play one workforce off against another in the pursuit of the cheapest and most compliant labour (which gives the misleading appearance of greater efficiency)…. [I]t has compelled regions and nations to compete with one another to try and attract investment by offering tax incentives, labour discipline, relaxed environmental and other regulations and publicly subsidised infrastructure … Thus has emerged the great paradox of our age, according to which those nations that prosper most (attract corporate investment) by most readily lowering their standard of living (wages, benefits, quality of life, political freedom). The net result of this system of extortion is a universal lowering of conditions and expectations in the name of competitiveness and prosperity."* [**Progress Without People**, pp. 91-92]

And, we must note, even when a country **does** lower its standard of living to attract investment or encourage its own business class to invest (as the USA and UK did by means of recession to discipline the workforce by high unemployment) it is no guarantee that capital will stay. US workers have seen their companies' profits rise while their wages have stagnated and (in reward) hundreds of thousands have been "down-sized" or seen their jobs moved to Mexico or South East Asia sweatshops. In the far east, Japanese, Hong Kong, and South Korean workers have also seen their manufacturing jobs move to low wage (and more repressive/authoritarian) countries such as China and Indonesia.

As well as the mobility of capital, there is also the threat posed by public debt. As Doug Henwood notes, *"[p]ublic debt is a powerful way of assuring that the state remains safely in capital's hands. The higher a government's debt, the more it must please its bankers. Should bankers grow displeased, they will refuse to roll over old debts or to extend new financing on any but the most punishing terms (if at all). The explosion of [US] federal debt in the 1980s vastly increased the power of creditors to demand austere fiscal and monetary policies to dampen the US economy as it recovered … from the 1989-92 slowdown."* [**Wall Street**, pp. 23-24] And, we must note, Wall street made a fortune on the debt, directly and indirectly.

This analysis applies within countries as well. Commenting on Clinton's plans for the devolution of welfare programmes from

Federal to State government in America, Noam Chomsky makes the important point that *"under conditions of relative equality, this could be a move towards democracy. Under existing circumstances, devolution is intended as a further blow to the eroding democratic processes. Major corporations, investment firms, and the like, can constrain or directly control the acts of national governments and can set one national workforce against another. But the game is much easier when the only competing player that might remotely be influenced by the 'great beast' is a state government, and even middle-sized enterprise can join in. The shadow cast by business [over society and politics] can thus be darker, and private power can move on to greater victories in the name of freedom."* [Noam Chomsky, *"Rollback III"*, **Z Magazine**, March, 1995]

Economic blackmail is a very useful weapon in deterring freedom. Little wonder Proudhon argued that the *"Revolutionary principle … is Liberty. In other words, no more government of man by man through the accumulation of capital."* [quoted by Jack Hayward, **After the French Revolution**, p. 177]

D.2.1 Is capital flight really that powerful?

Yes. By capital flight, business can ensure that any government which becomes too independent and starts to consider the interests of those who elected it will be put back into its place. Therefore we cannot expect a different group of politicians to react in different ways to the same institutional influences and interests. It's no coincidence that the Australian Labour Party and the Spanish Socialist Party introduced "Thatcherite" policies at the same time as the "Iron Lady" implemented them in Britain. The New Zealand Labour government is a case in point, where *"within a few months of re-election [in 1984], finance minister Roger Douglas set out a programme of economic 'reforms' that made Thatcher and Reagan look like wimps…. [A]lmost everything was privatised and the consequences explained away in marketspeak. Division of wealth that had been unknown in New Zealand suddenly appeared, along with unemployment, poverty and crime."* [John Pilger, *"Breaking the one party state,"* **New Statesman**, 16/12/94]

An extreme example of capital flight being used to "discipline" a naughty administration can be seen from Labour governments in Britain during the 1960s and 1970s. Harold Wilson, the Labour Prime Minister between 1964 and 1970, recorded the pressures his government was under from "the markets":

> *"We were soon to learn that decisions on pensions and taxation were no longer to be regarded, as in the past, as decisions for parliament alone. The combination of tax increases with increased social security benefits provoked the first of a series of attacks on sterling, by speculators and others, which beset almost every section of the government for the next five years."* [**The Labour Government 1964-1970**, p. 31]

He also had to *"listen night after night to demands that there should be cuts in government expenditure, and particularly in those parts of government expenditure which related to social services. It was not long before we were being asked, almost at pistol-point to cut back on expenditure"* by the Governor of the Bank of England, the stock exchange's major mouthpiece. [**Op. Cit.**, p. 34] One attempt to pressurise Wilson resulted in him later reflecting:

> *"Not for the first time, I said that we had now reached the situation where a newly elected government with a mandate from the people was being told, not so much by the Governor of the Bank of England but by international speculators, that the policies on which we had fought the election could not be implemented; that the government was to be forced into the adoption of Tory policies to which it was fundamentally opposed. The Governor confirmed that that was, in fact, the case."* [**Op. Cit.**, p. 37]

Only the bluff of threatening to call another general election allowed Wilson to win that particular battle but his government was constrained. It implemented only some of the reforms it had won the election on while implementing many more policies which reflected the wishes of the capitalist class (for example, attempts to shackle the rank and file of the unions).

A similar process was at work against the 1974 to 1979 Labour government. In January, 1974, the FT Index for the London Stock Exchange stood at 500 points. In February, the Miner's went on strike, forcing Heath (the Tory Prime Minister) to hold (and lose) a general election. The new Labour government (which included some left-wingers in its cabinet) talked about nationalising the banks and much heavy industry. In August, 1974, Tony Benn announced plans to nationalise the ship building industry. By December, the FT index had fallen to 150 points. [John Casey, *"The Seventies"*, **The Heavy Stuff**, no. 3, p. 21] By 1976 the Treasury was *"spending $100 million a day buying back its own money on the markets to support the pound."* [**The Times**, 10/6/76]

The Times [27/5/76] noted that *"the further decline in the value of the pound has occurred despite the high level of interest rates. … [D]ealers said that selling pressure against the pound was not heavy or persistent, but there was an almost total lack of interest amongst buyers. The drop in the pound is extremely surprising in view of the unanimous opinion of bankers, politicians and officials that the currency is undervalued."* While there was much talk of private armies and military intervention, this was not needed. As anarchist John Casey argues, the ruling class *"chose to play the economic card…. They decided to subdue the rogue Labour administration by pulling the financial plugs out of the economy…. This resulted in the stock market and the pound plummeting…. This was a much neater solution than bullets and forced the Wilson government to clean up the mess by screwing the working class with public spending cuts and a freeze on wage claims…. The whole process of economic sabotage was neatly engineering through third parties like dealers in the currency markets."* [**Op. Cit.**, p. 23]

The Labour government, faced with the power of international capital, ended up having to receive a temporary "bailing out" by the IMF, which imposed a package of cuts and controls, to which Labour's response was, in effect, *"We'll do anything you say,"* as one economist described it. The social costs of these policies were disastrous, with unemployment rising to the then unheard-of-height of one million. And let's not forget that they *"cut expenditure by twice the amount the IMF were promised"* in an attempt to appear business-friendly. [Peter Donaldson, **A Question of Economics**, p. 89] By capital flight, a slightly radical Labour government was brought to heel.

Capital will not invest in a country that does not meet its approval. In 1977, the Bank of England failed to get the Labour government to abolish its exchange controls. Between 1979 and 1982 the Tories abolished them and ended restrictions on lending for banks and building societies:

> *"The result of the abolition of exchange controls was visible almost immediately: capital hitherto invested in the U.K. began going abroad. In the **Guardian** of 21 September, 1981, Victor Keegan noted that 'Figures published last week by the Bank of England show that pension funds are now investing 25% of their money abroad (compared with almost nothing a few years ago) and there has been no investment at all (net) by unit trusts in the UK since exchange controls were abolished.'"* [Robin Ramsay, *"Mrs Thatcher, North Sea and the Hegemony of the City"*, pp. 2-9, **Lobster**, no. 27, p. 3]

This contributed to the general mismanagement of the economy by Thatcher's Monetarist government. While Milton Friedman had predicted *"only a modest reduction in output and employment will be a side effect of reducing inflation to single figures by 1982,"* the actual results of applying his ideas were drastically different. [quoted by Michael Stewart, **Keynes and After**, p. 179] Britain experienced its deepest recession since the 1930s, with unemployment nearly tripling between 1979 and 1985 (officially, from around 5% to 13% but the real figure was even higher as the government changed the method of measuring it to reduce the figures!). Total output fell by 2.5% in 1980 and another 1.5% in 1981. By 1984 manufacturing investment was still 30% lower in 1979. [Steward, **Op. Cit.**, p. 180] Poverty and inequality soared as unemployment and state repression broke the back of the labour movement and working class resistance.

Eventually, capital returned to the UK as Thatcher's government had subdued a militant working class, shackled the trade unions by law and made the welfare state difficult to live on. It reversed many of the partial gains from previous struggles and ended a situation where people had enough dignity not to accept any job offered or put up with an employer's authoritarian practices. These factors created "inflexibility" in the labour market, so that the working class had to be taught a lesson in "good" economics (in part, ironically, by mismanaging the economy by applying neoclassical dogmas in their Monetarist form!).

Needless to say, the situation in the 21st century has become worse. There has been a *"huge rise in international borrowing … in international capital markets since the liberalisation moves of the 1970s, and [a] significant increase in foreign penetration of national central government bond markets."* This means that it is *"obvious that no central government today may follow economic policies that are disapproved of by the capital markets, which have the power to create an intolerable economic pressure on the respective country's borrowing ability, currency value and investment flows."* [Takis

Fotopoulos, **Toward an Inclusive Democracy**, p. 42] We discuss globalisation in more detail in section D.5.

Unsurprisingly, when left-wing governments have been elected into office after the 1980s, they have spent a lot of time during the election showing how moderate they are to the capitalist class ("the markets"). This moderation continued once in office and any reforms implemented have been of a minor nature and placed within a general neo-liberal context. This was the fate of the British Labour government of Tony Blair, while in Brazil the government of Lula (a former lathe operator, labour union leader and Brazil's first working-class president) was termed "Tropical Blairism" by left-wing critics. Rather than use popular mandate to pursue social justice, they have governed for the rich. Given the role of the state and the pressures governments experience from capital, anarchists were not surprised.

Of course, exceptions can occur, with popular governments implementing significant reforms when economic and political circumstances are favourable. However, these generally need popular movements at the same time to be really effective and these, at some stage, come into conflict with the reformist politicians who hold them back. Given the need for such extra-parliamentary movements to ensure reforms anarchists consider their time better spent building these than encouraging illusions about voting for radical politicians to act for us (see section J.2 for details).

D.2.2 How extensive is business propaganda?

Business spends a lot of money to ensure that people accept the status quo. Referring again to the US as an example (where such techniques are common), various means are used to get people to identify "free enterprise" (meaning state-subsidised private power with no infringement of managerial prerogatives) as "the American way." The success of these campaigns is clear, since many American working people (for example) now object to unions having too much power or irrationally reject all radical ideas as "Communism" (i.e. Stalinism) regardless of their content. By the 1990s, it had even made "liberal" (i.e. mildly reformist centre-left policies) into a swear word in some parts of the country.

This is unsurprising and its roots can be found in the success of the sort of popular movements business propaganda was created to combat. As Chomsky argues, due to popular struggles, *"the state has limited capacity to coerce"* in the advanced capitalist countries (although it is always there, to be used when required). This meant that *"elite groups – the business world, state managers and so on – recognised early on that they are going to have to develop massive methods of control of attitude and opinion, because you cannot control people by force anymore and therefore you have to modify their consciousness so that they don't perceive that they are living under conditions of alienation, oppression, subordination and so on. In fact, that's what probably a couple trillion dollars are spent on each year in the US, very self-consciously, from the framing of television advertisements for two-year olds to what you are taught in graduate school economics programs. It's designed to create a consciousness of subordination and it's also intended specifically and pretty consciously to suppress normal human emotions."* [**Chomsky on Anarchism**, p. 223]

This process became apparent in the 1960s. In the words of Edward Herman:

> *"The business community of the United States was deeply concerned over the excesses of democracy in the United States in the 1960s, and it has tried hard to rectify this problem by means of investments in both politicians and informing public opinion. The latter effort has included massive institutional advertising and other direct and indirect propaganda campaigns, but it has extended to attempts to influence the content of academic ideas … [With] a significant portion of academic research coming from foundations based on business fortunes … [and money] intended to allow people with preferred viewpoints to be aided financially in obtaining academic status and influence and in producing and disseminating books."* [*"The Selling of Market Economics,"* pp. 173-199, **New Ways of Knowing**, Marcus G. Raskin and Herbert J. Bernstein (eds.), p. 182]

Wealth, in other words, is employed to shape the public mind and ensure that challenges to that wealth (and its source) are reduced. These include funding private foundations and institutes ("think-tanks") which can study, promote and protect ways to advance the interests of the few. It can also include the private funding of university chairs as well as the employment of PR companies to attack opponents and sell to the public the benefits not only of specific companies their activities but also the whole socio-economic system. In the words of Australian Social Scientist Alex Carey the *"twentieth century has been characterised by three developments of great political importance: the growth of democracy, the growth of corporate power, and the growth of corporate propaganda as a means of protecting corporate power against democracy."* [quoted by Noam Chomsky, **World Orders, Old and New**, p. 89]

By 1978, American business was spending $1 billion a year on grassroots propaganda. [Chomsky, **Op. Cit.**, p. 93] This is known as *"Astroturf"* by PR insiders, to reflect the appearance of popular support, without the substance, and *"grasstops"* whereby influential citizens are hired to serve as spokespersons for business interests. In 1983, there existed 26 general purpose foundations for this purpose with endowments of $100 million or more, as well as dozens of corporate foundations. One extremely wealth conservative, Richard Mellon Scaife, was giving $10 million a year through four foundations and trusts. [G. William Domhoff, **Who Rules America Now?**, p. 92 and p. 94] These, along with media power, ensure that force – always an inefficient means of control – is replaced by (to use a term associated with Noam Chomsky) the *"manufacture of consent"*: the process whereby the limits of acceptable expression are defined by the wealthy.

Various institutions are used to get Big Business's message across, for example, the Joint Council on Economic Education, ostensibly a charitable organisation, funds economic education for teachers and provides books, pamphlets and films as teaching aids. In 1974, 20,000 teachers participated in its workshops. The aim is to induce teachers to present corporations in an uncritical light to their students. Funding for this propaganda machine comes from the American Bankers Association, AT&T, the Sears Roebuck Foundation and the Ford Foundation. As Domhoff points out, *"[a]lthough it [and other bodies like it] has not been able to bring about active acceptance of all power elite policies and perspectives, on economic or other domestic issues, it has been able to ensure that opposing opinions have remained isolated, suspect and only partially developed."* [**Op. Cit.**, pp. 103-4]

In other words, "unacceptable" ideas are marginalised, the limits of expression defined, and all within a society apparently based on "the free marketplace of ideas."

This process has been going on for some time. For example *"[i]n April 1947, the Advertising Council announced a $100 million campaign to use all media to 'sell' the American economic system – as they conceived it – to the American people; the program was officially described as a 'major project of educating the American people about the economic facts of life.' Corporations 'started extensive programs to indoctrinate employees,' the leading business journal* **Fortune** *reported, subjected their captive audiences to 'Courses in Economic Education' and testing them for commitment to the 'free enterprise system – that is, Americanism.' A survey conducted by the American Management Association (AMA) found that many corporate leaders regarded 'propaganda' and 'economic education' as synonymous, holding that 'we want our people to think right' … [and that] 'some employers view … [it] as a sort of 'battle of loyalties' with the unions' – a rather unequal battle, given the resources available."* These huge PR campaigns *"employed the media, cinema, and other devices to identify 'free enterprise' – meaning state-subsidised private power with no infringement on managerial prerogatives – as 'the American way,' threatened by dangerous subversives."* [Noam Chomsky, **Op. Cit.**, pp. 89-90 and p. 89]

By 1995, $10 billion was considered a *"conservative estimate"* on how much money was spent on public relations. The actual amount is unknown, as the PR industry (and their clients, of course) *"carefully conceals most of its activities from public view. This invisibility is part of a deliberate strategy for manipulating public opinion and government policy."* The net effect is that the wealth of *"large corporations, business associations and governments"* is used to *"out-manoeuvre, overpower and outlast true citizen reformers."* In other words: *"Making the World Safe from Democracy."* [John Stauber and Sheldon Rampton, **Toxic Sludge is Good for You!**, p. 13, p. 14 and p. 13] The public relations industry, as Chomsky notes, is a means by which *"the oppressors … instil their assumptions as the perspective from which you [should] look at the world"* and is *"done extremely consciously."* [**Propaganda and the Public Mind**, p. 166]

The effects of this business propaganda are felt in all other aspects of life, ensuring that while the US business class is extremely class conscious, the rest of the American population considers "class" a swear word! It does have an impact. The rise of, say, "supply-side" economics in the late 1970s can be attributed to the sheer power of its backers rather than its intellectual or scientific merit (which, even in terms of mainstream economics, were slim). Much the same can be said for Monetarism and other discredited free-market dogmas. Hence the usual targets for these campaigns: taxes, regulation of business, welfare (for the poor, not for business), union corruption (when facing organising drives), and so on. All, of course, wrapped up in populist rhetoric which hides the real beneficiaries of the policies (for example, tax cut campaigns which strangely fail to mention that the elite will benefit most, or entirely, from the proposed legislation).

Ironically, the apparent success of this propaganda machine shows the inherent contradiction in the process. Spin and propaganda, while influential, cannot stop people experiencing the grim consequences when the business agenda is applied. While corporate propaganda has shaped the American political scene significantly to the right since the 1970s, it cannot combat the direct experience of stagnating wages, autocratic bosses, environmental degradation, economic insecurity and wealth polarisation indefinitely. The actual objective reality of neo-liberal capitalism will always come into glaring contrast with the propaganda used to justify and extend it. Hence the rising budgets for these activities cannot counteract the rising unease the American people feel about the direction their country is taking. The task of anarchists is to help the struggle, in America and across the globe, by which they can take their country and lives back from the elite.

D.3

How does wealth influence the mass media?

In a word, massively. This, in turn, influences the way people see the world and, as a result, the media is a key means by which the general population come to accept, and support, *"the arrangements of the social, economic, and political order."* The media, in other words *"are vigilant guardians protecting privilege from the threat of public understanding and participation."* This process ensures that state violence is not necessary to maintain the system as *"more subtle means are required: the manufacture of consent, [and] deceiving the masses with 'necessary illusions."* [Noam Chomsky, **Necessary Illusions**, pp. 13-4 and p. 19] The media, in other words, are a key means of ensuring that the dominant ideas within society are those of the dominant class.

Noam Chomsky has helped develop a detailed and sophisticated analysis of how the wealthy and powerful use the media to propagandise in their own interests behind a mask of objective news reporting. Along with Edward Herman, he has developed the *"Propaganda Model"* of how the media works. Herman and Chomsky expound this analysis in their book **Manufacturing Consent: The Political Economy of the Mass Media**, whose main theses we will summarise in this section (unless otherwise indicated all quotes are from this work). We do not suggest that we can present anything other than a summary here and, as such, we urge readers to consult **Manufacturing Consent** itself for a full description and extensive supporting evidence. We would also recommend Chomsky's **Necessary Illusions** for a further discussion of this model of the media.

Chomsky and Herman's "propaganda model" of the media postulates a set of five *"filters"* that act to screen the news and other material disseminated by the media. These *"filters"* result in a media that reflects elite viewpoints and interests and mobilises *"support for the special interests that dominate the state and private activity."* [**Manufacturing Consent**, p. xi] These *"filters"* are: (1) the size, concentrated ownership, owner wealth, and profit orientation of the dominant mass-media firms; (2) advertising as the primary income source of the mass media; (3) the reliance of the media on information provided by government, business, and "experts" funded and approved by these primary sources and agents of power; (4) *"flak"* (negative responses to a media report) as a means of disciplining the media; and (5) *"anticommunism"* as a national religion and control mechanism. It is these filters which ensure that genuine objectivity is usually lacking in the media (needless to say, some media, such as Fox news and the right-wing newspapers like the UK's Sun, Telegraph and Daily Mail, do not even try to present an objective perspective).

"The raw material of news must pass through successive filters leaving only the cleansed residue fit to print," Chomsky and Herman maintain. The filters *"fix the premises of discourse and interpretation, and the definition of what is newsworthy in the first place, and they explain the basis and operations of what amount to propaganda campaigns."* [p. 2] We will briefly consider the nature of these five filters below before refuting two common objections to the model. As with Chomsky and Herman, examples are mostly from the US media. For more extensive analysis, we would recommend two organisations which study and critique the performance of the media from a perspective informed by the "propaganda model." These are the American **Fairness & Accuracy In Reporting** (FAIR) and the UK based **MediaLens** (neither, it should be pointed out, are anarchist organisations).

Before discussing the "propaganda model", we will present a few examples by FAIR to show how the media reflects the interests of the ruling class. War usually provides the most obvious evidence for the biases in the media. For example, Steve Rendall and Tara Broughel analysed the US news media during the first stage of the 2003 invasion of Iraq and found that official voices dominated it *"while opponents of the war have been notably underrepresented,"* Nearly two-thirds of all sources were pro-war, rising to 71% of US guests. Anti-war voices were a mere 10% of all sources, but just 6% of non-Iraqi sources and 3% of US sources. *"Thus viewers were more than six times as likely to see a pro-war source as one who was anti-war; with U.S. guests alone, the ratio increases to 25 to 1."* Unsurprisingly, official voices, *"including current and former government employees, whether civilian or military, dominated network newscasts"* (63% of overall sources). Some analysts did criticise certain aspects of the military planning, but such *"the rare criticisms were clearly motivated by a desire to see U.S. military efforts succeed."* While dissent was quite visible in America, *"the networks largely ignored anti-war opinion."* FAIR found that just 3% of US sources represented or expressed opposition to the war in spite of the fact more than one in four Americans opposed it. In summary, *"none of the networks offered anything resembling proportionate coverage of anti-war voices".* [*"Amplifying Officials, Squelching Dissent"*, **Extra!** May/June 2003]

This perspective is common during war time, with the media's rule of thumb being, essentially, that to support the war is to be objective, while to be anti-war is to carry a bias. The media repeats the sanitised language of the state, relying on official sources to inform the public. Truth-seeking independence was far from the media agenda and so they made it easier for governments to do what they always do, that is lie. Rather than challenge the agenda of the state, the media simply foisted them onto the general population. Genuine criticism only starts to appear when the costs of a conflict become so high that elements of the ruling class start to question tactics and strategy. Until that happens, any criticism is minor (and within a generally pro-war perspective) and the media acts essentially as the fourth branch of the government rather than a Fourth Estate. The Iraq war, it should be noted, was an excellent example of this process at work. Initially, the media simply amplified elite needs, uncritically reporting the Bush Administration's pathetic "evidence" of Iraqi WMD (which quickly became exposed as the nonsense it was). Only when the war became too much of a burden did critical views start being heard and then only in a context of being supportive of the goals of the operation.

This analysis applies as much to domestic issues. For example, Janine Jackson reported how most of the media fell in step with the Bush Administration's attempts in 2006 to trumpet a "booming" U.S. economy in the face of public disbelief. As she notes, there were *"obvious reasons [for] the majority of Americans dissent…. Most American households are not, in fact, seeing their economic fortunes improve. GDP is up, but virtually all the growth has gone into corporate profits and the incomes of the highest economic brackets. Wages and incomes for average workers, adjusted for inflation, are down in recent years; the median income for non-elderly households is down 4.8 percent since 2000…. The poverty rate is rising, as is the number of people in debt."* Yet *"rather than confront these realities, and explore the implications of the White House's efforts to deny them, most mainstream media instead assisted the Bush team's PR by themselves feigning confusion over the gap between the official view and the public mood."* They did so by presenting *"the majority of Americans' understanding of their own economic situation … as somehow disconnected from reality, ascribed to 'pessimism,' ignorance or irrationality…. But why these ordinary workers, representing the majority of households, should not be considered the arbiters of whether or not 'the economy' is good is never explained."* Barring a few exceptions, the media did not *"reflect the concerns of average salaried workers at least as much as those of the investor class."* Needless to say, while capitalist economists were allowed space to discuss their ideas, progressive economists were not. [*"Good News! The Rich Get Richer: Lack of applause for falling wages is media mystery,"* **Extra!**, March/April 2006] Given the nature and role of the media, this reporting comes as no surprise. We stress again, before continuing, that this is a **summary** of Herman's and Chomsky's thesis and we cannot hope to present the wealth of evidence and argument available in either **Manufacturing Consent** or **Necessary Illusions**. We recommend either of these books for more information on and evidence to support the "propaganda model" of the media. Unless otherwise indicated, all quotes in this section of the FAQ are from Herman and Chomsky's **Manufacturing Consent**.

D.3.1 How does the structure of the media affect its content?

Even a century ago, the number of media with any substantial outreach was limited by the large size of the necessary investment, and this limitation has become increasingly effective over time. As in any well developed market, this means that there are very effective **natural** barriers to entry into the media industry. Due to this process of concentration, the ownership of the major media has become increasingly concentrated in fewer and fewer hands. As Ben Bagdikian stresses in his 1987 book **Media Monopoly**, the 29 largest media systems account for over half of the output of all newspapers, and most of the sales and audiences in magazines, broadcasting, books, and movies. The *"top tier"* of these – somewhere between 10 and 24 systems – along with the government and wire services, *"defines the news agenda and supplies much of the national and international news to the lower tiers of the media, and thus for the general public."* [p. 5] Since then, media concentration has increased, both nationally and on a global level. Bagdikian's 2004 book, **The New Media Monopoly**, showed that since 1983 the number of corporations controlling most newspapers, magazines, book publishers, movie studios, and electronic media have shrunk from 50 to five global-dimension firms, operating with many of the characteristics of a cartel – Time-Warner, Disney, News Corporation, Viacom and Germany-based Bertelsmann.

These *"top-tier companies are large, profit-seeking corporations, owned and controlled by very wealthy people … Many of these companies are fully integrated into the financial market"* which means that *"the pressures of stockholders, directors and bankers to focus on the bottom line are powerful."* [p. 5] These pressures have intensified in recent years as media stocks have become market favourites and as deregulation has increased profitability and so the threat of take-overs. These ensure that these *"control groups obviously have a special take on the status quo by virtue of their wealth and their strategic position in one of the great institutions of society. And they exercise the power of this strategic position, if only by establishing the general aims of the company and choosing its top management."* [p. 8]

The media giants have also diversified into other fields. For example GE and Westinghouse, both owners of major television networks, are huge, diversified multinational companies heavily involved in the controversial areas of weapons production and nuclear power. GE and Westinghouse depend on the government to subsidise their nuclear power and military research and development, and to create a favourable climate for their overseas sales and investments. Similar dependence on the government affect other media.

Because they are large corporations with international investment interests, the major media tend to have a right-wing political bias. In addition, members of the business class own most of the mass media, the bulk of which depends for their existence on advertising revenue (which in turn comes from private business). Business also provides a substantial share of "experts" for news programmes and generates massive "flak." Claims that the media are "left-leaning" are sheer disinformation manufactured by the "flak" organisations described below (in section D.3.4). Thus Herman and Chomsky:

> "the dominant media forms are quite large businesses; they are controlled by very wealthy people or by managers who are subject to sharp constraints by owners and other market-profit-oriented forces; and they are closely interlocked, and have important common interests, with other major corporations, banks, and government. This is the first powerful filter that effects news choices." [p. 14]

Needless to say, reporters and editors will be selected based upon how well their work reflects the interests and needs of their employers. Thus a radical reporter and a more mainstream one both of the same skills and abilities would have very different careers within the industry. Unless the radical reporter toned down their copy, they are unlikely to see it printed unedited or unchanged. Thus the structure within the media firm will tend to penalise radical viewpoints, encouraging an acceptance of the status quo in order to further a career. This selection process ensures that owners do not need to order editors or reporters what to do – to be successful they will have to internalise the values of their employers.

D.3.2 What is the effect of advertising on the mass media?

The main business of the media is to sell audiences to advertisers. Advertisers thus acquire a kind of de facto licensing authority, since without their support the media would cease to be economically viable. And it is **affluent** audiences that get advertisers interested. As Chomsky and Herman put it, the "idea that the drive for large audiences makes the mass media 'democratic' thus suffers from the initial weakness that its political analogue is a voting system weighted by income!" [p.16]

As regards TV, in addition to "discrimination against unfriendly media institutions, advertisers also choose selectively among programs on the basis of their own principles. With rare exceptions these are culturally and politically conservative. Large corporate advertisers on television will rarely sponsor programs that engage in serious criticisms of corporate activities." Accordingly, large corporate advertisers almost never sponsor programs that contain serious criticisms of corporate activities, such as negative ecological impacts, the workings of the military-industrial complex, or corporate support of and benefits from Third World dictatorships. This means that TV companies "learn over time that such programs will not sell and would have to be carried at a financial sacrifice, and that, in addition, they may offend powerful advertisers." More generally, advertisers will want "to avoid programs with serious complexities and disturbing controversies that interfere with the 'buying mood.'" [p. 17]

Political discrimination is therefore structured into advertising allocations by wealthy companies with an emphasis on people with money to buy. In addition, "many companies will always refuse to do business with ideological enemies and those whom they perceive as damaging their interests." Thus overt discrimination adds to the force of the "voting system weighted by income." This has had the effect of placing working class and radical papers at a serious disadvantage. Without access to advertising revenue, even the most popular paper will fold or price itself out of the market. Chomsky and Herman cite the British pro-labour and pro-union **Daily Herald** as an example of this process. At its peak, the **Daily Herald** had almost double the readership of **The Times**, the **Financial Times** and **The Guardian** combined, yet even with 8.1% of the national circulation it got 3.5% of net advertising revenue and so could not survive on the "free market." As Herman and Chomsky note, a "mass movement without any major media support, and subject to a great deal of active press hostility, suffers a serious disability, and struggles against grave odds." With the folding of the **Daily Herald**, the labour movement lost its voice in the mainstream media. [pp. 17-8 and pp. 15-16]

Thus advertising is an effective filter for news choice (and, indeed, survival in the market).

D.3.3 Why do the media rely on government and business "experts" for information?

As Herman and Chomsky stress, basic economics explains why the mass media "are drawn into a symbiotic relationship with powerful sources of information" as well as "reciprocity of interest." The media need "a steady, reliable flow of raw material of news. They have daily news demands and imperative news schedules that they must meet." They cannot afford to have reporters and cameras at all locations and so economics "dictates that they concentrate their resources where significant news often occurs." [p. 18] This means that bottom-line considerations dictate that the media concentrate their resources where news, rumours and leaks are plentiful, and where regular press conferences are held. The White House, Pentagon, and the State Department, in Washington, D.C., are centres of such activity on a national scale, while city hall and police departments are their local equivalents. In addition, trade groups, businesses and corporations also provide regular stories that are deemed as newsworthy and from credible sources.

In other words, government and corporate sources have the great merit of being recognisable and credible by their status and prestige; moreover, they have the most money available to produce a flow of news that the media can use. For example, the Pentagon has a public-information service employing many thousands of people, spending hundreds of millions of dollars every year, and far outspending not only the public-information resources of any dissenting individual or group but the **aggregate** of such groups. Only the corporate sector has the resources to produce public information and propaganda on the scale of the Pentagon and other government bodies. The Chamber of Commerce, a business collective, had a 1983 budget for research, communications, and political activities of $65 million. Besides the US Chamber of Commerce, there are thousands of state and local chambers of commerce and trade associations also engaged in public relations and lobbying activities. As we noted in section D.2, the corporate funding of PR is massive. Thus "business corporations and trade groups are also regular purveyors of stories deemed newsworthy. These bureaucracies turn out a large volume of material that meets the demands of news organisations for reliable, scheduled flows." [p. 19]

To maintain their pre-eminent position as sources, government and business-news agencies expend much effort to make things easy for news organisations. They provide the media organisations with facilities in which to gather, give journalists advance copies of speeches and upcoming reports; schedule press conferences at hours convenient for those needing to meet news deadlines; write press releases in language that can be used with little editing; and carefully organise press conferences and photo-opportunity sessions. This means that, in effect, *"the large bureaucracies of the powerful* **subsidise** *the mass media, and gain special access by their contribution to reducing the media's costs of acquiring the raw materials of, and producing, news."* [p. 22]

This economic dependency also allows corporations and the state to influence the media. The most obvious way is by using their *"personal relationships, threats, and rewards to further influence and coerce the media. The media may feel obligated to carry extremely dubious stories and mute criticism in order not to offend sources and disturb a close relationship. It is very difficult to call authorities on whom one depends for daily news liars, even if they tell whoppers."* Critical sources may be avoided not only due to the higher costs in finding them and establishing their credibility, but because the established *"primary sources may be offended and may even threaten the media with using them."* [p. 22] As well as refusing to co-operate on shows or reports which include critics, corporations and governments may threaten the media with loss of access if they ask too many critical questions or delve into inappropriate areas.

In addition, *"more important, powerful sources regularly take advantage of media routines and dependency to 'manage' the media, to manipulate them into following a special agenda and framework ... Part of this management process consists of inundating the media with stories, which serve sometimes to foist a particular line and frame on the media ... and at other times to chase unwanted stories off the front page or out of the media altogether."* [p. 23]

The dominance of official sources would, of course, be weakened by the existence of highly respectable unofficial sources that gave dissident views with great authority. To alleviate this problem, the power elite uses the strategy of *"co-opting the experts"* – that is, putting them on the payroll as consultants, funding their research, and organising think tanks that will hire them directly and help disseminate the messages deemed essential to elite interests. "Experts" on TV panel discussions and news programs are often drawn from such organisations, whose funding comes primarily from the corporate sector and wealthy families – a fact that is, of course, never mentioned on the programs where they appear. This allows business, for example, to sell its interests as objective and academic while, in fact, they provide a thin veneer to mask partisan work which draws the proper conclusions desired by their pay masters.

This process of creating a mass of experts readily available to the media *"has been carried out on a deliberate and a massive scale."* These ensure that *"the corporate viewpoint"* is effectively spread

as the experts work is *"funded and their outputs ... disseminated to the media by a sophisticated propaganda effort. The corporate funding and clear ideological purpose in the overall effort had no discernible effect on the credibility of the intellectuals so mobilised; on the contrary, the funding and pushing of their ideas catapulted them into the press."* [p. 23 and p. 24]

D.3.4 How is "flak" used as a means of disciplining the media?

"Flak" is a term used by Herman and Chomsky to refer *"to negative responses to a media statement or program."* Such responses may be expressed as phone calls, letters, telegrams, e-mail messages, petitions, lawsuits, speeches, bills before Congress, or *"other modes of complaint, threat, or punishment."* Flak may be generated centrally, by organisations, or it may come from the independent actions of individuals (sometimes encouraged to act by media hacks such as right-wing talk show hosts or newspapers). *"If flak is produced on a large-scale, or by individuals or groups with substantial resources, it can be both uncomfortable and costly to the media."* [p. 26]

This is for many reasons. Positions need to be defended within and outwith an organisation, sometimes in front of legislatures and (perhaps) in the courts. Advertisers are very concerned to avoid offending constituencies who might produce flak, and their demands for inoffensive programming exerts pressure on the media to avoid certain kinds of facts, positions, or programs that are likely to call forth flak. This can have a strong deterrence factor, with media organisations avoiding certain subjects and sources simply to avoid having to deal with the inevitable flak they will receive from the usual sources. The ability to produce flak *"is related to power,"* as it is expensive to generate on scale which is actually effective. [p. 26] Unsurprisingly, this means that the most effective flak comes from business and government who have the funds to produce it on a large scale.

The government itself is *"a major producer of flak, regularly assailing, threatening, and 'correcting' the media, trying to contain any deviations from the established line in foreign or domestic policy."* However, the right-wing plays a major role in deliberately creating flak. For example, during the 1970s and 1980s, the corporate community sponsored the creation of such institutions as the American Legal Foundation, the Capital Legal Foundation, the Media Institute, the Center for Media and Public Affairs, and Accuracy in Media (AIM), which may be regarded as organisations designed for the specific purpose of producing flak. Freedom House is an older US organisation which had a broader design but whose flak-producing activities became a model for the more recent organisations. The Media Institute, for instance, was set up in 1972 and is funded by wealthy corporate patrons, sponsoring media monitoring projects, conferences, and studies of the media. The main focus of its studies and conferences has been the alleged failure of the media to portray business accurately and to give adequate weight to the business point of view, but it also sponsors works which "expose" alleged left-wing bias in the mass media. [p. 28 and pp. 27-8]

And, it should be noted, while the flak machines *"steadily attack the media, the media treats them well. They receive respectful attention, and their propagandistic role and links to a large corporate program are rarely mentioned or analysed."* [p. 28] Indeed, such attacks *"are often not unwelcome, first because response is simple or superfluous; and second, because debate over this issue helps entrench the belief that the media are … independent and objective, with high standards of professional integrity and openness to all reasonable views"* which is *"quite acceptable to established power and privilege – even to the media elites themselves, who are not averse to the charge that they may have gone to far in pursuing their cantankerous and obstreperous ways in defiance of orthodoxy and power."* Ultimately, such flak *"can only be understood as a demand that the media should not even reflect the range of debate over tactical questions among the dominant elites, but should serve only those segments that happen to manage the state at a particular moment, and should do so with proper enthusiasm and optimism about the causes – noble by definition – in which state power is engaged."* [Chomsky, **Necessary Illusions**, p. 13 and p. 11]

D.3.5 Why is "anticommunism" used as control mechanism?

The final filter which Herman and Chomsky discuss is the ideology of anticommunism. "Communism" is of course regarded as the ultimate evil by the corporate rich, since the ideas of collective ownership of productive assets *"threatens the very root of their class position and superior status."* As the concept is *"fuzzy,"* it can be widely applied and *"can be used against anybody advocating policies that threaten property interests."* [p. 29] Hence the attacks on third-world nationalists as "socialists" and the steady expansion of "communism" to apply to any form of socialism, social democracy, reformism, trade unionism or even "liberalism" (i.e. any movement which aims to give workers more bargaining power or allow ordinary citizens more voice in public policy decisions).

Hence the ideology of anticommunism has been very useful, because it can be used to discredit anybody advocating policies regarded as harmful to corporate interests. It also helps to divide the Left and labour movements, justifies support for pro-US fascist regimes abroad as "lesser evils" than communism, and discourages liberals from opposing such regimes for fear of being branded as heretics from the national religion. This process has been aided immensely by the obvious fact that the "communist" regimes (i.e. Stalinist dictatorships) have been so terrible.

Since the collapse of the USSR and related states in 1989, the utility of anticommunism has lost some of its power. Of course, there are still a few official communist enemy states, like North Korea, Cuba, and China, but these are not quite the threat the USSR was. North Korea and Cuba are too impoverished to threaten the world's only super-power (that so many Americans think that Cuba was ever a threat says a lot about the power of propaganda). China is problematic, as Western corporations now have access to, and can exploit, its resources, markets and cheap labour. As such, criticism of China will be mooted, unless it starts to hinder US corporations

or become too much of an economic rival.

So we can still expect, to some degree, abuses or human rights violations in these countries are systematically played up by the media while similar abuses in client states are downplayed or ignored. Chomsky and Herman refer to the victims of abuses in enemy states as **worthy victims,** while victims who suffer at the hands of US clients or friends are **unworthy victims.** Stories about worthy victims are often made the subject of sustained propaganda campaigns, to score political points against enemies. For example:

> *"If the government or corporate community and the media feel that a story is useful as well as dramatic, they focus on it intensively and use it to enlighten the public. This was true, for example, of the shooting down by the Soviets of the Korean airliner KAL 007 in early September 1983, which permitted an extended campaign of denigration of an official enemy and greatly advanced Reagan administration arms plans."*

> *"In sharp contrast, the shooting down by Israel of a Libyan civilian airliner in February 1973 led to no outcry in the West, no denunciations for 'cold-blooded murder,' and no boycott. This difference in treatment was explained by the **New York Times** precisely on the grounds of utility: 'No useful purpose is served by an acrimonious debate over the assignment of blame for the downing of a Libyan airliner in the Sinai peninsula last week.' There **was** a very 'useful purpose' served by focusing on the Soviet act, and a massive propaganda campaign ensued."* [p. 32]

As noted, since the end of the Cold War, anti-communism has not been used as extensively as it once was to mobilise support for elite crusades. Other enemies have to be found and so the "Drug War" or "anti-terrorism" now often provide the public with "official enemies" to hate and fear. Thus the Drug War was the excuse for the Bush administration's invasion of Panama, and "fighting narco-terrorists" has more recently been the official reason for shipping military hardware and surveillance equipment to Mexico (where it's actually being used against the Zapatista rebels in Chiapas, whose uprising is threatening to destabilise the country and endanger US investments). After 9/11, terrorism became the key means of forcing support for policies. The mantra *"you are either with us or with the terrorists"* was used to bolster support and reduce criticism for both imperial adventures as well as a whole range of regressive domestic policies.

Whether any of these new enemies will prove to be as useful as anticommunism remains to be seen. It is likely, particularly given how "communism" has become so vague as to include liberal and social democratic ideas, that it will remain the bogey man of choice – particularly as many within the population both at home and abroad continue to support left-wing ideas and organisations. Given the track record of neo-liberalism across the globe, being able to tar its opponents as "communists" will remain a useful tool.

D.3.6 Isn't the "propaganda model" a conspiracy theory?

No, far from it. Chomsky and Herman explicitly address this charge in **Manufacturing Consent** and explain why it is a false one:

> "Institutional critiques such as we present in this book are commonly dismissed by establishment commentators as 'conspiracy theories,' but this is merely an evasion. We do not use any kind of 'conspiracy' hypothesis to explain mass-media performance. In fact, our treatment is much closer to a 'free market' analysis, with the results largely an outcome of the workings of market forces." [p. xii]

They go on to suggest what some of these "market forces" are. One of the most important is the weeding-out process that determines who gets the journalistic jobs in the major media: "Most biased choices in the media arise from the preselection of right-thinking people, internalised preconceptions, and the adaptation of personnel to the constraints of ownership, organisation, market, and political power." This is the key, as the model "helps us to understand how media personnel adapt, and are adapted, to systemic demands. Given the imperatives of corporate organisation and the workings of the various filters, conformity to the needs and interests of privileged sectors is essential to success." This means that those who do not display the requisite values and perspectives will be regarded as irresponsible and/or ideological and, consequently, will not succeed (barring a few exceptions). In other words, those who "adapt, perhaps quite honestly, will then be able to assert, accurately, that they perceive no pressures to conform. The media are indeed free ... for those who have internalised the required values and perspectives." [p. xii and p. 304]

In other words, important media employees learn to internalise the values of their bosses: "Censorship is largely self-censorship, by reporters and commentators who adjust to the realities of source and media organisational requirements, and by people at higher levels within media organisations who are chosen to implement, and have usually internalised, the constraints imposed by proprietary and other market and governmental centres of power." But, it may be asked, isn't it still a conspiracy theory to suggest that media leaders all have similar values? Not at all. Such leaders "do similar things because they see the world through the same lenses, are subject to similar constraints and incentives, and thus feature stories or maintain silence together in tacit collective action and leader-follower behaviour." [p. xii]

The fact that media leaders share the same fundamental values does not mean, however, that the media are a solid monolith on all issues. The powerful often disagree on the tactics needed "to attain generally shared aims, [and this gets] reflected in media debate. But views that challenge fundamental premises or suggest that the observed modes of exercise of state power are based on systemic factors will be excluded from the mass media even when elite controversy over tactics rages fiercely." [p. xii] This means that viewpoints which question the legitimacy of elite aims or suggest that state power is being exercised in elite interests rather than the

"national" interest will be excluded from the mass media. As such, we would expect the media to encourage debate within accepted bounds simply because the ruling class is not monolithic and while they agree on keeping the system going, they disagree on the best way to do so.

Therefore the "propaganda model" has as little in common with a "conspiracy theory" as saying that the management of General Motors acts to maintain and increase its profits. As Chomsky notes, "[t]o confront power is costly and difficult; high standards of evidence and argument are imposed, and critical analysis is naturally not welcomed by those who are in a position to react vigorously and to determine the array of rewards and punishments. Conformity to a 'patriotic agenda,' in contrast, imposes no such costs." This means that "conformity is the easy way, and the path to privilege and prestige ... It is a natural expectation, on uncontroversial assumptions, that the major media and other ideological institutions will generally reflect the perspectives and interests of established power." [**Necessary Illusions**, pp. 8-9 and p. 10]

D.3.7 Isn't the model contradicted by the media reporting government and business failures?

As noted above, the claim that the media are "adversarial" or (more implausibly) that they have a "left-wing bias" is due to right-wing PR organisations. This means that some "inconvenient facts" are occasionally allowed to pass through the filters in order to give the **appearance** of "objectivity" – precisely so the media can deny charges of engaging in propaganda. As Chomsky and Herman put it: "the 'naturalness' of these processes, with inconvenient facts allowed sparingly and within the proper framework of assumptions, and fundamental dissent virtually excluded from the mass media (but permitted in a marginalised press), makes for a propaganda system that is far more credible and effective in putting over a patriotic agenda than one with official censorship." [p. xiv]

To support their case against the "adversarial" nature of the media, Herman and Chomsky look into the claims of such right-wing media PR machines as Freedom House. However, it is soon discovered that "the very examples offered in praise of the media for their independence, or criticism of their excessive zeal, illustrate exactly the opposite." Such flak, while being worthless as serious analysis, does help to reinforce the myth of an "adversarial media" and so is taken seriously by the media. By saying that both right and left attack them, the media presents themselves as neutral, balanced and objective – a position which is valid only if both criticisms are valid and of equal worth. This is not the case, as Herman and Chomsky prove, both in terms of evidence and underlying aims and principles. Ultimately, the attacks by the right on the media are based on the concern "to protect state authority from an intrusive public" and so "condemn the media for lack of sufficient enthusiasm in supporting official crusades." In other words, that the "existing level of subordination to state authority is often deemed unsatisfactory." [p. xiv and p. 301] The right-wing notion that the media are "liberal" or "left-wing" says far more about the authoritarian vision and aims of the right than the reality of the media.

Therefore the "adversarial" nature of the media is a myth, but this is not to imply that the media does not present critical analysis. Herman and Chomsky in fact argue that the *"mass media are not a solid monolith on all issues."* and do not deny that it does present facts (which they do sometimes themselves cite). This *"affords the opportunity for a classic **non sequitur**, in which the citations of facts from the mainstream press by a critic of the press is offered as a triumphant 'proof' that the criticism is self-refuting, and that media coverage of disputed issues is indeed adequate."* But, as they argue, *"[t]hat the media provide some facts about an issue … proves absolutely nothing about the adequacy or accuracy of that coverage. The mass media do, in fact, literally suppress a great deal…. But even more important in this context is the question given to a fact – its placement, tone, and repetitions, the framework within which it is presented, and the related facts that accompany it and give it meaning (or provide understanding) … there is no merit to the pretence that because certain facts may be found by a diligent and sceptical researcher, the absence of radical bias and de facto suppression is thereby demonstrated."* [p. xii and pp xiv-xv]

As they stress, the media in a democratic system is different from one in a dictatorship and so they *"do not function in the manner of the propaganda system of a totalitarian state. Rather, they permit – indeed, encourage – spirited debate, criticism, and dissent, as long as these remain faithfully within the system of presuppositions and principles that constitute an elite consensus, a system so powerful as to be internalised largely without awareness."* Within this context, *"facts that tend to undermine the government line, if they are properly understood, can be found."* Indeed, it is *"possible that the volume of inconvenient facts can expand, as it did during the Vietnam War, in response to the growth of a critical constituency (which included elite elements from 1968). Even in this exceptional case, however, it was very rare for news and commentary to find their way into the mass media if they failed to conform to the framework of established dogma (postulating benevolent U.S aims, the United States responding to aggression and terror, etc.)"* While during the war and after, *"apologists for state policy commonly pointed to the inconvenient facts, the periodic 'pessimism' of media pundits, and the debates over tactics as showing that the media were 'adversarial' and even 'lost' the war,"* in fact these *"allegations are ludicrous."* [p. 302 and p. xiv] A similar process, it should be noted, occurred during the invasion and occupation of Iraq.

To summarise, as Chomsky notes *"what is essential is the power to set the agenda."* This means that debate *"cannot be stilled, and indeed, in a properly functioning system of propaganda, it should not be, because it has a system-reinforcing character if constrained within proper bounds. What is essential is to set the bounds firmly. Controversy may rage as long as it adheres to the presuppositions that define the consensus of elites, and it should furthermore be encourages within these bounds, this helping to establish these doctrines as the very condition of thinkable thought while reinforcing the belief that freedom reigns."* [**Necessary Illusions**, p. 48]

D.4

What is the relationship between capitalism and the ecological crisis?

Environmental damage has reached alarming proportions. Almost daily there are new upwardly revised estimates of the severity of global warming, ozone destruction, topsoil loss, oxygen depletion from the clearing of rain forests, acid rain, toxic wastes and pesticide residues in food and water, the accelerating extinction rate of natural species, etc., etc. Almost all scientists now recognise that global warming may soon become irreversible, with devastating results for humanity. Those few who reject this consensus are usually paid by corporations with a vested interest in denying the reality of what their companies are doing to the planet (such as oil companies). That sections of the ruling class have become aware of the damage inflicted on the planet's eco-systems suggests that we have only a few decades before they are irreparably damaged.

Most anarchists see the ecological crisis as rooted in the psychology of domination, which emerged with the rise of hierarchy (including patriarchy, classes, and the first primitive states) during the Late Neolithic. Murray Bookchin, one of the pioneers of eco-anarchism, points out that *"[t]he hierarchies, classes, propertied forms, and statist institutions that emerged with social domination were carried over conceptually into humanity's relationship with nature. Nature too became increasingly regarded as a mere resource, an object, a raw material to be exploited as ruthlessly as slaves on a latifundium."* [**Toward an Ecological Society** p. 41] In his view, without uprooting the psychology of domination, all attempts to stave off ecological catastrophe are likely to be mere palliatives and so doomed to failure.

Bookchin argues that *"the conflict between humanity and nature is an extension of the conflict between human and human. Unless the ecology movement encompasses the problem of domination in all its aspects, it will contribute **nothing** toward eliminating the root causes of the ecological crisis of our time. If the ecology movement stops at mere reformism in pollution and conservation control – at mere 'environmentalism' – without dealing radically with the need for an expanded concept of revolution, it will merely serve as a safety value for the existing system of natural and human exploitation."* [**Op. Cit.**, p. 43] Since capitalism is the vehicle through which the psychology of domination finds its most ecologically destructive outlet, most eco-anarchists give the highest priority to dismantling it:

> *"Literally, the system in its endless devouring of nature will reduce the entire biosphere to the fragile simplicity of our desert and arctic biomes. We will be reversing the process of organic evolution which has differentiated flora and fauna into increasingly complex forms and relationships, thereby creating a simpler and less stable world of life. The consequences of this appalling regression are predictable enough in the long run – the biosphere will become so fragile that it will eventually collapse from the*

standpoint human survival needs and remove the organic preconditions for human life. That this will eventuate from a society based on production for the sake of production is ... merely a matter of time, although when it will occur is impossible to predict." [**Op. Cit.**, p. 68]

This is not to say that ecological destruction did not exist before the rise of capitalism. This is not the case. Social problems, and the environmental destruction they create, *"lie not only in the conflict between wage labour and capital"* they also *"lie in the conflicts between age-groups and sexes within the family, hierarchical modes of instruction in the schools, the bureaucratic usurpation of power within the city, and ethnic divisions within society. Ultimately, they stem from a hierarchical sensibility of command and obedience that begins with the family and merely reaches its most visible social form in the factory, bureaucracy and military. I cannot emphasise too strongly that these problems emerged long before capitalism."* However, capitalism is the dominant economic form today and so the *"modern urban crisis largely reflects the divisions that capitalism has produced between society and nature."* [**Op. Cit.**, p. 29 and p. 28]

Capitalism, unlike previous class and hierarchical systems, has an expansionist nature which makes it incompatible with the planet's ecology. So it is important to stress that capitalism must be **eliminated** because it **cannot** reform itself so as to become "environment friendly," contrary to the claims of so-called "green" capitalists. This is because *"[c]apitalism not only validates precapitalist notions of the domination of nature, ... it turns the plunder of nature into society's law of life. To quibble with this kind of system about its values, to try to frighten it with visions about the consequences of growth is to quarrel with its very metabolism. One might more easily persuade a green plant to desist from photosynthesis than to ask the bourgeois economy to desist from capital accumulation."* [**Op. Cit.**, p. 66]

Thus capitalism causes ecological destruction because it is based upon domination (of human over human and so humanity over nature) and continual, endless growth (for without growth, capitalism would die). This can be seen from the fact that industrial production has increased fifty fold between 1950 and the 1990s. Obviously such expansion in a finite environment cannot go on indefinitely without disastrous consequences. Yet it is impossible **in principle** for capitalism to kick its addiction to growth. It is important to understand why.

Capitalism is based on production for profit. In order to stay profitable, a firm needs to make a profit. In other words, money must become more money. This can be done in two ways. Firstly, a firm can produce new goods, either in response to an existing need or (by means of advertising) by creating a new one. Secondly, by producing a new good more cheaply than other firms in the same industry in order to successfully compete. If one firm increases its productivity (as all firms must try to do), it will be able to produce more cheaply, thus undercutting its competition and capturing more market share (until eventually it forces less profitable firms into bankruptcy). Hence, constantly increasing productivity is essential for survival.

There are two ways to increase productivity, either by passing on costs to third parties (externalities) or by investing in new means of production. The former involves, for example, polluting the surrounding environment or increasing the exploitation of workers (e.g. longer hours and/or more intense work for the same amount of pay). The latter involves introducing new technologies that reduce the amount of labour necessary to produce the same product or service. Due to the struggle of workers to prevent increases in the level of their exploitation and by citizens to stop pollution, new technologies are usually the main way that productivity is increased under capitalism (though of course capitalists are always looking for ways to avoid regulations and to increase the exploitation of workers on a given technology by other means as well).

But new technologies are expensive, which means that in order to pay for continuous upgrades, a firm must continually sell **more** of what it produces, and so must keep expanding its capital. To stay in the same place under capitalism is to tempt crisis – thus a firm must always strive for more profits and thus must always expand and invest. In order to survive, a firm must constantly expand and upgrade its capital and production levels so it can sell enough to **keep** expanding and upgrading its capital – i.e. "grow or die," or *"production for the sake of production"* (to use Marx's term). This means that the accumulation of capital is at the heart of the system and so it is impossible in principle for capitalism to solve the ecological crisis, because "grow or die" is inherent in its nature:

> *"To speak of 'limits to growth' under a capitalistic market economy is as meaningless as to speak of limits of warfare under a warrior society. The moral pieties, that are voiced today by many well-meaning environmentalists, are as naive as the moral pieties of multinationals are manipulative. Capitalism can no more be 'persuaded' to limit growth than a human being can be 'persuaded' to stop breathing. Attempts to 'green' capitalism, to make it 'ecological', are doomed by the very nature of the system as a system of endless growth."* [Bookchin, **Remaking Society**, pp. 93-94]

As long as capitalism exists, it will **necessarily** continue its *"endless devouring of nature,"* until it removes the *"organic preconditions for human life."* For this reason there can be no compromise with capitalism: We must destroy it before it destroys us. And time is running out.

Capitalists, of course, do not accept this conclusion. Many simply ignore the evidence or view the situation through rose-coloured spectacles, maintaining that ecological problems are not as serious as they seem or that science will find a way to solve them before it's too late. Some are aware of the problem, but they fail to understand its roots and, as such, advocate reforms which are based on either regulation or (more usually in these neo-liberal days) on "market" based solutions. In section E we will show why these arguments are unsound and why libertarian socialism is our best hope for preventing ecological catastrophe.

D.5

What causes imperialism?

In a word: power. Imperialism is the process by which one country dominates another directly, by political means, or indirectly, by economic means, in order to steal its wealth (either natural or produced). This, by necessity, means the exploitation of working people in the dominated nation. Moreover, it can also aid the exploitation of working people in the imperialist nation itself. As such, imperialism cannot be considered in isolation from the dominant economic and social system. Fundamentally the cause is the same inequality of power, which is used in the service of exploitation.

While the rhetoric used for imperial adventures may be about self-defence, defending/exporting "democracy" and/or "humanitarian" interests, the reality is much more basic and grim. As Chomsky stresses, *"deeds consistently accord with interests, and conflict with words – discoveries that must not, however, weaken our faith in the sincerity of the declarations of our leaders."* This is unsurprising as states are always *"pursuing the strategic and economic interests of dominant sectors to the accompaniment of rhetorical flourishes about its exceptional dedication to the highest values"* and so *"the evidence for … the proclaimed messianic missions reduces to routine pronouncements"* (faithfully repeated by the media) while *"counter-evidence is mountainous."* [**Failed States**, p. 171 and pp. 203-4]

We must stress that we are concentrating on the roots of imperialism here. We do not, and cannot, provide a detailed history of the horrors associated with it. For US imperialism, the works of Noam Chomsky are recommended. His books **Turning the Tide** and **The Culture of Terrorism** expose the evils of US intervention in Central America, for example, while **Deterring Democracy, Rogue States: The Rule of Force in World Affairs** and **Failed States: The Abuse of Power and the Assault on Democracy** present a wider perspective. **Killing Hope: US Military and CIA Interventions Since World War II** and **Rogue State: A Guide to the World's Only Superpower** by William Blum are also worth reading. For post-1945 British imperialism, Mark Curtis's **Web of Deceit: Britain's Real Role in the World** and **Unpeople: Britain's Secret Human Rights Abuses** are recommended.

As we will discuss in the following sections, imperialism has changed over time, particularly during the last two hundred years (where its forms and methods have evolved with the changing needs of capitalism). But even in the pre-capitalist days of empire building, imperialism was driven by economic forces and needs. In order to make one's state secure, in order to increase the wealth available to the state, its ruling bureaucracy and its associated ruling class, it had to be based on a strong economy and have a sufficient resource base for the state and ruling elite to exploit (both in terms of human and natural resources). By increasing the area controlled by the state, one increased the wealth available.

States by their nature, like capital, are expansionist bodies, with those who run them always wanting to increase the range of their power and influence (this can be seen from the massive number of wars that have occurred in Europe over the last 500 years). This process was began as nation-states were created by Kings declaring lands to be their private property, regardless of the wishes of those who actually lived there. Moreover, this conflict did not end when monarchies were replaced by more democratic forms of government. As Bakunin argued:

> *"we find wars of extermination, wars among races and nations; wars of conquest, wars to maintain equilibrium, political and religious wars, wars waged in the name of 'great ideas'…, patriotic wars for greater national unity…. And what do we find beneath all that, beneath all the hypocritical phrases used in order to give these wars the appearance of humanity and right? Always the same economic phenomenon:* **the tendency on the part of some to live and prosper at the expense of others.** *All the rest is mere humbug. The ignorant and naive, and the fools are entrapped by it, but the strong men who direct the destinies of the State know only too well that underlying all those wars there is only one motive: pillage, the seizing of someone else's wealth and the enslavement of someone else's labour."* [**The Political Philosophy of Bakunin**, p. 170]

However, while the economic motive for expansion is generally the same, the economic system which a nation is based on has a definite impact on what drives that motive as well as the specific nature of that imperialism. Thus the empire building of ancient Rome or Feudal England has a different economic base (and so driving need) than, say, the imperialism of nineteenth century Germany and Britain or twentieth and twenty-first century United States. Here we will focus mainly on modern capitalist imperialism as it is the most relevant one in the modern world.

Capitalism, by its very nature, is growth-based and so is characterised by the accumulation and concentration of capital. Companies **must** expand in order to survive competition in the marketplace. This, inevitably, sees a rise in international activity and organisation as a result of competition over markets and resources within a given country. By expanding into new markets in new countries, a company can gain an advantage over its competitors as well as overcome limited markets and resources in the home nation. In Bakunin's words:

> *"just as capitalist production and banking speculation, which in the long run swallows up that production, must, under the threat of bankruptcy, ceaselessly expand at the expense of the small financial and productive enterprises which they absorb, must become universal, monopolistic enterprises extending all over the world – so this modern and necessarily military State is driven on by an irrepressible urge to become a universal State. … Hegemony is only a modest manifestation possible under the circumstances, of this unrealisable urge inherent in every State. And the first condition of this hegemony is the relative impotence and subjection of all the neighbouring States."* [**Op. Cit.**, p. 210]

Therefore, economically and politically, the imperialistic activities of

both capitalist and state-capitalist (i.e. the Soviet Union and other "socialist" nations) comes as no surprise. Capitalism is inevitably imperialistic and so *"[w]ar, capitalism and imperialism form a veritable trinity,"* to quote Dutch pacifist-syndicalist Bart de Ligt [**The Conquest of Violence**, p. 64] The growth of big business is such that it can no longer function purely within the national market and so they have to expand internationally to gain advantage in and survive. This, in turn, requires the home state of the corporations also to have global reach in order to defend them and to promote their interests. Hence the economic basis for modern imperialism, with *"the capitalistic interests of the various countries fight[ing] for the foreign markets and compete with each other there"* and when they *"get into trouble about concessions and sources of profit,"* they *"call upon their respective governments to defend their interests … to protect the privileges and dividends of some … capitalist in a foreign country."* [Alexander Berkman, **What is Anarchism?**, p. 31] Thus a capitalist class needs the power of nation states not only to create internal markets and infrastructure but also to secure and protect international markets and opportunities in a world of rivals and **their** states.

As power depends on profits within capitalism, this means that modern imperialism is caused more by economic factors than purely political considerations (although, obviously, this factor does play a role). Imperialism serves capital by increasing the pool of profits available for the imperialistic country in the world market as well as reducing the number of potential competitors. As Kropotkin stressed, *"capital knows no fatherland; and if high profits can be derived from the work of Indian coolies whose wages are only one-half of those of English workmen [or women], or even less, capital will migrate to India, as it has gone to Russia, although its migration may mean starvation for Lancashire."* [**Fields, Factories and Workshops**, p. 57]

Therefore, capital will travel to where it can maximise its profits – regardless of the human or environmental costs at home or abroad. This is the economic base for modern imperialism, to ensure that any trade conducted benefits the stronger party more than the weaker one. Whether this trade is between nations or between classes is irrelevant, the aim of imperialism is to give business an advantage on the market. By travelling to where labour is cheap and the labour movement weak (usually thanks to dictatorial regimes), environmental laws few or non-existent, and little stands in the way of corporate power, capital can maximise its profits. Moreover, the export of capital allows a reduction in the competitive pressures faced by companies in the home markets (at least for short periods).

This has two effects. Firstly, the industrially developed nation (or, more correctly corporation based in that nation) can exploit less developed nations. In this way, the dominant power can maximise for itself the benefits created by international trade. If, as some claim, trade always benefits each party, then imperialism allows the benefits of international trade to accrue more to one side than the other. Secondly, it gives big business more weapons to use to weaken the position of labour in the imperialist nation. This, again, allows the benefits of trade (this time the trade of workers liberty for wages) to accrue to more to business rather than to labour.

How this is done and in what manner varies and changes, but the aim is always the same – exploitation.

This can be achieved in many ways. For example, allowing the import of cheaper raw materials and goods; the export of goods to markets sheltered from foreign competitors; the export of capital from capital-rich areas to capital-poor areas as the investing of capital in less industrially developed countries allows the capitalists in question to benefit from lower wages; relocating factories to countries with fewer (or no) social and environmental laws, controls or regulations. All these allow profits to be gathered at the expense of the working people of the oppressed nation (the rulers of these nations generally do well out of imperialism, as would be expected). The initial source of exported capital is, of course, the exploitation of labour at home but it is exported to less developed countries where capital is scarcer and the price of land, labour and raw materials cheaper. These factors all contribute to enlarging profit margins:

> *"The relationship of these global corporations with the poorer countries had long been an exploiting one … Whereas U.S. corporations in Europe between 1950 and 1965 invested $8.1 billion and made $5.5 billion in profits, in Latin America they invested $3.8 billion and made $11.2 billion in profits, and in Africa they invested $5.2 billion and made $14.3 bullion in profits."* [Howard Zinn, **A People's History of the United States**, p. 556]

Betsy Hartman, looking at the 1980s, concurs. *"Despite the popular Western image of the Third World as a bottomless begging bowl,"* she observes, *"it today gives more to the industrialised world than it takes. Inflows of official 'aid' and private loans and investments are exceeded by outflows in the form of repatriated profits, interest payments, and private capital sent abroad by Third World Elites."* [quoted by George Bradford, **Woman's Freedom: Key to the Population Question**, p. 77]

In addition, imperialism allows big business to increase its strength with respect to its workforce in the imperialist nation by the threat of switching production to other countries or by using foreign investments to ride out strikes. This is required because, while the "home" working class are still exploited and oppressed, their continual attempts at organising and resisting their exploiters proved more and more successful. As such, *"the opposition of the white working classes to the … capitalist class continually gain[ed] strength, and the workers … [won] increased wages, shorter hours, insurances, pensions, etc., the white exploiters found it profitable to obtain their labour from men [,women and children] of so-called inferior race … Capitalists can therefore make infinitely more out there than at home."* [Bart de Ligt, **Op. Cit.**, p. 49]

As such, imperialism (like capitalism) is not only driven by the need to increase profits (important as this is, of course), it is also driven by the class struggle – the need for capital to escape from the strength of the working class in a particular country. From this perspective, the export of capital can be seen in two ways. Firstly, as a means of disciplining rebellious workers at home by an "investment strike" (capital, in effect, runs away, so causing unemployment which disciplines the rebels). Secondly, as a way to increase the 'reserve army' of the unemployed facing working people in the imperialist nations by creating new competitors for their jobs (i.e. dividing, and so ruling, workers by playing one set of workers against another).

Both are related, of course, and both seek to weaken working class power by the fear of unemployment. This process played a key role in the rise of globalisation – see section D.5.3 for details.

Thus imperialism, which is rooted in the search from surplus profits for big business, is also a response to working class power at home. The export of capital is done by emerging and established transnational companies to overcome a militant and class consciousness working class which is often too advanced for heavy exploitation, and finance capital can make easier and bigger profits by investing productive capital elsewhere. It aids the bargaining position of business by pitting the workers in one country against another, so while they are being exploited by the same set of bosses, those bosses can use this fictional "competition" of foreign workers to squeeze concessions from workers at home.

Imperialism has another function, namely to hinder or control the industrialisation of other countries. Such industrialisation will, of course, mean the emergence of new capitalists, who will compete with the existing ones both in the "less developed" countries and in the world market as a whole. Imperialism, therefore, attempts to reduce competition on the world market. As we discuss in the next section, the nineteenth century saw the industrialisation of many European nations as well as America, Japan and Russia by means of state intervention. However, this state-led industrialisation had a drawback, namely that it created more and more competitors on the world market. Moreover, as Kropotkin noted, they had the advantage that the *"new manufacturers … begin where"* the old have *"arrived after a century of experiments and groupings"* and so they *"are built according to the newest and best models which have been worked out elsewhere."* [**Op. Cit.**, p. 32 and p. 49] Hence the need to stop new competitors and secure raw materials and markets, which was achieved by colonialism:

> *"Industries of all kinds decentralise and are scattered all over the globe; and everywhere a variety, an integrated variety, of trades grows, instead of specialisation … each nation becomes in its turn a manufacturing nation…. For each new-comer the first steps only are difficult…. The fact is so well felt, if not understood, that the race for colonies has become the distinctive feature of the last twenty years [Kropotkin is writing in 1912]. Each nation will have her own colonies. But colonies will not help."* [**Op. Cit.**, p. 75]

Imperialism hinders industrialisation in two ways. The first way was direct colonisation, a system which has effectively ended. The second is by indirect means – namely the extraction of profits by international big business. A directly dominated country can be stopped from developing industry and be forced to specialise as a provider of raw materials. This was the aim of "classic" imperialism, with its empires and colonial wars. By means of colonisation, the imperialist powers ensure that the less-developed nation stays that way – so ensuring one less competitor as well as favourable access to raw materials and cheap labour. French anarchist Elisée Reclus rightly called this a process of creating *"colonies of exploitation."* [quoted by John P Clark and Camille Martin (eds.), **Anarchy, Geography, Modernity**, p. 92]

This approach has been superseded by indirect means (see next section). Globalisation can be seen as an intensification of this process. By codifying into international agreements the ability of corporations to sue nation states for violating "free trade," the possibility of new competitor nations developing is weakened. Industrialisation will be dependent on transnational corporations and so development will be hindered and directed to ensure corporate profits and power. Unsurprisingly, those nations which **have** industrialised over the last few decades (such as the East Asian Tiger economies) have done so by using the state to protect industry and control international finance.

The new attack of the capitalist class ("globalisation") is a means of plundering local capitalists and diminishing their power and area of control. The steady weakening and ultimate collapse of the Eastern Block (in terms of economic/political performance and ideological appeal) also played a role in this process. The end of the Cold War meant a reduction in the space available for local elites to manoeuvre. Before this local ruling classes could, if they were lucky, use the struggle between US and USSR imperialism to give them a breathing space which they could exploit to pursue their own agenda (within limits, of course, and with the blessing of the imperialist power in whose orbit they were in). The Eastern Tiger economies were an example of this process at work. The West could use them to provide cheap imports for the home market as well as in the ideological conflict of the Cold War as an example of the benefits of the "free market" (not that they were) and the ruling elites, while maintaining a pro-west and pro-business environment (by force directed against their own populations, of course), could pursue their own economic strategies. With the end of the Cold War, this factor is no longer in play and the newly industrialised nations are now an obvious economic competitor. The local elites are now "encouraged" (by economic blackmail via the World Bank and the IMF) to embrace US economic ideology. Just as neo-liberalism attacks the welfare state in the Imperialist nations, so it results in a lower tolerance of local capital in "less developed" nations.

However, while imperialism is driven by the needs of capitalism it cannot end the contradictions inherent in that system. As Reclus put it in the late nineteenth century, *"the theatre expands, since it now embraces the whole of the land and seas. But the forces that struggled against one another in each particularl state are precisely those that fight across the earth. In each country, capital seeks to subdue the workers. Similarly, on the level of the broadest world market, capital, which had grown enormously, disregards all the old borders and seeks to put the entire mass of producers to work on behalf of its profits, and to secure all the consumers in the world."* [Reclus, quoted by Clark and Martin (eds.), **Op. Cit.**, p. 97]

This struggle for markets and resources does, by necessity, lead to conflict. This may be the wars of conquest required to initially dominate an economically "backward" nation (such as the US invasion of the Philippines, the conquest of Africa by West European states, and so on) or maintain that dominance once it has been achieved (such as the Vietnam War, the Algerian War, the Gulf War and so on). Or it may be the wars between major imperialist powers once the competition for markets and colonies reaches a point when they cannot be settled peacefully (as in the First and Second World Wars). As Kropotkin argued:

"men no longer fight for the pleasure of kings, they fight for the integrity of revenues and for the growing wealth … [for the] benefit of the barons of high finance and industry … [P]olitical preponderance … is quite simply a matter of economic preponderance in international markets. What Germany, France, Russia, England, and Austria are all trying to win … is not military preponderance: it is economic domination. It is the right to impose their goods and their customs tariffs on their neighbours; the right to exploit industrially backward peoples; the privilege of building railroads … to appropriate from a neighbour either a port which will activate commerce, or a province where surplus merchandise can be unloaded…. When we fight today, it is to guarantee our great industrialists a profit of 30%, to assure the financial barons their domination at the Bourse [stock-exchange], and to provide the shareholders of mines and railways with their incomes."
[**Words of a Rebel**, pp. 65-6]

In summary, current imperialism is caused by, and always serves, the needs and interests of Capital. If it did not, if imperialism were bad for business, the business class would oppose it. This partly explains why the colonialism of the 19th century is no more (the other reasons being social resistance to foreign domination, which obviously helped to make imperialism bad for business as well, and the need for US imperialism to gain access to these markets after the second world war). There are now more cost-effective means than direct colonialism to ensure that "underdeveloped" countries remain open to exploitation by foreign capital. Once the costs exceeded the benefits, colonialist imperialism changed into the neo-colonialism of multinationals, political influence, and the threat of force. Moreover, we must not forget that any change in imperialism relates to changes in the underlying economic system and so the changing nature of modern imperialism can be roughly linked to developments within the capitalist economy.

Imperialism, then, is basically the ability of countries to globally and locally dictate trade relations and investments with other countries in such a way as to gain an advantage over the other countries. When capital is invested in foreign nations, the surplus value extracted from the workers in those nations are not re-invested in those nations. Rather a sizeable part of it returns to the base nation of the corporation (in the form of profits for that company). Indeed, that is to be expected as the whole reason for the investment of capital in the first place was to get more out of the country than the corporation put into it. Instead of this surplus value being re-invested into industry in the less-developed nation (as would be the case with home-grown exploiters, who are dependent on local markets and labour) it ends up in the hands of foreign exploiters who take them out of the dominated country. This means that industrial development has less resources to draw on, making the local ruling class dependent on foreign capital and its whims.

This can be done directly (by means of invasion and colonies) or indirectly (by means of economic and political power). Which method is used depends on the specific circumstances facing the countries in question. Moreover, it depends on the balance of class forces within each country as well (for example, a nation with a militant working class would be less likely to pursue a war policy due to the social costs involved). However, the aim of imperialism is always to enrich and empower the capitalist and bureaucratic classes.

D.5.1 How has imperialism changed over time?

The development of Imperialism cannot be isolated from the general dynamics and tendencies of the capitalist economy. Imperialist capitalism, therefore, is not identical to pre-capitalist forms of imperialism, although there can, of course, be similarities. As such, it must be viewed as an advanced stage of capitalism and not as some kind of deviation of it. This kind of imperialism was attained by some nations, mostly Western European, in the late 19th and early 20th-century. Since then it has changed and developed as economic and political developments occurred, but it is based on the same basic principles. As such, it is useful to describe the history of capitalism in order to fully understand the place imperialism holds within it, how it has changed, what functions it provides and, consequently, how it may change in the future.

Imperialism has important economic advantages for those who run the economy. As the needs of the business class change, the forms taken by imperialism also change. We can identify three main phases: classic imperialism (i.e. conquest), indirect (economic) imperialism, and globalisation. We will consider the first two in this section and globalisation in section D.5.3. However, for all the talk of globalisation in recent years, it is important to remember that capitalism has always been an international system, that the changing forms of imperialism reflect this international nature and that the changes within imperialism are in response to developments within capitalism itself.

Capitalism has always been expansive. Under mercantilism, for example, the "free" market was nationalised **within** the nation state while state aid was used to skew international trade on behalf of the home elite and favour the development of capitalist industry. This meant using the centralised state (and its armed might) to break down "internal" barriers and customs which hindered the free flow of goods, capital and, ultimately, labour. We should stress this as the state has always played a key role in the development and protection of capitalism. The use of the state to, firstly, protect infant capitalist manufacturing and, secondly, to create a "free" market (i.e. free from the customs and interference of society) should not be forgotten, particularly as this second ("internal") role is repeated "externally" through imperialism. Needless to say, this process of "internal" imperialism within the country by the ruling class by means of the state was accompanied by extensive violence against the working class (also see section F.8).

So, state intervention was used to create and ensure capital's dominant position at home by protecting it against foreign competition and the recently dispossessed working class. This transition from feudal to capitalist economy enjoyed the active promotion of the state authorities, whose increasing centralisation ran parallel with the growing strength and size of merchant capital.

It also needed a powerful state to protect its international trade, to conquer colonies and to fight for control over the world market. The absolutist state was used to actively implant, help and develop capitalist trade and industry.

The first industrial nation was Britain. After building up its industrial base under mercantilism and crushing its rivals in various wars, it was in an ideal position to dominate the international market. It embraced free trade as its unique place as the only capitalist/industrialised nation in the world market meant that it did not have to worry about competition from other nations. Any free exchange between unequal traders will benefit the stronger party. Thus Britain, could achieve domination in the world market by means of free trade. This meant that goods were exported rather than capital.

Faced with the influx of cheap, mass produced goods, existing industry in Europe and the Americas faced ruin. As economist Nicholas Kaldor notes, *"the arrival of cheap factory-made English goods **did** cause a loss of employment and output of small-scale industry (the artisanate) both in European countries (where it was later offset by large-scale industrialisation brought about by protection) and even more in India and China, where it was not so offset."* [**Further Essays on Applied Economics**, p. 238] The existing industrial base was crushed, industrialisation was aborted and unemployment rose. These countries faced two possibilities: turn themselves into providers of raw materials for Britain or violate the principles of the market and industrialise by protectionism.

In many nations of Western Europe (soon to be followed by the USA and Japan), the decision was simple. Faced with this competition, these countries utilised the means by which Britain had industrialised – state protection. Tariff barriers were raised, state aid was provided and industry revived sufficiently to turn these nations into successful competitors of Britain. This process was termed by Kropotkin as *"the consecutive development of nations"* (although he underestimated the importance of state aid in this process). No nation, he argued, would let itself become specialised as the provider of raw materials or the manufacturer of a few commodities but would diversify into many different lines of production. Obviously no national ruling class would want to see itself be dependent on another and so industrial development was essential (regardless of the wishes of the general population). Thus a nation in such a situation *"tries to emancipate herself from her dependency ... and rapidly begins to manufacture all those goods she used to import."* [**Fields, Factories and Workshops**, p. 49 and p. 32]

Protectionism may have violated the laws of neo-classical economics, but it proved essential for industrialisation. While, as Kropotkin argued, protectionism ensured *"the high profits of those manufacturers who do not improve their factories and chiefly rely upon cheap labour and long hours,"* it also meant that these profits would be used to finance industry and develop an industrial base. [**Op. Cit.**, p. 41] Without this state aid, it is doubtful that these countries would have industrialised (as Kaldor notes, *"all the present 'developed' or 'industrialised' countries established their industries through 'import substitution' by means of protective tariffs and/or differential subsidies."* [**Op. Cit.**, p. 127]).

Within the industrialising country, the usual process of competition

driving out competitors continued. More and more markets became dominated by big business (although, as Kropotkin stressed, without totally eliminating smaller workshops within an industry and even creating more around them). Indeed, as Russian anarchist G. P. Maximoff stressed, the *"specific character of Imperialism is ... the concentration and centralisation of capital in syndicates, trusts and cartels, which ... have a decisive voice, not only in the economic and political life of their countries, but also in the life of the nations of the worlds a whole."* [**Program of Anarcho-Syndicalism**, p. 10] The modern multi-national and transnational corporations are the latest expression of this process.

Simply put, the size of big business was such that it had to expand internationally as their original national markets were not sufficient and to gain further advantages over their competitors. Faced with high tariff barriers and rising international competition, industry responded by exporting capital as well as finished goods. This export of capital was an essential way of beating protectionism (and even reap benefits from it) and gain a foothold in foreign markets (*"protective duties have no doubt contributed ... towards attracting German and English manufacturers to Poland and Russia"* [Kropotkin, **Op. Cit.**, p. 41]). In addition, it allowed access to cheap labour and raw materials by placing capital in foreign lands As part of this process colonies were seized to increase the size of "friendly" markets and, of course, allow the easy export of capital into areas with cheap labour and raw materials. The increased concentration of capital this implies was essential to gain an advantage against foreign competitors and dominate the international market as well as the national one.

This form of imperialism, which arose in the late nineteenth century, was based on the creation of larger and larger businesses and the creation of colonies across the globe by the industrialised nations. Direct conquest had the advantage of opening up more of the planet for the capitalist market, thus leading to more trade and exploitation of raw materials and labour. This gave a massive boost to both the state and the industries of the invading country in terms of new profits, so allowing an increase in the number of capitalists and other social parasites that could exist in the developed nation. As Kropotkin noted at the time, *"British, French, Belgian and other capitalists, by means of the ease with which they exploit countries which themselves have no developed industry, today control the labour of hundreds of millions of those people in Eastern Europe, Asia, and Africa. The result is that the number of those people in the leading industrialised countries of Europe who live off the work of others doesn't gradually decrease at all. Far from it."* [*"Anarchism and Syndicalism"*, **Black Flag**, no. 210, p. 26]

As well as gaining access to raw materials, imperialism allows the dominating nation to gain access to markets for its goods. By having an empire, products produced at home can be easily dumped into foreign markets with less developed industry, undercutting locally produced goods and consequently destroying the local economy (and so potential competitors) along with the society and culture based on it. Empire building is a good way of creating privileged markets for one's goods. By eliminating foreign competition, the imperialist nation's capitalists can charge monopoly prices in the dominated country, so ensuring high profit margins for capitalist business. This adds with the problems associated with the over-production of goods:

> "The workman being unable to purchase with their wages the riches they are producing, industry must search for new markets elsewhere, amidst the middle classes of other nations. It must find markets, in the East, in Africa, anywhere; it must increase, by trade, the number of its serfs in Egypt, in India, on the Congo. But everywhere it finds competitors in other nations which rapidly enter into the same line of industrial development. And wars, continuous wars, must be fought for the supremacy in the world-market – wars for the possession of the East, wars for getting possession of the seas, wars for the right of imposing heavy duties on foreign merchandise."
> [Kropotkin, **Anarchism**, pp. 55-6]

This process of expansion into non-capitalist areas also helps Capital to weather both the subjective and objective economic pressures upon it which cause the business cycle (see section C.7 for more details). As wealth looted from less industrially developed countries is exported back to the home country, profit levels can be protected both from working-class demands and from any relative decline in surplus-value production caused by increased capital investment (see section C.2 for more on surplus value). In fact, the working class of the imperialist country could receive improved wages and living conditions as the looted wealth was imported into the country and that meant that the workers could fight for, and win, improvements that otherwise would have provoked intense class conflict. And as the sons and daughters of the poor emigrated to the colonies to make a living for themselves on stolen land, the wealth extracted from those colonies helped to overcome the reduction in the supply of labour at home which would increase its market price. This loot also helps reduce competitive pressures on the nation's economy. Of course, these advantages of conquest cannot totally **stop** the business cycle nor eliminate competition, as the imperialistic nations soon discovered.

Therefore, the "classic" form of imperialism based on direct conquest and the creation of colonies had numerous advantages for the imperialist nations and the big business which their states represented.

These dominated nations were, in the main, pre-capitalist societies. The domination of imperialist powers meant the importation of capitalist social relationships and institutions into them, so provoking extensive cultural and physical resistance to these attempts of foreign capitalists to promote the growth of the free market. However, peasants', artisans' and tribal people's desires to be "left alone" was never respected, and "civilisation" was forced upon them "for their own good." As Kropotkin realised, "force is necessary to continually bring new 'uncivilised nations' under the same conditions [of wage labour]." [**Anarchism and Anarchist Communism**, p. 53] Anarchist George Bradford also stresses this, arguing that we "should remember that, historically, colonialism, bringing with it an emerging capitalist economy and wage system, destroyed the tradition economies in most countries. By substituting cash crops and monoculture for forms of sustainable agriculture, it destroyed the basic land skills of the people whom it reduced to plantation workers." [**How Deep is Deep Ecology**, p. 40] Indeed,

this process was in many ways similar to the development of capitalism in the "developed" nations, with the creation of a class of landless workers who formed the nucleus of the first generation of people given up to the mercy of the manufacturers.

However, this process had objective limitations. Firstly, the expansion of empires had the limitation that there were only so many potential colonies out there. This meant that conflicts over markets and colonies was inevitable (as the states involved knew, and so they embarked on a policy of building larger and larger armed forces). As Kropotkin argued before the First World War, the real cause of war at the time was "the competition for markets and the right to exploit nations backward in industry." [quoted by Martin Miller, **Kropotkin**, p. 225] Secondly, the creation of trusts, the export of goods and the import of cheap raw materials cannot stop the business cycle nor "buy-off" the working class indefinitely (i.e. the excess profits of imperialism will never be enough to grant more and more reforms and improvements to the working class in the industrialised world). Thus the need to overcome economic slumps propelled business to find new ways of dominating the market, up to and including the use of war to grab new markets and destroy rivals. Moreover, war was a good way of side tracking class conflict at home – which, let us not forget, had been reaching increasingly larger, more militant and more radical levels in all the imperialist nations (see John Zerzan's "Origins and Meaning of WWI" in his **Elements of Refusal**).

Thus this first phase of imperialism began as the growing capitalist economy started to reach the boundaries of the nationalised market created by the state within its own borders. Imperialism was then used to expand the area that could be colonised by the capital associated with a given nation-state. This stage ended, however, once the dominant powers had carved up the planet into different spheres of influence and there was nowhere left to expand into. In the competition for access to cheap raw materials and foreign markets, nation-states came into conflict with each other. As it was obvious that a conflict was brewing, the major European countries tried to organise a "balance of power." This meant that armies were built and navies created to frighten other countries and so deter war. Unfortunately, these measures were not enough to countermand the economic and power processes at play ("Armies equipped to the teeth with weapons, with highly developed instruments of murder and backed by military interests, have their own dynamic interests," as Goldman put it [**Red Emma Speaks**, p. 353]). War did break out, a war over empires and influence, a war, it was claimed, that would end all wars. As we now know, of course, it did not because it did not fight the root cause of modern wars, capitalism.

After the First World War, the identification of nation-state with national capital became even more obvious, and can be seen in the rise of extensive state intervention to keep capitalism going – for example, the rise of Fascism in Italy and Germany and the efforts of "national" governments in Britain and the USA to "solve" the economic crisis of the Great Depression. However, these attempts to solve the problems of capital did not work. The economic imperatives at work before the first world war had not gone away. Big business still needed markets and raw materials and the statification of industry under fascism only aided to the problems associated with imperialism. Another war was only a matter of time and when it came most anarchists, as they had during the first world war, opposed both sides and called for revolution:

> "the present struggle is one between rival Imperialisms and for the protection of vested interests. The workers in every country, belonging to the oppressed class, have nothing in common with these interests and the political aspirations of the ruling class. Their immediate struggle is their **emancipation. Their** front line is the workshop and factory, not the Maginot Line where they will just rot and die, whilst their masters at home pile up their ill-gotten gains." ["*War Commentary*", quoted Mark Shipway, **Anti-Parliamentary Communism**, p. 170]

After the Second World War, the European countries yielded to pressure from the USA and national liberation movements and granted many former countries "independence" (often after intense conflict). As Kropotkin predicted, such social movements were to be expected for with the growth of capitalism "*the number of people with an interest in the capitulation of the capitalist state system also increases.*" ["*Anarchism and Syndicalism*", **Op. Cit.**, p. 26] Unfortunately these "liberation" movements transformed mass struggle from a potential struggle against capitalism into movements aiming for independent capitalist nation states (see section D.7). Not, we must stress, that the USA was being altruistic in its actions, independence for colonies weakened its rivals as well as allowing US capital access to those markets.

This process reflected capital expanding even more **beyond** the nation-state into multinational corporations. The nature of imperialism and imperialistic wars changed accordingly. In addition, the various successful struggles for National Liberation ensured that imperialism had to change itself in face of popular resistance. These two factors ensured that the old form of imperialism was replaced by a new system of "neo-colonialism" in which newly "independent" colonies are forced, via political and economic pressure, to open their borders to foreign capital. If a state takes up a position which the imperial powers consider "bad for business," action will be taken, from sanctions to outright invasion. Keeping the world open and "free" for capitalist exploitation has been America's general policy since 1945. It springs directly from the expansion requirements of private capital and so cannot be fundamentally changed. However, it was also influenced by the shifting needs resulting from the new political and economic order and the rivalries existing between imperialist nations (particularly those of the Cold War). As such, which method of intervention and the shift from direct colonialism to neo-colonialism (and any "anomalies") can be explained by these conflicts.

Within this basic framework of indirect imperialism, many "developing" nations did manage to start the process of industrialising. Partly in response to the Great Depression, some former colonies started to apply the policies used so successfully by imperialist nations like Germany and America in the previous century. They followed a policy of "import substitution" which meant that they tried to manufacture goods like, for instance, cars that they had previously imported. Without suggesting this sort of policy offered a positive alternative (it was, after all, just local capitalism) it did have one big disadvantage for the imperialist powers: it tended to deny them

both markets and cheap raw materials (the current turn towards globalisation was used to break these policies). As such, whether a nation pursued such policies was dependent on the costs involved to the imperialist power involved.

So instead of direct rule over less developed nations (which generally proved to be too costly, both economically and politically), indirect forms of domination were now preferred. These are rooted in economic and political pressure rather than the automatic use of violence, although force is always an option and is resorted to if "business interests" are threatened. This is the reality of the expression "the international community" – it is code for imperialist aims for Western governments, particularly the U.S. and its junior partner, the U.K. As discussed in section D.2.1, economic power can be quite effective in pressuring governments to do what the capitalist class desire even in advanced industrial countries. This applies even more so to so-called developing nations.

In addition to the stick of economic and political pressure, the imperialist countries also use the carrot of foreign aid and investment to ensure their aims. This can best be seen when Western governments provide lavish funds to "developing" states, particularly petty right-wing despots, under the pseudonym "foreign aid." Hence the all too common sight of US Presidents supporting authoritarian (indeed, dictatorial) regimes while at the same time mouthing nice platitudes about "liberty" and "progress." The purpose of this foreign aid, noble-sounding rhetoric about freedom and democracy aside, is to ensure that the existing world order remains intact and that US corporations have access to the raw materials and markets they need. Stability has become the watchword of modern imperialists, who see **any** indigenous popular movements as a threat to the existing world order. The U.S. and other Western powers provide much-needed war material and training for the military of these governments, so that they may continue to keep the business climate friendly to foreign investors (that means tacitly and overtly supporting fascism around the globe).

Foreign aid also channels public funds to home based transnational companies via the ruling classes in Third World countries. It is, in other words, a process where the poor people of rich countries give their money to the rich people of poor countries to ensure that the investments of the rich people of rich countries is safe from the poor people of poor countries! Needless to say, the owners of the companies providing this "aid" also do very well out of it. This has the advantage of securing markets as other countries are "encouraged" to buy imperialist countries' goods (often in exchange for "aid", typically military "aid") and open their markets to the dominant power's companies and their products.

Thus, the Third World sags beneath the weight of well-funded oppression, while its countries are sucked dry of their native wealth, in the name of "development" and in the spirit of "democracy" and "freedom". The United States leads the West in its global responsibility (another favourite buzzword) to ensure that this peculiar kind of "freedom" remains unchallenged by any indigenous movements. The actual form of the regime supported is irrelevant, although fascist states are often favoured due to their stability (i.e. lack of popular opposition movements). As long as the fascist regimes remain compliant and obedient to the West and capitalism thrives unchallenged then they can commit any crime against their own people while being praised for making progress towards "democracy." However, the moment they step out of line and act in ways which clash with the interests of the imperialist powers then their short-comings will used to justify intervention (the example of Saddam Hussein is the most obvious one to raise here). As for "democracy," this can be tolerated by imperialism as long as its in *"the traditional sense of 'top-down' rule by elites linked to US power, with democratic forms of little substance – unless they are compelled to do so, by their own populations in particular."* This applies *"internally"* as well as abroad, for *"democracy is fine as long as it … does not risk popular interference with primary interests of power and wealth."* Thus the aim is to ensure *"an obedient client state is firmly in place, the general preference of conquerors, leaving just military bases for future contingencies."* [**Failed States**, p. 171, p. 204 and p. 148]

In these ways, markets are kept open for corporations based in the advanced nations all without the apparent use of force or the need for colonies. However, this does not mean that war is not an option and, unsurprisingly, the post-1945 period has been marked by imperialist conflict. These include old-fashioned direct war by the imperialist nation (such as the Vietnam and Iraq wars) as well as new-style imperialistic wars by proxy (such as US support for the Contras in Nicaragua or support for military coups against reformist or nationalist governments). As such, if a regime becomes too independent, military force always remains an option. This can be seen from the 1990 Gulf War, when Saddam invaded Kuwait (and all his past crimes, conducted with the support of the West, were dragged from the Memory Hole to justify war).

Least it be considered that we are being excessive in our analysis, let us not forget that the US *"has intervened well over a hundred times in the internal affairs of other nations since 1945. The rhetoric has been that we have done so largely to preserve or restore freedom and democracy, or on behalf of human rights. The reality has been that [they] … have been consistently designed and implemented to further the interests of US (now largely transnational) corporations, and the elites both at home and abroad who profit from their depredations."* [Henry Rosemont, Jr., *"U.S. Foreign Policy: the Execution of Human Rights"*, pp. 13-25, **Social Anarchism**, no. 29 p. 13] This has involved the overthrow of democratically elected governments (such as in Iran, 1953; Guatemala, 1954; Chile, 1973) and their replacement by reactionary right-wing dictatorships (usually involving the military). As George Bradford argues, *"[i]n light of [the economic] looting [by corporations under imperialism], it should become clearer … why nationalist regimes that cease to serve as simple conduits for massive U.S. corporate exploitation come under such powerful attack – Guatemala in 1954, Chile in 1973 … Nicaragua [in the 1980s] … [U.S.] State Department philosophy since the 1950s has been to rely on various police states and to hold back 'nationalistic regimes' that might be more responsive to 'increasing popular demand for immediate improvements in the low living standards of the masses,' in order to 'protect our resources' – in their countries!"* [**How Deep is Deep Ecology?**, p. 62]

This is to be expected, as imperialism is the only means of defending the foreign investments of a nation's capitalist class, and by allowing the extraction of profits and the creation of markets, it also safeguards the future of private capital.

This process has not come to an end and imperialism is continuing to evolve based on changing political and economic developments. The most obvious political change is the end of the USSR. During the cold war, the competition between the USA and the USSR had an obvious impact on how imperialism worked. On the one hand, acts of imperial power could be justified in fighting "Communism" (for the USA) or "US imperialism" (for the USSR). On the other, fear of provoking a nuclear war or driving developing nations into the hands of the other side allowed more leeway for developing nations to pursue policies like import substitution. With the end of the cold-war, these options have decreased considerably for developing nations as US imperialism how has, effectively, no constraints beyond international public opinion and pressure from below. As the invasion of Iraq in 2003 shows, this power is still weak but sufficient to limit some of the excesses of imperial power (for example, the US could not carpet bomb Iraq as it had Vietnam).

The most obvious economic change is the increased global nature of capitalism. Capital investments in developing nations have increased steadily over the years, with profits from the exploitation of cheap labour flowing back into the pockets of the corporate elite in the imperialist nation, not to its citizens as a whole (though there are sometimes temporary benefits to other classes, as discussed in section D.5.4). With the increasing globalisation of big business and markets, capitalism (and so imperialism) is on the threshold of a new transformation. Just as direct imperialism transformed into in-direct imperialism, so in-direct imperialism is transforming into a global system of government which aims to codify the domination of corporations over governments. This process is often called "globalisation" and we discuss it in section D.5.3. First, however, we need to discuss non-private capitalist forms of imperialism associated with the Stalinist regimes and we do that in the next section.

D.5.2 Is imperialism just a product of private capitalism?

While we are predominantly interested in **capitalist** imperialism, we cannot avoid discussing the activities of the so-called "socialist" nations (such as the Soviet Union, China, etc.). Given that modern imperialism has an economic base caused in developed capitalism by, in part, the rise of big business organised on a wider and wider scale, we should not be surprised that the state capitalist ("socialist") nations are/were also imperialistic. As the state-capitalist system expresses the logical end point of capital concentration (the one big firm) the same imperialistic pressures that apply to big business and its state will also apply to the state capitalist nation.

In the words of libertarian socialist Cornelius Castoriadis:

> *"But if imperialist expansion is the necessary expression of an economy in which the process of capital concentration has arrived at the stage of monopoly domination, this is true a fortiori for an economy in which this process of concentration has arrived at its natural limit … In other words, imperialist expansion is even more necessary for*

a totally concentrated economy.... That they are realised through different modes (for example, capital exportation plays a much more restricted role and acts in a different way than is the case with monopoly domination) is the result of the differences separating bureaucratic capitalism from monopoly capitalism, but at bottom this changes nothing.

"We must strongly emphasise that the imperialistic features of capital are not tied to 'private' or 'State' ownership of the means of production ... the same process takes place if, instead of monopolies, there is an exploiting bureaucracy; in other words, this bureaucracy also can **exploit***, but only on the condition that it* **dominates.***"* [**Political and Social Writings**, vol. 1, p. 159]

Given this, it comes as no surprise that the state-capitalist countries also participated in imperialist activities, adventures and wars, although on a lesser scale and for slightly different reasons than those associated with private capitalism. However, regardless of the exact cause the USSR *"has always pursued an imperialist foreign policy, that it is the state and not the workers which owns and controls the whole life of the country."* Given this, it is unsurprising that *"world revolution was abandoned in favour of alliances with capitalist countries. Like the bourgeois states the USSR took part in the manoeuvrings to establish a balance of power in Europe."* This has its roots in its internal class structure, as *"it is obvious that a state which pursues an imperialist foreign policy cannot itself be revolutionary"* and this is shown in *"the internal life of the USSR"* where *"the means of wealth production"* are *"owned by the state which represents, as always, a privileged class – the bureaucracy."* [*"USSR – Anarchist Position,"* pp. 21-24, Vernon Richards (ed.), **The Left and World War II**, p. 22 and p. 23]

This process became obvious after the defeat of Nazi Germany and the creation of Stalinist states in Eastern Europe. As anarchists at the time noted, this was *"the consolidation of Russian imperialist power"* and their *"incorporation ... within the structure of the Soviet Union."* As such, *"all these countries behind the Iron Curtain are better regarded as what they really [were] – satellite states of Russia."* [*"Russia's Grip Tightens"*, pp. 283-5, Vernon Richards (ed.), **World War – Cold War**, p. 285 and p. 284] Of course, the creation of these satellite states was based on the inter-imperialist agreements reached at the Yalta conference of February 1945.

As can be seen by Russia's ruthless policy towards her satellite regimes, Soviet imperialism was more inclined to the defence of what she already had and the creation of a buffer zone between herself and the West. This is not to deny that the ruling elite of the Soviet Union did not try to exploit the countries under its influence. For example, in the years after the end of the Second World War, the Eastern Block countries paid the USSR millions of dollars in reparations. As in private capitalism, the *"satellite states were regarded as a source of raw materials and of cheap manufactured goods. Russia secured the satellites exports at below world prices. And it exported to them at above world prices."* Thus trade *"was based on the old imperialist principle of buying cheap and selling dear – very, very dear!"* [Andy Anderson, **Hungary '56**, pp. 25-6

and p. 25] However, the nature of the imperialist regime was such that it discouraged too much expansionism as *"Russian imperialism [had] to rely on armies of occupation, utterly subservient quisling governments, or a highly organised and loyal political police (or all three). In such circumstances considerable dilution of Russian power occur[red] with each acquisition of territory."* [*"Russian Imperialism"*, pp. 270-1, Vernon Richards (ed.), **Op. Cit.**, p. 270] Needless to say, the form and content of the state capitalist domination of its satellite countries was dependent on its own economic and political structure and needs, just as traditional capitalist imperialism reflected its needs and structures. While direct exploitation declined over time, the satellite states were still expected to develop their economies in accordance with the needs of the Soviet Bloc as a whole (i.e., in the interests of the Russian elite). This meant the forcing down of living standards to accelerate industrialisation in conformity with the requirements of the Russian ruling class. This was because these regimes served not as outlets for excess Soviet products but rather as a means of *"plugging holes in the Russian economy, which [was] in a chronic state of underproduction in comparison to its needs."* As such, the *"form and content"* of this regimes' *"domination over its satellite countries are determined fundamentally by its own economic structure"* and so it would be *"completely incorrect to consider these relations identical to the relations of classical colonialism."* [Castoriadis, **Op. Cit.**, p. 187] So part of the difference between private and state capitalism was driven by the need to plunder these countries of commodities to make up for shortages caused by central planning (in contrast, capitalist imperialism tended to export goods). As would be expected, within this overall imperialist agenda the local bureaucrats and elites feathered their own nests, as with any form of imperialism.

As well as physical expansionism, the state-capitalist elites also aided "anti-imperialist" movements when it served their interests. The aim of this was to place such movements and any regimes they created within the Soviet or Chinese sphere of influence. Ironically, this process was aided by imperialist rivalries with US imperialism as American pressure often closed off other options in an attempt to demonise such movements and states as "communist" in order to justify supporting their repression or for intervening itself. This is **not** to suggest that Soviet regime was encouraging "world revolution" by this support. Far from it, given the Stalinist betrayals and attacks on genuine revolutionary movements and struggles (the example of the Spanish Revolution is the obvious one to mention here). Soviet aid was limited to those parties which were willing to subjugate themselves and any popular movements they influenced to the needs of the Russian ruling class. Once the Stalinist parties had replaced the local ruling class, trade relations were formalised between the so-called "socialist" nations for the benefit of both the local and Russian rulers. In a similar way, and for identical needs, the Western Imperialist powers supported murderous local capitalist and feudal elites in their struggle against their own working classes, arguing that it was supporting "freedom" and "democracy" against Soviet aggression.

The turning of Communist Parties into conduits of Soviet elite interests became obvious under Stalin, when the twists and turns of the party line were staggering. However, it actually started under

Lenin and Trotsky and *"almost from the beginning"* the Communist International (Comintern) *"served primarily not as an instrument for World Revolution, but as an instrument of Russian Foreign Policy."* This explains *"the most bewildering changes of policy and political somersaults"* it imposed on its member parties. Ultimately, *"the allegedly revolutionary aims of the Comintern stood in contrast to the diplomatic relations of the Soviet Union with other countries."* [Marie-Louise Berneri, **Neither East Nor West**, p. 64 and p. 63] As early as 1920, the Dutch Council Communist Anton Pannekoek was arguing that the Comintern opposition to anti-parliamentarianism was rooted *"in the needs of the Soviet Republic"* for *"peaceful trade with the rest of the world."* This meant that the Comintern's policies were driven *"by the political needs of Soviet Russia."* [*"Afterword to World Revolution and Communist Tactics,"* D.A. Smart (ed.), **Pannekoek and Gorter's Marxism**, p. 143 and p. 144] This is to be expected, as the regime had always been state capitalist and so the policies of the Comintern were based on the interests of a (state) capitalist regime.

Therefore, imperialism is not limited to states based on private capitalism – the state capitalist regimes have also been guilty of it. This is to be expected, as both are based on minority rule, the exploitation and oppression of labour and the need to expand the resources available to it. This means that anarchists oppose all forms of capitalist imperialism and raise the slogan *"Neither East nor West."* We *"cannot alter our views about Russia [or any other state capitalist regime] simply because, for imperialist reasons, American and British spokesmen now denounce Russia totalitarianism. We know that their indignation is hypocritical and that they may become friendly to Russia again if it suits their interests."* [Marie-Louise Berneri, **Op. Cit.**, p. 187] In the clash of imperialism, anarchists support neither side as both are rooted in the exploitation and oppression of the working class.

Finally, it is worthwhile to refute two common myths about state capitalist imperialism. The first myth is that state-capitalist imperialism results in a non-capitalist regimes and that is why it is so opposed to by Western interests. From this position, held by many Trotskyists, it is argued that we should support such regimes against the West (for example, that socialists should have supported the Russian invasion of Afghanistan). This position is based on a fallacy rooted in the false Trotskyist notion that state ownership of the means of production is inherently socialist.

Just as capitalist domination saw the transformation of the satellite countries social relations from pre-capitalist forms in favour of capitalist ones, the domination of "socialist" nations meant the elimination of traditional bourgeois social relations in favour of state capitalist ones. As such, the nature and form of imperialism was fundamentally identical and served the interests of the appropriate ruling class in each case. This transformation of one kind of class system into another explains the root of the West's very public attacks on Soviet imperialism. It had nothing to do with the USSR being considered a "workers' state" as Trotsky, for example, argued. *"Expropriation of the capitalist class,"* argued one anarchist in 1940, *"is naturally terrifying"* to the capitalist class *"but that does not prove anything about a workers' state … In Stalinist Russia expropriation is carried out … by, and ultimately for the benefit of, the bureaucracy, not by the workers at all. The bourgeoisie are afraid of expropriation,*

of power passing out of their hands, whoever seizes it from them. They will defend their property against any class or clique. The fact that they are indignant [about Soviet imperialism] proves their fear – it tells us nothing at all about the agents inspiring that fear." [J.H., *"The Fourth International"*, pp. 37-43, Vernon Richards (ed.), **Op. Cit.**, pp. 41-2] This elimination of traditional forms of class rule and their replacement with new forms is required as these are the only economic forms compatible with the needs of the state capitalist regimes to exploit these countries on a regular basis.

The second myth is the notion that opposition to state-capitalist imperialism by its subject peoples meant support for Western capitalism. In fact, the revolts and revolutions which repeatedly flared up under Stalinism almost always raised genuine socialist demands. For example, the 1956 Hungarian revolution *"was a social revolution in the fullest sense of the term. Its object was a fundamental change in the relations of production, and in the relations between ruler and ruled in factories, pits and on the land."* Given this, unsurprisingly Western political commentary *"was centred upon the nationalistic aspects of the Revolution, no matter how trivial."* This was unsurprising, as the West was *"opposed both to its methods and to its aims … What capitalist government could genuinely support a people demanding 'workers' management of industry' and already beginning to implement this on an increasing scale?"* The revolution *"showed every sign of making both them and their bureaucratic counterparts in the East redundant."* The revolt itself was rooted *"[n]ew organs of struggle,"* workers' councils *"which embodied, in embryo, the new society they were seeking to achieve."* [Anderson, **Op. Cit.**, p.6, p. 106 and p. 107]

The ending of state capitalism in Eastern Europe in 1989 has ended its imperialist domination of those countries. However, it has simply opened the door for private-capitalist imperialism as the revolts themselves remained fundamentally at the political level. The ruling bureaucracy was faced with both popular pressure from the streets and economic stagnation flowing from its state-run capitalism. Being unable to continue as before and unwilling, for obvious reasons, to encourage economic and political participation, it opted for the top-down transformation of state to private capitalism. Representative democracy was implemented and state assets were privatised into the hands of a new class of capitalists (often made up of the old bureaucrats) rather than the workers themselves. In other words, the post-Stalinist regimes are still class systems and now subject to a different form of imperialism – namely, globalisation.

D.5.3 Does globalisation mean the end of imperialism?

No. While it is true that the size of multinational companies has increased along with the mobility of capital, the need for nation-states to serve corporate interests still exists. With the increased mobility of capital, i.e. its ability to move from one country and invest in another easily, and with the growth in international money markets, we have seen what can be called a "free market" in states developing. Corporations can ensure that governments do as they are told simply by threatening to move elsewhere (which they will do anyway, if it results in more profits).

Therefore, as Howard Zinn stresses, *"it's very important to point out that globalisation is in fact imperialism and that there is a disadvantage to simply using the term 'globalisation' in a way that plays into the thinking of people at the World Bank and journalists … who are agog at globalisation. They just can't contain their joy at the spread of American economic and corporate power all over the world … it would be very good to puncture that balloon and say 'This is imperialism.'"* [**Bush Drives us into Bakunin's Arms**]

Globalisation is, like the forms of imperialism that preceded it, a response to both objective economic forces and the class struggle. Moreover, like the forms that came before, it is rooted in the economic power of corporations based in a few developed nations and political power of the states that are the home base of these corporations. These powers influence international institutions and individual countries to pursue neo-liberal policies, the so-called "Washington Consensus" of free market reforms, associated with globalisation.

Globalisation cannot be understood unless its history is known. The current process of increasing international trade, investment and finance markets started in the late 60s and early 1970s. Increased competition from a re-built Europe and Japan challenged US domination combined with working class struggle across the globe to leave the capitalist world feeling the strain. Dissatisfaction with factory and office life combined with other social movements (such as the women's movement, anti-racist struggles, anti-war movements and so on) which demanded more than capitalism could provide. The near revolution in France, 1968, is the most famous of these struggles but it occurred all across the globe.

For the ruling class, the squeeze on profits and authority from ever-increasing wage demands, strikes, stoppages, boycotts, squatting, protests and other struggles meant that a solution had to be found and the working class disciplined (and profits regained). One part of the solution was to "run away" and so capital flooded into certain areas of the "developing" world. This increased the trends towards globalisation. Another solution was the embrace of Monetarism and tight money (i.e. credit) policies. It is a moot point whether those who applied Monetarism actually knew it was nonsense and, consequently, sought an economic crisis or whether they were simply incompetent ideologues who knew little about economics and mismanaged the economy by imposing its recommendations, the outcome was the same. It resulted in increases in the interest rate, which helped deepen the recessions of the early 1980s which

broke the back of working class resistance in the U.K. and U.S.A. High unemployment helped to discipline a rebellious working class and the new mobility of capital meant a virtual "investment strike" against nations which had a "poor industrial record" (i.e. workers who were not obedient wage slaves). Moreover, as in any economic crisis, the "degree of monopoly" (i.e. the dominance of large firms) in the market increased as weaker firms went under and others merged to survive. This enhanced the tendencies toward concentration and centralisation which always exist in capitalism, so ensuring an extra thrust towards global operations as the size and position of the surviving firms required wider and larger markets to operate in.

Internationally, another crisis played its role in promoting globalisation. This was the Debit Crisis of the late 1970s and early 1980s. Debt plays a central role for the western powers in dictating how their economies should be organised. The debt crisis proved an ideal leverage for the western powers to force "free trade" on the "third world." This occurred when third world countries faced with falling incomes and rising interest rates defaulted on their loans (loans that were mainly given as a bribe to the ruling elites of those countries and used as a means to suppress the working people of those countries – who now, sickenly, are expected to repay them!).

Before this, as noted in section D.5.1, many countries had followed a policy of "import substitution." This tended to create new competitors who could deny transnational corporations both markets and cheap raw materials. With the debt crisis, the imperialist powers could end this policy but instead of military force, the governments of the west sent in the International Monetary Fund (IMF) and World Bank (WB). The loans required by "developing" nations in the face of recession and rising debt repayments meant that they had little choice but to agree to an IMF-designed economic reform programme. If they refused, not only were they denied IMF funds, but also WB loans. Private banks and lending agencies would also pull out, as they lent under the cover of the IMF – the only body with the power to both underpin loans and squeeze repayment from debtors. These policies meant introducing austerity programmes which, in turn, meant cutting public spending, freezing wages, restricting credit, allowing foreign multinational companies to cherry pick assets at bargain prices, and passing laws to liberalise the flow of capital into and out of the country. Not surprisingly, the result was disastrous for the working population, but the debts were repaid and both local and international elites did very well out of it. So while workers in the West suffered repression and hardship, the fate of the working class in the "developing" world was considerably worse.

Leading economist Joseph Stiglitz worked in the World Bank and described some of dire consequences of these policies. He notes how the neo-liberalism the IMF and WB imposed has, *"too often, not been followed by the promised growth, but by increased misery"* and workers *"lost their jobs [being] forced into poverty"* or *"been hit by a heightened sense of insecurity"* if they remained in work. For many *"it seems closer to an unmitigated disaster."* He argues that part of the problem is that the IMF and WB have been taken over by true believers in capitalism and apply market fundamentalism in all cases. Thus, they *"became the new missionary institutions"* of *"free market ideology"* through which *"these ideas were pushed on* reluctant poor countries." Their policies were *"based on an ideology – market fundamentalism – that required little, if any, consideration of a country's particular circumstances and immediate problems. IMF economists could ignore the short-term effects their policies might have on [a] country, content in the belief **in the long run** the country would be better off"* – a position which many working class people there rejected by rioting and protest. In summary, globalisation *"as it has been practised has not lived up to what its advocates promised it would accomplish … In some cases it has not even resulted in growth, but when it has, it has not brought benefits to all; the net effect of the policies set by the Washington Consensus had all too often been to benefit the few at the expense of the many, the well-off at the expense of the poor."* [**Globalisation and Its Discontents**, p. 17, p. 20, p. 13, p. 36 and p. 20]

While transnational companies are, perhaps, the most well-known representatives of this process of globalisation, the power and mobility of modern capitalism can be seen from the following figures. From 1986 to 1990, foreign exchange transactions rose from under $300 billion to $700 billion daily and were expected to exceed $1.3 trillion in 1994. The World Bank estimates that the total resources of international financial institutions at about $14 trillion. To put some kind of perspective on these figures, the Basel-based Bank for International Settlement estimated that the aggregate daily turnover in the foreign exchange markets at nearly $900 billion in April 1992, equal to 13 times the Gross Domestic Product of the OECD group of countries on an annualised basis [**Financial Times**, 23/9/93]. In Britain, some $200-300 billion a day flows through London's foreign exchange markets. This is the equivalent of the UK's annual Gross National Product in two or three days. Needless to say, since the early 1990s, these amounts have grown to even higher levels (daily currency transactions have risen from a mere $80 billion in 1980 to $1.26 trillion in 1995. In proportion to world trade, this trading in foreign exchange rose from a ration of 10:1 to nearly 70:1 [Mark Weisbrot, **Globalisation for Whom?**]).

Little wonder that a **Financial Times** special supplement on the IMF stated that *"Wise governments realise that the only intelligent response to the challenge of globalisation is to make their economies more acceptable."* [**Op. Cit.**] More acceptable to business, that is, not their populations. As Chomsky put it, *"free capital flow creates what's sometimes called a 'virtual parliament' of global capital, which can exercise veto power over government policies that it considers irrational. That means things like labour rights, or educational programmes, or health, or efforts to stimulate the economy, or, in fact, anything that might help people and not profits (and therefore irrational in the technical sense)."* [**Rogue States**, pp. 212-3]

This means that under globalisation, states will compete with each other to offer the best deals to investors and transnational companies – such as tax breaks, union busting, no pollution controls, and so forth. The effects on the countries' ordinary people will be ignored in the name of future benefits (not so much pie in the sky when you die, more like pie in the future, maybe, if you are nice and do what you are told). For example, such an "acceptable" business climate was created in Britain, where *"market forces have deprived workers of rights in the name of competition."* [**Scotland on Sunday**, 9/1/95] Unsurprisingly the number of people with less than half the

average income rose from 9% of the population in 1979 to 25% in 1993. The share of national wealth held by the poorer half of the population has fallen from one third to one quarter. However, as would be expected, the number of millionaires has increased, as has the welfare state for the rich, with the public's tax money being used to enrich the few via military Keynesianism, privatisation and funding for Research and Development. Like any religion, the free-market ideology is marked by the hypocrisy of those at the top and the sacrifices required from the majority at the bottom.

In addition, the globalisation of capital allows it to play one work force against another. For example, General Motors plans to close two dozen plants in the United States and Canada, but it has become the largest employer in Mexico. Why? Because an *"economic miracle"* has driven wages down. Labour's share of personal income in Mexico has *"declined from 36 percent in the mid-1970's to 23 percent by 1992."* Elsewhere, General Motors opened a $690 million assembly plant in the former East Germany. Why? Because there workers are willing to *"work longer hours than their pampered colleagues in western Germany"* (as the **Financial Times** put it) at 40% of the wage and with few benefits. [Noam Chomsky, **World Orders, Old and New**, p. 160]

This mobility is a useful tool in the class war. There has been *"a significant impact of NAFTA on strikebreaking. About half of union organising efforts are disrupted by employer threats to transfer production abroad, for example … The threats are not idle. When such organising drives succeed, employers close the plant in whole or in part at triple the pre-NAFTA rate (about 15 percent of the time). Plant-closing threats are almost twice as high in more mobile industries (e.g. manufacturing vs. construction)."* [**Rogue States**, pp. 139-40] This process is hardly unique to America, and takes place all across the world (including in the "developing" world itself). This process has increased the bargaining power of employers and has helped to hold wages down (while productivity has increased). In the US, the share of national income going to corporate profits increased by 3.2 percentage points between 1989 and 1998. This represents a significant redistribution of the economic pie. [Mark Weisbrot, **Op. Cit.**] Hence the need for **international** workers' organisation and solidarity (as anarchists have been arguing since Bakunin [**The Political Philosophy of Bakunin**, pp. 305-8]).

This means that such agreements such as NAFTA and the Multilateral Agreement on Investment (shelved due to popular protest and outrage but definitely not forgotten) considerably weaken the governments of nation-states – but only in one area, the regulation of business. Such agreements restrict the ability of governments to check capital flight, restrict currency trading, eliminate environment and labour protection laws, ease the repatriation of profits and anything else that might impede the flow of profits or reduce business power. Indeed, under NAFTA, corporations can sue governments if they think the government is hindering its freedom on the market. Disagreements are settled by unelected panels outside the control of democratic governments. Such agreements represent an increase in corporate power and ensure that states can only intervene when it suits corporations, not the general public.

The ability of corporations to sue governments was enshrined in chapter 11 of NAFTA. In a small town in the Mexican state of San Luis Potosi, a California firm – Metalclad – a commercial purveyor of hazardous wastes, bought an abandoned dump site nearby. It proposed to expand on the dumpsite and use it to dump toxic waste material. The people in the neighbourhood of the dump site protested. The municipality, using powers delegated to it by the state, rezoned the site and forbid Metalclad to extend its land holdings. Metalclad, under Chapter 11 of NAFTA, then sued the Mexican government for damage to its profit margins and balance sheet as a result of being treated unequally by the people of San Luis Potosi. A trade panel, convened in Washington, agreed with the company. [Naomi Klein, **Fences and Windows**, pp. 56-59] In Canada, the Ethyl corporation sued when the government banned its gasoline additive as a health hazard. The government settled "out of court" to prevent a public spectacle of a corporation overruling the nation's Parliament.

NAFTA and other Free Trade agreements are designed for corporations and corporate rule. Chapter 11 was not enshrined in the NAFTA in order to make a better world for the people of Canada, any more than for the people of San Luis Potosi but, instead, for the capitalist elite. This is an inherently imperialist situation, which will "justify" further intervention in the "developing" nations by the US and other imperialist nations, either through indirect military aid to client regimes or through outright invasion, depending on the nature of the *"crisis of democracy"* (a term used by the Trilateral Commission to characterise popular uprisings and a politicising of the general public).

However, force is always required to protect private capital. Even a globalised capitalist company still requires a defender. After all, *"[a]t the international level, U.S. corporations need the government to insure that target countries are 'safe for investment' (no movements for freedom and democracy), that loans will be repaid, contracts kept, and international law respected (but only when it is useful to do so)."* [Henry Rosemont, Jr., **Op. Cit.**, p. 18] For the foreseeable future, America seems to be the global rent-a-cop of choice – particularly as many of the largest corporations are based there.

It makes sense for corporations to pick and choose between states for the best protection, blackmailing their citizens to pay for the armed forces via taxes. It is, in other words, similar to the process at work within the US when companies moved to states which promised the most favourable laws. For example, New Jersey repealed its anti-trust law in 1891-2 and amended its corporation law in 1896 to allow companies to be as large as they liked, to operate anywhere and to own other corporations. This drew corporations to it until Delaware offered even more freedoms to corporate power until other states offered similar laws. In other words, competed for revenue by writing laws to sell to corporations and the mobility of corporations meant that they bargained from a superior position. Globalisation is simply this process on a larger scale, as capital will move to countries whose governments supply what it demands (and punish those which do not). Therefore, far from ending imperialism, globalisation will see it continue, but with one major difference: the citizens in the imperialist countries will see even fewer benefits from imperialism than before, while, as ever, still having to carry the costs.

So, in spite of claims that governments are powerless in the face of global capital, we should never forget that state power has increased

drastically in one area – in state repression against its own citizens. No matter how mobile capital is, it still needs to take concrete form to generate surplus value. Without wage salves, capital would not survive. As such, it can never permanently escape from its own contradictions – wherever it goes, it has to create workers who have a tendency to disobey and do problematic things like demand higher wages, better working conditions, go on strike and so on (indeed, this fact has seen companies based in "developing" nations move to less "developed" to find more compliant labour).

This, of course, necessitates a strengthening of the state in its role as protector of property and as a defence against any unrest provoked by the inequalities, impoverishment and despair caused by globalisation (and, of course, the hope, solidarity and direct action generated by that unrest within the working class). Hence the rise of the neo-liberal consensus in both Britain and the USA saw an increase in state centralisation as well as the number of police, police powers and in laws directed against the labour and radical movements.

As such, it would be a mistake (as many in the anti-globalisation movement do) to contrast the market to the state. State and capital are not opposed to each other – in fact, the opposite is the case. The modern state exists to protect capitalist rule, just as every state exists to defend minority rule, and it is essential for nation states to attract and retain capital within their borders to ensure their revenue by having a suitably strong economy to tax. Globalisation is a state-led initiative whose primary aim is to keep the economically dominant happy. The states which are being "undermined" by globalisation are not horrified by this process as certain protestors are, which should give pause for thought. States are complicit in the process of globalisation – unsurprisingly, as they represent the ruling elites who favour and benefit from globalisation. Moreover, with the advent of a "global market" under GATT, corporations still need politicians to act for them in creating a "free" market which best suits their interests. Therefore, by backing powerful states, corporate elites can increase their bargaining powers and help shape the "New World Order" in their own image.

Governments may be, as Malatesta put it, the property owners **gendarme**, but they can be influenced by their subjects, unlike multinationals. NAFTA was designed to reduce this influence even more. Changes in government policy reflect the changing needs of business, modified, of course, by fear of the working population and its strength. Which explains globalisation – the need for capital to strengthen its position vis-à-vis labour by pitting one labour force against another – and our next step, namely to strengthen and globalise working class resistance. Only when it is clear that the costs of globalisation – in terms of strikes, protests, boycotts, occupations, economic instability and so on – is higher than potential profits will business turn away from it. Only international working class direct action and solidarity will get results. Until that happens, we will see governments co-operating in the process of globalisation.

So, for better or for worse, globalisation has become the latest buzz word to describe the current stage of capitalism and so we shall use it here. Its use does have two positive side effects though. Firstly, it draws attention to the increased size and power of transnational corporations and their impact on global structures of governance **and** the nation state. Secondly, it allows anarchists and other protesters to raise the issue of international solidarity and a globalisation from below which respects diversity and is based on people's needs, not profit.

After all, as Rebecca DeWitt stresses, anarchism and the WTO *"are well suited opponents and anarchism is benefiting from this fight. The WTO is practically the epitome of an authoritarian structure of power to be fought against. People came to Seattle because they knew that it was wrong to let a secret body of officials make policies unaccountable to anyone except themselves. A non-elected body, the WTO is attempting to become more powerful than any national government…. For anarchism, the focus of global capitalism couldn't be more ideal."* [*"An Anarchist Response to Seattle,"* pp. 5-12, **Social Anarchism**, no. 29, p. 6]

To sum up, globalisation will see imperialism change as capitalism itself changes. The need for imperialism remains, as the interests of private capital still need to be defended against the dispossessed. All that changes is that the governments of the imperialistic nations become even more accountable to capital and even less to their populations.

D.5.4 What is the relationship between imperialism and the social classes within capitalism?

The two main classes within capitalist society are, as we indicated in section B.7, the ruling class and the working class. The grey area between these two classes is sometimes called the middle class. As would be expected, different classes have different positions in society and, therefore, different relationships with imperialism. Moreover, we have to also take into account the differences resulting from the relative positions of the nations in question in the world economic and political systems. The ruling class in imperialist nations will not have identical interests as those in the dominated ones, for example. As such, our discussion will have to indicate these differences as well.

The relationship between the ruling class and imperialism is quite simple: It is in favour of it when it supports its interests and when the benefits outweigh the costs. Therefore, for imperialist countries, the ruling class will always be in favour of expanding their influence and power as long as it pays. If the costs outweigh the benefits, of course, sections of the ruling class will argue against imperialist adventures and wars (as, for example, elements of the US elite did when it was clear that they would lose both the Vietnam war and, perhaps, the class war at home by continuing it).

There are strong economic forces at work as well. Due to capital's need to grow in order to survive and compete on the market, find new markets and raw materials, it needs to expand (as we discussed in section D.5). Consequently, it needs to conquer foreign markets and gain access to cheap raw materials and labour. As such, a nation with a powerful capitalist economy will need an aggressive and expansionist foreign policy, which it achieves by buying politicians, initiating media propaganda campaigns, funding right-wing think tanks, and so on, as previously described.

Thus the ruling class benefits from, and so usually supports, imperialism – only, we stress, when the costs out-weight the benefits will we see members of the elite oppose it. Which, of course, explains the elites support for what is termed "globalisation." Needless to say, the ruling class has done **very** well over the last few decades. For example, in the US, the gaps between rich and poor **and** between the rich and middle income reaching their widest point on record in 1997 (from the **Congressional Budget Office** study on Historic Effective Tax Rates 1979-1997). The top 1% saw their after-tax incomes rise by $414,200 between 1979-97, the middle fifth by $3,400 and the bottom fifth fell by -$100. The benefits of globalisation are concentrated at the top, as is to be expected (indeed, almost all of the income gains from economic growth between 1989 and 1998 accrued to the top 5% of American families).

Needless to say, the local ruling classes of the dominated nations may not see it that way. While, of course, local ruling classes do extremely well from imperialism, they need not **like** the position of dependence and subordination they are placed in. Moreover, the steady stream of profits leaving the country for foreign corporations cannot be used to enrich local elites even more. Just as the capitalist dislikes the state or a union limiting their power or taxing/ reducing their profits, so the dominated nation's ruling class dislikes imperialist domination and will seek to ignore or escape it whenever possible. This is because *"every State, in so far as it wants to live not only on paper and not merely by sufferance of its neighbours, but to enjoy real independence – inevitably must become a conquering State."* [Bakunin, **Op. Cit.**, p. 211] So the local ruling class, while benefiting from imperialism, may dislike its dependent position and, if it feels strong enough, may contest their position and gain more independence for themselves.

Many of the post-war imperialist conflicts were of this nature, with local elites trying to disentangle themselves from an imperialist power. Similarly, many conflicts (either fought directly by imperialist powers or funded indirectly by them) were the direct result of ensuring that a nation trying to free itself from imperialist domination did not serve as a positive example for other satellite nations. Which means that local ruling classes can come into conflict with imperialist ones. These can express themselves as wars of national liberation, for example, or just as normal conflicts (such as the first Gulf War). As competition is at the heart of capitalism, we should not be surprised that sections of the international ruling class disagree and fight each other.

The relationship between the working class and imperialism is more complex. In traditional imperialism, foreign trade and the export of capital often make it possible to import cheap goods from abroad and increase profits for the capitalist class, and in this sense, workers can gain because they can improve their standard of living without necessarily coming into system threatening conflict with their employers (i.e. struggle can win reforms which otherwise would be strongly resisted by the capitalist class). Thus living standard may be improved by low wage imports while rising profits may mean rising wages for some key workers (CEOs giving themselves higher wages because they control their own pay rises does not, of course, count!). Therefore, in imperialistic nations during economic boom times, one finds a tendency among the working class (particularly the unorganised sector) to support foreign military adventurism and an aggressive foreign policy. This is part of what is often called the "embourgeoisement" of the proletariat, or the co-optation of labour by capitalist ideology and "patriotic" propaganda. Needless to say, those workers made redundant by these cheap imports may not consider this as a benefit and, by increasing the pool of unemployment and the threat of companies outsourcing work and moving plants to other countries, help hold or drive down wages for most of the working population (as has happened in various degrees in Western countries since the 1970s).

However, as soon as international rivalry between imperialist powers becomes too intense, capitalists will attempt to maintain their profit rates by depressing wages and laying people off in their own country. Workers' real wages will also suffer if military spending goes beyond a certain point. Moreover, if militarism leads to actual war, the working class has much more to lose than to gain as they will be fighting it and making the necessary sacrifices on the "home front" in order to win it. In addition, while imperialism can improve living conditions (for a time), it cannot remove the hierarchical nature of capitalism and therefore cannot stop the class struggle, the spirit of revolt and the instinct for freedom. So, while workers in the developed nations may sometimes benefit from imperialism, such periods cannot last long and cannot end the class struggle.

Rudolf Rocker was correct to stress the contradictory (and self-defeating) nature of working class support for imperialism:

> "No doubt some small comforts may sometimes fall to the share of the workers when the bourgeoisie of their country attain some advantage over that of another country; but this always happens at the cost of their own freedom and the economic oppression of other peoples. The worker ... participates to some extent in the profits which, without effort on their part, fall into the laps of the bourgeoisie of his country from the unrestrained exploitation of colonial peoples; but sooner or later there comes the time when these people too, wake up, and he has to pay all the more dearly for the small advantages he has enjoyed. ... Small gains arising from increased opportunity of employment and higher wages may accrue to the workers in a successful state from the carving out of new markets at the cost of others; but at the same time their brothers on the other side of the border have to pay for them by unemployment and the lowering of the standards of labour. The result is an ever widening rift in the international labour movement ... By this rift the liberation of the workers from the yoke of wage-slavery is pushed further and further into the distance. As long as the worker ties up his interests with those of the bourgeoisie of his country instead of with his class, he must logically also take in his stride all the results of that relationship. He must stand ready to fight the wars of the possessing classes for the retention and extension of their markets, and to defend any injustice they may perpetrate on other people ... Only when the workers in every country shall come to understand clearly that their interests are everywhere the same, and out of this understanding learn to act together, will the effective basis be laid for the international liberation of the working class." [**Anarcho-Syndicalism**, p. 71]

Ultimately, any *"collaboration of workers and employers ... can only result in the workers being condemned to ... eat the crumbs that fall from the rich man's table."* [Rocker, **Op. Cit.**, pp. 70-1] This applies to both the imperialist and the satellite state, of course. Moreover, as imperialism needs to have a strong military force available for it and as a consequence it required militarism at home. This has an impact at home in that resources which could be used to improve the quality of life for all are funnelled towards producing weapons (and profits for corporations). Moreover, militarism is directed not only at external enemies, but also against those who threaten elite role at home. We discuss militarism in more detail in section D.8.

However, under globalisation things are somewhat different. With the increase in world trade and the signing of "free trade" agreements like NAFTA, the position of workers in the imperialist nations need not improve. For example, since the 1970s, the wages – adjusted for inflation – of the typical American employee have actually fallen, even as the economy has grown. In other words, the majority of Americans are no longer sharing in the gains from economic growth. This is very different from the previous era, for example 1946-73, when the real wages of the typical worker rose by about 80 percent. Not that this globalisation has aided the working class in the "developing" nations. In Latin America, for example, GDP per capita grew by 75 percent from 1960-1980, whereas between 1981 and 1998 it has only risen 6 percent. [Mark Weisbrot, Dean Baker, Robert Naiman, and Gila Neta, **Growth May Be Good for the Poor – But are IMF and World Bank Policies Good for Growth?**]

As Chomsky noted, *"[t]o the credit of the **Wall Street Journal**, it points out that there's a 'but.' Mexico has 'a stellar reputation,' and it's an economic miracle, but the population is being devastated. There's been a 40 percent drop in purchasing power since 1994. The poverty rate is going up and is in fact rising fast. The economic miracle wiped out, they say, a generation of progress; most Mexicans are poorer than their parents. Other sources reveal that agriculture is being wiped out by US-subsidised agricultural imports, manufacturing wages have declined about 20 percent, general wages even more. In fact, NAFTA is a remarkable success: it's the first trade agreement in history that's succeeded in harming the populations of all three countries involved. That's quite an achievement."* In the U.S., *"the medium income (half above, half below) for families has gotten back now to what it was in 1989, which is below what it was in the 1970s."* [**Rogue States**, pp. 98-9 and p. 213]

An achievement which was predicted. But, of course, while occasionally admitting that globalisation may harm the wages of workers in developed countries, it is argued that it will benefit those in the "developing" world. It is amazing how open to socialist arguments capitalists and their supporters are, as long as its not their income being redistributed! As can be seen from NAFTA, this did not happen. Faced with cheap imports, agriculture and local industry would be undermined, increasing the number of workers seeking work, so forcing down wages as the bargaining power of labour is decreased. Combine this with governments which act in the interests of capital (as always) and force the poor to accept the costs of economic austerity and back business attempts to break unions and workers resistance then we have a situation where productivity can increase dramatically while wages fall behind (either relatively or absolutely). As has been the case in both the USA and Mexico, for example.

This reversal has had much to do with changes in the global "rules of the game," which have greatly favoured corporations and weakened labour. Unsurprisingly, the North American union movement has opposed NAFTA and other treaties which empower business over labour. Therefore, the position of labour within both imperialist and dominated nations can be harmed under globalisation, so ensuring international solidarity and organisation have a stronger reason to be embraced by both sides. This should not come as a surprise, however, as the process towards globalisation was accelerated by intensive class struggle across the world and was used as a tool against the working class (see last section).

It is difficult to generalise about the effects of imperialism on the "middle class" (i.e. professionals, self-employed, small business people, peasants and so on – **not** middle income groups, who are usually working class). Some groups within this strata stand to gain, others to lose (in particular, peasants who are impoverished by cheap imports of food). This lack of common interests and a common organisational base makes the middle class unstable and susceptible to patriotic sloganeering, vague theories of national or racial superiority, or fascist scapegoating of minorities for society's problems. For this reason, the ruling class finds it relatively easy to recruit large sectors of the middle class to an aggressive and expansionist foreign policy, through media propaganda campaigns. Since organised labour tends to perceive imperialism as being against its overall best interests, and thus usually opposes it, the ruling class is able to intensify the hostility of the middle class to the organised working class by portraying the latter as "unpatriotic" and "unwilling to sacrifice" for the "national interest." Sadly, the trade union bureaucracy usually accepts the "patriotic" message, particularly at times of war, and often collaborates with the state to further imperialistic interests. This eventually brings them into conflict with the rank-and-file, whose interests are ignored even more than usual when this occurs.

To summarise, the ruling class is usually pro-imperialism – as long as it is in their interests (i.e. the benefits outweigh the costs). The working class, regardless of any short term benefit its members may gain, end up paying the costs of imperialism by having to fight its wars and pay for the militarism it produces. So, under imperialism, like any form of capitalism, the working class will pay the bill required to maintain it. This means that we have a real interest in ending it – particularly as under globalisation the few benefits that used to accrue to us are much less.

D.6

Are anarchists against Nationalism?

Yes, anarchists are opposed to nationalism in all its forms. British anarchists Stuart Christie and Albert Meltzer simply point out the obvious: *"As a nation implies a state, it is not possible to be a nationalist and an anarchist."* [**The Floodgates of Anarchy**, p. 59fn]

To understand this position, we must first define what anarchists mean by nationalism. For many people, it is just the natural attachment to home, the place one grew up. Nationality, as Bakunin noted, is a *"natural and social fact,"* as *"every people and the smallest folk-unit has its own character, its own specific mode of existence, its own way of speaking, feeling, thinking, and acting; and it is this idiosyncrasy that constitutes the essence of nationality."* [**The Political Philosophy of Bakunin**, p. 325] These feelings, however, obviously do not exist in a social vacuum. They cannot be discussed without also discussing the nature of these groups and what classes and other social hierarchies they contain. Once we do this, the anarchist opposition to nationalism becomes clear.

This means that anarchists distinguish between **nationality** (that is, cultural affinity) and **nationalism** (confined to the state and government itself). This allows us to define what we support and oppose – nationalism, at root, is destructive and reactionary, whereas cultural difference and affinity is a source of community, social diversity and vitality.

Such diversity is to be celebrated and allowed to express it itself on its own terms. Or, as Murray Bookchin puts it, *"[t]hat specific peoples should be free to fully develop their own cultural capacities is not merely a right but a desideratum. The world would be a drab place indeed if a magnificent mosaic of different cultures does not replace the largely decultured and homogenised world created by modern capitalism."* [*"Nationalism and the 'National Question'"*, pp. 8-36. **Society and Nature**, No. 5, pp. 28-29] But, as he also warns, such cultural freedom and variety should **not** be confused with nationalism. The latter is far more (and ethically, a lot less) than simple recognition of cultural uniqueness and love of home. Nationalism is the love of, or the desire to create, a nation-state and for this reason anarchists are opposed to it, in all its forms.

This means that nationalism cannot and must not be confused with nationality. The later is a product of social processes while the former to a product of state action and elite rule. Social evolution cannot be squeezed into the narrow, restricting borders of the nation state without harming the individuals whose lives **make** that social development happen in the first place.

The state, as we have seen, is a centralised body invested with power and a social monopoly of force. As such it pre-empts the autonomy of localities and peoples, and in the name of the "nation" crushes the living, breathing reality of "nations" (i.e. peoples and their cultures) with one law, one culture and one "official" history. Unlike most nationalists, anarchists recognise that almost all "nations" are in fact not homogeneous, and so consider nationality to be far wider in application than just lines on maps, created by conquest. Hence we think that recreating the centralised state in a slightly smaller area, as nationalist movements generally advocate, cannot solve what is called the "national question."

Ultimately, as Rudolf Rocker argued, the *"nation is not the cause, but the result of the state. It is the state that creates the nation, not the nation the state."* Every state *"is an artificial mechanism imposed upon [people] from above by some ruler, and it never pursues any other ends but to defend and make secure the interests of privileged minorities within society."* Nationalism *"has never been anything but the political religion of the modern state."* [**Nationalism and Culture**, p. 200 and p. 201] It was created to reinforce the state by providing it with the loyalty of a people of shared linguistic, ethnic, and cultural affinities. And if these shared affinities do not exist, the state will create them by centralising education in its own hands, imposing an "official" language and attempting to crush cultural differences from the peoples within its borders.

This is because it treats groups of people not as unique individuals but rather *"as if they were individuals with definite traits of character and peculiar psychic properties or intellectual qualities"* which *"must irrevocably lead to the most monstrously deceptive conclusions."* [Rocker, **Op. Cit.**, p. 437] This creates the theoretical justification for authoritarianism, as it allows the stamping out of all forms of individuality and local customs and cultures which do not concur with the abstract standard. In addition, nationalism hides class differences within the "nation" by arguing that all people must unite around their supposedly common interests (as members of the same "nation"), when in fact they have nothing in common due to the existence of hierarchies and classes.

Malatesta recognised this when he noted that you cannot talk about states like they were *"homogeneous ethnographic units, each having its proper interests, aspirations, and mission, in opposition to the interests, aspirations, and mission of rival units. This may be true relatively, as long as the oppressed, and chiefly the workers, have no self-consciousness, fail to recognise the injustice of their inferior position, and make themselves the docile tools of the oppressors."* In that case, it is *"the dominating class only that counts"* and this *"owing to its desire to conserve and to enlarge its power ... may excite racial ambitions and hatred, and send its nation, its flock, against 'foreign' countries, with a view to releasing them from their present oppressors, and submitting them to its own political and economical domination."* Thus anarchists have *"always fought against patriotism, which is a survival of the past, and serves well the interests of the oppressors."* [**Errico Malatesta: His Life and Ideas**, p. 244]

Thus nationalism is a key means of obscuring class differences and getting those subject to hierarchies to accept them as "natural." As such, it plays an important role in keeping the current class system going (unsurprisingly, the nation-state and its nationalism arose at the same time as capitalism). As well dividing the working class internationally, it is also used within a nation state to turn working class people born in a specific nation against immigrants. By getting native-born workers to blame newcomers, the capitalist class weakens the resistance to their power as well as turning economic issues into racial/nationalist ones. In practice, however, nationalism is a *"state ideology"* which boils down to saying it is

*"'our country' as opposed to **theirs**, meaning **we** were the serfs of the government first."* [Christie and Meltzer, **Op. Cit.**, p. 71] It tries to confuse love of where you grow up or live with *"love of the State"* and so nationalism is *"not the faithful expression"* of this natural feeling but rather *"an expression distorted by means of a false abstraction, always for the benefit of an exploiting minority."* [Bakunin, **Op. Cit.**, p. 324]

Needless to say, the nationalism of the bourgeoisie often comes into direct conflict with the people who make up the nation it claims to love. Bakunin simply stated a truism when he noted that the capitalist class *"would rather submit"* to a *"foreign yoke than renounce its social privileges and accept economic equality."* This does not mean that the *"bourgeoisie is unpatriotic; on the contrary patriotism, in the narrowest sense, is its essential virtue. But the bourgeoisie love their country only because, for them, the country, represented by the State, safeguards their economic, political, and social privileges. Any nation withdrawing their protection would be disowned by them, therefore, for the bourgeoisie, the country **is** the State. Patriots of the State, they become furious enemies of the masses if the people, tired of sacrificing themselves, of being used as a passive footstool by the government, revolt against it. If the bourgeoisie had to choose between the masses who rebel against the State"* and a foreign invader, *"they would surely choose the latter."* [**Bakunin on Anarchism**, pp. 185-6] Given this, Bakunin would have not been surprised by either the rise of Fascism in Italy nor when the Allies in post-fascist Italy *"crush[ed] revolutionary movements"* and gave *"their support to fascists who made good by becoming Allied Quislings."* [Marie-Louise Berneri, **Neither East Nor West**, p. 97]

In addition, nationalism is often used to justify the most horrific crimes, with the Nation effectively replacing God in terms of justifying injustice and oppression and allowing individuals to wash their hands of their own actions. For *"under cover of the nation everything can be hid"* argues Rocker (echoing Bakunin, we must note). *"The national flag covers every injustice, every inhumanity, every lie, every outrage, every crime. The collective responsibility of the nation kills the sense of justice of the individual and brings man to the point where he overlooks injustice done; where, indeed, it may appear to him a meritorious act if committed in the interests of the nation."* [**Op. Cit.**, p. 252] So when discussing nationalism:

> *"we must not forget that we are always dealing with the organised selfishness of privileged minorities which hide behind the skirts of the nation, hide behind the credulity of the masses. We speak of national interests, national capital, national spheres of interest, national honour, and national spirit; but we forget that behind all this there are hidden merely the selfish interests of power-loving politicians and money-loving business men for whom the nation is a convenient cover to hide their personal greed and their schemes for political power from the eyes of the world."* [Rocker, **Op. Cit.**, pp. 252-3]

Hence we see the all too familiar sight of successful "national liberation" movements replacing foreign oppression with a home-based one. Nationalist governments introduce *"the worse features of the very empires from which oppressed peoples have tried to* shake loose. Not only do they typically reproduce state machines that are as oppressive as the ones that colonial powers imposed on them, but they reinforce those machines with cultural, religious, ethnic, and xenophobic traits that are often used to foster regional and even domestic hatreds and sub-imperialisms." [Bookchin, **Op. Cit.**, p. 30] This is unsurprising as nationalism delivers power to local ruling classes as it relies on taking state power. As a result, nationalism can never deliver freedom to the working class (the vast majority of a given "nation") as its function is to build a mass support base for local elites angry with imperialism for blocking their ambitions to rule and exploit "their" nation and fellow country people.

In fact, nationalism is no threat to capitalism or even to imperialism. It replaces imperialist domination with local elite and foreign oppression and exploitation with native versions. That sometimes the local elites, like imperial ones, introduce reforms which benefit the majority does not change the nature of the new regimes although this does potentially bring them into conflict with imperialist powers. As Chomsky notes, for imperialism the *"threat is not nationalism, but independent nationalism, which focuses on the needs of the population, not merely the wealthy sectors and the foreign investors to whom they are linked. Subservient nationalism that does not succumb to these heresies is quite welcome"* and it is *"quite willing to deal with them if they are willing to sell the country to the foreign master, as Third World elites (including now those in much of Eastern Europe) are often quite willing to do, since they may greatly benefit even as their countries are destroyed."* [*"Nationalism and the New World Order"* pp. 1-7, **Society and Nature**, No. 5, pp. 4-5] However, independent nationalism is like social democracy in imperialist countries in that it may, at best, reduce the evils of the class system and social hierarchies but it never gets rid of them (at worse, it creates new classes and hierarchies clustered around the state bureaucracy).

Anarchists oppose nationalism in all its forms as harmful to the interests of those who make up a given nation and their cultural identities. As Rocker put it, peoples and groups of peoples have *"existed long before the state put in its appearance"* and *"develop without the assistance of the state. They are only hindered in their natural development when some external power interferes by violence with their life and forces it into patterns which it has not known before."* A nation, in contrast, *"encompasses a whole array of different peoples and groups of peoples who have by more or less violent means been pressed together into the frame of a common state."* In other words, the *"nation is, then, unthinkable without the state."* [**Op. Cit.**, p. 201]

Given this, we do support nationality and cultural difference, diversity and self-determination as a natural expression of our love of freedom and support for decentralisation. This should not, however, be confused with supporting nationalism. In addition, it goes without saying that a nationality that take on notions of racial, cultural or ethnic "superiority" or "purity" or believe that cultural differences are somehow rooted in biology get no support from anarchists. Equally unsurprisingly, anarchists have been the most consistent foes of that particularly extreme form of nationalism, fascism (*"a politico-economic state where the ruling class of each country behaves towards its own people as … it has behaved to*

the colonial peoples under its heel." [Bart de Ligt, **The Conquest of Violence**, p. 74]). Moreover, we do not support those aspects of specific cultures which reflect social hierarchies (for example, many traditional cultures have sexist and homophobic tendencies). By supporting nationality, we do not advocate tolerating these. Nor do the negative aspects of specific cultures justify another state imposing its will on it in the name of "civilising" it. As history shows, such "humanitarian" intervention is just a mask for justifying imperialist conquest and exploitation and it rarely works as cultural change has to flow from below, by the actions of the oppressed themselves, in order to be successful.

In opposition to nationalism, Anarchists are *"proud of being internationalists."* We seek *"the end of all oppression and of all exploitation,"* and so aim *"to awaken a consciousness of the antagonism of interests between dominators and dominated, between exploiters and workers, and to develop the class struggle inside each country, and the solidarity among all workers across the frontiers, as against any prejudice and any passion of either race or nationality."* [Malatesta, **Op. Cit.**, p. 244]

We must stress that anarchists, being opposed to all forms of exploitation and oppression, are against a situation of external domination where the one country dominates the people and territory of another country (i.e., imperialism – see section D.5). This flows from our basic principles as *"[t]rue internationalism will never be attained except by the independence of each nationality, little or large, compact or disunited – just as anarchy is in the independence of each individual. If we say no government of man over man, how can [we] permit the government of conquered nationalities by the conquering nationalities?"* [Kropotkin, quoted by Martin A. Miller, **Kropotkin**, p. 231] As we discuss in the next section, while rejecting Nationalism anarchists do not necessarily oppose national liberation struggles against foreign domination.

D.7

Are anarchists opposed to National Liberation struggles?

Obviously, given the anarchist analysis of imperialism discussed in section D.5, anarchists are opposed to imperialism and wars it inevitably causes. Likewise, as noted in the last section, we are against any form of nationalism. Anarchists oppose nationalism just as much as they oppose imperialism – neither offer a way to a free society. While we oppose imperialism and foreign domination and support decentralisation, it does not mean that anarchists blindly support national liberation movements. In this section we explain the anarchist position on such movements.

Anarchists, it should be stressed, are not against globalisation or international links and ties as such. Far from it, we have always been internationalists and are in favour of ***"globalisation from below,"*** one that respects and encourages diversity and difference while sharing the world. However, we have no desire to live in a world turned bland by corporate power and economic imperialism. As such, we are opposed to capitalist trends that commodify culture as it commodifies social relationships. We want to make the world an interesting place to live in and that means opposing both actual (i.e. physical, political and economic) imperialism as well as the cultural and social forms of it.

However, this does not mean that anarchists are indifferent to the national oppression inherent within imperialism. Far from it. Being opposed to all forms of hierarchy, anarchists cannot be in favour of a system in which a country dominates another. The Cuban anarchists spoke for all of us when they stated that they were *"against all forms of imperialism and colonialism; against the economic domination of peoples ... against military pressure to impose upon peoples political and economic systems foreign to their national cultures, customs and social systems ... We believe that among the nations of the world, the small are as worthy as the big. Just as we remain enemies of national states because each of them hold its own people in subjection; so also are we opposed to the super-states that utilise their political, economic and military power to impose their rapacious systems of exploitation on weaker countries. As against all forms of imperialism, we declare for revolutionary internationalism; for the creation of great confederations of free peoples for their mutual interests; for solidarity and mutual aid."* [quoted by Sam Dolgoff, **The Cuban Revolution: A Critical Perspective**, p. 138]

It is impossible to be free while dependent on the power of another. If the capital one uses is owned by another country, one is in no position to resist the demands of that country. If you are dependent on foreign corporations and international finance to invest in your nation, then you have to do what they want (and so the ruling class will suppress political and social opposition to please their backers as well as maintain themselves in power). To be self-governing under capitalism, a community or nation must be economically independent. The centralisation of capital implied by imperialism means that power rests in the hands of a few others, not with those directly affected by the decisions made by that power. This power allows them to define and impose the rules and guidelines of the global market, forcing the many to follow the laws the few make. Thus capitalism soon makes a decentralised economy, and so a free society, impossible. As such, anarchists stress decentralisation of industry and its integration with agriculture (see section I.3.8) within the context of socialisation of property and workers' self-management of production. Only this can ensure that production meets the needs of all rather than the profits of a few.

Moreover, anarchists also recognise that economic imperialism is the parent of cultural and social imperialism. As Takis Fotopoulos argues, *"the marketisation of culture and the recent liberalisation and deregulation of markets have contributed significantly to the present cultural homogenisation, with traditional communities and their cultures disappearing all over the world and people converted to consumers of a mass culture produced in the advanced capitalist countries and particularly the USA."* [**Towards an Inclusive Democracy**, p. 40] Equally, we are aware, to quote Chomsky, that racism *"is inherent in imperial rule"* and that it is *"inherent in the relation of domination"* that imperialism is based on. [**Imperial Ambitions**, p. 48]

It is this context which explains the anarchist position on national liberation struggles. While we are internationalists, we are against all forms of domination and oppression – including national ones. This means that we are not indifferent to national liberation struggles. Quite the opposite. In the words of Bakunin:

> *"Fatherland and nationality are, like individuality, each a natural and social fact, physiological and historical at the same time; neither of them is a principle. Only that can be called a human principle which is universal and common to all men; and nationality separates men ... What is a principle is the respect which everyone should have for natural facts, real or social. Nationality, like individuality, is one of those facts ... To violate it is to commit a crime ... And that is why I feel myself always the patriot of all oppressed fatherlands."* [**The Political Philosophy of Bakunin**, p. 324]

This is because nationality *"is a historic, local fact, which, like all real and harmless facts, has the right to claim general acceptance."* This means that *"[e]very people, like every person, is involuntarily that which it is and therefore has a right to be itself. Therein lies the so-called national rights."* Nationality, Bakunin stressed, *"is not a principle; it is a legitimate fact, just as individuality is. Every nationality, great or small, has the incontestable right to be itself, to live according to its own nature. This right is simply the corollary of the general principal of freedom."* [**Op. Cit.** p. 325]

More recently Murray Bookchin has expressed similar sentiments. *"No left libertarian,"* he argued, *"can oppose the **right** of a subjugated people to establish itself as an autonomous entity – be it in a [libertarian] confederation ... or as a nation-state based in hierarchical and class inequities."* Even so, anarchists do not elevate the idea of national liberation *"into a mindless article of faith,"* as much of the Leninist-influenced left has done. We do not call for support for the oppressed nation without first inquiring into *"**what kind of society** a given 'national liberation' movement would likely produce."* To do so, as Bookchin points out, would be to *"support national liberation struggles for instrumental purposes, merely as a means of 'weakening' imperialism,"* which leads to *"a condition of moral bankruptcy"* as socialist ideas become associated with the authoritarian and statist goals of the "anti-imperialist" dictatorships in "liberated" nations. *"But to oppose an oppressor is not equivalent to calling for **support** for everything formerly colonised nation-states do."* [*"Nationalism and the 'National Question'"*, pp. 8-36, **Society and Nature**, No. 5, p. 31, p. 25, p. 29 and p. 31]

This means that anarchists oppose foreign oppression and are usually sympathetic to attempts by those who suffer it to end it. This does not mean that we necessarily support national liberation movements as such (after all, they usually desire to create a new state) but we cannot sit back and watch one nation oppress another and so act to stop that oppression (by, for example, protesting against the oppressing nation and trying to get them to change their policies and withdraw from the oppressed nations affairs). Nor does it mean we are uncritical of specific expressions of nationality and popular cultures. Just as we are against sexist, racist and homophobic individuals and seek to help them change their attitudes, we are also opposed to such traits within peoples and cultures and urge those who are subject to such popular prejudices to change them by their own efforts with the practical and moral solidarity of others (any attempt to use state force to end such discrimination rarely works and is often counter-productive as it entrenches such opinions). Needless to say, justifying foreign intervention or occupation by appeals to end such backward cultural traits is usually hypocritical in the extreme and masks more basic interests. An obvious example is the Christian and Republican right and its use of the position of women in Afghanistan to bolster support for the invasion of 2001 (the sight of the American Taliban discovering the importance of feminism – in other countries, of course – was surreal but not unexpected given the needs of the moment and their basis in "reasons of state").

The reason for this critical attitude to national liberation struggles is that they usually counterpoise the common interests of "the nation" to those of a (foreign) oppressor and assume that **class** and social hierarchies (i.e. internal oppression) are irrelevant. Although nationalist movements often cut across classes, they in practice seek to increase autonomy for certain parts of society (namely the local elites) while ignoring that of other parts (namely the working class who are expected to continue being subject to class and state oppression). For anarchists, a new national state would not bring any fundamental change in the lives of most people, who would still be powerless both economically and socially. Looking around the world at all the many nation-states in existence, we see the same gross disparities in power, influence and wealth restricting self-determination for working-class people, even if they are free "nationally." It seems hypocritical for nationalist leaders to talk of liberating their own nation from imperialism while advocating the creation of a capitalist nation-state, which will be oppressive to its own population (and, perhaps, eventually become imperialistic itself as it develops to a certain point and has to seek foreign outlets for its products and capital). The fate of all former colonies provides ample support for this conclusion.

As Bakunin stressed, nationalists do not understand that "the spontaneous and free union of the living forces of a nation has nothing in common with their artificial concentration at once mechanistic and forced in the political centralisation of the unitary state; and because [they] confused and identified these two very opposing things [they have] not only been the promoter of the independence of [their] country [they have] become at the same time … the promoter of its present slavery." [quoted by Jean Caroline Cahm, "Bakunin", pp. 22-49, Eric Cahm and Vladimir Claude Fisera (eds.), **Socialism and Nationalism**, vol. 1, p. 36]

In response to national liberation struggles, anarchists stress the self-liberation of the working class, which can be only achieved by its members' own efforts, creating and using their own organisations. In this process there can be no separation of political, social and economic goals. The struggle against imperialism cannot be separated from the struggle against capitalism. This has been the approach of most, if not all, anarchist movements in the face of foreign domination – the combination of the struggle against foreign domination with the class struggle against native oppressors. In many different countries (including Bulgaria, Mexico, Cuba and Korea) anarchists have tried, by their "propaganda, and above all **action**, [to] encourage the masses to turn the struggle for political independence into the struggle for the Social Revolution." [Sam Dolgoff, **Op. Cit.**, p. 41] In other words, a people will free only "by

the general uprising of the labouring masses." [Bakunin, quoted by Cahm, **Op. Cit.**, p. 36]

History has shown the validity of this argument, as well as the fears of Mexican anarchist Ricardo Flores Magón that it is "the duty of all the poor to work and to struggle to break the chains that enslave us. To leave the solution of our problems to the educated and the rich classes is to voluntarily put ourselves in the grasp of their claws." For "a simple change of rulers is not a fount of liberty" and "any revolutionary program that doesn't contain a clause concerning the taking of the lands [and workplaces] by the people is a program of the ruling classes, who will never struggle against their own interests." [**Dreams of Freedom**, p. 142 and p. 293] As Kropotkin stressed, the "failure of all nationalist movements … lies in this curse … that the economic question … remains on the side … In a word, it seems to me that in each national movement we have a major task: to set forth the question [of nationalism] on an economic basis and carry out agitation against serfdom [and other forms of exploitation] at one with the struggle against [oppression by] foreign nationality." [quoted by Martin A. Miller, **Kropotkin**, p. 230]

Moreover, we should point out that Anarchists in imperialist countries have also opposed national oppression by both words and deeds. For example, the prominent Japanese Anarchist Kotoku Shusi was framed and executed in 1910 after campaigning against Japanese expansionism. In Italy, the anarchist movement opposed Italian expansionism into Eritrea and Ethiopia in the 1880s and 1890s, and organised a massive anti-war movement against the 1911 invasion of Libya. In 1909, the Spanish Anarchists organised a mass strike against intervention in Morocco. More recently, anarchists in France struggled against two colonial wars (in Indochina and Algeria) in the late 50's and early 60's, anarchists world-wide opposed US aggression in Latin America and Vietnam (without, we must note, supporting the Cuban and Vietnamese Stalinist regimes), opposed the Gulf War (during which most anarchists raised the call of "No war but the class war") as well as opposing Soviet imperialism.

In practice national liberation movements are full of contradictions between the way the rank and file sees progress being made (and their hopes and dreams) and the wishes of their ruling class members/leaders. The leadership will always resolve this conflict in favour of the future ruling class, at best paying lip-service to social issues by always stressing that addressing them must be postponed to **after** the foreign power has left the country. That makes it possible for individual members of these struggles to realise the limited nature of nationalism and break from these politics towards anarchism. At times of major struggle and conflict this contradiction will become very apparent and at this stage it is possible that large numbers may break from nationalism in practice, if not in theory, by pushing the revolt into social struggles and changes. In such circumstances, theory may catch up with practice and nationalist ideology be rejected in favour of a wider concept of freedom, particularly **if** an alternative that addresses these concerns exists. Providing that anarchists do not compromise our ideals such movements against foreign domination can be wonderful opportunities to spread our politics, ideals and ideas – and to show up the limitations and dangers of nationalism itself and present a viable alternative.

For anarchists, the key question is whether freedom is for abstract concepts like "the nation" or for the individuals who make up the nationality and give it life. Oppression must be fought on all fronts, within nations and internationally, in order for working-class people to gain the fruits of freedom. Any national liberation struggle which bases itself on nationalism is doomed to failure as a movement for extending human freedom. Thus anarchists *"refuse to participate in national liberation fronts; they participate in class fronts which may or may not be involved in national liberation struggles. The struggle must spread to establish economic, political and social structures in the liberated territories, based on federalist and libertarian organisations."* [Alfredo M. Bonanno, **Anarchism and the National Liberation Struggle**, p. 12]

The Makhnovist movement in the Ukraine expressed this perspective well when it was fighting for freedom during the Russian Revolution and Civil War. The Ukraine at the time was a very diverse country, with many distinct national and ethnic groups living within it which made this issue particularly complex:

> *"Clearly, each national group has a natural and indisputable entitlement to speak its language, live in accordance with its customs, retain its beliefs and rituals … in short, to maintain and develop its national culture in every sphere. It is obvious that this clear and specific stance has absolutely nothing to do with narrow nationalism of the 'separatist' variety which pits nation against nation and substitutes an artificial and harmful separation for the struggle to achieve a natural social union of toilers in one shared social communion.*

> *"In our view, national aspirations of a natural, wholesome character (language, customs, culture, etc.) can achieve full and fruitful satisfaction only in the union of nationalities rather than in their antagonism …*

> *"The speedy construction of a new life on [libertarian] socialist foundations will ineluctably lead to development of the culture peculiar to each nationality. Whenever we Makhnovist insurgents speak of independence of the Ukraine, we ground it in the social and economic plane of the toilers. We proclaim the right of the Ukrainian people (and every other nation) to self-determination, not in the narrow, nationalist sense … but in the sense of the toilers' right to self-determination. We declare that the toiling folk of the Ukraine's towns and countryside have shown everyone through their heroic fight that they do not wish any longer to suffer political power and have no use for it, and that they consciously aspire to a libertarian society. We thus declare that all political power … is to be regarded … as an enemy and counter-revolutionary. To the very last drop of their blood they will wage a ferocious struggle against it, in defence of their entitlement to self-organisation."* [quoted by Alexandre Skirda, **Nestor Makhno Anarchy's Cossack**, pp. 377-8]

So while anarchists unmask nationalism for what it is, we do not disdain the basic struggle for identity and self-management which nationalism diverts. We encourage direct action and the spirit of revolt against all forms of oppression – social, economic, political, racial, sexual, religious and national. By this method, we aim to turn national liberation struggles into **human** liberation struggles. And while fighting against oppression, we struggle for anarchy, a free confederation of communes based on workplace and community assemblies. A confederation which will place the nation-state, all nation-states, into the dust-bin of history where it belongs. This struggle for popular self-determination is, as such, considered to be part of a wider, international movement for *"a social revolution cannot be confined to a single isolated country, it is by its very nature international in scope"* and so popular movements must *"link their aspirations and forces with the aspirations and forces of all other countries"* and so the *"only way of arriving at emancipation lies in the fraternity of oppressed peoples in an international alliance of all countries."* [Bakunin, quoted by Cahm, **Op. Cit.**, p. 40 and p. 36] And as far as "national" identity within an anarchist society is concerned, our position is clear and simple. As Bakunin noted with respect to the Polish struggle for national liberation during the last century, anarchists, as *"adversaries of every State, … reject the rights and frontiers called historic. For us Poland only begins, only truly exists there where the labouring masses are and want to be Polish, it ends where, renouncing all particular links with Poland, the masses wish to establish other national links."* [quoted by Jean Caroline Cahm, **Op. Cit.**, p. 43]

D.8

What causes militarism and what are its effects?

There are three main causes of capitalist militarism.

Firstly, there is the need to contain the domestic enemy – the oppressed and exploited sections of the population. As Emma Goldman argued, the military machine *"is not directed only against the external enemy; it aims much more at the internal enemy. It concerns that element of labour which has learned not to hope for anything from our institutions, that awakened part of the working people which has realised that the war of classes underlies all wars among nations, and that if war is justified at all it is the war against economic dependence and political slavery, the two dominant issues involved in the struggle of the classes."* In other words, the nation *"which is to be protected by a huge military force is not"* that *"of the people, but that of the privileged class; the class which robs and exploits the masses, and controls their lives from the cradle to the grave."* [**Red Emma Speaks**, p. 352 and p. 348]

The second, as noted in the section on imperialism, is that a strong military is necessary in order for a ruling class to pursue an aggressive and expansionist foreign policy in order to defend its interests globally. For most developed capitalist nations, this kind of foreign policy becomes more and more important because of economic forces, i.e. in order to provide outlets for its goods and capital to prevent the system from collapsing by expanding the market continually outward. This outward expansion of, and so competition between, capital needs military force to protect its interests (particularly those invested in other countries) and give it added clout in the economic jungle of the world market. This need has resulted in, for example, *"hundreds of US bases [being] placed all over the world to ensure global domination."* [Chomsky, **Failed States**, p. 11]

The third major reason for militarism is to bolster a state's economy. Capitalist militarism promotes the development of a specially favoured group of companies which includes *"all those engaged in the manufacture and sale of munitions and in military equipment for personal gain and profit."* [Goldman, **Op. Cit.**, p. 354] These armaments companies ("defence" contractors) have a direct interest in the maximum expansion of military production. Since this group is particularly wealthy, it exerts great pressure on government to pursue the type of state intervention and, often, the aggressive foreign policies it wants. As Chomsky noted with respect to the US invasion and occupation of Iraq:

> *"Empires are costly. Running Iraq is not cheap. Somebody's paying. Somebody's paying the corporations that destroyed Iraq and the corporations that are rebuilding it. in both cases, they're getting paid by the U.S. taxpayer. Those are gifts from U.S. taxpayers to U.S. Corporations ... The same tax-payers fund the military-corporate system of weapons manufacturers and technology companies that bombed Iraq ... It's a transfer of wealth from the general population to narrow sectors of the population."* [**Imperial Ambitions**, pp. 56-7]

This "special relationship" between state and Big Business also has the advantage that it allows the ordinary citizen to pay for industrial Research and Development. As Noam Chomsky points out in many of his works, the *"Pentagon System,"* in which the public is forced to subsidise research and development of high tech industry through subsidies to defence contractors, is a covert substitute in the US for the overt industrial planning policies of other "advanced" capitalist nations, like Germany and Japan. Government subsidies provide an important way for companies to fund their research and development at taxpayer expense, which often yields "spin-offs" with great commercial potential as consumer products (e.g. computers). Needless to say, all the profits go to the defence contractors and to the commercial companies who buy licences to patented technologies from them, rather than being shared with the public which funded the R&D that made the profits possible. Thus militarism is a key means of securing technological advances within capitalism.

It is necessary to provide some details to indicate the size and impact of military spending on the US economy:

> *"Since 1945 ... there have been new industries sparking investment and employment.... In most of them, basic research and technological progress were closely linked to the expanding military sector. The major innovation in the 1950s was electronics ... [which] increased its output 15 percent per year. It was of critical importance in workplace automation, with the federal government providing the bulk of the research and development (R&D) dollars for military-orientated purposes. Infrared*

instrumentation, pressure and temperature measuring equipment, medical electronics, and thermoelectric energy conversion all benefited from military R&D. By the 1960s indirect and direct military demand accounted for as much as 70 percent of the total output of the electronics industry. Feedbacks also developed between electronics and aircraft, the second growth industry of the 1950s. By 1960 ... [i]ts annual investment outlays were 5.3 times larger than their 1947-49 level, and over 90 percent of its output went to the military. Synthetics (plastics and fibres) was another growth industry owning much of its development to military-related projects. Throughout the 1950s and 1960s, military-related R&D, including space, accounted for 40 to 50 percent of total public and private R&D spending and at least 85% of federal government share." [Richard B. Du Boff, **Accumulation and Power**, pp. 103-4]

As another economist notes, it is *"important to recognise that the role of the US federal government in industrial development has been substantial even in the post-war period, thanks to the large amount of defence-related procurements and R&D spending, which have had enormous spillover effects. The share of the US federal government in total R&D spending, which was only 16 per cent in 1930, remained between one-half and two-thirds during the post-war years. Industries such as computers, aerospace and the internet, where the USA still maintains an international edge despite the decline in its overall technological leadership, would not have existed without defence-related R&D funding by the country's federal government."* Moreover, the state also plays a *"crucial role"* in supporting R&D in the pharmaceutical industry. [Ha-Joon Chang, **Kicking Away the Ladder**, p. 31]

Not only this, government spending on road building (initially justified using defence concerns) also gave a massive boost to private capital (and, in the process, totally transformed America into a land fit for car and oil corporations). The cumulative impact of the 1944, 1956 and 1968 Federal Highway Acts *"allowed $70 billion to be spent on the interstates without [the money] passing through the congressional appropriations board."* The 1956 Act *"[i]n effect wrote into law the 1932 National Highway Users Conference strategy of G[eneral] M[otors] chairman Alfred P. Sloan to channel gasoline and other motor vehicle-related excise taxes into highway construction."* GM also bought-up and effectively destroyed public transit companies across America, so reducing competition against private car ownership. The net effect of this state intervention was that by 1963-66 *"one in every six business enterprises was directly dependent on the manufacture, distribution, servicing, and the use of motor vehicles."* The impact of this process is still evident today – both in terms of ecological destruction and in the fact that automobile and oil companies still dominate the top twenty of the Fortune 500. [**Op. Cit.**, p. 102]

This system, which can be called military Keynesianism, has three advantages over socially-based state intervention. Firstly, unlike social programmes, military intervention does not improve the situation (and thus, hopes) of the majority, who can continue to be marginalised by the system, suffer the discipline of the labour market and feel the threat of unemployment. Secondly, it acts likes welfare for the rich, ensuring that while the many are subject to market forces, the few can escape that fate – while singing the praises of the "free market". And, thirdly, it does not compete with private capital – in fact, it supplements it.

Because of the connection between militarism and imperialism, it was natural after World War II that America should become the world's leading military state at the same time that it was becoming the world's leading economic power, and that strong ties developed between government, business, and the armed forces. American "military capitalism" is described in detail below, but the remarks also apply to a number of other "advanced" capitalist states.

In his farewell address, President Eisenhower warned of the danger posed to individual liberties and democratic processes by the *"military-industrial complex,"* which might, he cautioned, seek to keep the economy in a state of continual war-readiness simply because it is good business. This echoed the warning which had been made earlier by sociologist C. Wright Mills (in **The Power Elite**), who pointed out that since the end of World War II the military had become enlarged and decisive to the shape of the entire American economy, and that US capitalism had in fact become a military capitalism. This situation has not substantially changed since Mills wrote, for it is still the case that all US military officers have grown up in the atmosphere of the post-war military-industrial alliance and have been explicitly educated and trained to carry it on. Moreover, many powerful corporations have a vested interest in maintaining this system and will be funding and lobbying politicians and their parties to ensure its continuance.

That this interrelationship between corporate power and the state expressed by militarism is a key aspect of capitalism can be seen from the way it survived the end of the Cold War, the expressed rationale for this system:

> *"With the Cold war no longer available, it was necessary to reframe pretexts not only for [foreign] intervention but also for militarised state capitalism at home. The Pentagon budget presented to Congress a few months after the fall of the Berlin Wall remained largely unchanged, but was packaged in a new rhetorical framework, presented in the National Security Strategy of March 1990. Once priority was to support advanced industry in traditional ways, in sharp violation of the free market doctrines proclaimed and imposed on others. The National Security Strategy called for strengthening 'the defence industrial base' (essentially, high-tech industry) with incentives 'to invest in new facilities and equipment as well as in research and development.' As in the past, the costs and risks of the coming phases of the industrial economy were to be socialised, with eventual profits privatised, a form of state socialism for the rich on which much of the advanced US economy relies, particularly since World War II."* [**Failed States**, p. 126]

This means that US defence businesses, which are among the biggest lobbyists, cannot afford to lose this "corporate welfare." Unsurprisingly, they did not. So while many politicians asserted a "peace dividend" was at hand when the Soviet Bloc collapsed, this has not came to pass. Although it is true that some fat was trimmed from the defence budget in the early 1990s, both economic and political pressures have tended to keep the basic military-industrial complex intact, insuring a state of global war-readiness and continuing production of ever more advanced weapons systems into the foreseeable future. Various excuses were used to justify continued militarism, none of them particularly convincing due to the nature of the threat.

The first Gulf War was useful, but the quick defeat of Saddam showed how little a threat he actually was. The Iraq invasion of 2003 proved that his regime, while temporarily helpful to the Pentagon, was not enough of a menace to warrant the robust defence budgets of yore now given that his military machine had been smashed. This did not, of course, stop the Bush Administration spinning the threat and lying to the world about (non-existent) Iraqi "Weapons of Mass Destruction" (this is unsurprising, though, given how the Soviet military machine had also been hyped and its threat exaggerated to justify military spending). Other "threats" to the world's sole super-power such as Cuba, Iran, Libya and North Korea are equally unconvincing to any one with a firm grasp of reality. Luckily for the US state, a new enemy appeared in the shape of Islamic Terrorism.

The terrorist atrocity of 9/11 was quickly used to justify expanding US militarism (and expanding the power of the state and reducing civil liberties). In its wake, various government bureaucracies and corporations could present their wish-lists to the politicians and expect them to be passed without real comment all under the guise of "the war on terror." As this threat is so vague and so widespread, it is ideal to justify continuing militarism as well as imperial adventures across the global (any state can be attacked simply be declaring it is harbouring terrorists). It can also be used to justify attacks on existing enemies, such as Iraq and the other countries in the so-called "axis of evil" and related states. As such, it was not surprising to hear about the possible Iranian nuclear threat and about the dangers of Iranian influence even while the US military was bogged down in the quagmire of Iraq.

While the Bush Administration's doctrine of *"pre-emptive war"* (i.e. aggression) may have, as Chomsky noted, *"broken little new ground"* and have been standard (but unspoken) US policy from its birth, its does show how militarism will be justified for some time to come. [**Op. Cit.**, p. 85] It (and the threat of terrorism which is used to justify it) provides the Pentagon with more arguments for continued high levels of defence spending and military intervention. In a nutshell, then, the trend toward increasing militarism is not likely to be checked as the Pentagon has found a sufficiently dangerous and demonic enemy to justify continued military spending in the style to which it's accustomed.

Thus the demands of US military capitalism still take priority over the needs of the people. For example, Holly Sklar points out that Washington, Detroit, and Philadelphia have higher infant death rates than Jamaica or Costa Rica and that Black America as a whole has a higher infant mortality rate than Nigeria; yet the US still spends less public funds on education than on the military, and more on military bands than on the National Endowment for the Arts. [*"Brave New World Order,"* Cynthia Peters (ed.), **Collateral Damage**, pp. 3-46] But of course, politicians continue to maintain that education and social services must be cut back even further because there is "no money" to fund them. As Chomsky so rightly says:

> "It is sometimes argued that concealing development of high-tech industry under the cover of 'defence' has been a valuable contribution to society. Those who do not share that contempt for democracy might ask what decisions the population would have made if they had been informed of the real options and allowed to choose among them. Perhaps they might have preferred more social spending for health, education, decent housing, a sustainable environment for future generations, and support for the United Nations, international law, and diplomacy, as polls regularly show. We can only guess, since fear of democracy barred the option of allowing the public into the political arena, or even informing them about what was being done in their name." [**Op. Cit.**, p. 127]

Finally, as well as skewing resource allocation and wealth away from the general public, militarism also harms freedom and increases the threat of war. The later is obvious, as militarism cannot help but feed an arms race as countries hurry to increase their military might in response to the developments of others. While this may be good for profits for the few, the general population have to hope that the outcome of such rivalries do not lead to war. As Goldman noted about the First World War, war can be, in part, *"traced to the cut-throat competition for military equipment ... Armies equipped to the teeth with weapons, with highly developed instruments of murder backed by their military interests, have their own dynamic functions."* [**Op. Cit.**, p. 353]

As to freedom, as an institution the military is based on the *"unquestioning obedience and loyalty to the government."* (to quote, as Goldman did, one US General). The ideal soldier, as Goldman puts it, is *"a cold-blooded, mechanical, obedient tool of his military superiors"* and this position cannot be harmonised with individual liberty. Indeed, *"[c]an there be anything more destructive of the true genius of liberty than ... the spirit of unquestioning obedience?"* [**Op. Cit.**, pp. 52-4] As militarism becomes bigger, this spirit of obedience widens and becomes more dominant in the community. It comes to the fore during periods of war or in the run up to war, when protest and dissent are equated to treason by those in power and their supporters. The war hysteria and corresponding repression and authoritarianism which repeatedly sweeps so-called "free" nations shows that militarism has a wider impact than just economic development and wasted resources. As Bakunin noted, *"where military force prevails, there freedom has to take its leave – especially the freedom and well-being of the working people."* [**The Political Philosophy of Bakunin**, pp. 221-2]

Under capitalism, political power tends to become concentrated in the executive branch of government, along with a corresponding decline in the effectiveness of parliamentary institutions. As Kropotkin discussed in his account of *"Representative Government,"* parliaments grew out of the struggle of capitalists against the power of centralised monarchies during the early modern period. This meant that the function of parliaments was to check and control the exercise of executive power when it was controlled by another class (namely the aristocracy and landlords). The role of Parliaments flourished and reached the peak of their prestige in the struggle against the monarchy and immediately afterwards.

With the end of absolute monarchy, legislatures become battlegrounds of contending parties, divided by divergent class and group interests. This reduces their capacity for positive action, particularly when struggle outside parliament is pressurising representatives to take some interest in public concerns. The ruling class also needs a strong centralised state that can protect its interests internally and externally and which can ignore both popular demands and the vested interests of specific sections of the dominant economic and social elites in order to pursue policies required to keep the system as a whole going. This means that there will be a tendency for Parliament to give up its prerogatives, building up a centralised and uncontrolled authority in the form of an empowered executive against which, ironically, it had fought against at its birth.

This process can be seen clearly in the history of the United States. Since World War II, power has become centralised in the hands of the president to such an extent that some scholars now refer to an *"imperial presidency,"* following Arthur Schlesinger's 1973 book of that title. In the UK, Prime Minister Tony Blair has been repeatedly criticised for his *"presidential"* form of government, while Parliament has been repeatedly side-tracked. This builds on tendencies which flow back to, at least, the Thatcher government which started the neo-liberal transformation of the UK with its associated rise in inequality, social polarisation and increases in state centralisation and authority.

Contemporary US presidents' appropriation of congressional authority, especially in matters relating to national security, has paralleled the rise of the United States as the world's strongest and most imperialistic military power. In the increasingly dangerous and interdependent world of the 20th century, the perceived need for a leader who can act quickly and decisively, without possibly disastrous obstruction by Congress, has provided an impetus for ever greater concentration of power in the White House. This concentration has taken place in both foreign and domestic policy, but it has been catalysed above all by a series of foreign policy decisions in which modern US presidents have seized the most vital of all government powers, the power to make war. For example, President Truman decided to commit troops in Korea without prior congressional approval while the Eisenhower Administration established a system of pacts and treaties with nations all over the globe, making it difficult for Congress to limit the President's deployment of troops according to the requirements of treaty obligations and national security, both of which were left to presidential judgement. The CIA, a secretive agency accountable to Congress only after the fact, was made the primary instrument of US intervention in the internal affairs of other nations for national security reasons. This process of executive control over war reached a peak post-911, with Bush's nonsense of a *"pre-emptive"* war and public acknowledgement of a long standing US policy that the Commander-in-Chief was authorised to take "defensive" war measures without congressional approval or UN authorisation.

And as they have continued to commit troops to war without congressional authorisation or genuine public debate, the President's unilateral policy-making has spilled over into domestic affairs as well. Most obviously, thanks to Bush I and Clinton, important economic treaties (like GATT and NAFTA) can be rammed through Congress as *"fast-track"* legislation, which limits the time allowed for debate and forbids amendments. Thanks to Jimmy Carter, who reformed the Senior Executive Service to give the White House more control over career bureaucrats, and Ronald Reagan, who politicised the upper levels of the executive branch to an unprecedented degree, presidents can now pack government with their spoilsmen and reward partisan bureaucrats (the lack of response by FEMA during the Katrina hurricane is an example of this). Thanks to the first Bush, presidents now have a powerful new technique to enhance presidential prerogatives and erode the intent of Congress even further – namely, signing laws while announcing that they will not obey them. Fifth, thanks also to Bush, yet another new instrument of arbitrary presidential power has been created: the "tsar," a presidential appointee with vague, sweeping charges that overlap with or supersede the powers of department heads. [Michael Lind, *"The Case for Congressional Power: the Out-of-Control Presidency,"* **The New Republic**, Aug. 14, 1995]

Thus we find administrations bypassing or weakening official government agencies or institutions to implement policies that are not officially permitted. In the US, the Reagan Administration's Iran-Contra affair is an example. During that episode the National Security Council, an arm of the executive branch, secretly funded the Contras, a mercenary counter-revolutionary force in Central America, in direct violation of the Boland Amendment which Congress had passed for the specific purpose of prohibiting such funding. Then there is the weakening of government agencies to the point where they can no longer effectively carry out their mandate. Reagan's tenure in the White House again provides a number of examples. The Environmental Protection Agency, for instance, was for all practical purposes neutralised when employees dedicated to genuine environmental protection were removed and replaced with people loyal to corporate polluters. Such detours around the law are deliberate policy tools that allow presidents to exercise much more actual power than they appear to have on paper. Finally, there is the President's authority to determine foreign and domestic policy through National Security Directives that are kept secret from Congress and the American people. Such NSDs cover

a virtually unlimited field of actions, shaping policy that may be radically different from what is stated publicly by the White House and involving such matters as interference with First Amendment rights, initiation of activities that could lead to war, escalation of military conflicts, and even the commitment of billions of dollars in loan guarantees – all without congressional approval or even knowledge.

President Clinton's use of an Executive Order to bail out Mexico from its debt crisis after Congress failed to appropriate the money falls right into the authoritarian tradition of running the country by fiat, a process which accelerated with his successor George Bush (in keeping with the general tendencies of Republican administrations in particular). The second Bush took this disdain for democracy and the law even further. His administration has tried to roll back numerous basic liberties and rights as well. He has sought to strip people accused of crimes of rights that date as far back as the Magna Carta in Anglo-American jurisprudence: elimination of presumption of innocence, keeping suspects in indefinite imprisonment, ending trial by impartial jury, restricting access to lawyers and knowledge of evidence and charges against the accused. He has regularly stated when signing legislation that he will assert the right to ignore those parts of laws with which he disagrees. His administration has adopted policies which have ignored the Geneva Convention (labelled as *"quaint"*) and publicly tolerated torture of suspects and prisoners of war. That this underlying authoritarianism of politicians is often belied by their words should go without saying (an obvious fact, somehow missed by the mainstream media, which made satire redundant in the case of the second Bush).

Not that this centralisation of powers has bothered the representatives whom are being disempowered by it. Quite the reverse. This is unsurprising, for under a leader which *"guarantees 'order' – that is to say internal exploitation and external expansion – than the parliament submits to all his caprices and arms him with ever new powers … That is understandable: all government has tendency to become personal since that is its origin and its essence … it will always search for the man on whom it can unload the cares of government and to whom in turn it will submit. As long as we confide to a small group all the economic, political, military, financial and industrial prerogatives with which we arm them today, this small group will necessarily be inclined … to submit to a single chief."* [Kropotkin, **Op. Cit.**, p. 128] As such, there are institutional forces at work within the government organisational structure which encourage these tendencies and as long as they find favour with business interests they will not be challenged.

This is a key factor, of course. If increased authoritarianism and concentration of decision making were actually harming the interests of the economically dominant elite then more concern would be expressed about them in what passes for public discourse. However, the reduction of democratic processes fits in well with the neo-liberal agenda (and, indeed, this agenda is dependent on it). As Chomsky notes, *"democracy reduces to empty form"* when the votes of the general public have no impact or role in determining economic and social development. In other words, *"neoliberal reforms are antithetical to promotion of democracy. They are not designed to shrink the state, as often asserted, but to strengthen state institutions to serve even more than before the needs of the* substantial people." This has seen "extensive gerrymandering to prevent competition for seats in the House, the most democratic of government institutions and therefore the most worrisome," while congress has been "geared to implementing the pro-business policies" and the White House has been reconstructed into top-down systems, in a similar way to that of a corporation ("In structure, the political counterpart to a corporation is a totalitarian state.") [**Op. Cit.**, p. 218, p. 237 and p. 238]

The aim is to exclude the general politic from civil society, creating Locke's system of rule by property owners only. As one expert (and critic) on Locke argues in his scheme, the "labouring class, being without estate, are subject to, but not full members of civil society" and the "right to rule (more accurately, the right to control any government) is given to men of estate only." The working class will be in but not part of civil society in the same way that they are in but not part of a company. The labouring class may do the actual work in a capitalist firm, but they "cannot take part in the operation of the company at the same level as the owners." Thus the ideal (classical) "liberal" state is a "joint-stock company of owners whose majority decision binds not only themselves but also their employees." [C. B. MacPherson, **The Political Theory of Possessive Individualism**, p. 248, p. 249 and p. 251] The aim of significant sections of the right and the ruling class is to achieve this goal within the context of a nominally democratic state which, on paper, allows significant civil liberties but which, in practice, operates like a corporation. Liberty for the many will be reduced to market forms, the ability to buy and sell, within the rules designed by and for the property owners. Centralised state power within an overall authoritarian social culture is the best way to achieve this aim.

It should be stressed that the rise of inequality and centralised state power has came about by design, not by accident. Both trends delight the rich and the right, whose aim has always been to exclude the general population from the public sphere, eliminate taxation on wealth and income derived from owning it and roll back the limited reforms the general population have won over the years. In his book **Post-Conservative America** Kevin Phillips, one of the most knowledgeable and serious conservative ideologues, discusses the possibility of fundamental alterations that he regards as desirable in the US government. His proposals leave no doubt about the direction in which the Right wishes to proceed. "Governmental power is too diffused to make difficult and necessary economic and technical decisions," Phillips maintains. "[A]ccordingly, the nature of that power must be re-thought. Power at the federal level must be augmented, and lodged for the most part in the executive branch." [p. 218] He assures us that all the changes he envisions can be accomplished without altering the Constitution.

As one moderate British Conservative MP has documented, the "free-market" Conservative Thatcher government of the 1980s increased centralisation of power and led a sustained "assault on local government." One key reason was "dislike of opposition" which applied to "intermediate institutions" between the individual and the state. These "were despised and disliked because they got in the way of 'free-market forces' … and were liable to disagree with Thatcherite policies." Indeed, they simply abolished elected local governments (like the Greater London Council) which were opposed to the policies of the central government. They controlled the rest by removing their power to raise their own funds, which destroyed their local autonomy. The net effect of neo-liberal reforms was that Britain became "ever more centralised" and local government was "fragmenting and weakening." [**Dancing with Dogma**, p. 261, p. 262 and p. 269]

This reversal of what, traditionally, conservatives and even liberals had argued had its roots in the "free market" capitalist ideology. For "[n]othing is to stand in the way of the free market, and no such fripperies as democratic votes are to be allowed to upset it. The unadulterated free market is unalterable, and those who dislike it or suffer from it must learn to put up with it. In Rousseau's language, they must be forced to be free." as such there was "no paradox" to the "Thatcherite devotion to both the free market and a strong state" as the "establishment of individualism and a free-market state is an unbending if not dictatorial venture which demands the prevention of collective action and the submission of dissenting institutions and individuals." Thus rhetoric about "liberty" and rolling back the state can easily be "combined in practice with centralisation and the expansion of the state's frontiers." [**Op. Cit.**, pp. 273-4 and p. 273] A similar process occurred under Reagan in America.

As Chomsky stresses, the "antidemocratic thrust has precedents, of course, but is reaching new heights" under the current set of "reactionary statists" who "are dedicated warriors. With consistency and passion that approach caricature, their policies serve the substantial people – in fact, an unusually narrow sector of them – and disregard or harm the underlying population and future generations. They are also seeking to use their current opportunities to institutionalise these arrangements, so that it will be no small task to reconstruct a more humane and democratic society." [**Op. Cit.**, p. 238 and p. 236] As we noted in section D.1, the likes of Reagan, Thatcher and Bush do not appear by accident. They and the policies they implement reflect the interests of significant sectors of the ruling elite and their desires. These will not disappear if different, more progressive sounding, politicians are elected. Nor will the nature of the state machine and its bureaucracy, nor will the workings and needs of the capitalist economy.

This helps explain why the distinctions between the two major parties in the US have been, to a large extent, virtually obliterated. Each is controlled by the corporate elite, albeit by different factions within it. Despite many tactical and verbal disagreements, virtually all members of this elite share a basic set of principles, attitudes, ideals, and values. Whether Democrat or Republican, most of them have graduated from the same Ivy League schools, belong to the same exclusive social clubs, serve on the same interlocking boards of directors of the same major corporations, and send their children to the same private boarding schools (see G. William Domhoff, **Who Rules America Now?** and C. Wright Mills, **The Power Elite**). Perhaps most importantly, they share the same psychology, which means that they have the same priorities and interests: namely, those of corporate America. That the Democrats are somewhat more dependent on and responsive to progressive working class people while the Republicans are beholden to the rich and sections of the religious right come election time should not make us confuse rhetoric with the reality of policies pursued and underlying common assumptions and interests.

This means that in the USA there is really only one party – the

Business Party – which wears two different masks to hide its real face from the public. Similar remarks apply to the liberal democratic regimes in the rest of the advanced capitalist states. In the UK, Blair's "New Labour" has taken over the mantle of Thatcherism and have implemented policies based on its assumptions. Unsurprisingly, it received the backing of numerous right-wing newspapers as well as funding from wealthy individuals. In other words, the UK system has mutated into a more US style one of two Business parties, one of which gets more trade union support than the other (needless to say, it is unlikely that Labour will be changing its name to "Capital" unless forced to by the trading standards office nor does it look likely that the trade union bureaucracy will reconsider their funding in spite of the fact New Labour simply ignored them when not actually attacking them!). The absence of a true opposition party, which itself is a main characteristic of authoritarian regimes, is thus an accomplished fact already, and has been so for many years.

Besides the reasons noted above, another cause of increasing political centralisation under capitalism is that industrialisation forces masses of people into alienated wage slavery, breaking their bonds to other people, to the land, and to tradition, which in turn encourages strong central governments to assume the role of surrogate parent and to provide direction for their citizens in political, intellectual, moral, and even spiritual matters. (see Hannah Arendt, **The Origins of Totalitarianism**). And as Marilyn French emphasises in **Beyond Power**, the growing concentration of political power in the capitalist state can also be attributed to the form of the corporation, which is a microcosm of the authoritarian state, since it is based on centralised authority, bureaucratic hierarchy, antidemocratic controls, and lack of individual initiative and autonomy. Thus the millions of people who work for large corporations tend automatically to develop the psychological traits needed to survive and "succeed" under authoritarian rule: notably, obedience, conformity, efficiency, subservience, and fear of responsibility. The political system naturally tends to reflect the psychological conditions created at the workplace, where most people spend about half their time.

Reviewing such trends, Marxist Ralph Miliband concluded that *"it points in the direction of a regime in which democratic forms have ceased to provide effective constraints upon state power."* The *"distribution of power"* will become *"more unequal"* and so *"[h]owever strident the rhetoric of democracy and popular sovereignty may be, and despite the 'populist' overtones which politics must now incorporate, the trend is toward the ever-greater appropriation of power at the top."* [**Divided Societies**, p. 166 and p. 204] As such, this reduction in genuine liberty, and democracy, and growth in executive power does not flow simply from the intentions of a few bad apples. Rather, they reflect economic developments, the needs of the system as a whole plus the pressures associated with the way specific institutions are structured and operate as well as the need to exclude, control and marginalise the general population. Thus while we can struggle and resist specific manifestations of this process, we need to fight and eliminate their root causes within capitalism and statism themselves if we want to turn them back and, eventually, end them.

This increase in centralised and authoritarian rule may not result in obvious elimination of such basic rights as freedom of speech.

However, this is due to the success of the project to reduce genuine freedom and democracy rather than its failure. If the general population are successfully marginalised and excluded from the public sphere (i.e. turned into Locke's system of being within but not part of a society) then a legal framework which recognises civil liberties would still be maintained. That most basic liberties would remain relatively intact and that most radicals will remain unmolested would be a testimony to the lack of power possessed by the public at large in the existing system. That is, countercultural movements need not be a concern to the government until they become broader-based and capable of challenging the existing socio-economic order – only then is it "necessary" for the repressive, authoritarian forces to work on undermining the movement. So long as there is no effective organising and no threat to the interests of the ruling elite, people are permitted to say whatever they want. This creates the illusion that the system is open to all ideas, when, in fact, it is not. But, as the decimation of the Wobblies and anarchist movement after the First World War first illustrated, the government will seek to eradicate any movement that poses a significant threat.

D.9.1 What is the relationship between wealth polarisation and authoritarian government?

We have previously noted the recent increase in the rate of wealth polarisation, with its erosion of working-class living standards (see section B.7). This process has been referred to by Noam Chomsky as "Third-Worldisation." It is appearing in a particularly acute form in the US – the "richest" industrialised nation which also has the highest level of poverty, since it is the most polarised – but the process can be seen in other "advanced" industrial nations as well, particularly in the UK. As neo-liberalism has spread, so has inequality soared.

Third World governments are typically authoritarian, since harsh measures are required to suppress rebellions among their impoverished and discontented masses. Hence "Third-Worldisation" implies not only economic polarisation but also increasingly authoritarian governments. As Philip Slater puts it, a large, educated, and alert "middle class" (i.e. average income earners) has always been the backbone of democracy, and anything that concentrates wealth tends to weaken democratic institutions. [**A Dream Deferred**, p. 68] This analysis is echoed by left-liberal economist James K. Galbraith:

> *"As polarisation of wages, incomes and wealth develops, the common interests and common social programs of society fall into decline. We have seen this too, in this country over thirty years, beginning with the erosion of public services and public investments, particularly in the cities, with the assault on the poor and on immigrants and the disabled that led to the welfare bill of 1996, and continuing now manufactured crises of Medicare and the social security system. The haves are on the march. With*

growing inequality, so grows their power. And so also diminish the voices of solidarity and mutual reinforcement, the voices of civil society, the voices of a democratic and egalitarian middle class." [**Created Unequal: The Crisis in American Pay**, p. 265]

If this is true, then along with increasing wealth polarisation in the US we should expect to see signs of growing authoritarianism. This hypothesis is confirmed by numerous facts, including the following: continuing growth of an *"imperial presidency"* (concentration of political power); extralegal operations by the executive branch (e.g. the Iran-Contra scandal, the Grenada and Panama invasions); skyrocketing incarceration rates; more official secrecy and censorship; the rise of the Far Right; more police and prisons; FBI requests for massive wiretapping capability; and so on. Public support for draconian measures to deal with crime reflect the increasingly authoritarian mood of citizens beginning to panic in the face of an ongoing social breakdown, which has been brought about, quite simply, by ruling-class greed that has gotten out of hand – a fact that is carefully obscured by the media. The 911 attacks have been used to bolster these authoritarian trends, as would be expected.

One might think that representative democracy and constitutionally guaranteed freedoms would make an authoritarian government impossible in the United States and other liberal democratic nations with similar constitutional "protections" for civil rights. In reality, however, the declaration of a "national emergency" would allow the central government to ignore constitutional guarantees with impunity and set up what Hannah Arendt calls *"invisible government"* – mechanisms allowing an administration to circumvent constitutional structures while leaving them nominally in place. The erosion of civil liberties and increase in state powers post-911 in both the US and UK should show that such concerns are extremely valid.

In response to social breakdown or "terrorism," voters may turn to martial-style leaders (aided by the media). Once elected, and with the support of willing legislatures and courts, administrations could easily create much more extensive mechanisms of authoritarian government than already exist, giving the executive branch virtually dictatorial powers. Such administrations could escalate foreign militarism, further expand the funding and scope of the police, national guard units, secret police and foreign intelligence agencies, and authorise more widespread surveillance of citizens as well as the infiltration of dissident political groups (all of which happened in post-911 America). There would be a corresponding rise of government secrecy (as *"popular understanding of the workings of government is not conducive to instilling proper reverence for powerful leaders and their nobility."* [Chomsky, **Failed States**, p.238]). These developments would not occur all at once, but so gradually, imperceptibly, and logically – given the need to maintain "law and order" – that most people would not even be aware that an authoritarian take-over was underway. Indeed, there is substantial evidence that this is already underway in the US (see **Friendly Fascism** by Bertram Gross for details).

We will examine some of the symptoms of growing authoritarianism listed above, again referring primarily to the example of the United States. The general trend has been a hollowing out of even the limited democratic structures associated with representative states in favour of a purely formal appearance of elections which are used to justify ignoring the popular will, authoritarianism and "top-down" rule by the executive. While these have always been a feature of the state (and must be, if it is to do its function as we discussed in section B.2) the tendencies are increasing and should be of concern for all those who seek to protect, never mind, expand what human rights and civil liberties we have. While anarchists have no illusions about the nature of even so-called democratic states, we are not indifferent to the form of state we have to endure and how it changes. As Malatesta put it:

> *"there is no doubt that the worst of democracies is always preferable, if only from an educational point of view, than the best of dictatorships. Of course democracy, so-called government of the people, is a lie; but the lie always slightly binds the liar and limits the extent of his arbitrary power ... Democracy is a lie, it is oppression and is in reality, oligarchy; that is, government by the few to the advantage of a privileged class. But we can still fight it in the name of freedom and equality, unlike those who have replaced it or want to replace it with something worse."*
> [**The Anarchist Revolution**, p. 77]

We must stress that as long as governments exist, then this struggle against authoritarianism will continue. As Kropotkin argued, these tendencies *"do not depend on individuals; they are inherent in the institution."* We must always remember that *"[o]f its own accord, representative government does not offer real liberties, and it can accommodate itself remarkably well to despotism. Freedoms have to be seized from it, as much as they do from absolute kings; and once they have been gained they must be defended against parliament as much as they were against a king."* [**Words of a Rebel**, p. 137 and p. 123]

So we cannot assume that legal rights against and restrictions on state or economic power are enough in themselves. Liberty needs to be continually defended by the mass of the population who cannot leave it to others to act for them. *"If we want ... to leave the gates wide open to reaction,"* Kropotkin put it, *"we have only to confide our affairs to a representative government."* Only *"extra-parliamentary agitation"* will stop the state *"imping[ing] continually on the country's political rights"* or *"suppress[ing] them with a strike of the pen."* The state must always *"find itself faced by a mass of people ready to rebel."* [**Op. Cit.** p. 129 and p. 124]

D.9.2 Why is government surveillance of citizens on the increase?

Authoritarian governments are characterised by fully developed secret police forces, extensive government surveillance of civilians, a high level of official secrecy and censorship, and an elaborate system of state coercion to intimidate and silence dissenters. All of these phenomena have existed in the US since suppression of the anarchist inspired No-Conscription League and the IWW for its unionising and anti-war activity. The post-World War I Red Scare and Palmer raids continued this process of wartime jailings and intimidation, combined with the deportation of aliens (the arrest, trial and subsequent deportation of Alexander Berkman and Emma Goldman is but one example of this war on radicals). [Howard Zinn, **A People's History of America**, pp. 363-7]

However, since World War II these systems have taken more extreme forms, especially during the 1980s and 2000s. Indeed, one of the most disturbing revelations to emerge from the Iran-Contra affair was the Reagan administration's contingency plan for imposing martial law. Alfonso Chardy, a reporter for the Miami Herald, revealed in July 1987 that Lt. Col. Oliver North, while serving on the National Security Council's staff, had worked with the Federal Emergency Management Agency on a plan to suspend the Bill of Rights by imposing martial law in the event of *"national opposition to a US military invasion abroad."* [Richard O. Curry (ed.), **Freedom at Risk: Secrecy, Censorship, and Repression in the 1980s**] However, this rise in authoritarian-style government policies is not limited to just possibilities and so in this section we will examine the operations of the secret police in the USA since the 1950s. First, however, we must stress that these tendencies are hardly US specific. For example, the secret services in the UK have regularly spied on left-wing groups as well as being heavily involved in undermining the 1984-5 Miners strike. [S. Milne, **The Enemy Within**]

The creation of an elaborate US "national security" apparatus has come about gradually since 1945 through congressional enactments, numerous executive orders and national security directives, and a series of Supreme Court decisions that have eroded First Amendment rights. The policies of the Reagan administration, however, reflected radical departures from the past, as revealed not only by their comprehensive scope but by their institutionalisation of secrecy, censorship, and repression in ways that will be difficult, if not impossible, to eradicate. As Richard Curry points out, the Reagan administration's success stems *"from major structural and technological changes that have occurred in American society during the twentieth century – especially the emergence of the modern bureaucratic State and the invention of sophisticated electronic devices that make surveillance possible in new and insidious ways."* [**Op. Cit.**, p. 4]

The FBI has used *"countersubversive"* surveillance techniques and kept lists of people and groups judged to be potential national security threats since the days of the Red Scare in the 1920s. Such activities were expanded in the late 1930s when Franklin Roosevelt instructed the FBI to gather information about Fascist and Communist activities in the US and to conduct investigations into possible espionage and sabotage (although for most of the 1920s and 1930s, fascists and fascist sympathisers were, at best, ignored and, at worse, publicly praised while anti-fascists like anarchist Carol Tresca were spied on and harassed by the authorities. [Nunzio Pernicone, **Carlo Tresca**]). FBI chief J. Edgar Hoover interpreted these directives as authorising open-ended inquiries into a very broad category of potential "subversives"; and by repeatedly misinforming a succession of careless or indifferent presidents and attorneys general about the precise scope of Roosevelt's directives, Hoover managed for more than 30 years to elicit tacit executive approval for continuous FBI investigations into an ever-expanding class of political dissidents. [Geoffrey R. Stone, *"The Reagan Administration, the First Amendment, and FBI Domestic Security Investigations,"* Curry (ed.), **Op. Cit.**]

The advent of the Cold War, ongoing conflicts with the Soviet Union, and fears of the "international Communist conspiracy" provided justification not only for covert CIA operations and American military intervention in countries all over the globe, but also contributed to the FBI's rationale for expanding its domestic surveillance activities. Thus in 1957, without authorisation from Congress or any president, Hoover launched a highly secret operation called COINTELPRO:

> *"From 1957 to 1974, the bureau opened investigative files on more than half a million 'subversive' Americans. In the course of these investigations, the bureau, in the name of 'national security,' engaged in widespread wire-tapping, bugging, mail-openings, and break-ins. Even more insidious was the bureau's extensive use of informers and undercover operative to infiltrate and report on the activities and membership of 'subversive' political associations ranging from the Socialist Workers Party to the NAACP to the Medical Committee for Human Rights to a Milwaukee Boy Scout troop."* [Stone, **Op. Cit.**, p. 274]

But COINTELPRO involved much more than just investigation and surveillance. As Chomsky notes, it was *"one of its major programs of repression"* and was used to discredit, weaken, and ultimately destroy the New Left and Black radical movements of the sixties and early seventies, i.e. to silence the major sources of political dissent and opposition. It's aim was to *"disrupt"* a wide range of popular movements *"by instigating violence in the ghetto, direct participation in police assassination of a Black Panther organiser, burglaries and harassment of the Socialist Workers Party over many years, and other methods of defamation and disruption."* [**Necessary Illusions**, p. 189]

The FBI fomented violence through the use of agents provocateurs and destroyed the credibility of movement leaders by framing them, bringing false charges against them, distributing offensive materials published in their name, spreading false rumours, sabotaging equipment, stealing money, and other dirty tricks. By such means the Bureau exacerbated internal frictions within movements, turning members against each other as well as other groups. For example, during the civil rights movement, while the government was making concessions and verbally supporting the movement, the FBI was harassing and breaking up black groups. Between 1956 and 1971, the FBI took 295 actions against black groups as part of COLINTELPRO. [Zinn, **Op. Cit.**, p. 455]

Government documents show the FBI and police involved in creating acrimonious disputes which ultimately led to the break-up of such groups as Students for a Democratic Society, the Black Panther Party, and the Liberation News Service. The Bureau also played a part in the failure of such groups to form alliances across racial, class, and regional lines. The FBI is implicated in the assassination of Malcolm X, who was killed in a "factional dispute" that the Bureau bragged of having "developed" in the Nation of Islam. Martin Luther King, Jr., was the target of an elaborate FBI plot to drive him to suicide before he was conveniently killed by a lone sniper. Other radicals were portrayed as "Communists", criminals, adulterers, or government agents, while still others were murdered in phoney "shoot-outs" where the only shooting was done by the police.

These activities finally came to public attention because of the Watergate investigations, congressional hearings, and information obtained under the Freedom of Information Act (FOIA). In response to the revelations of FBI abuse, Attorney General Edward Levi in 1976 set forth a set of public guidelines governing the initiation and scope of the bureau's domestic security investigations, severely restricting its ability to investigate political dissidents.

The Levi guidelines, however, proved to be only a temporary reversal of the trend. Although throughout his presidency Ronald Reagan professed to be against the increase of state power in regard to domestic policy, he in fact expanded the power of the national bureaucracy for "national security" purposes in systematic and unprecedented ways. One of the most significant of these was his immediate elimination of the safeguards against FBI abuse that the Levi guidelines had been designed to prevent. This was accomplished through two interrelated executive branch initiatives: Executive Order 12333, issued in 1981, and Attorney General William French Smith's guidelines, which replaced Levi's in 1983. The Smith guidelines permitted the FBI to launch domestic security investigations if the facts *"reasonably indicated"* that groups or individuals were involved in criminal activity. More importantly, however, the new guidelines also authorised the FBI to *"anticipate or prevent crime."* As a result, the FBI could now investigate groups or individuals whose statements *"advocated"* criminal activity or indicated an **apparent intent** to engage in crime, particularly crimes of violence.

As Curry notes, the language of the Smith guidelines provided FBI officials with sufficient interpretative latitude to investigate virtually any group or individual it chose to target, including political activists who opposed the administration's foreign policy. Not surprisingly, under the new guidelines the Bureau immediately began investigating a wide variety of political dissidents, quickly making up for the time it had lost since 1976. Congressional sources show that in 1985 alone the FBI conducted 96 investigations of groups and individuals opposed to the Reagan Administration's Central American policies, including religious organisations who expressed solidarity with Central American refugees.

Since the 1980s, the state has used the threat of "terrorism" (both domestic and international) to bolster its means of repression. The aim has been to allow the President, on his own initiative and by his own definition, to declare any person or organisation "terrorist" and so eliminate any rights they may, in theory, have. The 911 attacks were used to pass in effect a "wish-list" (in the form of the PATRIOT act) of measures long sought by both the secret state and the right but which they had difficulty in passing previously due to public scrutiny. Post-911, as after the Oklahoma bombing, much opposition was muted while those that did raise their voices were dismissed as, at best, naive or, at worse, pro-terrorist.

Post-911, presidential rulings are considered as conclusive while the Attorney General was handed new enforcement powers, e.g. suspects would be considered guilty unless proven innocent, and the source or nature of the evidence brought against suspects would not have to be revealed if the Justice Department claimed a *"national security"* interest in suppressing such facts, as of course it would. Security agencies were given massive new powers to gather information on and act against suspected "terrorists" (i.e., any enemy of the state, dissident or critic of capitalism). As intended, the ability to abuse these powers is staggering. They greatly increased the size and funding of the FBI and gave it the power to engage in "anti-terrorist" activities all over the country, without judicial oversight. Unsurprisingly, during the run-up to the Iraq invasion of 2003, the anti-war movement was targeted with these new powers of surveillance. That the secret state, for example, seriously argued that potential "terrorists" could exist within Quaker peace groups says it all. Unsurprisingly, given the history of the secret state the new measures were turned against the Left, as COINTELPRO and similar laws were in the past.

If, as the Bush Administration continually asserted, the terrorists hate the west for our freedoms (rather than their self-proclaimed hatred of US foreign policy) then that government is the greatest appeaser the world has ever seen (not to mention the greatest recruiting agent they ever had). It has done more to undermine freedom and increase state power (along with the threat of terrorism) than the terrorists ever dreamed. However, it would be a mistake to draw the conclusion that it is simply incompetence, arrogance and ignorance which was at work (tempting as that may be). Rather, there are institutional factors at work as well (a fact that becomes obvious when looking at the history of the secret state and its activities). The fact that such draconian measures were even considered says volumes about the direction in which the US – and by implication the other "advanced" capitalist states – are headed.

D.9.3 What causes justifications for racism to appear?

The tendency toward social breakdown which is inherent in the growth of wealth polarisation, as discussed above, is also producing a growth in racism in the countries affected. As we have seen, social breakdown leads to the increasingly authoritarian government prompted by the need of the ruling class to contain protest and civil unrest among those at the bottom of the wealth pyramid. In the US those in the lowest economic strata belong mostly to racial minorities, while in several European countries there are growing populations of impoverished minorities from the Third World, often from former colonies. The desire of the more affluent strata to justify their superior economic positions is, as one would expect, causing racially based theories of privilege to become more popular.

That racist feelings are gaining strength in America is evidenced by the increasing political influence of the right, whose thinly disguised racism reflects the darkening vision of a growing segment of the conservative community. Further evidence can be seen in the growth of ultraconservative extremist groups preaching avowedly racist philosophies, such as the Ku Klux Klan, the Aryan Nations, the White Aryan Resistance, and others (see James Ridgeway's **Blood in the Face: The Ku Klux Klan, Aryan Nations, Nazi Skinheads, and the Rise of a New White Culture**). Much the same can be said of Europe, with the growth of parties like the BNP in Britain, the FN in France and similar organisations elsewhere.

Most conservative politicians have taken pains to distance themselves officially from the extreme right. Yet they are dependent on getting votes of those influenced by the right-wing media personalities and the extreme right. This means that this racism cannot help seep into their election campaigns and, unsurprisingly, mainstream conservative politicians have used, and continue to use, code words and innuendo ("welfare queens," "quotas," etc.) to convey a thinly veiled racist message. This allows mainstream right-wingers to exploit the budding racism of lower- and middle-class white youths, who must compete for increasingly scarce jobs with desperate minorities who are willing to work at very low wages. As Lorenzo Lom'boa Ervin notes:

"Basing themselves on alienated white social forces, the Nazis and Klan are trying to build a mass movement which can hire itself out to the Capitalists at the proper moment and assume state power…. Fascism is the ultimate authoritarian society when in power, even though it has changed its face to a mixture of crude racism and smoother racism in the modern democratic state.

"So in addition to the Nazis and the Klan, there are other Right-Wing forces that have been on the rise…. They include ultra-conservative rightist politicians and Christian fundamentalist preachers, along with the extreme right section of the Capitalist ruling class itself, small business owners, talk show hosts … along with the professors, economists, philosophers and others in academia who are providing the ideological weapons for the Capitalist offensive against the workers and oppressed people. So not all racists wear sheets. These are the 'respectable' racists, the New Right conservatives…. The Capitalist class has already shown their willingness to use this conservative movement as a smoke screen for an attack on the Labor movement, Black struggle, and the entire working class." [**Anarchism and the Black Revolution**, p. 18]

The expanding popularity of such racist groups in the US is matched by a similar phenomenon in Europe, where xenophobia and a weak economy have propelled extreme right-wing politicians into the limelight on promises to deport foreigners. This poisons the whole mainstream political spectrum, with centre and centre-left politicians pandering to racism and introducing aspects of the right's agenda under the rhetoric of "addressing concerns" and raising the prospect that by not doing what the right wants, the right will expand in influence. How legitimising the right by implementing its ideas is meant to undercut their support is never explained, but the "greater evil" argument does have its utility for every opportunistic politician (particularly one under pressure from the right-wing media whipping up scare stories about immigration and such like to advance the interests of their wealthy backers).

What easier way is there to divert people's anger than onto scapegoats? Anger about bad housing, no housing, boring work, no work, bad wages and conditions, job insecurity, no future, and so on. Instead of attacking the real causes of these (and other) problems, people are encouraged to direct their anger against people who face the same problems just because they have a different skin colour or come from a different part of the world! Little wonder politicians and their rich backers like to play the racist card – it diverts attention away from them and the system they run (i.e. the **real** causes of our problems).

Racism, in other words, tries to turn **class** issues into "race" issues. Little wonder that sections of the ruling elite will turn to it, as and when required. Their class interests (and, often, their personal bigotry) requires them to do so – a divided working class will never challenge their position in society. This means that justifications for racism appear for two reasons. Firstly, to try and justify the existing inequalities within society (for example, the infamous – and highly inaccurate – "Bell Curve" and related works). Secondly, to divide the working class and divert anger about living conditions and social problems away from the ruling elite and their system onto scapegoats in our own class. After all, "for the past fifty years American business has been organising a major class war, and they needed troops – there **are** votes after all, and you can't just come before the electorate and say, 'Vote for me, I'm trying to screw you.' So what they've had to do is appeal to the population on some other grounds. Well, there aren't a lot of other grounds, and everybody picks the same ones … – jingoism, racism, fear, religious fundamentalism: These are ways of appealing to people if you're trying to organise a mass base of support for policies that are really intended to crush them." [Chomsky, **Understanding Power**, pp. 294-5]

Part of the right-wing resurgence in the US and elsewhere has been the institutionalisation of the Reagan-Bush brand of conservatism, whose hallmark was the reinstatement, to some degree, of laissez-faire economic policies (and, to an even larger degree, of laissez-faire rhetoric). A "free market," Reagan's economic "experts" argued, necessarily produced inequality; but by allowing unhindered market forces to select the economically fittest and to weed out the unfit, the economy would become healthy again. The wealth of those who survived and prospered in the harsh new climate would ultimately benefit the less fortunate, through a "trickle-down" effect which was supposed to create millions of new high-paying jobs.

All this would be accomplished by deregulating business, reducing taxes on the wealthy, and dismantling or drastically cutting back federal programmes designed to promote social equality, fairness, and compassion. The aptly named Laffer Curve (although invented without the burden of any empirical research or evidence) alleged to illustrate how cutting taxes actually **raises** government revenue. When this program of pro-business policies was applied the results were, unsurprisingly, the opposite of that proclaimed, with wealth flooding upwards and the creation of low-paying, dead-end jobs (the biggest "Laffers" in this scenario were the ruling class, who saw unprecedented gains in wealth at the expense of the rest of us).

The Reaganites' doctrine of inequality gave the official seal of approval to ideas of racial superiority that right-wing extremists had used for years to rationalise the exploitation of minorities. If, on average, blacks and Hispanics earn only about half as much as whites; if more than a third of all blacks and a quarter of all Hispanics lived below the poverty line; if the economic gap between whites and non-whites was growing – well, that just proved that there was a racial component in the Social-Darwinian selection process, showing that minorities "deserved" their poverty and lower social status because they were "less fit." By focusing on individuals, laissez-faire economics hides the social roots of inequality and the effect that economic institutions and social attitudes have on inequality. In the words of left-liberal economist James K. Galbraith:

> "What the economists did, in effect, was to reason backward, from the troublesome effect to a cause that would rationalise and justify it … [I]t is the work of the efficient market [they argued], and the fundamental legitimacy of the outcome is not supposed to be questioned.

> "The **apologia** is a dreadful thing. It has distorted our understanding, twisted our perspective, and crabbed our politics. On the right, as one might expect, the winners on the expanded scale of wealth and incomes are given a reason for self-satisfaction and an excuse for gloating. Their gains are due to personal merit, the application of high intelligence, and the smiles of fortune. Those on the loosing side are guilty of sloth, self-indulgence, and whining. Perhaps they have bad culture. Or perhaps they have bad genes. While no serious economist would make that last leap into racist fantasy, the underlying structure of the economists' argument has undoubtedly helped to legitimise, before a larger public, those who promote such ideas." [**Op. Cit.**, p. 264]

The logical corollary of this social Darwinism is that whites who are "less fit" (i.e., poor) also deserve their poverty. But philosophies of racial hatred are not necessarily consistent. Thus the ranks of white supremacist organisations have been swollen in recent years by undereducated and underemployed white youths frustrated by a declining industrial labour market and a noticeably eroding social status. [Ridgeway, **Op. Cit.**, p.186] Rather than drawing the logical Social-Darwinian conclusion – that they, too, are "inferior" – they have instead blamed blacks, Hispanics, Asians, and Jews for "unfairly" taking their jobs. Thus the neo-Nazi skinheads, for example, have been mostly recruited from disgruntled working-class whites below the age of 30. This has provided leaders of right-wing extremist groups with a growing base of potential storm troopers.

Therefore, laissez-faire ideology helps create a social environment in which racist tendencies can increase. Firstly, it does so by increasing poverty, job insecurity, inequality and so on which right-wing groups can use to gather support by creating scapegoats in our own class to blame (for example, by blaming poverty on blacks "taking our jobs" rather than capitalists moving their capital to other, more profitable, countries or them cutting wages and conditions for **all** workers – and as we point out in section B.1.4, racism, by dividing the working class, makes poverty and inequality **worse** and so is self-defeating). Secondly, it abets racists by legitimising the notions that inequalities in pay and wealth are due to racial differences rather than a hierarchical system which harms **all** working class people (and uses racism to divide, and so weaken, the oppressed). By pointing to individuals rather than to institutions, organisations, customs, history and above all power – the relative power between workers and capitalists, citizens and the state, the market power of big business, etc. – laissez-faire ideology points analysis into a dead-end as well as apologetics for the wealthy, apologetics which can be, and are, utilised by racists to justify their evil politics.

D.10
How does capitalism affect technology?

Technology has an obvious effect on individual freedom, in some ways increasing it, in others restricting it. However, since capitalism is a social system based on inequalities of power, it is a truism that technology will reflect those inequalities as it does not develop in a social vacuum. As Bookchin puts it:

> "Along side its positive aspects, technological advance has a distinctly negative, socially regressive side. If it is true that technological progress enlarges the historical potentiality for freedom, it is also true that the bourgeois control of technology reinforces the established organisation of society and everyday life. Technology and the resources of abundance furnish capitalism with the means for assimilating large sections of society to the established system of hierarchy and authority … By their centralistic and bureaucratic tendencies, the resource of abundance reinforce the monopolistic, centralistic and bureaucratic tendencies in the political apparatus … [Technology can be used] for perpetuating hierarchy, exploitation and unfreedom." [**Post-Scarcity Anarchism**, p. 3]

No technology evolves and spreads unless there are people who benefit from it and have sufficient means to disseminate it. In a capitalist society, technologies useful to the rich and powerful are generally the ones that spread. This can be seen from capitalist industry, where technology has been implemented specifically to deskill the worker, so replacing the skilled, valued craftsperson with the easily trained and replaced "mass worker." By making any individual worker dispensable, the capitalist hopes to deprive workers of a means of controlling the relation between their effort on the job and the pay they receive. In Proudhon's words, the *"machine, or the workshop, after having degraded the labourer by giving him a master, completes his degeneracy by reducing him from the rank of artisan to that of common workman."* [**System of Economical Contradictions**, p. 202]

So, unsurprisingly, technology within a hierarchical society will tend to re-enforce hierarchy and domination. Managers/capitalists will select technology that will protect and extend their power (and profits), not weaken it. Thus, while it is often claimed that technology is "neutral" this is not (and can never be) the case. Simply put, "progress" within a hierarchical system will reflect the power structures of that system.

As sociologist George Reitzer notes, technological innovation under a hierarchical system soon results in *"increased control and the replacement of human with non-human technology. In fact, the replacement of human with non-human technology is very often motivated by a desire for greater control, which of course is motivated by the need for profit-maximisation. The great sources of uncertainty and unpredictability in any rationalising system are people … McDonaldisation involves the search for the means to exert increasing control over both employees and customers."* [**The McDonaldisation of Society**, p. 100] For Reitzer, capitalism is marked by the *"irrationality of rationality,"* in which this process of control results in a system based on crushing the individuality and humanity of those who live within it.

In this process of controlling employees for the purpose of maximising profit, deskilling comes about because skilled labour is more expensive than unskilled or semi-skilled and skilled workers have more power over their working conditions and work due to the difficulty in replacing them. Unskilled labour makes it easier to "rationalise" the production process with methods like Taylorism, a system of strict production schedules and activities based on the amount of time (as determined by management) that workers "need" to perform various operations in the workplace, thus requiring simple, easily analysed and timed movements. As companies are in competition, each has to copy the most "efficient" (i.e. profit maximising) production techniques introduced by the others in order to remain profitable, no matter how dehumanising this may be for workers. Thus the evil effects of the division of labour and deskilling becoming widespread. Instead of managing their own work, workers are turned into human machines in a labour process they do not control, instead being controlled by those who own the machines they use (see also Harry Braverman, **Labour and Monopoly Capital: The Degradation of Work in the Twentieth Century**).

As Max Stirner noted (echoing Adam Smith), this process of deskilling and controlling work means that *"[w]hen everyone is to cultivate himself into man, condemning a man to* **machine-like labour** *amounts to the same thing as slavery. … Every labour is to have the intent that the man be satisfied. Therefore he must become a* **master** *in it too, be able to perform it as a totality. He who in a pin-factory only puts on heads, only draws the wire, works, as it were mechanically, like a machine; he remains half-trained, does not become a master: his labour cannot* **satisfy** *him, it can only* **fatigue** *him. His labour is nothing by itself, has no object* **in itself,**

is nothing complete in itself; he labours only into another's hands, and is **used** *(exploited) by this other."* [**The Ego and Its Own**, p. 121] Kropotkin makes a similar argument against the division of labour (*"machine-like labour"*) in **The Conquest of Bread** (see chapter XV – *"The Division of Labour"*) as did Proudhon (see chapters III and IV of **System of Economical Contradictions**). Modern industry is set up to ensure that workers do not become "masters" of their work but instead follow the orders of management. The evolution of technology lies in the relations of power within a society. This is because *"the viability of a design is not simply a technical or even economic evaluation but rather a political one. A technology is deemed viable if it conforms to the existing relations of power."* [David Noble, **Progress without People**, p. 63]

This process of controlling, restricting, and de-individualising labour is a key feature of capitalism. Work that is skilled and controlled by workers is empowering to them in two ways. Firstly it gives them pride in their work and themselves. Secondly, it makes it harder to replace them or suck profits out of them. Therefore, in order to remove the "subjective" factor (i.e. individuality and worker control) from the work process, capital needs methods of controlling the workforce to prevent workers from asserting their individuality, thus preventing them from arranging their own lives and work and resisting the authority of the bosses. This need to control workers can be seen from the type of machinery introduced during the Industrial Revolution. According to Andrew Ure (author of **Philosophy of Manufactures**), a consultant for the factory owners at the time:

> *"In the factories for spinning coarse yarn … the mule-spinners [skilled workers] have abused their powers beyond endurance, domineering in the most arrogant manner … over their masters. High wages, instead of leading to thankfulness of temper and improvement of mind, have, in too many cases, cherished pride and supplied funds for supporting refractory spirits in strikes … During a disastrous turmoil of [this] kind … several of the capitalists … had recourse to the celebrated machinists … of Manchester … [to construct] a self-acting mule … This invention confirms the great doctrine already propounded, that when capital enlists science in her service, the refractory hand of labour will always be taught docility."* [quoted by Noble, **Op. Cit.**, p. 125]

Proudhon quotes an English Manufacturer who argues the same point:

> *"The insubordination of our workmen has given us the idea of dispensing with them. We have made and stimulated every imaginable effort to replace the service of men by tools more docile, and we have achieved our object. Machinery has delivered capital from the oppression of labour."* [**System of Economical Contradictions**, p. 189]

It is important to stress that technological innovation was not driven by reasons of economic efficiency as such but rather to break the power of workers at the point of production. Once that was done, initially uneconomic investments could become economically viable. As David Noble summarises, during the Industrial Revolution *"Capital invested in machines that would reinforce the system of domination [in the workplace], and this decision to invest, which might in the long run render the chosen technique economical, was not itself an economical decision but a political one, with cultural sanction."* [**Op. Cit.**, p. 6]

Needless to say, this use of technology within the class war continued. A similar process was at work in the US, where the rise in trade unionism resulted in *"industrial managers bec[oming] even more insistent that skill and initiative not be left on the shop floor, and that, by the same token, shop floor workers not have control over the reproduction of relevant skills through craft-regulated apprenticeship training. Fearful that skilled shop-floor workers would use their scare resources to reduce their effort and increase their pay, management deemed that knowledge of the shop-floor process must reside with the managerial structure."* [William Lazonick, **Organisation and Technology in Capitalist Development**, p. 273]

American managers happily embraced Taylorism (aka "scientific management"), according to which the task of the manager was to gather into his possession all available knowledge about the work he oversaw and reorganise it. Taylor himself considered the task for workers was *"to do what they are told to do promptly and without asking questions or making suggestions."* [quoted by David Noble, **American By Design**, p. 268] Taylor also relied exclusively upon incentive-pay schemes which mechanically linked pay to productivity and had no appreciation of the subtleties of psychology or sociology (which would have told him that enjoyment of work and creativity is more important for people than just higher pay). Unsurprisingly, workers responded to his schemes by insubordination, sabotage and strikes and it was *"discovered … that the 'time and motion' experts frequently knew very little about the proper work activities under their supervision, that often they simply guessed at the optimum rates for given operations … it meant that the arbitrary authority of management has simply been reintroduced in a less apparent form."* [David Noble, **Op. Cit.**, p. 272] Although, now, the power of management could hide behind the "objectivity" of "science."

Katherine Stone also argues that the *"transfer of skill [from the worker to management] was not a response to the necessities of production, but was, rather, a strategy to rob workers of their power"* by *"tak[ing] knowledge and authority from the skilled workers and creating a management cadre able to direct production."* Stone highlights that this deskilling process was combined by a *"divide and rule"* policy by management based on wage incentives and new promotion policies. This created a reward system in which workers who played by the rules would receive concrete gains in terms of income and status. Over time, such a structure would become to be seen as *"the natural way to organise work and one which offered them personal advancement"* even though, *"when the system was set up, it was neither obvious nor rational. The job ladders were created just when the skill requirements for jobs in the industry were diminishing as a result of the new technology, and jobs were becoming more and more equal as to the learning time and responsibility involved."* The modern structure of the capitalist workplace was created to break workers resistance to capitalist authority and was deliberately *"aimed at altering workers' ways of*

thinking and feeling – which they did by making workers' individual 'objective' self-interests congruent with that of the employers and in conflict with workers' collective self-interest." It was a means of *"labour discipline"* and of *"motivating workers to work for the employers' gain and preventing workers from uniting to take back control of production."* Stone notes that the *"development of the new labour system in the steel industry was repeated throughout the economy in different industries. As in the steel industry, the core of these new labour systems were the creation of artificial job hierarchies and the transfer of skills from workers to the managers."* [*"The Origins of Job Structure in the Steel Industry,"* pp. 123-157, Root & Branch (ed.), **Root and Branch: The Rise of the Workers' Movements**, p. 155, p. 153, p. 152 and pp. 153-4]

This process of deskilling workers was complemented by other factors – state protected markets (in the form of tariffs and government orders – the *"lead in technological innovation came in armaments where assured government orders justified high fixed-cost investments"*); the use of *"both political and economic power [by American Capitalists] to eradicate and diffuse workers' attempts to assert shop-floor control"*; and *"repression, instigated and financed both privately and publicly, to eliminate radical elements [and often not-so-radical elements as well, we must note] in the American labour movement."* [William Lazonick, **Competitive Advantage on the Shop Floor**, p. 218 and p. 303] Thus state action played a key role in destroying craft control within industry, along with the large financial resources of capitalists compared to workers. Bringing this sorry story up to date, we find *"many, if not most, American managers are reluctant to develop skills [and initiative] on the shop floor for the fear of losing control of the flow of work."* [William Lazonick, **Organisation and Technology in Capitalist Development**, pp. 279-280] Nor should we forget that many technologies are the product of state aid. For example, in the case of automation *"the state, especially the military, has played a central role. Not only has it subsidised extravagant developments that the market could not or refused to bear but it absorbed excessive costs and thereby kept afloat those competitors who would otherwise have sunk."* [**Op. Cit.**, p. 83]

Given that there is a division of knowledge in society (and, obviously, in the workplace as well) this means that capitalism has selected to introduce a management and technology mix which leads to inefficiency and waste of valuable knowledge, experience and skills. Thus the capitalist workplace is both produced by and is a weapon in the class struggle and reflects the shifting power relations between workers and employers. The creation of artificial job hierarchies, the transfer of skills away from workers to managers and technological development are all products of class struggle. Thus technological progress and workplace organisation within capitalism have little to do with "efficiency" and far more to do with profits and power. *"Capitalism does not utilise a socially neutral technology for capitalist ends,"* Cornelius Castoriadis correctly argued. It has *"created a capitalist technology, which is by no means neutral. The real intention of capitalist technology is not to develop production for production's sake: It is to subordinate and dominate the producers"* and *"to eliminate the human element in productive labour."* This means that capitalist technologies will evolve, that there is *"a process of 'natural selection,' affecting technical inventions as they are applied* to industry. Some are preferred to others" and will be "the ones that fit in with capitalism's basic need to deal with labour power as a measurable, supervisable, and interchangeable commodity." Thus technology will be selected "within the framework of its own class rationality." [**Social and Political Writings**, vol. 2, p. 104]

This means that while self-management has consistently proven to be more efficient (and empowering) than hierarchical management structures, capitalism actively selects **against** it. This is because capitalism is motivated purely by increasing the power and profits for the bosses, and both are best done by disempowering workers and empowering bosses (i.e. the maximisation of power) – even though this concentration of power harms efficiency by distorting and restricting information flow and the gathering and use of widely distributed knowledge within the firm (as in any command economy) as well as having a serious impact on the wider economy and social efficiency. Thus the last refuge of the capitalist or technophile (namely that the productivity gains of technology outweigh the human costs or the means used to achieve them) is doubly flawed. Firstly, disempowering technology may maximise profits, but it need not increase efficient utilisation of resources or workers' time, skills or potential. Secondly, "when investment does in fact generate innovation, does such innovation yield greater productivity? ... After conducting a poll of industry executives on trends in automation, **Business Week** concluded in 1982 that 'there is a heavy backing for capital investment in a variety of labour-saving technologies that are designed to fatten profits without necessary adding to productive output.'" David Noble concludes that "whenever managers are able to use automation to 'fatten profits' and enhance their authority (by eliminating jobs and extorting concessions and obedience from the workers who remain) without at the same time increasing social product, they appear more than ready to do so." [David Noble, **Progress Without People**, pp. 86-87 and p. 89] As we argue in greater detail later, in section J.5.12, efficiency and profit maximisation are two different things, with such deskilling and management control actually **reducing** efficiency – compared to workers' control – but as it allows managers to maximise profits the capitalist market selects it.

Of course the claim is that higher wages follow increased investment and technological innovation ("in the long run" – although usually "the long run" has to be helped to arrive by workers' struggle and protest!). Passing aside the question of whether slightly increased consumption really makes up for dehumanising and uncreative work, we must note that it is usually the capitalist who **really** benefits from technological change in money terms. For example, between 1920 and 1927 (a period when unemployment caused by technology became commonplace) the automobile industry (which was at the forefront of technological change) saw wages rise by 23.7%. Thus, claim supporters of capitalism, technology is in all our interests. However, capital surpluses rose by 192.9% during the same period – 8 times faster! Little wonder wages rose! Similarly, over the last 20 years the USA and many other countries have seen companies "down-sizing" and "right-sizing" their workforce and introducing new technologies. The result? Simply put, the 1970s saw the start of "no-wage growth expansions." Before the early 1970s, "real wage growth tracked the growth of productivity and production in the economy overall. After..., they ceased to do so ...

Real wage growth fell sharply below measured productivity growth." [James K. Galbraith, **Created Unequal**, p. 79] So while real wages have stagnated, profits have been increasing as productivity rises and the rich have been getting richer – technology yet again showing whose side it is on.

Overall, as David Noble notes (with regards to manufacturing in the early 1990s):

"U.S. Manufacturing industry over the last thirty years ... [has seen] the value of capital stock (machinery) relative to labour double, reflecting the trend towards mechanisation and automation. As a consequence ... the absolute output person hour increased 115%, more than double. But during this same period, real earnings for hourly workers ... rose only 84%, less than double. Thus, after three decades of automation-based progress, workers are now earning less relative to their output than before. That is, they are producing more for less; working more for their boss and less for themselves." [**Op. Cit.**, pp. 92-3]

Noble continues:

"For if the impact of automation on workers has not been ambiguous, neither has the impact on management and those it serves – labour's loss has been their gain. During the same first thirty years of our age of automation, corporate after tax profits have increased 450%, more than five times the increase in real earnings for workers." [**Op. Cit.**, p. 95]

But why? Because labour has the ability to produce a flexible amount of output (use value) for a given wage. Unlike coal or steel, a worker can be made to work more intensely during a given working period and so technology can be utilised to maximise that effort as well as increasing the pool of potential replacements for an employee by deskilling their work (so reducing workers' power to get higher wages for their work). Thus technology is a key way of increasing the power of the boss, which in turn can increase output per worker while ensuring that the workers' receive relatively less of that output back in terms of wages – "Machines," argued Proudhon, "promised us an increase of wealth they have kept their word, but at the same time endowing us with an increase of poverty. They promised us liberty ... [but] have brought us slavery." [**Op. Cit.**, p. 199]

But do not get us wrong, technological progress does not imply that we are victims. Far from it, much innovation is the direct result of our resistance to hierarchy and its tools. For example, capitalists turned to Taylorism and "scientific management" in response to the power of skilled craft workers to control their work and working environment (the famous 1892 Homestead strike, for example, was a direct product of the desire of the company to end the skilled workers' control and power on the shop-floor). Such management schemes never last in the long run nor totally work in the short run either – which explains why hierarchical management continues, as does technological deskilling. Workers always find ways of using new technology to increase their power within the workplace, undermining management decisions to their own advantage).

As left-wing economist William Lazonick puts it:

"Because it is the workers, not managers, who are actually doing the work, access to information on the effort-saving potential of a machine will be asymmetric, giving workers a distinct advantage in determining the pace of work. In addition, workers through their unions will attempt to exert industry-wide control over the relation between effort and pay on newly diffused technology. The resultant relation between effort and earnings will depend on the exercise of social power, not on abstract 'laws' of proportional change." [**Competitive Advantage on the Shop Floor**, pp. 66-7]

This means that the *"economic effectiveness of the factory as a mode of work organisation did not occur within a social vacuum but depend[s] on the historical evolution of conditions that determined the relative power of capitalists and workers to structure the relation between effort and pay."* As such, it is important not to overemphasise the *"independent influence of technology as opposed to the relations of production in the determination of work organisation. Because machinery does change the skill content of work, it can potentially serve as an instrument of social power. How and to what extent it does so, however, depends not only on the nature of the technology but also on the nature of the social environment into which it is introduced."* Thus the introduction of machinery into the capitalist labour process *"is only a necessary, not sufficient, condition for the displacement of worker control over the relation between effort and pay."* [Lazonick, **Op. Cit.**, p. 52 and p. 63] Needless to say, capitalists have always appealed to the state to help create a suitable social environment.

This analysis applies to both the formal and informal organisation of workers in workplace. Just as the informal structures and practices of working people evolve over time in response to new technology and practices, so does union organisation. In response to Taylorism, factory and other workers created a whole new structure of working class power – a new kind of unionism based on the industrial level. For example, the IWW was formed specifically to create industrial unions arguing that *"[l]abourers are no longer classified by difference in trade skill, but the employer assigns them according to the machine which they are attached. These divisions, far from representing differences in skill or interests among the labourers, are imposed by the employers that workers may be pitted against one another and spurred to greater exertion in the shop, and that all resistance to capitalist tyranny may be weakened by artificial distinctions."* [quoted by Stone, **Op. Cit.**, p. 157]

For this reason, anarchists and syndicalists argued for, and built, industrial unions – one union per workplace and industry – in order to combat these divisions and effectively resist capitalist tyranny. This can be seen in many different countries. In Spain, the C.N.T. (an anarcho-syndicalist union) adopted the **sindicato unico** (one union) in 1918 which united all workers of the same workplace in the same union (by uniting skilled and unskilled in a single organisation, the union increased their fighting power). In the UK, the shop stewards movement arose during the first world war based on workplace organisation (a movement inspired by the pre-war syndicalist revolt and which included many syndicalist activists). This movement was partly in response to the reformist TUC unions working with the state during the war to suppress class struggle. In Germany, the 1919 near revolution saw the creation of revolutionary workplace unions and councils (and a large increase in the size of the anarcho-syndicalist union FAU which was organised by industry).

This process was not limited to just libertarian unions. In the USA, the 1930s saw a massive and militant union organising drive by the C.I.O. based on industrial unionism and collective bargaining (inspired, in part, by the example of the I.W.W. and its broad organisation of unskilled workers). More recently, workers in the 1960s and 70s responded to the increasing reformism and bureaucratic nature of such unions as the CIO and TUC by organising themselves directly on the shop floor to control their work and working conditions. This informal movement expressed itself in wildcat strikes against both unions and management, sabotage and unofficial workers' control of production (see John Zerzan's essay *"Organised Labour and the Revolt Against Work"* in **Elements of Refusal**). In the UK, the shop stewards' movement revived itself, organising much of the unofficial strikes and protests which occurred in the 1960s and 70s. A similar tendency was seen in many countries during this period.

So in response to a new developments in technology and workplace organisation, workers' developed new forms of resistance which in turn provokes a response by management. Thus technology and its (ab)uses are very much a product of the class struggle, of the struggle for freedom in the workplace. With a given technology, workers and radicals soon learn to resist it and, sometimes, use it in ways never dreamed of to resist their bosses and the state (which necessitates a transformation of within technology again to try and give the bosses an upper hand!). The use of the Internet, for example, to organise, spread and co-ordinate information, resistance and struggles is a classic example of this process (see Jason Wehling, *"'Netwars' and Activists Power on the Internet"*, **Scottish Anarchist** no. 2 for details). There is always a "guerrilla war" associated with technology, with workers and radicals developing their own tactics to gain counter control for themselves. Thus much technological change reflects **our** power and activity to change our own lives and working conditions. We must never forget that.

While some may dismiss our analysis as "Luddite," to do so is to make "technology" an idol to be worshipped rather than something to be critically analysed. Indeed, it would be temping to argue that worshippers of technological progress are, in effect, urging us **not** to think and to sacrifice ourselves to a new abstraction like the state or capital. Moreover, such attacks misrepresent the ideas of the Luddites themselves – they never actually opposed **all** technology or machinery. Rather, they opposed *"all Machinery hurtful to Commonality"* (as a March 1812 letter to a hated Manufacturer put it). Rather than worship technological progress (or view it uncritically), the Luddites subjected technology to critical analysis and evaluation. They opposed those forms of machinery that harmed themselves or society. Unlike those who smear others as "Luddites," the labourers who broke machines were not intimidated by the modern notion of progress. As John Clark notes, they *"chose to smash the dehumanising machinery being imposed on them, rather than submit to domination and degradation in the name of technical progress."* [**The Anarchist Moment**, p. 102] Their sense of right and wrong was not clouded by the notion that technology was somehow inevitable, neutral or to be worshipped without question.

The Luddites did not think that **human** values (or their own interests) were irrelevant in evaluating the benefits and drawbacks of a given technology and its effects on workers and society as a whole. Nor did they consider their skills and livelihood as less important than the profits and power of the capitalists. In other words, they would have agreed with Proudhon's later comment that machinery *"plays the leading role in industry, man is secondary"* **and** they acted to change this relationship. [**Op. Cit.**, p. 204] The Luddites were an example of working people deciding what their interests were and acting to defend them by their own direct action – in this case opposing technology which benefited the ruling class by giving them an edge in the class struggle. Anarchists follow this critical approach to technology, recognising that it is not neutral nor above criticism. That this is simply sensible can be seen from the world around us, where capitalism has, to quote Rocker, made work *"soulless and has lost for the individual the quality of creative joy. By becoming a dreary end-in-itself it has degraded man into an eternal galley slave and robbed him of that which is most precious, the inner joy of accomplished work, the creative urge of the personality. The individual feels himself to be only an insignificant element of a gigantic mechanism in whose dull monotone every personal note dies out."* He has *"became the slave of the tool he created."* There has been a *"growth of technology at the expense of human personality."* [**Nationalism and Culture**, p. 253 and p. 254]

For capital, the source of problems in industry is people. Unlike machines, people can think, feel, dream, hope and act. The "evolution" of technology must, therefore, reflect the class struggle within society and the struggle for liberty against the forces of authority. Technology, far from being neutral, reflects the interests of those with power. Technology will only be truly our friend once we control it ourselves and **modify** it to reflect **human** values (this may mean that some forms of technology will have to be written off and replaced by new forms in a free society). Until that happens, most technological processes – regardless of the other advantages they may have – will be used to exploit and control people. Thus Proudhon's comments that *"in the present condition of society, the workshop with its hierarchical organisation, and machinery"* could only serve *"exclusively the interests of the least numerous, the least industrious, and the wealthiest class"* rather than *"be employed for the benefit of all."* [**Op. Cit.**, p. 205]

While resisting technological "progress" which is considered harmful to people or the planet (by means up to and including machine breaking) is essential in the here and now, the issue of technology can only be truly solved when those who use a given technology control its development, introduction and use. (*"The worker will only respect machinery* **on the day** *when it becomes his friend, shortening his work, rather than as* **today***, his enemy, taking away jobs, killing workers,"* in the words of French syndicalist Emile Pouget [quoted by David Noble, **Op. Cit.**, p. 15]). Little wonder, therefore, that anarchists consider workers' self-management as a key means of solving the problems created by technology. Proudhon, for example, argued that the solution to the problems created by the division of labour and technology could only be solved by *"association"*, and *"by a broad education, by the obligation of apprenticeship, and by the co-operation of all who take part in the collective work."* This would ensure that *"the division of labour can no longer be a cause of degradation for the workman [or workwoman]."* [**The General Idea of the Revolution**, p. 223]

While as far as technology goes, it may not be enough to get rid of the boss this is a necessary first step. Unless this is done, it will be impossible to transform existing technologies or create new ones which enhance freedom rather than controlling and shaping the worker (or user in general) and enhancing the power and profits of the capitalist. This means that in an anarchist society, technology would have to be transformed and/or developed which empowered those who used it, so reducing any oppressive aspects of it. In the words of Cornelius Castoriadis, the *"conscious transformation of technology will therefore be a central task of a society of free workers."* [**Op. Cit.**, p. 104] As German anarchist Gustav Landauer stressed, most are *"completely unaware of how fundamentally the technology of the socialists differs from capitalist technology … Technology will, in a cultured people, have to be directed to the psychology of free people who want to use it."* This will happen when *"the workers themselves determine under what conditions they want to work,"* step out of *"capitalism mentally and physically"*, and *"cease playing a role in it and begin to be men [and women]."* [*"For Socialism,"* pp. 184-6, **Anarchism**, Robert Graham (ed.), p. 285 and p. 286]

Thus most anarchists would agree with Bookchin's comment that technology *"is necessarily liberatory or consistently beneficial to man's development"* but we *"do not believe that man is destined to be enslaved by technology and technological modes of thought."* A free society *"will not want to negate technology precisely because it is liberated and can strike a balance"* and create a *"technology for life,"* a liberatory technology based on human and ecological needs. [**Op. Cit.**, p. 43 and p. 80] See section I.4.9 for more discussion on technology within an anarchist society.

D.11

Can politics and economics be separated from each other?

A key aspect of anarchism is the idea that the political and economic aspects of society cannot be separated. Section D has been an attempt to show how these two aspects of society interact and influence each other. This means that economic liberty cannot be separated from political liberty and vice versa. If working class people are subject to authoritarian political organisations then their economic liberty will likewise be restricted and, conversely, if their economic freedoms are limited then so, too, will their political freedoms. As Proudhon put it, *"industrial liberty is inseparable from political liberty."* [quoted by Alan Ritter, **The Political Thought of Pierre-Joseph Proudhon**, p. 188]

Some disagree, arguing that economic liberty is of primary importance. When Milton Friedman died in 2006, for example, many of his supporters parroted his defence of working with the Pinochet regime and noted that Chile had (eventually) become a democracy. For Friedman, this justified his praise for the "economic liberty" the regime had introduced and rationalised the advice he gave it. For him, Chile provided his earlier assertion that *"economic freedom is an indispensable means toward the achievement of political freedom."* For while Friedman stated that there was *"an intimate connection between economics and politics,"* he meant simply that capitalism was required to produce democracy (to use his words, *"capitalism is a necessary condition for political freedom"*). [**Capitalism and Freedom**, p. 8 and p. 10]

So it should first be stressed that by "economic liberty" Friedman meant capitalism and by "political liberty" he meant representative government and a democratic state. Anarchists would disagree that either of those institutions have much to do with genuine liberty. However, we will ignore this for the moment and take his general point. Sadly, such a position makes little sense. In fact, Friedman's separation of "economic" and "political" liberties is simply wrong as well as having authoritarian implications and lacking empirical basis.

The easiest way of showing that statism and capitalism cannot be separated is to look at a country where "economic liberty" (i.e. free market capitalism) existed but "political liberty" (i.e. a democratic government with basic human rights) did not. The most obvious example is Pinochet's Chile, an experiment which Friedman praised as an "economic miracle" shortly before it collapsed. In section C.11 we discussed the Chilean "economic miracle" at face value, refusing to discuss the issue of whether describing the regime as one of "economic liberty" could be justified. Rather, we exposed the results of applying what leading ideologues of capitalism have called "free market" policies on the country. As would be expected, the results were hardly an "economic miracle" if you were working class. Which shows how little our lives are valued by the elite and their "experts."

As to be expected with Friedman, the actual experience of implementing his economic dogmas in Chile refuted them. Much the same can be said of his distinction of "economic" and "political" liberty. Friedman discussed the Chilean regime in 1991, arguing that *"Pinochet and the military in Chile were led to adopt free market principles after they took over only because they did not have any other choice."* [**Economic Freedom, Human Freedom, Political Freedom**] This is an interesting definition of *"free market principles."* It seems to be compatible with a regime in which the secret police can seize uppity workers, torture them and dump their bodies in a ditch as a warning to others.

For Friedman, the economic and political regimes could be separated. As he put it, *"I have nothing good to say about the political regime that Pinochet imposed. It was a terrible political regime. The real miracle of Chile is not how well it has done economically; the real miracle of Chile is that a military junta was willing to go against its principles and support a free market regime designed by principled believers in a free market."* [**Op. Cit.**] How, exactly, could the political regime **not** impact on the economic one? How is a "free market" possible if people who make up the labour market are repressed and in fear of their lives? True, the Chilean workers could, as workers in Tsarist Russia, *"change their jobs without*

getting permission from political authorities" (as Friedman put it [**Capitalism and Freedom**, p. 10]), however this is only a small part of what anarchists consider to be genuine economic liberty.

To see why, it is useful to show a snapshot of what life was like under Friedman's "economic liberty" for working class people. Once this is done, it is easy to see how incredulous Friedman was being. Peter Winn gives a good description of what Chile's "economic liberty" was based on:

> *"In the wake of the coup, most of the 'revolutionary' leaders of the textile workers disappeared, some to unmarked graves, jails, or concentration camps, others to exile or the underground resistance. Moreover, when the textile factories resumed production, it was under military administration and with soldiers patrolling the plants. Authoritarian management and industrial discipline were reimposed at the point of a bayonet, and few workers dared to protest. Some feared for their lives or liberty; many more feared for their jobs. Military intelligence officers interrogated the workers one by one, pressing them to inform on each other and then firing those considered to be leftist activists. The dismissals often continued after the mills were returned to their former owners, at first for political reasons or for personal revenge, but, with the recession of 1975, for economic motives as well. The unions, decimated by their leadership losses, intimidated by the repression, and proscribed by military decree from collective bargaining, strikes, or other militant actions, were incapable of defending their members' jobs, wages, or working conditions. With wages frozen and prices rising rapidly, living standards fell precipitously, even for those fortunate enough to keep their jobs."* [*"No Miracle for Us"*, Peter Winn (ed.), **Victims of the Chilean Miracle: Workers and Neoliberalism in the Pinochet Era, 1973-2002**, p. 131]

In the copper mines, *"[h]undreds of leftist activists were fired, and many were arrested and tortured ... the military exercised a firm control over union leaders and activity within the unions remained dormant until the 1980s."* The *"decade following the military coup was defined by intense repression and a generalised climate of terror and fear."* Workers recalled that people who spoke at union meetings were detained and until 1980 police permission was required to hold a meeting, which was held under police supervision. At work, *"supervisors and foremen ruled with an authoritarian discipline"* while miners *"reported that spies denounced workers who talked politics or spoke at union meetings to the company administration and police."* [Thomas Miller Klubock, *"Class, Community, and Neoliberalism in Chile"*, Winn (ed.), **Op. Cit.**, p. 214 p. 216 and p. 217]

Over all, workers *"bore the brunt of the repression during the military take-over and throughout the Pinochet regime. The armed forces viewed workers – and the level of organisation they had achieved under previous governments – as the greatest threat to traditional power structure in Chile ... Armed troops went after workers in general and union members and leaders in particular with a virulence that contradicted their claim to be stamping out* 'class hatred.'" As for the relationship between "economic" and "political" liberty, the latter was dependent on the end of the former: *"Fear of repression was clearly essential to the implementation of free-market labour policies, but far more pervasive was the fear of unemployment"* generated by the so-called "economic miracle." [John Lear and Joseph Collins, *"Working in Chile's Free Market"*, pp. 10-29, **Latin American Perspectives**, vol. 22, No. 1, pp. 12-3 and p. 14]

Thus the ready police repression made strikes and other forms of protest both impractical and dangerous. When working class people did take to the streets after the economic crash of 1982, they were subject to intense state repression as Pinochet *"cracked down, sending in army troops to curb the demonstrators."* According to a report by the Roman Catholic Church 113 protesters had been killed during social protest, with several thousand detained for political activity and protests between May 1983 and mid-1984. Thousands of strikers were also fired and union leaders jailed. [Rayack, **Op. Cit.**, p. 70] In fact, the *"brutal government repression put even the militant copper miners on the defensive."* [Winn, *"The Pinochet Era"*, Winn (ed.), **Op. Cit.**, p. 43] Workers were aware that the regime *"was likely to use the full rigour of the law against workers who acted in defence of their interests. Moreover, even though the arbitrary actions of the secret police diminished in the last years of the dictatorship, they did not disappear, nor did their internalised legacy. Fear of becoming a target of repression still exercised a chilling effect on both workers and their leaders."* [Winn, *"No Miracle for Us"*, Winn (ed.), **Op. Cit.**, p. 133]

All of which puts into stark light Friedman's 1982 comment that *"Chile is an even more amazing political miracle. A military regime has supported reforms that sharply reduce the role of the state and replace control from the top with control from the bottom."* [quoted by Rayack, **Not so Free to Choose**, p. 37] Clearly Friedman had no idea what he was talking about. While the *"role of the state"* **was** reduced in terms of welfare for the masses, it was obviously massively **increased** in terms of warfare against them (we will address the *"control from the bottom"* nonsense shortly).

For anarchists, it is simply common-sense that "economic liberty" cannot exist within an authoritarian state for the mass of the population. In reality, the economic and political regime cannot be so easily compartmentalised. As Malatesta noted, *"every economic question of some importance automatically becomes a political question … Workers' organisations must therefore, of necessity, adopt a line of action in face of present as well as possible future government action."* [**Errico Malatesta: His Life and Ideas**, pp. 130-1] Such common-sense is sadly lacking with Friedman who seriously seems to believe that "economic liberty" could exist without the freedom of workers to take collective action if they so desired. In other words, the "economic miracle" Friedman praises was built on the corpses, fears and backs of working class people. Unlike Friedman, Chile's workers and bosses know that *"employers could count on the backing of the military in any conflict with workers."* [Lear and Collins, **Op. Cit.**, p. 13] As can be seen, Malatesta had a much firmer grasp of the question of liberty that Friedman, as expected as the latter equals it with capitalism and its hierarchies while the former spent much of his live in prison and exile trying to increase the freedom of working class people by fighting the former

and the state which maintains them.

As we argued in section D.1.4, laissez-faire capitalism does not end statism. Rather it focuses it on purely defending economic power (i.e. "economic liberty" for the capitalist class). The example of Chile's "economic liberty" proves this beyond doubt and shows that the separation of economic and political freedom is impossible and, consequently, both capitalism **and** the state need to be fought and, ultimately, abolished.

D.11.1 What does Chile tell us about the right and its vision of liberty?

The key to understanding how Friedman managed to ignore the obvious lack of "economic liberty" for the bulk of the population under Pinochet lies in remembering that he is a supporter of capitalism. As capitalism is a hierarchical system in which workers sell their liberty to a boss, it comes as no real surprise that Friedman's concern for liberty is selective.

Pinochet did introduce free-market capitalism, but this meant real liberty only for the rich. For the working class, "economic liberty" did not exist, as they did not manage their own work nor control their workplaces and lived under a fascist state. The liberty to take economic (never mind political) action in the forms of forming unions, going on strike, organising go-slows and so on was severely curtailed by the very likely threat of repression. Of course, the supporters of the Chilean "Miracle" and its "economic liberty" did not bother to question how the suppression of political liberty effected the economy or how people acted within it. They maintained that the repression of labour, the death squads, the fear installed in rebel workers could be ignored when looking at the economy. But in the real world, people will put up with a lot more if they face the barrel of a gun than if they do not. So the claim that "economic liberty" existed in Chile makes sense only if we take into account that there was only **real** liberty for one class. The bosses may have been "left alone" but the workers were not, unless they submitted to authority (capitalist or state). Hardly what most people would term as "liberty".

Beyond the ideologues of capitalism who term themselves "economists," it is generally admitted that the "labour market," if it exists, is a somewhat unique market. As "labour" cannot be separated from its owner, it means that when you "buy" labour you "buy" the time, and so liberty, of the individual involved. Rather than be bought on the market all at once, as with a slave, the wage slave's life is bought piecemeal. This is the key to understanding Friedman's nonsensical claims for never forget that by "economic freedom" he means capitalism. To understand the difference we need only compare two of Friedman's arguments to the reality of capitalism. Once we do that then his blindness to Chile's neo-liberal dictatorship's impact on genuine economic liberty becomes clear. The most obvious fallacy within his argument is this assertion:

> *"A characteristic feature of a free private market is that all parties to a transaction believe that they are going*

to be better off by that transaction. It is not a zero sum game in which some can benefit only at the expense of others. It is a situation in which everybody thinks he is going to be better off." [**Economic Freedom, Human Freedom, Political Freedom**]

Who can deny that the worker who sells her liberty to the autocrat of a capitalist firm is *"going to be better off"* than one starving to death? As we noted in section B.4.1, Friedman avoids the obvious fact that a capitalist economy is dependent on there being a class of people who have no means of supporting themselves **except** by selling their labour (i.e. liberty). While full employment will mitigate this dependency (and, as a result, bring the system to crisis), it never goes away. And given that Pinochet's *"free market regime designed by principled believers in a free market"* had substantial unemployment, it is unsurprising that the capitalist was *"better off"* than the worker as a result. As the experience of the *"free private market"* in Chile suggests, workers need to be free to organise without the fear of death squads otherwise they will be oppressed and exploited by their bosses. By denying that freedom, Pinochet's regime could only be considered "free" by the ideologues and savants of capitalism. The only positive thing that can be said is that it provided empirical evidence that the ideal neo-classical labour market would increase inequality and exploitation (see section C.11.3).

The problem with Friedman's argument is that he fails to recognise the hierarchical nature of capitalism and the limited liberty it produces. This can be seen from Friedman's comparison of military dictatorships to capitalism:

"Almost all military juntas are adverse to economic freedom for obvious reasons. The military is organised from the top down: the general tells the colonel, the colonel tells the captain, the captain tells the lieutenant, and so on. A market economy is organised from the bottom up: the consumer tells the retailer, the retailer tells the wholesaler, the wholesaler tells the producer, and the producer delivers. The principles underlying a military organisation are precisely the reverse of those underlying a market organisation." [**Op. Cit.**]

Obviously geometry was not Friedman's strong point. A "market economy" is characterised by **horizontal** links between workplaces and consumers, not vertical ones. However, the key issue is that the dominant *"market organisation"* under capitalism **is** marked by the *"principles underlying a military organisation."* To present a more accurate picture than Friedman, in the *"market organisation"* of a capitalist firm the boss tells the worker what to do. It is *"organised from the top down"* just as a military junta is. That Friedman ignores the organisational structure which 90% of the population have to operate within for most of their waking hours is significant. It shows how little he understands of capitalism and "economic freedom."

In Pinochet's Chile, the workplace **did** become more like *"a military organisation."* Without effective unions and basic human rights, the bosses acted like the autocrats they are. Discussing the textile industry, Peter Winn notes that *"most mill owners took full advantage of the regime's probusiness Labour Code … At many mills,*

sweatshop conditions prevailed, wages were low, and management was authoritarian, even tyrannical … Workers might resent these conditions, but they often felt powerless to oppose them. Informers and the threat of dismissal kept even alienated and discontented workers in line."* [*"No Miracle for Us"*, Winn (ed.), **Op. Cit.**, p. 132 and pp. 132-3] John Lear and Joseph Collins generalise the picture, noting that *"[i]n wake of the coup, factory owners suddenly had absolute control over their workers and could fire any worker without case. From 1973 through 1978, practically every labour right for organised and unorganised workers was suspended. All tools of collective bargaining, including of course the right to strike, were outlawed."* [**Op. Cit.**, p. 13] The Junta themselves had no illusions about the military-like regime they desired within the workplace, stating in 1974 its intention of *"imposing authority and discipline in production and labour relations."* [quoted by Joseph Collins and John Lear, **Chile's Free-Market Miracle: A Second Look**, p. 27]

The reality of life under Pinochet for working class people should make anyone with sense wary of praising the regime in any way, but Friedman argued that the *"results were spectacular. Inflation came down sharply. After a transitory period of recession and low output that is unavoidable in the course of reversing a strong inflation, output started to expand, and ever since, the Chilean economy has performed better than any other South American economy."* [**Op. Cit.**] Of course, by downplaying the deep recession caused by applying his recommended *"shock-treatment"* policies, Friedman can confuse the high growth resulting from coming out of the boom combined with ready repression on labour with sound economic policies. Strangely he failed to mention the *"spectacular"* recession of 1982 which wiped out the gains of 1976 to 1981. As indicated in section C.11, looking over the whole of the Pinochet period the results were hardly *"spectacular"* (unless you were rich) and the moderate gains were paid for by the working class in terms of longer hours, lower pay and political and economic oppression.

In other words, Friedman and the 'Chicago boys' provided an appearance of technical respectability to the dreams, greed and power of the landlords and capitalists who made up the Chilean oligarchy. The military simply applied the brutal force required to achieve those goals. As such, there is only an apparent contradiction between political tyranny and "economic liberty," not a real one. Repression for the working class and "economic liberty" for the elite are two sides of the same coin.

This should be common-sense and, as such, it is nonsensical for the likes of Friedman to support an economic policy while pretending to reject the system of terror it required to implement. After all, economic policies do not occur in a social and political vacuum. They are conditioned by, and at the same time modify, the social and political situation where they are put into practice. Thus there cannot be "economic liberty" for workers if they expect a visit from the secret police if they talk back to their boss. Yet for Friedman and those like him, there seems to be a lack of awareness of such basic and obvious facts. There is a necessary connection between economic policy (and its outcome) and the socio-political setting in which it is implemented.

Friedman exposes the utter hypocrisy of the supporters of capitalism. His myopia about the reality of the regime was expressed in articles which amount to little more than apologetics for the dictatorship. For example, in 1982 he noted in response to the economic problems of the previous year *"the opposition to the free-market policies that had been largely silenced by success is being given full voice."* [quoted by Rayack, **Op. Cit.**, p. p. 63] No mention that the real cause of the *"silence"* of the opposition was not the *"success"* of policies which had impoverished the working class and enriched the elite but, rather, the expectation of a visit by the secret police. Given that Pinochet had sent murder squads to kill prominent dissidents abroad, Friedman's comments are incredulous – particularly as Allende's former foreign minister, Orlando Letelier, was assassinated in Washington in 1976 by a car bomb.

The state terror, the violation of human rights and drastic control and suppression of every form of meaningful dissent is discussed (and often condemned) as something only indirectly linked, or indeed entirely unrelated, to the economic policies that the military imposed. To publicly praise and support the economic policies adopted by the dictatorship while regretting its political regime is simply illogical hypocrisy. However, it does expose the limited nature of the right's concept of liberty as well as its priorities and values.

D.11.2 But surely Chile proves that "economic freedom" creates political freedom?

As noted above, Friedman defended his praise for the Pinochet regime by arguing that its "economic liberty" helped produce the end of the dictatorship. In the words of Friedman:

> *"The economic development and the recovery produced by economic freedom in turn promoted the public's desire for a greater degree of political freedom ... In Chile, the drive for political freedom, that was generated by economic freedom and the resulting economic success, ultimately resulted in a referendum that introduced political democracy. Now, at long last, Chile has all three things: political freedom, human freedom and economic freedom. Chile will continue to be an interesting experiment to watch to see whether it can keep all three or whether, now that it has political freedom, that political freedom will tend to be used to destroy or reduce economic freedom."* [**Op. Cit.**]

It is hard to find an account so skewed by ideological blindness as this. The notion that Chile's "free market" capitalism provided the base for eliminating Pinochet's dictatorship is hard to defend. If it were true then we would expect Pinochet's rule to be substantially shorter than other military dictatorships in the region. However, this is **not** the case. For example, Argentina's Military Junta lasted from 1976 to 1983, 7 years; Peru's 12 years (1968 to 1980); Uruguay's 12 years (1973 to 1985); Bolivia's 18 years (1964 to 1982). Pinochet's lasted 17 years, exceeded by Brazil's 21 years (1964 to 1985). If Friedman's argument were valid then Pinochet would have fallen long before the rest. In fact, Chile was one of the last Latin American countries to return to democracy.

Nor can it be said that ending of the Pinochet regime was an automatic outcome of economic forces. Rather, it was a product of struggle by ordinary people who took to the streets in the early 1980s to protest in the face of state repression. The regime was subject to popular pressures from below and these, not capitalism, were the key factor. After all, it was not "economic liberty" which produced the desire for "political freedom." Working class people could remember what political freedom was before it was destroyed in order to create Friedman's "economic liberty" and tried to recreate it.

In the face of state terror, political activists and trade unionists fought the regime. The 1988 referendum Friedman alludes to was the product of this heroic activity, not some abstract economic force. As Cathy Schneider points out, the 1983-86 *"cycle of protests had set the stage for a negotiated transition to democracy in 1990."* These protests, it should be noted, were subject to extreme state repression (one demonstration saw Pinochet send 18,000 troops onto the streets, who shot 129 people, 29 fatally, and tortured some of the 1,000 arrested). [**Shantytown protest in Pinochet's Chile**, p. 194 and p. 165] Peter Winn, for example, notes *"the resistance of workers to both the dictatorship and its neoliberal policies, often against great odds and at great risks."* In fact, *"during the Pinochet era, with its repression and restrictions on union activism, Chile's workers displayed great creativity in devising new ways to resist ... Nor was this resistance confined to the workplace or workers' issues ... it was Chile's workers who first raised the flag of political resistance against the dictatorship in the 1970s and sustained it during the years when political parties were banned. And it was the copper miners who mobilised the social protests and political opposition to the military regime in the 1980s to demand an end to Pinochet's dictatorship and the restoration of democracy and civil liberties."* [*"Introduction"*, Winn (ed.), **Op. Cit.**, p. 11] This is confirmed by John Lear and Joseph Collins, who note that *"[d]uring the mid-1980s, unions were fundamental to organising the national protests that led eventually to the negotiations of the 1988 plebiscite."* [**Op. Cit.**, p. 20]

This, it should be noted, has always been the case. Political freedoms have **never** been given by the powers that be but rather won by long struggles by working class people. This has always been the case, as Kropotkin stressed basic political liberties were *"extorted from parliament by force, by agitations that threatened to become rebellions. It was by establishing trade unions and practising strike action despite the edicts of Parliament and the hangings"* that workers *"won the right to associate and strike"* in Britain for example. [**Words of a Rebel**, pp. 123-4] To ignore that often heroic struggle shows an ignorance about history which only matches an ignorance about liberty. The history of capitalism is important in this regard. It first developed under Absolutist states which used its power to bolster the position of their capitalist class within both national (against the working class) and international markets (against foreign competitors). As we discuss in section F.8, they actively intervened to create the pre-conditions for generalised wage slavery before becoming a handicap to the rising bourgeoisie. These regimes were generally replaced by liberal states with limited voting rights which generally lifted the burden of state regulation from the capitalist class. The working class had to fight long and hard to win basic civil liberties and the vote. As Chomsky notes, such progress *"didn't just happen; it happened through the struggles of the labour movement, and the Civil Rights Movement, and the women's movement, and everything else. It's the popular movements which expanded the domain of freedom of speech [and other liberties] until it began to be meaningful."* [**Understanding Power**, pp. 268-9]

Once these rights were won, the ruling elite has always turned to fascism to control them once they started to threaten their power and wealth. This obviously applies to Chile. Until the coup of 11 September 1973, Chile had been seen increasing participation of the working class in economic and social decision making. The coup was, simply, a massive class revenge of the wealthy against a working class which had dared to imagine that another world was possible. Unsurprisingly, given the key role of working class people in the struggle for freedom, *"Worker leaders and activists … were central targets of the military regime's state terror, whose goal was to intimidate them into passivity, in large part so that neoliberal policies could be imposed."* [Peter Winn, *"Introduction"*, **Op. Cit.**, p. 12]

Equally unsurprising, those who had taken to the streets aimed for political freedom in order to **end** the "economic liberty" imposed by the regime.

This means that Friedman's maxim that economic liberty is required to produce political liberty is a deeply flawed position to take. Not only does it ignore the popular struggles which have always had to be fought to end minority government, it also allows its advocates to justify and work with authoritarian regimes. At best, this position ensures that you will be indifferent to the destruction of political freedom as long as "economic liberty" (i.e. capitalism) was secured. At worse, it ensures that you would actively support such a destruction as you can justify it in terms of a return to "democracy" in the long run. Friedman and the "Chicago Boys" express both ends of that spectrum. That he can comment on *"the paradox that economic freedom produces political freedom but political freedom may destroy economic freedom"* in the context of Chile is staggering, as it was the destruction of "political freedom" that allowed "economic freedom" (for the rich) to be imposed. [**Op. Cit.**] In reality, Chile provides evidence to support the alternative argument that the introduction of free market capitalism requires the elimination or, at best, the reduction of "political liberty."

In other words, fascism was an ideal political environment to introduce "economic liberty" **because** it had destroyed political liberty. Perhaps we should conclude that the denial of political liberty is both necessary and sufficient in order to create (and preserve) "free market" capitalism? After all, the history of capitalism has been marked by the ruling class overthrowing "political liberty" when their power was threatened by popular movements. In other words, that Malatesta was right to argue that the *"capitalists can maintain the struggle in the economic field so long as workers demand small … improvements; but as soon as they see their profits seriously diminished and the very existence of their privileges threatened, they appeal to government and if it is not sufficiently understanding and not strong enough to defend them … they use their own wealth to finance new repressive forces and to set up a new government*

which will serve them better." [**Op. Cit.**, p. 131]

Friedman's argument implies that "economic liberty" is more important than "political liberty," so making people less concerned about dictatorships as long as they support the interests of the capitalist class. While the long list of capitalists, conservatives and right-wing ("classical") liberals who supported fascism or fascist-like regimes shows that giving them an ideological prop to justify it is unnecessary, it is hardly wise.

Then there is the question of whether Chile does, in fact, have genuine political liberty (i.e. a democratic government). The answer is, not quite. Chile's democracy is a "managed" one, constrained both by the political legacy of Pinochet's constitution and the threat of military intervention. Significantly, Friedman seems unconcerned about the quality of the post-Pinochet democracy Chile experiences. Simply put, the existence of an electoral regime cannot be confused with democracy or "political liberty."

It is clear that Pinochet went into the 1988 plebiscite expecting to win (particularly as he tried to rig it like the 1980 one). According to many reports from members of his cabinet and staff, he was absolutely furious and wanted to annul the results. The popular backlash this would have created ensured he abided by the result. Instead, he ensured that the new governments had to accept his authoritarian constitution and decree-laws. In other words, knowing he would be replaced he immediately took steps to limit the subsequent democratically elected governments as well as remaining as the head of the armed forces (as we discuss below, this obviously ensures the threat of a coup hung over the new governments).

This means that post-Pinochet Chile is not your typical "democracy." Pinochet became an unelected senator for life after his retirement as armed forces commander in March 1998 and 28% of the Senate is *"designated,"* including four retired military officers named by the National Security Council. Pinochet also imposed a *"unique binomial electoral law, [in] which to elect two deputies or senators from the same district, a party or electoral alliance needed to double its opponent's vote – a difficult feat – or else the opponent received an equal number of seats in congress."* This ensured rightist control of the Senate despite a decade of majority victories by the centre-left in elections and so *"Pinochet's 'designated senators' and undemocratic electoral law continued to frustrate the popular will and limit Chile's restored democracy."* The majority could not *"pass laws without the consent of its rightist opponents."* Pinochet used *"final months as president to decree laws that would hamstring his opponents, even if a majority of the electorate supported them."* In addition, any new government was *"confronted by a judiciary and government bureaucracy packed by Pinochet with his own adherents. Moreover, the Right enjoyed a near monopoly of the press and media that grew as the decade advanced."* [Winn, *"The Pinochet Era"*, **Op. Cit.**, p. 64 and p. 49]

Thus Chile is lumbered with Pinochet's legacy, *"the authoritarian constitution of 1980, which sought to create a 'protected democracy' under military tutelage. It was written so as to be difficult to amend and designed to handcuff a future opposition government and frustrate popular will."* It *"removed the military from civilian control, while submitting future elected governments to a military-dominated National Security Council with a vague but broad purview."* It also "banned measures against private property." With some "relative minor modifications of some of its most egregious features during the transition to democracy" it remained "in effect for the rest of the century" and in 2004 was "still Chile's fundamental charter." [Winn, **Op. Cit.**, p. 30] This constitution built upon the work of right-"libertarian" Friedrich von Hayek and, unsurprisingly aimed to insulate "economic liberty" from popular pressures, i.e. to limit and reduce democracy to secure the freedom of capitalism (and, of course, the capitalist class).

In addition, the threat of military intervention is always at the forefront of political discussions. For example, on 11 September 1990, Pinochet "warned that he would lead another coup if conditions warranted it. In 1993, when investigations into an arms procurement scandal implicated his son, Pinochet ordered combat-ready troops and tanks onto the streets for an 'exercise' ... Throughout the Aylwin presidency, Pinochet maintained an army 'shadow cabinet' that acted as a political pressure group." Unsurprisingly, the first post-Pinochet government "often backed down in practice for the sake of social peace – or out of fear of endangering the transition to democracy. As a result, Aylwin was unable to fulfil his promises of constitutional and institutional reforms that would reverse Pinochet's authoritarian legacy." This was because the new government thought that the coup and dictatorship "reflected the decision of business elites to call in the military, because they could not protect their core interests under Chile's radicalised democracy. The lesson that ... [they] drew ... was that to avoid its repetition in the 1990s it was necessary to reassure business that its interests would be protected." [Winn, **Op. Cit.**, p. 50 and p. 53]

The limited nature of Chile's democracy was seen in 1998, when Pinochet was arrested in Britain in regard of a warrant issued by a Spanish Judge for the murders of Spanish citizens during his regime. Commentators, particularly those on the right, stressed that Pinochet's arrest could undermine Chile's "fragile democracy" by provoking the military. In other words, Chile is only a democracy in-so-far as the military let it be. Of course, few commentators acknowledged the fact that this meant that Chile was not, in fact, a democracy after all.

All of which explains why subsequent governments have only tinkered with the free-market policies introduced by Pinochet. They have dared not reverse them not due to their popular nature but to the obvious fact that recent Chilean history shows that progressive politicians and their supporters have something to fear besides losing an election. Unsurprisingly, workers "socio-economic aspirations were postponed in the interest of not jeopardising the transition and their expectations of labour law reform were sacrificed on the same alter." [Winn, "Introduction", Winn (ed.), **Op. Cit.**, p. 10] While 2002 saw the election of the first socialist president since Allende, it is unlikely that Chile will experience anything beyond minor reforms – the legacy of fear and political restrictions will ensure that the ruling class will have little to fear from "political liberty" being used by politicians to curb their power and wealth.

Then there is the social legacy of 17 years of dictatorship. As one expert on Latin America, Cathy Scheider, noted in 1993, "the transformation of the economic and political system" under Pinochet "has had a profound impact on the world view of the typical Chilean," with most having "little contact with other workers or with their neighbours, and only limited time with their family. Their exposure to political or labour organisations is minimal ... they lack either the political resources or the disposition to confront the state. The fragmentation of opposition communities has accomplished what brute military repression could not. It has transformed Chile, both culturally and politically, from a country of active participatory grassroots communities, to a land of disconnected, apolitical individuals. The cumulative impact of this change is such that we are unlikely to see any concerted challenge to the current ideology in the near future." [quoted by Noam Chomsky, **World Orders, Old and New**, p. 184]

In such circumstances, political liberty can be re-introduced, as no one is in a position to effectively use it. In addition, Chileans live with the memory that challenging the state in the near past resulted in a fascist dictatorship murdering thousands of people as well as repeated and persistent violations of human rights by the junta, not to mention the existence of "anti-Marxist" death squads – for example in 1986 "Amnesty International accused the Chilean government of employing death squads." [P. Gunson, A. Thompson, G. Chamberlain, **Op. Cit.**, p. 86] According to one Human Rights group, the Pinochet regime was responsible for 11,536 human rights violations between 1984 and 1988 alone. [Calculation of "Comite Nacional de Defensa do los Derechos del Pueblo," reported in **Fortin**, September 23, 1988]

These facts that would have a strongly deterrent effect on people contemplating the use of political liberty to actually **change** the status quo in ways that the military and economic elites did not approve of. This does not mean, of course, that the Chilean people are not resisting oppression and exploitation and rebuilding their organisations, simply that using free speech, striking and other forms of social action is more difficult. That is protects and increases the power, wealth and authority of the employer and state over their wage slaves goes without sating – it was what was intended. As Kropotkin pointed out years ago, "freedom of press ... and all the rest, are only respected if the people do not make use of them against the privileged classes. But the day the people begin to take advantage of them to undermine those privileges, then the so-called liberties will be cast overboard." [**Op. Cit.**, p. 42] Chile is a classic example of this, a bloody example which helps deter genuine democracy in that country decades later.

Section E
What do anarchists think causes ecological problems?

Section E – What do anarchists think causes
ecological problems? 434

E.1 What are the root causes of our ecological problems? 436
E.1.1 Is industry the cause of environmental problems? 439
E.1.2 What is the difference between environmentalism and ecology? 440

E.2 What do eco-anarchists propose instead of capitalism? 442

E.3 Can private property rights protect the environment? 446
E.3.1 Will privatising nature save it? 449
E.3.2 How does economic power contribute to the ecological crisis? 453
E.3.3 Can capitalism's focus on short-term profitability deal with the ecological crisis? 458

E.4 Can laissez-faire capitalism protect the environment? 459
E.4.1 Will laissez-faire capitalism actually end pollution? 462
E.4.2 Can wilderness survive under laissez-faire capitalism? 464

E.5 Can ethical consumerism stop the ecological crisis? 467

E.6 What is the population myth? 471

Section E
What do anarchists think causes ecological problems?

This section of the FAQ expands upon section D.4 ("What is the relationship between capitalism and the ecological crisis?") in which we indicated that since capitalism is based upon the principle of "grow or die," a "green" capitalism is impossible. By its very nature capitalism must expand, creating new markets, increasing production and consumption, and so invading more ecosystems, using more resources, and upsetting the interrelations and delicate balances that exist within ecosystems. We have decided to include a separate section on this to stress how important green issues are to anarchism and what a central place ecology has in modern anarchism.

Anarchists have been at the forefront of ecological thinking and the green movement for decades. This is unsurprising, as many key concepts of anarchism are also key concepts in ecological thought. In addition, the ecological implications of many anarchist ideas (such as decentralisation, integration of industry and agriculture, and so forth) has meant that anarchists have quickly recognised the importance of ecological movements and ideas.

Murray Bookchin in particular has placed anarchist ideas at the centre of green debate as well as bringing out the links anarchism has with ecological thinking. His eco-anarchism (which he called **social ecology**) was based on emphasising the **social** nature of the ecological problems we face. In such classic works as **Post-Scarcity Anarchism**, **Toward an Ecological Society** and **The Ecology of Freedom** he has consistently argued that humanity's domination of nature is the result of domination **within** humanity itself.

However, anarchism has always had an ecological dimension. As Peter Marshall notes in his extensive overview of ecological thought, ecologists *"find in Proudhon two of their most cherished social principles: federalism and decentralisation."* He *"stands as an important forerunner of the modern ecological movement for his stress on the close communion between humanity and nature, for his belief in natural justice, for his doctrine of federalism and for his insight that liberty is the mother and not the daughter of order."* [**Nature's Web**, p. 307 and p. 308] For Proudhon, a key problem was that people viewed the land as *"something which enables them to levy a certain revenue each year. Gone is the deep feeling for nature."* People *"no longer love the soil. Landowners sell it, lease it, divide it into shares, prostitute it, bargain with it and treat it as an object of speculation. Farmers torture it, violate it, exhaust it and sacrifice it to their impatient desire for gain. They never become one with it."* We *"have lost our feeling for nature."* [**Selected Writings of Pierre-Joseph Proudhon**, p. 261]

Other precursors of eco-anarchism can be found in Peter Kropotkin's writings. For example, in his classic work **Fields, Factories and Workshops**, Kropotkin argued the case for *"small is beautiful"* 70 years before E. F. Schumacher coined the phase, advocating *"a*

harmonious balance between agriculture and industry. Instead of the concentration of large factories in cities, he called for economic as well as social decentralisation, believing that diversity is the best way to organise production by mutual co-operation. He favoured the scattering of industry throughout the country and the integration of industry and agriculture at the local level."* His vision of a decentralised commonwealth based on an integration of agriculture and industry as well as manual and intellectual work has obvious parallels with much modern green thought, as does his stress on the need for **appropriate** levels of technology and his recognition that the capitalist market distorts the development, size and operation of technology and industry. Through his investigations in geography and biology, Kropotkin discovered species to be interconnected with each other and with their environment. **Mutual Aid** is the classic source book on the survival value of co-operation within species which Kropotkin regarded as an important factor of evolution, arguing that those who claim competition within and between species is the chief or only factor have distorted Darwin's work. All this ensures that Kropotkin is *"a great inspiration to the modern ecological movement."* [Marshall, **Op. Cit.**, p. 311 and p. 312]

As well as Kropotkin's work, special note must be made of French anarchist Elisée Reclus. As Clark and Martin note, Reclus introduced *"a strongly ecological dimension into the tradition of anarchist and libertarian social theory".* He made *"a powerful contribution to introducing this more ecological perspective into anarchist thought,"* of *"looking beyond the project of planetary domination and attempting to restore humanity to its rightful place within, rather than above, nature."* Reclus, *"much more than Kropotkin, introduced into anarchist theory themes that were later developed in social ecology and eco-anarchism."* [John P. Clark and Camille Martin (ed.), **Anarchy, Geography, Modernity**, p. 19] For example, in 1866 Reclus argued as follows:

> *"Wild nature is so beautiful. Is it really necessary for man, in seizing it, to proceed with mathematical precision in exploiting each new conquered domain and then mark his possession with vulgar constructions and perfectly straight boundaries? If this continues to occur, the harmonious contrasts that are one of the beauties of the earth will soon give way to depressing uniformity …*

> *"The question of knowing which of the works of man serves to beautify and which contributes to the degradation of external nature can seem pointless to so-called practical minds; nevertheless, it is a matter of the greatest importance. Humanity's development is most intimately connected with the nature that surrounds it. A secret harmony exists between the earth and the peoples whom it nourishes, and when reckless societies allow themselves to meddle with that which creates the beauty of their domain, they always end up regretting it."* [quoted by Clark and Martin, **Op. Cit.**, pp. 125-6]

"Man," Reclus says, can find beauty in *"the intimate and deeply seated harmony of his work with that of nature."* Like the eco-anarchists a century later, he stressed the social roots of our environmental problems arguing that a *"complete union of Man with Nature can*

only be effected by the destruction of the frontiers between castes as well as between peoples." He also indicated that the exploitation of nature is part and parcel of capitalism, for "it matters little to the industrialist ... whether he blackens the atmosphere with fumes ... or contaminates it with foul-smelling vapours." "Since nature is so often desecrated by speculators precisely because of its beauty," Reclus argued, "it is not surprising that farmers and industrialists, in their own exploitative endeavours, fail to consider whether they contribute to defacing the land." The capitalist is "concerned not with making his work harmonious with the landscape." [quoted by Clark and Martin, **Op. Cit.**, p. 28, p. 30, p. 124 and p. 125] Few modern day eco-anarchists would disagree.

So, while a specifically ecological anarchism did not develop until the revolutionary work done by Murray Bookchin from the 1950's onwards, anarchist theory has had a significant "proto-green" content since at least the 1860s. What Bookchin and writers like him did was to make anarchism's implicit ecological aspects explicit, a work which has immensely enriched anarchist theory and practice. In addition to pointing out the key role ecology plays within anarchism, this section is required to refute some commonly proposed solutions to the ecological problems we face. While it is wonderful that green ideas have becoming increasingly commonplace, the sad fact is that many people have jumped on the green bandwagon whose basic assumptions and practices are deeply anti-ecological. Thus we find fascists expounding on their environmental vision or defenders of capitalism proposing "ecological" solutions based on expanding private property rights. Similarly, we find the notion of green consumerism raised as viable means of greening the planet (rather than as an addition to social struggle) or a focus on symptoms (such as population growth) rather than root causes. This section refutes many such flawed suggestions.

A key concept to remember in our discussion is the division between environmentalism and ecology. Following Bookchin, eco-anarchists contrast their ideas with those who seek to reform capitalism and make it more green (a position they term "environmentalism" rather than ecology). The latter "focus on specific issues like air and water pollution" while ignoring the social roots of the problems they are trying to solve. In other words, their outlook "rest[s] on an instrumental, almost engineering approach to solving ecological dislocations. To all appearances, they wanted to adapt the natural world to the needs of the existing society and its exploitative, capitalist imperatives by way of reforms that minimise harm to human health and well-being. The much-needed goals of formulating a project for radical social change and for cultivating a new sensibility toward the natural world tended to fall outside the orbit of their practical concerns." Eco-anarchists, while supporting such partial struggles, stress that "these problems originate in a hierarchical, class, and today, competitive capitalist system that nourishes a view of the natural world as a mere agglomeration of 'resources' for human production and consumption." [**The Ecology of Freedom**, pp. 15-6] This means that while some kind of environmentalism may be possible under capitalism or some other authoritarian system, an ecological approach is impossible. Simply put, the concerns of ecology cannot be squeezed into a hierarchical perspective or private property. Just as an eco-system cannot be commanded, divided and enclosed, nor can a truly ecological vision.

Attempts to do so will impoverish both.

As we discuss in the next section, for anarchists the root cause of our ecological problems is hierarchy in society compounded by a capitalist economy. For anarchists, the notion of an ecological capitalism is, literally, impossible. Libertarian socialist Takis Fotopoulous has argued that the main reason why the project of "greening" capitalism is just a utopian dream "lies in a fundamental contradiction that exists between the logic and dynamic of the growth economy, on the one hand, and the attempt to condition this dynamic with qualitative interests" on the other. ["Development or Democracy?", pp. 57-92, **Society and Nature**, No. 7, p. 82] Green issues, like social ones, are inherently qualitative in nature and, as such, it is unsurprising that a system based on profit would ignore them.

Under capitalism, ethics, nature and humanity all have a price tag. And that price tag is god. This is understandable as every hierarchical social system requires a belief-system. Under feudalism, the belief-system came from the Church, whereas under capitalism, it pretends to come from science, whose biased practitioners (usually funded by the state and capital) are the new priesthood. Like the old priesthoods, only those members who produce "objective research" become famous and influential – "objective research" being that which accepts the status quo as "natural" and produces what the elite want to hear (i.e. apologetics for capitalism and elite rule will always be praised as "objective" and "scientific" regardless of their actual scientific and factual content, the infamous "bell curve" and Malthus's "Law of Population" being classic examples). More importantly, capitalism needs science to be able to measure and quantify everything in order to sell it. This mathematical faith is reflected in its politics and economics, where quantity is more important than quality, where 5 votes are better than 2 votes, where $5 is better than $2. And like all religions, capitalism needs sacrifice. In the name of "free enterprise," "economic efficiency," "stability" and "growth" it sacrifices individuality, freedom, humanity, and nature for the power and profits of the few.

Understanding the social roots of the problems we face is the key. Many greens attack what they consider the "wrong ideas" of modern society, its "materialistic values" and counter-pose **new** ideas, more in tune with a green society. This approach, however, misses the point. Ideas and values do not "just happen", but are the **product** of a given set of social relationships and the struggles they produce. This means that it is not just a matter of changing our values in a way that places humanity in harmony with nature (important though that is), but also of understanding the **social** and **structural** origins of the ecological crisis. Ideas and values **do** need to be challenged, but unless the authoritarian social relationships, hierarchy and inequalities in power (i.e. what produces these values and ideas) are also challenged and, more importantly, **changed** an ecological society is impossible. So unless other Greens recognise that this crisis did not develop in a social vacuum and is not the "fault" of people as **people** (as opposed to people in a hierarchical society), little can be done root out the systemic causes of the problems that we and the planet face.

Besides its alliance with the ecology movement, eco-anarchism also finds allies in the feminist and peace movements, which it regards, like the ecology movement, as implying the need for anarchist principles. Thus eco-anarchists think that global competition between nation-states is responsible not only for the devouring of nature but is also the primary cause of international military tensions, as nations seek to dominate each other by military force or the threat thereof. As international competition becomes more intense and weapons of mass destruction spread, the seeds are being sown for catastrophic global warfare involving nuclear, chemical, and/or biological weapons. Because such warfare would be the ultimate ecological disaster, eco-anarchism and the peace movement are but two aspects of the same basic project. Similarly, eco-anarchists recognise that domination of nature and male domination of women have historically gone hand in hand, so that eco-feminism is yet another aspect of eco-anarchism. Since feminism, ecology, and peace are key issues of the Green movement, anarchists believe that many Greens are implicitly committed to anarchism, whether they realise it or not, and hence that they should adopt anarchist principles of direct action rather than getting bogged down in trying to elect people to state offices.

Here we discuss some of the main themes of eco-anarchism and consider a few suggestions by non-anarchists about how to protect the environment. In section E.1, we summarise why anarchists consider why a green society cannot be a capitalist one (and vice versa). Section E.2 presents a short overview of what an ecological society would be like. Section E.3 refutes the false capitalist claim that the answer to the ecological crisis is to privatise everything while section E.4 discusses why capitalism is anti-ecological and its defenders, invariably, anti-green. Then we indicate why green consumerism is doomed to failure in section E.5 before, in section E.6, refuting the myth that population growth is a **cause** of ecological problems rather than the **effect** of deeper issues.

Obviously, these are hardly the end of the matter. Some tactics popular in the green movement are shared by others and we discuss these elsewhere. For example, the issue of electing Green Parties to power will be addressed in section J.2.4 ("Surely voting for radical parties will be effective?") and so will be ignored here. The question of "single-issue" campaigns (like C.N.D. and Friends of the Earth) will be discussed in section J.1.4. Remember that eco-anarchists, like all anarchists, take a keen interest in many other issues and struggles and just because we do not discuss something here does not mean we are indifferent to it.

For anarchists, unless we resolve the underlying contradictions within society, which stem from domination, hierarchy and a capitalist economy, ecological disruption will continue and grow, putting our Earth in increasing danger. We need to resist the system and create new values based on quality, not quantity. We must return the human factor to our alienated society before we alienate ourselves completely off the planet.

Peter Marshall's **Nature's Web** presents a good overview of all aspects of green thought over human history from a libertarian perspective, including excellent summaries of such anarchists as Proudhon, Kropotkin and Bookchin (as well as libertarian socialist William Morris and his ecologically balanced utopia **News from Nowhere**).

E.1

What are the root causes of our ecological problems?

The dangers associated with environmental damage have become better known over the last few decades. In fact, awareness of the crisis we face has entered into the mainstream of politics. Those who assert that environmental problems are minor or non-existent have, thankfully, become marginalised (effectively, a few cranks and so-called "scientists" funded by corporations and right-wing think tanks). Both politicians and corporations have been keen to announce their "green" credentials. Which is ironic, as anarchists would argue that both the state and capitalism are key causes for the environmental problems we are facing.

In other words, anarchists argue that pollution and the other environmental problems we face are symptoms. The disease itself is deeply imbedded in the system we live under and need to be addressed alongside treating the more obvious results of that deeper cause. Otherwise, to try and eliminate the symptoms **by themselves** can be little more than a minor palliative and, fundamentally, pointless as they will simply keep reappearing until their root causes are eliminated.

For anarchists, as we noted in section A.3.3, the root causes for our ecological problems lie in social problems. Bookchin uses the terms *"first nature"* and *"second nature"* to express this idea. First nature is the environment while second nature is humanity. The latter can shape and influence the former, for the worse or for the better. How it does so depends on how it treats itself. A decent, sane and egalitarian society will treat the environment it inhabits in a decent, sane and respective way. A society marked by inequality, hierarchies and exploitation will trend its environment as its members treat each other. Thus *"all our notions of dominating nature stem from the very real domination of human by human."* The *"domination of human by human **preceded** the notion of dominating nature. Indeed, human domination of human gave rise to the very **idea** of dominating nature."* This means, obviously, that *"it is not until we eliminate domination in all its forms … that we will really create a rational, ecological society."* [**Remaking Society**, p. 44]

By degrading ourselves, we create the potential for degrading our environment. This means that anarchists *"emphasise that ecological degradation is, in great part, a product of the degradation of human beings by hunger, material insecurity, class rule, hierarchical domination, patriarchy, ethnic discrimination, and competition."* [Bookchin, *"The Future of the Ecology Movement,"* pp. 1-20, **Which Way for the Ecology Movement?**, p. 17] This is unsurprising, for *"nature, as every materialist knows, is not something merely external to humanity. We are a part of nature. Consequently, in dominating nature we not only dominate an 'external world' – we also dominate ourselves."* [John Clark, **The Anarchist Moment**, p. 114]

We cannot stress how important this analysis is. We cannot ignore *"the deep-seated division in society that came into existence with hierarchies and classes."* To do so means placing *"young people and* old, women and men, poor and rich, exploited and exploiters, people of colour and whites *all* on a par that stands completely at odds with social reality. Everyone, in turn, despite the different burdens he or she is obliged to bear, is given the same responsibility for the ills of our planet. Be they starving Ethiopian children or corporate barons, all people are held to be equally culpable in producing present ecological problems." These become *"de-socialised"* and so this perspective *"side-step[s] the profoundly social roots of present-day ecological dislocations"* and *"deflects* innumerable people from engaging in a practice that could yield effective social change." It *"easily plays into the hands of a privileged stratum who are only too eager to blame all the human victims of an exploitative society for the social and ecological ills of our time."* [**The Ecology of Freedom**, p. 33]

Thus, for eco-anarchists, hierarchy is the fundamental root cause of our ecological problems. Hierarchy, notes Bookchin includes economic class *"and even gives rise to class society historically"* but it *"goes beyond this limited meaning imputed to a largely economic form of stratification."* It refers to a system of *"command and obedience in which elites enjoy varying degrees of control over their subordinates without necessarily exploiting them."* [**Ecology of Freedom**, p. 68] Anarchism, he stressed, *"anchored ecological problems for the first time in hierarchy, not simply in economic classes."* [**Remaking Society**, p. 155]

Needless to say, the forms of hierarchy have changed and evolved over the years. The anarchist analysis of hierarchies goes *"well beyond economic forms of exploitation into cultural forms of domination that exist in the family, between generations and sexes, among ethnic groups, in institutions of political, economic, and social management, and very significantly, in the way we experience reality as a whole, including nature and non-human life-forms."* [**Op. Cit.**, p. 46] This means that anarchists recognise that ecological destruction has existed in most human societies and is not limited just to capitalism. It existed, to some degree, in all hierarchical pre-capitalist societies and, of course, in any hierarchical post-capitalist ones as well. However, as most of us live under capitalism today, anarchists concentrate our analysis to that system and seek to change it. Anarchists stress the need to end capitalism simply because of its inherently anti-ecological nature (*"The history of 'civilisation' has been a steady process of estrangement from nature that has increasingly developed into outright antagonism."*). Our society faces *"a breakdown not only of its values and institutions, but also of its natural environment. This problem is not unique to our times"* but previous environmental destruction *"pales before the massive destruction of the environment that has occurred since the days of the Industrial Revolution, and especially since the end of the Second World War. The damage inflicted on the environment by contemporary society encompasses the entire world … The exploitation and pollution of the earth has damaged not only the integrity of the atmosphere, climate, water resources, soil, flora and fauna of specific regions, but also the basic natural cycles on which all living things depend."* [Bookchin, **Ecology of Freedom**, p. 411 and p. 83]

This has its roots in the "grow-or-die" nature of capitalism we discussed in section D.4. An ever-expanding capitalism must inevitably come into collision with a finite planet and its fragile ecology. Firms whose aim is to maximise their profits in order to grow will happily exploit whoever and whatever they can to do so. As capitalism is based on exploiting people, can we doubt that it will also exploit nature? It is unsurprising, therefore, that this system results in the exploitation of the real sources of wealth, namely nature and people. It is as much about robbing nature as it is about robbing the worker. To quote Murray Bookchin:

> *"Any attempt to solve the ecological crisis within a bourgeois framework must be dismissed as chimerical. Capitalism is inherently anti-ecological. Competition and accumulation constitute its very law of life, a law … summarised in the phrase, 'production for the sake of production.' Anything, however hallowed or rare, 'has its price' and is fair game for the marketplace. In a society of this kind, nature is necessarily treated as a mere resource to be plundered and exploited. The destruction of the natural world, far being the result of mere hubristic blunders, follows inexorably from the very logic of capitalist production."* [**Post-Scarcity Anarchism**, pp. viii-ix]

So, in a large part, environmental problems derive from the fact that capitalism is a competitive economy, guided by the maxim "grow or die." This is its very law of life for unless a firm expands, it will be driven out of business or taken over by a competitor. Hence the capitalist economy is based on a process of growth and production for their own sake. *"No amount of moralising or pietising,"* stresses Bookchin, *"can alter the fact that rivalry at the most molecular base of society is a bourgeois law of life … Accumulation to undermine, buy out, or otherwise absorb or outwit a competitor **is a condition for existence in a capitalist economic order.**"* This means *"a capitalistic society based on competition and growth for its own sake must ultimately devour the natural world, just like an untreated cancer must ultimately devour its host. Personal intentions, be they good or bad, have little to do with this unrelenting process. An economy that is structured around the maxim, 'Grow or Die,' must **necessarily** pit itself against the natural world and leave ecological ruin in its wake as its works it way through the biosphere."* [**Remaking Society**, p. 93 and p. 15]

This means that good intentions and ideals have no bearing on the survival of a capitalist enterprise. There is a very simple way to be "moral" in the capitalist economy: namely, to commit economic suicide. This helps explain another key anti-ecological tendency within capitalism, namely the drive to externalise costs of production (i.e., pass them on to the community at large) in order to minimise private costs and so maximise profits and so growth. As we will discuss in more detail in section E.3, capitalism has an in-built tendency to externalise costs in the form of pollution as it rewards the kind of short-term perspective that pollutes the planet in order to maximise the profits of the capitalist. This is also driven by the fact that capitalism's need to expand also reduces decision making from the quantitative to the qualitative. In other words, whether something produces a short-term profit is the guiding maxim of decision making and the price mechanism itself suppresses the kind of information required to make ecologically informed decisions.

As Bookchin summarises, capitalism *"has made social evolution hopelessly incompatible with ecological evolution."* [**Ecology of**

Freedom, p. 14] It lacks a sustainable relation to nature not due to chance, ignorance or bad intentions but due to its very nature and workings.

Fortunately, as we discussed in section D.1, capitalism has rarely been allowed to operate for long entirely on its own logic. When it does, counter-tendencies develop to stop society being destroyed by market forces and the need to accumulate money. Opposition forces always emerge, whether these are in the form of state intervention or in social movements aiming for reforms or more radical social change (the former tends to be the result of the latter, but not always). Both force capitalism to moderate its worst tendencies.

However, state intervention is, at best, a short-term. This is because the state is just as much a system of social domination, oppression and exploitation as capitalism. Which brings us to the next key institution which anarchists argue needs to be eliminated in order to create an ecological society: the state. If, as anarchists argue, the oppression of people is the fundamental reason for our ecological problems then it logically follows that the state **cannot** be used to either create and manage an ecological society. It is a hierarchical, centralised, top-down organisation based on the use of coercion to maintain elite rule. It is, as we stressed in section B.2, premised on the monopolisation of power in the hands of a few. In other words, it is the opposite of commonly agreed ecological principles such as freedom to develop, decentralisation and diversity.

As Bookchin put it, the *"notion that human freedom can be achieved, much less perpetuated, through a state of **any** kind is monstrously oxymoronic – a contradiction in terms."* This is because *"statist forms"* are based on *"centralisation, bureaucratisation, and the professionalisation of power in the hands of elite bodies."* This flows from its nature for one of its **"essential functions is to confine, restrict, and essentially suppress local democratic institutions and initiatives."** It has been organised to reduce public participation and control, even scrutiny. [*"The Ecological Crisis, Socialism, and the need to remake society,"* pp. 1-10, **Society and Nature**, vol. 2, no. 3, p. 8 and p. 9] If the creation of an ecological society requires individual freedom and social participation (and it does) then the state by its very nature and function excludes both.

The state's centralised nature is such that it cannot handle the complexities and diversity of life. *"No administrative system is capable of representing"* a community or, for that matter, an eco-system argues James C. Scott *"except through a heroic and greatly schematised process of abstraction and simplification. It is not simply a question of capacity … It is also a question of purpose. State agents have no interest – nor should they – in describing an entire social reality … Their abstractions and simplifications are disciplined by a small number of objectives."* This means that the state is unable to effectively handle the needs of ecological systems, including human ones. Scott analyses various large-scale state schemes aiming at social improvement and indicates their utter failure. This failure was rooted in the nature of centralised systems. He urges us *"to consider the kind of human subject for whom all these benefits were being provided. This subject was singularly abstract."* The state was planning *"for generic subjects who needed so many square feet of housing space, acres of farmland, litres of clean water, and units of transportation and so much food, fresh*

air, and recreational space. Standardised citizens were uniform in their needs and even interchangeable. What is striking, of course, is that such subjects … have, for purposes of the planning exercise, no gender; no tastes; no history; no values; no opinions or original ideas, no traditions, and no distinctive personalities to contribute to the enterprise … The lack of context and particularity is not an oversight; it is the necessary first premise of any large-scale planning exercise. To the degree that the subjects can be treated as standardised units, the power of resolution in the planning exercise is enhanced … The same logic applies to the transformation of the natural world." [**Seeing like a State**, pp. 22-3 and p. 346]

A central power reduces the participation and diversity required to create an ecological society and tailor humanity's interaction with the environment in a way which respects local conditions and eco-systems. In fact, it helps creates ecological problems by centralising power at the top of society, limiting and repressing the freedom of individuals communities and peoples as well as standardising and so degrading complex societies and eco-systems. As such, the state is just as anti-ecological as capitalism is as it shares many of the same features. As Scott stresses, capitalism *"is just as much an agency of homogenisation, uniformity, grids, and heroic simplification as the state is, with the difference being that, for capitalists, simplification must pay. A market necessarily reduces quality to quantity via the price mechanism and promotes standardisation; in markets, money talks, not people … the conclusions that can be drawn from the failures of modern projects of social engineering are as applicable to market-driven standardisation as they are to bureaucratic homogeneity."* [**Op. Cit.**, p. 8]

In the short term, the state may be able to restrict some of the worse excesses of capitalism (this can be seen from the desire of capitalists to fund parties which promise to deregulate an economy, regardless of the social and environmental impact of so doing). However, the interactions between these two anti-ecological institutions are unlikely to produce long term environmental solutions. This is because while state intervention can result in beneficial constraints on the anti-ecological and anti-social dynamics of capitalism, it is always limited by the nature of the state itself. As we noted in section B.2.1, the state is an instrument of class rule and, consequently, extremely unlikely to impose changes that may harm or destroy the system itself. This means that any reform movement will have to fight hard for even the most basic and common-sense changes while constantly having to stop capitalists ignoring or undermining any reforms actually passed which threaten their profits and the accumulation of capital as a whole. This means that counterforces are always set into motion by ruling class and even sensible reforms (such as anti-pollution laws) will be overturned in the name of "deregulation" and profits.

Unsurprisingly, eco-anarchists, like all anarchists, reject appeals to state power as this *"invariably legitimates and strengthens the State, with the result that it disempowers the people."* They note that ecology movements *"that enter into parliamentary activities not only legitimate State power at the expense of popular power,"* they also are *"obligated to function **within** the State"* and *"must 'play the game,' which means that they must shape their priorities according to predetermined rules over which they have no control."* This results in *"an ongoing **process** of degeneration, a steady devolution* *of ideals, practices, and party structures"* in order to achieve *"very little"* in *"arrest[ing] environmental decay."* [**Remaking Society**, p. 161, p. 162 and p. 163] The fate of numerous green parties across the world supports that analysis.

That is why anarchists stress the importance of creating social movements based on direct action and solidarity as the means of enacting reforms under a hierarchical society. Only when we take a keen interest and act to create and enforce reforms will they stand any chance of being applied successfully. If such social pressure does not exist, then any reform will remain a dead-letter and ignored by those seeking to maximise their profits at the expense of both people and planet. As we discuss in section J, this involves creating alternative forms of organisation like federations of community assemblies (see section J.5.1) and industrial unions (see section J.5.2). Given the nature of both a capitalist economy and the state, this makes perfect sense.

In summary, the root cause of our ecological problems likes in hierarchy within humanity, particularly in the form of the state and capitalism. Capitalism is a "grow-or-die" system which cannot help destroy the environment while the state is a centralised system which destroys the freedom and participation required to interact with eco-systems. Based on this analysis, anarchists reject the notion that all we need do is get the state to regulate the economy as the state is part of the problem as well as being an instrument of minority rule. Instead, we aim to create an ecological society and end capitalism, the state and other forms of hierarchy. This is done by encouraging social movements which fight for improvements in the short term by means of direct action, solidarity and the creation of popular libertarian organisations.

E.1.1 Is industry the cause of environmental problems?

Some environmentalists argue that the root cause of our ecological crisis lies in industry and technology. This leads them to stress that "industrialism" is the problem and that needs to be eliminated. An extreme example of this is primitivism (see section A.3.9), although it does appear in the works of "deep ecologists" and liberal greens. However, most anarchists are unconvinced and agree with Bookchin when he noted that "cries against 'technology' and 'industrial society' [are] two very safe, socially natural targets against which even the bourgeoisie can inveigh in Earth Day celebrations, as long as minimal attention is paid to the social relations in which the mechanisation of society is rooted." Instead, ecology needs *a confrontational stance toward capitalism and hierarchical society"* in order to be effective and fix the root causes of our problems. [**The Ecology of Freedom**, p. 54]

Claiming that "industrialism" rather than "capitalism" is the cause of our ecological problems allowed greens to point to both the west and the so-called "socialist" countries and draw out what was common to both (i.e. terrible environmental records and a growth mentality). In addition, it allowed green parties and thinkers to portray themselves as being "above" the "old" conflicts between socialism and capitalism (hence the slogan *"Neither Right nor*

Left, but in front"). Yet this position rarely convinced anyone as any serious green thinker soon notes that the social roots of our environmental problems need to be addressed and that brings green ideas into conflict with the status quo (it is no coincidence that many on the right dismiss green issues as nothing more than a form of socialism or, in America, "liberalism"). However, by refusing to clearly indicate opposition to capitalism this position allowed many reactionary ideas (and people!) to be smuggled into the green movement (the population myth being a prime example). As for "industrialism" exposing the similarities between capitalism and Stalinism, it would have been far better to do as anarchists had done since 1918 and call the USSR and related regimes what they actually were, namely "state capitalism."

Some greens (like many defenders of capitalism) point to the terrible ecological legacy of the Stalinist countries of Eastern Europe and elsewhere. For supporters of capitalism, this was due to the lack of private property in these systems while, for greens, it showed that environmental concerns were above both capitalism and "socialism." Needless to say, by "capitalism" anarchists mean both private and state forms of that system. As we argued in section B.3.5, under Stalinism the state bureaucracy controlled and so effectively owned the means of production. As under private capitalism, an elite monopolised decision making and aimed to maximise their income by oppressing and exploiting the working class. Unsurprisingly, they had as little consideration for "first nature" (the environment) as they had for "second nature" (humanity) and dominated, oppressed and exploited both (just as private capitalism does).

As Bookchin emphasised the ecological crisis stems not only from private property but from the principle of domination itself – a principle embodied in institutional hierarchies and relations of command and obedience which pervade society at many different levels. Thus, *"[w]ithout changing the most molecular relationships in society – notably, those between men and women, adults and children, whites and other ethnic groups, heterosexuals and gays (the list, in fact, is considerable) – society will be riddled by domination even in a socialistic 'classless' and 'non-exploitative' form. It would be infused by hierarchy even as it celebrated the dubious virtues of 'people's democracies,' 'socialism' and the 'public ownership' of 'natural resources,' And as long as hierarchy persists, as long as domination organises humanity around a system of elites, the project of dominating nature will continue to exist and inevitably lead our planet to ecological extinction."* [**Toward an Ecological Society**, p. 76]

Given this, the real reasons for why the environmental record of Stalinist regimes is worse than private capitalism can easily be found. Firstly, any opposition was more easily silenced by the police state and so the ruling bureaucrats had far more lee-way to pollute than in most western countries. In other words, a sound environment requires freedom, the freedom of people to participate and protest. Secondly, such dictatorships can implement centralised, top-down planning which renders their ecological impact more systematic and widespread (James C. Scott explores this at great length in his excellent book **Seeing like a State**).

Fundamentally, though, there is no real difference between private and state capitalism. That this is the case can be seen from the willingness of capitalist firms to invest in, say, China in order to take advantage of their weaker environmental laws and regulations plus the lack of opposition. It can also be seen from the gutting of environmental laws and regulation in the west in order to gain competitive advantages. Unsurprisingly, laws to restrict protest have been increasingly passed in many countries as they have embraced the neo-liberal agenda with the Thatcher regime in the UK and its successors trail-blazing this process. The centralisation of power which accompanies such neo-liberal experiments reduces social pressures on the state and ensures that business interests take precedence.

As we argued in section D.10, the way that technology is used and evolves will reflect the power relations within society. Given a hierarchical society, we would expect a given technology to be used in repressive ways regardless of the nature of that technology itself. Bookchin points to the difference between the Iroquois and the Inca. Both societies used the same forms of technology, but the former was a fairly democratic and egalitarian federation while the latter was a highly despotic empire. As such, technology *"does not fully or even adequately account for the institutional differences"* between societies. [**The Ecology of Freedom**, p. 331] This means that technology does not explain the causes for ecological harm and it is possible to have an anti-ecological system based on small-scale technologies:

> *"Some of the most dehumanising and centralised social systems were fashioned out of very 'small' technologies; but bureaucracies, monarchies, and military forces turned these systems into brutalising cudgels to subdue humankind and, later, to try to subdue nature. To be sure, a large-scale technics will foster the development of an oppressively large-scale society; but every warped society follows the dialectic of its own pathology of domination, irrespective of the scale of its technics. It can organise the 'small' into the repellent as surely as it can imprint an arrogant sneer on the faces of the elites who administer it…. Unfortunately, a preoccupation with technical size, scale, and even artistry deflects our attention away from the most significant problems of technics – notably, its ties with the ideals and social structures of freedom."* [Bookchin, **Op. Cit.**, pp. 325-6]

In other words, "small-scale" technology will not transform an authoritarian society into an ecological one. Nor will applying ecologically friendly technology to capitalism reduce its drive to grow at the expense of the planet and the people who inhabit it. This means that technology is an aspect of a wider society rather than a socially neutral instrument which will **always** have the same (usually negative) results. As Bookchin stressed, a *"liberatory technology presupposes liberatory institutions; a liberatory sensibility requires a liberatory society. By the same token, artistic crafts are difficult to conceive without an artistically crafted society, and the 'inversion of tools' is impossible with a radical inversion of all social and productive relationships."* [**Op. Cit.**, pp. 328-9]

Finally, it should be stressed that attempts to blame technology or industry for our ecological problems have another negative effect than just obscuring the real causes of those problems and turning attention away from the elites who implement specific forms of technology to further their aims. It also means denying that technology can be transformed and new forms created which can help produce an ecologically balanced society:

> *"The knowledge and physical instruments for promoting a harmonisation of humanity with nature and of human with human are largely at hand or could easily be devised. Many of the physical principles used to construct such patently harmful facilities as conventional power plants, energy-consuming vehicles, surface-mining equipment and the like could be directed to the construction of small-scale solar and wind energy devices, efficient means of transportation, and energy-saving shelters."* [Bookchin, **Op. Cit.**, p. 83]

We must understand that *"the very **idea** of dominating first nature has its origins in the domination of human by human"* otherwise *"we will lose what little understanding we have of the social origin of our most serious ecological problems."* It this happens then we cannot solve these problems, as it *"will grossly distort humanity's potentialities to play a creative role in non-human as well as human development."* For *"the human capacity to reason conceptually, to fashion tools and devise extraordinary technologies"* can all *"be used for the good of the biosphere, not simply for harming it. What is of **pivotal** importance in determining whether human beings will creatively foster the evolution of first nature or whether they will be highly destructive to non-human and human beings alike is precisely the kind of **society** we establish, not only the kind of sensibility we develop."* [**Op. Cit.**, p. 34]

E.1.2 What is the difference between environmentalism and ecology?

As we noted in section A.3.3, eco-anarchists contrast ecology with environmentalism. The difference is important as it suggests both a different analysis of where our ecological problems come from and the best way to solve them. As Bookchin put it:

> *"By 'environmentalism' I propose to designate a mechanistic, instrumental outlook that sees nature as a passive habitat composed of 'objects' such as animals, plants, minerals, and the like that must merely be rendered more serviceable for human use … Within this context, very little of a social nature is spared from the environmentalist's vocabulary: cities become 'urban resources' and their inhabitants 'human resources' … Environmentalism … tends to view the ecological project for attaining a harmonious relationship between humanity and nature as a truce rather than a lasting equilibrium. The 'harmony' of the environmentalist centres around the development of new techniques for plundering the natural world with minimal disruption of the human 'habitat.' Environmentalism does not question the most basic premise of the present society, notably, that humanity must dominate nature; rather, it seeks to **facilitate***

that notion by developing techniques for diminishing the hazards caused by the reckless despoliation of the environment." [**The Ecology of Freedom**, p. 86]

So eco-anarchists call the position of those who seek to reform capitalism and make it more green "environmentalism" rather than ecology. The reasons are obvious, as environmentalists *"focus on specific issues like air and water pollution"* while ignoring the social roots of the problems they are trying to solve. In other words, their outlook *"rest[s] on an instrumental, almost engineering approach to solving ecological dislocations. To all appearances, they wanted to adapt the natural world to the needs of the existing society and its exploitative, capitalist imperatives by way of reforms that minimise harm to human health and well-being. The much-needed goals of formulating a project for radical social change and for cultivating a new sensibility toward the natural world tended to fall outside the orbit of their practical concerns."* Eco-anarchists, while supporting such partial structures, stress that *"these problems originate in a hierarchical, class, and today, competitive capitalist system that nourishes a view of the natural world as a mere agglomeration of 'resources' for human production and consumption."* [**Op. Cit.**, pp. 15-6]

This is the key. As environmentalism does not bring into question the underlying notion of the present society that man must dominate nature it cannot present anything other than short-term solutions for the various symptoms of the underlying problem. Moreover, as it does not question hierarchy, it simply adjusts itself to the status quo. Thus liberal environmentalism is so *"hopelessly ineffectual"* because *"it takes the present social order for granted"* and is mired in *"the paralysing belief that a market society, privately owned property, and the present-day bureaucratic nation-state cannot be changed in any basic sense. Thus, it is the prevailing order that sets the terms of any 'compromise' or 'trade-off'"* and so *"the natural world, including oppressed people, always loses something piece by piece, until everything is lost in the end. As long as liberal environmentalism is structured around the social status quo, property rights always prevail over public rights and power always prevails over powerlessness. Be it a forest, wetlands, or good agricultural soil, a 'developer' who owns any of these 'resources' usually sets the terms on which every negotiation occurs and ultimately succeeds in achieving the triumph of wealth over ecological considerations."* [Bookchin, **Remaking Society**, p. 15]

This means that a truly ecological perspective seeks to end the situation where a few govern the many, not to make the few nicer. As Chomsky once noted on the issue of *"corporate social responsibility"*, he could not discuss the issue as such because he did *"not accept some of its presuppositions, specifically with regard to the legitimacy of corporate power"* as he did not see any more *"justification for concentration of private power"* than *"in the political domain."* Both would *"act in a socially responsible way – as benevolent despots – when social strife, disorder, protest, etc., induce them to do so for their own benefit."* He stressed that in a capitalist society *"socially responsible behaviour would be penalised quickly in that competitors, lacking such social responsibility, would supplant anyone so misguided as to be concerned with something other than private benefit."* This explains why real capitalist systems

have always *"been required to safeguard social existence in the face of the destructive forces of private capitalism"* by means of *"substantial state control."* However, the *"central questions ... are not addressed, but rather begged"* when discussing corporate social responsibility. [**Language and Politics**, p. 275]

Ultimately, the key problem with liberal environmentalism (as with liberalism in general) is that it tends, by definition, to ignore class and hierarchy. The "we are all in this together" kind of message ignores that most of decisions that got us into our current ecological and social mess were made by the rich as they have control over resources and power structures (both private and public). It also suggests that getting us out of the mess must involve taking power and wealth back from the elite – if for no other reason because working class people do not, by themselves, have the resources to solve the problem.

Moreover, the fact is the ruling class do **not** inhabit quite the same polluted planet as everyone else. Their wealth protects them, to a large degree, from the problems that they themselves have created and which, in fact, they owe so much of that wealth to (little wonder, then, they deny there is a serious problem). They have access to a better quality of life, food and local environment (no toxic dumps and motorways are near their homes or holiday retreats). Of course, this is a short term protection but the fate of the planet is a long-term abstraction when compared to the immediate returns on one's investments. So it is not true to say that **all** parts of the ruling class are in denial about the ecological problems. A few are aware but many more show utter hatred towards those who think the planet is more important than profits.

This means that such key environmentalist activities such as education and lobbying are unlikely to have much effect. While these may produce **some** improvements in terms of our environmental impact, it cannot stop the long-term destruction of our planet as the ecological crisis is *"**systemic** – and not a matter of misinformation, spiritual insensitivity, or lack of moral integrity. The present social illness lies not only in the outlook that pervades the present society; it lies above all in the very **structure** and **law of life** in the system itself, in its imperative, which no entrepreneur or corporation can ignore without facing destruction: growth, more growth, and still more growth."* [Murray Bookchin, *"The Ecological Crisis, Socialism, and the need to remake society,"* pp. 1-10, **Society and Nature**, vol. 2, no. 3, pp. 2-3] This can only be ended by ending capitalism, not by appeals to consumers to buy eco-friendly products or to capitalists to provide them:

> *"Accumulation is determined not by the good or bad intentions of the individual bourgeois, but by the commodity relationship itself ... It is not the perversity of the bourgeois that creates production for the sake of production, but the very market nexus over which he presides and to which he succumbs. ... It requires a grotesque self-deception, or worse, an act of ideological social deception, to foster the belief that this society can undo its very law of life in response to ethical arguments or intellectual persuasion."* [**Toward an Ecological Society**, p. 66]

Sadly, much of what passes for the green movement is based on this kind of perspective. At worse, many environmentalists place their hopes on green consumerism and education. At best, they seek to create green parties to work within the state to pass appropriate regulations and laws. Neither option gets to the core of the problem, namely a system in which there are *"oppressive human beings who literally own society and others who are owned by it. Until society can be reclaimed by an undivided humanity that will use its collective wisdom, cultural achievements, technological innovations, scientific knowledge, and innate creativity for its own benefit and for that of the natural world, all ecological problems will have their roots in social problems."* [Bookchin, **Remaking Society**, p. 39]

E.2
What do eco-anarchists propose instead of capitalism?

Given what eco-anarchists consider to be the root cause of our ecological problems (as discussed in the last section), it should come as no surprise that they think that the current ecological crisis can only be really solved by eliminating those root causes, namely by ending domination within humanity and creating an anarchist society. So here we will summarise the vision of the free society eco-anarchists advocate before discussing the limitations of various non-anarchist proposals to solve environmental problems in subsequent sections.

However, before so doing it is important to stress that eco-anarchists consider it important to fight against ecological and social problems today. Like all anarchists, they argue for direct action and solidarity to struggle for improvements and reforms under the current system. This means that eco-anarchism *"supports every effort to conserve the environment"* in the here and now. The key difference between them and environmentalists is that eco-anarchists place such partial struggles within a larger context of changing society as a whole. The former is part of *"waging a delaying action against the rampant destruction of the environment"* the other is *"a creative movement to totally revolutionise the social relations of humans to each other and of humanity to nature."* [Murray Bookchin, **Toward an Ecological Society**, p. 43] This is one of the key differences between an ecological perspective and an environmental one (a difference discussed in section E.1.2). Finding ways to resist capitalism's reduction of the living world to resources and commodities and its plunder of the planet, our resistance to specific aspects of an eco-cidal system, are merely a starting point in the critique of the whole system and of a wider struggle for a better society. As such, our outline of an ecological society (or ecotopia) is not meant to suggest an indifference to partial struggles and reforms within capitalism. It is simply to indicate why anarchists are confident that ending capitalism and the state will create the necessary preconditions for a free and ecologically viable society.

This perspective flows from the basic insight of eco-anarchism, namely that ecological problems are not separate from social ones. As we are part of nature, it means that how we interact and shape ourselves

with it will be influenced by how we interact and shape ourselves. As Reclus put it *"every people gives, so to speak, new clothing to the surrounding nature. By means of its fields and roads, by its dwelling and every manner of construction, by the way it arranges the trees and the landscape in general, the populace expresses the character of its own ideals. If it really has a feeling for beauty, it will make nature more beautiful. If, on the other hand, the great mass of humanity should remain as it is today, crude, egoistic and inauthentic, it will continue to mark the face of the earth with its wretched traces. Thus will the poet's cry of desperation become a reality: 'Where can I flee? Nature itself has become hideous.'"* In order to transform how we interact with nature, we need to transform how we interact with each other. *"Fortunately,"* Reclus notes, *"a complete alliance of the beautiful and the useful is possible."* [quoted by Clark and Martin (eds.) , **Anarchy, Geography, Modernity**, p. 125 and p. 28]

Over a century later, Murray Bookchin echoed this insight:

"The views advanced by anarchists were deliberately called **social** *ecology to emphasise that major ecological problems have their roots in social problems – problems that go back to the very beginnings of patricentric culture itself. The rise of capitalism, with a law of life based on competition, capital accumulation, and limitless growth, brought these problems – ecological and social – to an acute point; indeed, one that was unprecedented in any prior epoch of human development. Capitalist society, by recycling the organic world into an increasingly inanimate, inorganic assemblage of commodities, was destined to simplify the biosphere, thereby cutting across the grain of natural evolution with its ages-long thrust towards differentiation and diversity.*

"To reverse this trend, capitalism had to be replaced by an ecological society based on non-hierarchical relationships, decentralised communities, eco-technologies like solar power, organic agriculture, and humanly scaled industries – in short, by face-to-face democratic forms of settlement economically and structurally tailored to the ecosystems in which they were located." [**Remaking Society**, pp. 154-5]

The vision of an ecological society rests on the obvious fact that people can have both positive and negative impacts on the environment. In current society, there are vast differences and antagonisms between privileged whites and people of colour, men and women, rich and poor, oppressor and oppressed. Remove those differences and antagonisms and our interactions with ourselves and nature change radically. In other words, there is a vast difference between free, non-hierarchical, class, and stateless societies on the one hand, and hierarchical, class-ridden, statist, and authoritarian ones and how they interact with the environment.

Given the nature of ecology, it should come as no surprise that social anarchists have been at the forefront of eco-anarchist theory and activism. It would be fair to say that most eco-anarchists, like most anarchists in general, envision an ecotopia based on communist-anarchist principles. This does not mean that individualist anarchists are indifferent to environmental issues, simply that most anarchists are unconvinced that such solutions will actually end the ecological crisis we face. Certain of the proposals in this section are applicable to individualist anarchism (for example, the arguments that co-operatives will produce less growth and be less likely to pollute). However, others are not. Most obviously, arguments in favour of common ownership and against the price mechanism are not applicable to the market based solutions of individualist anarchism. It should also be pointed out, that much of the eco-anarchist critique of capitalist approaches to ecological problems are also applicable to individualist and mutualist anarchism as well (particularly the former, as the latter does recognise the need to regulate the market). While certain aspects of capitalism would be removed in an individualist anarchism (such as massive inequalities of wealth, capitalist property rights as well as direct and indirect subsidies to big business), it is still has the informational problems associated with markets as well as a growth orientation.

Here we discuss the typical eco-anarchist view of a free ecological society, namely one rooted in social anarchist principles. Eco-anarchists, like all consistent anarchists advocate workers' self-management of the economy as a necessary component of an ecologically sustainable society. This usually means society-wide ownership of the means of production and all productive enterprises self-managed by their workers (as described further in section I.3). This is a key aspect of making a truly ecological society. Most greens, even if they are not anarchists, recognise the pernicious ecological effects of the capitalist "grow or die" principle; but unless they are also anarchists, they usually fail to make the connection between that principle and the **hierarchical form** of the typical capitalist corporation. The capitalist firm, like the state, is centralised, top-down and autocratic. These are the opposite of what an ecological ethos would suggest. In contrast, eco-anarchists emphasise the need for socially owned and worker self-managed firms.

This vision of co-operative rather than hierarchical production is a common position for almost all anarchists. Communist and non-communist social anarchists, like mutualists and collectivists, propose co-operative workplaces but differ in how best to distribute the products produced. The former urge the abolition of money and sharing according to need while the latter see income related to work and surpluses are shared equally among all members. Both of these systems would produce workplaces which would be under far less pressure toward rapid expansion than the traditional capitalist firm (as individualist anarchism aims for the abolition of rent, profit and interest it, too, will have less expansive workplaces).

The slower growth rate of co-operatives has been documented in a number of studies, which show that in the traditional capitalist firm, owners' and executives' percentage share of profits greatly increases as more employees are added to the payroll. This is because the corporate hierarchy is designed to facilitate exploitation by funnelling a disproportionate share of the surplus value produced by workers to those at the top of the pyramid (see section C.2) Such a design gives ownership and management a very strong incentive to expand, since, other things being equal, their income rises with every new employee hired. [David Schweickart, **Against Capitalism**, pp. 153-4] Hence the hierarchical form of the capitalist corporation is one of the main causes of runaway growth as well as

social inequality and the rise of big business and oligopoly in the so-called "free" market.

By contrast, in an equal-share worker co-operative, the addition of more members simply means more people with whom the available pie will have to be equally divided – a situation that immensely reduces the incentive to expand. Thus a libertarian-socialist economy will not be under the same pressure to grow. Moreover, when introducing technological innovations or facing declining decline for goods, a self-managed workplace would be more likely to increase leisure time among producers rather than increase workloads or reduce numbers of staff.

This means that rather than produce a few big firms, a worker-controlled economy would tend to create an economy with more small and medium sized workplaces. This would make integrating them into local communities and eco-systems far easier as well as making them more easily dependent on green sources of energy. Then there are the other ecological advantages to workers' self-management beyond the relative lack of expansion of specific workplaces and the decentralisation this implies. These are explained well by market socialist David Schweickart:

> "To the extent that emissions affect the workers directly on the job (as they often do), we can expect a self-managed firm to pollute less. Workers will control the technology; it will not be imposed on them from without.

> "To the extent that emissions affect the local community, they are likely to be less severe, for two reasons. Firstly, workers (unlike capitalist owners) will necessarily live nearby, and so the decision-makers will bear more of the environmental costs directly. Second … a self-managed firm will not be able to avoid local regulation by running away (or threatening to do so). The great stick that a capitalist firm holds over the head of a local community will be absent. Hence absent will be the macrophenomenon of various regions of the country trying to compete for firms by offering a 'better business climate' (i.e. fewer environmental restrictions)." [**Op. Cit.**, p. 145]

For an ecological society to work, it requires the active participation of those doing productive activity. They are often the first to be affected by industrial pollution and have the best knowledge of how to stop it happening. As such, workplace self-management is an essential requirement for a society which aims to live in harmony with its surrounds (and with itself, as a key aspect of social unfreedom would be eliminated in the form of wage slavery).

For these reasons, libertarian socialism based on producer co-operatives is essential for the type of economy necessary to solve the ecological crisis. These all feed directly into the green vision as *"ecology points to the necessity of decentralisation, diversity in natural and social systems, human-scale technology, and an end to the exploitation of nature."* [John Clark, **The Anarchist Moment**, p. 115] This can only be achieved in a society which bases itself on workers' self-management as this would facilitate the decentralisation of industries in ways which are harmonious with nature.

So far, all forms of social anarchism are in agreement. However, eco-anarchists tend to be communist-anarchists and oppose both mutualism and collectivism. This is because workers' ownership and self-management places the workers of an enterprise in a position where they can become a particularistic interest within their community. This may lead to these firms acting purely in their own narrow interests and against the local community. They would be, in other words, outside of community input and be solely accountable to themselves. This could lead to a situation where they become "collective capitalists" with a common interest in expanding their enterprises, increasing their "profits" and even subjecting themselves to irrational practices to survive in the market (i.e., harming their own wider and long-term interests as market pressures have a distinct tendency to produce a race to the bottom – see section I.1.3 for more discussion). This leads most eco-anarchists to call for a confederal economy and society in which communities will be decentralised and freely give of their resources without the use of money.

As a natural compliment to workplace self-management, eco-anarchists propose communal self-management. So, although it may have appeared that we focus our attention on the economic aspects of the ecological crisis and its solution, this is not the case. It should always be kept in mind that all anarchists see that a complete solution to our many ecological and social problems must be multi-dimensional, addressing all aspects of the total system of hierarchy and domination. This means that only anarchism, with its emphasis on the elimination of authority in **all** areas of life, goes to the fundamental root of the ecological crisis.

The eco-anarchist argument for direct (participatory) democracy is that effective protection of the planet's ecosystems requires that all people are able to take part at the grassroots level in decision-making that affects their environment, since they are more aware of their immediate eco-systems and more likely to favour stringent environmental safeguards than politicians, state bureaucrats and the large, polluting special interests that now dominate the "representative" system of government. Moreover, real change must come from below, not from above as this is the very source of the social and ecological problems that we face as it divests individuals, communities and society as a whole of their power, indeed right, to shape their own destinies as well as draining them of their material and "spiritual" resources (i.e., the thoughts, hopes and dreams of people).

Simply put, it should be hardly necessary to explore in any great depth the sound ecological and social reasons for decentralising decision making power to the grassroots of society, i.e. to the people who have to live with the decisions being reached. The decentralised nature of anarchism would mean that any new investments and proposed solutions to existing problems would be tailored to local conditions. Due to the mobility of capital, laws passed under capitalism to protect the environment have to be created and implemented by the central government to be effective. Yet the state, as discussed in section E.1, is a centralised structure unsuited to the task of collecting and processing the information and knowledge required to customise decisions to local ecological and social circumstances. This means that legislation, precisely due to its scope, cannot be finely tuned to local conditions (and so can generate local opposition, particularly if whipped up by corporate front organisations). In an eco-anarchist society, decentralisation

would not have the threat of economic power hanging over it and so decisions would be reached which reflected the actual local needs of the population. As they would be unlikely to want to pollute themselves or their neighbours, eco-anarchists are confident that such local empowerment will produce a society which lives with, rather than upon, the environment.

Thus eco-communities (or eco-communes) are a key aspect of an ecotopia. Eco-communes, Bookchin argued, will be *"networked confederally through ecosystems, bioregions, and biomes"* and be *"artistically tailored to their naturally surrounding. We can envision that their squares will be interlaced by streams, their places of assembly surrounded by groves, their physical contours respected and tastefully landscaped, their soils nurtured caringly to foster plant variety for ourselves, our domestic animals, and wherever possible the wildlife they may support on their fringes."* They would be decentralised and *"scaled to human dimensions,"* using recycling as well as integrating *"solar, wind, hydraulic, and methane-producing installations into a highly variegated pattern for producing power. Agriculture, aquaculture, stockraising, and hunting would be regarded as crafts – an orientation that we hope would be extended as much as possible to the fabrication of use-values of nearly all kinds. The need to mass-produce goods in highly mechanised installations would be vastly diminished by the communities' overwhelming emphasis on quality and permanence."* [**The Ecology of Freedom**, p. 444]

This means that local communities will generate social and economic policies tailored to their own unique ecological circumstances, in co-operation with others (it is important to stress that eco-communes do not imply supporting local self-sufficiency and economic autarchy as values in themselves). Decisions that have regional impact are worked out by confederations of local assemblies, so that everybody affected by a decision can participate in making it. Such a system would be self-sufficient as workplace and community participation would foster creativity, spontaneity, responsibility, independence, and respect for individuality – the qualities needed for a self-management to function effectively. Just as hierarchy shapes those subject to it in negative ways, participation would shape us in positive ways which would strengthen our individuality and enrich our freedom and interaction with others and nature.

That is not all. The communal framework would also impact on how industry would develop. It would allow eco-technologies to be prioritised in terms of R&D and subsidised in terms of consumption. No more would green alternatives and eco-technologies be left unused simply because most people cannot afford to buy them nor would their development be under-funded simply because a capitalist sees little profit from it or a politician cannot see any benefit from it. It also means that the broad outlines of production are established at the community assembly level while they are implemented in practice by smaller collective bodies which also operate on an egalitarian, participatory, and democratic basis. Co-operative workplaces form an integral part of this process, having control over the production process and the best way to implement any general outlines.

It is for these reasons that anarchists argue that common ownership combined with a use-rights based system of possession is better for the environment as it allows everyone the right to take action to stop pollution, not simply those who are directly affected by it. As a framework for ecological ethics, the communal system envisioned by social anarchists would be far better than private property and markets in protecting the environment. This is because the pressures that markets exert on their members would not exist, as would the perverse incentives which reward anti-social and anti-ecological practices. Equally, the anti-ecological centralisation and hierarchy of the state would be ended and replaced with a participatory system which can take into account the needs of the local environment and utilise the local knowledge and information that both the state and capitalism suppresses.

Thus a genuine solution to the ecological crisis presupposes communes, i.e. participatory democracy in the social sphere. This is a transformation that would amount to a political revolution. However, as Bakunin continually emphasised, a political revolution of this nature cannot be envisioned without a **socio-economic** revolution based on workers' self-management. This is because the daily experience of participatory decision-making, non-authoritarian modes of organisation, and personalistic human relationships would not survive if those values were denied during working hours. Moreover, as mentioned above, participatory communities would be hard pressed to survive the pressure that big business would subject them to.

Needless to say, the economic and social aspects of life cannot be considered in isolation. For example, the negative results of workplace hierarchy and its master-servant dynamic will hardly remain there. Given the amount of time that most people spend working, the political importance of turning it into a training ground for the development of libertarian values can scarcely be overstated. As history has demonstrated, political revolutions that are not based upon social changes and mass psychological transformation – that is, by a deconditioning from the master/slave attitudes absorbed from the current system – result only in the substitution of new ruling elites for the old ones (e.g. Lenin becoming the new "Tsar" and Communist Party aparatchiks becoming the new "aristocracy"). Therefore, besides having a slower growth rate, worker co-operatives with democratic self-management would lay the psychological foundations for the kind of directly democratic political system necessary to protect the biosphere. Thus "green" libertarian socialism is the only proposal radical enough to solve the ecological crisis.

Ecological crises become possible only within the context of social relations which weaken people's capacities to fight an organised defence of the planet's ecology and their own environment. This means that the restriction of participation in decision-making processes within hierarchical organisations such as the state and capitalism firms help create environmental along with social problems by denying those most affected by a problem the means of fixing it. Needless to say, hierarchy within the workplace is a prerequisite to accumulation and so growth while hierarchy within a community is a prerequisite to defend economic and social inequality as well as minority rule as the disempowered become indifferent to community and social issues they have little or no say in. Both combine to create the basis of our current ecological crisis and both need to be ended.

Ultimately, a free nature can only begin to emerge when we live in a fully participatory society which itself is free of oppression, domination and exploitation. Only then will we be able to rid ourselves of the idea of dominating nature and fulfil our potential as individuals and be a creative force in natural as well social evolution. That means replacing the current system with one based on freedom, equality and solidarity. Once this is achieved, *"social life will yield a sensitive development of human and natural diversity, falling together into a well balanced harmonious whole. Ranging from community through region to entire continents, we will see a colourful differentiation of human groups and ecosystems, each developing its unique potentialities and exposing members of the community to a wide spectrum of economic, cultural and behavioural stimuli. Falling within our purview will be an exciting, often dramatic, variety of communal forms – here marked by architectural and industrial adaptations to semi-arid ecosystems, there to grasslands, elsewhere by adaptation to forested areas. We will witness a creative interplay between individual and group, community and environment, humanity and nature."* [Bookchin, **Post-Scarcity Anarchism**, p. 39]

So, to conclude, in place of capitalism eco-anarchists favour ecologically responsible forms of libertarian socialism, with an economy based on the principles of complementarily with nature; decentralisation (where possible and desirable) of large-scale industries, reskilling of workers, and a return to more artisan-like modes of production; the use of eco-technologies and ecologically friendly energy sources to create green products; the use of recycled and recyclable raw materials and renewable resources; the integration of town and country, industry and agriculture; the creation of self-managed eco-communities which exist in harmony with their surroundings; and self-managed workplaces responsive to the wishes of local community assemblies and labour councils in which decisions are made by direct democracy and co-ordinated (where appropriate and applicable) from the bottom-up in a free federation. Such a society would aim to develop the individuality and freedom of all its members in order to ensure that we end the domination of nature by humanity by ending domination within humanity itself.

This is the vision of a green society put forth by Murray Bookchin. To quote him:

> *"We must create an ecological society – not merely because such a society is desirable but because it is direly necessary. We must begin to live in order to survive. Such a society involves a fundamental reversal of all the trends that mark the historic development of capitalist technology and bourgeois society – the minute specialisation of machines and labour, the concentration of resources and people in gigantic industrial enterprises and urban entities, the stratification and bureaucratisation of life, the divorce of town from country, the objectification of nature and human beings. In my view, this sweeping reversal means that we must begin to decentralise our cities and establish entirely new eco-communities that are artistically moulded to the ecosystems in which they are located ...*

"Such an eco-community ... would heal the split between town and country, indeed, between mind and body by fusing intellectual with physical work, industry with agriculture in a rotation or diversification of vocational tasks. An eco-community would be supported by a new kind of technology – or eco-technology – one composed of flexible, versatile machinery whose productive applications would emphasise durability and quality ... " [**Toward an Ecological Society**, pp. 68-9]

Lastly, we need to quickly sketch out how anarchists see the change to an ecological society happening as there is little point having an aim if you have no idea how to achieve it.

As noted above, eco-anarchists (like all anarchists) do not counterpose an ideal utopia to existing society but rather participate in current ecological struggles. Moreover, we see that struggle itself as the link between what is and what could be. This implies, at minimum, a two pronged strategy of neighbourhood movements and workplace organising as a means of both fighting and abolishing capitalism. These would work together, with the former targeting, say, the disposal of toxic wastes and the latter stopping the production of toxins in the first place. Only when workers are in a position to refuse to engage in destructive practices or produce destructive goods can lasting ecological change emerge. Unsurprisingly, modern anarchists and anarcho-syndicalists have been keen to stress the need for a green syndicalism which addresses ecological as well as economical exploitation. The ideas of community and industrial unionism are discussed in more detail in section J.5 along with other anarchist tactics for social change. Needless to say, such organisations would use direct action as their means of achieving their goals (see section J.2). It should be noted that some of Bookchin's social ecologist followers advocate, like him, greens standing in local elections as a means to create a counter-power to the state. As we discuss in section J.5.14, this strategy (called Libertarian Municipalism) finds few supporters in the wider anarchist movement.

This strategy flows, of course, into the structures of an ecological society. As we discuss in section I.2.3, anarchists argue that the framework of a free society will be created in the process of fighting the existing one. Thus the structures of an eco-anarchist society (i.e. eco-communes and self-managed workplaces) will be created by fighting the ecocidal tendencies of the current system. In other words, like all anarchists eco-anarchists seek to create the new world while fighting the old one. This means what we do now is, however imperfect, an example of what we propose instead of capitalism. That means we act in an ecological fashion today in order to ensure that we can create an ecological society tomorrow. For more discussion of how an anarchist society would work, see section I. We will discuss the limitations of various proposed solutions to the environmental crisis in the following sections.

Environmental issues have become increasingly important over the decades. When Murray Bookchin wrote his first works on our ecological problems in the 1950s, he was only one of a small band. Today, even right-wing politicians have to give at least some lip-service to environmental concerns while corporations are keen to present their green credentials to the general public (even if they do not, in fact, have any).

As such, there has been a significant change. This is better late than never, considering that the warnings made by the likes of Bookchin in the 1950s and 1960s have come true to a threateningly worrying degree. Sadly, eco-anarchist solutions are still ignored but that is unsurprising as they go to the heart of the ecological problem, namely domination within humanity as the precondition for the domination of nature and the workings of the capitalist economy. It is hardly likely that those who practice and benefit from that oppression and exploitation will admit that they are causing the problems! Hence the need to appear green in order to keep a fundamentally anti-green system going.

Of course, some right-wingers are totally opposed to ecological issues. They seriously seem to forget without a viable ecology, there would be no capitalism. Ayn Rand, for example, dismissed environmental concerns as being anti-human and had little problem with factory chimneys belching smoke into the atmosphere (her fondness for chimneys and skyscrapers would have made Freud reach for his notepad). As Bob Black once noted, *"Rand remarked that she **worshipped** smokestacks. For her ... they not only stood for, they **were** the epitome of human accomplishment. She must have meant it since she was something of a human smokestack herself; she was a chain smoker, as were the other rationals in her entourage. In the end she abolished her own breathing: she died of lung cancer."* [*"Smokestack Lightning,"* **Friendly Fire**, p. 62] The fate of this guru of capitalism is a forewarning for our collective one if we ignore the environment and our impact on it.

The key to understanding why so many on the right are dismissive of ecological concerns is simply that ecology cannot be squeezed into their narrow individualistic property based politics. Ecology is about interconnectiveness, about change and interaction, about the sources of life and how we interact with them and they with us. Moreover, ecology is rooted in the **quality** of life and does not automatically view quantity as the key factor. As such, the notion that more is better does not strike the ecologist as, in itself, a good thing. The idea that growth is good as such is the principle associated with cancer. Ecology also destroys the individualistic premise of capitalist economics. It exposes the myth that the market ensures everyone gets exactly what they want – for if you consume eco-friendly products but others do not then you are affected by their decisions as the environmental impact affects all. Equally, the notion that the solution to GM crops should be letting "the market" decide fails to take into account that such crops spread into local eco-systems and contaminate whole areas (not to mention the issue of corporate power enclosing another part of the commons). The market "solution" in this case would result in everyone, to some degree, consuming GM crops eventually. None of this can be fitted into the capitalist ideology.

However, while vocal irrational anti-green perspectives linger on in some sections of the right (particularly those funded by the heaviest polluters), other supporters of capitalism have considered the problems of ecological destruction in some degree. Some of this is, of course, simply greenwashing (i.e., using PR and advertising to present a green image while conducting business as usual). Some of it is funding think tanks which use green-sounding names, imagery and rhetoric to help pursue a decidedly anti-ecological practice and agenda. Some of is, to some degree, genuine. Al Gore's campaign to make the world aware of the dangers of climate change is obviously sincere and important work (although it is fair to point out the lack of green policies being raised during his 2000 Presidential election campaign and the poverty of his proposed solutions and means of change). Nicholas Stern's 2006 report on climate change produced for the UK government is another example and it gives an insight into the mentality of such environmentalists. The report did produce quite an impact (plus its dismissal by the usual suspects). The key reason for that was, undoubtedly, due to it placing a money sum on the dangers of environmental disruption. Such is capitalism – people and planet can go to the dogs, but any threat to profits must be acted upon. As the British PM at the time put it, any Climate Change Bill must be *"fully compatible with the interests of businesses and consumers as well."* Which is ironic, as it is the power of money which is causing the bulk of the problems we face.

Which is what we will discuss here, namely whether private property can be used to solve our environmental problems. Liberal environmentalists base their case on capitalist markets aided with some form of state intervention. Neo-liberal and right-"libertarian" environmentalists base their case purely on capitalist markets and reject any role for the state bar that of defining and enforcing private property rights. Both, however, assume that capitalism will remain and tailor their policies around it. Anarchists question that particular assumption particularly given, as we discussed in section E.1, the fundamental reason why capitalism cannot be green is its irrational "grow-or-die" dynamic. However, there are other aspects of the system which contribute to capitalism bringing ecological crisis sooner rather than later. These flow from the nature of private property and the market competition it produces (this discussion, we should stress, ignores such factors as economic power which will be addressed in section E.3.2).

The market itself causes ecological problems for two related reasons: externalities and the price mechanism. It is difficult making informed consumption decisions under capitalism because rather than provide enough information to make informed decisions, the market hinders the flow of relevant information and suppresses essential knowledge. This is particularly the case with environmental information and knowledge. Simply put, we have no way of knowing from a given price the ecological impact of the products we buy. One such area of suppressed information is that involving externalities. This is a commonly understood problem. The market actively rewards those companies which inflict externalities

on society. This is the *"routine and regular harms caused to **others** – workers, consumers, communities, the environment."* These are termed *"externalities"* in *"the coolly technical jargon of economics"* and the capitalist company is an *"externalising machine"* and it is *"no exaggeration to say that the corporation's built in compulsion to externalise its costs is at the root of many of the world's social and environmental ills."* [Joel Bakan, **The Corporation**, p. 60 and p. 61]

The logic is simple, by externalising (imposing) costs on others (be it workers, customers or the planet) a firm can reduce its costs and make higher profits. Thus firms have a vested interest in producing externalities. To put it crudely, pollution pays while ecology costs. Every pound a business spends on environmental protections is one less in profits. As such, it makes economic sense to treat the environment like a dump and externalise costs by pumping raw industrial effluent into the atmosphere, rivers, and oceans. The social cost of so doing weighs little against the personal profits that result from inflicting diffuse losses onto the general public. Nor should we discount the pressure of market forces in this process. In order to survive on the market, firms may have to act in ways which, while profitable in the short-run, are harmful in the long term. For example, a family-owned farm may be forced to increase production using environmentally unsound means simply in order to avoid bankruptcy.

As well as economic incentives, the creation of externalities flows from the price mechanism itself. The first key issue, as green economist E. F. Schumacher stressed, is that the market is based on *"total quantification at the expense of qualitative differences; for private enterprise is not concerned with what it produces but only what it gains from production."* This means that the *"judgement of economics … is an extremely **fragmentary** judgement; out of the large number of aspects which in real life have to be seen and judged together before a decision can be taken, economics supplies only one – whether a thing yields a profit **to those who undertake it** or not."* [**Small is Beautiful**, p. 215 and p. 28] This leads to a simplistic decision making perspective:

> *"Everything becomes crystal clear after you have reduced reality to one – one only – of its thousand aspects. You know what to do – whatever produces profits; you know what to avoid – whatever reduces them or makes a loss. And there is at the same time a perfect measuring rod for the degree of success or failure. Let no-one befog the issue by asking whether a particular action is conducive to the wealth and well-being of society, whether it leads to moral, aesthetic, or cultural enrichment. Simply find out whether it pays."* [**Op. Cit.**, p. 215]

This means that key factors in decision making are, at best, undermined by the pressing need to make profits or, at worse, simply ignored as a handicap. So *"in the market place, for practical reasons, innumerable qualitative distinctions which are of vital importance for man and society are suppressed; they are not allowed to surface. Thus the reign of quantity celebrates its greatest triumphs in 'The Market.'"* This feeds the drive to externalise costs, as it is *"based on a definition of cost which excludes all 'free goods,' that is to say, the entire God-given environment, except for those parts of it that* have been privately appropriated. This means that an activity can be economic although it plays hell with the environment, and that a competing activity, if at some cost it protects and conserves the environment, will be uneconomic." To summarise: "it is inherent in the methodology of economics to **ignore man's dependence on the natural world.**" [**Op. Cit.**, p. 30 and p. 29]

Ultimately, should our decision-making be limited to a single criteria, namely whether it makes someone a profit? Should our environment be handed over to a system which bases itself on confusing efficient resource allocation with maximising profits in an economy marked by inequalities of wealth and, consequently, on unequal willingness and ability to pay? In other words, biodiversity, eco-system stability, clean water and air, and so forth only become legitimate social goals when the market places a price on them sufficient for a capitalist to make money from them. Such a system can only fail to achieve a green society simply because ecological concerns cannot be reduced to one criteria ("The discipline of economics achieves its formidable resolving power by transforming what might otherwise be considered qualitative matters into quantitative issues with a single metric and, as it were, a bottom line: profit or loss." [James C. Scott, **Seeing like a State**, p. 346]). This is particularly the case when even economists admit that the market under-supplies public goods, of which a clean and aesthetically pleasing environment is the classic example. Markets may reflect, to some degree, individual consumer preferences distorted by income distribution but they are simply incapable of reflecting collective values (a clean environment and spectacular views are inherently collective goods and cannot be enclosed). As a result, capitalists will be unlikely to invest in such projects as they cannot make everyone who uses them pay for the privilege.

Then there is the tendency for the market to undermine and destroy practical and local knowledge on which truly ecological decisions need to be based. Indigenous groups, for example, have accumulated an enormous body of knowledge about local ecological conditions and species which are ignored in economic terms or eliminated by competition with those with economic power. Under markets, in other words, unarticulated knowledge of soil conditions and bio-diversity which have considerable value for long-term sustainability is usually lost when it meets agribusiness.

Practical knowledge, i.e. local and tacit knowledge which James C. Scott terms metis, is being destroyed and replaced "by standardised formulas legible from the centre" and this "is virtually inscribed in the activities of both the state and large-scale bureaucratic capitalism." The "logic animating the project ... is one of control and appropriation. Local knowledge, because it is dispersed and relatively autonomous, is all but unappropriable. The reduction or, more utopian still, the elimination of metis and the local control its entails are preconditions, in the case of the state, of administrative order and fiscal appropriation and, in the case of the large capitalism firm, of worker discipline and profit." [**Op. Cit.**, pp. 335-6] Green socialist John O'Neill provides a similar analysis:

"far from fostering the existence of practical and local knowledge, the spread of markets often appears to do the opposite: the growth of global markets is associated with the disappearance of knowledge that is local and practical, and the growth of abstract codifiable information ... the market as a mode of co-ordination appears to foster forms of abstract codifiable knowledge.... The knowledge of weak and marginal actors in markets, such as peasant and marginalised indigenous communities, tends to be lost to those who hold market power. The epistemic value of knowledge claims bear no direct relation to their market value. Local and often unarticulated knowledge of soil conditions and crop varieties that have considerable value for long-term sustainability of agriculture has no value in markets and hence is always liable to loss when it comes into contact with oil-based agricultural technologies of those who do have market power. The undermining of local practical knowledge in market economies has also been exacerbated by the global nature of both markets and large corporate actors who require knowledge that is transferable across different cultures and contexts and hence abstract and codifiable.... Finally, the demand for commensurability and calculability runs against the defence of local and practical knowledge. This is not just a theoretical problem but one with real institutional embodiments. The market encourages a spirit of calculability.... That spirit is the starting point for the algorithmic account of practical reason which requires explicit common measures for rational choice and fails to acknowledge the existence of choice founded upon practical judgement. More generally it is not amicable to forms of knowledge that are practical, local and uncodifiable." [**Markets, Deliberation and Environment**, pp. 192-3]

Thus the market tends to replace traditional forms of agriculture and working practices (and the complex knowledge and expertises associated with both) with standardised techniques which aim to extract as much profit in the short-term as possible by concentrating power into the hands of management and their appointed experts. That they cannot even begin to comprehend the local conditions and practical knowledge and skills required to effectively use the resources available in a sustainable manner should go without saying. Unfortunately, the economic clout of big business is such that it can defeat traditional forms of knowledge in the short-term (the long-term effect of such exploitation is usually considered someone else's problem).

So, given this analysis, it comes as no surprise to anarchists that private property has not protected the environment. In fact, it is one of the root causes of our ecological problems. Markets hide the ecological and health information necessary for environmentally sound decisions. Ultimately, environmental issues almost always involve value judgements and the market stops the possibility of producing a public dialogue in which these values can be discussed and enriched. Instead, it replaces this process by an aggregation of existing preferences (shaped by economic pressures and necessity) skewed in favour of this generation's property owners. An individual's interest, like that of the public as a whole, is not something which exists independently of the decision-making processes used but rather is something which is shaped by them. Atomistic processes focused on a simplistic criteria will produce simplistic decisions which have collectively irrational results. Collective decision making based on equal participation of all will produce decisions which reflect **all** the concerns of **all** affected in a process which will help produce empowered and educated individuals along with informed decisions.

Some disagree. For these the reason why there is environmental damage is not due to too much private property but because there is too little. This perspective derives from neo-classical and related economic theory and it argues that ecological harm occurs because environmental goods and bads are unpriced. They come free, in other words. This suggests that the best way to protect the environment is to privatise everything and to create markets in all areas of life. This perspective, needless to say, is entirely the opposite of the standard eco-anarchist one which argues that our environmental problems have their root in market mechanisms, private property and the behaviour they generate. As such, applying market norms even more rigorously and into areas of life that were previously protected from markets will tend to make ecological problems worse, not better.

As would be expected, the pro-property perspective is part of the wider turn to free(r) market capitalism since the 1970s. With the apparent success of Thatcherism and Reaganism (at least for the people who count under capitalism, i.e. the wealthy) and the fall of Stalinism in the Eastern Block, the 1980s and 1990s saw a period of capitalist triumphantism. This lead to an increase in market based solutions to every conceivable social problem, regardless of how inappropriate and/or insane the suggestions were. This applies to ecological issues as well. The publication of **Free Market Environmentalism** by Terry L. Anderson and Donald R. Leal in 1991 saw ideas previously associated with the right-"libertarian" fringe become more mainstream and, significantly, supported by corporate interests and the think-tanks and politicians they fund.

Some see it as a deliberate plan to counteract a growing ecological movement which aims to change social, political and economic structures in order to get at the root cases of our environmental problems. Activist Sara Diamond suggested that *"[s]ome farsighted corporations are finding that the best 'bulwark' against 'anti-corporation' environmentalism is the creation and promotion of an alternative model called 'free market environmentalism.'"* [*"Free Market Environmentalism,"* **Z Magazine**, December 1991] Whatever the case, the net effect of this reliance on markets is to depoliticise environmental debates, to transform issues which involve values and affect many people into ones in which the property owner is given priority and where the criteria for decision making becomes one of profit and loss. It means, effectively, ending debates over **why** ecological destruction happens and what we should do about it and accepting the assumptions, institutions and social relationships of capitalism as a given as well as privatising yet more of the world and handing it over to capitalists. Little wonder it is being proposed as an alternative by corporations concerned about their green image. At the very least, it is fair to say that the corporations who punt free market environmentalism as an alternative paradigm for environmental policy making are not expecting to pay more by internalising their costs by so doing.

As with market fundamentalism in general, private property based

environmentalism appears to offer solutions simply because it fails to take into account the reality of any actual capitalist system. The notion that all we have to do is let markets work ignores the fact that any theoretical claim for the welfare superiority of free-market outcomes falls when we look at any real capitalist market. Once we introduce, say, economic power, imperfect competition, public goods, externalities or asymmetric information then the market quickly becomes a god with feet of clay. This is what we will explore in the rest of this section while the next section will discuss a specific example of how laissez-faire capitalism cannot be ecological as proved by one of its most fervent ideologues. Overall, anarchists feel we have a good case on why is unlikely that private property can protect the environment.

E.3.1 Will privatising nature save it?

No, it will not. To see why, it is only necessary to look at the arguments and assumptions of those who advocate such solutions to our ecological problems.

The logic behind the notion of privatising the planet is simple. Many of our environmental problems stem, as noted in the last section, from externalities. According to the "market advocates" this is due to there being unowned resources for if someone owned them, they would sue whoever or whatever was polluting them. By means of private property and the courts, pollution would end. Similarly, if an endangered species or eco-system were privatised then the new owners would have an interest in protecting them if tourists, say, were willing to pay to see them. Thus the solution to environmental problems is simple. Privatise everything and allow people's natural incentive to care for their own property take over.

Even on this basic level, there are obvious problems. Why assume that **capitalist** property rights are the only ones, for example? However, the crux of the problem is clear enough. This solution only works if we assume that the "resources" in question make their owners a profit or if they are willing and able to track down the polluters. Neither assumption is robust enough to carry the weight that capitalism places on our planet's environment. There is no automatic mechanism by which capitalism will ensure that environmentally sound practices will predominate. In fact, the opposite is far more likely.

At its most basic, the underlying rationale is flawed. It argues that it is only by giving the environment a price can we compare its use for different purposes. This allows the benefits from preserving a forest to be compared to the benefits of cutting it down and building a shopping centre over it. Yet by "benefits" it simply means economic benefits, i.e. whether it is profitable for property owners to do so, rather than ecologically sensible. This is an important difference. If more money can be made in turning a lake into a toxic waste dump then, logically, its owners will do so. Similarly, if timber prices are not rising at the prevailing profit or interest rate, then a self-interested firm will seek to increase its profits and cut-down its trees as fast as possible, investing the returns elsewhere. They may even sell such cleared land to other companies to develop. This undermines any claim that private property rights and environmental protection go hand-in-hand.

As Glenn Albrecht argues, such a capitalist "solution" to environmental problems is only *"likely to be effective in protecting species [or ecosystems] which are commercially important only if the commercial value of that species [or ecosystem] exceeds that of other potential sources of income that could be generated from the same 'natural capital' that the species inhabits. If, for example, the conservation of species for ecotourism generates income which is greater than that which could be gained by using their habit for the growing of cash crops, then the private property rights of the owners of the habitat will effectively protect those species … However, this model becomes progressively less plausible when we are confronted with rare but commercially unimportant species [or ecosystems] versus very large development proposals that are inconsistent with their continual existence. The less charismatic the species, the more 'unattractive' the ecosystem, the more likely it will be that the development proposal will proceed. The 'rights' of developers will eventually win out over species and ecosystems since … bio-diversity itself has no right to exist and even if it did, the clash of rights between an endangered species and multi-national capital would be a very uneven contest."* ["Ethics, Anarchy and Sustainable Development", pp. 95-118, **Anarchist Studies**, vol. 2, no. 2, pp. 104-5]

So the conservation of endangered species or eco-systems is not automatically achieved using the market. This is especially the case when there is little, or no, economic value in the species or eco-system in question. The most obvious example is when there is only a limited profit to be made from a piece of land by maintaining it as the habitat of a rare species. If any alternative economic uses for that land yields a greater profit then that land will be developed. Moreover, if a species looses its economic value as a commodity then the property owners will become indifferent to its survival. Prices change and so an investment which made sense today may not look so good tomorrow. So if the market price of a resource decreases then it becomes unlikely that its ecological benefits will outweigh its economic ones. Overall, regardless of the wider ecological importance of a specific eco-system or species it is likely that their owner will prioritise short-term profits over environmental concerns. It should go without saying that threatened or endangered eco-systems and species will be lost under a privatised regime as it relies on the willingness of profit-orientated companies and individuals to take a loss in order to protect the environment.

Overall, advocates of market based environmentalism need to present a case that **all** plants, animals and eco-systems are valuable commodities in the same way as, say, fish are. While a case for market-based environmentalism can be made by arguing that fish have a market price and, as such, owners of lakes, rivers and oceans would have an incentive to keep their waters clean in order to sell fish on the market, the same cannot be said of all species and habitats. Simply put, not all creatures, plants and eco-systems with an ecological value will have an economic one as well.

Moreover, markets can send mixed messages about the environmental policies which should be pursued. This may lead to over investment in some areas and then a slump. For example, rising demand for recycled goods may inspire an investment boom which, in turn, may lead to over-supply and then a crash, with plants closing as the price falls due to increased supply. Recycling may then become economically unviable, even though it remains ecologically essential. In addition, market prices hardly provide an accurate signal regarding the "correct" level of ecological demands in a society as they are constrained by income levels and reflect the economic pressures people are under. Financial security and income level play a key role, for in the market not all votes are equal. A market based allocation of environmental goods and bads does not reflect the obvious fact the poor may appear to value environmental issues less than the wealthy in this scheme simply because their preferences (as expressed in the market) are limited by lower budgets.

Ultimately, market demand can change without the underlying demand for a specific good changing. For example, since the 1970s the real wages of most Americans have stagnated while inequality has soared. As a result, fewer households can afford to go on holidays to wilderness areas or buy more expensive ecologically friendly products. Does that imply that the people involved now value the environment less simply because they now find it harder to make ends meet? Equally, if falling living standards force people to take jobs with dangerous environmental consequences does than really provide an accurate picture of people's desires? It takes a giant leap of faith (in the market) to assume that falling demand for a specific environmental good implies that reducing environmental damage has become less valuable to people. Economic necessity may compel people to act against their best impulses, even strongly felt natural values (an obvious example is that during recessions people may be more willing to tolerate greenhouse gas emissions simply because they need the work).

Nor can it be claimed that all the relevant factors in ecological decision making can take the commodity form, i.e. be given a price. This means that market prices do not, in fact, actually reflect people's environmental values. Many aspects of our environment simply cannot be given a market price (how can you charge people to look at beautiful scenery?). Then there is the issue of how to charge a price which reflects the demand of people who wish to know that, say, the rainforest or wilderness exists and is protected but who will never visit either? Nor are future generations taken into account by a value that reflects current willingness to pay and might not be consistent with long-term welfare or even survival. And how do you factor in the impact a cleaner environment has on protecting or extending human lives? Surely a healthy environment is worth much more than simply lost earnings and the medical bills and clean-up activities saved? At best, you could factor this in by assuming that the wage premium of workers in dangerous occupations reflects it but a human life is, surely, worth more than the wages required to attract workers into dangerous working conditions. Wages are **not** an objective measure of the level of environmental risks workers are willing to tolerate as they are influenced by the overall state of the economy, the balance of class power and a whole host of other factors. Simply put, fear of unemployment and economic security will ensure that workers tolerate jobs that expose them and their communities to high levels of environmental dangers.

Economic necessity drives decisions in the so-called "free" market (given a choice between clean air and water and having a job, many people would choose the latter simply because they have to in order to survive). These factors can only be ignored which means that environmental values **cannot** be treated like commodities and market prices **cannot** accurately reflect environmental values. The key thing to remember is that the market does not meet demand, it meets **effective** demand (i.e. demands backed up with money). Yet people want endangered species and eco-systems protected even if there is no effective demand for them on the market (nor could be). We will return to this critical subject in the next section.

Then there are the practicalities of privatising nature. How, for example, do we "privatise" the oceans? How do we "privatise" whales and sharks in order to conserve them? How do we know if a whaling ship kills "your" whale? And what if "your" shark feeds on "my" fish? From whom do we buy these resources in the first place? What courts must be set up to assess and try crimes and define damages? Then there are the costs of defining and enforcing private rights by means of the courts. This would mean individual case-by-case adjudications which increase transaction costs. Needless to say, such cases will be influenced by the resources available to both sides. Moreover, the judiciary is almost always the least accountable and representative branch of the state and so turning environmental policy decisions over to them will hardly ensure that public concerns are at the foremost of any decision (such a move would also help undermine trial by jury as juries often tend to reward sizeable damages against corporations in such cases, a factor corporations are all too aware of).

This brings us to the problem of actually proving that the particles of a specific firm has inflicted a specific harm on a particular person and their property. Usually, there are multiple firms engaging in polluting the atmosphere and it would be difficult, if not impossible, to legally establish the liability of any particular firm. How to identify which particular polluter caused the smog which damaged your lungs and garden? Is it an individual company? A set of companies? All companies? Or is it transportation? In which case, is it the specific car which finally caused your cancer or a specific set of car uses? Or all car users? Or is it the manufacturers for producing such dangerous products in the first place?

Needless to say, even this possibility is limited to the current generation. Pollution afflicts future generations as well and it is impossible for their interests to be reflected in court for "future harm" is not the question, only present harm counts. Nor can non-human species or eco-systems sue for damage, only their owners can and, as noted above, they may find it more profitable to tolerate (or even encourage) pollution than sue. Given that non-owners cannot sue as they are not directly harmed, the fate of the planet will rest in the hands of the property-owning class and so the majority are effectively dispossessed of any say over their environment beyond what their money can buy. Transforming ecological concerns into money ensures a monopoly by the wealthy few:

> "In other words, the environment is assumed to be something that can be 'valued,' in a similar way that everything else is assigned a value within the market economy.

> "However, apart from the fact that there is no way to put an 'objective' value on most of the elements that constitute the environment (since they affect a subjective par excellence factor, i.e. the quality of life), the solution suggested … implies the extension of the marketisation process to the environment itself. In other words, it implies the assignment of a market value to the environment … so that the effects of growth onto it are 'internalised' … The outcome of such a process is easily predictable: the environment will either be put under the control of the economic elites that control the market economy (in case an actual market value be assigned to it) or the state (in case an imputed value is only possible). In either case, not only the arrest of the ecological damage is – at least – doubtful, but the control over Nature by elites who aim to dominate it – using 'green' prescriptions this time – is perpetuated." [Takis Fotopoulous, *"Development or Democracy?"*, pp. 57-92, **Society and Nature**, No. 7, pp. 79-80]

Another key problem with using private property in regard to environmental issues is that they are almost always reactive, almost never proactive. Thus the pollution needs to have occurred before court actions are taken as strict liability generally provides after-the-fact compensation for injuries received. If someone does successfully sue for damages, the money received can hardly replace an individual or species or eco-system. At best, it could be argued that the threat of being sued will stop environmentally damaging activities but there is little evidence that this works. If a company concludes that the damages incurred by court action is less than the potential profits to be made, then they will tolerate the possibility of court action (particularly if they feel that potential victims do not have the time or resources available to sue). This kind of decision was most infamously done by General Motors when it designed its Malibu car. The company estimated that the cost of court awarded damages per car was less than ensuring that the car did not explode during certain kinds of collusion and so allowed people to die in fuel-fed fires rather than alter the design. Unfortunately for GM, the jury was horrified (on appeal, the damages were substantially reduced). [Joel Bakan, **The Corporation**, pp. 61-5]

So this means that companies seeking to maximise profits have an incentive to cut safety costs on the assumption that the risk of so doing will be sufficiently low to make it worthwhile and that any profits generated will more than cover the costs of any trial and damages imposed. As eco-anarchist David Watson noted in regards to the Prudhoe Bay disaster, it *"should go without saying that Exxon and its allies don't try their best to protect the environment or human health. Capitalist institutions produce to accumulate power and wealth, not for any social good. Predictably, in order to cut costs, Exxon steadily dismantled what emergency safeguards it had throughout the 1980s, pointing to environmental studies showing a major spill as so unlikely that preparation was unnecessary. So when the inevitable came crashing down, the response was complete impotence and negligence."* [**Against the Megamachine**, p. 57] As such, it cannot be stressed too much that the only reason companies act any different (if and when they do) is because outside agitators – people who understand and care about the planet and people more than they do about company profits – eventually force them to.

So given all this, it is clear that privatising nature is no guarantee that environmental problems will be reduced. In fact, it is more likely to have the opposite effect. Even its own advocates suggest that their solution may produce **more** pollution than the current system of state regulation. Terry L. Anderson and Donald R. Leal put it this way:

> "If markets produce 'too little' clean water because dischargers do not have to pay for its use, then political solutions are equally likely to produce 'too much' clean water because those who enjoy the benefits do not pay the cost…. Just as pollution externalities can generate too much dirty air, political externalities can generate too much water storage, clear-cutting, wilderness, or water quality…. Free market environmentalism emphasises the importance of market process in determining optimal amounts of resource use." [**Free Market Environmentalism**, p. 23]

What kind of environmentalism considers the possibility of "too much" clean air and water? This means, ironically, that from the perspective of free-market "environmentalism" that certain ecological features may be over-protected as a result of the influence of non-economic goals and priorities. Given that this model is proposed by many corporate funded think tanks, it is more than likely that their sponsors think there is "too much" clean air and water, "too much" wilderness and "too much" environmental goods. In other words, the "optimal" level of pollution is currently too low as it doubtful that corporations are seeking to increase their costs of production by internalising even more externalities.

Equally, we can be sure that "too much" pollution *is where the company polluting the water has to pay too much to clean up the mess they make. It involves a judgement that costs to the company are somehow synonymous with costs to the community and therefore can be weighed against benefits to the community."* Such measures *"grant the highest decision-making power over environmental quality to those who currently make production decisions. A market system gives power to those most able to pay. Corporations and firms, rather than citizens or environmentalists, will have the choice about whether to pollute (and pay the charges or buy credits to do so)."* [Sharon Beder, **Global Spin**, p. 104]

The surreal notion of "too much" clean environment does indicate another key problem with this approach, namely its confusion of need and demand with **effective** demand. The fact is that people may desire a clean environment, but they may not be able to afford to pay for it on the market. In a similar way, there can be "too much" food while people are starving to death simply because people cannot afford to pay for it (there is no effective demand for food, but an obvious pressing need). Much the same can be said of environment goods. A lack of demand for a resource today does **not** mean it is not valued by individuals nor does it mean that it will not be valued in the future. However, in the short-term focus produced by the market such goods will be long-gone, replaced by more profitable investments.

The underlying assumption is that a clean environment is a luxury which we must purchase from property owners rather than a right we have as human beings. Even if we assume the flawed concept of self-ownership, the principle upon which defenders of capitalism tend to justify their system, the principle should be that our ownership rights in our bodies excludes it being harmed by the actions of others. In other words, a clean environment should be a basic right for all. Privatising the environment goes directly against this basic ecological insight.

The state's environmental record **has** often been terrible, particularly as its bureaucrats have been influenced by private interest groups when formulating and implementing environmental policies. The state is far more likely to be "captured" by capitalist interests than by environmental groups or even the general community. Moreover, its bureaucrats have all too often tended to weight the costs and benefits of specific projects in such a way as to ensure that any really desired ones will go ahead, regardless of what local people want or what the environmental impact will really be. Such projects, needless to say, will almost always have powerful economic interests behind them and will seek to ensure that "development" which fosters economic growth is pursued. This should be unsurprising. If we assume, as "market advocates" do, that state officials seek to further their own interests then classes with the most economic wealth are most likely to be able to do that the best. That the state will reflect the interests of those with most private property and marginalise the property-less should, therefore, come as no surprise.

Yet the state is not immune to social pressure from the general public or the reality of environmental degradation. This is proved, in its own way, by the rise of corporate PR, lobbying and think-tanks into multi-million pound industries. So while the supporters of the market stress its ability to change in the face of consumer demand, their view of the alternatives is extremely static and narrow. They fail, unsurprisingly, to consider the possibility of alternative forms of social organisation. Moreover, they also fail to mention that popular struggles can influence the state by means of direct action. For them, state officials will always pursue their own private interests, irrespective of popular pressures and social struggles (or, for that matter, the impact of corporate lobbying). While it is possible that the state will favour specific interests and policies, it does not mean that it cannot be forced to consider wider ones by the general public (until such time as it can be abolished, of course).

As we discussed in section D.1.5, the fact the state can be pressured by the general public is precisely why certain of its secondary functions have been under attack by corporations and the wealthy (a task which their well-funded think-tanks provide the rationales for). If all this is the case (and it is), then why expect cutting out the middle-person by privatising nature to improve matters? By its own logic, therefore, privatising nature is hardly going to produce a better environment as it is unlikely that corporations would fund policies which would result in more costs for themselves and less access to valuable natural resources. As free market environmentalism is premised on economic solutions to ecological problems and assumes that economic agents will act in ways which maximise their own benefit, such an obvious conclusion should come naturally to its advocates. For some reason, it does not.

Ultimately, privatising nature rests on the ridiculous notion that a clean environment is a privilege which we must buy rather than a right. Under "free market environmentalism" private property is assumed to be the fundamental right while there is no right to a clean and sustainable environment. In other words, the interests of property owners are considered the most important factor and the rest of us are left with the possibility of asking them for certain environmental goods which they may supply if they make a profit from so doing. This prioritisation and categorisation is by no means obvious and uncontroversial. Surely the right to a clean and liveable environment is more fundamental than those associated with property? If we assume this then the reduction of pollution, soil erosion, and so forth are not goods for which we must pay but rather rights to which we are entitled. In other words, protecting species and ecosystems as well as preventing avoidable deaths and illnesses are fundamental issues which simply transcend the market. Being asked to put a price on nature and people is, at best, meaningless, or, at worst, degrading. It suggests that the person simply does not understand why these things are important.

But why should we be surprised? After all, private property bases itself on the notion that we must buy access to land and other resources required for a fully human life. Why should a clean environment and a healthy body be any different? Yet again, we see the derived rights (namely private property) trumping the fundamental base right (namely the right of self-ownership which should automatically exclude harm by pollution). That this happens so consistently should not come as too great a surprise, given that the theory was invented to justify the appropriation of the fruits of the worker's labour by the property owner (see section B.4.2). Why should we be surprised that this is now being used to appropriate the rights of individuals to a clean environment and turn it into yet another means of expropriating them from their birthrights?

E.3.2 How does economic power contribute to the ecological crisis?

So far in this section we have discussed why markets fail to allocate environmental resources. This is due to information blocks and costs, lack of fully internalised prices (externalities) and the existence of public goods. Individual choices are shaped by the information available to them about the consequences of their actions, and the price mechanism blocks essential aspects of this and so information is usually partial at best within the market. Worse, it is usually distorted by advertising and the media as well as corporate and government spin and PR. Local knowledge is undermined by market power, leading to unsustainable practices to reap maximum short term profits. Profits as the only decision making criteria also leads to environmental destruction as something which may be ecologically essential may not be economically viable. All this means that the price of a good cannot indicate its environmental impact and so that market failure is pervasive in the environmental area. Moreover, capitalism is as unlikely to produce the fair distribution of environmental goods any more than any other good or resource due to differences in income and so demand (particularly as it takes the existing distribution of wealth as the starting point). The reality of our environmental problems provides ample evidence for this analysis.

During this discussion we have touched upon another key issue, namely how wealth can affect how environmental and other externalities are produced and dealt with in a capitalist system. Here we extend our critique by addressing an issue we have deliberately ignored until now, namely the distribution of wealth and its resulting economic power. The importance of this factor cannot be stressed too much, as "market advocates" at best downplay it or, at worse, ignore it or deny it exists. However, it plays the same role in environmental matters as it does in, say, evaluating individual freedom within capitalism. Once we factor in economic power the obvious conclusion is the market based solutions to the environment will result in, as with freedom, people selling it simply to survive under capitalism (as we discussed in section B.4, for example).

It could be argued that strictly enforcing property rights so that polluters can be sued for any damages made will solve the problem of externalities. If someone suffered pollution damage on their property which they had not consented to then they could issue a lawsuit in order to get the polluter to pay compensation for the damage they have done. This could force polluters to internalise the costs of pollution and so the threat of lawsuits can be used as an incentive to avoid polluting others.

While this approach could be considered as **part** of any solution to environmental problems under capitalism, the sad fact is it ignores the realities of the capitalist economy. The key phrase here is "not consented to" as it means that pollution would be fine if the others agree to it (in return, say, for money). This has obvious implications for the ability of capitalism to reduce pollution. For just as working class people "consent" to hierarchy within the workplace in return for access to the means of life, so to would they "consent" to pollution. In other words, the notion that pollution can be stopped by means of private property and lawsuits ignores the issue of class and economic inequality. Once these are factored in, it soon becomes clear that people may put up with externalities imposed upon them simply because of economic necessity and the pressure big business can inflict.

The first area to discuss is inequalities in wealth and income. Not all economic actors have equal resources. Corporations and the wealthy have far greater resources at their disposal and can spend millions of pounds in producing PR and advertising (propaganda), fighting court cases, influencing the political process, funding "experts" and think-tanks, and, if need be, fighting strikes and protests. Companies can use *"a mix of cover-up, publicity campaigns and legal manoeuvres to continue operations unimpeded."* They can go to court to try and *"block more stringent pollution controls."* [David Watson, **Against the Megamachine**, p. 56] Also while, in principle, the legal system offers equal protection to all in reality, wealthy firms and individuals have more resources than members of the general public. This means that they can employ large numbers of lawyers and draw out litigation procedures for years, if not decades.

This can be seen around us today. Unsurprisingly, the groups which bear a disproportionate share of environmental burdens are the poorest ones. Those at the bottom of the social hierarchy have less resources available to fight for their rights. They may not be aware of their rights in specific situations and not organised enough to resist. This, of course, explains why companies spend so much time attacking unions and other forms of collective organisation which change that situation. Moreover as well as being less willing to sue, those on lower incomes may be more willing to be bought-off due to their economic situation. After all, tolerating pollution in return for some money is more tempting when you are struggling to make ends meet.

Then there is the issue of effective demand. Simply put, allocation of resources on the market is based on money and not need. If more money can be made in, say, meeting the consumption demands of the west rather than the needs of local people then the market will "efficiently" allocate resources away from the latter to the former regardless of the social and ecological impact. Take the example of Biofuels which have been presented by some as a means of fuelling cars in a less environmentally destructive way. Yet this brings people and cars into direct competition over the most "efficient" (i.e. most profitable) use of land. Unfortunately, effective demand is on the side of cars as their owners usually live in the developed countries. This leads to a situation where land is turned from producing food to producing biofuels, the net effect of which is to reduce supply of food, increase its price and so produce an increased likelihood of starvation. It also gives more economic incentive to destroy rainforests and other fragile eco-systems in order to produce more biofuel for the market.

Green socialist John O'Neill simply states the obvious:

> "[The] treatment of efficiency as if it were logically independent of distribution is at best misleading, for the determination of efficiency already presupposes a given distribution of rights ... [A specific outcome] is always relative to an initial starting point.... If property rights are changed so also is what is efficient. Hence, the opposition between distributional and efficiency criteria is misleading. Existing costs and benefits themselves are the product of a given distribution of property rights. Since costs are not independent of rights they cannot guide the allocation of rights. Different initial distributions entail differences in whose preferences are to count. Environmental conflicts are often about who has rights to environment goods, and hence who is to bear the costs and who is to bear the benefits.... Hence, environmental policy and resource decision-making cannot avoid making normative choices which include questions of resource distribution and the relationships between conflicting rights claims.... The monetary value of a 'negative externality' depends on social institutions and distributional conflicts – willing to pay measures, actual or hypothetical, consider preferences of the higher income groups [as] more important than those of lower ones. If the people damaged are poor, the monetary measure of the cost of damage will be lower – 'the poor sell cheap.'" [**Markets, Deliberation and Environment**, pp. 58-9]

Economic power also impacts on the types of contracts people make. It does not take too much imagination to envision the possibility that companies may make signing waivers that release it from liability a condition for working there. This could mean, for example, a firm would invest (or threaten to move production) only on condition that the local community and its workers sign a form waiving the firm of any responsibility for damages that may result from working there or from its production process. In the face of economic necessity, the workers may be desperate enough to take the jobs and sign the waivers. The same would be the case for local communities, who tolerate the environmental destruction they are subjected to simply to ensure that their economy remains viable. This already happens, with some companies including a clause in their contracts which states the employee cannot join a union.

Then there is the threat of legal action by companies. *"Every year,"* records green Sharon Beder, *"thousands of Americans are sued for speaking out against governments and corporations. Multi-million dollar law suits are being filed against individual citizens and groups for circulating petitions, writing to public officials, speaking at, or even just attending, public meetings, organising a boycott and engaging in peaceful demonstrations."* This trend has spread to other countries and the intent is the same: to silence opposition and undermine campaigns. This tactic is called a SLAPP (for ***"Strategic Lawsuits Against Public Participation"***) and is a civil court action which does not seek to win compensation but rather aims *"to harass, intimidate and distract their opponents … They win the political battle, even when they lose the court case, if their victims and those associated with them stop speaking out against them."* This is an example of economic power at work, for the cost to a firm is just part of doing business but could bankrupt an individual or environmental organisation. In this way *"the legal system best serves those who have large financial resources at their disposal"* as such cases take *"an average of three years to be settled, and even if the person sued wins, can cost tens of thousands of dollars in legal fees. Emotional stress, disillusionment, diversion of time and energy, and even divisions within families, communities and groups can also result."* [**Global Spin**, pp. 63-7]

A SLAPP usually deters those already involved from continuing to freely participate in debate and protest as well as deterring others from joining in. The threat of a court case in the face of economic power usually ensures that SLAPPS do not go to trial and so its objective of scaring off potential opponents usually works quickly. The reason can be seen from the one case in which a SLAPP backfired, namely the McLibel trial. After successfully forcing apologies from major UK media outlets like the BBC, Channel 4 and the Guardian by threatening legal action for critical reporting of the company, McDonald's turned its attention to the small eco-anarchist group London Greenpeace (which is not affiliated with Greenpeace International). This group had produced a leaflet called *"What's Wrong with McDonald's"* and the company sent spies to its meetings to identify people to sue. Two of the anarchists refused to be intimidated and called McDonald's bluff. Representing themselves in court, the two unemployed activists started the longest trial in UK history. After three years and a cost of around £10 million, the trial judge found that some of the claims were untrue (significantly, McDonald's had successfully petitioned the judge not to have a jury for the case, arguing that the issues were too complex for the public to understand). While the case was a public relations disaster for the company, McDonald's keeps going as before using the working practices exposed in the trial and remains one of the world's largest corporations confident that few people would have the time and resources to fight SLAPPs (although the corporation may now think twice before suing anarchists!).

Furthermore, companies are known to gather lists of known "trouble-makers" These "black lists" of people who could cause companies "trouble" (i.e., by union organising or suing employers over "property rights" issues) would often ensure employee "loyalty," particularly if new jobs need references. Under wage labour, causing one's employer "problems" can make one's current and future position difficult. Being black-listed would mean no job, no wages, and little chance of being re-employed. This would be the result of continually suing in defence of one's property rights – assuming, of course, that one had the time and money necessary to sue in the first place. Hence working-class people are in a weak position to defend their rights under capitalism due to the power of employers both within and without the workplace. All these are strong incentives **not** to rock the boat, particularly if employees have signed a contract ensuring that they will be fired if they discuss company business with others (lawyers, unions, media, etc.).

Economic power producing terrible contracts does not affect just labour, it also effects smaller capitalists as well. As we discussed in section C.4, rather than operating "efficiently" to allocate resources within perfect competition any real capitalist market is dominated by a small group of big companies who make increased profits at the expense of their smaller rivals. This is achieved, in part, because their size gives such firms significant influence in the market, forcing smaller companies out of business or into making concessions to get and maintain contracts.

The negative environmental impact of such a process should be obvious. For example, economic power places immense pressures towards monoculture in agriculture. In the UK the market is dominated by a few big supermarkets. Their suppliers are expected to produce fruits and vegetables which meet the requirements of the supermarkets in terms of standardised products which are easy to transport and store. The large-scale nature of the operations ensure that farmers across Britain (indeed, the world) have to turn their farms into suppliers of these standardised goods and so the natural diversity of nature is systematically replaced by a few strains of specific fruits and vegetables over which the consumer can pick. Monopolisation of markets results in the monoculture of nature.

This process is at work in all capitalist nations. In America, for example, the *"centralised purchasing decisions of the large restaurant chains and their demand for standardised products have given a handful of corporations an unprecedented degree of power over the nation's food supply ... obliterating regional differences, and spreading identical stores throughout the country ... The key to a successful franchise ... can be expressed in one world: 'uniformity.'"* This has resulted in the industrialisation of food production, with the *"fast food chains now stand[ing] atop a huge food-industrial complex that has gained control of American agriculture ... large multinationals ... dominate one commodity market after another ... The fast food chain's vast purchasing power and their demand for a uniform product have encouraged fundamental changes in how cattle are raised, slaughter, and processed into ground beef. These changes have made meatpacking ... into the most dangerous job in the United States ... And the same meat industry practices that endanger these workers have facilitated the introduction of deadly pathogens ... into America's hamburger meat."* [Eric Schlosser, **Fast Food Nation**, p. 5 and pp. 8-9]

Award winning journalist Eric Schlosser has presented an excellent insight in this centralised and concentrated food-industrial complex in his book **Fast Food Nation**. Schlosser, of course, is not alone in documenting the fundamentally anti-ecological nature of capitalism and how an alienated society has created an alienated means of feeding itself. As a non-anarchist, he does fail to draw the obvious conclusion (namely abolish capitalism) but his book does present a good overview of the nature of the process at work and what drives it. Capitalism has created a world where even the smell and taste of food is mass produced as the industrialisation of agriculture and food processing has lead to the product (it is hard to call it food) becoming bland and tasteless and so chemicals are used to counteract the effects of producing it on such a scale. It is standardised food for a standardised society. As he memorably notes: *"Millions of ... people at that very moment were standing at the same counter, ordering the same food from the same menu, food that tasted everywhere the same."* The Orwellian world of modern corporate capitalism is seen in all its glory. A world in which the industry group formed to combat Occupational Safety and Health Administration regulation is called *"Alliance for Workplace Safety"* and where the processed food's taste has to have the correct *"mouthfeel."* Unsurprisingly, the executives of these companies talk about *"the very essence of freedom"* and yet their corporation's *"first commandant is that only production counts ... The employee's duty is to follow orders. Period."* In this irrational world, technology will solve all our problems, even the ones it generates itself. For example, faced with the serious health problems generated by the industrialisation of meat processing, the meatpacking industry advocated yet more technology to "solve" the problems caused by the existing technology. Rather than focusing on the primary causes of meat contamination, they proposed irradiating food. Of course the firms involved want to replace the word *"irradiation"* with the phrase *"cold pasteurisation"* due to the public being unhappy with the idea of their food being subject to radiation.

All this is achievable due to the economic power of fewer and fewer firms imposing costs onto their workers, their customers and, ultimately, the planet.

The next obvious factor associated with economic power are the pressures associated with capital markets and mobility. Investors and capitalists are always seeking the maximum return and given a choice between lower profits due to greater environmental regulation and higher profits due to no such laws, the preferred option will hardly need explaining. After all, the investor is usually concerned with the returns they get on their investment, **not** in its physical condition nor in the overall environmental state of the planet (which is someone else's concern). This means that investors and companies interest is in moving their capital to areas which return most money, not which have the best environmental impact and legacy. Thus the mobility of capital has to be taken into account. This is an important weapon in ensuring that the agenda of business is untroubled by social concerns and environmental issues. After all, if the owners and managers of capital consider a state's environmental laws too restrictive then it can simply shift investments to states with a more favourable business climate. This creates significant pressures on communities to minimise environmental protection both in order to retain existing business and attract new ones.

Let us assume that a company is polluting a local area. It is usually the case that capitalist owners rarely live near the workplaces they own, unlike workers and their families. This means that the decision makers do not have to live with the consequences of their decisions. The "free market" capitalist argument would be, again, that those affected by the pollution would sue the company. We will assume that concentrations of wealth have little or no effect on the social system (which is a **highly** unlikely assumption, but never mind). Surely, if local people did successfully sue, the company would be harmed economically – directly, in terms of the cost of the judgement, indirectly in terms of having to implement new, eco-friendly processes. Hence the company would be handicapped in competition, and this would have obvious consequences for the local (and wider) economy.

This gives the company an incentive to simply move to an area that would tolerate the pollution if it were sued or even threatened with a lawsuit. Not only would existing capital move, but fresh capital would not invest in an area where people stand up for their rights. This – the natural result of economic power – would be a "big stick" over the heads of the local community. And when combined with the costs and difficulties in taking a large company to court, it would make suing an unlikely option for most people. That such a result would occur can be inferred from history, where we see that multinational firms have moved production to countries with little or no pollution laws and that court cases take years, if not decades, to process.

This is the current situation on the international market, where there is competition in terms of environment laws. Unsurprisingly, industry tends to move to countries which tolerate high levels of pollution (usually because of authoritarian governments which, like the capitalists themselves, simply ignore the wishes of the general population). Thus we have a market in pollution laws which, unsurprisingly, supplies the ability to pollute to meet the demand for it. This means that developing countries *are nothing but a dumping ground and pool of cheap labour for capitalist corporations. Obsolete technology is shipped there along with the production of chemicals, medicines and other products banned in the developed world. Labour is cheap, there are few if any safety standards, and costs are cut. But the formula of cost-benefit still stands: the costs are simply borne by others, by the victims of Union Carbide, Dow, and Standard Oil."* [David Watson, **Op. Cit.**, p. 44] This, it should be noted, makes perfect economic sense. If an accident happened and the poor actually manage to successfully sue the company, any payments will reflect their lost of earnings (i.e., not very much).

As such, there are other strong economic reasons for doing this kind of pollution exporting. You can estimate the value of production lost because of ecological damage and the value of earnings lost through its related health problems as well as health care costs. This makes it more likely that polluting industries will move to low-income areas or countries where the costs of pollution are correspondingly less

(particularly compared to the profits made in selling the products in high-income areas). Rising incomes makes such goods as safety, health and the environment more valuable as the value of life is, for working people, based on their wages. Therefore, we would expect pollution to be valued less when working class people are affected by it. In other words, toxic dumps will tend to cluster around poorer areas as the costs of paying for the harm done will be much less. The same logic underlies the arguments of those who suggest that Third World countries should be dumping grounds for toxic industrial wastes since life is cheap there

This was seen in early 1992 when a memo that went out under the name of the then chief economist of the World Bank, Lawrence Summers, was leaked to the press. Discussing the issue of *"dirty"* industries, the memo argued that the World Bank should *"be encouraging MORE migration of the dirty industries"* to Less Developed Countries and provided three reasons. Firstly, the *"measurements of the costs of health impairing pollution depends on the foregone earnings from increased morbidity and mortality"* and so *"pollution should be done in the country with the lowest cost, which will be the country with the lowest wages."* Secondly, *"that under-populated countries in Africa are vastly UNDER-polluted, their air quality is probably vastly inefficiently low compared to Los Angeles or Mexico City."* Thirdly, the *"demand for a clean environment for aesthetic and health reasons is likely to have very high income elasticity."* Concern over pollution related illness would be higher in a country where more children survive to get them. *"Also, much of the concern over industrial atmosphere discharge is about visibility impairing particulates … Clearly trade in goods that embody aesthetic pollution concerns could be welfare enhancing. While production is mobile the consumption of pretty air is a non-tradable."* The memo notes *"the economic logic behind dumping a load of toxic waste in the lowest wage country is impeccable and we should face up to that"* and ends by stating that the *"problem with the arguments against all of these proposals for more pollution"* in the third world *"could be turned around and used more or less effectively against every Bank proposal for liberalisation."* [**The Economist**, 08/02/1992]

While Summers accepted the criticism for the memo, it was actually written by Lant Pritchett, a prominent economist at the Bank. Summers claimed he was being ironic and provocative. **The Economist**, unsurprisingly, stated *"his economics was hard to answer"* while criticising the language used. This was because clean growth may be slower than allowing pollution to occur and this would stop *"helping millions of people in the third world to escape their poverty."* [15/02/1992] So not only is poisoning the poor with pollution economically correct, it is in fact required by morality. Ignoring the false assumption that growth, any kind of growth, always benefits the poor and the utter contempt shown for both those poor themselves and our environment, what we have here is the cold logic that drives economic power to move location to maintain its right to pollute our common environment. Economically, it is perfectly logical but, in fact, totally insane (this helps explain why making people "think like an economist" takes so many years of indoctrination within university walls and why so few achieve it).

Economic power works in other ways as well. A classic example of this at work can be seen from the systematic destruction of public transport systems in America from the 1930s onwards (see David St. Clair's **The Motorization of American Cities** for a well-researched account of this). These systems were deliberately bought by automotive (General Motors), oil, and tyre corporations in order to eliminate a less costly (both economically **and** ecologically) competitor to the automobile. This was done purely to maximise sales and profits for the companies involved yet it transformed the way of life in scores of cities across America. It is doubtful that if environmental concerns had been considered important at the time that they would have stopped this from happening. This means that individual consumption decisions will be made within a market whose options can be limited simply by a large company buying out and destroying alternatives.

Then there is the issue of economic power in the media. This is well understood by corporations, who fund PR, think-tanks and "experts" to counteract environmental activism and deny, for example, that humans are contributing to global warming. Thus we have the strange position that only Americans think that there is a debate on the causes of global warming rather than a scientific consensus. The actions of corporate funded "experts" and PR have ensured **that** particular outcome. As Sharon Beder recounts in her book **Global Spin: The Corporate Assault on Environmentalism**, a large amount of money is being spent on a number of sophisticated techniques to change the way people think about the environment, what causes the problems we face and what we can and should do about it. Compared to the resources of environmental and green organisations, it is unsurprising that this elaborate multi-billion pound industry has poisoned public debate on such a key issue for the future of humanity by propaganda and dis-information.

Having substantial resources available means that the media can be used to further an anti-green agenda and dominate the debate (at least for a while). Take, as an example, **The Skeptical Environmentalist**, a book by Bjørn Lomborg (a political scientist and professor of statistics at the University of Aarhus in Denmark). When it was published in 2001, it caused a sensation with its claims that scientists and environmental organisations were making, at best, exaggerated and, at worst, false claims about the world's environmental problems. His conclusion was panglossian in nature, namely that there was not that much to worry about and we can continue as we are. That, of course, was music to the ears of those actively destroying the environment as it reduces the likelihood that any attempt will be made to stop them.

Unsurprisingly, the book was heavily promoted by the usual suspects and, as a result received significant attention from the media. However, the **extremely** critical reviews and critiques it subsequently produced from expert scientists on the issues Lomborg discussed were less prominently reviewed in the media, if at all. That critics of the book argued that it was hardly an example of good science based on objectivity, understanding of the underlying concepts, appropriate statistical methods and careful peer review goes without saying. Sadly, the fact that numerous experts in the fields Lomborg discussed showed that his book was seriously flawed, misused data and statistics and marred by flawed logic and hidden value judgements was not given anything like the same coverage even though this information is far more important in terms of shaping public perception. Such works and their orchestrated media blitz provides those with a vested interest in the status quo with arguments that they should be allowed to continue their anti-environmental activities and agenda. Moreover, it takes up the valuable time of those experts who have to debunk the claims rather than do the research needed to understand the ecological problems we face and propose possible solutions.

As well as spin and propaganda aimed at adults, companies are increasingly funding children's education. This development implies obvious limitations on the power of education to solve ecological problems. Companies will hardly provide teaching materials or fund schools which educate their pupils on the **real** causes of ecological problems. Unsurprisingly, a 1998 study in the US by the Consumers Union found that 80% of teaching material provided by companies was biased and provided students with incomplete or slanted information that favoured its sponsor's products and views [Schlosser, **Op. Cit.**, p. 55] The more dependent a school is on corporate funds, the less likely it will be to teach its students the necessity to question the motivations and activities of business. That business will not fund education which it perceives as anti-business should go without saying. As Sharon Beder summarises, *"the infiltration of school curricula through banning some texts and offering corporate-based curriculum material and lesson plans in their place can conflict with educational objectives, and also with the attainment of an undistorted understanding of environmental problems."* [**Op. Cit.**, pp. 172-3]

This indicates the real problem of purely "educational" approaches to solving the ecological crisis, namely that the ruling elite controls education (either directly or indirectly). This is to be expected, as any capitalist elite must control education because it is an essential indoctrination tool needed to promote capitalist values and to train a large population of future wage-slaves in the proper habits of obedience to authority. Thus capitalists cannot afford to lose control of the educational system. And this means that such schools will not teach students what is really necessary to avoid ecological disaster: namely the dismantling of capitalism itself. And we may add, alternative schools (organised by libertarian unions and other associations) which used libertarian education to produce anarchists would hardly be favoured by companies and so be effectively black-listed – a real deterrent to their spreading through society. Why would a capitalist company employ a graduate of a school who would make trouble for them once employed as their wage slave?

Finally, needless to say, the combined wealth of corporations and the rich outweighs that of even the best funded environmental group or organisation (or even all of them put together). This means that the idea of such groups buying, say, rainforest is unlikely to succeed as they simply do not have the resources needed – they will be outbid by those who wish to develop wilderness regions. This is particularly the case once we accept the framework of economic self-interest assumed by market theory. This implies that organisations aiming to increase the income of individuals will be better funded than those whose aim is to preserve the environment for future generations. As recent developments show, companies can and do use superior resources to wage a war for hearts and minds in all aspects of society, starting in the schoolroom. Luckily no amount of spin can nullify reality or the spirit of freedom and so this propaganda war will continue as long as capitalism does.

In summary, market solutions to environmental problems under capitalism will always suffer from the fact that real markets are marked by economic inequalities and power.

E.3.3 Can capitalism's focus on short-term profitability deal with the ecological crisis?

In a word, no. This is another key problem associated with capitalism's ability to deal with the ecological crisis it helps create. Due to the nature of the market, firms are forced to focus on short-term profitability rather than long-term survival. This makes sense. If a company does not make money now, it will not be around later.

This, obviously, drives the creation of "externalities" discussed in previous sections. Harmful environmental effects such as pollution, global warming, ozone depletion, and destruction of wildlife habitat are not counted as "costs of production" in standard methods of accounting because they are borne by everyone in the society. This gives companies a strong incentive to ignore such costs as competition forces firms to cut as many costs as possible in order to boost short-term profits.

To give an obvious example, if a firm has to decide between installing a piece of costly equipment which reduces its pollution and continuing as it currently is, then it is more likely to do the latter. If the firm **does** invest then its costs are increased and it will lose its competitive edge compared to its rivals who do not make a similar investment. The "rational" decision is, therefore, not to invest, particularly if by externalising costs it can increase its profits or market share by cutting prices. In other words, the market rewards the polluters and this is a powerful incentive to maximise such activities. The market, in other words, provides incentives to firms to produce externalities as part their drive for short-term profitability. While this is rational from the firm's position, it is collectively irrational as the planet's ecology is harmed.

The short-term perspective can also be seen by the tendency of firms to under-invest in developing risky new technologies. This is because basic research may take years, if not decades, to develop and most companies are unwilling to take on that burden. Unsurprisingly, most advanced capitalist countries see such work funded by the state (as we noted in section D.8, over 50% of total R&D funding has been provided by the federal state in the USA). Moreover, the state has provided markets for such products until such time as markets have appeared for them in the commercial sector. Thus capitalism, by itself, will tend to under-invest in long term projects:

"in a competitive system you do **short-term planning only**.... Let's take corporate managers, where there's no real confusion about what they're doing. They are maximising profit and market share in the short term. In fact, if they were not to do that, they would no longer exist. Let's be concrete. Suppose that some automobile company, say General Motors, decides to devote their resources to planning for something that will be profitable ten years from now. Suppose that's where they divert their resources: they want to think in some long-term conception of market dominance. Their rivals are going to be maximising profit and power in the short term, and they're going to take over the market, and General Motors won't be in business. That's true for the owners and also for the managers. The managers want to stay managers. They can fight off hostile take-over bids, they can keep from being replaced, as long as they contribute to short-term profitability. As a result, long-term considerations are rarely considered in competitive systems." [Noam Chomsky, **Language and Politics**, p. 598]

This does not mean that firms will not look into future products nor do research and development. Many do (particularly if helped by the state). Nor does it imply that some industries do not have a longer-term perspective. It simply shows that such activity is not the normal state of affairs. Moreover, any such "long-term" perspective is rarely more than a decade while an ecological perspective demands much more than this. This also applies to agriculture, which is increasingly being turned into agribusiness as small farmers are being driven out of business. Short-termism means that progress in agriculture is whatever increases the current yield of a crop even if means destroying the sources of fertility in the long run in order to maintain current fertility by adding more and more chemicals (which run off into rivers, seep into the water table and end up in the food itself.

This kind of irrational short-term behaviour also afflicts capital markets as well. The process works in the same way Chomsky highlights. Suppose there are 3 companies, X, Y, and Z and suppose that company X invests in the project of developing a non-polluting technology within ten years. At the same time its competitors, Y and Z, will be putting their resources into increasing profits and market share in the coming days and months and over the next year. During that period, company X will be unable to attract enough capital from investors to carry out its plans, since investors will flock to the companies that are most immediately profitable. This means that the default position under capitalism is that the company (or country) with the lowest standards enjoys a competitive advantage, and drags down the standards of other companies (or countries). Sometimes though, capital markets experience irrational bubbles. During the dot.com boom of the 1990s, investors did plough money into internet start-ups and losses were tolerated for a few years in the expectation of high profits in the near future. When that did not happen, the stock market crashed and investors turned away from that market in droves. If something similar happened to eco-technologies, the subsequent aftermath may mean that funding essential for redressing our interaction with the environment would not be forthcoming until the memories of the crash had disappeared in the next bubble frenzy.

Besides, thanks to compound interest benefits far in the future have a very small present value. If $1 were left in a bank at 5% annual interest, it would be worth more than $2 million after 300 years. So if it costs $1 today to prevent ecological damage worth

$2 million in the 24th century then economic theory argues that our descendants would be better off with us putting that $1 in the bank. This would suggest that basing our responsibility to future generations on economics may not be the wisest course.

The supporter of capitalism may respond by arguing that business leaders are as able to see long-term negative environmental effects as the rest of us. But this is to misunderstand the nature of the objection. It is not that business leaders **as individuals** are any less able to see what's happening to the environment. It is that if they want to keep their jobs they have to do what the system requires, which is to concentrate on what is most profitable in the short term. Thus if the president of company X has a mystical experience of oneness with nature and starts diverting profits into pollution control while the presidents of Y and Z continue with business as usual, the stockholders of company X will get a new president who is willing to focus on short-term profits like Y and Z. As Joel Bakan stresses, managers of corporations *"have a legal duty to put shareholders' interests above all others ... Corporate social responsibility is thus illegal – at least when it is genuine."* Ones which *"choose social and environmental goals over profits – who try and act morally – are, in fact, immoral"* as their role in both the economy and economic ideology is to *"make much as much money as possible for shareholders."* [**The Corporation**, pp. 36-7 and p. 34]

In general, then, if one company tries to devote resources to develop products or processes that are ecologically responsible, they will simply be undercut by other companies which are not doing so (assuming such products or processes are more expensive, as they generally are as the costs are not inflicted on other people and the planet). While some products may survive in small niche markets which reflect the fact that many people are willing and able to pay more to protect their world, in general they will not be competitive in the market and so the ecologically damaging products will have the advantage. In other words, capitalism has a built-in bias toward short-term gain, and this bias – along with its inherent need for growth – means the planet will continue its free-fall toward ecological disaster so long as capitalism exists.

This suggests that attempts to address ecological problems like pollution and depletion of resources by calling for public education are unlikely to work. While it is true that this will raise people's awareness to the point of creating enough demand for environment-friendly technologies and products that they will be profitable to produce, it does not solve the problem that the costs involved in doing such research now cannot be met by a possible future demand. Moreover, the costs of such technology can initially be quite high and so the effective demand for such products may not be sufficient. For example, energy-saving light bulbs have been around for some time but have been far more expensive than traditional ones. This means that for those on lower-incomes who would, in theory, benefit most from lower-energy bills cannot afford them. Thus their short-term income constraints undermine long-term benefits.

Even if the research is completed, the market itself can stop products being used. For example, the ability to produce reasonably inexpensive solar photovoltaic power cells has existed for some time. The problem is that they are currently very expensive and so

there is a limited demand for them. This means that no capitalist wants to risk investing in a factory large enough to take advantage of the economies of scale possible. The net effect is that short-term considerations ensure that a viable eco-technology has been marginalised.

This means that no amount of education can countermand the effects of market forces and the short-term perspective they inflict on us all. If faced with a tight budget and relatively expensive "ecological" products and technology, consumers and companies may be forced to choose the cheaper, ecologically unfriendly product to make ends meet or survive in the market. Under capitalism, we may be free to choose, but the options are usually lousy choices, and not the only ones potentially available in theory (this is a key problem with green consumerism – see section E.5).

The short-termism of capitalism has produced, in effect, a system which is *"a massive pyramid scheme that will collapse somewhere down the line when all the major players have already retired from the game. Of course when the last of these hustlers cash in their chips, there won't be any place left to retire to."* [David Watson, **Op. Cit.**, p. 57]

E.4
Can laissez-faire capitalism protect the environment?

In a word, no. Here we explain why using as our example the arguments of a leading right-"libertarian."

As discussed in the last section, there is plenty of reason to doubt the claim that private property is the best means available to protect the environment. Even in its own terms, it does not do so and this is compounded once we factor in aspects of any real capitalist system which are habitually ignored by supporters of that system (most obviously, economic power derived from inequalities of wealth and income). Rather than the problem being too little private property, our environmental problems have their source not in a failure to apply market principles rigorously enough, but in their very spread into more and more aspects of our lives and across the world.

That capitalism simply cannot have an ecological nature can be seen from the work of right-"libertarian" Murray Rothbard, an advocate of extreme laissez-faire capitalism. His position is similar to that of other free market environmentalists. As pollution can be considered as an infringement of the property rights of the person being polluted then the solution is obvious. Enforce "absolute" property rights and end pollution by suing anyone imposing externalities on others. According to this perspective, only absolute private property (i.e. a system of laissez-faire capitalism) can protect the environment.

This viewpoint is pretty much confined to the right-"libertarian" defenders of capitalism and those influenced by them. However, given the tendency of capitalists to appropriate right-"libertarian" ideas to bolster their power much of Rothbard's assumptions and arguments have a wider impact and, as such, it is useful to discuss them and their limitations. The latter is made extremely easy as Rothbard himself has indicated why capitalism and the environment simply do not go together. While paying lip-service to environmental notions, his ideas (both in theory and in practice) are inherently anti-green and his solutions, as he admitted himself, unlikely to achieve their (limited) goals.

Rothbard's argument seems straight forward enough and, in theory, promises the end of pollution. Given the problems of externalities, of companies polluting our air and water resources, he argued that their roots lie not in capitalist greed, private property or the market rewarding anti-social behaviour but by the government refusing to protect the rights of private property. The remedy is simple: privatise everything and so owners of private property would issue injunctions and pollution would automatically stop. For example, if there were "absolute" private property rights in rivers and seas their owners would not permit their pollution:

> "if private firms were able to own the rivers and lakes ... then anyone dumping garbage ... would promptly be sued in the courts for their aggression against private property and would be forced by the courts to pay damages and to cease and desist from any further aggression. Thus, only private property rights will insure an end to pollution-invasion of resources. Only because rivers are unowned is there no owner to rise up and defend his precious resource from attack." [**For a New Liberty**, p. 255]

The same applies to air pollution:

> "The remedy against air pollution is therefore crystal clear.... The remedy is simply for the courts to return to their function of defending person and property rights against invasion, and therefore to enjoin anyone from injecting pollutants into the air.... The argument against such an injunctive prohibition against pollution that it would add to the costs of industrial production is as reprehensible as the pre-Civil War argument that the abolition of slavery would add to the costs of growing cotton, and therefore abolition, however morally correct, was 'impractical.' For this means that the polluters are able to impose all of the high costs of pollution upon those whose lungs and property rights they have been allowed to invade with impunity." [**Op. Cit.**, p. 259]

This is a valid point. Regulating or creating markets for emissions means that governments tolerate pollution and so allows capitalists to impose its often high costs onto others. The problem is that Rothbard's solution cannot achieve this goal as it ignores economic power. Moreover, this argument implies that the consistent and intellectually honest right-"libertarian" would support a zero-emissions environmental policy. However, as we discuss in the next section, Rothbard (like most right-"libertarians") turned to various legalisms like "provable harm" and ideological constructs to ensure that this policy would not be implemented. In fact, he argued extensively on how polluters **could** impose costs on other people under his system. First however, we need to discuss the limitations of his position before discussing how he later refuted his own arguments. Then in section E.4.2 we will indicate how his own theory cannot support the privatisation of water or the air nor the preservation of wilderness areas. Needless to say, much of the critique presented in section E.3 is also applicable here and so we will summarise the key issues in order to reduce repetition.

As regards the issue of privatising natural resources like rivers, the most obvious issue is that Rothbard ignores one major point: why **would** the private owner be interested in keeping it clean? What if the rubbish dumper is the corporation that owns the property? Why not just assume that the company can make more money turning the lakes and rivers into dumping sites, or trees into junk mail? This scenario is no less plausible. In fact, it is more likely to happen in many cases as there is a demand for such dumps by wealthy corporations who would be willing to pay for the privilege.

So to claim that capitalism will protect the environment is just another example of free market capitalists trying to give the reader what he or she wants to hear. In practice, the idea that extending property rights to rivers, lakes and so forth (if possible) will stop ecological destruction all depends on the assumptions used. Thus, for example, if it is assumed that ecotourism will produce more income from a wetland than draining it for cash crops, then, obviously, the wetlands are saved. If the opposite assumption is made, the wetlands are destroyed.

But, of course, the supporter of capitalism will jump in and say that if dumping were allowed, this would cause pollution, which would affect others who would then sue the owner in question. "Maybe" is the answer to this claim, for there are many circumstances where a lawsuit would be unlikely to happen. For example, what if the locals are slum dwellers and cannot afford to sue? What if they are afraid that their landlords will evict them if they sue (particularly if the landlords also own the polluting property in question)? What if many members of the affected community work for the polluting company and stand to lose their jobs if they sue? All in all, this argument ignores the obvious fact that resources are required to fight a court case and to make and contest appeals. In the case of a large corporation and a small group of even average income families, the former will have much more time and resources to spend in fighting any lawsuit. This is the case today and it seems unlikely that it will change in any society marked by inequalities of wealth and power. In other words, Rothbard ignores the key issue of economic power:

> "Rothbard appears to assume that the courts will be as accessible to the victims of pollution as to the owner of the factory. Yet it is not unlikely that the owner's resources will far exceed those of his victims. Given this disparity, it is not at all clear that persons who suffer the costs of pollution will be able to bear the price of relief.

> "Rothbard's proposal ignores a critical variable: power. This is not surprising. Libertarians [sic!] are inclined to view 'power' and 'market' as antithetical terms.... In Rothbard's discussion, the factory owner has no power over those who live near the factory. If we define power as comparative advantage under restricted circumstances, however, we can see that he may. He can exercise that power by stretching out the litigation until his opponent's financial resources are exhausted. In what is perhaps a worst case example, though by no means an unrealistic scenario,

the owner of an industry on which an entire community depends for its livelihood may threaten to relocate unless local residents agree to accept high levels of pollution. In this instance, the 'threat' is merely an announcement by the owner that he will move his property, as is his right, unless the people of the community 'freely' assent to his conditions ... There is no reason to believe that all such persons would seek injunctive relief ... Some might be willing to tolerate the pollution if the factory owner would provide compensation. In short, the owner could pay to pollute. This solution ... ignores the presence of power in the market. It is unlikely that the 'buyers' and 'sellers' of pollution will be on an equal footing." [Stephen L. Newman, **Liberalism at wits' end**, pp. 121-2]

There is strong reason to believe that some people may tolerate pollution in return for compensation (as, for example, a poor person may agree to let someone smoke in their home in return for $100 or accept a job in a smoke filled pub or bar in order to survive in the short term regardless of the long-term danger of lung cancer). As such, it is always possible that, due to economic necessity in an unequal society, that a company may pay to be able to pollute. As we discussed in section E.3.2, the demand for the ability to pollute freely has seen a shift in industries from the west to developing nations due to economic pressures and market logic:

"Questions of intergenerational equity and/or justice also arise in the context of industrial activity which is clearly life threatening or seriously diminishes the quality of life. Pollution of the air, water, soil and food in a way that threatens human health is obviously not sustainable, yet it is characteristic of much industrial action. The greatest burden of the life and health threatening by-products of industrial processes falls on those least able to exercise options that provide respite. The poor have risks to health **imposed** on them while the wealthy can afford to purchase a healthy lifestyle. In newly industrialising countries the poorest people are often faced with no choice in living close to plants which present a significant threat to the local population ... With the international trend toward moving manufacturing industry to the cheapest sources of labour, there is an increasing likelihood that standards in occupational health and safety will decline and damage to human and environmental health will increase." [Glenn Albrecht, "Ethics, Anarchy and Sustainable Development", pp. 95-118, **Anarchist Studies**, vol. 2, no. 2, pp. 107-8]

The tragedy at Bhopal in India is testimony to this process. This should be unsurprising, as there is a demand for the ability to pollute from wealthy corporations and this has resulted in many countries supplying it. This reflects the history of capitalism within the so-called developed countries as well. As Rothbard laments:

"[F]actory smoke and many of its bad effects have been known ever since the Industrial Revolution, known to the extent that the American courts, during the late – and as far back as the early – 19th century made the deliberate decision to allow property rights to be violated by industrial smoke. To do so, the courts had to – and did – systematically change and weaken the defences of property rights embedded in Anglo-Saxon common law ... the courts systematically altered the law of negligence and the law of nuisance to **permit** any air pollution which was not unusually greater than any similar manufacturing firm, one that was not more extensive than the customary practice of polluters." [**Op. Cit.**, p. 257]

Left-wing critic of right-"libertarianism" Alan Haworth points out the obvious by stating that "[i]n this remarkably – wonderfully – self-contradictory passage, we are invited to draw the conclusion that private property **must** provide the solution to the pollution problem from an account of how it clearly did **not**." In other words 19th-century America – which for many right-"libertarians" is a kind of "golden era" of free-market capitalism – saw a move "from an initial situation of well-defended property rights to a later situation where greater pollution was tolerated." This means that private property cannot provide a solution to the pollution problem. [**Anti-Libertarianism**, p. 113]

It is likely, as Haworth points out, that Rothbard and other free marketeers will claim that the 19th-century capitalist system was not pure enough, that the courts were motivated to act under pressure from the state (which in turn was pressured by powerful industrialists). But can it be purified by just removing the government and privatising the courts, relying on a so-called "free market for justice"? The pressure from the industrialists remains, if not increases, on the privately owned courts trying to make a living on the market. Indeed, the whole concept of private courts competing in a "free market for justice" becomes absurd once it is recognised that those with the most money will be able to buy the most "justice" (as is largely the case now). Also, this faith in the courts ignores the fact suing would only occur **after** the damage has already been done. It's not easy to replace ecosystems and extinct species. And if the threat of court action had a "deterrent" effect, then pollution, murder, stealing and a host of other crimes would long ago have disappeared.

To paraphrase Haworth, the characteristically "free market" capitalist argument that if X were privately owned, Y would almost certainly occur, is just wishful thinking.

Equally, it would be churlish to note that this change in the law (like so many others) was an essential part of the creation of capitalism in the first place. As we discuss in section F.8, capitalism has always been born of state intervention and the toleration of pollution was one of many means by which costs associated with creating a capitalist system were imposed on the general public. This is still the case today, with (for example) the **Economist** magazine happily arguing that the migration of dirty industries to the third world is "desirable" as there is a "trade-off between growth and pollution control." Inflicting pollution on the poorest sections of humanity is, of course, in their own best interests. As the magazine put it, "[i]f clean growth means slower growth, as it sometimes will, its human cost will be lives blighted by a poverty that would otherwise have been mitigated. That is why it is wrong for the World Bank or anybody else to insist upon rich-country standards of environmental practices in developing countries ... when a trade off between cleaner air and less poverty has to be faced, most poor countries will rightly want to tolerate more pollution than rich countries do in return for more growth." ["Pollution and the Poor", **The Economist**, 15/02/1992] That "poor countries" are just as state, class and hierarchy afflicted as "rich-country" ones and so it is **not** the poor who will be deciding to "tolerate" pollution in return for higher profits (to use the correct word rather than the economically correct euphemism). Rather, it will be inflicted upon them by the ruling class which runs their country. That members of the elite are willing to inflict the costs of industrialisation on the working class in the form of pollution is unsurprising to anyone with a grasp of reality and how capitalism develops and works (it should be noted that the magazine expounded this particular argument to defend the infamous Lawrence Summers memo discussed in section E.3.2).

Finally, let us consider what would happen if Rothbard's schema could actually be applied. It would mean that almost every modern industry would be faced with law suits over pollution. This would mean that the costs of products would soar, assuming production continued at all. It is likely that faced with demands that industry stop polluting, most firms would simply go out of business (either due to the costs involved in damages or simply because no suitable non-polluting replacement technology exists) As Rothbard here considers **all** forms of pollution as an affront to property rights, this also applies to transport. In other words, "pure" capitalism would necessitate the end of industrial society. While such a prospect may be welcomed by some deep ecologists and primitivists, few others would support such a solution to the problems of pollution.

Within a decade of his zero-emissions argument, however, Rothbard had changed his position and presented a right-"libertarian" argument which essentially allowed the polluters to continue business as usual, arguing for a system which, he admitted, would make it nearly impossible for individuals to sue over pollution damage. As usual, given a choice between individual freedom and capitalism Rothbard choose the latter. As such, as Rothbard himself proves beyond reasonable doubt, the extension of private property rights will be unable to protect the environment. We discuss this in the next section.

E.4.1 Will laissez-faire capitalism actually end pollution?

No, it will not. In order to show why, we need only quote Murray Rothbard's own arguments. It is worth going through his arguments to see exactly why "pure" capitalism simply cannot solve the ecological crisis.

As noted in the last section, Rothbard initially presented an argument that free market capitalism would have a zero-emissions policy. Within a decade, he had substantially changed his tune in an article for the right-"libertarian" think-tank the **Cato Institute**. Perhaps this change of heart is understandable once you realise that most free market capitalist propagandists are simply priests of a religion convenient to the interests of the people who own the marketplace.

Rothbard founded the think-tank which published this article along with industrialist Charles Koch in 1977. Koch companies are involved in the petroleum, chemicals, energy, minerals, fertilisers industries as well as many others. To advocate a zero-pollution policy would hardly be in the Institute's enlightened self-interest as its backers would soon be out of business (along with industrial capitalism as a whole).

Rothbard's defence of the right to pollute is as ingenious as it is contradictory to his original position. As will be discussed in section F.4, Rothbard subscribes to a "homesteading" theory of property and he utilises this not only to steal the actual physical planet (the land) from this and future generations but also our (and their) right to a clean environment. He points to "more sophisticated and modern forms of homesteading" which can be used to "homestead" pollution rights. If, for example, a firm is surrounded by unowned land then it can pollute to its hearts content. If anyone moves to the area then the firm only becomes liable for any excess pollution over this amount. Thus firms "can be said to have **homesteaded a pollution easement** of a certain degree and type." He points to an "exemplary" court case which rejected the argument of someone who moved to an industrial area and then sued to end pollution. As the plaintiff had voluntarily moved to the area, she had no cause for complaint. In other words, polluters can simply continue to pollute under free market capitalism. This is particularly the case as clean air acts would not exist in libertarian legal theory, such an act being "illegitimate and itself invasive and a criminal interference with the property rights of noncriminals." ["Law, Property Rights, and Air Pollution," pp. 55-99, **Cato Journal**, Vol. 2, No. 1, p. 77, p. 79 and p. 89]

In the last section, we showed how Rothbard had earlier argued that the solution to pollution was to privatise everything. Given that rivers, lakes and seas are currently **unowned** this implies that the current levels of pollution would be the initial "homesteaded" level and so privatisation will not, in fact, reduce pollution at all. At best, it may stop pollution getting worse but even this runs into the problem that pollution usually increases slowly over time and would be hard to notice and much harder to prove which incremental change produced the actual quantitative change.

Which leads to the next, obvious, problem. According to Rothbard you can sue provided that "the polluter has not previously established a homestead easement," "prove strict causality from the actions of the defendant ... beyond a reasonable doubt" and identify "**those who actually** commit the deed" (i.e. the employees involved, **not** the company). [**Op. Cit.**, p. 87] Of course, how do you know and prove that a specific polluter is responsible for a specific environmental or physical harm? It would be near impossible to identify which company contributed which particles to the smog which caused pollution related illnesses. Polluters, needless to say, have the right to buy-off a suit which would be a handy tool for wealthy corporations in an unequal society to continue polluting as economic necessity may induce people to accept payment in return for tolerating it.

Turning to the pollution caused by actual products, such as cars, Rothbard argues that "libertarian [sic!] principle" requires a return to **privity,** a situation where the manufacturers of a product are not responsible for any negative side-effects when it is used. In terms of transport pollution, the *"guilty polluter should be each individual car owner and not the automobile manufacturer, who is not responsible for the actual tort and the actual emission."* This is because the manufacturer does not know how the car will be used (Rothbard gives an example that it may not be driven but was bought *"mainly for aesthetic contemplation by the car owner"*!). He admits that *"the situation for plaintiffs against auto emissions might seem hopeless under libertarian law."* Rest assured, though, as *"the roads would be privately owned"* then the owner of the road could be sued for the emissions going *"into the lungs or airspace of other citizens"* and so *"would be liable for pollution damage."* This would be *"much more feasible than suing each individual car owner for the minute amount of pollutants he might be responsible for."* [**Op. Cit.**, p. 90 and p. 91]

The problems with this argument should be obvious. Firstly, roads are currently "unowned" under the right-"libertarian" perspective (they are owned by the state which has no right to own anything). This means, as Rothbard has already suggested, any new road owners would have already created a "homesteading" right to pollute (after all, who would buy a road if they expected to be sued by so doing?). Secondly, it would be extremely difficult to say that specific emissions from a specific road caused the problems and Rothbard stresses that there must be *"proof beyond reasonable doubt."* Road-owners as well as capitalist firms which pollute will, like the tobacco industry, be heartened to read that *"statistical correlation ... cannot establish causation, certainly not for a rigorous legal proof of guilt or harm."* After all, *"many smokers never get lung cancer"* and *"many lung cancer sufferers have never smoked."* [**Op. Cit.**, p. 92 and p. 73] So if illnesses cluster around, say, roads or certain industries then this cannot be considered as evidence of harm caused by the pollution they produce.

Then there is the question of who is responsible for the damage inflicted. Here Rothbard runs up against the contradictions within wage labour. Capitalism is based on the notion that a person's liberty/labour can be sold/alienated to another who can then use it as they see fit. This means that, for the capitalist, the worker has no claim on the products and services that labour has produced. Strangely, according to Rothbard, this alienation of responsibility suddenly is rescinded when that sold labour commits an action which has negative consequences for the employer. Then it suddenly becomes nothing to do with the employer and the labourer becomes responsible for their labour again.

Rothbard is quite clear that he considers that the owners of businesses are **not** responsible for their employee's action. He gives the example of an employer who hires an incompetent worker and suffers the loss of his wages as a result. However, *"there appears to be no legitimate reason for forcing the employer to bear the **additional** cost of his employee's tortious behaviour."* For a corporation *"does not act; only individuals act, and each must be responsible for his own actions and those alone."* He notes that employers are sued because they *"generally have more money than employees, so that it becomes more convenient ... to stick the wealthier class with the liability."* [**Op. Cit.**, p. 76 and p. 75]

This ignores the fact that externalities are imposed on others in order to maximise the profits of the corporation. The stockholders directly benefit from the "tortious behaviour" of their wage slaves.

For example, if a manager decides to save £1,000,000 by letting toxic waste damage to occur, then the owners benefit by a higher return on their investment. To state that it is the manager who must pay for any damage means that the owners of a corporation or business are absolved for any responsibility for the actions of those hired to make money for them. In other words, they accumulate the benefits in the form of more income but not the risks or costs associated with, say, imposing externalities onto others. That the "wealthier class" would be happy to see such a legal system should go without saying.

The notion that as long as *"the tort is committed by the employee in the course of furthering, even only in part, his employer's business, then the employer is also liable"* is dismissed as *"a legal concept so at war with libertarianism, individualism, and capitalism, and suited only to a precapitalist society."* [**Op. Cit.**, p. 74 and p. 75] If this principle is against "individualism" then it is simply because capitalism violates individualism. What Rothbard fails to appreciate is that the whole basis of capitalism is that it is based on the worker selling his time/liberty to the boss. As Mark Leier puts it in his excellent biography of Bakunin:

> *"The primary element of capitalism is wage labour It is this that makes capitalism what it is ... The employer owns and controls the coffee shop or factory where production takes place and determines who will be hired and fired and how things will be produced; that's what it means to be a 'boss.' Workers produce goods or services for their employer. Everything they produce on the job belongs to the capitalist: workers have no more right to the coffee or cars they produce than someone off the street. Their employer, protected by law and by the apparatus of the state, owns all they produce. The employer then sells the goods that have been produced and gives the workers a portion of the value they have created. Capitalists and workers fight over the precise amounts of this portion, but the capitalist system is based on the notion that the capitalist owns everything that is produced and controls how everything is produced."* [**Bakunin: The Creative Passion**, p. 26]

This is clearly the case when a worker acts in a way which increases profits without externalities. The most obvious case is when workers' produce more goods than they receive back in wages (i.e. the exploitation at the heart of capitalism – see section C.2). Why should that change when the action has an externality? While it may benefit the boss to argue that he should gain the profits of the worker's actions but not the costs it hardly makes much logical sense. The labour sold becomes the property of the buyer who is then entitled to appropriate the produce of that labour. There is no reason for this to suddenly change when the product is a negative rather than a positive. It suggests that the worker has sold both her labour and its product to the employer unless it happens to put her employer in court, then it suddenly becomes her's again!

And we must note that it is Rothbard's own arguments which are *"suited only to a precapitalist society."* As David Ellerman notes, the slave was considered a piece of property under the law **unless** he or she committed a crime. Once that had occurred, the slave became an autonomous individual in the eyes of the law and, as a result, could be prosecuted as an individual rather than his owner. This exposed a fundamental inconsistency *"in a legal system that treats the same individual as a thing in normal work and legally as a person when committing a crime."* Much the same applies to wage labour as well. When an employee commits a negligent tort then *"the tortious servant emerges from the cocoon of non-responsibility metamorphosed into a responsible human agent."* In other words, *"the employee is said to have stepped outside the employee's role."* [**Property and Contract in Economics**, p. 125, p. 128 and p. 133] Rothbard's argument is essentially the same as that of the slave-owner, with the boss enjoying the positive fruits of their wage slaves activities but not being responsible for any negative results.

So, to summarise, we have a system which will allow pollution to continue as this right has been "homesteaded" while, at the same time, making it near impossible to sue individual firms for their contribution to the destruction of the earth. Moreover, it rewards the owners of companies for any externalities inflicted while absolving them of any responsibility for the actions which enriched them. And Rothbard asserts that *"private ownership"* can solve *"many 'externality' problems"*! The key problem is, of course, that for Rothbard the *"overriding factor in air pollution law, as in other parts of the law, should be libertarian and property rights principles"* rather than, say, stopping the destruction of our planet or even defending the right of individual's not to die of pollution related diseases. [**Op. Cit.**, p. 91 and p. 99] Rothbard shows that for the defender of capitalism, given a choice between property and planet/people the former will always win.

To conclude, Rothbard provides more than enough evidence to disprove his own arguments. This is not a unique occurrence. As discussed in the next section he does the same as regards owning water and air resources.

E.4.2 Can wilderness survive under laissez-faire capitalism?

No. This conclusion comes naturally from the laissez-faire capitalist defence of private property as expounded by Murray Rothbard. Moreover, ironically, he also destroys his own arguments for ending pollution by privatising water and air.

For Rothbard, labour is the key to turning unowned natural resources into private property. As he put it, *"before the homesteader, no one really used and controlled – and hence owned – the land. The pioneer, or homesteader, is the man who first brings the valueless unused natural objects into production and use."* [**The Ethics of Liberty**, p. 49]

Starting with the question of wilderness (a topic close to many eco-anarchists' and other ecologists' hearts) we run into the usual problems and self-contradictions which befalls right-"libertarian" ideology. Rothbard states clearly that *"libertarian theory must invalidate [any] claim to ownership"* of land that has *"never been transformed from its natural state"* (he presents an example of an owner who has left a piece of his *"legally owned"* land untouched). If another person appears who **does** transform the land, it becomes *"justly owned by another"* and the original owner cannot stop her (and should the original owner *"use violence to prevent another settler from entering this never-used land and transforming it into use"* they also become a *"criminal aggressor"*). Rothbard also stresses that he is **not** saying that land must continually be in use to be valid property. [**Op. Cit.**, pp. 63-64] This is unsurprising, as that would justify landless workers seizing the land from landowners during a depression and working it themselves and we cannot have that now, can we?

Now, where does that leave wilderness? In response to ecologists who oppose the destruction of the rainforest, many supporters of capitalism suggest that they put their money where their mouth is and **buy** rainforest land. In this way, it is claimed, rainforest will be protected (see section B.5 for why such arguments are nonsense). As ecologists desire the rainforest **because it is wilderness** they are unlikely to "transform" it by human labour (its precisely what they want to stop). From Rothbard's arguments it is fair to ask whether logging companies have a right to "transform" the virgin wilderness owned by ecologists, after all it meets Rothbard's criteria (it is still wilderness). Perhaps it will be claimed that fencing off land "transforms" it (hardly what you imagine "mixing labour" with to mean, but never mind) – but that allows large companies and rich individuals to hire workers to fence in vast tracts of land (and recreate the land monopoly by a "libertarian" route). But as discussed in section F.4.1, fencing off land does not seem to imply that it becomes property in Rothbard's theory. And, of course, fencing in areas of rainforest disrupts the local eco-system – animals cannot freely travel, for example – which, again, is what ecologists desire to stop. Would Rothbard have accepted a piece of paper as "transforming" land? We doubt it (after all, in his example the wilderness owner **did** legally own it) – and so most ecologists will have a hard time in pure capitalism (wilderness is just not an option).

Moreover, Rothbard's "homesteading" theory actually violates his support for unrestricted property rights. What if a property owner **wants** part of her land to remain wilderness? Their desires are violated by the "homesteading" theory (unless, of course, fencing things off equals "transforming" them, which it apparently does not). How can companies provide wilderness holidays to people if they have no right to stop settlers (including large companies) "homesteading" that wilderness? Then there is the question of wild animals. Obviously, they can only become owned by either killing them or by domesticating them (the only possible means of "mixing your labour" with them). Does it mean that someone only values, say, a polar bear when they kill it or capture it for a zoo?

At best, it could be argued that wilderness would be allowed **if** the land was transformed first then allowed to return to the wild. This flows from Rothbard's argument that there is no requirement that land continue to be used in order for it to continue to be a person's property. As he stresses, *"our libertarian [sic!] theory holds that land needs only be transformed **once** to pass into private ownership."* [**Op. Cit.**, p. 65] This means that land could be used and then allowed to fall into disuse for the important thing is that once labour is mixed with the natural resources, it remains owned in perpetuity. However, destroying wilderness in order to recreate it is simply an insane position to take as many eco-systems are extremely fragile and will not return to their previous state. Moreover, this process takes a long time during which access to the land will be restricted to all but those the owner consents to.

And, of course, where does Rothbard's theory leave hunter-gatherer or nomad societies. They **use** the resources of the wilderness, but they do not "transform" them (in this case you cannot easily tell if virgin land is empty or being used). If a group of nomads find its traditionally used, but natural, oasis appropriated by a homesteader what are they to do? If they ignore the homesteaders claims he can call upon the police (public or private) to stop them – and then, in true Rothbardian fashion, the homesteader can refuse to supply water to them unless they pay for the privilege. And if the history of the United States and other colonies are anything to go by, such people will become "criminal aggressors" and removed from the picture.

As such, it is important to stress the social context of Rothbard's Lockean principles. As John O'Neill notes, Locke's labour theory of property was used not only to support enclosing common land in England but also as a justification for stealing the land of indigenous population's across the world. For example, the *"appropriation of America is justified by its being brought into the world of commerce and hence cultivation … The Lockean account of the 'vast wilderness' of America as land uncultivated and unshaped by the pastoral activities of the indigenous population formed part of the justification of the appropriation of native land."* [**Markets, Deliberation and Environment**, p. 119] That the native population was **using** the land was irrelevant as Rothbard himself noted. As he put it, the Indians *"laid claim to vast reaches of land which they hunted but which they did not transform by cultivation."* [**Conceived in Liberty**, vol. 1, p. 187]. This meant that *"the bulk of Indian-claimed land was not settled and transformed by the Indians"* and so settlers were *"at least justified in ignoring vague, abstract claims."* The Indian hunting based claims were *"dubious."* [**Op. Cit.**, vol. 2, p. 54 and p. 59] The net outcome, of course, was that the *"vague, abstract"* Indian claims to hunting lands were met with the concrete use of force to defend the newly appropriated (i.e. stolen) land (force which quickly reached the level of genocide).

So unless people bestowed some form of transforming labour over the wilderness areas then any claims of ownership are unsubstantiated. At most, tribal people and nomads could claim the wild animals they killed and the trails that they cleared. This is because a person would *"have to use the land, to 'cultivate' it in some way, before he could be asserted to own it."* This cultivation is not limited to *"tilling the soil"* but also includes clearing it for a house or pasture or caring for some plots of timber. [**Man, Economy, and State, with Power and Market**, p. 170] Thus game preserves or wilderness areas could **not** exist in a pure capitalist society. This has deep ecological implications as it automatically means the replacement of wild, old-growth forests with, at best, managed ones. These are **not** an equivalent in ecological terms even if they have approximately the same number of trees. As James C. Scott stresses:

*"Old-growth forests, polycropping, and agriculture with open-pollinated landraces **may** not be as productive, in the short run, as single-species forests and fields or identical hybrids. But they are demonstrably more stable,*

more self-sufficient, and less vulnerable to epidemics and environmental stress…. Every time we replace 'natural capital' (such as wild fish stocks or old-growth forests) with what might be termed 'cultivated natural capital' (such as fish farms or tree plantations), we gain ease of appropriation and in immediate productivity, but at the cost of more maintenance expenses and less 'redundancy, resiliency, and stability'…. Other things being equal … the less diverse the cultivated natural capital, the more vulnerable and nonsustainable it becomes. The problem is that in most economic systems, the external costs (in water or air pollution, for example, or the exhaustion of non-renewable resources, including a reduction in biodiversity) accumulate long before the activity becomes unprofitable in a narrow profit-and-loss sense." [**Seeing like a State**, p. 353]

Forests which are planned as a resource are made ecologically simplistic in order to make them economically viable (i.e., to reduce the costs involved in harvesting the crop). They tend to be monocultures of one type of tree and conservationists note that placing all eggs in one basket could prompt an ecological disaster. A palm oil monoculture which replaces rainforest to produce biofuel, for example, would be unable to support the rich diversity of wildlife as well as leaving the environment vulnerable to catastrophic disease. Meanwhile, local people dependent on the crop could be left high and dry if it fell out of favour on the global market.

To summarise, capitalism simply cannot protect wilderness and, by extension, the planet's ecology. Moreover, it is no friend to the indigenous population who use but do not "transform" their local environment.

It should also be noted that the underlying assumption behind this and similar arguments is that other cultures and ways of life, like many eco-systems and species, are simply not worth keeping. While lip-service is made to the notion of cultural diversity, the overwhelming emphasis is on universalising the capitalist model of economic activity, property rights and way of life (and a corresponding ignoring of the role state power played in creating these as well as destroying traditional customs and ways of life). Such a model for development means the replacement of indigenous customs and communitarian-based ethics by a commercial system based on an abstract individualism with a very narrow vision of what constitutes self-interest. These new converts to the international order would be forced, like all others, to survive on the capitalist market. With vast differences in wealth and power such markets have, it is likely that the net result would simply be that new markets would be created out of the natural 'capital' in the developing world and these would soon be exploited.

As an aside, we must note that Rothbard fails to realise – and this comes from his worship of capitalism and his "Austrian economics" – is that people value many things which do not, indeed cannot, appear on the market. He claims that wilderness is *"valueless unused natural objects"* for it people valued them, they would use – i.e. transform – them. But unused things may be of **considerable** value to people, wilderness being a classic example. And if something **cannot** be transformed into private property, does that mean people do not value it? For example, people value community, stress-free working environments, meaningful work – if the market cannot provide these, does that mean they do not value them? Of course not (see Juliet Schor's **The Overworked American** on how working people's desire for shorter working hours was not transformed into options on the market).

So it should be remembered that in valuing impacts on nature, there is a difference between use values (i.e. income from commodities produced by a resource) and non-use values (i.e., the value placed on the existence of a species or wilderness). The former are usually well-defined, but often small while the latter are often large, but poorly defined. For example, the Exxon Valdez oil spill in Alaska resulted in losses to people who worked and lived in the affected area of an estimated $300 million. However, the existence value of the area to the American population was $9 billion. In other words, the amount that American households were reportedly willing to pay to prevent a similar oil spill in a similar area was 30 times larger. Yet this non-use value cannot be taken into account in Rothbard's schema as nature is not considered a value in itself but merely a resource to be exploited.

Which brings us to another key problem with Rothbard's argument: he simply cannot justify the appropriation of water and atmosphere by means of his own principles. To show why, we need simply consult Rothbard's own writings on the subject.

Rothbard has a serious problem here. As noted above, he subscribed to a Lockean vision of property. In this schema, property is generated by mixing labour with unowned resources. Yet you simply cannot mix your labour with water or air. In other words, he is left with a system of property rights which cannot, by their very nature, be extended to common goods like water and air. Let us quote Rothbard on this subject:

> "it is true that the high seas, in relation to shipping lanes, are probably inappropriable, because of their abundance in relation to shipping routes. This is **not** true, however, of **fishing** rights. Fish are definitely not available in unlimited quantities, relatively to human wants. Therefore, they are appropriable…. In a free [sic!] society, fishing rights to the appropriate areas of oceans would be owned by the first users of these areas and then useable or saleable to other individuals. Ownership of areas of water that contain fish is directly analogous to private ownership of areas of land or forests that contain animals to be hunted … water can definitely be marked off in terms of latitudes and longitudes. These boundaries, then would circumscribe the area owned by individuals, in the full knowledge that fish and water can move from one person's property to another." [**Man, Economy, and State, with Power and Market**, pp. 173-4]

In a footnote to this surreal passage, he added that it "is rapidly becoming evident that air lanes for planes are becoming scare and, in a free [sic!] society, would be owned by first users."

So, travellers crossing the sea gain no property rights by doing so but those travelling through the air do. Why this should be the case is hard to explain as, logically, both acts "transform" the commons by "labour" in exactly the same manner (i.e. not at all). Why **should**

fishing result in absolute property rights in oceans, seas, lakes and rivers? Does picking a fruit give you property rights in the tree or the forest it stands in? Surely, at best, it gives you a property right in the fish and fruit? And what happens if an area of water is so polluted that there are no fish? Does that mean that this body of water is impossible to appropriate? How does it become owned? Surely it cannot and so it will always remain a dumping ground for waste?

Looking at the issue of land and water, Rothbard asserts that owning water is *"directly analogous"* to owning land for hunting purposes. Does this mean that the landowner who hunts cannot bar travellers from their land? Or does it mean that the sea-owner can bar travellers from crossing their property? Ironically, as shown above, Rothbard later explicitly rejected the claims of Native Americans to own their land because they hunted animals on it. The same, logically, applies to his arguments that bodies of water can be appropriated.

Given that Rothbard is keen to stress that labour is required to transform land into private property, his arguments are self-contradictory and highly illogical. It should also be stressed that here Rothbard nullifies his criteria for appropriating private property. Originally, only labour being used on the resource can turn it into private property. Now, however, the only criteria is that it is scarce. This is understandable, as fishing and travelling through the air cannot remotely be considered "mixing labour" with the resource.

It is easy to see why Rothbard produced such self-contradictory arguments over the years as each one was aimed at justifying and extending the reach of capitalist property rights. Thus the Indians' hunting claims could be rejected as these allowed the privatising of the land while the logically identical fishing claims could be used to allow the privatisation of bodies of water. Logic need not bother the ideologue when seeking ways to justify the supremacy of the ideal (capitalist private property, in this case).

Finally, since Rothbard (falsely) claims to be an anarchist, it is useful to compare his arguments to that of Proudhon's. Significantly, in the founding work of anarchism Proudhon presented an analysis of this issue directly opposite to Rothbard's. Let us quote the founding father of anarchism on this important matter:

> "A man who should be prohibited from walking in the highways, from resting in the fields, from taking shelter in caves, from lighting fires, from picking berries, from gathering herbs and boiling them in a bit of baked clay, – such a man could not live. Consequently the earth – like water, air, and light – is a primary object of necessity which each has a right to use freely, without infringing another's right. Why, then, is the earth appropriated? … [An economist] assures us that it is because it is not INFINITE. The land is limited in amount. Then … it ought to be appropriated. It would seem, on the contrary, that he ought to say, Then it ought not to be appropriated. Because, no matter how large a quantity of air or light any one appropriates, no one is damaged thereby; there always remains enough for all. With the soil, it is very different. Lay hold who will, or who can, of the sun's rays, the passing breeze, or the sea's billows; he has my

consent, and my pardon for his bad intentions. But let any living man dare to change his right of territorial possession into the right of property, and I will declare war upon him, and wage it to the death!" [**What is Property?**, p. 106]

Unlike Locke who at least paid lip-service to the notion that the commons can be enclosed when there is enough and as good left for others to use, Rothbard turn this onto its head. In his "Lockean" schema, a resource can be appropriated only when it is scarce (i.e. there is **not** enough and as good left for others). Perhaps it comes as no surprise that Rothbard rejects the ***"Lockean proviso"*** (and essentially argues that Locke was not a consistent Lockean as his work is *"riddled with contradictions and inconsistencies"* that have been *"expanded and purified"* by his followers. [**The Ethics of Liberty**, p. 22]).

Rothbard is aware of what is involved in accepting the Lockean Proviso – namely the existence of private property (*"Locke's proviso may lead to the outlawry of **all** private property of land, since one can always say that the reduction of available land leaves everyone else ... worse off"* [**Op. Cit.**, p. 240]). The Proviso **does** imply the end of capitalist property rights which is why Rothbard, and other right-"libertarians", reject it while failing to note that Locke himself simply assumed that the invention of money transcended this limitation. [C.B. MacPherson, **The Political Theory of Individualism**, pp. 203-20] As we discussed in section B.3.4, it should be stressed that this limitation is considered to be transcended purely in terms of material wealth rather than its impact on individual liberty or dignity which, surely, should be of prime concern for someone claiming to favour "liberty." What Rothbard failed to understand is that Locke's Proviso of apparently limiting appropriation of land as long as there was enough and as good for others was a ploy to make the destruction of the commons palatable to those with a conscience or some awareness of what liberty involves. This can be seen from the fact this limitation could be transcended at all (in the same way, Locke justified the exploitation of labour by arguing that it was the property of the worker who sold it to their boss – see section B.4.2 for details). By getting rid of the Proviso, Rothbard simply exposes this theft of our common birthright in all its unjust glory.

It is simple. Either you reject the Proviso and embrace capitalist property rights (and so allow one class of people to be dispossessed and another empowered at their expense) or you take it seriously and reject private property in favour of possession and liberty. Anarchists, obviously, favour the latter option. Thus Proudhon:

> *"Water, air, and light are **common** things, not because they are **inexhaustible**, but because they are **indispensable**; and so indispensable that for that very reason Nature has created them in quantities almost infinite, in order that their plentifulness might prevent their appropriation. Likewise the land is indispensable to our existence, – consequently a common thing, consequently unsusceptible of appropriation; but land is much scarcer than the other elements, therefore its use must be regulated, not for the profit of a few, but in the interest and for the security of all.*

> *"In a word, equality of rights is proved by equality of needs. Now, equality of rights, in the case of a commodity which is limited in amount, can be realised only by equality of possession ... From whatever point we view this question of property – provided we go to the bottom of it – we reach equality."* [**Op. Cit.**, p. 107]

To conclude, it would be unfair to simply quote Keynes evaluation of one work by von Hayek, another leading "Austrian Economist," namely that it *"is an extraordinary example of how, starting with a mistake, a remorseless logician can end up in bedlam."* This is only partly true as Rothbard's account of property rights in water and air is hardly logical (although it is remorseless once we consider its impact when applied in an unequal and hierarchical society). That this nonsense is in direct opposition to the anarchist perspective on this issue should not come as a surprise any more than its incoherence. As we discuss in section F, Rothbard's claims to being an "anarchist" are as baseless as his claim that capitalism will protect the environment.

E.5
Can ethical consumerism stop the ecological crisis?

No. At best, it can have a limited impact in reducing environmental degradation and so postpone the ecological crisis. At worst, it could accelerate that crisis by creating new markets and thus increasing growth.

Before discussing why and just so there is no misunderstanding, we must stress that anarchists fully recognise that using recycled or renewable raw materials, reducing consumption and buying "ecologically friendly" products and technologies **are** very important. As such, we would be the last to denounce such a thing. But such measures are of very limited use as solutions to the ecological problems we face. At best they can only delay, not prevent, capitalism's ultimate destruction of the planet's ecological base.

Green consumerism is often the only thing capitalism has to offer in the face of mounting ecological destruction. Usually it boils down to nothing more than slick advertising campaigns by big corporate polluters to hype band-aid measures such as using a few recycled materials or contributing money to a wildlife fund, which are showcased as "concern for the environment" while off camera the pollution and devouring of non-renewable resources goes on. They also engage in "greenwashing", in which companies lavishly fund PR campaigns to paint themselves "green" without altering their current polluting practices!

This means that apparently "green" companies and products actually are not. Many firms hire expensive Public Relations firms and produce advertisements to paint a false image of themselves as being ecologically friendly (i.e. perform "greenwashing"). This indicates a weakness of market economies – they hinder (even distort) the flow of information required for consumers to make informed decisions. The market does not provide enough information for consumers to determine whether a product **is** actually green or not – it just gives them a price supplemented by (often deliberately misleading) advertising designed to manipulate the consumer and present an appropriate corporate image. Consumers have to rely on other sources, many of which are minority journals and organisations and so difficult to find, to provide them with the accurate information required to countermand the power and persuasion of advertising and the work of PR experts. This helps explain why, for example, *"large agribusiness firms are now attempting, like Soviet commissars, to stifle criticism of their policies"* by means of *"veggie libel laws."* These laws, which in 2001 had been passed in 13 American states (*"backed by agribusiness"*) *"make it illegal to criticise agricultural commodities in a manner inconsistent with 'reasonable' scientific evidence. The whole concept of 'veggie libel' laws is probably unconstitutional; nevertheless, these laws remain on the books."* [Eric Schlosser, **Fast Food Nation**, p. 266]

We should not discount the impact of PR experts in shaping the way people see the world or decide to consume. A lot of resources are poured into corporate Public Relations in order to present a green image. *"In the perverse world of corporate public relations,"* note critics John Stauber and Sheldon Rampton, *"propagandising and lobbying **against** environmental protection is called 'environmental' or 'green' PR. 'Greenwashing' is a more accurate pejorative now commonly used to describe the ways that polluters employ deceptive PR to falsely paint themselves an environmentally responsible public image ... Today a virulent, pro-industry, **anti**-environmentalism is on the rise ... PR experts ... are waging and winning a war against environmentalists on behalf of corporate clients in the chemical, energy, food, automobile, forestry and mining industries."* A significant amount of cash is spent (an estimated $1 billion a year by the mid-1990s) *"on the services of anti-environmental PR professionals and on 'greenwashing' their corporate image."* [**Toxic Sludge is Good for You!**, p. 125] See the chapter called *"Silencing Spring"* in Stauber's and Rampton's book **Toxic Sludge is Good for You!** for a good summary of this use of PR firms.

Even apparently ecologically friendly firms like "The Body Shop" can present a false image of what they do. For example, journalist Jon Entine investigated that company in 1994 and discovered that only a minuscule fraction of its ingredients came from **Trade Not Aid** (a program claimed to aid developing countries). Entine also discovered that the company also used many outdated, off-the-shelf product formulas filled with non-renewable petrochemicals as well as animal tested ingredients. When Entine contacted the company he received libel threats and it hired a PR company to combat his story. [Stauber and Rampton, **Op. Cit.**, pp. 74-5] This highlights the dangers of looking to consumerism to solve ecological problems. As Entine argued:

> "The Body Shop is a corporation with the privileges and power in society as all others. Like other corporations it makes products that are unsustainable, encourages consumerism, uses non-renewable materials, hires giant PR and law firms, and exaggerates its environment policies. If we are to become a sustainable society, it is crucial that we have institutions ... that are truly sustainable. The Body Shop has deceived the public by trying to make us think that they are a lot further down the road to sustainability than they really are. We should ... no longer ... lionise the Body Shop and others who claim to be something they are not." [quoted by Stauber and Rampton, **Op. Cit.**, p. 76]

Even ignoring the distorting influence of advertising and corporate-paid PR, the fundamental issue remains of whether consumerism can actually fundamentally influence how business works. One environmental journalist puts the arguments well in his excellent book on "Fast Food" (from the industrialisation of farming, to the monopolisation of food processing, to the standardisation of food consumption). As he puts it corporations will *"sell free-range, organic, grass-fed hamburgers if you demand it. They will sell whatever sells at a profit."* [Eric Schlosser, **Op. Cit.**, p. 269] He complements this position by suggesting various regulations and some role for trade unions.

Which, of course, is true. It is equally true that we are not forced to buy any specific product, which is why companies spend so much in convincing us to buy their products. Yet even ignoring the influence of advertising, it is unlikely that using the market will make capitalism nicer. Sadly, the market rewards the anti-social activities that Schlosser and other environmentalists chronicle. As he himself notes, the *"low price of a fast food hamburger does not reflect its real cost ... The profits of the fast food chains have been made possible by the losses imposed on the rest of society."* [**Op. Cit.**, p. 261] This means that the idea that by using the market we can "reform" capitalism is flawed simply because even "good" companies have to make a profit and so will be tempted to cut costs, inflict them on third parties (such as workers, consumers and the planet). The most obvious form of such externalities is pollution. Such anti-social and anti-ecological behaviour makes perfect business sense as prices fall when costs are passed on to others in the form of externalities. Thus firms which employ debt-slaves in sweatshops while polluting the atmosphere in a third-world dictatorship will have lower costs and so prices than those employing unionised workers under eco-friendly regulations.

The amazing thing is that being concerned about such issues is considered as a flaw in economics. In fact, seeking the lowest price and ignoring the social and ecological impact of a product is *"considered virtuousness"* by the market and by economists for, as green economist E. F. Schumacher, pointed out *"[i]f a buyer refused a good bargain because he suspected that the cheapness of the goods in question stemmed from exploitation or other despicable practices (except theft), he would be open to criticism of behaving 'uneconomically' which is viewed as nothing less than a fall from grace. Economists and others are wont to treat such eccentric behaviour with derision if not indignation. The religion of economics has its own code of ethics, and the First Commandment is to behave 'economically.'"* [**Small is Beautiful**, p. 30] And, of course, such a consumer would face numerous competitors who will happily take advantage of such activities.

Then there is the issue of how the market system hides much more information than it gives (a factor we will return to in section I.1.2). Under the price system, customers have no way of knowing the ecological (or social) impact of the products they buy. All they have is a price and that simply does not indicate how the product was produced and what costs were internalised in the final price and which were externalised. Such information, unsurprisingly, is usually supplied **outside** the market by ecological activists, unions, customer groups and so on. Then there is the misinformation provided by the companies themselves in their adverts and PR campaigns. The skilfully created media images of advertising can easily swamp the efforts of these voluntary groups to inform the public of the facts of the social and environmental costs of certain products. Besides, any company has the threat of court action to silence their critics as the cost in money, resources, energy and time to fight for free speech in court is an effective means to keep the public ignorant about the dark side of capitalism.

This works the other way too. Simply put, a company has no idea whether you not buying a product is based on ethical consumption decisions or whether it is due to simple dislike of the product. Unless there is an organised consumer boycott, i.e. a collective campaign, then the company really has no idea that it is being penalised for its anti-ecological and/or anti-social actions. Equally, corporations are so interlinked that it can make boycotts ineffective. For example, unless you happened to read the business section on the day McDonalds bought a sizeable share in Pret-a-Manger you would have no idea that going there instead of McDonalds would be swelling the formers profits.

Ultimately, the price mechanism does not provide enough information for the customer to make an informed decision about the impact of their purchase and, by reducing prices, actively rewards the behaviour Schlosser condemns. After all, what is now "organic" production was just the normal means of doing it. The pressures of the market, the price mechanism so often suggested as a tool for change, ensured the industrialisation of farming which so many now rightly condemn. By reducing costs, market demand increased for the cheaper products and these drove the other, more ecologically and socially sound, practices out of business.

Which feeds into the issue of effective demand and income limitations. The most obvious problem is that the market is **not** a consumer democracy as some people have more votes than others (in fact, the world's richest people have more "votes" than the poorest billions, combined!). Those with the most "votes" (i.e. money) will hardly be interested in changing the economic system which placed them in that position. Similarly, those with the least "votes" will be more willing to buy ecologically destructive products simply to make ends meet rather than any real desire to do so. In addition, one individual's decision **not** to buy something will easily be swamped by others seeking the best deal, i.e. the lowest prices, due to economic necessity or ignorance. Money (quantity) counts in the market, not values (quality).

Then there is the matter of sourcing of secondary products. After all, most products we consume are made up of a multitude of other goods and it is difficult, if not impossible, to know where these component parts come from. Thus we have no real way of knowing whether your latest computer has parts produced in sweatshops in third-world countries nor would a decision not to buy it be communicated that far back down the market chain (in fact, the company would not even know that you were even **thinking** about buying a product unless you used non-market means to inform them and then they may simply dismiss an individual as a crank).

So the notion that consumerism can be turned to pressurising companies is deeply flawed. This is **not** to suggest that we become unconcerned about how we spend our money. Far from it. Buying greener products rather than the standard one does have an impact. It just means being aware of the limitations of green consumerism, particularly as a means of changing the world. Rather, we must look to changing how goods are produced. This applies, of course, to shareholder democracy as well. Buying shares in a firm rarely results in an majority at the annual meetings nor, even if it did, does it allow an effective say in the day-to-day decisions management makes.

Thus green consumerism is hindered by the nature of the market – how the market reduces everything to price and so hides the information required to make truly informed decisions on what to consume. Moreover, it is capable of being used to further ecological damage by the use of PR to paint a false picture of the companies and their environmental activities. In this way, the general public think things are improving while the underlying problems remain (and, perhaps, get worse). Even assuming companies are honest and do minimise their environmental damage they cannot face the fundamental cause of the ecological crisis in the "grow-or-die" principle of capitalism ("green" firms need to make profits, accumulate capital and grow bigger), nor do they address the pernicious role of advertising or the lack of public control over production and investment under capitalism. Hence it is a totally inadequate solution.

As green Sharon Beder notes, green marketing aims at *"increasing consumption, not reducing it. Many firms [seek] to capitalise on new markets created by rising environmental consciousness"* with such trends prompting *"a surge of advertisements and labels claiming environmental benefits. Green imagery was used to sell products, and caring for the environment became a marketing strategy"* and was a *"way of redirecting a willingness to spend less into a willingness to buy green products."* This means that firms can *"expand their market share to include consumers that want green products. Since manufacturers still make environmentally damaging products and retailers still sell non-green products on shelves next to green ones, it is evident that green marketing is merely a way of expanding sales. If they were genuinely concerned to protect the environment they would replace the unsound products with sound ones, not just augment their existing lines."* Moreover, green marketing *"does not necessarily mean green products, but false and misleading claims can be hard for consumers to detect"* while the *"most cynical marketers simply use environmental imagery to conjure up the impression that a product is good for the environment without making any real claims at all."* Ultimately, green consumerism *"reduces people to consumers. Their power to influence society is reduced to their purchasing power."* It *"does not deal with issues such as economic growth on a finite planet, the power of transnational corporations, and the way power is structured in our society."* [**Global Spin**, pp. 176-80]

Andrew Watson sums up green consumerism very eloquently as follows:

> *"green consumerism, which is largely a cynical attempt to maintain profit margins, does not challenge capital's eco-*

cidal accumulation, but actually facilitates it by opening a new market. All products, no matter how 'green', cause some pollution, use some resources and energy, and cause some ecological disturbance. This would not matter in a society in which production was rationally planned, but in an exponentially expanding economy, production, however 'green', would eventually destroy the Earth's environment. Ozone-friendly aerosols, for example, still use other harmful chemicals; create pollution in their manufacture, use and disposal; and use large amounts of resources and energy. Of course, up to now, the green pretensions of most companies have been exposed largely as presenting an acceptably green image, with little or no substance. The market is presented as the saviour of the environment. Environmental concern is commodified and transformed into ideological support for capitalism. Instead of raising awareness of the causes of the ecological crisis, green consumerism mystifies them. The solution is presented as an individual act rather than as the collective action of individuals struggling for social change. The corporations laugh all the way to the bank."
[**From Green to Red**, pp. 9-10]

"Ethical" consumerism, like "ethical" investment, is still based on profit making, the extraction of surplus value from others. This is hardly "ethical," as it cannot challenge the inequality in exchange and power that lies at the heart of capitalism nor the authoritarian social relationships it creates. Therefore it cannot really undermine the ecologically destructive nature of capitalism.

In addition, since capitalism is a world system, companies can produce and sell their non-green and dangerous goods elsewhere. Many of the products and practices banned or boycotted in developed countries are sold and used in developing ones. For example, Agent Orange (used to defoliate forests during the Vietnam War by the US) is used as an herbicide in the Third World, as is DDT. Agent Orange contains one of the most toxic compounds known to humanity and was responsible for thousands of deformed children in Vietnam. Ciba-Geigy continued to sell Enterovioform (a drug which caused blindness and paralysis in at least 10,000 Japanese users of it) in those countries that permitted it to do so. Many companies have moved to developing countries to escape the stricter pollution and labour laws in the developed countries.

Neither does green consumerism question why it should be the ruling elites within capitalism that decide what to produce and how to produce it. Since these elites are driven by profit considerations, if it is profitable to pollute, pollution will occur. Moreover, green consumerism does not challenge the (essential) capitalist principle of consumption for the sake of consumption, nor can it come to terms with the fact that "demand" is created, to a large degree, by "suppliers," specifically by advertising agencies that use a host of techniques to manipulate public tastes, as well as using their financial clout to ensure that "negative" (i.e. truthful) stories about companies' environmental records do not surface in the mainstream media.

Because ethical consumerism is based **wholly** on market solutions to the ecological crisis, it is incapable even of recognising a key **root**

cause of that crisis, namely the atomising nature of capitalism and the social relationships it creates. Atomised individuals ("soloists") cannot change the world, and "voting" on the market hardly reduces their atomisation. As Murray Bookchin argues, *"[t]ragically, these millions [of "soloists"] have surrendered their social power, indeed, their very personalities, to politicians and bureaucrats who live in a nexus of obedience and command in which they are normally expected to play subordinate roles.* **Yet this is precisely the immediate cause of the ecological crisis of our time** – *a cause that has its historic roots in the market society that engulfs us."* [**Toward an Ecological Society**, p. 81] This means that fighting ecological destruction today must be a **social** movement rather than one of individual consumption decisions or personalistic transformation. These can go on without questioning the ecocidal drive of capitalism which *"will insidiously simplify the biosphere (making due allowances for 'wilderness' reserves and theme parks), steadily reduce the organic to the inorganic and the complex to the simple, and convert soil into sand – all at the expense of the biosphere's integrity and viability. The state will still be an ever-present means for keeping oppressed people at bay and will 'manage' whatever crises emerge as best it can. Ultimately, society will tend to become more and more authoritarian, public life will atrophy."* [Bookchin, *"The Future of the Ecology Movement,"* pp. 1-20, **Which Way for the Ecology Movement?**, p. 14]

All this is not to suggest that individual decisions on what to consume are irrelevant, far from it. Nor are consumer boycotts a waste of time. If organised into mass movements and linked to workplace struggle they can be very effective. It is simply to point out that individual actions, important as they are, are no solution to **social** problems. Thus Bookchin:

"The fact is that we are confronted by a thoroughly irrational social system, not simply by predatory individuals who can be won over to ecological ideas by moral arguments, psychotherapy, or even the challenges of a troubled public to their products and behaviour…. One can only commend the individuals who by virtue of their consumption habits, recycling activities. and appeals for a new sensibility undertake public activities to stop ecological degradation. Each surely does his or her part. But it will require a much greater effort – and organised, clearly conscious, and forward-looking political **movement** *– to meet the basic challenges posed by our aggressively* **anti**-*ecological society.*

"Yes, we as individuals should change our lifestyles as much as possible, but it is the utmost short-sightedness to believe that that is all or even primarily what we have to do. We need to restructure the entire society, even as we engage in lifestyle changes and single-issue struggles against pollution, nuclear power plants, the excessive use of fossil fuels, the destruction of soil, and so forth. We must have a coherent analysis of the deep-seated hierarchical relationships and systems of domination, as well as class relationships and economic exploitation, that degrade people as well as the environment." ["The*

Ecological Crisis, Socialism, and the need to remake society," pp. 1-10, **Society and Nature**, vol. 2, no. 3, p. 4]

Using the capitalist market to combat the effects produced by that same market is no alternative. Until capitalism and the state are dismantled, solutions like ethical consumerism will be about as effective as fighting a forest fire with a water pistol. Such solutions are doomed to failure because they promote individual responses to social problems, problems that by their very nature require collective action, and deal only with the symptoms, rather than focusing on the cause of the problem in the first place. Real change comes from collective struggle, not individual decisions within the market place which cannot combat the cancerous growth principle of the capitalist economy. As such, ethical consumerism does not break from the logic of capitalism and so is doomed to failure.

E.6
What is the population myth?

The idea that population growth is the **key** cause of ecological problems is extremely commonplace. Even individuals associated with such radical green groups as **Earth First!** have promoted it. It is, however, a gross distortion of the truth. **Capitalism** is the main cause of both overpopulation **and** the ecological crisis.

Firstly, we should point out that all the "doomsday" prophets of the "population bomb" have been proved wrong time and time again. The dire predictions of Thomas Malthus, the originator of the population myth, have not come true, yet neo-Malthusians continue to mouth his reactionary ideas. In fact Malthus wrote his infamous *"Essay on the Principles of Population"* which inflicted his *"law of population"* onto the world in response to the anarchist William Godwin and other social reformers. In other words, it was explicitly conceived as an attempt to "prove" that social stratification, and so the status quo, was a "law of nature" and that poverty was the fault of the poor themselves, not the fault of an unjust and authoritarian socio-economic system. As such, the "theory" was created with political goals in mind and as a weapon in the class struggle (as an aside, it should be noted that Darwin argued his theory of natural selection was *"the doctrine of Malthus applied to the whole animal and vegetable kingdom."* [quoted by Peter Marshall, **Nature's Web**, p. 320] In other words, anarchism, indirectly, inspired the theory of evolution. Perhaps unsurprisingly, in the form of Social Darwinism this was also used against working class people and social reform).

As Kropotkin summarised, Malthus work was *"pernicious"* in its influence. It *"summed up ideas already current in the minds of the wealth-possessing minority"* and arose to combat the *"ideas of equality and liberty"* awakened by the French and American revolutions. Malthus asserted against Godwin *"that no equality is possible; that the poverty of the many is not due to institutions, but is a natural **law.**"* This meant he *"thus gave the rich a kind of scientific argument against the ideas of equality."* However, it was simply *"a pseudo-scientific"* assertion which reflected *"the*

secret desires of the wealth-possessing classes" and not a scientific hypothesis. This is obvious as technology has ensured that Malthus's fears are *"groundless"* while they are continually repeated. [**Fields, Factories and Workshops Tomorrow**, p. 77, p. 78 and p. 79]

That the theory was fundamentally ideological in nature can be seen from Malthus himself. It is interesting to note that in contrast, and in direct contradiction to his population "theory," as an economist Malthus was worried about the danger of **over-production** within a capitalist economy. He was keen to defend the landlords from attacks by Ricardo and had to find a reason for their existence. To do this, he attacked Say's Law (the notion that over-production was impossible in a free market economy). Utilising the notion of effective demand, he argued that capitalist saving caused the threat of over-production and it was the landlords luxury consumption which made up the deficit in demand this caused and ensured a stable economy. As Marxist David McNally points out, the *"whole of this argument is completely at odds with the economic analysis"* of his essay on population. According to that, the *"chronic … danger which confronts society is **underproduction** of food relative to people."* In his economics book, the world *"is threatened by **overproduction.** Rather than there being too little supply relative to demand, there is now too little demand relative to supply."* In fact, Malthus even went so far as to argue for the poor to be employed in building roads and public works! No mention of "excess" population there, which indicates well the ideological nature of his over-population theory. As McNally shows, it was the utility of Malthus's practical conclusions in his "Essay on the Principles of Population" for fighting the poor law and the right to subsistence (i.e. welfare provisions) which explained his popularity: *"he made classical economics an open enemy of the working class."* [*"The Malthusian Moment: Political Economy versus Popular Radicalism"*, pp. 62-103, **Against the Market**, p. 85 and p. 91]

So it is easy to explain the support Malthus and his assertions got in spite of the lack of empirical evidence and the self-contradictory utterances of its inventor. Its support rests simply in its utility as a justification for the inhuman miseries inflicted upon the British people by "its" ruling class of aristocrats and industrialists was the only reason why it was given the time of day. Similarly today, its utility to the ruling class ensures that it keeps surfacing every so often, until forced to disappear again once the actual facts of the case are raised. That the population myth, like "genetic" justifications for race-, class- and gender-based oppression, keeps appearing over and over again, even after extensive evidence has disproved it, indicates its usefulness to the ideological guardians of the establishment.

Neo-Malthusianism basically blames the victims of capitalism for their victimisation, criticising ordinary people for "breeding" or living too long, thus ignoring (at best) or justifying (usually) **privilege** – the social root of hunger. To put it simply, the hungry are hungry because they are excluded from the land or cannot earn enough to survive. In Latin America, for example, 11% of the population was landless in 1961, by 1975 it was 40%. Approximately 80% of all Third World agricultural land is owned by 3% of landowners. As anarchist George Bradford stresses, Malthusians *"do not consider the questions of land ownership, the history of colonialism, and where social power lies. So when the poor demand their rights,* the Malthusians see 'political instability' growing from population pressure." [**Woman's Freedom: Key to the Population Question**, p. 77] Bookchin makes a similar critique:

> "the most sinister feature about neo-Malthusianism is the extent to which it actively deflects us from dealing with the social origins of our ecological problems – indeed, the extent to which it places the blame for them on the victims of hunger rather than those who victimise them. Presumably, if there is a 'population problem' and famine in Africa, it is the ordinary people who are to blame for having too many children or insisting on living too long – an argument advanced by Malthus nearly two centuries ago with respect to England's poor. The viewpoint not only justifies privilege; it fosters brutalisation and degrades the neo-Malthusians even more than it degrades the victims of privilege." ["The Population Myth", pp. 30-48, **Which Way for the Ecology Movement?**, p. 34]

Increased population is not the cause of landlessness, it is the result of it. If a traditional culture, its values, and its sense of identity are destroyed, population growth rates increase dramatically. As in 17th- and 18th-century Britain, peasants in the Third World are kicked off their land by the local ruling elite, who then use the land to produce cash crops for export while their fellow country people starve. Like Ireland during the Potato Famine, the Third World nations most affected by famine have also been exporters of food to the developed nations. Malthusianism is handy for the wealthy, giving them a "scientific" excuse for the misery they cause so they can enjoy their blood-money without remorse. It is unwise for greens to repeat such arguments:

> "It's a betrayal of the entire message of social ecology to ask the world's poor to deny themselves access to the necessities of life on grounds that involve long-range problems of ecological dislocation, the shortcomings of 'high' technology, and very specious claims of natural shortages in materials, while saying nothing at all about the artificial scarcity engineered by corporate capitalism." [**The Ecology of Freedom**, p. 350]

In a country that is being introduced to the joys of capitalism by state intervention (the usual means by which traditional cultures and habits are destroyed to create a "natural system of liberty"), population soon explodes as a result of the poor social and economic conditions in which people find themselves. In the inner-city ghettos of the First World, social and economic conditions similar to those of the Third World give rise to similarly elevated birth rates. When ghetto populations are composed mostly of minorities, as in countries like the US, higher birth rates among the minority poor provides a convenient extra excuse for racism, "proving" that the affected minorities are "inferior" because they "lack self-control," are "mere animals obsessed with procreation," etc. Much the same was said of Irish Catholics in the past and, needless to say, such an argument ignores the fact that slum dwellers in, for example, Britain during the Industrial Revolution were virtually all white but still had high birth rates.

Population growth, far from being the cause of poverty, is in fact a result of it. There is an inverse relationship between per capita income and the fertility rate – as poverty decreases, so do the population rates. When people are ground into the dirt by poverty, education falls, women's rights decrease, and contraception is less available. Having children then becomes virtually the only survival means, with people resting their hopes for a better future in their offspring. Therefore social conditions have a major impact on population growth. In countries with higher economic and cultural levels, population growth soon starts to fall off. Today, for example, much of Europe has seen birth rates fall beyond the national replacement rate. This is the case even in Catholic countries, which one would imagine would have religious factors encouraging large families.

To be clear, we are **not** saying that overpopulation is not a very serious problem. Obviously, population growth **cannot** be ignored or solutions put off until capitalism is eliminated. We need to immediately provide better education and access to contraceptives across the planet as well as raising cultural levels and increasing women's rights in order to combat overpopulation **in addition to** fighting for land reform, union organising and so on. Overpopulation only benefits the elite by keeping the cost of labour low. This was the position of the likes of Emma Goldman and other radicals of her time:

> "Many working-class radicals accepted the logic that excessive numbers were what kept the poor in their misery. During the nineteenth century there were courageous attempts to disseminate birth-control information both to promote lower population and to make it possible for women to control their own reproductivity and escape male domination. Birth control was the province of feminism, radical socialism and anarchism." [Bradford, **Op. Cit.**, p. 69]

Unlike many neo-Malthusians Goldman was well aware that **social** reasons explained why so many people went hungry. As she put it, "if the masses of people continue to be poor and the rich grow ever richer, it is not because the earth is lacking in fertility and richness to supply the need of an excessive race, but because the earth is monopolised in the hands of the few to the exclusion of the many." She noted that the promotion of large families had vested interests behind it, although working class people "have learned to see in large families a millstone around their necks, deliberately imposed upon them by the reactionary forces in society because a large family paralyses the brain and benumbs the muscles of the masses … [The worker] continues in the rut, compromises and cringes before his master, just to earn barely enough to feed the many little mouths. He dare not join a revolutionary organisation; he dare not go on strike; he dare not express an opinion." ["The Social Aspects of Birth Control", **Anarchy! An Anthology of Emma Goldman's Mother Earth**, p. 135 and pp. 136-7] This support for birth control, it should be stressed, resulted in Goldman being arrested. Malthus, like many of his followers "opposed contraception as immoral, preferring to let the poor starve as a 'natural' method of keeping numbers down. For him, only misery, poverty, famine, disease, and war would keep population from expanding beyond the carrying capacity of the land." [Bradford, **Op. Cit.**, p. 69]

Unsurprisingly, Goldman linked the issue of birth control to that of women's liberation arguing that *"I never will acquiesce or submit to authority, nor will I make peace with a system which degrades woman to a mere incubator and which fattens on her innocent victims. I now and here declare war upon this system."* The key problem was that woman *"has been on her knees before the altar of duty imposed by God, by Capitalism, by the State, and by Morality"* for ages. Once that changed, the issue of population would solve itself for *"[a]fter all it is woman whom is risking her health and sacrificing her youth in the reproduction of the race. Surely she ought to be in a position to decide how many children she should bring into world, whether they should be brought into the world by the man she loves and because she wants the child, or should be born in hatred and loathing."* [**Op. Cit.**, p. 140 and p. 136]

Other anarchists have echoed this analysis. George Bradford, for example, correctly notes that *"the way out of the [ecological] crisis lies in the practical opening toward freedom of self-expression and selfhood for women that is the key to the destruction of hierarchy."* In other words, women's *"freedom and well-being are at the centre of the resolution to the population problem, and that can only be faced within the larger social context."* That means *"real participation in social decision-making, real health concerns, access to land, and the overthrow of patriarchal domination."* [**Op. Cit.**, p. 68 and p. 82] Bookchin makes the same point, noting that population growth rates have fallen in developed countries because *"of the **freedom** that women have acquired over recent decades to transcend the role that patriarchy assigned to them as mere reproductive factories."* [*"The Future of the Ecology Movement,"* pp. 1-20, **Which Way for the Ecology Movement?**, p. 19]

This means that an **increase** of freedom will solve the population question. Sadly, many advocates of neo-Malthusianism extend control over people from women to all. The advocates of the "population myth," as well as getting the problem wrong, also (usually) suggest very authoritarian "solutions" – for example, urging an increase in state power with a "Bureau of Population Control" to "police" society and ensure that the state enters the bedroom and our most personal relationships. Luckily for humanity and individual freedom, since they misconceive the problem, such "Big Brother" solutions are not required.

So, it must be stressed the "population explosion" is not a neutral theory, and its invention reflected class interests at the time and continual use since then is due to its utility to vested interests. We should not be fooled into thinking that overpopulation is the main cause of the ecological crisis, as this is a strategy for distracting people from the root-cause of both ecological destruction and population growth today: namely, the capitalist economy and the inequalities and hierarchical social relationships it produces. As such, those who stress the issue of population numbers get it backward. Poverty causes high birth rates as people gamble on having large families so that some children will survive in order to look after the parents in their old age. Eliminate economic insecurity and poverty, then people have less children.

Some Greens argue that it is impossible for **everyone** to have a high standard of living, as this would deplete available resources and place too much pressure on the environment. However, their use of statistics hides a sleight of hand which invalidates their

argument. As Bookchin correctly argues:

> *"Consider the issue of population and food supply in terms of mere numbers and we step on a wild merry-go-round that does not support neo-Malthusian predictions of a decade ago, much less a generation ago. Such typically neo-Malthusian stunts as determining the 'per capita consumption' of steel, oil, paper, chemicals, and the like of a nation by dividing the total tonnage of the latter by the national population, such that every man, women, and child is said to 'consume' a resultant quantity, gives us a picture that is blatantly false and functions as a sheer apologia for the upper classes. The steel that goes into a battleship, the oil that is used to fuel a tank, and the paper that is covered by ads hardly depicts the human consumption of materials. Rather, it is stuff consumed by all the Pentagons of the world that help keep a 'grow-or-die economy in operation – goods, I may add, whose function is to destroy and whose destiny is to be destroyed."* [*"The Population Myth"*, pp. 30-48, **Which Way for the Ecology Movement?**, pp. 34-5]

Focusing on averages, in other words, misses out the obvious fact we live in a highly unequal societies which results in a few people using many resources. To talk about consumption and not to wonder how many Rolls Royces and mansions the "average" person uses means producing skewed arguments. Equally, it is possible to have more just societies with approximately the same living standards with significantly **less** consumption of resources and **less** pollution and waste produced. We need only compare America with Europe to see this. One could point out, for example, that Europeans enjoy more leisure time, better health, less poverty, less inequality and thus more economic security, greater intergenerational economic mobility, better access to high-quality social services like health care and education, and manage to do it all in a far more environmentally sustainable way (Europe generates about half the CO2 emissions for the same level of GDP) compared to the US.

In fact, even relatively minor changes in how we work can have significant impact. For example, two economists at the Center for Economic and Policy Research produced a paper comparing U.S. and European energy consumption and related it to hours worked. They concluded that if Americans chose to take advantage of their high level of productivity by simply shortening the workweek or taking longer holidays rather than producing more, there would follow a number of benefits. Specifically, if the U.S. followed Western Europe in terms of work hours then not only would workers find themselves with seven additional weeks of time off, the US would consume some 20% less energy and if this saving was directly translated into lower carbon emissions then it would have emitted 3% less carbon dioxide in 2002 than in 1990 (this level of emissions is only 4% above the negotiated target of the Kyoto Protocol). If Europe followed IMF orthodoxy and increased working hours, this would have a corresponding negative impact on energy use and emissions (not to mention quality of life). [David Rosnick and Mark Weisbrot, **Are Shorter Work Hours Good for the Environment?**] Of course, any such choice is influenced by social institutions and pressures and, as such, part of a wider social struggle for change.

In other words, we must question the underlying assumption of the neo-Malthusians that society and technology are static and that the circumstances that produced historic growth and consumption rates will remain unchanged. This is obviously false, since humanity is not static. To quote Bookchin again:

"by reducing us to studies of line graphs, bar graphs, and statistical tables, the neo-Malthusians literally freeze reality as it is. Their numerical extrapolations do not construct any reality that is new; they mere extend, statistic by statistic, what is basically old and given.... We are taught to accept society, behaviour, and values as they **are**, *not as they should be or even* **could** *be. This procedure places us under the tyranny of the status quo and divests us of any ability to think about radically changing the world. I have encountered very few books or articles written by neo-Malthusians that question whether we should live under any kind of money economy at all, any statist system of society, or be guided by profit oriented behaviour. There are books and articles aplenty that explain 'how to' become a 'morally responsible' banker, entrepreneur, landowner, 'developer,' or, for all I know, arms merchant. But whether the whole system called capitalism (forgive me!), be it corporate in the west or bureaucratic in the east, must be abandoned if we are to achieve an ecological society is rarely discussed."* [**Op. Cit.**, p. 33]

It is probably true that an "American" living standard is not possible for the population of the world at its present level (after all, the US consumes 40% of the world's resources to support only 5% of its population). For the rest of the world to enjoy that kind of standard of living we would require the resources of multiple Earths! Ultimately, anything which is not renewable is exhaustible. The real question is when will it be exhausted? How? Why? And by whom? As such, it is important to remember that this "standard of living" is a product of an hierarchical system which produces an alienated society in which consumption for the sake of consumption is the new god. In a grow-or-die economy, production and consumption must keep increasing to prevent economic collapse. This need for growth leads to massive advertising campaigns to indoctrinate people with the capitalist theology that more and more must be consumed to find "happiness" (salvation), producing consumerist attitudes that feed into an already-present tendency to consume in order to compensate for doing boring, pointless work in a hierarchical workplace. Unless a transformation of values occurs that recognises the importance of **living** as opposed to **consuming,** the ecological crisis **will** get worse. It is impossible to imagine such a radical transformation occurring under capitalism and so a key aim of eco-anarchists is to encourage people to consider what they need to live enriched, empowering and happy lives rather than participate in the rat race capitalism produces (even if you do win, you remain a rat).

Nor it cannot be denied that developments like better health care, nutrition, and longer lifespans contribute to overpopulation and are made possible by "industry." But to see such developments as primary causes of population growth is to ignore the central role played by poverty, the disruption of cultural patterns, and the need for cheap labour due to capitalism. There are always elevated birth rates associated with poverty, whether or not medical science improves significantly (for example, during the early days of capitalism). "Industrialism" is in fact a term used by liberal Greens (even when they call themselves "deep") who do not want to admit that the ecological crisis cannot be solved without the complete overthrow of capitalism, pretending instead that the system can become "green" through various band-aid reforms. "Controlling population growth" is always a key item on such liberals' agendas, taking the place of "eliminating capitalism," which should be the centrepiece. *"Population control is substituted for social justice, and the problem is actually aggravated by the Malthusian 'cure',"* points out feminist Betsy Hartmann. [quoted by Bradford, **Op. Cit.**, p. 77]

After all, there **is** enough food to feed the world's population but its distribution reflects inequalities in wealth, power and effective demand (this is most obviously seen when food is exported from famine areas as there is no effective demand for it there, a sadly regular occurrence). The *"myth that population increases in places like the Sudan, for example, result in famine"* can only survive if we ignore *"the notorious fact that the Sudanese could easily feed themselves if they were not forced by the American-controlled World Bank and International Monetary Fund to grow cotton instead of grains."* [Bookchin, **Remaking Society**, p. 11] Hence the importance of class analysis and an awareness of hierarchy. We can hardly talk of "our" resources when those resources are owned by a handful of giant corporations. Equally, we cannot talk about "our" industrial impact on the planet when the decisions of industry are made by bosses and most of us are deliberately excluded from the decision making process. While it makes sense for the ruling elite to ignore such key issues, it is counter-productive for radicals to do so and blame "people" or their numbers for social and environmental problems:

"The most striking feature of such a way of thinking is not only that it closely parallels the way of thinking that is found in the corporate world. What is more serious is that it serves to deflect our attention from the role society plays in producing ecological breakdown. If 'people' as a **species** *are responsible for environmental dislocations, these dislocations cease to be the result of* **social** *dislocations. A mythic 'Humanity' is created – irrespective of whether we are talking about oppressed minorities, women, Third World people, or people in the First World – in which everyone is brought into complicity with powerful corporate elites in producing environmental dislocations. In this way, the social roots of ecological problems are shrewdly obscured ... [W]e can dismiss or explain away hunger, misery, or illness as 'natural checks' that are imposed on human beings to retain the 'balance of nature.' We can comfortably forget that much of the poverty and hunger that afflicts the world has its origins in the corporate exploitation of human beings and nature – in agribusiness and social oppression."* [**Op. Cit.**, pp. 9-10]

Looking at population numbers simply misses the point. As Murray Bookchin argues, this *"arithmetic mentality which disregards the social context of demographics is incredibly short-sighted. Once we accept without any reflection or criticism that we live in a 'grow-or-die' capitalistic society in which accumulation is literally a law of economic survival and competition is the motor of 'progress,' anything we have to say about population is basically meaningless. The biosphere will eventually be destroyed whether five billion or fifty million live on the planet. Competing firms in a 'dog-eat-dog' market must outproduce each other if they are to remain in existence. They must plunder the soil, remove the earth's forests, kill off its wildlife, pollute its air and waterways not because their intentions are necessarily bad, although they usually are ... but because they must simply survive. Only a radical restructuring of society as a whole, including its anti-ecological sensibilities, can remove this all commanding social compulsion."* [*"The Population Myth"*, pp. 30-48, **Op. Cit.**, p. 34] A sane society would not be driven by growth for the sake of growth and would aim to reduce production by reducing the average working week to ensure both an acceptable standard of living **plus** time to enjoy it. So it is not a case that the current industrial system is something we need to keep. Few anarchists consider a social revolution as simply expropriating current industry and running it more or less as it is now. While expropriating the means of life is a necessary first step, it is only the start of a process in which we transform the way we interact with nature (which, of course, includes people).

To conclude, as Bradford summarises the *"salvation of the marvellous green planet, our Mother Earth, depends on the liberation of women – and children, and men – from social domination, exploitation and hierarchy. They must go together."* [**Op. Cit.**, p. 68] By focusing attention away from the root causes of ecological and social disruption – i.e. capitalism and hierarchy – and onto their victims, the advocates of the "population myth" do a great favour to the system that creates mindless growth. Hence the population myth will obviously find favour with ruling elites, and this – as opposed to any basis for the myth in scientific fact – will ensure its continual re-appearance in the media and education.

Section F
Is "anarcho"-capitalism a type of anarchism?

Section F – Is "anarcho"-capitalism a type of anarchism? 478

F.1 Are "anarcho"-capitalists really anarchists? 481

F.2 What do "anarcho"-capitalists mean by freedom? 486
F.2.1 How does private property affect freedom? 488
F.2.2 Do "libertarian"-capitalists support slavery? 490

F.3 Why do "anarcho"-capitalists place little or no value on equality? 493
F.3.1 Why is this disregard for equality important? 497
F.3.2 Can there be harmony of interests in an unequal society? 499

F.4 What is the right-"libertarian" position on private property? ... 503
F.4.1 What is wrong with a "homesteading" theory of property? 506

F.5 Will privatising "the commons" increase liberty? 508

F.6 Is "anarcho"-capitalism against the state? 510
F.6.1 What's wrong with this "free market" justice? 511
F.6.2 What are the social consequences of such a system? 514
F.6.3 But surely market forces will stop abuses by the rich? 515
F.6.4 Why are these "defence associations" states? 518

F.7 How does the history of "anarcho"-capitalism show that it is not anarchist? 519
F.7.1 Are competing governments anarchism? 521
F.7.2 Is government compatible with anarchism? 523
F.7.3 Can there be a "right-wing" anarchism? 526

F.8 What role did the state take in the creation of capitalism? 528
F.8.1 What social forces lay behind the rise of capitalism? 533
F.8.2 What was the social context of the statement "laissez-faire"? 534
F.8.3 What other forms did state intervention in creating capitalism take? 536
F.8.4 Aren't the enclosures a socialist myth? 539
F.8.5 What about the lack of enclosures in the Americas? 541
F.8.6 How did working people view the rise of capitalism? 545

Section F
Is "anarcho"-capitalism a type of anarchism?

Anyone who has followed political discussion on the net has probably come across people calling themselves "libertarians" but arguing from a right-wing, pro-capitalist perspective. For most people outside of North America, this is weird as the term *"libertarian"* is almost always used in conjunction with *"socialist"* or *"communist"* (particularly in Europe and, it should be stressed, historically in America). In the US, though, the Right has partially succeeded in appropriating the term "libertarian" for itself. Even stranger is that a few of these right-wingers have started calling themselves "anarchists" in what must be one of the finest examples of an oxymoron in the English language: "Anarcho-capitalist"!!!

Arguing with fools is seldom rewarded, but to let their foolishness to go unchallenged risks allowing them to deceive those who are new to anarchism. This is what this section of the FAQ is for, to show why the claims of these "anarchist" capitalists are false. Anarchism has always been anti-capitalist and any "anarchism" that claims otherwise cannot be part of the anarchist tradition. It is important to stress that anarchist opposition to the so-called capitalist "anarchists" does **not** reflect some kind of debate within anarchism, as many of these types like to pretend, but a debate between anarchism and its old enemy, capitalism. In many ways this debate mirrors the one between Peter Kropotkin and Herbert Spencer (an English capitalist minimal statist) at the turn the 19th century and, as such, it is hardly new.

At that time, people like Spencer tended to call themselves "liberals" while, as Bookchin noted, *"libertarian"* was *"a term created by nineteenth-century European anarchists, not by contemporary American right-wing proprietarians."* [**The Ecology of Freedom**, p. 57] David Goodway concurs, stating that *"libertarian"* has been *"frequently employed by anarchists"* as an alternative name for our politics for over a century. However, the *"situation has been vastly complicated in recent decades with the rise of ... extreme right-wing laissez-faire philosophy ... and [its advocates] adoption of the words 'libertarian' and 'libertarianism.' It has therefore now become necessary to distinguish between their right libertarianism and the left libertarianism of the anarchist tradition."* [**Anarchist Seeds Beneath the Snow**, p. 4] This appropriation of the term "libertarian" by the right not only has bred confusion, but also protest as anarchists have tried to point out the obvious, namely that capitalism is marked by **authoritarian** social relationships and so there are good reasons for anarchism being a fundamentally anti-capitalist socio-political theory and movement. That a minority of the right "libertarians" have also tried to appropriate "anarchist" to describe their authoritarian politics is something almost all anarchists reject and oppose.

That the vast majority of anarchists reject the notion of "anarcho"-capitalism as a form of anarchism is an inconvenient fact for its supporters. Rather than address this, they generally point to the fact that some academics state that "anarcho"-capitalism is a form of anarchism and include it in their accounts of our movement and ideas. That some academics do this is true, but irrelevant. What counts is what anarchists think anarchism is. To place the opinions of academics above that of anarchists implies that anarchists know nothing about anarchism, that we do not really understand the ideas we advocate but academics do! Yet this is the implication. As such the near universal rejection of "anarcho"-capitalism as a form of anarchism within anarchist circles is significant. However, it could be argued that as a few anarchists (usually individualist ones, but not always) **do** admit "anarcho"-capitalism into our movement that this (very small) minority shows that the majority are "sectarian." Again, this is not convincing as some individuals in any movement will hold positions which the majority reject and which are, sometimes, incompatible with the basic principles of the movement (Proudhon's sexism and racism are obvious examples). Equally, given that anarchists and "anarcho"-capitalists have fundamentally **different** analyses and goals it is hardly "sectarian" to point this out (being "sectarian" in politics means prioritising differences and rivalries with politically close groups).

Some scholars do note the difference. For example, Jeremy Jennings, in his excellent overview of anarchist theory and history, argues that it is *"hard not to conclude that these ideas ["anarcho"-capitalism] – with roots deep in classical liberalism – are described as anarchist only on the basis of a misunderstanding of what anarchism is."* [*"Anarchism"*, **Contemporary Political Ideologies**, Roger Eatwell and Anthony Wright (eds.), p. 142] Barbara Goodwin reaches a similar conclusion, noting that the "anarcho"-capitalists' *"true place is in the group of right-wing libertarians"* not in anarchism for *"[w]hile condemning absolutely state coercion, they tacitly condone the economic and interpersonal coercion which would prevail in a totally **laissez-faire** society. Most anarchists share the egalitarian ideal with socialists: anarcho-capitalists abhor equality and socialism equally."* [**Using Political Ideas**, p. 138]

Sadly, these seem to be the minority in academic circles as most are happy to discuss right-"libertarian" ideology as a subclass of anarchism in spite of there being so little in common between the two. Their inclusion does really seem to derive from the fact that "anarcho"-capitalists **call** themselves anarchists and the academics take this at face value. Yet, as one anarchist notes, having a *"completely fluid definition of anarchism, allows for anyone and anything to be described as such, no matter how authoritarian and anti-social."* [Benjamin Franks, *"Mortal Combat"*, pp. 4-6, **A Touch of Class**, no. 1, p. 5] Also, given that many academics approach anarchism from what could be termed the "dictionary definition" methodology rather than as a political movement approach there is a tendency for "anarcho"-capitalist claims to be taken at face value. As such, it is useful to stress that anarchism is a social movement with a long history and while its adherents have held divergent views, it has never been limited to simply opposition to the state (i.e. the dictionary definition).

The "anarcho"-capitalist argument that it is a form of anarchism hinges on using the dictionary definition of "anarchism" and/or "anarchy." They try to define anarchism as being "opposition to government," and nothing else. Of course, many (if not most) dictionaries "define" anarchy as "chaos" or "disorder" but we never see "anarcho"-capitalists use those particular definitions! Moreover, and this should go without saying, dictionaries are hardly politically sophisticated and their definitions rarely reflect the wide range of ideas associated with political theories and their history. Thus the dictionary "definition" of anarchism will tend to ignore its consistent views on authority, exploitation, property and capitalism (ideas easily discovered if actual anarchist texts are read). And for this strategy to work, a lot of "inconvenient" history and ideas from all branches of anarchism must be ignored. From individualists like Tucker to communists like Kropotkin all have considered anarchism as part of the wider socialist movement. Therefore "anarcho"-capitalists are not anarchists in the same sense that rain is not dry.

Significantly, the inventor of the term "anarcho"-capitalism, Murray Rothbard had no impact on the anarchist movement even in North America. His influence, unsurprisingly, was limited to the right, particularly in so-called "libertarian" circles. The same can be said of "anarcho"-capitalism in general. This can be seen from the way Rothbard is mentioned in Paul Nursey-Bray's bibliography on anarchist thinkers. This is an academic book, a reference for libraries. Rothbard is featured, but the context is very suggestive. The book includes Rothbard in a section titled *"On the Margins of Anarchist Theory."* His introduction to the Rothbard section is worth quoting:

> *"Either the inclusion or the omission of Rothbard as an anarchist is likely, in one quarter or another, to be viewed as contentious. Here, his Anarcho-Capitalism is treated as marginal, since, while there are linkages with the tradition of individualist anarchism, there is a dislocation between the mutualism and communitarianism of that tradition and the free market theory, deriving from Ludwig von Mises and Friedrich von Hayek, that underpins Rothbard's political philosophy, and places him in the modern Libertarian tradition."* [**Anarchist Thinkers and Thought**, p. 133]

This is important, for while Rothbard (like other "anarcho"-capitalists) appropriates **some** aspects of individualist anarchism he does so in a highly selective manner and places what he does take into an utterly different social environment and political tradition. So while there are similarities between both systems, there are important differences as we will discuss in detail in section G along with the anti-capitalist nature of individualist anarchism (i.e. those essential bits which Rothbard and his followers ignore or dismiss). Needless to say, Nursey-Bray does not include "anarcho"-capitalism in his discussion of anarchist schools of thought in the bibliography's introduction.

Of course, we cannot stop the "anarcho"-capitalists using the words "anarcho", "anarchism" and "anarchy" to describe their ideas. The democracies of the west could not stop the Chinese Stalinist state calling itself the People's Republic of China. Nor could the social democrats stop the fascists in Germany calling themselves "National Socialists". Nor could the Italian anarcho-syndicalists stop the fascists using the expression "National Syndicalism". This does not mean their names reflected their content – China is a dictatorship, not a democracy; the Nazi's were not socialists (capitalists made fortunes in Nazi Germany because it crushed the labour movement); and the Italian fascist state had nothing in common with anarcho-

syndicalist ideas of decentralised, "from the bottom up" unions and the abolition of the state and capitalism.

It could be argued (and it has) that the previous use of a word does not preclude new uses. Language changes and, as such, it is possible for a **new** kind of "anarchism" to develop which has little, or no, similarities with what was previously known as anarchism. Equally, it could be said that new developments of anarchism have occurred in the past which were significantly different from old versions (for example, the rise of communist forms of anarchism in opposition to Proudhon's anti-communist mutualism). Both arguments are unconvincing. The first just makes a mockery of the concept of language and breeds confusion. If people start calling black white, it does not make it so. Equally, to call an ideology with little in common with a known and long established socio-political theory and movement the same name simply results in confusion. No one takes, say, fascists seriously when they call their parties "democratic" nor would we take Trotskyists seriously if they started to call themselves "libertarians" (as some have started to do). The second argument fails to note that developments within anarchism built upon what came before and did not change its fundamental (socialistic) basis. Thus communist and collectivist anarchism are valid forms of anarchism because they built upon the key insights of mutualism rather than denying them.

A related defence of "anarcho"-capitalism as a form of anarchism is the suggestion that the problem is one of terminology. This argument is based on noting that "anarcho"-capitalists are against "actually existing" capitalism and so *"we must distinguish between 'free-market capitalism' … and 'state capitalism' … The two are as different as day and night."* [Rothbard, **The Logic of Action II,** p. 185] It would be churlish indeed to point out that the **real** difference is that one exists while the other has existed only in Rothbard's head. Yet point it out we must, for the simple fact is that not only do "anarcho"-capitalists use the word anarchism in an unusual way (i.e. in opposition to what has always been meant by the term), they also use the word capitalism in a like manner (i.e., to refer to something that has never existed). It should go without saying that using words like "capitalism" and "anarchism" in ways radically different to traditional uses cannot help but provoke confusion. Yet is it a case that "anarcho"-capitalists have simply picked a bad name for their ideology? Hardly, as its advocates will quickly rush to defend exploitation (non-labour income) and capitalist property rights as well as the authoritarian social structures produced with them. Moreover, as good capitalist economists the notion of an economy without interest, rent and profit is considered highly inefficient and so unlikely to develop. As such, their ideology is rooted in a perspective and an economy marked by wage labour, landlords, banking and stock markets and so hierarchy, oppression and exploitation, i.e. a capitalist one.

So they have chosen their name well as it shows in clear light how far they are from the anarchist tradition. As such, almost all anarchists would agree with long-time anarchist activist Donald Rooum's comment that *"self-styled 'anarcho-capitalists' (not to be confused with anarchists of any persuasion) [simply] want the state abolished as a regulator of capitalism, and government handed over to capitalists."* They are *"wrongly self-styled 'anarchists'"* because they *"do not oppose capitalist oppression"* while genuine anarchists are *"extreme libertarian socialists."* [**What Is Anarchism?**, p. 7, pp. 12-13 and p. 10] As we stress in section F.1, "anarcho"-capitalists do not oppose the hierarchies and exploitation associated with capitalism (wage labour and landlordism) and, consequently, have no claim to the term "anarchist." Just because someone uses a label it does not mean that they support the ideas associated with that label and this is the case with "anarcho"-capitalism – its ideas are at odds with the key ideas associated with all forms of traditional anarchism (even individualist anarchism which is often claimed, usually by "anarcho"-capitalists, as being a forefather of the ideology).

We are covering this topic in an anarchist FAQ for three reasons. Firstly, the number of "libertarian" and "anarcho"-capitalists on the net means that those seeking to find out about anarchism may conclude that they are "anarchists" as well. Secondly, unfortunately, some academics and writers have taken their claims of being anarchists at face value and have included their ideology in general accounts of anarchism (the better academic accounts do note that anarchists generally reject the claim). These two reasons are obviously related and hence the need to show the facts of the matter. The last reason is to provide other anarchists with arguments and evidence to use against "anarcho"-capitalism and its claims of being a new form of "anarchism."

So this section of the FAQ does not, as we noted above, represent some kind of "debate" within anarchism. It reflects the attempt by anarchists to reclaim the history and meaning of anarchism from those who are attempting to steal its name. However, our discussion also serves two other purposes. Firstly, critiquing right "libertarian" theories allows us to explain anarchist ones at the same time and indicate why they are better. Secondly, and more importantly, it shares many of the same assumptions and aims of neo-liberalism. This was noted by Bob Black in the early 1980s, when a *"wing of the Reaganist Right … obviously appropriated, with suspect selectivity, such libertarian themes as deregulation and voluntarism. Ideologues indignate that Reagan has travestied their principles. Tough shit! I notice that it's **their** principles, not mine, that he found suitable to travesty."* ["The Libertarian As Conservative", pp. 141-8, **The Abolition of Work and Other Essays**, pp. 141-2] This was echoed by Noam Chomsky two decades later when he stated that *"nobody takes [right-wing libertarianism] seriously"* (as *"everybody knows that a society that worked by … [its] principles would self-destruct in three seconds"*). The *"only reason"* why some people in the ruling elite *"pretend to take it seriously is because you can use it as a weapon"* in the class struggle [**Understanding Power**, p. 200] As neo-liberalism is being used as the ideological basis of the current attack on the working class, critiquing "anarcho"-capitalism also allows us to build theoretical weapons to use to resist this attack and aid our side in the class war.

The results of the onslaught of free(r) market capitalism along with anarchist criticism of "anarcho"-capitalism has resulted in some "anarcho"-capitalists trying to re-brand their ideology as "market anarchism." This, from their perspective, has two advantages. Firstly, it allows them to co-opt the likes of Tucker and Spooner (and, sometimes, even Proudhon!) into their family tree as all these supported markets (while systematically attacking capitalism). Secondly, it allows them to distance their ideology from the grim

reality of neo-liberalism and the results of making capitalism more "free market." Simply put, going on about the benefits of "free market" capitalism while freer market capitalism is enriching the already wealthy and oppressing and impoverishing the many is hard going. Using the term "market anarchism" to avoid both the reality of anarchism's anti-capitalist core and the reality of the freer market capitalism they have helped produce makes sense in the marketplace of ideas (the term "blackwashing" seems appropriate here). The fact is that however laudable its stated aims, "anarcho"-capitalism is deeply flawed due to its simplistic nature and is easy to abuse on behalf of the economic oligarchy that lurks behind the rhetoric of economic textbooks in that "special case" so ignored by economists, namely reality.

Anarchism has always been aware of the existence of "free market" capitalism, particularly its extreme (minimal state) wing, and has always rejected it. As we discuss in section F.7, anarchists from Proudhon onwards have rejected it (and, significantly, vice versa). As academic Alan Carter notes, anarchist concern for equality as a necessary precondition for genuine freedom *"is one very good reason for not confusing anarchists with liberals or economic 'libertarians' – in other words, for not lumping together everyone who is in some way or another critical of the state. It is why calling the likes of Nozick 'anarchists' is highly misleading."* ["Some notes on 'Anarchism'", pp. 141-5, **Anarchist Studies**, vol. 1, no. 2, p. 143] So anarchists have evaluated "free market" capitalism and rejected it as non-anarchist since the birth of anarchism and so attempts by "anarcho"-capitalism to say that their system is "anarchist" flies in the face of this long history of anarchist analysis. That some academics fall for their attempts to appropriate the anarchist label for their ideology is down to a false premise: it *"is judged to be anarchism largely because some anarcho-capitalists **say** they are 'anarchists' and because they criticise the State."* [Peter Sabatini, **Social Anarchism**, no. 23, p. 100]

More generally, we must stress that most (if not all) anarchists do not want to live in a society **just like this one** but without state coercion and (the initiation of) force. Anarchists do not confuse "freedom" with the "right" to govern and exploit others nor with being able to change masters. It is not enough to say we can start our own (co-operative) business in such a society. We want the abolition of the capitalist system of authoritarian relationships, not just a change of bosses or the possibility of little islands of liberty within a sea of capitalism (islands which are always in danger of being flooded and our freedom destroyed). Thus, in this section of the FAQ, we analyse many "anarcho"-capitalist claims on their own terms (for example, the importance of equality in the market or why replacing the state with private defence firms is simply changing the name of the state rather than abolishing it) but that does not mean we desire a society nearly identical to the current one. Far from it, we want to transform this society into one more suited for developing and enriching individuality and freedom.

Finally, we dedicate this section of the FAQ to those who have seen the real face of "free market" capitalism at work: the working men and women (anarchist or not) murdered in the jails and concentration camps or on the streets by the hired assassins of capitalism.

F.1

Are "anarcho"-capitalists really anarchists?

In a word, no. While "anarcho"-capitalists obviously try to associate themselves with the anarchist tradition by using the word "anarcho" or by calling themselves "anarchists" their ideas are distinctly at odds with those associated with anarchism. As a result, any claims that their ideas are anarchist or that they are part of the anarchist tradition or movement are false.

"Anarcho"-capitalists claim to be anarchists because they say that they oppose government. As noted in the last section, they use a dictionary definition of anarchism. However, this fails to appreciate that anarchism is a **political theory**. As dictionaries are rarely politically sophisticated things, this means that they fail to recognise that anarchism is more than just opposition to government, it is also marked a opposition to capitalism (i.e. exploitation and private property). Thus, opposition to government is a necessary but not sufficient condition for being an anarchist – you also need to be opposed to exploitation and capitalist private property. As "anarcho"-capitalists do not consider interest, rent and profits (i.e. capitalism) to be exploitative nor oppose capitalist property rights, they are not anarchists.

Part of the problem is that Marxists, like many academics, also tend to assert that anarchists are simply against the state. It is significant that both Marxists and "anarcho"-capitalists tend to define anarchism as purely opposition to government. This is no co-incidence, as both seek to exclude anarchism from its place in the wider socialist movement. This makes perfect sense from the Marxist perspective as it allows them to present their ideology as the only serious anti-capitalist one around (not to mention associating anarchism with "anarcho"-capitalism is an excellent way of discrediting our ideas in the wider radical movement). It should go without saying that this is an obvious and serious misrepresentation of the anarchist position as even a superficial glance at anarchist theory and history shows that no anarchist limited their critique of society simply at the state. So while academics and Marxists seem aware of the anarchist opposition to the state, they usually fail to grasp the anarchist critique applies to all other authoritarian social institutions and how it fits into the overall anarchist analysis and struggle. They seem to think the anarchist condemnation of capitalist private property, patriarchy and so forth are somehow superfluous additions rather than a logical position which reflects the core of anarchism:

> "Critics have sometimes contended that anarchist thought, and classical anarchist theory in particular, has emphasised opposition to the state to the point of neglecting the real hegemony of economic power. This interpretation arises, perhaps, from a simplistic and overdrawn distinction between the anarchist focus on political domination and the Marxist focus on economic exploitation ... there is abundant evidence against such

a thesis throughout the history of anarchist thought." [John P. Clark and Camille Martin, **Anarchy, Geography, Modernity**, p. 95]

So Reclus simply stated the obvious when he wrote that "the anti-authoritarian critique to which the state is subjected applies equally to all social institutions." [quoted by Clark and Martin, **Op. Cit.**, p. 140] Proudhon, Bakunin, Kropotkin, Goldman and so on would all agree with that. While they all stressed that anarchism was against the state they quickly moved on to present a critique of private property and other forms of hierarchical authority. So while anarchism obviously opposes the state, "sophisticated and developed anarchist theory proceeds further. It does not stop with a criticism of political organisation, but goes on to investigate the authoritarian nature of economic inequality and private property, hierarchical economic structures, traditional education, the patriarchal family, class and racial discrimination, and rigid sex- and age-roles, to mention just a few of the more important topics." For the "essence of anarchism is, after all, not the theoretical opposition to the state, but the practical and theoretical struggle against domination." [John Clark, **The Anarchist Moment**, p. 128 and p. 70]

This is also the case with individualist anarchists whose defence of certain forms of property did stop them criticising key aspects of **capitalist** property rights. As Jeremy Jennings notes, the "point to stress is that all anarchists, and not only those wedded to the predominant twentieth-century strain of anarchist communism have been critical of private property to the extent that it was a source of hierarchy and privilege." He goes on to state that anarchists like Tucker and Spooner "agreed with the proposition that property was legitimate only insofar as it embraced no more than the total product of individual labour." ["Anarchism", **Contemporary Political Ideologies**, Roger Eatwell and Anthony Wright (eds.), p. 132] This is acknowledged by the likes of Rothbard who had to explicitly point how that his position on such subjects was fundamentally different (i.e., at odds) with individualist anarchism.

As such, it would be fair to say that most "anarcho"-capitalists are capitalists first and foremost. If aspects of anarchism do not fit with some element of capitalism, they will reject that element of anarchism rather than question capitalism (Rothbard's selective appropriation of the individualist anarchist tradition is the most obvious example of this). This means that right-"libertarians" attach the "anarcho" prefix to their ideology because they believe that being against government intervention is equivalent to being an anarchist (which flows into their use of the dictionary definition of anarchism). That they ignore the bulk of the anarchist tradition should prove that there is hardly anything anarchistic about them at all. They are not against authority, hierarchy or the state – they simply want to privatise them.

Ironically, this limited definition of "anarchism" ensures that "anarcho"-capitalism is inherently self-refuting. This can be seen from leading "anarcho"-capitalist Murray Rothbard. He thundered against the evil of the state, arguing that it "arrogates to itself a monopoly of force, of ultimate decision-making power, over a given territorial area." In and of itself, this definition is unremarkable. That a few people (an elite of rulers) claim the right to rule others must be **part** of any sensible definition of the state or government.

Is "anarcho"-capitalism a type of anarchism?

However, the problems begin for Rothbard when he notes that "[o]bviously, in a free society, Smith has the ultimate decision-making power over his own just property, Jones over his, etc." [**The Ethics of Liberty**, p. 170 and p. 173] The logical contradiction in this position should be obvious, but not to Rothbard. It shows the power of ideology, the ability of mere words (the expression *"private property"*) to turn the bad (*"ultimate decision-making power over a given area"*) into the good (*"ultimate decision-making power over a given area"*).

Now, this contradiction can be solved in only **one** way – the users of the *"given area"* are also its owners. In other words, a system of possession (or "occupancy and use") as favoured by anarchists. However, Rothbard is a capitalist and supports private property, non-labour income, wage labour, capitalists and landlords. This means that he supports a divergence between ownership and use and this means that this *"ultimate decision-making power"* extends to those who **use,** but do not own, such property (i.e. tenants and workers). The statist nature of private property is clearly indicated by Rothbard's words – the property owner in an "anarcho"-capitalist society possesses the *"ultimate decision-making power"* over a given area, which is also what the state has currently. Rothbard has, ironically, proved by his own definition that "anarcho"-capitalism is not anarchist.

Of course, it would be churlish to point out that the usual name for a political system in which the owner of a territory is also its ruler is, in fact, monarchy. Which suggests that while "anarcho"-capitalism may be called "anarcho-statism" a far better term could be "anarcho-monarchism." In fact, some "anarcho"-capitalists have made explicit this obvious implication of Rothbard's argument. Hans-Hermann Hoppe is one.

Hoppe prefers monarchy to democracy, considering it the superior system. He argues that the monarch is the **private** owner of the government – all the land and other resources are **owned** by him. Basing himself on Austrian economics (what else?) and its notion of time preference, he concludes that the monarch will, therefore, work to maximise both current income and the total capital value of his estate. Assuming self-interest, his planning horizon will be farsighted and exploitation be far more limited. Democracy, in contrast, is a publicly-owned government and the elected rulers have use of resources for a short period only and **not** their capital value. In other words, they do not own the country and so will seek to maximise their short-term interests (and the interests of those they think will elect them into office). In contrast, Bakunin stressed that if anarchism rejects democracy it was *"hardly in order to reverse it but rather to advance it,"* in particular to extend it via *"the great economic revolution without which every right is but an empty phrase and a trick."* He rejected wholeheartedly *"the camp of aristocratic ... reaction."* [**The Basic Bakunin**, p. 87]

However, Hoppe is not a traditional monarchist. His ideal system is one of **competing** monarchies, a society which is led by a *"voluntarily acknowledged 'natural' elite – a **nobilitas naturalis**"* comprised of *"families with long-established records of superior achievement, farsightedness, and exemplary personal conduct."* This is because *"a few individuals quickly acquire the status of an elite"* and their inherent qualities will *"more likely than not [be] passed on within a few – noble – families."* The sole "problem"

with traditional monarchies was *"with **monopoly**, not with elites or nobility,"* in other words the King monopolised the role of judge and their subjects could not turn to other members of the noble class for services. [*"The Political Economy of Monarchy and Democracy and the Idea of a Natural Order,"* pp. 94-121, **Journal of Libertarian Studies**, vol. 11, no. 2, p. 118 and p. 119]

Which simply confirms the anarchist critique of "anarcho"-capitalism, namely that it is **not** anarchist. This becomes even more obvious when Hoppe helpfully expands on the reality of "anarcho"-capitalism:

"In a covenant concluded among proprietor and community tenants for the purpose of protecting their private property, no such thing as a right to free (unlimited) speech exists, not even to unlimited speech on one's own tenant-property. One may say innumerable things and promote almost any idea under the sun, but naturally no one is permitted to advocate ideas contrary to the very purpose of the covenant of preserving private property, such as democracy and communism. There can be no tolerance towards democrats and communists in a libertarian social order. They will have to be physically separated and expelled from society. Likewise in a covenant founded for the purpose of protecting family and kin, there can be no tolerance toward those habitually promoting lifestyles incompatible with this goal. They – the advocates of alternative, non-family and kin-centred lifestyles such as, for instance, individual hedonism, parasitism, nature-environment worship, homosexuality, or communism – will have to be physically removed from society, too, if one is to maintain a libertarian order." [**Democracy: the God that Failed**, p. 218]

Thus the proprietor has power/authority over his tenants and can decree what they can and cannot do, excluding anyone whom they consider as being subversive (in the tenants' own interests, of course). In other words, the autocratic powers of the boss are extended into **all** aspects of society – all under the mask of advocating liberty. Sadly, the preservation of property rights destroys liberty for the many (Hoppe states clearly that for the "anarcho"-capitalist the *"natural outcome of the voluntary transactions between various private property owners is decidedly non-egalitarian, hierarchical and elitist."* [*"The Political Economy of Monarchy and Democracy and the Idea of a Natural Order,"* **Op. Cit.**, p. 118]). Unsurprisingly, Chomsky argued that right-wing "libertarianism" has *"no objection to tyranny as long as it is private tyranny."* In fact it (like other contemporary ideologies) *"reduce[s] to advocacy of one or another form of illegitimate authority, quite often real tyranny."* [**Chomsky on Anarchism**, p. 235 and p. 181] As such, it is hard not to conclude that "anarcho"-capitalism is little more than a play with words. It is not anarchism but a cleverly designed and worded surrogate for elitist, autocratic conservatism. Nor is too difficult to conclude that genuine anarchists and libertarians (of all types) would not be tolerated in this so-called *"libertarian social order."*

Some "anarcho"-capitalists do seem dimly aware of this glaringly obvious contradiction. Rothbard, for example, does present an argument which could be used to solve it, but he utterly fails. He simply ignores the crux of the matter, that capitalism is based on hierarchy and, therefore, cannot be anarchist. He does this by arguing that the hierarchy associated with capitalism is fine as long as the private property that produced it was acquired in a "just" manner. Yet in so doing he yet again draws attention to the identical authority structures and social relationships of the state and property. As he puts it:

> "**If** the State may be said to properly **own** its territory, then it is proper for it to make rules for everyone who presumes to live in that area. It can legitimately seize or control private property because there **is** no private property in its area, because it really owns the entire land surface. **So long** as the State permits its subjects to leave its territory, then, it can be said to act as does any other owner who sets down rules for people living on his property." [**Op. Cit.**, p. 170]

Obviously Rothbard argues that the state does not "justly" own its territory. He asserts that *"our homesteading theory"* of the creation of private property *"suffices to demolish any such pretensions by the State apparatus"* and so the problem with the state is that it *"claims and exercises a compulsory monopoly of defence and ultimate decision-making over an area larger than an individual's justly-acquired property."* [**Op. Cit.**, p. 171 and p. 173] There are four fundamental problems with his argument.

First, it assumes his "homesteading theory" is a robust and libertarian theory, but neither is the case (see section F.4.1). Second, it ignores the history of capitalism. Given that the current distribution of property is just as much the result of violence and coercion as the state, his argument is seriously flawed. It amounts to little more than an **"immaculate conception of property"** unrelated to reality. Third, even if we ignore these issues and assume that private property could be and was legitimately produced by the means Rothbard assumes, it does not justify the hierarchy associated with it as current and future generations of humanity have, effectively, been excommunicated from liberty by previous ones. If, as Rothbard argues, property is a natural right and the basis of liberty then why should the many be excluded from their birthright by a minority? In other words, Rothbard denies that liberty should be universal. He chooses property over liberty while anarchists choose liberty over property. Fourthly, it implies that the fundamental problem with the state is **not**, as anarchists have continually stressed, its hierarchical and authoritarian nature but rather the fact that it does not justly own the territory it claims to rule.

Even worse, the possibility that private property can result in **more** violations of individual freedom (at least for non-proprietors) than the state of its citizens was implicitly acknowledged by Rothbard. He uses as a hypothetical example a country whose King is threatened by a rising "libertarian" movement. The King responds by *"employ[ing] a cunning stratagem,"* namely he *"proclaims his government to be dissolved, but just before doing so he arbitrarily parcels out the entire land area of his kingdom to the 'ownership' of himself and his relatives."* Rather than taxes, his subjects now pay rent and he can *"regulate the lives of all the people who presume to live on"* his property as he sees fit. Rothbard then asks:

> "Now what should be the reply of the libertarian rebels to this pert challenge? If they are consistent utilitarians, they must bow to this subterfuge, and resign themselves to living under a regime no less despotic than the one they had been battling for so long. Perhaps, indeed, **more** despotic, for now the king and his relatives can claim for themselves the libertarians' very principle of the absolute right of private property, an absoluteness which they might not have dared to claim before." [**Op. Cit.**, p. 54]

It should go without saying that Rothbard argues that we should reject this *"cunning stratagem"* as a con as the new distribution of property would not be the result of "just" means. However, he failed to note how his argument undermines his own claims that capitalism can be libertarian. As he himself argues, not only does the property owner have the same monopoly of power over a given area as the state, it is **more** despotic as it is based on the *"absolute right of private property"*! And remember, Rothbard is arguing **in favour** of "anarcho"-capitalism (*"if you have unbridled capitalism, you will have all kinds of authority: you will have **extreme** authority."* [Chomsky, **Understanding Power**, p. 200]). The fundamental problem is that Rothbard's ideology blinds him to the obvious, namely that the state and private property produce identical social relationships (ironically, he opines the theory that the state owns its territory *"makes the State, as well as the King in the Middle Ages, a feudal overlord, who at least theoretically **owned** all the land in his domain"* without noticing that this makes the capitalist or landlord a King and a feudal overlord within "anarcho"-capitalism. [**Op. Cit.**, p. 171]).

One group of Chinese anarchists pointed out the obvious in 1914. As anarchism *"takes opposition to authority as its essential principle,"* anarchists aim to *"sweep away all the evil systems of present society which have an authoritarian nature"* and so *"our ideal society"* would be *"without landlords, capitalists, leaders, officials, representatives or heads of families."* [quoted by Arif Dirlik, **Anarchism in the Chinese Revolution**, p. 131] Only this, the elimination of all forms of hierarchy (political, economic and social) would achieve genuine anarchism, a society without authority (anarchy). In practice, private property is a major source of oppression and authoritarianism within society – there is little or no freedom subject to a landlord or within capitalist production (as Bakunin noted, *"the worker sells his person and his liberty for a given time"*). In stark contrast to anarchists, "anarcho"-capitalists have no problem with landlords and factory fascism (i.e. wage labour), a position which seems highly illogical for a theory calling itself libertarian. If it were truly libertarian, it would oppose all forms of domination, not just statism (*"Those who reject authoritarianism will require nobody's permission to breathe. The libertarian ... is not grateful to get permission to reside anywhere on his own planet and denies the right of any one to screen off bits of it for their own use or rule."* [Stuart Christie and Albert Meltzer, **Floodgates of Anarchy**, p. 31]). This illogical and self-contradictory position flows from the "anarcho"-capitalist definition of freedom as the absence of coercion and will be discussed in section F.2 in more detail. The ironic thing is that "anarcho"-capitalists implicitly prove the anarchist critique of their own ideology.

Of course, the "anarcho"-capitalist has another means to avoid the obvious, namely the assertion that the market will limit the abuses of the property owners. If workers do not like their ruler then they can seek another. Thus capitalist hierarchy is fine as workers and tenants "consent" to it. While the logic is obviously the same, it is doubtful that an "anarcho"-capitalist would support the state just because its subjects can leave and join another one. As such, this does not address the core issue – the authoritarian nature of capitalist property (see section A.2.14). Moreover, this argument completely ignores the reality of economic and social power. Thus the "consent" argument fails because it ignores the social circumstances of capitalism which limit the choice of the many.

Anarchists have long argued that, as a class, workers have little choice but to "consent" to capitalist hierarchy. The alternative is either dire poverty or starvation. "Anarcho"-capitalists dismiss such claims by denying that there is such a thing as economic power. Rather, it is simply freedom of contract. Anarchists consider such claims as a joke. To show why, we need only quote (yet again) Rothbard on the abolition of slavery and serfdom in the 19th century. He argued, correctly, that the *"bodies of the oppressed were freed, but the property which they had worked and eminently deserved to own, remained in the hands of their former oppressors. With economic power thus remaining in their hands, the former lords soon found themselves virtual masters once more of what were now free tenants or farm labourers. The serfs and slaves had tasted freedom, but had been cruelly deprived of its fruits."* [**Op. Cit.**, p. 74]

Contrast this with the standard "anarcho"-capitalist claim that if market forces ("voluntary exchanges") result in the creation of *"tenants or farm labourers"* then they are free. Yet labourers dispossessed by market forces are in exactly the same social and economic situation as the ex-serfs and ex-slaves. If the latter do not have the fruits of freedom, neither do the former. Rothbard sees the obvious *"economic power"* in the latter case, but denies it in the former (ironically, Rothbard dismissed economic power under capitalism in the same work. [**Op. Cit.**, pp. 221-2]). It is only Rothbard's ideology that stops him from drawing the obvious conclusion – identical economic conditions produce identical social relationships and so capitalism is marked by *"economic power"* and *"virtual masters."* The only solution is for "anarcho"-capitalists to simply say that the ex-serfs and ex-slaves were actually free to choose and, consequently, Rothbard was wrong. It might be inhuman, but at least it would be consistent!

Rothbard's perspective is alien to anarchism. For example, as individualist anarchist William Bailie noted, under capitalism there is a class system marked by *"a dependent industrial class of wage-workers"* and *"a privileged class of wealth-monopolisers, each becoming more and more distinct from the other as capitalism advances."* This has turned property into *"a social power, an economic force destructive of rights, a fertile source of injustice, a means of enslaving the dispossessed."* He concluded: *"Under this system equal liberty cannot obtain."* Bailie notes that the modern *"industrial world under capitalistic conditions"* have *"arisen under the **regime** of status"* (and so *"law-made privileges"*) however, it seems unlikely that he would have concluded that such a class

system would be fine if it had developed naturally or the current state was abolished while leaving that class structure intact. [**The Individualist Anarchists**, p. 121] As we discuss in section G.4, Individualist Anarchists like Tucker and Yarrows ended up recognising that even the freest competition had become powerless against the enormous concentrations of wealth associated with corporate capitalism.

Therefore anarchists recognise that "free exchange" or "consent" in unequal circumstances will reduce freedom as well as increasing inequality between individuals and classes. As we discuss in section F.3, inequality will produce social relationships which are based on hierarchy and domination, **not** freedom. As Noam Chomsky put it:

> *"Anarcho-capitalism, in my opinion, is a doctrinal system which, if ever implemented, would lead to forms of tyranny and oppression that have few counterparts in human history. There isn't the slightest possibility that its (in my view, horrendous) ideas would be implemented, because they would quickly destroy any society that made this colossal error. The idea of 'free contract' between the potentate and his starving subject is a sick joke, perhaps worth some moments in an academic seminar exploring the consequences of (in my view, absurd) ideas, but nowhere else."* [**Noam Chomsky on Anarchism**, interview with Tom Lane, December 23, 1996]

Clearly, then, by its own arguments "anarcho"-capitalism is not anarchist. This should come as no surprise to anarchists. Anarchism, as a political theory, was born when Proudhon wrote **What is Property?** specifically to refute the notion that workers are free when capitalist property forces them to seek employment by landlords and capitalists. He was well aware that in such circumstances property *"violates equality by the rights of exclusion and increase, and freedom by despotism … [and has] perfect identity with robbery."* He, unsurprisingly, talks of the *"proprietor, to whom [the worker] has sold and surrendered his liberty."* For Proudhon, anarchy was *"the absence of a master, of a sovereign"* while *"proprietor"* was *"synonymous"* with *"sovereign"* for he *"imposes his will as law, and suffers neither contradiction nor control."* This meant that *"property engenders despotism,"* as *"each proprietor is sovereign lord within the sphere of his property."* [**What is Property**, p. 251, p. 130, p. 264 and pp. 266-7] It must also be stressed that Proudhon's classic work is a lengthy critique of the kind of apologetics for private property Rothbard espouses to salvage his ideology from its obvious contradictions.

So, ironically, Rothbard repeats the same analysis as Proudhon but draws the **opposite** conclusions and expects to be considered an anarchist! Moreover, it seems equally ironic that "anarcho"-capitalism calls itself "anarchist" while basing itself on the arguments that anarchism was created in opposition to. As shown, "anarcho"-capitalism makes as much sense as "anarcho-statism" – an oxymoron, a contradiction in terms. The idea that "anarcho"-capitalism warrants the name "anarchist" is simply false. Only someone ignorant of anarchism could maintain such a thing. While you expect anarchist theory to show this to be the case, the wonderful thing is that "anarcho"-capitalism itself does the same. Little wonder Bob Black argues that *"[t]o demonise state* *authoritarianism while ignoring identical albeit contract-consecrated subservient arrangements in the large-scale corporations which control the world economy is fetishism at its worst."* ["The Libertarian As Conservative", **The Abolition of Work and Other Essays**, pp. 142] Left-liberal Stephen L. Newman makes the same point:

> *"The emphasis [right-wing] libertarians place on the opposition of liberty and political power tends to obscure the role of authority in their worldview ... the authority exercised in private relationships, however – in the relationship between employer and employee, for instance – meets with no objection. ... [This] reveals a curious insensitivity to the use of private authority as a means of social control. Comparing public and private authority, we might well ask of the [right-wing] libertarians: When the price of exercising one's freedom is terribly high, what practical difference is there between the commands of the state and those issued by one's employer? ... Though admittedly the circumstances are not identical, telling disgruntled employees that they are always free to leave their jobs seems no different in principle from telling political dissidents that they are free to emigrate."* [**Liberalism at Wit's End**, pp. 45-46]

As Bob Black pointed out, right libertarians argue that *"'one can at least change jobs.' But you can't avoid having a job – just as under statism one can at least change nationalities but you can't avoid subjection to one nation-state or another. But freedom means more than the right to change masters."* [**Op. Cit.**, p. 147] The similarities between capitalism and statism are clear – and so why "anarcho"-capitalism cannot be anarchist. To reject the authority (the *"ultimate decision-making power"*) of the state and embrace that of the property owner indicates not only a highly illogical stance but one at odds with the basic principles of anarchism. This whole-hearted support for wage labour and capitalist property rights indicates that "anarcho"-capitalists are not anarchists because they do not reject all forms of **archy.** They obviously support the hierarchy between boss and worker (wage labour) and landlord and tenant. Anarchism, by definition, is against all forms of archy, including the hierarchy generated by capitalist property. To ignore the obvious archy associated with capitalist property is highly illogical and trying to dismiss one form of domination as flowing from "just" property while attacking the other because it flows from "unjust" property is not seeing the wood for the trees.

In addition, we must note that such inequalities in power and wealth will need "defending" from those subject to them ("anarcho"-capitalists recognise the need for private police and courts to defend property from theft – and, anarchists add, to defend the theft and despotism associated with property!). Due to its support of private property (and thus authority), "anarcho"-capitalism ends up retaining a state in its "anarchy": namely a **private** state whose existence its proponents attempt to deny simply by refusing to call it a state, like an ostrich hiding its head in the sand. As one anarchist so rightly put it, "anarcho"-capitalists *"simply replaced the state with private security firms, and can hardly be described as anarchists as the term is normally understood."* [Brian Morris, "Global Anti-Capitalism", pp. 170-6, **Anarchist Studies**, vol. 14,

no. 2, p. 175] As we discuss more fully in section F.6 this is why "anarcho"-capitalism is better described as "private state" capitalism as there would be a functional equivalent of the state and it would be just as skewed in favour of the propertied elite as the existing one (if not more so). As Albert Meltzer put it:

> *"Common-sense shows that any capitalist society might dispense with a 'State' ... but it could not dispense with organised government, or a privatised form of it, if there were people amassing money and others working to amass it for them. The philosophy of 'anarcho-capitalism' dreamed up by the 'libertarian' New Right, has nothing to do with Anarchism as known by the Anarchist movement proper. It is a lie ... Patently unbridled capitalism ... needs some force at its disposal to maintain class privileges, either from the State itself or from private armies. What they believe in is in fact a limited State – that is, one in which the State has one function, to protect the ruling class, does not interfere with exploitation, and comes as cheap as possible for the ruling class. The idea also serves another purpose ... a moral justification for bourgeois consciences in avoiding taxes without feeling guilty about it."* [**Anarchism: Arguments For and Against**, p. 50]

For anarchists, this need of capitalism for some kind of state is unsurprising. For *"Anarchy without socialism seems equally as impossible to us [as socialism without anarchy], for in such a case it could not be other than the domination of the strongest, and would therefore set in motion right away the organisation and consolidation of this domination; that is to the constitution of government."* [Errico Malatesta, **Errico Malatesta: His Life and Ideas**, p. 148] Because of this, the "anarcho"-capitalist rejection of the anarchist critique of capitalism and our arguments on the need for equality, they cannot be considered anarchists or part of the anarchist tradition. To anarchists it seems bizarre that "anarcho"-capitalists want to get rid of the state but maintain the system it helped create and its function as a defender of the capitalist class's property and property rights. In other words, to reduce the state purely to its function as (to use Malatesta's apt word) the gendarme of the capitalist class is **not** an anarchist goal.

Thus anarchism is far more than the common dictionary definition of "no government" – it also entails being against all forms of **archy**, including those generated by capitalist property. This is clear from the roots of the word "anarchy." As we noted in section A.1, the word anarchy means "no rulers" or "contrary to authority." As Rothbard himself acknowledges, the property owner is the ruler of their property and, therefore, those who use it. For this reason "anarcho"-capitalism cannot be considered as a form of anarchism – a real anarchist must logically oppose the authority of the property owner along with that of the state. As "anarcho"-capitalism does not explicitly (or implicitly, for that matter) call for economic arrangements that will end wage labour and usury it cannot be considered anarchist or part of the anarchist tradition. While anarchists have always opposed capitalism, "anarcho"-capitalists have embraced it and due to this embrace their "anarchy" will be marked by relationships based upon subordination and hierarchy (such as wage labour), **not** freedom (little wonder that Proudhon argued that *"property is despotism"* – it creates authoritarian and hierarchical relationships between people in a similar way to statism). Their support for "free market" capitalism ignores the impact of wealth and power on the nature and outcome of individual decisions within the market (see sections F.2 and F.3 for further discussion). Furthermore, any such system of (economic and social) power will require extensive force to maintain it and the "anarcho"-capitalist system of competing "defence firms" will simply be a new state, enforcing capitalist power, property rights and law.

Thus the "anarcho"-capitalist and the anarchist have different starting positions and opposite ends in mind. Their claims to being anarchists are bogus simply because they reject so much of the anarchist tradition as to make what little they do pay lip-service to be non-anarchist in theory and practice. Little wonder Peter Marshall said that *"few anarchists would accept the 'anarcho-capitalists' into the anarchist camp since they do not share a concern for economic equality and social justice."* As such, "anarcho"-capitalists, *"even if they do reject the State, might therefore best be called right-wing libertarians rather than anarchists."* [**Demanding the Impossible**, p. 565]

F.2
What do "anarcho"-capitalists mean by freedom?

For "anarcho"-capitalists, the concept of freedom is limited to the idea of *"freedom from."* For them, freedom means simply freedom from the *"initiation of force,"* or the *"non-aggression against anyone's person and property."* [Murray Rothbard, **For a New Liberty**, p. 23] The notion that real freedom must combine both freedom *"to"* **and** freedom *"from"* is missing in their ideology, as is the social context of the so-called freedom they defend.

Before continuing, it is useful to quote Alan Haworth when he notes that *"[i]n fact, it is surprising how **little** close attention the concept of freedom receives from libertarian writers. Once again **Anarchy, State, and Utopia** is a case in point. The word 'freedom' doesn't even appear in the index. The word 'liberty' appears, but only to refer the reader to the 'Wilt Chamberlain' passage. In a supposedly 'libertarian' work, this is more than surprising. It is truly remarkable."* [**Anti-Libertarianism**, p. 95] Why this is the case can be seen from how the right-"libertarian" defines freedom.

In right-"libertarian" and "anarcho"-capitalist ideology, freedom is considered to be a product of property. As Murray Rothbard puts it, *"the libertarian defines the concept of 'freedom' or 'liberty' … [as a] condition in which a person's ownership rights in his body and his legitimate material property rights are not invaded, are not aggressed against. … Freedom and unrestricted property rights go hand in hand."* [**Op. Cit.**, p.41]

This definition has some problems, however. In such a society, one cannot (legitimately) do anything with or on another's property if the owner prohibits it. This means that an individual's only **guaranteed** freedom is determined by the amount of property that he or she owns. This has the consequence that someone with no property

has no guaranteed freedom at all (beyond, of course, the freedom not to be murdered or otherwise harmed by the deliberate acts of others). In other words, a distribution of property is a distribution of freedom, as the right-"libertarians" themselves define it. It strikes anarchists as strange that an ideology that claims to be committed to promoting freedom entails the conclusion that some people should be more free than others. Yet this is the logical implication of their view, which raises a serious doubt as to whether "anarcho"-capitalists are actually interested in freedom at all.

Looking at Rothbard's definition of "liberty" quoted above, we can see that freedom is actually no longer considered to be a fundamental, independent concept. Instead, freedom is a derivative of something more fundamental, namely the *"legitimate rights"* of an individual, which are identified as property rights. In other words, given that "anarcho"-capitalists and right-"libertarians" in general consider the right to property as "absolute," it follows that freedom and property become one and the same. This suggests an alternative name for the right Libertarian, namely **"Propertarian."** And, needless to say, if we do not accept the right-libertarians' view of what constitutes "legitimate rights," then their claim to be defenders of liberty is weak.

Another important implication of this "liberty as property" concept is that it produces a strangely alienated concept of freedom. Liberty, as we noted, is no longer considered absolute, but a derivative of property – which has the important consequence that you can "sell" your liberty and still be considered free by the ideology. This concept of liberty is usually termed "self-ownership." But, to state the obvious, I do not "own" myself, as if were an object somehow separable from my subjectivity – I **am** myself (see section B.4.2). However, the concept of "self-ownership" is handy for justifying various forms of domination and oppression – for by agreeing (usually under the force of circumstances, we must note) to certain contracts, an individual can "sell" (or rent out) themselves to others (for example, when workers sell their labour power to capitalists on the "free market"). In effect, "self-ownership" becomes the means of justifying treating people as objects – ironically, the very thing the concept was created to stop! As anarchist L. Susan Brown notes, *"[a]t the moment an individual 'sells' labour power to another, he/she loses self-determination and instead is treated as a subjectless instrument for the fulfilment of another's will."* [**The Politics of Individualism**, p. 4]

Given that workers are paid to obey, you really have to wonder which planet Murray Rothbard was on when he argued that a person's *"labour service is alienable, but his **will** is not"* and that he *"cannot alienate his **will**, more particularly his control over his own mind and body."* He contrasts private property and self-ownership by arguing that *"[a]ll physical property owned by a person is alienable … I can give away or sell to another person my shoes, my house, my car, my money, etc. But there are certain vital things which, in natural fact and in the nature of man, are **in**alienable … [his] will and control over his own person are inalienable."* [**The Ethics of Liberty**, p. 40, p. 135 and pp. 134-5] Yet *"labour services"* are unlike the private possessions Rothbard lists as being alienable. As we argued in section B.1 a person's *"labour services"* and *"will"* cannot be divided – if you sell your labour services, you also have to give control of your body and mind to another person. If a worker does not obey the commands of her employer, she is fired. That Rothbard denied this indicates a total lack of common-sense. Perhaps Rothbard would have argued that as the worker can quit at any time she does not really alienate their will (this seems to be his case against slave contracts – see section F.2.2). But this ignores the fact that between the signing and breaking of the contract and during work hours (and perhaps outside work hours, if the boss has mandatory drug testing or will fire workers who attend union or anarchist meetings or those who have an "unnatural" sexuality and so on) the worker **does** alienate his will and body. In the words of Rudolf Rocker, *"under the realities of the capitalist economic form … there can … be no talk of a 'right over one's own person,' for that ends when one is compelled to submit to the economic dictation of another if he does not want to starve."* [**Anarcho-Syndicalism**, p. 10]

Ironically, the rights of property (which are said to flow from an individual's self-ownership of themselves) becomes the means, under capitalism, by which self-ownership of non-property owners is denied. The foundational right (self-ownership) becomes denied by the derivative right (ownership of things). *"To treat others and oneself as property,"* argues L. Susan Brown, *"objectifies the human individual, denies the unity of subject and object and is a negation of individual will … [and] destroys the very freedom one sought in the first place. The liberal belief in property, both real and in the person, leads not to freedom but to relationships of domination and subordination."* [**Op. Cit.**, p. 3] Under capitalism, a lack of property can be just as oppressive as a lack of legal rights because of the relationships of domination and subjection this situation creates. That people "consent" to this hierarchy misses the point. As Alexander Berkman put it:

> *"The law says your employer does not steal anything from you, because it is done with your consent. You have agreed to work for your boss for certain pay, he to have all that you produce …*
>
> *"But did you really consent?*
>
> *"When the highway man holds his gun to your head, you turn your valuables over to him. You 'consent' all right, but you do so because you cannot help yourself, because you are **compelled** by his gun.*
>
> *"Are you not **compelled** to work for an employer? Your need compels you just as the highwayman's gun. You must live … You can't work for yourself … The factories, machinery, and tools belong to the employing class, so you **must** hire yourself out to that class in order to work and live. Whatever you work at, whoever your employer may be, it always comes to the same: you must work **for him**. You can't help yourself. You are **compelled**."* [**What is Anarchism?**, p. 11]

Due to this class monopoly over the means of life, workers (usually) are at a disadvantage in terms of bargaining power – there are more workers than jobs (see section C.9). Within capitalism there is no equality between owners and the dispossessed, and so property

is a source of **power.** To claim that this power should be "left alone" or is "fair" is *"to the anarchists … preposterous. Once a State has been established, and most of the country's capital privatised, the threat of physical force is no longer necessary to coerce workers into accepting jobs, even with low pay and poor conditions. To use* [right-"libertarian"] *Ayn Rand's term, 'initial force' has **already taken place,** by those who now have capital against those who do not. … In other words, if a thief died and willed his 'ill-gotten gain' to his children, would the children have a right to the stolen property? Not legally. So if 'property is theft,' to borrow Proudhon's quip, and the fruit of exploited labour is simply legal theft, then the only factor giving the children of a deceased capitalist a right to inherit the 'booty' is the law, the State. As Bakunin wrote, 'Ghosts should not rule and oppress this world, which belongs only to the living.'"* [Jeff Draughn, **Between Anarchism and Libertarianism**]

Or, in other words, right-Libertarianism fails to *"meet the charge that normal operations of the market systematically places an entire class of persons (wage earners) in circumstances that compel them to accept the terms and conditions of labour dictated by those who offer work. While it is true that individuals are formally free to seek better jobs or withhold their labour in the hope of receiving higher wages, in the end their position in the market works against them; they cannot live if they do not find employment. When circumstances regularly bestow a relative disadvantage on one class of persons in their dealings with another class, members of the advantaged class have little need of coercive measures to get what they want."* [Stephen L. Newman, **Liberalism at Wit's End**, p. 130] Eliminating taxation does not end oppression, in other words. As Tolstoy put it:

> *"in Russia serfdom was only abolished when all the land had been appropriated. When land was granted to the peasants, it was burdened with payments which took the place of the land slavery. In Europe, taxes that kept the people in bondage began to be abolished only when the people had lost their land, were unaccustomed to agricultural work, and … quite dependent on the capitalists … [They] abolish the taxes that fall on the workers … only because the majority of the people are already in the hands of the capitalists. One form of slavery is not abolished until another has already replaced it."* [**The Slavery of Our Times**, p. 32]

So Rothbard's argument (as well as being contradictory) misses the point (and the reality of capitalism). Yes, **if** we define freedom as *"the absence of coercion"* then the idea that wage labour does not restrict liberty is unavoidable, but such a definition is useless. This is because it hides structures of power and relations of domination and subordination. As Carole Pateman argues, *"the contract in which the worker allegedly sells his labour power is a contract in which, since he cannot be separated from his capacities, he sells command over the use of his body and himself … To sell command over the use of oneself for a specified period … is to be an unfree labourer. The characteristics of this condition are captured in the term **wage slave**."* [**The Sexual Contract**, p. 151]

In other words, contracts about property in the person inevitably create subordination. "Anarcho"-capitalism defines this source

Is "anarcho"-capitalism a type of anarchism?

of unfreedom away, but it still exists and has a major impact on people's liberty. For anarchists freedom is better described as "self-government" or "self-management" – to be able to govern ones own actions (if alone) or to participate in the determination of join activity (if part of a group). Freedom, to put it another way, is not an abstract legal concept, but the vital concrete possibility for every human being to bring to full development all their powers, capacities, and talents which nature has endowed them. A key aspect of this is to govern ones own actions when within associations (self-management). If we look at freedom this way, we see that coercion is condemned but so is hierarchy (and so is capitalism for during working hours people are not free to make their own plans and have a say in what affects them. They are order takers, **not** free individuals).

It is because anarchists have recognised the authoritarian nature of capitalist firms that they have opposed wage labour and capitalist property rights along with the state. They have desired to replace institutions structured by subordination with institutions constituted by free relationships (based, in other words, on self-management) in **all** areas of life, including economic organisations. Hence Proudhon's argument that the *"workmen's associations … are full of hope both as a protest against the wage system, and as an affirmation of* **reciprocity***"* and that their importance lies *"in their denial of the rule of capitalists, money lenders and governments."* [**The General Idea of the Revolution**, pp. 98-99]

Unlike anarchists, the "anarcho"-capitalist account of freedom allows an individual's freedom to be rented out to another while maintaining that the person is still free. It may seem strange that an ideology proclaiming its support for liberty sees nothing wrong with the alienation and denial of liberty but, in actual fact, it is unsurprising. After all, contract theory is a *"theoretical strategy that justifies subjection by presenting it as freedom"* and has *"turned a subversive proposition [that we are born free and equal] into a defence of civil subjection."* Little wonder, then, that contract *"creates a relation of subordination"* and not of freedom [Carole Pateman, **Op. Cit.**, p. 39 and p. 59] Little wonder, then, that Colin Ward argued that, as an anarchist, he is *"by definition, a socialist"* and that *"[w]orkers' control of industrial production"* is *"the only approach compatible with anarchism."* [**Talking Anarchy**, p. 25 and p. 26]

Ultimately, any attempt to build an ethical framework starting from the abstract individual (as Rothbard does with his *"legitimate rights"* method) will result in domination and oppression between people, **not** freedom. Indeed, Rothbard provides an example of the dangers of idealist philosophy that Bakunin warned about when he argued that while *"[m]aterialism denies free will and ends in the establishment of liberty; idealism, in the name of human dignity, proclaims free will, and on the ruins of every liberty founds authority."* [**God and the State**, p. 48] That this is the case with "anarcho"-capitalism can be seen from Rothbard's wholehearted support for wage labour, landlordism and the rules imposed by property owners on those who use, but do not own, their property. Rothbard, basing himself on abstract individualism, cannot help but justify authority over liberty. This, undoubtedly, flows from the right-liberal and conservative roots of his ideology. Individualist anarchist Shawn Wilbar once defined Wikipedia as *"the most successful modern experiment in promoting*

obedience to authority as freedom." However, Wikipedia pales into insignificance compared to the success of liberalism (in its many forms) in doing precisely that. Whether politically or economically, liberalism has always rushed to justify and rationalise the individual subjecting themselves to some form of hierarchy. That "anarcho"-capitalism does this under the name "anarchism" is deeply insulting to anarchists.

Overall, we can see that the logic of the right-"libertarian" definition of "freedom" ends up negating itself because it results in the creation and encouragement of **authority,** which is an **opposite** of freedom. For example, as Ayn Rand pointed out, *"man has to sustain his life by his own effort, the man who has no right to the product of his effort has no means to sustain his life. The man who produces while others dispose of his product, is a slave."* [**The Ayn Rand Lexicon: Objectivism from A to Z**, pp. 388-9] But, as was shown in section C.2, capitalism is based on, as Proudhon put it, workers working *"for an entrepreneur who pays them and keeps their products,"* and so is a form of **theft.** Thus, by "libertarian" capitalism's **own** logic, capitalism is based not on freedom, but on (wage) slavery; for interest, profit and rent are derived from a worker's **unpaid** labour, i.e. *"others dispose of his [sic] product."*

Thus it is debatable that a right-"libertarian" or "anarcho" capitalist society would have less unfreedom or authoritarianism in it than "actually existing" capitalism. In contrast to anarchism, "anarcho"-capitalism, with its narrow definitions, restricts freedom to only a few areas of social life and ignores domination and authority beyond those aspects. As Peter Marshall points out, their *"definition of freedom is entirely negative. It calls for the absence of coercion but cannot guarantee the positive freedom of individual autonomy and independence."* [**Demanding the Impossible**, p. 564] By confining freedom to such a narrow range of human action, "anarcho"-capitalism is clearly **not** a form of anarchism. Real anarchists support freedom in every aspect of an individual's life.

In short, as French anarchist Elisée Reclus put it there is *"an abyss between two kinds of society,"* one of which is *"constituted freely by men of good will, based on a consideration of their common interests"* and another which *"accepts the existence of either temporary or permanent masters to whom [its members] owe obedience."* [quoted by Clark and Martin, **Anarchy, Geography, Modernity**, p. 62] In other words, when choosing between anarchism and capitalism, "anarcho"-capitalists pick the latter and call it the former.

F.2.1 How does private property affect freedom?

The right-"libertarian" either does not acknowledge or dismisses as irrelevant the fact that the (absolute) right of private property may lead to extensive control by property owners over those who use, but do not own, property (such as workers and tenants). Thus a free-market capitalist system leads to a very selective and class-based protection of "rights" and "freedoms." For example, under capitalism, the "freedom" of employers inevitably conflicts with the "freedom" of employees. When stockholders or their managers exercise their "freedom of enterprise" to decide how their company will operate, they violate their employee's right to decide how their labouring capacities will be utilised and so under capitalism the "property rights" of employers will conflict with and restrict the "human right" of employees to manage themselves. Capitalism allows the right of self-management only to the few, not to all. Or, alternatively, capitalism does not recognise certain human rights as **universal** which anarchism does.

This can be seen from Austrian Economist W. Duncan Reekie's defence of wage labour. While referring to *"intra-firm labour markets"* as *"hierarchies"*, Reekie (in his best *ex cathedra* tone) states that *"[t]here is nothing authoritarian, dictatorial or exploitative in the relationship. Employees order employers to pay them amounts specified in the hiring contract just as much as employers order employees to abide by the terms of the contract."* [**Markets, Entrepreneurs and Liberty**, p. 136 and p. 137]. Given that *"the terms of contract"* involve the worker agreeing to obey the employers orders and that they will be fired if they do not, its pretty clear that the ordering that goes on in the *"intra-firm labour market"* is decidedly **one way**. Bosses have the power, workers are paid to obey. And this begs the question: **if** the employment contract creates a free worker, why must she abandon her liberty during work hours?

Reekie actually recognises this lack of freedom in a "round about" way when he notes that *"employees in a firm at any level in the hierarchy can exercise an entrepreneurial role. The area within which that role can be carried out increases the more authority the employee has."* [**Op. Cit.**, p. 142] Which means workers **are** subject to control from above which restricts the activities they are allowed to do and so they are **not** free to act, make decisions, participate in the plans of the organisation, to create the future and so forth within working hours. And it is strange that while recognising the firm as a hierarchy, Reekie tries to deny that it is authoritarian or dictatorial – as if you could have a hierarchy without authoritarian structures or an unelected person in authority who is not a dictator. His confusion is shared by Austrian guru Ludwig von Mises, who asserted that the *"entrepreneur and capitalist are not irresponsible autocrats"* because they are *"unconditionally subject to the sovereignty of the consumer"* while, **on the next page**, admitting there was a *"managerial hierarchy"* which contains *"the average subordinate employee."* [**Human Action**, p. 809 and p. 810] It does not enter his mind that the capitalist may be subject to some consumer control while being an autocrat to their subordinated employees. Again, we find the right-"libertarian" acknowledging that the capitalist managerial structure is a hierarchy and workers are subordinated while denying it is autocratic to the workers! Thus we have "free" workers within a relationship distinctly **lacking** freedom – a strange paradox. Indeed, if your personal life were as closely monitored and regulated as the work life of millions of people across the world, you would rightly consider it the worse form of oppression and tyranny.

Somewhat ironically, right-wing liberal and "free market" economist Milton Friedman contrasted *"central planning involving the use of coercion – the technique of the army or the modern totalitarian state"* with *"voluntary co-operation between individuals – the technique of the marketplace"* as two distinct ways of co-ordinating the economic activity of large groups (*"millions"*) of people. [**Capitalism and Freedom**, p. 13] However, this misses the key issue of the internal nature of the company. As right-"libertarians" themselves note, the internal structure of a capitalist company is hierarchical. Indeed, the capitalist company **is** a form of central planning and so shares the same "technique" as the army. As Peter Drucker noted in his history of General Motors, *"[t]here is a remarkably close parallel between General Motors' scheme of organisation and those of the two institutions most renowned for administrative efficiency: that of the Catholic Church and that of the modern army."* [quoted by David Engler, **Apostles of Greed**, p. 66] Thus capitalism is marked by a series of totalitarian organisations. Dictatorship does not change much – nor does it become less fascistic – when discussing economic structures rather than political ones. To state the obvious, *"the employment contract (like the marriage contract) is not an exchange; both contracts create social relations that endure over time – social relations of subordination."* [Carole Pateman, **The Sexual Contract**, p. 148]

Perhaps Reekie (like most right-"libertarians") will maintain that workers voluntarily agree ("consent") to be subject to the bosses dictatorship (he writes that *"each will only enter into the contractual agreement known as a firm if each believes he will be better off thereby. The firm is simply another example of mutually beneficial exchange."* [**Op. Cit.**, p. 137]). However, this does not stop the relationship being authoritarian or dictatorial (and so exploitative as it is **highly** unlikely that those at the top will not abuse their power). Representing employment relations as voluntary agreement simply mystifies the existence and exercise of power within the organisation so created.

As we argue further in the section F.3, in a capitalist society workers have the option of finding a job or facing abject poverty and/or starvation. Little wonder, then, that people "voluntarily" sell their labour and "consent" to authoritarian structures! They have little option to do otherwise. So, **within** the labour market workers **can** and **do** seek out the best working conditions possible, but that does not mean that the final contract agreed is "freely" accepted and not due to the force of circumstances, that both parties have equal bargaining power when drawing up the contract or that the freedom of both parties is ensured.

Which means to argue (as right-"libertarians" do) that freedom cannot be restricted by wage labour because people enter into relationships they consider will lead to improvements over their initial situation totally misses the point. As the initial situation is not considered relevant, their argument fails. After all, agreeing to work in a sweatshop 14 hours a day **is** an improvement over starving to death – but it does not mean that those who so agree are free when working there or actually **want** to be there. They are not and it is the circumstances, created and enforced by the law (i.e., the state), that have ensured that they "consent" to such a regime (given the chance, they would desire to **change** that regime but cannot as this would violate their bosses property rights and they would be repressed for trying).

So the "libertarian" right is interested only in a narrow concept of freedom (rather than in freedom or liberty as such). This can be seen in the argument of Ayn Rand that *"**Freedom**, in a political context, means freedom from government coercion. It does **not** *mean freedom from the landlord, or freedom from the employer, or freedom from the laws of nature which do not provide men with automatic prosperity. It means freedom from the coercive power of the state – and nothing else!"* [**Capitalism: The Unknown Ideal**, p. 192] By arguing in this way, right-"libertarians" ignore the vast number of authoritarian social relationships that exist in capitalist society and, as Rand does here, imply that these social relationships are like *"the laws of nature."* However, if one looks at the world without prejudice but with an eye to maximising freedom, the major coercive institutions are the state **and** capitalist social relationships (and the latter relies on the former). It should also be noted that, unlike gravity, the power of the landlord and boss depends on the use of force – gravity does not need policemen to make things fall! The right "libertarian," then, far from being a defender of freedom, is in fact a keen defender of certain forms of authority. As Kropotkin argued against a forerunner of right-"libertarianism":

> *"The modern Individualism initiated by Herbert Spencer is, like the critical theory of Proudhon, a powerful indictment against the dangers and wrongs of government, but its practical solution of the social problem is miserable – so miserable as to lead us to inquire if the talk of 'No force' be merely an excuse for supporting landlord and capitalist domination."* [**Act For Yourselves**, p. 98]

To defend the "freedom" of property owners is to defend authority and privilege – in other words, statism. So, in considering the concept of liberty as "freedom from," it is clear that by defending private property (as opposed to possession) the "anarcho"-capitalist is defending the power and authority of property owners to govern those who use "their" property. And also, we must note, defending all the petty tyrannies that make the work lives of so many people frustrating, stressful and unrewarding.

Anarchism, by definition, is in favour of organisations and social relationships which are non-hierarchical and non-authoritarian. Otherwise, some people are more free than others. Failing to attack hierarchy leads to massive contradictions. For example, since the British Army is a volunteer one, it is an "anarchist" organisation! Ironically, it can also allow a state to appear "libertarian" as that, too, can be considered a voluntary arrangement as long as it allows its subjects to emigrate freely. So equating freedom with (capitalist) property rights does not protect freedom, in fact it actively denies it. This lack of freedom is only inevitable as long as we accept capitalist private property rights. If we reject them, we can try and create a world based on freedom in all aspects of life, rather than just in a few.

F.2.2 Do "libertarian" -capitalists support slavery?

Yes. It may come as a surprise to many people, but right-"Libertarianism" is one of the few political theories that justifies slavery. For example, Robert Nozick asks whether *"a free system would allow [the individual] to sell himself into slavery"* and he answers *"I believe that it would."* [**Anarchy, State and Utopia**, p. 371] While some right-"libertarians" do not agree with Nozick, there is no logical basis in their ideology for such disagreement.

This can be seen from "anarcho"-capitalist Walter Block, who, like Nozick, supports voluntary slavery. As he puts it, *"if I own something, I can sell it (and should be allowed by law to do so). If I can't sell, then, and to that extent, I really don't own it."* Thus agreeing to sell yourself for a lifetime *"is a bona fide contract"* which, if *"abrogated, theft occurs."* He critiques those other right-wing "libertarians" (like Murray Rothbard) who oppose voluntary slavery as being inconsistent to their principles. Block, in his words, seeks to make *"a tiny adjustment"* which *"strengthens libertarianism by making it more internally consistent."* He argues that his position shows *"that contract, predicated on private property [can] reach to the furthest realms of human interaction, even to voluntary slave contracts."* [*"Towards a Libertarian Theory of Inalienability: A Critique of Rothbard, Barnett, Smith, Kinsella, Gordon, and Epstein,"* pp. 39-85, **Journal of Libertarian Studies**, vol. 17, no. 2, p. 44, p. 48, p. 82 and p. 46]

So the logic is simple, you cannot really own something unless you can sell it. Self-ownership is one of the cornerstones of laissez-faire capitalist ideology. Therefore, since you own yourself you can sell yourself.

This defence of slavery should not come as a surprise to any one familiar with classical liberalism. An elitist ideology, its main rationale is to defend the liberty and power of property owners and justify unfree social relationships (such as government and wage labour) in terms of "consent." Nozick and Block just take it to its logical conclusion. This is because their position is not new but, as with so many other right-"libertarian" ones, can be found in John Locke's work. The key difference is that Locke refused the term *"slavery"* and favoured *"drudgery"* as, for him, slavery meant a relationship *"between a lawful conqueror and a captive"* where the former has the power of life and death over the latter. Once a *"compact"* is agreed between them, *"an agreement for a limited power on the one side, and obedience on the other … slavery ceases."* As long as the master could not kill the slave, then it was *"drudgery."* Like Nozick, he acknowledges that *"men did sell themselves; but, it is plain, this was only to drudgery, not to slavery: for, it is evident, the person sold was not under an absolute, arbitrary, despotical power: for the master could not have power to kill him, at any time, whom, at a certain time, he was obliged to let go free out of his service."* [Locke, **Second Treatise of Government**, Section 24] In other words, voluntary slavery was fine but just call it something else.

Not that Locke was bothered by **involuntary** slavery. He was heavily involved in the slave trade. He owned shares in the **"Royal Africa Company"** which carried on the slave trade for England, making a profit when he sold them. He also held a significant share in another slave company, the **"Bahama Adventurers."** In the *"Second Treatise"*, Locke justified slavery in terms of *"Captives taken in a just war,"* a war waged against aggressors. [Section 85] That, of course, had nothing to do with the **actual** slavery Locke profited from (slave raids were common, for example). Nor did his "liberal" principles stop him suggesting a constitution that would ensure that *"every freeman of Carolina shall have absolute power and authority over his Negro slaves."* The constitution itself was typically autocratic and hierarchical, designed explicitly to *"avoid erecting a numerous democracy."* [**The Works of John Locke**, vol. X, p. 196]

So the notion of contractual slavery has a long history within right-wing liberalism, although most refuse to call it by that name. It is of course simply embarrassment that stops many right-"libertarians" calling a spade a spade. They incorrectly assume that slavery has to be involuntary. In fact, historically, voluntary slave contracts have been common (David Ellerman's **Property and Contract in Economics** has an excellent overview). Any new form of voluntary slavery would be a "civilised" form of slavery and could occur when an individual would "agree" to sell their lifetime's labour to another (as when a starving worker would "agree" to become a slave in return for food). In addition, the contract would be able to be broken under certain conditions (perhaps in return for breaking the contract, the former slave would have pay damages to his or her master for the labour their master would lose – a sizeable amount no doubt and such a payment could result in debt slavery, which is the most common form of "civilised" slavery. Such damages may be agreed in the contract as a "performance bond" or "conditional exchange."

In summary, right-"libertarians" are talking about "civilised" slavery (or, in other words, civil slavery) and not forced slavery. While some may have reservations about calling it slavery, they agree with the basic concept that since people own themselves they can sell themselves, that is sell their labour for a lifetime rather than piecemeal.

We must stress that this is no academic debate. "Voluntary" slavery has been a problem in many societies and still exists in many countries today (particularly third world ones where bonded labour – i.e. where debt is used to enslave people – is the most common form). With the rise of sweat shops and child labour in many "developed" countries such as the USA, "voluntary" slavery (perhaps via debt and bonded labour) may become common in all parts of the world – an ironic (if not surprising) result of "freeing" the market and being indifferent to the actual freedom of those within it.

Some right-"libertarians" are obviously uneasy with the logical conclusion of their definition of freedom. Murray Rothbard, for example, stressed the *"unenforceability, in libertarian theory, of voluntary slave contracts."* Of course, **other** "libertarian" theorists claim the exact opposite, so *"libertarian theory"* makes no such claim, but never mind! Essentially, his objection revolves around the assertion that a person *"cannot, in nature, sell himself into slavery and have this sale enforced – for this would mean that his future will over his own body was being surrendered in advance"* and that if a *"labourer remains totally subservient to his master's will*

voluntarily, he is not yet a slave since his submission is voluntary." However, as we noted in section F.2, Rothbard's emphasis on quitting fails to recognise the actual denial of will and control over ones own body that is explicit in wage labour. It is this failure that pro-slave contract "libertarians" stress – they consider the slave contract as an extended wage contract. Moreover, a modern slave contract would likely take the form of a *"performance bond,"* on which Rothbard laments about its *"unfortunate suppression"* by the state. In such a system, the slave could agree to perform X years labour or pay their master substantial damages if they fail to do so. It is the threat of damages that enforces the contract and such a "contract" Rothbard does agree is enforceable. Another means of creating slave contracts would be *"conditional exchange"* which Rothbard also supports. As for debt bondage, that too, seems acceptable. He surreally notes that paying damages and debts in such contracts is fine as *"money, of course, **is** alienable"* and so forgets that it needs to be earned by labour which, he asserts, is **not** alienable! [**The Ethics of Liberty**, pp. 134-135, p. 40, pp. 136-9, p. 141 and p. 138]

It should be noted that the slavery contract cannot be null and void because it is unenforceable, as Rothbard suggests. This is because the doctrine of specific performance applies to all contracts, not just to labour contracts. This is because **all** contracts specify some future performance. In the case of the lifetime labour contract, then it can be broken as long as the slave pays any appropriate damages. As Rothbard puts it elsewhere, *"if A has agreed to work for life for B in exchange for 10,000 grams of gold, he will have to return the proportionate amount of property if he terminates the arrangement and ceases to work."* [**Man, Economy, and State**, vol. I , p. 441] This is understandable, as the law generally allows material damages for breached contracts, as does Rothbard in his support for the *"performance bond"* and *"conditional exchange."* Needless to say, having to pay such damages (either as a lump sum or over a period of time) could turn the worker into the most common type of modern slave, the debt-slave.

And it is interesting to note that even Murray Rothbard is not against the selling of humans. He argued that children are the property of their parents who can (bar actually murdering them by violence) do whatever they please with them, even sell them on a *"flourishing free child market."* [**The Ethics of Liberty**, p. 102] Combined with a whole hearted support for child labour (after all, the child can leave its parents if it objects to working for them) such a "free child market" could easily become a "child slave market" – with entrepreneurs making a healthy profit selling infants and children or their labour to capitalists (as did occur in 19th century Britain). Unsurprisingly, Rothbard ignores the possible nasty aspects of such a market in human flesh (such as children being sold to work in factories, homes and brothels). But this is besides the point.

Of course, this theoretical justification for slavery at the heart of an ideology calling itself "libertarianism" is hard for many right-"libertarians" to accept and so they argue that such contracts would be very hard to enforce. This attempt to get out of the contradiction fails simply because it ignores the nature of the capitalist market. If there is a demand for slave contracts to be enforced, then companies will develop to provide that "service" (and it would be interesting to see how two "protection" firms, one defending slave

Is "anarcho"-capitalism a type of anarchism?

contracts and another not, could compromise and reach a peaceful agreement over whether slave contracts were valid). Thus we could see a so-called "free" society producing companies whose specific purpose was to hunt down escaped slaves (i.e. individuals in slave contracts who have not paid damages to their owners for freedom). Of course, perhaps Rothbard would claim that such slave contracts would be "outlawed" under his *"general libertarian law code"* but this is a denial of market "freedom". If slave contracts **are** "banned" then surely this is paternalism, stopping individuals from contracting out their "labour services" to whom and however long they "desire". You cannot have it both ways.

So, ironically, an ideology proclaiming itself to support "liberty" ends up justifying and defending slavery. Indeed, for the right-"libertarian" the slave contract is an exemplification, not the denial, of the individual's liberty! How is this possible? How can slavery be supported as an expression of liberty? Simply, right-"libertarian" support for slavery is a symptom of a **deeper** authoritarianism, namely their uncritical acceptance of contract theory. The central claim of contract theory is that a contract is the means to secure and enhance individual freedom. Slavery is the antithesis to freedom and so, in theory, contract and slavery must be mutually exclusive. However, as indicated above, some contract theorists (past and present) have included slave contracts among legitimate contracts. This suggests that contract theory cannot provide the theoretical support needed to secure and enhance individual freedom.

As Carole Pateman argues, *"contract theory is primarily about a way of creating social relations constituted by subordination, not about exchange."* Rather than undermining subordination, contract theorists justify modern subjection – *"contract doctrine has proclaimed that subjection to a master – a boss, a husband – is freedom."* [**The Sexual Contract**, p. 40 and p. 146] The question central to contract theory (and so right-Libertarianism) is not "are people free" (as one would expect) but "are people free to subordinate themselves in any manner they please." A radically different question and one only fitting to someone who does not know what liberty means.

Anarchists argue that not all contracts are legitimate and no free individual can make a contract that denies his or her own freedom. If an individual is able to express themselves by making free agreements then those free agreements must also be based upon freedom internally as well. Any agreement that creates domination or hierarchy negates the assumptions underlying the agreement and makes itself null and void. In other words, voluntary government is still government and a defining characteristic of an anarchy must be, surely, "no government" and "no rulers."

This is most easily seen in the extreme case of the slave contract. John Stuart Mill stated that such a contract would be "null and void." He argued that an individual may voluntarily choose to enter such a contract but in so doing *"he abdicates his liberty; he foregoes any future use of it beyond that single act. He therefore defeats, in his own case, the very purpose which is the justification of allowing him to dispose of himself ... The principle of freedom cannot require that he should be free not to be free. It is not freedom, to be allowed to alienate his freedom."* He adds that *"these reasons, the force of which is so conspicuous in this particular case, are evidently of far wider application."* [quoted by Pateman, **Op. Cit.**, pp. 171-2]

And it is such an application that defenders of capitalism fear (Mill did in fact apply these reasons wider and unsurprisingly became a supporter of a market syndicalist form of socialism). If we reject slave contracts as illegitimate then, logically, we must also reject **all** contracts that express qualities similar to slavery (i.e. deny freedom) including wage slavery. Given that, as David Ellerman points out, *"the voluntary slave ... and the employee cannot in fact take their will out of their intentional actions so that they could be 'employed' by the master or employer"* we are left with *"the rather implausible assertion that a person can vacate his or her will for eight or so hours a day for weeks, months, or years on end but cannot do so for a working lifetime."* [**Property and Contract in Economics**, p. 58] This is Rothbard's position.

The implications of supporting voluntary slavery are quite devastating for all forms of right-wing "libertarianism." This was proven by Ellerman when he wrote an extremely robust defence of it under the pseudonym "J. Philmore" called **The Libertarian Case for Slavery** (first published in **The Philosophical Forum**, xiv, 1982). This classic rebuttal takes the form of "proof by contradiction" (or **reductio ad absurdum**) whereby he takes the arguments of right-libertarianism to their logical end and shows how they reach the memorable conclusion that the *"time has come for liberal economic and political thinkers to stop dodging this issue and to critically re-examine their shared prejudices about certain voluntary social institutions ... this critical process will inexorably drive liberalism to its only logical conclusion: libertarianism that finally lays the true moral foundation for economic and political slavery."* Ellerman shows how, from a right-"libertarian" perspective there is a *"fundamental contradiction"* in a modern liberal society for the state to prohibit slave contracts. He notes that there *"seems to be a basic shared prejudice of liberalism that slavery is inherently involuntary, so the issue of genuinely voluntary slavery has received little scrutiny. The perfectly valid liberal argument that involuntary slavery is inherently unjust is thus taken to include voluntary slavery (in which case, the argument, by definition, does not apply). This has resulted in an abridgement of the freedom of contract in modern liberal society."* Thus it is possible to argue for a *"civilised form of contractual slavery."* ["J. Philmore,", **Op. Cit.**]

So accurate and logical was Ellerman's article that many of its readers were convinced it **was** written by a right-"libertarian" (including, we have to say, us!). One such writer was Carole Pateman, who correctly noted that *"[t]here is a nice historical irony here. In the American South, slaves were emancipated and turned into wage labourers, and now American contractarians argue that all workers should have the opportunity to turn themselves into civil slaves."* [**Op. Cit.**, p. 63]).

The aim of Ellerman's article was to show the problems that employment (wage labour) presents for the concept of self-government and how contract need not result in social relationships based on freedom. As "Philmore" put it, *"[a]ny thorough and decisive critique of voluntary slavery or constitutional nondemocratic government would carry over to the employment contract – which is the voluntary contractual basis for the free-market free-enterprise system. Such a critique would thus be a **reductio ad absurdum**."* As "contractual slavery" is an *"extension of the employer-employee contract,"* he shows that the difference between wage labour and slavery is the time scale rather than the principle or social relationships involved. [**Op. Cit.**] This explains why the early workers' movement called capitalism **"wage slavery"** and why anarchists still do. It exposes the unfree nature of capitalism and the poverty of its vision of freedom. While it is possible to present wage labour as "freedom" due to its "consensual" nature, it becomes much harder to do so when talking about slavery or dictatorship (and let us not forget that Nozick also had no problem with autocracy – see section B.4). Then the contradictions are exposed for all to see and be horrified by.

All this does not mean that we must reject free agreement. Far from it! Free agreement is **essential** for a society based upon individual dignity and liberty. There are a variety of forms of free agreement and anarchists support those based upon co-operation and self-management (i.e. individuals working together as equals). Anarchists desire to create relationships which reflect (and so express) the liberty that is the basis of free agreement. Capitalism creates relationships that deny liberty. The opposition between autonomy and subjection can only be maintained by modifying or rejecting contract theory, something that capitalism cannot do and so the right-wing "libertarian" rejects autonomy in favour of subjection (and so rejects socialism in favour of capitalism).

So the real contrast between genuine libertarians and right-"libertarians" is best expressed in their respective opinions on slavery. Anarchism is based upon the individual whose individuality depends upon the maintenance of free relationships with other individuals. If individuals deny their capacities for self-government through a contract the individuals bring about a qualitative change in their relationship to others – freedom is turned into mastery and subordination. For the anarchist, slavery is thus the paradigm of what freedom is **not**, instead of an exemplification of what it is (as right-"libertarians" state). As Proudhon argued:

> "If I were asked to answer the following question: What is slavery? and I should answer in one word, It is murder, my meaning would be understood at once. No extended argument would be required to show that the power to take from a man his thought, his will, his personality, is a power of life and death; and that to enslave a man is to kill him." [**What is Property?**, p. 37]

In contrast, the right-"libertarian" effectively argues that "I support slavery because I believe in liberty." It is a sad reflection of the ethical and intellectual bankruptcy of our society that such an "argument" is actually proposed by some people under the name of liberty. The concept of "slavery as freedom" is far too Orwellian to warrant a critique – we will leave it up to right-"libertarians" to corrupt our language and ethical standards with an attempt to prove it.

From the basic insight that slavery is the opposite of freedom, the anarchist rejection of authoritarian social relations quickly follows:

> "Liberty is inviolable. I can neither sell nor alienate my liberty; every contract, every condition of a contract, which has in view the alienation or suspension of liberty, is null: the slave, when he plants his foot upon the soil of liberty, at that moment becomes a free man ... Liberty

is the original condition of man; to renounce liberty is to renounce the nature of man: after that, how could we perform the acts of man?" [P.J. Proudhon, **Op. Cit.**, p. 67]

The employment contract (i.e. wage slavery) abrogates liberty. It is based upon inequality of power and "exploitation is a consequence of the fact that the sale of labour power entails the worker's subordination." [Carole Pateman, **Op. Cit.**, p. 149] Hence Proudhon's support for self-management and opposition to capitalism – any relationship that resembles slavery is illegitimate and no contract that creates a relationship of subordination is valid. Thus in a truly anarchistic society, slave contracts would be unenforceable – people in a truly free (i.e. non-capitalist) society would **never** tolerate such a horrible institution or consider it a valid agreement. If someone was silly enough to sign such a contract, they would simply have to say they now rejected it in order to be free – such contracts are made to be broken and without the force of a law system (and private defence firms) to back it up, such contracts will stay broken.

The right-"libertarian" support for slave contracts (and wage slavery) indicates that their ideology has little to do with liberty and far more to do with justifying property and the oppression and exploitation it produces. Their theoretical support for permanent and temporary voluntary slavery and autocracy indicates a deeper authoritarianism which negates their claims to be libertarians.

F.3

Why do "anarcho"-capitalists place little or no value on equality?

Murray Rothbard argued that "the 'rightist' libertarian is not opposed to inequality." [**For a New Liberty**, p. 47] In contrast, genuine libertarians oppose inequality because it has harmful effects on individual liberty. Part of the reason "anarcho"-capitalism places little or no value on "equality" derives from their definition of that term. "A and B are 'equal,'" Rothbard argued, "if they are identical to each other with respect to a given attribute ... There is one and only one way, then, in which any two people can really be 'equal' in the fullest sense: they must be identical in **all** their attributes." He then pointed out the obvious fact that "men are not uniform ... the species, mankind, is uniquely characterised by a high degree of variety, diversity, differentiation: in short, inequality." [**Egalitarianism as a Revolt against Nature and Other Essays**, p. 4 and p.5]

In others words, every individual is unique – something no egalitarian has ever denied. On the basis of this amazing insight, he concludes that equality is impossible (except "equality of rights") and that the attempt to achieve "equality" is a "revolt against nature." The utility of Rothbard's sophistry to the rich and powerful should be obvious as it moves analysis away from the social system we live in and onto biological differences. This means that because we are all unique, the outcome of our actions will not be identical and so

Is "anarcho"-capitalism a type of anarchism?

social inequality flows from natural differences and is not due to the economic system we live under. Inequality of endowment, in this perspective, implies inequality of outcome and so social inequality. As individual differences are a fact of nature, attempts to create a society based on "equality" (i.e. making everyone identical in terms of possessions and so forth) is impossible and "unnatural." That this would be music to the ears of the wealthy should go without saying.

Before continuing, we must note that Rothbard is destroying language to make his point and that he is not the first to abuse language in this particular way. In George Orwell's **1984**, the expression *"all men are created equal"* could be translated into Newspeak *"but only in the same sense in which **All men are redhaired** is a possible Oldspeak sentence. It did not contain a grammatical error, but it expressed a palpable untruth – i.e. that all men are of equal size, weight, or strength."* [*"Appendix: The Principles of Newspeak"*, **1984**, p. 246] It is nice to know that "Mr. Libertarian" is stealing ideas from Big Brother, and for the same reason: to make critical thought impossible by restricting the meaning of words.

"Equality," in the context of political discussion, does not mean "identical," it means equality of rights, respect, worth, power and so forth. It does not imply treating everyone identically (for example, expecting an eighty year old man to do identical work as an eighteen violates treating both equally with respect as unique individuals). Needless to say, no anarchist has ever advocated such a notion of equality as being identical. As discussed in section A.2.5, anarchists have always based our arguments on the need for social equality on the fact that, while people are different, we all have the same right to be free and that inequality in wealth produces inequalities of liberty. For anarchists:

> "equality does not mean an equal amount but equal **opportunity** … Do not make the mistake of identifying equality in liberty with the forced equality of the convict camp. True anarchist equality implies freedom, not quantity. It does not mean that every one must eat, drink, or wear the same things, do the same work, or live in the same manner. Far from it: the very reverse, in fact. Individual needs and tastes differ, as appetites differ. It is **equal** opportunity to satisfy them that constitutes true equality. Far from levelling, such equality opens the door for the greatest possible variety of activity and development. For human character is diverse, and only the repression of this free diversity results in levelling, in uniformity and sameness. Free opportunity and acting out your individuality means development of natural dissimilarities and variations. … Life in freedom, in anarchy will do more than liberate man merely from his present political and economic bondage. That will be only the first step, the preliminary to a truly human existence." [**What is Anarchism?**, pp. 164-5]

So it is precisely the diversity of individuals (their uniqueness) which drives the anarchist support for equality, not its denial. Thus anarchists reject the Rothbardian-Newspeak definition of equality as meaningless. No two people are identical and so imposing "identical" equality between them would mean treating them as **unequals**, i.e. not having equal worth or giving them equal respect as befits them as human beings and fellow unique individuals.

So what should we make of Rothbard's claim? It is tempting just to quote Rousseau when he argued *"it is … useless to inquire whether there is any essential connection between the two inequalities [social and natural]; for this would be only asking, in other words, whether those who command are necessarily better than those who obey, and if strength of body or of mind, wisdom, or virtue are always found in particular individuals, in proportion to their power or wealth: a question fit perhaps to be discussed by slaves in the hearing of their masters, but highly unbecoming to reasonable and free men in search of the truth."* [**The Social Contract and Discourses**, p. 49] This seems applicable when you see Rothbard proclaim that inequality of individuals will lead to inequalities of income as *"each man will tend to earn an income equal to his 'marginal productivity.'"* This is because *"some men"* (and it is always men!) are *"more intelligent, others more alert and farsighted, than the remainder of the population"* and capitalism will *"allow the rise of these natural aristocracies."* In fact, for Rothbard, all government, in its essence, is a conspiracy against the superior man. [**The Logic of Action II,** p. 29 and p. 34] But a few more points should be raised.

The uniqueness of individuals has always existed but for the vast majority of human history we have lived in very egalitarian societies. If social inequality did, indeed, flow from natural inequalities then **all** societies would be marked by it. This is not the case. Indeed, taking a relatively recent example, many visitors to the early United States noted its egalitarian nature, something that soon changed with the rise of capitalism (a rise dependent upon state action, we must add). This implies that the society we live in (its rights framework, the social relationships it generates and so forth) has far more of a decisive impact on inequality than individual differences. Thus certain rights frameworks will tend to magnify "natural" inequalities (assuming that is the source of the initial inequality, rather than, say, violence and force). As Noam Chomsky argues:

> "Presumably it is the case that in our 'real world' some combination of attributes is conducive to success in responding to 'the demands of the economic system.' Let us agree, for the sake of discussion, that this combination of attributes is in part a matter of native endowment. Why does this (alleged) fact pose an 'intellectual dilemma' to egalitarians? Note that we can hardly claim much insight into just what the relevant combination of attributes may be…. One might suppose that some mixture of avarice, selfishness, lack of concern for others, aggressiveness, and similar characteristics play a part in getting ahead and 'making it' in a competitive society based on capitalist principles…. Whatever the correct collection of attributes may be, we may ask what follows from the fact, if it is a fact, that some partially inherited combination of attributes tends to material success? All that follows … is a comment on our particular social and economic arrangements…. The egalitarian might respond, in all such cases, that the social order should be changed so that the collection of attributes that tends to bring success no

longer do so. He might even argue that in a more decent society, the attributes that now lead to success would be recognised as pathological, and that gentle persuasion might be a proper means to help people to overcome their unfortunate malady." [**The Chomsky Reader**, p. 190]

So if we change society then the social inequalities we see today would disappear. It is more than probable that natural difference has long ago been replaced with **social** inequalities, especially inequalities of property. And as we argue in section F.8 these inequalities of property were initially the result of force, **not** differences in ability. Thus to claim that social inequality flows from natural differences is false as most social inequality has flown from violence and force. This initial inequality has been magnified by the framework of capitalist property rights and so the inequality within capitalism is far more dependent upon, say, the existence of wage labour rather than "natural" differences between individuals.

This can be seen from existing society: we see that in workplaces and across industries many, if not most, unique individuals receive identical wages for identical work (although this often is not the case for women and blacks, who receive less wages than male, white workers for identical labour). Similarly, capitalists have deliberately introduced wage inequalities and hierarchies for no other reason that to divide and so rule the workforce (see section D.10). Thus, if we assume egalitarianism **is** a revolt against nature, then much of capitalist economic life is in such a revolt and when it is not, the "natural" inequalities have usually been imposed artificially by those in power either within the workplace or in society as a whole by means of state intervention, property laws and authoritarian social structures. Moreover, as we indicated in section C.2.5, anarchists have been aware of the **collective** nature of production within capitalism since Proudhon wrote **What is Property?** in 1840. Rothbard ignores both the anarchist tradition and reality when he stresses that individual differences produce inequalities of outcome. As an economist with a firmer grasp of the real world put it, the *"notion that wages depend on personal skill, as expressed in the value of output, makes no sense in any organisation where production is interdependent and joint – which is to say it makes no sense in virtually any organisation."* [James K. Galbraith, **Created Unequal**, p. 263]

Thus "natural" differences do not necessarily result in inequality as such nor do such differences have much meaning in an economy marked by joint production. Given a different social system, "natural" differences would be encouraged and celebrated far wider than they are under capitalism (where hierarchy ensures the crushing of individuality rather than its encouragement) without any reduction in social equality. At its most basic, the elimination of hierarchy within the workplace would not only increase freedom but also reduce inequality as the few would not be able to monopolise the decision making process and the fruit of joint productive activity. So the claim that "natural" differences generate social inequalities is question begging in the extreme – it takes the rights framework of capitalism as a given and ignores the initial source of inequality in property and power. Indeed, inequality of outcome or reward is more likely to be influenced by social conditions rather than individual differences (as would be expected in a society based on

wage labour or other forms of exploitation).

Rothbard is at pains to portray egalitarians as driven by envy of the rich. It is hard to credit "envy" as the driving force of the likes of Bakunin and Kropotkin who left the life of wealthy aristocrats to become anarchists, who suffered imprisonment in their struggles for liberty for all rather than an elite. When this is pointed out, the typical right-wing response is to say that this shows that **real** working class people are not socialists. In other words if you are a working class anarchist then you are driven by envy and if not, if you reject your class background, then you show that socialism is not a working class movement! So driven by this assumption and hatred for socialism Rothbard went so far as to distort Karl Marx's words to fit it into his own ideological position. He stated that *"Marx concedes the truth of the charge of anti-communists then and now"* that communism was the expression of envy and a desire to reduce all to a common level. Except, of course, Marx did nothing of the kind. In the passages Rothbard presented as evidence for his claims, Marx is critiquing what he termed "crude" communism (the *"this type of communism"* in the passage Rothbard quoted but clearly did not understand) and it is, therefore, not surprising Marx *"clearly did not stress this dark side of communist revolution in his later writings"* as he explicitly **rejected** this type of communism! For Rothbard, all types of socialism seem to be identical and identified with central planning – hence his bizarre comment that *"Stalin established socialism in the Soviet Union."* [**The Logic of Action II,** pp. 394-5 and p. 200]

Another reason for "anarcho"-capitalist lack of concern for equality is that they think that (to use Robert Nozick's expression) *"liberty upsets patterns"*. It is argued that equality (or any *"end-state principle of justice"*) cannot be *"continuously realised without continuous interference with people's lives,"* i.e. can only be maintained by restricting individual freedom to make exchanges or by taxation of income. [**Anarchy, State, and Utopia**, pp. 160-3] However, what this argument fails to acknowledge is that inequality also restricts individual freedom and that the capitalist property rights framework is not the only one possible. After all, money is power and inequalities in terms of power easily result in restrictions of liberty and the transformation of the majority into order takers rather than free producers. In other words, once a certain level of inequality is reached property does not promote, but actually conflicts with, the ends which render private property legitimate. As we argue in the next section, inequality can easily led to the situation where self-ownership is used to justify its own negation and so unrestricted property rights will undermine the meaningful self-determination which many people intuitively understand by the term "self-ownership" (i.e., what anarchists would usually call "freedom" rather than self-ownership). Thus private property itself leads to continuous interference with people's lives, as does the enforcement of Nozick's "just" distribution of property and the power that flows from such inequality. Moreover, as many critics have noted Nozick's argument assumes what it sets out to prove. As one put it, while Nozick may *"wish to defend capitalist private property rights by insisting that these are founded in basic liberties,"* in fact he *"has produced ... an argument for unrestricted private property using unrestricted private property, and thus he begs the question he tries to answer."* [Andrew Kerhohan, *"Capitalism and*

Self-Ownership", pp. 60-76, **Capitalism**, Ellen Frankel Paul, Fred D. Miler, Jr, Jeffrey Paul and John Ahrens (eds.), p. 71]

So in response to the claim that equality could only be maintained by continuously interfering with people's lives, anarchists would say that the inequalities produced by capitalist property rights also involve extensive and continuous interference with people's lives. After all, as Bob Black notes *"it is apparent that the source of greatest direct duress experienced by the ordinary adult is **not** the state but rather the business that employs him [or her]. Your foreman or supervisor gives you more or-else orders in a week than the police do in a decade."* [*"The Libertarian As Conservative"*, **The Abolition of Work and Other Essays**, p. 145] For example, a worker employed by a capitalist cannot freely exchange the machines or raw materials they have been provided with to use but Nozick does not class this distribution of "restricted" property rights as infringing liberty (nor does he argue that wage slavery itself restricts freedom, of course). Thus claims that equality involves infringing liberty ignores the fact that inequality also infringes liberty (never mind the significant negative effects of inequality, both of wealth and power, we discussed in section B.1). A reorganisation of society could effectively minimise inequalities by eliminating the major source of such inequalities (wage labour) by self-management. We have no desire to restrict free exchanges (after all, most anarchists desire to see the "gift economy" become a reality sooner or later) but we argue that free exchanges need not involve the unrestricted capitalist property rights Nozick assumes (see section I.5.12 for a discussion of "capitalistic acts" within an anarchist society).

Rothbard, ironically, is aware of the fact that inequality restricts freedom for the many. As he put it *"inequality of control"* is an *"inevitable corollary of freedom"* for in any organisation *"there will always be a minority of people who will rise to the position of leaders and others who will remain as followers in the rank and file."* [**Op. Cit.**, p. 30] To requote Bob Black: *"Some people giving orders and others obeying them: this is the essence of servitude."* [**Op. Cit.**, p. 147] Perhaps if Rothbard had spent some time in a workplace rather than in a tenured academic post he may have realised that bosses are rarely the natural elite he thought they were. Like the factory owner Engels, he was blissfully unaware that it is the self-activity of the non-"elite" on the shop floor (the product of which the boss monopolises) that keeps the whole hierarchical structure going (as we discuss in section H.4.4, the work to rule – where workers do **exactly** what the boss orders them to do – is a devastating weapon in the class struggle). It does seem somewhat ironic that the anti-Marxist Rothbard should has recourse to the same argument as Engels in order to refute the anarchist case for freedom within association! It should also be mentioned that Black has also recognised this, noting that right-"libertarianism" and mainstream Marxism *"are as different as Coke and Pepsi when it comes to consecrating class society and the source of its power, work. Only upon the firm foundation of factory fascism and office oligarchy do libertarians and Leninists dare to debate the trivial issues dividing them."* [**Op. Cit.**, p. 146]

So, as Rothbard admits, inequality produces a **class** system and authoritarian social relationships which are rooted in ownership and control of private property. These produce specific areas of conflict over liberty, a fact of life which Rothbard (like other "anarcho"-

capitalists) is keen to deny as we discuss in section F.3.2. Thus, for anarchists, the "anarcho"-capitalist opposition to equality misses the point and is extremely question begging. Anarchists do not desire to make people "identical" (which would be impossible and a total denial of liberty **and** equality) but to make the social relationships between individuals equal in **power.** In other words, they desire a situation where people interact together without institutionalised power or hierarchy and are influenced by each other "naturally," in proportion to how the (individual) **differences** between (social) **equals** are applicable in a given context. To quote Michael Bakunin, *"[t]he greatest intelligence would not be equal to a comprehension of the whole. Thence results ... the necessity of the division and association of labour. I receive and I give – such is human life. Each directs and is directed in his turn. Therefore there is no fixed and constant authority, but a continual exchange of mutual, temporary, and, above all, voluntary authority and subordination."* [**God and the State**, p. 33]

Such an environment can only exist within self-managed associations, for capitalism (i.e. wage labour) creates very specific relations and institutions of authority. It is for this reason anarchists are socialists. In other words, anarchists support equality precisely **because** we recognise that everyone is unique. If we are serious about "equality of rights" or "equal freedom" then conditions must be such that people can enjoy these rights and liberties. If we assume the right to develop one's capacities to the fullest, for example, then inequality of resources and so power within society destroys that right simply because most people do not have the means to freely exercise their capacities (they are subject to the authority of the boss, for example, during work hours).

So, in direct contrast to anarchism, right-"libertarianism" is unconcerned about any form of equality except "equality of rights". This blinds them to the realities of life; in particular, the impact of economic and social power on individuals within society and the social relationships of domination they create. Individuals may be "equal" before the law and in rights, but they may not be free due to the influence of social inequality, the relationships it creates and how it affects the law and the ability of the oppressed to use it. Because of this, all anarchists insist that equality is essential for freedom, including those in the Individualist Anarchist tradition the "anarcho"-capitalist tries to co-opt (*"Spooner and Godwin insist that inequality corrupts freedom. Their anarchism is directed as much against inequality as against tyranny"* and so *"[w]hile sympathetic to Spooner's individualist anarchism, they [Rothbard and David Friedman] fail to notice or conveniently overlook its egalitarian implications."* [Stephen L. Newman, **Liberalism at Wit's End**, p. 74 and p. 76]). Without social equality, individual freedom is so restricted that it becomes a mockery (essentially limiting freedom of the majority to choosing **which** master will govern them rather than being free).

Of course, by defining "equality" in such a restrictive manner, Rothbard's own ideology is proved to be nonsense. As L.A. Rollins notes, *"Libertarianism, the advocacy of 'free society' in which people enjoy 'equal freedom' and 'equal rights,' is actually a specific form of egalitarianism. As such, Libertarianism itself is a revolt against nature. If people, by their very biological nature, are unequal in all the attributes necessary to achieving, and preserving* 'freedom' and 'rights' ... then there is no way that people can enjoy 'equal freedom' or 'equal rights'. If a free society is conceived as a society of 'equal freedom,' then there ain't no such thing as 'a free society'." [**The Myth of Natural Law**, p. 36] Under capitalism, freedom is a commodity like everything else. The more money you have, the greater your freedom. "Equal" freedom, in the Newspeak-Rothbardian sense, **cannot** exist! As for "equality before the law", its clear that such a hope is always dashed against the rocks of wealth and market power. As far as rights go, of course, both the rich and the poor have an "equal right" to sleep under a bridge (assuming the bridge's owner agrees of course!); but the owner of the bridge and the homeless have **different** rights, and so they cannot be said to have "equal rights" in the Newspeak-Rothbardian sense either. Needless to say, poor and rich will not "equally" use the "right" to sleep under a bridge, either.

As Bob Black observed: "The time of your life is the one commodity you can sell but never buy back. Murray Rothbard thinks egalitarianism is a revolt against nature, but his day is 24 hours long, just like everybody else's." [**Op. Cit.**, p. 147]

By twisting the language of political debate, the vast differences in power in capitalist society can be "blamed" not on an unjust and authoritarian system but on "biology" (we are all unique individuals, after all). Unlike genes (although biotechnology corporations are working on this, too!), human society **can** be changed, by the individuals who comprise it, to reflect the basic features we all share in common – our humanity, our ability to think and feel, and our need for freedom.

F.3.1 Why is this disregard for equality important?

Simply because a disregard for equality soon ends with liberty for the majority being negated in many important ways. Most "anarcho"-capitalists and right-Libertarians deny (or at best ignore) market power. Rothbard, for example, claims that economic power does not exist under capitalism; what people call "economic power" is "simply the right under freedom to refuse to make an exchange" and so the concept is meaningless. [**The Ethics of Liberty**, p. 222]

However, the fact is that there are substantial power centres in society (and so are the source of hierarchical power and authoritarian social relations) which are **not the state.** As Elisée Reclus put it, the "power of kings and emperors has limits, but that of wealth has none at all. The dollar is the master of masters." Thus wealth is a source of power as "the essential thing" under capitalism "is to train oneself to pursue monetary gain, with the goal of commanding others by means of the omnipotence of money. One's power increases in direct proportion to one's economic resources." [quoted by John P. Clark and Camille Martin (eds.), **Anarchy, Geography, Modernity**, p. 95 and pp. 96-7] Thus the central fallacy of "anarcho"-capitalism is the (unstated) assumption that the various actors within an economy have relatively equal power. This assumption has been noted by many readers of their works. For example, Peter Marshall notes that "'anarcho-capitalists' like Murray Rothbard assume individuals would have equal bargaining

power in a [capitalist] market-based society." [**Demanding the Impossible**, p. 46] George Walford also makes this point in his comments on David Friedman's **The Machinery of Freedom**:

"The private ownership envisaged by the anarcho-capitalists would be very different from that which we know. It is hardly going too far to say that while the one is nasty, the other would be nice. In anarcho-capitalism there would be no National Insurance, no Social Security, no National Health Service and not even anything corresponding to the Poor Laws; there would be no public safety-nets at all. It would be a rigorously competitive society: work, beg or die. But as one reads on, learning that each individual would have to buy, personally, all goods and services needed, not only food, clothing and shelter but also education, medicine, sanitation, justice, police, all forms of security and insurance, even permission to use the streets (for these also would be privately owned), as one reads about all this a curious feature emerges: everybody always has enough money to buy all these things.

"There are no public casualty wards or hospitals or hospices, but neither is there anybody dying in the streets. There is no public educational system but no uneducated children, no public police service but nobody unable to buy the services of an efficient security firm, no public law but nobody unable to buy the use of a private legal system. Neither is there anybody able to buy much more than anybody else; no person or group possesses economic power over others.

"No explanation is offered. The anarcho-capitalists simply take it for granted that in their favoured society, although it possesses no machinery for restraining competition (for this would need to exercise authority over the competitors and it is an **anarcho**- capitalist society) competition would not be carried to the point where anybody actually suffered from it. While proclaiming their system to be a competitive one, in which private interest rules unchecked, they show it operating as a co-operative one, in which no person or group profits at the cost of another." [**On the Capitalist Anarchists**]

This assumption of (relative) equality comes to the fore in Murray Rothbard's "Homesteading" concept of property (discussed in section F.4.1). "Homesteading" paints a picture of individuals and families going into the wilderness to make a home for themselves, fighting against the elements and so forth. It does **not** invoke the idea of transnational corporations employing tens of thousands of people or a population without land and resources and selling their labour to others. Rothbard as noted argued that economic power does not exist (at least under capitalism, as we saw in section F.1 he does make – highly illogical – exceptions). Similarly, David Friedman's example of a pro-death penalty and anti-death penalty "defence" firm coming to an agreement (see section F.6.3) implicitly assumes that the firms have equal bargaining powers and resources – if

Is "anarcho"-capitalism a type of anarchism?

not, then the bargaining process would be very one-sided and the smaller company would think twice before taking on the larger one in battle (the likely outcome if they cannot come to an agreement on this issue) and so compromise.

However, the right-"libertarian" denial of market power is unsurprising. The *"necessity, not the redundancy, of the assumption about natural equality* is required *"if the inherent problems of contract theory are not to become too obvious."* If some individuals **are** assumed to have significantly more power are more capable than others, and if they are always self-interested, then a contract that creates equal partners is impossible – the pact will establish an association of masters and servants. Needless to say, the strong will present the contract as being to the advantage of both: the strong no longer have to labour (and become rich, i.e. even stronger) and the weak receive an income and so do not starve. [Carole Pateman, **The Sexual Contract**, p. 61] So if freedom is considered as a function of ownership then it is very clear that individuals lacking property (outside their own body, of course) lose effective control over their own person and labour (which was, least we forget, the basis of their equal natural rights). When ones bargaining power is weak (which is typically the case in the labour market) exchanges tend to magnify inequalities of wealth and power over time rather than working towards an equalisation.

In other words, "contract" need not replace power if the bargaining position and wealth of the would-be contractors are not equal (for, if the bargainers had equal power it is doubtful they would agree to sell control of their liberty/labour to another). This means that "power" and "market" are not antithetical terms. While, in an abstract sense, all market relations are voluntary in practice this is not the case within a capitalist market. A large company has a comparative advantage over smaller ones, communities and individual workers which will definitely shape the outcome of any contract. For example, a large company or rich person will have access to more funds and so stretch out litigations and strikes until their opponents resources are exhausted. Or, if a company is polluting the environment, the local community may put up with the damage caused out of fear that the industry (which it depends upon) would relocate to another area. If members of the community **did** sue, then the company would be merely exercising its property rights when it threatened to move to another location. In such circumstances, the community would "freely" consent to its conditions or face massive economic and social disruption. And, similarly, *"the landlords' agents who threatened to discharge agricultural workers and tenants who failed to vote the reactionary ticket"* in the 1936 Spanish election were just exercising their legitimate property rights when they threatened working people and their families with economic uncertainty and distress. [Murray Bookchin, **The Spanish Anarchists**, p. 260]

If we take the labour market, it is clear that the "buyers" and "sellers" of labour power are rarely on an equal footing (if they were, then capitalism would soon go into crisis – see section C.7). As we stressed in section C.9, under capitalism competition in labour markets is typically skewed in favour of employers. Thus the ability to refuse an exchange weighs most heavily on one class than another and so ensures that "free exchange" works to ensure the domination (and so exploitation) of one by the other. Inequality in the market ensures that the decisions of the majority of people

within it are shaped in accordance with that needs of the powerful, not the needs of all. It was for this reason, for example, that the Individualist Anarchist J.K. Ingalls opposed Henry George's proposal of nationalising the land. Ingalls was well aware that the rich could outbid the poor for leases on land and so the dispossession of the working class would continue.

The market, therefore, does not end power or unfreedom – they are still there, but in different forms. And for an exchange to be truly voluntary, both parties must have equal power to accept, reject, or influence its terms. Unfortunately, these conditions are rarely meet on the labour market or within the capitalist market in general. Thus Rothbard's argument that economic power does not exist fails to acknowledge that the rich can out-bid the poor for resources and that a corporation generally has greater ability to refuse a contract (with an individual, union or community) than vice versa (and that the impact of such a refusal is such that it will encourage the others involved to compromise far sooner). In such circumstances, formally free individuals will have to "consent" to be unfree in order to survive. Looking at the tread-mill of modern capitalism, at what we end up tolerating for the sake of earning enough money to survive it comes as no surprise that anarchists have asked whether the market is serving us or are we serving it (and, of course, those who have positions of power within it).

So inequality cannot be easily dismissed. As Max Stirner pointed out, free competition *"is not 'free,' because I lack the **things** for competition."* Due to this basic inequality of wealth (of "things") we find that *"[u]nder the **regime** of the commonality the labourers always fall into the hands of the possessors ... of the capitalists, therefore. The labourer cannot **realise** on his labour to the extent of the value that it has for the customer ... The capitalist has the greatest profit from it."* [**The Ego and Its Own**, p. 262 and p. 115] It is interesting to note that even Stirner recognised that capitalism results in exploitation and that its roots lie in inequalities in property and so power. And we may add that value the labourer does not *"realise"* goes into the hands of the capitalists, who invest it in more "things" and which consolidates and increases their advantage in "free" competition. To quote Stephan L. Newman:

> *"Another disquieting aspect of the libertarians' refusal to acknowledge power in the market is their failure to confront the tension between freedom and autonomy.... Wage labour under capitalism is, of course, formally free labour. No one is forced to work at gun point. Economic circumstance, however, often has the effect of force; it compels the relatively poor to accept work under conditions dictated by owners and managers. The individual worker retains freedom [i.e. negative liberty] but loses autonomy [positive liberty]."* [**Liberalism at Wit's End**, pp. 122-123]

If we consider "equality before the law" it is obvious that this also has limitations in an (materially) unequal society. Brian Morris notes that for Ayn Rand, *"[u]nder capitalism ... politics (state) and economics (capitalism) are separated ... This, of course, is pure ideology, for Rand's justification of the state is that it 'protects' private property, that is, it supports and upholds the economic power of capitalists by coercive means."* [**Ecology & Anarchism**, p. 189] The same can be said of "anarcho"-capitalism and its "protection agencies" and *"general libertarian law code."* If within a society a few own all the resources and the majority are dispossessed, then any law code which protects private property **automatically** empowers the owning class. Workers will **always** be initiating force if they rebel against their bosses or act against the code and so "equality before the law" reflects and reinforces inequality of power and wealth. This means that a system of property rights protects the liberties of some people in a way which gives them an unacceptable degree of power over others. And this critique cannot be met merely by reaffirming the rights in question, we have to assess the relative importance of the various kinds of liberty and other values we hold dear.

Therefore right-"libertarian" disregard for equality is important because it allows "anarcho"-capitalism to ignore many important restrictions of freedom in society. In addition, it allows them to brush over the negative effects of their system by painting an unreal picture of a capitalist society without vast extremes of wealth and power (indeed, they often construe capitalist society in terms of an ideal – namely artisan production – that is **pre**-capitalist and whose social basis has been eroded by capitalist development). Inequality shapes the decisions we have available and what ones we make:

> *"An 'incentive' is always available in conditions of substantial social inequality that ensure that the 'weak' enter into a contract. When social inequality prevails, questions arise about what counts as voluntary entry into a contract. This is why socialists and feminists have focused on the conditions of entry into the employment contract and the marriage contract. Men and women … are now juridically free and equal citizens, but, in unequal social conditions, the possibility cannot be ruled out that some or many contracts create relationships that bear uncomfortable resemblances to a slave contract."* [Carole Pateman, **Op. Cit.**, p. 62]

This ideological confusion of right-libertarianism can also be seen from their opposition to taxation. On the one hand, they argue that taxation is wrong because it takes money from those who "earn" it and gives it to the poor. On the other hand, "free market" capitalism is assumed to be a more equal society! If taxation takes from the rich and gives to the poor, how will "anarcho"-capitalism be more egalitarian? That equalisation mechanism would be gone (of course, it could be claimed that all great riches are purely the result of state intervention skewing the "free market" but that places all their "rags to riches" stories in a strange position). Thus we have a problem: either we have relative equality or we do not. Either we have riches, and so market power, or we do not. And its clear from the likes of Rothbard, "anarcho"-capitalism will not be without its millionaires (there is, according to him, apparently nothing un-libertarian about *"hierarchy, wage-work, granting of funds by libertarian millionaires, and a libertarian party"* [quoted by Black, **Op. Cit.**, p. 142]). And so we are left with market power and so extensive unfreedom.

Thus, for an ideology that denounces egalitarianism as a *"revolt against nature"* it is pretty funny that they paint a picture of "anarcho"-capitalism as a society of (relative) equals. In other words, their propaganda is based on something that has never existed, and never will: an egalitarian capitalist society. Without the implicit assumption of equality which underlies their rhetoric then the obvious limitations of their vision of "liberty" become too obvious. Any real laissez-faire capitalism would be unequal and *"those who have wealth and power would only increase their privileges, while the weak and poor would go to the wall … Right-wing libertarians merely want freedom for themselves to protect their privileges and to exploit others."* [Peter Marshall, **Op. Cit.**, p. 653]

F.3.2 Can there be harmony of interests in an unequal society?

Like the right-liberalism it is derived from, "anarcho"-capitalism is based on the concept of *"harmony of interests"* which was advanced by the likes of Frédéric Bastiat in the 19th century and Rothbard's mentor Ludwig von Mises in the 20th. For Rothbard, *"all classes live in harmony through the voluntary exchange of goods and services that mutually benefits them all."* This meant that capitalists and workers have no antagonistic class interests [**Classical Economics: An Austrian Perspective on the History of Economic Thought**, Vol. 2, p. 380 and p. 382]

For Rothbard, class interest and conflict does not exist within capitalism, except when it is supported by state power. It was, he asserted, *"fallacious to employ such terms as 'class interests' or 'class conflict' in discussing the market economy."* This was because of two things: *"harmony of interests of different groups"* **and** *"lack of homogeneity among the interests of any one social class."* It is only in *"relation to* **state** *action that the interests of different men become welded into 'classes'."* This means that the *"homogeneity* **emerges from** *the interventions of the government into society."* [**Conceived in Liberty**, vol. 1, p. 261] So, in other words, class conflict is impossible under capitalism because of the wonderful coincidence that there are, simultaneously, both common interests between individuals and classes and lack of any!

You do not need to be an anarchist or other socialist to see that this argument is nonsense. Adam Smith, for example, simply recorded reality when he noted that workers and bosses have *"interests [which] are by no means the same. The workmen desire to get as much, the masters to give as little as possible. The former are disposed to combine in order to raise, the latter to lower the wages of labour."* [**The Wealth of Nations**, p. 58] The state, Smith recognised, was a key means by which the property owning class maintained their position in society. As such, it **reflects** economic class conflict and interests and does not **create** it (this is **not** to suggest that economic class is the only form of social hierarchy of course, just an extremely important one). American workers, unlike Rothbard, were all too aware of the truth in Smith's analysis. For example, one group argued in 1840 that the bosses *"hold us then at their mercy, and make us work solely for their profit … The capitalist has no other interest in us, than to get as much labour out of us as possible. We are hired men, and hired men, like hired horses, have no souls."* Thus *"their interests as capitalist, and ours as labourers, are directly opposite"* and *"in the nature of things, hostile, and irreconcilable."* [quoted by Christopher L. Tomlins,

Law, Labor, and Ideology in the Early American Republic, p. 10] Then there is Alexander Berkman's analysis:

"It is easy to understand why the masters don't want you to be organised, why they are afraid of a real labour union. They know very well that a strong, fighting union can compel higher wages and better conditions, which means less profit for the plutocrats. That is why they do everything in their power to stop labour from organising ...

*The masters have found a very effective way to paralyse the strength of organised labour. They have persuaded the workers that they have the same interests as the employers ... and what is good for the employer is also good for his employees ... If your interests are the same as those of your boss, then why should you fight him? That is what they tell you ... It is good for the industrial magnates to have their workers believe [this] ... [as they] will not think of fighting their masters for better conditions, but they will be patient and wait till the employer can 'share his prosperity' with them ... If you listen to your exploiters and their mouthpieces you will be 'good' and consider only the interests of your masters ... but no one cares about **your** interests ... 'Don't be selfish,' they admonish you, while the boss is getting rich by your being good and unselfish. And they laugh in their sleeves and thank the Lord that you are such an idiot.*

"But ... the interests of capital and labour are not the same. No greater lie was ever invented than the so-called 'identity of interests'.... It is clear that ... they are entirely opposite, in fact antagonistic to each other." [**What is Anarchism?**, pp. 74-5]

That Rothbard denies this says a lot about the power of ideology. Rothbard was clear what unions do, namely limit the authority of the boss and ensure that workers keep more of the surplus value they produce. As he put it, unions *"attempt to persuade workers that they can better their lot at the expense of the employer. Consequently, they invariably attempt as much as possible to establish work rules that hinder management's directives ... In other words, instead of agreeing to submit to the work orders of management in exchange for his pay, the worker now set up not only minimum wages, but also work rules without which they refuse to work."* This will *"lower output."* [**The Logic of Action II,** p. 40 and p. 41] Notice the assumption, that the income of and authority of the boss are sacrosanct.

For Rothbard, unions lower productivity and harm profits because they contest the authority of the boss to do what they like on their property (apparently, laissez-faire was not applicable for working class people during working hours). Yet this implicitly acknowledges that there **are** conflicts of interests between workers and bosses. It does not take too much thought to discover possible conflicts of interests which could arise between workers who seek to maximise their wages and minimise their labour and bosses who seek to minimise their wage costs and maximise the output their workers produce. It could be argued that if workers do win this conflict of

interests then their bosses will go out of business and so they harm themselves by not obeying their industrial masters. The rational worker, in this perspective, would be the one who best understood that his or her interests have become the same as the interests of the boss because his or her prosperity will depend on how well their firm is doing. In such cases, they will put the interest of the firm before their own and not hinder the boss by questioning their authority. If that is the case, then "harmony of interests" simply translates as "bosses know best" and "do what you are told" – and such obedience is a fine "harmony" for the order giver we are sure!

So the interesting thing is that Rothbard's perspective produces a distinctly servile conclusion. If workers do not have a conflict of interests with their bosses then, obviously, the logical thing for the employee is to do whatever their boss orders them to do. By serving their master, they automatically benefit themselves. In contrast, anarchists have rejected such a position. For example, William Godwin rejected capitalist private property precisely because of the *"spirit of oppression, the spirit of servility, and the spirit of fraud"* it produced. [**An Enquiry into Political Justice**, p. 732]

Moreover, we should note that Rothbard's diatribe against unions also implicitly acknowledges the socialist critique of capitalism which stresses that it is being subject to the authority of boss during work hours which makes exploitation possible (see section C.2). If wages represented the workers' "marginal" contribution to production, bosses would not need to ensure their orders were followed. So any real boss fights unions precisely because they limit their ability to extract as much product as possible from the worker for the agreed wage. As such, the hierarchical social relations within the workplace ensure that there are no *"harmony of interests"* as the key to a successful capitalist firm is to minimise wage costs in order to maximise profits. It should also be noted that Rothbard has recourse to another concept "Austrian" economists claim to reject during his anti-union comments. Somewhat ironically, he appeals to equilibrium analysis as, apparently, *"wage rates on the non-union labour market will always tend toward equilibrium in a smooth and harmonious manner"* (in another essay, he opines that *"in the Austrian tradition ... the entrepreneur harmoniously adjusts the economy in the direction of equilibrium"*). [**Op. Cit.**, p. 41 and p. 234] True, he does not say that the wages will reach equilibrium (and what stops them, unless, in part, it is the actions of entrepreneurs disrupting the economy?) however, it is strange that the labour market can approximate a situation which Austrian economists claim does not exist! However, as noted in section C.1.6 this fiction is required to hide the obvious economic power of the boss class under capitalism.

Somewhat ironically, given his claims of *"harmony of interests,"* Rothbard was well aware that landlords and capitalists have always used the state to further their interests. However, he preferred to call this *"mercantilism"* rather than capitalism. As such, it is amusing to read his short article *"Mercantilism: A Lesson for Our Times?"* as it closely parallels Marx's classic account of *"Primitive Accumulation"* contained in volume 1 of **Capital**. [Rothbard, **Op. Cit.**, pp. 43-55] The key difference is that Rothbard simply refused to see this state action as creating the necessary preconditions for his beloved capitalism nor does it seem to impact on his mantra of *"harmony* of interests" between classes. In spite of documenting exactly how the capitalist and landlord class used the state to enrich themselves at the expense of the working class, he refuses to consider how this refutes any claim of *"harmony of interests"* between exploiter and exploited.

Rothbard rightly notes that mercantilism involved the *"use of the state to cripple or prohibit one's competition."* This applies to both foreign capitalists and to the working class who are, of course, competitors in terms of how income is divided. Unlike Marx, he simply failed to see how mercantilist policies were instrumental for building an industrial economy and creating a proletariat. Thus he thunders against mercantilism for *"lowering interest rates artificially"* and promoting inflation which *"did not benefit the poor"* as *"wages habitually lagged behind the rise in prices."* He describes the *"desperate attempts by the ruling classes to coerce wages below their market rates."* Somewhat ironically, given the "anarcho"-capitalist opposition to legal holidays, he noted the mercantilists *"dislike of holidays, by which the 'nation' was deprived of certain amounts of labour; the desire of the individual worker for leisure was never considered worthy of note."* So why were such "bad" economic laws imposed? Simply because the landlords and capitalists were in charge of the state. As Rothbard notes, *"this was clearly legislation for the benefit of the feudal landlords and to the detriment of the workers"* while Parliament *"was heavily landlord-dominated."* In Massachusetts the upper house consisted *"of the wealthiest merchants and landowners."* The mercantilists, he notes but does not ponder, *"were frankly interested in exploiting [the workers'] labour to the utmost."* [**Op. Cit.**, p. 44, p. 46, p. 47, p. 51, p. 48, p. 51, p. 47, p. 54 and p. 47] Yet these policies made perfect sense from their class perspective, they were essential for maximising a surplus (profits) which was subsequently invested in developing industry. As such, they were very successful and laid the foundation for the industrial capitalism of the 19th century. The key change between mercantilism and capitalism proper is that economic power is greater as the working class has been successfully dispossessed from the means of life and, as such, political power need not be appealed to as often and can appear, in rhetoric at least, defensive.

Discussing attempts by employers in Massachusetts in 1670 and 1672 to get the state to enforce a maximum wage Rothbard opined that there *"seemed to be no understanding of how wages are set in an unhampered market."* [**Conceived in Liberty**, vol. 2, p. 18] On the contrary, dear professor, the employers were perfectly aware of how wages were set in a market where workers have the upper hand and, consequently, sought to use the state to hamper the market. As they have constantly done since the dawn of capitalism as, unlike certain economists, they are fully aware of the truth of *"harmony of interests"* and acted accordingly. As we document in section F.8, the history of capitalism is filled with the capitalist class using the state to enforce the kind of *"harmony of interests"* which masters have always sought – obedience. This statist intervention has continued to this day as, in practice, the capitalist class has never totally relied on economic power to enforce its rule due to the instability of the capitalist market – see section C.7 – as well as the destructive effects of market forces on society and the desire to bolster its position in the economy at the expense of the working

class – see section D.1. That the history and current practice of capitalism was not sufficient to dispel Rothbard of his *"harmony of interests"* position is significant. But, as Rothbard was always at pains to stress as a good "Austrian" economist, empirical testing does not prove or disprove a theory and so the history and practice of capitalism matters little when evaluating the pros and cons of that system (unless its history confirms Rothbard's ideology then he does make numerous empirical statements).

For Rothbard, the obvious **class** based need for such policies is missing. Instead, we get the pathetic comment that only *"certain"* merchants and manufacturers *"benefited from these mercantilist laws."* [**The Logic of Action II,** p. 44] He applied this same myopic perspective to "actually existing" capitalism as well, of course, lamenting the use of the state by certain capitalists as the product of economic ignorance and/or special interests specific to the capitalists in question. He simply could not see the forest for the trees. This is hardly a myopia limited to Rothbard. Bastiat formulated his *"harmony of interests"* theory precisely when the class struggle between workers and capitalists had become a threat to the social order, when socialist ideas of all kinds (including anarchism, which Bastiat explicitly opposed) were spreading and the labour movement was organising illegally due to state bans in most countries. As such, he was propagating the notion that workers and bosses had interests in common when, in practice, it was most obviously the case they had not. What "harmony" that did exist was due to state repression of the labour movement, itself a strange necessity if labour and capital **did** share interests.

The history of capitalism causes problems within "anarcho"-capitalism as it claims that everyone benefits from market exchanges and that this, not coercion, produces faster economic growth. If this **is** the case, then why did some individuals reject the market in order to enrich themselves by political means and, logically, impoverish themselves in the long run (and it has been an **extremely** long run)? And why have the economically dominant class generally also been the ones to control the state? After all, if there are no class interests or conflict then why has the property owning classes always sought state aid to skew the economy in its interests? If the classes **did** have harmonious interests then they would have no need to bolster their position nor would they seek to. Yet state policy has always reflected the needs of the property-owning elite – subject to pressures from below, of course (as Rothbard rather lamely notes, without pondering the obvious implications, the *"peasantry and the urban labourers and artisans were never able to control the state apparatus and were therefore at the bottom of the state-organised pyramid and exploited by the ruling groups."* [**Conceived in Liberty**, vol. 1, p. 260]). It is no coincidence that the working classes have not been able to control the state nor that legislation is *"grossly the favourer of the rich against the poor."* [William Godwin, **Op. Cit.**, p. 93] They **are** the ones passing the laws, after all. This long and continuing anti-labour intervention in the market does, though, place Rothbard's opinion that government is a conspiracy against the superior man in a new light!

So when right-"libertarians" assert that there are *"harmony of interests"* between classes in an unhampered market, anarchists simply reply by pointing out that the very fact we have a "hampered" market shows that no such thing exists within capitalism. It will be argued, of course, that the right-"libertarian" is against state intervention for the capitalists (beyond defending their property which is a significant use of state power in and of itself) and that their political ideas aim to stop it. Which is true (and why a revolution would be needed to implement it!). However, the very fact that the capitalist class has habitually turned to the state to bolster its economic power is precisely the issue as it shows that the right-"libertarian" harmony of interests (on which they place so much stress as the foundation of their new order) simply does not exist. If it did, then the property owning class would never have turned to the state in the first place nor would it have tolerated "certain" of its members doing so.

If there were harmony of interests between classes, then the bosses would not turn to death squads to kill rebel workers as they have habitually done (and it should be stressed that libertarian union organisers have been assassinated by bosses and their vigilantes, including the lynching of IWW members and business organised death squads against CNT members in Barcelona). This use of private and public violence should not be surprising, for, at the very least, as Mexican anarchist Ricardo Flores Magón noted, there can be no real fraternity between classes *"because the possessing class is always disposed to perpetuate the economic, political, and social system that guarantees it the tranquil enjoyment of its plunders, while the working class makes efforts to destroy this iniquitous system."* [**Dreams of Freedom**, p. 139]

Rothbard's obvious hatred of unions and strikes can be explained by his ideological commitment to the *"harmony of interests."* This is because strikes and the need of working class people to organise gives the lie to the doctrine of *"harmony of interests"* between masters and workers that apologists for capitalism like Rothbard suggested underlay industrial relations. Worse, they give credibility to the notion that there exists opposed interests between classes. Strangely, Rothbard himself provides more than enough evidence to refute his own dogmas when he investigates state intervention on the market.

Every ruling class seeks to deny that it has interests separate from the people under it. Significantly those who deny class struggle the most are usually those who practice it the most (for example, Mussolini, Pinochet and Thatcher all proclaimed the end of class struggle while, in America, the Republican-right denounces anyone who points out the results of **their** class war on the working class as advocating "class war"). The elite has long been aware, as Black Nationalist Steve Biko put it, that the *"most potent weapon in the hands of the oppressor is the mind of the oppressed."* Defenders of slavery and serfdom presented it as god's will and that the master's duty was to treat the slave well just as the slave's duty was to obey (while, of course, blaming the slave if the master did not hold up his side of the covenant). So every hierarchical system has its own version of the *"harmony of interests"* position and each hierarchical society which replaces the last mocks the previous incarnations of it while, at the same time, solemnly announcing that **this** society truly does have harmony of interests as its founding principle. Capitalism is no exception, with many economists repeating the mantra that every boss has proclaimed from the dawn of time, namely that workers and their masters have common interests. As usual, it is worthwhile to quote Rothbard on this matter. He (rightly)

takes to task a defender of the slave master's version of *"harmony of interests"* and, in so doing, exposes the role of economics under capitalism. To quote Rothbard:

> *"The increasing alienation of the slaves and the servants led … the oligarchy to try to win their allegiance by rationalising their ordeal as somehow natural, righteous, and divine. So have tyrants always tried to dupe their subjects into approving – or at least remaining resigned to – their fate…. Servants, according to the emphatically non-servant [Reverend Samuel] Willard, were duty-bound to revere and obey their masters, to serve them diligently and cheerfully, and to be patient and submissive even to the cruellest master. A convenient ideology indeed for the masters! … All the subjects must do, in short, was to surrender their natural born gift of freedom and independence, to subject themselves completely to the whims and commands of others, who could then be blindly trusted to 'take care' of them permanently …*

> *"Despite the myths of ideology and the threats of the whip, servants and slaves found many ways of protest and rebellion. Masters were continually denouncing servants for being disobedient, sullen, and lazy."* [**Conceived in Liberty**, vol. 2, pp. 18-19]

Change Reverend Samuel Willard to the emphatically non-worker Professor Murray Rothbard and we have a very succinct definition of the role his economics plays within capitalism. There are differences. The key one was that while Willard wanted permanent servitude, Rothbard sought a temporary form and allowed the worker to change masters. While Willard turned to the whip and the state, Rothbard turned to absolute private property and the capitalist market to ensure that workers had to sell their liberty to the boss class (unsurprisingly, as Willard lived in an economy whose workers had access to land and tools while in Rothbard's time the class monopolisation of the means of life was complete and workers have little alternative but to sell their liberty to the owning class).

Rothbard did not seek to ban unions and strikes. He argued that his system of absolute property rights would simply make it nearly impossible for unions to organise or for any form of collective action to succeed. Even basic picketing would be impossible for, as Rothbard noted many a time, the pavement outside the workplace would be owned by the boss who would be as unlikely to allow picketing as he would allow a union. Thus we would have private property and economic power making collective struggle **de facto** illegal rather than the **de jure** illegality which the state has so enacted on behalf of the capitalists. As he put it, while unions were *"theoretically compatible with the existence of a purely free market"* he doubted that it would be possible as unions relied on the state to be "neutral" and tolerate their activities as they *"acquire almost all their power through the wielding of force, specifically force against strike-beakers and against the property of employers."* [**The Logic of Action II**, p. 41] Thus we find right-"libertarians" in favour of "defensive" violence (i.e., that limited to defending the property and power of the capitalists and landlords) while denouncing as violence any action of those subjected to it.

Rothbard, of course, allowed workers to leave their employment in order to seek another job if they felt exploited. Yet for all his obvious hatred of unions and strikes, Rothbard does not ask the most basic question – if there is not clash of interests between labour and capital then why do unions even exist and why do bosses always resist them (often brutally)? And why has capital always turned to the state to bolster its position in the labour market? If there were really harmony of interests between classes then capital would not have turned repeatedly to the state to crush the labour movement. For anarchists, the reasons are obvious as is why the bosses always deny any clash of interests for *"it is to the interests of capital to keep the workers from understanding that they are wage slaves. The 'identity of interest'; swindle is one of the means of doing it … All those who profit from wage slavery are interested in keeping up the system, and all of them naturally try to prevent the workers from understanding the situation."* [Berkman, **Op. Cit.**, p. 77]

Rothbard's vociferous anti-unionism and his obvious desire to make any form of collective action by workers impossible in practice if not in law shows how economics has replaced religion as a control mechanism. In any hierarchical system it makes sense for the masters to indoctrinate the servant class with such self-serving nonsense but only capitalists have the advantage that it is proclaimed a "science" rather than, say, a religion. Yet even here, the parallels are close. As Colin Ward noted in passing, the *"so-called Libertarianism of the political Right"* is simply *"the worship of the market economy."* [**Talking Anarchy**, p. 76] So while Willard appealed to god as the basis of his natural order, Rothbard's appeal to "science" was nothing of the kind given the ideological apriorism of "Austrian" economics. As a particularly scathing reviewer of one of his economics books rightly put it, the *"main point of the book is to show that the never-never land of the perfectly free market economy represents the best of all conceivable worlds giving maximum satisfaction to all participants. Whatever is, is right in the free market … It would appear that Professor Rothbard's book is more akin to systematic theology than economics … its real interest belongs to the student of the sociology of religion."* [D.N. Winch, **The Economic Journal**, vol. 74, No. 294, pp. 481-2]

To conclude, it is best to quote Emma Goldman's biting dismissal of the right-liberal individualism that Rothbard's ideology is just another form of. She rightly attacked that *"'rugged individualism' which is only a masked attempt to repress and defeat the individual and his individuality. So-called Individualism is the social and economic **laissez-faire**: the exploitation of the masses by classes by means of trickery, spiritual debasement and systematic indoctrination of the servile spirit … That corrupt and perverse 'individualism' is the strait-jacket of individuality … This 'rugged individualism' has inevitably resulted in the greatest modern slavery, the crassest class distinctions … 'Rugged individualism' has meant all the 'individualism' for the masters, while the people are regimented into a slave caste to serve a handful of self-seeking 'supermen' … [and] in whose name political tyranny and social oppression are defended and held up as virtues while every aspiration and attempt of man to gain freedom and social opportunity to live is denounced as … evil in the name of that same individualism."* [**Red Emma Speaks**, p. 112]

So, to conclude. Both the history and current practice of capitalism shows that there can be no harmony of interests in an unequal society. Anyone who claims otherwise has not been paying attention.

F.4

What is the right-"libertarian" position on private property?

Right-"libertarians" are not interested in eliminating capitalist private property and thus the authority, oppression and exploitation which goes with it. They make an idol of private property and claim to defend "absolute" and "unrestricted" property rights. In particular, taxation and theft are among the greatest evils possible as they involve coercion against "justly held" property. It is true that they call for an end to the state, but this is not because they are concerned about the restrictions of liberty experienced by wage slaves and tenants but because they wish capitalists and landlords not to be bothered by legal restrictions on what they can and cannot do on their property. Anarchists stress that the right-"libertarians" are not opposed to workers being exploited or oppressed (in fact, they deny that is possible under capitalism) but because they do not want the state to impede capitalist "freedom" to exploit and oppress workers even more than is the case now! Thus they *"are against the State simply because they are capitalists first and foremost."* [Peter Marshall, **Demanding the Impossible**, p. 564]

It should be obvious **why** someone is against the state matters when evaluating claims of a thinker to be included within the anarchist tradition. For example, socialist opposition to wage labour was shared by the pro-slavery advocates in the Southern States of America. The latter opposed wage labour as being worse than its chattel form because, it was argued, the owner had an incentive to look after his property during both good and bad times while the wage worker was left to starve during the latter. This argument does not place them in the socialist camp any more than socialist opposition to wage labour made them supporters of slavery. As such, "anarcho"-capitalist and right-"libertarian" opposition to the state should not be confused with anarchist and left-libertarian opposition. The former opposes it because it restricts capitalist power, profits and property while the latter opposes it because it is a bulwark of all three.

Moreover, in the capitalist celebration of property as the source of liberty they deny or ignore the fact that private property is a source of "tyranny" in itself (as we have indicated in sections B.3 and B.4, for example). As we saw in section F.1, this leads to quite explicit (if unaware) self-contradiction by leading "anarcho"-capitalist ideologues. As Tolstoy stressed, the *"retention of the laws concerning land and property keeps the workers in slavery to the landowners and the capitalists, even though the workers are freed from taxes."* [**The Slavery of Our Times**, pp. 39-40] Hence Malatesta:

> *"One of the basic tenets of anarchism is the abolition of [class] monopoly, whether of the land, raw materials or the means of production, and consequently the abolition*

of exploitation of the labour of others by those who possess the means of production. The appropriation of the labour of others is from the anarchist and socialist point of view, theft." [**Errico Malatesta: His Life and Ideas**, pp. 167-8]

As much anarchists may disagree about other matters, they are united in condemning capitalist property. Thus Proudhon argued that property was *"theft"* and *"despotism"* while Stirner indicated the religious and statist nature of private property and its impact on individual liberty when he wrote:

> *"Property in the civic sense means* **sacred** *property, such that I must* **respect** *your property. 'Respect for property!' ... The position of affairs is different in the egoistic sense. I do not step shyly back from your property, but look upon it always as* **my** *property, in which I respect nothing. Pray do the like with what you call my property!*
>
> *"With this view we shall most easily come to an understanding with each other.*
>
> *"The political liberals are anxious that ... every one be free lord on his ground, even if this ground has only so much area as can have its requirements adequately filled by the manure of one person.... Be it ever so little, if one only has somewhat of his own – to wit, a* **respected** *property: The more such owners ... the more 'free people and good patriots' has the State.*
>
> *"Political liberalism, like everything religious, counts on* **respect,** *humaneness, the virtues of love. Therefore does it live in incessant vexation. For in practice people respect nothing, and everyday the small possessions are bought up again by greater proprietors, and the 'free people' change into day labourers.*
>
> *"If, on the contrary, the 'small proprietors' had reflected that the great property was also theirs, they would not have respectively shut themselves out from it, and would not have been shut out.... Instead of owning the world, as he might, he does not even own even the paltry point on which he turns around."* [**The Ego and Its Own**, pp. 248-9]

While different anarchists have different perspectives on what comes next, we are all critical of the current capitalist property rights system. Thus "anarcho"-capitalists reject totally one of the common (and so defining) features of all anarchist traditions – the opposition to capitalist property. From Individualist Anarchists like Tucker to Communist-Anarchists like Bookchin, anarchists have been opposed to what William Godwin termed *"accumulated property."* This was because it was in *"direct contradiction"* to property in the form of *"the produce of his [the worker's] own industry"* and so it allows *"one man ... [to] dispos[e] of the produce of another man's industry."* [**The Anarchist Reader**, pp. 129-131]

For anarchists, capitalist property is a source of exploitation and domination, **not** freedom (it undermines the freedom associated with possession by creating relations of domination between owner and employee). Hardly surprising then, that according to Murray Bookchin, Murray Rothbard *"attacked me as an anarchist with vigour because, as he put it, I am opposed to private property."* Bookchin, correctly, dismisses "anarcho-capitalists as *"proprietarians"* [*"A Meditation on Anarchist Ethics"*, pp. 328-346, **The Raven**, no. 28, p. 343]

We will discuss Rothbard's "homesteading" justification of private property in the next section. However, we will note here one aspect of right-"libertarian" absolute and unrestricted property rights, namely that it easily generates evil side effects such as hierarchy and starvation. As economist and famine expert Amartya Sen notes:

> *"Take a theory of entitlements based on a set of rights of 'ownership, transfer and rectification.' In this system a set of holdings of different people are judged to be just (or unjust) by looking at past history, and not by checking the consequences of that set of holdings. But what if the consequences are recognisably terrible? ... [R]efer[ing] to some empirical findings in a work on famines ... evidence [is presented] to indicate that in many large famines in the recent past, in which millions of people have died, there was no over-all decline in food availability at all, and the famines occurred precisely because of shifts in entitlement resulting from exercises of rights that are perfectly legitimate. ... [Can] famines ... occur with a system of rights of the kind morally defended in various ethical theories, including Nozick's[?] I believe the answer is straightforwardly yes, since for many people the only resource that they legitimately possess, viz. their labour-power, may well turn out to be unsaleable in the market, giving the person no command over food ... [i]f results such as starvations and famines were to occur, would the distribution of holdings still be morally acceptable despite their disastrous consequences? There is something deeply implausible in the affirmative answer."* [**Resources, Values and Development**, pp. 311-2]

Thus "unrestricted" property rights can have seriously bad consequences and so the existence of "justly held" property need not imply a just or free society – far from it. The inequalities property can generate can have a serious effect on individual freedom (see section F.3). Indeed, Murray Rothbard argued that the state was evil not because it restricted individual freedom but because the resources it claimed to own were not "justly" acquired. If they were, then the state could deny freedom within its boundaries just as any other property owner could. Thus right-"libertarian" theory judges property **not** on its impact on current freedom but by looking at past history. This has the interesting side effect, as we noted in section F.1, of allowing its supporters to look at capitalist and statist hierarchies, acknowledge their similar negative effects on the liberty of those subjected to them but argue that one is legitimate and the other is not simply because of their history. As if this changed the domination and unfreedom that both inflict on people living today! This flows from the way "anarcho"-capitalists define "freedom," namely so that only **deliberate** acts which violate your (right-

"libertarian" defined) rights by other humans beings that cause unfreedom (*"we define freedom ... as the **absence of invasion** by another man of a man's person or property."* [Rothbard, **The Ethics of Liberty**, p. 41]). This means that if no-one deliberately coerces you then you are free. In this way the workings of the capitalist private property can be placed alongside the "facts of nature" and ignored as a source of unfreedom. However, a moments thought shows that this is not the case. Both deliberate and non-deliberate acts can leave individuals lacking freedom. A simply analogy will show why.

Let us assume (in an example paraphrased from Alan Haworth's excellent book **Anti-Libertarianism** [p. 49]) that someone kidnaps you and places you down a deep (naturally formed) pit, miles from anyway, which is impossible to climb up. No one would deny that you are unfree. Let us further assume that another person walks by and accidentally falls into the pit with you. According to right-"libertarianism", while you are unfree (i.e. subject to deliberate coercion) your fellow pit-dweller is perfectly free for they have been subject to the "facts of nature" and not human action (deliberate or otherwise). Or, perhaps, they "voluntarily choose" to stay in the pit, after all, it is "only" the "facts of nature" limiting their actions. But, obviously, both of you are in **exactly the same position,** have **exactly the same choices** and so are **equally** unfree! Thus a definition of "liberty" that maintains that only deliberate acts of others – for example, coercion – reduces freedom misses the point totally. In other words, freedom is path independent and the *"forces of the market cannot provide genuine conditions for freedom any more than the powers of the State. The victims of both are equally enslaved, alienated and oppressed."* [Peter Marshall, **Demanding the Impossible**, p. 565]

It is worth quoting Noam Chomsky at length on this subject:

> *"Consider, for example, the [right-'libertarian'] 'entitlement theory of justice' ... [a]ccording to this theory, a person has a right to whatever he has acquired by means that are just. If, by luck or labour or ingenuity, a person acquires such and such, then he is entitled to keep it and dispose of it as he wills, and a just society will not infringe on this right.*

> *"One can easily determine where such a principle might lead. It is entirely possible that by legitimate means – say, luck supplemented by contractual arrangements 'freely undertaken' under pressure of need – one person might gain control of the necessities of life. Others are then free to sell themselves to this person as slaves, if he is willing to accept them. Otherwise, they are free to perish. Without extra question-begging conditions, the society is just.*

> *"The argument has all the merits of a proof that 2 + 2 = 5 ... Suppose that some concept of a 'just society' is advanced that fails to characterise the situation just described as unjust.... Then one of two conclusions is in order. We may conclude that the concept is simply unimportant and of no interest as a guide to thought or action, since it fails to apply properly even in such an elementary case*

as this. Or we may conclude that the concept advanced is to be dismissed in that it fails to correspond to the pretheorectical notion that it intends to capture in clear cases. If our intuitive concept of justice is clear enough to rule social arrangements of the sort described as grossly unjust, then the sole interest of a demonstration that this outcome might be 'just' under a given 'theory of justice' lies in the inference by **reductio ad absurdum** to the conclusion that the theory is hopelessly inadequate. While it may capture some partial intuition regarding justice, it evidently neglects others.*

> *"The real question to be raised about theories that fail so completely to capture the concept of justice in its significant and intuitive sense is why they arouse such interest. Why are they not simply dismissed out of hand on the grounds of this failure, which is striking in clear cases? Perhaps the answer is, in part, the one given by Edward Greenberg in a discussion of some recent work on the entitlement theory of justice. After reviewing empirical and conceptual shortcomings, he observes that such work 'plays an important function in the process of ... 'blaming the victim,' and of protecting property against egalitarian onslaughts by various non-propertied groups.' An ideological defence of privileges, exploitation, and private power will be welcomed, regardless of its merits.*

> *"These matters are of no small importance to poor and oppressed people here and elsewhere."* [**The Chomsky Reader**, pp. 187-188]

The glorification of property rights has always been most strongly advocated by those who hold the bulk of property in a society. This is understandable as they have the most to gain from this. Those seeking to increase freedom in society would be wise to understand why this is the case and reject it.

The defence of capitalist property does have one interesting side effect, namely the need arises to defend inequality and the authoritarian relationships inequality creates. Due to (capitalist) private property, wage labour would still exist under "anarcho"-capitalism (it is capitalism after all). This means that "defensive" force, a state, is required to "defend" exploitation, oppression, hierarchy and authority from those who suffer them. Inequality makes a mockery of free agreement and "consent" as we have continually stressed. As Peter Kropotkin pointed out long ago:

> *"When a workman sells his labour to an employer ... it is a mockery to call that a free contract. Modern economists may call it free, but the father of political economy – Adam Smith – was never guilty of such a misrepresentation. As long as three-quarters of humanity are compelled to enter into agreements of that description, force is, of course, necessary, both to enforce the supposed agreements and to maintain such a state of things. Force – and a good deal of force – is necessary to prevent the labourers from taking possession of what they consider unjustly appropriated by the few.... The Spencerian party [proto-*

right-'libertarians'] perfectly well understand that; and while they advocate no force for changing the existing conditions, they advocate still more force than is now used for maintaining them. As to Anarchy, it is obviously as incompatible with plutocracy as with any other kind of -cracy." [**Anarchism and Anarchist Communism**, pp. 52-53]

Because of this need to defend privilege and power, "anarcho"-capitalism is best called "private-state" capitalism. As anarchists Stuart Christie and Albert Meltzer argue, the *"American oil baron, who sneers at any form of State intervention in his manner of conducting business – that is to say, of exploiting man and nature – is also able to 'abolish the State' to a certain extent. But he has to build up a repressive machine of his own (an army of sheriffs to guard his interests) and takes over as far as he can, those functions normally exercised by the government, excluding any tendency of the latter that might be an obstacle to his pursuit of wealth."* [**Floodgates of Anarchy**, p. 12] Unsurprising "anarcho"-capitalists propose private security forces rather than state security forces (police and military) – a proposal that is equivalent to bringing back the state under another name. This will be discussed in more detail in section F.6.

By advocating private property, right-"libertarians" contradict many of their other claims. For example, they tend to oppose censorship and attempts to limit freedom of association within society when the state is involved yet they will wholeheartedly support the right of the boss or landlord when they ban unions or people talking about unions on their property. They will oppose closed shops when they are worker created but have no problems when bosses make joining the company union a mandatory requirement for taking a position. Then they say that they support the right of individuals to travel where they like. They make this claim because they assume that only the state limits free travel but this is a false assumption. Owners must agree to let you on their land or property (*"people only have the right to move to those properties and lands where the owners desire to rent or sell to them."* [Murray Rothbard, **The Ethics of Liberty**, p. 119]. There is no "freedom of travel" onto private property (including private roads). Therefore immigration may be just as hard under "anarcho"-capitalism as it is under statism (after all, the state, like the property owner, only lets people in whom it wants to let in). Private property, as can be seen from these simple examples, is the state writ small. Saying it is different when the boss does it is not convincing to any genuine libertarian.

Then there is the possibility of alternative means of living. Right-"libertarians" generally argue that people can be as communistic as they want on their own property. They fail to note that all groups would have no choice about living under laws based on the most rigid and extreme interpretation of property rights invented and surviving within the economic pressures such a regime would generate. If a community cannot survive in the capitalist market then, in their perspective, it deserves its fate. Yet this Social-Darwinist approach to social organisation is based on numerous fallacies. It confuses the market price of something with how important it is; it confuses capitalism with productive activity in general; and it confuses profits with an activities contribution to social and individual well being; it

confuses freedom with the ability to pick a master rather than as an absence of a master. Needless to say, as they consider capitalism as the most efficient economy ever the underlying assumption is that capitalist systems will win out in competition with all others. This will obviously be aided immensely under a law code which is capitalist in nature.

F.4.1 What is wrong with a "homesteading" theory of property?

So how do "anarcho"-capitalists justify property? Looking at Murray Rothbard, we find that he proposes a *"homesteading theory of property"*. In this theory it is argued that property comes from occupancy and mixing labour with natural resources (which are assumed to be unowned). Thus the world is transformed into private property, for *"title to an unowned resource (such as land) comes properly only from the expenditure of labour to transform that resource into use."* [**The Ethics of Liberty**, p. 63]

His theory, it should be stressed, has its roots in the same Lockean tradition as Robert Nozick's (which we critiqued in section B.3.4). Like Locke, Rothbard paints a conceptual history of individuals and families forging a home in the wilderness by the sweat of their labour (it is tempting to rename his theory the **"immaculate conception of property"** as his conceptual theory is so at odds with actual historical fact). His one innovation (if it can be called that) was to deny even the rhetorical importance of what is often termed the Lockean Proviso, namely the notion that common resources can be appropriated only if there is enough for others to do likewise. As we noted in section E.4.2 this was because it could lead (horror of horrors!) to the outlawing of all private property.

Sadly for Rothbard, his "homesteading" theory of property was refuted by Proudhon in **What is Property?** in 1840 (along with many other justifications of property). Proudhon rightly argued that *"if the liberty of man is sacred, it is equally sacred in all individuals; that, if it needs property for its objective action, that is, for its life, the appropriation of material is equally necessary for all ... Does it not follow that if one individual cannot prevent another ... from appropriating an amount of material equal to his own, no more can he prevent individuals to come."* And if all the available resources are appropriated, and the owner *"draws boundaries, fences himself in ... Here, then, is a piece of land upon which, henceforth, no one has a right to step, save the proprietor and his friends ... Let [this] ... multiply, and soon the people ... will have nowhere to rest, no place to shelter, no ground to till. They will die at the proprietor's door, on the edge of that property which was their birthright."* [**What is Property?**, pp. 84-85 and p. 118]

Proudhon's genius lay in turning apologies for private property against it by treating them as absolute and universal as its apologists treated property itself. To claims like Rothbard's that property was a natural right, he explained that the essence of such rights was their universality and that private property ensured that this right could not be extended to all. To claims that labour created property, he simply noted that private property ensured that most people have no property to labour on and so the outcome of that labour was owned by those who did. As for occupancy, he simply noted that most owners do not occupancy all the property they own while those who do use it do not own it. In such circumstances, how can occupancy justify property when property excludes occupancy? Proudhon showed that the defenders of property had to choose between self-interest and principle, between hypocrisy and logic. Rothbard picks the former over the latter and his theory is simply a rationale for a specific class based property rights system (*"[w]e who belong to the proletaire class, property excommunicates us!"* [P-J Proudhon, **Op. Cit.**, p. 105]). As Rothbard **himself** admitted in respect to the aftermath of slavery and serfdom, not having access to the means of life places one in the position of unjust dependency on those who do and so private property creates economic power as much under his beloved capitalism as it did in post-serfdom (see section F.1). Thus, Rothbard's account, for all its intuitive appeal, ends up justifying capitalist and landlord domination and ensures that the vast majority of the population experience property as theft and despotism rather than as a source of liberty and empowerment (which possession gives).

It also seems strange that while (correctly) attacking social contract theories of the state as invalid (because *"no past generation can bind later generations"* [**Op. Cit.**, p. 145]) he fails to see he is doing **exactly that** with his support of private property (similarly, Ayn Rand argued that *"[a]ny alleged 'right' of one man, which necessitates the violation of the right of another, is not and cannot be a right"* but, obviously, appropriating land does violate the rights of others to walk, use or appropriate that land [**Capitalism: The Unknown Ideal**, p. 325]). Due to his support for appropriation and inheritance, Rothbard is clearly ensuring that future generations are **not** born as free as the first settlers were (after all, they cannot appropriate any land, it is all taken!). If future generations cannot be bound by past ones, this applies equally to resources and property rights. Something anarchists have long realised – there is no defensible reason why those who first acquired property should control its use and exclude future generations.

Even if we take Rothbard's theory at face value we find numerous problems with it. If title to unowned resources comes via the *"expenditure of labour"* on it, how can rivers, lakes and the oceans be appropriated? The banks of the rivers can be transformed, but can the river itself? How can you mix your labour with water? "Anarcho"-capitalists usually blame pollution on the fact that rivers, oceans, and so forth are unowned but as we discussed in section E.4, Rothbard provided no coherent argument for resolving this problem nor the issue of environmental externalities like pollution it was meant to solve (in fact, he ended up providing polluters with sufficient apologetics to allow them to continue destroying the planet).

Then there is the question of what equates to "mixing" labour. Does fencing in land mean you have "mixed labour" with it? Rothbard argues that this is not the case (he expresses opposition to *"arbitrary claims"*). He notes that it is **not** the case that *"the first discoverer ... could properly lay claim to"* a piece of land by *"laying out a boundary for the area."* He thinks that *"their claim would still be no more than the boundary **itself**, and not to any of the land within, for only the boundary will have been transformed and used

by men"* However, if the boundary **is** private property and the owner refuses others permission to cross it, then the enclosed land is inaccessible to others! If an "enterprising" right-"libertarian" builds a fence around the only oasis in a desert and refuses permission to cross it to travellers unless they pay his price (which is everything they own) then the person **has** appropriated the oasis without "transforming" it by his labour. The travellers have the choice of paying the price or dying (and any oasis owner is well within his rights letting them die). Given Rothbard's comments, it is probable that he could claim that such a boundary is null and void as it allows "arbitrary" claims – although this position is not at all clear. After all, the fence builder **has** transformed the boundary and "unrestricted" property rights is what the right-"libertarian" is all about. One thing is true, if the oasis became private property by some means then refusing water to travellers would be fine as *"the owner is scarcely being 'coercive'; in fact he is supplying a vital service, and should have the right to refuse a sale or charge whatever the customers will pay. The situation may be unfortunate for the customers, as are many situations in life."* [**Op. Cit.**, p. 50f and p. 221] That the owner is providing *"a vital service"* only because he has expropriated the common heritage of humanity is as lost on Rothbard as is the obvious economic power that this situation creates.

And, of course, Rothbard ignores the fact of economic power – a transnational corporation can "transform" far more virgin resources in a day by hiring workers than a family could in a year. A transnational "mixing" the labour it has bought from its wage slaves with the land does not spring into mind reading Rothbard's account of property but in the real world that is what happens. This is, perhaps, unsurprising as the whole point of Locke's theory was to justify the appropriation of the product of other people's labour by their employer.

Which is another problem with Rothbard's account. It is completely ahistoric (and so, as we noted above, is more like an *"immaculate conception of property"*). He has transported "capitalist man" into the dawn of time and constructed a history of property based upon what he is trying to justify. He ignores the awkward historic fact that land was held in common for millennium and that the notion of "mixing" labour to enclose it was basically invented to justify the expropriation of land from the general population (and from native populations) by the rich. What **is** interesting to note, though, is that the **actual** experience of life on the US frontier (the historic example Rothbard seems to want to claim) was far from the individualistic framework he builds upon it and (ironically enough) it was destroyed by the development of capitalism.

As Murray Bookchin notes, in rural areas there *"developed a modest subsistence agriculture that allowed them to be almost wholly self-sufficient and required little, if any, currency."* The economy was rooted in barter, with farmers trading surpluses with nearby artisans. This pre-capitalist economy meant people enjoyed *"freedom from servitude to others"* and *"fostered"* a *"sturdy willingness to defend [their] independence from outside commercial interlopers. This condition of near-autarchy, however, was not individualistic; rather it made for strong community interdependence ... In fact, the independence that the New England yeomanry enjoyed was itself a function of the co-operative social base from which it emerged. To barter home-grown goods and objects, to share tools and implements, to engage in common labour during harvesting time in a system of mutual aid, indeed, to help new-comers in barn-raising, corn-husking, log-rolling, and the like, was the indispensable cement that bound scattered farmsteads into a united community." Bookchin quotes David P. Szatmary (author of a book on Shay's Rebellion) stating that it was a society based upon "co-operative, community orientated interchanges" and not a "basically competitive society." [**The Third Revolution**, vol. 1, p. 233]

Into this non-capitalist society came capitalist elements. Market forces and economic power soon resulted in the transformation of this society. Merchants asked for payment in specie (gold or silver coin), which the farmers did not have. In addition, money was required to pay taxes (taxation has always been a key way in which the state encouraged a transformation towards capitalism as money could only be made by hiring oneself to those who had it). The farmers "were now cajoled by local shopkeepers" to "make all their payments and meet all their debts in money rather than barter. Since the farmers lacked money, the shopkeepers granted them short-term credit for their purchases. In time, many farmers became significantly indebted and could not pay off what they owed, least of all in specie." The creditors turned to the courts and many of the homesteaders were dispossessed of their land and goods to pay their debts. In response Shay's rebellion started as the "urban commercial elites adamantly resisted [all] peaceful petitions" while the "state legislators also turned a deaf ear" as they were heavily influenced by these same elites. This rebellion was an important factor in the centralisation of state power in America to ensure that popular input and control over government were marginalised and that the wealthy elite and their property rights were protected against the many ("Elite and well-to-do sectors of the population mobilised in great force to support an instrument that clearly benefited them at the expense of the backcountry agrarians and urban poor.") [Bookchin, **Op. Cit.**, p. 234, p. 235 and p. 243]). Thus the homestead system was, ironically, undermined and destroyed by the rise of capitalism (aided, as usual, by a state run by and for the rich).

So while Rothbard's theory has a certain appeal (reinforced by watching too many Westerns, we imagine) it fails to justify the "unrestricted" property rights theory (and the theory of freedom Rothbard derives from it). All it does is to end up justifying capitalist and landlord domination (which is what it was intended to do).

F.5

Will privatising "the commons" increase liberty?

"Anarcho"-capitalists aim for a situation in which "no land areas, no square footage in the world shall remain 'public,'" in other words **everything** will be "privatised." [Murray Rothbard, **Nations by Consent**, p. 84] They claim that privatising "the commons" (e.g. roads, parks, etc.) which are now freely available to all will increase liberty. Is this true? Here we will concern ourselves with private ownership of commonly used "property" which we all take for granted (and often pay for with taxes).

Its clear from even a brief consideration of a hypothetical society based on "privatised" roads (as suggested by Murray Rothbard [**For a New Liberty**, pp. 202-203] and David Friedman [**The Machinery of Freedom**, pp. 98-101]) that the only increase of liberty will be for the ruling elite. As "anarcho"-capitalism is based on paying for what one uses, privatisation of roads would require some method of tracking individuals to ensure that they pay for the roads they use. In the UK, for example, during the 1980s the British Tory government looked into the idea of toll-based motorways. Obviously having toll-booths on motorways would hinder their use and restrict "freedom," and so they came up with the idea of tracking cars by satellite. Every vehicle would have a tracking device installed in it and a satellite would record where people went and which roads they used. They would then be sent a bill or have their bank balances debited based on this information (in the fascist city-state/company town of Singapore such a scheme **has** been introduced). In London, the local government has introduced a scheme which allowed people to pay for public transport by electronic card. It also allowed the government to keep a detailed record of where and when people travelled, with obvious civil liberty implications.

If we extrapolate from these to a system of **fully** privatised "commons," it would clearly require all individuals to have tracking devices on them so they could be properly billed for use of roads, pavements, etc. Obviously being tracked by private firms would be a serious threat to individual liberty. Another, less costly, option would be for private guards to randomly stop and question car-owners and individuals to make sure they had paid for the use of the road or pavement in question. "Parasites" would be arrested and fined or locked up. Again, however, being stopped and questioned by uniformed individuals has more in common with police states than liberty. Toll-boothing **every** street would be highly unfeasible due to the costs involved and difficulties for use that it implies. Thus the idea of privatising roads and charging drivers to gain access seems impractical at best and distinctly freedom endangering at worse. Would giving companies that information for all travellers, including pedestrians, **really** eliminate all civil liberty concerns?

Of course, the option of owners letting users have free access to the roads and pavements they construct and run would be difficult for a profit-based company. No one could make a profit in that case. If companies paid to construct roads for their customers/employees to use, they would be financially hindered in competition with other companies that did not, and thus would be unlikely to do so. If they restricted use purely to their own customers, the tracking problem appears again. So the costs in creating a transport network and then running it explains why capitalism has always turned to state aid to provide infrastructure (the potential power of the owners of such investments in charging monopoly prices to other capitalists explains why states have also often regulated transport).

Some may object that this picture of extensive surveillance of individuals would not occur or be impossible. However, Murray Rothbard (in a slightly different context) argued that technology would be available to collate information about individuals. He argued that *"[i]t should be pointed out that modern technology makes even more feasible the collection and dissemination of information about people's credit ratings and records of keeping or violating their contracts or arbitration agreements. Presumably, an anarchist [sic!] society would see the expansion of this sort of dissemination of data."* [**Society Without A State"**, p. 199] So with the total privatisation of society we could also see the rise of private Big Brothers, collecting information about individuals for use by property owners. The example of the **Economic League** (a British company which provided the "service" of tracking the political affiliations and activities of workers for employers) springs to mind.

And, of course, these privatisation suggestions ignore differences in income and market power. If, for example, variable pricing is used to discourage road use at times of peak demand (to eliminate traffic jams at rush-hour) as is suggested both by Murray Rothbard and David Friedman, then the rich will have far more "freedom" to travel than the rest of the population. And we may even see people having to go into debt just to get to work or move to look for work.

Which raises another problem with notion of total privatisation, the problem that it implies the end of freedom of travel. Unless you get permission or (and this seems more likely) pay for access, you will not be able to travel **anywhere.** As Rothbard **himself** makes clear, "anarcho"-capitalism means the end of the right to roam. He states that *"it became clear to me that a totally privatised country would not have open borders at all. If every piece of land in a country were owned … no immigrant could enter there unless invited to enter and allowed to rent, or purchase, property."* What happens to those who cannot **afford** to pay for access or travel (i.e., exit) is not addressed (perhaps, being unable to exit a given capitalist's land they will become bonded labourers? Or be imprisoned and used to undercut workers' wages via prison labour? Perhaps they will just be shot as trespassers? Who can tell?). Nor is it addressed how this situation actually **increases** freedom. For Rothbard, a *"totally privatised country would be as closed as the particular inhabitants and property owners [**not** the same thing, we must point out] desire. It seems clear, then, that the regime of open borders that exists **de facto** in the US really amounts to a compulsory opening by the central state … and does not genuinely reflect the wishes of the proprietors."* [**Nations by Consent**, p. 84 and p. 85] Of course, the wishes of **non**-proprietors (the vast majority) do not matter in the slightest. Thus, it is clear, that with the privatisation of "the commons" the right to roam, to travel, would become a privilege, subject to the laws and rules of the property owners. This can hardly be said to **increase** freedom for anyone bar the capitalist class.

Rothbard acknowledges that *"in a fully privatised world, access rights would obviously be a crucial part of land ownership."* [**Op. Cit.**, p. 86] Given that there is no free lunch, we can imagine we would have to pay for such "rights." The implications of this are obviously unappealing and an obvious danger to individual freedom. The problem of access associated with the idea of privatising the roads can only be avoided by having a "right of passage" encoded into the "general libertarian law code." This would mean that road owners would be required, by law, to let anyone use them. But where are "absolute" property rights in this case? Are the owners of roads not to have the same rights as other owners? And if "right of passage" is enforced, what would this mean for road owners when people sue them for car-pollution related illnesses? (The right of those injured by pollution to sue polluters is the main way "anarcho"-capitalists propose to protect the environment – see section E.4). It is unlikely that those wishing to bring suit could find, never mind sue, the millions of individual car owners who could have potentially caused their illness. Hence the road-owners would be sued for letting polluting (or unsafe) cars onto "their" roads. The road-owners would therefore desire to restrict pollution levels by restricting the right to use their property, and so would resist the "right of passage" as an "attack" on their "absolute" property rights. If the road-owners got their way (which would be highly likely given the need for "absolute" property rights and is suggested by the variable pricing way to avoid traffic jams mentioned above) and were able to control who used their property, freedom to travel would be **very** restricted and limited to those whom the owner considered "desirable." Indeed, Murray Rothbard supports such a regime (*"In the free [sic!] society, they [travellers] would, in the first instance, have the right to travel only on those streets whose owners agree to have them there."* [**The Ethics of Liberty**, p. 119]). The threat to liberty in such a system is obvious – to all but Rothbard and other right-"libertarians", of course.

To take another example, let us consider the privatisation of parks, streets and other public areas. Currently, individuals can use these areas to hold political demonstrations, hand out leaflets, picket and so on. However, under "anarcho"-capitalism the owners of such property can restrict such liberties if they desire, calling such activities "initiation of force" (although they cannot explain how speaking your mind is an example of "force"). Therefore, freedom of speech, assembly and a host of other liberties we take for granted would be eliminated under a right-"libertarian" regime. Or, taking the case of pickets and other forms of social struggle, its clear that privatising "the commons" would only benefit the bosses. Strikers or political activists picketing or handing out leaflets in shopping centres are quickly ejected by private security even today. Think about how much worse it would become under "anarcho"-capitalism when the whole world becomes a series of malls – it would be impossible to hold a picket when the owner of the pavement objects (as Rothbard himself gleefully argued. [**Op. Cit.**, p. 132]). If the owner of the pavement also happens to be the boss being picketed, which Rothbard himself considered most likely, then workers' rights would be zero. Perhaps we could also see capitalists suing working class organisations for littering their property if they do hand out leaflets (so placing even greater stress on limited resources).

The I.W.W. went down in history for its rigorous defence of freedom of speech because of its rightly famous "free speech" fights in numerous American cities and towns. The city bosses worried by the wobblies' open air public meetings simply made them illegal. The I.W.W. used direct action and carried on holding them. Violence was inflicted upon wobblies who joined the struggle by "private citizens," but in the end the I.W.W. won (for Emma Goldman's account of the San Diego struggle and the terrible repression inflicted on the libertarians by the "patriotic" vigilantes see **Living My Life** [vol. 1, pp. 494-503]). Consider the case under "anarcho"-capitalism. The wobblies would have been "criminal aggressors" as the owners of the streets have refused to allow "subversives" to use them to argue their case. If they refused to acknowledge the decree of the property owners, private cops would have taken them away. Given that those who controlled city government in the historical example were the wealthiest citizens in town, its likely that the same people would have been involved in the fictional ("anarcho"-capitalist) account. Is it a good thing that in the real account the wobblies are hailed as heroes of freedom but in the fictional one they are "criminal aggressors"? Does converting public spaces into private property **really** stop restrictions on free speech being a bad thing? Of course, Rothbard (and other right-"libertarians") are aware that privatisation will not remove restrictions on freedom of speech, association and so on (while, at the same time, trying to portray themselves as supporters of such liberties!). However, for them such restrictions are of no consequence. As Rothbard argues, any *"prohibitions would not be state imposed, but would simply be requirements for residence or for use of some person's or community's land area."* [**Nations by Consent**, p. 85] Thus we yet again see the blindness of right-"libertarians" to the commonality between private property and the state we first noted in section F.1. The state also maintains that submitting to its authority is the requirement for taking up residence in its territory. As Tucker noted, the state can be defined as (in part) *"the assumption of sole authority over a given area and all within it."* [**The Individualist Anarchists**, p. 24] If the property owners can determine "prohibitions" (i.e. laws and rules) for those who use the property then they are the *"sole authority over a given area and all within it,"* i.e. a state. Thus privatising "the commons" means subjecting the non-property owners to the rules and laws of the property owners – in effect, privatising the state and turning the world into a series of monarchies and oligarchies without the pretence of democracy and democratic rights.

These examples can hardly be said to be increasing liberty for society as a whole, although "anarcho"-capitalists seem to think they would. So far from **increasing** liberty for all, then, privatising the commons would only increase it for the ruling elite, by giving them yet another monopoly from which to collect income and exercise their power over. It would **reduce** freedom for everyone else. Ironically, therefore, Rothbard 'sideology provides more than enough evidence to confirm the anarchist argument that private property and liberty are fundamentally in conflict. *"It goes without saying that th[e] absolute freedom of thought, speech, and action"* anarchists support *"is incompatible with the maintenance of institutions that restrict free thought, rigidify speech in the form of a final and irrevocable vow, and even dictate that the worker*

fold his arms and die of hunger at the owners' command." [Elisée Reclus, quoted by John P. Clark and Camille Martin (eds.), **Anarchy, Geography, Modernity**, p. 159] As Peter Marshall notes, *"[i]n the name of freedom, the anarcho-capitalists would like to turn public spaces into private property, but freedom does not flourish behind high fences protected by private companies but expands in the open air when it is enjoyed by all."* [**Demanding the Impossible**, p. 564]

Little wonder Proudhon argued that *"if the public highway is nothing but an accessory of private property; if the communal lands are converted into private property; if the public domain, in short, is guarded, exploited, leased, and sold like private property – what remains for the proletaire? Of what advantage is it to him that society has left the state of war to enter the regime of police?"* [**System of Economic Contradictions**, p. 371]

F.6

Is "anarcho"-capitalism against the state?

No. Due to its basis in private property, "anarcho"-capitalism implies a class division of society into bosses and workers. Any such division will require a state to maintain it. However, it need not be the same state as exists now. Regarding this point, "anarcho"-capitalism plainly advocates "defence associations" to protect property. For the "anarcho"-capitalist these private companies are not states. For anarchists, they most definitely are. As Bakunin put it, the state *"is authority, domination, and force, organised by the property-owning and so-called enlightened classes against the masses."* [**The Basic Bakunin**, p. 140] It goes without saying that "anarcho"-capitalism has a state in the anarchist sense.

According to Murray Rothbard [**Society Without A State**, p. 192], a state must have one or both of the following characteristics:

(1) The ability to tax those who live within it.
(2) It asserts and usually obtains a coerced monopoly of the provision of defence over a given area.

He makes the same point elsewhere. [**The Ethics of Liberty**, p. 171] Significantly, he stresses that *"our definition of anarchism"* is a system which *"provides no legal sanction"* for aggression against person and property rather than, say, being against government or authority. [**Society without a State**, p. 206]

Instead of this, the "anarcho"-capitalist thinks that people should be able to select their own "defence companies" (which would provide the needed police) and courts from a free market in "defence" which would spring up after the state monopoly has been eliminated. These companies *"all ... would have to abide by the basic law code,"* [**Op. Cit.**, p. 206] Thus a *"general libertarian law code"* would govern the actions of these companies. This "law code" would prohibit coercive aggression at the very least, although to do so it would have to specify what counted as legitimate property, how said can be owned and what actually constitutes aggression. Thus the law code would be quite extensive.

How is this law code to be actually specified? Would these laws be democratically decided? Would they reflect common usage (i.e. custom)? "Supply and demand"? "Natural law"? Given the strong dislike of democracy shown by "anarcho"-capitalists, we think we can safely say that some combination of the last two options would be used. Murray Rothbard argued for "Natural Law" and so the judges in his system would *not [be] making the law but finding it on the basis of agreed-upon principles derived either from custom or reason."* [**Op. Cit.**, p. 206] David Friedman, on the other hand, argues that different defence firms would sell their own laws. [**The Machinery of Freedom**, p. 116] It is sometimes acknowledged that non-"libertarian" laws may be demanded (and supplied) in such a market although the obvious fact that the rich can afford to pay for more laws (either in quantity or in terms of being more expensive to enforce) is downplayed.

Around this system of "defence companies" is a free market in "arbitrators" and "appeal judges" to administer justice and the *"basic law code."* Rothbard believes that such a system would see *"arbitrators with the best reputation for efficiency and probity"* being *"chosen by the various parties in the market"* and *"will come to be given an increasing amount of business."* Judges *"will prosper on the market in proportion to their reputation for efficiency and impartiality."* [**Op. Cit.**, p. 199 and p. 204] Therefore, like any other company, arbitrators would strive for profits and the most successful ones would *"prosper"*, i.e. become wealthy. Such wealth would, of course, have no impact on the decisions of the judges, and if it did, the population (in theory) are free to select any other judge. Of course, the competing judges would **also** be striving for profits and wealth – which means the choice of character may be somewhat limited! – and the laws which they were using to guide their judgements would be enforcing capitalist rights.

Whether or not this system would work as desired is discussed in the following sections. We think that it will not. Moreover, we will argue that "anarcho"-capitalist "defence companies" meet not only the criteria of statehood we outlined in section B.2, but also Rothbard's own criteria for the state. As regards the anarchist criterion, it is clear that "defence companies" exist to defend private property; that they are hierarchical (in that they are capitalist companies which defend the power of those who employ them); that they are professional coercive bodies; and that they exercise a monopoly of force over a given area (the area, initially, being the property of the person or company who is employing the company). Not only that, as we discuss in section F.6.4 these "defence companies" also match the right-libertarian and "anarcho"-capitalist definition of the state. For this (and other reasons), we should call the "anarcho"-capitalist defence firms "private states" – that is what they are – and "anarcho"-capitalism "private state" capitalism.

F.6.1 What's wrong with this "free market" justice?

It does not take much imagination to figure out whose interests prosperous arbitrators, judges and defence companies would defend: their own as well as those who pay their wages – which is to say, other members of the rich elite. As the law exists to defend property, then it (by definition) exists to defend the power of capitalists against their workers. Rothbard argued that the *"judges"* would *"not [be] making the law but finding it on the basis of agreed-upon principles derived either from custom or reason."* [**Society without a State**, p. 206] However, this begs the question: **whose** reason? **whose** customs? Do individuals in different classes share the same customs? The same ideas of right and wrong? Would rich and poor desire the same from a *"basic law code"*? Obviously not. The rich would only support a code which defended their power over the poor.

Rothbard does not address this issue. He stated that "anarcho"-capitalism would involve *"taking the largely libertarian common law, and correcting it by the use of man's reason, before enshrining it as a permanently fixed libertarian law code."* [*"On Freedom and the Law"*, **New Individualist Review**, Winter 1962, p. 40] Needless to say, *"man"* does not exist – it is an abstraction (and a distinctly collectivist one, we should note). There are only individual men and women and so individuals and **their** reason. By *"man's reason"* Rothbard meant, at best, the prejudices of those individuals with whom he agreed with or, at worst, his own value judgements. Needless to say, what is considered acceptable will vary from individual to individual and reflect their social position. Similarly, as Kropotkin stressed, "common law" does not develop in isolation of class struggles and so is a mishmash of customs genuinely required by social life and influences imposed by elites by means of state action. [**Anarchism**, pp. 204-6] This implies what should be *"corrected"* from the "common law" will also differ based on their class position and their general concepts of what is right and wrong. History is full of examples of lawyers, jurists and judges (not to mention states) *"correcting"* common law and social custom in favour of a propertarian perspective which, by strange co-incidence, favoured the capitalists and landlords, i.e. those of the same class as the politicians, lawyers, jurists and judges (see section F.8 for more details). We can imagine the results of similar "correcting" of common law by those deemed worthy by Rothbard and his followers of representing both "man" and "natural law."

Given these obvious points, it should come as no surprise that Rothbard solves this problem by explicitly excluding the general population from deciding which laws they will be subject to. As he put it, *"it would not be a very difficult task for Libertarian lawyers and jurists to arrive at a rational and objective code of libertarian legal principles and procedures … This code would then be followed and applied to specific cases by privately-competitive and free-market courts and judges, all of whom would be pledged to abide by the code."* [*"The Spooner-Tucker Doctrine: An Economist's View"*, pp. 5-15, **Journal of Libertarian Studies**, Vol. 20, No. 1, p. 7] By jurist Rothbard means a professional or an expert who studies, develops, applies or otherwise deals with the law, i.e. a lawyer or a judge. That is, law-making by privately-competitive judges and lawyers. And not only would the law be designed by experts, so would its interpretation:

> "If legislation is replaced by such judge-made law fixity and certainty ... will replace the capriciously changing edicts of statutory legislation. The body of judge-made law changes very slowly ... decisions properly apply only to the particular case, judge-made law – in contrast to legislation – permits a vast body of voluntary, freely-adapted rules, bargains, and arbitrations to proliferate as needed in society. The twin of the free market economy, then, is ... a proliferation of voluntary rules interpreted and applied by experts in the law." ["On Freedom and the Law", **Op. Cit.** p. 38]

In other words, as well as privatising the commons in land he also seeks to privatise "common law." This will be expropriated from the general population and turned over to wealthy judges and libertarian scholars to "correct" as they see fit. Within this mandatory legal regime, there would be "voluntary" interpretations yet it hardly taxes the imagination to see how economic inequality would shape any "bargains" made on it. So we have a legal system created and run by judges and jurists within which specific interpretations would be reached by "bargains" conducted between the rich and the poor. A fine liberation indeed!

So although only *"finding"* the law, the arbitrators and judges still exert an influence in the "justice" process, an influence not impartial or neutral. As the arbitrators themselves would be part of a profession, with specific companies developing within the market, it does not take a genius to realise that when *"interpreting"* the *"basic law code,"* such companies would hardly act against their own interests as companies. As we noted in section F.3.2, the basic class interest of keeping the current property rights system going will still remain – a situation which wealthy judges would be, to say the least, happy to see continue. In addition, if the "justice" system was based on "one dollar, one vote," the "law" would best defend those with the most "votes" (the question of market forces will be discussed in section F.6.3). Moreover, even if "market forces" would ensure that "impartial" judges were dominant, all judges would be enforcing a **very** partial law code (namely one that defended **capitalist** property rights). Impartiality when enforcing partial laws hardly makes judgements less unfair.

Thus, due to these three pressures – the interests of arbitrators/judges, the influence of money and the nature of the law – the terms of "free agreements" under such a law system would be tilted in favour of lenders over debtors, landlords over tenants, employers over employees, and in general, the rich over the poor just as we have today. This is what one would expect in a system based on "unrestricted" property rights and a (capitalist) free market.

Some "anarcho"-capitalists, however, claim that just as cheaper cars were developed to meet demand, so cheaper defence associations and "people's arbitrators" would develop on the market for the working class. In this way impartiality will be ensured. This argument overlooks a few key points.

Firstly, the general "libertarian" law code would be applicable to **all** associations, so they would have to operate within a system determined by the power of money and of capital. The law code would reflect, therefore, property **not** labour and so "socialistic" law codes would be classed as "outlaw" ones. The options then facing working people is to select a firm which best enforced the **capitalist** law in their favour. And as noted above, the impartial enforcement of a biased law code will hardly ensure freedom or justice for all. This means that saying the possibility of competition from another judge would keep them honest becomes meaningless when they are all implementing the **same** capitalist law!

Secondly, in a race between a Jaguar and a Volkswagen Beetle, who is more likely to win? The rich would have "the best justice money can buy," even more than they do now. Members of the capitalist class would be able to select the firms with the best lawyers, best private cops and most resources. Those without the financial clout to purchase quality "justice" would simply be out of luck – such is the "magic" of the marketplace.

Thirdly, because of the tendency toward concentration, centralisation, and oligopoly under capitalism (due to increasing capital costs for new firms entering the market, as discussed in section C.4), a few companies would soon dominate the market – with obvious implications for "justice." Different firms will have different resources and in a conflict between a small firm and a larger one, the smaller one is at a disadvantage. They may not be in a position to fight the larger company if it rejects arbitration and so may give in simply because, as the "anarcho"-capitalists so rightly point out, conflict and violence will push up a company's costs and so they would have to be avoided by smaller ones (it is ironic that the "anarcho"-capitalist implicitly assumes that every "defence company" is approximately of the same size, with the same resources behind it and in real life this would clearly **not** the case). Moreover, it seems likely that a Legal-Industrial complex would develop, with other companies buying shares in "defence" firms as well as companies which provide lawyers and judges (and vice versa). We would also expect mergers to develop as well as cross-ownership between companies, not to mention individual judges and security company owners and managers having shares in other capitalist firms. Even if the possibility that the companies providing security and "justice" have links with other capitalist firms is discounted then the fact remains that these firms would hardly be sympathetic to organisations and individuals seeking to change the system which makes them rich or, as property owners and bosses, seeking to challenge the powers associated with both particularly if the law is designed from a propertarian perspective.

Fourthly, it is **very** likely that many companies would make subscription to a specific "defence" firm or court a requirement of employment and residence. Just as today many (most?) workers have to sign no-union contracts (and face being fired if they change their minds), it does not take much imagination to see that the same could apply to "defence" firms and courts. This was/is the case in company towns (indeed, you can consider unions as a form of "defence" firm and these companies refused to recognise them). As the labour market is almost always a buyer's market, it is not enough to argue that workers can find a new job without this condition. They may not and so have to put up with this situation. And if (as seems likely) the laws and rules of the property-owner will take precedence in any conflict, then workers and tenants will be at a disadvantage no matter how "impartial" the judges.

Ironically, some "anarcho"-capitalists (like David Friedman) have pointed to company/union negotiations as an example of how different defence firms would work out their differences peacefully. Sadly for this argument, union rights under "actually existing capitalism" were hard fought for, often resulting in strikes which quickly became mini-wars as the capitalists used the full might associated with their wealth to stop them getting a foothold or to destroy them if they had. In America the bosses usually had recourse to private defence firms like the Pinkertons to break unions and strikes. Since 1935 in America, union rights have been protected by the state in direct opposition to capitalist "freedom of contract." Before the law was changed (under pressure from below, in the face of business opposition and violence), unions were usually crushed by force – the companies were better armed, had more resources and had the law on their side (Rothbard showed his grasp of American labour history by asserting that union *"restrictions and strikes"* were the *"result of government privilege, notably in the Wagner Act of 1935."* [**The Logic of Action II,** p. 194]). Since the 1980s and the advent of the free(r) market, we can see what happens to "peaceful negotiation" and "co-operation" between unions and companies when it is no longer required and when the resources of both sides are unequal. The market power of companies far exceeds those of the unions and the law, by definition, favours the companies. As an example of how competing "protection agencies" will work in an "anarcho"-capitalist society, it is far more insightful than originally intended!

Now let us consider Rothbard's *"basic law code"* itself. For Rothbard, the laws in the *"general libertarian law code"* would be unchangeable, selected by those considered as "the voice of nature" (with obvious authoritarian implications). David Friedman, in contrast, argues that as well as a market in defence companies, there will also be a market in laws and rights. However, there will be extensive market pressure to unify these differing law codes into one standard one (imagine what would happen if every CD manufacturer created a unique CD player, or every computer manufacturer different sized floppy-disk drivers – little wonder, then, that over time companies standardise their products). Friedman himself acknowledges that this process is likely (and uses the example of standard paper sizes to illustrate it). Which suggests that competition would be meaningless as **all** firms would be enforcing the same (capitalist) law.

In any event, the laws would not be decided on the basis of "one person, one vote"; hence, as market forces worked their magic, the "general" law code would reflect vested interests and so be very hard to change. As rights and laws would be a commodity like everything else in capitalism, they would soon reflect the interests of the rich – particularly if those interpreting the law are wealthy professionals and companies with vested interests of their own. Little wonder that the individualist anarchists proposed "trial by jury" as the only basis for real justice in a free society. For, unlike professional "arbitrators," juries are ad hoc, made up of ordinary people and do not reflect power, authority, or the influence of wealth. And by being able to judge the law as well as a conflict, they can ensure a populist revision of laws as society progresses.

Rothbard, unsurprisingly, is at pains to dismiss the individualist anarchist idea of juries judging the law as well as the facts, stating it would give each free-market jury *"totally free rein over judicial decisions"* and this *"could not be expected to arrive at just or even libertarian decisions."* [*"The Spooner-Tucker Doctrine: An Economist's View"*, **Op. Cit.**, p.7] However, the opposite is the case as juries made up of ordinary people will be more likely to reach just decisions which place genuinely libertarian positions above a law dedicated to maintaining capitalist property and power. History is full of examples of juries acquitting people for so-called crimes against property which are the result of dire need or simply reflect class injustice. For example, during the Great Depression unemployed miners in Pennsylvania *"dug small mines on company property, mined coal, trucked it to cities and sold it below the commercial rate. By 1934, 5 million tons of this 'bootleg' coal were produced by twenty thousand men using four thousand vehicles. When attempts were made to prosecute, local juries would not convict, local jailers would not imprison."* [Howard Zinn, **A People's History of the United States**, pp. 385-6] It is precisely this outcome which causes Rothbard to reject that system.

Thus Rothbard postulated a **judge** directed system of laws in stark contrast to individualist anarchism's **jury** directed system. It is understandable that Rothbard would seek to replace juries with judges, it is the only way he can exclude the general population from having a say in the laws they are subjected to. Juries allow the general public to judge the law as well as any crime and so this would allow those aspects "corrected" by right-"libertarians" to seep back into the "common law" and so make private property and power accountable to the general public rather than vice versa. Moreover, concepts of right and wrong evolve over time and in line with changes in socio-economic conditions. To have a "common law" which is unchanging means that social evolution is considered to have stopped when Murray Rothbard decided to call his ideology "anarcho"-capitalism.

In a genuinely libertarian system, social customs (common law) would evolve based on what the general population thought was right and wrong based on changing social institutions and relationships between individuals. That is why ruling classes have always sought to replace it with state determined and enforced laws. Changing social norms and institutions can be seen from property. As Proudhon noted, property *"changed its nature"* over time. Originally, *"the word **property** was synonymous with ... **individual possession**"* but it became more *"complex"* and turned into **private property** – *"the right to use it by his neighbour's labour."* [**What is Property?**, p. 395] The changing nature of property created relations of domination and exploitation between people absent before. For the capitalist, however, both the tools of the self-employed artisan and the capital of a transnational corporation are both forms of "property" and so basically identical. Changing social relations impact on society and the individuals who make it up. This would be reflected in any genuinely libertarian society, something right-"libertarians" are aware of. They, therefore, seek to freeze the rights framework and legal system to protect institutions, like property, no matter how they evolve and come to replace whatever freedom enhancing features they had with oppression. Hence we find Rothbard's mentor, Ludwig von Mises asserting that *"[t]here* may possibly be a difference of opinion about whether a particular institution is socially beneficial or harmful. But once it has been judged [by whom?] beneficial, one can no longer contend that, for some inexplicable reason, it must be condemned as immoral." [**Liberalism**, p. 34] Rothbard's system is designed to ensure that the general population cannot judge whether a particular institution has changed is social impact. Thus a system of "defence" on the capitalist market will continue to reflect the influence and power of property owners and wealth and not be subject to popular control beyond choosing between companies to enforce the capitalist laws.

Ultimately, such an "anarcho"-capitalist system would be based on simple absolute principles decided in advance by a small group of ideological leaders. We are then expected to live with the consequences as best we can. If people end up in a worse condition than before then that is irrelevant as that we have enforced the eternal principles they have proclaimed as being in our best interests.

F.6.2 What are the social consequences of such a system?

The "anarcho" capitalist imagines that there will be police agencies, "defence associations," courts, and appeals courts all organised on a free-market basis and available for hire. As David Wieck points out, however, the major problem with such a system would not be the corruption of "private" courts and police forces (although, as suggested above, this could indeed be a problem):

> "There is something more serious than the 'Mafia danger', and this other problem concerns the role of such 'defence' institutions in a given social and economic context.
>
> "[The] context … is one of a free-market economy with no restraints upon accumulation of property. Now, we had an American experience, roughly from the end of the Civil War to the 1930's, in what were in effect private courts, private police, indeed private governments. We had the experience of the (private) Pinkerton police which, by its spies, by its **agents provocateurs,** and by methods that included violence and kidnapping, was one of the most powerful tools of large corporations and an instrument of oppression of working people. We had the experience as well of the police forces established to the same end, within corporations, by numerous companies … (The automobile companies drew upon additional covert instruments of a private nature, usually termed vigilante, such as the Black Legion). These were, in effect, private armies, and were sometimes described as such. The territories owned by coal companies, which frequently included entire towns and their environs, the stores the miners were obliged by economic coercion to patronise, the houses they lived in, were commonly policed by the private police of the United States Steel Corporation or whatever company owned the properties. The chief practical function of these police was, of course, to prevent labour organisation and preserve a certain balance of 'bargaining.' … These complexes were a law unto themselves, powerful enough to ignore, when they did not purchase, the governments of various jurisdictions of the American federal system. This industrial system was, at the time, often characterised as feudalism." [**Anarchist Justice**, pp. 223-224]

For a description of the weaponry and activities of these private armies, the Marxist economic historian Maurice Dobb presents an excellent summary in **Studies in Capitalist Development**. [pp. 353-357] According to a report on "Private Police Systems" quoted by Dobb, in a town dominated by Republican Steel the "civil liberties and the rights of labour were suppressed by company police. Union organisers were driven out of town." Company towns had their own (company-run) money, stores, houses and jails and many corporations had machine-guns and tear-gas along with the usual shot-guns, rifles and revolvers. The "usurpation of police powers by privately paid 'guards and 'deputies', often hired from detective agencies, many with criminal records" was "a general practice in many parts of the country."

The local (state-run) law enforcement agencies turned a blind-eye to what was going on (after all, the workers **had** broken their contracts and so were "criminal aggressors" against the companies) even when union members and strikers were beaten and killed. The workers own defence organisations (unions) were the only ones willing to help them, and if the workers seemed to be winning then troops were called in to "restore the peace" (as happened in the Ludlow strike, when strikers originally cheered the troops as they thought they would defend them; needless to say, they were wrong).

Here we have a society which is claimed by many "anarcho"-capitalists as one of the closest examples to their "ideal," with limited state intervention, free reign for property owners, etc. What happened? The rich reduced the working class to a serf-like existence, capitalist production undermined independent producers (much to the annoyance of individualist anarchists at the time), and the result was the emergence of the corporate America that "anarcho"-capitalists (sometimes) say they oppose.

Are we to expect that "anarcho"-capitalism will be different? That, unlike before, "defence" firms will intervene on behalf of strikers? Given that the "general libertarian law code" will be enforcing capitalist property rights, workers will be in exactly the same situation as they were then. Support of strikers violating property rights would be a violation of the law and be costly for profit making firms to do (if not dangerous as they could be "outlawed" by the rest). This suggests that "anarcho"-capitalism will extend extensive rights and powers to bosses, but few if any rights to rebellious workers. And this difference in power is enshrined within the fundamental institutions of the system. This can easily be seen from Rothbard's numerous anti-union tirades and his obvious hatred of them, strikes and pickets (which he habitually labelled as violent). As such it is not surprising to discover that Rothbard complained in the 1960s that, because of the Wagner Act, the American police "commonly remain 'neutral' when strike-breakers are molested or else blame the strike-breakers for 'provoking' the attacks on them

... *When unions are permitted to resort to violence, the state or other enforcing agency has implicitly delegated this power to the unions. The unions, then, have become 'private states.'"* [**The Logic of Action II,** p. 41] The role of the police was to back the property owner against their rebel workers, in other words, and the state was failing to provide the appropriate service (of course, that bosses exercising power over workers provoked the strike is irrelevant, while private police attacking picket lines is purely a form of "defensive" violence and is, likewise, of no concern).

In evaluating "anarcho"-capitalism's claim to be a form of anarchism, Peter Marshall notes that *"private protection agencies would merely serve the interests of their paymasters."* [**Demanding the Impossible**, p. 653] With the increase of private "defence associations" under "really existing capitalism" today (associations that many "anarcho"-capitalists point to as examples of their ideas), we see a vindication of Marshall's claim. There have been many documented experiences of protesters being badly beaten by private security guards. As far as market theory goes, the companies are only supplying what the buyer is demanding. The rights of others are **not a factor** (yet more "externalities," obviously). Even if the victims successfully sue the company, the message is clear – social activism can seriously damage your health. With a reversion to *"a general libertarian law code"* enforced by private companies, this form of "defence" of "absolute" property rights can only increase, perhaps to the levels previously attained in the heyday of US capitalism, as described above by Wieck.

F.6.3 But surely market forces will stop abuses by the rich?

Unlikely. The rise of corporations within America indicates exactly how a *"general libertarian law code"* would reflect the interests of the rich and powerful. The laws recognising corporations as "legal persons" were **not** primarily a product of "the state" but of private lawyers hired by the rich. As Howard Zinn notes:

> *"the American Bar Association, organised by lawyers accustomed to serving the wealthy, began a national campaign of education to reverse the [Supreme] Court decision [that companies could not be considered as a person].... By 1886, they succeeded ... the Supreme Court had accepted the argument that corporations were 'persons' and their money was property protected by the process clause of the Fourteenth Amendment.... The justices of the Supreme Court were not simply interpreters of the Constitution. They were men of certain backgrounds, of certain [class] interests."* [**A People's History of the United States**, p. 255]

Of course it will be argued that the Supreme Court is chosen by the government and is a state enforced monopoly and so our analysis is flawed. Yet this is not the case. As Rothbard made clear, the *"general libertarian law code"* would be created by lawyers and jurists and everyone would be expected to obey it. Why expect **these** lawyers and jurists to be any less class conscious then those in the 19th century? If the Supreme Court *"was doing its bit for the ruling elite"* then why would those creating the law system be any different? *"How could it be neutral between rich and poor,"* argues Zinn, *"when its members were often former wealthy lawyers, and almost always came from the upper class?"* [**Op. Cit.**, p. 254] Moreover, the corporate laws came about because there was a demand for them. That demand would still have existed in "anarcho"-capitalism. Now, while there may nor be a Supreme Court, Rothbard does maintain that *"the basic Law Code ... would have to be agreed upon by all the judicial agencies"* but he maintains that this *"would imply no unified legal system"*! Even though *"[a]ny agencies that transgressed the basic libertarian law code would be open outlaws"* and soon crushed this is **not**, apparently, a monopoly. [**The Ethics of Liberty**, p. 234] So, you either agree to the law code or you go out of business. And that is **not** a monopoly! Therefore, we think, our comments on the Supreme Court are valid (see also section F.7.2).

If all the available defence firms enforce the same laws, then it can hardly be called "competitive"! And if this is the case (and it is) *"when private wealth is uncontrolled, then a police-judicial complex enjoying a clientele of wealthy corporations whose motto is self-interest is hardly an innocuous social force controllable by the possibility of forming or affiliating with competing 'companies.'"* [Wieck, **Op. Cit.**, p. 225] This is particularly true if these companies are themselves Big Business and so have a large impact on the laws they are enforcing. If the law code recognises and protects capitalist power, property and wealth as fundamental **any** attempt to change this is "initiation of force" and so the power of the rich is written into the system from the start!

And, we must add, if there is a general libertarian law code to which all must subscribe, where does that put customer demand? If people demand a non-libertarian law code, will defence firms refuse to supply it? If so, will not new firms, looking for profit, spring up that will supply what is being demanded? And will that not put them in direct conflict with the existing, pro-general law code ones? And will a market in law codes not just reflect economic power and wealth? David Friedman, who is for a market in law codes, argues that *"[i]f almost everyone believes strongly that heroin addiction is so horrible that it should not be permitted anywhere under any circumstances anarcho-capitalist institutions will produce laws against heroin. Laws are being produced on the market, and that is what the market wants."* And he adds that *"market demands are in dollars, not votes. The legality of heroin will be determined, not by how many are for or against but how high a cost each side is willing to bear in order to get its way."* [**The Machinery of Freedom**, p. 127] As the market is less than equal in terms of income and wealth, such a position will mean that the capitalist class will have a higher effective demand than the working class and more resources to pay for any conflicts that arise. Thus any law codes that develop will tend to reflect the interests of the wealthy.

Which brings us nicely on to the next problem regarding market forces.

As well as the obvious influence of economic interests and differences in wealth, another problem faces the "free market" justice of "anarcho"-capitalism. This is the *"general libertarian law code"* itself. Even if we assume that the system actually works like it should in theory, the simple fact remains that these "defence companies" are enforcing laws which explicitly defend capitalist property (and so social relations). Capitalists own the means of production upon which they hire wage-labourers to work and this is an inequality established **prior** to any specific transaction in the labour market. This inequality reflects itself in terms of differences in power within (and outside) the company and in the "law code" of "anarcho"-capitalism which protects that power against the dispossessed.

In other words, the law code within which the defence companies work assumes that capitalist property is legitimate and that force can legitimately be used to defend it. This means that, in effect, "anarcho"-capitalism is based on a monopoly of law, a monopoly which explicitly exists to defend the power and capital of the wealthy. The major difference is that the agencies used to protect that wealth will be in a weaker position to act independently of their pay-masters. Unlike the state, the "defence" firm is not remotely accountable to the general population and cannot be used to equalise even slightly the power relationships between worker and capitalist (as the state has, on occasion done, due to public pressure and to preserve the system as a whole). And, needless to say, it is very likely that the private police forces **will** give preferential treatment to their wealthier customers (which business does not?) and that the law code will reflect the interests of the wealthier sectors of society (particularly if prosperous judges administer that code) in reality, even if not in theory. Since, in capitalist practice, "the customer is always right," the best-paying customers will get their way in "anarcho"-capitalist society.

For example, in chapter 29 of **The Machinery of Freedom**, David Friedman presents an example of how a clash of different law codes could be resolved by a bargaining process (the law in question is the death penalty). This process would involve one defence firm giving a sum of money to the other for them accepting the appropriate (anti/pro capital punishment) court. Friedman claims that *"[a]s in any good trade, everyone gains"* but this is obviously not true. Assuming the anti-capital punishment defence firm pays the pro one to accept an anti-capital punishment court, then, yes, both defence firms have made money and so are happy, so are the anti-capital punishment consumers but the pro-death penalty customers have only (perhaps) received a cut in their bills. Their desire to see criminals hanged (for whatever reason) has been ignored (if they were not in favour of the death penalty, they would not have subscribed to that company). Friedman claims that the deal, by allowing the anti-death penalty firm to cut its costs, will ensure that it *"keep its customers and even get more"* but this is just an assumption. It is just as likely to loose customers to a defence firm that refuses to compromise (and has the resources to back it up). Friedman's assumption that lower costs will automatically win over people's passions is unfounded as is the assumption that both firms have equal resources and bargaining power. If the pro-capital punishment firm demands more than the anti can provide and has larger weaponry and troops, then the anti defence firm may have to agree to let the pro one have its way. So, all in all, it is **not** clear that *"everyone gains"* – there may be a sizeable percentage of those involved who do not "gain" as their desire for capital punishment is traded away by those who claimed they would enforce it. This may, in turn, produce a demand for defence firms which do **not**

compromise with obvious implications for public peace.

In other words, a system of competing law codes and privatised rights does not ensure that **all** individual interests are meet. Given unequal resources within society, it is clear that the "effective demand" of the parties involved to see their law codes enforced is drastically different. The wealthy head of a transnational corporation will have far more resources available to him to pay for **his** laws to be enforced than one of his employees on the assembly line. Moreover, as we noted in section F.3.1, the labour market is usually skewed in favour of capitalists. This means that workers have to compromise to get work and such compromises may involve agreeing to join a specific "defence" firm or not join one at all (just as workers are often forced to sign non-union contracts today in order to get work). In other words, a privatised law system is very likely to skew the enforcement of laws in line with the skewing of income and wealth in society. At the very least, unlike every other market, the customer is **not** guaranteed to get exactly what they demand simply because the product they "consume" is dependent on others within the same market to ensure its supply. The unique workings of the law/defence market are such as to deny customer choice (we will discuss other aspects of this unique market shortly). Wieck summed up by pointing out the obvious:

> *"any judicial system is going to exist in the context of economic institutions. If there are gross inequalities of power in the economic and social domains, one has to imagine society as strangely compartmentalised in order to believe that those inequalities will fail to reflect themselves in the judicial and legal domain, and that the economically powerful will be unable to manipulate the legal and judicial system to their advantage. To abstract from such influences of context, and then consider the merits of an abstract judicial system … is to follow a method that is not likely to take us far. This, by the way, is a criticism that applies … to any theory that relies on a rule of law to override the tendencies inherent in a given social and economic system"* [**Op. Cit.**, p. 225]

There is another reason why "market forces" will not stop abuse by the rich, or indeed stop the system from turning from private to public statism. This is due to the nature of the "defence" market (for a similar analysis of the "defence" market see right-"libertarian" economist Tyler Cowen's *Law as a Public Good: The Economics of Anarchy"* [**Economics and Philosophy**, no. 8 (1992), pp. 249-267] and *"Rejoinder to David Friedman on the Economics of Anarchy"* [**Economics and Philosophy**, no. 10 (1994), pp. 329-332]). In "anarcho"-capitalist theory it is assumed that the competing "defence companies" have a vested interest in peacefully settling differences between themselves by means of arbitration. In order to be competitive on the market, companies will have to co-operate via contractual relations otherwise the higher price associated with conflict will make the company uncompetitive and it will go under. Those companies that ignore decisions made in arbitration would be outlawed by others, ostracised and their rulings ignored. By this process, it is argued, a system of competing "defence" companies will be stable and not turn into a civil war between agencies with each enforcing the interests of their clients against others by force.

However, there is a catch. Unlike every other market, the businesses in competition in the "defence" industry **must** co-operate with its fellows in order to provide its services for its customers. They need to be able to agree to courts and judges, agree to abide by decisions and law codes and so forth. In economics there are other, more accurate, terms to describe co-operative activity between companies: collusion and cartels. These are when companies in a specific market agree to work together (co-operate) to restrict competition and reap the benefits of monopoly power by working to achieve the same ends in partnership with each other. By stressing the co-operative nature of the "defence" market, "anarcho"-capitalists are implicitly acknowledging that collusion is built into the system. The necessary contractual relations between agencies in the "protection" market require that firms co-operate and, by so doing, to behave (effectively) as one large firm (and so resemble a normal state even more than they already do). Quoting Adam Smith seems appropriate here: *"People of the same trade seldom meet together, even for merriment and diversion, but the conversation ends in a conspiracy against the public, or in some contrivance to raise prices."* [**The Wealth of Nations**, p. 117] Having a market based on people of the same trade co-operating seems, therefore, an unwise move.

For example, when buying food it does not matter whether the supermarkets visited have good relations with each other. The goods bought are independent of the relationships that exist between competing companies. However, in the case of private states this is **not** the case. If a specific "defence" company has bad relationships with other companies in the market then it is against a customer's self-interest to subscribe to it. Why subscribe to a private state if its judgements are ignored by the others and it has to resort to violence to be heard? This, as well as being potentially dangerous, will also push up the prices that have to be paid. Arbitration is one of the most important services a defence firm can offer its customers and its market share is based upon being able to settle interagency disputes without risk of war or uncertainty that the final outcome will not be accepted by all parties. Lose that and a company will lose market share.

Therefore, the market set-up within the "anarcho"-capitalist "defence" market is such that private states **have to co-operate** with the others (or go out of business fast) and this means collusion can take place. In other words, a system of private states will have to agree to work together in order to provide the service of "law enforcement" to their customers and the result of such co-operation is to create a cartel. However, unlike cartels in other industries, the "defence" cartel will be a stable body simply because its members **have** to work with their competitors in order to survive.

Let us look at what would happen after such a cartel is formed in a specific area and a new "defence company" desired to enter the market. This new company will have to work with the members of the cartel in order to provide its services to its customers (note that "anarcho"-capitalists already assume that they *"will have to"* subscribe to the same law code). If the new defence firm tries to under-cut the cartel's monopoly prices, the other companies would refuse to work with it. Having to face constant conflict or the possibility of conflict, seeing its decisions being ignored by other agencies and being uncertain what the results of a dispute

would be, few would patronise the new "defence company." The new company's prices would go up and it would soon face either folding or joining the cartel. Unlike every other market, if a "defence company" does not have friendly, co-operative relations with other firms in the same industry then it will go out of business.

This means that the firms that are co-operating have simply to agree not to deal with new firms which are attempting to undermine the cartel in order for them to fail. A "cartel busting" firm goes out of business in the same way an outlaw one does – the higher costs associated with having to solve all its conflicts by force, not arbitration, increases its production costs much higher than the competitors and the firm faces insurmountable difficulties selling its products at a profit (ignoring any drop of demand due to fears of conflict by actual and potential customers). Even if we assume that many people will happily join the new firm in spite of the dangers to protect themselves against the cartel and its taxation (i.e. monopoly profits), enough will remain members of the cartel so that co-operation will still be needed and conflict unprofitable and dangerous (and as the cartel will have more resources than the new firm, it could usually hold out longer than the new firm could). In effect, breaking the cartel may take the form of an armed revolution – as it would with any state.

The forces that break up cartels and monopolies in other industries (such as free entry – although, of course the "defence" market will be subject to oligopolistic tendencies as any other and this will create barriers to entry) do not work here and so new firms have to co-operate or loose market share and/or profits. This means that "defence companies" will reap monopoly profits and, more importantly, have a monopoly of force over a given area.

It is also likely that a multitude of cartels would develop, with a given cartel operating in a given locality. This is because law enforcement would be localised in given areas as most crime occurs where the criminal lives (few criminals would live in Glasgow and commit crimes in Paris). However, as defence companies have to co-operate to provide their services, so would the cartels. Few people live all their lives in one area and so firms from different cartels would come into contact, so forming a cartel of cartels. This cartel of cartels may (perhaps) be less powerful than a local cartel, but it would still be required and for exactly the same reasons a local one is. Therefore "anarcho"-capitalism would, like "actually existing capitalism," be marked by a series of public states covering given areas, co-ordinated by larger states at higher levels. Such a set up would parallel the United States in many ways except it would be run directly by wealthy shareholders without the sham of "democratic" elections. Moreover, as in the USA and other states there will still be a monopoly of rules and laws (the *"general libertarian law code"*).

Hence a monopoly of private states will develop in addition to the existing monopoly of law and this is a de facto monopoly of force over a given area (i.e. some kind of public state run by share holders). New companies attempting to enter the "defence" industry will have to work with the existing cartel in order to provide the services it offers to its customers. The cartel is in a dominant position and new entries into the market either become part of it or fail. This is exactly the position with the state, with "private agencies" free to operate as long as they work to the state's guidelines. As with the monopolist *"general libertarian law code"*, if you do not toe the line, you go out of business fast.

"Anarcho"-capitalists claim that this will not occur, but that the co-operation needed to provide the service of law enforcement will somehow **not** turn into collusion between companies. However, they are quick to argue that renegade "agencies" (for example, the so-called "Mafia problem" or those who reject judgements) will go out of business because of the higher costs associated with conflict and not arbitration. Yet these higher costs are ensured because the firms in question do not co-operate with others. If other agencies boycott a firm but co-operate with all the others, then the boycotted firm will be at the same disadvantage – regardless of whether it is a cartel buster or a renegade. So the "anarcho"-capitalist is trying to have it both ways. If the punishment of non-conforming firms cannot occur, then "anarcho"-capitalism will turn into a war of all against all or, at the very least, the service of social peace and law enforcement cannot be provided. If firms cannot deter others from disrupting the social peace (one service the firm provides) then "anarcho"-capitalism is not stable and will not remain orderly as agencies develop which favour the interests of their own customers and enforce their own law codes at the expense of others. If collusion cannot occur (or is too costly) then neither can the punishment of non-conforming firms and "anarcho"-capitalism will prove to be unstable.

So, to sum up, the "defence" market of private states has powerful forces within it to turn it into a monopoly of force over a given area. From a privately chosen monopoly of force over a specific (privately owned) area, the market of private states will turn into a monopoly of force over a general area. This is due to the need for peaceful relations between companies, relations which are required for a firm to secure market share. The unique market forces that exist within this market ensure collusion and the system of private states will become a cartel and so a public state – unaccountable to all but its shareholders, a state of the wealthy, by the wealthy, for the wealthy.

F.6.4 Why are these "defence associations" states?

It is clear that "anarcho"-capitalist defence associations meet the criteria of statehood outlined in section B.2 ("Why are anarchists against the state"). They defend property and preserve authority relationships, they practice coercion, and are hierarchical institutions which govern those under them on behalf of a "ruling elite," i.e. those who employ both the governing forces and those they govern. Thus, from an anarchist perspective, these "defence associations" are most definitely states.

What is interesting, however, is that by their own definitions a very good case can be made that these "defence associations" are states in the "anarcho"-capitalist sense too. Capitalist apologists usually define a "government" (or state) as something which has a monopoly of force and coercion within a given area. Relative to the rest of the society, these defence associations would have a monopoly of force and coercion of a given piece of property: thus,

by the "anarcho"-capitalists' **own definition** of statehood, these associations would qualify!

If we look at Rothbard's definition of statehood, which requires (a) the power to tax and/or (b) a *"coerced monopoly of the provision of defence over a given area"*, "anarcho"-capitalism runs into trouble. In the first place, the costs of hiring defence associations will be deducted from the wealth created by those who use, but do not own, the property of capitalists and landlords. Let us not forget that a capitalist will only employ a worker or rent out land and housing if they make a profit from so doing. Without the labour of the worker, there would be nothing to sell and no wages to pay for rent and so a company's or landlord's "defence" firm will be paid from the revenue gathered from the capitalists power to extract a tribute from those who use, but do not own, a property. In other words, workers would pay for the agencies that enforce their employers' authority over them via the wage system and rent – taxation in a more insidious form.

In the second, under capitalism most people spend a large part of their day on other people's property – that is, they work for capitalists and/or live in rented accommodation. Hence if property owners select a "defence association" to protect their factories, farms, rental housing, etc., their employees and tenants will view it as a *"coerced monopoly of the provision of defence over a given area."* For certainly the employees and tenants will not be able to hire their own defence companies to expropriate the capitalists and landlords. So, from the standpoint of the employees and tenants, the owners do have a monopoly of "defence" over the areas in question. Of course, the "anarcho"-capitalist will argue that the tenants and workers "consent" to **all** the rules and conditions of a contract when they sign it and so the property owner's monopoly is not "coerced." However, the "consent" argument is so weak in conditions of inequality as to be useless (see section F.3.1, for example) and, moreover, it can and has been used to justify the state. In other words, "consent" in and of itself does not ensure that a given regime is not statist. So an argument along these lines is deeply flawed and can be used to justify regimes which are little better than "industrial feudalism" (such as, as indicated in section B.4, company towns, for example – an institution which right-"libertarians" have no problem with). Even the *"general libertarian law code,"* could be considered a "monopoly of government over a particular area," particularly if ordinary people have no real means of affecting the law code, either because it is market-driven and so is money-determined, or because it will be "natural" law and so unchangeable by mere mortals.

In other words, **if** the state *"arrogates to itself a monopoly of force, of ultimate decision-making power, over a given area territorial area"* then its pretty clear that the property owner shares this power. As we indicated in section F.1, Rothbard agrees that the owner is, after all, the *"ultimate decision-making power"* in their workplace or on their land. If the boss takes a dislike to you (for example, you do not follow their orders) then you get fired. If you cannot get a job or rent the land without agreeing to certain conditions (such as not joining a union or subscribing to the "defence firm" approved by your employer) then you either sign the contract or look for something else. Rothbard fails to draw the obvious conclusion and instead refers to the state *"prohibiting the voluntary purchase and* *sale of defence and judicial services."* [**The Ethics of Liberty**, p. 170 and p. 171] But just as surely as the law of contract allows the banning of unions from a property, it can just as surely ban the sale and purchase of defence and judicial services (it could be argued that market forces will stop this happening, but this is unlikely as bosses usually have the advantage on the labour market and workers have to compromise to get a job). After all, in the company towns, only company money was legal tender and company police the only law enforcers.

Therefore, it is obvious that the "anarcho"-capitalist system meets the Weberian criteria of a monopoly to enforce certain rules in a given area of land. The *"general libertarian law code"* is a monopoly and property owners determine the rules that apply on their property. Moreover, if the rules that property owners enforce are subject to rules contained in the monopolistic *"general libertarian law code"* (for example, that they cannot ban the sale and purchase of certain products – such as defence – on their own territory) then "anarcho"-capitalism **definitely** meets the Weberian definition of the state (as described by Ayn Rand as an institution *"that holds the exclusive power to **enforce** certain rules of conduct in a given geographical area"* [**Capitalism: The Unknown Ideal**, p. 239]) as its "law code" overrides the desires of property owners to do what they like on their own property.

Therefore, no matter how you look at it, "anarcho"-capitalism and its "defence" market promotes a *"monopoly of ultimate decision making power"* over a *"given territorial area"*. It is obvious that for anarchists, the "anarcho"-capitalist system is a state system. And, as we note, a reasonable case can be made for it also being a state in the "anarcho"-capitalist sense as well. So, in effect, "anarcho"-capitalism has a **different** sort of state, one in which bosses hire and fire the policeman. As anarchist Peter Sabatini notes:

> *"Within [right] Libertarianism, Rothbard represents a minority perspective that actually argues for the total elimination of the state. However Rothbard's claim as an anarchist is quickly voided when it is shown that he only wants an end to the public state. In its place he allows countless private states, with each person supplying their own police force, army, and law, or else purchasing these services from capitalist vendors ... Rothbard sees nothing at all wrong with the amassing of wealth, therefore those with more capital will inevitably have greater coercive force at their disposal, just as they do now."* [**Libertarianism: Bogus Anarchy**]

Far from wanting to abolish the state, then, "anarcho"-capitalists only desire to privatise it – to make it solely accountable to capitalist wealth. Their "companies" perform the same services as the state, for the same people, in the same manner. However, there is one slight difference. Property owners would be able to select between competing companies for their "services." Because such "companies" are employed by the boss, they would be used to reinforce the totalitarian nature of capitalist firms by ensuring that the police and the law they enforce are not even slightly accountable to ordinary people. Looking beyond the "defence association" to the defence market itself (as we argued in the last section), this will become a cartel and so become some kind of public state. The very nature of the private state, its need to co-operate with others in the same industry, push it towards a monopoly network of firms and so a monopoly of force over a given area. Given the assumptions used to defend "anarcho"-capitalism, its system of private statism will develop into public statism – a state run by managers accountable only to the share-holding elite.

To quote Peter Marshall again, the "anarcho"-capitalists *"claim that all would benefit from a free exchange on the market, it is by no means certain; any unfettered market system would most likely sponsor a reversion to an unequal society with defence associations perpetuating exploitation and privilege."* [**Demanding the Impossible**, p. 565] History, and current practice, prove this point.

In short, "anarcho"-capitalists are not anarchists at all, they are just capitalists who desire to see private states develop – states which are strictly accountable to their paymasters without even the sham of democracy we have today. Hence a far better name for "anarcho"-capitalism would be "private-state" capitalism. At least that way we get a fairer idea of what they are trying to sell us. Bob Black put it well: *"To my mind a right-wing anarchist is just a minarchist who'd abolish the state to his own satisfaction by calling it something else ... They don't denounce what the state does, they just object to who's doing it."* ["The Libertarian As Conservative", **The Abolition of Work and Other Essays**, p. 144]

F.7

How does the history of "anarcho"-capitalism show that it is not anarchist?

Of course, "anarcho"-capitalism does have historic precedents and "anarcho"-capitalists spend considerable time trying to co-opt various individuals into their self-proclaimed tradition of "anti-statist" liberalism. That, in itself, should be enough to show that anarchism and "anarcho"-capitalism have little in common as anarchism developed in opposition to liberalism and its defence of capitalism. Unsurprisingly, these "anti-state" liberals tended to, at best, refuse to call themselves anarchists or, at worst, explicitly deny they were anarchists.

One "anarcho"-capitalist overview of their tradition is presented by David M. Hart. His perspective on anarchism is typical of the school, noting that in his essay anarchism or anarchist *"are used in the sense of a political theory which advocates the maximum amount of individual liberty, a necessary condition of which is the elimination of governmental or other organised force."* ["Gustave de Molinari and the Anti-statist Liberal Tradition: Part I", pp. 263-290, **Journal of Libertarian Studies**, vol. V, no. 3, p. 284] Yet anarchism has **never** been solely concerned with abolishing the state. Rather, anarchists have always raised economic and social demands and goals along with their opposition to the state. As such, anti-statism may be a necessary condition to be an anarchist, but not a sufficient one to count a specific individual or theory as anarchist.

Specifically, anarchists have turned their analysis onto private property noting that the hierarchical social relationships created by inequality of wealth (for example, wage labour) restricts individual freedom. This means that if we do seek *"the maximum of individual liberty"* then our analysis cannot be limited to just the state or government. Thus a libertarian critique of private property is an essential aspect of anarchism. Consequently, to limit anarchism as Hart does requires substantial rewriting of history, as can be seen from his account of William Godwin.

Hart tries to co-opt William Godwin into the ranks of "anti-state" liberalism, arguing that he *"defended individualism and the right to property."* [**Op. Cit.**, p. 265] He, of course, quotes from Godwin to support his claim yet strangely truncates Godwin's argument to exclude his conclusion that *"[w]hen the laws of morality shall be clearly understood, their excellence universally apprehended, and themselves seen to be coincident with each man's private advantage, the idea of property in this sense will remain, but no man will have the least desire, for purposes of ostentation or luxury, to possess more than his neighbours."* In other words, personal property (possession) would still exist but not private property in the sense of capital or inequality of wealth. For Godwin, *"it follows, upon the principles of equal and impartial justice, that the good things of the world are a common stock, upon which one man has a valid a title as another to draw for what he wants."* [**An Enquiry into Political Justice**, p. 199 and p. 703] Rather than being a liberal Godwin moved beyond that limited ideology to provide the first anarchist critique of private property and the authoritarian social relationships it created. His vision of a free society would, to use modern terminology, be voluntary (**libertarian**) communism.

This analysis is confirmed in book 8 of Godwin's classic work, entitled ***"On Property."*** Needless to say, Hart fails to mention this analysis, unsurprisingly as it was later reprinted as a socialist pamphlet. Godwin thought that the *"subject of property is the keystone that completes the fabric of political justice."* Like Proudhon, he subjected property as well as the state to an anarchist analysis. For Godwin, there were *"three degrees"* of property. The first is possession of things you need to live. The second is *"the empire to which every man is entitled over the produce of his own industry."* The third is *"that which occupies the most vigilant attention in the civilised states of Europe. It is a system, in whatever manner established, by which one man enters into the faculty of disposing of the produce of another man's industry."* He notes that it is *"clear therefore that the third species of property is in direct contradiction to the second."* [**Op. Cit.**, p. 701 and p. 710-2] The similarities with Proudhon's classic analysis of private property are obvious (and it should be stressed that the two founders of the anarchist tradition independently reached the same critique of private property).

Godwin, unlike classical liberals, saw the need to *"point out the evils of accumulated property,"* arguing that the *"spirit of oppression, the spirit of servility, and the spirit of fraud … are the immediate growth of the established administration of property. They are alike hostile to intellectual and moral improvement."* Thus private property harms the personality and development those subjected to the authoritarian social relationships it produces, for *"accumulation brings home a servile and truckling spirit"* and such accumulated property *"treads the powers of thought in the dust, extinguishes the sparks of genius, and reduces the great mass of mankind to*

be immersed in sordid cares." This meant that the *"feudal spirit still survives that reduced the great mass of mankind to the rank of slaves and cattle for the service of a few."* Like the socialist movement he inspired, Godwin argued that *"it is to be considered that this injustice, the unequal distribution of property, the grasping and selfish spirit of individuals, is to be regarded as one of the original sources of government, and, as it rises in its excesses, is continually demanding and necessitating new injustice, new penalties and new slavery."* He stressed, *"let it never be forgotten that accumulated property is usurpation"* and considered the evils produced by monarchies, courts, priests, and criminal laws to be *"imbecile and impotent compared to the evils that arise out of the established administration of property."* [**Op. Cit.**, p. 732, p. 725, p. 730, p. 726, pp. 717-8, p. 718 and p. 725]

Unsurprisingly given this analysis, Godwin argued against the current system of property and in favour of *"the justice of an equal distribution of the good things of life."* This would be based on *"[e]quality of conditions, or, in other words, an equal admission to the means of improvement and pleasure"* as this *"is a law rigorously enjoined upon mankind by the voice of justice."* [**Op. Cit.**, p. 725 and p. 736] Thus his anarchist ideas were applied to private property, noting like subsequent anarchists that economic inequality resulted in the loss of liberty for the many and, consequently, an anarchist society would see a radical change in property and property rights. As Kropotkin noted, Godwin *"stated in 1793 in a quite definite form the political and economic principle of Anarchism."* Little wonder he, like so many others, argued that Godwin was *"the first theoriser of Socialism without government – that is to say, of Anarchism."* [**Environment and Evolution**, p. 62 and p. 26] For Kropotkin, anarchism was by definition not restricted to purely political issues but also attacked economic hierarchy, inequality and injustice. As Peter Marshall confirms, *"Godwin's economics, like his politics, are an extension of his ethics."* [**Demanding the Impossible**, p. 210]

Godwin's theory of property is significant because it prefigured what was to become standard nineteenth century socialist thought on the matter. In Britain, his ideas influenced Robert Owen and, as a result, the early socialist movement in that country. His analysis of property, as noted, was identical to and predated Proudhon's classic anarchist analysis. As such, to state, as Hart did, that Godwin simply *"concluded that the state was an evil which had to be reduced in power if not eliminated completely"* while not noting his analysis of property gives a radically false presentation of his ideas. [**Op. Cit.**, p. 265] However, it does fit into his flawed assertion that anarchism is purely concerned with the state. Any evidence to the contrary is simply ignored.

F.7.1 Are competing governments anarchism?

No, of course not. Yet according to "anarcho"-capitalism, it is. This can be seen from the ideas of Gustave de Molinari.

Hart is on firmer ground when he argues that the 19th century economist Gustave de Molinari is the true founder of "anarcho"-capitalism. With Molinari, he argues, *"the two different currents of anarchist thought converged: he combined the political anarchism of Burke and Godwin with the nascent economic anarchism of Adam Smith and Say to create a new form of anarchism"* that has been called *"anarcho-capitalism, or free market anarchism."* [**Op. Cit.**, p. 269] Of course, Godwin (like other anarchists) did not limit his anarchism purely to "political" issues and so he discussed *"economic anarchism"* as well in his critique of private property (as Proudhon also did). As such, to artificially split anarchism into political and economic spheres is both historically and logically flawed. While some dictionaries limit "anarchism" to opposition to the state, anarchists did and do not.

The key problem for Hart is that Molinari refused to call himself an anarchist. He did not even oppose government, as Hart himself notes Molinari proposed a system of insurance companies to provide defence of property and *"called these insurance companies 'governments' even though they did not have a monopoly within a given geographical area."* As Hart notes, Molinari was the sole defender of such free-market justice at the time in France. [David M. Hart, *"Gustave de Molinari and the Anti-statist Liberal Tradition: Part II"*, pp. 399-434, **Journal of Libertarian Studies**, vol. V, no. 4, p. 415 and p. 411] Molinari was clear that he wanted *"a regime of free government,"* counterpoising *"monopolist or communist governments"* to *"free governments."* This would lead to *"freedom of government"* rather than its abolition (i.e., not freedom **from** government). For Molinari the future would not bring *"the suppression of the state which is the dream of the anarchists ... It will bring the diffusion of the state within society. That is ... 'a free state in a free society.'"* [quoted by Hart, **Op. Cit.**, p. 429, p. 411 and p. 422] As such, Molinari can hardly be considered an anarchist, even if "anarchist" is limited to purely being against government.

Moreover, in another sense Molinari was in favour of the state. As we discuss in section F.6, these companies would have a monopoly within a given geographical area – they have to in order to enforce the property owner's power over those who use, but do not own, the property in question. The key contradiction can be seen in Molinari's advocating of company towns, privately owned communities (his term was a *"proprietary company"*). Instead of taxes, people would pay rent and the *"administration of the community would be either left in the hands of the company itself or handled by special organisations set up for this purpose."* Within such a regime *"those with the most property had proportionally the greater say in matters which affected the community."* If the poor objected then they could simply leave. [**Op. Cit.**, pp. 421-2 and p. 422]

Given this, the idea that Molinari was an anarchist in any form can be dismissed. His system was based on privatising government, not abolishing it (as he himself admitted). This would be different from the current system, of course, as landlords and capitalists would be hiring police directly to enforce their decisions rather than relying on a state which they control indirectly. This system would not be anarchist as can be seen from American history. There capitalists and landlords created their own private police forces and armies, which regularly attacked and murdered union organisers and strikers. As an example, there is Henry Ford's Service Department (private police force):

> *"In 1932 a hunger march of the unemployed was planned to march up to the gates of the Ford plant at Dearborn.... The machine guns of the Dearborn police and the Ford Motor Company's Service Department killed [four] and wounded over a score of others ... Ford was fundamentally and entirely opposed to trade unions. The idea of working men questioning his prerogatives as an owner was outrageous ... [T]he River Rouge plant ... was dominated by the autocratic regime of Bennett's service men. Bennett ... organise[d] and train[ed] the three and a half thousand private policemen employed by Ford. His task was to maintain discipline amongst the work force, protect Ford's property [and power], and prevent unionisation ... Frank Murphy, the mayor of Detroit, claimed that 'Henry Ford employs some of the worst gangsters in our city.' The claim was well based. Ford's Service Department policed the gates of his plants, infiltrated emergent groups of union activists, posed as workers to spy on men on the line.... Under this tyranny the Ford worker had no security, no rights. So much so that any information about the state of things within the plant could only be freely obtained from ex-Ford workers."* [Huw Beynon, **Working for Ford**, pp. 29-30]

The private police attacked women workers handing out pro-union leaflets and gave them *"a severe beating."* At Kansas and Dallas *"similar beatings were handed out to the union men."* This use of private police to control the work force was not unique. General Motors *"spent one million dollars on espionage, employing fourteen detective agencies and two hundred spies at one time [between 1933 and 1936]. The Pinkerton Detective Agency found anti-unionism its most lucrative activity."* [**Op. Cit.**, p. 34 and p. 32] We must also note that the Pinkerton's had been selling their private police services for decades before the 1930s. For over 60 years the Pinkerton Detective Agency had *"specialised in providing spies, agent provocateurs, and private armed forces for employers combating labour organisations."* By 1892 it *"had provided its services for management in seventy major labour disputes, and its 2,000 active agents and 30,000 reserves totalled more than the standing army of the nation."* [Jeremy Brecher, **Strike!**, p. 55] With this force available, little wonder unions found it so hard to survive in the USA.

Only an "anarcho"-capitalist would deny that this is a private government, employing private police to enforce private power. Given that unions could be considered as "defence" agencies for workers, this suggests a picture of how "anarcho"-capitalism may work in practice radically different from than that produced by its advocates. The reason is simple, it does not ignore inequality and subjects property to an anarchist analysis. Little wonder, then, that Proudhon stressed that it *"becomes necessary for the workers to form themselves into democratic societies, with equal conditions for all members, on pain of a relapse into feudalism."* Anarchism, in other words, would see *"[c]apitalistic and proprietary exploitation stopped everywhere, the wage system abolished"* and so *"the economic organisation [would] replac[e] the governmental and military system."* [**The General Idea of the Revolution**, p. 227 and p. 281] Clearly, the idea that Proudhon shared the same political goal as Molinari is a joke. He would have dismissed such a system as little more than an updated form of feudalism in which the property owner is sovereign and the workers subjects (also see section B.4).

Unsurprisingly, Molinari (unlike the individualist anarchists) attacked the jury system, arguing that its obliged people to *"perform the duties of judges. This is pure communism."* People would *"judge according to the colour of their opinions, than according to justice."* [quoted by Hart, **Op. Cit.**, p. 409] As the jury system used amateurs (i.e. ordinary people) rather than full-time professionals it could not be relied upon to defend the power and property rights of the rich. As we noted in section F.6.1, Rothbard criticised the individualist anarchists for supporting juries for essentially the same reasons.

But, as is clear from Hart's account, Molinari had little concern that working class people should have a say in their own lives beyond consuming goods and picking bosses. His perspective can be seen from his lament that in those *"colonies where slavery has been abolished without the compulsory labour being replaced with an equivalent quantity of free [sic!] labour [i.e., wage labour], there has occurred the opposite of what happens everyday before our eyes. Simple workers have been seen to exploit in their turn the industrial* **entrepreneurs,** *demanding from them wages which bear absolutely no relation to the legitimate share in the product which they ought to receive. The planters were unable to obtain for their sugar a sufficient price to cover the increase in wages, and were obliged to furnish the extra amount, at first out of their profits, and then out of their very capital. A considerable number of planters have been ruined as a result ... It is doubtless better that these accumulations of capital should be destroyed than that generations of men should perish [Marx: 'how generous of M. Molinari'] but would it not be better if both survived?"* [quoted by Karl Marx, **Capital**, vol. 1, p. 937f]

So workers exploiting capital is the *"opposite of what happens everyday before our eyes"*? In other words, it is normal that entrepreneurs *"exploit"* workers under capitalism? Similarly, what is a *"legitimate share"* which workers *"ought to receive"*? Surely that is determined by the eternal laws of supply and demand and not what the capitalists (or Molinari) thinks is right? And those poor former slave drivers, they really do deserve our sympathy. What horrors they face from the impositions subjected upon them by their ex-chattels – they had to reduce their profits! How dare their ex-slaves refuse to obey them in return for what their ex-owners think was their *"legitimate share in the produce"*! How *"simple"* these workers were, not understanding the sacrifices their former masters suffer nor appreciating how much more difficult it is for their ex-masters to create *"the product"* without the whip and the branding iron to aid them! As Marx so rightly comments: *"And*

what, if you please, is this 'legitimate share', which, according to [Molinari's] own admission, the capitalist in Europe daily neglects to pay? Over yonder, in the colonies, where the workers are so 'simple' as to 'exploit' the capitalist, M. Molinari feels a powerful itch to use police methods to set on the right road that law of supply and demand which works automatically everywhere else."* [**Op. Cit.**, p. 937f]

An added difficulty in arguing that Molinari was an anarchist is that he was a contemporary of Proudhon, the first self-declared anarchist, and lived in a country with a vigorous anarchist movement. Surely if he was really an anarchist, he would have proclaimed his kinship with Proudhon and joined in the wider movement. He did not, as Hart notes as regards Proudhon:

> *"their differences in economic theory were considerable, and it is probably for this reason that Molinari refused to call himself an anarchist in spite of their many similarities in political theory. Molinari refused to accept the socialist economic ideas of Proudhon ... in Molinari's mind, the term 'anarchist' was intimately linked with socialist and statist economic views."* [**Op. Cit.**, p. 415]

Yet Proudhon's economic views, like Godwin's, flowed from his anarchist analysis and principles. They cannot be arbitrarily separated as Hart suggests. So while arguing that *"Molinari was just as much an anarchist as Proudhon,"* Hart forgets the key issue. Proudhon was aware that private property ensured that the proletarian did not exercise *"self-government"* during working hours, i.e. that he was ruled by another. As for Hart claiming that Proudhon had *"statist economic views"* it simply shows how far an *"anarcho"*-capitalist perspective is from genuine anarchism. Proudhon's economic analysis, his critique of private property and capitalism, flowed from his anarchism and was an integral aspect of it.

By restricting anarchism purely to opposition to the state, Hart is impoverishing anarchist theory and denying its history. Given that anarchism was born from a critique of private property as well as government, this shows the false nature of Hart's claim that *"Molinari was the first to develop a theory of free-market, proprietary anarchism that extended the laws of the market and a rigorous defence of property to its logical extreme."* [**Op. Cit.**, p. 415 and p. 416] Hart shows how far from anarchism Molinari was as Proudhon had turned his anarchist analysis to property, showing that *"defence of property"* lead to the oppression of the many by the few in social relationships identical to those which mark the state. Moreover, Proudhon, argued the state would always be required to defend such social relations. Privatising it would hardly be a step forward.

Unsurprisingly, Proudhon dismissed the idea that the laissez faire capitalists shared his goals. *"The school of Say,"* Proudhon argued, was *"the chief focus of counter-revolution next to the Jesuits"* and *"has for ten years past seemed to exist only to protect and applaud the execrable work of the monopolists of money and necessities, deepening more and more the obscurity of a science [economics] naturally difficult and full of complications"* (much the same can be said of *"anarcho"*-capitalists, incidentally). For Proudhon, *"the disciples of Malthus and of Say, who oppose with all their might* any intervention of the State in matters commercial or industrial, do not fail to avail themselves of this seemingly liberal attitude, and to show themselves more revolutionary than the Revolution. More than one honest searcher has been deceived thereby." However, this apparent "anti-statist" attitude of supporters of capitalism is false as pure free market capitalism cannot solve the social question, which arises because of capitalism itself. As such, it was impossible to abolish the state under capitalism. Thus *"this inaction of Power in economic matters was the foundation of government. What need should we have of a political organisation, if Power once permitted us to enjoy economic order?"* Instead of capitalism, Proudhon advocated the *"constitution of Value,"* the *"organisation of credit,"* the elimination of interest, the *"establishment of workingmen's associations"* and *"the use of a just price."* [**The General Idea of the Revolution**, p. 225, p. 226 and p. 233]

Clearly, then, the claims that Molinari was an anarchist fail as he, unlike his followers, was aware of what anarchism actually stood for. Hart, in his own way, acknowledges this:

> "In spite of his protestations to the contrary, Molinari should be considered an anarchist thinker. His attack on the state's monopoly of defence must surely warrant the description of anarchism. His reluctance to accept this label stemmed from the fact that the socialists had used it first to describe a form of non-statist society which Molinari definitely opposed. Like many original thinkers, Molinari had to use the concepts developed by others to describe his theories. In his case, he had come to the same political conclusions as the communist anarchists although he had been working within the liberal tradition, and it is therefore not surprising that the terms used by the two schools were not compatible. It would not be until the latter half of the twentieth century that radical, free-trade liberals would use the word 'anarchist' to describe their beliefs." [**Op. Cit.**, p. 416]

It should be noted that Proudhon was **not** a communist-anarchist, but the point remains (as an aside, Rothbard also showed his grasp of anarchism by asserting that *"the demented Bakunin"* was a *"leading anarcho-communist,"* who *"emphasised [the lumpenproletariat] in the 1840s."* [**The Logic of Action II**, p. 388 and p. 381] Which would have been impressive as not only did Bakunin become an anarchist in the 1860s, anarcho-communism, as anyone with even a basic knowledge of anarchist history knows, developed after his death nor did Bakunin emphasise the lumpenproletariat as the agent of social change, Rothbardian and Marxian inventions not withstanding). The aims of anarchism were recognised by Molinari as being inconsistent with his ideology. Consequently, he (rightly) refused the label. If only his self-proclaimed followers in the *"latter half of the twentieth century"* did the same then anarchists would not have to bother with them!

It does seem ironic that the founder of "anarcho"-capitalism should have come to the same conclusion as modern day anarchists on the subject of whether his ideas are a form of anarchism or not!

Of course not, but ironically this is the conclusion arrived at by Hart's analysis of the British "voluntaryists," particularly Auberon Herbert. Voluntaryism was a fringe part of the right-wing individualist movement inspired by Herbert Spencer, a leading spokesman for free market capitalism in the later half of the nineteenth century. Like Hart, leading "anarcho"-capitalist Hans-Hermann Hoppe believes that Herbert *"develop[ed] the Spencerian idea of equal freedom to its logically consistent anarcho-capitalist end."* [**Anarcho-Capitalism: An Annotated Bibliography**]

Yet, as with Molinari, there is a problem with presenting this ideology as anarchist, namely that its leading light, Herbert, explicitly rejected the label "anarchist" and called for both a government and a democratic state. Thus, apparently, both state and government are *"logically consistent"* with "anarcho"-capitalism and vice versa! Herbert was clearly aware of individualist anarchism and distanced himself from it. He argued that such a system would be *"pandemonium."* He thought that we should *"not direct our attacks – as the anarchists do – **against all government**, against government in itself"* but *"only against the overgrown, the exaggerated, the insolent, unreasonable and indefensible forms of government, which are found everywhere today."* Government should be *"strictly limited to its legitimate duties in defence of self-ownership and individual rights."* He stressed that *"we are governmentalists … formally constituted by the nation, employing in this matter of force the majority method."* Moreover, Herbert knew of, and rejected, individualist anarchism, considering it to be *"founded on a fatal mistake."* [**Essay X: The Principles Of Voluntaryism And Free Life**] He repeated this argument in other words, stating that anarchy was a *"contradiction,"* and that the Voluntaryists *"reject the anarchist creed."* He was clear that they *"believe in a national government, voluntary supported … and only entrusted with force for protection of person and property."* He called his system of a national government funded by non-coerced contributions *"the Voluntary State."* [*"A Voluntaryist Appeal"*, **Herbert Spencer and the Limits of the State**, Michael W. Taylor (ed.), p. 239 and p. 228] As such, claims that Herbert was an anarchist cannot be justified.

Hart is aware of this slight problem, quoting Herbert's claim that he aimed for *"regularly constituted government, generally accepted by all citizens for the protection of the individual."* [quoted by Hart, **Op. Cit.**, p. 86] Like Molinari, Herbert was aware that anarchism was a form of socialism and that the political aims could not be artificially separated from its economic and social aims. As such, he was right **not** to call his ideas anarchism as it would result in confusion (particularly as anarchism was a much larger movement than his). As Hart acknowledges, *"Herbert faced the same problems that Molinari had with labelling his philosophy. Like Molinari, he rejected the term 'anarchism,' which he associated with the socialism of Proudhon and … terrorism."* While *"quite tolerant"* of individualist anarchism, he thought they *"were mistaken in their rejections of 'government.'"* However, Hart knows better than

Herbert about his own ideas, arguing that his ideology *"is in fact a new form of anarchism, since the most important aspect of the modern state, the monopoly of the use of force in a given area, is rejected in no uncertain terms by both men."* [**Op. Cit.**, p. 86] He does mention that Benjamin Tucker called Herbert a *"true anarchist in everything but name,"* but Tucker denied that Kropotkin was an anarchist suggesting that he was hardly a reliable guide. [quoted by Hart, **Op. Cit.**, p. 87] As it stands, it seems that Tucker (unlike other anarchists) was mistaken in his evaluation of Herbert's politics.

While there were similarities between Herbert's position and individualist anarchism, *"the gulf"* between them *"in other respects was unbridgeable"* notes historian Matthew Thomas. *"The primary concern of the individualists was with the preservation of existing property relations and the maintenance of some form of organisation to protect these relations ... Such a vestigial government was obviously incompatible with the individualist anarchist desire to abolish the state. The anarchists also demanded sweeping changes in the structure of property relations through the destruction of the land and currency monopolies. This they argued, would create equal opportunities for all. The individualists however rejected this and sought to defend the vested interests of the property-owning classes. The implications of such differences prevented any real alliance."* [**Anarchist Ideas and Counter-Cultures in Britain, 1880-1914**, p. 20] Anarchist William R. McKercher, in his analysis of the libertarian (socialist) movement of late 19th century Britain, concludes (rightly) that Herbert *"was often mistakenly taken as an anarchist"* but *"a reading of Herbert's work will show that he was not an anarchist."* [**Freedom and Authority**, p. 199fn and p. 73fn] The leading British social anarchist journal of the time noted that the *"Auberon Herbertites in England are sometimes called Anarchists by outsiders, but they are willing to compromise with the inequity of government to maintain private property."* [**Freedom**, Vol. II, No. 17, 1888]

Some non-anarchists **did** call Herbert an anarchist. For example, J. A. Hobson, a left-wing liberal, wrote a critique of Herbert's politics called *"A Rich Man's Anarchism."* Hobson argued that Herbert's support for exclusive private property would result in the poor being enslaved to the rich. Herbert, *"by allowing first comers to monopolise without restriction the best natural supplies"* would allow them *"to thwart and restrict the similar freedom of those who come after."* Hobson gave the *"extreme instance"* of an island *"the whole of which is annexed by a few individuals, who use the rights of exclusive property and transmission ... to establish primogeniture."* In such a situation, the bulk of the population would be denied the right to exercise their faculties or to enjoy the fruits of their labour, which Herbert claimed to be the inalienable rights of all. Hobson concluded: *"It is thus that the 'freedom' of a few (in Herbert's sense) involves the 'slavery' of the many."* [quoted by M. W. Taylor, **Men Versus the State**, pp. 248-9] M. W. Taylor notes that *"of all the points Hobson raised ... this argument was his most effective, and Herbert was unable to provide a satisfactory response."* [**Op. Cit.**, p. 249]

The ironic thing is that Hobson's critique simply echoed the **anarchist** one and, moreover, simply repeated Proudhon's arguments in **What is Property?**. As such, from an anarchist perspective, Herbert's inability to give a reply was unsurprising given the power of Proudhon's libertarian critique of private property. In fact, Proudhon used a similar argument to Hobson's, presenting *"a colony ... in a wild district"* rather than an island. His argument and conclusions are the same, though, with a small minority becoming *"proprietors of the whole district"* and the rest *"dispossessed"* and *"compelled to sell their birthright."* He concluded by saying *"[i]n this century of bourgeoisie morality ... the moral sense is so debased that I should not be at all surprised if I were asked, by many a worthy proprietor, what I see in this that is unjust and illegitimate? Debased creature! galvanised corpse! how can I expect to convince you, if you cannot tell robbery when I show it to you?"* [**What is Property?**, pp. 125-7] Which shows how far Herbert's position was from genuine anarchism – and how far "anarcho"-capitalism is.

So, economically, Herbert was not an anarchist, arguing that the state should protect Lockean property rights. Of course, Hart may argue that these economic differences are not relevant to the issue of Herbert's anarchism but that is simply to repeat the claim that anarchism is solely concerned with government, a claim which is hard to support. This position cannot be maintained, particularly given that both Herbert and Molinari defended the right of capitalists and landlords to force their employees and tenants to follow their orders. Their "governments" existed to defend the capitalist from rebellious workers, to break unions, strikes and occupations. In other words, they were a monopoly of the use of force in a given area to enforce the monopoly of power in a given area (namely, the wishes of the property owner). While they may have argued that this was "defence of liberty," in reality it is defence of power and authority.

What about if we just look at the political aspects of his ideas? Did Herbert actually advocate anarchism? No, far from it. He clearly demanded a minimal state based on voluntary taxation. The state would not use force of any kind, *"except for purposes of restraining force."* He argued that in his system, while *"the state should compel no services and exact no payments by force,"* it *"should be free to conduct many useful undertakings ... in competition with all voluntary agencies ... in dependence on voluntary payments."* [Herbert, **Essay X: The Principles Of Voluntaryism And Free Life**] As such, *"the state"* would remain and unless he is using the term "state" in some highly unusual way, it is clear that he means a system where individuals live under a single elected government as their common law maker, judge and defender within a given territory.

This becomes clearer once we look at how the state would be organised. In his essay **"A Politician in Sight of Haven,"** Herbert does discuss the franchise, stating it would be limited to those who paid a voluntary *"income tax"* and anyone *"paying it would have the right to vote; those who did not pay it would be – as is just – without the franchise. There would be no other tax."* The law would be strictly limited, of course, and the *"government ... must confine itself simply to the defence of life and property, whether as regards internal or external defence."* In other words, Herbert was a minimal statist, with his government elected by a majority of those who choose to pay their income tax and funded by that (and by any other voluntary taxes they decided to pay). Whether individuals and companies could hire their own private police in such a regime is irrelevant in determining whether it is an anarchy.

This can be best seen by comparing Herbert with Ayn Rand. No one would ever claim Rand was an anarchist, yet her ideas were extremely similar to Herbert's. Like Herbert, Rand supported laissez-faire capitalism and was against the "initiation of force." Like Herbert, she extended this principle to favour a government funded by voluntary means [*"Government Financing in a Free Society,"* **The Virtue of Selfishness**, pp. 116-20] Moreover, like Herbert, she explicitly denied being an anarchist and, again like Herbert, thought the idea of competing defence agencies ("governments") would result in chaos. The similarities with Herbert are clear, yet no "anarcho"-capitalist would claim that Rand was an anarchist, yet some do claim that Herbert was.

This position is, of course, deeply illogical and flows from the non-anarchist nature of "anarcho"-capitalism. Perhaps unsurprisingly, when Rothbard discusses the ideas of the "voluntaryists" he fails to address the key issue of who determines the laws being enforced in society. For Rothbard, the key issue was **who** is enforcing the law, not where that law comes from (as long, of course, as it is a law code he approved of). The implications of this is significant, as it implies that "anarchism" need not be opposed to either the state nor government! This can be clearly seen from Rothbard's analysis of Herbert's voluntary taxation position.

Rothbard, correctly, notes that Herbert advocated voluntary taxation as the means of funding a state whose basic role was to enforce Lockean property rights. The key point of his critique was **not** who determines the law but who enforces it. For Rothbard, it should be privatised police and courts and he suggests that the *"voluntary taxationists have never attempted to answer this problem; they have rather stubbornly assumed that no one would set up a competing defence agency within a State's territorial limits."* If the state **did** bar such firms, then that system is not a genuine free market. However, *"if the government **did** permit free competition in defence service, there would soon no longer be a central government over the territory. Defence agencies, police and judicial, would compete with one another in the same uncoerced manner as the producers of any other service on the market."* [**Power and Market**, p. 122 and p. 123]

Obviously this misses the point totally. What Rothbard ignores is who determines the laws which these private "defence" agencies would enforce. If the laws are made by a central government then the fact that citizen's can hire private police and attend private courts does not stop the regime being statist. We can safely assume Rand, for example, would have had no problem with companies providing private security guards or the hiring of private detectives within the context of her minimal state. Ironically, Rothbard stresses the need for such a monopoly legal system:

> *"While 'the government' would cease to exist, the same cannot be said for a constitution or a rule of law, which, in fact, would take on in the free society a far more important function than at present. For the freely competing judicial agencies would have to be guided by a body of absolute law to enable them to distinguish objectively between defence and invasion. This law, embodying elaborations upon the basic injunction to defend person and property from acts of invasion, would be codified in the basic legal*

> *code. Failure to establish such a code of law would tend to break down the free market, for then defence against invasion could not be adequately achieved."* [**Op. Cit.**, p. 123-4]

So if you violate the *"absolute law"* defending (absolute) property rights then you would be in trouble. The problem now lies in determining who sets that law. For Rothbard, as we noted in section F.6.1, his system of monopoly laws would be determined by judges, Libertarian lawyers and jurists. The "voluntaryists" proposed a different solution, namely a central government elected by the majority of those who voluntarily decided to pay an income tax. In the words of Herbert:

> *"We agree that there must be a central agency to deal with crime – an agency that defends the liberty of all men, and employs force against the uses of force; but my central agency rests upon voluntary support, whilst Mr. Levy's central agency rests on compulsory support."* [quoted by Carl Watner, *"The English Individualists As They Appear In Liberty,"* pp. 191-211, **Benjamin R. Tucker and the Champions of Liberty**, p. 194]

And all Rothbard is concerned about is whether private cops would exist or not! This lack of concern over the existence of the state and government flows from the strange fact that "anarcho"-capitalists commonly use the term "anarchism" to refer to any philosophy that opposes all forms of initiatory coercion. Notice that government does not play a part in this definition, thus Rothbard can analyse Herbert's politics without commenting on who determines the law his private "defence" agencies enforce. For Rothbard, *"an anarchist society"* is defined *"as one where there is no legal possibility for coercive aggression against the person and property of any individual."* He then moved onto the state, defining that as an *"institution which possesses one or both (almost always both) of the following properties: (1) it acquires its income by the physical coercion known as 'taxation'; and (2) it acquires and usually obtains a coerced monopoly of the provision of defence service (police and courts) over a given territorial area."* [**Society without a State**, p. 192]

This is highly unusual definition of "anarchism," given that it utterly fails to mention or define government. This, perhaps, is understandable as any attempt to define it in terms of *"monopoly of decision-making power"* results in showing that capitalism is statist (see section F.1 for a summary). The key issue here is the term *"legal possibility."* That suggests a system of laws which determine what is *"coercive aggression"* and what constitutes what is and what is not legitimate "property." Herbert is considered by some "anarcho"-capitalists as one of them. Which brings us to a strange conclusion that, for "anarcho"-capitalists you can have a system of "anarchism" in which there is a government and state – as long as the state does not impose taxation nor stop private police forces from operating!

As Rothbard argues *"if a government based on voluntary taxation permits free competition, the result will be the purely free-market system … The previous government would now simply be one competing defence agency among many on the market."* [**Power and Market**, p. 124] That the government is specifying what is and is not legal does not seem to bother him or even cross his mind. Why should it, when the existence of government is irrelevant to his definition of anarchism and the state? That private police are enforcing a monopoly law determined by the government seems hardly a step in the right direction nor can it be considered as anarchism. Perhaps this is unsurprising, for under his system there would be *"a basic, common Law Code"* which *"all would have to abide by"* as well as *"some way of resolving disputes that will gain a majority consensus in society … whose decision will be accepted by the great majority of the public."* [**Society without a State**, p. 205]

That this is simply a state under a different name can be seen from looking at other right-wing liberals. Milton Friedman, for example, noted (correctly) that the *"consistent liberal is not an anarchist."* He stated that government *"is essential"* for providing a *"legal framework"* and provide *"the definition of property rights."* In other words, to *"determine, arbitrate and enforce the rules of the game."* [**Capitalism and Freedom**, p. 34, p. 15, p. 25, p. 26 and p. 27] For Ludwig von Mises *"liberalism is not anarchism, nor has it anything whatsoever to do with anarchism."* Liberalism *"restricts the activity of the state in the economic sphere exclusively to the protection of property."* [**Liberalism**, p. 37 and p. 38] The key difference between these liberals and Rothbard's brand of liberalism is that rather than an elected parliament making laws, "anarcho"-capitalism would have a general law code produced by "libertarian" lawyers, jurists and judges. Both would have laws interpreted by judges. Rothbard's system is also based on a legal framework which would both provide a definition of property rights and determine the rules of the game. However, the means of enforcing and arbitrating those laws would be totally private. Yet even this is hardly a difference, as it is doubtful if Friedman or von Mises (like Rand or Herbert) would have barred private security firms or voluntary arbitration services as long as they followed the law of the land. The only major difference is that Rothbard's system explicitly excludes the general public from specifying or amending the laws they are subject to and allows (prosperous) judges to interpret and add to the (capitalist) law. Perhaps this dispossession of the general public is the only means by which the minimal state will remain minimal (as Rothbard claimed) and capitalist property, authority and property rights remain secure and sacrosanct, yet the situation where the general public has no say in the regime and the laws they are subjected to is usually called dictatorship, not "anarchy."

At least Herbert is clear that his politics was a governmental system, unlike Rothbard who assumes a monopoly law but seems to think that this is not a government or a state. As David Wieck argued, this is illogical for according to Rothbard *"all 'would have to' conform to the same legal code"* and this can only be achieved by means of *"the forceful action of adherents to the code against those who flout it"* and so *"in his system **there would stand over against every individual the legal authority of all the others.** An individual who did not recognise private property as legitimate would surely perceive this as a tyranny of law, a tyranny of the majority or of the most powerful – in short, a hydra-headed state. If the law code is itself unitary, then this multiple state might be said to have properly a single head – the law … But it looks as though one might still call this 'a state,' under Rothbard's definition,* by satisfying **de facto** one of his pair of sufficient conditions: 'It asserts and usually obtains a coerced monopoly of provision of defence service (police and courts) over a given territorial area' … Hobbes's individual sovereign would seem to have become many sovereigns – with but one law, however, and in truth, therefore, a single sovereign in Hobbes's more important sense of the latter term. One might better, and less confusingly, call this a libertarian state than an anarchy."* [**Anarchist Justice**, pp. 216-7]

The obvious recipients of the coercion of the new state would be those who rejected the authority of their bosses and landlords, those who reject the Lockean property rights Rothbard and Herbert hold dear. In such cases, the rebels and any "defence agency" (like, say, a union) which defended them would be driven out of business as it violated the law of the land. How this is different from a state banning competing agencies is hard to determine. This is a *"difficulty"* argues Wieck, which *"results from the attachment of a principle of private property, and of unrestricted accumulation of wealth, to the principle of individual liberty. This increases sharply the possibility that many reasonable people who respect their fellow men and women will find themselves outside the law because of dissent from a property interpretation of liberty."* Similarly, there are the economic results of capitalism. *"One can imagine,"* Wieck continues, *"that those who lose out badly in the free competition of Rothbard's economic system, perhaps a considerable number, might regard the legal authority as an alien power, a state for them, based on violence, and might be quite unmoved by the fact that, just as under nineteenth century capitalism, a principle of liberty was the justification for it all."* [**Op. Cit.**, p. 217 and pp. 217-8]

F.7.3 Can there be a "right-wing" anarchism?

In a word, no. This can be seen from "anarcho"-capitalism itself as well as its attempts to co-opt the US individualist anarchists into its family tree.

Hart mentions the individualist anarchists, calling Tucker's ideas *"laissez faire liberalism."* [**Op. Cit.**, p. 87] However, Tucker called his ideas *"socialism"* and presented a left-wing critique of most aspects of liberalism, particularly its Lockean based private property rights. Tucker based much of his ideas on property on Proudhon, so if Hart dismisses the latter as a socialist then this must apply to Tucker as well. Given that he notes that there are *"two main kinds of anarchist thought,"* namely *"communist anarchism which denies the right of an individual to seek profit, charge rent or interest and to own property"* and a *"'right-wing' proprietary anarchism, which vigorously defends these rights"* then Tucker, like Godwin, would have to be placed in the *"left-wing"* camp. [*"Gustave de Molinari and the Anti-statist Liberal Tradition: Part II"*, **Op. Cit.**, p. 427] Tucker, after all, argued that he aimed for the end of profit, interest and rent and attacked private property in land and housing beyond "occupancy and use." It is a shame that Hart was so ignorant of anarchism to ignore all the other forms of anarchism which, while anti-capitalist, were not communist.

As has been seen, Hart's account of the history of "anti-state" liberalism is flawed. Godwin is included only by ignoring his views on property, views which in many ways reflects the later "socialist" (i.e. anarchist) analysis of Proudhon. He then discusses a few individuals who were alone in their opinions even within the extreme free market right and all of whom knew of anarchism and explicitly rejected that name for their respective ideologies. In fact, they preferred the term *government* or *state* to describe their systems which, on the face of it, would be hard to reconcile with the usual "anarcho"-capitalist definition of anarchism as being "no government" or simply "anti-statism." Hart's discussion of individualist anarchism is equally flawed, failing to discuss their economic views (just as well, as its links to "left-wing" anarchism would be obvious).

However, the similarities of Molinari's views with what later became known as "anarcho"-capitalism are clear. Hart notes that with Molinari's death in 1912, *"liberal anti-statism virtually disappeared until it was rediscovered by the economist Murray Rothbard in the late 1950's"* [*"Gustave de Molinari and the Anti-statist Liberal Tradition: Part III"*, **Op. Cit.**, p. 88] While this fringe is somewhat bigger than previously, the fact remains that the ideas expounded by Rothbard are just as alien to the anarchist tradition as Molinari's. It is a shame that Rothbard, like his predecessors, did not call his ideology something other than anarchism. Not only would it have been more accurate, it would also have led to much less confusion and no need to write this section of the FAQ! It is a testament to their lack of common sense that Rothbard and other "anarcho"-capitalists failed to recognise that, given a long-existing socio-political theory and movement called anarchism, they could not possibly call themselves "anarchists" without conflating their own views with those of the existing tradition. Yet rather than introducing a new term into political vocabulary (or using Molinari's terminology) they preferred to try fruitlessly to appropriate a term used by others. They seemed to have forgotten that political vocabulary and usage are path dependent. Hence we get subjected to articles which talk about the new "anarchism" while trying to disassociate "anarcho"-capitalism from the genuine anarchism found in media reports and history books. As it stands, the only reason why "anarcho"-capitalism is considered a form of "anarchism" by some is because one person (Rothbard) decided to steal the name of a well established and widespread political and social theory and movement in the 1950s and apply it to an ideology with little, if anything, in common with it.

As Hart inadvertently shows, it is not a firm base to build a claim. That anyone can consider "anarcho"-capitalism as anarchist simply flows from a lack of knowledge about anarchism – as numerous anarchists have argued. For example, *"Rothbard's conjunction of anarchism with capitalism,"* according to David Wieck, *"results in a conception that is entirely outside the mainstream of anarchist theoretical writings or social movements ... this conjunction is a self-contradiction."* He stressed that *"the main traditions of anarchism are entirely different. These traditions, and theoretical writings associated with them, express the perspectives and the aspirations, and also, sometimes, the rage, of the oppressed people in human society: not only those economically oppressed, although the major anarchist movements have been mainly movements of workers and peasants, but also those oppressed by power in all those social dimensions ... including of course that of political power*

expressed in the state." In other words, anarchism represents *"a moral commitment"* which Rothbard's position is *"diametrically opposite"* to. [**Anarchist Justice**, p. 215, p. 229 and p. 234]

It is a shame that some academics consider only the word Rothbard uses as relevant rather than the content and its relation to anarchist theory and history. If they did, they would soon realise that the expressed opposition of so many anarchists to "anarcho"-capitalism is something which cannot be ignored or dismissed. In other words, a "right-wing" anarchist cannot and does not exist, no matter how often sections of the right try to use that word to describe their ideology.

The reason is simple. Anarchist economics and politics cannot be artificially separated. They are intrinsically linked. Godwin and Proudhon did not stop their analysis at the state. They extended it to the social relationships produced by inequality of wealth, i.e. economic power as well as political power. To see why, we need only consult Rothbard's work. As noted in the last section, for Rothbard the key issue with the "voluntary taxationists" was not who determined the *"body of absolute law"* but rather who enforced it. In his discussion, he argued that a democratic "defence agency" is at a disadvantage in his "free market" system. As he put it:

> *"It would, in fact, be competing at a severe disadvantage, having been established on the principle of 'democratic voting.' Looked at as a market phenomenon, 'democratic voting' (one vote per person) is simply the method of the consumer 'co-operative.' Empirically, it has been demonstrated time and again that co-operatives cannot compete successfully against stock-owned companies, especially when both are equal before the law. There is no reason to believe that co-operatives for defence would be any more efficient. Hence, we may expect the old co-operative government to 'wither away' through loss of customers on the market, while joint-stock (i.e., corporate) defence agencies would become the prevailing market form."* [**Power and Market**, p. 125]

Notice how he assumes that both a co-operative and corporation would be *"equal before the law."* But who determines that law? Obviously **not** a democratically elected government, as the idea of "one person, one vote" in determining the common law all are subject to is *"inefficient."* Nor does he think, like the individualist anarchists, that the law would be judged by juries along with the facts. As we note in section F.6.1, he rejected that in favour of it being determined by *"Libertarian lawyers and jurists."* Thus the law is unchangeable by ordinary people and enforced by private defence agencies hired to protect the liberty and property of the owning class. In the case of a capitalist economy, this means defending the power of landlords and capitalists against rebel tenants and workers.

This means that Rothbard's *"common Law Code"* will be determined, interpreted, enforced and amended by corporations based on the will of the majority of shareholders, i.e. the rich. That hardly seems likely to produce equality before the law. As he argues in a footnote:

> *"There is a strong **a priori** reason for believing that corporations will be superior to co-operatives in any*

Is "anarcho"-capitalism a type of anarchism?

given situation. For if each owner receives only one vote regardless of how much money he has invested in a project (and earnings are divided in the same way), there is no incentive to invest more than the next man; in fact, every incentive is the other way. This hampering of investment militates strongly against the co-operative form." [**Op. Cit.**, p. 125]

So **if** the law is determined and interpreted by defence agencies and courts then it will be done so by those who have invested most in these companies. As it is unlikely that the rich will invest in defence firms which do not support their property rights, power, profits and definition of property, it is clear that agencies which favour the wealthy will survive on the market. The idea that market demand will counter this class rule seems unlikely, given Rothbard's own argument. In order to compete successfully you need more than demand, you need sources of investment. If co-operative defence agencies do form, they will be at a market disadvantage due to lack of investment. As argued in section J.5.12, even though co-operatives are more efficient than capitalist firms lack of investment (caused by the lack of control by capitalists Rothbard notes) stops them replacing wage slavery. Thus capitalist wealth and power inhibits the spread of freedom in production. If we apply Rothbard's argument to his own system, we suggest that the market in "defence" will also stop the spread of more libertarian associations thanks to capitalist power and wealth. In other words, like any market, Rothbard's "defence" market will simply reflect the interests of the elite, not the masses.

Moreover, we can expect any democratic defence agency (like a union) to support, say, striking workers or squatting tenants, to be crushed. This is because, as Rothbard stresses, **all** "defence" firms would be expected to apply the *"common"* law, as written by *"Libertarian lawyers and jurists."* If they did not they would quickly be labelled "outlaw" agencies and crushed by the others. Ironically, Tucker would join Bakunin and Kropotkin in an "anarchist" court accused of violating "anarchist" law by practising and advocating "occupancy and use" rather than the approved Rothbardian property rights. Even if these democratic "defence" agencies could survive and not be driven out of the market by a combination of lack of investment and violence due to their "outlaw" status, there is another problem. As we discussed in section F.1, landlords and capitalists have a monopoly of decision making power over their property. As such, they can simply refuse to recognise any democratic agency as a legitimate defence association and use the same tactics perfected against unions to ensure that it does not gain a foothold in their domain.

Clearly, then, a "right-wing" anarchism is impossible as any system based on capitalist property rights will simply be an oligarchy run by and for the wealthy. As Rothbard notes, any defence agency based on democratic principles will not survive in the "market" for defence simply because it does not allow the wealthy to control it and its decisions. Little wonder Proudhon argued that laissez-faire capitalism meant *"the victory of the strong over the weak, of those who own property over those who own nothing."* [quoted by Peter Marshall, **Demanding the Impossible**, p. 259]

F.8

What role did the state take in the creation of capitalism?

If the "anarcho"-capitalist is to claim with any plausibility that "real" capitalism is non-statist or that it can exist without a state, it must be shown that capitalism evolved naturally, in opposition to state intervention. In reality, the opposite is the case. Capitalism was born from state intervention. In the words of Kropotkin, *"the State … and capitalism … developed side by side, mutually supporting and re-enforcing each other."* [**Anarchism**, p. 181]

Numerous writers have made this point. For example, in Karl Polanyi's flawed masterpiece **The Great Transformation** we read that *"the road to the free market was opened and kept open by an enormous increase in continuous, centrally organised and controlled interventionism"* by the state. [p. 140] This intervention took many forms – for example, state support during "mercantilism," which allowed the "manufactures" (i.e. industry) to survive and develop, enclosures of common land, and so forth. In addition, the slave trade, the invasion and brutal conquest of the Americas and other "primitive" nations, and the looting of gold, slaves, and raw materials from abroad also enriched the European economy, giving the development of capitalism an added boost. Thus Kropotkin:

> "The history of the genesis of capital has already been told by socialists many times. They have described how it was born of war and pillage, of slavery and serfdom, of modern fraud and exploitation. They have shown how it is nourished by the blood of the worker, and how little by little it has conquered the whole world…. Law … has followed the same phases as capital … they have advanced hand in hand, sustaining one another with the suffering of mankind." [**Op. Cit.**, p. 207]

This process is what Karl Marx termed ***"primitive accumulation"*** and was marked by extensive state violence. Capitalism, as he memorably put it, *"comes dripping from head to toe, from every pore, with blood and dirt"* and the *"starting-point of the development that gave rise both to the wage-labourer and to the capitalist was the enslavement of the worker."* [**Capital**, vol. 1, p. 926 and p. 875] Or, if Kropotkin and Marx seem too committed to be fair, we have John Stuart Mill's summary that the *"social arrangements of modern Europe commenced from a distribution of property which was the result, not of just partition, or acquisition by industry, but of conquest and violence."* [**Principles of Political Economy**, p. 15]

The same can be said of all countries. As such, when supporters of "libertarian" capitalism say they are against the "initiation of force," they mean only **new** initiations of force: for the system they support was born from numerous initiations of force in the past (moreover, it also requires state intervention to keep it going – section D.1 addresses this point in some detail). Indeed, many thinkers have argued that it was precisely this state support and coercion (particularly the separation of people from the land) that played the **key** role in allowing capitalism to develop rather than the theory that *"previous savings"* did so. As left-wing German thinker Franz Oppenheimer (whom Murray Rothbard selectively quoted) argued, *"the concept of a 'primitive accumulation,' or an original store of wealth, in land and in movable property, brought about by means of purely economic forces"* while *"seem[ing] quite plausible"* is in fact *"utterly mistaken; it is a 'fairly tale,' or it is a class theory used to justify the privileges of the upper classes."* [**The State**, pp. 5-6] As Individualist anarchist Kevin Carson summarised as part of his excellent overview of this historic process:

> *"Capitalism has never been established by means of the free market. It has always been established by a revolution from above, imposed by a ruling class with its origins in the Old Regime ... by a pre-capitalist ruling class that had been transformed in a capitalist manner. In England, it was the landed aristocracy; in France, Napoleon III's bureaucracy; in Germany, the Junkers; in Japan, the Meiji. In America, the closest approach to a 'natural' bourgeois evolution, industrialisation was carried out by a mercantilist aristocracy of Federalist shipping magnates and landlords."* [*"Primitive Accumulation and the Rise of Capitalism,"* **Studies in Mutualist Political Economy**]

This, the actual history of capitalism, will be discussed in the following sections. So it is ironic to hear right-"libertarians" sing the praises of a capitalism that never existed and urge its adoption by all nations, in spite of the historical evidence suggesting that only state intervention made capitalist economies viable – even in that Mecca of "free enterprise," the United States. As Noam Chomsky argues, *"who but a lunatic could have opposed the development of a textile industry in New England in the early nineteenth century, when British textile production was so much more efficient that half the New England industrial sector would have gone bankrupt without very high protective tariffs, thus terminating industrial development in the United States? Or the high tariffs that radically undermined economic efficiency to allow the United States to develop steel and other manufacturing capacities? Or the gross distortions of the market that created modern electronics?"* [**World Orders, Old and New**, p. 168] Such state interference in the economy is often denounced and dismissed by right-"libertarians" as mercantilism. However, to claim that "mercantilism" is not capitalism makes little sense. Without mercantilism, "proper" capitalism would never have developed, and any attempt to divorce a social system from its roots is ahistoric and makes a mockery of critical thought (particularly as "proper" capitalism turns to mercantilism regularly).

Similarly, it is somewhat ironic when "anarcho"-capitalists and other right "libertarians" claim that they support the freedom of individuals to choose how to live. After all, the working class was not given **that** particular choice when capitalism was developing. Instead, their right to choose their own way of life was constantly violated and denied – and justified by the leading capitalist economists of the time. To achieve this, state violence had one overall aim, to dispossess the labouring people from access to the means of life (particularly the land) and make them dependent on landlords and capitalists to earn a living. The state coercion *"which creates the capital-relation can be nothing other than the process*

which divorces the worker from the ownership of the conditions of his own labour; it is a process which operates two transformations, whereby the social means of subsistence and production are turned into capital, and the immediate producers are turned into wage-labourers. So-called primitive accumulation, therefore, is nothing else than the historical process of divorcing the producer from the means of production." [Marx, **Op. Cit.**, pp. 874-5] So to claim that **now** (after capitalism has been created) we get the chance to try and live as we like is insulting in the extreme. The available options we have are not independent of the society we live in and are decisively shaped by the past. To claim we are "free" to live as we like (within the laws of capitalism, of course) is basically to argue that we are able (in theory) to "buy" the freedom that every individual is due from those who have stolen it from us in the first place. It ignores the centuries of state violence required to produce the "free" worker who makes a "voluntary" agreement which is compelled by the social conditions that this created.

The history of state coercion and intervention is inseparable from the history of capitalism: it is contradictory to celebrate the latter while claiming to condemn the former. In practice capitalism has **always** meant intervention in markets to aid business and the rich. That is, what has been called by supporters of capitalism "laissez-faire" was nothing of the kind and represented the political-economic program of a specific fraction of the capitalist class rather than a set of principles of "hands off the market." As individualist anarchist Kevin Carson summaries, *"what is nostalgically called 'laissez-faire' was in fact a system of continuing state intervention to subsidise accumulation, guarantee privilege, and maintain work discipline."* [**The Iron Fist behind the Invisible Hand**] Moreover, there is the apparent unwillingness by such "free market" advocates (i.e. supporters of "free market" capitalism) to distinguish between historically and currently unfree capitalism and the other truly free market economy that they claim to desire. It is common to hear "anarcho"-capitalists point to the state-based capitalist system as vindication of their views (and even more surreal to see them point to **pre**-capitalist systems as examples of their ideology). It should be obvious that they cannot have it both ways.

In other words, Rothbard and other "anarcho"-capitalists treat capitalism as if it were the natural order of things rather than being the product of centuries of capitalist capture and use of state power to further their own interests. The fact that past uses of state power have allowed capitalist norms and assumptions to become the default system by their codification in property law and justified by bourgeois economics does not make it natural. The role of the state in the construction of a capitalist economy cannot be ignored or downplayed as government has always been an instrument in creating and developing such a system. As one critic of right-"libertarian" ideas put it, Rothbard *"completely overlooks the role of the state in building and maintaining a capitalist economy in the West. Privileged to live in the twentieth century, long after the battles to establish capitalism have been fought and won, Rothbard sees the state solely as a burden on the market and a vehicle for imposing the still greater burden of socialism. He manifests a kind of historical nearsightedness that allows him to collapse many centuries of human experience into one long night of tyranny that ended only with the invention of the free market and* its 'spontaneous' triumph over the past. It is pointless to argue, as Rothbard seems ready to do, that capitalism would have succeeded without the bourgeois state; the fact is that all capitalist nations have relied on the machinery of government to create and preserve the political and legal environments required by their economic system." That, of course, has not stopped him "critis[ing] others for being unhistorical." [Stephen L. Newman, **Liberalism at Wit's End**, pp. 77-8 and p. 79]

Thus we have a key contradiction within "anarcho"-capitalism. While they bemoan state intervention in the market, their underlying assumption is that it had no real effect on how society has evolved over the centuries. By a remarkable coincidence, the net effect of all this state intervention was to produce a capitalist economy identical in all features as one which would have been produced if society had been left alone to evolve naturally. It does seem strange that state violence would happen to produce the same economic system as that produced by right-"libertarians" and Austrian economists logically deducing concepts from a few basic axioms and assumptions. Even more of a coincidence, these conclusions also happen to be almost exactly the same as what those who have benefited from previous state coercion want to hear – namely, that private property is good, trade unions and strikes are bad, that the state should not interfere with the power of the bosses and should not even think about helping the working class (employed or unemployed). As such, while their advice and rhetoric may have changed, the social role of economists has not. State action was required to dispossess the direct producers from the means of life (particularly the land) and to reduce the real wage of workers so that they have to provide regular work in a obedient manner. In this, it and the capitalists received much advice from the earliest economists as Marxist economic historian Michael Perelman documents in great detail. As he summarises, "classical political economy was concerned with promoting primitive accumulation in order to foster capitalist development, even though the logic of primitive accumulation was in direct conflict with the classical political economists' purported adherence to the values of laissez-faire." [**The Invention of Capitalism**, p. 12] The turn to "laissez-faire" was possible because direct state power could be mostly replaced by economic power to ensure the dependency of the working class.

Needless to say, some right-"libertarians" recognise that the state played **some** role in economic life in the rise and development of capitalism. So they contrast "bad" business people (who took state aid) and "good" ones (who did not). Thus Rothbard's comment that Marxists have "made no particular distinction between 'bourgeoisie' who made use of the state, and bourgeoisie who acted on the free market." [**The Ethics of Liberty**, p. 72] But such an argument is nonsense as it ignores the fact that the "free market" is a network (and defined by the state by the property rights it enforces). This means that state intervention in one part of the economy will have ramifications in other parts, particularly if the state action in question is the expropriation and/or protection of productive resources (land and workplaces) or the skewing of the labour market in favour of the bosses. In other words, the individualistic perspective of "anarcho"-capitalism blinds its proponents to the obvious collective nature of working class exploitation and oppression which flows from the

collective and interconnected nature of production and investment in any real economy. State action supported by sectors of the capitalist class has, to use economic jargon, positive externalities for the rest. They, in general, benefit from it **as a class** just as working class people suffers from it collectively as it limits their available choices to those desired by their economic and political masters (usually the same people). As such, the right-"libertarian" fails to understand the **class** basis of state intervention.

For example, the owners of the American steel and other companies who grew rich and their companies big behind protectionist walls were obviously "bad" bourgeoisie. But were the bourgeoisie who supplied the steel companies with coal, machinery, food, "defence" and so on not also benefiting from state action? And the suppliers of the luxury goods to the wealthy steel company owners, did they not benefit from state action? Or the suppliers of commodities to the workers that laboured in the steel factories that the tariffs made possible, did they not benefit? And the suppliers to these suppliers? And the suppliers to these suppliers? Did not the users of technology first introduced into industry by companies protected by state orders also not benefit? Did not the capitalists who had a large pool of landless working class people to select from benefit from the "land monopoly" even though they may not have, unlike other capitalists, directly advocated it? It increased the pool of wage labour for **all** capitalists and increased their bargaining position/power in the labour market at the expense of the working class. In other words, such a policy helped maintain capitalist market power, irrespective of whether individual capitalists encouraged politicians to vote to create/maintain it. And, similarly, **all** American capitalists benefited from the changes in common law to recognise and protect capitalist private property and rights that the state enforced during the 19th century (see section B.2.5).

Rothbard, in other words, ignores class theft and the accumulative effect of stealing both productive property and the products of the workers who use it. He considered the "moral indignation" of socialism arose from the argument "that the capitalists have stolen the rightful property of the workers, and therefore that existing titles to accumulated capital are unjust." He argued that given "this hypothesis, the remainder of the impetus for both Marxism and anarchosyndicalism follow quite logically." However, Rothbard's "solution" to the problem of past force seems to be (essentially) a justification of existing property titles and not a serious attempt to understand or correct past initiations of force that have shaped society into a capitalist one and still shape it today. This is because he is simply concerned with returning property which has been obviously stolen and can be returned to those who have been directly dispossessed or their descendants (for example, giving land back to peasants or tenant farmers). If this cannot be done then the "title to that property, belongs properly, justly and ethically to its current possessors." [**Op. Cit.**, p. 52 and p. 57] At best, he allows nationalised property and any corporation which has the bulk of its income coming from the state to be "homesteaded" by their workers (which, according to Rothbard's arguments for the end of Stalinism, means they will get shares in the company). The end result of his theory is to leave things pretty much as they are. This is because he could not understand that the exploitation of the working class was/is collective in nature and, as such, is simply impossible to redress it in his individualistic term of reference.

To take an obvious example, if the profits of slavery in the Southern states of America were used to invest in factories in the Northern states (as they were), does giving the land to the freed slaves in 1865 **really** signify the end of the injustice that situation produced? Surely the products of the slaves work were stolen property just as much as the land was and, as a result, so is any investment made from it? After all, investment elsewhere was based on the profits extracted from slave labour and *"much of the profits earned in the northern states were derived from the surplus originating on the southern plantations."* [Perelman, **Op. Cit.**, p. 246] In terms of the wage workers in the North, they have been indirectly exploited by the existence of slavery as the investment this allowed reduced their bargaining power on the market as it reduced their ability to set up business for themselves by increasing the fixed costs of so doing. And what of the investment generated by the exploitation of these wage workers? As Mark Leier points out, the capitalists and landlords *"may have purchased the land and machinery, but this money represented nothing more than the expropriated labour of others."* [**Bakunin**, p. 111] If the land should be returned to those who worked it as Rothbard suggests, why not the industrial empires that were created on the backs of the generations of slaves who worked it? And what of the profits made from the generations of wage slaves who worked on these investments? And what of the investments which these profits allowed? Surely if the land should be given to those who worked it then so must any investments it generated? And assuming that those currently employed can rightly seize their workplaces, what about those previously employed and **their** descendants? Why should they be excluded from the riches their ancestors helped create?

To talk in terms of individuals misses all this and the net result is to ensure that the results of centuries of coercion and theft are undisturbed. This is because it is the working class **as a whole** who have been expropriated and whose labour has been exploited. The actual individuals involved and their descendants would be impossible to identify nor would it be possible to track down how the stolen fruits of their labour were invested. In this way, the class theft of our planet and liberty as well as the products of generations of working class people will continue safely.

Needless to say, some governments interfere in the economy more than others. Corporations do not invest in or buy from suppliers based in authoritarian regimes by accident. They do not just happen to be here, passively benefiting from statism and authoritarianism. Rather they choose **between** states to locate in based precisely on the cheapness of the labour supply. In other words, they prefer to locate in dictatorships and authoritarian regimes in Central America and Southeast Asia **because** those regimes interfere in the labour market the most – while, of course, talking about the very "free market" and "economic liberty" those regimes deny to their subjects. For Rothbard, this seems to be just a coincidence or a correlation rather than systematic for the collusion between state and business is the fault, not of capitalism, but simply of particular capitalists. The system, in other words, is pure; only individuals are corrupt. But, for anarchists, the origin of the modern capitalist system lies not in the individual qualities of capitalists as such but in the dynamic and evolution of capitalism itself – a complex interaction of class interest, class struggle, social defence against the destructive actions of the market, individual qualities and so forth. In other words, Rothbard's claims are flawed – they fail to understand capitalism as a **system**, its dynamic nature and the authoritarian social relationships it produces and the need for state intervention these produce and require.

So, when the right suggests that "we" be "left alone," what they mean by "we" comes into clear focus when we consider how capitalism developed. Artisans and peasants were only "left alone" to starve (sometimes not even that, as the workhouse was invented to bring vagabonds to the joy of work), and the working classes of industrial capitalism were only "left alone" outside work and for only as long as they respected the rules of their "betters." As Marx memorably put it, the *"newly freed men became sellers of themselves only after they had been robbed of all their own means of production, and all the guarantees of existence afforded by the old feudal arrangements. And this history, the history of their expropriation, is written in the annals of mankind in letters of blood and fire."* [**Op. Cit.**, p. 875] As for the other side of the class divide, they desired to be "left alone" to exercise their power over others as we will see. That modern "capitalism" is, in effect, a kind of "corporate mercantilism," with states providing the conditions that allow corporations to flourish (e.g. tax breaks, subsidies, bailouts, anti-labour laws, etc.) says more about the statist roots of capitalism than the ideologically correct definition of capitalism used by its supporters.

In fact, if we look at the role of the state in creating capitalism we could be tempted to rename "anarcho"-capitalism "marxian-capitalism". This is because, given the historical evidence, a political theory can be developed by which the "dictatorship of the bourgeoisie" is created and that this capitalist state "withers away" into "anarchy". That this means replacing the economic and social ideas of Marxism and their replacement by their direct opposite should not mean that we should reject the idea (after all, that is what "anarcho"-capitalism has done to Individualist Anarchism!). But we doubt that many "anarcho"-capitalists will accept such a name change (even though this would reflect their politics far better; after all they do not object to past initiations of force, just current ones and many do seem to think that the modern state **will** wither away due to market forces).

This is suggested by the fact that Rothbard did not advocate change from below as the means of creating "anarchy." He helped found the so-called Libertarian Party in 1971 which, like Marxists, stands for political office. With the fall of Stalinism in 1989, Rothbard faced whole economies which could be "homesteaded" and he argued that *"desocialisation"* (i.e., de-nationalisation as, like Leninists, he confused socialisation with nationalisation) *"necessarily involves the action of that government surrendering its property to its private subjects ... In a deep sense, getting rid of the socialist state requires that state to perform one final, swift, glorious act of self-immolation, after which it vanishes from the scene."* (compare to Engels' comment that *"the taking possession of the means of production in the name of society"* is the state's *"last independent act as a state."* [**Selected Works**, p. 424]). He considered the *"capital goods built by the State"* as being *"philosophically unowned"* yet failed to note whose labour was exploited and taxed to build them in the first place (needless to say, he rejected the ideas of shares to all as this would be *"egalitarian handouts ... to undeserving citizens,"* presumably the ill, the unemployed, retirees, mothers, children, and future generations). [**The Logic of Action II,** p. 213, p. 212 and p. 209]

Industrial plants would be transferred to workers currently employed there, but not by their own direct action and direct expropriation. Rather, the state would do so. This is understandable as, left to themselves, the workers may not act quite as he desired. Thus we see him advocating the transfer of industry from the state bureaucracy to workers by means of *"private, negotiable shares"* as ownership was *"not to be granted to collectives or co-operatives or workers or peasants holistically, which would only bring back the ills of socialism in a decentralised and chaotic syndicalist form."* His "homesteading" was not to be done by the workers themselves rather it was a case of *"granting shares to workers"* by the state. He also notes that it should be a *"priority"* for the government *"to return all stolen, confiscated property to its original owners, or to their heirs."* This would involve *"finding original landowners"* – i.e., the landlord class whose wealth was based on exploiting the serfs and peasants. [**Op. Cit.**, p. 210 and pp. 211-2] Thus expropriated peasants would have their land returned but not, apparently, any peasants working land which had been taken from their feudal and aristocratic overlords by the state. Thus those who had just been freed from Stalinist rule would have been subjected to "libertarian" rule to ensure that the transition was done in the economically correct way. As it was, the neo-classical economists who did oversee the transition ensured that ownership and control transferred directly to a new ruling class rather than waste time issuing "shares" which would eventually end up in a few hands due to market forces (the actual way it was done could be considered a modern form of "primitive accumulation" as it ensured that capital goods did not end up in the hands of the workers).

But this is beside the point. The fact remains that state action was required to create and maintain capitalism. Without state support it is doubtful that capitalism would have developed at all. So the only "capitalism" that has existed is a product of state support and intervention, and it has been characterised by markets that are considerably less than free. Thus, serious supporters of truly free markets (like the American Individualist Anarchists) have not been satisfied with "capitalism" – have, in fact, quite rightly and explicitly opposed it. Their vision of a free society has always been at odds with the standard capitalist one, a fact which "anarcho"-capitalists bemoan and dismiss as "mistakes" and/or the product of "bad economics." Apparently the net effect of all this state coercion has been, essentially, null. It has **not**, as the critics of capitalism have argued, fundamentally shaped the development of the economy as capitalism would have developed naturally by itself. Thus an economy marked by inequalities of wealth and power, where the bulk of the population are landless and resourceless and where interest, rent and profits are extracted from the labour of working people would have developed anyway regardless of the state coercion which marked the rise of capitalism and the need for a subservient and dependent working class by the landlords and capitalists which drove these policies simply accelerated the process towards "economic liberty." However, it is more than mere coincidence that capitalism and state coercion are so intertwined both in history and in current practice.

In summary, like other apologists for capitalism, right-wing "libertarians" advocate that system without acknowledging the means that were necessary to create it. They tend to equate it with any market system, failing to understand that it is a specific kind of market system where labour itself is a commodity. It is ironic, of course, that most defenders of capitalism stress the importance of markets (which have pre-dated capitalism) while downplaying the importance of wage labour (which defines it) along with the violence which created it. Yet as both anarchists and Marxists have stressed, money and commodities do not define capitalism any more than private ownership of the means of production. So it is important to remember that from a socialist perspective capitalism is **not** identical to the market. As we stressed in section C.2, both anarchists and Marxists argue that where people produce for themselves, it is not capitalist production, i.e. when a worker sells commodities this is not capitalist production. Thus the supporters of capitalism fail to understand that a great deal of state coercion was required to transform pre-capitalist societies of artisans and peasant farmers selling the produce of their labour into a capitalist society of wage workers selling themselves to bosses, bankers and landlords.

Lastly, it should be stressed that this process of primitive accumulation is not limited to private capitalism. State capitalism has also had recourse to such techniques. Stalin's forced collectivisation of the peasantry and the brutal industrialisation involved in five-year plans in the 1930s are the most obvious example. What took centuries in Britain was condensed into decades in the Soviet Union and other state capitalist regimes, with a corresponding impact on its human toil. However, we will not discuss these acts of state coercion here as we are concerned primarily with the actions required to create the conditions required for private capitalism.

Needless to say, this section cannot hope to go into all the forms of state intervention across the globe which were used to create or impose capitalism onto an unwilling population. All we can do is provide a glimpse into the brutal history of capitalism and provide enough references for those interested to pursue the issue further. The first starting point should be Part VIII (*"So-Called Primitive Accumulation"*) of volume 1 of Marx's **Capital**. This classic account of the origins of capitalism should be supplemented by more recent accounts, but its basic analysis is correct. Marxist writers have expanded on Marx's analysis, with Maurice Dobb's **Studies in the Development of Capitalism** and David McNally's **Against the Market** are worth consulting, as is Michael Perelman's **The Invention of Capitalism**. Kropotkin's **Mutual Aid** has a short summary of state action in destroying communal institutions and common ownership of land, as does his **The State: It's Historic Role**. Rudolf Rocker's **Nationalism and Culture** is also essential reading. Individualist Anarchist Kevin Carson's **Studies in Mutualist Political Economy** provides an excellent summary (see part 2, *"Capitalism and the State: Past, Present and Future"*) as does his essay **The Iron Fist behind the Invisible Hand**.

F.8.1 What social forces lay behind the rise of capitalism?

Capitalist society is a relatively recent development. For Marx, while markets have existed for millennia *"the capitalist era dates from the sixteenth century."* [**Capital**, vol. 1, p. 876] As Murray Bookchin pointed out, for a *"long era, perhaps spanning more than five centuries,"* capitalism *"coexisted with feudal and simple commodity relationships"* in Europe. He argues that this period *"simply cannot be treated as 'transitional' without reading back the present into the past."* [**From Urbanisation to Cities**, p. 179] In other words, capitalism was not a inevitable outcome of "history" or social evolution.

Bookchin went on to note that capitalism existed *"with growing significance in the mixed economy of the West from the fourteenth century up to the seventeenth"* but that it *"literally exploded into being in Europe, particularly England, during the eighteenth and especially nineteenth centuries."* [**Op. Cit.**, p. 181] The question arises, what lay behind this *"growing significance"*? Did capitalism *"explode"* due to its inherently more efficient nature or were there other, non-economic, forces at work? As we will show, it was most definitely the second – capitalism was born not from economic forces but from the political actions of the social elites which its usury enriched. Unlike artisan (simple commodity) production, wage labour generates inequalities and wealth for the few and so will be selected, protected and encouraged by those who control the state in their own economic and social interests.

The development of capitalism in Europe was favoured by two social elites, the rising capitalist class within the degenerating medieval cities and the absolutist state. The medieval city was *"thoroughly changed by the gradual increase in the power of commercial capital, due primarily to foreign trade … By this the inner unity of the commune was loosened, giving place to a growing caste system and leading necessarily to a progressive inequality of social interests. The privileged minorities pressed ever more definitely towards a centralisation of the political forces of the community … Mercantilism in the perishing city republics led logically to a demand for larger economic units [i.e. to nationalise the market]; and by this the desire for stronger political forms was greatly strengthened … Thus the city gradually became a small state, paving the way for the coming national state."* [Rudolf Rocker, **Nationalism and Culture**, p. 94] Kropotkin stressed that in this destruction of communal self-organisation the state not only served the interests of the rising capitalist class but also its own. Just as the landlord and capitalist seeks a workforce and labour market made up of atomised and isolated individuals, so does the state seek to eliminate all potential rivals to its power and so opposes *"all coalitions and all private societies, whatever their aim."* [**The State: It's Historic role**, p. 53]

The rising economic power of the proto-capitalists conflicted with that of the feudal lords, which meant that the former required help to consolidate their position. That aid came in the form of the monarchical state which, in turn, needed support against the feudal lords. With the force of absolutism behind it, capital could start the process of increasing its power and influence by expanding the "market" through state action. This use of state coercion was required because, as Bookchin noted, *"[i]n every pre-capitalist society, countervailing forces … existed to restrict the market economy. No less significantly, many pre-capitalist societies raised what they thought were insuperable obstacles to the penetration of the State into social life."* He noted the *"power of village communities to resist the invasion of trade and despotic political forms into society's abiding communal substrate."* State violence was required to break this resistance and, unsurprisingly the *"one class to benefit most from the rising nation-state was the European bourgeoisie … This structure … provided the basis for the next great system of labour mobilisation: the factory."* [**The Ecology of Freedom**, pp. 207-8 and p. 336] The absolutist state, noted Rocker, *"was dependent upon the help of these new economic forces, and vice versa* and so it *"at first furthered the plans of commercial capital"* as its coffers were filled by the expansion of commerce. Its armies and fleets *"contributed to the expansion of industrial production because they demanded a number of things for whose large-scale production the shops of small tradesmen were no longer adapted. Thus gradually arose the so-called manufactures, the forerunners of the later large industries."* [**Op. Cit.**, pp. 117-8] As such, it is impossible to underestimate the role of state power in creating the preconditions for both agricultural and industrial capitalism.

Some of the most important state actions from the standpoint of early industry were the so-called Enclosure Acts, by which the "commons" – the free farmland shared communally by the peasants in most rural villages – was "enclosed" or incorporated into the estates of various landlords as private property (see section F.8.3). This ensured a pool of landless workers who had no option but to sell their labour to landlords and capitalists. Indeed, the widespread independence caused by the possession of the majority of households of land caused the rising class of capitalists to complain, as one put it, *"that men who should work as wage-labourers cling to the soil, and in the naughtiness of their hearts prefer independence as squatters to employment by a master."* [quoted by Allan Engler, **The Apostles of Greed**, p. 12] Once in service to a master, the state was always on hand to repress any signs of *"naughtiness"* and *"independence"* (such as strikes, riots, unions and the like). For example, Seventeenth century France saw a *"number of decrees … which forbade workers to change their employment or which prohibited assemblies of workers or strikes on pain of corporal punishment or even death. (Even the Theological Faculty of the University of Paris saw fit to pronounce solemnly against the sin of workers' organisation)."* [Maurice Dobb, **Studies in the Development of Capitalism**, p. 160]

In addition, other forms of state aid ensured that capitalist firms got a head start, so ensuring their dominance over other forms of work (such as co-operatives). A major way of creating a pool of resources that could be used for investment was the use of mercantilist policies which used protectionist measures to enrich capitalists and landlords at the expense of consumers and their workers. For example, one of most common complaints of early capitalists was that workers would not turn up to work regularly. Once they had worked a few days, they disappeared as they had earned enough money to live on. With higher prices for food, caused by protectionist

Is "anarcho"-capitalism a type of anarchism?

measures, workers had to work longer and harder and so became accustomed to factory labour. In addition, mercantilism allowed native industry to develop by barring foreign competition and so allowed industrialists to reap excess profits which they could then use to increase their investments. In the words of Marxist economic historian Maurice Dobb:

> "In short, the Mercantile System was a system of State-regulated exploitation through trade which played a highly important rule in the adolescence of capitalist industry: it was essentially the economic policy of an age of primitive accumulation." [**Op. Cit.**, p. 209]

As Rocker summarises, "when absolutism had victoriously overcome all opposition to national unification, by its furthering of mercantilism and economic monopoly it gave the whole social evolution a direction which could only lead to capitalism." [**Op. Cit.**, pp. 116-7]

Mercantilist policies took many forms, including the state providing capital to new industries, exempting them from guild rules and taxes, establishing monopolies over local, foreign and colonial markets, and granting titles and pensions to successful capitalists. In terms of foreign trade, the state assisted home-grown capitalists by imposing tariffs, quotas, and prohibitions on imports. They also prohibited the export of tools and technology as well as the emigration of skilled workers to stop competition (this applied to any colonies a specific state may have had). Other policies were applied as required by the needs of specific states. For example, the English state imposed a series of Navigation Acts which forced traders to use English ships to visit its ports and colonies (this destroyed the commerce of Holland, its chief rival). Nor should the impact of war be minimised, with the demand for weapons and transportation (including ships) injecting government spending into the economy. Unsurprisingly, given this favouring of domestic industry at the expense of its rivals and the subject working class population the mercantilist period was one of generally rapid growth, particularly in England.

As we discussed in section C.10, some kind of mercantilism has always been required for a country to industrialise. Over all, as economist Paul Ormerod puts it, the "advice to follow pure free-market polices seems ... to be contrary to the lessons of virtually the whole of economic history since the Industrial Revolution ... every country which has moved into ... strong sustained growth ... has done so in outright violation of pure, free-market principles." These interventions include the use of "tariff barriers" to protect infant industries, "government subsidies" and "active state intervention in the economy." He summarises: "The model of entrepreneurial activity in the product market, with judicious state support plus repression in the labour market, seems to be a good model of economic development." [**The Death of Economics**, p. 63]

Thus the social forces at work creating capitalism were a combination of capitalist activity and state action. But without the support of the state, it is doubtful that capitalist activity would have been enough to generate the initial accumulation required to start the economic ball rolling. Hence the necessity of Mercantilism in Europe and its modified cousin of state aid, tariffs and "homestead acts" in America.

F.8.2 What was the social context of the statement "laissez-faire"?

The honeymoon of interests between the early capitalists and autocratic kings did not last long. "This selfsame monarchy, which for weighty reasons sought to further the aims of commercial capital and was ... itself aided in its development by capital, grew at last into a crippling obstacle to any further development of European industry." [Rudolf Rocker, **Nationalism and Culture**, p. 117]

This is the social context of the expression "laissez-faire" – a system which has outgrown the supports that protected it in its early stages. Just as children eventually rebel against the protection and rules of their parents, so the capitalists rebelled against the over-bearing support of the absolutist state. Mercantilist policies favoured some industries and harmed the growth of others. The rules and regulations imposed upon those it did favour reduced the flexibility of capitalists to changing environments. As Rocker argues, "no matter how the absolutist state strove, in its own interest, to meet the demands of commerce, it still put on industry countless fetters which became gradually more and more oppressive ... [it] became an unbearable burden ... which paralysed all economic and social life." [**Op. Cit.**, p. 119] All in all, mercantilism became more of a hindrance than a help and so had to be replaced. With the growth of economic and social power by the capitalist class, this replacement was made easier. As Errico Malatesta notes:

> "The development of production, the vast expansion of commerce, the immeasurable power assumed by money ... have guaranteed this supremacy [of economic power over political power] to the capitalist class which, no longer content with enjoying the support of the government, demanded that government arise from its own ranks. A government which owed its origin to the right of conquest ... though subject by existing circumstances to the capitalist class, went on maintaining a proud and contemptuous attitude towards its now wealthy former slaves, and had pretensions to independence of domination. That government was indeed the defender, the property owners' gendarme, but the kind of gendarmes who think they are somebody, and behave in an arrogant manner towards the people they have to escort and defend, when they don't rob or kill them at the next street corner; and the capitalist class got rid of it ... and replac[ed] it by a government of its own choosing, at all times under its control and specifically organised to defend that class against any possible demands by the disinherited." [**Anarchy**, pp. 22-3]

Malatesta here indicates the true meaning of "leave us alone," or "laissez-faire." The **absolutist** state (not "the state" per se) began to interfere with capitalists' profit-making activities and authority, so they determined that it had to go – which the rising capitalist class did when they utilised such popular movements as the English, French and American revolutions. In such circumstances, when the state is not fully controlled by the capitalist class, then it makes perfect sense to oppose state intervention no matter how useful it may have been in the past – a state run by aristocratic and feudal landlords does not produce class legislation in quite the right form. That changes when members of the capitalist class hold state power and when the landlords start acting more like rural capitalists and, unsurprisingly, laissez-faire was quickly modified and then abandoned once capitalists could rely on a **capitalist** state to support and protect its economic power within society.

When capitalism had been rid of unwanted interference by the hostile use of state power by non-capitalist classes then laissez-faire had its utility (just as it has its utility today when attacking social welfare). Once this had been accomplished then state intervention in society was encouraged and applauded by capitalists. *"It is ironic that the main protagonists of the State, in its political and administrative authority, were the middle-class Utilitarians, on the other side of whose Statist banner were inscribed the doctrines of economic Laissez Faire."* [E.P. Thompson, **The Making of the English Working Class**, p. 90] Capitalists simply wanted **capitalist** states to replace monarchical states, so that heads of government would follow state economic policies regarded by capitalists as beneficial to their class as a whole. And as development economist Lance Taylor argues:

> *"In the long run, there are no laissez-faire transitions to modern economic growth. The state has always intervened to create a capitalist class, and then it has to regulate the capitalist class, and then the state has to worry about being taken over by the capitalist class, but the state has always been there."* [quoted by Noam Chomsky, **Year 501**, p. 104]

In order to attack mercantilism, the early capitalists had to ignore the successful impact of its policies in developing industry and a "store of wealth" for future economic activity. As William Lazonick points out, *"the political purpose of [Adam Smith's] the **Wealth of Nations** was to attack the mercantilist institutions that the British economy had built up over the previous two hundred years. Yet in proposing institutional change, Smith lacked a dynamic historical analysis. In his attack on these institutions, Smith might have asked why the extent of the world market available to Britain in the late eighteenth century was **so uniquely under British control.** If Smith had asked this 'big question,' he might have been forced to grant credit for Britain's extent of the world market to the very mercantilist institutions he was attacking."* Moreover, he *"might have recognised the integral relation between economic and political power in the rise of Britain to international dominance."* Overall, *"[w]hat the British advocates of laissez-faire neglected to talk about was the role that a system of national power had played in creating conditions for Britain to embark on its dynamic development path … They did not bother to ask how Britain had attained th[e] position [of 'workshop of the world'], while they conveniently ignored the on going system of national power – the British Empire – that … continued to support Britain's position."* [**Business Organisation and the Myth of the Market Economy**, p. 2, p. 3 and p.5]

Similar comments are applicable to American supporters of laissez faire who fail to notice that the "traditional" American support for world-wide free trade is quite a recent phenomenon. It started only at the end of the Second World War (although, of course, **within** America military Keynesian policies were utilised). While American industry was developing, the state and capitalist class had no time for laissez-faire (see section F.8.5 for details). After it had grown strong, the United States began preaching laissez-faire to the rest of the world – and began to kid itself about its own history, believing its slogans about laissez-faire as the secret of its success. Yet like all other successful industrialisers, the state could aid capitalists directly and indirectly (via tariffs, land policy, repression of the labour movement, infrastructure subsidy and so on) and it would "leave them alone" to oppress and exploit workers, exploit consumers, build their industrial empires and so forth.

Takis Fotopoulos indicates that the social forces at work in "freeing" the market did not represent a "natural" evolution towards freedom:

> "Contrary to what liberals and Marxists assert, marketisation of the economy was not just an evolutionary process, following the expansion of trade under mercantilism … modern [i.e. capitalist] markets did not evolve out of local markets and/or markets for foreign goods … the nation-state, which was just emerging at the end of the Middle Ages, played a crucial role creating the conditions for the 'nationalisation' of the market … and … by freeing the market from effective social control." ["The Nation-state and the Market", pp. 37-80 Society and Nature, Vol. 2, No. 2, pp. 44-45]

The "freeing" of the market means freeing those who "own" most of the market (i.e. the wealthy elite) from "effective social control," but the rest of society was not as lucky. Kropotkin makes a similar point: "While giving the capitalist any degree of free scope to amass his wealth at the expense of the helpless labourers, the government has nowhere and never … afforded the labourers the opportunity 'to do as they pleased'." [**Anarchism**, p. 182]

So, the expression "laissez-faire" dates from the period when capitalists were objecting to the restrictions that helped create them in the first place. It has little to do with freedom as such and far more to do with the needs of capitalist power and profits. It should also be remembered that at this time the state was run by the rich and for the rich. Elections, where they took place, involved the wealthiest of male property owners. This meant there were two aspects in the call for laissez-faire. On the one hand, by the elite to eliminate regulations and interventions they found burdensome and felt unnecessary as their social position was secure by their economic power (mercantilism evolved into capitalism proper when market power was usually sufficient to produce dependency and obedience as the working class had been successfully dispossessed from the land and the means of production). On the other, serious social reformers (like Adam Smith) who recognised that the costs of such elite inspired state regulations generally fell on working class people. The moral authority of the latter was used to bolster the desire of the former to maximise their wealth by imposing costs on others (workers, customers, society and the planet's eco-system) with the state waiting in the wings to support them as and when required.

Unsurprising, working class people recognised the hypocrisy of

Is "anarcho"-capitalism a type of anarchism?

this arrangement (even if most modern-day right-"libertarians" do not and provide their services justifying the actions and desires of repressive and exploitative oligarchs seeking monopolistic positions). They turned to political and social activism seeking to change a system which saw economic and political power reinforce each other. Some (like the Chartists and Marxists) argued for political reforms to generalise democracy into genuine one person, one vote. In this way, political liberty would be used to end the worse excesses of so-called "economic liberty" (i.e., capitalist privilege and power). Others (like mutualists) aimed at economic reforms which ensure that the capitalist class would be abolished by means of genuine economic freedom. Finally, most other anarchists argued that revolutionary change was required as the state and capitalism were so intertwined that both had to be ended at the same time. However, the struggle against state power always came from the general population. As Murray Bookchin argued, it is an error to depict this "revolutionary era and its democratic aspirations as 'bourgeois,' an imagery that makes capitalism a system more committed to freedom, or even ordinary civil liberties, than it was historically." [**From Urbanisation to Cities**, p. 180f] While the capitalist class may have benefited from such popular movements as the English, American and French revolutions these revolutions were not led, never mind started or fought, by the bourgeoisie.

Not much has changed as capitalists are today seeking maximum freedom from the state to ensure maximum authority over their wage slaves and society. The one essential form of support the "Libertarian" right wants the state (or "defence" firms) to provide capitalism is the enforcement of property rights – the right of property owners to "do as they like" on their own property, which can have obvious and extensive social impacts. What "libertarian" capitalists object to is attempts by others – workers, society as a whole, the state, etc. – to interfere with the authority of bosses. That this is just the defence of privilege and power (and not freedom) has been discussed in section B and elsewhere in section F, so we will not repeat ourselves here. Samuel Johnson once observed that *"we hear the loudest **yelps** for liberty among the drivers of Negroes."* [quoted by Noam Chomsky, **Year 501**, p. 141] Our modern "libertarian" capitalist drivers of wage-slaves are yelping for exactly the same kind of "liberty."

F.8.3 What other forms did state intervention in creating capitalism take?

Beyond being a paymaster for new forms of production and social relations as well as defending the owners' power, the state intervened economically in other ways as well. As we noted in section B.2.5, the state played a key role in transforming the law codes of society in a capitalistic fashion, ignoring custom and common law when it was convenient to do so. Similarly, the use of tariffs and the granting of monopolies to companies played an important role in accumulating capital at the expense of working people, as did the breaking of unions and strikes by force.

However, one of the most blatant of these acts was the enclosure

of common land. In Britain, by means of the Enclosure Acts, land that had been freely used by poor peasants was claimed by large landlords as private property. As socialist historian E.P. Thompson summarised, *"the social violence of enclosure consisted … in the drastic, total imposition upon the village of capitalist property-definitions."* [**The Making of the English Working Class**, pp. 237-8] Property rights, which favoured the rich, replaced the use rights and free agreement that had governed peasants use of the commons. Unlike use rights, which rest in the individual, property rights require state intervention to create and maintain. *"Parliament and law imposed capitalist definitions to exclusive property in land,"* Thompson notes. This process involved ignoring the wishes of those who used the commons and repressing those who objected. Parliament was, of course, run by and for the rich who then simply *"observed the rules which they themselves had made."* [**Customs in Common**, p. 163]

Unsurprisingly, many landowners would become rich through the enclosure of the commons, heaths and downland while many ordinary people had a centuries old right taken away. Land enclosure was a gigantic swindle on the part of large landowners. In the words of one English folk poem written in 1764 as a protest against enclosure:

> They hang the man, and flog the woman,
> That steals the goose from off the common;
> But let the greater villain loose,
> That steals the common from the goose.

It should be remembered that the process of enclosure was not limited to just the period of the industrial revolution. As Colin Ward notes, *"in Tudor times, a wave of enclosures by land-owners who sought to profit from the high price of wool had deprived the commoners of their livelihood and obliged them to seek work elsewhere or become vagrants or squatters on the wastes on the edges of villages."* [**Cotters and Squatters**, p. 30] This first wave increased the size of the rural proletariat who sold their labour to landlords. Nor should we forget that this imposition of capitalist property rights did not imply that it was illegal. As Michael Perelman notes, *"[f]ormally, this dispossession was perfectly legal. After all, the peasants did not have property rights in the narrow sense. They only had traditional rights. As markets evolved, first land-hungry gentry and later the bourgeoisie used the state to create a legal structure to abrogate these traditional rights."* [**The Invention of Capitalism**, pp. 13-4]

While technically legal as the landlords made the law, the impact of this stealing of the land should not be under estimated. Without land, you cannot live and have to sell your liberty to others. This places those with capital at an advantage, which will tend to increase, rather than decrease, the inequalities in society (and so place the landless workers at an increasing disadvantage over time). This process can be seen from early stages of capitalism. With the enclosure of the land an agricultural workforce was created which had to travel where the work was. This influx of landless ex-peasants into the towns ensured that the traditional guild system crumbled and was transformed into capitalistic industry with bosses and wage slaves rather than master craftsmen and their journeymen. Hence the enclosure of land played a key role, for *"it is clear that economic inequalities are unlikely to create a division of society into an employing master class and a subject wage-earning class, unless access to the means of production, including land, is by some means or another barred to a substantial section of the community."* [Maurice Dobb, **Studies in Capitalist Development**, p. 253]

The importance of access to land is summarised by this limerick by the followers of Henry George (a 19th century writer who argued for a *"single tax"* and the nationalisation of land). The Georgites got their basic argument on the importance of land down to these few, excellent, lines:

> *A college economist planned*
> *To live without access to land*
> *He would have succeeded*
> *But found that he needed*
> *Food, shelter and somewhere to stand.*

Thus anarchists concern over the *"land monopoly"* of which the Enclosure Acts were but one part. The land monopoly, to use Tucker's words, *"consists in the enforcement by government of land titles which do not rest upon personal occupancy and cultivation."* [**The Anarchist Reader**, p. 150] So it should be remembered that common land did **not** include the large holdings of members of the feudal aristocracy and other landlords. This helped to artificially limit available land and produce a rural proletariat just as much as enclosures.

It is important to remember that wage labour first developed on the land and it was the protection of land titles of landlords and nobility, combined with enclosure, that meant people could not just work their own land. The pressing economic circumstances created by enclosing the land and enforcing property rights to large estates ensured that capitalists did not have to point a gun at people's heads to get them to work long hours in authoritarian, dehumanising conditions. In such circumstances, when the majority are dispossessed and face the threat of starvation, poverty, homelessness and so on, "initiation of force" is **not required.** But guns **were** required to enforce the system of private property that created the labour market in the first place, to enclosure common land and protect the estates of the nobility and wealthy.

By decreasing the availability of land for rural people, the enclosures destroyed working-class independence. Through these Acts, innumerable peasants were excluded from access to their former means of livelihood, forcing them to seek work from landlords or to migrate to the cities to seek work in the newly emerging factories of the budding industrial capitalists who were thus provided with a ready source of cheap labour. The capitalists, of course, did not describe the results this way, but attempted to obfuscate the issue with their usual rhetoric about civilisation and progress. Thus John Bellers, a 17th-century supporter of enclosures, claimed that commons were *"a hindrance to Industry, and ... Nurseries of Idleness and Insolence."* The *"forests and great Commons make the Poor that are upon them too much like the **Indians.**"* [quoted by Thompson, **Op. Cit.**, p. 165] Elsewhere Thompson argues that the commons *"were now seen as a dangerous centre of indiscipline*

... Ideology was added to self-interest. It became a matter of public-spirited policy for gentlemen to remove cottagers from the commons, reduce his labourers to dependence." [**The Making of the English Working Class**, pp. 242-3] David McNally confirms this, arguing *"it was precisely these elements of material and spiritual independence that many of the most outspoken advocates of enclosure sought to destroy."* Eighteenth-century proponents of enclosure *"were remarkably forthright in this respect. Common rights and access to common lands, they argued, allowed a degree of social and economic independence, and thereby produced a lazy, dissolute mass of rural poor who eschewed honest labour and church attendance ... Denying such people common lands and common rights would force them to conform to the harsh discipline imposed by the market in labour."* [**Against the Market**, p. 19]

The commons gave working-class people a degree of independence which allowed them to be "insolent" to their betters. This had to be stopped, as it undermined to the very roots of authority relationships within society. The commons **increased** freedom for ordinary people and made them less willing to follow orders and accept wage labour. The reference to "Indians" is important, as the independence and freedom of Native Americans is well documented. The common feature of both cultures was communal ownership of the means of production and free access to it (usufruct). This is discussed further in section I.7 (Won't Libertarian Socialism destroy individuality?). As Bookchin stressed, the factory *"was not born from a need to integrate labour with modern machinery,"* rather it was to regulate labour and make it regular. For the *"irregularity, or 'naturalness,' in the rhythm and intensity of traditional systems of work contributed more towards the bourgeoisie's craze for social control and its savagely anti-naturalistic outlook than did the prices or earnings demanded by its employees. More than any single technical factor, this irregularity led to the rationalisation of labour under a single ensemble of rule, to a discipline of work and regulation of time that yielded the modern factory ... the initial goal of the factory was to dominate labour and destroy the worker's independence from capital."* [**The Ecology of Freedom** p. 406]

Hence the pressing need to break the workers' ties with the land and so the *"loss of this independence included the loss of the worker's contact with food cultivation ... To live in a cottage ... often meant to cultivate a family garden, possibly to pasture a cow, to prepare one's own bread, and to have the skills for keeping a home in good repair. To utterly erase these skills and means of a livelihood from the worker's life became an industrial imperative."* Thus the worker's *"complete dependence on the factory and on an industrial labour market was a compelling precondition for the triumph of industrial society ... The need to destroy whatever independent means of life the worker could garner ... all involved the issue of reducing the proletariat to a condition of total powerlessness in the face of capital. And with that powerlessness came a supineness, a loss of character and community, and a decline in moral fibre."* [Bookchin, **Op. Cit.**, pp. 406-7] Unsurprisingly, there was a positive association between enclosure and migration out of villages and a *"definite correlation ... between the extent of enclosure and reliance on poor rates ... parliamentary enclosure resulted in out-migration and a higher level of pauperisation."* Moreover, *"the standard of living was generally much higher in those areas where labourers*

Is "anarcho"-capitalism a type of anarchism?

managed to combine industrial work with farming ... Access to commons meant that labourers could graze animals, gather wood, stones and gravel, dig coal, hunt and fish. These rights often made the difference between subsistence and abject poverty." [David McNally, **Op. Cit.**, p. 14 and p. 18] Game laws also ensured that the peasantry and servants could not legally hunt for food as from the time of Richard II (1389) to 1831, no person could kill game unless qualified by estate or social standing.

The enclosure of the commons (in whatever form it took – see section F.8.5 for the US equivalent) solved both problems – the high cost of labour, and the freedom and dignity of the worker. The enclosures perfectly illustrate the principle that capitalism requires a state to ensure that the majority of people do not have free access to any means of livelihood and so must sell themselves to capitalists in order to survive. There is no doubt that if the state had "left alone" the European peasantry, allowing them to continue their collective farming practices ("collective farming" because, as Kropotkin shows, the peasants not only shared the land but much of the farm labour as well), capitalism could not have taken hold (see **Mutual Aid** for more on the European enclosures [pp. 184-189]). As Kropotkin notes, *"[i]nstances of commoners themselves dividing their lands were rare, everywhere the State coerced them to enforce the division, or simply favoured the private appropriation of their lands"* by the nobles and wealthy. Thus *"to speak of the natural death of the village community [or the commons] in virtue of economical law is as grim a joke as to speak of the natural death of soldiers slaughtered on a battlefield."* [**Mutual Aid**, p. 188 and p. 189]

Once a labour market **was** created by means of enclosure and the land monopoly, the state did **not** passively let it work. When market conditions favoured the working class, the state took heed of the calls of landlords and capitalists and intervened to restore the "natural" order. The state actively used the law to lower wages and ban unions of workers for centuries. In Britain, for example, after the Black Death there was a "servant" shortage. Rather than allow the market to work its magic, the landlords turned to the state and the result was *"the Statute of Labourers"* of 1351:

> *"Whereas late against the malice of servants, which were idle, and not willing to serve after the pestilence, without taking excessive wages, it was ordained by our lord the king ... that such manner of servants ... should be bound to serve, receiving salary and wages, accustomed in places where they ought to serve in the twentieth year of the reign of the king that now is, or five or six years before; and that the same servants refusing to serve in such manner should be punished by imprisonment of their bodies ... now forasmuch as it is given the king to understand in this present parliament, by the petition of the commonalty, that the said servants having no regard to the said ordinance, ... to the great damage of the great men, and impoverishing of all the said commonalty, whereof the said commonalty prayeth remedy: wherefore in the said parliament, by the assent of the said prelates, earls, barons, and other great men, and of the same commonalty there assembled, to refrain the malice of*

the said servants, be ordained and established the things underwritten."

Thus state action was required because labourers had increased bargaining power and commanded higher wages which, in turn, led to inflation throughout the economy. In other words, an early version of the NAIRU (see section C.9). In one form or another this statute remained in force right through to the 19th century (later versions made it illegal for employees to "conspire" to fix wages, i.e., to organise to demand wage increases). Such measures were particularly sought when the labour market occasionally favoured the working class. For example, *"[a]fter the Restoration [of the English Monarchy],"* noted Dobb, *"when labour-scarcity had again become a serious complaint and the propertied class had been soundly frightened by the insubordination of the Commonwealth years, the clamour for legislative interference to keep wages low, to drive the poor into employment and to extend the system of workhouses and 'houses of correction' and the farming out of paupers once more reached a crescendo."* The same occurred on Continental Europe. [**Op. Cit.**, p. 234]

So, time and again employers called on the state to provide force to suppress the working class, artificially lower wages and bolster their economic power and authority. While such legislation was often difficult to enforce and often ineffectual in that real wages did, over time, increase, the threat and use of state coercion would ensure that they did not increase as fast as they may otherwise have done. Similarly, the use of courts and troops to break unions and strikes helped the process of capital accumulation immensely. Then there were the various laws used to control the free movement of workers. *"For centuries,"* notes Colin Ward, *"the lives of the poor majority in rural England were dominated by the Poor law and its ramifications, like the Settlement Act of 1697 which debarred strangers from entering a parish unless they had a Settlement Certificate in which their home parish agreed to take them back if they became in need of poor relief. Like the Workhouse, it was a hated institution that lasted into the 20th century."* [**Op. Cit.**, p. 31]

As Kropotkin stressed, *"it was the State which undertook to settle ... griefs"* between workers and bosses *"so as to guarantee a 'convenient' livelihood"* (convenient for the masters, of course). It also acted *"severely to prohibit all combinations ... under the menace of severe punishments ... Both in the town and in the village the State reigned over loose aggregations of individuals, and was ready to prevent by the most stringent measures the reconstitution of any sort of separate unions among them."* Workers who formed unions *"were prosecuted wholesale under the Master and Servant Act – workers being summarily arrested and condemned upon a mere complaint of misbehaviour lodged by the master. Strikes were suppressed in an autocratic way ... to say nothing of the military suppression of strike riots ... To practice mutual support under such circumstances was anything but an easy task ... After a long fight, which lasted over a hundred years, the right of combing together was conquered."* [**Mutual Aid**, p. 210 and p. 211] It took until 1813 until the laws regulating wages were repealed while the laws against combinations remained until 1825 (although that did not stop the Tolpuddle Martyrs being convicted of "administering an illegal oath" and deported to Tasmania in 1834). Fifty years later, the provisions of the statues of labourers which made it a civil action if the boss broke his contract but a criminal action if the worker broke it were repealed. Trade unions were given legal recognition in 1871 while, at the same time, another law limited what the workers could do in a strike or lockout. The British ideals of free trade never included freedom to organise.

(Luckily, by then, economists were at hand to explain to the workers that organising to demand higher wages was against their own self-interest. By a strange coincidence, all those laws against unions had actually **helped** the working class by enforcing the necessary conditions for perfect competition in the labour market! What are the chances of that? Of course, while considered undesirable from the perspective of mainstream economists – and, by strange co-incidence, the bosses – unions are generally not banned these days but rather heavily regulated. The freedom loving, deregulating Thatcherites passed six Employment Acts between 1980 and 1993 restricting industrial action by requiring pre-strike ballots, outlawing secondary action, restricting picketing and giving employers the right to seek injunctions where there is doubt about the legality of action – in the workers' interest, of course as, for some reason, politicians, bosses and economists have always known what's best for trade unionists rather than the trade unionists themselves. And if they objected, well, that was what the state was for.)

So to anyone remotely familiar with working class history the notion that there could be an economic theory which ignores power relations between bosses and workers is a particularly self-serving joke. Economic relations always have a power element, even if only to protect the property and power of the wealthy – the Invisible Hand always counts on a very visible Iron Fist when required. As Kropotkin memorably put it, the rise of capitalism has always seen the State *"tighten the screw for the worker"* and *"impos[ing] industrial serfdom."* So what the bourgeoisie *"swept away as harmful to industry"* was anything considered as *"useless and harmful"* but that class *"was at pains not to sweep away was the power of the State over industry, over the factory serf."* Nor should the role of public schooling be overlooked, within which *"the spirit of voluntary servitude was always cleverly cultivated in the minds of the young, and still is, in order to perpetuate the subjection of the individual to the State."* [**The State: Its Historic Role**, pp. 52-3 and p. 55] Such education also ensured that children become used to the obedience and boredom required for wage slavery.

Like the more recent case of fascist Chile, "free market" capitalism was imposed on the majority of society by an elite using the authoritarian state. This was recognised by Adam Smith when he opposed state intervention in **The Wealth of Nations**. In Smith's day, the government was openly and unashamedly an instrument of wealth owners. Less than 10 per cent of British men (and no women) had the right to vote. When Smith opposed state interference, he was opposing the imposition of wealth owners' interests on everybody else (and, of course, how "liberal", never mind "libertarian", is a political system in which the many follow the rules and laws set-down in the so-called interests of all by the few? As history shows, any minority given, or who take, such power **will** abuse it in their own interests). Today, the situation is reversed, with neo-liberals and right-"libertarians" opposing state interference in the economy (e.g. regulation of Big Business) so as to prevent the public from

having even a minor impact on the power or interests of the elite. The fact that "free market" capitalism always requires introduction by an authoritarian state should make all honest "Libertarians" ask: How "free" is the "free market"?

F.8.4 Aren't the enclosures a socialist myth?

The short answer is no, they are not. While a lot of historical analysis has been spent in trying to deny the extent and impact of the enclosures, the simple fact is (in the words of noted historian E.P. Thompson) enclosure *"was a plain enough case of class robbery, played according to the fair rules of property and law laid down by a parliament of property-owners and lawyers."* [**The Making of the English Working Class**, pp. 237-8]

The enclosures were one of the ways that the *"land monopoly"* was created. The land monopoly referred to feudal and capitalist property rights and ownership of land by (among others) the Individualist Anarchists. Instead of an *"occupancy and use"* regime advocated by anarchists, the land monopoly allowed a few to bar the many from the land – so creating a class of people with nothing to sell but their labour. While this monopoly is less important these days in developed nations (few people know how to farm) it was essential as a means of consolidating capitalism. Given the choice, most people preferred to become independent farmers rather than wage workers (see next section). As such, the *"land monopoly"* involves more than simply enclosing common land but also enforcing the claims of landlords to areas of land greater than they can work by their own labour.

Needless to say, the titles of landlords and the state are generally ignored by supporters of capitalism who tend to concentrate on the enclosure movement in order to downplay its importance. Little wonder, for it is something of an embarrassment for them to acknowledge that the creation of capitalism was somewhat less than "immaculate" – after all, capitalism is portrayed as an almost ideal society of freedom. To find out that an idol has feet of clay and that we are still living with the impact of its origins is something pro-capitalists must deny. So **are** the enclosures a socialist myth? Most claims that it is flow from the work of the historian J.D. Chambers' famous essay *"Enclosures and the Labour Supply in the Industrial Revolution."* [**Economic History Review**, 2nd series, no. 5, August 1953] In this essay, Chambers attempts to refute Karl Marx's account of the enclosures and the role it played in what Marx called *"primitive accumulation."*

We cannot be expected to provide an extensive account of the debate that has raged over this issue (Colin Ward notes that *"a later series of scholars have provided locally detailed evidence that reinforces"* the traditional socialist analysis of enclosure and its impact. [**Cotters and Squatters**, p. 143]). All we can do is provide a summary of the work of William Lazonick who presented an excellent reply to those who claim that the enclosures were an unimportant historical event (see his *"Karl Marx and Enclosures in England."* [**Review of Radical Political Economy**, no. 6, pp. 1-32]). Here, we draw upon his subsequent summarisation of his critique provided in his books **Competitive Advantage on the Shop Floor** and **Business Organisation and the Myth of the Market Economy**.

There are three main claims against the socialist account of the enclosures. We will cover each in turn.

Firstly, it is often claimed that the enclosures drove the uprooted cottager and small peasant into industry. However, this was never claimed. As Lazonick stresses while some economic historians *"have attributed to Marx the notion that, in one fell swoop, the enclosure movement drove the peasants off the soil and into the factories. Marx did not put forth such a simplistic view of the rise of a wage-labour force … Despite gaps and omission in Marx's historical analysis, his basic arguments concerning the creation of a landless proletariat are both important and valid. The transformations of social relations of production and the emergence of a wage-labour force in the agricultural sector were the critical preconditions for the Industrial Revolution."* [**Competitive Advantage on the Shop Floor**, pp. 12-3]

It is correct, as the critics of Marx stress, that the agricultural revolution associated with the enclosures **increased** the demand for farm labour as claimed by Chambers and others. And this is the whole point – enclosures created a pool of dispossessed labourers who had to sell their time/liberty to survive and whether this was to a landlord or an industrialist is irrelevant (as Marx himself stressed). As such, the account by Chambers, ironically, *"confirms the broad outlines of Marx's arguments"* as it implicitly acknowledges that *"over the long run the massive reallocation of access to land that enclosures entailed resulted in the separation of the mass of agricultural producers from the means of production."* So the *"critical transformation was not the level of agricultural employment before and after enclosure but the changes in employment relations caused by the reorganisation of landholdings and the reallocation of access to land."* [**Op. Cit.**, p. 29, pp. 29-30 and p. 30] Thus the key feature of the enclosures was that it created a supply for farm labour, a supply that had no choice but to work for another. Once freed from the land, these workers could later move to the towns in search for better work:

> *"Critical to the Marxian thesis of the origins of the industrial labour force is the transformation of the social relations of agriculture and the creation, in the first instance, of an agricultural wage-labour force that might eventually, perhaps through market incentives, be drawn into the industrial labour force."* [**Business Organisation and the Myth of the Market Economy**, p. 273]

In summary, when the critics argue that enclosures increased the demand for farm labour they are not refuting Marx but confirming his analysis. This is because the enclosures had resulted in a transformation in employment relations in agriculture with the peasants and farmers turned into wage workers for landlords (i.e., rural capitalists). For if wage labour is the defining characteristic of capitalism then it matters little if the boss is a farmer or an industrialist. This means that the *"critics, it turns out, have not differed substantially with Marx on the facts of agricultural transformation. But by ignoring the historical and theoretical significance of the resultant changes in the social relations of*

agricultural production, the critics have missed Marx's main point."* [**Competitive Advantage on the Shop Floor**, p. 30]

Secondly, it is argued that the number of small farm owners increased, or at least did not greatly decline, and so the enclosure movement was unimportant. Again, this misses the point. Small farm owners can still employ wage workers (i.e. become capitalist farmers as opposed to "yeomen" – an independent peasant proprietor). As Lazonick notes, *"[i]t is true that after 1750 some petty proprietors continued to occupy and work their own land. But in a world of capitalist agriculture, the yeomanry no longer played an important role in determining the course of capitalist agriculture. As a social class that could influence the evolution of British economy society, the yeomanry had disappeared."* Moreover, Chambers himself acknowledged that for the poor without legal rights in land, then enclosure injured them. For *"the majority of the agricultural population … had only customary rights. To argue that these people were not treated unfairly because they did not possess legally enforceable property rights is irrelevant to the fact that they were dispossessed by enclosures. Again, Marx's critics have failed to address the issue of the transformation of access to the means of production as a precondition for the Industrial Revolution."* [**Op. Cit.**, p. 32 and p. 31]

Thirdly, it is often claimed that it was population growth, rather than enclosures, that caused the supply of wage workers. So was population growth more important than enclosures? Given that enclosure impacted on the individuals and social customs of the time, it is impossible to separate the growth in population from the social context in which it happened. As such, the population argument ignores the question of whether the changes in society caused by enclosures and the rise of capitalism have an impact on the observed trends towards earlier marriage and larger families after 1750. Lazonick argues that *"[t]here is reason to believe that they did."* [**Op. Cit.**, p. 33] Overall, Lazonick notes that *"[i]t can even be argued that the changed social relations of agriculture altered the constraints on early marriage and incentives to childbearing that contributed to the growth in population. The key point is that transformations in social relations in production can influence, and have influenced, the quantity of wage labour supplied on both agricultural and industrial labour markets. To argue that population growth created the industrial labour supply is to ignore these momentous social transformations"* associated with the rise of capitalism. [**Business Organisation and the Myth of the Market Economy**, p. 273]

In other words, there is good reason to think that the enclosures, far from being some kind of socialist myth, in fact played a key role in the development of capitalism. As Lazonick notes, *"Chambers misunderstood"* the *"argument concerning the 'institutional creation' of a proletarianised (i.e. landless) workforce. Indeed, Chamber's own evidence and logic tend to support the Marxian [and anarchist!] argument, when it is properly understood."* [**Op. Cit.**, p. 273]

Lastly, it must be stressed that this process of dispossession happened over hundreds of years. It was not a case of simply driving peasants off their land and into factories. In fact, the first acts of expropriation took place in agriculture and created a rural proletariat which had to sell their labour/liberty to landlords and it was the second wave of enclosures, in the eighteenth and nineteenth centuries, that was closely connected with the process of industrialisation. The enclosure movement, moreover, was imposed in an uneven way, affecting on different areas at different times, depending on the power of peasant resistance and the nature of the crops being grown (and other objective conditions). Nor was it a case of an instant transformation – for a long period this rural proletariat was not totally dependent on wages, still having some access to the land and wastes for fuel and food. So while rural wage workers did exist throughout the period from 1350 to the 1600s, capitalism was not fully established in Britain yet as such people comprised only a small proportion of the labouring classes. The acts of enclosure were just one part of a long process by which a proletariat was created.

F.8.5 What about the lack of enclosures in the Americas?

The enclosure movement was but one part of a wide-reaching process of state intervention in creating capitalism. Moreover, it is just one way of creating the *"land monopoly"* which ensured the creation of a working class. The circumstances facing the ruling class in the Americas were distinctly different than in the Old World and so the "land monopoly" took a different form there. In the Americas, enclosures were unimportant as customary land rights did not really exist (at least once the Native Americans were eliminated by violence). Here the problem was that (after the original users of the land were eliminated) there were vast tracts of land available for people to use. Other forms of state intervention were similar to that applied under mercantilism in Europe (such as tariffs, government spending, use of unfree labour and state repression of workers and their organisations and so on). All had one aim, to enrich and power the masters and dispossess the actual producers of the means of life (land and means of production).

Unsurprisingly, due to the abundance of land, there was a movement towards independent farming in the early years of the American colonies and subsequent Republic and this pushed up the price of remaining labour on the market by reducing the supply. Capitalists found it difficult to find workers willing to work for them at wages low enough to provide them with sufficient profits. It was due to the difficulty in finding cheap enough labour that capitalists in America turned to slavery. All things being equal, wage labour **is** more productive than slavery but in early America all things were **not** equal. Having access to cheap (indeed, free) land meant that working people had a choice, and few desired to become wage slaves and so because of this, capitalists turned to slavery in the South and the "land monopoly" in the North.

This was because, in the words of Maurice Dobb, it *"became clear to those who wished to reproduce capitalist relations of production in the new country that the foundation-stone of their endeavour must be the restriction of land-ownership to a minority and the exclusion of the majority from any share in [productive] property."* [**Studies in Capitalist Development**, pp. 221-2] As one radical historian puts it, *"[w]hen land is 'free' or 'cheap'. as it was in different regions of the United States before the 1830s, there was no compulsion*

for farmers to introduce labour-saving technology. As a result, 'independent household production' ... hindered the development of capitalism ... [by] allowing large portions of the population to escape wage labour." [Charlie Post, *"The 'Agricultural Revolution' in the United States"*, pp. 216-228, **Science and Society**, vol. 61, no. 2, p. 221]

It was precisely this option (i.e. of independent production) that had to be destroyed in order for capitalist industry to develop. The state had to violate the holy laws of "supply and demand" by controlling the access to land in order to ensure the normal workings of "supply and demand" in the labour market (i.e. that the bargaining position favoured employer over employee). Once this situation became the typical one (i.e., when the option of self-employment was effectively eliminated) a more (protectionist based) "laissez-faire" approach could be adopted, with state action used indirectly to favour the capitalists and landlords (and readily available to protect private property from the actions of the dispossessed).

So how was this transformation of land ownership achieved?

Instead of allowing settlers to appropriate their own farms as was often the case before the 1830s, the state stepped in once the army had cleared out (usually by genocide) the original users. Its first major role was to enforce legal rights of property on unused land. Land stolen from the Native Americans was sold at auction to the highest bidders, namely speculators, who then sold it on to farmers. This process started right *"after the revolution, [when] huge sections of land were bought up by rich speculators"* and their claims supported by the law. [Howard Zinn, **A People's History of the United States**, p. 125] Thus land which should have been free was sold to land-hungry farmers and the few enriched themselves at the expense of the many. Not only did this increase inequality within society, it also encouraged the development of wage labour – having to pay for land would have ensured that many immigrants remained on the East Coast until they had enough money. Thus a pool of people with little option but to sell their labour was increased due to state protection of unoccupied land. That the land usually ended up in the hands of farmers did not (could not) countermand the shift in class forces that this policy created.

This was also the essential role of the various "Homesteading Acts" and, in general, the *"Federal land law in the 19th century provided for the sale of most of the public domain at public auction to the higher bidder ... Actual settlers were forced to buy land from speculators, at prices considerably above the federal minimal price."* (which few people could afford anyway). [Charlie Post, **Op. Cit.**, p. 222] This is confirmed by Howard Zinn who notes that 1862 Homestead Act *"gave 160 acres of western land, unoccupied and publicly owned, to anyone who would cultivate it for five years ... Few ordinary people had the $200 necessary to do this; speculators moved in and bought up much of the land. Homestead land added up to 50 million acres. But during the Civil War, over 100 million acres were given by Congress and the President to various railroads, free of charge."* [**Op. Cit.**, p. 233] Little wonder the Individualist Anarchists supported an *"occupancy and use"* system of land ownership as a key way of stopping capitalist and landlord usury as well as the development of capitalism itself.

This change in the appropriation of land had significant effects on agriculture and the desirability of taking up farming for immigrants.

As Post notes, *"[w]hen the social conditions for obtaining and maintaining possession of land change, as they did in the Midwest between 1830 and 1840, pursuing the goal of preserving [family ownership and control] … produced very different results. In order to pay growing mortgages, debts and taxes, family farmers were compelled to specialise production toward cash crops and to market more and more of their output."* [**Op. Cit.**, p. 221-2]

So, in order to pay for land which was formerly free, farmers got themselves into debt and increasingly turned to the market to pay it off. Thus, the *"Federal land system, by transforming land into a commodity and stimulating land speculation, made the Midwestern farmers dependent upon markets for the continual possession of their farms."* Once on the market, farmers had to invest in new machinery and this also got them into debt. In the face of a bad harvest or market glut, they could not repay their loans and their farms had to be sold to so do so. By 1880, 25% of all farms were rented by tenants, and the numbers kept rising. In addition, the *"transformation of social property relations in northern agriculture set the stage for the 'agricultural revolution' of the 1840s and 1850s … [R]ising debts and taxes forced Midwestern family farmers to compete as commodity producers in order to maintain their land-holding … The transformation … was the central precondition for the development of industrial capitalism in the United States."* [Charlie Post, **Op. Cit.**, p. 223 and p. 226]

It should be noted that feudal land owning was enforced in many areas of the colonies and the early Republic. Landlords had their holdings protected by the state and their demands for rent had the full backing of the state. This lead to numerous anti-rent conflicts. [Howard Zinn, **A People's History of the United States**, p. 84 and pp. 206-11] Such struggles helped end such arrangements, with landlords being "encouraged" to allow the farmers to buy the land which was rightfully theirs. The wealth appropriated from the farmers in the form of rent and the price of the land could then be invested in industry so transforming feudal relations on the land into capitalist relations in industry (and, eventually, back on the land when the farmers succumbed to the pressures of the capitalist market and debt forced them to sell).

This means that Murray Rothbard's comment that *"once the land was purchased by the settler, the injustice disappeared"* is nonsense – the injustice was transmitted to other parts of society and this, the wider legacy of the original injustice, lived on and helped transform society towards capitalism. In addition, his comment about *"the establishment in North America of a truly libertarian land system"* would be one the Individualist Anarchists of the period would have seriously disagreed with! [**The Ethics of Liberty**, p. 73] Rothbard, at times, seems to be vaguely aware of the importance of land as the basis of freedom in early America. For example, he notes in passing that *"the abundance of fertile virgin land in a vast territory enabled individualism to come to full flower in many areas."* [**Conceived in Liberty**, vol. 2, p. 186] Yet he did not ponder the transformation in social relationships which would result when that land was gone. In fact, he was blasé about it. *"If latecomers are worse off,"* he opined, *"well then that is their proper assumption of risk in this free and uncertain world. There is no longer a vast frontier in the United States, and there is no point crying over the fact."* [**The Ethics of Liberty**, p. 240] Unsurprisingly we also find Murray Rothbard

commenting that Native Americans *"lived under a collectivistic regime that, for land allocation, was scarcely more just than the English governmental land grab."* [**Conceived in Liberty**, vol. 1, p. 187] That such a regime made for **increased** individual liberty and that it was precisely the independence from the landlord and bosses this produced which made enclosure and state land grabs such appealing prospects for the ruling class was lost on him.

Unlike capitalist economists, politicians and bosses at the time, Rothbard seemed unaware that this *"vast frontier"* (like the commons) was viewed as a major problem for maintaining labour discipline and appropriate state action was taken to reduce it by restricting free access to the land in order to ensure that workers were dependent on wage labour. Many early economists recognised this and advocated such action. Edward Wakefield was typical when he complained that *"where land is cheap and all are free, where every one who so pleases can easily obtain a piece of land for himself, not only is labour dear, as respects the labourer's share of the product, but the difficulty is to obtain combined labour at any price."* This resulted in a situation were few *"can accumulate great masses of wealth"* as workers *"cease … to be labourers for hire; they … become independent landowners, if not competitors with their former masters in the labour market."* Unsurprisingly, Wakefield urged state action to reduce this option and ensure that labour become cheap as workers had little choice but to seek a master. One key way was for the state to seize the land and then sell it to the population. This would ensure that *"no labourer would be able to procure land until he had worked for money"* and this *"would produce capital for the employment of more labourers."* [quoted by Marx, **Op. Cit.**, , p. 935, p. 936 and p. 939] Which is precisely what did occur.

At the same time that it excluded the working class from virgin land, the state granted large tracts of land to the privileged classes: to land speculators, logging and mining companies, planters, railroads, and so on. In addition to seizing the land and distributing it in such a way as to benefit capitalist industry, the *"government played its part in helping the bankers and hurting the farmers; it kept the amount of money – based in the gold supply – steady while the population rose, so there was less and less money in circulation. The farmer had to pay off his debts in dollars that were harder to get. The bankers, getting loans back, were getting dollars worth more than when they loaned them out – a kind of interest on top of interest. That was why so much of the talk of farmers' movements in those days had to do with putting more money in circulation."* [Zinn, **Op. Cit.**, p. 278] This was the case with the Individualist Anarchists at the same time, we must add.

Overall, therefore, state action ensured the transformation of America from a society of independent workers to a capitalist one. By creating and enforcing the "land monopoly" (of which state ownership of unoccupied land and its enforcement of landlord rights were the most important) the state ensured that the balance of class forces tipped in favour of the capitalist class. By removing the option of farming your own land, the US government created its own form of enclosure and the creation of a landless workforce with little option but to sell its liberty on the "free market". They was nothing "natural" about it. Little wonder the Individualist Anarchist J.K. Ingalls attacked the "land monopoly" with the following words:

"The earth, with its vast resources of mineral wealth, its spontaneous productions and its fertile soil, the free gift of God and the common patrimony of mankind, has for long centuries been held in the grasp of one set of oppressors by right of conquest or right of discovery; and it is now held by another, through the right of purchase from them. All of man's natural possessions ... have been claimed as property; nor has man himself escaped the insatiate jaws of greed. The invasion of his rights and possessions has resulted ... in clothing property with a power to accumulate an income." [quoted by James Martin, **Men Against the State**, p. 142]

Marx, correctly, argued that *"the capitalist mode of production and accumulation, and therefore capitalist private property, have for their fundamental condition the annihilation of that private property which rests on the labour of the individual himself; in other words, the expropriation of the worker."* [**Capital**, Vol. 1, p. 940] He noted that to achieve this, the state is used:

"How then can the anti-capitalistic cancer of the colonies be healed? ... Let the Government set an artificial price on the virgin soil, a price independent of the law of supply and demand, a price that compels the immigrant to work a long time for wages before he can earn enough money to buy land, and turn himself into an independent farmer." [**Op. Cit.**, p. 938]

Moreover, tariffs were introduced with *"the objective of manufacturing capitalists artificially"* for the *"system of protection was an artificial means of manufacturing manufacturers, or expropriating independent workers, of capitalising the national means of production and subsistence, and of forcibly cutting short the transition ... to the modern mode of production,"* to capitalism [**Op. Cit.**, p. 932 and pp. 921-2]

So mercantilism, state aid in capitalist development, was also seen in the United States of America. As Edward Herman points out, the *"level of government involvement in business in the United States from the late eighteenth century to the present has followed a U-shaped pattern: There was extensive government intervention in the pre-Civil War period (major subsidies, joint ventures with active government participation and direct government production), then a quasi-laissez faire period between the Civil War and the end of the nineteenth century [a period marked by "the aggressive use of tariff protection" and state supported railway construction, a key factor in capitalist expansion in the USA], followed by a gradual upswing of government intervention in the twentieth century, which accelerated after 1930."* [**Corporate Control, Corporate Power**, p. 162]

Such intervention ensured that income was transferred from workers to capitalists. Under state protection, America industrialised by forcing the consumer to enrich the capitalists and increase their capital stock. *"According to one study, if the tariff had been removed in the 1830s 'about half the industrial sector of New England would have been bankrupted' ... the tariff became a near-permanent political institution representing government assistance to manufacturing. It kept price levels from being driven down by foreign competition*

and thereby shifted the distribution of income in favour of owners of industrial property to the disadvantage of workers and customers." This protection was essential, for the *"end of the European wars in 1814 ... reopened the United States to a flood of British imports that drove many American competitors out of business. Large portions of the newly expanded manufacturing base were wiped out, bringing a decade of near-stagnation."* Unsurprisingly, the *"era of protectionism began in 1816, with northern agitation for higher tariffs."* [Richard B. Du Boff, **Accumulation and Power**, p. 56, p. 14 and p. 55] Combined with ready repression of the labour movement and government "homesteading" acts (see section F.8.5), tariffs were the American equivalent of mercantilism (which, after all, was above all else a policy of protectionism, i.e. the use of government to stimulate the growth of native industry). Only once America was at the top of the economic pile did it renounce state intervention (just as Britain did, we must note).

This is **not** to suggest that government aid was limited to tariffs. The state played a key role in the development of industry and manufacturing. As John Zerzan notes, the *"role of the State is tellingly reflected by the fact that the 'armoury system' now rivals the older 'American system of manufactures' term as the more accurate to describe the new system of production methods"* developed in the early 1800s. [**Elements of Refusal**, p. 100] By the middle of the nineteenth century *"a distinctive 'American system of manufactures' had emerged ... The lead in technological innovation [during the US Industrial Revolution] came in armaments where assured government orders justified high fixed-cost investments in special-pursue machinery and managerial personnel. Indeed, some of the pioneering effects occurred in government-owned armouries."* Other forms of state aid were used, for example the textile industry *"still required tariffs to protect [it] from ... British competition."* [William Lazonick, **Competitive Advantage on the Shop Floor**, p. 218 and p. 219] The government also *"actively furthered this process [of 'commercial revolution'] with public works in transportation and communication."* In addition to this "physical" aid, *"state government provided critical help, with devices like the chartered corporation"* [Richard B. Du Boff, **Op. Cit.**, p. 15] As we noted in section B.2.5, there were changes in the legal system which favoured capitalist interests over the rest of society.

Nineteenth-century America also went in heavily for industrial planning – occasionally under that name but more often in the name of national defence. The military was the excuse for what is today termed rebuilding infrastructure, picking winners, promoting research, and co-ordinating industrial growth (as it still is, we should add). As Richard B. Du Boff points out, the "anti-state" backlash of the 1840s onwards in America was highly selective, as the general opinion was that *"[h]enceforth, if governments wished to subsidise private business operations, there would be no objection. But if public power were to be used to control business actions or if the public sector were to undertake economic initiatives on its own, it would run up against the determined opposition of private capital."* [**Op. Cit.**, p. 26] State intervention was not limited to simply reducing the amount of available land or enforcing a high tariff. *"Given the independent spirit of workers in the colonies, capital understood that great profits required the use of unfree labour."* [Michael Perelman, **The Invention of Capitalism**, p. 246] It was also applied in the labour market as well. Most obviously, it enforced the property rights of slave owners (until the civil war, produced when the pro-free trade policies of the South clashed with the pro-tariff desires of the capitalist North). The evil and horrors of slavery are well documented, as is its key role in building capitalism in America and elsewhere so we will concentrate on other forms of obviously unfree labour. Convict labour in Australia, for example, played an important role in the early days of colonisation while in America indentured servants played a similar role.

Indentured service was a system whereby workers had to labour for a specific number of years usually in return for passage to America with the law requiring the return of runaway servants. In theory, of course, the person was only selling their labour. In practice, indentured servants were basically slaves and the courts enforced the laws that made it so. The treatment of servants was harsh and often as brutal as that inflicted on slaves. Half the servants died in the first two years and unsurprisingly, runaways were frequent. The courts realised this was a problem and started to demand that everyone have identification and travel papers.

It should also be noted that the practice of indentured servants also shows how state intervention in one country can impact on others. This is because people were willing to endure indentured service in the colonies because of how bad their situation was at home. Thus the effects of primitive accumulation in Britain impacted on the development of America as most indentured servants were recruited from the growing number of unemployed people in urban areas there. Dispossessed from their land and unable to find work in the cities, many became indentured servants in order to take passage to the Americas. In fact, between one half to two thirds of all immigrants to Colonial America arrived as indentured servants and, at times, three-quarters of the population of some colonies were under contracts of indenture. That this allowed the employing class to overcome their problems in hiring "help" should go without saying, as should its impact on American inequality and the ability of capitalists and landlords to enrich themselves on their servants labour and to invest it profitably.

As well as allowing unfree labour, the American state intervened to ensure that the freedom of wage workers was limited in similar ways as we indicated in section F.8.3. *"The changes in social relations of production in artisan trades that took place in the thirty years after 1790,"* notes one historian, *"and the ... trade unionism to which ... it gave rise, both replicated in important respects the experience of workers in the artisan trades in Britain over a rather longer period ... The juridical responses they provoked likewise reproduced English practice. Beginning in 1806, American courts consciously seized upon English common law precedent to combat journeymen's associations."* Capitalists in this era tried to *"secure profit ... through the exercise of disciplinary power over their employees."* To achieve this *"employers made a bid for legal aid"* and it is here *"that the key to law's role in the process of creating an industrial economy in America lies."* As in the UK, the state invented laws and issued proclamations against workers' combinations, calling them conspiracies and prosecuting them as such. Trade unionists argued that laws which declared unions as illegal combinations should be repealed as against the Constitution of the USA while *"the specific cause of trademens protestations of their right to*

organise was, unsurprisingly, the willingness of local authorities to renew their resort to conspiracy indictments to countermand the growing power of the union movement." Using criminal conspiracy to counter combinations among employees was commonplace, with the law viewing a *"collective quitting of employment [as] a criminal interference"* and combinations to raise the rate of labour *"indictable at common law."* [Christopher L. Tomlins, **Law, Labor, and Ideology in the Early American Republic**, p. 113, p. 295, p. 159 and p. 213] By the end of the nineteenth century, state repression for conspiracy was replaced by state repression for acting like a trust while actual trusts were ignored and so laws, ostensibly passed (with the help of the unions themselves) to limit the power of capital, were turned against labour (this should be unsurprising as it was a capitalist state which passed them). [Howard Zinn, **A People's History of the United States**, p. 254]

Another key means to limit the freedom of workers was denying departing workers their wages for the part of the contract they had completed. This *"underscored the judiciary's tendency to articulate their approval"* of the hierarchical master/servant relationship in terms of its *"social utility: It was a necessary and desirable feature of the social organisation of work ... that the employer's authority be reinforced in this way."* Appeals courts held that *"an employment contract was an entire contract, and therefore that no obligation to pay wages existed until the employee had completed the agreed term."* Law suits *"by employers seeking damages for an employee's departure prior to the expiry of an agreed term or for other forms of breach of contract constituted one form of legally sanctioned economic discipline of some importance in shaping the employment relations of the nineteenth century."* Thus the boss could fire the worker without paying their wages while if the worker left the boss he would expect a similar outcome. This was because the courts had decided that the *"employer was entitled not only to receipt of the services contracted for in their entirety prior to payment but also to the obedience of the employee in the process of rendering them."* [Tomlins, **Op. Cit.**, pp. 278-9, p. 274, p. 272 and pp. 279-80] The ability of workers to seek self-employment on the farm or workplace or even better conditions and wages were simply abolished by employers turning to the state.

So, in summary, the state could remedy the shortage of cheap wage labour by controlling access to the land, repressing trade unions as conspiracies or trusts and ensuring that workers had to obey their bosses for the full term of their contract (while the bosses could fire them at will). Combine this with the extensive use of tariffs, state funding of industry and infrastructure among many other forms of state aid to capitalists and we have a situation were capitalism was imposed on a pre-capitalist nation at the behest of the wealthy elite by the state, as was the case with all other countries.

F.8.6 How did working people view the rise of capitalism?

The best example of how hated capitalism was can be seen by the rise and spread of the labour and socialist movements, in all their many forms, across the world. It is no coincidence that the development of capitalism also saw the rise of socialist theories. Nor was it a coincidence that the rising workers movement was subjected to extensive state repression, with unions, strikes and other protests being systematically repressed. Only once capital was firmly entrenched in its market position could economic power come to replace political force (although, of course, that always remained ready in the background to defend capitalist property and power).

The rise of unions, socialism and other reform movements and their repression was a feature of **all** capitalist countries. While America is sometime portrayed as an exception to this, in reality that country was also marked by numerous popular movements which challenged the rise of capitalism and the transformation of social relationships within the economy from artisanal self-management to capitalist wage slavery. As in other countries, the state was always quick to support the capitalist class against their rebellious wage slaves, using first conspiracy and then anti-trust laws against working class people and their organisations. So, in order to fully understand how different capitalism was from previous economic systems, we will consider early capitalism in the US, which for many right-"libertarians" is **the** example of the "capitalism-equals-freedom" argument.

Early America was pervaded by artisan production – individual ownership of the means of production. Unlike capitalism, this system is **not** marked by the separation of the worker from the means of life. Most people did not have to work for another, and so did not. As Jeremy Brecher notes, in 1831 the *"great majority of Americans were farmers working their own land, primarily for their own needs. Most of the rest were self-employed artisans, merchants, traders, and professionals. Other classes – employees and industrialists in the North, slaves and planters in the South – were relatively small. The great majority of Americans were independent and free from anybody's command."* [**Strike!**, p. xxi] So the availability of land ensured that in America, slavery and indentured servants were the only means by which capitalists could get people to work for them. This was because slaves and servants were not able to leave their masters and become self-employed farmers or artisans. As noted in the last section this material base was, ironically, acknowledged by Rothbard but the implications for freedom when it disappeared was not. While he did not ponder what would happen when that supply of land ended and whether the libertarian aspects of early American society would survive, contemporary politicians, bosses, and economists did. Unsurprisingly, they turned to the state to ensure that capitalism grew on the grave of artisan and farmer property.

Toward the middle of the 19th century the economy began to change. Capitalism began to be imported into American society as the infrastructure was improved by state aid and tariff walls were constructed which allowed home-grown manufacturing companies to develop. Soon, due to (state-supported) capitalist competition, artisan production was replaced by wage labour. Thus "evolved" modern capitalism. Many workers understood, resented, and opposed their increasing subjugation to their employers, which could not be reconciled with the principles of freedom and economic independence that had marked American life and had sunk deeply into mass consciousness during the days of the early economy. In 1854, for example, a group of skilled piano makers hoped that *"the day is far distant when they [wage earners] will so far forget what is due to manhood as to glory in a system forced upon them by their necessity and in opposition to their feelings of independence and self-respect. May the piano trade be spared such exhibitions of the degrading power of the day [wage] system."* [quoted by Brecher and Costello, **Common Sense for Hard Times**, p. 26] Clearly the working class did not consider working for a daily wage, in contrast to working for themselves and selling their own product, to be a step forward for liberty or individual dignity. The difference between selling the product of one's labour and selling one's labour (i.e. oneself) was seen and condemned (*"[w]hen the producer ... sold his product, he retained himself. But when he came to sell his labour, he sold himself ... the extension [of wage labour] to the skilled worker was regarded by him as a symbol of a deeper change."* [Norman Ware, **The Industrial Worker, 1840-1860**, p. xiv]). Indeed, one group of workers argued that they were *"slaves in the strictest sense of the word"* as they had *"to toil from the rising of the sun to the going down of the same for our masters – aye, masters, and for our daily bread."* [quoted by Ware, **Op. Cit.**, p. 42] Another group argued that *"the factory system contains in itself the elements of slavery, we think no sound reasoning can deny, and everyday continues to add power to its incorporate sovereignty, while the sovereignty of the working people decreases in the same degree."* [quoted by Brecher and Costello, **Op. Cit.**, p. 29] For working class people, free labour meant something radically different than that subscribed to by employers and economists. For workers, free labour meant economic independence through the ownership of productive equipment or land. For bosses, it meant workers being free of any alternative to consenting to authoritarian organisations within their workplaces – if that required state intervention (and it did), then so be it.

The courts, of course, did their part in ensuring that the law reflected and bolstered the power of the boss rather than the worker. *"Acting piecemeal,"* summarises Tomlins, *"the law courts and law writers of the early republic built their approach to the employment relationship on the back of English master/servant law. In the process, they vested in the generality of nineteenth-century employers a controlling authority over the employees founded upon the pre-industrial master's claim to property in his servant's personal services."* Courts were *"having recourse to master/servant's language of power and control"* as the *"preferred strategy for dealing with the employment relation"* and so advertised their conclusion that *"employment relations were properly to be conceived of as generically hierarchical."* [**Op. Cit.**, p. 231 and p. 225] As we noted in the last section the courts, judges and jurists acted to outlaw unions as conspiracies and force workers to work the full length of their contracts. In addition, they also reduced employer liability in industrial accidents (which, of course, helped lower the costs of investment as well as operating costs).

Artisans and farmers correctly saw this as a process of downward mobility toward wage labour and almost as soon as there were wage workers, there were strikes, machine breaking, riots, unions and many other forms of resistance. John Zerzan's argument that a *"relentless assault on the worker's historical rights to free time, self-education, craftsmanship, and play was at the heart of the rise of the factory system"* is extremely accurate. [**Elements of Refusal**, p. 105] And it was an assault that workers resisted with all their might. In response to being subjected to the wage labour, workers rebelled and tried to organise themselves to fight the powers that be and to replace the system with a co-operative one. As the printer's union argued, its members *"regard such an organisation [a union] not only as an agent of immediate relief, but also as an essential to the ultimate destruction of those unnatural relations at present subsisting between the interests of the employing and the employed classes … when labour determines to sell itself no longer to speculators, but to become its own employer, to own and enjoy itself and the fruit thereof, the necessity for scales of prices will have passed away and labour will be forever rescued from the control of the capitalist."* [quoted by Brecher and Costello, **Op. Cit.**, pp. 27-28]

Little wonder, then, why wage labourers considered capitalism as a modified form of slavery and why the term *"wage slavery"* became so popular in the labour and anarchist movements. It was just reflecting the feelings of those who experienced the wages system at first hand and who created the labour and socialist movements in response. As labour historian Norman Ware notes, the *"term 'wage slave' had a much better standing in the forties [of the 19th century] than it has today. It was not then regarded as an empty shibboleth of the soap-box orator. This would suggest that it has suffered only the normal degradation of language, has become a **cliché**, not that it is a grossly misleading characterisation."* [**Op. Cit.**, p. xvf] It is no coincidence that, in America, the first manufacturing complex in Lowell was designed to symbolise its goals and its hierarchical structure nor that its design was emulated by many of the penitentiaries, insane asylums, orphanages and reformatories of the period. [Bookchin, **The Ecology of Freedom**, p. 392]

These responses of workers to the experience of wage labour is important as they show that capitalism is by no means "natural." The fact is the first generation of workers tried to avoid wage labour if at all possible – they hated the restrictions of freedom it imposed upon them. Unlike the bourgeoisie, who positively eulogised the discipline they imposed on others. As one put it with respect to one corporation in Lowell, New England, the factories at Lowell were *"a new world, in its police it is **imperium in imperio**. It has been said that an absolute despotism, justly administered … would be a perfect government … For at the same time that it is an absolute despotism, it is a most perfect democracy. Any of its subjects can depart from it at pleasure … Thus all the philosophy of mind which enter vitally into government by the people … is combined with a set of rule which the operatives have no voice in forming or administering, yet of a nature not merely perfectly just, but human, benevolent, patriarchal in a high degree."* Those actually subjected to this *"benevolent"* dictatorship had a somewhat different

perspective. Workers, in contrast, were perfectly aware that wage labour was wage slavery – that they were decidedly **unfree** during working hours and subjected to the will of another. The workers therefore attacked capitalism precisely because it was despotism (*"monarchical principles on democratic soil"*) and thought they *"who work in the mills ought to own them."* Unsurprisingly, when workers did revolt against the benevolent despots, the workers noted how the bosses responded by marking *"every person with intelligence and independence … He is a suspected individual and must be either got rid of or broken in. Hundreds of honest labourers have been dismissed from employment … because they have been suspected of knowing their rights and daring to assert them."* [quoted by Ware, **Op. Cit.**, p. 78, p. 79 and p. 110]

While most working class people now are accustomed to wage labour (while often hating their job) the actual process of resistance to the development of capitalism indicates well its inherently authoritarian nature and that people were not inclined to accept it as "economic freedom." Only once other options were closed off and capitalists given an edge in the "free" market by state action did people accept and become accustomed to wage labour. As E. P. Thompson notes, for British workers at the end of the 18th and beginning of the 19th centuries, the *"gap in status between a 'servant,' a hired wage-labourer subject to the orders and discipline of the master, and an artisan, who might 'come and go' as he pleased, was wide enough for men to shed blood rather than allow themselves to be pushed from one side to the other. And, in the value system of the community, those who resisted degradation were in the right."* [**The Making of the English Working Class**, p. 599]

Opposition to wage labour and factory fascism was/is widespread and seems to occur wherever it is encountered. *"Research has shown"*, summarises William Lazonick, *"that the 'free-born Englishman' of the eighteenth century – even those who, by force of circumstance, had to submit to agricultural wage labour – tenaciously resisted entry into the capitalist workshop."* [**Competitive Advantage on the Shop Floor**, p. 37] British workers shared the dislike of wage labour of their American cousins. A *"Member of the Builders' Union"* in the 1830s argued that the trade unions *"will not only strike for less work, and more wages, but will ultimately **abolish wages**, become their own masters and work for each other; labour and capital will no longer be separate but will be indissolubly joined together in the hands of workmen and work-women."* [quoted by E. P. Thompson, **Op. Cit.**, p. 912] This perspective inspired the **Grand National Consolidated Trades Union** of 1834 which had the *"two-fold purpose of syndicalist unions – the protection of the workers under the existing system and the formation of the nuclei of the future society"* when the unions *"take over the whole industry of the country."* [Geoffrey Ostergaard, **The Tradition of Workers' Control**, p. 133] As Thompson noted, *"industrial syndicalism"* was a major theme of this time in the labour movement. *"When Marx was still in his teens,"* he noted, British trade unionists had *"developed, stage by stage, a theory of syndicalism"* in which the *"unions themselves could solve the problem of political power"* along with wage slavery. This vision was lost *"in the terrible defeats of 1834 and 1835."* [**Op. Cit.**, p. 912 and p. 913] In France, the mutualists of Lyons had come to the same conclusions, seeking *"the formation of a series of co-operative associations"* which would *"return to the workers control of their industry."* Proudhon would take up this theme, as would the anarchist movement he helped create. [K. Steven Vincent, **Pierre-Joseph Proudhon and the Rise of French Republican Socialism**, pp. 162-3] Similar movements and ideas developed elsewhere, as capitalism was imposed (subsequent developments were obviously influenced by the socialist ideas which had arisen earlier and so were more obviously shaped by anarchist and Marxist ideas).

This is unsurprising, the workers then, who had not been swallowed up whole by the industrial revolution, could make critical comparisons between the factory system and what preceded it. *"Today, we are so accustomed to this method of production [capitalism] and its concomitant, the wage system, that it requires quite an effort of imagination to appreciate the significance of the change in terms of the lives of ordinary workers ... the worker became **alienated** ... from the means of production and the products of his labour ... In these circumstances, it is not surprising that the new socialist theories proposed an alternative to the capitalist system which would avoid this alienation."* While wage slavery may seem "natural" today, the first generation of wage labourers saw the transformation of the social relationships they experienced in work, from a situation in which they controlled their own work (and so themselves) to one in which **others** controlled them, and they did not like it. However, while many modern workers instinctively hate wage labour and having bosses, without the awareness of some other method of working, many put up with it as "inevitable." The first generation of wage labourers had the awareness of something else (although a flawed and limited something else as it existed in a hierarchical and class system) and this gave then a deep insight into the nature of capitalism and produced a deeply radical response to it and its authoritarian structures. Anarchism (like other forms of socialism) was born of the demand for liberty and resistance to authority which capitalism had provoked in its wage slaves. With our support for workers' self-management of production, *"as in so many others, the anarchists remain guardians of the libertarian aspirations which moved the first rebels against the slavery inherent in the capitalist mode of production."* [Ostergaard, **Op. Cit.**, p. 27 and p. 90]

State action was required produce and protect the momentous changes in social relations which are central to the capitalist system. However, once capital **has** separated the working class from the means of life, then it no longer had to rely as much on state coercion. With the choice now between wage slavery or starving, then the appearance of voluntary choice could be maintained as economic power was/is usually effective enough to ensure that state violence could be used as a last resort. Coercive practices are still possible, of course, but market forces are usually sufficient as the market is usually skewed against the working class. However, the role of the state remains a key to understanding capitalism as a system rather than just specific periods of it. This is because, as we stressed in section D.1, state action is not associated only with the past, with the transformation from feudalism to capitalism. It happens today and it will continue to happen as long as capitalism continues.

Far from being a "natural" development, then, capitalism was imposed on a society by state action, by and on behalf of ruling elites. Those working class people alive at the time viewed it as *"unnatural relations"* and organised to overcome it. It is from such movements that all the many forms of socialism sprang, including anarchism. This is the case with the European anarchism associated with Proudhon, Bakunin and Kropotkin as well as the American individualist anarchism of Warren and Tucker. The links between anarchism and working class rebellion against the autocracy of capital and the state are reflected not only in our theory and history, but also in our anarchist symbols. The Black Flag, for example, was first raised by rebel artisans in France and its association with labour insurrection was the reason why anarchists took it up as our symbol (see the appendix on "The Symbols of Anarchy"). So given both the history of capitalism and anarchism, it becomes obvious any the latter has always opposed the former. It is why anarchists today still seek to encourage the desire and hope for political **and** economic freedom rather than the changing of masters we have under capitalism. Anarchism will continue as long as these feelings and hopes still exist and they will remain until such time as we organise and abolish capitalism and the state.

Appendix
The Symbols of Anarchy

Appendix – The Symbols of Anarchy 550

Introduction

Introduction 550
1 What is the history of the Black Flag? 550
2 Why the red-and-black flag? 554
3 Where does the circled-A come from? 555

Introduction

Anarchism has always stood deliberately for a broad, and at times vague, political platform. The reasoning is sound; blueprints create rigid dogma and stifle the creative spirit of revolt. Along the same lines and resulting in the same problems, Anarchists have rejected the "disciplined" leadership that is found in many other political groupings on the Left. The reasoning for this is also sound; leadership based on authority is inherently hierarchical.

It seems to follow logically that since Anarchists have shied away from anything static, that we would also shy away from the importance of symbols and icons. Yet the fact is Anarchists have used symbolism in our revolt against the State and Capital, the most famous of which are the circled-A, the black flag and the red-and-black flag. This appendix tries to show the history of these three iconic symbols and indicate why they were taken up by anarchists to represent our ideas and movement.

Ironically enough, one of the original anarchist symbols was the *red* flag. As anarchist Communard Louise Michel put it, *"Lyon, Marseille, Narbonne, all had their own Communes, and like ours [in Paris], theirs too were drowned in the blood of revolutionaries. That is why our flags are red. Why are our red banners so terribly frightening to those persons who have caused them to be stained that colour?"* [**The Red Virgin: Memoirs of Louise Michel**, p. 65] March 18th, 1877, saw Kropotkin participate in a protest march in Berne which involved the anarchists *"carrying the red flag in honour of the Paris Commune"* for *"in Switzerland federal law prohibited public display of the red flag."* [Martin A. Miller, **Kropotkin**, p. 137] Anarchist historians Nicolas Walter and Heiner Becker note that *"Kropotkin always preferred the red flag."* [Peter Kropotkin, **Act for Yourselves**, p. 128] On Labour Day in 1899, Emma Goldman gave lectures to miners in Spring Valley, Illinois, which ended in a demonstration which she headed *"carrying a large red flag."* [**Living My Life**, vol. 1, p. 245] According to historian Caroline Waldron Merithew, the 300 marchers *"defied police orders to haul down the 'red flag of anarchy.'"* [**Anarchist Motherhood**, p. 236]

This should be unsurprising as anarchism is a form of socialism and came out of the general socialist and labour movements. Common roots would imply common imagery. However, as mainstream socialism developed in the nineteenth century into either reformist social democracy or the state socialism of the revolutionary Marxists, anarchists developed their own images of revolt based upon those raised by working class people in struggle. As will be shown, they come from the revolutionary anarchism most directly associated with the wider labour and socialist movements, i.e., the dominant, mainstream social anarchist tradition. As Nicholas Walter put it:

"[The] serious study of anarchism should be based on fact rather than fantasy, and concentrate on people and movements that actually used the word. However old and wide the ideas of anarchism may be ... no one called himself an anarchist before [Proudhon in] 1840, and no movement called itself anarchist before the 1870s.... The actual anarchist movement was founded ... by the anti-authoritarian sections of the First International ... This was certainly the first anarchist movement, and this movement was certainly based on a libertarian version of the concept of the class struggle." [**The Anarchist Past and other essays**, pp. 60-1]

Unsurprisingly, the first anarchist symbols reflected the origins and ideas of this class struggle movement. Both the black and red-and-black flags were first used by revolutionary anarchists. The black flag was popularised in the 1880s by Louise Michel, a leading French communist-anarchist militant. From Europe it spread to America when the communist-anarchists of the **International Working People's Association** raised it in their struggle against capitalism before being taken up by other revolutionary class struggle anarchists across the globe. The red-and-black flag was first used by the Italian section of the First International and this had been the first to move from collectivist to communist-anarchism in October 1876. [Nunzio Pernicone, **Italian Anarchism, 1864-1892**, p. 111] From there, it spread to Mexico and was used by anarchist labour militants there before being re-invented by the Spanish anarcho-syndicalists in the 1930s. Like anarchism itself, the anarchist flags are a product of the social struggle against capitalism and statism.

We would like to point out that this appendix is partly based on Jason Wehling's 1995 essay **Anarchism and the History of the Black Flag**. Needless to say, this appendix does not cover all anarchists symbols. For example, recently the red-and-black flag has become complemented by the green-and-black flag of eco-anarchism (the symbolism of the green should need no explanation). Other libertarian popular symbols include the IWW inspired *"Wildcat"* (representing, of course, the spontaneity, direct action, solidarity and militancy of a wildcat strike), the *"Black Rose"* (inspired, no doubt, by the demand of striking IWW women workers in Lawrence, 1912, for not only bread, but for roses too) and the ironic *"little black bomb"* (among others). Here we concentrate on the three most famous ones.

1 What is the history of the Black Flag?

As is well known, the black flag is the symbol of anarchism. Howard Ehrlich has a great passage in his book **Reinventing Anarchy, Again** on why anarchists use it. It is worth quoting at length:

"Why is our flag black? Black is a shade of negation. The black flag is the negation of all flags. It is a negation of nationhood which puts the human race against itself and denies the unity of all humankind. Black is a mood of anger and outrage at all the hideous crimes against

humanity perpetrated in the name of allegiance to one state or another. It is anger and outrage at the insult to human intelligence implied in the pretences, hypocrisies, and cheap chicaneries of governments.... Black is also a colour of mourning; the black flag which cancels out the nation also mourns its victims the countless millions murdered in wars, external and internal, to the greater glory and stability of some bloody state. It mourns for those whose labour is robbed (taxed) to pay for the slaughter and oppression of other human beings. It mourns not only the death of the body but the crippling of the spirit under authoritarian and hierarchic systems; it mourns the millions of brain cells blacked out with never a chance to light up the world. It is a colour of inconsolable grief.

"But black is also beautiful. It is a colour of determination, of resolve, of strength, a colour by which all others are clarified and defined. Black is the mysterious surrounding of germination, of fertility, the breeding ground of new life which always evolves, renews, refreshes, and reproduces itself in darkness. The seed hidden in the earth, the strange journey of the sperm, the secret growth of the embryo in the womb all these the blackness surrounds and protects.

"So black is negation, is anger, is outrage, is mourning, is beauty, is hope, is the fostering and sheltering of new forms of human life and relationship on and with this earth. The black flag means all these things. We are proud to carry it, sorry we have to, and look forward to the day when such a symbol will no longer be necessary." ["Why the Black Flag?", Howard Ehrlich (ed.), **Reinventing Anarchy, Again**, pp. 31-2]

Here we discuss when and why anarchists first took up the black flag as our symbol.

There are ample accounts of the use of black flags by anarchists. Probably the most famous was Nestor Makhno's partisans during the Russia Revolution. Under the black banner, his army routed a dozen armies and kept a large portion of the Ukraine free from concentrated power for a good couple of years. On the black flag was embroidered *"Liberty or Death"* and *"The Land to the Peasant, The Factories to the Workers."* [Voline, **The Unknown Revolution**, pp. 607-10] In 1925, the Japanese anarchists formed the **Black Youth League** and, in 1945, when the anarchist federation reformed, their journal was named **Kurohata** (**Black Flag**). [Peter Marshall, **Demanding the Impossible**, pp. 525-6] In 1968, students carried black (and red) flags during the street fighting and General Strike in France, bringing the resurgence of anarchism in the 1960s into the view of the general public. The same year saw the black flag being raised at the American **Students for a Democratic Society** national convention. Two years later the British based magazine **Black Flag** was started and is still going strong. At the turn of the 21st century, the Black Flag was at the front of the so-called anti-globalisation protests. Today, if you go to any sizeable demonstration you will usually see the Black Flag raised by the anarchists present.

However, the anarchists' black flag originated much earlier than this. Louise Michel, famous participant in the Paris Commune of 1871, was instrumental in popularising the use of the black flag in anarchist circles. At a March 18th public meeting in 1882 to commemorate the Paris Commune she proclaimed that the *"red flag was no longer appropriate; [the anarchists] should raise the black flag of misery."* [Edith Thomas, **Louise Michel**, p. 191] The following year she put her words into action. According to anarchist historian George Woodcock, Michel flew the black flag on March 9, 1883, during a demonstration of the unemployed in Paris, France. An open air meeting of the unemployed was broken up by the police and around 500 demonstrators, with Michel at the front carrying a black flag and shouting *"Bread, work, or lead!"* marched off towards the Boulevard Saint-Germain. The crowd pillaged three baker's shops before the police attacked. Michel was arrested and sentenced to six years solitary confinement. Public pressure soon forced the granting of an amnesty. [**Anarchism**, pp. 251-2] August the same year saw the publication of the anarchist paper **Le Drapeau Noir** (**The Black Flag**) in Lyon which suggests that it had become a popular symbol within anarchist circles. [*"Sur la Symbolique anarchiste"*, **Bulletin du CIRA**, no. 62, p. 2] However, anarchists had been using red-and-black flags a number of years previously (see next section) so Michel's use of the colour black was not totally without precedence.

Not long after, the black flag made its way to America. Paul Avrich reports that on November 27, 1884, it was displayed in Chicago at an anarchist demonstration. According to Avrich, August Spies, one of the Haymarket martyrs, *"noted that this was the first occasion on which [the black flag] had been unfurled on American soil."* By January the following year, *"[s]treet parades and mass outdoor demonstrations, with red and black banners ... were the most dramatic form of advertisement"* for the revolutionary anarchist movement in America. April 1885 saw Lucy Parsons and Lizzie Holmes at the head of a protest march *"each bearing a flag, one black, the other red."* [**The Haymarket Tragedy**, p. 145, pp. 81-2 and p. 147] The black flag continued to be used by anarchists in America, with one being seized by police at an anarchist organised demonstration for the unemployed in 1893 at which Emma Goldman spoke. [**Emma Goldman: A Documentary History of the American Years**, vol. 1, p. 144] Twenty one years later, Alexander Berkman reported on another anarchist inspired unemployed march in New York which raised the black flag in *"menacing defiance in the face of parasitic contentment and self-righteous arrogance"* of the *"exploiters and well-fed idlers."* [*"The Movement of the Unemployed"*, **Anarchy! An Anthology of Emma Goldman's Mother Earth**, p. 341]

It seems that black flags did not appear in Russia until the founding of the **Chernoe Znamia** (**"black banner"**) movement in 1905. With the defeat of that year's revolution, anarchism went underground again. The black flag, like anarchism in general, re-emerged during the 1917 revolution. Anarchists in Petrograd took part in the February demonstrations which brought down Tsarism carrying black flags with *"Down with authority and capitalism!"* on them. As part of their activity, anarchists organised armed detachments in most towns and cities called *"Black Guards"* to defend themselves against counter-revolutionary attempts by the provisional government. As noted above, the Makhnovists fought Bolshevik and White dictatorship under black flags. On a more dreary note, February 1921 saw the end of black flags in Soviet Russia. That month saw Peter Kropotkin's funeral take place in Moscow. Twenty thousand people marched in his honour, carrying black banners that read: *"Where there is authority there is no freedom."* [Paul Avrich, **The Russian Anarchists**, p. 44, p. 124, p. 183 and p. 227] Only two weeks after Kropotkin's funeral march, the Kronstadt rebellion broke out and anarchism was erased from Soviet Russia for good. With the end of Stalinism, anarchism with its black flag re-emerged all across Eastern Europe, including Russia.

While the events above are fairly well known, as has been related, the exact origin of the black flag is not. What is known is that a large number of Anarchist groups in the early 1880s adopted titles associated with black. In July of 1881, the Black International was founded in London. This was an attempt to reorganise the Anarchist wing of the recently dissolved First International. In October 1881, a meeting in Chicago lead to the **International Working People's Association** being formed in North America. This organisation, also known as the **Black International**, affiliated to the London organisation. [Woodcock, **Op. Cit.**, pp. 212-4 and p. 393] These two conferences were immediately followed by Michel's demonstration (1883) and the black flags in Chicago (1884).

Thus it was around the early 1880s that anarchism and the black flag became inseparably linked. Avrich, for example, states that in 1884, the black flag *"was the new anarchist emblem."* [**The Haymarket Tragedy**, p. 144] In agreement, Murray Bookchin reports that *"in later years, the Anarchists were to adopt the black flag"* when speaking of the Spanish Anarchist movement in 1870. [**The Spanish Anarchists**, p. 57] Walter and Heiner also note that *"it was adopted by the anarchist movement during the 1880s."* [Kropotkin, **Act for Yourselves**, p. 128]

Now the question becomes why, exactly, black was chosen. The Chicago *"Alarm"* stated that the black flag is *"the fearful symbol of hunger, misery and death."* [quoted by Avrich, **Op. Cit.**, p. 144] Bookchin asserts that anarchists were *"to adopt the black flag as a symbol of the workers misery and as an expression of their anger and bitterness."* [**Op. Cit.**, p. 57] Historian Bruce C. Nelson also notes that the black flag was considered *"the emblem of hunger"* when it was unfurled in Chicago in 1884. [**Beyond the Martyrs**, p. 141 and p. 150] While it *"was interpreted in anarchist circles as the symbol of death, hunger and misery"* it was *"also said to be the 'emblem of retribution'"* and in a labour procession in Cincinnati in January 1885, *"it was further acknowledged to be the banner of working-class intransigence, as demonstrated by the words 'No Quarter' inscribed on it."* [Donald C. Hodges, **Sandino's Communism**, p. 21] For Berkman, it was the *"symbol of starvation and desperate misery."* [**Op. Cit.**, p. 341] Louise Michel stated that the *"black flag is the flag of strikes and the flag of those who are hungry."* [**Op. Cit.**, p. 168]

Along these lines, Albert Meltzer maintains that the association between the black flag and working class revolt *"originated in Rheims [France] in 1831 ('Work or Death') in an unemployed demonstration."* [**The Anarcho-Quiz Book**, p. 49] He went on to assert that it was Michel's action in 1883 that solidified the association. The links from revolts in France to anarchism are even stronger. As Murray Bookchin records, in Lyon *"[i]n 1831, the silk-*

weaving artisans ... rose in armed conflict to gain a better **tarif**, or contract, from the merchants. For a brief period they actually took control of the city, under red and black flags – which made their insurrection a memorable event in the history of revolutionary symbols. Their use of the word **mutuelisme** to denote the associative disposition of society that they preferred made their insurrection a memorable event in the history of anarchist thought as well, since Proudhon appears to have picked up the word from them during his brief stay in the city in 1843-4."* [**The Third Revolution**, vol. 2, p. 157] Sharif Gemie confirms this, noting that a police report sent to the Lyon prefect that said: *"The silk-weavers of the Croix-Rousse have decided that tomorrow they will go down to Lyon, carrying a black flag, calling for work or death."* The revolt saw the black flag raised:

> *"At eleven a.m. the silk-weavers' columns descended the slops of the Croix-Rousse. Some carried black flags, the colour of mourning and a reminder of their economic distress. Others pushed loaves of bread on the bayonets of their guns and held them aloft. The symbolic force of this action was reinforced by a repeatedly-shouted slogan: 'bread or lead!': in other words, if they were not given bread which they could afford, then they were prepared to face bullets. At some point during the rebellion, a more eloquent expression was devised: 'Vivre en travaillant ou mourir en combattant!' – 'Live working or die by fighting!'. Some witnesses report seeing this painted on a black flag."* [Sharif Gemie, **French Revolutions, 1815-1914**, pp. 52-53]

Kropotkin himself states that its use continued in the French labour movement after this uprising. He notes that the Paris Workers *"raised in June [1848] their black flag of 'Bread or Labour'"* [**Act for Yourselves**, p. 100] Black flags were also hung from windows in Paris on the 1st of March, 1871, in defiance of the Prussians marching through the city after their victory in the Franco-Prussian War. [Stewart Edwards, **The Communards of Paris, 1871**, p. 25]

The use of the black flag by anarchists, therefore, is an expression of their roots and activity in the labour movement in Europe, particularly in France. The anarchist adoption of the black flag by the movement in the 1880s reflects its use as *"the traditional symbol of hunger, poverty and despair"* and that it was *"raised during popular risings in Europe as a sign of no surrender and no quarter."* [Walter and Becker, **Act for Yourselves**, p. 128] This is confirmed by the first anarchist journal to be called **Black Flag**: *"On the heights of the city [of Lyon] in la Croix-Rousse and Vaise, workers, pushed by hunger, raised for the first time this sign of mourning and revenge [the black flag], and made therefore of it the emblem of workers' demands."* [**Le Drapeau Noir**, no. 1, 12th August 1883] This was echoed by Louise Michel:

> *"How many wrathful people, young people, will be with us when the red and black banners wave in the wind of anger! What a tidal wave it will be when the red and black banners rise around the old wreck!*

"The red banner, which has always stood for liberty, frightens the executioners because it is so red with our blood. The black flag, with layers of blood upon it from those who wanted to live by working or die by fighting, frightens those who want to live off the work of others. Those red and black banners wave over us mourning our dead and wave over our hopes for the dawn that is breaking." [**The Red Virgin: Memoirs of Louise Michel**, pp. 193-4]

The mass slaughter of Communards by the French ruling class after the fall of the Paris Commune of 1871 could also explain the use of the black flag by anarchists at this time. Black *"is the colour of mourning [at least in Western cultures], it symbolises our mourning for dead comrades, those whose lives were taken by war, on the battlefield (between states) or in the streets and on the picket lines (between classes)."* [Chico, "letters", **Freedom**, vol. 48, No. 12, p. 10] Given the 25 000 dead in the Commune, many of them anarchists and libertarian socialists, the use of the black flag by anarchists afterwards would make sense. Sandino, the Nicaraguan libertarian socialist (whose use of the red-and-black colours we discuss below) also said that black stood for mourning (*"Red for liberty; black for mourning; and the skull for a struggle to the death"* [Donald C. Hodges, **Sandino's Communism**, p. 24]).

Regardless of other meanings, it is clear that anarchists took up the black flag in the 1880s because it was, like the red flag, a recognised symbol of working class resistance to capitalism. This is unsurprising given the nature of anarchist politics. Just as anarchists base our ideas on actual working class practice, we would also base our symbols on those created by that self-activity. For example, Proudhon as well as taking the term *"mutualism"* from radical workers also argued that co-operative *"labour associations"* had *"spontaneously, without prompting and without capital been formed in Paris and in Lyon ... the proof of it [mutualism, the organisation of credit and labour] ... lies in current practice, revolutionary practice."* [**No Gods, No Masters**, vol. 1, pp. 59-60] He considered his ideas, in other words, to be an expression of working class self-activity. Indeed, according to K. Steven Vincent, there was *"close similarity between the associational ideal of Proudhon ... and the program of the Lyon Mutualists"* and that there was *"a remarkable convergence [between the ideas], and it is likely that Proudhon was able to articulate his positive program more coherently because of the example of the silk workers of Lyon. The socialist ideal that he championed was already being realised, to a certain extent, by such workers."* [**Pierre-Joseph Proudhon and the Rise of French Republican Socialism**, p. 164] Other anarchists have made similar arguments concerning anarchism being the expression of tendencies within working class struggle against oppression and exploitation and so the using of a traditional workers symbol would be a natural expression of this aspect of anarchism.

Similarly, perhaps it is Louise Michel's comment that the black flag was the *"flag of strikes"* which could explain the naming of the **Black International** founded in 1881 (and so the increasing use of the black flag in anarchist circles in the early 1880s). Around the time of its founding congress Kropotkin was formulating the idea that this organisation would be a *"Strikers' International"* (**Internationale**

Greviste) – it would be *"an organisation of resistance, of strikes."* [quoted by Martin A. Miller, **Kropotkin**, p. 147] In December 1881 he discussed the revival of the International Workers Association as a **Strikers' International** for to *"be able to make the revolution, the mass of workers will have to organise themselves. Resistance and strikes are excellent methods of organisation for doing this."* He stressed that the *"strike develops the sentiment of solidarity"* and argued that the First International *"was born of strikes; it was fundamentally a strikers' organisation."* [quoted by Caroline Cahm, **Kropotkin and the Rise of Revolutionary Anarchism, 1872-1886**, p. 255 and p. 256]

A *"Strikers International"* would need the strikers flag and so, perhaps, the **Black International** got its name. This, of course, fits perfectly with the use of the black flag as a symbol of workers' resistance by anarchism, a political expression of that resistance. However, the black flag did not instantly replace the red flag as the main anarchist symbol. The use of the red flag continued for some decades in anarchist circles. Thus we find Kropotkin writing in the early 1880s of *"anarchist groups ... rais[ing] the red flag of revolution."* As Woodcock noted, the *"black flag was not universally accepted by anarchists at this time. Many, like Kropotkin, still thought of themselves as socialists and of the red flag as theirs also."* [**Words of a Rebel**, p. 75 and p. 225] In addition, we find the Chicago anarchists using both black and red flags all through the 1880s. French Anarchists carried three red flags at the funeral of Louise Michel's mother in 1885 as well as at her own funeral in January 1905. [Louise Michel, **Op. Cit.**, p. 183 and p. 201] Anarchists in Japan, for example, demonstrated under red flags bearing the slogans *"Anarchy"* and *"Anarchist Communism"* in June, 1908. [John Crump, **Hatta Shuzo and Pure Anarchism in Interwar Japan**, p. 25] Three years later, the Mexican anarchists declared that they had *"hoisted the Red Flag on Mexico's fields of action"* as part of their *"war against Authority, war against Capital, and war against the Church."* They were *"fighting under the Red Flag to the famous cry of 'Land and Liberty.'"* [Ricardo Flores Magon, **Land and Liberty**, p. 98 and p. 100]

So for a considerable period of time anarchists used red as well as black flags as their symbol. The general drift away from the red flag towards the black must be placed in the historical context. During the 1880s the socialist movement was changing. Marxist social democracy was becoming the dominant socialist trend, with libertarian socialism going into relative decline in many areas. Thus the red flag was increasingly associated with the authoritarian and statist (and increasingly reformist) side of the socialist movement. In order to distinguish themselves from other socialists, the use of the black flag makes perfect sense as it was an accepted symbol of working class revolt like the red flag.

After the Russian Revolution and its slide into dictatorship (first under Lenin, then Stalin) anarchist use of the red flag decreased as it no longer *"stood for liberty."* Instead, it had become associated, at worst, with the Communist Parties or, at best, bureaucratic, reformist and authoritarian social democracy. This change can be seen from the Japanese movement. As noted above, before the First World War anarchists there had happily raised the red flag but in the 1920s they unfurled the black flag. Organised in the **Kokushoku Seinen Renmei** (Black Youth League), they published **Kokushoku**

Seinen (Black Youth). By 1930, the anarchist theoretical magazine **Kotushoku Sensen** (Black Battlefront) had been replaced by two journals called **Kurohata** (Black Flag) and **Kuhusen** (Black Struggle). [John Crump, **Op. Cit.**, pp. 69-71 and p. 88]

According to historian Candace Falk, *"[t]hough black has been associated with anarchism in France since 1883, the colour red was the predominant symbol of anarchism throughout this period; only after the First World War was the colour black widely adopted."* [**Emma Goldman: A Documentary History of the American Years**, vol. 1, p. 208fn] As this change did not occur overnight, it seems safe to conclude that while anarchism and the black flag had been linked, at the latest, from the early 1880s, it did not become the definitive anarchist symbol until the 1920s (Carlo Tresca in America was still talking of standing *"beneath the red flag that is the immaculate flag of the anarchist idea"* in 1925. [quoted by Nunzio Pernicone, **Carlo Tresca: Portrait of a Rebel**, p. 161]). Before then, anarchists used both it and the red flag as their symbols of choice. After the Russian Revolution, anarchists would still use red in their flags, but only when combined with black. In this way they would not associate themselves with the tyranny of the USSR or the reformism and statism of the mainstream socialist movement.

2 Why the red-and-black flag?

The red-and-black flag has been associated with anarchism for some time. Murray Bookchin placed the creation of this flag in Spain:

"The presence of black flags together with red ones became a feature of Anarchist demonstrations throughout Europe and the Americas. With the establishment of the CNT, a single flag on which black and red were separated diagonally, was adopted and used mainly in Spain." [**The Spanish Anarchists**, p. 57]

George Woodcock also stressed the Spanish origin of the flag:

"The anarcho-syndicalist flag in Spain was black and red, divided diagonally. In the days of the [First] International the anarchists, like other socialist sects, carried the red flag, but later they tended to substitute for it the black flag. The black-and-red flag symbolised an attempt to unite the spirit of later anarchism with the mass appeal of the International." [**Anarchism**, p. 325fn]

According to Abel Paz, anarchist historian and CNT militant in the 1930s, the 1st of May 1931 was, *"the first time in history [that] the red and black flag flew over a CNT-FAI rally."* This was the outcome of an important meeting of CNT militants and anarchist groups to plan the May Day demonstrations in Barcelona. One of the issues to be resolved was *"under what flag to march."* One group was termed the *"Red Flag"* anarchists (who *"put greater emphasis on labour issues"*), the other *"Black Flag"* anarchists (who were *"more distant (at the time) from economic questions"*). However, with the newly proclaimed Republic there were *"tremendous opportunities for mass mobilisations"* which made disagreements on how much

emphasis to place on labour issues *"meaningless."* This allowed an accord to be reached with its *"material expression"* being *"making the two flags into one: the black and red flag."* [**Durruti in the Spanish Revolution**, p. 206]

However, the red-and-black flag was used by anarchists long before 1931, indeed decades before the CNT was even formed. In fact, it, rather than the black flag, may well have been the first specifically anarchist flag.

The earliest recorded use of the red-and-black colours was during the attempted Bologna insurrection of August 1874 where participants were *"sporting the anarchists' red and black cockade."* [Nunzio Pernicone, **Italian Anarchism, 1864-1892**, p. 93] In April 1877, a similar attempt at provoking rebellion saw anarchists enter the small Italian town of Letino *"wearing red and black cockades"* and carrying a *"red and black banner."* These actions helped to *"captur[e] national attention"* and *"draw considerable notice to the International and its socialist programme."* [Nunzio Pernicone, **Op. Cit.**, pp. 124-5 and pp. 126-7] Significantly, another historian notes that the insurgents in 1874 were *"decked out in the red and black emblem of the International"* while three years later they were *"prominently displaying the red and black anarchist flag."* [T. R. Ravindranathan, **Bakunin and the Italians**, p. 208 and p. 228] Thus the black-and-red flag, like the black flag, was a recognised symbol of the labour movement (in this case, the Italian section of the First International) before becoming linked to anarchism.

The red-and-black flag was used by anarchists a few years later in Mexico. At an anarchist protest meeting on December 14th, 1879, at Columbus Park in Mexico City *"[s]ome five thousand persons gathered replete with numerous red-and-black flags, some of which bore the inscription 'La Social, Liga International del Jura.' A large black banner bearing the inscription 'La Social, Gran Liga International' covered the front of the speaker's platform."* The links between the Mexican and European anarchist movements were strong, as the *"nineteenth-century Mexican urban labour-movement maintained direct contact with the Jura branch of the … European-based First International Workingmen's Association and at one stage openly affiliated with it."* [John M. Hart, **Anarchism and the Mexican Working Class, 1860-1931**, p. 58 and p. 17] One year after it was founded, the anarchist influenced **Casa del Obrero Mundial** organised Mexico's first May Day demonstration in 1913 and *"between twenty and twenty-five thousand workers gathered behind red and black flags"* in Mexico City. [John Lear, **Workers, Neighbors, and Citizens**, p. 236]

Augusto Sandino, the radical Nicaraguan national liberation fighter was so inspired by the example of the Mexican anarcho-syndicalists that he based his movement's flag on their red-and-black ones (the Sandinista's flag is divided horizontally, rather than diagonally). As historian Donald C. Hodges notes, Sandino's *"red and black flag had an anarcho-syndicalist origin, having been introduced into Mexico by Spanish immigrants."* Unsurprisingly, his flag was considered a *"workers' flag symbolising their struggle for liberation."* (Hodges refers to Sandino's *"peculiar brand of anarcho-communism"* suggesting that his appropriation of the flag indicated a strong libertarian theme to his politics). [**Intellectual Foundations of the Nicaraguan Revolution**, p. 49, p. 137 and p. 19]

This suggests that the red-and-black flag was rediscovered by the Spanish Anarchists in 1931 rather than being invented by them. However, the CNT-FAI seem to have been the first to bisect their flags diagonally black and red (but other divisions, such as horizontally, were also used). In the English speaking world though, the use of the red-and-black flag by anarchists seems to spring from the world-wide publicity generated by the Spanish Revolution in 1936. With CNT-FAI related information spreading across the world, the use of the CNT inspired diagonally split red-and-black flag also spread until it became a common anarchist and anarcho-syndicalist symbol in all countries.

For some, the red-and-black flag is associated with anarcho-syndicalism more than anarchism. As Albert Meltzer put it, *"[t]he flag of the labour movement (not necessarily only of socialism) is red. The CNT of Spain originated the red-and-black of anarchosyndicalism (anarchism plus the labour movement)."* [**Anarcho-Quiz Book**, p. 50] Donald C. Hodges makes a similar point, when he states that *"[o]n the insignia of the Mexico's House of the World Worker [the Mexican anarcho-syndicalist union], the red band stood for the economic struggle of workers against the proprietary classes, and the black for their insurrectionary struggle."* [**Sandino's Communism**, p. 22]

This does not contradict its earliest uses in Italy and Mexico as those anarchists took it for granted that they should work within the labour movement to spread libertarian ideas. Therefore, it is not surprising we find movements in Mexico and Italy using the same flags. Both were involved in the First International and its anti-authoritarian off-spring. Both, like the Jura Federation in Switzerland, were heavily involved in union organising and strikes. Given the clear links and similarities between the collectivist anarchism of the First International (the most famous advocate of which was Bakunin) and anarcho-syndicalism, it is not surprising that they used similar symbols. As Kropotkin argued, *"Syndicalism is nothing other than the rebirth of the International – federalist, worker, Latin."* [quoted by Martin A. Miller, **Kropotkin**, p. 176] So a rebirth of symbols would not be a co-incidence.

Thus the red-and-black flag comes from the experience of anarchists in the labour movement and is particularly, but not exclusively, associated with anarcho-syndicalism. The black represents libertarian ideas and strikes (i.e. direct action), the red represents the labour movement. Over time association with anarcho-syndicalism has become less noted, with many non-syndicalist anarchists happy to use the red-and-black flag (many anarcho-communists use it, for example). It would be a good generalisation to state that social anarchists are more inclined to use the red-and-black flag than individualist anarchists just as social anarchists are usually more willing to align themselves with the wider socialist and labour movements than individualists (in modern times at least). However, both the red and black flags have their roots in the labour movement and working class struggle which suggests that the combination of both flags into one was a logical development. Given that the black **and** red flags were associated with the Lyon uprising of 1831, perhaps the development of the red-and-black flag is not too unusual. Similarly, given that the black flag was the *"flag of strikes"* (to quote Louise Michel – see above) its use with the red flag of the labour movement seems a natural development for a movement like anarchism and anarcho-syndicalism which bases

itself on direct action and the importance of strikes in the class struggle.

So while associated with anarcho-syndicalism, the red-and-black flag has become a standard anarchist symbol as the years have gone by, with the black still representing anarchy and the red, social co-operation or solidarity. Thus the red-and-black flag more than any one symbol symbolises the aim of anarchism (*"Liberty of the individual and social co-operation of the whole community"* [Peter Kropotkin, **Act for Yourselves**, p. 102]) as well as its means (*"[t]o make the revolution, the mass of workers will have to organise themselves. Resistance and the strike are excellent means of organisation for doing this"* and *"the strike develops the sentiment of solidarity."* [Kropotkin, quoted by Caroline Cahm, **Kropotkin and the Rise of Revolutionary Anarchism: 1872-1186**, p. 255 and p. 256]).

3 Where does the circled-A come from?

The circled-A is, perhaps, even more famous than the black and red-and-black flags as an anarchist symbol (probably because it lends itself so well to graffiti). According to Peter Marshall the *"circled-A"* represents Proudhon's maxim *"Anarchy is Order."* [**Demanding the Impossible** p. 558] Peter Peterson also adds that the circle is *"a symbol of unity and determination"* which *"lends support to the oft-proclaimed idea of international anarchist solidarity."* [*"Flag, Torch, and Fist: The Symbols of Anarchism"*, **Freedom**, vol. 48, No. 11, pp. 8]

However, the origin of the "circled-A" as an anarchist symbol is less clear. Many think that it started in the 1970s punk movement, but it goes back to a much earlier period. According to Peter Marshall, *"[i]n 1964 a French group, **Jeunesse Libertaire**, gave new impetus to Proudhon's slogan 'Anarchy is Order' by creating the circled-A a symbol which quickly proliferated throughout the world."* [**Op. Cit.**, p. 445] This is not the earliest sighting of this symbol. On November 25 1956, at its foundation in Brussels, the **Alliance Ouvriere Anarchiste** (AOA) adopted this symbol. Going even further, a BBC documentary on the Spanish Civil War shows an anarchist militia member with a "circled-A" clearly on the back of his helmet. Other than this, there is little known about the "circled-A"s origin.

Today the circled-A is one of the most successful images in the whole field of political symbolising. Its *"incredible simplicity and directness led [it] to become the accepted symbol of the restrengthened anarchist movement after the revolt of 1968"* particularly as in many, if not most, of the world's languages the word for anarchy begins with the letter A. [Peter Peterson, **Op. Cit.**, p. 8]

AFAQ volume two
contents

Introduction to Volume 2

Section G – Is individualist anarchism capitalistic?

Section H – Why do anarchists oppose state socialism?

Section I – What would an anarchist society look like?

Section J – What do anarchists do?

Bibliography

selected AK PRESS titles

ACKELSBERG, Martha
Free Women of Spain – Anarchism and the Struggle for the Emancipation of Women
paperback £12.00
1902593960

AVRICH, Paul
Anarchist Voices – An Oral History of Anarchism in America
paperback £16.00
1904859275

AVRICH, Paul
Modern School Movement – Anarchism & Education in the United States
paperback £13.95
9781904859093

AVRICH, Paul
Russian Anarchists
paperback £11.95
9781904859482

BERKMAN, Alexander (ed.)
The Blast
paperback £15.00
9781904859086

BERKMAN, Alexander
What is Anarchism?
paperback £10.00
9781902593708

BOOKCHIN, Murray
Social Anarchism Or Lifestyle Anarchism – An Unbridgable Chasm?
paperback £5.95
9781873176832

BOOKCHIN, Murray
Post-Scarcity Anarchism
paperback £10.00
9781904859062

BRINTON, Maurice
For Workers' Power – Selected Writings
paperback £12.00
1904859070

CHOMSKY, Noam
Chomsky On Anarchism
paperback £11.00
1904859208

CHOMSKY, Noam
Radical Priorities
paperback £10.00
9781902593692

COHN-BENDIT, Daniel
Obsolete Communism – the Leftwing Alternative
paperback £10.00
1902593251

DE CLEYRE, Voltairine
Voltairine de Cleyre Reader
paperback £10.00
9781902593876

FRANKS, Benjamin
Rebel Alliances
paperback £15.00
9781904859406

FREMION, Yves
Orgasms of History – 3000 Years of Spontaneous Insurrection
paperback £12.00
9781902593340

GUERIN, Daniel (ed.)
No Gods No Masters – An Anthology of Anarchism
paperback £16.95
1904859259

KATSIAFICAS, George
Subversion of Politics
paperback £12.00
9781904859536

KROPOTKIN, Peter
Conquest of Bread
paperback £10.00
9781904859109

MacPHEE, Josh, & REULAND, Erik
Realizing the Impossible – Art Against Authority
paperback £16.00
9781904859321

MAGON, Ricardo Flores
Dreams of Freedom – A Ricardo Flores Magon Reader
paperback £12.00
1904859240

MELTZER, Albert
Anarchism – Arguments For and Against
paperback £3.95
9781873176573

PANNEKOEK, Anton
(Introduction by Noam Chomsky)
Workers' Councils
paperback £9.00
9781902593562

PAZ, Abel
Durruti In The Spanish Revolution
paperback £20.00
9781904859505

PORTER, David (ed.)
Vision on Fire – Emma Goldman on the Spanish Revolution
paperback £13.00
9781904859574

ROCKER, Rudolf
Anarcho-Syndicalism – Theory and Practice
paperback £9.00
9781902593920

SHUKAITIS, S. & GRAEBER, D. (eds.)
Constituent Imagination – Militant Investigations, Collective Theorization
paperback £12.00
9781904859352

SITRIN, Marina (Ed)
Horizontalism – Voices of Popular Power in Argentinia
paperback £12.00
9781904859581

SKIRDA, Alexandre.
Translator – SHARKEY, Paul
Facing the Enemy – a History of Anarchist Organization from Proudhon to May 1968
paperback £12.00
1902593197